The Routledge Handbook of Discourse Analysis

'This discourse analysis handbook wins hands down as the most intellectually responsible in the field – both in terms of the comprehensiveness of the topics considered and the international spectrum of specialists involved.'

James Martin, *University of Sydney, Australia*

'*The Routledge Handbook of Discourse Analysis* is accessible to undergraduates and yet a state-of-the-art introduction for graduate students and practicing researchers in a wide-range of fields. There are many introductions to or handbooks of Discourse Analysis available today. This is the most comprehensive, up-to-date, and internationally representative of them all.'

Sarah Michaels, *Clark University, USA*

The Routledge Handbook of Discourse Analysis covers the major approaches to Discourse Analysis from Critical Discourse Analysis to Multimodal Discourse Analysis and their applications in key educational and institutional settings. The handbook is divided into six sections: Approaches to Discourse Analysis, Approaches to Spoken Discourse, Genres and Practices, Educational Applications, Institutional Applications, and Identity, Culture and Discourse.

The chapters are written by a wide range of contributors from around the world, each a leading researcher in their respective field. All chapters have been closely edited by James Paul Gee and Michael Handford. With a focus on the application of discourse analysis to real-life problems, the contributors introduce the reader to a topic, and analyse authentic data.

The Routledge Handbook of Discourse Analysis is vital reading for linguistics students as well as students of communication and cultural studies, social psychology and anthropology.

James Paul Gee is the Mary Lou Fulton Presidential Professor of Literacy Studies at Arizona State University. He is the author of many titles, including *An Introduction to Discourse Analysis* (1999, Third Edition 2011); *How to do Discourse Analysis* (2011) and *Language and Learning in the Digital Age* (2011), all published by Routledge.

Michael Handford is Associate Professor in English Language at the University of Tokyo. He is the author of *The Language of Business Meetings* (2010).

Routledge Handbooks in Applied Linguistics

Routledge Handbooks in Applied Linguistics provide comprehensive overviews of the key topics in applied linguistics. All entries for the handbooks are specially commissioned and written by leading scholars in the field. Clear, accessible and carefully edited *Routledge Handbooks in Applied Linguistics* are the ideal resource for both advanced undergraduates and postgraduate students.

The Routledge Handbook of Forensic Linguistics
Edited by Malcolm Coulthard and Alison Johnson

The Routledge Handbook of Corpus Linguistics
Edited by Anne O'Keeffe and Mike McCarthy

The Routledge Handbook of World Englishes
Edited by Andy Kirkpatrick

The Routledge Handbook of Applied Linguistics
Edited by James Simpson

The Routledge Handbook of Discourse Analysis
James Paul Gee and Michael Handford

The Routledge Handbook of Second Language Acquisition
Edited by Susan Gass and Alison Mackey

The Routledge Handbook of Multilingualism
Edited by Marilyn Martin-Jones, Adrian Blackledge and Angela Creese

The Routledge Handbook of Translation Studies
Edited by Carmen Millan Varela and Francesca Bartrina

The Routledge Handbook of Language Testing
Edited by Glenn Fulcher and Fred Davidson

The Routledge Handbook of Language and Intercultural Communication
Edited by Jane Jackson

The Routledge Handbook of Language and Health Communication
Edited by Heidi Hamilton and Wen-ying Sylvia Chou

The Routledge Handbook of Language and Professional Communication
Edited by Vijay Bhatia and Stephen Bremner

The Routledge Handbook of Discourse Analysis

Edited by James Paul Gee and Michael Handford

LONDON AND NEW YORK

First published in paperback 2014
First published 2012
by Routledge
2 Park Square, Milton Park, Abingdon, Oxon OX14 4RN

Simultaneously published in the USA and Canada
by Routledge
711 Third Avenue, New York, NY 10017

Routledge is an imprint of the Taylor & Francis Group, an informa business

British Library Cataloguing in Publication Data
A catalogue record for this book is available from the British Library

Library of Congress Cataloging in Publication Data
   The Routledge handbook of discourse analysis / edited by
James Paul Gee and Michael Handford.
      p. cm. -- (Routledge handbooks in applied linguistics)
   Includes bibliographical references and index.
   1. Discourse analysis--Handbooks, manuals, etc. I. Gee, James Paul.
   II. Handford, Michael, 1969-
   P302.R68 2011
   401'.41--dc22   2011000560

ISBN: 978-0-415-55107-6 (hbk)
ISBN: 978-0-415-70978-1 (pbk)
ISBN: 978-0-203-80906-8 (ebk)

Typeset in Bembo
by Integra Software Services Pvt. Ltd, Pondicherry, India

Printed and bound by CPI Group (UK) Ltd, Croydon, CR0 4YY

Contents

Contents

Contents

Contents

Illustrations

Figures

Tables

Acknowledgments

The Cambridge and Nottingham Business English Corpus (CANBEC), which forms part of the Cambridge International Corpus, is a collection of samples of spoken business English in use today. It collects recordings of people in everyday working life settings formal and informal meetings, presentations, chats over lunch, and so on. These conversations are then entered onto a computer and analysed. This helps the Corpus team to find out how real people speak and use English in a work environment, how language really works, how to teach it better, and how to make better dictionaries and language learning materials for people learning Business English.

This publication has made use of the Cambridge and Nottingham Corpus of Discourse in English (CANCODE). CANCODE was funded by Cambridge University Press (CUP) and is a 5 million-word computerized corpus of spoken English, made up of recordings from a variety of settings in the United Kingdom and Ireland. The corpus is designed with a substantial, organized database, giving information on participants, settings and conversational goals. CANCODE was built by CUP and the University of Nottingham and forms part of the Cambridge International Corpus (CIC). It provides insights into language use and offers a resource to supplement what is already known about English from other, non-corpus-based research, thereby providing valuable and accurate information for researchers and those preparing teaching materials. Sole copyright of the Corpus resides with CUP, from which all permissions to reproduce material must be obtained.

Contributors

Svenja Adolphs is Professor of English Language and Linguistics at the University of Nottingham, UK. Her research interests are in corpus linguistics, discourse analysis, and pragmatics, and she has published widely in these areas. Her recent books include *Introducing Electronic Text Analysis* (2006) and *Corpus and Context: Investigating Pragmatic Functions in Spoken Discourse* (2008). She has particular interests in the development and analysis of multimodal corpora of spoken English and the investigation of different domains of discourse, including health communication and business communication.

Sarah Atkins is a postgraduate research student in Applied Linguistics at the University of Nottingham. Her research interests lie in healthcare communication and the sociolinguistics of the Internet and new media, particularly the use of metaphor, deictic and spatial markers, and creative language in forming online communities. Her ESRC-funded Ph.D. research focuses on the importance of such online community interactions in the context of disseminating healthcare information. She has carried out and published work on other research projects in applied linguistics, including an ESRC-funded placement for the British Library investigating the language of science in the news media, a study on the use of vague language in healthcare consultations for Professor Svenja Adolphs, University of Nottingham, a research project on language and gender in a corpus of business discourse for Dr Louise Mullany, University of Nottingham, and work for Professor Ron Carter on creative language use in everyday contexts.

Francesca Bargiela-Chiappini has published widely on business discourse. She has co-authored the first advanced textbook *Business Discourse* (with C. Nickerson and B. Planken; 2007) and edited *The Handbook of Business Discourse* (2009). She is currently an honorary associate professor at the University of Warwick.

Charles Bazerman is Professor of Education at the University of California, Santa Barbara, and recent Chair of the Conference on College Composition and Communication. His interests lie in the social dynamics of writing, rhetorical theory, and the rhetoric of knowledge production and use. His recently edited *Handbook of Research on Writing* won the 2009 CCCC Outstanding Book Award. His other recent books include a collection of essays co-edited with David Russell on writing and activity theory, *Writing Selves/Writing Societies* (available online at http://wac.colostate.edu/books/selves_societies/), and a methods book on textual analysis co-edited with Paul Prior, *What Writing Does and How It Does It*. His book *The Languages of Edison's of Edison's Light* won the American Association of Publisher's Award for the best scholarly book of 1999 in the History of Science and Technology. His previous books include *Constructing Experience, Shaping*

Written Knowledge: The Genre and Activity of the Experimental Article in Science, *The Informed Writer: Using Sources in the Disciplines*, and *Involved: Writing for College*, and *Writing for Your Self*. His co-edited volumes include *Textual Dynamics of the Professions* and *Landmark Essays in Writing across the Curriculum*.

Vijay Bhatia is a visiting professor in the Department of English at the City University of Hong Kong. He has been in the teaching profession for more than 45 years. Before joining the City University in 1993, he worked at the National University of Singapore from 1983 to 1993. Some of his recent research projects include *Analyzing Genre-Bending in Corporate Disclosure Documents* and *International Arbitration Practice: A Discourse Analytical Study*, in which he leads research teams from more than 20 countries. He is a member of the editorial boards of several internationally refereed journals. His research interests include genre analysis of academic and professional discourses, including legal, business, newspaper, and advertising genres; ESP and professional communication; simplification of legal and other public documents; and cross-cultural and cross-disciplinary variations in professional genres. His international publications are numerous and include journal articles, book chapters, and edited and individually written books. Two of his books, *Analysing Genre: Language Use in Professional Settings* and *Worlds of Written Discourse: A Genre-Based View*, are widely used in genre theory and practice.

Douglas Biber is Regents' Professor of English (Applied Linguistics) at Northern Arizona University. His research efforts have focused on corpus linguistics, English grammar, and register variation (in English and cross-linguistically, synchronically, and diachronically). He has written numerous books and monographs, including academic books published by Cambridge University Press (1988, 1995, 1998, 2009) and John Benjamins (2006, 2007), the co-authored *Longman Grammar of Spoken and Written English* (1999), and three grammar textbooks published by Longman.

Adrian Blackledge is Professor of Bilingualism in the School of Education, University of Birmingham, UK. His research interests include the politics of multilingualism, linguistic ethnography, education of linguistic minority students, negotiation of identities in multilingual contexts, and language testing, citizenship, and immigration. His publications include *Multilingualism, A Critical Perspective* (with Angela Creese; 2010), *Discourse and Power in a Multilingual World* (2005), *Negotiation of Identities in Multilingual Contexts* (with Aneta Pavlenko; 2004), *Multilingualism, Second Language Learning and Gender* (co-edited with Aneta Pavlenko, Ingrid Piller, and Marya Teutsch-Dwyer; 2001), and *Literacy, Power, and Social Justice* (2001).

Paula Buttery is a senior research associate in the Computation Cognition and Language group at the Research Centre for English and Applied Linguistics, University of Cambridge; a senior technical officer for Information Extraction and Data-Mining Engineering at the European BioInformatics Institute; and an associate researcher in the Natural Language and Information Processing Group at the University of Cambridge Computer Laboratory. Her current work involves statistical language modelling (with focus on language acquisition), automated corpus analysis, as well as the application of natural language processing techniques for research into the neurocognition of language.

Lynne Cameron is Professor of Applied Linguistics at the Open University. Her research interests center around metaphor in discourse activity, developing theory and methodology from a series of empirical studies. She has been granted a fellowship (for 2009–2012) by ESRC as Research Fellow in the Global Uncertainties program in the *Living with Uncertainty* project, which extends metaphor analysis to the study of the dynamics of social empathy. She was Founder Chair of the international association Researching and Applying Metaphor, and Founder co-editor of the new journal *Metaphor and the Social World*. Her recent publications include *Metaphor Analysis: Research practice in Applied Linguistics, Social Sciences and the Humanities*, (co-edited with R. Maslen; 2010) and *Metaphor and Reconciliation* (2011).

Ronald Carter is Professor of Modern English Language at the University of Nottingham. He has written and edited more than 50 books and has published over 100 academic papers in the fields of literary-linguistics, language and education, applied linguistics, and the teaching of English. He has taught, lectured, and given consultancies to government agencies and ministries in over thirty countries worldwide. In the UK he has worked as linguistic advisor to the UK Ministry of Education and to Qualifications and Curriculum Authority (QCA) on English in the National Curriculum and the Adult ESOL Core Curriculum. His recent books include *Language and Creativity: The Art of Common Talk* (2004), *From Corpus to Classroom: Language Use and Language Teaching* (with Anne O'Keeffe and Michael McCarthy; 2007), and *Cambridge Grammar of English: A Comprehensive Guide to Spoken and Written Grammar and Usage* (with Michael McCarthy; 2006), which won the 2007 British Council International English Language Innovation Award. *English Grammar Today* (reference and workbook) (with Michael McCarthy, Geraldine Mark, and Anne O'Keeffe) will be published in 2011. Professor Carter is a fellow of the Royal Society of Arts and a fellow of the British Academy for Social Sciences, and was Chair of the British Association for Applied Linguistics (2003–2006).

Wallace Chafe was employed by the Smithsonian Institution in Washington as a specialist in Native American languages before moving in 1962 to the University of California, Berkeley. In 1986 he was transferred to the Santa Barbara campus, where he is now Research Professor Emeritus. His work has focused on several Native American languages, differences between speaking and writing, the functions of prosody, the relation between language and thought, and the relation between linguistics and literature. Few among his many writings are *Meaning and the Structure of Language* (1970), *Discourse, Consciousness, and Time* (1994), and *The Importance of Not Being Earnest* (2007).

Winnie Cheng is Professor of English and Director of the Research Centre for Professional Communication in English (RCPCE), Department of English, the Hong Kong Polytechnic University. Her main research interests include ESP, intercultural business and professional communication, intercultural pragmatics, corpus linguistics, conversational analysis, discourse analysis, discourse intonation, outcome-based education, work-integrated education, and collaborative learning and assessment. Her publications include *Intercultural Conversation* (2003) and *A Corpus-driven Analysis of Discourse Intonation* (co-authored with Chris Greaves and Martin Warren, 2008), both published by John Benjamins, and *Professional Communication: Collaboration between Academics and Practitioners* (co-edited with Kenneth C.C. Kong, 2009) published by Hong Kong University Press. She has published in a wide range of journals.

Steven E. Clayman is Professor of Sociology at the University of California, Los Angeles (UCLA). His research concerns the organization of human interaction, both as a phenomenon in its own right and as a medium for the interface between individuals and institutions. He is particularly interested in forms of broadcast talk such as news interviews and presidential news conferences, and what they can reveal about journalism, political communication, and the public sphere. His articles have appeared in the leading journals in sociology, communication studies, and linguistics, as well as edited collections worldwide. He is the co-author (with John Heritage) of *Talk in Action: Interactions, Identities, and Institutions* (2010) and *The News Interview: Journalists and Public Figures on the Air* (2002).

Jennifer Coates is Emeritus Professor of English Language and Linguistics at Roehampton University in London, UK. Her published work includes *Women, Men and Language* (originally published, 1986; third edition 2004), *Women Talk. Conversation between Women Friends* (1996), *Men Talk: Stories in the Making of Masculinities* (2003), and *The Sociolinguistics of Narrative* (edited with Joanna Thornborrow, 2005). A second revised edition of her *Language and Gender: A Reader* is due in 2011. She has given lectures at universities all over the world and has held visiting professorships in universities in Australia, New Zealand, the USA, Germany, Switzerland, Spain, and Italy. She became a fellow of the English Association in 2002.

Julia de Bres is a sociolinguist with research interests in multilingualism, language in the workplace, language attitudes and ideologies, minority languages, and language policy and planning. She holds a Ph.D. in linguistics from Victoria University of Wellington, in which she addressed the topic of language planning targeting the attitudes and behaviors of non-Māori New Zealanders toward the Māori language. She has worked as part of the Language in the Workplace Project at Victoria University of Wellington and is currently undertaking a research project at the University of Luxembourg on the language ideologies and practices of cross-border workers in Luxembourg.

Teun A. van Dijk was Professor of Discourse Studies at the University of Amsterdam until 2004, and is at present visiting professor at the Universitat Pompeu Fabra, Barcelona, until his retirement in 2013. He is the author of several books in most of these areas, and he edited *The Handbook of Discourse Analysis* (1985) the introductory book *Discourse Studies* (1997; new one-volume edition, 2011) as well as the reader *The Study of Discourse* (2007). He founded six international journals, *Poetics*, *Text* (now *Text and Talk*), *Discourse and Society*, *Discourse Studies*, *Discourse and Communication*, and the Internet journal in Spanish *Discurso and Sociedad* (www.dissoc.org), of which he still edits the latter four. His recent monographs in English are *Ideology* (1998), *Racism and Discourse in Spain and Latin America* (2005), *Discourse and Context* (2008), and *Society and Discourse* (2009). His latest edited books are *Racism at the Top* (with Ruth Wodak; 2000) and *Racism and Discourse in Latin America* (2009). Teun van Dijk holds two honorary doctorates and has lectured widely in many countries. For a list of publications, recent articles, resources for discourse studies, and other information, see his homepage: www.discourses.org.

Norman Fairclough was Professor of Language in Social Life at Lancaster University, UK, until he retired in 2004, and he is now Emeritus Professor and Honorary Research Fellow in the Institute for Advanced Studies, and Deputy Director of the Centre for Cultural Political Economy Research. He has written many books and articles on critical approaches to discourse analysis, including, most recently, *Critical Discourse Analysis* (extensively revised second edition, 2010), *Language and Globalization* (2006), and *Analyzing Discourse: Textual Analysis for Social Research* (2003). He is currently working with Isabela Fairclough on a book to be published by Routledge on political discourse analysis, focusing upon argumentation and especially practical argumentation in political discourse.

Edward Finegan is Professor Emeritus of Linguistics and Law at the University of Southern California, where he continues to teach, carry out research, and play an active role in administrative responsibilities. He has a long-standing interest in the discourses of various legal registers, especially transactional matters, defamation, and the expression of stance in appellate court opinions. He has served on the editorial boards of *English Language and Linguistics*, *American Speech*, and *Discourse Processes*, and as general editor of Oxford Studies in Sociolinguistics. For more than three decades he has served as a forensic linguistic in scores of US federal and state cases. He has lectured and written about ethical practices among expert consultants and expert witnesses and has lectured on the history and character of legal language in judicial education sessions.

Lynne Flowerdew works at the Hong Kong University of Science and Technology. She has published widely in different areas of corpus linguistics in international journals and refereed edited collections. Her most recent authored book is *Corpus-Based Analyses of the Problem–Solution Pattern* (2008). Her two forthcoming books include a co-edited volume with Ana Frankenberg-Garcia and Guy Aston entitled *New Trends in Corpora and Language Learning* (Continuum) and an authored volume *Corpora and Language Education* (Palgrave Macmillan). She is a member of the editorial board of *TESOL Quarterly*, *English for Specific Purposes*, *Journal of English for Academic Purposes*, and *Text Construction*.

James Paul Gee is the Mary Lou Fulton Presidential Professor of Literacy Studies in Arizona State University. He is a member of the National Academy of Education. His book *Sociolinguistics and Literacies* (1990; third edition, 2007) was one of the founding documents in the formation of the "New Literacy Studies," an interdisciplinary field devoted to studying language, learning, and literacy in an integrated way, in the full range of their cognitive, social, and cultural contexts. His book *An Introduction to Discourse Analysis* (1999; 2005; 2011) brings together his work on a methodology for studying communication in its cultural settings, an approach that has been widely influential over the last two decades. Two of his recent books deal with video games, language, and learning. *What Video Games Have to Teach Us About Learning and Literacy* (2003; 2007) argues that good video games are designed to enhance learning through effective learning principles supported by research in the Learning Sciences. *Situated Language and Learning* (2004) places video games within an overall theory of learning and literacy and shows how they can help us in thinking about the reform of schools. His most recent books are *Good Video Games and Good Learning: Collected Essays* (2007), and *Woman as Gamers: The Sims and 21st Century Learning* (2010) and *Language and Learning in the Digital World* (to appear), both written with Elizabeth Hayes. Gee has published widely in journals on linguistics, psychology, the social sciences, and education.

Virginia Teas Gill is Professor in the Department of Sociology and Anthropology at Illinois State University. Her research focuses on the organization of social interaction in medical settings, especially lay members' practices for exerting agency during clinic visits. She has examined how patients offer and rule out causal explanations for illness, request medical interventions, and pursue physicians' responses to their initiatives. She has also examined how clinicians in a clinic for childhood developmental disabilities deliver diagnostic news to parents, and the methods parents use to resist labels that are applied to their children. Her work has been published in journals such as *Social Psychology Quarterly*, *Research on Language and Social Interaction*, and *Sociology of Health and Illness*. She is the co-editor of *Communication in Healthcare Settings: Policy, Participation and New Technologies* (with Alison Pilnick and Jon Hindmarsh; 2010).

Yueguo Gu has an MA and a Ph.D. from Lancaster University, and is Research Professor and the Head of the Contemporary Linguistics Department in the Chinese Academy of Social Sciences. He is also Research Professor of Linguistics and the Founding Dean of the Institute of Beiwai

Online Education. His research interests include pragmatics, discourse analysis, corpus linguistics, rhetoric, and online education. He has published research papers quite extensively both at home and abroad. He has also authored and edited several series of textbooks covering linguistics, rhetoric, ELT methodology, action research, across-cultural communication, and teaching English to Chinese learners. He is a co-chief editor of the *Journal of Contemporary Linguistics* and is on the advisory editorial boards of ten International Journals. He is the winner of five national top research prizes and was awarded a K. C. Wong Fellow of the British Academy in 1997. He is a holder of many honorary posts, most noticeably the special professorship of the University of Nottingham (2004–2011) and an honorary doctorate from Lancaster University, UK, in 2011.

Michael Handford is Associate Professor of English Language at the University of Tokyo. He gained his Ph.D. in Applied Linguistics in 2007 from the University of Nottingham, where he also lectured for four years on language teaching, corpus linguistics, and discourse analysis. He teaches and has published on English for specific purposes, professional communication, discourse analysis, genre analysis, corpus linguistics, pragmatics, and intercultural communication. He is particularly interested in using corpora to unearth discursive practices in professional spoken contexts; he constructed the CANBEC corpus, and is in the process of developing a new corpus on international professional spoken English. He regularly works as a communications consultant with international companies, and is a columnist on intercultural and business issues, for example for *Newsweek Japan*. He is the author of *The Language of Business Meetings* (2010).

Kenji Hakuta is the Lee J. Jacks Professor of Education at Stanford University. He has been at Stanford since 1989, except for three years when he left to start the new University of California at Merced as its Founding Dean of the School of Social Sciences, Humanities and Arts. Hakuta received his Ph.D. in Experimental Psychology from Harvard University, and began his career as a developmental psychologist at Yale University. He is the author of many research papers and books, including *Mirror of Language: The Debate on Bilingualism* (1986). Hakuta is active in education policy. He has testified to Congress and other public bodies on language policy, the education of language minority students, affirmative action in higher education, and improvement of quality in educational research. Hakuta is an elected member of the National Academy of Education, a fellow of the American Educational Research Association, and a fellow of the American Association for the Advancement of Science, and is recognized for his accomplishments in Linguistics and Language Sciences. He has served on the board of various organizations, including the Educational Testing Service, the Spencer Foundation, and the New Teacher Center.

Kevin Harvey is a lecturer in Sociolinguistics at the University of Nottingham. His principal research specialities lie in the fields of applied sociolinguistics, discourse analysis, and corpus linguistics. Broadly speaking, he is interested in interdisciplinary approaches to professional communication, with his present research, for example, focusing on multimodal approaches to medical discourse and its practical implications for healthcare deliveries. Specifically, this work involves a corpus linguistic exploration of electronic health messages: an examination of the health concerns communicated by contributors to medical professionals online.

Janet Holmes holds a personal chair in Linguistics at Victoria University of Wellington. She teaches sociolinguistics courses, specializing in workplace discourse, New Zealand English, and language and gender. She is the Director of the *Wellington Language in the Workplace* project (see www.victoria.ac.nz/lals/lwp) and a fellow of the Royal Society of New Zealand. Her books include *Gendered Talk at Work* (2006), *An Introduction to Sociolinguistics* (1992), now in its third edition, and the Blackwell *Handbook of Language and Gender* (with Miriam Meyerhoff, 2003). She has also published numerous articles in international journals on topics ranging from gendered discourse, through socio-pragmatic aspects of interaction, to variationist features of New Zealand English. Her recent work focuses on leadership discourse and the relevance of gender and ethnicity in the workplace, and with the *Language in the Workplace* project team she is currently exploring the relevance of socio-pragmatic skills for new migrants in professional workplaces.

Paul J. Hopper holds the Paul Mellon Distinguished Chair of the Humanities at Carnegie Mellon University in Pittsburgh. He has a Ph.D. in Linguistics from the University of Texas. He studied at the University of Reading, England, and at the University of Erlangen, Germany. He has been Visiting Professor of Linguistics at the University of Köln and Directeur d'Études at the École Pratique des Hautes Études, the Sorbonne. He is a recipient of the Medal of the Collège de France. He was a fellow of the Guggenheim Foundation (1985) and was the Hermann and Klara Collitz Professor of Comparative Philology at the Linguistic Society of America Linguistics Institute in UCLA in 1984. His publications include works on Germanic and Indo-European linguistics, Malay and Indonesian, grammaticalization, and discourse analysis.

Ken Hyland is Chair Professor of Applied Linguistics and Director of the Centre for Applied English Studies at the University of Hong Kong. He has taught applied linguistics and EAP for over 30 years in Asia, Australasia, and the UK, where he was Professor of Applied Linguistics in Education at the Institute of Education, London. He has published over 150 articles and 14 books on language education and academic writing, of which the most recent are *Academic Discourse* (2009), a second edition of *Teaching and Researching Writing* (2009), and *Academic Evaluation* (edited with Giuliana Diani; 2009). He is currently working on a book on disciplinary identity for CUP and editing a book on discourse analysis and on corpus applications for Continuum. He was Founding Co-editor of the *Journal of English for Academic Purposes* and is now the co-editor of *Applied Linguistics* and editor of the Continuum Discourse Series.

Hale Işık-Güler is Assistant Professor in the Department of Foreign Language Education at Middle East Technical University, Turkey. Her major research interests include (im)politeness conceptualizations across languages, corpus approaches to politeness research, and cross-cultural and intercultural communication. She has co-authored articles on face, relational work, and emotion in the *Journal of Pragmatics* and *Intercultural Pragmatics*.

Jürgen Jaspers currently holds a postdoctoral fellowship from the Research Foundation Flanders and teaches at the University of Antwerp, Belgium. He researches linguistic interaction ethnographically in relation to education, urban multilingualism, and linguistic policy, with publications in *Language and Communication*, *Linguistics and Education*, and *International Journal of Bilingualism*. Recently he became the co-editor of *Society and Language Use* (2010) and *Multilingual Structures and Agencies* (special issue of *Journal of Pragmatics*, in press).

Mary M. Juzwik is an associate professor of Language and Literacy in the Department of Teacher Education at Michigan State University. She teaches undergraduate and graduate courses in writing, discourse, and English education, and coordinates the Secondary English Education program. She is affiliated with the Rhetoric, Writing, and American Cultures Program and the English department at Michigan State University and is a principal investigator at the Literacy Achievement Research Center. She studies issues related to literacy teaching and learning, including linguistic and cultural diversity in English classrooms; writing theory and instruction; teacher identity; ways of reading, writing, and talking about the Holocaust; and ways of supporting dialogically organized instructional practices in teaching and teacher preparation. Juzwik's work engages with diverse scholarly traditions such as narrative studies, interactional sociolinguistics, and rhetorical theory. She has published her research in numerous journals She received the 2010 Edward P. Fry award from the Literacy Research Association for her book *The Rhetoric of Teaching: Understanding the Dynamics of Holocaust Narratives in an English Classroom* (2009).

Andy Kirkpatrick is Chair Professor of English as an International Language at the Hong Kong Institute of Education (HKIEd) and Director of the Institute's Research Centre into Language Education and Acquisition in Multilingual Societies. His research interests include the development of regional varieties of English, with a particular focus on Asian Englishes and the history of Chinese rhetoric. He is the editor of the *Routledge Handbook of World Englishes* (2010) and the author of *English as a Lingua Franca in ASEAN: The Multilingual Model* (Hong Kong University Press, 2010) and *World Englishes: Implications for International Communication and ELT* (CUP, 2007).

Almut Koester is Senior Lecturer in English Language in the School of English, Drama and American and Canadian Studies at the University of Birmingham, where she teaches courses in English Language, Discourse Analysis, Genre Analysis, Business English and Applied Linguistics. Her research focuses on spoken workplace discourse, using a combination of corpus linguistic and discourse analytic methods, and her publications have examined genre, modality, relational language, vague language and idioms. She is author of three books, *The Language of Work* (2004), *Investigating Workplace Discourse* (2006) and *Workplace Discourse* (2010) and she has written for international journals and contributed to edited volumes. She actively promotes the application of research in discourse analysis and corpus research to English Language Teaching through presentations at ELT conferences, workshops for teachers and Business English materials writing. She is currently involved in the development of a corpus-informed Business English course with an ELT publisher.

Gunther Kress is Professor of Semiotics and Education at the Institute of Education, University of London. His interests are in meaning-making and communication in contemporary environments as well as in developing a social semiotic theory of multimodal communication. His books include *Social Semiotics* (with R Hodge; 1988); *Before Writing: Rethinking the Paths to Literacy* (1996); *Reading Images: The Grammar of Graphic Design* (1996/2006) and *Multimodal Discourse: The Modes and Media of Contemporary Communication* (2002) both with T. van Leeuwen; *Multimodal Learning and Teaching: The Rhetorics of the Science Classroom* (2001); *Literacy in the New Media Age* (2003); and *Multimodality: A Social Semiotic Approach to Contemporary Communication* (2010).

Phoenix Lam is an assistant professor at the Department of English Language and Literature in Hong Kong Baptist University. Her research interests include corpus linguistics, discourse analysis, discourse intonation, pragmatics, and sociolinguistics.

William L. Leap is Professor of Anthropology at American University (Washington, DC) His recent writings on language and sexuality explore the uneven connections between sexual sameness, discursive practice, masculinity, and privilege in US and South African settings. He coordinates the annual American University Conference on Lavender Languages and Linguistics (www.american.edu/lavenderlanguages), the longest-running lesbian/gay/queer studies conference in the USA (and perhaps the world), and a site where queer linguistics themes have been explored freely and frankly since 1993. He outlines his commitments to scholarship and social justice in the introductory essay in *Out in Public: Reinventing Lesbian and Gay Anthropology in a Globalizing World* (edited by Lewin and Leap; 2010).

Jay L. Lemke is Senior Research Scientist in the Laboratory of Comparative Human Cognition (LCHC) at the University of California, San Diego. He is the author of *Talking Science: Language, Learning, and Values* (1990) and of *Textual Politics: Discourse and Social Dynamics* (1995) as well as of over 100 publications in the fields of discourse linguistics, multimedia semiotics, and science and literacy education. His current research focus is on the integration of feeling and meaning in multimedia activity systems. Jay has been the co-editor of *Linguistics and Education: An International Journal* (1993–2003) and is currently the co-editor of *Critical Discourse Studies*, as well as a member of the editorial boards of numerous other journals and a reviewer for faculty promotions and honors at more than a dozen universities internationally. He has been a visiting scholar and/or invited lecturer at the Universities of London, Sydney, Melbourne, Vienna, Barcelona, Copenhagen, Oslo, and Utrecht, among many others.

Michael McCarthy is Emeritus Professor of Applied Linguistics, University of Nottingham, UK, Adjunct Professor of Applied Linguistics, Pennsylvania State University, USA, and Adjunct Professor of Applied Linguistics, University of Limerick, Ireland. He is the author/co-author/editor of more than 40 books and more than 80 academic papers. He is the Co-Director (with Ronald Carter) of the 5 million word CANCODE spoken English corpus project, and the one-million-word CANBEC spoken business English corpus. His current research involves the creation and analysis of spoken learner corpora in connection with the English Profile project. He is a fellow of the Royal Society of Arts. He has lectured on language and language teaching in 40 countries and has been actively involved in language teaching and applied linguistics for 45 years.

James McLellan is a senior lecturer in General and Applied Linguistics at the University of Waikato, Aotearoa (New Zealand), teaching Sociolinguistics and English for Academic Purposes at undergraduate level, and postgraduate papers in Applied Linguistics. He has a Ph.D. from Curtin University of Technology, Australia. He was previously at the University of Brunei, Darussalam, from 1989 to 2002, serving as Head of Department of English Language and Applied Linguistics in 2001. He has also taught languages at secondary level in France, the UK, Malaysia, and Brunei. Major research interests include the online revitalization of Borneo indigenous languages, language policy in education in Southeast Asia, Malay–English code-switching in online environments, and Asian varieties of English. He has published journal articles and book chapters on all these topics.

Louise Mullany is Associate Professor of Sociolinguistics in the School of English Studies, University of Nottingham, UK. Her research focuses on sociolinguistic and pragmatic approaches to discourse in professional and institutional contexts. She has conducted studies in business, medical, and media settings. Her recent publications include *Gendered Discourse in the Professional Workplace* (2007), *Introducing English Language* (with P. Stockwell; 2010), and *Language, Gender and Feminism: Theory and Methodology* (with S. Mills; 2011). She is currently working on her next monograph, *The Sociolinguistics of Gender in Public Life* (2012).

Anne O'Keeffe is Senior Lecturer at Mary Immaculate College, University of Limerick, Ireland. She has written numerous journal articles and book chapters on corpus linguistics, media discourse, and language teaching. She has published six books, including: *Investigating Media Discourse* (2006), *From Corpus to Classroom* (with Ronald Carter and Michael McCarthy; 2007), *The Vocabulary Matrix* (with Michael McCarthy and Steve Walsh; 2009), *Introducing Pragmatics in Use* (with Brian Clancy and Svenja Adolphs; 2011). Also, she has edited the Routledge *Handbook of Corpus Linguistics* (with Michael McCarthy; 2010) and has guest-edited *Teanga* (the Irish Yearbook of Applied Linguistics), *Language Awareness* and *The International Journal of Corpus Linguistics*.

David R. Olson is University Professor Emeritus of the Ontario Institute for Studies in Education, University of Toronto. He has published extensively on language, literacy, and cognition, including the widely anthologized article "From utterance to text: the bias of language in speech and writing" (*Harvard Educational Review*, 1977). His book *The World on Paper* (1994) has been translated into several languages. He is the co-editor of *The Cambridge Handbook of Literacy* (with Nancy Torrance, 2009), *The Handbook of Education and Human Development* (with Nancy Torrance; 1996), *Technology, Literacy and the Evolution of Society: Implications of the* work *of Jack Goody* (with Michael Cole; 2006), *Developing Theories of Mind* (with Janet Astington and Paul Harris, 1988), *Developing Theories of Intention* (with Janet Astington and Philip Zelazo; 1999), *Literacy and Orality* (with Nancy Torrance; 1991), and *Literacy, Language and Learning* (with Nancy Torrance and Angela Hildyard; 1985). His most recent books are *Psychological Theory and Educational Reform: How School Remakes Mind and Society* (2003) and *Jerome Bruner: The Cognitive Revolution in Educational Theory* (2007).

Jonathan Potter is Professor of Discourse Analysis and Dean of Social, Political and Geographical Sciences at Loughborough University. He has studied racism, argumentation, fact construction, and topics in social science theory and method. His most recent books include *Representing Reality* (1996), which attempted to provide a systematic overview, integration, and critique of constructionist research in social psychology, postmodernism, rhetoric, and ethno-methodology; and *Conversation and Cognition* (with Hedwig te Molder; 2005), in which a range of different researchers consider the implication of studies of interaction for understanding cognition. He is one of the founders of discursive psychology.

Justin B. Richland is Associate Professor of Law and Anthropology at the University of California, Irvine, and also Vice-Chair of the Department of Criminology, Law and Society. He holds a J.D. from the University of California at Berkeley School of Law and a Ph.D. in Anthropology from UCLA. Professor Richland's areas of research interest include legal semiotics and linguistic anthropology, anthropology of law, contemporary Native American law and politics, and North American colonialism. He is the author of several works on the legal discourses and practices of Native American nations, including *Arguing with Tradition: The Language of Law in Hopi Tribal Court* (2008) and, with Sarah Deer, *Introduction to Tribal Legal Studies* (2010). His articles have appeared in numerous leading peer review outlets. From 2005 to 2009 he served as Justice Pro Tempore of the Hopi Appellate Court, the Hopi Nation's highest court. He currently serves as co-editor (with John Conley and Elizabeth Mertz) of *PoLAR: Political and Legal Anthropology Review*.

David Rose is the director of *Reading to Learn*, an international literacy program that trains teachers across school and university sectors. He is Associate of the Department of Linguistics and the Faculty of Education and Social Work at the University of Sydney. His work has been particularly concerned with Indigenous Australian communities, languages, and education programs, with which he has worked for 25 years. He is a speaker of Pitjantjatjara, a language of

Australia's Western Desert, and is a member of the Western Desert Indigenous Ceremonial Law. His research interests include language and cultural contexts, literacy pedagogy, and teacher education. He is the author of *The Western Desert Code: An Australian Cryptogrammar* (2001), *Working with Discourse: Meaning beyond the Clause* (with J. R. Martin; 2007), *Genre Relations: Mapping Culture* (with J. R. Martin; 2008), and *Learning to Write, Reading to Learn: Genre, Knowledge and Pedagogy* (with J. R. Martin; in press).

Ingrid de Saint-Georges is Associate Professor in the Faculty for Language and Literature, Humanities, Arts and Education at the University of Luxembourg. Her research is in the field of language and work, vocational education and training, multimodal approaches to discourse, time, and unemployment, with publications in *Langage et Société*, the *European Journal of Psychology of Education*, *Visual Sociology*, *Vocations and Learning*. She has a special interest in prospective critique and in the study of anticipatory discourses. She is the co-editor of *Les objets dans la formation et les apprentissages* (2010) and "Linguistic competences in education and at work. Transitions and Transformations" (special issue, forthcoming), as well as the co-author of "Vos mains sont intelligentes": Interactions en formation professionnelle initiale" (2008).

Mary J. Schleppegrell earned a Ph.D. in Linguistics from Georgetown University and is currently Professor of Education at the University of Michigan, Ann Arbor, USA. Her research uses systemic functional linguistics to explore language and meaning in ways that illuminate issues in education, and she is currently leading a project to introduce teachers to functional grammar approaches that support reading comprehension and writing development. She is the author of *The Language of Schooling* (2004); co-author, with Zhihui Fang, of *Reading in Secondary Content Areas: A Language-Based Pedagogy* (2008); and co-editor, with Cecilia Colombi, of *Developing Advanced Literacy in First and Second Languages: Meaning with Power* (2002). Her work has appeared in *Discourse Processes, Journal of Pragmatics, Functions of Language, Written Communication, Linguistics and Education*, and other journals and edited volumes. She teaches courses in discourse analysis and linguistics in education.

Suzie Wong Scollon is an independent scholar based in Seattle, Washington, where she continues the multiple discourses project that has evolved over four decades of her partnership with Ron Scollon to investigate to what extent intertextuality and, more importantly, interdiscursivity across discourses can be achieved, to what extent, therefore, identities can be flexibly constructed, and to what extent incompatibilities of practice, cultural tools, and habitus show the idealized sociocultural movement of the post-modern dream to be an ideologized vision of a neoliberal society. She also continues the joint enterprise of integrating the study of anticipatory discourse with bringing about social change through mediated discourse analysis, the study of geosemiotics, narrative social analysis, and discourses of food, climate change, and energy.

Shi-xu has a Ph.D. from the University of Amsterdam and was Research Fellow at the University of Amsterdam, Lecturer at the National University of Singapore, and Reader at the University of Ulster. His books in English include *Cultural Representations*, *A Cultural Approach to Discourse*, *Read the Cultural Other* (lead-editor), and *Discourse as Cultural Struggle* (editor). He is founding Editor-in-Chief of *Journal of Multicultural Discourses* and series editor of *Studying Multicultural Discourses*. Currently he is Changjiang Distinguished Professor (Ministry of Education appointment, China), Director of the Centre for Contemporary Chinese Discourse Studies, Zhejiang University; and Qiantang Distinguished Professor, Director of the Centre for Discourse and Cultural Studies, Hangzhou Normal University. His central scholarly position is that contemporary language/communication/discourse must be studied as a site of cultural contest, cooperation and transformation.

Elsa Simões Lucas Freitas has a Ph.D. in Linguistics (Advertising Discourse) from Lancaster University and an MA in English and American literature from the University of Porto. She is an associate professor at Fernando Pessoa University (Portugal), where she teaches advertising, literature, English, and translation. She has published extensively in the fields of advertising and intersemiotic translation and her previous works include *Taboo in Advertising* (2008) and a chapter in Guy Cook's *The Language of Advertising* (2007). She has also published a number of articles on these subjects in international journals.

Graham Smart is an associate professor in the School of Linguistics and Language Studies at Carleton University, Ottawa, Canada. He has published numerous studies of writing and texts in workplace and academic settings. His book *Writing the Economy: Activity, Genre and Technology in the World of Banking* (2006) is an ethnographic study of the discourse practices and collaborative intellectual work of economists at the Bank of Canada, the country's central bank. The book explores the role that the economists' writing and texts play, in combination with economic models and other technologies, in the activities of knowledge-building, policy-making, and public communication. His current research focuses on environmental discourse, exploring the broad and complex body of discourse jointly created by government, business, and civil-society organizations as these groups construct and communicate arguments regarding the reality, impacts, and remediation of global climate change. Part of this research looks at how social actors on all sides of the climate-change debate employ different representations of science for rhetorical purposes in constructing their arguments.

Helen Spencer-Oatey is Director of the Centre for Applied Linguistics at the University of Warwick. Her primary research interests are in intercultural interaction, intercultural discourse, cross-cultural pragmatics, and cross-cultural psychology. She has published extensively in the field of intercultural communication. She is the editor of *Culturally Speaking* (2000/2008) and *e-Learning Initiatives in China* (2007), and co-editor of the *Handbook of Intercultural Communication* (2007). Her latest book, co-authored with Peter Franklin, is *Intercultural Interaction: A Multidisciplinary Approach to Intercultural Communication* (2009). Helen has published articles on pragmatics and intercultural communication in a wide range of journals. Since 2007, Helen has been leading the Global People project, funded by the Higher Education Funding Council for England. This researches the intercultural competencies needed for effective interaction in different contexts, such as international projects and international study.

Stefanie Stadler trained as a linguist and English language teacher and, in 2007, she graduated with a jointly awarded Ph.D. on the multimodal expression of (im)politeness, from the University of Auckland and the Universität Hamburg. With a background in intercultural communication studies and cultural anthropology as well as linguistics, Stefanie has a long-standing professional interest in the linguistic, social, and professional aspects of interacting in intercultural contexts. Having lived, studied, and worked in seven different countries across Europe, Asia, and Oceania, her interest in constructing and negotiating discourse and mutual understanding is as much motivated by personal interests and needs as by professional concernment. In 2010, Stefanie joined Nanyang Technological University, where she is actively engaged in research and teaching on intercultural communication, discourse analysis, pragmatics, multimodality, and cognitive sociolinguistics.

Peter K. W. Tan is Senior Lecturer at the Department of English Language and Literature in the National University of Singapore. His research interests include the development of Non-Anglo Englishes in Southeast Asia, including their literary and computer-mediated forms and discourses and how they have influenced naming conventions. He is the author of *A Stylistics of Drama* (1994) and has co-edited *Language as Commodity: Global Structures, Local Marketplaces* (with Rani Rubdy; 2008). He has also published in a wide range of journals, and in the books *Advances in Corpus Linguistics* (edited by Aijmer and Altenberg), *English in the World* (edited by Rubdy and Saraceni), *Complicities: Connections and Divisions* (edited by Sankaran *et al.*), *Evolving Identities* (edited by Ooi), *Language as Commodity* (edited by Tan and Rubdy), *Exploring the Language of Drama* (edited by Culpeper *et al.*), *Engineering Earth* (edited by Brunn), and *Singapore: The Encyclopedia* (the first two book chapters were co-authored with Vincent Ooi and Andy Chiang).

Hiromasa Tanaka is Professor at the School of Humanities and Social Sciences at Meisei University, Tokyo. He received his Ed.D. in curriculum, instruction, and technology in education from Temple University. His research interests are in the area of business discourse analysis and critical pedagogy with a special focus on English as a lingua franca. In Meisei University, he has initiated a socio-cultural theory-based teacher development program involving multinational pre-service and in-service teachers using English as lingua franca. Previously Hiro was a managing consultant of SNNO Institute of Management. He participated in several corporate change initiatives and training curriculum development projects for multinational employees in Japanese and non-Japanese companies in Korea, China, and the United States. Currently, he helps hydro-chemical and alternative energy industry companies in Japan, Iran, and Saudi Arabia develop training curricula. Recently he has contributed chapters to *The Handbook of Business Discourse* (2009) and *Language and Life in Japan* (2010).

Karen Thompson is a doctoral candidate in Educational Linguistics at the Stanford University School of Education. Prior to her time at Stanford, she worked for more than a decade in California public schools as a bilingual teacher, school reform consultant, and after-school program coordinator. Her research focuses on education policy, curriculum, and instruction for English learners in US schools.

Joanna Thornborrow is Reader at the Centre for Language and Communication Research in Cardiff University. Her main research interests are in discourse and conversation analysis, with a particular focus on institutional interaction and broadcast talk. Publications include *The Sociolinguistics of Narrative* (2005), co-edited with Jennifer Coates, and Power Talk: Language and Interaction in Institutional Discourse', in the 'Real Language' Series (2002). She has also published many journal articles and book chapters on media and institutional discourse, co-editing most recently with Martin Montgomery a special issue of *Discourse and Communication* (2010), on personalisation in broadcast news.

Amy B. M. Tsui is Pro-Vice-Chancellor and Vice-President of the University of Hong Kong. She assists the Vice-Chancellor in setting the direction and policy for the university's undergraduate curriculum reform, quality assurance of the undergraduate and postgraduate curricula, and promotion of teaching excellence at the university. Professor Tsui concurrently holds the position of Chair Professor in the Faculty of Education. She obtained her Ph.D. in linguistics in 1986 at the University of Birmingham, UK, and has published seven books and numerous journal papers in the areas of classroom discourse analysis, conversational analysis, teacher education, and language policy. She has also given numerous keynotes in international conferences and serves on the editorial/advisory board of a number of international refereed journals. Her recent publications are *Understanding Expertise in Teaching: Case Studies of ESL Teachers* (2003), and *Learning in School–University Partnership: Sociocultural Perspectives* (2009, as lead author) and *Language, Culture and Identity in Asian Contexts* (2007, as co-editor).

Ruth Wodak is Distinguished Professor of Discourse Studies at Lancaster University since 2004 and has remained affiliated with the University of Vienna, where she became full professor of Applied Linguistics in 1991. She is currently President of the *Societas Linguistica Europea*. In 2010 she was awarded an honorary doctorate by Örebro University, Sweden. Her research interests focus on discourse studies, identity politics and politics of the past, language and/in politics, racism and discrimination, and ethnographic methods of linguistic field work. She is a member of the editorial board of a range of linguistic journals and co-editor of the journals *Discourse and Society*, *Critical Discourse Studies*, and *Language and Politics*, and co-editor of the book series Discourse Approaches to Politics, Society and Culture. Her recent publications include *Qualitative Discourse Analysis in the Social Sciences* (with M. Krzyżanowski; 2008), *Migration, Identity and Belonging* (with G. Delanty and P. Jones; 2008; second revised edition, 2011), *The Discursive Construction of History. Remembering the Wehrmacht's War of Annihilation* (with H. Heer, W. Manoschek, and A. Pollak; 2008), *The Politics of Exclusion* (with M. Krzyżanowski; 2009), *Gedenken im Gedankenjahr* (with R. de Cillia; 2009), *The Discursive Construction of National Identity* (with R. de Cillia, M. Reisigl, and K. Liebhart; second revised edition, 2009), *The SAGE Handbook of Sociolinguistics* (with B. Johnstone and P. Kerswill, 2010) and *The Discourse of Politics in Action: Politics as Usual* (second revised edition, 2011).

Introduction

James Paul Gee and Michael Handford

Discourse analysis is the study of language in use. It is the study of the meanings we give language and the actions we carry out when we use language in specific contexts. Discourse analysis is also sometimes defined as the study of language above the level of a sentence, of the ways sentences combine to create meaning, coherence, and accomplish purposes. However, even a single sentence or utterance can be analyzed as a "communication" or as an "action," and not just as a sentence structure whose "literal meaning" flows from the nature of grammar. Grammar can tell us what "I pronounce you man and wife" literally means, but not when and where it actually means you are married.

Sometimes the term "pragmatics" is used for the study of language in use (Levinson, 1983), and people reserve the phrase "discourse analysis" for studying how the sentences in an oral or written "text" pattern together to create meaning and coherence and to define different genres (e.g. dialogues, narratives, reports, descriptions, explanations, and so forth). In this book, the phrase "discourse analysis" covers both pragmatics (the study of contextually specific meanings of language in use) and the study of "texts" (the study of how sentences and utterances pattern together to create meaning across multiple sentences or utterances).

We do not just mean things with language: we also do things with language. We accomplish actions, goals, and purposes. When a minister says "I pronounce you man and wife," he or she is marrying two people, not just communicating something to them. When a person calls the union of two gay men a "marriage," the speaker is helping to create or re-create the institution of marriage in a certain way, as an institutionally sanctioned union between two committed people, and not necessarily a man and a woman. When another person refuses to use the word for the union of two gay men, that speaker is helping to create or re-create a different institution of marriage.

Linguists make an important distinction between two types of meaning, a distinction that has relevance for discourse analysis. They distinguish between *utterance-type meaning* and *utterance-token meaning* (Levinson, 2000). Any word, phrase, or structure has a general range of possible meanings, what we might call its "meaning range." This is its utterance-type meaning. For example, the word "cat" has to do, broadly, with felines, and the (syntactic) structure "subject of a sentence" has to do, broadly, with naming a "topic" in the sense of "that which is being talked about."

However, words and phrases take on much more specific meanings in actual contexts of use. These are utterance-token meanings, or what we can also call "situated meanings." Thus, in a situation where we say something like "The world's big cats are all endangered," "cat" means things like lions and tigers; in a situation where we are discussing mythology and say something like "The cat was a sacred symbol to the ancient Egyptians," "cat" means real and pictured cats as symbols; and in a situation where we are discussing breakable decorative objects on our mantel and say something like "The cat broke," "cat" means the statue of a cat.

Subjects of sentences are always "topic-like" (this is their utterance-type meaning); in different situations of use, subjects take on a range of more specific meanings. In a debate, if I say, "The constitution only protects the rich," the subject of the sentence ("the constitution") is an entity about which a claim is being made; if a friend of yours has just arrived and I usher her in saying "Mary's here," the subject of the sentence ("Mary") is a center of interest or attention; and in a situation where I am commiserating with a friend and say something like "You really got cheated by that guy," the subject of the sentence ("you") is a center of empathy (signaled also by the fact that the normal subject of the active version of the sentence—"That guy really cheated you"—has been "demoted" from subject position through use of the "get-passive").

Discourse analysis can undertake one or both of two tasks, one related to utterance-type (general) meaning and one related to situated meaning. One task is what we can call the *utterance-type meaning task*. This task involves the study of correlations between form and function in language at the level of utterance-type meanings (general meanings). "Form" here means things like morphemes, words, phrases, or other syntactic structures (e.g. the subject position of a sentence). "Function" means meaning or the communicative purpose a form carries out.

The other task is what we can call *the utterance-token meaning or situated meaning task*. This task involves the study of correlations between form and function in language at the level of utterance-token meanings. Essentially, this task involves discovering the situation-specific or situated meanings of forms used in specific contexts of use.

Failing to distinguish between these two tasks can be dangerous, since very different issues of validity for discourse analysis come up with each of these tasks, as we will see below. Let's start with an example of the utterance-type meaning task. Specific forms in a language are prototypically used as tools to carry out certain communicative functions (that is, to express certain meanings). For example, consider the sentence labeled (1) below (adapted from Gagnon, 1987: 65).

> Though the Whig and Tory parties were both narrowly confined to the privileged classes, they represented different factions and tendencies.

This sentence is made up of two clauses, an *independent* (or *main*) clause ("they represented different factions and tendencies") and a *dependent* clause ("Though the Whig and Tory parties were both narrowly confined to the privileged classes"). These are statements about form. An independent clause has as one of its functions (at the utterance-type level) that it expresses an *assertion*; that is, it expresses a *claim* that the speaker/writer is making. A dependent clause has as one of its functions that it expresses information that is not asserted, but rather *assumed* or *taken for granted*. These are statements about function (meaning).

Normally (that is, technically speaking, in the "unmarked" case), in English, dependent clauses follow independent clauses. Thus, sentence (1) above might more normally appear as: "The Whig and Tory parties represented different factions, though they were both narrowly confined to the privileged classes." In (1) the dependent clause has been *fronted* (placed in front of the whole sentence). This is a statement about form. Such fronting has as one of its functions that the information in the clause is *thematized* (Halliday, 1994), that is, the information is treated as a launching off point or thematically important context from which to consider the claim in the following dependent clause. This is a statement about function.

To sum up, in respect to form-functioning mapping at the utterance-type level, we can say that sentence (1) renders its dependent clause ("Though the Whig and Tory parties were both narrowly confined to the privileged classes") a taken-for-granted, assumed, unargued for (i.e. unasserted), though important (thematized) context from which to consider the main claim in the independent clause ("they represented different factions and tendencies"). The dependent clause is, we might say, a concession. Other historians might prefer to make this concession the main asserted point, and thus they would use a different grammar, perhaps saying something like: "Though they represented different factions and tendencies, the Whig and Tory parties were both narrowly confined to the privileged classes."

At a fundamental level, all types of discourse analysis involve claims (however tacitly they may be acknowledged) about form–function matching at the utterance-type level. This is so because, if one is making claims about a piece of language even at a much more situated and contextualized level (which we will see in a moment), yet these claims violate what we know about how form and function are related to each other in language at the utterance-type level, these claims are quite suspect, unless there is evidence the speaker or writer is trying to violate these sorts of basic grammatical relationships in the language (e.g. in poetry).

As we have already said, the meanings with which forms are correlated at the utterance-type level are rather general (meanings like "assertion," "taken-for-granted information," "contrast," etc.). In reality, they represent only the meaning potential or meaning range of a form or structure, as we have said. The more specific or situated meanings that a form carries in a given context of use must be figured out through an engagement with our next task, the utterance-token or situated meaning task.

A second task that discourse analysis can undertake is what we called above the utterance-token or situated meaning task. When we actually utter or write a sentence, it has a *situated meaning* (Gee, 2010, 2011). Situated meanings arise because particular language forms take on specific or situated meanings in different, specific contexts of use.

Consider the word "coffee" as a very simple example of how situated meaning differs from utterance-type meaning. "Coffee" is an arbitrary form (other languages use different sounding words for coffee) that correlates with meanings having to do with the substance coffee (this is its meaning potential). At a more specific level, however, we have to use context to determine what the word means in any situated way. In one context, "coffee" may mean a brown liquid ("The coffee spilled, go get a mop"); in another one it may mean grains of a certain sort ("The coffee spilled, go get a broom"); in another it may mean containers ("The coffee spilled, stack it again"); and it can mean other things in other contexts, e.g. berries of a certain sort, a certain flavor, or a skin color. We can even use the word with a novel situated meaning, as in "You give me a coffee high" or "Big Coffee is as bad as Big Oil as corporate actors."

To see a further example of situated meanings at work, consider sentence (1) again ("Though the Whig and Tory parties were both narrowly confined to the privileged classes, they represented different factions"). We said above that an independent clause represents an assertion (a claim that something is true). But this general form–function correlation can mean different specific things in actual contexts of use, and can indeed be even mitigated, or altogether undercut.

For example, in one context, say between two like-minded historians, the claim that the Whig and Tory parties represented different factions may just be taken as a *reminder* of a "fact" they both agree on. On the other hand, between two quite diverse historians, the same claim may be taken as a *challenge* (despite YOUR claim that shared class interests mean no real difference in political parties, the Whig and Tory parties in seventeenth-century England were really different). And, of course, on stage as part of a drama, the claim about the Whig and Tory parties is not even a "real" assertion, but a "pretended" one.

Furthermore, the words "privileged," "contending," and "factions" will take on different specific meanings in different contexts. For example, in one context, "privileged" might mean "rich," while in another context it might mean "educated" or "cultured" or "politically connected" or "born into a family with high status" or some combination of the above or something else altogether.

To analyze Gagnon's sentence or his whole text, or any part of it, at the level of situated meanings—that is, in order to carry out the situated meaning task—would require a close study of some of the relevant contexts within which that text is placed and which it, in turn, helps to create. This might mean inspecting the parts of Gagnon's text that precede or follow a part of the text we want to analyze. It might mean inspecting other texts related to Gagnon's. It might mean studying debates among different types of historians and debates about educational standards and policy (since Gagnon's text was meant to argue for a view about what history ought to be taught in schools). It might mean studying these debates historically, across time, and in terms of the actual situations Gagnon and his text were caught up in (e.g. debates about new school history standards in Massachusetts, a state where Gagnon once helped write a version of the standards). It might mean many other things as well. Obviously, there is no space in a paper of this scope to develop such an analysis.

The issue of validity for analyses of situated meaning is quite different from the issue of validity for analyses of utterance-type meanings. We saw above that the issue of validity for analyses of utterance-type meanings basically comes down to choosing and defending a particular grammatical theory of how form and function relate in language at the level of utterance-type meanings, as well as, of course, offering correct grammatical and semantic descriptions of one's data. On the other hand, the issue of validity for analyses of situated meaning is much harder. In fact, it involves a very deep problem, known as "the frame problem" (Gee, 2010).

The frame problem is this: Any aspect of context can affect the meaning of an (oral or written) utterance. Context, however, is indefinitely large, ranging from local matters like the positioning of bodies and eye gaze, through people's beliefs, to historical, institutional, and cultural settings. No matter how much of the context we have considered in offering an interpretation of an utterance, there is always the possibility of considering other and additional aspects of the context, and these new considerations may change how we interpret the utterance. Where do we cut off consideration of context? How can we be sure any interpretation is "right," if considering further aspects of the context might well change that interpretation?

Let us give an example of a case where changing how much of the context of an utterance we consider changes significantly the interpretation we give to that utterance. Take a claim like: "Many children die in Africa before they are five years old because they get infectious diseases like malaria." What is the appropriate amount of context within which to assess this claim? We could consider just medical facts, a narrow context. And in the context the claim seems unexceptional. But widen the context and consider the context described below:

> Malaria, an infectious disease, is one of the most severe public health problems worldwide. It is a leading cause of death and disease in many developing countries, where young children and pregnant women are the groups most affected. Worldwide, one death in three is from an infectious or communicable disease. However, almost all these deaths occur in the non-industrialized world. Health inequality effects not just how people live, but often dictates how and at what age they die. (See http://www.cdc.gov/malaria/impact/index.htm and http://ucatlas.ucsc.edu/cause.php)

This context would seem to say that so many children in Africa die early not because of infectious diseases but because of poverty and economic underdevelopment. While this widening of the context does not necessarily render the claim "Many children die in Africa before they are five years old because they get infectious diseases like malaria" false, at least it suggests that a narrow construal of "because" here (limiting it to physical and medical causes) effaces the workings of poverty and economics.

The frame problem is both a problem and a tool. It is problem because our discourse analytic interpretations (just like people's everyday interpretations of language) are always vulnerable to changing as we widen the context within which we interpret a piece of language. It is a tool because we can use it—by widening the context—to see what information and values are being left unsaid or effaced in a piece of language.

The frame problem, of course, raises problems about validity for discourse analysis. We cannot really argue that an analysis is valid unless we keep widening the context in which we consider a piece of language until the widening appears to make no difference to our interpretation. At that point, we can stop and make our claims (which are open, of course, to later falsification, as in all empirical inquiry).

It should be clear now that discourse analysis involves studying language in the context of society, culture, history, institutions, identity formation, politics, power, and all the other things that language helps us to create and which, in turn, render language meaningful in certain ways and able to accomplish certain purposes. As such, discourse analysis is both a branch of linguistics and a contribution to the social sciences. Because of its relevance to so many social and cultural issues, discourse analysis of one form or another is used in a great many disciplines, for example history, anthropology, psychiatry, sociology, political science, or education.

There are many different types of discourse analysis. Some forms are closely tied to linguistics and tie their claims closely to facts about grammar and about the way different grammatical structures function in different contexts of use. Other forms are less closely tied to linguistics or grammar and focus on the development of themes or images across the sentences or utterances in an oral or written text. Some forms of discourse analysis are primarily interested in description and explanation. Others are also interested in tying language to politically, socially, or culturally contentious issues and in intervening in these issues in some way. These latter forms of discourse analysis are often called "critical discourse analysis" (Fairclough, 2003; see Fairclough, this volume).

People do not make meaning just as individuals. They do so as parts of social groups which agree on, contest, or negotiate norms and values about how language ought to used and what things ought to mean. Many forms of discourse analysis are thus connected to views about and studies of different types of social groups. These groups are called by different names, depending on the aspects of social activity that the discourse analyst wants to stress: discourse communities, speech communities, communities of practice, activity systems, discourses ("big D Discourses"), networks, and cultures. Whatever term is used, discourse analysis is always, at heart, simultaneously an analysis of language and one of practices in society.

The main importance of discourse analysis lies in the fact that, through speaking and writing in the world, we make the world meaningful in certain ways and not in others. We shape, produce, and reproduce the world through language in use. In turn the world we shape and help to create works in certain ways to shape us as humans. This mutual shaping process can have profound consequences for people's lives. In the end, discourse analysis matters because discourse matters. We, discourse analysts, want to expose to light the often taken-for-granted workings of discourse, because, like in the study of atoms, cells, and stars, there is here a great wealth scientific knowledge to be gained. But there is also insight to be gained into how to make the world a better and more humane place.

This collection contains 46 chapters, which are separated into six sections: *approaches to discourse analysis, genre and register, developments in spoken discourse, educational applications, institutional applications*, and *identity, culture and discourse*. As with all such categorizations, other groupings are possible, and certain chapters may seem more prototypical of the category than others. Moreover, some chapters may easily fit in two or three categories simultaneously; for instance Vijay Bhatia's chapter on professional written genres is in the *genre and register* section, but would be equally comfortable in the institutional applications section. Janet Holmes and Julia deBres' chapter on ethnicity and humour in the workplace could have been placed in the spoken discourse or culture and discourse sections. Therefore we suggest that the reader use the categorizations merely as guide; also, each author suggests related chapters and areas at the end of his or her chapter, which the reader is encouraged to explore. Further material for certain chapters is also available on the Routledge website.

In designing this handbook, we intended it to be accessible and relevant for the widest possible audience. Discourse analysis is indeed an interdisciplinary approach, and this book should allow readers from various academic backgrounds and disciplines to understand how discourse analysis is done, and why it might be relevant to them. With this in mind, nearly all the chapters contain expository analysis of real data. Readers should be able to see how the tools of discourse analysis are used, and on what types of data. A quick glance through the list of authors will show that the handbook contains many of the leading figures in their fields, who continue to produce groundbreaking work. Such researchers have been encouraged to give a more personal account of their research and of their motivations than is typical in publications of this sort, and to place their research in the academic wider context. The handbook is, we believe, also unusual in the geographical spread of the contributors and in the range of topics covered. In these ways we hope to have assembled a collection that, in the words of one contributor, not only defines the field but also helps to drive it forward.

References

Fairclough, N. (2003) *Analysing Discourse: Textual Analysis for Social Research*. London: Routledge.

Gagnon, P. (1987) *Democracy's Untold Story: What World History Textbooks Neglect*. Washington, DC: American Federation of Teachers.

Gee, J. P. (2010) *An Introduction to Discourse Analysis: Theory and Method*. Third Edition. London: Routledge.

Gee, J. P. (2011) *Social Linguistics and Literacies: Ideology in Discourses*. Fourth Edition. London: Taylor & Francis.

Halliday, M. A. K. (1994) *An Introduction to Functional Grammar*. Second Edition. London: Edward Arnold.

Levinson, S. C. (1983) *Pragmatics*. Cambridge: Cambridge University Press.

Levinson, S. C. (2000) *Presumptive Meanings: The Theory of Generalized Conversational Implicature*. Cambridge, MA: MIT Press.

Part I
Approaches to discourse analysis

1

Critical discourse analysis

Norman Fairclough

Introduction

Critical discourse analysis (CDA) brings the critical tradition of social analysis into language studies and contributes to critical social analysis a particular focus on discourse and on relations between discourse and other social elements (power relations, ideologies, institutions, social identities, and so forth). Critical social analysis can be understood as normative and explanatory critique. It is normative critique in that does not simply describe existing realities but also evaluates them, assesses the extent to which they match up to various values, which are taken (more or less contentiously) to be fundamental for just or decent societies (e.g. certain standards – material but also political and cultural – of human well-being). It is explanatory critique in that it does not simply describe existing realities but seeks to explain them, for instance by showing them to be effects of structures or mechanisms or forces that the analyst postulates and whose reality s/he seeks to test out (e.g. inequalities in wealth, income and access to various social goods might be explained as an effect of mechanisms and forces associated with 'capitalism').

There is a long tradition within critical social analysis, evident for instance in Marx (Marsden, 1999), of viewing social reality as 'conceptually mediated', as we might put it – meaning that there are no social events or practices without representations, construals, conceptualizations or theories of these events and practices; or, to put it in different terms, that social realities have a reflexive character, i.e. the way people see and represent and interpret and conceptualize them is a part of these realities. So the 'objects' of critical social analysis are, we might say, 'material–semiotic' (Jessop, 2004), that is, simultaneously material and semiotic in character, and a central concern is with relations between the material and the semiotic (or 'discourse'), which I would see as dialectical relations (Fairclough, 2006). A consequence is that critical social analysis has an interdisciplinary character, since the nature of its 'objects' requires it to bring together disciplines whose primary concern is with material facets of social realities and disciplines whose primary concern is with semiotic facets. I will argue that it has, more specifically, a 'trans-disciplinary' character, in that dialogue across different disciplines is seen as the source for the theoretical and methodological development of each of them (see Jessop and Sum, 2001 on 'post-disciplinary or 'trans-disciplinary' research as – in a sense – a return to the 'pre-disciplinary' positions of Karl Marx or Adam Smith, for instance; see also Fairclough and Graham, 2002). In these terms, CDA contributes a semiotic emphasis and a 'point of entry' into trans-disciplinary critical social analysis (Fairclough, 2009b).

The chapter will be structured as follows. First I shall elaborate what I have said so far about critical social analysis and I shall further discuss CDA as a part of critical social analysis. Second, I shall present one version of CDA, and, third, a trans-disciplinary research methodology associated with it. Fourth and finally, I shall illustrate CDA through a discussion of aspects of the current financial and economic crisis. The version of CDA is the one which I have been developing and using in my recent work. It differs in various respects from versions in earlier publications (e.g. Fairclough, 1989, 1992, 2010).

Critical analysis of discourse as a part of critical social analysis

What distinguishes critical social analysis from forms of social analysis that are not critical is its emphasis upon existing social realities as humanly produced constraints, which in certain respects unnecessarily reduce human flourishing or well-being and increase human suffering; upon historical explanation of how and why such social realities have come into being; and upon possibilities for transforming existing realities in ways that enhance well-being and reduce suffering. I suggested above that this critique is normative and explanatory, concerned with both values and causes. Some versions of critique are only normative or moral, but I take the (Marxist) view that changing the world for the better depends upon being able to explain how it has come to be the way it is. It is one thing to critique people's language and practices on the grounds that they are racist, but another thing to explain why and how racism emerges or becomes virulent amongst certain people in certain circumstances. A purely normative or moral critique is not enough if the aim is to change social realities for the better; but values, evaluation and moral critique are a necessary part of critical social science (Sayer, 2003).

I referred above to the tradition in critical social science of viewing social reality as 'conceptually mediated', such that the 'objects' of critical social analysis are simultaneously material and semiotic in character. This means that dialectical relations between the material and the semiotic are a necessary focus in both normative and explanatory critique. The version of CDA which I outline below is well placed to bring a focus on these material–semiotic relations into trans-disciplinary critical social research.

CDA has for instance addressed the ideological character of discourse (Fairclough, 1989). Take for example the commonsensical construal of public finances as being in all essentials analogous to household budgets, a construal beloved by former British Prime Minister Margaret Thatcher and by many other politicians, so that for instance governments have to 'budget and save' just as households do. This is open to normative critique as a false claim, in that the analogy does not stand up to serious economic scrutiny, and as an ideological one, in the sense that it is a discourse that can contribute to sustaining an unjust and inequitable socio-economic order. Currently, in the UK for instance, one finds it in practical reasoning by politicians who are in favour of cutting public expenditure and public services to restore public finances in the aftermath of government use of public money to rescue the banks, which not only threatens to turn the recession into depression but arguably places on the general public most of the burden of paying for the (bankers') crisis. To explain the strategy of off-loading onto the public the costs of rescuing the markets from themselves, of which there are many other historical instances, we need to bring in material–structural factors associated with the character of capitalism, but also semiotic factors – including examples of the causal power of common sense and of commonsensical construals in bringing about material effects (particular trajectories within and out of the crisis). Causes can be semiotic as well as material, and CDA can contribute to the project, within critical social science, of showing the relationships between the two.

One version of CDA

In this section I shall briefly present the primary concepts, categories and relations associated with the version of CDA I have recently worked with.

Discourse is commonly used in various senses, including (a) meaning-making as an element of the social process; (b) the language associated with a particular social field or practice (e.g. 'political discourse'); (c) a way of construing aspects of the world associated with a particular social perspective (e.g. a 'neo-liberal discourse of globalization'). It is easy to confuse them, so I prefer to use *semiosis* for the first, most abstract and general sense (Fairclough *et al.*, 2004) – which has the further advantage of suggesting that discourse analysis is concerned with various 'semiotic modalities', of which language is only one (others are visual images and 'body language').

Semiosis is viewed here as an element of the social process, which is *dialectically* related to others. Relations between elements are dialectical in the sense of being different but not 'discrete', i.e. fully separate; each one 'internalizes' the others without being reducible to them (Harvey, 1996). So social relations, power, institutions, beliefs and cultural values are in part semiotic, i.e. they internalize semiosis without being reducible to it. This means for example that, although we should analyse political institutions or business organizations as partly semiotic objects, it would be a mistake to treat them as purely semiotic, if only because then we couldn't ask the key question: what is the relationship between semiotic and other elements? CDA focuses not just upon semiosis as such, but on *relations between semiotic and other social elements*. The nature of this relationship varies between institutions and organizations and according to time and place, and it needs to be established through analysis.

The social process can be seen as the interplay between three levels of social reality: social *structures*, *practices* and *events* (Chouliaraki and Fairclough, 1999). Social practices 'mediate' the relationship between general and abstract social structures and particular and concrete social events; social fields, institutions and organizations are constituted as networks of social practices. In this approach to CDA, analysis is focused on two dialectical relations: between structure (especially social practices as an intermediate level of structuring) and events (or: structure and action, structure and strategy); and, within each, between semiotic and other elements. There are three major ways in which semiosis relates to other elements of social practices and of social events: as a facet of action; in the construal (representation) of aspects of the world; and in the constitution of identities. And there are three semiotic (or discourse-analytical) categories corresponding to these: genre, discourse and style.

Genres are semiotic ways of acting and interacting such as news or job interviews, reports or editorials in newspapers, or advertisements on TV or the internet. Part of doing a job, or running a country, is to interact semiotically or communicatively in certain ways, and such activities have distinctive sets of genres associated with them. *Discourses* are semiotic ways of construing aspects of the world (physical, social or mental) that can generally be identified with different positions or perspectives of different groups of social actors. For instance, the lives of poor people are construed not only through different discourses associated with different social practices (in politics, medicine, social welfare, academic sociology), but through different discourses in each, which correspond to differences of position and perspective. I use 'construe' in preference to 'represent' in order to emphasize an active and often difficult process of 'grasping' the world from a particular perspective (Fairclough, 2009a). *Styles* are identities, or 'ways of being', in their semiotic aspect – for instance, being a 'manager' in the currently fashionable way, in business or in universities, is partly a matter of developing the right semiotic style.

The semiotic dimension of (networks of) social practices that constitute social fields, institutions, organizations etc. is *orders of discourse* (Fairclough, 1992); the semiotic dimension of events is *texts*. Orders of discourse are particular configurations of different genres, different discourses, and different styles. An order of discourse is a social structuring of semiotic difference, a particular social ordering of relationships between different ways of making meaning – different genres, discourses and styles. So for example the network of social practices that constitutes the field of education, or a particular educational organization such as a university, is constituted semiotically as an order of discourse. Texts are to be understood in an inclusive sense: they are not only written texts but also e.g. conversations and interviews, as well as the 'multi-modal' texts (mixing language and visual images) of television and the internet. Some events consist almost entirely of texts (e.g. a lecture or an interview), in others texts have a relatively small part (e.g. a game of chess).

Discourses that originate in some particular social field or institution (to anticipate the example, neo-liberal economic discourse, which originated within academic economics and business) may be *recontextualized* in others (e.g. in the political field, or in the wider educational field). Recontextualization has an ambivalent character (Chouliaraki and Fairclough, 1999): it can be seen as 'colonization' of one field or institution by another, but also as 'appropriation' of 'external' discourses, often incorporation of discourses into strategies pursued by particular groups of social agents within the recontextualizing field.

Discourses may under certain conditions be *operationalized*, 'put into practice' – a dialectical process with three aspects: they may be *enacted* as new ways of (inter)acting, they may be *inculcated* as new ways of being (identities), or they may be physically *materialized*, e.g. as new ways of organizing space in architecture. Enactment and inculcation may themselves take semiotic forms: a new management discourse (e.g. the discourse of marketized 'new public management', which has invaded public sector fields like education and health) may be enacted as management procedures, which include new genres of interaction between managers and workers, or it may be inculcated as identities which semiotically include the styles of the new type of managers. The modality is important: I have formulated these processes of operationalization as possibilities ('may'), because they are not necessary but contingent processes, which may or may not take place depending upon a range of factors and conditions, both material and semiotic (Fairclough *et al.*, 2004).

CDA oscillates as I have indicated, between a focus on *structures* (especially the intermediate level of structuring of social practices) and a focus on *strategies*, a focus on shifts in the structuring of semiotic difference (orders of discourse) and a focus on strategies of social agents that manifest themselves in texts. In both perspectives, a central concern is shifting relations between genres, between discourses and between styles: change in social structuring of relations between them that achieves relative permanence and stability in orders of discourse, and the ongoing working of relations between them in texts. The term *interdiscursivity* is reserved for the latter: the inter-discursivity of a text is a part of its intertextuality (Fairclough, 1992) – a question of what genres, discourses and styles it draws upon, and how it works them into particular articulations. Textual analysis also includes linguistic analysis, and analysis – where appropriate – of visual images and 'body language'; and these features of texts can be seen as realizing their interdiscursive features.

A trans-disciplinary research methodology

The focus I have just indicated on relations between semiosis and other elements calls for interdisciplinary research – more exactly, it requires CDA to be integrated within frameworks for *trans-disciplinary* research. An example is the framework I have used in recent publications – 'cultural political economy', which combines elements from three disciplines: a form of economic analysis, a theory of the state, and CDA (Jessop, 2004; Fairclough, 2006). What distinguishes trans-disciplinary from other forms of interdisciplinary research is that, in bringing disciplines and theories together to address research issues, it sees 'dialogue' between them as a source for the theoretical and methodological development of each of them. For example, *recontextualization* was introduced as a concept and as a category in CDA through a dialogue with Basil Bernstein's sociology of pedagogy, where it originated (Chouliaraki and Fairclough, 1999).

I refer to a 'methodology' rather than a 'method.' Methodology is to be understood as a trans-disciplinary process of theoretically constructing the *object of research* (Bourdieu and Wacquant, 1992) for a research project; particular methods are selected according to how the *object of research* is constructed. So it is not just a matter of 'applying methods' in the usual sense, and we cannot so sharply separate theory and method. This version of CDA is associated with a *general* method, which I briefly indicated in the final paragraph of the last section; but the specific methods used for a particular piece of research arise from the theoretical process of constructing its object.

We can identify 'steps' or 'stages' in the methodology: these are essential parts of the methodology (a matter of its 'theoretical order'), and, while it does make partial sense to proceed from one to the next (a matter of the 'procedural order'), the relationship between them in doing research is not simply that of sequential order. For instance, the 'step' I refer to below, of constructing the 'object of research' (Step 2 of Stage 1), does need to precede subsequent steps, but it also makes sense to 'loop' back to it in the light of subsequent steps, seeing the formulation of the object of research as a preoccupation throughout. It is also helpful to distinguish 'theoretical' and 'procedural' from the 'presentational' order one chooses to follow in writing a paper, for instance – other generally rhetorical factors will affect the order in which one presents one's analysis.

The methodology can be seen as a variant of Bhaskar's 'explanatory critique' (Bhaskar 1986, Chouliaraki and Fairclough, 1999), which can be formulated in four 'stages' that can be further elaborated as 'steps'.

Stage 1: Focus upon a social wrong, in its semiotic aspects.
Stage 2: Identify obstacles to addressing the social wrong.
Stage 3: Consider whether the social order 'needs' the social wrong.
Stage 4: Identify possible ways past the obstacles.

Stage 1: Focus upon a social wrong, in its semiotic aspect

CDA is a form of critical social science geared to the better understanding of the nature and sources of social wrongs, the obstacles to addressing them, and possible ways of overcoming those obstacles. 'Social wrongs' can be understood in broad terms as aspects of social systems, forms or orders that are detrimental to human well-being and could in principle be ameliorated if not eliminated, though perhaps only through major changes in these systems, forms or orders. Examples might be poverty, forms of inequality, lack of freedom or racism. Of course, what constitutes a 'social wrong' is a controversial matter, and CDA is inevitably involved in debates and arguments about this that go on all the time.

We can elaborate Stage 1 in two steps:

> *Step 1*: Select a research topic that relates to, or points up, a social wrong and that can productively be approached in a trans-disciplinary way, with a particular focus on dialectical relations between semiotic and other 'moments'.

We might for instance conclude that such an approach is potentially 'productive' because there are significant semiotic features of the topic that have not been sufficiently attended to. A topic might attract our interest because it has been prominent in the relevant academic literature, or because it is a focus of practical attention in the domain or field at issue (the current crisis, for instance, is both). Topics are often 'given', and they sometimes virtually select themselves – who could doubt for instance that 'immigration', 'terrorism', 'globalization' or 'security' are important contemporary topics, with significant implications for human well-being, which researchers should attend to? Selecting such topics has the advantage of ensuring that research is relevant to the issues, problems and wrongs of the day, but it also has the danger that their very obviousness can lead us to take them too much at face value. We cannot assume that such topics are coherent research objects; to 'translate' topics into objects, we need to theorize them:

> *Step 2*: Construct objects of research for initially identified research topics by theorizing them in a trans-disciplinary way.

Let me anticipate the example I shall discuss in the next section: the initially identified research topic is the current financial and economic crisis. This is a huge topic, various aspects of which might productively be approached with a focus on dialectical relations between semiotic and material moments. Constructing objects of research is a trans-disciplinary process, so we would need to decide which relevant bodies of social science and theory to engage with. The 'cultural political economy' framework I mentioned above is a good choice in this case, though one might well want to combine it with other approaches (e.g. on 'moral economy', see Sayer, 2004). Social wrongs we might focus upon include: the largely unquestioned dominance of a 'neo-liberal' economic order that turned out to be deeply flawed, with dire consequences for a great many people; the greed of people like bankers, which contributed to the crisis and to increasing inequalities of wealth and income that have various negative social consequences; the policies of certain governments to make ordinary people bear most of the burden of repairing public finances, depleted as these are as a result of support given to the banks, for instance. Each of these has significant semiotic aspects. One possible construction of an object of research associated with the first of them might be to focus on the neo-liberal 'ideas' (semiotically, discourses) that informed, shaped and were used to legitimize the economic order and on the material effects of these ideas/ discourses.

Stage 2: Identify obstacles to addressing the social wrong

Stage 2 approaches the social wrong in a rather indirect way, by asking what it is about the way in which social life is structured and organized that prevents the social wrong from being addressed. This requires bringing in analyses of the social order, and one 'point of entry' into this process can be semiotic, which entails selecting and analysing relevant 'texts' and addressing dialectical relations between semiosis and other social elements.

Steps 1–3 can be formulated as follows:

1. Analyse dialectical relations between semiosis and other social elements: between orders of discourse and other elements of social practices, between texts and other elements of events.
2. Select texts, and points of focus and categories for their analysis, in the light of, and appropriately to, the constitution of the object of research.
3. Carry out analysis of texts – both interdiscursive analysis and linguistic/semiotic analysis.

Taken together, these three steps indicate an important feature of this version of CDA: textual analysis is only a part of semiotic analysis (discourse analysis), and the former must be adequately framed within the latter. The aim is to develop a specifically semiotic 'point of entry' into objects of research that are constituted in a trans-disciplinary way, through dialogue between different theories and disciplines. Analysis of texts can effectively contribute to this only in so far as it is located within a wider analysis of the object of research, in terms of dialectical relations between semiotic and other elements – an analysis that comprehends relations between the level of social practices and the level of events (and between orders of discourse and texts).

Stage 3: Consider whether the social order 'needs' the social wrong

It is not awfully obvious what this means, and I shall try to clarify it by again anticipating the example, with respect to a social wrong I identified above: governments trying to make ordinary people pay for the public costs of the crisis. In what sense might the social order 'need' this? A broad answer might be to show that capitalism has historically not only asserted the supreme worth of markets and, to varying degrees, the need for them to operate with minimal political and social control, but has also claimed that it is the job of the state to bail them out when periodic (but regular and predictable) crises occur. Stage 3 leads us to consider whether the social wrong in focus is inherent to the social order, whether it can be addressed within it, or only by changing it. Stage 3 is a way of linking 'is' to 'ought': if a social order can be shown inherently to give rise to major social wrongs, that is a reason for thinking that perhaps it should be changed. This stage also connects with questions of ideology: discourse is ideological in so far as it contributes to sustaining particular relations of power and domination.

Stage 4: Identify possible ways past the obstacles

Stage 4 moves the analysis from negative to positive critique: identifying, with a focus on dialectical relations between semiosis and other elements, possibilities within the existing social process for overcoming obstacles to addressing the social wrong in question. This includes developing a semiotic 'point of entry' into research on the ways in which these obstacles are actually tested, challenged and resisted, be it within organized political or social groups or move-ments or, more informally, by people in the course of their ordinary working, social and domestic lives. A specifically semiotic focus would include, in the case of the crisis, ways in which the discourses, narratives, arguments etc. of business and governments are being contested and replaced by others, as part of struggles against mainstream strategies and in support of alternatives.

Illustration – critical research on the financial and economic crisis

The events of the financial and economic crisis are relatively clear, but its causes are more contentious. There are numerous explanatory accounts of it that differ, for instance in the relative weight they give to structural causes (e.g. recurrent economic 'cycles') as opposed to agential or 'subjective' causes (e.g. the failures – greed, incompetence etc – of key agents such as bankers, government ministers or regulators). Most explanatory accounts directly or indirectly recognize that semiosis, or discourse, needs to figure in explanations. For instance Roger Bootle, a respected British economist and consultant, after identifying eight major causal factors, concludes that it is nevertheless possible to identify a single cause that underlies them: the impact of economic *ideas* (Bootle, 2009), most especially the 'efficient market hypothesis' – the idea, in its extreme form, that markets are always right, which in many cases ceased to be treated as a hypothesis and came to be treated as an established fact. What Bootle calls 'ideas' amounts to semiosis or discourse – and, more specifically, we might say a Discourse of (or about) economic (including financial) activities (a 'big' Discourse that subsumes a number of 'small' discourses – Gee, 1999), which (amongst other things) construes 'markets' in certain ways (as 'knowing best', as efficient, as rational, etc). So potent and prestigious was this Discourse that key players in business, government and financial governance failed to see or refused to see what were for some more perceptive commentators the extreme dangers of the levels of debt that were building up, some of the so-called 'innovations' in finance, and so forth. The Discourse, we might say, became dogma. It was also extensively recontextualized, for instance within the International Monetary Fund (IMF)/World Bank 'Washington Consensus', which was internationally promoted, if not imposed, as part of a model for capitalism that informed processes of 'transition' from socialism to capitalism in Central and Eastern Europe. And it was operationalized, enacted in practices (and, semiotically, genres) such as those associated with the 'light-touch' regulation of banks and other financial institutions, and inculcated (though workplace disciplines, the mass media and education) in the identities of economic 'subjects' (producers and consumers) and, semiotically, into their styles.

Analysing, interpreting and explaining these processes might be part of one possible piece of research oriented towards the crisis, which might seek to assess the impact of this Discourse and its operationalizations in the establishment, maintenance and legitimation of the neo-liberal order, but also to address the question of how the Discourse might have contributed to the apparent incapacity of bankers, regulators, governments and so on to understand the dangers of that order and to anticipate its crises. But it follows from what I have said above that the object of such a piece of research should be constructed in a trans-disciplinary way. For instance, from cultural political economy (CPE) one might take a theory of structuration that focuses on dialectical relations between structures and strategies and includes a framework for explaining how, from a variety of strategies, certain ones come to be selected and retained (and, in CDA terms, recontextualized and operationalized). What are the factors and conditions (both semiotic and material/structural) that led to the selection and retention of neo-liberal strategy (from the 1970s onwards) and of its semiotic moments (including the Discourse discussed above) rather than of other strategies (Fairclough et al., 2004)? CPE also includes ways of addressing the processes of systemic and governance failure, which link this historical account of neo-liberalism to the current crisis.

These observations roughly address issues related to Stage 1 of the methodology, identifying a social wrong (the predominance of a flawed economic order, whose failure has caused serious damage to many) with a significant semiotic aspect and construction of research objects for addressing it. If we turn to Stage 2, the primary question is: what obstacles have there been, and are there still, to addressing the social wrong? Let us focus on the current period. Trans-disciplinary analysis of the contemporary political–economic situation might suggest that the neo-liberal order, and Discourse, have been weakened to the point that the obstacles to surpassing it that one might have identified a few years ago are much less daunting. But this does not mean that any new strategy for replacing neo-liberalism, whatever that may be, would necessarily address in its essentials the central wrong at issue – a new strategy may not overcome the problems of an economic order with unjust effects (e.g. in terms of inequalities of wealth and income) and a liability to devastating crises. Analysis of recent and current texts, for instance from the coverage of, commentary on and debate over the crisis in the political public sphere of countries like Britain and the USA, can be used to identify the range and positioning of discourses (or Discourses), and can be integrated within a trans-disciplinary framework based upon CPE which, amongst other things, maps d/Discourses onto strategies for responding to the crisis and for moving towards an economic order that may facilitate economic recovery. One tendency that might be focused upon, for instance, is for certain governments, including the British one, to pursue a strategy for the restitution of the *status quo ante* with only relatively minor modifications of regulatory systems.

Here is, for example, a short extract from a speech by British Prime Minister Gordon Brown to the Foreign Press Association in London, January 2009:

> We know now that financial institutions are international, that capital flows are global, but their regulators and supervisors have remained so far only national. So we have highly

interdependent financial flows which dwarf wor
policing them. And as the downturn spreads acro
cross-border flows growing more slowly than
favouring their domestic lending over foreign l
halted if we are to avoid the risk of a damaging
deglobalisation with adverse consequences for all
for an open global economy where countries
finance faster development which benefits us all
responding when these markets fail.

social control of the fu
parts of the banking
environmental cri
of possibility a
Here is a s
March 2

A short extract can only give a partial impressio
'globalisation' that Brown wishes to defend is
globalisation', and he is effectively defending th
(implicitly therefore construing the crisis as a crisis *in* rather than *of* neo-liberalism,
speech incorporates without modification the established legitimizing narrative for this form
of globalization, 'globalisation produces growth which produces prosperity for all and reduces
poverty', despite the flaws that have been exposed in this model (e.g. long-term tendencies to
reduce wages and to increase the gap between rich and poor), which he does not address, and
despite its failure and the consequential crisis. He construes features of this model ('financial
institutions are international', 'capital flows are global', 'highly interdependent financial flows
which dwarf world GDP') as simply the way the world now is, and condemns 'deleveraging',
which might be seen (in an appropriate form and within appropriate limits) as a reasonable
response to the excessive 'leveraging' which was widely seen as a cause of the financial crisis, as
a 'risk' and as a 'damaging spiral', which would have 'adverse consequences for all our
economies'. At the same time he implies that 'consensus' for such an 'open global economy'
could be at risk. His solution to this danger is international regulation, 'which can provide a
means of responding when these markets fail', presupposing that they do and will fail. From
this speech and other evidence it seems that the British government is committed to restoring
the *status quo ante* with minor modifications, in some cases drawing upon the d/Discourses and
narratives of the more triumphant years of neo-liberalism in the reasons they give for the
actions and policies they propose. (See Fairclough and Fairclough, forthcoming, for an
approach to the analysis of practical reasoning in political discourse applied to political
responses to the crisis.)

Stage 3, addressing the question of whether the social order needs the social wrong, gives rise to
the question of whether it is possible within a capitalist system to develop and implement a new
strategy, which can overcome the injustices and the dangers of crisis. Although one might argue
that these are to an extent endemic in all forms of capitalism, one might also argue that forms of
capitalism have differed markedly in the extent to which they have mitigated these tendencies
and dangers, which would indicate that it is in principle possible for a new form of capitalism,
which mitigates the wrongs of neo-liberalism, to emerge, though that leaves open the question of
whether it is practicable in existing conditions. For instance, different forms of capitalism share a
commitment to constant 'growth', yet arguably the environmental and resource (oil, water) crises,
which co-exist with the current financial and economic crisis, render this commitment deeply
problematic and raise the question of whether capitalism as such can provide real solutions to our
multiple crises.

Let me turn to Stage 4. The sort of analysis I am suggesting should include strategies and
associated D/discourses for transforming the existing financial and economic order in ways that
might begin to address the social wrongs at issue, including more radical strategies for a substantive

...ctioning of markets (and in some cases permanent nationalization of key ...ystem, for instance) and strategies for a 'Green New Deal' that address also the ...is. The aim of trans-disciplinary analysis would include identifying the conditions ...nd the obstacles to such strategies and D/discourses being selected and retained. ...ort extract from Neil Lawson and John Harris 'No turning back' (*New Statesman*, ...009):

> The starting point for a better future is the simple recognition that the Good Society is incompatible with market fundamentalism. … Markets never contain themselves. Instead, they always look for new opportunities to make more profit. This leads to no end of disastrous and dysfunctional outcomes: among them, the commercialisation of the lives of our children and the rise of the kinds of complex financial instruments that have brought the whole house down. To turn society in a different direction, markets will have to be regulated and trammeled by social forces – the state and civil society. We must put in place the institutions that allow society to make the market its servant.

The authors represent, or imagine, a society in which markets are the 'servant' of social aspirations and goals for 'the Good Society', and they are 'regulated and trammeled' by 'the state and civil society'. Ways to achieve this are only indicated in the most general terms ('put in place … institutions'), but the strategy of mobilizing 'civil society' as well as the state in order to force markets into serving societal rather than just economic (e.g. 'growth') ends is a radical one compared with Brown's and others'. Embedding CDA within CPE allows us to explore both the semiotic and the material conditions of possibility for, and obstacles to, such a strategy and Discourse being selected and retained – the obstacles in this case would seem to be currently very severe.

These comments draw only upon a part of the version of CDA presented earlier. An issue that can be brought into the analysis is the recontextualization of d/Discourses, which is relevant to the resonance and impact that are germane to the selection of certain d/Discourses, but not others. For example, in the summer of 2009 media coverage of the crisis in Britain came to be dominated by 'repairing public finances' and 'reducing government debt' and by the 'cuts' in public spending, which were portrayed as the main necessary means of achieving this. The question of what 'cuts' the competing political parties would make, how deeply and how quickly, came to dominate the front pages of much of the press. There is a good case for arguing that it was Conservative Party agitation on this issue that was extensively recontextualized, not only in the news, but also in the editorial columns of much of the press, and succeeded in focusing the crisis agenda on the willingness to make deep and speedy cuts. When Gordon Brown's speech at the Labour Party conference in October 2009 partially took up this 'cuts' agenda at the expense of his previous construal of public spending during the crisis as an 'investment', these sections of the press were triumphant – 'At last Brown uses the c-word!' The issue of operationalization (and the associated questions of how d/Discourses come to be enacted in practices and, semiotically, in genres, inculcated in identities and, semiotically, in styles, and materialized in the physical world) will on the other hand become particularly significant as the process of selecting particular d/Discourses, and achieving a measure of hegemony for them, advances. Thus, since the elections of May 2010 in the UK, a coalition government (Conservatives plus Liberal Democrats) has begun to operationalize the 'cuts' agenda by substantially changing and reducing the provision of welfare and public services. (See Chiapello and Fairclough (2002) for a discussion of the operationalization of discourses in the process of emergence of the 'new capitalism' from the 1970s.)

Conclusion

I have focused here on one version of CDA that differs both from versions I have used myself in earlier work and from versions developed and used by other CDA practitioners (see Fairclough and Wodak, 1997 and Meyer and Wodak, 2009 for a number of these). CDA is a loosely interconnected set of different approaches, which differ for instance in the relative weight given to social as opposed to cognitive issues, or in the relative centrality given to social change (and therefore to concepts and categories such as interdiscursivity and recontextualization).

The version of CDA I have briefly presented here, and its precursors in earlier publications (e.g. Fairclough, 1992; Chouliaraki and Fairclough, 1999), are strongly focused upon shifting articulations of genres, discourses and styles in texts (interdiscursivity) and in orders of discourse. The interdiscursive analysis of texts has been seen to have a crucial mediating role between the linguistic analysis of texts (and, where appropriate, the 'multi-modal' analysis of relations between language, body language, visual images, etc.) and whatever forms of social analysis are germane to the particular piece of research being undertaken. On the one hand, shifts in the articulation of genres, discourses and styles in texts (or: the 'hybridisation' or 'mixing' of different genres, different discourses, different styles) are realized in changes in linguistic (and multi-modal) features of texts; on the other hand, these interdiscursive shifts are the semiotic element or 'moment' of social changes, and they are dialectically interconnected with other, non-semiotic elements or 'moments'. Of course, not every interdiscursive novelty in texts amounts to social change in a substantive sense. There is a huge amount of variation in texts, but which variants come to be selected and retained (Jessop, 2004) depends upon a range of non-semiotic as well as semiotic factors and conditions. Where interdiscursive shifts are selected and retained, we can identify changes in the orders of discourse, i.e. changes in social practices in their semiotic aspect. To put the point in different terms, changes that occur in concrete events (texts) are selectively and contingently retained as changes in structures, changes in semiotic structures (orders of discourse) that are dialectically operationalized in changes in non-semiotic structures.

Further reading

Fairclough, N. (2000) *New Labour, New Language?* London: Routledge.

An accessible application of CDA to analysis of political discourse, written for a general, non-specialized readership.

Fairclough, N. (2003) *Analysing Discourse: Textual Analysis for Social Research*. London: Routledge.

Discusses in some detail methods of textual analysis in CDA, which I have not said much about in this paper. It also shows how textual analysis can be selectively used to strengthen social research on a variety of issues.

Lemke, J. (1995) *Textual Politics: Discourse and Social Dynamics*. London and Bristol, PA: Taylor and Francis.

A powerful presentation of an approach to CDA that differs in various ways from the one I have presented here.

References

Bootle, R. (2009) *The Trouble with Markets: Saving Capitalism From Itself*. London: Nicholas Brealey.

Bourdieu, P. and Wacquant, L. (1992) *An Invitation to Reflexive Sociology*. Cambridge: Polity Press.

Chiapello, E. and Fairclough, N. (2002) 'Understanding the new management ideology: a transdisciplinary contribution from critical discourse analysis and new sociology of capitalism', *Discourse & Society*, 13 (2).

Chouliaraki, L. and Fairclough, N. (1999) *Discourse in Late Modernity*. Edinburgh: Edinburgh University Press.

Fairclough, I. and Fairclough, N. (Forthcoming) *Political Discourse Analysis*. London: Routledge.

Fairclough, N. (1989) *Language and Power*. London: Longman.

Fairclough, N. (1992) *Discourse and Social Change*. Cambridge: Polity Press.

Fairclough, N. (2006) *Language and Globalization*. London: Routledge.

Fairclough, N. (2009a) 'Language, reality and power', in J. Culpeper *et al.* (eds.) *English Language: Description, Variation and Contex*. London: Palgrave Macmillan.

Fairclough, N. (2009b) 'A dialectical–relational approach to critical discourse analysis in social research', in R. Wodak and M. Meyer (eds.) *Methods of Critical Discourse Analysis*. Second Edition. London: Sage, pp. 162–186.

Fairclough, N. (2010) *Critical Discourse Analysis*. Second Edition. London: Longman.

Fairclough, N. and Graham, P. (2002) 'Marx as critical discourse analyst: the genesis of a critical method and its relevance to the critique of global capital', *Estudios de Sociolinguistica*, 3 (1): 185–229.

Fairclough, N., Jessop, B., and Sayer, A. (2004) 'Critical realism and semiosis', in J. Joseph and J. Roberts (eds.) *Realism, Discourse and Deconstruction*. London: Routledge.

Fairclough, N. and Wodak, R. (1997) 'Critical discourse analysis', in T. van Dijk (ed.) *Discourse as Social Interaction*. London: Sage.

Gee, J. (1999) *An Introduction to Discourse Analysis*. London: Routledge.

Harvey, D. (1996) *Justice, Nature and the Geography of Difference*. Oxford: Blackwell.

Jessop, B. (2004) 'Critical semiotic analysis and cultural political economy', *Critical Discourse Studies*, 1 (2): 159–175.

Jessop, B. and Sum, N.-L. (2001) 'Pre-disciplinary and post-disciplinary perspectives in political economy', *New Political Economy*, 6: 89–101.

Marsden, R. (1999) *The Nature of Capital: Marx After Foucault*. London: Routledge.

Meyer, M. and Wodak, R. (2009) *Methods in Critical Discourse Analysis*. Second Edition. London: Sage.

Sayer, A. (2003) 'Restoring the moral dimension in critical social science'. Available online at: http://www.lancs.ac.uk/fass/sociology/papers/sayer-restoring-the-moral-dimension.pdf (accessed 21 June 2010).

Sayer, A. (2004) 'Moral economy'. Available online at: http://www.lancs.ac.uk/fass/sociology/papers/sayer-moral-economy.pdf (accessed 21 June 2010).

2

Systemic functional linguistics

Mary J. Schleppegrell

Discourse analysis seeks patterns in linguistic data. Systemic functional linguistics (SFL) offers a means of exploring meaning in language and of relating language use to social contexts so as to contribute to our understanding of language in social life. This chapter provides an overview of SFL theory and its constructs and describes studies that have used SFL to explore meaning in discourse in a variety of contexts.

What is systemic functional linguistics?

SFL is the linguistic theory developed by Michael Halliday (Halliday, 1978, 1994; Halliday and Matthiessen, 2004). SFL recognizes the powerful role language plays in our lives and sees meaning-making as a process through which language shapes, and is shaped by, the contexts in which it is used. Every language offers its speakers/writers a wealth of options for construing meaning. SFL facilitates exploration of meaning in context through a comprehensive text-based grammar that enables analysts to recognize the choices speakers and writers make from linguistic *systems* and to explore how those choices are *functional* for construing meanings of different kinds. SFL describes three abstract functions (*metafunctions*) that are simultaneously realized in every clause we speak or write, and relates our linguistic choices to the contexts that the language participates in. The three metafunctions are the *ideational, interpersonal*, and *textual*, as in every clause our language simultaneously construes some kind of experience (ideational metafunction), enacts a role relationship with a listener or reader (interpersonal metafunction), and relates our messages to the prior and following text and context (textual metafunction). SFL provides constructs and tools for exploring these three kinds of meanings and their interaction in discourse.

For example, in the first sentence of this chapter, *Discourse analysis seeks patterns in linguistic data*, I simultaneously used linguistic resources that present information, construct a particular relationship with the reader, and move the text along. Ideationally, this clause construes *discourse analysis* as an *actor* in the process of *seeking*; what is sought are *patterns in linguistic data*. Interpersonally, this is stated assertively, with no indeterminacy and no negotiation or interaction with the reader (compare, for example, beginning with *What are the goals of discourse analysis?*). Textually, the clause takes *discourse analysis* as its point of departure, connecting this chapter with the topic of the handbook as a whole, and makes *seeks patterns in linguistic data* the point of the clause—the "new" information that the sentence presents. Different choices might have been made in any of these areas of meaning, and SFL offers a comprehensive framework for exploring variation and for relating it to the discourse context.

SFL describes linguistic systems and the functions they enable, revealing the ways social actors construe their experiences and enact relationships.[1] From the *systemic* perspective, language is seen as a network of dynamic and open systems from which speakers and writers are constantly selecting as they use language, thereby maintaining or changing the systems over time through their choices. The system of *transitivity*, for example, offers a range of options for ideational (content) meaning that is comprehensive of the ways language varies in presenting experience: as *doing, sensing, saying,* or *being.*[2] SFL analysis of transitivity describes the grammatical differences between, for example, a clause with an *actor* in a *doing* process (*Discourse analysis seeks patterns in linguistic data*) and a clause with a *senser* in a *sensing* process (*We can think of discourse analysis as a process of seeking patterns in linguistic data*). This enables the analyst to consider how the choices a speaker/ writer has made from the transitivity system construe the experience presented in the text. (For example, analysis of transitivity patterns in literary texts often reveals that authors represent characters' feelings in their actions.)

SFL uses the abstract categories *field, tenor,* and *mode* to refer to the relationship between language and context. Ideational resources point to the topic/content (*field*); interpersonal resources enact relationships and convey attitudes (*tenor*); and textual resources indicate the role language plays in the context (*mode*), for example, whether the language constitutes or accompanies activity. Field, tenor, and mode vary as the speaker/writer's lexical and grammatical choices respond to, and at the same time help construct, the context in which language is used. Selections from the transitivity system are one element of *field.* Every clause also has grammatical features that contribute to the construal of *tenor*—for example through selection from the *mood* system (each clause is declarative, interrogative, or imperative) and from other resources for interpersonal meaning. *Mode* is also simultaneously construed in each clause through, among other systems, selections from the *theme/rheme* system, as the speaker/writer makes choices about the point of departure of each clause and the new information that it will present. The SFL grammar describes the choices available to speakers/writers in these and other systems of English and other languages, and the analysis can also be extended to other modalities, to enable the discourse analyst to describe the different constellations of meanings that emerge from different choices within each system (*choice* here means *selection*, not entailing conscious/ deliberate choice). From this perspective, SFL discourse analysis can answer the question: *How does this text mean what it does?*

Variation in linguistic choices with respect to context is captured in SFL in the notion of *register.* Drawing on different systems of language in different combinations realizes different registers, because the particular language choices, and so the meanings we make, vary according to social and cultural context. Language is a vast resource for meaning-making, and speakers/ writers draw on this resource in different ways, depending on what is going on, whom we are interacting with, and the role language is playing. Analyzing language choices can reveal important differences in how content, role relationships, and information flow are constructed in different contexts, as these differences realize and reveal different registers. This suggests the second question that SFL analysis can help answer, namely: *How does this text contribute to shaping the social context?*

Differences in the configurations of meaning that emerge from different choices in the grammar can be compared to recognize differences in register, as the grammatical choices evoke for listeners/readers the social meanings that the language helps instantiate. Each of the linguistic systems described in SFL grammar enables comprehensive analysis of an area of meaning in the language, and analyzing the linguistic choices that realize different meanings tells us something about how the text means what it does and how it participates in social life.

Reasoning with patterns of grammar and meaning

One of Halliday's contributions to SFL discourse analysis has been a description of the evolution of scientific English (Halliday, 1993a). Analyzing texts written by fourteenth through to twentieth century scientists, Halliday shows how science discourse evolved in its grammatical choices, drawing increasingly on nominalization (his *grammatical metaphor*: see below) as new kinds of knowledge and interpersonal relationships developed in science over time. The focus he takes and the insights he presents are a good example of what SFL discourse analysis can illuminate.

Halliday illustrates how, over time, scientists adapted the grammatical resources available in English to create discourse that develops an argument through logical steps—the kind of argumentation needed to share the results of experiments in physical science. He describes how the ideational and textual resources used by scientists changed as they began developing technical taxonomies and theorizing in new ways. At the same time, the tenor of scientific discourse also evolved into the impersonal stance typical of science today. Halliday reports how Newton, for example, wrote in very direct ways about the experiments he conducted, telling what he did, observed, and thought about it: "I held the prism ... observed the length of its refracted Image ... it appears that ...". This is quite different from the discourse of today's experimental report, and Halliday describes how scientists began to exploit the potential of the nominal group (noun phrase) to distill and repackage the processes scientists were writing about so that they could be related to each other. For example:

> The rate of crack growth depends not only on the chemical environment but also on the magnitude of the applied stress. The development of a complete model for the kinetics of fracture requires an understanding of how stress accelerates the bond-rupture reaction.
>
> *(Michalske and Bunker 1987, p. 81 cited in Halliday, 1993a)*

Here the nominal group *The rate of crack growth* distills the process of *cracking slowly/quickly*. The nominal group *the magnitude of the applied stress* repackages information from the process of *applying much/little stress*. These are the experimental processes that the scientist has engaged in, but the process is not reported in the way Newton did (e.g., *how quickly the [glass] cracks depends on how much stress [I] apply*).

It is not only the physical processes, but also the scientists' thinking processes that can be presented in these nominal group structures. *The development of a complete model for the kinetics of fracture* is a nominal group that repackages the process *We want to develop a model*. The nominal group *an understanding of how stress accelerates the bond-rupture reaction* repackages the process *We need to understand how*. ... These are "internal" processes: processes that the scientists engage in through their thinking (*If we want to develop a model ..., we need to understand how ...*).

Through analyses of the nominal groups used by scientists over time and of the role the nominal groups play in experimental discourse, Halliday shows how the ideational resources of the grammar have developed to enable a kind of texture in which, as we see in this text, a process (*glass cracking*) is presented as a thing (*the rate of crack growth*) that can then participate further in the discourse. Halliday points out that using the nominalization *the rate of crack growth* at the beginning of the passage is only possible because the text has already talked about the speed at which glass cracks. Halliday calls nominalizations like these *grammatical metaphors*. He points out that, in the registers of everyday life, we typically express meanings in structures that relate *congruently* to those meanings. We present meanings about *things* in nouns; meanings about *processes* in verbs; meanings about *connections* in conjunctions, meanings about *qualities* in adjectives. Grammatical metaphor enables the presentation of meaning in a structure that is not congruent with the grammatical form, and this is one of the ways in which technical and academic discourses have evolved.

Grammatical metaphor enables meanings to be distilled and compacted. Presenting processes as things enabled scientists to create chains of reasoning and argumentation that facilitated the development and presentation of theories, enabling science discourse to evolve in ways that facilitated the presentation of new knowledge.[3] For example, a whole argument can be summed up in a few words, which make it possible to examine the argument in relation to other arguments or perspectives; or a new scientific process can be distilled into a few words, so that it can be used as a participant in yet another process. Grammatical metaphor is a key feature of scientific discourse today, but it was not always so, and Halliday shows how this linguistic technology changed the *tenor* and *mode* of science discourse as scientists increasingly drew on interpersonal and textual options that construe more distanced interpersonal relationships, but that enable the text to be organized to efficiently present an explanation or build an argument.

As this discussion exemplifies, the functional grammar is the basis for SFL discourse analysis, and understanding how every clause can be analyzed from the three metafunctional perspectives to reveal the complexity of meanings always construed in each use of language is the foundation of analyzing a text from an SFL perspective.

Approaches to SFL discourse analysis

Halliday and Hasan's (1976) seminal work on cohesion describes non-syntactic relations that make a text hang together (*reference, ellipsis, substitution, conjunction,* and *lexical cohesion*) and enable a text to evolve from clause to clause. The description of cohesion in text was an important foundation for further work on the semantics of texts and the development of SFL discourse analysis tools. Today there are two major branches of SFL discourse analysis, generated from the work of Ruqaiya Hasan and J. R. Martin. Each of them has proposed a set of tools and approaches to discourse that have been taken up by analysts in different contexts. "Text" is the unit of SFL discourse analysis; it refers to "any passage, spoken or written, of whatever length, that forms a unified whole" (Halliday and Hasan, 1976: 1). Texts are approached with different analytic tools, depending on the goals of the analysis.

Hasan has developed SFL discourse analysis through the constructs *generic structure potential* (Hasan, 1996a), *cohesive harmony analysis* (Hasan, 1984), and *semantic networks* (Hasan, 1996b). SFL is often associated with an interest in *genre*, and Hasan's *generic structure potential* and *cohesive harmony analysis* are tools for recognizing the moves that may occur within a genre (e.g., Hasan, 1996a). In analyzing *generic structure potential*, multiple examples of a genre are reviewed in order to identify elements that are obligatory and optional and the ordering possibilities for those elements. Togher *et al.* (2004), for example, use analysis of generic structure potential to compare "typical" encounters with police with encounters the police have with people with traumatic brain injury, who often do not engage in the genre of this encounter in the same ways as people who are not injured. They show how the structure of the encounters with brain-injured people departs from what police typically expect, and their analysis is contributing to a more effective interaction with brain-injured people. *Cohesive harmony analysis* (Hasan, 1984) is another approach to recognizing how a discourse evolves, helping an analyst describe connections across a text by "identifying the lexical and referential chains formed in a text and then examining the ways in which these chains interact" (Cloran *et al.*, 2007: 651). Cloran *et al.* show how analysis of cohesive chains helps identify boundaries within texts, as the appearance and disappearance of chains reveals the text's structure. This is illustrated in Cloran (1999), where she uses an analysis of cohesion to identify how particular moves are embedded in larger discourse units.

Ruqaiya Hasan has also initiated a productive strand of SFL discourse analysis in her study of the discursive practices of mothers interacting with young children in contexts of everyday life (see Hasan *et al.*, 2007 for a history of this work). Drawing on SFL's notion of *system networks*, Hasan developed the construct *semantic network*, to show at a very detailed level differences in the meanings speakers construe in what might otherwise be seen as the "same" context; for example in bathing a child (Hasan, 1996b; Hasan *et al.*, 2007). In analyzing semantic networks, transcripts are divided into *messages* (similar to a clause), and the messages are compared to identify different linguistic realizations. For example, Hasan (1996b) discusses how some utterances from mother to child incorporate the semantic option *assumptive*. Selecting the option *assumptive* presents the implication that the speaker has a view of what the situation should have been. This is realized through negation, in clauses such as: *Didn't you see me? Why don't you love Rosemary?* Or: *You didn't eat it?* (the child *ought to have seen her; should love Rosemary, should have eaten it*). A *semantic network* is an attempt to account for "systematic variation in the meanings people select in similar contexts as a function of their social positioning" (Williams, 2005: 457).

Hasan (2009) reports on how this analysis has enabled exploration of variation in the ways mothers who are positioned in different ways in the social structure ask and answer their children's questions, in the ways they reason with their children, and in the ways gender and class ideologies are construed in everyday talk between parent and child (see also Cloran, 2000). Williams (2005) also analyzes this corpus by using the statistical techniques of principal components and cluster analysis. He shows that mothers vary in the frequency with which they select different options as they read aloud to their children – for example, in how frequently they foreground the expression of individual points of view vs. taking for granted that they know the child's experience or state of knowledge.

J. R. Martin has also developed an approach to the analysis of discourse that builds on the notion of cohesion as discourse structure, analysis of discourse semantics and genre being his point of departure. He has developed analytic tools that provide a framework for "tackling a text" (Martin, 1992; Martin and Rose, 2003), offering those unfamiliar with SFL grammar a set of tools for engaging in analysis through exploration of six discourse-level systems: *appraisal, ideation, identification, conjunction, periodicity,* and *negotiation* (Martin and Rose, 2003). The analysis of each system affords different possibilities for exploring meaning in text, the basis for analysis being an understanding that language participates in social life through *genres.*

Martin's approach sees genre as a level of context above and beyond field, tenor, and mode, and makes genre central to describing the role of culture in language use (Martin, 1999a). He defines genre as a staged, goal-directed social process, and his early work in educational contexts developed a description of a range of genres that are typical of and expected in different disciplinary pedagogies (Martin, 1993, 1999b). Martin and his colleagues analyzed more than 2,000 texts in different school subjects, as described in Rothery (1996), developing descriptions of linguistic pathways into disciplinary literacies—descriptions that have been highly influential (see Christie and Martin (1997); Martin (2002) offers an example from history). For more on SFL and genre, see Martin and Rose (2008); Rose (this volume). For a recent application of this approach, see Macken-Horarik *et al.*'s (2006) analysis of the linguistic demands of a pre-service teacher education program.

Two of the discourse semantic systems developed in Martin and Rose (2003) will be described here: *ideation* and *appraisal. Ideation* analysis explores the linguistic resources that construe experience and construct the field of discourse. Similar to the analysis of cohesive harmony described above, ideation analysis focuses on the semantics of each clause and tracks meaning across a text to reveal sequences of activities, the people and things involved in them, and their associated places and qualities. This analysis can show how texts of different types, in different contexts, unfold in different ways. For example, Martin (2006: 292) uses ideation analysis to show how agency is construed in a text aimed at reconciling Australian and Japanese war experiences, where he argues that representing Australians as more agentive "can perhaps be read as balancing the more commonly promulgated (in Australia) 'Japan as aggressor, Australia as victim' motif." Through analysis of lexical relations within the clause and chains of relationships between lexical elements, ideation analysis can reveal the sequences of activity that make up different stages of a genre (see also Martin, 2001).

Appraisal analysis explores how interpersonal meaning permeates a text, enabling exploration of resources for evaluative meaning, "the kinds of attitudes that are negotiated in a text, the strength of the feelings involved and the ways in which values are sourced and readers aligned" (Martin and Rose, 2003: 25). A related development in SFL discourse analysis is the elaboration of the *engagement* system, a sub-system of appraisal, to identify the sources of attitudes and evaluative meaning (Martin and White, 2005). The appraisal tools are currently informing SFL discourse analyses across a range of contexts (e.g. White, 2003a; Martin, 2004; Arkoudis, 2005; Hood, 2006; and the special issue of Text (2003, Vol. 23 n. 2)). Hood, for example, uses appraisal analysis of research paper introductions to illustrate how different configurations of attitudinal meanings are relevant to accomplishing different purposes: for instance for presenting a rationale, arguing for new knowledge, or presenting one's own work as valuable. Arkoudis (2005) uses appraisal analysis to reveal tensions and power relationships around teachers' collaboration.

Martin's recent work explores how texts about the same event draw on different linguistic systems to instantiate different perspectives (e.g. Martin, 2008a). In analyzing three accounts of events in a novel, he shows how authors present and combine meanings in different ways, the different instantiations of the story affording different readings. Martin draws implications from this for understanding the affordances of translation, the use of different modalities, and summarizing. In a related chapter, Martin (2008b) explores the same texts to show how differences in the dialogism of the texts construct the speakers as more or less authoritative. This and other features of the discourse construe the characters' identities and position them in ways that different readers may align with. These chapters provide detailed examples of how analyses of genre, periodicity, appraisal, conjunction, and ideation offer insights for discourse analysis.

Tools for meaning-based discourse analysis, based on close attention to linguistic realization, have proliferated within SFL. The approaches offer ways to track a range of meanings across texts, as analysts recognize elements of text structure, identify and track participants in the text, recognize and explore the kinds of processes they are engaged in, look at the attitudes and judgments that are infused, and explore differences in the ways texts move from clause to clause. The close focus on the choices speakers and writers make reveals the contexts they are participating in and the ways language contributes to construing those contexts.

Contexts that SFL analysts have explored

SFL analyses have described features of the registers and genres of different disciplines (e.g. Halliday and Martin (1993) on science; O'Halloran (2005) on mathematics; Coffin (2006) on history; Christie (1999) on subject English; Wignell (2007) on social science; see Christie (2007) for analysis of the role of disciplinary differences in the recontextualization of knowledge for education). Education has been an especially important and fruitful area of SFL discourse analysis (Christie and Unsworth (2005) provide a history), and Frances Christie has been an important contributor, informing educational theory and practice in significant ways. Christie (2002) provides a methodology for the analysis of classroom discourse that shows how instructional content and regulation of students are simultaneously managed by teachers. She illustrates how to distinguish the *content* or *instructional register* from the *regulative* or *pedagogical register* that projects the content, and analyzes these registers in interaction with each other to explore the knowledge being made available to students through classroom discourse as well as the ways students are positioned as learners. Christie shows how, in the early grades, the regulative register is foregrounded, but, as students move into the higher grades, it becomes more implicit. For example, teachers use fewer direct imperatives and more modality in directing behavior (e.g., "*So you're probably best to sit next to somebody that you will work with*" (p. 165)), and abstractions take the place of overt expressions of authority (e.g., "*The main requirement is…*") (p. 166)). The regulative register in this sense "appropriates" the instructional register, which is projected through it. Christie also illustrates how learning occurs at different phases of a lesson and how students' language develops as they work with new ideas and technical language. She shows that, where teaching is successful, students are enabled to reason in particular ways that reflect the values of the disciplines they are studying.

In recent work, Christie and Derewianka (2008) draw on a database of 2,000 texts from studies over the past 20 years to offer extensive and detailed descriptions of the developmental trajectories through which children gain control of written language in English, history, and science. This discourse analysis of children's written development across the school years in different subject areas shows the importance of grammatical metaphor to academic achievement and describes the linguistic resources through which abstraction, generalization, value judgment and opinion come to be expressed as students' writing matures.

Schleppegrell (2004) offers an analysis of the register features of the texts encountered in schooling in order to highlight the linguistic challenges of different genres and disciplines, describing the "language of schooling" as a register that enables students to display knowledge authoritatively in texts that have certain expectations for their structuring. Oteíza and Pinto (2008) use analyses of transitivity and appraisal to show how the dictatorships and subsequent transitions to democracy are portrayed in pedagogical texts used in Chile and Spain, illustrating how the authors silence some social actors while giving prominence to others as they present historical explanations to students. Achugar and Schleppegrell (2005) analyze very different ways in which causality is construed in history textbooks, showing how implicit causality puts in the background information important for critical reading of history texts. In an investigation of expository school history writing and teachers' expectations for this type of writing, de Oliveira (2010) explores thematic development, evaluation, and elaboration in secondary students' writing. Morgan's (2005) analysis of mathematics texts uses an analysis of transitivity to reveal how they represent the nature of mathematics and how they construe power and authority in particular ways. She shows, for example, that pedagogical texts obscure agency in mathematics far more than professional mathematicians do. Macken-Horarik (2006) analyzes exemplars of students' performance on high-stakes examinations to show what really matters to evaluators, highlighting linguistic aspects of high-scoring essays that are seldom acknowledged or explicitly taught.

Other SFL analyses have explored spoken discourse in science (Lemke, 1990) and mathematics (Chapman, 1995) classrooms, to show how teachers and students are often construing knowledge in different ways, revealing that students may not understand certain concepts. O'Halloran (2004) demonstrates how analysis of mood and modality can shed light on interpersonal relationships in the mathematics classroom and reveal how students are positioned as learners. Gibbons (2006) analyzes spoken interaction and students' written texts to illustrate how teachers can support the development of language and content learning in classrooms with diverse students, including some who are learning English as a second language. She argues that teachers need to understand language from a functional perspective in order to move students along a "mode continuum," from everyday into more specialized ways of construing knowledge. Zolkower and Shreyer (2007) use analysis of mood and speech function, supplemented by comments on modality, to analyze the ways a teacher "commands" her students in a sixth grade algebra lesson to "think verbally," showing how "thinking" is constructed in language as the teacher organizes and scaffolds instruction.

SFL has enabled advanced second and foreign language instruction to develop pathways into the kinds of discourse and language use that is needed for engagement in academic and professional contexts (see special issue of *Linguistics and Education* (Byrnes, 2009, Vol. 20 n. 1)). Byrnes (2009), for example, analyzes the writing development of 14 students of German as a foreign language over three curricular levels, providing quantitative and qualitative measures of the development of grammatical metaphor in second language writing, and suggests how such analyses can contribute to a deeper understanding of contrastive rhetoric and of the relationship between first and second language writing development (see also Ryshina-Pankova, 2010). Hood (2010) analyzes how published researchers and second language writers draw on the resources of English to introduce their own research and to critique the research of others, and provides an elaboration of the networks within the appraisal system to account for differences in the evaluation strategies of writers along several dimensions. Lee (2010) analyzes what she calls the "commanding strategies of 'shouldness'" in undergraduate second language writers' texts, focusing on metaphors of mood and modulation. SFL analysis has also been extended to languages other than English (e.g. Colombi, 2002; Oteiza, 2006; see Martin, 2009, for other references), and is used by researchers around the world. Children's language development has been a foundational area of focus in SFL discourse analysis, with important work presented in Halliday (1975, 1993b) and Painter (1999).

Clinical contexts have also been frequent sites for SFL discourse analysis, which is used in studying and treating language disorders such as aphasia, traumatic brain injury, dementia, and developmental disorders (Armstrong, 2005; Armstrong *et al.*, 2005). Bartlett *et al.* (2005) describe studies that have used cohesion analysis to understand autism, where this kind of analysis enables consideration of interpersonal resources for meaning-making and "allows the researcher to develop a linguistic theory linking the linguistic resources to the social roles and identity of the individuals" (p. 211). Mortensen (2005) analyzes the genre structure and semantics of personal letters written by writers with brain impairment and discusses the variation in this corpus, as well as the challenges of comparing patterns of variation. Thompson (2001) illustrates how cohesive harmony analysis helps track the progress of a patient with schizophrenia. Togher (2001) provides a case study illustrating how SFL analysis helps the clinician/researcher explore relationships between discourse context and the language realized in that context, pointing to the power relations underlying therapeutic interactions and treatment goals focused on assisting the client in achieving autonomy and choice. She suggests that SFL analysis "can unveil some of the mystery of why people with communication difficulties and their communication partners find everyday interactions awkward or unrewarding. It allows the clinician to tease out how the words being used, the way information is exchanged, and the structure of interactions are linked to context" (pp. 145–146). (See also Fine, 2006; and the 2005 special issue of *Clinical Linguistics and Phonetics*, 9 (3)). Körner (2010) uses appraisal categories to describe how patients and physicians adopt different intersubjective stances in discussing challenging treatments for hepatitis C.

SFL has been a popular tool for critical discourse analysis (see e.g. Fairclough, 2003; Gee, 2004; Rogers *et al.*, 2005), with ongoing dialogue (e.g. Billig, 2008, and responses; Martin and Veel, 1998; Martin, 2000; Martin and Wodak, 2003). Achugar (2008) uses genre and register analysis as well as analysis of intertextuality and appraisal resources to show how the actions of the Uruguayan military were construed in various discourses at the time they occurred and afterward, legitimating and then transforming the official memory while constructing a positive institutional identity. Oteiza Silva (2006) offers a multimodal analysis of the ways the overthrow of Allende and the resulting Pinochet regime are represented in Chilean history textbooks. Bonnin (2009) explores nominalization and grammatical metaphor in an analysis of the historical relationship between religious and political discourse in Argentina. Butt *et al.* (2004) analyze speeches given in Iraq prior to the war, in order to uncover the various ideologies at play in discourse at that time. Young and Harrison (2004) show how SFL analysis can raise awareness of the power of language to naturalize certain ways of thinking and can help us recognize how different positions are constructed in language, so that those positions might be challenged or queried.

Media analyses have also drawn on SFL (e.g. White, 2003b). Moore (2006), for example, analyzes how articles in the *Economist* magazine use similar genre structures and semantic relations in their reporting on Cambodia, and relates these findings to the cultural and situational context. Literary texts have also been a frequent focus of SFL discourse analysis – one that illustrates how the grammatical choices of an author redound with the themes and motifs of a text, enabling that author to create particular effects (Halliday, 2002; see Lukin and Webster, 2005 for a history and exemplification of SFL in literary analysis). Lukin (2008) offers a comprehensive SFL treatment of a poem by Edna St. Vincent Millay, illustrating how a linguistic analysis can afford insights that enable students to engage in critique rather than just rely on personal response.

Recent developments in SFL discourse analysis include tools for creating corpora coded for SFL grammar and discourse features that allow large-scale semantic analyses, and multimodal and multi-semiotic analyses that draw on SFL theory to explore how other modalities and semiotic systems interact with language in making meaning (Kress and van Leeuwen, 1996; Royce and Bowcher, 2007; O'Halloran, 2008; van Leeuwen, 2008; see Martin, 2009 for other references).)

Contributions of SFL to discourse analysis

As this review indicates, the tools of SFL can be drawn on in a variety of ways to explore the linguistic systems through which social actors instantiate meaning. This makes SFL a valuable resource for research across fields. Deciding how to approach authentic language in context, in spoken or written form, is often a challenging task. SFL offers a "way in" by providing concrete tools for exploring language comprehensively and for making sense of discourse data. Its flexible set of tools can be adapted to working with multimodal texts, and the results of SFL analyses can be presented in qualitative discussions as well as used in quantitative studies. In fields where discourse data are collected and analyzed, the functional grammar of SFL offers grounded ways to explore meaning in such data.

Christie (2002: 16) notes that "language does not just passively reflect a pre-existing social reality. It is an active agent in constructing that reality." SFL discourse analysis recognizes the dialectical nature of the relationship between language and context. By enabling the analyst to reveal how every text shapes and is shaped by social situations, SFL offers powerful tools for comprehensively exploring meaning in language at the levels of genre, register, and clause and for accounting for differences between speakers, differences over time, or differences in context. The variety of contexts to which SFL discourse analysis contributes testifies to its flexibility and utility in meeting the needs of analysts from different disciplines and settings. Furthermore, as the most elaborated meaning-based grammar available to discourse analysts, SFL can be used by sociolinguists and discourse analysts in conjunction with other analytic tools, providing a means of attending closely to the linguistic realization of meanings in spoken and written discourse, to supplement exploration of other aspects of interaction in context.

Acknowledgment

I would like to thank Mariana Achugar, Cecilia Colombi, and J. R. Martin for insightful comments on an earlier version of this chapter, without holding them in any way responsible for the final version.

Further reading

Halliday, M. A. K. (1994) *An Introduction to Functional Grammar*. Second Edition. London: Edward Arnold.
A good introduction to SFL grammar.

Halliday, M. A. K. and Matthiessen, C. M. I. M. (2004) *An Introduction to Functional Grammar*. Third Edition. London: Arnold.
Expands the grammatical description with more detail and examples.

Martin, J. R. and Rose, D. (2003) *Working with Discourse: Meaning Beyond the Clause*. First and Second Editions. London: Continuum.
Introduces SFL discourse analysis tools, illustrated with analysis of a range of genres.[4]

Eggins, S. and Slade, D. (1997) *Analysing Casual Conversation*. London: Cassell.
Illustrates spoken discourse analysis of casual conversation with SFL.

Martin, J. R. (1999c) 'Grace: the logogenesis of freedom', *Discourse Studies*, 1 (1): 29–56.

Uses many of the tools and constructs described here to analyze an excerpt from Nelson Mandela's autobiography that illustrates how Mandela uses his life story to develop a deep understanding of the meaning of freedom and to inspire the reader. This is a good introduction to what the SFL tools afford the analyst.

Notes

1 This chapter focuses on the grammatical and discourse semantic systems, but SFL analysts have also worked with phonological/graphological systems and systems from different modalities, such as visual display and gesture (see Martin (2009) for references).
2 Different SFL analysts carve up the meaning spaces in different systems in different ways. Martin and Rose (2003) use these four categories of processes, while Halliday (1994) describes six: *material, behavioural, mental, verbal, relational,* and *existential*. This variation reflects the fact that language is a complex system and categories are ineffable (Halliday, 1984); but, whichever set of categories an analyst uses, the categories are meant to cover the entire meaning space of the system.
3 Grammatical metaphor has become an important construct in the analysis of language development in the individual as well (see e.g. Christie and Derewianka, 2008; Halliday, 1993b).
4 There are significant differences between the two editions, as a chapter on negotiation and analysis of spoken language was added and the chapter on ideation was revised so as to take an ergative rather than a transitive perspective on the clause.

References

Achugar, M. (2008) *What We Remember: The Construction of Memory in Military Discourse*. Amsterdam: John Benjamins.
Achugar, M. and Schleppegrell, M. J. (2005) 'Beyond connectors: the construction of *cause* in history textbooks', *Linguistics and Education*, 16 (3): 298–318.
Arkoudis, S. (2005) 'Fusing pedagogic horizons: language and content teaching in the mainstream', *Linguistics and Education*, 16: 173–187.
Armstrong, E. (2005) 'Language disorder: a functional linguistic perspective', *Clinical Linguistics and Phonetics*, 19 (3): 137–153.
Armstrong, E., Ferguson, A., Mortensen, L., and Togher, L. (2005) 'Acquired language disorders: some functional insights', in R. Hasan, C. M. I. M. Matthiessen, and J. Webster (eds.) *Continuing Discourse on Language*. London: Equinox, pp. 383–412.

Bartlett, S. C., Armstrong, E., and Roberts, J. (2005) 'Linguistic resources of individuals with Asperger syndrome', *Clinical Linguistics and Phonetics*, 19 (3): 203–213.

Billig, M. (2008) 'The language of critical discourse analysis: the case of nominalization', *Discourse and Society*, 19 (6): 783–800.

Bonnin, J. E. (2009) 'Religious and political discourse in Argentina: the case of reconciliation', *Discourse and Society*, 20 (3): 327–343.

Butt, D., Lukin, A., and Matthiessen, C. M. I. M. (2004) 'Grammar – the first covert operation of war', *Discourse and Society*, 15 (2–3): 267–290.

Byrnes, H. (2009) 'Emergent L2 German writing ability in a curricular context: A longitudinal study of grammatical metaphor', *Linguistics and Education*, 20: 50–66.

Chapman, A. (1995) 'Intertextuality in school mathematics: the case of functions', *Linguistics and Education*, 7 (3): 243–262.

Christie, F. (1999) 'The pedagogic device and the teaching of English', in F. Christie (ed.) *Pedagogy and the Shaping of Consciousness: Linguistic and Social Processes*. London: Continuum, pp. 156–184.

Christie, F. (2002) *Classroom Discourse Analysis: A Functional Perspective*. London: Continuum.

Christie, F. (2007) 'Ongoing dialogue: functional linguistic and Bernsteinian sociological perspectives on education', in F. Christie and J. R. Martin (eds.) *Language, Knowledge, and Pedagogy: Functional Linguistic and Sociological Perspectives*. London: Continuum, pp. 3–13.

Christie, F. and Derewianka, B. (2008) *School Discourse: Learning to Write Across the Years of Schooling*. London: Continuum.

Christie, F. and Martin J. R. (eds.) (1997) *Genre and Institutions: Social Processes in the Workplace and School*. London: Cassell.

Christie, F. and Unsworth, L. (2005) 'Developing dimensions of an educational linguistics', in R. Hasan, C. M. I. M. Matthiessen, and J. Webster (eds.) *Continuing Discourse on Language: A Functional Perspective*. London: Equinox, pp. 217–250.

Cloran, C. (1999) 'Contexts for learning', in F. Christie (ed.) *Pedagogy and the Shaping of Consciousness: Linguistic and Social Processes*. London: Continuum, pp. 31–65.

Cloran, C. (2000) 'Socio-semantic variation: different wordings, different meanings', in L. Unsworth (ed.) *Researching Language in Schools and Communities: Functional Linguistic Perspectives*. London: Cassell, pp. 152–183.

Cloran, C., Stuart-Smith, V., and Young, L. (2007) 'Models of discourse', in R. Hasan, C. M. I. M. Matthiessen, and J. Webster (eds.) *Continuing Discourse on Language: A Functional Perspective*. Vol. 2. London: Equinox, pp. 647–670.

Coffin, C. (2006) *Historical Discourse: The Language of Time, Cause, and Evaluation*. London: Continuum.

Colombi, M. C. (2002) 'Academic language development in Latino students' writing in Spanish', in M. J. Schleppegrell and M. C. Colombi (eds.) *Developing Advanced Literacy in First and Second Languages: Meaning with Power*. Mahwah, NJ: Lawrence Erlbaum, pp. 67–86.

de Oliveira, L. C. (2010) *Knowing and Writing School History: The Language of Students' Expository Writing and Teachers' Expectations*. Charlotte, NC: Information Age Publishing.

Eggins, S. and Slade, D. (1997) *Analysing Casual Conversation*. London: Cassell.

Fairclough, N. (2003) *Analysing Discourse: Textual Analysis for Social Research*. London and New York: Routledge.

Fine, J. (2006) *Language in Psychiatry: A Handbook of Clinical Practice*. London: Equinox.

Gee, J. P. (2004) 'Discourse analysis: what makes it critical?', in R. Rogers (ed.) *An Introduction to Critical Discourse Analysis in Education*. Mahwah, NJ: Lawrence Erlbaum, pp. 19–50.

Gibbons, P. (2006) *Bridging Discourses in the ESL Classroom: Students, Teachers and Researchers*. London: Continuum.

Halliday, M. A. K. (1975) *Learning How to Mean: Explorations in the Development of Language*. London: Edward Arnold.

Halliday, M. A. K. (1978) *Language as Social Semiotic*. London: Edward Arnold.

Halliday, M. A. K. (1984) 'On the ineffability of grammatical categories', in A. Manning, P. Martin, and K. McCalla (eds.) *The Tenth LACUS Forum*. Amsterdam: John Benjamins, pp. 3–18.

Halliday, M. A. K. (1993a) 'On the language of physical science', in M. A. K. Halliday and J. R. Martin (eds.) *Writing Science: Literacy and Discursive Power*. Pittsburgh: University of Pittsburgh Press, pp. 54–68.

Halliday, M. A. K. (1993b) 'Towards a language-based theory of learning', *Linguistics and Education*, 5 (2): 93–116.

Halliday, M. A. K. (1994) *An Introduction to Functional Grammar*. Second Edition. London: Edward Arnold.

Halliday, M. A. K. (2002) *Linguistic Studies of Text and Discourse*. Vol. 2. London: Continuum.

Halliday, M. A. K. and Hasan, R. (1976) *Cohesion in English*. London: Longman.

Halliday, M. A. K. and Martin, J. R. (eds.) (1993) *Writing Science: Literacy and Discursive Power*. Pittsburgh, PA: University of Pittsburgh Press.

Halliday, M. A. K. and Matthiessen, C. M. I. M. (2004) *An Introduction to Functional Grammar*. Third Edition. London: Arnold.

Hasan, R. (1984) 'Coherence and cohesive harmony', in J. Flood (ed.) *Understanding Reading Comprehension: Cognition, Language, and the Structure of Prose*. Newark, DE: International Reading Association, pp. 181–219.

Hasan, R. (1996a) 'The nursery tale as a genre', in C. Cloran, D. Butt, and G. Williams (eds.) *Ways of Saying: Ways of Meaning*. London: Cassell, pp. 51–72.

Hasan, R. (1996b) 'Semantic networks: A tool for the analysis of meaning', in C. Cloran, D. Butt, and G. Williams (eds.) *Ways of Saying: Ways of Meaning*. London: Cassell, pp. 104–131.

Hasan, R. (2009) *Semantic Variation: The Collected Works of Ruqaiya Hasan*. Vol. 2. London: Equinox.

Hasan, R., Cloran, C., Williams, G., and Lukin, A. (2007) 'Semantic networks: the description of linguistic meaning in SFL', in R. Hasan, C. M. I. M. Matthiessen, and J. Webster (eds.) *Continuing Discourse on Language: A Functional Perspective*. Vol. 2. London: Equinox, pp. 697–738.

Hood, S. (2006) 'The persuasive power of prosodies: radiating values in academic writing', *Journal of English for Academic Purposes*, 5: 37–49.

Hood, S. (2010) *Appraising Research: Evaluation in Academic Writing*. London: Palgrave Macmillan.

Körner, H. (2010) 'Negotiating treatment for hepatitis C: interpersonal alignment in the clinical encounter', *Health*, 14 (3): 272–291.

Kress, G. and van Leeuwen, T. (1996) *Reading Images: A Grammar of Visual Design*. London: Routledge.

Lee, S. H. S. (2010) 'Command strategies for balancing respect and authority in undergraduate expository essays', *Journal of English for Academic Purposes*, 9: 61–75.

Lemke, J. (1990) *Talking Science: Language, Learning, and Values*. Norwood, NJ: Ablex.

Lukin, A. (2008) 'Reading literary texts: Beyond personal response', in Z. Fang and M. J. Schleppegrell *Reading in Secondary Content Areas: A Language-Based Pedagogy*. Ann Arbor, MI: University of Michigan Press, pp. 84–103.

Lukin, A. and Webster, J. (2005) 'SFL and the study of literature', in R. Hasan, C. M. I. M. Matthiessen, and J. Webster (eds.) *Continuing Discourse on Language: A Functional Perspective*. London: Equinox, pp. 413–456.

Macken-Horarik, M. (2006) 'Recognizing and realizing "what counts" in examination English', *Functions of Language*, 13 (1): 1–35.

Macken-Horarik, M., Devereux, L., Trimingham-Jack, C., and Wilson, K. (2006) 'Negotiating the territory of tertiary literacies: a case study of teacher education', *Linguistics and Education*, 17: 240–257.

Martin, J. R. (1992) *English Text*. Philadelphia, PA: John Benjamins.

Martin, J. R. (1993) 'Genre and literacy – modeling context in educational linguistics', *Annual Review of Applied Linguistics*, 13: 141–172.

Martin, J. R. (1999a) 'Modelling context: a crooked path of progress in contextual linguistics', in M. Ghadessy (ed.) *Text and Context in Functional Linguistics*. Amsterdam: John Benjamins, pp. 25–61.

Martin, J. R. (1999b) 'Mentoring semogenesis: "Genre-based" literacy pedagogy', in F. Christie (ed.) *Pedagogy and the Shaping of Consciousness: Linguistic and Social Processes*. London: Continuum, pp. 123–155.

Martin, J. R. (1999c) 'Grace: the logogenesis of freedom', *Discourse Studies*, 1 (1): 29–56.

Martin, J. R. (2000) 'Close reading: functional linguistics as a tool for critical discourse analysis', in L. Unsworth (ed.) *Researching Language in Schools and Communities: Functional Linguistic Perspectives*. London: Cassell, pp. 275–302.

Martin, J. R. (2001) 'Cohesion and texture', in D. Schiffrin, D. Tannen, and H. Hamilton (eds.) *Handbook of Discourse Analysis*. Oxford: Blackwell, pp. 35–53.

Martin, J. R. (2002) 'Writing history: construing time and value in discourses of the past', in M. J. Schleppegrell and M. C. Colombi (eds.) *Developing Advanced Literacy in First and Second Languages: Meaning with Power*. Mahwah, NJ: Lawrence Erlbaum Assoc, pp. 87–118.

Martin, J. R. (2004) 'Mourning: how we get aligned', *Discourse and Society*, 15 (2–3): 321–344.

Martin, J. R. (2006) 'Genre, ideology and intertextuality: a systemic functional perspective', *Language and the Human Sciences*, 2 (2): 275–298.

Martin, J. R. (2008a) 'Tenderness: realisation and instantiation in a Botswanan town', in N. Nørgaard (ed.) *Odense Working Papers in Language and Communication* (Special Issue of Papers from 34th International Systemic Functional Congress), pp. 30–62.

Martin, J. R. (2008b) 'Innocence: realisation, instantiation and individuation in a Botswanan town', in N. Knight and A. Mahboob (eds.) *Questioning Linguistics*. Cambridge: Cambridge Scholars Publishing, pp. 27–54.

Martin, J. R. (2009) 'Discourse studies', in M. A. K. Halliday and J. Webster (eds.) *Continuum Companion to Systemic Functional Linguistics*. London: Continuum, pp. 154–165.

Martin, J. R. and Rose, D. (2003) *Working with Discourse: Meaning Beyond the Clause*. First and Second Editions. London: Continuum.

Martin, J. R. and Rose, D. (2008) *Genre Relations: Mapping Culture*. London: Equinox.

Martin, J. R. and Veel, R. (eds.) (1998) *Reading Science: Critical and Functional Perspectives on Discourses of Science*. London: Routledge.

Martin, J. R. and White, P. R. R. (2005) *The Language of Evaluation*. New York: Palgrave Macmillan.

Martin, J. R. and Wodak, R. (eds.) (2003) *Re/Reading the Past: Critical and Functional Perspectives on Time and Value*. Amsterdam: John Benjamins.

Moore, S. H. (2006) 'Managing rhetoric in "smart" journalism: generic and semantic contours', *Text and Talk*, 26 (3): 351–381.

Morgan, C. (2005) 'Word, definitions and concepts in discourses of mathematics, teaching and learning', *Language and Education*, 19 (2): 103–117.

Mortensen, L. (2005) 'Written discourse and acquired brain impairment: evaluation of structural and semantic features of personal letters from a systemic functional linguistic perspective', *Clinical Linguistics and Phonetics*, 19 (3): 227–247.

Oteíza, T. and Pinto, D. (2008) 'Agency, responsibility and silence in the construction of contemporary history in Chile and Spain', *Discourse and Society*, 19 (3): 333–358.

Oteíza Silva, T. (2006) *El Discurso Pedagógico De La Historia: Un Análisis Lingüístico Sobre La Construcción Ideológica De La Historia De Chile (1970–2001)*. Santiago: Frasis.

O'Halloran, K. (2004) 'Discourses in secondary school mathematics classrooms according to social class and gender', in J. A. Foley (ed.) *Language, Education and Discourse: Functional Approaches*. London: Continuum, pp. 191–225.

O'Halloran, K. (2005) *Mathematical Discourse: Language, Symbolism and Visual Images*. London: Continuum.

O'Halloran, K. (2008) 'Systemic functional–multimodal discourse analysis (SF–DA): Constructing ideational meaning using language and visual imagery', *Visual Communication*, 7 (4): 443–473.

Painter, C. (1999) *Learning Through Language in Early Childhood*. London: Continuum.

Rogers, R., Malancharuvil-Berkes, E., Mosley, M., Hui, D., and Joseph, G. O. G. (2005) 'Critical discourse analysis in education: a review of the literature', *Review of Educational Research*, 75 (3): 365–416.

Rothery, J. (1996) 'Making changes: developing an educational linguistics', in R. Hasan and G. Williams (eds.) *Literacy in Society*. Harlow, Essex: Addison Wesley Longman, pp. 86–123.

Royce, T. D. and Bowcher, W. L. (eds.) (2007) *New Directions in the Analysis of Multimodal Discourse*. Mahwah, NJ: Erlbaum.

Ryshina-Pankova, M. (2010) 'Toward mastering the discourses of reasoning: Use of grammatical metaphor at advanced levels of foreign language acquisition', *Modern Language Journal*, 94 (2): 181–197.

Schleppegrell, M. J. (2004) *The Language of Schooling: A Functional Linguistics Perspective*. Mahwah, NJ: Lawrence Erlbaum.

Thompson, I. (2001) 'Discourse analysis in psychiatry', in J. France and S. Kramer (eds.) *Communication and Mental Illness: Theoretical and Practical Approaches*. London: Jessica Kingsley Publishers, pp. 393–406.

Togher, L. (2001) 'Discourse sampling in the 21st century', *Journal of Communication Disorders*, 34 (1–2): 131–150.

Togher, L., McDonald, S., Code, C., and Grant, S. (2004) 'Training communication partners of people with traumatic brain injury: a randomised controlled trial', *Aphasiology*, 18 (4): 313–335.

van Leeuwen, T. (2008) *Discourse and Practice: New Tools for Critical Discourse Analysis*. Oxford: Oxford University Press.

White, P. R. R. (2003a) 'Beyond modality and hedging: a dialogic view of the language of intersubjective stance', *Text*, 23 (2): 259–284.

White, P. R. R. (2003b) 'News as history: your daily gossip', in J. R. Martin and R. Wodak (eds.) *Re/Reading the Past: Critical and Functional Perspectives on Time and Value*. Amsterdam: John Benjamins, pp. 61–89.

Wignell, P. (2007) *On the Discourse of Social Science*. Darwin: Charles Darwin University Press.

Williams, G. (2005) 'Semantic variation', in R. Hasan, C. M. I. M. Matthiessen, and J. Webster (eds.) *Continuing Discourse on Language: A Functional Perspective.* London: Equinox, pp. 457–480.

Young, L. and Harrison, C. (2004) *Systemic Functional Linguistics and Critical Discourse Analysis: Studies in Social Change.* London: Continuum.

Zolkower, B. and Shreyar, S. (2007) 'A teacher's mediation of a thinking-aloud discussion in a 6th grade mathematics classroom', *Educational Studies in Mathematics,* 65: 177–202.

3

Multimodal discourse analysis

Gunther Kress

What is multimodal discourse analysis?

The history of *discourse analysis* is beset by a vagueness around the homonym 'discourse'. The term names a large territory, located somewhere between two 'markers', which might, generally speaking, be something like 'providing accounts of connected stretches of language in use' and 'uncovering salient social, political, psychological features in text-like entities'. In sociolinguistics, by and large, the major emphasis has been on understanding the link between (environments of) *language use* and (features of) the *language used* (Hymes, 1964; Labov, 1966, 1972; Bernstein, 1984). In such work, 'the social' and its meanings and effects are foregrounded: who speaks, to whom, when, with what purposes, in what ways. These factors and the purposes leave traces – whether the details of pronunciation in Labov's early work or the regularity of use of a certain range of linguistic resources, leading to the development of the notion of 'codes' in Bernstein's theory.

In more *linguistically* rather than *sociolinguistically* or *sociologically* oriented approaches, the emphasis has been on seeing whether regularities of a 'formal' kind could be discerned in 'stretches' of speech and writing 'above' the sentence, somewhat akin to those that linguistics had been able to establish in relation to the sentence in the 1970s – whether in mid-century American structuralism or in Chomskyan conceptions of the organization of language at or below the level of the sentence. For that latter kind of work, the term *text-linguistics* – rather than *discourse analysis* – has been commonly used in the 'mainstream' of linguistics (van Dijk, 1977; Wodak and Meyer, 2001). In between these there are countless positions, as the distinct takes – and histories – of contributors to this volume show. There were those who, like myself, had become interested in the expression of power, 'knowledge' in and through language (Kress and Hodge, 1979; Fowler *et al.*, 1979; Hodge and Kress, 1993), for whom Foucault's use of the term *discourse* (Foucault, 1981; Kress, 1984/1989; Fairclough, 1992; Gee, 1999, 2008) provided an important means of extending the investigation of the relation of 'social givens' and language. In the writings of Foucault, *discourse* as institutionally produced 'knowledge' is a *social* rather than a *linguistic* category; the *social* is taken as the generative 'source' of meaning.

Given the range of uses just described, the terms *text* and *discourse* have frequently been used more or less interchangeably, as names for 'extended stretches of speech or writing' as well as pointing to the social meanings 'inherent' in such texts. *Discourse* has been readily used in relation to the (political/philosophical) approach of Foucault (Foucault, 1981; Kress, 1984/1989; Fairclough, 1992; Gee, 1999, 2008); or as a characterization of social interaction as the means to establish consensual knowledge, as in the work of Habermas (1984); or to name meanings of the social much more generally (as in the work of Labov, or of Hymes); or in the relatively formal approach of Sinclair and Coulthard (1975) to the organization of linguistic interaction in classrooms. The plethora of uses has blurred the meanings of the term *discourse* (and of the phrase *discourse analysis*) and has made its use as a descriptive and analytical tool problematic.

That leaves a question about two other terms: *ideology* and *text*. I use the former as the name for the specific configuration of discourses present in any one text. *Text*, in my approach, is the material *site of emergence* of immaterial *discourse(s)*. The etymology of the word *text* draws attention to the *result* of processes of 'weaving' together differing 'threads' – usually assumed to be either *speech* or *writing* – into a coherent whole. 'Weaving' implies a 'weaver' who has a sense of coherence. In multimodal discourse analysis (MMDA) – as in others – the question of who the 'weaver' is, and what forms of 'coherence' are shaped by her, him, or them, is a significant issue at all times.

In MMDA the textual 'threads' are many and they are materially diverse: *gesture, speech, image* (still or moving), *writing, music* (on a website or in a film). These, as well as three-dimensional entities, can be drawn into one textual/semiotic whole. *Text*, in MMDA, is a *multimodal semiotic entity* in two, three or four dimensions: as when students in a science classroom make a 3D model of a plant cell, or when they perform a play scripted by them in a literature classroom (Franks, 1995, 1997; Franks and Jewitt, 2001). *Texts*, of whatever kind, are the result of the semiotic work of *design*, and of processes of *composition* and *production*. They result in *ensembles* composed of different *modes*, resting on the agentive semiotic work of the maker of such texts.

Texts realize the interests of their makers. A *text* is (made) *coherent* through the use of semiotic resources that establish *cohesion* both internally, among the elements of the text, and externally, with elements of the environment in which *texts* occur (Halliday and Hasan, 1976; van Leeuwen, 2005; Bezemer and Kress, 2008; Kress and Bezemer, 2009). In the semiotic work of *interpretation*, the internal re-making the text, the interpreter of a semiotic entity also produces a coherent, newly made *text*, the result of her or his *interpretation*. There is no guarantee that the kind of coherence of the new *text* will be as it was in the prompting *text*.

Coherence is a defining characteristic of *text*. The *principles of coherence* are social in their origins and, being social, they point to meanings about 'social order'. The coherence of a text derives from the coherence of the social environment in which it is produced, or which it projects; it is realized by semiotic means. Nevertheless, the decision to select particular aspects of coherence, to shape coherence, to attribute coherence to a textual/semiotic entity or to deny it the status of coherence is always the act of a socially located maker and re-maker of a text. Power is involved in the making, recognition and attribution of coherence in a text.

Implicitly, 'coherence' as a textual characteristic gives rise to questions such as: *How is 'the social' organized? What are its salient entities and how are they configured in this instance?* and from there to the more semiotically oriented *What links with what, in what ways? What belongs where, in the ensemble of entities in a text?* As coherence is social and therefore 'tracks' social changes, *texts* exhibit the conceptions of order of the community that has elaborated these principles of order, and which uses them as a resource for establishing and maintaining cohesion and coherence in the community. In *texts*, these *social* principles appear as *semiotic* principles, made material, manifest, visible, tangible.

Being socially made, the *principles of coherence* differ from community to community and for different groups in communities. The principles held by a group defined by *generation* (as the social construction of age), teachers, let's say, are unlikely to be the same as those of a younger generation, their students. As structures of power now no longer necessarily work across *generation*, there is at the moment an ever-growing gap between the principles of (social and semiotic) order held by a younger generation and those 'before them'.

In part, *texts* are constitutive of social institutions; in part they are traces of (inter-)actions in such institutions and, in this, they provide means of 'reading' the interests and purposes of those involved in the making of *texts* in an institution. That makes the category of *text* essential and significant in discourse analysis (DA); and it makes *text* clearly distinct, socially and semiotically, from *discourse*.

In broad terms, the aim of MMDA is to elaborate tools that can provide insight into the relation of the meanings of a community and its semiotic manifestations. In MMDA, the *apt* use of modes for the realization of *discourses* in *text* in a specific situation is a central question. A multimodal approach assumes that language, whether as *speech* or as writing, is one means among many available for representation and for making meaning. That assumes that the meanings revealed by forms of DA relying on an analysis of writing or speech are only ever 'partial' meanings. The meanings of the maker of a text as a *whole* reside in the meanings made jointly by all the modes in a text. If I am interested in understanding the meanings at large in a community, speech or writing – alone or even jointly – will provide a part of the meaning only.

The category of *discourse* (in the Foucauldian sense) does not deal with all meanings at issue in social (inter-)action that emerge in *text*. *Genre*, the category that realizes the organization of social participants involved in the making and re-making of a text, operates at the same level as *discourse*: jointly they are the social foundations of text (Kress, 1984/1989). Other meanings, beyond those of *discourse* and *genre*, need to be accounted for in a full description of social interaction – large or small, formal or informal, meanings about generation or region, for instance. Power is expressed in all these, everywhere, in a multiplicity of ways. Looking at *discourse* alone is not sufficient to provide a full account of meaning in social situations and practices in the texts that are produced there. A comprehensive account of power and meaning requires further semiotic categories.

So, for instance, irrespective of the discourses invoked, a speaker or writer will need to deal with a general social–semiotic category such as 'proximity' and 'distance' and to have the semiotic means to realize meanings of what Brown and Gilman called 'power' and 'solidarity' (Brown and Gilman, 1968): in English, the use of past as against present tense (Kress, 1975; Kress and Hodge, 1979), or of deictics of distance, such as 'this' vs 'that'; and any number of other devices, different in different modes and different cultures. If a major issue in MMDA is a full account of power for instance, then it is entirely plausible to call that more comprehensive enterprise MMDA, even though in the scope of categories drawn into the 'toolkit' it goes beyond the description of the use of discourses. MMDA names the description and analysis of any text – as a complete and coherent semiotic entity – which aims at describing and analyzing what 'goes on' in a text, including the working of power in social interaction. In MMDA, an understanding of any text assumes understanding the selection of discourses, of their 'arrange-ments' – which one is dominant, what functions does each have. Other meanings are present, and they are framed by the discourses present in the text, in an ideological arrangement. MMDA, as do other forms of discourse analysis, sets out to develop tools that can be used in such a task.

In this chapter I try to elaborate on five questions. What are (some of) the key issues that MMDA has brought to light? Closely connected and central is: What is multimodal MMDA? Then there is the following issue: What does the theoretical frame of *social semiotics* entail for a view of communication and (inter-)action? Given my professional location in an educational institu-tion, what I want to know is: What can MMDA tell us about learning and social life? And a question collecting up the responses to the preceding questions is: Why is a social semiotic MMDA important?

What are the key issues that multimodal discourse analysis has brought to light?

'Multimodality' names the field in which semiotic work takes place, a domain for enquiry, a description of the space and of the resources that enter into *meaning* in some way or another (see also Jewitt, 2009). In the perspectives of different theories and approaches – psychology, media-studies, pedagogy, museum studies, archeology, sociology of different kinds – differently constituted questions lead to distinct theoretical and methodological tools, elaborated for the needs of each case. As mentioned, the theoretical approach presented here is that of a theory of meaning and communication, social semiotics, so the tools developed are shaped by that theory.

Multimodality asserts that 'language' is just one among the many resources for making meaning. That implies that the modal resources available in a culture need to be seen as one coherent, integral field, of – nevertheless distinct – resources for making meaning. The point of a *multimodal approach* is to get beyond approaches where *mode* was integrally linked, often in a mutually defining way, with a theory and a discipline. In such approaches writing was dealt with by linguistics; image by art history; and so on. In a multimodal approach, all modes are framed as one field, as one domain. Jointly they are treated as one connected cultural resource for (representation as) meaning-*making* by members of a social group at a particular moment. All are seen as equal, potentially, in their capacity to contribute meaning to a complex semiotic entity, a text, and each is treated as distinct in its material potential and social shaping. Each therefore needs to be dealt with as requiring apt descriptive categories which arise from that difference.

This means that MMDA needs to encompass all modes used in any *text* or *text-like entity*, with each described both in terms specific to its material and historical affordances *and* in terms shared by all modes.

While this constitutes a profound challenge to dominant views about the place of language, by itself it does not constitute a theory. Rather it projects the domain in which a theory – in this case, social semiotics; in other cases, say psychology or anthropology – find its application. Multimodality and social semiotics, together, make it possible to ask questions around *meaning* and meaning-*making*; about the *agency* of meaning-*makers*, the constitution of *identity* in sign- and meaning-making; about the (social) constraints they face in *making* meaning; around *social semiosis* and *knowledge*; how 'knowledge' is produced, shaped and constituted distinctly in different modes; and by whom. Multimodality includes questions around the potentials – the *affordances* – of the resources that are available in any one society for the *making* of meaning; and how, therefore, 'knowledge' appears differently in different modes.

MMDA (and social semiotic theory) deepen and expand issues which concern other forms of DA more generally. At the same time it has brought to light issues which extend beyond the scope of DA as more usually conceived. I will draw attention to four of these.

One, mentioned just above, is the *partiality of language*. A second issue is the central one of the *logics* and *affordances of modes*, with their effects on ontology and epistemology and in terms of *rhetoric*, *selection* and *design*; a third issue is a move beyond the deeply pervasive notion of *implicit meanings*; and fourth, there is the matter of *recognition*: *recognition of semiotic work*, both in terms of who does such work – the question of *agency* – and in terms of the means by which such work is done – the issue of *modes*.

Recognizing the *partiality of language* entails that all modes in a *multimodal ensemble* are treated as contributing to the meaning of that ensemble; language is always a *partial* bearer of the meaning of a textual/semiotic whole. It problematizes the notion of 'language' in two ways: first, in the context of MMDA, language can no longer be treated as providing a full account of meaning but is seen as only ever providing a partial account. Consequently the other means of making meaning must be given full recognition and attention in theories of meaning. Second, given the entirely distinct materiality of speech and writing and their different shaping in different social places, it becomes highly problematic to treat 'language' as a mode. It seems essential now to speak of the two linguistic modes of *speech* and *writing*: and to 'retire' the use of the term 'language' from the theoretical vocabulary of MMDA. So in MMDA *speech* and *writing* are treated as different modes; their meaning potentials and their discursive (and ideological) affordances are used in that way and are open for investigation. While the former view held sway, meanings expressed in other modes could be treated as marginal at best, or could remain invisible. In MMDA we are required to look seriously at all modes.

Closely allied to the partiality of language is that of *'implicit' meanings*. If all modes carry meaning, even if differently, then such meanings cannot be treated as 'implicit'. For MMDA, a notion such as 'implicitness' is an (ideologically exploitable) barrier to transparency, including meanings around power. In MMDA attention is drawn to the part all modes have in constituting the meaning of a text: differently because of their different materiality and because of the affordances which derive from that. In a multimodal approach, all meanings, in any mode in a culture are *explicit* meanings – even though there may at any one moment exist a limited vocabulary for their description – a problem of means for transcription – either in 'common parlance' or in theoretical accounts. Discourses, crucially, as I will show just below, are realized in all modes.

Modes are distinct on the basis of their material characteristics and of the social shaping of the social–semiotic affordances of that material over (often) long periods of time. *Speech* and *writing* differ both on the basis of their materiality and on the basis of their different social shaping – differently in different societies – as for instance *writing* and *image* do, leading in all cases to distinct cultural–semiotic resources. This has one further consequence in this train of reasoning around materiality, social–semiotic work and mode. Materially, nothing links *speech* and *writing* – sound and inscriptions are materially distinct. Over long periods of social–semiotic work, in some societies – though clearly not in all – links have been forged between speech and (what became) writing, so that forms of image representation have become means of representing (aspects only of) speech – as in alphabetic scripts.

'Recognition' of *semiotic work*, both in terms of *agency* and in terms of *mode*, becomes a crucial matter in MMDA. It leads to two constant questions: Whose semiotic work? And what modes are involved in that work? The first is a matter of recognizing *agency*; the second a matter of recognizing the *mode* in which work was done. In institutional situations where power-difference is marked, work done in a *mode* that is not 'recognized' is easily disregarded. School is a paradigm example, but so are examples of bureaucratic uses of language.

In the first two examples – two signs that give directions to drivers on how to get into the car-parks of two supermarkets – these four issues are brought into view. The signs are about four metres up on two buildings, one on each side of a major urban road, located just before a large and complicated intersection. The signs are unremarkable; they serve to illustrate points about multimodality and multimodal discourse analysis more generally (Figures 3.1 and 3.2).

While there are 'dictionaries' of visual signs, they are quite unlike those for language, usually as inventories of quite abstract visual entities – 'icons'. There are no dictionaries to look up for something like 'directions into car-parks', from which such signs could be taken. These signs, like the vast majority of visual signs – images – are 'newly made' from readily available, socially shaped cultural modal resources: here of *layout, colour, writing, image, font*. Each of the signs makes a specialized use of these five modes to construct an *ensemble* of modes to shape the meaning intended. Each mode plays its specific part: writing *tells*, image *shows*, colour *frames* and *highlights*; *layout* and *font* are used in part for reasons of compositional arrangements, and, as the other modes,

Figure 3.1 Morrison's car park

Figure 3.2 Waitrose car park

too, always for reasons of 'taste'. To *write* what the image *shows* would take too much space, and it would take too much time to read for motorists, who need to concentrate on the traffic at this busy intersection.

What is the meaning, overall, of each of the two signs? How is that meaning constituted? Does the meaning of one sign differ from the meaning of the other, and, if so, in what ways? How do the two signs function as messages? Who is being addressed and how?

The two signs use the same compositional elements and use them in similar arrangements. Yet they also differ: in *how font is used* – as capital letters alone on one sign, and as capital and lower case letters on the other; in type of font; in drawing style; in colour. The category of *style* is useful here to get a plausible account of that difference: style as the effect of the sum of choices made (Kress and Aers, 1982): choice of a colour palette, of individual colours, and of colour saturation;

of font-type; of drawing style and of layout. Choice points to the *semiotic work* of *selection*, to preference: this colour rather than those others; this font as better for the designer's purposes here than others. Every choice of a signifier in each of the modes (colour, font, lettering, drawing) points to a decision *made* about an apt match of 'what is to be meant' with 'what can best express that meaning'. The thick, heavy lines of one sign to carry a meaning of 'no nonsense shopping', of shoppers with 'feet on the ground', who care about 'value for money'; the lighter lines of the other sign to carry a meaning of 'we are, and we know *you* are, interested in elegance, in taste, in a light touch'. And so with all of the signs that make up the two multimodal ensembles.

The makers of each sign have constructed specific *knowledge* about this matter in this specific site, using the affordances of the modes in each ensemble. We may ask about *design*: How was this text designed? and about *interpretation*: How does this text here work, for anyone who engages with it?' All 'readers' of these texts, each one in turn, make their new sign for themselves in their interpretation, drawing on all the modes in the ensemble. In *writing* and *image* – ideationally – the signs seem designed to answer the question: How do I get into the car-park of this supermarket? In *font, colour, image* – interpersonally – the signs seem designed to answer another question: *Which* of these supermarkets is the one I would prefer to go to? If the driver's/reader's interpretation in response to the prompting (see Kress, 2010) turns out to have been misleading, he or she will find themselves grumpily in the supermarket which matches neither their sense of what this supermarket is or of who they are.

In other words, the meanings of the signs are about 'directions' in two ways: about 'geographical' directions in the mode of *writing* and *image*, and about 'social directions' in the modes of *font, colour, image*: about 'where you belong' in terms of taste and social affiliation. Along with the practical directions – 'This is how you can get into the car park' – the signs carry meanings about identity: about the store's 'brand' and what that stands for. They project an image of its assumed customers – 'This is who you are, this is the place for you.' 'Directions' to lifestyle, identity, taste and dispositions, to the 'social place' where 'I' will feel at home, are expressed in these two signs. The affordances of modes go well beyond their ideational function alone.

To return to the notions of 'explicit' and 'implicit' just for a moment. The misconception that speech or writing provides explicit information and that other modes 'leave things implicit' can be used for ideological purposes. Instead of writing or saying (what would, at the moment at least, be unspeakable or impossible to write) 'here in this store we appeal to a more discerning class of customers, the middle classes' or 'we appeal to a class of customers of coarser tastes or to people who do not care, the lower classes', these messages are given *explicitly*, but in modes that, for the moment. are less subject to social policing. This ensures that power of certain kinds is much more difficult to challenge.

Such meanings are clearly in the domain of *discourse*. The banality of the two texts does not exclude *discourse* as a shaping influence: discourses around taste, identity, a position in life; and they have shaped the signs. The multiplicity of modal resources for the realization of the meanings in the text requires the *selection* of semiotic resources apt for this task: 'choice' of *modal resources*, of *genre* and of other forms of textual organization and arrangements.

Choice leads to *selection*, and both necessitate acknowledging *design* as part of a set of theoretical tools, as a means of answering questions such as: What mode is apt here? These are questions of design, themselves deriving from a rhetorical disposition to communication. *Design* assumes the prior action of the rhetor. The task of the rhetor is to assess and describe the salient aspects of the environment of communication. The rhetor's questions seek to establish the conditions for communication: who are the participants and what are their characteristics – for instance, are they 7-year-old school children or adult participants in a public debate? What are their relations of power; what are the semiotic requirements from the matter to be communicated – for instance, is it better to show the complexity of an elbow joint in a diagram, or to show it as a 3D model, or to describe it in writing, or to imitate it gesturally, supported by speech? And there are the rhetor's intent and purposes in communicating. The agency of the rhetor shapes the actions of the designer, whose agency in turn shapes the realization of the rhetor's intent. In that conception, *rhetoric* is the politics of communication, *style* is the politics of choice; *aesthetics* is the politics of style; and *ethics* is the politics of (e)valuation.

In a multimodal environment the possibilities for *choice* and *selection* multiply well beyond those in a monomodal one. My second example aims to show how the stance on *recognition* just outlined – of semiotic work, of agency and modes, of explicitness – makes possible a different take on 'reading', 'reception' and communication generally. The example comes from a research project on museum visitor studies, 'The museum, the exhibition and the visitor', funded by the Swedish National Science Foundation and conducted at the National History Museum; in an exhibition of Swedish prehistory; at the East Asia Museum in Stockholm; and at the Museum of London, in two exhibitions: 'London before London' and 'Roman London'.

In the project, one aim was to understand how visitors 'made sense of' a specific exhibition. Visitors were invited to participate as couples (grandparent and grandchild, friends, married couples), in order for a sense of their *interaction* with the exhibition to be captured, at least in part. Participants were given wearable voice-recorders; they were given a camera to take whatever images they wished; and they were videoed as they made their way through the exhibition. At the conclusion of their visit they were asked to 'draw a map' that represented their sense of the exhibition, and they were asked to participate in a brief interview about the visit, prompted by their 'map'. All of these – video, photos, voice-recording, interview and 'map' – were seen as means of documenting the visitors' sense of the exhibition, as 'signs of learning'.

Museums have an interest in knowing what the visitors 'take' from their visits. They cannot usually exercise over their visitors the kind of power that schools (attempt to) exercise over their students, whether in relation to communication or to learning. Hence an 'assessment' of under-standing, based on the principle of *interpretation* (Kress, 2010), suggests itself as preferable. Here are two maps made by a member of two of the participating 'couples', both from the Museum of London and both from the exhibition 'London before London'.

Curators (as designers) of an exhibition have specific aims and purposes – social, aesthetic or pedagogic, ideological. These are rarely stated overtly in the exhibition, though in interviews with curators or curatorial teams it was clear that much discussion around aims and purposes precedes the construction of an exhibition – discussion framed by the interests of curators, policies of the museum, of governments. Given the absence, usually, of overt accounts, and also the need to link such accounts where they were available with features of the exhibition, MMDA seemed an ideal tool for gaining an understanding – as a hypothesis – of what meanings had been made by the curators/designers and of what meanings visitors, in their turn, made from the exhibition.

Semiotically speaking, an exhibition is a complex multimodal text/message. It provides a complex set of signs for the visitors who come to engage with it, and from it they construct for themselves an infinite series of promptings for interpretation. In that context, the 'maps' made by the visitors at the conclusion of their visit can give some indication of which aspects of the overall design/message engaged the visitor's interest and how. None of the signs, singly or together, provides, by any means, a full account of the meanings made by any of the visitors; and that applies to these two visitors (an 18-year-old woman and an 11-year-old boy), but they certainly do give a clear sense of a difference in *interest*.

Most immediately, the two examples show a specific – and we might say unusual – sense of what a 'map' is or does, with specific conceptions of what 'mapping' means and what is to be mapped. In both cases the notion of 'map' is a 'conceptual' – rather than a 'spatial' – one. Signs

Figure 3.3 Map of a museum exhibition (Heathrow)

make the sign-maker's *interest* and *interpretation* material and evident; in that sense, the maps-as-signs give an insight, hypothetically, into an implicit question: What was the interest? In the case of Figure 3.3, the question seemingly was: What, for me, were (the) salient elements of this exhibition, and in what arrangement shall I present them? In Figure 3.4, what seems to be mapped is the map-maker's sense: This is what their life was like. Both are *interpretations* of the exhibition overall for these visitors; the maps represent (an aspect) of the knowledge made and of what had been learned by them.

If *interest* guides selection, attention, framing, interpretation, we need to ask about that 'interest': who are the map-makers, what shaped their interests; what principles of selection,

Figure 3.4 Map of a museum exhibition (integrated display)

attention, seem to be evident in these maps? As a shorthand account, it may help, to understand these two *signs*–maps, to know that the 'map' in Figure 3.4 was made by one of two 18-year-old German women who were spending a week in London to get to know England. The other map was made by an 11-year-old boy from London who had come – reluctantly – with his mother for a 'day of activities' (which did not eventuate) at the museum. His attention had been drawn by a model airplane at a display representing a neolithic campsite uncovered at the site of the present Heathrow airport, as well as by an African mask and some tools and weapons.

Questions of *rhetoric* and *design* in the use of *modes* goes to initial conceptions of the exhibition, and from there to the overall 'shaping' of the exhibition: it is evident in the selection of its objects and in the salience given to particular themes and to the modes chosen in representing specific meanings – for instance in the layout of the exhibition, in its lighting, in the use of written text or of image or of 3D objects. Are 3D objects more salient, more 'attractive', more noticeable than written captions? Is movement more salient as a means of explanation than long written accounts? Are painted scenes more engaging than 3D tableaux? What effect does lighting have in creating affect and mood? Is the distance at which visitors are able to engage with objects, or whether they are able to touch an object, a significant matter? The question of *affect* has to be addressed in the case of the exhibition: the 'wrong' affect will inhibit or detract the attention of visitors. But affect is equally significant in all sites of learning, institutional or not. With all modal resources, *discourse, power, forms of knowledge*, are constantly at issue.

In all this there is another core issue, that of the *affordances* and *logics* of modes and their effects, communicationally, in *rhetoric, selection* and *design* and in terms of the differential shaping of knowledge in *ontology* and *epistemology*.

Here is a simple example, on the issue of *knowledge* and *mode*, from a science classroom for 13–14-year-olds. In the fourth lesson, on cells, the teacher asks the children: 'What can you tell me about a plant cell?' A child says: '*Miss, a cell has a nucleus.*' The teacher asks her to come to the front and to *draw* on the whiteboard what she has just *said*. She takes a felt-tip pen and draws something, as in Figure 3.5.

In drawing the image, the young woman is faced with (implicit) questions, which she had not faced in making her spoken comment. She has to decide what shape the cell(-wall) is; what the nucleus looks like; how large it is; whether it is a circle or a dot; and she has to make a decision as to where in the circle she needs to place the nucleus. The results of the decisions she has made are realized in a drawing such as that of Figure 3.5. Having drawn the circular shape and placed the dot or circle, the maker of this sign has made an *epistemological commitment*: 'this is what it is like, and this is the relation between the entities 'cell(-wall)' and 'nucleus'. A student who looks at a teacher's

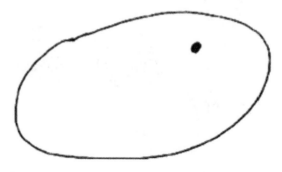

Figure 3.5 Cell with nucleus

drawing on the board or at a drawing in a text-book is entitled to take that as 'the facts of the matter'.

Whatever the mode, *epistemological commitment* cannot be avoided: a shape of some kind has to be drawn to indicate the cell-wall and the cell; a dot or a circle of some size has to be made as a representation of the nucleus; and the dot or circle has to be placed somewhere. Yet in speech there is also an *epistemological commitment*: that there are two object-like things, a 'cell' and a 'nucleus', which are joined in a relation of possession – 'has'; while the so-called 'universal present tense' of 'has' guarantees its factuality: it indicates that this is always the case. The *drawing* carries no suggestion of possession or of a timeless truth; in the drawing, the relation is one of spatial co-locations of a specific kind: proximate or distant, central or marginal. Epistemological commitment cannot be avoided, no matter what the mode. It varies in line with the affordances of each mode: here in a contrast of *speech* and *image* – of *lexis* vs *depiction*; of *possession* vs *proximity* or *distance*, of *centrality* or *marginality*; as a *verb-form* vs *spatial co-location*; *sequence* (as *temporal succession* in speech or *linearity* in writing) vs *simultaneity* (of appearance and arrangement) of the entities.

Both these signs were newly made. Both drawing and spoken utterance are based on the *interest* of the student,– manifested for instance in selecting 'nucleus' as the salient feature. Both the spoken utterance and the drawing represent this student's selection from a large variety of curricular material, encountered in the course of four lessons. Both signs represent a selection, transformation/interpretation and encapsulation of the student's knowledge at that moment. In making the signs, she is making *knowledge* for herself and for others. Both signs declare: 'This is what I *know*.'

The two representations materialize (curricular) 'knowledge' about this topic differently: ontologically the two are different accounts of the world in focus. For learning and teaching, in the construction and presentation of a curriculum for a specific group, this matters. Until 'knowledge' is 'made material' in a specific mode, it has no 'shape': we cannot 'get at it'. To me it is not at all clear what knowledge *is* before it is made material in a representation. In *speech*, knowledge is represented in a mode shaped by the underlying logic of sequence of elements *in time*; as *image*, it is shaped by the logic of simultaneity of elements *in space*. Each *logic*, with the social shaping of each in long histories of social and semiotic work, imposes its ontology and epistemology on what is represented through the organization of elements in arrangements.

To make a sign is to *make* knowledge. *Knowledge* is shaped in the use, by a social agent, of distinct representational affordances of specific modes at the point of making of the sign. Another student might have regarded 'cytoplasms' as most significant, or might have focused on the functions of the membrane of the cell; and in each case they could have written or drawn or represented in 3D what they had wanted to represent (Kress *et al.*, 2001).

What can multimodal discourse analysis tell us about learning and social life?

Modes are the result of social shaping and bear the traces of that work of constant *selection* in many environments. Why were these materials selected and not others? And why have these aspects of the materials been emphasized and those others ignored? These are traces of *work done* in response to social concerns, focus, interest, need, and so on. That can tell us much about the histories of the groups of those who use the modes. It can also tells us why two cultures may share a mode and yet make profoundly different use of that mode semiotically. That means that the 'reach' of a mode is not the same across different societies and their cultures. As a simple yet stark example, we know that all societies use the mode of *gesture*; yet how that mode is used differs vastly between, say, communities of the speech impaired and communities of people who are not affected this way.

The insistence that the linguistic modes of speech and writing are – like all modes – partial means of making meaning forces attention onto the role of other modes in meaning-making. With that comes not just the potential, but the necessity for the recognition of the meaning made by those who, for whatever reasons, use writing – and maybe even speech – less than others, yet who are highly 'articulate' in all sorts of domains of social, personal, professional life. The same emphasis forces us to rethink from bottom up the notion of 'implicitness' and, with that, of 'knowledge' and its widely differing materializations. In short, this opens up a view on a much fuller sense of meaning and knowing.

The meanings of social and professional life – of the snooker player or the surgeon, of the child playing in a sandpit or of the amateur cook at home, re-creating a dish encountered on vacation – now appear everywhere, and all are becoming amenable to descriptions and accounts. In principle, this opens the windows to an encompassing and generous view of the meanings of all members of a social group, without the restricting perspective of linguistic lenses. The recognition of semiotic work – as agency and in all modes – has the same potentially freeing effect. The potentials of that for rethinking forms of assessment in all domains, and in schools in particular, are entirely untapped and hugely promising.

The central place accorded to *materiality* in MMDA – even though subject to constant social and semiotic work – remains: MMDA opens the possibility of moving against the reductiveness of twentieth-century generalization and abstraction (in much of linguistics for instance), and toward a full account – in conjunction with other theories and disciplines – of the impact of the fact that, as humans, we are physical, material bodies and that meaning cannot be understood outside the recognition of this materiality.

At one level, this is not much more than what many of us know 'in our bodies': for instance, that in switching from one language to another the musculature of our body, the muscles of the chest and head in particular, take on distinct configurations, which express and realize distinct, deeply embodied forms of identity, meanings of a deep kind. The 'lazy drawl' of the mythic Australian stockman is more than a mere manner of talking: it speaks of a far-reaching disposition to life and to the world.

What does a social semiotic multimodal discourse analysis of communication/(inter-)action and of semiotic entities/texts entail?

If 'multimodality' names the field of work and 'social semiotics' names the theory with which that field is approached, then a number of points arise in relation to each. Multimodality, first and foremost, refuses the idea of the 'priority' of the linguistic modes; it regards them as partial means of making meaning. In principle, any mode may be 'prior' in its use in a particular environment. Modes shape our encounter with the world and our means of re-making the world in semiotic entities of any kind. This is so both in terms of the 'logics' of modes – temporal or spatial – and in terms of the consequences which flow from that in the social development of modes in a particular community over time; and it is so in terms of affordances of other kinds, for example of (still) *image* compared to *writing*. The entities of *writing* – lexical, syntactic, textual – are entirely different from those of *image*: *words* work differently from *depictions*, and spatial means of showing 'connection' and 'relation' are quite unlike those of the syntax of writing.

Social semiotics serves to emphasize what is shared communicationally: that there need to be resources for showing connection and relation in any mode, even though they will be different in each mode; that features of meaning are shared among all modes – *intensity, framing, foregrounding, highlighting, coherence* and *cohesion*, forms of *genre*, etc. – even though they will differ from mode to mode. *Intensity* may be materialized as *loudness* in *speech* and as *saturation* in *colour*, or as *thickness* or *bolding* in *writing* or in *image*.

Communicationally, social semiotic theory brings a *rhetorical approach*: that is, rhetoric as the politics of communication demands an attitude that enquires about the social environment of communication and its participants, about their relations in terms of power and their social characteristics. It focuses on what is to be communicated and on the means available for materializing the meanings at issue and the means most apt in terms of the social environment and of the characteristics of the audience. The *designer*, usually the same person as the *rhetor*, then has the task of turning the rhetorical assessment of the environment, of the audience and of the means for materializing these into a design most likely to meet the political aims of the rhetor.

The availability of modes founded on the different logics of time and space – or of both, as in *sign languages*, or *dance* – is particularly useful as a resource for *design*, for instance in designing texts or other semiotic objects on the differing principles of modularity or linearity – or to use the insights of the theory to provide descriptions of how these principles work in different modes, as much as in different cultures. A theory that includes that distinction is essential in 'the West', where linear forms of semiotic organization are now challenged intensely by modular forms – to some extent as an effect of the 'transport' of one principle from a social cultural site where it has been dominant to a site where it has not been so hitherto, as much as of the displacement of one site of appearance and display – the page – by another – the screen.

In areas of cross-cultural communication a multimodal approach is an essential prerequisite, and it affects all forms of composition, everywhere, though differently in different sites.

Why is a social semiotic multimodal discourse analysis important?

Whatever view one takes of the social, economic, cultural, political and technological world, it is a world in rapid transition and a world where the pace of 'transport' in all these dimensions has accelerated – out of control nearly. The pace of transport, the instantaneity of access in many domains, have changed the social and political and economic framings of the world and, with that, the framings around – and of – the cultural resources at issue in the semiotic domain, the domain of meaning-*making*.

This entails that more adequate, sharper tools are needed, tools that are apt for the multiplicity of semiotic resources as much as for the intensely varying appearances and effects of power in a largely unbounded and barely framed semiotic world. *Rhetoric* is essential when every occasion of communication is likely to be new and often profoundly different.

Design, similarly, is at the forefront of essential semiotic dispositions in a world of vastly varying resources, many instantly accessible, needed and used. *Design* is needed for forms of social interaction as much as for the 'content' of messages. Both the need and the potentials for designing have increased and have moved centre stage. Notions of (in-)coherence are hugely more problematic and difficult: coherence and incoherence have become more visible with the ubiquity of screens and more difficult to establish with a move to horizontally organized power.

In a world of much greater variety and variability, the wide range of available modes increases the possibilities and potentials of apt representations of the world framed. This makes the 'transcriptional possibilities' of modes into desirable or essential characteristics: the world 'transcribed' in writing as *narrative* differs from the world 'transcribed' in several modes with different affordances, distinct logics and genres.

My use here of the term 'transcription' points to an urgent problem for MMDA: the terminology available to describe a multimodally constituted and recognized semiotic world is no longer apt, and that world urgently needs renaming. The labels we have come from a world that was founded on the pre-eminence of language, and of writing in particular. Using terms that carry a heavy freight of past theory designed for different tasks, now congealed into commonsense, is likely to skew the new enterprise in its development. There is a large agenda of work here. There is also the promise of seeing and doing better. Both will be essential in dealing with the problems that currently define the world of meaning.

Further reading

Jewitt, C. (2008) *Technology, Literacy, Learning.* London: RoutledgeFalmer.

The book introduces central concepts multimodal analysis and provides analyses of texts in different media from three areas of the secondary curriculum: English, mathematics and science.

Jewitt, C. (2009) *The Routledge Handbook of Multimodal Analysis.* London: RoutledgeFalmer.

Definitional chapters from leading theoreticians and practitioners in different domains of multimodal work, in the frame of a broad theoretical 'location' of the work by the editor.

Hodge, R. I. V. and G. R. Kress (1988) *Social Semiotics.* Cambridge: Polity Press.

A wide range of materials – photographs, sculpture, newspapers, paintings, literary texts – are used to develop a socially grounded, encompassing account of semiosis, not derived from linguistic theories.

Kress, G. R. (2010) *Multimodality: A Social Semiotic Take on Contemporary Communication.* London and New York: RoutledgeFalmer.

Multimodality approached in the encompassing frame of social semiosis, with a wide range of materials exemplifying meaning-making in contemporary sites and media.

Mavers, D. (2010) *Children's Writing and Drawing: The Remarkable in the Unremarkable.* New York and London: RoutledgeFalmer.

A meticulously detailed account documenting meaning-making in the visual–graphic domain, with a sharp focus on the means for recognition of semiotic work.

Norris, S. (2004) *Analysing Multimodal Interaction: A Methodological Framework.* London and New York: RoutledgeFalmer.

A closely detailed setting out of the intricacies of multimodal interaction, providing methodologies for dealing with the complexities of handling such materials in research.

References

Bernstein, B. (1984) *Class, Codes and Control: Theoretical Studies Towards a Sociology of Language.* Vol.1. London, Routledge and Kegan Paul.
Bezemer, J. and Kress, G. (2008) 'Writing in multimodal texts: a social semiotic account of designs for learning', *Written Communication*, 25 (2): 166–195 (Special Issue on Writing and New Media).
Bezemer, J. and Kress, G. (2009) 'Visualizing English: a social semiotic history of a school subject', *Visual Communication*, 8: 247–262 (Special Issue on Information Environments).
Brown, R. and Gilman, A. (1968) 'The pronouns of power and solidarity', in Thomas A. Sebeok (ed.) *Style in Language*. Cambridge, MA: MIT Press, pp. 253–276.
Chomsky, N. A. (1957) *Syntactic Structures.* The Hague: Mouton.
Chomsky, N. A. (1965) *Aspects of the Theory of Syntax.* Harvard, MA: MIT Press.
Fairclough, N. (1989) *Language and Power.* London: Longman.
Fairclough, N. (1992) *Discourse and Social Change.* Cambridge: Polity Press.
Foucault, M. (1981) 'The Order of discourse', in R Young (ed.) *Untying the Text: A Post-Structuralist Reader.* London and New York: Routledge and Kegan Paul, pp. 48–78.
Fowler, R., Hodge, B., Kress, G., and Trew, T. (eds.) (1979). *Language and control.* London: Routledge and Kegan Paul.

Franks, A. (1995) 'The Body as a Form of Representation¹, *Social Semiotics*, 5 (1): 1–21.

Franks, A. (1997) 'Drama, desire and schooling', *Changing English*, 4 (1): 131–148.

Franks, A. and Jewitt, C. (2001) 'The meaning of action in learning and teaching', *British Educational Research Journal*, 27 (2): 201–221.

Gee, J. P. (1999) *Introduction to Discourse Analysis*. New York: Routledge.

Gee, J. P. (2008) *Social Linguistics and Literacies: Ideologies in Discourses*. Abingdon: Routledge.

Gibson, J. J. (1986) *The Ecological Approach to Visual Perception*. Hillsdale, NJ: Lawrence Erlbaum.

Gumperz, J. (1982) *Discourse Strategies*. Cambridge: Cambridge University Press.

Habermas, J. (1984) *The Theory of Communicative Action: Reason and the Rationalization of Society*. Boston, MA: Beacon Press.

Halliday, M. A. K. and Hasan, R. (1976) *Cohesion in English*. London: Longman.

Hodge, R. and Kress, G. (1988) *Social Semiotics*. Cambridge: Polity Press.

Hodge, R. and Kress, G. (1993) *Language as Ideology*, 2nd edn. London: Routledge.

D. Hymes, (ed.) (1964) *Language in Culture and Society: A Reader in Linguistics and Anthropology*. New York: Harper and Row.

Insulander, E. (2008) 'The museum as a semi-formal site for learning'. Medien Journal. Lernen. Ein zentraler Begriff für die Kommunikationswissenschaft. 32. Jahrgang. Nr. 1/2008.

Insulander, E. and Lindstrand, F. (2008) 'Past and present – multimodal constructions of identity in two exhibitions', Paper for Comparing National Museums: Territories, Nation-Building and Change, NaMu IV 18–20 February 2008, Linköping University, Norrköping, Sweden.

Jewitt, C. (2008) *Technology, Literacy, Learning*. London: RoutledgeFalmer.

Jewitt, C. (2009) *The Routledge Handbook of Multimodal Analysis*. London: RoutledgeFalmer.

Jewitt, C. and Kress, G. (2003) 'Multimodal research in education', in S. Goodman, T. Lillis, J. Maybin, and N. Mercer (eds.) *Language, Literacy and Education: A Reader*. Stoke on Trent: Trentham Books /Open University, pp. 277–292.

Kress, G. R. (1975) 'Tense as Modality', *UEA Papers in Linguistics*, 3.

Kress, G. R. (1982) *Learning to Write*. London: Routledge and Kegan Paul.

Kress, G. R. (1984/1989) *Linguistic Processes in Sociocultural Practices*. Geelong: Deakin University Press, Oxford: Oxford University Press.

Kress, G. R. (2001) *Early Spelling. From Creativity to Convention*. London: RoutledgeFalmer.

Kress, G. R. (2003) *Literacy in the New Media Age*. London: RoutledgeFalmer.

Kress, G. R. (2009) 'What is mode?', in C. Jewitt (ed.) *Routledge Handbook of Multimodal Analysis*. London: Routledge, pp. 54–67.

Kress, G. R. (2010) *Multimodality: A Social Semiotic Approach to Contemporary Communication*. London: RoutledgeFalmer.

Kress, G. and Aers, D. (1982) 'The politics of style in measure for measure', *Style* 16(1): 22–37.

Kress, G. and Bezemer, J. (2009) 'Writing in a multimodal world of representation', in R. Beard, D. Myhill, M. Nystrand, and J. Riley (eds.) *SAGE Handbook of Writing Development*. London: Sage, pp. 167–181.

Kress, G. R., Bourne, J., Franks, A., Hardcastle, J., Jewitt, C., and Jones, K. (2004) *English in Urban Classrooms: A Multimodal Perspective on Teaching and Learning*. London: RoutledgeFalmer.

Kress, G. R. and Hodge, R. I. V. (1979) *Language as Ideology*. London: Routledge and Kegan Paul.

Kress, G., Jewitt, C., Ogborn, J., and Tsatsarelis, C. (2001) *Multimodal Teaching and Learning: The Rhetorics of the Science Classroom*. London: Continuum.

Kress, G. R. and van Leeuwen, T. (1996/2006) *Reading Images: The Grammar of Graphic Design*. London: RoutledgeFalmer.

Labov, W. (1966) *The Social Stratification of English in New York City*. Cambridge: Cambridge University Press.

Labov, W. (1972) *Language in the Inner City*. Philadelphia: University of Pennsylvania Press.

Lindstrand, F. (2010) 'Transformed meanings – multimodal meaning-making at the museum', in Selander, S. (2008b). 'Designs for learning – A theoretical perspective'. *Designs for Learning*, 1 (1): 10–24.

Mavers, D. (2007) 'Semiotic resourcefulness: a young child's email exchange as design', *Journal of Early Childhood Literacy*, 7 (2): 155–176.

Mavers, D. (2009) 'Student text-making as semiotic work', *Journal of Early Childhood Literacy*, 9 (2): 141–155.

Mavers, D. (2010) *Children's Writing and Drawing: The Remarkable in the Unremarkable*. New York and London: RoutledgeFalmer.

Rorty, R. (1967) *The Linguistic Turn. Essays in Philosophical Method*. Chicago and London: The University of Chicago Press.

Sinclair, J. M. H. and Coulthard, R. M. (1975) *Towards an Analysis of Discourse: The English Used by Teachers and Pupils*. Oxford: Oxford University Press.

van Dijk, T. (1977) *Text and context. Explorations in the semantics and pragmatics of discourse*. London: Longman.

van Dijk, T. and Kintsch, W. (1983) *Strategies of Discourse Comprehension*. London: Academic Press.

van Leeuwen, T. (2005) *Introduction to Social Semiotics*. London: RoutledgeFalmer.

R. Wodak and M. Meyer (eds.) (2001) *Methods of Critical Discourse Analysis*. London: Sage Publications

4

Narrative analysis

Joanna Thornborrow

Introduction: why analyse narratives?

Narrative discourse is pervasive in most contexts for social interaction. Storytelling is integral to the way we structure, account for and display our understanding of our human condition and experience; therefore analysing narrative as a genre, or particular form of talk activity, has become one of the central areas of inquiry within the broad field of discourse analysis. Narrative analysis has been approached from many different angles across the social sciences, and from a variety of analytical perspectives and methodologies, depending on disciplinary priorities and research foci (see particularly Juzwik this volume). In this chapter I will limit my discussion of narrative analysis to an overview of the principle methods and findings taken from the related fields of interactional sociolinguistics, discourse pragmatics and conversation analysis. The scope of this work means that some forms of narrative discourse cannot be addressed here, for instance fictional, text-based, or 'news' narratives, nor will I be dealing with the more abstract sense of 'big' stories, sometimes called social, macro- or 'meta-narratives', which tend to emerge as conceptual frameworks within the fields of social and cultural studies. However, there is now a considerable body of research that deals primarily with largely unscripted, naturally occurring, spoken narrative discourse. This includes both informal storytelling, the 'small' stories (Georgakopoulou, 2007) that are woven into the fabric of everyday talk and conversational interaction, and more formal, institutional contexts for narrative discourse, from the media to the courtroom, from research interviews to therapeutic encounters. I will look at examples of both conversational and institutional narratives in this chapter. But the first step in narrative analysis is to establish a framework for identifying narrative discourse, which is to say that we need to be able to describe a story formally, before addressing the issue of what storytelling means and how it functions across different contexts for talk.

Theorizing narrative as a discursive activity

Discourse analytic research on narrative has produced some important insights into how stories are structured – that is, into their formal features – into what makes stories tellable – that is, into their cultural resonance and meaningfulness – and into what kind of work is involved in how stories are told – that is, into their interactional design and situated tellings. I outline below some of the key theoretical and conceptual approaches to narrative.

Modelling narrative discourse

That it's a story, anybody knows.

(Sacks, 1995, Vol. II: 21)

What is it that marks out stories as distinctive from other forms of talk? Stories have a recognizable shape, in the Aristotelian sense of having a beginning, a middle, and an end. How they begin, what happens in the middle, and how they end are questions that sociolinguists and discourse and conversation analysts have been concerned with for some time. In their pioneering work on the structure of oral narratives, Labov and Waletzky (1967) and subsequently Labov (1972) found that, in stories elicited in the context of sociolinguistic research interviews, there emerged an identifiable 'syntax' for narrative discourse, a structural model that, one way or another, has provided the basis for much narrative analysis over the past four decades (see Juzwik, this volume).

According to this model, a story consists minimally of two narrative past tense clauses, sequentially ordered. If the order of those clauses changes, then the story changes too. Michael Toolan (2001) provides a neat example of the importance of sequence when he points out that 'John fell in the river and had two whiskies' is not at all the same story as 'John had two whiskies and fell in the river'. In addition to the 'core' narrative clauses, there are further components that routinely occur in oral storytelling. I illustrate these components (italicized below) by using an example taken from Norrick (2005: 112). This story is told among a group of friends, three of whom are German university students, on a visit to two friends in the UK.

An *abstract* (which is an 'optional' element, as not all narratives have abstracts) can provide a summary of the upcoming story. The example below does contain an abstract of 'the story of the proposal' (line 50), which Emma develops in lines 8–10:

Example 1

```
 5   Emma:      and you should, you should hear the story of the ehm proposal
 6   Cordelia:  {laughing} yeah that,
 7   Emma:      I mean this is so funny,
 8              'cause the two of them were proposed to
 9              within I don't know, [three]
10   Lois:      [twenty-four hours]
11   Emma:      two days, yeah
```

Here Emma provides the gist of what the story will be about, i.e. two marriage proposals within two days, before the full story is told. In the lead into this story we also find an *evaluation* (line 7), which signals the value or *point* of the story, what it is that makes it 'tellable' (Thornborrow and Coates, 2005, Juzwik this volume). 'I mean this is so funny' (line 7) orients the story recipients to expect an amusing, out of the ordinary tale about what might otherwise be considered an unexceptional event (that is, to anyone other than those immediately involved in the proposal). Finding a marriage proposal 'funny' is not perhaps the most conventional assessment of such an event (romantic, unexpected, or even awkward may be more likely assessments), so this story promises to break some canonic cultural script (Bruner, 1991). Furthermore, this is a known-about story for some of the participants – two of whom contribute to building up the narrative as one worth telling (see contributions from Cordelia 'yeah that' in line 6, and Lois 'twenty four hours' in line 10). In terms of *orientation* – the 'who, where and when' aspects of the narrative – all we are given here is 'the two of them' (line 8). The identity of the 'two' is contextually recoverable to the participants, who are friends of the protagonists. Much more relevant orientation detail is produced as this story progresses:

Example 2

```
40   Cordelia:  yeah, and then,
41              he proposed in a park in Stuttgart,
42              it was really cute,
```

43		in a little hut,
44		on a ehm children's
45		what is it?
46	Emma:	[playground]
47	Lois:	[playground]
48	Cordelia:	yeah, on a playground,

The setting, the little hut on a children's playground, turns out to be a significant part of the story, and contributes to Cordelia's own assessment of the narrative as 'dramatic': they had met to talk things through, it was raining, they had taken candles, their dog had to stand outside getting wet in the rain – all, details that make the narrative of this proposal 'tellable'. The proposal itself (line 41) is the *resolution* to a *complicating action* that precedes it in the story, as we can see now in line 35:

Example 3

35		anyway, he moved out,
36		and then (3 sec.)
37		well, he realized it was the wrong idea
38		{laughing} to move out
39	James:	yeah, yeah
40	Cordelia:	yeah, and then,
41		he proposed in a park in Stuttgart,

The last of Labov's components is the *coda*, which, like the abstract, is 'optional'. This is the part of the story that signals the end of the narrative and forms a bridge out of the story time and back into the conversational present. After Cordelia's story of the proposal, we can see an explicit evaluation of the narrative by recipient James (Example 4, line 83): 'that's a great story', followed by Lois's evaluation: 'in the end, it turned out to be really romantic, didn't it?' This is similar to the 'happy ever after' endings that typically characterize fairytale romances. But it is not yet 'funny'. So, while ending the first proposal story, this coda leads into the telling of the second one (line 89) which needs to be told to fulfil the initial pitch for the proposal story as 'so funny':

Example 4

83	James:	Oh God, that's a great [story.]
84	Cordelia:	[mmh,] well, it was (2 sec.)
85	Lois:	yeah, in the end,
86		it turned out to be
87		really romantic, didn't it?
88	James:	{laughs}
89	Emma:	and then it really spoiled [Hank's plan to propose to Lois]

The second proposal story is then told by Lois, which did turn out to be funny as she thought Hank was only proposing to her because of Ernie and Cordelia and didn't take him seriously.

While Labov's model has proved to be a robust one in terms of providing a starting point for the analysis of narrative discourse in a range of different contexts (and I return to some of these contexts in more detail in the section 'Chapter Summary'), it is firmly rooted in a traditional sociolinguistic, and primarily variationist, approach to language. Labov was studying the linguistic forms used by speakers of a variety of English known as Black English Vernacular (BEV), as well as the linguistic techniques of narrative evaluation and how these developed according to age. The narratives he analysed were elicited from pre-adolescents (9–13) and adolescents (14–19) in

Joanna Thornborrow

Harlem, and were produced in response to the now famous 'danger of death' interview question (Labov, 1972: 354), which was designed to produce unselfconscious, casual vernacular speech from informants. So, while his method is useful as a descriptive model of narratives elicited during a research interview, what it doesn't deal with so well is the locally 'situated' nature of narrative discourse – that is to say, how stories emerge within the context of ongoing talk in interaction (see Schegloff, 1997 for a critique of Labov's narrative model). To explore the situated production of narratives in more detail, we need to turn to the conversation analytic tradition of research, which provides an alternative account of how and why narratives are shaped they way they are.

Narrative as an interactional phenomenon

Sacks observed that (1) people tell stories in particular ways to particular recipients; and (2) stories are so designed that recipients are aware of what it will take for a story to be told, and what kind of story it is going to be:

> Stories are 'about' – have to do with – the people who are telling them and hearing them.
>
> *(Sacks, 1995, Vol. I: 768)*

> There are ways to begin, which inform a hearer – and intendedly inform a hearer – how to listen so as to find when it will have ended, in such a way that when it will have ended they can signal that they see it has ended in a way that is related to the way it began.
>
> *(Sacks, 1995, Vol. I: 766)*

Let's examine these two fundamental points about narrative as an interactional accomplishment in relation to the proposal story above. We can see how it is set up for the listener, in this case the primary recipient James, in precisely the way Sacks describes, from the lead in or 'preface' to the story as 'so funny' in line 7, to the lead on to the second proposal narrative needed to complete the story in line 89: 'it really spoiled Hank's plan'. Furthermore, the narrative emerges within a specific context, where some of those present already know the story, elicit it from a storyteller for a specific recipient, and also participate in its telling.

Stories also need to contain 'news'; telling someone something they already know is a risk speakers don't normally take. One routine way of opening up narrative space in a conversation is through a 'story preface' (Sacks, 1995, Vol II: 18), where a potential storyteller will ask: 'Hey did I tell you about X?' or 'Have you heard Y?'.

> A story preface does a lot of work. It indicates what it will take for the thing to be finished, and it suggests what sort of thing should be done at the end. And that's one order of the things involved in 'telling a story'.
>
> *(Sacks, 1995, Vol II: 18)*

Sacks gives an oft-quoted example of a story preface where the storyteller specifically orients to the other as recipient. 'Say did you see anything in the paper last night?' he points out, is 'a request for help, where the other is then put in the position of one who might give help' (1995: 765). So, before it gets told, this story of 'the most gosh-awful wreck' begins with a request for information about the event and what the recipient knows.

Stories are shaped by the local, situated context in which they occur. They require one speaker occupying more, and extended, turns at talk, while the other speaker(s) hold off taking a turn until the story is over, but signal their involvement in the storytelling through displays of recipiency, usually in the form of minimal responses (e.g. 'oh no!', 'what?', 'did they?'). When the story is over, recipients display that they know this through an alignment with the storyteller's assessment

54

of the story: 'that's so funny/wonderful/awful' – or perhaps, if a story is judged to lack 'tellability' (Polanyi, 1985), a disalignment, or, in Labov's (1972) terms, a 'so what' assessment.

I now turn to a different example to illustrate the situated nature of conversational storytelling. In the next extract I show how a story emerges in an ongoing conversation among a group of 11-year-olds. The children are outside, walking down a street, ostensibly measuring out its length in paces for a school maths project, but chatting as they go about a well-known children's author (Roald Dahl). Below is the full transcript of this rather complex multi-party conversation, which, although it is not fully decipherable from the recording, nevertheless contains two distinct and bounded narratives (in that each has a clear beginning, middle and end).

Example 5

```
 1   Tasha:    when did he die
 2   JT:       [(about]     [x      [x)]
 3   Sophie:   [(in nineteen eighty nine]
 4   JT:       (x x x [x about) ten years ago
 5   Boy:                [it's not-
 6             (0.8)
 7   Tasha:    ye[ah yeah roughly]
 8   JT:         [(x x x x x x] x)
 9   Tasha:    it's so annoying like cos he's my favourite author now:
10             [>one of my favourite< authors
11   Pupil:    [yea::h
12   Tasha:    [and then he goes and die:s (x) and you never meet him or
13   Boy:      [(x x x)
14   Tasha:    [yeah [WHEN you're like one year old
15   Boy:            [(my favourite author's (x x x x)
16   Tasha:    [(x x x x x x x x x x x x x)]
17   Sophie:   [but there was this girl right]
18   Sophie:   there was this man (.) and um (0.9) this girl (0.5)
19   Sophie:   (ok)
20   Sophie:   [elvis presley]
21   Boy:      [(x x x x] x x I [(told him)
22   Pupil:                    [SH::::
23   Sophie:   right this (.) um (0.4) lay- this little girl
24             when she was little (0.3) she wrote to elvis presley
25             and somebody forgot to post it
26             and then they found it like forty years later
27             and po- um (0.3) and posted it
28             and it got to her house=
29   Boy:      [one hundred and forty five [that's what I had        ]
30   Sophie:   =[(x x x) elvis's actual home [(x x) >and everything<]
31   Pupil:                                  [(x x)
32   Sophie:   it was [like he only wrote three letters personal on]es
33   Pupil:          [(x x x x x-) one hundred and fifty]
34   Sophie:   one (>for each of them<)
35   Sophie:   and that was one of them
36   JT:       [okay
37   Sophie:   [and it [got there after all that time
```

```
38   Pupil:     [(x x x x x x x x)=
39   Pupil:     =(x x x)]                    [(x x x)
40   Sophie:    cos she was] still living [in the same place
41              she lived as a little girl
42              (0.7)
43   Sophie:    (isn't that really cool) hh
44   Pupil:     °oh:°
45   Sophie:    I read that in the paper
46              and there was this man right (.) and he-
47              he saw it in an old oxfam ↑shop↓
48              he found this (.) uh fil- a camera film (.) undeveloped
49              he developed it
50              and it was the person who he used to go fishing with
51              a little boy (.) and him as a [little boy.hh
52              was sitting in the middle of it (0.4)
53              can you imagine finding that
54   Boy:       that [must be so wei[rd
55   Sophie:         [it's like [I know (.) (oh x x x x)
56              (0.5)
57   Girl:      we're ↑he:re
58              (2.2)
59   Boy:       (we are near the gate)
60   Girl:      here we are
```

The narratives are embedded within another activity: counting out paces to measure the length of the street. (This ongoing task can be overheard in the exchange between two pupils in lines 29 and 33 in overlap with Sophie's narration.) The story seems to be triggered by Tasha's prior topic: her annoyance at not being able to meet her favourite author, who is now dead (lines 9–14). This talk sparks off Sophie's first story about the little girl and Elvis Presley (also dead) in line 17:

```
17   Sophie:    [but there was this girl right]
18   Sophie:    there was this man (.) and um (0.9) this girl (0.5)
19   Sophie:    (ok)
20   Sophie:    [elvis presley]
21   Boy:       [(x x x x] x x I [(told him)
22   Pupil:                      [SH::::
23   Sophie:    right this (.) um (0.4) lay- this little girl
```

It takes Sophie three attempts to get to a point where her story can be told, in other words for an upcoming story to be announced, and for the co-participants to cede the conversational space for her to tell it. Storytelling in conversational contexts takes time, in that a story is incrementally built by one speaker taking an extended turn, or turns, at talk, while the other(s) stop speaking and listen. This puts other participants in the position of being story recipients, and in a multi-party conversation such as this one this position needs to be worked up interactionally between the teller and the potential recipients. We can note Sophie's use of what Sacks (1995, Vol. I: 680) termed a 'floor seeker': 'there was this girl right' in line 17 (and similarly in line 23), and 'there was this man and um this girl ok' (lines 18–19) as an attempt to gain access to an extended turn at talk by signalling that she has a story to be told. In line 22 someone goes 'SH' which opens up that access and positions the others as recipients (although ongoing overlapping talk occurs between some in the group who are engaged in counting).

Sophie's story is not a personal narrative; it is one she has 'read in the paper' but deems relevant and tellable at this particular moment. Her evaluation of it in line 43, framed as an agreement-oriented question addressed to the recipients, 'Isn't that really cool?', provides her own warrant both for telling it and for continuing straightaway, in a similar vein, with the next story, which concerns 'the man' she has already mentioned in the floor-seeking turn in line 18. This second story ends with a coda that brings the talk back into the present time, and is again directly addressed as a question addressed to the story recipients: 'can you imagine finding that'. In the next turn, one of them provides an evaluation of the story event (line 54): 'that must be so weird':

53   can you imagine <u>find</u>ing that
54   Boy: that [must be so wei[rd
55   Sophie: [it's like [I <u>know</u> (.) (oh x x x x)

Here we can see that the two stories emerge out of the talk as topically relevant (triggered by death, fame, childhood and highly unlikely events in later life). As Sacks observed, they are designed from the beginning to let recipients know what it will take for the storytelling to be over, and indeed that there will in fact be two stories, as Sophie indicates two potential narrative subjects at the beginning of this narrative sequence:

18   Sophie: there was this <u>man</u> (.) and um (0.9) this girl (0.5)

The final assessment of the second story as 'so weird' brings the narrative to a close, just as the group arrives back at the school gate.

In my analysis of these two examples, I have used the first to exemplify Labov's model of narrative syntax, and the second to show some of the interactional work done by storytellers and recipients in the situated accomplishment of what Blum-Kulka (1997) calls a 'narrative event'. It is also important to note that the first example was an elicited story, i.e. one initiated by someone other than the teller, while the second was initiated by the teller herself, and the two narrative events involved different types of actions in each case (notably work around accessing the inter-actional narrative space). In the next section I review some more key research on the situated production of narratives which has informed our understanding of the design and function of narrative discourse in both conversational and institutional settings.

Social contexts and participant roles

In an investigation of Jewish and American/Israeli family interaction, Blum-Kulka (1997) includes an account of storytelling that takes place during family mealtimes. In her analysis of these narrative events she makes the useful distinction between three facets of narration: the 'tale', the 'teller(s)' and the 'telling'. The 'tale' refers to the story materials, the events, the chronology and the participants in the story (which we can relate to Labov's narrative components of orientation, complicating action and resolution). 'Teller' refers to a participant who takes part in the act of storytelling. Stories sometimes have multiple, collaborating tellers and it is analytically useful to be able to examine the roles and relationships of co-tellers within the narrative event. The 'telling' is the situated act of narration, the performance of the story as an interactional event. So the same story (the tale) can be told by different tellers on different occasions (tellings).

When analysing narrative discourse, researchers have drawn on these distinctions to examine the formal differences between 'tellings' – for example what happens when two tellers have competing versions of the same 'tale' (Thornborrow, 2000), or when the same 'tale' is told consecutively to two different recipients (see Norrick, 1997, 1998, 2005). Blum-Kulka has identified three main forms of collaborative narratives: monologic (with one main teller), dialogic (with question/answer participation and elicited narrative) and polyphonic, where the narrative is co-constructed by several participants. The findings from her own research into narrative activity in Israeli and Jewish American family settings showed cultural differences between the two groups in terms of ownership of the tale and performance rights. Israeli families tended to tell unshared events polyphonically, while Jewish American families tended to tell shared events monologically (see Blum-Kulka, 1997: 122–136).

In relation to what he calls 'interlaced stories' in conversational contexts, Norrick shows how the co-tellers of a marriage proposal story (a fragment of which has been discussed above) design its subsequent retelling through an interactional recontextualization of the 'tale' to produce a more unitary, humorous and more performed 'telllng' for a new recipient. His analysis demonstrates a kind of 'team performance' of the narrative discourse involved in producing 'a co-ordinated telling which lies between response stories [- - -] and collaborative narration' (Norrick, 2005: 125).

Finally, in their analysis of narrative discourse in a family context, Ochs and Taylor (1992) observed that participants in the narrative event took up different positions, or narrative roles, in the storytelling. These were identified as *introducer, narrator, protagonist, primary recipient, problematizer* (of protagonists or other co-narrators) and *problematizee*. They suggested that the asymmetry in the distribution of these roles amongst participants had a particular function for producing political order within the family. Mothers did most of the narrative introducing, or eliciting, while children were most often the protagonists. Fathers tended to be the primary recipients of the story, and also the main problematizers of the protagonists and co-narrators. Furthermore, they observed that children 'sometimes resisted family narrative activity, which suggested a certain awareness of the politics of narrative and its potential to expose them as objects of scrutiny' (Ochs and Taylor, 1992: 301). Similar narrative roles have also been identified in other social contexts, for instance in TV talk show discourse where guests' stories of personal experience are elicited by the host as introducer and sometimes co-narrator, problematized by the recipients (i.e. host and the studio audience) and where the narrator/protagonist becomes the problematizee. In addition, hosts have an additional role in such contexts as *dramatizers*, shaping the telling appropriately for the TV studio and viewing audience (Thornborrow, 2001). In the following section I examine mediated narratives further, as an example of storytelling in institutional discourse.

Narrative analysis in institutional discourse

The relevance of narrative analysis in institutional contexts, where narrative discourse takes on a more public, front stage format than the stories in the data extracts presented thus far, can be demonstrated in a range of work addressing the role and function of narratives in specific institutional settings. First I discuss some of my own research into storytelling in media discourse contexts, then I look at research on narratives produced in legal settings, drawing on work by Harris (2005) and Johnson (2008). In both contexts, I illustrate how narrative design is shaped by and through its contextual production as institutional talk, in public settings, for a particular array of participants and to accomplish particular goals.

Narrative in TV talk shows

The stories produced on television talk or chat shows are different from naturally occurring narratives in conversation in a variety of ways. Firstly, they are often elicited stories, where a TV host asks a participant to tell a personal experience narrative which contributes to the topical discussion, so the entry into narrative space is organized differently from many conversational narratives that contain a story preface or other interactional work (see section 'Narrative as an interactional phenomenon' above). Secondly, the 'tale' is likely to be already known to the elicitor and primary recipient, the host, but it is not known to other participants in the broadcast event, the studio and viewing audience. The participation framework in terms of roles – the tellers, co-tellers, protagonists and recipients – is thus configured differently and shapes the telling of the story on that occasion (Thornborrow, 2001).

In a study of competing narratives produced in public participation television broadcasts (talk shows and a small claims television courtroom), where members of the public are often called upon to produce accounts of events which are then contested or challenged by another participant, I identified a tendency for the second teller to routinely shift into the conversational historic present tense (CHP) in the second version, or 'telling' of the story (Thornborrow, 2000). These narratives can be either personal stories, relevant to the topic under discussion, which are offered as examples of particular forms of behaviour (in talk shows), or justifying accounts, elicited as evidence of actions that are being disputed (in the TV courtroom). In both contexts, the design of the second 'telling', which occurs straight after the first but is given from a different, conflicting perspective, is marked by the teller's shift into the CHP at key points in the narrative.

Here are two versions of the same story, taken from the talk show 'Esther', where the topic is how to deal with jealousy in relationships. The couple are Maria and Tony, who each give an account of the same incident at a party where Tony's behaviour had caused problems for the family:

Example 6

1	Maria:	well we can't go (down)the pub (1.0) like we could
2		never go to a night club (.) could never go in a pub
3		r (.hh) like we went to a party (.) and there was a bit
4		of an incident (.hh) like Kelly (.)that's my daughter
5		in the blonde hair (1.0)(.hh) a young chap(1.0) had
6		fancied her n'asked for her telephone number (1.0)
7		(.hh) n'it caused a bit of an argument over it Tony
8		thought (.) that I was taking the young chap's
9		telephone number (1.0) so it was quite embarrassing (.)
10		an'we had to leave the party

Example 7

1	Host:	do you think this is making (2.0) everyone's lives
2		a bit miserable (.) Tony
3		(2.0)
4	Tony:	yeah they say th'it does (1.0) makes my life miserable
5		as well really (.hh) but like (.) other things th–
6		at the party it was a different (.) situation there we
7		was all just (.) sitting having a drink n'I was I was
8		told why don't you go (.) to the bar (.) an'the
9		r minute I was at the bar n'I looked round she's talking
10		to someone else an'straight away (.hh) the old
11		jealousy comes in an' gets you n'I think what's going
12		on then she come up and said get a pen get a pen (.hh)

```
13              I gotta give that fella the number
14              [n'I'm like what? it's not for me] it's for Kelly (.)
15    Aud:      [((laughter------------------))]
16    Tony:     so I went hold on n'I'm s– [march across the dance
17    Maria:                                [((laughs------------------
18    Tony:     floor don'I]
19    Maria:    ------------].))
20    Tony:     an'Kelly's behind goin' no no no not me not me so
21              straight away I'm thinking (.) [well what's] going on
```

We can see in these consecutive tellings that, while Maria's story is narrated entirely in the past tense, Tony's is narrated using predominantly the CHP, from the second clause of the complicating action sequence in line 9: 'I looked round/*she's talking* to someone else' to his evaluation of the events at line 21: 'so straight away *I'm thinking* (.) well *what's going on*'. Furthermore, Tony uses direct rather than reported speech in his account, for instance in line 20, he reports his daughter Kelly's words 'an' Kelly's behind goin' no no no not me not me', another significant use of present tense forms.

Why does the second version contain such a high-level use of CHP, when the first does not? I suggest that the reasons for this difference are the stories' sequential relationship and what the second teller is doing in telling it this way. Wolfson (1978, 1981) described the use of the CHP as signalling a shift from narrative discourse into 'performance', and indeed Tony's version is more highly 'performed' in its telling than Maria's. In this media context, where the second teller has already figured (and in an unfavourable light) in the first teller's story, I argued that the CHP is a resource not only for producing a more performed account of the same story, but for telling it in a way that makes their version more believable than the previous one the audience have just heard.

In his discussion of Goffman's theory of 'footing', the 'production format' of utterances, Levinson (1988) noted that there are clear grammaticalized forms in many languages for displaying a speaker's level of personal commitment to what is being said, as well as for distinguishing the role of relayer or transmitter of a story from its informational source. The CHP functions here as such an 'evidential' form (Jakobson, 1971), displaying the second teller's commitment to the events by foregrounding their 'principalship' (Goffman, 1981), and presenting their actions as justifiable and accountable. Commitment and accountability are both crucial in sympathetically aligning the recipients to the second teller's position and in producing a version of the story that functions to some extent as a convincing rebuttal or counter to the previous teller's version. The use of CHP is thus significant in the design of these second tellings in the public construction of believable alternative versions.

Narrative in legal discourse

I now turn from media discourse to the analysis of narratives that occur in legal contexts. The centrality of narrative as a discourse activity in legal settings has been well documented (see for example Conley and O'Barr, 1998; Harris, 2001; Heffer, 2002). I draw on two recent examples to illustrate how narrative discourse analysis can provide insights into the way stories are shaped through their institutional context, and understanding the consequences of that shaping for the participants. I'll look first at Johnson's (2008) account of narrative negotiation in police interviews, then at Harris's (2005) study of narrative discourse as evidence in witness cross-examination.

Narrative and evidentiality

In her analysis of how suspects' 'free' narratives (a free narrative being the story first produced in lay terms on arrest for some criminal act) are transformed into institutional accounts of events where clear attributions of guilt or innocence can be articulated or resisted, Johnson (2008) describes the interactional process through which a narrative that is 'unevaluated in terms of culpability and responsibility' (2008: 328) becomes recontextualized in an institutional frame of police interview practices. The two short extracts below illustrate the differences between the start point and the renegotiated end point of a suspect's story:

Example 8

8a(start)
1   POL: so you've hit him, he's fallen back, lost his
2   balance and he's banged his head on one of the
3   wooden beams, is that right?

8b(end)
45 POL: But you admit that erm you stood up and
46   punched him in the side of the face?
47 SUS: yeah.
48 POL: Which caused him to lose his balance, fall
49   backwards, bang his head, which resulted in him
50   receiving a fractured skull in two places.
51 SUS: Yeah.

(Johnson, 2008: 339)

The renegotiated story becomes evidentially more valuable in terms of establishing the responsibility of the suspect and of moving the suspect from a position in the narrative 'where culpability is resisted to one where it is recognized and acknowledged' (2008: 331) – in other words, it occasions a more detailed story, with clear attribution of responsibility for suspects' actions. The shift of responsibility from the first 'free' version of the story to the second, negotiated version, produced through police questioning, is clearly demonstrated in this example. Johnson notes that the shift in frame from a suspect's initial story to an institutionally valuable version of events involves three main transformations: a shift of audience (the story must stand up in a court room), a shift of participation and role (establishing clear actors and victims) and a shift of evaluation into evidentiality.

My second example is Harris's (2005) study of witness cross examinations, which also uses narrative analysis to examine a particular form of narrative activity involved in giving evidence in a courtroom trial. Harris notes that witness testimony, including that of expert witnesses, consists of a significant amount of non-narrative discourse even in interrogation sequences that recapitulate past events (2005: 226). However, she also notes that in such contexts it is important to distinguish between narrative and non-narrative discourse, and she proposes a modified version of Labov's model consisting of 'orientation', 'core narrative' 'elaboration' and 'point', which she uses to analyse data from a US rape trial. 'Point', most crucially, 'establishes the significance of the narrative account for the larger trial narrative, i.e. the guilt or innocence of the defendant in criminal trials, and addressed directly to the jury' (2005: 219). In witness examination, narratives are produced in order to establish putative versions of events, to explore what did (and did not happen), and to present a version as believable to the jury.

The extract below shows a sequence where the defence lawyer tries to subvert the plaintiff's account of events, summarized as a 'telling' (lines 31–33), with his alternative account, which he presents as a 'fact' (lines 35–36). The first 17 lines consist of orientation details, and the core narrative starts from line 19:

Example 9

(DL: Defence lawyer; W: Plaintiff Vanessa Perhach; PL: Prosecution lawyer)

1	DL:	Well, let me ask you then about the beginning. The beginning is
2		in September of 1986. Correct?
3	W:	Yes.
4	DL:	When he checks into the Miami Airport Hilton. Is that right?
5	W:	Yes.
6	DL:	And you were working at the Airport Hilton at that time. Is that
7		correct?
8	W:	Yes.
9	DL:	You said that at that time you were having problems in your
10		home life. Is that correct?
11	W:	Yes.
12	DL:	As well as you were just finishing up a four-year relationship
13		with a man named Jack Reynolds. Isn't that correct?
14	PL:	Objection.
15	Judge:	Sustained.
16	DL:	And you say that you were working as a telephone operator.
17		Is that correct?
18	W:	Yes.
19	DL:	Now, of course, you found out from this registration form that
20		Mr Albert worked for NBC. Isn't that correct?
21	W:	Yes.
22	DL:	And you knew that NBC was a television network. Isn't that
23		correct?
24	W:	Yes.
25	DL:	Isn't it a fact – did you stop by his room?
26	W:	Yes, I did.
27	DL:	Is that after you found out that he worked for NBC?
28	W:	Yes.
29	DL:	And did you knock on his door?
30	W:	He asked me to come up.
31	DL:	You're telling us that he calls up on the phone and talks to
32		you and likes your voice, so he asked you to come up to his room.
33		Is that correct?
34	W:	Yes
35	DL:	Isn't it a fact that you just went and knocked on his door after you
36		found out that he was employed by NBC?
38	W:	Absolutely not.

(Harris, 2005: 230)

The 'narrative hybridity' that Harris identifies in this sequence emerges through a tension between two competing narratives: one is presented as a 'telling' and one is presented as 'fact'. In terms of its 'telling', this story is a long way from the conversational narrative discourse described in section 'Theorizing narrative as a discursive activity' above. Witness (cross-)examination is, however, a form of institutional interaction that turns crucially on the presentation of sequences of events, and its function is to establish a coherent narrative point for the jury – in this instance, to establish whether or not the plaintiff went to the defendant's room because she found out he was a well known TV presenter or because he had asked her to go up there. The relevance of this 'point' becomes clear as the trial progresses, as Harris shows in her analysis of the final examination of a witness for the prosecution. Here another hotel employee gives an account of a similar experience, which corroborates the plaintiff's narrative and results in a change of the defendant's plea to guilty:

Example 10

15	PL:	Did you hear from him after that?
16	W:	About 15 minutes later I got a page on my pager and there was
17		a call waiting and I responded to the call and it was him.
18	PL:	Why was he calling?
19	W:	He called to say that he needed a fax sent and could I send a fax
20		and help him with a fax. And I said sure.
21	PL:	Is that something that you do as part of your job?
22	W:	All the time I send faxes, and I deliver Fed Ex packages. That's part of
23		my job
24	PL:	What did you do?
25	W:	I went up to the suite and the door was – the bolt was open on the door
26		so it wasn't shut; it was ajar.
27	PL:	What kind of suite was it?
28	W:	It was a two-room suite with a bedroom off to one side and a
29		living room and a bar area.
30	PL:	And when you found the door ajar, what did you do?
31	W:	I knocked on the door and I said, It's PJ – and – that's the name I go under.
32		And he said, come on in. And he wasn't in the room, so I just walked over
33		He called from the bedroom and said he would be right out.
34	PL:	Where did you go when you got into the room?
35	W:	I walked over to the window and I was looking out the window, because
36		the hotel was right at the airport and I was watching the planes land.
37	PL:	What happened after that?
38	W:	I heard the door close behind me and I turned around I saw him
39		standing there.
40	PL:	What did you see?
41	W:	I saw him standing in white panties and a garter belt.
42	PL:	And what else did you see, if anything?
43	W:	He was exposed and he was aroused.
44	PL:	What did you do at that point?
45	W:	I was in shock. I didn't know what to do. I was in shock. I just stood there.

(Harris 205: 234–235)

Harris argues that this account is more strongly narrative than the one in example 9, because it is produced predominantly in the witness's own words, as a response to a different type of questioning. Rather than the narrative emerging through a series of either yes/no or declarative tag questions by the defence lawyer (e.g. 'You found out from this registration form that Mr Albert worked for NBC. Isn't that correct?), the story in example 10 emerges in response to information eliciting questions (what did you do? where did you go? what did you see? what happened after that?). However, in each of these examples, the narrative 'point' is not made explicitly, but is there to be inferred by the jury.

From this discussion we can see the centrality of narrative in relation to issues of evidentiality. These analyses, among other things, show how powerful narrative is in the context of producing believable and coherent versions of events through witness testimony. As both Harris and Johnson make clear, in interview and courtroom interaction there is a considerable level of activity which produces narrative in various forms and transforms raw, personal experience stories into institutionally functional discourses with coherent and persuasive cultural 'points'. Questions of blame, guilt and innocence are crucially tied to the evidential nature of courtroom narratives.

Summary

In this chapter I have aimed to make the case for the relevance of analysing narrative discourse by using a selection of examples taken from both conversational and institutional contexts. I began with a discussion of narrative form, based on the work of Labov and Sacks. These are two of the most influential accounts of narrative as a genre of spoken discourse and as organized social interaction – accounts that underpin much of the research on narrative analysis over the last four decades. Then, working through the examples, I illustrated some of the key concepts of narrative analysis and some of the ways in which narrative discourse is implicated in social action. Whether this is manifested in the ongoing accomplishment of building and maintaining social relationships through the 'small stories' of conversational talk, or in the institutional work of convincing an audience or structuring experience as evidence in a courtroom, there can be little doubt that narrative is a primary discursive resource across many contexts for human social interaction.

Further reading

A 'how-to' chapter:

Gimenez, J. (2010) 'Narrative analysis in linguistic research', in L. Litosseliti (ed.) *Research Methods in Linguistics*. London: Continuum, pp. 198–215.

Collections of recent work that illustrate the scope of narrative analysis:

De Fina, A. and Georgopoulou, A. (eds.) (2008) 'Narrative analysis in the shift from texts to practices', *Text and Talk*, 28 (3): 275–282 (special issue).

Thornborrow, J. and Jennifer, C. (eds.) (2005) *The Sociolinguistics of Narrative*. Amsterdam: John Benjamins.

References

Blum-Kulka, S. (1997) *Dinner Talk*. Mahwah, NJ: Erlbaum.
Bruner, J. (1991) 'The narrative construction of reality', *Critical Enquiry*, 18: 1–21.
Conley, J. and O'Barr, W. (1998) *Just Words: Law, Language and Power*. Chicago, IL: University of Chicago Press.
Georgakopolou, A. (2007) *Small Stories, Interaction and Identities*. Amsterdam/Philadelphia, PA: John Benjamins.
Goffman, E. (1981) *Forms of Talk*. Oxford: Blackwell.
Harris, S. (2001) 'Fragmented narratives and multiple tellers: Witness and defendant accounts in trials', *Discourse Studies*, 3 (1): 53–74.

Harris, S. (2005) 'Telling stories and giving evidence: the hybridization of narrative and non-narrative modes of discourse in a sexual assault trial', in J. Thornborrow and J. Coates (eds.), *The Sociolinguistics of Narrative*. Amsterdam: John Benjamins, pp. 215–238.

Heffer, C. (2002) ' "If you were standing in Marks and Spencers": Narrativization and comprehension in the English summing up', in J. Cotterill (ed.) *Language in the Legal Process*. London: Palgrave, pp. 228–245.

Jakobson, R. (1971) *Collected Papers*. Vol. 1. The Hague: Mouton.

Johnson, A. (2008) ' "From where we're sat ...": negotiating narrative transformation through interaction in police interviews with suspects', *Text and Talk*, 28 (3): 327–350.

Labov, W. (1972) *Language in the Inner City*. Philadelphia, PA: University of Pennsylvania Press.

Labov, W. and Waletzky, J. (1967) 'Narrative analysis: oral versions of personal experience', in J. Helms (ed.) *Essays on the Verbal and Visual Arts*. Seattle, WA: University of Washington Press.

Levinson, S. (1988) 'Putting linguistics on a proper footing', in P. Drew and T. Wootton (eds) *Erving Goffman: Exploring the Interaction Order*. Cambridge: Polity Press, pp. 161–227.

Norrick, N. (1997) 'Twice-told tales: collaborative narration of familiar stories', *Language in Society*, 26: 199–220.

Norrick, N. (1998) 'Retelling stories in spontaneous conversation', *Discourse Processes*, 22: 75–97.

Norrick, N. (2005) 'Contextualising and recontextualising interlaced stories in conversation', in J. Thornborrow and J. Coates (eds.) *The Sociolinguistics of Narrative*. Amsterdam: John Benjamins, pp. 107–128.

Ochs, E. and Taylor, C. (1992) 'Family narrative as political activity', *Discourse and Society*, 3 (3): 199–220.

Polanyi, L. (1985) 'Conversational storytelling', in T. A. van Dijk (ed.) *Handbook of Discourse Analysis 3: Discourse and Dialogue*. London: Academic Press, pp. 183–201.

Sacks, H. (1995) *Lectures on Conversation*. Vols 1 and II. Oxford: Blackwell.

Schegloff, E. (1997) 'Narrative analysis: thirty years later', *Journal of Narrative and Life History*, 7: 97–106.

Thornborrow, J. (2000) 'The construction of conflicting accounts in public participation TV', *Language in Society*, 29: 357–377.

Thornborrow, J. (2001) ' "Has this ever happened to you?": talk show narratives as mediated performance', in A. Tolson (ed.) *TV Talk Shows: Discourse, Performance, Spectacle*. Mahwah, NJ: Erlbaum, pp. 117–137.

Thornborrow, J. and Coates, J. (2005) *The Sociolinguistics of Narrative*. Amsterdam: John Benjamins.

Toolan, M. (2001) *Narrative: A Critical Linguistic Introduction*. Third Edition. London: Routledge.

Wolfson, N. (1978) 'A feature of performed narrative: the conversational historical present', *Language in Society*, 7: 215–237.

Wolfson, N. (1981) 'Tense switching in narrative', *Language and Style*, 14: 226–231.

5

Mediated discourse analysis

Suzie Wong Scollon and Ingrid de Saint-Georges

In December 1972 Ron and Suzie Scollon lived in Honolulu under the flight path of tankers flying to Guam to refuel B-52 bombers headed for Vietnam. From December 18th through the 29th, especially on Christmas Day, they noticed a great increase in the number of tankers. Ron reported this to friends who were active in protesting the war, but they did not believe his report, saying they had not read about it in the IF Stone weekly. This event marked an early stage in Ron's thinking about mediated discourse, as he observed that highly educated and well informed people would not believe what they could see with their own eyes and hear with their own ears had they chosen to do so. One, a professor of syntax, telephoned Senator Patsy Mink, who denied any knowledge of escalation. Not until they read about the operation in print did they believe it was happening. We now know that there was a secret "Operation Linebacker II," a massive bombing of Hanoi and Haiphong.

Mediated discourse analysis (MDA) is an approach to discourse analysis developed by Ron Scollon and colleagues around the turn of the millennium. As a theoretical position, it focuses on linkages between discourse and action and how these play out in complex social situations. It examines two broad kinds of questions that have been left under-theorized by other approaches. It investigates what part texts play in actions undertaken by social actors on the one hand and how texts arise as the outcomes of social interactive processes of production on the other hand. It will often start by asking (R. Scollon, 2001a, 2002):

- What is/are the action(s) going on here? What is someone doing here and why?
- What is the role of discourse in this/those actions? By whom is it produced, why is it used, and what motives are behind it?

By beginning with action rather than discourse or utterance meaning, MDA questions the idea that you can always "read" the meaning of a text from studying the text alone (Jones and Norris, 2005: 9). It prefers instead to pay attention to texts as they are used to mediate the real-time concrete actions of agents in actual social interactions and to examine their relevance to these actions. By doing this, MDA "seeks to develop a theoretical remedy for discourse analysis that operates without reference to social actions on the one hand, or social analysis that operates without reference to discourse on the other" (R. Scollon, 2001a: 1).

The core ideas of MDA were first articulated by Ron Scollon in the late 1990s (R. Scollon, 1997, 1998, 1999) on the basis of thinking and research dating back 50 years, when he read Nishida (1958), then used himself as an informant to study literacy, also using Spanish as a means to learning to play classical guitar and using guitar lessons as a means to learn Spanish. As a graduate student in linguistics in the early 1970s, he observed how people were so influenced by news media that printed accounts overrode what they could see and hear with their own eyes and ears. Back in December 1972, Scollon was trying to inform his fellow protestors that the war in Vietnam was escalating, with the intention perhaps of provoking joint action of some kind. He was dismayed that, because of the lack of media reportage, his friends did not believe what he told them, thus the first action of informing was derailed. The role of discourse was that, pending confirmation of the first action of informing, no further action could be taken. Scollon compared newspaper accounts of a bombing, showing how different details were selected to support varying ideologies.

Scollon's interest in narrative led to work in the ethnography of communication (Scollon and Scollon, 1979) and to new literacy studies (Scollon and Scollon, 1981). These were followed by work reported in *Nexus Analysis* (Scollon and Scollon, 2004) and in a study of media discourse (R. Scollon, 1998) and to a reworking of earlier work on first language acquisition (R. Scollon, 2001a), which theorized the nexus of practice. Thus MDA is in part a culmination of a theorization of research conducted from 1978 to 1983 in Alaska, reported in *Nexus Analysis*, and of research conducted from 1992 to 1997, largely in Hong Kong, theorized in *Mediated Discourse as Social Interaction* (R. Scollon, 1998).

Key studies

Scollon (1998) is usually credited for being the springboard from which scholars began doing what came to be known as mediated discourse analysis. It has led a number of them to engage in concrete, careful attempts at making visible for analysis the connections between discourse and action—a relatively daunting task, as actions are rather complex phenomena. They are complex at the time of their occurrence, and even more so if we take into account the historical circumstances that have led to them.

To disentangle these relations in the spirit of R. Scollon (2001a) in detailing the ontogenesis of language in a one-year-old child, some researchers have found it useful to pay attention to the ontogeny of social practices.[1] S. Scollon (2001), Shroyer (2004), and Castillo-Ayometzi (2007), for instance, have asked not only how social practices come about, but what happens when individuals can no longer operate according to the established norms and to practices embodied in their habitus[2] (Bourdieu 1977), and new practices need to replace the old ones (S. Scollon, 2001). Shroyer (2004) takes up the study of the practices through which children in America become "connected" with the American heritage in their early school years (daily pledge of allegiance, reading of text books, enacting of landmark events). This study raises the question of how children might develop the patriotic dispositions that might elicit strong commitment and loyalty to the nation in later years. Castillo-Ayometzi (2007) discusses adaptation and resilience in undocumented immigrants to the USA. Analyzing how, looking for a network of social support, they fall prey to the proselytizing practices of Baptist church missionaries, she documents how they are forced to embrace new narratives of the self, despite finding vivid contradictions between these and their own beliefs and experience. S. Scollon (2003) looks at the adjustments that take place among a group of friends practicing Taijiquan together in a Hong Kong park during the Taiwan Missile Crisis in March 1996, as different actors identify with different political stances. Exploring the links between social practice, habitus and ideology, these studies attempt to clarify how individuals "carry or are carried by political, social or cultural discourses" (S. Scollon, 2001) and to understand how broad macro-social–political discourses (e.g. religious or nationalist discourse) become part of our embodied life—one prime area of concern in MDA.

Other attempts to render apparent the dialogic connection between discourse and action consider the role of embodied actions in anticipating or producing certain events, action or states. With regard to political discourse, again, there was interest in showing that broad policies and regulations do not come out of nowhere but really arise out of a series of embodied actions at the micro-interactional level, with the corollary that these policies and regulations can also be impacted by acting at this level (R. Scollon, 2008). While Al Zidjaly (2006) discusses the strategic uses of narratives and anticipatory discourses through which a quadriplegic man in Oman manages to have his caregivers act on his behalf and transform a law affecting him as a handicapped person, Dunne (2003) studies the making and shaping of Egyptian President Mubarak's speeches by multiple stakeholders and the particular meanings of "democracy" they impart. Both studies show that "politics" and regulations result from a host of local actions and practices, which then circulate on larger timescales to affect the lives of others. Al Zidjaly also advanced the efforts of others (S. Scollon, 2001; de Saint-Georges, 2003, 2012) to study the anticipatory stances individuals take toward their capacity to effect change in the future.

But focus on broad discourses and actions can also point to situations when discourses *fail* to be relevant to the actors targeted by them and on the consequences of the failure to integrate one group's practices and discourses with another's. Jones (1999, 2007), presenting the key findings of the first extended study in MDA, shows the all but unbridgeable gap between what public media say about AIDS/HIV and the actions and identities of social actors engaged in non-safe sex behavior or drug use. The official stance that "quality" people do not get AIDS/HIV creates "imaginary protections," encouraging people to disconnect their sexual behavior from possible infection. This gap makes public health discourses largely irrelevant in producing effective changes in behavior, with easily anticipated consequences. This study and others also show powerfully the nexus of social practices by which individuals build their social identities, impute identities to others or renegotiate the scripts associated with their social roles (R. Scollon, 1997, 1998, 2001a; Jones, 1999, 2007; S. Scollon, 2001; Wohlwend, 2009b); they also show how this nexus selects or leaves out bits of circulating discourses to piece together these identities (Norris, 2005), sometimes with dire consequences.

Transverse to many of the studies in MDA is thus a fundamental interest in human action not just as a theoretical issue, but as the "root of social change" (Johnston, 2004) as well as of individual transformation. Thus many MDA scholars have addressed social issues. They have focused on public health and AIDS/HIV prevention (Jones, 1999, 2007). They have examined the grounds on which officers of the immigration and naturalization services approve or deny granting a green card to non-US citizens (Johnston, 2004). They have discussed food, commerce and commodity discourses in the global age (de Saint-Georges and Norris, 2000; Scollon and Scollon, 2005; R. Scollon, 2005a), literacy, assessment and inclusiveness in the classroom (Wohlwend, 2009b), or processes of marginalization of minority cultures in real-time interactions as well as in urban landscapes (Lou, 2010a). They have considered the practices of "translating" a child from one continent and one world of practices to another, as in international adoptions cases (Raudaskoski, 2010). They have also explored issues linked to learning and the individual transformations that occur when going through new "semiotic apprenticeships" (Wells, 1999) or identity shifts. This has most clearly been shown perhaps in the work of Jocuns (2007, 2009) focusing on the learning of gamelan, a traditional Balinese form of music in which learning how to be an active participant in how gamelan is learned is part of becoming a gamelan player in its own right. Learning has been equally studied in Norris (2005) or Jones (2009), who look at the means through which individuals find, in their environments and technologies available around them, material for articulating new discourses about themselves—as when a woman needs to rethink her notion of family and agency as a recently divorced individual, or when skaters use video technology to perfect their acrobatic figures.

Although the projects mentioned above may vary greatly in the issues they take up or the aspects of MDA they stress, they have a number of characteristics in common. Firstly, they share a broad definition of discourse, including not only written and spoken texts, but also the broader social and historical "discourses" (Gee, 1996: 132) embodied in the built environment, in people's demeanor and beliefs, in objects and artifacts, and reflecting sets of beliefs, attitudes, representations and so on. Secondly, since the authors usually explore complex issues and networks of practices, they also tend to solicit and blend a variety of methodological tools, mobilizing the ones they deem most fit to address the issue under analysis. Lou (2010a, b) or Wohlwend (2009a, b) illustrate this in an exemplary way as they solicit multiple approaches for data gathering and data analysis (linguistic landscaping, multimodal analysis, discourse analysis, ethnographic observations, sociolinguistics interviews, etc.) by using some methodologies to strengthen the potential weaknesses of others—a process called, in MDA, "methodological interdiscursivity" (R. Scollon, 2000; de Saint-Georges and Norris, 2000). Finally, because complex issues usually extend in space and time, the research overviewed often looks beyond the here and now, considering how present discourse relates to past or future ones. They thus "enlarge the classical circumference of discourse analysis" (R. Scollon, 2001b; de Saint-Georges, 2005), a perspective that few other approaches to discourse have taken thus far.

Theoretical underpinnings

From a theoretical point of view, MDA is wide-ranging and deeply interdisciplinary in orientation, with roots in at least the following frameworks: interactional sociolinguistics, conversation analysis, anthropological linguistics or the ethnography of communication, critical discourse analysis, practice theory, mediated action and activity theory, social semiotics, multimodal discourse analysis, the new literacy studies and, more recently, cultural geography (Jensen, 2007). MDA does not hesitate to combine frameworks (even if some of them are not always considered compatible elsewhere), for the reasons we hinted at above: if social issues are complex, it does not seem viable to approach them by limiting oneself to one particular angle. The frameworks mentioned above are all important pillars of the MDA perspective because each of them illuminates in specific ways the study of social practices.

For example, MDA shares with critical discourse analysis (CDA) the goal of understanding societal issues and conflict, both contending that discourse analysis opens a window on social problems largely constituted in discourse, with power relations grounded in social practice. MDA sees discursive practices as *one form of social practice*, not the foundational or constitutive form of practice out of which the rest of society and the resulting power relations arise. MDA takes it that discourse is *among the means* by which society and culture are constituted. MDA also argues that society and culture are constituted in the material products of that society as well as in its non-discursive practices—e.g. handing (R. Scollon, 2001a), photography, skateboarding (Jones, 2009).

MDA also incorporates the frameworks of the new literacy studies (NLS; Scollon and Scollon, 1981; Street, 1984; Gee, 1996; Barton and Hamilton, 1998). Much prior research reified literacy as an ontological object independent of human action; one "had" or "did not have" literacy. NLS scholars on the contrary have shown literacy to be itself a form of practice, giving off information about individuals' identities and affiliations. For example, in Singapore citizens are schooled in literacy in English and Chinese, Malay or Tamil, each with a different writing system, depending on family origins. Researchers have discussed how different literacies have different currency on the "literacy market" of a community and thus are sensitive to the power relations dominant in the community. MDA seeks to extend this conceptualization to all other mediational means. It is not just literacy that is constituted within practices, but all mediators of actions. Mediational means always index certain identities and express belonging and membership (as in the amateur use of the chisel by the occasional woodcarver or its expert manipulation by the professional cabinetmaker).

From anthropological linguistics and intercultural communication analysis, MDA takes the concern to explicate the sociocultural production of group identities, boundaries, and the discursive process of "othering." From interactional sociolinguistics and ethnomethodology, MDA takes its focus on real-time actions and on the "practical" inference that individuals need to make as they construct and interpret meanings. From "cultural geography" and multimodal semiotics, it borrows an interest in place and in the way we interpret the meaning of public texts as they are materially placed in the world (Scollon and Scollon, 2003). For MDA, many useful theoretical tools and concepts have been provided by other traditions, and they can usefully be brought together to illuminate the study of human actions.

Unit of analysis

While firmly anchored in the various frameworks briefly highlighted above, MDA has also developed a toolkit to focus attention on its own issues. We thus spell out key notions and ontological entities mobilized by researchers working within that frame. In general, social theory takes social groups or social classes as the primary focus of analysis. They are considered the "social units" that constitute the world and society, and individual humans who make up social groups are largely taken as interchangeable. Central questions typically have to do with how struggles between classes or groups form a dialectic so as to produce ideology, which is then absorbed by or embodied by individual members, giving groups a relatively permanent or stable existence. Social institutions, then, are primarily ontological entities where these struggles take place; individual humans become interesting only as they come to represent social institutions (Wertsch, 1991).

In contrast to this "social theory ontology" is an "individual ontology"—often called cognitive— that sees everything as being built up out of the actions or values or will of individuals. Struggles or conflicts, or even successful interactions, are primarily thought of as individual or interindividual, though some individuals "borrow" on the power of aggregates of people who have a common goal or interest. For example, a union as an aggregate of individuals may strike in order to obtain higher wages. Within that ontology, cognitive psychology is the primary discipline from which everything else derives.

Instead, in MDA researchers take the primary entity to be the *social action*, taken by a social actor through the use of some *mediational means* (Wertsch, 1991). These are all the physical and symbolic "objects," carriers of history and culture, that mediate people's actions and interactions, from technical tools and objects such as drills, bottle openers, pen and papers to the representational tools of language, diagrams, mnemonic techniques, pitch and intonation or genres. Mediational means have both inherent affordances and constraints: they enable certain actions better than others, and, to be useful, their usage needs to have been internalized at some point in the life cycle of the individual. As R. Scollon (2005b: 20) notes, focusing on the mediated action as the unit of analysis is a way of positioning the focus at a point that is not the individual social actor, nor the social groups or institutions, nor the mediational means, but a point at which these are brought concretely into engagement.

In MDA researchers further distinguish between social action and *social practice*. The former stresses the fact that each action is always unique and irreversible. This action at 5.30 pm is different from that action at 5.31 pm. Observation of everyday life makes it obvious that there are also kinds of actions that recur more or less frequently in the lifetime of an individual. These recurring actions, usually learned by participating in the everyday social life of a specific community, are called "practice" in MDA. Bourdieu (1977) defines a practice as an action with a history. R. Scollon defines a practice as "a historical accumulation within the habitus/historical body of the social actor of mediated actions taken over his or her life (experience) and which are recognizable to other social actors as 'the same' social action" (2001b: 149). Unlike its use in sociology and social theory, practice in MDA is understood in a rather narrow sense. MDA focuses not on "nationalism" as a practice, but on the myriad local actions that come to constitute, over time, a nationalist attitude in a particular individual located in a specific community. For example, putting the right hand over the heart, standing and saying the pledge of allegiance every morning in the classroom will be recognized by Americans as such a practice. It might coexist with cooking turkey in a certain way every November, or with wearing small flags and ribbons on one's jacket's lapel and the like.

The material entities constitutive of a mediated action

Some might argue that starting from such concrete units as the fleeting social action or the repeatable social practice is too narrow a focus to address the important social issues of our time (Jones and Norris, 2005; R. Scollon, 2008: 11). The stance taken by MDA, however, is that the broad social discourses of contemporary life circulate through all moments of human action, so in that sense looking at practice might be more meaningful than might seem at first glance. These broader social discourses may be most visible when one starts to unpack three essential material entities constitutive of any mediated action (see Figure 5.1):

1) the historical body of the social actor(s) engaged in the mediated action
2) the interaction order (the configuration of people present and the social structuring of their relationships)
3) the discourses in place (the complex set of discourses at the intersection of which the social action is carried out).

The *historical body* (Nishida, 1958), or what others, following Mauss (1936) and Bourdieu (1977), refer to as "habitus," could be defined as the abstraction of the aggregation of social practices or repeated experiences of the social actor in the course of life. It corresponds to the accumulation of

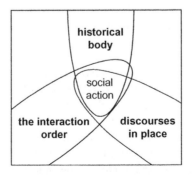

Figure 5.1 The material entities constitutive of a mediated action (reproduced from Scollon and Scollon, 2003).

experience that makes people perform actions with greater or lesser facility or dexterity. A lifetime of personal habits feel so natural that one's body carries out actions seemingly without being told. For example, a person might automatically squish ants on her desk. Another might get a spider or a ladybug to crawl onto a piece of paper and then shake it out a window. These actions reveal to spectators a lifetime of habits. Though the same person might do one for decades and then change to the other, the actions are linked by belonging to specific networks, and ultimately they are forms of embodied ideology.

The notion of *interaction order* comes from sociologist Erving Goffman (1971). It refers to the social configuration in which actors find themselves: the individuals who are present, the attention they pay to each other, the ecology of the situation. The concern is to identify in what kind of interactional configuration an action is carried out or inscribes itself. As R. Scollon (2008: 19) emphasizes, reading a statement criticizing some new regulation constitutes a very different kind of action (and thus carries very different meanings) depending on whether someone is reading this statement alone at his desk, in front of a television camera, or out loud among a group of activist friends sharing the same outlook on the regulation. The impact of the reading will be very different depending on the participants' roles in the situation: whether one is a ratified participant in a talk-show or voices his opinion as a non-invited guest will likely make a big difference in the reception and interpretation of this discourse. As R. Scollon remarks, the meaning of the text being read might at first have a potential for interpretation that we assume would not vary greatly from one situation to another, but the actual act of reading might transform that meaning given the interactional configuration in which it is accomplished (2008: 19).

The third material entity requiring attention is the arrays of texts actually present in the situation, as well as the mediational means available at the point of taking action: which texts or tools are being attended to? Which ones are being ignored or sidelined? The role of the analyst is to identify which discourses are present and used at the moment of performing a social action. Studying the discourses in place in a classroom for example might include attention to the posters on the walls, the spatial organization of desks and the perspective on instruction they materialize, the words written on the board, presidential portraits or religious crucifix, the text-books, the "play corner," the architecture of the school, its location in a wealthy or poor urban suburb and the way the sun shining through the windows changes the atmosphere and level of concentration. Besides studying these components, the researcher will need to listen to the overt discourses circulating in that space: the private chat pupils have hiding from the teacher's attention, the group discussions in collaborative moments of learning, the way the teacher words his explanations and instructions, the essays written by the pupils or the poems recited by them. She will also need to pay attention to the discourses "submerged" in the historical bodies of participants. A mediated discourse analysis does not seek to make an inventory of the discourses aggregating in one place, but rather to identify which ones constrain the actions of interest to the researcher and which ones seem, on the contrary, to facilitate their accomplishment or give them impetus.

Attending to these three interrelated aspects of any mediated action is a way to avoid uprooting words and actions from the historical bodies of the individuals performing them, or disconnecting the discourses and actions from the sociocultural context of their formation and realization, or ignoring the history of these actions and discourses for the individual and in the situation. These three entities—historical bodies, interaction order, discourses in place—are indeed not static entities but "processes in motion over time" (Wortham, 2006). The individual accumulates experience in the course of his/her trajectory across time and space, social orders open up and close and are rearranged, discourses in place are transformed as buildings are refashioned, inno-vative technologies are introduced, new texts and discourses circulate. The trajectory of these changes is unpredictable. Successfully developing a mediated discourse analysis means trying to map when these somewhat autonomous trajectories intersect and meet.

Given this complexity, one last issue that needs to be addressed concerns how researchers can be in a position to identify and analyze the actions most likely to give them a grip on the issue they are investigating. That question is taken up in the next section, as we report in a brief example what an MDA research project might look like.

Doing a mediated discourse analysis: nexus analysis

The historical, ethnographic and methodological arm of MDA is called "nexus analysis." A nexus analysis consists in opening up the circumference of analysis around moments of human action to begin to see the lines, sometimes visible and sometimes obscured, of historical and social processes by which discourses come together at particular moments of human action, as well as to make visible the ways in which outcomes such as transformations in those discourses, social actors and mediational means emanate from those moments of action.

Nexus analyses can take many forms (compare for example Jones, 2007, Wohlwend, 2009a, b, Raudaskoski, 2010, and Lou, 2010a, b). The research may involve close analysis of texts (or not), semiotic analyses of visuals, study of the interaction order, ethnographic observations and the like—or any combinations of these. This variety proceeds from nexus analysis as a form of action research, intimately bound to the specifics of situation studied and issue researched. The researcher in MDA is considered an integral part of the nexus she studies. She uses scientific inquiry to engage with the nexus—sometimes even to transform it.

A nexus analysis usually centers on three main tasks or activities: (1) engaging the nexus of practice; (2) navigating the nexus of practice; (3) changing the nexus of practice.[3] The following report on a project carried out by one of the authors (together with Yuling Pan; see S. Scollon, 2005) on census enumeration illustrates very briefly what is involved.

The opening task, "engaging the nexus of practice," consists in establishing a "zone of identification" with the nexus—that is, the researcher must place herself as part of the nexus of practice under study. When and how to identify oneself as part of the nexus is thus an important part of "engaging the nexus." We examine how this step is taken in the "census enumeration project."

A census consists of a series of closely related activities through which information about the members of a given population is acquired and recorded for statistical purposes for research, marketing or planning. Pan and Scollon sought to understand the moment of enumeration involving Chinese immigrants to the United States, uncovering sociopolitical discourses embodied in census forms and census enumerators, as well as immigrants. In particular, they wanted to find out why certain recent immigrants were reluctant to engage in the process. A preliminary step was to enter the nexus of practice. The focus was on determining the kind of interactional configurations in which enumeration happens (interaction order), the history of experience individuals had with census enumeration (historical body), and the aggregates of discourses coming into play at the moment when individuals engaged with a governmental discourse such as census enumeration ("discourses in place"). At this early stage, the authors identified the door-to-door interviews carried out by census enumerators as key moments of the process. They decided to observe the small "withs" (Goffman, 1971) or configurations of actors in which the process takes place, the history of practice of Chinese immigrants with the forms, and the discourses in place in homes where census enumeration typically occurs. It was relatively simple for the researchers, sponsored as they were by the US Census Bureau, to identify themselves as participants in interviews of Chinese immigrants and thus to start establishing themselves in a zone of identification with the residents of Washington DC urban neighborhoods. This position not only provided a good look-out post from where to study the practices of census enumeration, but also allowed them to engage in this practice themselves.

The second stage and main phase of a nexus analysis, "navigating the nexus of practice," consists, beyond identifying key sites and action, in working your way through the "trajectories of participants, places and situations both back in time historically and forward through actions and anticipations to see if crucial discourse cycles or semiotic cycles can be identified" (R. Scollon, 2008).

To understand why some people might be reluctant to engage in door-to-door interviews, researchers needed to go beyond local actions to open up the circumference of analysis. This is akin to providing what literary critics term the "backstory"—a narrative of what has happened in the character's life before the current narrative begins. In the census study the researchers set out to study how the habits of residents related to forms, languages, gadgets such as clipboards, as part of the discourses circulating at the moment of filling out the form. They attended to the interactional configuration in which enumeration takes place. They also paid attention to the historical bodies of individuals, their different ethnicity or their gender and occupational roles.

Looking at door-to-door interviews, the researchers identified a number of potential obstacles. Even before such an action can take place, the enumerator must gain access to a respondent by ringing a doorbell. No questioning can take place if a resident does not recognize the enumerator and open the door. The enumerator must present an adequate "personal front" (Goffman, 1971). She must take care to look professional and somewhat official, but unlike a solicitor. But, to understand this simple action, we also need to understand the habits of residents. In many big cities it may not be considered safe to open the door to strangers, and, in the experience of many residents, this may simply never have been done.

Navigating the nexus of practice also entailed interviewing a social worker with ten years of experience in working with Chinatown immigrants and in helping them deal with the census. Participants also taught English to recent immigrants, interviewing them in the process. The social worker highlighted that in Chinatown the census workers were typically African American males who had difficulty gaining entry into homes where Chinese immigrant women were home alone. The researchers also found out that recent immigrants from China are accustomed to having forms being filled out by census takers and thus have limited experience with deciphering questions or filling out forms, answering multiple choice questions or interacting with strangers or representatives of the government. This historical memory, as well the inability to speak or read English or Census form Chinese (that is, to speak Mandarin and to read simplified rather than complex characters), made them reluctant to engage in census enumeration (see Figure 5.2).

Navigating the nexus of practice thus resulted in studying discourse on three different levels. Firstly, it consisted in studying discourse as the complex aggregates of discourses in place, including the discourse on the census forms, the ways of dressing of census enumerators, their technological front (with personal digital assistants, notebook computers and the like), the design of the form,

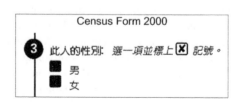

Figure 5.2 The census form in 2000

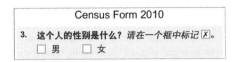

Census Form 2010

3. 这个人的性别是什么？ 请在一个框中标记 X 。
　　□ 男　　□ 女

Figure 5.3 The census form in 2010

the characters chosen and so on. Secondly, it included studying discourse as, and in, the bodies of individual social actors and how they embodied consciously or unconsciously a history of socio-cultural processes (opening doors to stranger, filling a form oneself or having it filled by someone else and so on). Thirdly, navigating the nexus consisted in analyzing discourse as distributed in the bodies of other social actors (the exchanges between census enumerator and residents, between social workers and residents, identity displays and so on). This analysis allowed the unpacking of various aspects of census enumeration as a situated and mediated process.

The third stage in a nexus analysis is called *changing the nexus of practice* and consists in re-engaging the product of the analysis back into the nexus of practice where it originates. The researcher has now contributed "time and skills in analysis to open up and make visible links and connections among the many trajectories of the historical bodies, discourses in place, and inter-action order," which constitutes the issue under investigation (Scollon and Scollon, 2004: 178), and the work of analyzing and disentangling practices and discourses has now become an integral part of the nexus. In the census project, changing the nexus of practice consisted in recommending changes at various levels on the basis of the results of the analysis. These included changes in the discourses in place, such as the Chinese characters printed on census forms (see Figure. 5.3), the place of enumeration and the interactional configuration. Many Chinatown residents were now being enumerated by a trusted social worker at a nearby social service center rather than by strangers at their home. Doing discourse analysis was thus transformative of the nexus of practice.

It may not be evident to the reader how this simple change in the way the US Census Bureau goes about its work constitutes activist sociolinguistics. It is conceivable that, taken together with Johnston's work with the immigration and naturalization services, Castillo-Ayometzi's work with narratives of undocumented immigrants crossing the Rio Grande into Texas, Shroyer's work on patriotism and recent moves by the State of Arizona to allow detention of citizens or documented immigrants without cause, changes in enumeration may be less than trivial. When door-to-door enumeration becomes a form of gatekeeping encounter in which the census taker has power to define significant outcomes for respondents who must account for themselves, it might be important that the respondents keep some agency in the process.

Conclusion

We see discourse analysis as a fundamentally active force. As Ron Scollon concludes in his book *Analyzing public discourse*, "in democratic public discourse positions are stated, positions are argued, positions are negotiated and the actions which are taken and which become policy and practice are the outcome of this dialectic" (2008: 162). Linguists have a role to play in society because they are adept at using and interpreting language, and language is the means of setting, consolidating or undermining sociopolitical positions. Being part of the process and part of the dialectic, they too can aspire to affect processes in the social world. But this cannot be done without seeing one's own trajectory altered in the process, and they must keep their wits about them to pay attention to the roar of tankers or clouds of petroleum when others are ignoring them.

Further reading

Scollon, R. (1998) *Mediated Discourse as Social Interaction*. London: Longman.

This book is the springboard from which scholars began doing what became known as MDA. In that work Scollon argues that, in the production of texts of mediated discourse, the texts, objects or images are secondary to social interactions among the producers of the texts.

Scollon, R. (2001a) *Mediated Discourse: The Nexus of Practice*. London: Routledge.

This further developed the above-mentioned conceptual core and detailed the ontogeny of the practice of handing an object in a child in the second year of life. The phrase "mediated discourse analysis" is first found here.

Scollon, R. and Scollon, S. B. K. (2004) *Nexus Analysis: Discourse and the Emerging Internet*. London: Routledge.

This outlined the method of nexus analysis retrospectively, by using data from projects conducted in Alaska from 1979 through to 1984. This is the methodological arm of MDA.

Norris, S. and Jones, R. H. (2005) *Discourse in Action: Introducing Mediated Discourse Analysis*. London: Routledge.

This edition of chapters introduces MDA and addresses real contemporary social issues, explicating key notions by showing actions taken with texts and their consequences.

Scollon, R. (2008) *Analyzing Public Discourse: Discourse Analysis in the Making of Public Policy*. London and New York: Routledge.

The book returns to Alaska, the site of the first nexus analysis, showing how MDA can be used to bring about change in the selling of oil leases off the Arctic coast to major oil companies, detailing how the analysis itself can be submitted as public input that the government bureau is obliged to pay attention to. It is an example of "activist sociolinguistics."

Notes

1 We discuss in the section "Unit of Analysis" below the distinction MDA makes between social actions and social practices.
2 Bourdieu's notion of habitus is further discussed below, under the heading "Unit of Analysis." It refers to the dispositions et predispositions an actor has by virtue of his previous conditions and experience and which are generative of specific ways of acting, perceiving or behaving in the world.
3 These activities are described in more detail in Scollon and Scollon (2004).

References

Al Zidjaly, N. (2006) 'Disability and anticipatory discourse: the interconnectedness of local and global aspects of talk,' *Communication and Medicine*, 3 (2): 101–112.

Barton, D. and Hamilton, M. (1998) *Local Literacies: Reading and Writing in One Community*. London: Routledge.

Bourdieu, P. (1977 [original in French 1972]) *Outline of a Theory of Practice*. Cambridge: Cambridge University Press.

Castillo-Ayometzi, C. (2007) 'Storying as becoming: Identity through the telling of conversion', in A. De Fina and M. Bamberg (eds.) *Selves and Identities in Narrative and Discourse*. Philadelphia, PA: John Benjamins, pp. 41–70.

de Saint-Georges, I. (2003). "Anticipatory discourses: constructing futures of action in a vocational program for long-term unemployed," unpublished PhD thesis, Georgetown University.

de Saint-Georges, I. (2005) 'From anticipation to performance: sites of engagement as process', in S. Norris and R. H. Jones (eds.) *Discourse in Action: Introduction to Mediated Discourse Analysis*. London: Routledge, pp. 155–165.

de Saint-Georges, I. (forthcoming) 'Anticipatory discourse', in C. A. Chappelle (ed.), *The Encyclopedia of Applied Linguistics*. Malden, MA: Wiley-Blackwell.

de Saint-Georges, I. and Norris, S. (2000) 'Nationality and the European Union: competing identities in the visual design of four European cities', *Visual Studies*, 15 (1): 65–78.

Dunne, M. D. (2003) *Democracy in Contemporary Egyptian Political Discourse*. Amsterdam/Philadelphia, PA: John Benjamins.

Gee, J. P. (1996) *Social Linguistics and Literacies: Ideology in Discourses*. Second Edition. London: Taylor and Francis.

Goffman, E. (1971) *Relations in Public: Microstudies of the Public Order*. New York: Basic Books.

Jensen, O. B. (2007) 'Culture stories: understanding cultural urban branding', *Planning Theory*, 6 (3): 211–236.

Jocuns, A. (2007) 'Semiotics and classroom interaction: mediated discourse, distributed cognition, and the multimodal semiotics of Maguru Panggul pedagogy in two Balinese Gamelan classrooms in the United States', *Semiotica*, 164 (1/4): 123–151.

Jocuns, A. (2009) 'Participation structures as mediational means: learning Balinese Gamelan in the United States through intent participation, mediated discourse, and distributed cognition', *Mind, Culture and Activity*, 16 (1): 48–63.

Johnston, A. (2004) 'Files, forms and fonts: mediational means and identity negotiation in immigration interviews', in P. Levine and R. Scollon (eds.) *Discourse and Technology: Multimodal Discourse Analysis*. Washington, DC: Georgetown University Press, pp.116–127.

Jones, R. H. (1999) 'Mediated action and sexual risk: searching for 'culture' in discourses of homosexuality and AIDS prevention in China', *Culture, Health and Sexuality*, 1 (2): 161–180.

Jones, R. H. (2007) 'Imagined comrades and imaginary protections: identity, community and sexual risks among men who have sex with men in China', *Journal of Homosexuality*, 53 (3): 83–115.

Jones, R. H. (2009) 'Dancing, skating and sex: action and text in the digital age', *Journal of Applied Linguistics*, 6 (3): 283–302.

Jones, R. H. and Norris, S. (2005) 'Discourse as action/discourse in action', in S. Norris and R. H. Jones (eds.) *Discourse in Action: Introduction to Mediated Discourse Analysis*. London: Routledge, pp. 3–14.

Lou, J. L. (2010a) 'Chinese on the side: the marginalization of Chinese in the linguistic and social landscape of Chinatown in Washington, DC', in E. Shohamy, E. Ben-Rafael, and M. Barni (eds.) *Linguistic Landscape in the City*. Bristol, Buffalo and Toronto: Multilingual Matters, pp. 96–114.

Lou, J. L. (2010b) 'Chinatown transformed: ideology, power and resources in narrative place-making', *Discourse Studies*, 12 (5): 625–647.

Mauss, M. (1936) 'Les Techniques du corps', *Journal de Psychologie*, 32 (3–4): 271–293.

Nishida, K. (1958) *Intelligibility and the Philosophy of Nothingness*. Tokyo: Maruzen Co. Ltd.

Norris, S. (2005) 'Habitus, social identity, the perception of male domination – and agency?', in S. Norris and R. H. Jones (eds.) *Discourse in Action: Introducing Mediated Discourse Analysis*. London: Routledge, pp. 183–196.

Norris, S. and Jones, R. H. (2005) *Discourse in Action: Introducing Mediated Discourse Analysis*. London: Routledge.

Raudaskoski, P. (2010) '"Hi father, Hi mother": a multimodal analysis of a significant, identity changing phone call mediated on TV', *Journal of Pragmatics*, 42 (2): 426–442.

Scollon, R. (1997) 'Handbills, tissues and condoms: a site of engagement for the construction of identity in public discourse', *Journal of Sociolinguistics*, 1 (1): 39–61.

Scollon, R. (1998) *Mediated Discourse as Social Interaction*. London: Longman.

Scollon, R. (1999) 'Mediated discourse and social interaction', *Research on Language and Social Interaction*, 32 (1, 2): 149–154.

Scollon, R. (2000) 'Methodological interdiscursivity: an ethnographic understanding of unfinalisability', in S. Sarangi and M. Coulthard (eds.) *Discourse and Social Life*. London: Pearson, pp. 138–154.

Scollon, R. (2001a) *Mediated Discourse: The Nexus of Practice*. London: Routledge.

Scollon, R. (2001b) 'Action and text: toward an integrated understanding of the place of text in social (inter) action', in R. Wodak and M. Meyer (eds.) *Methods of Critical Discourse Analysis*. London: Sage, pp. 139–183.

Scollon, R. (2002) "Nexus analysis: toward an ethnography of motives," paper presented at the Martin Spector Lecture in Applied Linguistics, Center for Language Acquisition, Pennsylvania State University, Pennsylvania, USA, October 2002.

Scollon, R. (2005a) 'The discourses of food in the world system: toward a nexus analysis of a world problem', *Journal of Language and Politics*, 4 (3): 467–490.

Scollon, R. (2005b) 'The rhythmic integration of action and discourse: work, the body and the earth', in S. Norris and R. H. Jones (eds.) *Discourse in Action: Introduction to Mediated Discourse Analysis*. London: Routledge, pp. 20–31.

Scollon, R. (2008) *Analyzing Public Discourse: Discourse Analysis in the Making of Public Policy*. London and New York: Routledge.

Scollon, R. and Scollon, S. B. K. (1979) *Linguistic Convergence: An Ethnography of Speaking at Fort Chipewyan, Alberta*. New York: Academic Press.

Scollon, R. and Scollon, S. B. K. (1981) *Narrative, Literacy, and Face in Interethnic Communication*. Norwood, NJ: Ablex Publishing Corporation.

Scollon, R. and Scollon, S. W. (2003) *Discourses in Place: Language in the Material World*. London: Routledge.

Scollon, R. and Scollon, S. W. (2004) *Nexus Analysis: Discourse and the Emerging Internet*. London: Routledge.

Scollon, R. and Scollon, S. B. K. (2005) 'Fast English, slow food, and intercultural exchanges: Social problems and problems for discourse analysis', in G. Cortese and A. Duszak (eds.) *Identity, Community, Discourse: English in Intercultural Settings*. London: Peter Lang, pp. 1–16.

Scollon, S. (2001) 'Habitus, consciousness, agency and the problem of intention: How we carry and are carried by political discourses', *Folia Linguistica*, 35 (1–2): 97–129.

Scollon, S. (2003) 'Political and somatic alignment: habitus, ideology and social practice', in R. Wodak and G. Weiss (eds.) *Theory and Interdisciplinarity in Critical Discourse Analysis*. London: Palgrave, pp. 167–198.

Scollon, S. W. (2005) 'Agency distributed through time, space and tools: Bentham, Babbage and the census', in S. Norris and R. H. Jones (eds.) *Discourse in Action: Introduction to Mediated Discourse Analysis*. London: Routledge, pp.172–182.

Shroyer, G. (2004) 'The presence of the past: enacting time, the nation, and the social self', *Essays in Arts and Sciences*, 33 (2): 67–84.

Street, B. (1984) *Literacy in Theory and Practice*. New York: Cambridge University Press.

Wells, G. (1999) *Dialogic Inquiry: Toward a Sociocultural Practice and Theory of Education*. New York: Cambridge University Press.

Wertsch, J. W. (1991) *Voices of the Mind: A Sociocultural Approach to Mediated Action*. Cambridge, MA: Harvard University Press.

Wohlwend, K. E. (2009a) 'Damsels in discourse: girls consuming and producing identity texts through Disney Princess play', *Reading Research Quarterly*, 44 (1): 57–83.

Wohlwend, K. E. (2009b) 'Dilemmas and discourses of learning to write: Assessment as a contested site', *Language Arts*, 86: 341–351.

Wortham, S. (2006) 'Review of Ron Scollon and Suzie Wong Scollon, *Nexus Analysis: Discourse and the Emerging Internet*', *Journal of Sociolinguistics*, 10 (1): 127–131.

6

Multimedia and discourse analysis

Jay L. Lemke

Discourse and me: a short history

What is discourse analysis? And what does it have to do with multimedia? In my view, discourse analysis is a set of techniques for making connections between texts and their meanings. Originally formulated for the analysis of purely linguistic texts, discourse analysis methods have come to form the basis for analyzing "texts" that consist not just of words, but also of visual forms such as images and diagrams (static or animated), full-motion video, sound effects and music, and various interactive features.

There are a number of different intellectual traditions that contribute to discourse and multimedia analysis. I came to this field before it really had a name, because I wanted to understand how physicists came to think and talk and write the way we did, and it seemed to me that we learned these things mostly through verbal and non-verbal communication with people who were already doing it. In the 1970s I was a student and junior researcher in theoretical physics, and it was pretty obvious that I was learning to frame and solve problems, to mobilize theory, and even to tell jokes like a physicist from sitting in classes, reading books, talking with other students and with physics faculty members, and watching the occasional video or display on a computer screen.

Would it be possible, I wondered, to videotape other students doing what I was doing and from the videos to figure out how the ideas and practices of physicists were being "transmitted" or learned? How would you analyze a videotape to achieve this?

As a theoretical physicist, I dealt mostly with text, mathematics, diagrams, and talk about them. I was less concerned about operating experimental apparatus. It seemed to me that most of what I was learning I had to be learning from talk and writing (whether in books, articles, or just on the chalkboard), so I asked around among my friends whether linguistics or anthropology had anything useful to offer on this subject. By good luck I was pointed in the direction of the work of Michael Halliday, a British linguist who was interested in how we make meaning with words (Halliday, 1978). This was not the dominant focus in linguistics at the time, when most linguists were following Noam Chomsky's lead and ignoring meaning in favor of purely formal analysis of grammatical structures.

I had also been reading the work of Lev Vygotsky, a Russian psychologist of the 1920s, who presented a theory of learning and intellectual development based on the hypothesis that people internalized the cultural meanings around them, largely through the medium of language (Vygotsky, 1963, 1978). And I had an interest in cultural anthropology, where there was a prevailing notion that people acquired the habits and values of their communities by active social participation. It was fashionable at that time to see all forms of cultural meaning as being similar to language in that they formed semiotic systems (Levi-Strauss, 1963).

What would we discover, I wondered, if we applied Halliday's analysis of the relationship between wording and meaning to what students and teachers said in a physics class? Extending this idea to the learning of science in general, I persuaded some people at the National Science Foundation in the US to fund a project to videotape science classes in secondary schools and at a university, to transcribe the talk in its contexts of classroom activity, and to apply Halliday's methods of analysis. The funding also allowed me to go to visit Halliday, who had recently moved to the University of Sydney in Australia, and also to go to England, where other people were engaged in similar efforts to do linguistically based discourse analysis (Sinclair and Coulthard, 1975).

It was an exciting time, because what we call discourse analysis today was just being created then (in the late 1970s and early 1980s). There was also, at that time, what later became known as the "linguistic turn" in the social sciences, led by people like the anthropologist Claude Lévi-Strauss and the historian and social theorist Michel Foucault. Lévi-Strauss followed an essentially semiotic approach to the analysis of the texts of myths from indigenous peoples, mainly in South America, but he had much wider influence with his philosophy of "structuralism" (Levi-Strauss, 1963, 1969). Foucault had a somewhat less semiotic and more cultural–historical approach to the analysis of archives of texts from earlier historical periods, which supported his inquiries into intellectual and institutional history (Foucault, 1969). Textual data were becoming the focus of important work in the human sciences.

Discourse analysis was shaped by the kinds of questions people were asking and by the kinds of uses to which this new discipline was being put. It was being developed as a tool for specific purposes, and its different variants reflect the variety of questions being posed. Lévi-Strauss wanted to know if the many different versions of the same myth across different indigenous groups could be seen as systematic variants of one another, rather as Chomsky was showing that different grammatical constructions could be transformed into one another by a set of simple rules (Chomsky, 1965). Foucault wanted to know what kinds of discourses were possible about a given topic in a given historical period, how they changed across the centuries, and how this was related to changing social institutions. Halliday wanted to know what kinds of meanings it was possible to make in the English language and how different grammatical resources were deployed in different contexts to make those meanings.

Today it is easy to see how these different enterprises could support one another, but at the time it was just a leap of imagination. There were also other pieces to the puzzle. The Russian literary theorist Mikhail Bakhtin and his linguist collaborator Valentin Voloshinov had developed in the 1920s and 1930s a theory of the inherent *dialogism* of texts—that is, of the sense in which anything said or written tended to situate its meanings in an implicit dialogue with other texts (Voloshinov, 1986; Bakhtin, 1973). This led to a general principle of *intertextuality*, which connected the work of Lévi-Strauss and Foucault to the *social semiotics* of Halliday. Pierre Bourdieu was combining traditional quantitative sociology with an interest in the development of a social or cultural habitus, a mostly unconscious disposition to do and say things in particular ways, which were like those of others in the same social position (Bourdieu, 1972). Basil Bernstein was connecting a kind of linguistic habitus to social class differences in learning in schools and primary socialization in families and turning to Halliday's linguistic methods to find supporting evidence (Bernstein, 1971).

In 1981 I found myself with a hundred pages of transcript of dialogue in science classrooms, a number of sociocultural frameworks for making sense of the general phenomena, and a set of specific linguistic tools for analyzing various aspects of the meanings being made. I had the overhead lights and the floor tiles, but the task of furnishing the room remained. What lies between the general theories of social learning (Vygotsky, Bernstein) and sociocultural structure (Lévi-Strauss, Foucault, Bourdieu) on the one hand, and, on the other, the line-by-line, clause-by-clause analysis of the meaning of what was being said and done in these classrooms?

Everything. Discourse analysis and its multimedia successors are about filling in the gap between macro-social theory and micro-social data. It is about construing patterns of various kinds, at some intermediate levels between what Halliday called the "system"—what is possible—and the "instance"—what actually happened this time – in order to say something about what is *typical*. And not just what is typical in general, but what is typical *for whom, when, and why* (Lemke, 1995).

Most of Halliday's work was a description of the grammar of English as a set of possibilities, linking each option that the grammatical resources of the language make available (such as singular or plural, past or future, transitive or intransitive, interrogative or imperative) to the kinds of meanings we make with it. But he did this within a larger theoretical framework, which he and the group in Sydney called "social semiotics" (Halliday, 1978; Hodge and Kress, 1988). In brief, it was a model of the relationship of language to society and it held that meaning was made by language in use in a context of situation and in a context of culture. Every different social setting evoked a different meaning potential, a different set of probabilities that particular meanings would be made by using particular resources from the grammar of the language.

This entailed a theory of which features of the setting were related to which kinds of meaning that could be made with the language. And it went both ways; that is, using language in part made or changed the nature of the setting, just as a given setting evoked the use of certain sorts of language. In this way it was possible to understand such notions as *register* (the kind of language typical for a particular kind of setting or activity) and *genre* (the forms of sequential discourse that people in a community use for particular purposes).

I had a setting—the classroom—and within it a variety of activities, from going over homework to explaining new concepts to having a dialogue about the best answer to a question. There were spoken genres, such as extended sequential dialogue in which teachers posed questions and evaluated student answers to them, and written genres, such as textbook chapters and student lab reports.

But there was also a great deal more. There were patterns of semantic relationships among technical terms—patterns that were worded differently but remained essentially the same across textbooks, classroom dialogues, and tests or curriculum documents. There were typical rhetorical patterns of reasoning and logical justification that appeared again and again. There were regularities across different sessions and different classes in how lessons started and ended. The room began to fill with furniture (Lemke, 1990).

I had begun from an interest in seeing how the conceptual content of physics was embodied in the dialogue between teacher and student. Over the course of a few years of analysis of the data, I came to see that this was just one part of a much more complex social process, linked to such matters as power, control, authority, and respect in the social relationships of the classroom, and to wider beliefs and values about the nature and role of science in society. People were expressing feelings and evaluations that were inseparable from the process of learning. Students were learning not just facts and theories from science, but ways of behaving in classrooms and beliefs and values about science, society, and themselves. The meanings being made in the classroom could often not be understood apart from other meanings and texts, which were not present in the classroom. The learning process and its stumbles were also part of longer-term developmental processes of students' (and teachers') identities, careers, and lives outside school.

The discourse of the science classroom was a window on much more than science education; it was a window on a society and a culture, just as social semiotics was claiming that this had to be the case for any use of language.

The importance of discourse analysis was not just as a tool to see what was happening in some event. It was a tool that could enable us to look far beyond the immediate events, whatever they were. Indeed you had to look beyond in order to understand what was in front of you.

From discourse analysis to multimedia semiotics

These were *science* classrooms. Meaning was being made all the time with media other than language: diagrams, mathematical and chemical symbols and formulae, pantomimes of natural processes, physical demonstrations of scientific phenomena, slide shows and films, 3D physical models, and so on. Teachers and students were not just talking and writing, they were also pointing, drawing, pouring, connecting wires and batteries, using calculators, and passing notes, and staring out the windows.

Science is an integrated description of the natural world in words, symbols, numbers, and diagrams. The language of science is a multimedia "language" or, more precisely, a multimodal semiotic system (Lemke, 1998b, 2002a). A semiotic system is an interrelated collection of signs or symbols that can be deployed to construct more complex meanings (or at least assemblages of signs to which meanings can be assigned by some system of conventions of use). Each separate semiotic system is a resource for making meanings, and, for historical and physical reasons, these different resources can be combined. They have evolved from one another (as mathematics evolved from language), or as partners of one another (writing and drawing, or speaking and gesturing), and in real life we simply cannot physically make meaning with only one semiotic system at a time.

If you write, you are deploying a linguistic meaning resource and a visual semiotic system (fonts, alphabets, paragraphing, etc.) together. If you speak, you are probably also gesturing; but, even if the gestures are not visible, there are other auditory–acoustic meaning systems in play (tone of voice, local accent, voice qualities that reflect health and mood, etc.). If you draw or see a picture, you cannot help, at least subvocally, naming some parts of what you see, and hence interpreting the image, in part, through language—as well as through the visual semiotic system of depiction. Every abstract sign that occupies some niche in a formal semiotic system has to be realized as some physical material signifier, and that in turn can always also be "read" according to other semiotic systems, in addition to the one that may have originally motivated its presence.

So all meaning-making is in fact multimodal. We can make a formal distinction between modes (different semiotic resource systems) and media (different technologies for realizing meanings that are made possible by these systems). We often also classify multimedia phenomena according to the sensory channels used by the technologies (auditory–acoustic, visual, tactile, etc.). This multimodal, multimedia character of meaning-making happens to be particularly obvious in the case of scientific communication, teaching, and learning.

Very early on I analyzed the role of gestures and chalkboard drawings in my classroom data, using videos and fieldnotes as well as transcripts (Lemke, 1987). Making multimodal transcripts is an art in itself, and one that requires and implies many theoretical choices (Ochs, 1979; Baldry and Thibault, 2005). But there was at that time (in the early to mid-1980s) no formal analogue of Halliday's meaning-centered grammar yet available for analyzing gestures or drawings and diagrams.

A number of us realized that there was no reason why the general principles of social semiotics could not be applied to other semiotic resource systems in addition to language. Michael O'Toole (1990, 1994) and Gunther Kress and Theo van Leeuwen (1996) were among the first to extend the theory to visual semiotics. Later, O'Toole's student, Kay O'Halloran (2005), tackled the extension to basic mathematics. Van Leeuwen has also worked on the semiotics of music and sound effects (1999), and on physical objects like toys and Lego blocks (van Leeuwen and Caldas-Coulthard, 2001).

From my own earliest work, I had always considered that action itself was in some sense the overarching or primary semiotic system. Human acts are meaningful and they do form a semiotic resource system. This approach converged with the Vygotskyan tradition, specifically with the work of A. N. Leontiev (1978) on cultural–historical activity theory. Speech, gesture, writing, and drawing are all integral parts of meaningful human activity, and that is really what I was looking at in the videos of science classrooms, even if I could only analyze them piecemeal, and with a primary focus on language.

Video is a multimedia and multi-channel technology. Its content is multimodal, meaningful through the combination of (usually) action, language, non-speech sound effects, and various visual semiotics. In my classroom recordings bells would ring, students would make rude noises, things would go pop, people would move around the room, teachers would draw on the board while talking about what they were drawing, students would gesture when they couldn't find the right word, and so on.

What is more important to realize than just the simple fact that there are multiple media and semiotic systems in play is that they are usually tightly integrated with one another in real time. Meanings are made through the co-deployment of different modalities, both consciously and unconsciously (or automatically). To make sense of what is going on, you need to be able to integrate all the different modes of meaning-making, and that is a very complex task, which most of us learn to do very well, at least in some settings. Unfortunately it is not something we are explicitly taught to do, even when the genres and conventions of meaning-making are as unfamiliar as those of the culture of science are for most students (Lemke, 1998a).

How does the integration work? In each case the details are somewhat different, but there are some common general principles (Lemke, 1997, 2002b). One of the most important is the combinatorial or multiplicative principle, which derives from information theory. In essence, each semiotic mode contributes a set of possible meanings, only one of which usually actually occurs at a particular moment or point in the multimedia text. In information theory, the informative value of that one depends on its not being any of the others, and the more others there could have been, the more informative, in principle, the one that does occur is. The informativeness of a cluster of such signs from many different semiotic systems, and therefore from many different sets of alternative possibilities (one word vs. other words, combined with one image vs. other images and one sound vs. other possible sounds, etc.) is again in principle the multiplicative product of the contributions from each semiotic system. Specific instances are more complicated, because often combinations of signs are so typical and predictable that their informativeness has to count more nearly like one unified sign than as two or more independent ones.

But we are not interested here in quantifying multimedia information, but in figuring out how joint meaning results from the meanings we can describe for each sign in its own semiotic system. Each sign, on its own, has a range of potential meanings or interpretations. In general that range gets narrowed down by what is typical in a particular context or setting. And in multimedia the signs in the other modalities (i.e. semiotic systems) are primary contexts for each other's inter-pretation. The interpretation of the whole multimodal complex of signs has to make consistent sense, in a way that fits with the normal range of potential meanings for each component sign separately. In practice, consistency is established among clusters of typically linked (collocated) groups of signs. Human beings happen to very good at this sort of pattern construing. We get a whole lot of pieces and we see a whole, a consistent meaningful whole arising from the heterogeneous elements.

Of course, this effort can still result in several different possible holistic or joint meanings for a multimodal cluster of signs. Which is why we also depend on typicality: on knowing what is most likely being meant, given the situation and setting, the culture and subculture, the field, the discipline, the topic, the attitudes of the producers, and so on. We use our knowledge of persons, settings, expectations, genres, registers, and especially of other "texts" that have something in common with the one we are figuring out (or constructing) at the moment. In fact there are many kinds of intertextuality, many principles according to which one text or multimedia production is considered relevant to the interpretation of another one. (For a related view of the extension of discourse analysis to multimedia, see Iedema, 2003.)

Multimedia and transmedia: who is Harry Potter?

Let's consider an example. Who is Harry Potter? That is, how do we form our sense of what this imaginary fictional character is like as a person? We can begin from the original verbal descriptions in J. K. Rowling's novels, and also consider what the narrative text tells us about Harry by means of what he says and does, how others react to him, and so on. But the odds are that the book will have come with a jacket or a printed cover with a full-color drawing of Harry Potter. How do we integrate our image of Harry from the text with the actual image of Harry on the cover?

This example was chosen because Harry Potter is not just a fictional character or a set of novels. Harry Potter is a transmedia franchise, a brand, an industry. Fans of Potter will know him not just from the books and their covers, but from the films, where he is portrayed by a particular young actor. And perhaps also from the computer games, where they themselves can play Harry's role, or that of one of his friends or enemies. In the films we hear Harry's voice, we see how he moves his body, and we see his facial expressions. In the games we can get a sense of what it might feel like to fly on his broomstick or to wave a wand and execute a magical spell. And we can buy a replica of the wand that is seen in the movies, we can even eat a commercial version of the fictional candies in his world.

This is multimedia with a vengeance. It is systematic intertextuality on a vast scale, across media as diverse as books, films, games, visual art, and commercial artifacts. And all of these potentially contribute to the formation of our sense of who Harry Potter is, to a complex meaning that can, nevertheless, feel to us like a single sense of him, a holistic compound meaning much like the sense we have of who persons in our own lives are. How do we do it?

There is certainly as yet no complete or satisfactory answer to that question, but it represents the kind of inquiry that multimedia analysis is about. If our example were not Harry Potter but, say, Richard Nixon or Ronald Reagan, we would be doing multimedia analysis not in the field of popular culture studies, but in that of journalism or political science. Again, there would be textual sources, films, both fictional and documentary, video and archival footage, print cartoons, and no doubt photographs, figurines, and maybe even a computer game.

Nor are these phenomena limited to persons, real or imaginary. Places also have their meanings, constructed for them across texts and media: Harry's Hogwarts School, or television's New York or Baghdad. How do you construct a sense of a place you have been to, but have also seen represented over and over again in photographs, films, books, and the like? These may not always converge to a unified sense of the place (or the person), but they are always the product of multimodal meaning-making across semiotic systems, media, and "texts."

Phenomenology and affect: complementing semiotic approaches

It should be apparent by now that I am trying to expand and complicate our sense of what is involved in discourse and multimedia analysis. It is not just what is in the text or in the video, but what we need to know about the context and culture that helps give it meaning. It is not just about one text at a time, but about extended complexes of potential intertexts, which may be seen as relevant to any one text's interpretation.

Every text and multimedia product is not just a window on what they present, but a window on the society and culture in which they were created. How we interpret them is also a mirror of and a window on our own society and culture. Politics, economics, and ideology are never irrelevant to interpretation. Nor is history, nor is an understanding of how the texts were constructed and of how and why they were published, distributed, bought and sold, legally encumbered, and so on.

Good, persuasive, insightful discourse and multimedia analysis is always *critical* analysis. Not simply in the basic sense of considering alternative interpretations and grounds for various claims, as all good reasoning does, but in the more specific sense of critical theory: applying a skepticism toward the justice of institutions and the moral status of beliefs and values, including our own. Why?

Because interpretation (and construction or authoring) of meanings is always selective contextualization, is always deploying a sign within a field of interpretive conventions that belong to some social order, complete with its history and its politics; that is, complete with the covert as well as the overt social, political, economic, and ideological functions of the typical discourses and conventions for interpreting meanings and deploying signs in a community—or at the intersection of various communities. For the intersection of discourse analysis and critical theory, see Fairclough (1995).

Bakhtin's principle of dialogism, the inspiration for seeing intertextuality as central to meaning-making, led him to recognize that meanings are made within systems of diverse social voices and that texts may ventriloquate multiple voices and speak as if in dialogue with multiple voices. Not the voices of persons as such, but the voices of social viewpoints: of men vs. women, of working-class vs. middle-class families, of fundamentalists and atheists, physicians and physicists, reactionaries and radicals. The organized diversity of social voices, which he called society's heteroglossia, is a key part of the context of culture within which every meaning is made (Bakhtin, 1981).

Bakhtin characterizes these social voices or viewpoints not only by their ways of representing the world—that is, by what they pay attention to and how they speak of these things—but also by their value judgments and moral stances. It is not just how we see the world that matters, but how we feel about it.

And here is yet another dimension that needs to be added to make discourse and multimedia analysis faithful to the world of meaning: seeing that there is no meaning without feeling. We do not just form a picture of Harry Potter, we get an impression of him, a sense of him, which would not be complete without our sense of how we feel about him. If a great many people did not feel strongly, and mostly positively, about Harry, they would not be devoting many, many hours to reading these books, watching these movies, and even playing the computer games, putting posters of Harry on their walls, and chewing on candy that sports his recommendation. And equally, if in some respects oppositely, regarding Richard Nixon or Ronald Reagan.

Where do these feelings come from? In the case of Potter we know that they cannot come from anywhere other than the multimedia representations of his character and the opinions of others about what they see represented there. This is no different, for most of us, from the sources of our feelings about politicians, celebrities, places we have never been to, or activities we have never performed. Even if we have had direct experience, it's pretty clear that our longer-term sense of such matters combines that experience with the many, many media representations and discourse viewpoints about them that we have encountered.

How we feel about something also clearly influences how we interpret its meaning. There is no easy way to separate the feeling of love or hatred, fear or pride, anxiety or desire from the meaning we attach to a representation of an action, a person, a place, an event. Meaning and feeling are two words for a single experiential reality. One emphasizes the descriptive, the other the evaluative aspect of our sense of something. Contrary to some traditional beliefs, we also know that extended reasoning is not possible without feeling-based choices and decisions (Damasio, 1994), and that feeling, like meaning, is actively constructed and arises in our participation in extended (situated, distributed) interactions.

We inherit, however, the biases of our intellectual ancestors, who lived in times when there was little separation between partisan politicking and adherence to intellectual (including religious) dogmas, and when violent feuds and wars, foreign and civil, were fought because of passionate feelings about matters of meaning. From those times came the eventual denigration of feeling as something opposed to reason, something proper only to women and children and serfs and laborers, and not to gentlemen of sober dedication to intellectual pursuits.

So feeling was prised away from meaning, affect separated from cognition, emotions opposed to reason, and their experiential unity denied and replaced by formal, analytic representations.

In today's world we need to understand that unity. We cannot blame passion alone for extremist violence without understanding the meanings that support and give rise to that passion. Nor can we hope to persuade people to take constructive courses of action if we do not address their feelings as well as their rational interests.

Mass media, popular culture media, even elite media cultivate feelings along with meanings, when they are successful. Meanings are made in part as expressions of feelings, and they are interpreted in part through how we feel about them and about alternatives to them. Discourse and multimedia analysis cannot succeed in their aims if they do not consider both meaning and feeling, both in relation to production/authorship and in relation to reception/interpretation.

Feeling and meaning meet in evaluation, and we are beginning to accumulate some systematic knowledge of how evaluations and appraisals operate, at least linguistically (Lemke, 1998c; Martin and White, 2005). By comparison with our extensive understanding of semiotic processes of meaning-making in language and other semiotics, we still know relatively little about affect, emotion, and feeling. But I think we at least know that they are important, indeed crucial, to the analysis of how we gain a sense of what is presented to us in media, how we react, and what kinds of meanings and feelings we in turn construct as our own next moves in the never-ending dialogues of life and art.

Trajectories and traversals: time, space, and media

I want to conclude with some discussion of basic questions of method in discourse and multimedia analysis.

In our transmedia example of the Harry Potter franchise, we considered the problem of how meanings are made not just across different texts, but across very different semiotic media. It was also clear then that these meanings are being made across time and space. To read all the Harry Potter novels, and to see all the films, much less to participate in any other aspects of the franchise, takes an extended time and more or less requires activity in different places. Certainly in their original versions the books were published about a year apart over seven years or more, and the films were released over an even longer period, extending well beyond the publication of the final novel.

Meanings were being made across long intervals of time, both by producers and by consumers. The same is also the case if we re-read the same book years apart, or if we watch episodes of a television series in re-runs again and again over many years. Meanings are made on different timescales. There is the meaning we make when initially reading a line or paragraph of text, or viewing a scene of a few minutes in a film or video. There is the meaning we make thinking back or reading back to that bit after we have gone on much further in the same text, or in a relevant intertext. There are meanings (and feelings) we make over years, and even over a lifetime of engagement with some set of texts (and, of course, by "text" here I am understanding an entity that includes paintings, symphonies, films, games, etc.).

So far I have raised this issue of extended encounters with a single work, a serialized work, or a set of works in a connected franchise. But the experience of life, day by day, is itself heterogeneous across media and genres. We move from one encounter to another, from a conversation to an email, to a sales transaction, to a meal, to a piece of music, to the gym, to the bookstore, to a few hours of channel-surfing on the television.

And yet we make some sort of coherent sense, meaning-with-feeling, of our days and of our lives. Along traversals of experience that cross boundaries of genres, activities, and media, we are always making some sort of cumulative sense of things. We are connecting the meanings and feelings of a few minutes to those of a day, a week, a decade, a lifetime. And we are using discourses and other semiotic media resources to do this (personal diaries, favorite books and programs, etc.).

How do the meanings of minutes add up to the meaning of a lifetime? Every distinct experience we have, every activity we engage in, lasts or takes place over a relatively short timescale, minutes to hours. A few projects we undertake may extend, with long interruptions, over months or years. The continuities we construct for lifelong ambitions or agendas, or even those that just take years, are retrospective "meanings made" far more than they are actually on-going processes with any coherence on those long timescales.

To what extent do our lives add up, then? Certainly there is coherence of meaning and feeling over long timescales, even if it is constituted from many separate events and activities, as with long-term personal relationships, careers, research agendas, hobbies, and so on. How do we use discursive and semiotic resources to construct these cumulations and continuities? And how do texts and media both aid and emulate this process, making longer-term wholes out of sentences and scenes?

Time figures importantly in all media, whether it is the durational time of reading or viewing, the actional timescales of writing and producing media, or the phenomena of pacing, interruption and resumption, multiple nested rhythms of activity, repetition and variation, and so on. Temporal considerations and temporal phenomena are fundamental to both meaning and feeling in texts and media.

So also, though at this point perhaps even less well understood, are matters of space and place. The fact that many media, such as semiotic technologies, are portable (and more so now than ever before) means that we use them in a far wider range of places, and across much longer separations in space, than in the past. Where we read or write or make photos and videos matters in some way to the meanings made. The advent of immersive-world computer games has called our attention once again to what Bakthin called the "chronotopes" of narrative fiction, and now also of interactive adventures. We move, or the characters and action we follow and identify with move, from place to place in the course of the story or adventure, and we/they spend varying amounts of time in each place. Some places are sites of important action, others are merely scenery we pass through. There is a rhythm of movement and action on the scales of travel or traversal through fictional and simulated worlds (Lemke, 2005b). Places themselves are filled with, and define, contexts of interpretation for texts and other semiotic media (Scollon and Scollon, 2003).

And there are spaces other than physical space, real or virtual. In hypertext we jump from one frame or media display to another through an informational space, a way of making sense metaphorically of links in a relational database, but one that succeeds because of its similarities to travel through physical space. As we move from place to place, seeing and doing different things, so we jump from scene to scene in hypertext or hypermedia, while making meaning-and-feeling connections along the trajectory we create as we move. The more heterogeneous the scenes or media presentations we encounter, as when we surf the web casually, jumping from website to website, from media genre to media genre, the less this resembles jumping around within a single text or work, and the more it resembles the kinds of meanings we make from the heterogeneous experiences of a day in our lives.

I tend to distinguish these terminologically as *trajectories*, within relatively homogeneous meaning domains, vs. *traversals*, crossing multiple boundaries of heterogeneous genres, institutions, and activities (Lemke, 2005a). Discourse and media analysis provide us with potential tools for delineating the nature of the homogeneities and heterogeneities in detail, and for identifying the kinds of semiotic resources and practices involved in constructing meaning along these experiential paths.

Discourse, and multimedia analysis itself, occur along such trajectories and traversals. It is part of the life of the analyst, and, while our analyses may be collaborative and in broad agreement with those of others, they remain views from somewhere, reflecting the focus of our interests and the selection of our tools. You should be able to see yourself, and not just your object of study, in the analysis you make. You should be able to see your cultures and histories as well as its. If you can, you will never have made the journey in vain, and your traveler's tale may help the rest of us make better sense of the country we all travel through. As I hope my tale here has done for you.

Further reading

Halliday, M. A. K. (1978) *Language as Social Semiotic*. London: Arnold.

Influential essays situating linguistic discourse analysis within a wider theory of language, society, and culture.

Lemke, J. L. (1995) *Textual Politics*. London: Taylor and Francis.

Discusses how discourse mediates between micro-social activity and macro-social system dynamics, with extended examples.

Kress, G. and van Leeuwen, T. (2001) *Multimodal Discourse*. London: Arnold.

An introduction to fundamental concepts for multimodal analysis in social context.

Lemke, J. L. (2002) 'Travels in hypermodality', *Visual Communication*, 1 (3): 299–325.

Gives examples and a theoretical synthesis of analyses of hypermedia.

O'Halloran, K. (ed.). (2004) *Multimodal Discourse Analysis: Systemic–Functional Perspectives*. London/New York: Continuum.

An edited collection of studies applying Halliday's model to multimodal analysis.

References

Bakhtin, M. (1973) *Problems of Dostoevsky's Poetics*. Ann Arbor, MI: Ardis.
Bakhtin, M. (1981) 'Discourse in the novel', in M. Holquist (ed.) *The Dialogic Imagination*. Austin, TX: University of Texas Press. pp. 259–422.
Baldry, A. and Thibault, P. (2005) *Multimodal Transcription and Text Analysis*. London: Equinox Publishing.

Bernstein, B. (1971) *Class, Codes, and Control*. Vol. 1. London: Routledge.

Bourdieu, P. (1972) *Outline of a Theory of Practice*. Cambridge: Cambridge University Press.

Chomsky, N. (1965) *Aspects of the Theory of Syntax*. Cambridge, MA: MIT Press.

Damasio, A. (1994) *Descartes' Error: Emotion, Reason, and the Human Brain*. New York: HarperCollins.

Fairclough, N. (1995) *Critical Discourse Analysis*. London: Longman.

Foucault, M. (1969) *The Archeology of Knowledge*. New York: Random House.

Halliday, M. A. K. (1978) *Language as Social Semiotic*. London: Edward Arnold.

Hodge, R. and Kress, G. (1988) *Social Semiotics*. Ithaca, NY: Cornell University Press.

Iedema, R. (2003) 'Multimodality, resemiotization: extending the analysis of discourse as a multi-semiotic practice', *Visual Communication*, 2 (1): 29–57.

Kress, G. and van Leeuwen, T. (1996) *Reading Images: The Grammar of Visual Design*. London: Routledge.

Lemke, J. L. (1987) 'Strategic deployment of speech and action: a sociosemiotic analysis', in J. Evans and J. Deely (eds.) *Semiotics 1983: Proceedings of the Semiotic Society of America 'Snowbird' Conference*. New York: University Press of America, pp. 67–79.

Lemke, J. L. (1990) *Talking Science: Language, Learning, and Values*. Norwood, NJ: Ablex.

Lemke, J. L. (1995) *Textual Politics: Discourse and Social Dynamics*. London: Taylor and Francis.

Lemke, J. L. (1997). Visual and verbal resources for evaluative meaning in political cartoons. Available online at: http://www-personal.umich.edu/~jaylemke/papers/polcart.htm (accessed 1 April 2011).

Lemke, J. L. (1998a) 'Multimedia demands of the scientific curriculum', *Linguistics and Education*, 10 (3): 247–272.

Lemke, J. L. (1998b) 'Multiplying meaning: visual and verbal semiotics in scientific text', in J. R. Martin and R. Veel (eds.) *Reading Science*. London: Routledge, pp. 87–113.

Lemke, J. L. (1998c) 'Resources for attitudinal meaning: evaluative orientations in text semantics', *Functions of Language*, 5 (1): 33–56.

Lemke, J. L. (2002a) 'Mathematics in the middle: measure, picture, gesture, sign, and word', in M. Anderson, A. Saenz-Ludlow, S. Zellweger, and V. Cifarelli (eds.) *Educational Perspectives on Mathematics as Semiosis: From Thinking to Interpreting to Knowing*. Ottawa: Legas Publishing, pp. 215–234.

Lemke, J. L. (2002b) 'Travels in hypermodality', *Visual Communication*, 1 (3): 299–325.

Lemke, J. L. (2005a) 'Multimedia genres and traversals', *Folia Linguistica*, 39 (1–2): 45–56.

Lemke, J. L. (2005b) 'Place, pace, and meaning: multimedia chronotopes', in S. Norris and R. Jones (eds.) *Discourse in Action*. London: Routledge, pp. 110–122.

Leontiev, A. N. (1978) *Activity, Consciousness, and Personality*. Englewood Cliffs, NJ: Prentice-Hall.

Lévi-Strauss, C. (1963) *Structural Anthropology*. New York: Basic Books.

Lévi-Strauss, C. (1969) *The Raw and the Cooked: Introduction to a Science of Mythology*. Vol. 1. New York: Harper and Row.

Martin, J. R. and White, P. R. R. (2005) *The Language of Evaluation: The Appraisal Framework*. New York: Palgrave Macmillan.

Ochs, E. (1979) 'Transcription as theory', in E. Ochs and B. Schieffelin, (eds.) *Developmental Pragmatics*. New York: Academic Press, pp. 43–72.

O'Halloran, K. (2005) *Mathematical Discourse: Language, Symbolism and Visual Images*. London: Continuum.

O'Toole, L. M. (1990) 'A systemic-functional semiotics of art', *Semiotica*, 82: 185–209.

O'Toole, L. M. (1994) *The Language of Displayed Art*. London: Leicester University Press.

Scollon, R. and Scollon, S. W. (2003) *Discourses in Place: Language in the Material World*. London: Routledge.

Sinclair, J. and Coulthard, M. (1975) *Towards an Analysis of Discourse*. London: Oxford University Press.

van Leeuwen, T. (1999) *Speech, Music, Sound*. New York: St. Martin's Press.

van Leeuwen, T. and Caldas-Coulthard, C. (2001) *Social Semiotics of Toys: Final Report on the Toys as Communication Project*. Halmstad: Halmstad University, Nordic Center for Research on Toys and Educational Media (NCFL).

Voloshinov, V. N. (1986 [1929]) *Marxism and the Philosophy of Language*. Cambridge, MA: Harvard University Press.

Vygotsky, L. S. (1963) *Thought and Language*. Cambridge, MA: MIT Press.

Vygotsky, L. S. (1978) *Mind in Society: The Development of Higher Psychological Processes*. Cambridge, MA: Harvard University Press.

Gender and discourse analysis

Jennifer Coates

Language and gender

One of the most striking phenomena in language study in the 1970s and 1980s was the development of the field of research known as 'language and gender'. This area of research continues to grow: the International Gender and Language Association was founded in 1999 and holds biennial conferences, and a new journal – *Gender and Language* – was launched in 2007, dedicated to the publication of research in this area.

The language and gender field consists of two main strands. The first developed as part of quantitative sociolinguistics: sociolinguists analysing the co-variation of language and variables such as social class began to notice that their data also revealed gender differences. Peter Trudgill (1974, 1983), for example, examining the pronunciation of a wide range of speakers living in Norwich, UK, realized that women and men of the same social class patterned differently. Women on average used forms closer to Standard English, while male speakers used a higher proportion of vernacular forms. Trudgill's analysis demonstrates that use of non-standard forms of language seems to be associated not only with working-class speakers, but also with *male* speakers, and thus with masculinity. This strand continues to flourish, with more recent research taking a communities of practice approach (see for example Eckert, 1998; Mallinson and Childs, 2007).

The second strand of language and gender research, which will be the subject of this paper, focuses not on phonological, morphological, or lexical features of language but on language as a 'concrete living totality' (Bakhtin, 1981) – in other words, on *discourse*. The move in linguistics from the micro-analysis of phonemes and syntactic structure to a more macro-analytic approach, looking at language in a more holistic way, was undoubtedly a paradigm shift with significant consequences. The freedom to think about talk in general and to analyse whole conversations has led to new understanding of the relationship between discourse and social life. Huge emphasis was placed on using authentic language data and on analysing these data in their social context.

At the same time as attention was shifting from isolated grammatical sentences to discourse, the old term 'sex' was replaced by 'gender'. In the early 1970s, 'gender' was a linguistic category referring to a morphological characteristic of nouns, and sociolinguists referred to *sex differences*. So linguistic analysis was oriented to the binary male/female, a binary based on biology. But by the late 1980s linguists and discourse analysts had adopted the new term 'gender' from the social sciences, and with it a new understanding that gender was not a given, but was culturally constructed and malleable.

The turn to discourse

The turn to discourse in sociolinguistics and in social psychology, combined with growing synergies with anthropological research, led to a huge creative burst in research and writing on language and gender. Researchers studied a wide variety of conversational data, encompassing talk in both mixed and single-sex groups and in both public and private contexts. Family talk, friendship talk, and workplace talk were all interrogated in the quest to understand how gender is constructed and maintained in everyday life.

Over the last thirty odd years, there have been three main approaches to language and gender research: the *dominance* approach, the *difference* approach, and the *social constructionist* approach. These developed in a historical sequence, but the emergence of a new approach did not mean that an earlier approach was superseded. It is probably true to say, though, that most researchers now adopt a social constructionist approach. Research that takes a dominance perspective interprets the differences between women's and men's linguistic usage as reflexes of the dominant–subordinate relationship holding between women and men. Research that takes a difference perspective, by contrast, sees the differences between women's linguistic usage and men's linguistic usage as arising from the different subcultures in which, it claims, women and men are socialized (this approach is sometimes called the subcultural or two-cultures approach). Research taking a social constructionist perspective sees language use as constitutive of social reality and gender not as a given but as accomplished through talk. In the rest of this section I will give a brief sketch of work done using the first two of these approaches (the social constructionist approach will be the focus of the following section).

The discursive construction of dominance

Early work on language and gender was inspired by the feminist movement of the 1970s and 1980s. In the book widely acknowledged as marking the beginnings of the new field, *Language and Woman's Place* (1975), Robin Lakoff was concerned to make people aware of the ways in which language use helped to keep women in their (subordinate) place. The feminist concern to expose discrimination against women meant that much early language and gender work analysed everyday interaction to reveal the ways in which male speakers dominated female speakers through talk. The classic example is the study carried out by Don Zimmerman and Candace West (1975) on the campus of the University of California, examining the use of interruptions.[1] They observed two-party interactions and demonstrated that interrupting – that is, starting to talk before another speaker finishes their turn – was rare in conversation involving two women or two men, but more common in talk involving a woman and a man. In mixed dyads, interruptions were nearly all made by the male speaker (46 out of a total of 48 interruptions). The following are typical examples:

(1) [*Two university students*]

FEMALE: so you really can't bitch when you've got all those on the same day (4.2) but I uh *asked* my physics professor if I couldn't chan[ge that]
MALE: [don't touch that
(1.2)
FEMALE: what?
MALE: I've got everything just how I want it in that notebook (#)
        You'll screw it up leafin' *through* it like that

(from West and Zimmerman, 1977)

(2)   [*brother and sister discussing wild rice*]

Anna: wild rice is nice/ you've never tasted it [so ((xx))–
Bill: [well the Indians don't eat

Anna:
Bill: it so why the bloody hell should you?

(from Coates, 2004)

In both these examples, the female speaker is prevented from continuing her turn by the male speaker's interruption. (Also note the 4.2 second pause in the first example, where the female student waits for a response from the other speaker – pauses of this length are a sign of a malfunctioning conversation.) As these examples make clear, '[g]ender relations are power relations' (Osmond and Thorne, 1993: 593). (For more on discourse and power, see Blackledge, this volume.)

Interruptions are not the only linguistic form involved in conversational dominance. Speakers may also dominate by holding the floor for lengthy periods or taking many turns. Joan Swann's (1989) research on classroom talk, in which she analysed videotapes of sessions in two different English primary schools, revealed that boys dominated discussion: on average, boys contributed more to the sessions, both in terms of the number of turns taken and in terms of the number of words uttered. A research project exploring conversational dominance in a very different context was Herring, Johnson, and Benedetto's (1992) analysis of interactive behaviour on the Internet. Susan Herring (1992) had observed that participation on the e-mail discussion list known as Linguist (subscribed to by professional linguists worldwide) was highly asymmetrical, with male participants contributing 80% of the total discussion. Herring, Johnson, and Benedetto therefore undertook an investigation of a smaller, more woman-friendly list, to see if a less adversarial environment would facilitate more symmetrical patterns of participation. In fact, women still only contributed 30 per cent of the discussion. But during the five weeks of discussion chosen for analysis, there were two days when women's contributions exceeded men's. The resulting disruption, when men claimed they were being 'silenced' and threatening to 'unsubscribe' from the network, suggests that there is an underlying cultural assumption that women and men do not have equal rights to speak.

A very different dominance strategy can be non-response or silence. Victoria DeFrancisco's (1991) study of seven married couples in the USA focused on non-cooperation in interaction. DeFrancisco asked the couples to record themselves at home for a week or more, using the method developed by Pamela Fishman (1980). She found that, although the women talked more than the men and introduced more topics, this was not associated with dominance. In fact the women were less successful than the men in getting their topics accepted. The men used various non-cooperative strategies to control conversation: no response, interruption, inadequate or delayed response, and silence. DeFrancisco concludes that men have the power to establish the norms of everyday conversation in the home, and that women have to adapt to these norms.

More recently, the dominance approach has fallen out of favour: there has been less research in this area – particularly on talk in the private sphere – as a result of the tension between the postmodern idea that 'woman' cannot be treated as a uniform social category and the awareness that there continues to be systematic discrimination against women. However, interest in discourse patterns in the workplace has grown dramatically, and, although these studies draw explicitly on a social constructionist framework, they are also implicitly drawing on ideas of conversational dominance. Large studies, such as the Wellington Language in the Workplace Project (see Holmes, 2000; Holmes and Stubbe, 2003), have revealed how complex power relations can be in the workplace, with women as well as men in powerful positions. However, overall the picture is not encouraging, as the following two examples show. Sylvia Shaw (2006) carried out research which looked at the experience of women MPs (members of parliament in the UK). Parliament has been, until very recently, an arena reserved for the male voice. An important way to 'do' power in parliamentary debate is to hold the floor. Shaw analysed floor apportionment and established that women MPs had trouble holding the floor, even when it was legally theirs, because male MPs frequently break the rules, making illegal comments (such as 'Rubbish') without being censored by the Speaker (who moderates parliamentary behaviour). In five debates, male participants made 90 per cent of all individual illegal utterances, which suggests that this kind of rule breaking is seen as normal by male MPs, while women MPs are disadvantaged because they are reluctant to break the rules. Another example comes from Ostermann (2003), who compares two institutions that work with victims of domestic violence in Brazil. Both workplaces are all-female, but the interactional patterns found in them are very different. Ostermann shows how female police officers, working in a male-dominated system, use more distancing and controlling interactional strategies, in part because they fear that using interactional patterns seen as more typical of women will disadvantage them in the symbolic market of the police system.

As Judith Baxter comments: 'Women still struggle for acceptance within institutional settings such as government, politics, law, education, the church, the media and the business world' (Baxter, 2006: xiv). Women are expected to adapt to androcentric norms, for example to use the more adversarial, information-focused style characteristic of all-male talk, and typical of talk in the public domain. But women who successfully adapt to characteristically male linguistic norms run the risk of being perceived as aggressive and confrontational, as un-feminine, while those who choose to use a more affiliative, cooperative style risk being marginalized.

Discourse patterns in same-sex talk

While the dominance approach proved helpful in analysing mixed talk, some researchers began to question the wisdom of focusing exclusively on talk involving both women and men. In the '80s and '90s, these researchers increasingly turned their attention to same-sex interaction and to the conversational strategies adopted by speakers in everyday talk. They adopted a theoretical framework known as the *difference* or *two cultures* approach. The idea of linguistic differences arising simply from boys and girls growing up in different subcultures (see Maltz and Borker, 1982) may seem simplistic now, but the difference approach was a breakthrough: it allowed researchers to show the strengths of linguistic strategies characteristic of same-sex talk. This meant, in particular, demonstrating the strengths of linguistic strategies characteristic of all-female talk and celebrating women's ways of talking.

Coates' work on the talk of women friends (1989, 1996, 1997a) focused on groups of close women friends in a single context: informal gatherings where the main aim is 'to talk' Talk is revealed as highly cooperative, with hedges, questions, and turn-taking strategies all used to promote symmetry and cohesion in the group. Topics tended to be personal, and topic shift was gradual. In the case of turn-taking, Coates argues that women prefer to establish a collaborative, or all-in-together floor, rather than the more conventional single, or one-at-a-time floor (the terms 'collaborative floor' and 'single floor' come from Edelsky, 1993). This means that women's friendly talk is characterized by repetition, overlap, and the joint construction of utterances, as well as by frequent laughter, as illustrated in the following examples:

(3) *[Pat tells Karen about her neighbour's attack of acute indigestion]*

P: he and his wife obviously thought he'd had a |heart attack/
K: |heart attack/

(4) *[talking about aging parents]*

Liz: and I mean it's a really weird situation because all

Sue: |you become a parent/ yeah/
Liz: of a sudden the |roles are all reversed/

(5) *[Amanda, Jody and Clare talk about a friend's mother's dubious boyfriend]*

A: I mean <u>the man has a mobile phone</u> <LAUGHING> so |one thing leads to
J: |he's an architect/
C: <LAUGHS----------------->

A: another […]   <LOW LAUGH>
J: […]   would you want to marry this man?=   would you want
C: =no

A: =would you want to bloody.
J: to be in the same room as this man?=
C: =no

A: |USE THIS MAN'S MOBILE PHONE? <LAUGHS>
J: |<LAUGHS--------------------------------->
C: |yeah <LAUGHS--------------------------->

These characteristics have also been found in subsequent research looking at a range of all-female groups, for example, teenage school students in the north of England (Davies, 2003); deaf friends at university in Bristol using British Sign Language (Coates and Sutton–Spence, 2001); elderly Austrian Jewish refugees living in London, code-switching between German and English (Eppler, 2009).

   This is in contrast with what we find in all-male talk. Analysing the talk of a range of all-male groups, Coates (2003) found that men talked about topics such as sport, politics, cars, and avoided introspective topics. Their talk was characterized by fewer hedges than were found in women's talk (a direct consequence of topic choice), questions tended to be information-focused, and turn-taking followed a one-at-a-time pattern. Male speakers like to play the expert and take it in turn to hold the floor, which leads to a pattern of serial monologues. The following is a typical male monologue[2]:

(6) *[Chris and Geoff are talking over lunch. Chris introduces the topic of mobile phones and proceeds to hold forth about mobile phone technology. Minimal responses from Geoff in italics.]*

   Cos you know we've got BT internet at home (*mhm*) and I've set it up so that (.) um through the BT internet WAP portal so that Kate can read (.) her email that she gets (.) um her phone (*oh right*) which is qui- which is quite useful if you're kinda not behind a computer but I was musing the other day on (.) on how funny it is that the sort of graphics you get on WAP phones now (.) is like you used to get on the ZX81 (*yeah*) and every-everything's having to adapt to that kind of LCSD based stuff (*that's right*) um computers have got to the point they've got to (.) and now they've gone all the way back with WAP technology

                                                                 (Coates, 2004: 134)

At other times, and in other groups, men enjoy the cut and thrust of more adversarial, bantering talk, as illustrated in the following example:

(7) *[Men working in a bakery in New Zealand]*

Ray: crate!
Sam: case!

Ray: what?
Sam: they come in cases Ray not crates
Ray: oh same thing if you must be picky over every one thing
Sam: just shut your fucking head Ray!
Ray: don't tell me to fuck off fuck (…)
Sam: I'll come over and shut yo-
Jim: yeah I'll have a crate of apples thanks [*laughingly using a thick sounding voice*]
Ray: no fuck off Jim
Jim: a dozen…
Dan: shitpicker! [*amused*].

(From Pilkington, 1998: 265)

Deborah Cameron (1997) analysed the conversation of a group of male students, recorded while they watched sport on television. One of the ways that these men perform gender in their talk is through their comments on the basketball game they are watching. Cameron suggests that 'sportstalk' is a typically masculine conversational genre. Besides sport, these friends talk about women and about alcohol, topics stereotypically associated with all-male conversation. But they also gossip about non-present others: they discuss in great detail certain males of their acquaintance, accusing them of being gay. Overall, the talk displays solidarity: the five friends are bonded through their shared denigration of the supposedly gay outsiders. Interestingly, Cameron shows how the talk of these men involves several features normally associated with 'cooperative' women's talk – hedges, overlapping speech, latching. But it also displays more competitive features – two speakers dominate the talk, and speakers vie for the floor. She argues that cooperation and competition as styles of talking cannot be simplistically attributed to one gender or the other.

While the cooperative/competitive divide is not neatly isomorphic with femininity and masculinity, there are still arenas where discourse styles are strikingly gendered. One of these arenas is the classroom. Julia Davies (2003) worked in three different secondary schools in the north of England, focusing on small discussion groups involving 14-year-old pupils dealing with specific tasks, such as answering questions about a poem or carrying out a role play of teachers dealing with bullying. In this paper Davies focuses on all-boy and all-girl discussion groups. She describes the girls' ways of talking as being characterized by 'polyphony' (borrowing the metaphor from Coates, 1996) and the boys' ways by 'cacophony'. Girls' discourse styles in the discussion groups involved both personal narrative and collaborative, jointly constructed text. Talk was highly cohesive, with lexical and grammatical repetition and the use of similar pitch levels and intonation patterns. By contrast, the boys' talk was full of interruptions, joking asides, insults, and was frequently off-topic. The chief goal of boys in classroom discussion was to demonstrate that they were 'real boys'. Classroom goals of cooperation and focus on the task in hand were seen as non-macho or 'gay', which made it very difficult for boys who wanted to engage with academic work. This is an important study, in that it not only demonstrates significant differences in discourse style between male and female speakers, but also draws attention to the conflict between the discourse of learning and expressions of heterosexual masculinity. (For more on classroom discourse, see Tsui, this volume.)

The discussion about male–female differences was popularized by Deborah Tannen's (1990) book *You Just Don't Understand*, which (following Maltz and Borker, 1982) linked gender differences to cross-gender miscommunication. This has led to the difference approach falling out of favour, because it became associated with a political stance which ignores male dominance. However, interesting work on same-sex talk continues to be carried out which implicitly draws on a difference or subcultural approach. But in many areas researchers have moved on, assimilating ideas from European social theory. Not only does more recent work view gender as fluid and malleable, but masculinity and femininity are no longer viewed as singular: analysts explore a range of femininities and masculinities.

Competing discourses: multiple femininities, multiple masculinities

Social constructionism is now the prevailing paradigm in discourse analysis and sociolinguistics. Gender is understood as a social construct rather than a 'given' social category, and speakers are seen as 'doing' gender – doing femininity or doing masculinity – in everyday interaction. Besides challenging the idea of a singular femininity or masculinity, current research takes the view that speakers have available to them a whole range of (often conflicting) discourses (see Weedon, 1987; Fairclough, 1992; Lee, 1992; Coates, 1997b). This use of the term 'discourse' is derived from the work of Michel Foucault. Discourse, in this sense, can be conceptualized as a 'system of statements which cohere around common meanings and values' (Hollway, 1983: 131). So, for example, in contemporary Britain there are discourses that can be labelled 'conservative' – that is, discourses that emphasize values and meanings where the status quo is cherished – and there are discourses that could be labelled 'patriarchal' – that is, discourses that emphasize meanings and values that assume the superiority of males. Dominant discourses such as these appear 'natural': they are powerful precisely because they are able to make invisible the fact that they are just one among many different discourses.

Thus at any one time there is a wide range of femininities and masculinities available to speakers. The next two examples, which both come from conversations about mothers, demonstrate how these discourses can conflict:

(8) [*talking about the function of funerals*]

MEG: I would see it [*mother's funeral*] as honouring her memory in some way/

(9) [*Sue is complaining that she phones her mother but her mother never phones her*]

SUE: | ((xx)) I'm not very close to my mother really/
LIZ: |cos most mothers are a pain in the bum/

In the first example Meg positions herself as a loving and dutiful daughter. She and her friends discuss whether it would be taboo to miss your mother's funeral. They draw on a dominant discourse where the family is revered and parents are to be honoured, a discourse that upholds the taboo against missing your mother's funeral. The second example represents mothers in a very different way. Here Sue and Liz resist dominant discourses of the family and express feelings that reveal a different picture of mother–daughter relations. This discourse challenges the hegemonic idea that all families are happy and all parents benevolent. Most people have probably experienced both positions, and may even hold both views simultaneously. This is possible because of the existence of alternative discourses, alternative ways of thinking about the world.

Just as there is a range of discourses encoding femininity today, so there is a range of discourses encoding masculinity. The following examples (from Coates, 2003) illustrate contemporary hegemonic masculinity:

(10) [*Julian tells 2 friends a story of a sporting triumph*]

so I took it on the half-volley, and it just went flying, [...] and it was just the most beautiful ball I've ever ever ever seen <EMPHATIC>

(11) [*Max tells Rick about the state of his car – Rick's words are in italics*]

can't believe my car, it's ((2 sylls)) [*really*] mhm, speedo's fucked [*oh no*] [...] wind[screen]wipers are fucked [*oh right*] and now the fucker won't start [*oh no*]

(12) [*Rob tells his friends about a fight at work*]

what he did was he threw this knife at me, this is honest truth, threw a knife at me, and then – and there was this cable [...] he fucking chased me with it, and I thought 'Fuck this', and he kept like having a go and teasing me, and I just smashed him straight round the face with a bell box in front of the boss

The men in these examples align themselves with hegemonic masculinity through their choice of topics (sport, cars, fights), through their emphasis on achievement (in sport or fighting), through their construction of a tough image through the use of swear words and (in the case of the third example) the appeal to violence. These men also construct a masculinity characterized by emotional restraint. Male inexpressivity is recognized as a major feature of contemporary masculinity, and is increasingly seen as problematic: as Vic Seidler puts it, 'we have learnt to use our language to set a safe distance from our felt experience' (Seidler, 1989: 63).

Alternative masculinities represent a challenge to the hegemonic form. Some men, in some conversations, construct themselves as more reflective, as having experienced fear or pain. But there is a constant awareness that this exposes them to ridicule or to accusations of deviance – in particular, to the accusation of being gay. The two men in the next example met in the pub after work and began to discuss what it means to try to be more open with each other.[3] This discussion began because one of their friends had talked about some difficult aspects of his life the previous week, and Pete and Tony agreed that this is something they admired. Tony says he is trying to be more open in his relationships with other people:

(13) *Tony*: I think it's because I decided that– . that (1.0) I ((really)) didn't like this way of relating to people very much and that . life actually would be . improved by . people being more open with each other . not that I'm . brilliant at it <QUIET LAUGH>

    Pete: makes you vulnerable though don't you think? . um don't don't you feel vulnerable? . sometimes?

    Tony: yeah but . I suppose that . that's a useful reminder really isn't it ((I mean)) vulnerability is er– (1.0) all the– all the– the– the masks and so on are supposed to keep vulnerability at bay but . .hh they only do this at a very high cost

(From Coates, 2001)

But even when they do discuss more personal issues and thus potentially challenge masculine norms, in most contexts men will choose to use linguistic strategies that neutralize this by aligning themselves with conventional masculinity. The following exchange comes from a conversation between four male friends talking about the infidelity of a friend's girlfriend:

(11) [*four men in a flat in Manchester, Northern England*]

Dave: fucking 'ell, harsh that...

Chaz: bit harsh that, innit?

> *Dave*: yeah, it's a bit heavy innit?
> *George*: blues big time
> *Ewan*: I'd be fucking gutted…

(From Gough and Edwards, 1998: 419)

The young men's use of taboo words here performs dominant masculinity and thus maintains masculine norms, despite the (more sensitive) topic. But note the use of repetition and tag questions (*innit?*) in this brief exchange – linguistic strategies more often associated with all-female talk.

Queering the study of gender and discourse

One of the key stimuli to fresh thinking about gender has been the new field of queer linguistics. In a recent paper, William Leap, for example, explicitly addresses the question: What do queer theories have to offer researchers of gender and language? (Leap, 2008; see also Chapter 39, this volume). This new field 'has the sexual and gender deviance of previous generations at its centre' (Hall, 2003: 354). Language in queer linguistics is studied from the twin perspectives of gender and sexuality, so research focusing on the language of gay, lesbian, bisexual, and transgender communities is at its heart. The notion of gender as fluid and multiple is intrinsic to queer linguistics, since binary categories like *man/woman* are unhelpful when studying communities like these. Recent examples include a study of British gay slang, known as *Polari* (Lucas, 2006), of the use of sexual insults by *hijras*, a class of transgendered individuals in India (Hall, 1997), of the language use of *travestis* (transvestite prostitutes) in Brazil (Kulick, 1998), and of lesbian coming-out stories in the UK (Saunston, 2007).

A seminal paper was that by Rusty Barrett (1999), which focused on a very particular subgroup of gay men – drag queens. Like female impersonators, drag queens dress in women's clothes and entertain people in clubs and bars, but, unlike female impersonators, who are straight, drag queens are gay. The drag queens that Barrett's paper concentrates on are 'glam queens' – that is, glamour-oriented drag queens who aim to produce a physical representation of hyperfeminine womanhood. He explores the way that speakers draw on a multiplicity of identities, and in particular shows how the drag queens he studied use language to index their identities as African Americans and gay men, as well as drag queens. Speakers exploit different speaking styles, switching between white–woman style, African American Vernacular English (AAVE), and gay male speech. The white-woman style indexes 'ideal' feminine behaviour and contrasts with other styles: in their performances, drag queens will use a stereotypically feminine speaking style but will deliberately subvert this by using taboo words or by switching into a stereotypically masculine voice. As Barrett puts it: 'The polyphony of stylistic voices and the identities they index serve to convey multiple meanings …' (1999: 327).

More recently, research into the discursive construction of gender and sexuality has broadened to other cultures and to other languages. A good example is Hideko Abe's (2006) paper 'Lesbian bar talk in Shinjuku, Tokyo'. Abe investigates the naming and identity construction of lesbian women in Tokyo and the linguistic patterns typical of their interactions. These women self-identify as belonging to two different groups: *rezubian* and *onabe*. *Rezubian* are women who are attracted to other women and who identify as female; *onabe*, by contrast, are women who are attracted to other women but whose social and emotional identity is male. These two groups are catered for by two different kinds of bar: *rezubian* bars and *onabe* bars. Abe's fieldwork involved frequent visits to these bars in a small area of Tokyo over a ten-month period. Among other things she analysed pronoun usage. In Japanese, first-person pronouns are gendered (just like third-person pronouns in English: *he/she*). Abe established that the general pattern was that *rezubian* use the first-person pronoun *watashi* (a pronoun available to both women and men) while *onabe* use *jibun* (a reflexive pronoun associated with men in sports or in the army). But the same speaker can use multiple first-person forms depending on the context, demonstrating the fluidity of lesbian identity in this community. Research like this shows very clearly how constricting a binary approach can be. Here all the people being studied are biologically female, but some identify as female and some as male. It would be all too easy to expect that first-person pronoun usage would correlate neatly with these two kinds of gay woman, but Abe's research shows that this is not the case.

The first book devoted to the subject of language and sexuality appeared in 2003 (Cameron and Kulick, 2003). We can anticipate growing interest in this area, the preoccupation with gay and lesbian language being overtaken by wider concerns such as the linguistic representation of erotic desire, the politics of sexual consent, and the language of sexual prejudice. Case studies like the ones discussed here have been invaluable not only in breaking the stranglehold of simplistic understandings of gender but also in opening up research into non-English-speaking cultures. The new focus on language and sexuality has also served to problematize heterosexuality and to make more visible the way language is used to impose heteronormativity. The aim of queer theory to disentangle sexuality from gender has proved to be less achievable. In particular, dominant norms of masculinity are intrinsically heterosexual (see Cameron, 1997; Kiesling, 2002; Coates, 2007). As Cameron and Kulick (2003: 141) put it: 'Since desiring subjects and desired objects are never genderless, you cannot "do sexuality" without at the same time "doing gender".'

Ideologies of gender and discourse

The last twenty years in language and gender research have been marked by battles over essentialism. Early researchers relied on a biologically based binary – male/female – and used the term 'sex' rather than gender. The realization that gender was culturally constructed meant that the original biologically based binary was replaced by a new cultural binary: masculine/feminine. But in the 1990s binaries of all kinds came under fierce attack. The argument was that binaries relied on an essentialist view of gender, reducing the complexities of masculinity and femininity to a homogeneous duality. The terms 'woman' and 'man' were seen as intrinsically flawed, since they appealed to an essentialist and binary notion of gender.

With the turn of the century came a new awareness of the role played by *ideology* in structuring society. Even though researchers talk in terms of the fluidity and plurality of gender, it is important to acknowledge the power of the social ideology of gender as dichotomous. Most people in most cultures align themselves with this ideology. Gender is seen as a simple mapping onto sex, and sex is construed as binary (male/female). And the ideology has force because gender is not just a cultural construct – it is also a physical reality. 'There is an irreducible bodily dimension in experience and practice' (Connell, 1995: 51)

When speakers perform gender, they are inevitably influenced by prevailing ideologies of gender (see Cameron, 2003; Talbot, 2003). Ideologies of gender and language have varied over the last 200 years, but one thing that is constant is 'the insistence that in any identifiable social group, women and men are *different*' (Cameron, 2003: 452, italics in original). These ideologies of gender and language maintain gender distinctions and help to naturalize the idea that there are two 'opposite' sexes.

Recent work in the language and gender field is increasingly paying attention to the ideologies of gender and language underpinning everyday interaction. For example, Susan Ehrlich (2006) looks at the language used in a Canadian court room, in a trial about sexual assault, and shows how dominant ideologies of gender and of sexual behaviour make it very difficult for the woman complainant to be heard. A second example is research done by Sylvia Shaw (2006) (discussed briefly in section 'The discursive construction of dominance'), who looked at the experience of women members of Parliament in England. Women have trouble making themselves heard in Parliament, a problem arising from an ideology that still sees Parliament as a male arena and women as outsiders. Jie Yang's (2007) research looks at the impact sexist ideology can have on women's everyday lives. Yang identifies a meta-pragmatic discourse on domestic violence in China around the term *zuiqian*, meaning 'deficient mouth'. This discourse includes a series of terms such as *zuisui* 'broken mouth' (talking about trivial things in great detail) or *chang shetou* 'long tongue' (being too inquisitive and nosey). In effect this discourse blames women's 'deviant' speaking styles for the serious social problem of domestic violence. The Chinese terms for women imply there are lots of different sorts of women with different (deviant) ways of speaking. But a feminist analysis makes clear that the true basis of violence against women is simply the fact that they are women.

Cameron (2003: 448) argues that we need to understand the way ideologies work if we are to understand the way ideological representations of language and gender 'inform everyday linguistic and social practice among real women and men'. She looks at how language and gender ideologies vary through time and in different cultures. She argues that the role of ideologies is to make the (unequal) relationship between women and men in any society appear natural, rather than unjust. She also charts what she calls 'the fall and rise of women's language', arguing that women's language skills are no longer seen as deficient, but as superior to men's. However, this new ideology of women as great communicators has not resulted in better pay or higher-status jobs for women, who are simply seen as doing what they are 'naturally' good at. Interestingly, Cameron shows how, while working class males are disadvantaged by these new ideologies, powerful men combine the new 'feminine' communicative skills (emotional expressiveness, good listening, rapport) with traditionally masculine ones (authority, enterprise and leadership). Good examples of such men in the recent past are Bill Clinton, ex-president of the USA, and Tony Blair, ex-prime minister of the UK. Cameron points out that, while men who combine the masculine and the feminine like this are widely admired, women in senior positions are not rewarded for developing masculine characteristics: 'Nobody ever said approvingly of Margaret Thatcher that she was "in touch with her masculine side" ' (Cameron, 2003: 463).

Gender and discourse: the case for strategic essentialism?

The last twenty years have been tumultuous, with researchers disagreeing on the goals of language and gender research and on the theoretical frameworks and methodologies best suited to achieving these goals. During these last twenty years, ideas about language and gender have changed considerably. What used to be called 'language' is now seen instead as a heterogeneous collection of competing discourses. Gender is no longer viewed as monolithic or static but as multiple and fluid. Researchers have moved on to observing the discursive production of a wide range of femininities and masculinities, and have broadened the range of communities investigated, both geographically and in terms of gay, lesbian, bisexual and transgender speakers.

However, in the twenty-first century there has been a re-appraisal of the roots of language and gender research, and some researchers have begun to argue explicitly for a revival of feminist awareness in language and gender research (see Baxter, 2003; McElhinny, 2003; Swann, 2003; Holmes, 2007). While it is not true to say that there is now consensus, there is a sense that a more pragmatic approach needs to prevail. Some are arguing for 'strategic essentialism', a phrase coined by the post-colonial theorist Gayatri Chakravorty Spivak (1987) to refer to the careful and temporary use of essentialism when the main goal is to expose discrimination against subaltern (subordinate) groups. As Holmes (2007) argues, the category of 'women' as a group (and some level of generalization about this category) is still 'strategically indispensable' if the aim of the scholar is to explore the 'gender order', that is, the 'ways in which women are the victims of repressive ideologies and discriminatory behaviour' (p. 56).

What this means for research in the area of discourse and gender is that there is currently a sense that researchers are now free to analyse talk in whatever way seems to make sense of the data; the fear of being accused of essentialism, which inhibited many researchers, has now begun to dissipate. Post-structuralist ideas have led to a loosening of ideas about gender, while at the same time a new understanding of the role of ideology has led to the re-emergence of binaries when used strategically. The discursive reproduction of gender is being explored all over the world and in a wide range of contexts, from the family dinner table to the twenty-first century global workplace. It seems likely that research in this area will continue to flourish and that our interest in the relationship between gender and discourse will continue unabated.

Further reading

Cameron, Deborah (2003) 'Gender and language ideologies', in J. Holmes and M. Meyerhoff (eds.) *The Handbook of Language and Gender*. Oxford: Blackwell, pp. 447–467.

A key paper – Cameron argues clearly that speakers are not free agents but are constrained in their language choices and in their sense of themselves as gendered by current ideologies.

Coates, Jennifer (2004) *Women, Men and Language*. Third Edition.

This comprehensive survey of the language and gender field covers all aspects of the subject. This edition contains several new chapters, including one on contemporary developments.

Davies, Julia (2003) 'Expressions of gender: an analysis of pupils' gendered discourse styles in small group classroom discussions', *Discourse and Society* 14 (2): 115–132.

This paper demonstrates very clearly how the discursive strategies of boys and girls in the classroom differ widely. It draws attention to the conflict between the discourse of learning and expressions of heterosexual masculinity.

Janet Holmes (2007) 'Social constructionism, postmodernism and feminist sociolinguistics', *Gender and Language*, 1 (1): 51–66.

A key paper, arguing for less rigidity in approaches to language and gender and emphasizing the importance of a feminist approach.

Pichler, Pia and Eppler, Eva (eds.) (2009) *Gender and Spoken Interaction*. London: Palgrave.

An important collection of up-to-date papers by researchers in the field covering a wide range of topics, with a theoretical introduction by Deborah Cameron.

Notes

1 Some commentators are less convinced about the role of interruption in conversational dominance; see for example James and Clarke (1993). Analysis of so-called 'interruptions' has not always distinguished clearly between supportive overlap, typical of collaborative talk, and simultaneous speech resulting from one speaker taking an illegitimate – and often adversarial – turn while another speaking is still talking. It is only the latter that is involved in conversational dominance.
2 Thanks to Kate Harrington, who collected the conversation this extract comes from and who allowed me to include the conversation in my database.
3 Most conversations in my database involved three or more male friends. This conversation was unusual in that one member of the group arrived late at the pub, which resulted in a short spell of two-party talk. It seems that talk among two men only is far more likely to involve self-disclosure than talk among larger numbers, a contrast not found so clearly in all-female conversation.

References

Abe, H. (2006) 'Lesbian bar talk in Shinjuku, Tokyo', in D. Cameron and D. Kulick (eds.) *The Language and Sexuality Reader*. London: Routledge, pp. 132–140.
Bakhtin, M. (1981) *The Dialogic Imagination: Four Essays*. Austin, TX: University of Texas Press.

Barrett, R. (1999) 'Indexing polyphonous identity in the speech of African American drag queens', in M. Bucholtz *et al.* (eds.) *Reinventing Identities.* New York: Oxford University Press, pp. 313–331.

Baxter, J. (2003) *Positioning Discourse in Gender: A Feminist Methodology.* Basingstoke: Palgrave Macmillan.

Baxter, J. (2006) 'Introduction', in J. Baxter (ed.) *Speaking Out: The Female Voice in Public Contexts.* Basingstoke: Palgrave Macmillan, pp. xiii–xviii.

Cameron, D. (1997) 'Performing gender identity: young men's talk and the construction of heterosexual masculinity', in S. Johnson and U. Meinhof (eds.) *Language and Masculinity.* Oxford: Blackwell, pp. 47–64

Cameron, D. (2003) 'Gender and language ideologies', in J. Holmes and M. Meyerhoff (eds.) *The Handbook of Language and Gender.* Oxford: Blackwell, pp. 447–467.

Cameron, D. and Kulick, D. (2003) *Language and Sexuality.* Cambridge: Cambridge University Press.

Coates, J. (1989) 'Gossip revisited: language in all-female groups', in J. Coates and D. Cameron (eds.) *Women in Their Speech Communities.* London: Longman, pp. 94–122.

Coates, J. (1996) *Women Talk: Conversation Between Women Friends.* Oxford: Blackwell.

Coates, J. (1997a) 'The construction of a collaborative floor in women's friendly talk', in T. Givon (ed.) *Conversation: Cognitive, Communicative and Social Perspectives.* Philadelphia, PA: John Benjamins, pp. 55–89.

Coates, J. (1997b) 'Competing discourses of femininity', in H. Kotthoff and R. Wodak (eds.) *Communicating Gender in Context.* Amsterdam: John Benjamins, pp. 285–314.

Coates, J. (2001) 'Pushing at the boundaries: the expression of alternative masculinities', in J. Cotterill and A. Ife (eds.) *Language Across Boundaries.* London: BAAL/Continuum, pp. 1–24.

Coates, J. (2003) *Men Talk: Stories in the Making of Masculinities.* Oxford: Blackwell.

Coates, J. (2004) *Women: Men and Language.* London: Londgmn.

Coates, J. (2007) ' "Everyone was convinced that we were closet fags": the role of heterosexuality in the construction of hegemonic masculinity', in H. Sauntson and S. Kyratzis (eds.) *Language, Sexualities and Desires: Cross-Cultural Perspectives.* Basingstoke: Palgrave Macmillan, pp. 41–67.

Coates, J. and Sutton-Spence, R. (2001) 'Turn-taking patterns in Deaf friends' talk', *Journal of Sociolinguistics*, 4 (4): 507–529.

Connell, R. W. (1995) *Masculinities.* Cambridge: Polity Press.

Davies, J. (2003) 'Expressions of gender: an analysis of pupils' gendered discourse styles in small group classroom discussions', *Discourse and Society*, 14 (2): 115–132.

DeFrancisco, V. (1991) 'The sounds of silence: how men silence women in marital relations', *Discourse and Society*, 2 (4): 413–424.

Eckert, P. (1998) 'Gender and sociolinguistic variation', in J. Coates (ed.) *Language and Gender: A Reader.* Oxford: Blackwell, pp. 64–75.

Edelsky, C. (1993) 'Who's got the floor?', in D. Tannen (ed.) *Gender and Conversational Interaction.* New York: Oxford University Press, pp. 189–227.

Ehrlich, S. (2006) 'Trial discourse and judicial decision-making: constraining the boundaries of gendered identities', in J. Baxter (ed.) *Speaking Out: The Female Voice in Public Contexts.* Basingstoke: Palgrave Macmillan, pp. 139–158.

Eppler, E. (2009) 'Four women, two codes, and one (crowded) floor: the joint construction of a bilingual collaborative floor', in P. Pichler and E. Eppler (eds.) *Gender and Spoken Interaction.* Basingstoke: Palgrave Macmillan, pp. 211–234.

Fairclough, N. (1992) *Discourse and Social Change.* Cambridge: Polity Press.

Fishman, P. (1980) 'Conversational insecurity', in H. Giles, W. P. Robinson, and P. M. Smith (eds.) *Language: Social Psychological Perspectives.* Oxford: Pergamon Press, pp. 127–132.

Gough, B. and Edwards, G. (1998) 'The beer talking: four lads, a carry out and the reproduction of masculinities', *The Sociological Review*, August 1998, pp. 409–435.

Hall, K. (1997) ' "Go suck your husband's sugarcane!": Hijras and the use of sexual insults', in A. Livia and K. Hall (eds.) *Queerly Phrased: Language, Gender and Sexuality.* New York: Oxford University Press, pp. 430–460.

Hall, K. (2003) 'Exceptional speakers: contested and problematised gender identities', in J. Holmes and M. Meyerhoff (eds.) *The Handbook of Language and Gender.* Oxford: Blackwell, pp. 353–380.

Herring, S. (1992) *Gender and Participation in Computer-Mediated Linguistic Discourse*, Washington, DC: ERIC Clearinghouse on Languages and linguistics. Document no. ED345552.

Herring, S. *et al.* (1992) 'Participation in electronic discourse in a "feminist" field', in K. Hall (ed.) *Locating Power.* Proceedings of the Second Berkeley Women and Language Conference. Berkeley, CA: BWLG, pp. 250–262.

Hollway, W. (1983) 'Heterosexual sex: power and desire for the other', in S. Cartledge and J. Ryan (eds.) *Sex and Love: New Thoughts on Old Contradictions.* London: Women's Press, pp. 124–140.

Holmes, J. (2000) 'Women at work: analyzing women's talk in New Zealand workplaces', *Australian Review of Applied Linguistics*, 22 (2): 1–17.

Holmes, J. (2007) 'Social constructionism, postmodernism and feminist sociolinguistics', *Gender and Language*, 1 (1): 51–66.

Holmes, J. and Stubbe, M. (2003) 'Feminine' workplaces: stereotypes and reality', in J. Holmes and M. Meyerhoff (eds.) *Handbook of Language and Gender*. Oxford: Blackwell, pp. 573–599.

James, D. and Clarke, S. (1993) 'Women, men and interruptions: a critical review', in D. Tannen(ed.) *Gender and Conversational Interaction*. New York: Oxford University Press, pp. 231–280.

Jie, Yang (2007) 'Zuiqian "deficient mouth": discourse, gender and domestic violence in urban China', *Gender and Language*, 1 (1): 107–118.

Kiesling, S. (2002) 'Playing the straight man: displaying and maintaining male heterosexuality in discourse', in K. Campbell-Kibler, R. Podevsa, S. J. Roberts, and A. Wong (eds.) *Language and Sexuality: Contesting Meaning in Theory and Practice*. Stanford, CA: CSLI Publications, pp. 2–10.

Kulick, D. (1998) *Travesti: Sex, Gender and Culture Among Brazilian Transgendered Prostitutes*. Chicago, IL: Chicago University Press.

Lakoff, R. (1975) *Language and Woman's Place*. New York: Harper and Row.

Leap, W. L. (2008) 'Queering gay men's English', in K. Harrington *et al.* (eds.) *Gender and Language Research Methodologies*. Basingstoke: Palgrave Macmillan, pp. 283–296.

Lee, D. (1992) *Competing Discourses: Perspective and Ideology in Language*. London: Longman.

Lucas, I. (2006) 'The colour of his eyes: Polari and the sisters of perpetual indulgence', in D. Cameron and D. Kulick (eds.) *Language and Sexuality Reader*. London: Routledge, pp. 85–94.

Mallinson, C. and Childs, B. (2007) 'Communities of practice in sociolinguistic description: analysing language and identity practices among black women in Appalachia', *Gender and Language*, 1 (2): 173–206.

Maltz, D. and Borker, R. (1982) 'A cultural approach to male-female communication', in J. Gumperz (ed.) *Language and Identity*. Cambridge: Cambridge University Press, pp. 195–216.

McElhinny, B. (2003) 'Theorising gender in sociolinguistics and linguistic anthropology', in J. Holmes and M. Meyerhoff (eds.) *The Handbook of Language and Gender*. Oxford: Blackwell, pp. 21–42.

Osmond, M. W. and Thorne, B. (1993) 'Feminist theories: the social construction of gender in families and society', in P. Boss *et al.* (eds.) *Sourcebook of Family Theories and Methods*. New York: Plenum, pp. 591–622.

Ostermann, A. C. (2003) 'Communities of practice at work: gender, facework and the power of habitus at an all-female police station and a feminist crisis interventions centre in Brazil', *Discourse and Society*, 14 (4): 473–505.

Pilkington, J. (1998) ' "Don't try and make out that I'm nice": The different strategies women and men use when gossiping', in J. Coates (ed.) *Language and Gender: A Reader*. Oxford: Blackwell, pp. 254–269.

Saunston, H. (2007) 'Education, culture and the construction of sexual identity: an APPRAISAL analysis of lesbian coming out narratives', in H. Saunston and S. Kyrakis (eds.) *Language, Sexualities and Desires: Cross-Cultural Perspectives*. Basingstoke: Palgrave Macmillan, pp. 140–164.

Seidler, V. (1989) *Rediscovering Masculinity: Reason, Language and Sexuality*. London: Routledge.

Shaw, S. (2006) 'Governed by the rules? the female voice in parliamentary debates', in J. Baxter (ed.) *Speaking Out: The Female Voice in Public Contexts*. Basingstoke: Palgrave Macmillan, pp. 81–102.

Spivak, G. C. (1987) *In Other Worlds: Essays in Cultural Politics*. New York: Routledge.

Swann, J. (1989) 'Talk control: an illustration from the classroom of problems in analysing male dominance in conversation', in J. Coates and D. Cameron (eds.) *Women in Their Speech Communities*. London: Longman, pp. 122–140.

Swann, J. (2003) 'Schooled language: language and gender in educational settings', in J. Holmes and M. Meyerhoff (eds.) *The Handbook of Language and Gender*. Oxford: Blackwell, 624–644.

Talbot, M. (2003) 'Gender stereotypes: reproduction and challenge', in J. Holmes and M. Meyerhoff (eds.) *The Handbook of Language and Gender*. Oxford: Blackwell, pp. 468–486.

Tannen, D. (1990) *You just Don't Understand: Women and Men in Conversation*. New York: William Morrow.

Trudgill, P. (1974) *The Social Differentiation of English in Norwich*. Cambridge: Cambridge University Press.

Trudgill, P. (1983) 'Sex and covert prestige', in P. Trudgill (ed.) *On Dialect*. Oxford: Blackwell, pp. 169–177.

Weedon, C. (1987) *Feminist Practice and Poststructuralist Theory*. Oxford: Blackwell.

West, C. and Zimmerman, D. (1977) 'Women's place in everyday talk: reflections on parent–child interaction', *Social Problems*, 24: 521–529.

Zimmerman, D. and West, C. (1975) 'Sex roles, interruptions and silences in conversation', in B. Thorne and N. Henley (eds.) *Language and Sex: Difference and Dominance*. Rowley, MA: Newbury House, pp. 105–129.

8

Discursive psychology and discourse analysis

Jonathan Potter

Discursive psychology is an approach that addresses psychological matters in terms of how they figure in discourse – in conversations over family mealtimes, in therapy sessions, in witness statements. It begins with psychology, as it confronts people as they live their lives. How does a speaker show that they are not prejudiced, while developing a derogatory version of an entire cultural group? How is upset displayed, understood and receipted in a call to a child protection helpline? How does a parent show that they care for a disabled daughter while they close down a phone call? How does a police officer move between technical and mundane notions of intention when interviewing a suspect? The point here is that psychology is something that is live and visible as it appears in and through discourse, as actions are performed and receipted. This is not just through psychological language – psychological predicates and avowals – although that is interesting and important, but through styles of speaking, through inflection and prosody, through descriptions that invoke and suggest psychological states and dispositions and through the apparatus of accountability that builds motivation and intention. All of this works through, and is dependent on, the normative organization of conversation, whose operations are themselves a major resource for psychological display and understanding. This is why discourse analysis must be at the heart of a reconfigured psychology.

Discursive psychology (henceforth DP) is a systematic and comprehensive alternative perspective to more traditional psychological approaches such as psychoanalysis, behaviourism and social cognition. It is focused on how psychological objects, orientations and displays are parts of discourse practices. The focus is on discourse practices as they appear naturally in everyday and institutional settings. These practices involve talk, but that talk is coordinated with embodied action and often responsive to, or reworking, texts (documents, files, computer fields and so on). Developing this perspective has necessarily involved a radical reworking of the nature and boundaries of the 'psychological'; part of its excitement has been the way an entirely new vision of psychology has started to crystallize.

It has also required a shift in methodology to an approach that takes seriously the nature of human discourse. It has been crucial to move away from the 'telementation' picture of language as a conduit sending ideas from one mind to another, as Harris (1981) so memorably described it, to a view that starts with the practical, action oriented role of discourse. The methodological principles of DP follow from its conceptualization of discourse as a basic medium of action rather than as an abstract system of description. This methodological innovation has built on more familiar critiques of experimental and survey methods in psychological research, but has taken methodological development in rather different directions. In particular, DP has increasingly drawn on the methods and conceptualizations of conversation analysis as they provide the most powerful approach available for analysing the way actions are performed in talk.

DP starts to address psychology in this way because discourse is the primary currency for action, understanding and intersubjectivity. DP is very different from the psychology of language, which tends to treat language as one variable among many. It starts with a view of people as social and relational and with psychology as a domain of practice rather than abstract contemplation. Although discourse research is often stimulated by broader theoretical considerations, one of the ironies of DP is that in its careful, descriptive focus on discourse it offers something of the observational science that classic experimental psychology often claims as its own.

This chapter will introduce the perspective of discursive psychology. It will start by offering a brief history of DP and its relationship to discourse analysis more broadly, as well as to the contemporary discipline of psychology. It will then outline some of the basic elements of a DP approach, highlighting links to the perspective of constructionism and conversation analysis. Following this, it will briefly sketch the basic methodological principles of DP and describe three research studies that highlight what is distinctive about this approach with respect to key psychological topics that fall within the more familiar psychological categories of cognition, attitudes and emotion. It will end with a brief review of contemporary debates and future developments.

The development of discursive psychology out of discourse analysis

Discursive psychology emerged from Potter and Wetherell's (1987) influential volume *Discourse and Social Psychology*. This in turn drew on, and offered an integration of, conversation analytic work (Atkinson and Drew, 1979; Levinson, 1983), post-structuralist arguments from Barthes, Derrida and Foucault and, crucially, work in the analysis of scientific discourse that was part of the broader sociology of scientific knowledge (Gilbert and Mulkay, 1984). These disparate strands were held together through an emphasis on: (a) the careful empirical study of discourse; (b) the manner in which discourse is oriented to action; and (c) the way representations are built to support actions.

Many of the features that are central to discursive psychology were outlined in Potter and Wetherell (1987). However, there are two important differences from that earlier work. First, Potter and Wetherell had as their major focus the identification and nature of the structured resources that underlie and sustain interaction. These include membership categories (Hester and Eglin, 1997), rhetorical commonplaces (Billig, 1987 [1996]) and, most notably, interpretative repertoires. Potter and Wetherell refined the notion of interpretative repertoires from Gilbert and Mulkay's (1984) earlier work on scientific discourse. Interpretative repertoires are clusters of terms organized around a central metaphor, often used with particular grammatical regularities. They are drawn on to support different actions. In Lawes' (1999) work on marriage talk, for example, speakers used a 'romantic' repertoire to justify their commitment to marriage, while they used a 'realist' repertoire to justify and explain marriage breakdown and divorce. The same speaker might draw inconsistently on both repertoires at different times to support different practices. The notion of interpretative repertoire has now been used in a large number of research studies (see, for recent examples, Stevens and Harper, 2007; Hernandez-Martinez *et al.*, 2008; Juhila, 2009).

The virtue of this analytic notion is its ability to capture complex, historically developed organizations of ideas that could be identified through research. Interpretative repertoires accommodate to the flexible requirements of social practice and thus offer greater analytic purchase than some neo-Foucaultian notions of discourse, which are more brittle and tectonic. The ideological role of this flexibility was highlighted by Billig *et al.* (1988), who noted the way flexible and dilemmatic forms of accounting can be ideologically more powerful than more crystallized alternatives. For example, they studied the way educational ideologies work in classroom situations. Although traditional approaches that stress learned outcomes seem very different from progressive approaches that value the way pupils come to their own understandings of the world, Billig *et al.*'s analysis shows that teachers work with both ideas of education as they manage classes and work toward specific outcomes. Techniques are used that generate specific outcomes (e.g. cueing certain kinds of answer, ignoring others) but the whole practice is described as pupil-centred and progressive. The contradictions at the level of ideology in the abstract become central, flexible strengths at the level of practice. For methods-focused pieces on the analysis of repertoires, see Edley (2001) and Potter (2004) and the original how-to-do-it chapter in Potter and Wetherell (1987).

Despite the virtues of this analytic notion, Wooffitt (2005) has suggested that the notion of interpretative repertoires misses the full complexity of human conduct. In particular, he raises the question of whether the way repertoires are patterned is a consequence of preformed conceptual organizations or a by-product of the pragmatic organization of practices (see Potter, 1996, ch. 6). Furthermore, the original repertoire notion required a series of procedures and criteria for the reliable identification of forms of talk and text as a repertoire. Yet current studies sometimes offer only a vague account of how repertoires are identified and of how they relate to a corpus of data (Potter, 2003).

The second area of difference between Potter and Wetherell's (1987) conception of discourse analysis and the later discursive psychology is the use of open-ended interviews. The majority of the many studies using interpretative repertoires have used open-ended interviews to generate data. Such interviews lend themselves to the production of talk that can be analysed for interpretative repertoires; so they can be part of a productive research strategy. However, discursive psychology is distinct from the earlier tradition of discourse analysis in almost completely abandoning open-ended interviews in favour of a focus on records of talk in natural settings. In part, this was a consequence of the profound problems that arise in the production and analysis of open-ended interviews (Potter and Hepburn, 2005). Most importantly, however, it is due to the excitement and creativity that comes from working with records of people actually living their lives in either everyday or institutional settings. I will say more about this below.

Despite these major differences, there are some important continuities between Potter and Wetherell (1987) and discursive psychology. Both draw heavily on the constructionist sociology of scientific knowledge and on the revitalized rhetoric of Billig (Billig 1987 [1996]). Both focus on categories and descriptions and on the way these are involved in actions. And both offer a respecification of basic psychological notions.

Theoretical principles of discursive psychology

Discursive psychology is usefully understood as working with three fundamental observations about the nature of discourse. Discourse is (1) oriented to action; (2) situated sequentially, institutionally and rhetorically; and (3) constructed and constructive. These observations structure analytic work in DP. I will take them in turn.

Discourse is action orientation

DP starts with a focus on discourse as a central resource for performing action. These may be relatively discrete actions, which have speech act verbs associated with them – invitation, complaint, say – or they may be complex, institutionally embedded practices where no speech act verb exists – using questions to give 'person centred' advice, perhaps. Often actions are done indirectly, via descriptions of some kind that provide a different kind of accountability for the speaker than an 'on-the-record' speech act. The key point is that discourse is studied for how action is done rather than treated as a medium for access to putative mental objects (intentions, dislikes). This is a very different startpoint from that of cognitive psychology, which was largely born out of an engagement with linguistics, and more specifically out of a concern with grammatical structure and abstract semantics (Potter and te Molder, 2005).

Discourse is situated

A central recognition of DP is that actions are situated. The most profound way that action is situated is in terms of the here and now of conversational sequence. Talk is *occasioned*. This point is at the heart of discursive psychological research practice. When we move from language as an abstract system that has a static and abstract relation to the world and to mental organizations to an action-focused approach, we are immediately considering the way events unfold in real time. As Heritage (1984) emphasized, talk is context dependent in that it picks up from, and responds to, the immediate conversational context; and it is also context reproducing in that it builds a new context for whatever talk is immediately following. For example, when an offer is issued, this sets up the environment for various relevant next actions, most relevantly acceptance or rejection. Note that, if the offer is ignored, this will be the action of ignoring the offer; it will be heard in relation to the offer. Moreover, by doing acceptance or rejection, the speaker is displaying an understanding of the offer as an offer. Conversation analysis has highlighted the extraordinary detail and specificity in which interaction is organized (Schegloff, 2007).

A second major way in which an action is situated is institutionally. DP does not adopt a position of contextual determinism; it does not treat all interaction in a doctor's surgery, say, as intrinsically medical. Nor does it treat institutional talk as organized into coherent, conceptually organized discourses, such that medical settings will implicate a medical discourse or register. Instead DP focuses on the way the coherence of medical talk, say, comes from the regular collection of interactional tasks that are being managed. However, these institutional tasks are often dependent on broader practices that have been utilized or refined in institutional settings (Potter, 2005). However, institutional talk is typically oriented to pervasive institutional identities, which in turn may be invoked, oriented to or subverted in different ways.

A third major way in which an action is situated is rhetorically. This came out of the early engagement with Billig's (1996) rhetorical psychology. It highlights the way that descriptions are often organized to counter actual or potential alternatives – and organized in ways that manage actual or possible attempts to undermine them (Potter, 1996). A major theme in DP is the way epistemic issues are managed using a wide range of conversational and rhetorical resources (Potter and Hepburn, 2008).

Discourse is constructed and constructive

Discourse is constructed from a range of resources – words, categories, rhetorical commonplaces, grammatical structures, repertoires, conversational practices and so on, all of which may be delivered in real time, with prosody and timing, or is built into documents with specific layouts, fonts and so on. These resources, their use and their conditions of assembly can become topics of DP study. They are both resources for action and challenges that may require management in order for one to work round their specific affordances.

Discourse is constructive in the sense that it is used to build versions of psychological worlds, of social organizations and action, and of histories and broader structures. Such versions are an integral part of different actions. DP research can be focused on the way constructions are built and stabilized and on the way they are made neutral, objective and independent of the speaker. People are skilled builders of descriptions; they have spent a lifetime learning how to do it. Part of the analytic art of DP is to reveal the complex and delicate work that goes into this seemingly effortless building. For example, how does one party in a relationship counselling session construct a version that presents the breakdown of a long-term relationship as primarily the responsibility of the other party; that is, how might one party produce the other as the one most in need of counselling and therefore under most pressure to change (Edwards, 1995)?

This kind of constructionism is different from cognitive constructionisms, which focus on the way mental images of the world are assembled through processes of information processing. It is also distinct from a range of social constructionisms, which focus on the way individuals are produced with particular constellations of subjectivity through processes of socialization and through the internalization of social relations. In DP the procedures of production are treated as analysable elements in themselves – they do not require the analyst to delve into a putative mental space. Whereas cognitive constructionisms tend to focus on purported mental entities and processes and social constructionists tend to focus on social relationships and social perception, the constructionist focus in discursive psychology is on people's practices, and particularly on how versions are constructed.

A further major principle of DP is that the space of psychology itself is not a natural object in the world, but is a major issue that participants manage. Consider the topic of evaluations (tradition-ally, attitudes and opinions in classic social science approaches). An evaluation can be built as a personal preference, something that the speaker is accountable for, or as a feature of how the world is – not something that the speaker feels or wants but a feature of the world that they notice. For example, a negative evaluation of a minority group can be built using descriptions that present that group's actions as negative, but present the speaker as actually sympathetically disposed. In this way speakers can manage possible attributions of racism. In contrast, a strongly positive assessment of some food that has been cooked by the host can be built as a personal attitude or disposition. Edwards (2007) calls these 'object side' and 'subject side constructions'. A major part of the production of talk and of the psychological attributions that go along with it can have the function of managing the production of object and subject side. Before illustrating some of these principles with research examples I will outline some of the basic methodological procedures of DP.

Methodological procedures of discursive psychology

Although there are some differences of emphasis, contemporary DP draws heavily on the methods and approach of conversation analysis (for more detail, see Chapter 3 in this volume). A typical DP study will work with a set of audio or video recordings collected in some setting. Recent work has used phone calls to neighbour dispute mediation service, calls to a child protection helpline, video records of family mealtimes. Researchers often draw on more familiar sets of mundane records of phone interaction to do primary or comparative work.

Such materials will be digitized and often transcribed in one pass by a transcription service that is meant to capture the basic words and speaker transitions. This can facilitate searches through material for particular themes or events of interest. Often these are generated through data sessions in which a number of researchers engage with a single example, with repeated viewings or listenings, and this stimulates preliminary ideas that lead to a search for new examples. Such a search can start to build a preliminary corpus of examples. These are typically transcribed using the system developed by Gail Jefferson (2004), which captures features of delivery that are oriented to by participants – overlap, volume, prosody – in a way that makes them visible on the page (see 'Transcription Conventions' at the end of this chapter and Hepburn and Bolden, in press, for a fuller account). Analysis and data sessions, however, typically work with both video/audio and transcript; the latter is not intended to replace the former. Unlike in more traditional social psychological work, specific research questions are rarely developed prior to the research; rather, the research often takes the setting as the key driver of questions (what kind of practices go on in a neighbour mediation helpline?) or works with a broad orientation to materials (in what sense can we find practices of advice giving in these helpline calls?).

A study will commonly work with a flexible corpus of examples. As analysis develops, the corpus will be refined. Some examples will be abandoned and new examples will be recognized, and therefore included in the corpus. The corpus will often start with standard cases and try to explicate them, and then consider deviant or counter cases, which may provide further specification of the phenomena. With interactional materials the orientations of the participants themselves are a primary analytic resource, as these display their understanding of what is going on in its most basic way. Heritage (2004) suggests that participants orient towards interaction in at least three ways. First, they address themselves to immediately preceding talk. Second, they set up the conditions for the action or actions that will come next. Third, in the production of next actions, participants show a set of understandings of the prior action: that it is complete, that it was addressed to them rather than someone else, what kind of action it was and so on. This matrix provides for the intelligibility of interaction that is crucial for participants and offers an extraordinarily rich resource for analysts.

In what follows I will take two contemporary discursive psychological studies. I will use them to illustrate the various theoretical and analytic features of this style of research. They will also, very loosely, illustrate the way DP respecifies basic phenomena of cognition and attitudes.

Studies in discursive psychology

Intention: institutions and practices

Ideas of intention have had a range of different roles in the social sciences. One of the most influential is probably in the field social cognition, where the theory of planned behaviour (Ajzen, 1991) has been associated with more than a thousand articles in the last two decades. This theory treats intentions as the product of a number of different elements, which work in combination to affect behavioural outcomes. Intention is treated as a kind of mental push that will result in the person engaging in the actual behaviour, unless something intervenes to prevent it. Some philosophers have criticized this kind of approach to intentions by offering a conceptual analytic picture of intentions as a language game for making distinctions between different kinds of actions (e.g. Austin, 1961).

Rather than engage in such conceptual analysis, Derek Edwards (2008) opts for an approach that considers intentions through considering the practical use of attributions of intention, of the term intention, and of intentional language more broadly. He notes that actually there is a very wide range of semantic and grammatical resources that can be used to denote that something was intended or done intentionally. Thus words such as *kick* imply agency, while words such as *fall* imply passivity or something that happened without intending. And the different grammatical resources can upgrade, cancel or modify the agency in some way. To limit analysis further as a basis for developing a collection of examples, he chose to focus on cases where the intentionality of an action was specifically topicalized by reference to a mental state. Edwards' first search is through a corpus of everyday UK mundane telephone conversations in which family members (and friends and acquaintances) chat to one another, make arrangements and transact their day-to-day business.

As a first observation, Edwards notes that intentionality is rarely topicalized in everyday talk of this kind, except where there is some difficulty – something has been impeded or has had to be postponed. Take the following example.

```
(Holt:1:4:2)
1  Les:  →    What time did you inten' getting here Keith.
2              (0.3)
3  Kei:       Uh:: (1.4) pr'obly about uh::: ten o'clock.
4              h's [train   co]mes[in
5  Les:            [Well the-]    [the trouble is you see uhm (1.1)
6              uhh! (0.2) You better haa- (0.3) There's a- uh- (.)
7              aga:p,h (0.2) when: I'm out'n she's out but if you're
8              early enough you c'n go with her I thi:nk, (…)
```

Leslie's query about Keith's arrival time (line 1) can be seen to be prompted by the prospect of trouble, which is introduced in line 5. However, Leslie signals the potential for trouble right in line 1 by using the term intention – things would be very different if she has simply said 'what time are you getting in?'. As Edwards puts it:

> The very notion of an intention to do something, as something worth formulating, makes relevant a potential a gap between thought and action.
>
> *(2008: 180)*

And Keith has clearly picked up that there is a looming problem as he delivers the time of arrival in a softened, delayed and hedged manner, preparing the way, perhaps, for a cooperative modification in plans. Edwards goes through a range of further examples that use terms that suggest intentional mental states (think, like), concluding that the formulation of baulked preferences or intentions is part of a standard conversational organization, familiar in conversation analysis, where invitations and offers are routinely declined. His conclusion is that intentionality is a major element in the building of accountability for failed actions (or ones that have been, or are, likely not to be realized) and is a resource that people use for the performance of conversational actions done in the telling (2008: 182).

This is the backdrop for an examination of the way notions of intentionality figure in police interrogation. The data here are a collection of British police interrogations recorded by the police themselves, as part of their process of evidence gathering and case building. His first observation is that, in contrast to the mundane materials, intentionality is a pervasive concern, and a concern that is not restricted to a focus on failed or baulked actions. Typically some degree of intent is a key criterion for the status of the suspect's action as a crime. However, the notion of intent is interestingly extended. In English law there is a distinction between *actus reus* (the actual illegal action) and *mens rea* (the criminal intent); conviction will depend on the prosecution showing both of these things. And the *mens rea* can vary from full premeditation to recklessness with regards to consequences. Edwards suggests that recklessness would not be part of a more everyday notion of intention; yet in legal settings 'recklessness is raised and negotiated alongside, and in terms of, intent and intentional states' (2008: 183).

Take the following example. The suspect has been accused of damaging a car following a row, and he has already admitted that he 'smashed the car up'.

(PN:2:2)

```
 1  P:       You said, (.) smashed the car up.
 2  S:       Well. (.) smashed the back window.
 3  P:       What'd (y'hit.)
 4           (1.3)
 5  S:       I [punched the window.]
 6  P:         [    (To get into)     ] the car.
 7           (0.3)
 8  P:       Punched the back window.=
 9  S:       =Yeh.
10           (3.7)
11  P:       Hh okha:yh h
12           (2.0)
13  P: →     What was y'r pur:pose when y'punched the window,hhh
14           (0.6)
15  S:       Take th'temper outa me.
16           (0.2)
17  S:       (_Th*at's *all_)
18           (1.9)
19  P:       *R:*ight
20           (0.7)
21  P: →     Did you inte:nd to cause any damage to the
22           window of the car,
23           (0.4)
24  S:       *No not really,*
25           (0.3)
26  P:       No,
```

Edwards suggests that across the range of interrogation examples the police work to parse events into action, effect and intent. The interrogator works to establish not only what the suspect did (in this case, punch the window), but also what the effects were (the window was broken) and what degree of intent there was with regard to those effects. Note how, having established a description of the action, the police officer moves to the issue of intent. The design of the question presupposes that the punching was done for some purpose. The suspect in this case avoids this presupposition by citing the role of the punching in terms of managing his mental state – it was to 'take the temper out' of him. Having unsuccessfully established intent with a relatively open WH-question, the interrogator pursues the issues of intent with a yes/no interrogative on 21. This move from open to closed forms of questions was recurrent in the corpus.

In this case the questions have not succeeded in eliciting the required admission of intent from the suspect. The police officer moves to an approach that, Edwards notes, is also recurrent in the corpus, which involves the use of normative and hypothetical reasoning.

(continued from previous)

```
27           (0.4)
28  P:       Ri*:ght*
29           (2.1) ((papers rustling))
30  P: →     What d'you think the likely outcome is if you punch
31           a window of a carhh.
```

```
32              (0.5)
33    S:        °Could sma:sh,°
34              (0.3)
35    P:        It could sma:sh
36              (1.7) ((papers rustling))
37    P: →      °'Kay.° Did you think about that risk before you-
38              punched it,
39    S:        *Didn't think about anythin:*
40              (0.5)
41    S:        (*Punched it.*)
42              (0.3)
43    P:        Righ'.
44              (1.1)
45    P:        But you're aWA:RE that by punching something
46              there's a risk.
47              (.)
48    P:        By punchin' a window there's a risk of it breakin'.
49    S:        °*>Ye:h<*°
```

Note the way in line 30, after the suspect has denied having the intention to break the window, the police officer builds a normative and hypothetical question – what is the likely outcome *if* you punch *a* window? Moreover, the question asks about the suspect's mental state – what do you *think*? As in the earlier extract, the officer moves from an open WH-question to a yes/no interrogative in 37–38. When this is unsuccessful, the interrogator again issues a hypothetical that links punching a window to it breaking, this time eliciting agreement.

Edwards' general observation is that the interrogations are an institutional setting that draw on, but refine, everyday practices of managing intentionality. Thus they go beyond the everyday appearance of intention when actions are baulked to being an overt topic closely related to issues of criminal responsibility. The analysis highlights some of the practices through which such intent is built: separating action, intention and effect; moving from open WH-questions to yes/no interrogatives; asking hypothetical questions. Unlike in the theory of planned behaviour, intention here is not treated by the analyst as the driver of behaviour, but is taken as a member's resource within particular everyday and institutional settings. That is, rather than being a practice of cognitive analysis, the discursive psychological analysis here is focused on participants' cognitive ascribing of practices.

Attitude: caring and closing

One of the major areas of historical and contemporary social psychology is the study of attitudes. Indeed attitudes are a commonplace of work from across the social sciences. The discursive psychological critique of the way attitudes were conceptualized was developed right from the start (Potter and Wetherell, 1987, 1988; Potter, 1998). It emphasized that evaluations were part of practices embedded in interaction, where they played particular roles. And it emphasized that evaluations are often produced by constituting the 'attitudinal object' in particular ways rather than by claiming a personal psychological position. Indeed it highlighted the importance of producing neutralism rather than an attitudinal stance for some, socially particularly controversial, topics (Potter, 1998). We have already touched on this above.

Another feature of this developing critique of attitude work is that it starts to break up the idea of a single underlying attitudinal dimension in favour of considering the way different kinds of evaluations can be produced for different purposes. For example, Wiggins and Potter (2003) highlighted the different roles of 'objective' and 'subjective' food evaluations – 'that pasta is lovely' vs 'I love that pasta.' And, as I have already noted, Edwards (2007) has highlighted the possibilities of people constructing subject side or object side descriptions.

This move to break up unitary dimensions of evaluation in favour of considering specific kinds of evaluative practice can be developed further. I will consider a particular example, where certain kinds of evaluation are at stake. Specifically, how does a parent show he or she *cares* in conversations with a young adult with a learning disability?

This study by Anne Patterson and Jonathan Potter (2009) worked with a corpus of more than 50 calls between a young adult with a diagnosed learning disability and different family members (mother, father, grandmother). The young adult was staying in a residential place-ment. While the young adult was away from home, these phone calls were her main way of staying in touch. The particular focus was the way the calls closed. This had two virtues. First, call closings are a site where the issue of the relationship between parties may become live. When a speaker initiates call closings, this is a potentially disaffiliative action where the 'motives' of the speaker may become relevant – are they bored? Do they dislike the other party? Closings are an occasion that may require delicate management. Second, call closings have been a topic of standard conversation analytic scrutiny. Conversation analysts have identified a robust set of organizational features that contribute to the orderly nature of closings (Schegloff and Sacks, 1973). From a discursive psychological point of view, this normative organization can provide a kind of natural laboratory in which to study the trickling of psychological matters into talk.

An initial observation about this corpus is the way the calls unfold differently from the typical closings in the literature. Schegloff and Sacks (1973) found a robust pattern of closings, built out of two adjacency pairs:

1	**A:**	Oright	*Offer to close*
2	**B:**	Okay [honey	*Acceptance*
3	**A:**	[bye dear=	*Terminal exchange*
4	**B:**	=bye	*Terminal exchange*

The first (lines 1 and 2) comprises an offer to close and an acceptance. The offer to close indicates that the speaker has nothing else to add and it offers a free turn to the other, should that person wish to add anything. The acceptance indicates that the second speaker has nothing to add either, and so participants can move to terminal exchanges, which is the second adjacency pair shown here in lines 3 and 4. Crucially, this organization allows both for the smooth transition to closing and for the insertion of further talk. At the point where the offer to close has been delivered, the recipient can add more talk, and this addition of further material can go through a number of iterations, each orderly provided for by the offer to close.

The collection of calls that Patterson and Potter studied was immediately striking in three ways. First, it maintained the general form identified by Sacks and Schegloff. Second, it showed a massive recycling of the closings. The authors compared the number of offers to close in their corpus and in a standard mundane corpus, widely used in conversation analysis research. They found that in the mundane corpus most of the calls had one or no sequences in which offers to close were made; however, in the family corpus most of the calls had three or four initiations of closings that did not result in an immediate closing but rather in the insertion of more talk. Third, the closings typically had a considerable amount of material inserted into them not found in standard mundane closings. Most commonly what was inserted were accounts for leaving the call.

Take the following simple example.

(R210505)

1	**Sue:**	Carrie ↓went with me	
2	**Dad:**	Good.	
3		(4.5)	
4	**Dad:**	right. >well	
5		I'm going to go now< darlin'.	*Announcement*
6 →		>cus I've got lots of< teeth to make.	*Account*
7	**Sue:**	yea::h	
8 →		I've got to finish ma cards off=	*Account*

In this extract, after a brief delay (the kind of thing that often prefigures a pre-closing), Dad announces his intention to go and therefore close the call. However, unlike in the more minimal standard form, this announcement is accompanied by an account. Note the detail here. Dad specifies a task that he has to accomplish (he is a dentist). The strength of the account is marked by the 'got' construction. Moreover, it is built, as is common in this corpus, from conventional resources that specify the constraining role of work, school, meal preparation, or the television schedules. Accounts of this kind make leaving the call a *requirement*, and in this way the speaker reflexively produces him or herself as *reluctant* to do so. Accounts do delicate relationship sustaining work. In particular, they build the speaker's care for the other.

The example above has a simple pattern; often the closings were built with a much more complex relational structure, in which the parent or aunt would build an account for call closure by focusing on material in the recipient's environment.

(A220505)

1	**Mum:**	>You're going to be an idn-< indep↑endent?	
2		young la:dy aren't yer an' i- it's great	
3		to talk to mum: but there'll be times	
4		when y-.h you'll think,	
5		↓(ooh:? I want to ↓do my own ↑thin:g:,	
6		(1.7) ((TV in background))	
7	**Sue:**	↓Yea:h:.	
8		(0.3)	
9	**Mum:**	↑Ye:ah?	
10		(1.5) ((TV noise in background))	
12	**Sue:**	Strictly- >is it?< the uh:m:, is i' th- a-	
13		>I can hear it in the< backgrou:nd:.=	
14	**Mum:**	O:kay- >did you want to go	*Interrogative*
15 →		and try and< wa:tch i:t.	*Candidate Account*
16		(0.9)	
17	**Mum:**	[D'y' want ↑to::?]	*Interrogative*
18	**Sue:**	[M u m: m y:.I ↓h]aven't voted for Sadie,	
19		I haven:'t.	

What is striking here is that Mum, who initiates the closing, provides an account for some action that Sue will need to perform. In this case, the interrogative form allows the offer to close to be built as an orientation to the *other*'s requirement to go. Material is available in the call that *could* be used to account for closing, but has not *yet* been formulated in this way. Thus Sue appears to be fending off a request from a party outside the call for her to go to supper. Mum follows this with an interrogative that asks Sue if she wants to leave the call to get supper and watch the rest of a TV programme.

In psychological terms, a complex piece of relational business is transacted here. Mum builds a candidate account for Sue to leave the call. She displays care for the Sue's 'wants'. Both parties are built as wanting to stay in the call, but required by television and food timetables to leave the call. This is particularly delicate business, as there is a strong emphasis in interaction on parties having rights over their own psychological states (Heritage and Raymond, 2005). There is a further feature of the design of accounts for the other. They construct reasons for going that focus on the needs and interests of the other party. In the example given the focus is on a favourite television programme. This adds a further element of caring. It is not just that pre-closing is treated as accountable and that one party produces an account for the other, it is that the account is built as responsive to, and protective of, the needs and interests of the other.

What we see in these examples is the way 'caring' is built interactionally. Pre-closing is an environment where motivation and other psychological states become alive. Participants orient to this both through the placement of accounts just at the point where closing is projected as the next action and through the form of accounts (highlighting the obligations on each party).

Standing back, we can see the difference of approach here from the standard psychological and social cognition take on attitudes. Rather than seeing Mum, say, as having a particular attitude to Sue, we see that the issue of her stance or evaluation becomes alive at key interactional moments, such as when a phone call is being ended. At this point accounts can be produced (for self and for other) for closing the call that build a stance of caring. This discursive psychological approach starts with psychological matters as they are built and displayed in discourse. The analysis focuses on action orientations (to close a phone call), on how these actions unfold sequentially (in a structural position in the call), on how they are constructed (out of a range of conventional and linguistic resources) and on how they construct features of speaker's and recipient's psychology.

Contemporary debates and prospects

Discursive psychology has stimulated, or been part of, a series of debates in the last decade. These can helpfully provide further definition for the approach. These debates focus on the status of interview data in comparison to studies of naturalistic records, the possibility of combining different methods, the epistemic basis of discourse research, the status of ethnographic work, and the place of the psychological subject in discursive psychology. They are cross-cutting and raise a wide variety of fundamental issues, only some of which can be addressed here.

The relative status of interviews as opposed to naturalistic records has been a source of controversy in the last decade, as researchers increasingly explored the use of naturalistic materials inspired by conversation analysis and the idea of the open-ended qualitative interview as the default option for much of qualitative and discursive research came to be questioned (Silverman, 2009).

There is a cluster of related issues with respect to the analysis of interviews for discursive psychological research and the status of interviews data. The virtues of interviews as a method for accessing participants' interpretative repertoires are: (a) they allows the researcher to focus on particular topics or themes; (b) questions can be designed to provoke the use of different interpretative resources in relation to a single topic or theme; (c) they allow a degree of standardization of questions across different participants; (d) they allow for more control in sampling. Clearly, these virtues are not negligible. However, there is a range of limitations and problems: (a) they are inevitably flooded by the expectations and categories of particular pre-existing social science agendas; (b) interviews abstract participants from their location in particular settings, where they have a specific stake and interest in ongoing actions; (c) they are hard to analyse, as the footing of the participants (as representative category member, as objective observer) is often unclear (this is partly a local analytic challenge and partly a function of the 'offstage' recruitment process, which is often crucial for setting up relevant memberships). These advantages and limitations are explored in two illuminating debates (see Potter and Hepburn, 2005 and responses; and Griffin, 2007 and responses; see also Potter and Hepburn, in press).

It is important to emphasise that the main thrust of discursive psychology since its origins as a specific variant on discourse analysis has been to work with naturalistic materials. The reason for this is not that qualitative interviews have been found wanting. Indeed, some of the most striking critical observations about qualitative interviews have been developed after the founding of the discursive psychological project. Instead discursive psychology has been invigorated by the excitement and surprise of working directly on records of people living their lives. Social life is organized with more granularity and is ordered much more profoundly than many alternative social and discursive approaches assumed. In addition, people show a more subtle practical understanding of one another than other traditions of work suggested; and these understandings are often lost in the process of analysis in the typical study of open-ended interviews.

Hammersley (2003) has argued that both conversation analysis and work in the tradition of Potter and Wetherell (1987) have epistemic commitments at odds with most other forms of social science and reject a focus on the individual actor and on his/her powers and competences. He argues that both of these traditions should best be seen as supplements to other styles and methods of work, notably ethnography. More recently Corcoran (2009) has developed some similar points about the epistemic commitments. In both cases, the critics have failed to appreciate the thoroughgoing constructionism in discursive psychological work. This is attentive to the complex role of descriptions, glosses, accounts, formulations, categories and so on as a basic element in social practices, and as such it retains a methodologically sceptical stance with respect to the simple, referential nature of these things (Potter, 2003, 2010). In its reflexive attention to methodological issues and its close coordination of theory, object and analysis, the constructionism of discursive psychology has developed a distinct methodological position. This strives to bestow the same careful attention to participants' business in all its specifics as they evidently display themselves.

Although Corcoran (2009) and others have suggested that discursive psychology fails to offer a full picture of the psychological subject, this is comparing the project of discursive psychology with earlier psychological approaches and failing to appreciate how radical the current project is. It is a radical social psychological perspective that starts with discourse – actions done through talk, gesture and texts – and puts participants' own practices and understandings at the centre of its project. It aims to explicate the subtleties of emotion (Edwards, 1997; Hepburn and Potter, 2010), for example, and the way subjectivity can be a contested space (Hepburn and Potter, 2011). It is unpacking psychology as a lived practice from the outside in.

Transcription Conventions

Um: :	Colons represent lengthening of the preceding sound; the more colons, the greater the lengthening.
What it i:s	Underscoring represents words or parts of words delivered with stress or emphasis
I've-	A hyphen represents the cut-off of the preceding sound, often by a stop.
↑Mm↓hmm	Vertical arrows precede marked pitch movement, over and above normal rhythms of speech.
.,?	Punctuation marks show 'normal' intonation, not grammar; period, comma and 'question mark' indicate downward, 'continuative', and upward contours respectively.
hhh hh .hhP (h)ut	An 'h' represents aspiration, sometimes simply hearable breathing, sometimes laughter, etc.; when preceded by a superimposed dot, it marks in-breath; in parenthesis inside a word it represents interpolated laughter.
hhh[hh .hhh] er[I just]	Left brackets represent point of overlap onset; right brackets represent point of overlap resolution.
(certainly) ((slurred voice))	Single parentheses mark problematic or uncertain hearings; double parentheses include additional transcriber's comments.
(0.2) (.)	Numbers in parentheses represent silence in tenths of a second; a dot in parentheses represents a micro-pause, less than a tenth of a second, hearable but too short to easily measure.
°mm hmm°	Degree signs enclose significantly lowered volume.
Ri*:ght*	Stars enclose talk delivered with 'creaky' voice.
Th*at's *all	Underlines enclose talk that is delivered with flat intonation.

Note: For full details on the transcription see Jefferson (2004).

Further reading

Edwards, D. (1997). *Discourse and Cognition*. London and Beverly Hills, CA: Sage.

This book highlights the interplay of discursive psychology, ethnomethodology and conversation analysis with a range of analyses of psychological matters. A major work that outlines the basic features of discursive psychology by reference to how it manages topics such as categories, scripts, emotions, narratives and shared knowledge. It rewards close study.

McKinlay, A. and McVittie, C. (2008). *Social Psychology and Discourse*. Oxford: Wiley-Blackwell.

This is an up-to-date and comprehensive exploration of the relationship of discursive psychology to social psychology. It follows the format of a major social psychology textbook, but provides an alternative approach to each topic area. It is extremely clear.

Potter, J. and Hepburn, A. (2008) 'Discursive constructionism', in J. A. Holstein, and J. F. Gubrium (eds.) *Handbook of Constructionist Research*. New York: Guildford, pp. 275–293.

This highlights the constructionist elements of discursive psychology. It shows the way discursive psychology and conversation analysis can be combined to address constructionist issues in a systematic manner.

Hepburn A. and Wiggins S. (eds) (2007). *Discursive Research in Practice: New Approaches to Psychology and Interaction*. Cambridge: Cambridge University Press.

This collection showcases a range of interaction analysts addressing psychological questions. It includes basic pieces on issues such as emotion and subjectivity and particular studies that address topics such as medical communication, sex offender therapy gender reassignment and troubled eating. Taken together, the contributions illustrate a different way of going about psychology.

Wooffitt, R. (2005). *Conversation Analysis and Discourse Analysis: A Comparative and Critical Introduction.* London: Sage.

An excellent critical overview of these two traditions of work and of how they relate to one another. It offers useful background to the above and clarifies tricky and confusing issues about the range of approaches that make up discourse analysis and how conversation analysis and discursive psychology sit with them.

References

Ajzen, I. (1991) 'The theory of planned behaviour', *Organizational Behavior and Human Decision Processes*, 50: 179–211.

Atkinson, J. M. and Drew, P. (1979) *Order in Court: The Organization of Verbal Interaction in Judicial Settings.* London: Macmillan.

Austin, J. L. (1961) *Philosophical Papers*, Oxford: Oxford University Press.

Billig, M. (1987 [1996]) *Arguing and Thinking: A Rhetorical Approach to Social Psychology.* Second Edition. Cambridge: Cambridge University Press.

Billig, M., Condor, S., Edwards, D., Gane, M., Middleton, D. J., and Radley, A. R. (1988) *Ideological Dilemmas: A Social Psychology of Everyday Thinking.* London: Sage.

Corcoran, T. (2009) 'Second nature', *British Journal of Social Psychology*, 48: 375–388.

Edley, N. (2001) 'Analysing masculinity: interpretative repertoires, ideological dilemmas and subject positions', in M. Wetherell, S. Taylor, and S. J. Yates (eds.) *Discourse as Data: A Guide to Analysis.* London: Sage, pp. 198–228.

Edwards, D. (1995) 'Two to Tango: script formulations, dispositions, and rhetorical symmetry in relationship troubles talk', *Research on Language and Social Interaction*, 28: 319–350.

Edwards, D. (1997) *Discourse and Cognition.* London and Beverly Hills, CA: Sage.

Edwards, D. (2007) 'Managing subjectivity in talk', in A. Hepburn and S. Wiggins (eds.) *Discursive Research in Practice: New Approaches to Psychology and Interaction.* Cambridge: Cambridge University Press, pp. 31–49.

Edwards, D. (2008) 'Intentionality and *mens rea* in police interrogations: the production of actions as crimes', *Intercultural Pragmatics*, 5: 177–199.

Gilbert, G. N. and Mulkay, M. (1984) *Opening Pandora's Box: A Sociological Analysis of Scientists' Discourse.* Cambridge: Cambridge University Press.

Griffin, C. (2007) 'Being dead and being there: Research interviews, sharing hand cream and the preference for analysing "naturally occurring data" ', *Discourse Studies*, 9: 246–269.

Hammersley, M. (2003) 'Conversation analysis and discourse analysis: methods or paradigms', *Discourse and Society*, 14: 751–781.

Harris, R. (1981) *The Language Myth.* London: Duckworth.

Hepburn, A. and Bolden, G. (in press) 'Transcription for conversation analysis', in J. Sidnell and T. Stivers (eds.) *Blackwell Handbook of Conversation Analysis.* Oxford: Blackwell.

Hepburn, A. and Potter, J. (2010) 'Interrogating tears: some uses of "tag questions" in a child protection helpline', in A. F. Freed and S. Ehrlich (eds.) *"Why Do You Ask?": The Function of Questions in Institutional Discourse.* Oxford: Oxford University Press, pp. 69–86.

Hepburn, A. and Potter, J. (2011) 'Designing the recipient: Some practices that manage advice resistance in institutional settings', *Social Psychology Quarterly*, 74: 216–241.

Heritage, J. (1984) *Garfinkel and Ethnomethodology.* Englewood Cliffs, NJ: Prentice-Hall.

Heritage, J. and Raymond, G. (2005) 'The terms of agreement: indexing epistemic authority and subordination in assessment sequences', *Social Psychology Quarterly*, 68: 15–38.

Heritage, J. C. (2004) 'Conversation analysis and institutional talk', in D. Silverman (ed.) *Qualitative Research: Theory, Method and Practice.* London: Sage, pp. 222–245.

Hernandez-Martinez, P., Black, L., Williams, J., Davis, P., Pampaka, M., and Wake, G. (2008) 'Mathematics students' aspirations for higher education: class, ethnicity, gender and interpretative repertoire styles', *Research Papers in Education*, 23: 153–165.

Hester, S. and Eglin, P. (eds) (1997) *Culture in Action: Studies in Membership Categorization Analysis.* Washington, DC: International Institute for Ethnomethodology and Conversation Analysis & University Press of America.

Jefferson, G. (2004) 'Glossary of transcript symbols with an introduction', in G. H. Lerner (ed.) *Conversation Analysis: Studies from the First Generation.* Amsterdam/Philadelphia: John Benjamins, pp. 13–31.

Juhila, K. (2009) 'From care to fellowship and back: interpretative repertoires used by the social welfare workers when describing their relationship with homeless women', *British Journal of Social Work*, 39: 128–143.

Lawes, R. (1999) 'Marriage: an analysis of discourse', *British Journal of Social Psychology*, 38: 1–20.

Levinson, S. C. (1983) *Pragmatics*. Cambridge: Cambridge University Press.

Patterson, A. and Potter, J. (2009) 'Caring: building a "psychological disposition" in pre-closing sequences in phone calls with a young adult with a learning disability', *British Journal of Social Psychology*, 48: 447–465.

Potter, J. (1996) *Representing Reality: Discourse, Rhetoric and Social Construction*. London: Sage.

Potter, J. (1998) 'Discursive social psychology: from attitudes to evaluations', *European Review of Social Psychology*, 9: 233–266.

Potter, J. (2003) 'Discursive psychology: between method and paradigm', *Discourse and Society*, 14: 783–794.

Potter, J. (2004) 'Discourse analysis', in M. Hardy and A. Bryman (eds.) *Handbook of Data Analysis*. London: Sage, pp. 607–624.

Potter, J. (2005) 'A discursive psychology of institutions', *Social Psychology Review*, 7: 25–35.

Potter, J. (2010) 'Contemporary discursive psychology: issues, prospects and Corcoran's awkward ontology', *British Journal of Social Psychology*, 49: 691–701.

Potter, J. and Hepburn, A. (2005) 'Qualitative interviews in psychology: problems and possibilities', *Qualitative Research in Psychology*, 2: 281–307.

Potter, J. and Hepburn, A. (2008) 'Discursive constructionism', in J. A. Holstein and J. F. Gubrium (eds) *Handbook of Constructionist Research*. New York: Guildford, pp. 275–293.

Potter, J. and Hepburn, A. (in press) 'Eight challenges for interview researchers', in J. F. Gubrium and J. A. Holstein (eds.) *Handbook of Interview Research*. Second Edition. London: Sage.

Potter, J. and te Molder, H. (2005) 'Talking cognition: mapping and making the terrain', in H. te Molder and J. Potter (eds) *Conversation and Cognition*. Cambridge: Cambridge University Press, pp. 1–54.

Potter, J. and Wetherell, M. (1987) *Discourse and Social Psychology: Beyond Attitudes and Behaviour*. London: Sage.

Potter, J. and Wetherell, M. (1988) 'Accomplishing attitudes: fact and evaluation in racist discourse', *Text*, 8: 51–68.

Schegloff, E. A. (2007) *Sequence Organization in Interaction. Volume 1: A Primer in Conversation Analysis*. Cambridge: Cambridge University Press.

Schegloff, E. A. and Sacks, H. (1973) 'Opening up closings', *Semiotica*, 7: 289–327.

Silverman, D. (2009) *A Very Short, Fairly Interesting and Reasonably Cheap Book About Qualitative Research*. London: Sage.

Stevens, P. and Harper, D. J. (2007) 'Professional accounts of electroconvulsive therapy: a discourse analysis', *Social Science and Medicine*, 64: 1475–1486.

Wiggins, S. and Potter, J. (2003) 'Attitudes and evaluative practices: Category vs. item and subjective vs. objective constructions in everyday food assessments', *British Journal of Social Psychology*, 42: 513–531.

Wooffitt, R. (2005) *Conversation Analysis and Discourse Analysis: A Comparative and Critical Introduction*. London: Sage.

9

Conversation analysis

Steven E. Clayman and Virginia Teas Gill

Introduction

Conversation analysis is an approach to the study of human interaction in society. Its name might be taken to imply a concern with informal and purely sociable talk, but the approach encompasses interactions of all sorts, ranging from informal to formal, from sociable to task-focused, and from face-to-face to synchronous technologically mediated interactions such as telephone talk and videoconferences. Although conversation analysis is wide-ranging in scope, the focus on the organization of conduct *within interaction* distinguishes this field from other forms of discourse analysis concerned with narratives, speeches, or texts. Conversation analysis is also distinguished by a methodology that exploits the affordances provided by recorded interaction as a form of data.

Conversation analysis (or CA) was developed by Harvey Sacks in collaboration with Emanuel Schegloff and Gail Jefferson. It emerged within sociology at a time—the 1960s—when that discipline was dominated by abstract theorizing and a concern with large-scale structural phenomena. Against the sociological mainstream, certain intellectual cross-currents had begun to address the specifics of social conduct in everyday life. Erving Goffman was exploring what he would later call "the interaction order" (1983): the domain of direct interaction between people. Goffman argued that this domain is a type of social institution in its own right, one that intersects with other, more familiar societal institutions but has its own organizational principles, motivational imperatives, and norms of conduct. In a related but distinct development, Harold Garfinkel (1967) was examining the procedures of commonsense reasoning that people use to make sense of one another and the circumstances in which they are embedded. Garfinkel challenged the mainstream view that social conduct is regulated by internalized norms, arguing instead that organized conduct emerges through the use of commonsense reasoning practices. These practices inform how actors implement norms in specific situations, and more generally how they produce actions and render them intelligible.

CA can be understood as a partial synthesis of these ideas concerning the institution of interaction, norms of interactional conduct, and the methods of reasoning implicated in the production and recognition of action. The research enterprise that emerged from this synthesis has generated a substantial and cumulative body of empirical findings. Some researchers work with data drawn primarily from ordinary conversation and seek to describe general interactional practices and systems of practice such as turn-taking, the sequencing of action, the repair of misunderstandings, the relationship between vocal and nonvocal behaviors, and so on (e.g. Atkinson and Heritage, 1984; Lerner, 2004; Schegloff, 2007). Others focus on data drawn from institutional settings—doctors' offices, courts of law, newsrooms—with the aim of exploring how generic practices of talk get mobilized and adapted for specific institutional tasks (Boden and

Zimmerman, 1991; Drew and Heritage, 1992b; Heritage and Maynard, 2006; Heritage and Clayman, 2010) and how speaking practices affect bureaucratic and professional outcomes (Maynard, 1984; Boyd, 1998; Clayman and Reisner, 1998; Heritage and Stivers, 1999; Gill, 2005; Stivers, 2007). Still others have addressed the relationship between interaction and racial and gender identities (e.g. West and Zimmerman, 1983; M. Goodwin, 1990; Kitzinger, 2005; Lerner and Whitehead, 2009; Speer and Stokoe, 2010); cultural difference and historical change (Houtkoop-Steenstra, 1991; Lindström 1994; Clayman et al., 2006); and the conduct of social scientific inquiry itself (Maynard et al., 2002; Drew et al., 2006).

The productivity of CA hinges in part on its distinctive methodology, which differs from both the ethnographic methods employed by Goffman and the demonstrations favored by Garfinkel. The aim of this paper is to provide a brief introduction to the methods of conversation analysis.[1]

Generating data: recording and transcribing

Conversation analysts work almost exclusively with naturally occurring interaction as it has been captured in audio and videorecordings and rendered into detailed transcripts.

Naturally occurring Interaction

Conversation analysts avoid role-playing and experimentally induced interactions, as well as hypothetical and invented examples. Past research has demonstrated that such data yield over-simplified and misleading representations of interactional processes. Specimens of actual interaction can generate astonishing discoveries, which, in Sacks' (1984: 25) words, "we could not, by imagination, assert were there."

What constitutes "natural" interaction is, however, by no means straightforward. Because of the "observer's paradox" (Labov, 1972), a researcher can never know whether an interaction unfolded as it would have, had it not been externally observed (ten Have, 1999). Indeed, the recording equipment itself may become a topic of conversation for participants (ten Have, 1999: 49).

However, such observer effects are less significant than they might seem at first glance. Sensitivity to being observed is a commonplace and "natural" feature of interaction. As Goodwin (1981: 44) notes, "participants never behave as if they were unobserved; it is clear that they organize their behavior in terms of the observation it will receive from their coparticipants." Moreover, these effects tend to be limited to the surface content of the talk, leaving its underlying interactional structure intact. Thus, while the participants may refer to the presence of the recording machine, they will do so via processes—ways of taking turns, building actions, and organizing them into sequences—that are not markedly different from the rest of their talk (ten Have, 1999). In any case, hyper-consciousness about the recording machine tends to be short-lived, receding into the background as the participants become enmeshed in the practical concerns of their daily lives.

A note on sampling

Unlike many fields, CA addresses a domain of phenomena whose components are not yet fully known or understood. Sacks (1984: 21) called this domain "the methods people use in doing social life." Until these methods are formally described—until their identifying features are catalogued and their local environments of occurrence are charted—it is premature to ask how prevalent they are within some larger population or how they are distributed in relation to exogenous psychological or sociological variables.

Because the objective of CA is to describe the endogenous organization of interactional phenomena rather than to determine their distribution, the issue of sampling is approached rather differently here from other fields. Conversation analysts typically follow the "naturalist's strategy" of gathering specimens of phenomena from as many settings of interaction as possible, for the purposes of systematic analysis and comparison (Heritage, 1988: 131; ten Have, 1999: 51).

As sources of data, not all settings are created equal. Ordinary conversation appears to represent the richest and most varied source of interactional practices, while interactions in bureaucratic, occupational, and other institutional contexts tend to contain a narrower range of practices, which are specialized or adapted for those contexts (Drew and Heritage, 1992a). It is thus important to bear in mind the social context from which data are drawn. For researchers interested in institutional forms of talk, it is often useful to use ordinary conversation as a comparative frame of reference (Schegloff, 1987).

While the naturalist's strategy remains primary within CA, quantitative extensions and applications have become increasingly common in recent years (e.g. Clayman *et al.*, 2006; Heritage *et al.*, 2007, Stivers, 2007). Although not embraced by all within the field, this is a natural development. Once interactional practices have been thoroughly explicated, this can provide a foundation for the development of validated measures and for analyses of frequency and association.

Audio and video recording

The decision to study conversation was originally a practical one for Harvey Sacks, whose main concern as a sociologist was to formally describe and analyze actual, real-time social events with a degree of rigor (Sacks, 1984). The availability of audio recording technology in the early 1960s made it possible to capture and preserve a particular type of social event, namely conversational interaction. Given the centrality of interaction in the life of society, Sacks' ostensibly practical decision turned out to be fortunate.

Audio recordings have now been augmented with video, which captures both vocal and nonvocal behaviors. But recordings still offer the same basic service as they did for Sacks in the 1960s: access to social interaction at a level of detail that approaches what is available to the participants themselves, and the capacity for repeated examination. The importance of recordings in CA can be likened to that of slow-motion "instant replay" during televised sporting events (Atkinson, 1984). While spectators in the stands may have only a vague grasp of the fleeting events within a particular play, television viewers can—by virtue of instant replay—achieve a more precise understanding of the specific sequence of behaviors that led to the play's outcome.

Transcribing data

Transcripts serve both analytical and presentational functions. For the purposes of analysis, when used in conjunction with the recording itself, a good transcript helps the researcher get a stronger purchase on the organization of interactional practices. Transcript excerpts, together with video "framegrabs," also serve as a resource in publications and presentations. They enable readers to assess independently the validity of analytic claims by reference to the key empirical instances on which they are based.

Gail Jefferson developed the transcription system commonly used within CA (see Appendix). This system balances two objectives: (1) preserving the details of talk as it was actually produced, while (2) remaining simple enough to yield transcripts that are accessible to a general audience.

Thus a full phonological system was avoided in favor of one that uses standard orthography, supplemented with additional symbols to capture features such as overlapping speech, silences, various forms of emphasis, and so on. Over the years, other investigators have built upon Jefferson's system, most notably Goodwin (1981), who developed transcription symbols to represent nonvocal activities such as gaze and gesture.

Audio transcribing has traditionally been done with the aid of a transcribing machine, by using a foot pedal to start, stop, and rewind a cassette tape. If the original data are on videotape, they can be inspected later to add aspects of nonvocal behavior. More recently, technological advances have made it possible to digitize and store data files on CD, DVD, or hard drive. A computer can now serve as a transcribing machine, with software programs enabling the researcher to transcribe in a word-processing program while simultaneously watching the video. Some programs can also time silences. The future of data is undoubtedly digital, a medium that is more compact, accessible, and durable than analog tapes.

The level of detail in a CA transcript may initially strike non-CA researchers as excessive. However, since the objective is to understand how interactants build mutually intelligible courses of action, any detail that is available to the interactants is potentially relevant for the researcher. For instance, Jefferson (1985) demonstrates the importance of seemingly trivial details surrounding the articulation of laughter. In the following excerpt, Louise laughs during the utterance "playing with his organ" (line 7). This transcript simply notes the laughter in line 8 rather than transcribing it beat by beat.

(1)

1	Ken:	And he came home and decided he was gonna play with
2		his orchids from then on in.
3	Roger:	With his <u>what</u>?
4	Louise:	heh heh heh heh
5	Ken:	With his orchids. [He has an orchid-
6	Roger:	[Oh heh hehheh
7	Louise:	→ Playing with his organ yeah I thought the same thing!
8		((spoken through laughter))
9	Ken:	Because he's got a great big [glass house-
10	Roger:	[I can see him playing with
11		his organ ((laughing)).

(Jefferson, 1985: 28, simplified transcript)

Such simplification obscures the way Louise employs laughter as a resource. In the more detailed transcript below, it becomes apparent that Louise precisely places her laughter in the key phrase "PLAYN(h)W(h)IZ O(h)R'N" (line 8), stopping abruptly when she moves on to the next utterance ("ya:h I thought the same"). Roger subsequently laughs in a strikingly similar way (line 14).

(2)

1	Ken:	An'e came <u>h</u>om'n decided'e wz gonna play with iz o:rchids.
2		from then on i:n.
3	Roger:	With iz <u>what</u>?
4	Louise:	mh hih <u>hih</u> [huh
5	Ken:	[With iz <u>o</u>rchids.=
6	Ken:	=Ee[z got an <u>o</u>rch[id-
7	Roger:	[Oh:. [hehh[hah.he:h].<u>h</u>eh
8	Louise: →	[heh huh.<u>hh</u>]PLAYN(h)W(h)IZ O(h)R'N
9		ya:h I[thought the[same

```
10   Roger:           [uh::        [.hunhh.hh.hh
11   Ken:                          [Cz eez gotta great big [gla:ss house]=
12   Roger:                                               [I c'n s(h)ee ]=
13   Ken:       =[(  )
14   Roger:  →  =[im pl(h)ay with iz o(h)r(h)g.(h)n.uh.
```

(Jefferson, 1985: 29, Detailed Transcript)

Deployed in this way, laughter displays recognition of an alternate "obscene" hearing of the phrase "playing with his orchids," even as it partially obscures its articulation.

Accordingly, researchers should strive to preserve as much detail as possible. At the same time, because transcribing is labor-intensive and time-consuming, the amount of time invested in a transcript will inevitably vary according to the size of the dataset and the interests of the researcher. One practical strategy is to transcribe in varying amounts of detail, reserving the highest level of detail for segments that will receive the greatest analytic attention.

Analyzing data

Getting started

Once data have been gathered and prepared, how should analysis begin? Since interaction is largely uncharted territory whose topography is only partially understood, CA seeks to map this topography by examining specimens of its contours and analyzing how they were systematically produced. This type of investigation requires holding in abeyance questions about *why* a social activity is organized in a particular way, focusing instead on *what* is being done and on *how* it is accomplished.

Interactional activities can be investigated at different levels of granularity. There are overarching *activity frameworks* that organize extended interactional episodes, such as "getting acquainted" or "talking about personal problems" or "seeing a doctor for medical help" or "cross-examining a witness." One step below this is represented by discrete *sequences of action*, which may be analyzed for their relatively generic sequential properties (e.g. as paired actions, story-telling sequences, etc.) or for type-specific characteristics (e.g. as question–answer sequences, invitation sequences, news delivery sequences, etc.). Next come the *actions* that comprise sequences, actions commonly accomplished through a single turn at talk such as questioning, requesting, announcing news, responding to these various actions, and so on. Finally there are *features mobilized within turns at talk*, such as lexical choices, intonation contours, nonvocal behaviors, etc.

As should be apparent from the preceding list, virtually everything that happens in interaction is fair game for analysis. While one might be tempted to dismiss familiar details of conduct as random noise or insignificant "manners of speaking," conversation analysts proceed from the assumption that all elements of interaction are potentially orderly and socially meaningful for the participants (Sacks, 1984). This attitude opens up a wealth of possibilities for analysis. But where to begin? Drawing on Schegloff (1996: 172) we suggest two pathways into the data.

Begin with a "noticing"

One can begin with relatively unmotivated observation. The analyst simply notices how an interactant says or does something at a given juncture, a bit of conduct that seems in some way "interesting." Of course, purely unmotivated observation is an unattainable ideal, as experienced analysts have an established conceptual foundation, grounded in previous research, which affects what they are inclined to notice and what strikes them as interesting. Nevertheless, it is possible to approach data without a specific agenda in mind, thereby remaining open to the prospect of discovery. Having noticed a given practice, the analyst can then explicate what it might be "doing" or accomplishing. This typically involves examining where it is placed in the stream of interaction and how it operates within that local context, focusing on the actions that immediately preceded it and the responses it attracts.

For example, Sacks ([1966] (1992): 256–257) observed that, when children speak to adults, they commonly begin by asking a question such as "You know what, Daddy?" Anyone who has been around children for any length of time will be familiar with this recurrent feature of children's talk. What is accomplished with this practice? One clue can be gleaned from the response it elicits. Adults typically respond to the "You know what" question with another question—namely "What?" This type of response not only invites the child to speak again and say what motivated the original question, but by so doing it simultaneously aligns the adult as one who is prepared to listen to the ensuing talk. Thus the child's original query sets in motion a chain of events that culminates in the child gaining a ratified speaking "slot" and an attentive recipient. When children use this practice, they may be addressing certain basic interactional problems, such as their diminished rights to talk and adults' preoccupation with other matters.

Heritage (1998) took a similar tack when analyzing a particular way of designing answers to questions. Heritage initially observed that some answers to questions are prefaced with "oh," as in line 6 of the following example, taken from a radio interview with Sir Harold Acton, a noted British aesthete.

```
(3)
  1   Act:       ....hhhh and some of thuh- (0.3) some of my students
  2              translated Eliot into Chine::se. I think thuh very
  3              first.
  4              (0.2)
  5   Har:       Did you learn to speak (.) Chine[:se.
  6   Act: →                                     [.hh Oh yes.
  7              (0.7)
  8   Act:       .hhhh You ca::n't live in thuh country without speaking
  9              thuh lang[uage it's impossible .hhhhh=
 10   Har:                [Not no: cour:se.
```

(Heritage, 1998: 294)

This practice, far from being random or insignificant, turns out to be socially meaningful and consequential. By prefacing an answer with "oh," the answerer implies that the prior question "came from left field" and is thus of questionable relevance. In this particular case, the ongoing discussion concerns Acton's experience teaching modern poetry at Beijing University, and it is in the context of this discussion that he is asked (at line 5) if he learned to speak Chinese. He treats the answer to the question as obvious or self-evident. He expresses this explicitly at lines 8–9, but he also does so implicitly in his initial response to the question (line 6) via the oh-prefaced affirmative answer.

With this pathway into the data, an initial noticing is "pursued by asking what—if anything—such a practice of talking has as its outcome" (Schegloff, 1996: 172). Not every observed practice will turn out to have a systematic import, but many core findings of CA have their origins in unmotivated noticings of just this sort.

Begin with a vernacular action

Another pathway into the data is to focus on a particular type of action that is already part of the vernacular culture—asking questions, giving advice, delivering news, and so on. Here the analytic challenge is to transcend what is already intuitively known about the action in question. This can be accomplished by exploring specific ways that a given action is designed and implemented, focusing again on the sequential environments in which speakers deploy each form and on the responses they receive.

For example, using announcements of news as a starting point, Maynard (2003) has uncovered a range of practices associated specifically with the telling of bad news in both everyday and clinical settings, while also demonstrating that they operate as solutions to specific problems associated with this difficult interpersonal task. One set of practices involves forecasting the news in advance of its delivery. Maynard demonstrates that forecasting, by providing some advance warning of what is to come, maximizes the likelihood that recipients will be prepared to register and accept the news. In a similar vein, studies have explored various methods for designing requests (Curl and Drew, 2008), presenting medical symptoms (Halkowski, 2006), and offering explanations for illness to doctors (Gill, 1998; Gill and Maynard, 2006). In each case, the analyst explores how participants deploy and respond to familiar actions and their varying forms.

Grounding an analysis

Once a possible phenomenon has been located, how should analysis proceed? In the broad tradition of interpretive social science, CA seeks analyses that are grounded in the understandings and orientations of the participants themselves. Within interaction, the understandings that matter most are those that participants display, act on, and thus render consequential for the interaction's subsequent development (Schegloff and Sacks, 1973).

The response as an analytic resource

One central resource for tapping into such understandings is embodied in how recipients respond to the phenomenon in question. Consider that interaction ordinarily unfolds as a series of contributions or "moves," each move being normally addressed to, and to some extent conditioned by, the move that preceded it. Given this, each move will normally display that speaker's understanding of what came before (Sacks *et al.*, 1974). Interactants themselves rely on such retrospective displays of understanding to ascertain whether and how they were understood, and this "architecture for intersubjectivity" (Heritage, 1984b) is also a resource for analysts.

To illustrate, consider the utterance: "Somebody just vandalized my car." As Whalen and Zimmerman (1987) have observed, while the lexical meaning of this utterance is transparent, the type of action that it implements—what it is "doing" from the standpoint of the participants—cannot be determined by considering the utterance in isolation. It could be a straightforward *announcement of news*, with no agenda other than that of conveying information to an uninformed recipient. If this were the case, one would expect it to generate an initial response along the lines of "Oh" or "Oh really" or "My goodness"—that is, a response that attends to it as new and perhaps surprising information (Jefferson and Lee, 1981; Heritage, 1984a). Alternatively, this item of news could be a vehicle for *requesting help* or assistance of some sort, in which case one would expect a response that either accepts or rejects the request, or at least proceeds in that direction. In actuality, the utterance was produced by a caller to a 911 emergency service, and it was responded to as follows (arrowed below).

(4)
1	Dispatcher:		Midcity Emergency
2	Caller:		Um yeah (.) somebody jus' vandalized my car,
3	Dispatcher:	→	What's your address.
4	Caller:		Sixteen seventy Redland Road.

(Whalen and Zimmerman, 1987: 174)

Notice that the dispatcher's response in line 3—a question about the caller's address—is a purely instrumental query and a necessary prerequisite for sending assistance. It clearly treats the prior utterance as a request for help rather than a news announcement, an interpretation that is routine in the institutional environment of a 911 helpline (Whalen and Zimmerman, 1987). The general point is that recipients' own understandings are displayed publicly in their responses, and are thus available as an analytic resource.

Responses can also be informative in more subtle ways. Beyond revealing participant understandings of the type of action produced previously, they can also shed light on its valence. For instance, news announcements may be understood by recipients as either good or bad, and this too is displayed though subsequent talk (Maynard, 1997). Thus the following birth announcement is receipted not only as news ("Oh"), but specifically as good news ("how lovely").

(5)
1   Carrie: I: thought you'd like to know I've got a little gran'daughter
2   Leslie: →   thlk Oh: how lovely.

(Maynard, 1997: 111)

In other cases the valence of a given news announcement may be unclear to the recipient, resulting in a more cautious mode of receipt. Contrast the birth announcement sequence above with a similar announcement in the next example. This time the announcement generates an initial response ("Oh my goodness" at line 2) that registers it as surprising, but specifically avoids evaluating the news in an explicit way.

(6)
1   Andi: hhhh! Bob and I are going to have a baby.
2   Betty: →   Oh my goodness hhow- (1.0)
3   did you have a reversal- he have a reversal?
4   Andi: Yea:h.
.
.
.
5   Andi: It was [very successful,][very quickly] hh::h.hhh
6   Betty: →   [OH I'M SO   ][HAPPY.   ]

(Maynard, 1997: 116, simplified)

In this case the announcement is being issued by the expectant mother (Andi) whose husband (Bob) had previously undergone a vasectomy, raising the spectre of an unplanned pregnancy. Moreover, the recipient of the news (Betty) is aware of this fact, as evidenced by her subsequent query about a reversal (line 3). Only when subsequent talk reveals that the husband's vasectomy had indeed been reversed and that the pregnancy was fully planned does Betty receipt it unequivocally as good news ("Oh I'm so happy," line 6).

At a still more subtle level, responses can shed light on the import of momentary silences in interaction (Davidson, 1984; Pomerantz, 1984). In the next example, C invites B and a third party to stay with him at the beach (line 1). This invitation makes relevant a response that either accepts or declines the invitation, but what initially follows is silence (line 2). A silence at this juncture is ordinarily understood as "belonging" to the recipient of the invitation (Sacks *et al.*, 1974) and it could, in principle, arise for a number of reasons. B may have a problem hearing or understanding the invitation, or B may have heard/understood the invitation but is having some problem with accepting it. The difficulty, in short, could be either in the intelligibility or in the acceptability of the invitation.

```
(7)
1   C:       Well you can both sta:y.
2            (0.4)
3   C: →     [Got plenty a' roo:m, hh[hh
4   B:       [Oh I-                  [Oh(h)o(h)o,
5            (.)
6   B:       Please don't tempt me,
```

(Davidson, 1984: 105, simplified)

C's response to the silence (line 3) clearly treats it as indicating the latter type of problem. Instead of repeating or reformulating the invitation—the usual way of handling a problem of intelligibility (Schegloff *et al.*, 1977)—C offers an argument for accepting it. This move presupposes the invitation's intelligibility and displays C's understanding that B is reluctant to accept. Moreover, the substance of C's argument displays his inference regarding the reason for B's reluctance (concern about insufficient room and the inconvenience this might entail)—a reason that he counters in an effort to nudge her toward an acceptance.

At varying levels of detail, then, successive contributions to interaction shed light on how the participants understand preceding events. Of course, it is possible for a respondent to misunderstand what a speaker originally intended, and such misunderstandings may come to light through subsequent repair efforts (Schegloff, 1992). More often, subsequent talk implicitly confirms previously displayed understandings. In any event, the sequential organization of interaction provides a running index of the participants' own mutual understandings and is thus a key methodological resource.

Deployment as an analytic resource

The response to an utterance is an extremely useful resource, particularly when analyzing utterances that *initiate* sequences (e.g. news announcements, requests, invitations). However, it is not always a sufficient basis upon which to build an analysis. Responses may be less than transparent, and at times designedly opaque in the understandings they exhibit. Fortunately, other analytic resources are available that center not on the *recipient* but on the *producer* of the talk in question. Examining in detail how speakers recurrently deploy a given practice—in particular sequential environments and in particular positions within the speaker's own turn, and in conjunction with other practices—can provide important clues about that practice's meaning and import.

To illustrate, consider the various bits of talk that are used to receipt prior talk—items such as *mm hm*, *yeah*, *oh*, and *okay*. These were long assumed to comprise an undifferentiated set of "acknowledgment tokens" or "backchannel" communications. However, it has been demonstrated, largely on the basis of the selective manner in which these tokens are deployed, that each performs a somewhat distinct interactional function (Heritage, 1984a; Jefferson, 1984; Beach, 1993). The contrast between *mm hm* and *yeah* provides a useful case in point (Jefferson, 1984). In the following excerpt, notice how B deploys these receipt tokens (arrowed) in the course of M's extended telling.

```
(8)
1   M:       and she's been very thrifty.
2   B: →     Mm hm,
3   M:       .hhhhh So: (.) I said it- it a:dds up to one thing
4            money somepla:ce
5   B: →     M hm,
6   M:       .hhhh=
```

```
 7   B: →   Mm [hm,
 8   M:        [But ish (.) she tn- transacts all her business in
 9             Lo:s Angeles you know and people like this are so secretive
10             it's a(m) really it's almost a mental state
11   B: →   Yeah .hh Well .hh uh:m (0.9) y- there's something wrong too
12             if she doesn't pay her bills ....
```
(Jefferson, 1984: 205)

Although B uses both forms of receipt, she deploys them in different ways. One point of difference is the prior sequential environment: the *mm hm* tokens (lines 2, 5, and 7) appear in the midst of M's extended telling as it unfolds, while the *yeah* token (line 11) appears at the completion of the telling. Correspondingly, there are differences in what B does next. Each *mm hm* token stands alone within B's turn at talk, while B follows the *yeah* token with further talk that responds more substantially to M's telling. Accordingly, these tokens embody different interactional stances, *mm hm* displaying "passive recipiency" and *yeah* displaying "incipient speakership" (Jefferson, 1984). This conclusion is based on the systematic manner in which they are deployed.

The distinct functions of such tokens are further revealed when the tokens are used in sequentially incongruous ways. Thus, when speaker G finishes an extended telling and explicitly marks it as complete ("So that's the story," line 10, below), B receipts the story with "*Mm hm*" (line 11).

```
(9)
 1   G:    I'd li:ke to have the mirrors. But if she wants them? (.)
 2         .hh why that's: I-th-tha:t's fi::ne.
 3   B:    Mm hm,
 4   G:    If she's going to use them you kno:w.
 5   B:    Mm [hm,
 6   G:        [.hhhhhh I'm not going to uh,hh maybe queer the dea:l
 7         just by wanting this that and the othe[r (you know),
 8   B:                                          [NO:.
 9         (0.2)
10   G:    .hhhh s:So: uhm,h (.) tha:t's the story.
11   B: →  Mm hm,
12         (0.2)
13   G:    An:d uh (0.6) uhm,hhh (1.0) .hhhh u-Then I have a ma:n
14         coming Tue:sday...
```
(Jefferson, 1984: 209)

This display of passive recipiency appears strikingly misfitted to such an obvious story completion. And yet it seems to have been produced and understood as embodying just such a passive stance—subsequently, B falls silent and offers no further talk (line 12), whereas G searches for and eventually finds something further to say (lines 13–14). Here, then, an interactant exploits the passivity of "*mm hm*" as a resource for resisting the speakership role, which in turn prompts the prior speaker to continue.

The analytic resources sketched here are based on the insight that the import of a given practice is observable in the manner in which it is deployed and responded to. By exploiting these resources, the researcher moves beyond speculation to generate analytic claims that are grounded in the displayed understandings and orientations of the interactional participants themselves.

Working through collections

The primary objective of CA is to elucidate the methods people use to build interaction together. Although analysis often begins by examining a single fragment of talk, this is normally the first step in a deeper analysis, which transcends that particular fragment and sheds light on practices that operate across a range of participants and social contexts. As Sacks has observed:

> Thus it is not any particular conversation, as an object, that we are primarily interested in. Our aim is to get into a position to transform … our view of "what happened," from a matter of a particular interaction done by particular people, to a matter of interactions as products of a machinery. We are trying to find the machinery. In order to do so we have to get access to its products.
>
> *(Sacks, 1984: 26–27)*

This requires the systematic analysis of numerous cases. Working with collections can flesh out and enrich an analysis initially arrived at through a single case, illuminating such matters as the practice's various forms, the boundaries that separate it from related practices, and its scope and normativity.

When building a collection of candidate instances of a given phenomenon, it is useful to begin by casting a wide net. One should include what appear to be clear cases of the phenomenon in question, cases in which the phenomenon is present in an atypical form, and also what appear to be outright negative or "deviant" cases. Analyzing such cases rather than dismissing them as random error almost always yields a richer and more powerful analysis.

Once a collection is assembled, analysis proceeds on a case-by-case basis, with the aim of developing a comprehensive account that encompasses all relevant instances in the collection. The process is roughly analogous to analytic induction (Katz, 1983), although in CA the objective is not causal explanation but an analysis that will encompass a practice's varying occurrences across a range of interactional contexts and exigencies.

Central to this process is the analysis of problematic or deviant cases. Some such cases are shown, upon analysis, to result from interactants' orientation to the same considerations that produce the "regular" cases. We've already seen an illustration of this in the discussion of excerpt 9 above, in which an *mm hm* token was placed in an unusual sequential environment, but was nonetheless shown to function much like other such tokens as a display of passive recipiency. Cases of this sort are, in effect, exceptions that prove the rule.

In other instances, deviant cases can prompt the researcher to revise the initial analysis in favor of a more general formulation, one that encompasses both the regular cases and the anomalous departure. Perhaps the clearest example of this process can be found in Schegloff's (1968) analysis of telephone call openings. In a corpus of 500 telephone calls, Schegloff found that a straightforward rule—"answerer speaks first" —adequately described all but one of the call openings. In that one unusual case, the caller speaks first (line 3):

```
(10)
1                  ((ring))
2                  ((receiver is lifted, and there is a one-second silence))
3    Caller:       Hello.
4    Answerer:     American Red Cross.
5    Caller:       Hello, this is police headquarters….
```
(Schegloff, 1968: 1079)

Rather than ignoring this instance or explaining it away in an ad hoc fashion, Schegloff returned to the drawing board and developed a more general analysis, which accounted for all 500 cases and revealed the organization of (what would later be termed) adjacency pairs (Schegloff and Sacks, 1973). Schegloff realized that the ringing of the telephone launches a special kind of adjacency pair sequence, namely a summons–answer sequence. The rule "answerer speaks first" actually reflects the more general principle that, once a summons (here, a ringing phone) has been issued, an appropriate response is due. The deviant case also can be explained by reference to summons–answer sequences. The ring (line 1 above) was followed by silence (line 2), during which the caller heard the relevant response to be absent. Caller then spoke first (line 3) as a way of renewing the summons, soliciting the missing response, and thereby completing the incomplete sequence. The end result is a more analytically powerful account, which encompasses both regular and atypical cases.

Finally, some deviant cases may, upon analysis, turn out to fall beyond the parameters of the phenomenon being investigated. Such cases are not genuinely "deviant" at all, and clarifying how this is so furthers understanding of the core phenomenon and its boundaries. For instance, consider how personal troubles are discussed in conversation (Jefferson and Lee, 1981; Jefferson, 1988). When speakers disclose their troubles, recipients commonly respond with affiliative displays of understanding. However, in contrast to this typical pattern, recipients may instead offer advice and thereby transform the situation from a "troubles-telling" to a "service encounter." This line of analysis, unlike the previous one, does not result in a single analytic formulation encompassing "regular" and "deviant" cases. Rather it recognizes *differences* between cases and the phenomena they instantiate.

Discussion

CA addresses a domain of phenomena, the endogenous organization of talk-in-interaction, in a manner that has proven to be both illuminating and productive. Much has been learned about the basic objects that comprise this domain.

Progress on this front has made it possible for researchers to use CA methods and findings to address questions extending beyond the organization of interaction per se, including questions about how this domain intersects with, and can illuminate, other aspects of the social world. As we noted at the beginning of this chapter, some researchers have examined the impact of interactional practices on bureaucratic and professional decision-making in medical, legal, educational, journalistic, and other contexts. Others have done comparative analyses of interactional practices to elucidate large-scale cultural differences and processes of historical change. Some of this work involves formal quantification, correlating interactional practices with other variables of interest. The utility of CA in this context is that it identifies previously unknown practices, establishes and validates their meaning and import, and thus provides a solid foundation for analyses of frequency and association.

As progress is made in these various applied areas, it is important to bear in mind that such work would not be possible without the basic research on which it rests. Talk in interaction remains a rich and compelling phenomenon in its own right, one in which human agency is exercised, intersubjectivity is achieved, and contexts of the social world are brought to life. Notwithstanding what has already been accomplished, much remains to be discovered about how human interaction actually works.

Transcription conventions

[ ]	Square brackets show beginning and ending of overlapping talk
(0.5)	Numbers in parentheses are silences timed to tenths of a second
(.)	Period in parentheses is a very brief silence (less than .1 sec.)

((quiet))	Transcribers' comments are enclosed in double parentheses
( )	Empty parentheses denote indecipherable utterance
(text)	Text within parentheses is transcriber's "best guess" as to a speaker's utterance
.	Period indicates downward intonation, not necessarily the end of a sentence
?	Question mark indicates upward intonation, not necessarily a question
,	Commas indicate slightly rising or "continuing" intonation
:	Colon(s) indicate that a sound is stretched. The more colons, the longer the sound
.hh	h's with preceding period indicate audible inbreath; the more h's, the longer the inbreath
hh	h's with no preceding period indicate audible outbreath; the more h's, the longer the outbreath
(h)	Parenthesized "h" indicates plosiveness, often associated with laughter, crying, breathlessness, etc.
>word<	Enclosed talk is spoken more quickly than surrounding talk
WORD	Upper case indicates greater loudness than surrounding talk
°Yes°	Words inside degree signs are spoken softly or whispered
every	Underlines indicate sounds that are stressed
Yes::	Colons indicate stretching of the preceding sound
n–	Dash indicates a cut-off of the preceding sound
=	Equal sign indicates utterances before and after have no intervening silence.

(Adapted from Jefferson, 1974)

Further reading

ten Have, P. (1999) *Doing Conversation Analysis: A Practical Guide*. London: Sage.
Provides a comprehensive discussion of the methodology of CA.

Heritage, J. (1984b) *Garfinkel and Ethnomethodology*. Cambridge: Polity Press.
Surveys the theoretical background to CA in the work of Harold Garfinkel and provides a useful overview of some of the main areas of research.

Schegloff, E. A. (2007) *Sequence Organization in Interaction*. Cambridge: Cambridge University Press.
Offers a focused analysis of a central feature of interactional organization.

John Heritage and Steven Clayman's *Talk in Action* (2010).
Surveys research on interaction in a variety of institutional settings.

Note

1 For a much more elaborated discussion of CA methods, see ten Have (1999).

References

Atkinson, J. M. (1984) *Our Masters' Voices: The Language and Body Language of Politics*. London: Methuen.

Atkinson, J. M. and Heritage, J. (eds.) (1984) *Structures of Social Action: Studies in Conversation Analysis*. Cambridge: Cambridge University Press.

Beach, W. A. (1993) 'Transitional regularities for casual "okay" usages', *Journal of Pragmatics*, 19: 325–352.

Boden, D. and Zimmerman, D. H. (ed.) (1991) *Talk and Social Structure*. Cambridge: Polity Press.

Boyd, E. (1998) 'Bureaucratic authority in the "company of equals": initiating discussion during medical peer review', *American Sociological Review*, 63: 200–224.

Clayman, S. E., Elliott, M. N., Heritage, J., and McDonald, L. (2006) 'Historical trends in questioning presidents 1953–2000', *Presidential Studies Quarterly*, 36: 561–583.

Clayman, S. E. and Reisner, A. (1998) 'Gatekeeping in action: editorial conferences and assessments of newsworthiness', *American Sociological Review*, 63: 178–199.

Curl, T. S. and Drew, P. (2008) 'Contingency and action: a comparison of two forms of requesting', *Research on Language and Social Interaction*, 41 (2): 129–153.

Davidson, J. (1984) 'Subsequent versions of invitations, offers, requests, and proposals dealing with potential or actual rejection', in J. M. Atkinson and J. Heritage (ed.) *Structures of Social Action*. Cambridge: Cambridge University Press, pp. 102–128.

Drew, P. and Heritage, J. (1992a) 'Analyzing talk at work: an introduction', in P. Drew and J. Heritage (eds.) *Talk at Work*. Cambridge: Cambridge University Press, pp. 3–65.

Drew, P. and Heritage, J. (eds.) (1992b) *Talk at Work*. Cambridge: Cambridge University Press.

Drew, P., Raymond, G., and Weinberg, D. (2006) *Talk and Interaction in Social Research Methods*. London: Sage.

Garfinkel, H. (1967) *Studies in Ethnomethodology*. Englewood Cliffs, NJ: Prentice-Hall.

Gill, V. T. (1998) 'Doing attributions in medical interaction: patients' explanations for illness and doctors' responses', *Social Psychology Quarterly*, 61 (4): 342–360.

Gill, V. T. (2005) 'Patient "demand" for medical interventions: exerting pressure for an offer in a primary care clinic visit', *Research on Language and Social Interaction*, 38 (4): 451–479.

Gill, V. T. and Maynard, D. W. (2006) 'Patients' explanations for health problems and physicians' responsiveness in the medical interview', in J. Heritage and D. W. Maynard (eds.) *Communication in Medical Care: Interaction Between Primary Care Physicians and Patients*. Cambridge: Cambridge University Press, pp. 115–150.

Goffman, E. (1983) 'The interaction order', *American Sociological Review*, 48: 1–17.

Goodwin, C. (1981) *Conversational Organization: Interaction Between Speakers and Hearers*. New York: Academic Press.

Goodwin, M. (1990) *He-Said-She-Said: Talk as Social Organization among Black Children*. Bloomington, IN: Indiana University Press.

Halkowski, T. (2006) 'Realizing the illness: patients' reports of symptom discovery in primary care visits', in J. Heritage and D. W. Maynard (eds.) *Communication in Medical Care: Interaction between Primary Care Physicians and Patients*. Cambridge: Cambridge University Press, pp. 86–114.

Heritage, J. (1984a) 'A change-of-state token and aspects of its sequential placement', in J. M. Atkinson and J. Heritage (ed.) *Structures of Social Action*. Cambridge: Cambridge University Press, pp. 299–345.

Heritage, J. (1984b) *Garfinkel and Ethnomethodology*. Cambridge: Polity Press.

Heritage, J. (1988) 'Explanations as accounts: a conversation analytic perspective', in C. Antaki (ed.) *Analyzing Everyday Explanation: A Casebook of Methods*. London: Sage, pp. 127–44.

Heritage, J. (1998) 'Oh-prefaced responses to inquiry', *Language in Society*, 27 (3): 291–334.

Heritage, J. and Clayman, S. (2010) *Talk in Action: Interactions, Identities, and Institutions*. Oxford: Wiley-Blackwell.

Heritage, J. and Maynard, D. W. (eds.) (2006) *Communication in Medical Care: Interaction between Primary Care Physicians and Patients*. Cambridge: Cambridge University Press.

Heritage, J., Robinson, J. D., Elliott, M. N., Beckett, M., and Wilkes, M. (2007). 'Reducing patients' unmet concerns in primary care: The difference one word can make', *Journal of General Internal Medicine*, 22 (10): 1429–1433.

Heritage, J. and Stivers, T. (1999) 'Online commentary in acute medical visits: a method of shaping patient expectations', *Social Science and Medicine*, 49 (11): 1501–1517.

Houtkoop-Steenstra, H. (1991) 'Opening sequences in Dutch telephone conversations', in D. Boden and D. H. Zimmerman (eds.) *Talk and Social Structure*. Berkeley, CA: University of California Press, pp. 232–250.

Jefferson, G. (1974) 'Error correction as an interactional resource', *Language in Society*, 2: 181–199.

Jefferson, G. (1984) 'Notes on a systematic deployment of the acknowledgement tokens "Yeah" and "Mm hm" ', *Papers in Linguistics*, 17: 197–216.

Jefferson, G. (1985) 'An exercise in the transcription and analysis of laughter', in T. A. Dijk (ed.) *Handbook of Discourse Analysis*, Volume 3. New York: Academic Press, pp. 25–34.

Jefferson, G. (1988) 'On the sequential organization of troubles-talk in ordinary conversation', *Social Problems*, 35 (4): 418–441.

Jefferson, G. and Lee, J. R. E. (1981) 'The rejection of advice: managing the problematic convergence of a "troubles-telling" and a "service encounter" ', *Journal of Pragmatics*, 5: 399–422.

Katz, J. (1983) 'A theory of qualitative methodology: the social system of analytic fieldwork', in R. M. Emerson (ed.) *Contemporary Field Research*. Boston, MA: Little Brown, pp. 127–148.

Kitzinger, C. (2005) 'Speaking as a heterosexual: (How) does sexuality matter for talk-in-interaction', *Research on Language and Social Interaction*, 38 (3): 221–265.

Labov, W. (1972) *Language in the Inner City: Studies in the Black English Vernacular*. Philadelphia, PA: University of Pennsylvania Press.

Lerner, G. (2004) *Conversation Analysis: Studies from the First Generation*. Amsterdam: John Benjamins.

Lerner, G. and Whitehead, K. (2009) ' "Categorizing the Categorizer": the management of racial common sense in interaction', *Social Psychology Quarterly*, 72 (4): 325–342.

Lindström, A. (1994) 'Identification and recognition in Swedish telephone conversation openings', *Language in Society*, 23 (2): 231–252.

Maynard, D. W. (1984) *Inside Plea Bargaining: The Language of Negotiation*. New York: Plenum.

Maynard, D. W. (1997) 'The news delivery sequence: bad news and good news in conversational interaction', *Research on Language and Social Interaction*, 30 (2): 93–130.

Maynard, D. W. (2003) *Bad News, Good News: Conversational Order in Everyday Talk and Clinical Settings*. Chicago: University of Chicago Press.

Maynard, D. W., Houtkoop-Steenstra, H., Schaeffer, N. C. and van der Zouwen, J. (eds) (2002) *Standardization and Tacit Knowledge: Interaction and Practice in the Survey Interview*. New York: John Wiley and Sons.

Pomerantz, A. (1984) 'Agreeing and disagreeing with assessments: some features of preferred/dispreferred turn shapes', in J. M. Atkinson and J. Heritage (ed.) *Structures of Social Action: Studies in Conversation Analysis*. Cambridge: Cambridge University Press, pp. 57–101.

Sacks, H. (1984) 'Notes on methodology', in J. M. Atkinson and J. Heritage (ed.) *Structures of Social Action*. Cambridge: Cambridge University Press, pp. 21–27.

Sacks, H. (1992) *Lectures on Conversation*. Oxford: Blackwell.

Sacks, H., Schegloff, E. A., and Jefferson, G. (1974) 'A simplest systematics for the organization of turn-taking for conversation', *Language*, 50: 696–735.

Schegloff, E. A. (1968) 'Sequencing in conversational openings', *American Anthropologist*, 70: 1075–1095.

Schegloff, E. A. (1987) 'Between macro and micro: contexts and other connections', in J. Alexander, B. Giessen, R. Munch and N. Smelser (eds.) *The Micro–Macro Link*. Berkeley, CA: University of California Press, pp. 207–234.

Schegloff, E. A. (1992) 'Repair after next turn: the last structurally provided for place for the defence of intersubjectivity in conversation', *American Journal of Sociology*, 95 (5): 1295–1345.

Schegloff, E. A. (1996) 'Confirming allusions: toward an empirical account of action', *American Journal of Sociology*, 102 (1): 161–216.

Schegloff, E. A. (2007) *Sequence Organization in Interaction*. Cambridge: Cambridge University Press.

Schegloff, E. A., Jefferson, G., and Sacks, H. (1977) 'The preference for self-correction in the organization of repair in conversation', *Language*, 53: 361–382.

Schegloff, E. A. and Sacks, H. (1973) 'Opening up closings', *Semiotica*, 8: 289–327.

Speer, S. A. and Stokoe, E. (eds.) (2010) *Conversation and Gender*. Cambridge: Cambridge University Press.

Stivers, T. (2007) *Prescribing Under Pressure: Physician–Parent Conversations and Antibiotics*. London: Oxford.

ten Have, P. (1999) *Doing Conversation Analysis: A Practical Guide*. London: Sage.

West, C. and Zimmerman, D. (1983) 'Small insults: a study of interruptions in cross-sex conversations with unacquainted persons', in B. Thorne, C. Kramarae, and N. Henley (eds.) *Language, Gender and Society*. Rowley, MA: Newbury House, pp. 102–117.

Whalen, M. and Zimmerman, D. H. (1987) 'Sequential and institutional contexts in calls for help', *Social Psychology Quarterly*, 50: 172–185.

10

Interactional sociolinguistics and discourse analysis

Jürgen Jaspers

What is interactional sociolinguistics?

Interactional sociolinguistics (IS) studies the language use of people in face-to-face interaction. It is a theoretical and methodological perspective on language use with eclectic roots in a wide variety of disciplines such as dialectology, ethnomethodology, conversation analysis, pragmatics, linguistic anthropology, microethnography and sociology. Basically IS starts from the finding that, when people talk, they are unable to say explicitly enough everything they mean. As a result, to appreciate what is meant, they cannot simply rely on the words that are used but must also depend on background knowledge, to discover what others assumed the relevant context was for producing words in. In fact people can get very angry when they are put to the test and asked to explain precisely what they meant. Imagine telling a colleague that you had a flat tire while driving to work, after which that colleague replies: 'What do you mean, you had a flat tire?' Or suppose you ask an acquaintance: 'How are you?', and you are being asked in return: 'How am I in regard to what? My health, my finance, my school work, my peace of mind, my …'. In both cases you might experience surprise or confusion because you feel no extra explanation is necessary. You may even consider such questions improper and angrily retort: 'Look! I was just trying to be polite. Frankly, I don't give a damn how you are!' (see, for these examples, Garfinkel, 1963: 221–222). Such reactions indicate that people expect each other to treat talk as incomplete and to fill in what is left unsaid; but also that people trust each other to provide a suitable interpretation of their words, that is, they expect one another to be aware of the social world that extends beyond the actual setting and of the norms for the use of words that apply there.

Put in another way, IS holds that, because of the incompleteness of talk, all language users must rely on extracommunicative knowledge to infer, or make hypotheses about, how what is said relates to the situation at hand and what a speaker possibly intends to convey by saying it. Interactional sociolinguists in principle try to describe how meaningful contexts are implied via talk, how and if these are picked up by relevant others, and how the production and reception of talk influences subsequent interaction. As the examples above show, misinterpreting or failing to make hypotheses frustrates others' expectations that you may be willing to share the same view on what background knowledge is relevant, and this may cost you a friend. Below, we will see that misinterpreting may result in even greater social damage, but before we go into this it is necessary to take a closer look at how speakers flag, or index, meaningful contexts by using only a limited but suggestive set of tools.

Jürgen Jaspers

If talk is incomplete, interactants need to do completion work. They have to find out what unstated context a certain word flags or points at for it to be made sense of. Consequently words can be said to have indexical meaning, and it is this meaning that interactants need to bring to bear when they interpret talk. This is obvious with terms such as 'this', 'there', 'you' or 'soon', terms that have been traditionally called indexical or 'deictic' in linguistics: every 'this' and 'soon' points at the specific context in which it is used, where each time one has to complete its new and specific meaning. But other words can be considered indexical as well. An utterance like 'That's a really awesome dog' still leaves interactants the work of discovering the precise meaning of 'awesome' (is the dog frightening? beautiful? can it do tricks and is it particularly friendly? or what else was said about the dog just before it was called awesome?), which can only be grasped by drawing upon contextual knowledge of who utters the words when and where (see Heritage, 1984: 142–144) 'Far from introducing vagueness', Verschueren therefore argues (1999: 111), 'allowing context into linguistic analysis is a prerequisite for precision'. In addition to words, whole utterances can be indexical of a contextually specific non-literal meaning that needs to be discovered for (polite) communication to succeed: 'It's a bit cold in here' often means: 'Is there any chance you could close the window?' (see Grice, 1989; Gumperz, 2001). Simply put, in order to describe and explain meaningful communication, we need to look at what indexical meanings are implied by the words in a particular context rather than only at the words themselves. Naturally, it's not impossible to work out the wrong meaning of 'awesome' and to realize your first inference was wrong. Inferencing thus inevitably entails improvisation and uncertainty, so that the meaning of a word can shift over the course of an encounter at the same time as the context it was thought to make sense in is adjustable, 'plastic and contestable' (Chilton, 2004: 154). Finding out what unstated extracommunicative knowledge contributes to or disambiguates the meaning of what it said, or the process of selecting, rejecting, moulding and/or (re)negotiating the relevant context is what is called 'contextualization' (Verschueren, 1999: 111).

If this makes you wonder how people manage to make the right inferences at all, it is necessary to know that much talk is quite conventional, or that it tends to produce typical sequences of words and appropriate contexts for producing them in. There aren't dozens of ways of casually greeting one another, so you can be safe to assume that 'how are you?' indexes just that and is not to be regarded as an invitation for starting up a lengthy monologue, unless of course the question is asked at the beginning of a therapeutic session. Knowing that a general question on someone's well-being can be used for casual greeting is itself learned through socialization. Next to this, one of the important contributions of IS to the study of language and social interaction is its finding that interactants employ many other signalling channels than words to make aspects of context available. These channels are used in co-occurrence with words and can be vocal (prosodic features such as intonation or accent, code-switches, style-shifts) or non-vocal (gaze, gesture, mimics, posture). Their signs are typically called 'contextualization cues', hints or signals that help put the talk in context, or that 'steer the interpretation of the words they accompany' (Auer, 1992: 3).[1] For example, when we intend to say something ironical, we often make a contrast between the words of our utterance and the 'colour' of our voice by using a different accent, an unusual pitch level or a particular intonation pattern, maybe in concert with a raising of the eyebrows. In musical terms, contextualization cues provide extra staffs on the score of conversation, as if they orchestrate the verbal activity (see Auer, 1992). These cues are not necessarily contrastive. Often they are in harmony with words, as when a formal accent, a loud(er) voice and a raising of the hand cluster together and accompany a public announcement. In this way, cues create a redundancy of meaning and so facilitate interpretation. It would be tiresome and inefficient to put all of this indirectly given information into explicit words.

In principle, contextualization can be flagged explicitly and directly, as when people say 'I'm only joking' or 'Welcome to this meeting.' But IS has been drawn to the implicit or indirect (and usually only vocal) signalling devices, given their much more subtle character, high user efficiency and complex interpretive consequences.[2] After all, loudness, intonation, pitch or articulation rate do not mean anything by themselves, but they acquire meaning when interpreted in a specific context – a long pause can hint at deference, modesty or possibly anger. Even so, these interpretations depend on the fact that most cues, just as 'how are you?' questions, have a conventional social indexicality due to their frequent use in specific places, communities, relationships or activities. A final rising intonation for example, at least in the West, is conventionally associated with tentativeness, whereas a falling intonation usually invokes definiteness and finality (Gumperz, 1982a: 169). Consequently, in the same way as 'how are you' is available for indicating the opening of a brief chat, cues can signal social contexts and the identities, relations or stances they involve: tentative intonations are convenient for suggesting friendliness and politeness, while a definite intonation is handy for issuing commands. Likewise, accents or whole languages may point at localities or educatedness, such that a shift to a standard accent may suggest that one wishes to shift from personal communication to taking up a public or professional social role, whereas a code-switch to a common heritage language may hint at the reverse. Usually words and cues operate in clusters to help build a social persona or a social role, as with the public announcement above. It enhances the chance of getting recognized as a persuasive announcer, a really friendly person, an authentic resident or a tough manager. The continual operation of such clusters eventually gives rise to what we call registers or styles, such as manager talk, youthful talk, local talk, etc. These registers in their turn colour the words and phrases that are typically used in them, such that 'perpetuate', 'gangsta' or 'LOL' hint at their typical users and user contexts. Needless to say, these social personae and styles can be produced both for real and for pleasure.

It should be added, however, that social personae, styles and the indexically meaningful resources they are made up of are not free-floating but are part of a longer-standing but thoroughly hierarchized social world, where elites are distinguished from non-elites and semi-elites (Blommaert, 2007). These distinctions are made according to widespread and ideologized standards of appropriateness, articulateness, educatedness and beauty, which assign all available resources and their users a higher/lower, better/worse place vis-à-vis the standard; and this exerts a formidable influence on what it means to talk like (and be recognized as) 'a woman', 'a lecturer', 'a job applicant', 'a manager', 'a local'. In particular, it sets limits to the freedom one has to employ words and cues and it imposes penalties for those who are seen to use resources inappropriately or over-ambitiously: one may laugh at a lousy attempt at producing hip hop style, or a tough female CEO may find that what she does to index the suitable context for others to interpret her words in – namely a frequently falling intonation in combination with directives, a hard gaze, a lower or loud voice, and so on – gets interpreted by her male staff as unsexy, since dominant views picture women as submissive and insecure, which needs to be flagged by using rising intonation, a high pitch, and by smiling invitingly – among other things (see Jaspers, 2010). Thus, even if interpretation poses no problems, one may be understood as going off the standard and be presented with the consequences.

In sum, making inferences on the basis of talk is inextricably bound up with evaluation and identity in an unequally rewarding social world. We've already seen that there are social repercussions when misunderstandings occur: one may be found unintelligible or impolite. These repercussions only magnify when interactants find themselves in unequal social positions (imagine saying 'How am I in regard to what?' to your boss's friendly greeting) and in stressful situations such as job application interviews. Things start to look even bleaker when interactants have culturally different inferencing habits or contextualization styles, in other words when they interpret cues differently or produce cues that the other party does not pick up. It is with such recipes for disaster that a number of classic IS studies have been concerned with, and I turn to these in the next section.

What are the key studies in the area?

A central theme in IS has been (mis)communication in western urban workplace settings. Specifically, a lot of attention has been devoted to gatekeeping encounters between people with different ethnic backgrounds, in which clients or lay people have to interact with inter-viewers and experts who have different interpretive premises. Key studies in this regard are Gumperz (1982a, b) and Roberts *et al.* (1992). Here is an example from a mid-70s selection interview where an applicant applies for paid traineeship and training in skills that were in short supply on the labour market (Gumperz, 2001: 224):

a. Interviewer: and you've put here, that you want to apply for that course because there are more jobs in … the *trade*.
b. Applicant: yeah (low).
c. Interviewer: so perhaps you could explain to Mr C. *apart* from *that* reason, *why* else you want to apply for *electrical* work.
d. Applicant: I think I like … this job in my-, as a profession.
e. Instructor: and *why* do you think you'll *like* it?
f. Applicant: why?
g. Instructor: could you explain to me why?
h. Applicant: why do I like it? I think it is more job *prospect*.

As Gumperz notes, by emphasizing the word 'trade' in (a), the interviewer is asking the applicant indirectly to say more about what he wrote in a questionnaire he filled out before the interview in reply to questions about his interest in electrical work. Yet the applicant seems to treat what the interviewer says as a literal yes/no question (b). The interviewer goes on and uses the same device – stress – to draw the applicant's attention to what needs to be gone into detail about, but the applicant simply rephrases the information he has already given in the questionnaire (d). Then the instructor takes over (e), using the same accenting device to elicit extra information, but again the applicant does not recognize this as an invitation to comment on what he wrote. Rather the applicant appears to be perplexed and once more paraphrases what he has already said (h). In sum, he does not recognize the interviewers' verbal tactics, which employs emphasizing to draw attention to issues she thinks need to be elaborated, and he is not seen to speak as a suitable candidate. Such misunderstandings are not uncommon, Gumperz remarks. Research among British-resident South Asians bears out that, 'as native speakers of languages that employ other linguistic means to highlight information in discourse, South Asians often fail to recognize that accenting is used in English to convey key informa-tion, and thus do not recognize the significance of the interviewers' contextualization cues' (2001: 224). Furthermore, ethnographic data also show that South Asians have been socialized to enter interview settings 'as hierarchical encounters, where candidates are expected to show reluctance to dwell on personal likes or preferences and avoid giving the appearance of being too forward or assertive' (2001: 224). This is only one fragment of the interview, which contained numerous other miscommunications. But it comes as no surprise that the applicant eventually did not gain admission, in spite of the fact that he did possess a reasonable skill in doing electrical work.

To the extent that such conversations shipwreck, it is easy to see how different inferencing habits may disadvantage certain social groups, damage workplace relations and confirm dominant stereotypes and race inequality. All the more so as the interpretive processes involved are highly automatized and difficult to name or remember, which is the reason why participants usually do not ascribe their misunderstanding to contextualization styles but to the other's attitude or personal characteristics. In fact IS has maintained that indirect contextualization cues, such as emphasis, are extremely susceptible to (sub)cultural influences, since the meanings attached to them are usually learnt in close-knit networks (peer group, family) where speakers can be sure that background knowledge is shared and indirect signalling will be picked up and understood. They are therefore extremely vulnerable for misinterpreting and subsequent social or intercultural conflict (see, e.g., Scollon and Scollon, 1981). In this regard also the multi-ethnic classroom has been pointed out as a place where misinterpretation can be far-reaching. Consider a primary school pupil responding 'I don't wanna read' to a teacher's invitation to do so, after which the teacher gets annoyed and says: 'Alright then, sit down.' Obviously, the teacher interpreted the pupil's response as a refusal, but when such interactions were played to others, it emerged that, for black informants, the (black) pupils' rising intonation suggested that she wanted encouragement – and it was added that, if she had wanted to refuse, she would have emphasized 'wanna' – whereas white informants followed the (white) teacher's line of interpretation (see Gumperz, 1982a: 147). Comparable differences in cueing and inferencing in the classroom have been noted with regard to gaze (gaze aversion as a sign of deference versus a display of non-involvement) or information organization during story-telling (attunement to chronological coherence versus topical coherence; see Erickson, 1996; Gee, 2004; and see Michaels 1981 in Schiffrin, 1996).

An important strand in IS has pointed out, however, that misunderstanding does not automatically follow from contrastive cueing habits. Thus Erickson and Shultz (1982) have described that 'situational comembership' may prevent trouble occurring between two interlocutors from different backgrounds: when both parties in the interaction decided to make relevant a shared identity (both being football fans, classical music devotees or coming from the same town), 'the interviewer and interviewee seemed willing to overlook the momentary difficulties in understanding and negative impression that may have been due to cultural differences in communication style. In the absence of comembership, communication style difference often became more and more troublesome as the interview progressed' (Erickson, 1996: 296). Even the relation between miscommunication and stereotypification can be less than straightforward. In non-native communication the parties involved often recognize their shared incompetence and easily volunteer to negotiate meaning beyond first-level incomprehension (Varonis and Gass, 1985). And in his discussion of non-native communication in English between Flemish engineers and groups of Korean and Tanzanian students, Meeuwis (1994) shows that, although many more communicative problems arose with Korean students, the engineers were much more forthcoming towards the latter than towards Tanzanian students, and also looked least favourably on Tanzanian students after the training course. Findings such as these point to the fact that differences, diverging habits and communicative problems are still negotiable and do not inevitably lead to conflict and stereotyping. Specific community memberships are, in other words, not omnirelevant or inescapable, but can be put on hold or ignored in favour of a situational construction of belonging. These studies also show, however, that stereotypes that exist before the actual interaction may help communication go awry even in the absence of real problems, inviting us to consider the strongly shaping influence of extra-situational orders and relations on how micro-interactions are worked out (compare the ideologized standards mentioned in section 'What is interactional sociolinguistics?'; for a similar perspective, see Gee's distinction between 'Discourse' and 'discourse' in Gee, 2005).

This invitation has been accepted by much interactional sociolinguistic work of the last 10 or 15 years. In this work, interest has not been so much in miscommunication or in invisible, routine cues that may cause confusion, but rather in how small-scale interaction reveals a constant tension between people's here-and-now concerns and more established routines and views on how things should be done. Analysts usually study friendship groups or practice communities both in leisure time and in school contexts where the potential for shared background knowledge is high, and they have a critical interest in how people in these contexts 'invoke, avoid or reconfigure the cultural and symbolic capital attendant on lines and identities with different degrees of accessibility and purchase in different situations' (Rampton, 2001: 97) and in how, as a result, they position themselves in a group and in wider-scale contexts. This has led to various descriptions of playful, creative and resistant-like practices that reconfigure and challenge widespread conventions or put them temporarily on hold (see e.g. Rampton, 1995, 2006; Heller, 1999; Jaspers, 2005; Reyes and Lo, 2009). This attention for the relation between micro-interaction and its reproduction of, as well as its possible challenge to, wider or dominant social contexts is indicative of how current IS helps to approach discourse.

How does IS help to approach discourse?

IS is greatly inspired by a social constructionist view of discourse as an arrangement of habitual social (rather than only verbal) practices. Principally within this line of thinking, people are seen neither as the victims of powers they do not comprehend or understand nor as omnipotent creators of their own circumstances, but as intensely socialized beings who at least partly create or actualize their (unequal, socially stratified) societies anew in their daily interactions. Rather than the mere reflection of pre-existing social structures, language use is seen as one of the primary resources for social actors to shape and re-shape their social surroundings actively and creatively. A crucial point is that these interactions do not take place in a vacuum. They are streamlined by longer-standing and larger-scale habits that restrict the range of possible new interactions. A potent motive for this is that habits provide recognizable frames, identities and relationships and so assure the ontological security – that is, the sense of stability and continuity about one's experiences – of those involved (Giddens, 1984). Conversely, as we have seen in Garfinkel's examples at the beginning of this chapter, deviating from routine behaviour causes confusion and indignation; it puts existing knowledge (such as knowing what a flat tire is, knowing how to greet someone casually) and identities (being a knowledgeable colleague or an acquaintance) under pressure and suggests they cannot be taken for granted any longer. The work of Garfinkel and also Goffman (1967) has shown that those who (potentially) deviate tend consequently to be held in check, over and above mere indignation, with a variety of delicate reproaches but also less subtle social penalties, as was the case for the female CEO above. Of course, those at the top of social hierarchies will applaud the reproduction of the world as it is, while those with less influence may often feel ill at ease or apprehensive about leaving the social paths in which they have learned to think, feel and act, so that, although social actors are constantly re-creating the social world, they will mostly (feel encouraged to) reproduce established discourses.

Yet, even though social interactions gravitate towards reproducing them, the fact that these established structures need to be actualized in interaction means that they are inescapably influenced by interaction and so constantly vulnerable to innovation and potential change. There is thus a two-way connection between local happenings and larger-scale processes. For, if social interaction is a construction zone (Erickson, 2004: 143) where it is necessary to keep other builders in check and to restrict the range of new creations, this means that habits do not totally determine what social actors can do but they still allow for actions that deviate, resist, question, by-pass or negotiate these habits. Needless to say, from this perspective social interaction becomes a privileged site for the study of society. It is the arena where customary ways of doing are confronted with the unpredictability of interaction, or the window through which we can observe social actors maintaining their own and others' identities at the same time as they are creatively reworking older or past traditions, which may eventually impact on larger-scale social patterns. Daily interactions could in this way be viewed as the small cogwheels of the broader social (and also linguistic) mechanism that interactants, through their talk, constantly grease or may throw sand into. For these reasons, and following Goffman (1983), IS argues that social interaction needs to be viewed as a distinct and intermediate level of organization, the workings of which cannot be explained by the rules of grammar alone, nor from a macro-social viewpoint. In sum, IS approaches discourse 'through the worm's eye, not the bird's' (Rampton, 2001: 84). It looks at small-scale interaction (rather than at public texts such as newspaper language or advertising) in order to provide a microscopic and insider view on larger social processes that crucially depend on these small-scale actions.

One danger here is to prioritize recordable verbal interaction or conversation as the only reliable empirical basis for studying how interactants 'do' discourse, as is often the case in conversation analysis, and to neglect the contextualizing procedures mentioned in sections 'What is interactional sociolinguistics?' and 'What are the key studies in the area?' (see Coupland, 2001: 12–15). Another danger is that analyses of interaction may remain at micro-level and may fail to situate it in larger-scale processes. In such cases, there is the risk that analysts describe how established practices and meanings are evoked in local interaction and possibly reworked or playfully contested, but they overemphasize the resistant quality of actions that in the end do not even ripple the surface of larger scale discourses. The challenge is thus to provide an intimate view of the interplay between reproduction and creativity in small-scale interaction, but also to relate what goes on at microscopic level to the determining influences of higher-order social processes – among other things, by exploring how local interactions are linked to others and by investigating what visible or non-visible traces they leave on institutional or other public records (Meeuwis, 1994; Heller, 2001; Rampton, 2001)

How do you make an IS analysis?

If you want to make an IS analysis, you will need first-hand data that are as rich as possible. This usually implies doing long-term ethnographic fieldwork in one setting during which you familiarize yourself with the local communicative ecology, appreciate how it is related to broader social structures and assemble as much commentary from participants as possible. Without this ethnographic knowledge, it will be difficult to pick up the background knowledge that interactants in that setting only display via subtle references. Recordings (digital or otherwise) of naturally occurring speech are a must-have, since it is next to impossible to reconstruct interactions from memory in the amount of detail you need in order to discover their moment-to-moment organization. It is not always easy to make recordings, but, once you have them, they will allow you to revisit the recorded scene as much as you like so as to check hypotheses. Making a transcript of your recordings is the following indispensable and quite time-intensive step. It is possible to leave this step out, but it will usually be much more practical to mark off important extracts on paper (see Schiffrin, 1996; Rampton, 2001).

Which extracts are important clearly depends on your research goals. But it is typical for ethnographic research that these may sometimes slightly shift focus when you arrive at the scene. This was also the case in my own research, in which I have been interested in the linguistic behaviour of students at a multi-ethnic secondary school in Antwerp, Belgium (Jaspers, 2005).

Initially I expected to find adolescents from different ethnic backgrounds playing around with each other's heritage languages and finding an interactional common ground in spite of their ethnic differences (cf. Rampton, 1995). But such behaviour was hard to find, and instead I noticed that ethnic minority students dominated the classroom floor and silenced most other voices by excelling in what they called 'doing ridiculous', that is, slowing down and parodying the lesson (and later on also research interviews) in not entirely unruly ways. Furthermore, in spite of the fact that these students are widely noted in Belgium as incompetent or unwilling speakers of Dutch, it turned out that they regularly switched from one Dutch variety to another for special effect, and I felt that bringing out such versatile language skills would help me to rub against common stereotypes. Therefore I started identifying all occasions in my data where such playful behaviour could be found and then categorized them according to variety (examples of playful Antwerp dialect, Standard Dutch, mock English, mock Turkish, etc.). I replayed extracts to these students for retrospective commentary, and I worked on the analysis of extracts, keeping an eye on how interaction and language use related, challenged, or diverged from widespread interactional conventions.

Here is one (translated) data-sample (see Jaspers, 2006, for more details). It is from an interview with Mourad, Adnan and Moumir (20, 19 and 21 years of age, respectively), all of Moroccan descent and in their last year of secondary education. I've just asked them in which cases they think they'll be needing Standard Dutch.

1	JJ:	and what exactly will you be needing from it?
2	A:	(you learn) to talk better or something [.] when you go
3		and apply for a for a job or something [..] then at least you
4		won't be making a fool of yourself
5	Mr:	that was last year () also uh [..] could write a letter
6		like that I've done such- such such an application letter [..]
7	JJ:	yeah
8	Mr:	and uh [.] and this year we're also going to be seeing this
9		isn't it? [viz: the letter] [..] isn't it guys? and uh [.] so uh [..] yeah
10	Md&A:	[laughing] [2.0]
11	Md:	[close to microphone, smile voice:] **so you are a repeater**
12		[laughter]
13	A:	Moumir Talhaoui [laughs]
14	Mr:	( )
15		[laughter]
16	Md:	22 YEARS OLD
17	JJ:	| (and do you have)
18		[laughter]
19	JJ:	but [.] but [.] right when you uh when you take a look at [etc.]

There is no miscommunication here, except perhaps between Moumir and his friends as to whether the latter know what Moumir is talking about. We notice Moumir suffer face-loss, having his nose rubbed into it by Mourad and Adnan, who find this highly amusing, and after a short while I try and put the interview back on track. If we look more closely, we can see that in lines 8–9, Moumir is seeking confirmation for his story ('isn't it guys?'), but then seems to realize that they are not repeating the year as he is, and thus cannot confirm if they are going to write a job application letter. This realization is clear in Moumir's second question for confirmation, which this time also involves an address ('guys'), whereas before he only used a 'we' to which he also counted himself. Moumir is in other words putting himself in a different position than his two classmates, and suddenly becomes someone who's addressing them about what they can expect this year in class. Moumir's story halts in line 9 and is followed by laughter in line 10, which suggests that Moumir is suffering face-loss and stops speaking because of this. Mourad discloses the precise content of Moumir's face-loss quite explicitly in line 11: the latter has unexpectedly and much to the amusement of his mates given himself away as a grade repeater, and as someone who is ashamed of this (or who is biting his tongue, since he has now given his classmates the opportunity to start teasing him about it again). Mourad does this in a stylized Standard Dutch: he uses careful pronunciation and the formal pronoun 'u' [you],[3] and in this way provides the other participants with a sudden piece of showcase behaviour that acts as a special cue for the others to appreciate the relevance of.

What could this relevance be? Obviously, it is not impossible that Mourad's stylization was invited by the interview questions on the use of Standard Dutch. But categorizing it as mere sound play would overlook the fact that the interview itself formed a special occasion, given that I diverged from my typical bystander or onlooker role and was now visibly taking up the position of a question-asking and turn-allocating authority who was taping everything they said. The unexpected focus on Moumir's status as a grade repeater only added to emphasizing the differences between them and myself, given our quite dissimilar educational histories (a university researcher versus students on a less than prestigious educational trajectory). Unusual moments such as these are what Goffman calls ritually sensitive moments (1967). Quite often, on such occasions people increase the symbolic quality of their behaviour and use special linguistic material, which has significance beyond the practical requirements of the here-and-now (Rampton, 2006). Here we find Standard Dutch, the variety in comparison to which all other varieties are 'lower' on the social ladder and which, for these students and in society at large, is strongly associated with high educational success and intellectual authority (and thus, for these students, also with nerdiness). In addition, this linguistic material is produced by Mourad right at that sequential position (line 11), a self-selected turn after Moumir's answer, which is usually only the prerogative of turn-allocating authorities such as teachers and interviewers (see Sacks et al., 1978: 45; Macbeth, 1991: 285).

It is therefore not unreasonable to claim that Mourad, aptly and humorously – or at least to his own and Adnan's enjoyment – rises to the occasion to disclose a failed school identity we all already know of in a teacher-like, educationally successful, voice – which, because of its sequential position, seems to ventriloquize that I would presumably find this important or worth mentioning in the interview; which is perhaps why Mourad assures the acoustic audibility of his stylization (by speaking very closely into the table-top microphone) and why we find the extra, but unnecessary, biographical information about Moumir in lines 13 and 16. Hence, in this extract we find (1) a playful reconfiguration of the interview's intentions (registering school failure rather than opinions on language); (2) inauthentic use of Standard Dutch, which throws its ideologically neutral character into comical relief; and (3) an intuition of how small-scale interactions at school, such as a research interview, can contribute to more macro-discursive processes that position people differently in hierarchical social patterns.

Why is IS important?

IS is important because it draws our attention to the existence of subtle cultural differences in the systematic combination of verbal and non-verbal signs which signal contexts and construct meaning, differences that are often hard to pin down by those who use them. IS can claim credit for having shown in great detail that disastrous consequences may follow if such different styles remain hidden and lead to miscommunication in gatekeeping encounters: applicants do not only fail to get a job or admission to a course, but often find their personal and ethnic background targeted as the cause for communication failure. IS has thus managed to uncover meaning and reason behind communicative styles that are regularly identified as inarticulate and incoherent, and the social relevance of this cannot be underestimated. It has shown that seemingly unintelligible job applicants or uninterested children are in fact sensible and involved if you (are willing to) read their contextualization cues in an appropriate way or you are prepared to accept their different cueing habits.

IS has also illustrated that technically differing styles do not necessarily lead to miscommunication, just as miscommunication itself does not automatically lead to conflict or stereotyping. As mentioned above, a readiness for observing and acknowledging differences can overcome even seriously diverging communication styles, or, conversely, the absence of difference does not always prevent negative identification or wilful misunderstanding from taking place. These findings invite us to look beyond the actual interactional setting and observe how interactants approach and evaluate one another as differently positioned social beings who may, depending on the circumstances, see each other as problematically or delightfully different. Even when the odds are unfavourable, interactants may find other identities, qualities or actions of a person valuable that may overrule communication difficulties and the effect of stereotyping (a talented football player's almost non-existent English will be passed over much more easily than that of an illegal refugee, who in her turn may find that her English is found cute and perfectly acceptable by her neighbours for whom she does babysitting). In other words, IS shows that communication is irrevocably a social happening where identities and relations matter, and which as such stands in close connection with wider social patterns and conventions that are also affected by it. This brings me to a third reason why IS is important.

IS offers an excellent tool for analysing the tension between here-and-now interaction and more established discursive practices. In putting a microscope on interaction, IS makes clear that communication can never be taken for granted but always involves collaboration, collusion and negotiation. As the discussion in section 'How do you make an IS analysis?' illustrated, traces of these processes can be extremely subtle and may go unnoticed when looked at from a further distance, or their relevance may not be fully appreciated when discussed in isolation from the established practices that facilitated their production. IS, on the other hand, is well capable of attending to such subtle traces and to the accompanying perspectives of 'participants who are compelled by their subordinate positions to express their commitments in ways that are indirect, off-record and relatively opaque to those in positions of dominance' (Rampton, 2001: 99). Consequently, IS can help to pinpoint those moments when established frames are called into question, reconfigured or otherwise transformed, and in this way it can also indicate when creative restructurings give rise to emergent and potentially habitualizing social configurations. In short, IS can contribute to our understanding of larger social evolutions.

Further reading

Auer, P. and Di Luzio, A. (eds.) (1992) *The Contextualization of Language*. Amsterdam and Philadelphia, PA: John Benjamins.

This edited volume is often referred to because it critically revisits Gumperz' concept of contextualization and also contains a number of interesting empirical studies on gesture and prosody (rhythm, tempo and intonation).

Erickson, F. (2004) *Talk and Social Theory: Ecologies of Speaking and Listening in Everyday Life*. Cambridge: Polity Press.

Erickson in this book re-analyses examples of everyday linguistic behaviour from his earlier work, before reviewing key perspectives in social theory. It is a very accessible book: the first chapter is in lay language; the following ones gradually introduce technical and theoretical terms necessary for reading the chapters on social theory.

Gumperz, J. (1982a) *Discourse Strategies*. Cambridge: Cambridge University Press.

This book is a landmark in interactional sociolinguistics. It is an eloquent introduction to Gumperz' main theoretical and methodological concepts. A must-read for any student of interactional sociolinguistics.

Rampton, B. (2006) *Language in Late Modernity: Interaction in an Urban School*. Cambridge: Cambridge University Press.

This book is referred to in many works because of its impressive empirical depth and theoretical width in describing adolescent linguistic practices in relation to various topics (popular culture, foreign language, playful and less playful uses of Cockney and 'posh' English).

Notes

1 Although words themselves can of course also function as cues.
2 Non-vocal cues (body posture, gesture, mimicry) have been given a lot of prominence in micro-ethnography (see McDermott *et al.*, 1978; Erickson, 2004).
3 Dutch has two forms for second person address: 'jij' [you] in informal situations, 'u' [you] in formal ones (cf. *tu* and *vous* in French).

References

Auer, P. (1992) 'Introduction: John Gumperz' approach to contextualization', in P. Auer and A. Di Luzio (eds.) *The Contextualization of Language*. Amsterdam/Philadelphia, PA: John Benjamins, pp. 1–37.

Blommaert, J. (2007) 'Sociolinguistics and discourse: orders of indexicality and polycentricity', *Journal of Multilingual Discourses*, 2: 115–130.

Chilton, P. (2004) *Analysing Political Discourse: Theory and Practice*. London: Routledge.

Coupland, N. (2001) 'Introduction: sociolinguistic theory and social theory', in N. Coupland, S. Sarangi, and Candlin, C. N. (eds.) *Sociolinguistics and Social Theory*. Harlow: Longman.

Erickson, F. (1996) 'Ethnographic microanalysis', in N. Hornberger and S. McKay (eds.) *Sociolinguistics and Language Teaching*. Cambridge: Cambridge University Press, pp. 283–306.

Erickson, F. (2004) *Talk and Social Theory: Ecologies of Speaking and Listening in Everyday Life*. Cambridge: Polity Press.

Erickson, F. and Shultz, J. (1982) *The Counsellor as Gatekeeper: Social Interaction in Interviews*. New York: Academic Press.

Garfinkel, H. (1963) 'A conception of, and experiments with, "trust" as a condition of stable concerted actions', in O. J. Harvey (ed.) *Motivation and Social Interaction*. New York: Ronald Press, pp. 187–238.

Gee, J. P. (2004) *Situated Language and Learning: A Critique of Traditional Schooling*. New York: Routledge.

Gee, J. P. (2005) *An Introduction to Discourse Analysis: Theory and Method*. Second Edition. New York: Routledge.

Giddens, A. (1984) *The Constitution of Society: Outline of the Theory of Structuration*. Cambridge: Polity Press.

Goffman, E. (1967) *Interaction Ritual: Essays on Face-to-Face Behaviour*. London: Penguin.

Goffman, E. (1983) 'The interaction order', *American Sociological Review*, 48: 1–17.

Grice, P. (1989) *Studies in the Ways of Words*. Cambridge, MA: Harvard University Press.

Gumperz, J. J. (1982a) *Discourse Strategies*, Cambridge: Cambridge University Press.

Gumperz, J. J. (ed.) (1982b) *Language and Social Identity*. Cambridge: Cambridge University Press.

Gumperz, J. J. (2001) 'Interactional sociolinguistics: a personal perspective', in D. Schiffrin, D. Tannen, and E. Hamilton (eds.) *The Handbook of Discourse Analysis*. Malden/Oxford: Blackwell, pp. 215–228.

Heller, M. (1999) *Linguistic Minorities and Modernity: A Sociolinguistic Ethnography*. London: Longman.

Heller, M. (2001) 'Discourse and interaction', in D. Schiffrin, D. Tannen, and E. Hamilton (eds.) *The Handbook of Discourse Analysis*. Malden/Oxford: Blackwell, pp. 250–264.

Heritage, J. (1984) *Garfinkel and Ethnomethodology*. Cambridge: Polity Press.

Jaspers, J. (2005) 'Linguistic sabotage in a context of monolingualism and standardization', *Language and Communication*, 25: 279–297.

Jaspers, J. (2006) 'Stylizing standard Dutch by Moroccan boys in Antwerp', *Linguistics and Education*, 17: 131–56.

Jaspers, J. (2010) 'Style and styling', in N. Hornberger and S. McKay (eds.) *Sociolinguistics and Language Education*. Clevedon: Multilingual Matters, pp. 177–204.

Macbeth, D. (1991) 'Teacher authority as practical action', *Linguistics and Education*, 3: 281–313.

McDermott, R., Gospodinoff, K., and Aron, J. (1978) 'Criteria for an ethnographically adequate description of concerted activities and their contexts', *Semiotica*, 24: 245–275.

Meeuwis, M. (1994) 'Leniency and testiness in intercultural communication: remarks on ideology and context in interactional sociolinguistics', *Pragmatics* 4: 391–408.

Rampton, B. (1995) *Crossing. Language and Ethnicity among Adolescents*. London: Longman.

Rampton, B. (2001) 'Critique in interaction', *Critique of Anthropology*, 21: 83–107.

Rampton, B. (2006) *Language in Late Modernity: Interaction in an Urban School*. Cambridge: Cambridge University Press.

Reyes, A. and Lo, A. (2009) *Beyond Yellow English: Toward a Linguistic Anthropology of Asian Pacific America*. Oxford: Oxford University Press.

Roberts, C., Davies, E., and Jupp, T. (1992) *Language and Discrimination*. London: Longman.

Sacks, H., Schegloff, E., and Jefferson, G. (1978) 'A simplest systematics for the organization of turn-taking for conversation', in J. N. Schenkein (ed.) *Studies in the Organization of Conversational Interaction*. New York: Academic Press, pp. 7–55.

Schiffrin, D. (1996) 'Interactional sociolinguistics', in N. Hornberger and S. McKay (eds.) *Sociolinguistics and Language Teaching*. Cambridge: Cambridge University Press, pp. 307–328.

Scollon, R. and Scollon, S. B. K. (1981) *Narrative, Literacy and Face in Interethnic Communication*. Norwood, NJ: Ablex.

Varonis E. M. and Gass, S. M. (1985) 'Non-native/non-native conversations: a model for negotiation of meaning', *Applied Linguistics*, 6: 71–90.

Verschueren, J. (1999) *Understanding Pragmatics*. London: Edward Arnold.

11

Discourse-oriented ethnography

Graham Smart

This chapter discusses two widely practised traditions of ethnography that each offer researchers a methodology for investigating a social group's culture and discourse practices: interpretive ethnography and ethnography of communication. Here I would make an initial distinction between ethnography and case study research. While both methodologies involve 'naturalistic' or 'field' research and the intention of both is to observe and explain the social world as it is, without intervention or manipulation (to the degree that this is possible), a case study typically focuses on the experience of a small number of informants or on a single event, and an ethnography investigates the local culture of a particular social group, viewed as a collective, with the goal of producing a holistic account of its shared conceptual world. And I use the term 'methodology' rather than 'method' here with meaningful intent. While some researchers use the two terms interchangeably, others find it useful to make a distinction between them. In the latter view, a research method is a set of procedures for collecting and analysing research data, while a research methodology is a method *as well as* an implicit set of assumptions regarding the nature of reality (ontology) and knowledge (epistemology).

The chapter begins with a section providing background on the emergence of ethnography in the fields of anthropology and sociology and on its subsequent evolution into a research methodology employed by various disciplines in the social sciences. The next section focuses on the two discourse-oriented approaches to ethnography, discussing each in turn. The chapter concludes with an account of how the author analyzed interview data in an ethnographic study of the discourse practices and intellectual work of economists at the Bank of Canada, the country's central bank.

Origins and brief history of ethnography

What we might view as a precursor to ethnography originated in the fifteenth and sixteenth centuries as a response to Europeans' encounters with culturally and racially diverse peoples during early voyages to the western hemisphere and South Pacific (Vidich and Lyman, 1998). These European travellers were prompted to ask questions about the origins, histories, languages, and ways of life of the varied groups of peoples they met – questions motivated both by an epistemological urge to situate unfamiliar cultures within the traditional worldview and received knowledge of western Europe and by the colonizer's need to organize and justify the exploitation of these cultures for their labour and natural resources (Asad, 1973). As a consequence, early proto-ethnographic accounts can be found in texts produced by European explorers, missionaries, and colonial administrators for readers in governments and other institutions.

Ethnography in its academic guise emerged in the late nineteenth century and early twentieth century, as a research methodology employed by cultural anthropologists for conducting extended in-depth investigations of the cultures of newly encountered peoples – again, for the most part in the 'New World' and South Pacific. Prominent examples of this genre are the field studies of Franz Boas (1897) in the north-western coastal regions of North America, Bronislaw Malinowkski (1922) in the Trobriand Islands, Margaret Mead in Samoa (1928), and Gregory Bateson (1936) in New Guinea.

In the following decades, a number of American sociologists took up the methodology, turning an 'ethnographic gaze' (Clifford and Marcus, 1986) on the social practices of urban subcultures within their own society, as with the field work of Helen Lynd and Robert Lynd (1937) among residents of Muncie, Indiana; of Nels Anderson (1940) among homeless 'hobos' in Chicago; of William Foote Whyte (1943) on an Italian community in Boston; and of Elliot Liebow (1966) among African Americans in a Washington, DC neighbourhood

In the years since, ethnography has been adopted by a range of other disciplines, including science studies (Latour and Woolgar, 1986), education (Goetz and Breneman, 1988), human geography (Mountz and Wright, 1996), and organizational studies (Orr, 1996). At the same time ethnography has been appropriated for applied purposes in industry (Richardson and Walker, 1948) and management (Jackell, 1988) as well as in policy areas such as education (Hess, 1991), public health (Jafarey, 2009), and criminology (Auty and Briggs, 2004). Recent decades have also seen the emergence of postmodern and other alternative forms of ethnography, such as critical ethnography, feminist ethnography, auto-ethnography, performance ethnography, video ethnography, and virtual Web-based ethnography.[1] As ethnography has migrated across these various academic disciplines, professional fields, and alternative forms and as researchers have adapted it to their own ends, the methodology has undergone a diversification of goals, epistemologies, and methods, while still retaining its larger purpose of investigating the culture and social reality of a particular community or group.

One direction that ethnography has taken since the mid-twentieth century is to focus its inquiry on the discourse practices of particular social groups – as these discourse practices are instantiated in writing, speaking, or other symbolic forms. The next section of the chapter describes two such approaches.

Discourse-oriented ethnography: two approaches

This section discusses two discourse-oriented approaches to ethnography: 'interpretive ethnography' and 'ethnography of communication', the first introduced by Clifford Geertz and the second by Dell Hymes. With both approaches, a researcher undertakes to investigate the relationship between the culture of a particular social group and its language or other symbolic resources in order to learn something of how members of the group live, interact, and communicate.

Interpretive ethnography

Interpretive ethnography (also referred to as symbolic or semiotic ethnography), as conceived by cultural anthropologist Clifford Geertz (1983, 1973) during his field studies in Southeast Asia – in Bali, most famously – and in North Africa from the 1950s to the 1980s, is a methodology that enables a researcher to study the discourse practices through which a particular social group constructs, maintains, and reproduces a shared social world. The methodology has been practiced and further developed by other researchers such as Michael Agar (1980), John Van Maanen (1988), Martin Hammersley and Paul Atkinson (1985), and Norman Denzin (1997).

Geertz's (1973) vision of ethnography rests on a semiotic notion of culture: '[a culture] is an historically transmitted pattern of meanings embodied in symbols, a system of inherited conceptions expressed in symbolic forms by means of which men [*sic*] communicate, perpetuate, and develop their knowledge about and their attitudes toward life' (p. 89). For Geertz, the task of the ethnographer is to spend an extended period of time within the group under study as a participant-observer and to chart the network of explicitly and tacitly shared meanings that constitute the group's social reality, as seen from the viewpoint of a quasi-insider. Geertz articulates this perspective on culture and ethnography below:

> Believing ... that man is an animal suspended in webs of significance he himself [*sic*] has spun, I take culture to be those webs, and the [ethnographic] analysis of it to be therefore not an experimental science in search of law but an interpretive one in search of meaning. ... The whole point of a semiotic approach to culture is... to aid us in gaining access to the conceptual world in which our subjects live.
>
> *(1973: 5, 24)*

For Geertz (1983), then, human cognition is largely social in nature – a 'matter of trafficking in the symbolic forms available within a particular community' (153) – and the work of an ethnographer is to investigate the life-world (Schütz, 1974) of a particular social group, mapping out its 'systems of symbols' (182) as 'modes of thought, idiom to be interpreted' (120).

Accordingly, for Geertz (1973), the ultimate aim of interpretive ethnography is to develop a 'thick description'[2] (6) of a social group's 'interworked systems of construable signs' (14) as 'structures of meaning' (182). Geertz (1973) describes this task as follows: 'What the ethnographer is in fact faced with [...] is a multiplicity of complex conceptual structures, many of them superimposed upon or knotted into one another, which are at once strange, irregular, and inexplicit, and which he [*sic*] must contrive somehow first to grasp and then to render' (9). The result of this rendering is a broad portrait of a social group's distinctive world of concepts and symbol systems.

Thus interpretive ethnography offers the researcher a methodology for exploring the discourse practices of a particular group of people – as their discourse is instantiated in writing, speaking, or other symbol systems – with the goal of learning how members of the group perceive, function and learn within their collectively created and maintained 'conceptual world'. The eventual outcome of such research is a 'thick description' of the group's culture, a description inscribed in an ethnographic account conveying a quasi-insider's understanding of how members of the group communicate and interact with one another, what they believe and value, how they define and solve common problems, how they construct and apply knowledge, and how they accomplish other meaningful communal activities.

Interpretive ethnography, in undertaking to explore and produce a representation of the shared meanings that constitute the discursively constructed conceptual world of a given social group, relies heavily on the practice of eliciting and presenting 'displays of members' thoughts, theories, and world views' (Van Maanen, 1988). To this end, the ethnographer collects a variety of data including field-notes from observations, interviews with informants, texts in different symbol systems, and in some cases data from surveys and focus groups. Using an iterative procedure referred to as 'recursive analysis' (Merriam, 1988; LeCompte and Preissle, 1993), the ethnographer moves through repeated cycles of data collection, analysis of the data, reflection on the results of the analysis, possible redirection of the research in light of the analysis and reflection, and then more data collection, analysis, reflection, and so on. With its iterative cyclical pattern of data collection, analysis, and reflection, 'recursive analysis' has a family resemblance to the 'grounded theory' approach introduced by sociologists Barney Glaser and Anselm Strauss (1967) and further developed in the decades since by these two scholars and other methodologists working in the same tradition (Strauss and Corbin, 1998; Glaser, 2001; Charmaz, 2006).

Throughout the process of data collection, analysis, and reflection the ethnographer strives to develop provisional mini-theories – what Geertz (1983) refers to as 'low-hovering theories': theories that remain very close to informants' 'first-order constructs of reality' as found in the data (1973) – gradually working towards the production of an ethnographic account – a 'thick description' of the 'conceptual world' constructed and maintained by the social group under study.

During this ongoing cyclical process, the ethnographer works with social theories of two kinds: what Geertz (1973) calls 'experience-near' concepts (another term for the informants' 'first-order constructs of reality' mentioned above) and the 'experience-distant' concepts of disciplinary theorists. He distinguishes between the two below:

> An experience-near concept is, roughly, one which someone – a patient, a subject, in our case an informant – might himself [sic] naturally and effortlessly use to define what he or his fellows see, feel, think, imagine and so on, and which he would readily understand when similarly applied by others. An experience-distant concept is one which specialists of one sort or another – an analyst, an experimenter, an ethnographer – employ to forward their scientific, philosophical, or practical aims.
>
> (p. 57)

For Geertz, then, an essential part of the ethnographer's work is to identify within his or her data concepts that have been created locally by the social group under study – 'experience-near concepts' – and to 'place them in illuminating connection' with the 'concepts [that] theorists have fashioned to capture the general features of social life'. The aim here, according to Geertz (1973), is to produce 'an interpretation of the way a people lives which is neither imprisoned within their mental horizons, […] nor systematically deaf to the distinctive tonalities of their existence' (p. 57). As mentioned earlier, the desired outcome of this work is a 'thick description' – an account of the group's collective meaning-making activities and resultant conceptual world, as theorized through the disciplinary concepts employed by the researcher in the analysis.

A researcher might well ask, however, how one is to go about identifying key 'experience-near concepts' in one's data and mapping out the conceptual world of the social group under study. In his methodological writings, Geertz (1983) offers the researcher three favoured analytical strategies: the '[search for] convergent data; the explication of linguistic classifications; and the examination of the life cycle' (p. 156). According to Geertz, in looking for 'convergent data', a researcher should seek, within the data collected for a study, instances of common perspectives shared among the 'multiply connected individuals' within the group – 'a mutually reinforcing network of social understandings' (pp. 156–157). The 'explication of linguistic classifications' is the strategy of seeking frequently used terms in the vernacular of the group and of probing these terms as markers of shared meanings, which, taken together, can be seen to suggest 'a whole way of going at the world' (p. 157). Finally, in referring to the 'examination of the life cycle', Geertz is talking about searching in the data for stories from informants describing significant episodes in the group's shared history or pointing to important lines of communal development, and then analysing these stories as symbolic artefacts, potentially rich in meaning. Such stories, once analysed, may cast light on the group's history as 'a structure of hope, fear, desire, and disappointment' (pp. 159–160).

Examples of book-length research studies using interpretive ethnography include Bruno Latour and Steve Woolgar's *Laboratory Life: The Construction of Social Facts* (1979), Shirley Brice Heath's *Ways with Words: Language, Life and Work in Communities and Classrooms* (1980), John Swales's *Other Floors, Other Voices: A Textography of a Small University Building* (1998), Paul Prior's *Writing/Disciplinarity: A Sociohistoric Account of Literate Activity in the Academy* (1998), and the author's own *Writing the Economy: Activity, Genre and Technology in the World of Banking* (2006). The diversity of these studies reflects the versatility offered by interpretive ethnography for investigating the cultures and discourse practices of different social groups within school, workplace, and community settings.

Ethnography of communication

The 'ethnography of communication', introduced by anthropologist and sociolinguist Dell Hymes in a seminal 1962 paper, is a methodology that enables a researcher to explore the distinctive configuration of verbal routines, conventions, and genres that structures communication within any given social group. As with Clifford Geertz, it was Hymes' experience in the field as a cultural anthropologist – in his case, among the Aboriginal peoples of the north-western coastal area of North America, in work inspired by Franz Boas' (1897) earlier work in the same region – that provided the impetus for methodological innovation.

An approach that combines ethnography – the description and analysis of culture – with linguistics – the description and analysis of language – the ethnography of communication takes as its scholarly remit the study of the 'speech community' (Bloomfield, 1933; Labov, 1966) – a group of people sharing linguistic resources as well as norms of interaction, expression, and interpretation – along with the 'speech situations', 'speech events', and 'speech acts' that serve to organize communicative interaction within the group. Researchers have used the approach to describe and analyze the 'rules of speaking' in a wide range of speech communities, while at the same time contributing concepts and theories to a larger meta-understanding of patterns of communication across human cultures (Saville-Troike, 1982).

While Hymes originally referred to his methodology as the 'ethnography of speaking', reflecting a focus on spoken language, he and John Gumperz later reconceived the approach along broader lines as the 'ethnography of communication' (Gumperz and Hymes, 1964), expanding the possible objects of study so as to include 'the various available channels, and their modes of use, speaking, writing, printing, drumming, blowing, whistling, singing, face and body motion as visually perceived, smelling, tasting, and tactile sensation [along with] the various codes shared by various participants, linguistic, paralinguistic, kinesic, musical, and other. ...' (13). Indeed, later on in his career Hymes (1981, 2003) further adapted the ethnography of communication into a specialized approach that he termed 'ethnopoetics', which Hymes used in order to identify poetic elements in written texts, transcriptions, and artefacts conveying the folklore and myths of North American Aboriginal peoples. Most of the researchers who have contributed to the development of the ethnography of communication, however, have retained the original focus on spoken language; these include John Gumperz (1972), Joel Sherzer (1974), Gerry Philipsen (1992), Iffat Farah (1992), Dan Slobin (1967), Richard Bauman (1974), Susan Philips (1983), Susan Irvin-Tripp (1964), and Muriel Saville-Troike (1982).

As conceived by Hymes, the ethnography of communication is founded on the theoretical assumption that structured patterns of language use within speech communities are co-terminous and interactive with patterns of social action and social organization. Farah (1998, cited in Johnstone and Marcellino, 2010) elaborates on Hymes' theoretical perspective, which was, at least in part, a reaction against the primacy of Noam Chomsky's (1957) formal linguistics, with its focus on a universal context-free grammar and ideal speaker-listeners (Keating, 2001):

> [T]he study of language must concern itself with describing and analyzing the ability of the native speakers to use language for communication in real situations (communicative competence) rather than limiting itself to describing the potential ability of the ideal speaker/

listener to produce grammatically correct sentences (linguistic competence). Speakers of a language in particular communities are able to communicate with each other in a manner which is not only correct but also appropriate to the sociocultural context. This ability involves a shared knowledge of the linguistic code as well as of the socio-cultural rules, norms and values which guide the conduct and interpretation of speech and other channels of communication in a community.

(p. 125)

In coining the term 'communicative competence' to describe what an individual needs to know and be capable of doing, both linguistically and socially, in order to communicate effectively within a particular speech community, Hymes contributed a concept that would become widely used in language education from the late 1970s onward, particularly in second-language and foreign-language teaching (Canale and Swain, 1980; Savignon, 1983; Candlin, 2001). Hymes (1972) describes what such communicative competence involves, using the experience of a child as an example:

We have to account for the fact that a normal child acquires knowledge of sentences not only as grammatical but also as appropriate. He or she acquires competence as to when to speak, when not, and as to what to talk about with whom, when, where and in what manner. In short, a child becomes able to accomplish a repertoire of speech acts, to take part in speech events, and to evaluate their accomplishment by others. This competence, moreover, is integral with attitudes, values, and motivations concerning language, its features and uses, and integral with competence for, and attitudes towards, the interrelation of language with the other code of communicative conduct [viz. social interaction].

(pp. 277–278)

For practitioners of the ethnography of communication, then, the central question to pursue in investigating the communicative norms of a speech community is the following (Saville-Troike, 1982): 'What does a speaker need to know in order to communicate appropriately within a particular speech community, and how does he or she learn?' (p. 2). Hymes (1967) elaborates on this question to offer a guide to researchers intending to investigate a speech community's 'rules of speaking':

What [forms of language] are used, where and when, among whom, and for what purpose and with what result, to say what, in what way; subject to what norms of interaction and of interpretation; as instances of what speech acts and genres of speaking? How do community and personal beliefs, values and practices impinge upon the use of language, and upon the acquisition of such language by children?

(p. 8)

For an ethnographer of communication undertaking to explore the rules of speaking that organize communicative interaction within a particular speech community, two kinds of research are necessary – emic and etic. A significant part of the culture-specific knowledge needed if one is to answer Hymes' questions above requires an emic, or insider-like, perspective, which can only be gained through extended experience as a participant-observer within the group under study, with a year of participant observation within the speech community being sometimes mentioned as a minimum duration (Saville-Troike, 1982). Depending on the ethnographer's status within the speech community and access to reliable informants, the data to be collected might include observational field-notes, interviews with a variety of different individuals, artistic and other material artefacts, as well as secondary sources providing background on the history, demographics, and social organization of the group.

For the second kind of inquiry – conducted from an etic, or outsider, position – Hymes (1972) offers researchers a heuristic acronym for identifying the various facets of a speech event: SPEAKING. Hymes points to eight such facets – *s*etting, *p*articipants, *e*nds, *a*ct sequences, *k*ey, *i*nstrumentalities, *n*orms, and *g*enre. Farah (1998: 26) describes the components of this heuristic in useful detail:

> **(S)** Setting including the time and place, physical aspects of the situation such as arrangement of furniture in the classroom; **(P)** participant identity including personal characteristics such as age and sex, social status, relationship with each other; **(E)** ends including the purpose of the event itself as well as the individual goals of the participants; **(A)** act, sequence or how speech acts are organized within a speech event and what topic/s are addressed; **(K)** key or the tone and manner in which something is said or written; **(I)** instrumentalities or the linguistic code i.e. language, dialect, variety and channel i.e. speech or writing; **(N)** norm or the standard socio-cultural rules of interaction and interpretation; and **(G)** genre or type of event such as lecture, poem, letter.
>
> *(p. 127)*

Hymes' acronym is reminiscent of literary critic and rhetorician Kenneth Burke's (1989) 'dramatistic pentad' – act, scene, agent, agency, and purpose – which Burke proposed as an analytical tool for examining discursive events – an influence that Hymes (2003) readily acknowledged. Indeed, Hymes studied under Burke at Indiana University, and the two scholars subsequently maintained a decades-long correspondence and had a mutual influence on one another's work (Jordan, 2005).

Notable book-length studies employing the ethnography of communication as a methodology include those of Gerry Philipsen (1992), *Speaking Culturally: Explorations in Social Communication*; Joel Sherzer (1983), *Kuna Ways of Speaking: An Ethnographic Perspective*; Richard Bauman (1983), *Let Your Words Be Few: Symbolism and Silence among Seventeenth Century Quakers*; Ron Scollon and Suzanne Wong Scollon (1979), *Linguistic Convergence: An Ethnography of Speaking at Fort Chipewyan*; Iffat Farah (1992), *Literacy Practices in a Rural Community in Pakistan*; and Cazden, John, and Hymes (1972), *Functions of Language in the Classroom*.

Analysing interview data in an ethnographic study

In this section of the chapter I describe two episodes that occurred when I was analyzing interview transcripts during the preparation of my book *Writing the Economy: Activity, Genre and Technology in the World of Banking*, an ethnographic study of the intellectual work and discourse practices of economists at the Bank of Canada that explores the role of writing and texts, used in combination with computer-run economic models, in the collaborative activities of knowledge-building, policy-making, and public communication. Earlier in the chapter I mentioned Clifford Geertz's (1973: 56–57) suggestion to ethnographers that they search in their data for instances of 'experience-near' concepts – local concepts created by the social group under study – and that they attempt to 'place [these experience-near concepts] in illuminating connection' with 'concepts [that] theorists have fashioned to capture the general features of social life' – referred to by Geertz as 'experience-distant' concepts. For Geertz, making such 'illuminating connections' was an integral part of producing a 'thick description' of the group's meaning-making activities and shared conceptual world.

At one point, as I was analysing the transcript of an interview with a senior Bank of Canada executive, I recognized an 'experience-near concept' – in this case, a characterization of the bank as an 'information-processing factory' – a place where the bank's economists collaborate in interpreting, through the medium of writing and texts, the meanings of statistical data, these meanings eventually being converted into specialized economic knowledge, which in turn is conveyed in non-mathematical written discourse to the governor of the bank and his senior colleagues for use in making decisions about the country's monetary policy. Here is how the executive described this collaborative knowledge-building:[3]

> What this place is when it comes to monetary policy is a big information-processing factory, structured like a pyramid. Enormous amounts of information come in at the bottom – all sorts of statistics covering a wide range of territory: financial markets, product markets, factor markets, and so on. And what we do is channel this information upwards through the different levels in the organization, distilling and synthesizing it. As the information moves upwards, through increasingly senior staff, it's analyzed in ways that are more and more pertinent to the decisions the Governing Council has to take, with people asking themselves: 'What are the implications of this information? What does it mean for the job that we do, *for conducting monetary policy?* And given that the analysis has to get transported from level to level, the question is, 'Well, how's it going to get done?' And there's been a very great reliance put on the written page around this institution.

When I saw this passage in the transcript, representing, in Geertz's terms, an experience-near concept, I was struck by its resonance with an experience-distant concept conceived by Bruno Latour and Steve Woolgar (1979): the 'inscription' of scientific knowledge, a concept derived from Latour's observations of the work of scientists and technicians in a research laboratory in California, observations conducted over a two-year period. Latour and Woolgar used the term 'inscription' to refer to the process of collaborative knowledge-building that occurs in many research-intensive professional organizations. Within this type of organization, empirical data reflecting some aspect of the external world relevant to the organization's mandate is progressively analysed, collaboratively and with the use of relevant theories, in a sequence of texts – here taken to include both documents and other semiotic forms such as graphs and numerical tables. During this collaborative work, successive interpretations of the data are negotiated among members of the organization, which eventually leads to a consensual knowledge claim that is presented in a research report, published in a scientific journal and possibly accepted in due course by the larger research community.

What I find significant about this parallel between, on the one hand, the bank executive's metaphorical description of the collaborative process of analysing statistical data and of trans-forming it, through the medium of writing and texts, into specialized knowledge used by the Bank's the senior executives in making monetary policy decisions and, on the other hand, Latour and Woolgar's notion of the inscription of knowledge is how this 'illuminating con-nection' helped me, as a non-specialist, to begin establishing a bridge into the conceptual world of the bank's economists. The association that I was able to make between the 'experience-near' concept articulated by the executive – the metaphor of the bank as an 'information-processing factory' – and Latour and Woolgar's 'experience-distant' concept of knowledge inscription gave me a foothold to begin exploring the conceptual landscape of the economists' work environment.

A related episode occurred a little later in my research. It began as I transcribed three interviews with senior economists. In each interview, I had asked the economist to talk about the Bank of Canada's work of monitoring the country's economy and directing its monetary policy. As I compared their respective descriptions of this work, I recognized a common theme: each of the economists talked of the institution's role as one of steering the economy on a course into the future, towards a particular goal:

When you're conducting monetary policy, you have to think of three questions: First, where's the economy currently? Second, where do you want the economy to go? And third, how are you going to get there?

(Economist 1)

Decisions on monetary policy are taken in a forward-looking way. The whole process is about how to get the economy from where we are now, with the current inflation rate, to where we want to be, the inflation-control targets. To do this, we have to make decisions about the appropriate path of interest rates. So all the economic analysis coming up to us from the staff is used to address one question: 'Are we on track?' As new information comes in, it changes one's views, and if evidence piles up that we're not on track, then at some point the [senior decision-makers] will have to make a decision about changing the policy.

(Economist 2)

Essentially, what the monetary-policy process does is this: you've got an objective; you say, for example: 'Here's where we want the economy to be in three years, at 2 per cent inflation.' So each quarter there are some new events. And you say, 'OK, given these events, given what we think is going to happen over the near term, and given how we figure the economy works, what path for interest rates will get us to our target?' Now obviously there could be several paths. But we want a smooth landing when we get to the target point; we'd like the economy to come in at that point, not run past it.

(Economist 3)

I found this common theme in the three interviews to be significant in two ways. The first is that it serves as a prime example of what Geertz (1983) calls 'convergent data': shared perspectives among the 'multiply connected individuals' within a social group – part of 'a mutually reinforcing network of social understandings' (pp. 156–157). Such instances of convergent data often point to an important constituent of a group's shared conceptual world.

Second, I was struck by another theoretical parallel, this time involving a passage from Edwin Hutchins' (1993) paper 'Learning to navigate', in which he discusses the concept of the 'activity system' (Cole and Engeström, 1993): a local, historically and culturally situated sphere of collaborative endeavour, in which thinking, knowing, and learning are distributed across a number of people and their work practices and, at the same time, mediated by a repertoire of culturally constructed tools, all with the larger aim of accomplishing communally defined goals (Smart, 2003). In the relevant passage from Hutchins' paper that I remembered, he gives the example of an activity system known as the 'fix cycle', which is enacted collaboratively by crew members of a large ship as it heads into a harbour. Several crew members located in different parts of the ship simultaneously take the bearings of landmarks in the harbour entrance; this information is then reported by telephone to the pilot house, where another crew member records it on a navigation chart and performs directional calculations to guide the ship's helmsman. Hutchins elaborates upon the larger aim of the fix cycle:

The central computations in navigation answer the questions, Where are we? and If we proceed in a certain way for a specified time, where will we be? Answering the first question is called 'fixing the position' or getting a fix. Answering the second is called 'dead reckoning'. It is necessary to answer the first in order to answer the second, and it is necessary to answer the second to keep the ship out of danger. This is especially true for large ships that lack maneuverability. In order to make a turn in restricted waters in a big ship, it is not good enough to know when one has reached the point where the ship is to make the turn. Because of the lag in maneuvering response of such a massive object, when a ship reaches the turn point, if it has not already taken action to make the turn, it is too late to do so.

(p. 39)

Again, I was able to make an 'illuminating connection' between the 'experience-near' concept used by the three economists in describing the bank's role of directing Canada's monetary policy as one of steering the country's economy on a course into the future and the 'experience-distant' concept of the activity system, as illustrated by Hutchins' example of the ship and its navigational 'fix cycle'. Just as Hutchins used the theoretical idea of the activity system to depict how knowledge required for navigating a large ship into harbour was collaboratively created and applied through multi-individual observations and acts of reasoning mediated by cultural tools, so the notion of the activity system offers a way of conceptualizing the bank's activity of knowledge-building and policy-making. The conduct of monetary policy can be viewed as an activity system in which bank economists collaborate in repeatedly taking 'sightings' of significant trends in statistical data on the Canadian economy and then interpreting these trends by using a set of written genres, together with analytical tools such as computer-run economic models, to produce specialized knowledge that is applied by the Bank's senior decision-makers in taking actions to influence the future course of the nation's economy. This was an important step in my research, in that looking at the bank's monetary policy process as an activity system, together with the recognition of the institution's collaborative analytical activity as a process of knowledge inscription, allowed me to see, and then to describe in an ethnographic account, important aspects of the bank's approach to knowledge-building and policy-making, while also providing a framework for analysing other related data as I collected it.

Further reading

Farah, I. (1998) 'The ethnography of communication', in N. Hornberger and P. Corson (eds.) *Encyclopedia of Language and Education*. Volume 8: *Research Methods in Language and Education*. Dordrecht: Kluwer, pp. 125–127.

Hammersley, M., and Atkinson, P. (1985) *Ethnography: Principles and Practice*. Second Edition. London: Routledge.

Geertz, C. (1983) *Local Knowledge*. New York: Basic Books.

Geertz, C. (1973) *The Interpretation of Cultures*. New York: Basic Books.

Gumperz, J. and Hymes, D. (eds.) *Directions in Sociolinguistics*. New York: Holt, Rinehart & Winston.

Clifford, J. and Marcus, G. (1986) *Writing Culture: The Poetics and Politics of Ethnography*.

Saville-Troike, M. (1982). *The Ethnography of Communication: An Introduction*. Oxford, UK: Basil Blackford.

Notes

1 Descriptions of these alternative approaches to ethnography can be found in *The Handbook of Qualitative Research* (Eds. Norman Denzin and Yvonne Lincoln, 2000).
2 The phrase "thick description" has been taken by some methodologists and researchers to refer simply to a highly detailed account of a particular culture – an understandable inference, given the face meaning of the phrase. However, a close look at Geertz's methodological writing and his own ethnographic accounts reveals his intention to give the phrase the more specific meaning ascribed to it in this chapter.
3 The excerpts of interview transcripts included in the chapter have been edited to remove false starts, hesitations, fillers, and redundancy.

References

Agar, M. (1980) *The Professional Stranger: An Informal Introduction to Ethnography*. New York: Academic Press.
Anderson, N. (1940) *Men on the Move*. Chicago, IL: University of Chicago Press.

Asad, T. (1973) *Anthropology and the Colonial Encounter*. Dryden, NY: Ithaca Press.

Auty, K. and Briggs, D. (2004) 'Koori court, Victoria: magistrates court (Koori Court) Act 2002', *Law, Text, Culture*, 8: 7–37.

Bateson, G. (1936) *Naven: A Survey of the Problems Suggested by a Composite Picture of the Culture of a New Guinea Tribe Drawn From Three Points of View*. Palo Alto, CA: Stanford University Press.

Bauman, R. (1974) 'Speaking in the light: The role of the Quaker minister', in R. Bauman and J. Sherzer (eds.) *Explorations in the Ethnography of Speaking*. Cambridge: Cambridge University Press, pp. 144–162.

Bauman, R. (1983) *Let Your Words Be Few: Symbolism and Silence among Seventeenth Century Quakers*. Cambridge: Cambridge University Press.

Bloomfield, L. (1933) *Language*. New York: Holt, Rinehart & Winston.

Boas, F. (1897) 'The social organization and the secret societies of the Kwakiutl Indians', *Report of the U.S. National Museum for 1897*, Washington, DC: Smithsonian Institution, pp. 311–738.

Burke, K. (1989) *On Symbols and Society*. Chicago, IL: University of Chicago Press.

Canale, M. and Swain, M. (1980) 'Theoretical bases of communicative approaches to second language teaching and testing', *Applied Linguistics*, 1: 1–47.

Candlin, C. and Mercer, N. (eds) (2001) *English Language Teaching in Its Social Context: A Reader*. London: Routledge.

Cazden, C., John, V., and Hymes, D. (eds.) (1972) *Functions of Language in the Classroom*. New York: Teachers College Press.

Charmaz, K. (2006) *Constructing Grounded Theory: A Practical Guide Through Qualitative Analysis*. Thousand Oaks, CA: Sage Publications.

Chomsky, N. (1957) *Syntactic Structures*. The Hague/Paris: Mouton.

Clifford, J. and Marcus, G. (eds.) (1986) *Writing Culture: The Poetics and Politics of Ethnography*. Berkeley, CA: University of California Press.

Denzin, N. (1997) *Interpretive Ethnography: Ethnographic Practices for the 21st Century*. Thousand Oaks, CA: Sage Publications.

Denzin, N. and Lincoln, Y. (eds.) (2000) *The Handbook of Qualitative Research*. Second Edition. Thousand Oaks, CA: Sage Publications.

Ervin-Tripp, S. (1964) 'An analysis of the interaction of language, topic, and listener', *American Anthropologist*, 66: 86–102.

Farah, I. (1992) *Literacy Practices in a Rural Community in Pakistan*. Unpublished doctoral dissertation, University of Pennsylvania, PA, USA.

Farah, I. (1998) 'The ethnography of communication', in N. Hornberger and P. Corson (eds.) *Encyclopedia of Language and Education: Volume 8: Research Methods in Language and Education*. Dordrecht: Kluwer, pp. 125–127.

Geertz, C. (1973) *The Interpretation of Cultures*. New York: Basic Books.

Geertz, C. (1983) *Local Knowledge*. New York: Basic Books.

Glaser, B. (2001) *The Grounded Theory Perspective: Conceptualization Contrasted with Description*. Mill Valley, CA: Sociology Press.

Glaser, B. and Strauss, A. (1967) *The Discovery of Grounded Theory: Strategies for Qualitative Research*. New York: Aldine.

Goetz, J. and Breneman, E. (1988) 'Desegregation and black students' experiences in two rural southern elementary schools', *Elementary School Journal*, 88: 489–502.

Gumperz, J. (1972) *Language in Social Groups*. Palo Alto, CA: University of Stanford Press.

Gumperz J. and Hymes, D. (eds.) (1964) Special issue of *American Anthropologist*, 66.

Hammersley, M. and Atkinson, P. (1985) *Ethnography: Principles and Practice*. Second Edition. London: Routledge.

Heath, S. B. (1980) *Ways with Words: Language, Life and Work in Communities and Classrooms*. Cambridge: Cambridge University Press.

Hess, G. (1991) *School Restructuring, Chicago Style*. Newbury Park, CA: Sage Publications.

Hutchins, E. (1983) 'Learning to navigate', in S. Chaiklin and J. Lave (eds.) *Understanding Practice: Perspectives on Activity and Context*. Cambridge: Cambridge University, pp. 35–63.

Hymes, D. (1962) 'The ethnography of speaking', in T. Gladwin and W. Sturtevant (eds.) *Anthropology and Human Behavior*. Washington, DC: The Anthropology Society of Washington, pp. 13–53.

Hymes, D. (1967) 'Models of the interaction of language and social setting', *Journal of Social Issues*, 23: 8–28.

Hymes, D. (1972) 'Models of the interactions of language and social life', in J. Gumperz and D. Hymes (eds.) *Directions in Sociolinguistics*. New York: Holt, Rinehart & Winston, pp. 35–71.

Hymes, D. (1981) *In Vain I Tried to Tell You: Essays in Native American Ethnopoetics*. Philadelphia, PA: University of Pennsylvania Press.

Hymes, D. (2003) *Now I Know Only So Far: Essays in Ethnopoetics*. Lincoln, NE: University of Nebraska Press.

Irvin-Tripp, S. (1964) 'An analysis of the interaction of language, topic, and listener', *American Anthropologist*, 66: 86–102.

Jackell, R. (1988) *Moral Mazes: The World of Corporate Managers*. New York: Oxford University Press.

Jafarey, A. (2009) 'Conversations with kidney vendors in Pakistan: an ethnographic study', *Hastings Center Report*, 39: 29–44.

Johnstone, B. and Marcellino, W. (2010) 'Dell Hymes and the ethnography of communication', in B. Johnstone, R. Wodak, and P. Kerswill (eds.) *The Sage Handbook of Sociolinguistics*. London: Sage Publications, pp. 57–66.

Jordan, J. (2005) 'Dell Hymes, Kenneth Burke's "identification", and the birth of sociolinguistics', *Rhetoric Review*, 24: 264–279.

Keating, E. (2001) 'The ethnography of communication', in P. Atkinson, A. Coffey, S. Delamont, J., L. Lofland, and L. Lofland (eds.) *Handbook of Ethnography*. London: Sage Publications, pp. 285–301.

Labov, W. (1966) *The Social Stratification of English in New York City*. Washington, DC: Center for Applied Linguistics.

Latour, B. and Woolgar, S. (1979) *Laboratory Life: The Social Construction of Scientific Facts*. Beverly Hills, CA: Sage.

LeCompte, M. and Preissle, J. (1993) *Ethnography and Qualitative Design in Educational Research*. Second Edition. New York: Academic Press.

Liebow, E. (1966) *Tally's Corner: A Study of Negro Streetcorner Men*. Boston, MA: Little, Brown & Company.

Lynd, H. and Lynd, R. (1937) *Middletown in Transition: A Study in Cultural Conflicts*. New York: Harcourt, Brace & Company.

Malinowkski, B. (1922) *Argonauts of the Western Pacific*. New York: Holt, Rinehart & Winston.

Mead, M. (1928) *Coming of Age in Samoa*. New York: Morrow.

Merriam, S. (1988) *Case Study Research in Education: A Qualitative Approach*. San Francisco, CA: Jossey-Bass.

Mountz, A. and Wright, R. (1996) 'Daily life in the transnational migrant community of San Agustín, Oaxaca and Poughkeepsie, New York', *Diaspora*, 5: 403–428.

Orr, J. (1996) *Talking About Machines: An Ethnography of a Modern Job*. Ithaca, NY: Cornell University Press.

Philips, S. (1983) *The Invisible Culture: Communication in Classroom and Community on the Warm Springs Reservation*. New York: Longman.

Philipsen, G. (1992) *Speaking Culturally: Explorations in Social Communication*. Albany, NY: State University of New York Press.

Prior, P. (1998) *Writing/Disciplinarity: A Sociohistoric Account of Literate Activity in the Academy*. Mahwah, NJ: Lawrence Erlbaum Associates.

Richardson, F. and Walker, C. (1948) *Human Relations in an Expanding Company: A Study of the Manufacturing Departments in the Endicott Plant of the International Business Machines Corporation*. New Haven, CT: Yale University Labor Management Center.

Savignon, S. (1983) *Communicative Competence: Theory and Classroom Practice*. Reading, MA: Addison-Wesley.

Saville-Troike, M. (1982) *The Ethnography of Communication: An Introduction*. Oxford, UK: Basil Blackford.

Schütz, A. (1974) *Collected Papers: The Problem of Social Reality*. New York: Springer.

Scollon, R. and Scollon, S. (1979) *Linguistic Convergence: An Ethnography of Speaking at Fort Chipewyan*. Alberta. New York: Academic Press.

Sherzer, J. (1974) 'Namakke, Sunmakke, Kormakki: Three types of cuna speech event', in R. Bauman and J. Sherzer (eds.) *Explorations in the Ethnography of Speaking*. Cambridge: Cambridge University Press, pp. 263–282.

Sherzer, J. (1983) *Kuna Ways of Speaking: An Ethnographic Perspective in Contemporary Israel*. Austin, TX: University of Texas Press.

Slobin, D. (1967) *A Field Manual for Cross-Cultural Study of the Acquisition of Communicative Competence*. Berkeley, CA: Language Behavior Research Lab.

Smart, G. (2003) 'A central bank's "communications strategy": the interplay of activity, discourse genres and technology in a time of organizational change', in C. Bazerman and D. Russell (eds.) *Writing Selves/Writing Societies: Research From Activity Perspectives*. Fort Collins, CO: The WAC Clearinghouse and *Mind, Culture, & Activity*.

Smart, G. (2006) *Writing the Economy: Activity, Genre and Technology in the World of Banking*. London: Equinox.

Strauss, A. and Corbin, J. (1998) *Basics of Qualitative Research: Techniques and Procedures for Developing Grounded Theory*. Thousand Oaks, CA: Sage Publications.

Swales, J. (1998) *Other Floors, Other Voices: A Textography of a Small University Building*. Mahwah, NJ: Lawrence Erlbaum.

Van Maanen, J. (1988) *Tales of the Field: On Writing Ethnography*. Chicago, IL: University of Chicago Press.

Vidich, A. and Lyman, S. (1998) 'Qualitative methods: their history in sociology and anthropology', in N. Denzin and Y. Lincoln (eds.) *The Landscape of Qualitative Research: Theories and Issues*. Thousand Oaks, CA: Sage Publications, pp. 41–110.

Whyte, W. F. (1943) *Street Corner Society: The Social Structure of an Italian Slum*. Chicago, IL: University of Chicago Press.

12

Discourse analysis and linguistic anthropology

Justin B. Richland

Introduction

Pick up the latest volumes of any of the leading linguistic anthropology and discourse analysis journals—*The Journal of Linguistic Anthropology, Language in Society, The Journal of Pragmatics*, and *Discourse and Society*, to name a few—and you might be struck by the broad diversity of analytic practices and objects of inquiry comfortably gathered in each. All will undoubtedly be essays that revolve around an exploration of the norms, structures, and practices of communication and of the ways in which these inform and/or are informed by the sociocultural and political–economic events and forces of which they are a part. And they will do so in ways that span the full analytic and methodological spectrum. Some of the studies will be centrally concerned with describing the most micro-interactional syntactic and grammatical details of contextually situated language practices. But they will be published side by side with others which endeavor to account for the most macro-sociological forces that inform communication and for the degree to which those forces naturalize the differential political–economic power and authority of some gendered, racialized, nationalized practices and of the social actors who use them.

In many ways the offerings of these journals seem interchangeable. And yet it might be surprising to know that the rapprochement between linguistic anthropology and discourse analysis is a relatively recent phenomenon, and one that is not as nearly complete as might first appear. Of course there is considerable overlap, particularly given the influence that interactional socio-linguistics, conversation analysis, the ethnography of communication, and semiotics have played in both fields, at least since the last quarter of the twentieth century. Nonetheless, in speaking directly to the relationship between discourse analysis and linguistic anthropology, Blommaert *et al.* (2001) note that, in "the absence of any dialogue between [the two fields], the differences are more striking than the similarities" (p. 5). While acknowledging the commitment that both have in teasing out the manifold and complex relationships between language, culture, and society, Blommaert and his co-authors note a tendency in the former to be concerned more with deconstructing the political forces informing texts and discourses, usually of the mass-mediated variety, while the latter takes as its mission the ethnographic investigation of face-to-face inter-action and, when it is oriented to the political, the exploration of the ways in which broader cultural norms shape beliefs about language and about its uses.

Of course this is a vast oversimplification, as the authors acknowledge. But, despite this and despite the fact that today the two fields may be mutually influencing each other more than ever before, it is still the case, I would argue, that a discernable divide separates them.

This chapter is offered in the same spirit in which Blommaert and his co-authors put forward their exploration of the analytic space between linguistic anthropology and discourse analysis, namely to improve "the transatlantic contact between the traditions" (Blommaert *et al.*, 2001: 5). To accomplish this, I will argue that some of the enduring incompatibilities between discourse analysis and linguistic anthropology stem, at least partly, from the historical foundations of the two fields and their rather different sociopolitical and cultural milieux. I will suggest that these foundations shape the research produced in each, an influence that, while increasingly muted, nonetheless compels a central analytic trajectory, which pulls at least some new scholarship from each field in different directions.

It is undoubtedly true that both fields are concerned with the nexus between language, culture, and society, and scholars in both would generally subscribe to the image that Silverstein (2004) offers of that nexus as one "forever in dialectical process" (p. 645). Still, I will argue that the particular sociohistoric contingencies informing the development of linguistic anthropology in North America and of discourse analysis in Europe continue to assert an influence on how scholars raised in each tradition orient to the exploration of that dialectic—a process that results, inadvertently or not, in a relatively different emphasis on one part of that dialectic over the other. More specifically, linguistic anthropology has been shaped by a set of interests—including a Boasian concern with "salvaging" dying languages and cultures (a broader disciplinary division of labor that keeps sociocultural phenomena within the scope of other, larger, anthropological subdisciplines) and with challenging the supremacy of Bloomfieldian and Chomskian formal linguistics—that have long oriented the discipline more toward revealing and exploring the sociocultural dimensions of language than toward exploring the role that language plays in the constitution of culture or society. Discourse analysis, on the other hand, and not just in its most critical modalities, locates its foundations less in linguistics than in the social sciences, particularly sociology—whether that be interactionist, ethnomethodological, processual, or critical–theoretical—and in the challenges they offered to various forms of macro-sociological structural functionalism and/or historical materialism (see e.g. Heritage, 1984; Slembrouck, 2001). As such, the analytic trajectories that shape the discourse analytic project have more often queried what language in use can tell us about society and culture, and only more rarely (and more recently) considered what culture and society can tell us about language.

Of course there are plenty of exceptions to these overgeneralizations, including very some long-standing and productive collaborations between individuals trained in each tradition, or trained in one but now read in both (e.g. Rampton, 2007; Collins *et al.*, 2008; van Dijk, 2009; Scollon, 2001). And yet I would argue that the influence of the histories of these two fields continue to shape them and help explain why it is that scholars of discourse analysis and linguistic anthropology are indeed converging around a common set of analytic interests commitments while at the same time, like sailors on passing ships, they find, on closer view, that gaps still separate them (Blommaert and Bulcaen, 2000; Blommaert *et al.*, 2001).

To explore the continued influence of the different teleological demands of linguistic anthropology and discourse analysis in the limited space that remains, I look first to some recapitulations of the scope and history of the two fields offered by leading scholars in each (Kroskrity, 2000; Slembrouck, 2001; Duranti, 2003; Gee, 2005). I offer these less for the truth value of the claims they make about the past, and more for what they might performatively reveal about the current analytic commitments and goals of both fields today. Because I am trained in linguistic anthropology, and others in this volume are far more qualified than I am to relate the history of discourse analysis, I will give greater attention to the side of this story offered by Duranti and Kroskrity, and particularly to the ways in which Duranti's vision of certain analytic incompatibilities within the linguistic anthropology can be extended to the on-going differences between discourse analysis and linguistic anthropology as well. As such, and depending on where you look, discourse analysis and linguistic anthropology can look increasingly similar or stubbornly different in their epistemological, teleological, and sociopolitical aims and trajectories.

Despite this, I am convinced that there is considerable opportunity for further rapprochement between linguistic anthropology and discourse analysis, a coming together that need not compromise the best aspects of each scholarly traditions or fail to meet what may likely endure as their differing analytic trajectories. In short, I believe there are solid examples of scholarship that gives equal weight to both sides of the language–culture/society dialectical process, inquiries that move analytically from language to culture/society and back again. Building on lessons from one such example (Silverstein, 1985, 2003), I will close with an analysis from my own research on the legal language of the contemporary Hopi tribal nation, to suggest the inroads that can be gained in our understanding of linguistic and sociocultural and political phenomena when we endeavor to move beyond the analytic boundaries that remain between discourse analysis and linguistic anthropology.

Origin stories, programmatic paradigms and analytic trajectories

Society in and through language: an origin story of discourse analysis

I would hazard that most linguistic anthropologists and discourse analysts would agree that origin stories—those interactional, textual and performative events in which the story of "how we got to here" is told—are analytically valuable as much for what they say about the present conditions of their expression as for what they do about the pasts they represent. They are useful for shedding light not only on what a narrator *intends* to say in telling the story at a given moment in social place and time, but also in discerning the various sociocultural norms, structures and practices that both shape and are shaped by the story performance.

Consider, then, the story that Stef Slembrouck (2001) offers for the origins of critical discourse analysis (CDA). As he tells it, critical discourse analysis, particularly as formulated by Norman Fairclough in the 1980s and 1990s, emerged in response to sociocultural and political economic events and trends occurring at the time in the global North. More specifically, Slembrouck points to events in Western Europe and the US, such as the rise to power of Thatcher and Regan styles of conservatism, the dismantling of the welfare state, and major increases of in-migrating populations, largely from Eastern Europe and the global South, which resulted in a period characterized by the author as Western Europe's "most radical post-war transformation" (2001: 34). Slembrouck couples these events with the rise, in European academia, of (post)structuralism and semiotics, the so-called "linguistic turn" of social science and its particular resonance within cultural studies and post-colonial scholarship, to argue that the context was ripe for a reinvigorated critical agenda that took discourse analysis as one of its key modalities (Slembrouck, 2001). Though he acknowledges that other "attempts at staging a critical agenda in language enquiry" also occurred at this time, it is nonetheless his contention that cultural studies, with "its interest in mass culture and consumer society … became a major source of inspiration for early work in the critical analysis of discourse" (Slembrouck, 2001: 35).

To that end Slembrouck points specifically to an April 1990 symposium organized by Teun van Dijk in Amsterdam as the watershed event where "perceptions … reflected an urgency about moving away from a predominantly descriptive … (socio)linguistics" (p. 35), and toward a mode of enquiry that "advocated a focus on the analysis and explanation of the constitutive role of language use within institutional practices and within the larger social ordering of institutional domains" (Slembrouck, 2001: 36). And thus, says Slembrouck, critical discourse analysis was born (see also van Dijk, 1993, Caldas-Coulthard and Coulthard, 1996; Fairclough and Wodak, 1997).

I offer this origin story as an example of the extent to which sociocultural phenomena and their explication rest not only (or even) at the foundation of CDA's development, but also at the center of its ongoing project today. It is telling, I would argue, that what Slembrouck sees as the signal contribution that CDA makes toward understanding the dialectic relationship between socio-cultural phenomena and language phenomena is its pointing up what language can tell us about society and its forces. Linguistics, as the descriptive analysis of language forms and practices, appears primarily as the alternative against which CDA defines itself and, later, as the modality by which the analysis shall be undertaken, rather than as something that contributes to the ultimate agenda of CDA itself.

Some may argue that this centering of sociocultural phenomena and considerations points more to the extent to which the deep analysis of language forms and practices constitutes the taken for granted (or otherwise presumed) baseline that necessarily informs CDA. Others might suggest that, by using a social history of critical discourse analysis, the most overtly political branch of discourse analysis, I am unduly weighting the evidence in support of my claims.

To both, however, I would suggest that the foregrounding of sociocultural and political economic problems as the ends of this scholarship, and the treatment of language primarily as a means to that end, is also observable in other, more general surveys of discourse analysis. Consider the second edition of James Paul Gee's widely read volume *An Introduction to Discourse Analysis* (2005). In the opening paragraphs, Gee first establishes that, for him, "a primary function of human language [is] to support the performance of social activities and social identities and to support human affiliation within cultures, social groups, and institutions" (p. 1). The book, and thus (by extension) the field of discourse analysis it introduces, "is concerned with a theory and a method for studying how language gets recruited … to enact specific social activities and social identities" (Gee, 2005). This, he then explains, requires arguing for and establishing that "language-in-use is everywhere and always 'political,' " a statement he immediately follows with a paragraph that explains what it is, precisely, that he means by the term "political" (Gee, 2005: 2). Of course, Gee's book spends ample time exploring various dimensions of linguistic structure and practice, from the micro-level details of syntax and grammar to the meso-level considerations of intertextuality, genre, interactional sequence, sociolinguistic variation and to the largest macro-level concerns with ("big D") "Discourse," habitus, and sign systems. And in numerous other works Gee has established how discourse analysis can help us better understand a variety of sociocultural practices that, we would undoubtedly acknowledge, are language-based, including (most notably) literacy and schooling (e.g. Gee, 1996, 2004, 2005, 2007). But, for all this attention to the language of discourse, the overriding telos of the kind of analysis called for by Gee is to demonstrate the ways in which broader sociological and cultural phenomena are presupposed and entailed by that "language-in-use." Like Slembrouck's history of CDA, so too with Gee's more generalized review of discourse analysis: both suggest that, in exploring, interpreting, and explaining the dialectic relationship between language and culture/society, the enduring analytic trajectory of discourse analysis, with some recent and noteworthy exceptions (e.g. van Dijk, 2009), resides in showing what language can tell us about society rather than the other way around.

Indeed some have argued that this analytic emphasis is implied in the very name of the field itself. Van Dijk points this out for critical discourse analysis, suggesting that, because the "critical study [of discourse] is not a ready made 'method' of analysis, but also has theoretical and applied dimensions" (Van Dijk, 2010), the field would be more aptly named "critical discourse studies."

Language in and through culture: a programmatic review of linguistic anthropology

Compare the way these discourse analysts explain the analytic trajectories of their field to similar efforts recently undertaken by some US based linguistic anthropologists, and the difference is striking. Take for example Alessandro Duranti's (2003) programmatic review of the field, where he identifies the diversity of linguistic anthropological scholarship today as constituting three paradigms, each of which holds out a different measure of the purposes and perspectives to be gained by viewing language in, through and as culture. Duranti's distinctions are productive given the purposes of this chapter, particularly insofar as he suggests that the field can be seen as constituting "a set of distinct and often not fully compatible practices," (Duranti, 2003: 323), an incompatibility grounded in different orientations to the language–culture relationship, which echoes the enduring differences observable between linguistic anthropology and discourse analysis more generally.

The earliest and first paradigm emerged in the late nineteenth and early twentieth century, and is characterized by the anthropological linguistics initiated by Boas (1911) and elaborated by the likes of Alfred Kroeber, Edward Sapir, and their first students. It was originally oriented to the project of descriptive linguistics for the purpose of salvaging non-Indo-European languages (particularly Native American languages) that were believed to be on their way to extinction. Work inspired by this original impulse can still be seen today in linguistic anthropology, particularly that which is dedicated to the documentation and revitalization of endangered languages. Significantly, while Boas was explicit in understanding that the value of these salvage efforts lay not just in preserving languages, but in the ways of life that they revealed, it was not long before this idea of language as a window onto cultural structures fell by the wayside. Indeed, most of the third generation of anthropological linguists entered a field largely understood through a kind of "service mentality," tolerated in anthropology departments only insofar as they could offer sociocultural anthropologists with field language training. Sapir is reported to have even started recommending potential graduate students to seek degrees in linguistics programs rather than in anthropology (Darnell, 1990). Nonetheless, this is also the paradigm that introduces the notion of linguistic relativity to the world, largely through the so-called "Sapir–Whorf Hypothesis" and through it the idea that the structures of different languages both presupposed and contributed to the structures of culture they lived in and from which they understood their world (see e.g. Whorf, 1956). Thus, while an enduring aspect of the first paradigm of anthropological linguistics was grounded in a view of language as shedding light on perduring structures of culture, this theoretical commitment, in the few instances where it was foregrounded, was marshaled to justify greater attention to the description of language rather than being marshaled for a deeper understanding of culture (Duranti, 2003).

The second paradigm, inaugurated in the 1960s by John Gumperz and Dell Hymes together with their students, argued for a mode of inquiry, sometimes captured with the moniker "interactional sociolinguistics," sometimes with the "ethnography of speaking" or just "linguistic anthropology". The latter reverses the name "anthropological linguistics," used by prior genera-tions, and in so doing attempts to recoup the distinctively anthropological character of this brand of language study as distinct from the formalist/generative linguistics à la Chomsky, which had come to dominate linguistics departments around the country. This second paradigm of linguistic anthropology emphasized the socioculturally informed quality of language as used and inaugu-rated a period of research dominated by inquiries into questions of verbal artistry and performance (e.g. Bauman, 1984), into the sociocultral dynamics of talk and interaction (Gumperz and Hymes, 1972; Goodwin and Duranti, 1992; Irvine and Hill, 1993), and even into theories of personhood and sociality as presupposed and entailed in language use (Rosaldo, 1982; Schieffelin and Ochs, 1986), to name just a few. This work brought linguists out from under the "service" position to which they had been relegated in anthropology and compelled recognition of the centrality of their inquiries to understanding culture, particularly in light of the rising tide of interpretivist and hermeneutic approaches championed by Clifford Geertz, among others. It also brought linguistic anthropology closer to, and in conversation with, similar efforts afoot in conversational analysis, variationist sociolinguistics, and pragmatics (e.g. Labov, 1972; Levinson, 1983; Atkinson and Heritage, 1984).

But, for all this, it is still the case that linguistic anthropology in this paradigm remains largely interested in what culture and society can tell us about language. Indeed, as Duranti explains, this is, at least partly, a product of its disciplinary positionality, caught between the "rock" of formal linguistics *and* the "hard place" of sociocultural anthropology. The need to be seen as different from both is what has continued to influence linguistic anthropologists operating in the second paradigm to focus on what is cultural about language. As Duranti writes: "Whereas sociocultural anthropologists tended to see language as a tool for describing and enacting culture, adherents of the second paradigm were trained to see the very organization of language use as 'cultural' and thus in need of linguistic and ethnographic description" (Duranti, 2003: 328).

It is in what Duranti describes as the third and most recent paradigm, beginning in the mid-1990s, that linguistic anthropological scholarship comes closest to aligning its analytic trajectory to those described for discourse analysis above. It is work in this vein, often by the students of Hymes and Gumperz and by their students' students, that has begun to explore what language practices can tell us about the everyday constitution and consequences of broader sociocultural forces such as identity formation, morality and normativity, political economy, and the like. As Duranti sees it, it is those working within this paradigm that have begun to "adopt theoretical perspectives developed outside anthropology or linguistics," (Duranti, 2003: 332)—including Bahktin's dialogism, Foucault's discourse, and Gidden's structuration, to name a few. Among the work Duranti sees as fitting most squarely within this third paradigm is that which has been grouped under the themes of "language ideology" (e.g. Schieffelin *et al.*, 1998, Kroskrity, 2000), intertextuality (Silverstein and Urban, 1996; Bauman and Briggs, 2003), and metadiscourse and metapragmatics (Silverstein, 1998, 2003). It is in this work that the sociocultural political economic forces that are presupposed and entailed by language practices are brought most fully to the forefront of linguistic anthropological analysis. Given these interests, it is perhaps little surprise that Duranti sees the scholars operating in this paradigm as sharing "a strong desire to use language studies to reach out to other disciplines" as well as "reconnecting with the rest of anthropology." It is also in them, Duranti contends, that "language [is] no longer the primary object of inquiry but … an instrument for gaining access to complex social processes" (Duranti, 2003: 332).

Indeed, in his introduction to *Regimes of Language*—one of two key linguistic anthropological volumes on language ideology—Paul Kroskrity starts by explaining how the collection was undertaken at a moment in sociopolitical history which he characterizes thus: "never before have the relations of language, politics, and identity seemed so relevant to so many" (Kroskrity, 2000: 1). In so doing, Kroskrity notes the extent to which the participants came together "to produce a more integrative, sociopolitically engaged linguistic anthropology" (p. 5).

But Kroskrity is also clear to point out that the research in the volume is squarely oriented toward further elucidation of language and linguistic phenomena as well. For example, he quotes an early formulation of the argument for studying language ideology in which Silverstein foregrounds the extent to which it is through norms about language that culture becomes inextricably part of a "total linguistic fact [that]… is irreducibly dialectic in nature" (p. 21). In such a formulation, through the study of language ideology, sociocultural forces are explored for what they can tell us about the forms and uses of language, rather than for how language is a window into culture and society.

It is perhaps not surprising that Duranti's programmatic review of linguistic anthropology misses these and other nuances of the extant research in the field. Indeed he himself recognizes this, acknowledging that his "three paradigms" vastly oversimplify a body of language research in which all three co-exist not only in the present scope of linguistic anthropological inquiry, but even within the oeuvres of individual scholars (e.g. Hill, 1985, 1993, 1998; Irvine, 1989, 1979, 2001; Kroskrity, 1993, 1997, 2000).

Nonetheless, what I believe is to good effect, he problematizes what he sees as linguistic anthropologists' failure to engage each other critically, across these paradigms, about their incompatibilities. He wonders whether he and others in his discipline are giving up, perhaps in the name of less troubled collegial waters, the possibility for "developing general models of language as culture that might be adopted, rejected, challenged, criticized, modified, or built upon" (Duranti, 2003: 335).

The point is, I believe, quite valid for a linguistic anthropological tradition that in some ways is following other anthropological sub fields in growing increasingly atomistic. Even more importantly, at least for this paper, Duranti's concern echoes the frustrations expressed by Blommaert and his co-authors, who were both linguistic anthropologists and discourse analysts, when they acknowledge the enduring differences between their respective analytic traditions.

What would these scholars, on both sides of the analytic divide, have us do? Duranti calls for greater reflection upon our most fundamental premises about language of/in/as society and culture, to see if we can't revisit and revise them in light of our different analytic trajectories, orientations and foci. Knowing what we all now know about the ways in which language is not just situated in contexts of culture, but actively contributes to the shape and force of those contexts and to the broader sociocultural and political–economic phenomena they presuppose and entail, how might we reframe our understanding of the structures and practices of the communicative media that are the objects and modes of our inquiry?

And, though Duranti is speaking mainly to linguistic anthropologists like myself, I believe his request is one in which our colleagues in discourse analysis should join us. I would argue that we both ought to be working to move our research agendas in even further alignment by considering the different analytic trajectories that our respective traditions impose on us, even though we claim to be studying the same language–culture dialectic. This would mean producing scholarship that poses, more radically, the question of what such scholarship might mean to scholars of language, culture, and society on both sides of the Atlantic, and to think of their objects of inquiry not merely as mutually informative, but as fundamentally and irreducibly all of a piece. What, then, could we learn from each other, if we were able to see all three as equally and at once the objects of our discourse analytic and linguistic anthropological inquires?

Certainly there already exists scholarship in both traditions that has proven the worth of such an endeavor (e.g. Schieffelin and Ochs, 1986; Silverstein and Urban, 1995; Rampton, 2007; van Dijk, 2009). And yet, as I have attempted to show here, a large segment of each field still views its goals in terms of analytic trajectories that, while similar, ultimately take them in opposite directions. In the space that remains, and by way of example, I shall briefly review a couple of insights I have gained into society, culture, and language by rethinking their irreducibility within the legal discourses and practices of the Tribal Court of the Hopi Indian Nation in northeastern Arizona. To do so in a way that attends to the different trajectories of our respective disciplines requires that my analysis move from language to law and back again, to show how we might give equal weight to the descriptive and explanatory power of both sides of the language–culture dialectical process.

From language to law …

Were my work to have been taken into account in Duranti's review (I was still an un-published graduate student in 2003), I believe he would have put me squarely in his third paradigm of linguistic anthropology. For my interest in the contemporary law and governance practices of American Indian tribes emerged while I was still a law student, before studying linguistic anthropology. But what particularly captured my attention was a group of pragmatic and theoretical impasses that I observed in the practice and study of tribal law—impasses that, I would later discover, were best accounted for via linguistic anthropological approaches.

Native American legal actors in the 1980s and 1990s strenuously argued for the centrality that tribal legal processes played in articulating and promoting their self-governance. Yet many also critiqued tribal courts for blindly adopting Anglo-adversarial legal norms in their rules and processes, and called for a "return" to the customs, traditions and unique cultural practices that, they argued, justified their status as nations (Pommershiem, 1995; Tsosie, 2002).

At the same time, social scientific concepts of the nation, sovereignty, culture, and tradition were being fundamentally reconsidered and deconstructed by anthropologists. The rise of post-structuralist and post-colonial theories led to ethnographic inquiries that cast doubt on once hoary representations of the independent, culturally coherent, self-governing nation–state. Indigenous claims to nationhood flew in the face of these critiques, and scholars who recognized this fact began taking aim at what they called the "invented," "inauthentic" character of indigenous claims to a sovereignty based on cultural identity and tradition (Miller, 2000; Dombrowski, 2004). Specifically, they argued that these claims, rather than resisting US hegemony, ironically worked more to constitute tribes in the essentializing images of otherness that reinscribe it (Biolsi, 2005).

At first glance the two sides to this debate made arguments that I found equally persuasive, but impossible to reconcile. It was only by focusing on the details of the actual communicative practices by and through which tribal law was being actively constituted by tribal legal actors—practices that had been entirely overlooked in the extant research—that I was able to account more fully for the political and juridical antinomies of native culture. What I discovered was that, when tribal actors presented notions of cultural identity, tradition, or custom in the language games of tribal courtroom interactions, they did so via meta-pragmatic and linguistic ideological practices, which *sometimes* worked to legitimate the Anglo influenced practices and powers of the court, but other times posed considerable challenges to that authority.

Thus, consider the following statement that a Hopi judge made to Hopi elders called as witnesses to testify about the traditions of property inheritance in their village. The case involved a dispute between a woman and her nieces over a piece a property that, the nieces claimed, she gave up when she married a non-Hopi and moved away from the Hopi reservation. The judge is asking the village elders to comment on whether a woman who marries a non-Hopi and relocates away from her village is still entitled to land. He poses his question in Hopi, this way:

(1) Questioning "In a Hopi way": Indefinite + HABITUAL

002 Judge: Pam   hapi pay **yephaqam   hak**   ayo'
In that way truly now somewhere here someone to there
In that manner someone may go over

003   Yangqw   ayo'   sen   naala   hoyok-hoyokni
From here   to there perhaps alone move- will move
S/he might move away from here alone

004   Niikyangw pi pay naat pi piptu**ngwu**
     But   truly now still truly return+ **HAB**
     But s/he continues to come back regularly

[NOTE: SOME LINES OMMITTED HERE]

007   **Hiisakis** sen pam pas pew pìpte'
     Sometime perhaps she much to here return
     How often must s/he return

008   Put pay naat
     It   now still
     And still -

010   Tutuyqaw**ngwu**   put tuutskwat
     maintain control over +**HAB** it land
     Ah…have the right over others in that land

011   Himu'yta**ngwu**
     Have as a posession+**HAB**
     To have ownership of it

Notice the judge's use of the Hopi indefinite terms *yephaqam* (somewhere here) and *hak* (someone) at line 2. Here the judge was framing the issues for elders to consider as hypothetical events of the same *type*, but not *identical to*, the factual events of the dispute. Then, in lines 7–11, he posed his question, employing at lines 10 and 11 verbs inflected with the habitual aspect marker *-ngwu*. This Indefinite + HABITUAL grammatical construction is in fact used repeatedly by this judge throughout his questioning of the elders.

As one native speaker explained to me, the form is typical of a genre of talk that Hopi call *ökwhanta*, "admonishing," a form of authoritative speech used in traditional contexts of Hopi interaction by which respected persons, even ritual performers, advise others to change some problematic behavior. A speaker invoking this genre reprimands recipients without directly naming them, explaining what *one should* do because of what has *always been* done. Such utterances thus project the generalized, "timeless" truths of the propositions they make about the world. Significantly, they project a kind of generalizing category of truth, very similarly to the way in which legal principles of Anglo-American-style jurisprudence are expressed and then discursively "applied" to the facts of particular disputes (Mertz, 1998, 2003).

I contend that the judge is employing the grammar and syntax of this authoritative genre of Hopi tradition discourse in an effort to get the witnesses to speak about generalized *principles of tradition*, in ways consistent with the Anglo-style discourses and practices of the Hopi court. The judge thus employs Hopi tradition in this interaction to authorize and legitimize tribal legal authority, in ways that subsume notions of Hopi cultural uniqueness to the legal discourses and knowledge practices that naturalize the hegemony of forms of law still recognized by many Hopi as the legacy of US colonization.

But, significantly, the elders do not easily capitulate to the judge's discursive demands. They make repeated efforts to speak not of general principles of tradition, but of their knowledge of the actual facts of the dispute between the woman and her nieces. The judge, however, interrupts them, insisting, "*Pay qa hakiy pas itam aw suuk aw taykyahkyàngw turta put yu'a'totani*" ("We are not to look at some one person as we talk about this").

After several such interruptions, the elders become frustrated. One comments: *Sùupan as itam pumuy- pay pumuysa engemyaqw, kur hapi pay pas itam sòosokmuy engemya* ("I thought we were doing this only for them, but it appears now we are doing this for everyone").

Another elder more pointedly challenges the judge, asking, explicitly, "*Um it kitsokit- um navotiyat uma hintsatsnaniqe oovi?*" ("What are you.-What are you going to do with the village's traditions?").

In posing these challenges, the Hopi elders are calling upon a wholly different set of ideologies about Hopi tradition discourses. Their discursive ideologies ground the authority of such genres of tradition talk, and those who control them, in their exclusive use in secret esoteric ceremonies, held in underground kivas and clan homes, and shared only among initiates and clan members. For Hopi individuals possessing such powerful traditional knowledge, to speak it publicly, in ways that proclaim a generalized authority over all Hopi people, regardless of ceremonial and clan affiliation, is not only to open themselves up to social sanction, but to make public, in reckless ways, very potent information that can be then appropriated and put to morally questionable ends. Someone's requesting that they do so, even a Hopi judge in Hopi court, raises serious questions about the legitimacy of the questioner's intentions with that traditional knowledge.

Thus, in the language practices and ideologies of these elders, notions of Hopi tradition are constituted in ways quite contradictory to those being employed by the judge—that is, by resisting instead of legitimizing his authority and by challenging the Anglo-style legal practices and ideologies that naturalize it.

Consequently, when we look at the actual discourses by which tribal legal actors constitute their tribal jurisprudence, we see that talk of tradition and culture emerges in multiple, complex, and even competing ways. As such, when we return to the ongoing debate about whether political notions of cultural identity and tradition work to reinscribe US authority or are anti-colonial in their effects, we must say that they are both and neither. Rather, by employing linguistic anthropological theories and methodologies to explore these issues, we begin to see how such notions operate as metadiscursive resources in Hopi tribal law—forms of law talk about law talk—which, whether they are reifying or resistant, are a crucial part of the warp and woof by which tribal law is actively made in the everyday practices of tribal jurisprudence. Failure to attend to the ways in which such sociocultural notions and political–economic forces inform everyday interaction can lead to intractable debates, as it does here, among those who would foreground only one side of what is an irreducibly more complex dialectic.

... And back again

Though this tells us something about what a linguistic anthropological approach can add to a sociocultural and political economic analysis of law, an answer to Duranti's call requires that I also explore what a sociocultural approach to legal discourse can add to our analyses of language. One answer comes from looking at the ways in which ideological and interpretive multiplicity have been addressed in both legal and linguistic anthropology.

Michael Silverstein's (e.g. 1979, 1993, 2001) analyses of the ways in which language ideology interfaces with language use through what he calls the meta-pragmatic function have always accounted for the fact that the meaning that certain language practices come to have for speakers shift over social space and time and are susceptible to multiple and ironically oppositional interpretations. As Silverstein explains, any moment of language use is only meaningful when language practices functioning meta-pragmatically (again, as instances of language use about language use) bring the ideologies that those speakers have about their language to their actual language practices, and in so doing key the interlocutors as to the meaning of the language activities by which they are engaging each other (1993, 1998, 2003). This is why almost all syntactic, grammatical, and lexical terms carry what Silverstein calls "indexical" significances that shift depending on the context of their use and on the different meta-pragmatic functions being

Justin B. Richland

employed by interlocutors to key those meanings to each other in each of those contexts of interaction (1976).

In addition, because of certain "limits of awareness" (2001[1981]) that we all have about our own language use, speaker's ideologies about language practices are distorted in ways that never fully capture all the possible social significances of that use. These distortions come to shape, in multiple and even ironic ways, the kinds of meanings that speakers understand those practices as carrying, and even how they then subsequently use those language practices in the future.

Silverstein (1985) offers an example of this distortion and shift in the historic loss of the informal English second person pronoun (*thee/thou*) as the unintended by-product of the political reaction to Quaker plain speech in seventeenth-century England. At the time, English possessed a formal/informal second person pronoun system, in which *Ye/You* was the form used between interlocutors to mark their social distance, while *Thee/Thou* was used to mark social proximity. As Silverstein explains, Quaker ideology about the essential equality of humans before God took a metadiscursive turn as Quaker activists began militating against the *Ye/You* form as a mark of elitism and insisted on using the *Thee/Thou* form even in situations of social distance and formality. By this first metapragmatic distortion (by virtue of a limit on Quaker metalinguistic "awareness") there emerges, in the Quaker conceptualization, a sense of the *Ye/You* form not as a marker of formality and social distance, but solely as one of social inequality. A second, ironic reversal of this metapragmatic distortion emerges, however, when, over time, it is the *Thee/Thou* form that is eventually lost in everyday English usage. This occurs, Silverstein explains, because non-Quaker English society orients now to this *Thee/Thou* form as a marker of Quaker social identity, and stops using it in order to avoid being labeled by that stigmatized and persecuted identity (Silverstein, 1985).

A critical element in Silverstein's understanding of this shifting of meaning is its temporal component. The extent to which the multiple and ironic meanings result from these metapragmatic distortions requires a certain kind of longitudinal perspective, tracing these interpretive shifts as they unfold over rather large scales of time.

However, an approach to these phenomena that takes into account perspectives gained from legal anthropology would argue that these multiplicities and ironies of meaning have their origins within spans of social time that are much more truncated, and may in some instances persist simultaneously. This is true insofar as one of the fundamental insights of legal anthropology is the recognition that multiple and competing cultural frames of interpretation regularly persist within the same community and that the dispute context is an ideal crucible within which to view those competing frames. Karl Llewellyn and E. Adamson Hoebel note this in their classic legal anthropological ethnography of the Cheyenne law, *The Cheyenne Way* (1941), in which they introduce their influential trouble-case method (Llewellyn and Hoebel 1941: 29; as they write, " if there be a portion of a society's life in which tensions of the culture come to an expression, in which the play of variant urges can be felt and seen … that portion of the life will concentrate in the case of trouble or disturbance").

Thus, just as we saw above how Hopi metadiscourses of tradition and cultural difference can be employed for multiple and competing sociolegal and cultural effects in tribal legal discourses, so too does this suggest the multiple and competing interpretations to which certain language practices can be susceptible, even between language users engaging each other, face to face, in the very same communicative event, over the relatively short span of social time in which it is accomplished.

Conclusion

Recently I submitted a manuscript to a leading cultural anthropology journal that explored some of the issues surrounding efforts to theorize the links between the micro-details of situated language use and the macro-sociological forces that are more often the purview of cultural anthropology. One of the reviewers commented that such concerns were unfamiliar to him, and likely more of an issue for linguists than for those cultural anthropologists who read the journal in question. Whether this is true or not, it is interesting to note that the paper, which considered aspects of Hopi probate law more generally, was one that I had thought would not have been good for a linguistic anthropology journal precisely because it was too much concerned with describing the sociocultural dimensions of certain legal texts rather than linguistic forms and practices that constitute them.

Whatever the fate of that manuscript, it is my hope that, with this chapter, I have brought to light the similar kinds of theoretical and methodological divisions that continue to endure between linguistic anthropology and discourse analysis, at least in some parts of their respective fields. And, while I am quite sure that, in the characterizations above, I have overstated the separation between the two, I nonetheless believe we have not yet reached the point when the differences identified by Blommaert and his co-authors in 2001 have been fully surmounted. I also hope to have, in some small way, offered a sense of the analytic value to be gained when we actively work at once toward acknowledging and moving beyond the analytic trajectories that continue to keep linguistic anthropology and discourse analysis apart. In so doing, I hope that this chapter may compel us to rethink fundamentally our respective analytic commitments in ways that are respectful to the legacy of each of our intellectual histories, while also being productive for our futures.

Further reading

Blommaert, J., Collins, J., Heller, M., Rampton, B., Slembrouck, S., and Verschueren, J. (eds.) (2001) 'Discourse and critique', *Critique of Anthropology* 21 (1–2): 5–183 (special issue).

Duranti, A. (2003) 'Language as culture in U.S. anthropology: three paradigms', *Current Anthropology*, 44: 323–335.

Duranti, A. (2001) *Key Terms in Language and Culture*. Oxford: Blackwell Publishing.

Silverstein, M. (2004) ' "Cultural" concepts and the language–culture nexus', *Current Anthropology*, 45: 621–652.

References

Atkinson, J. M. and Heritage, J. (eds.) (1984) *Structures of Social Action: Studies in Conversation Analysis*. Cambridge: Cambridge University Press.

Bauman, R. (1984) *Verbal Art as Performance*. Prospect Heights, IL: Waveland Press.

Biolsi, T. (2005) 'Imagined geographies: sovereignty, indigenous space, and American Indian struggle', *American Ethnologist*, 32: 239–259.

Blommaert, J. (2005) *Discourse: A Critical Introduction*. Cambridge: Cambridge University Press.

Blommaert, J. and Bulcaen, C. (2000) 'Critical discourse analysis', *Annual Review of Anthropology*, 29: 447–466.

Blommaert, J., Collins, J., Heller, M., Rampton, B., Slembrouck, S., and Verschueren, J. (eds.) (2001) 'Discourse and critique', *Critique of Anthropology*, 21 (1–2): 5–183 (special issue).

Boas, F. (1911) 'Introduction', in F. Boas (ed.) *Handbook of American Indian Languages*. Part 1. Washington, DC: Smithsonian Institution and Bureau of American Ethnology, Vol. BAE B 40.

Caldas-Coulthard, C. R. and Coulthard, M. (eds.) (1996) *Texts and Practices Readings in Critical Discourse Analysis*. London: Routledge.

Collins, J., Slembrouck, S., and Baynham, M. (2009) *Globalization and Language in Contact: Scale, Migration, and Communicative Practices*. London: Continuum.

Darnell, R. (1990) *Edward Sapir: Linguist, Anthropologist, Humanist*. Berkeley, CA: University of California Press.

Dombrowski, K. (2004) ' "The politics of native culture', in T. Biolsi (ed.) *A Companion to the Anthropology of American Indians*. Oxford: Blackwell Publishing California Press, pp. 360–382.

Duranti, A. (2001) 'An historical perspective on contemporary linguistic anthropology', *Teaching Anthropology: SACC Notes*, 7 (2) (Fall–Winter 2000–2001), 20–24.

Duranti, A. (2003) 'Language as culture in U.S. anthropology: three paradigms', *Current Anthropology*, 44: 323–335.

Fairclough, N. (1989) *Language and Power*. London: Longman.

Fairclough, N. (1995) *Critical Discourse Analysis: The Critical Study of Language*. London: Longman.

Fairclough, N. and Wodak, R. (1997) 'Critical discourse analysis', in T. Van Dijk (ed.) *Discourse Studies: A Multidisciplinary Introduction*. Vol. 2. London: Sage, pp. 258–284.

Gee, J. P. (1996) *Social Linguistics and Literacies Ideology in Discourse*. Second Edition. London: Falmer.

Gee, J. P. (2004) *Situated Language and Learning: A Critique of Traditional Schooling*. New York: Palgrave Macmillan.

Gee, J. P. (2005) *An Introduction to Discourse Analysis. Theory and Method*. Second Edition. Oxford: Routledge.

Gee, J. P. (2007) *What Video Games Have to Teach Us About Learning and Literacy*. Second Edition. New York: Palgrave Macmillan.

Goodwin, C. and Duranti, A. (eds.) (1992) *Rethinking Context: Language as an Interactive Phenomenon*. Cambridge: Cambridge University Press.

J. Gumperz and Hymes, D. (eds.) (1972) *Directions in Sociolinguistics: The Ethnography of Communication*. New York: Holt, Rinehart and Winson.

Heritage, J. (1984) *Garfinkel and Ethnomethodology*. Cambridge: Polity Press.

Hill, J. H. (1985) 'The grammar of consciousness and the consciousness of grammar', *American Ethnologist*, 12: 725–737.

Hill, J. H. (1993) 'Hasta la Vista, baby: Anglo Spanish in the American southwest', *Critique of Anthropology*, 13: 145–176.

Hill, J. H. (1998) ' "Today there is no respect": nostalgia, "respect", and oppositional discourse in Mexicano (Nahuatl) language ideology', in B. B. Schieffelin, K. A. Woolard, and P. B. Kroskrity (eds.) *Language Ideologies: Practice and Theory*. New York: Oxford University Press, pp. 68–86.

Irvine, J. T. (1979) 'Formality and informality in communicative events', *American Anthropologist*, 81: 773–790.

Irvine, J. T. (1989) "When talk isn't cheap: language and political economy', *American Ethnologist*, 16: 248–267.

Irvine, J. T. (2001) ' "Style" as distinctiveness: the culture and ideology of linguistic differentiation', in P. Eckert and J. R. Rickford (eds.) *Style and Sociolinguistic Variation*. Cambridge: Cambridge University Press, pp. 21–43.

Irvine, J. T. and Hill, J. (eds.) (1993) *Responsibility and Evidence in Oral Discourse*. Cambridge: Cambridge University Press.

Kroskrity, P. V. (1993) *Language, History, and Identity: Ethnolinguistic Studies of the Arizona Tewa*. Tucson, AZ: University of Arizona Press.

Kroskrity, P. V. (1997) "Discursive convergence with an evidential particle', in J. J. Hill, P. H., Mistry, and L. Campbell (eds.) *The Life of Language: Papers in Honor of William Bright*. Berlin: Mouton de Gruyter, pp. 25–34.

Kroskrity, P. V. (2000) 'Introduction', in P. V. Kroskrity (ed.) *Regimes of Language: Ideologies, Polities, and Identities*. Santa Fe, NM: School of American Research Press.

Labov, W. (1972) *Sociolinguistic Patterns*. Philadelphia, PA: University of Pennsylvania Press.

Levinson, S. (1983) *Pragmatics*. Cambridge: Cambridge University Press.

Miller, B. G. (2000) *The Problem of Justice: Tradition and Law in the Coast Salish World*. Lincoln and London: University of Nebraska Press.

Pommershiem, F. (1995) *Braid of Feathers: American Indian Law and Contemporary Tribal Life*. Berkeley, CA: University of California Press.

Rampton, B. (2007) 'Neo-Hymesian linguistic ethnography in the UK', *Journal of Sociolinguistics*, 11: 584–608.

Rosaldo, M. Z. (1982) 'The things we do with words: Ilongot speech acts and speech act theory in philosophy', *Language in Society*, 11: 203–237.

Schieffelin, B. and Ochs, E. (eds.) (1986) *Language Socialization Across Cultures*. Cambridge: Cambridge University Press.

Scollon, R. (2001) *Mediated Discourse: The Nexus of Practice*. New York: Routledge.

Silverstein, M. (1976) 'Shifters, linguistic categories, and cultural description', in K. H. Basso and H. A. Selby (eds.) *Meaning in Anthropology*. Alburquerque, NM: University of New Mexico Press, pp. 11–56.

Silverstein, M. (1985) 'Language and the culture of gender: at the intersection of structure, usage, and ideology', in E. Mertz and R. J. Parmentier (eds.) *Semioitic Mediation: Sociocultural and Psychological Perspectives*. Orlando, FL: Academic Press, pp. 219–259.

Silverstein, M. (1993) 'Metapragmatic discourse and metapragmatic function', in J. A. Lucy (ed.) *Reflexive Language: Reported Speech and Metapragmatics*. Cambridge: Cambridge University Press, pp. 33–58.

Silverstein, M. (2001[1981]) 'The limits of awareness', reprinted in A. Duranti (ed.) *Linguisitic Anthropology: A Reader*. Oxford: Blackwell, pp. 386–401.

Silverstein, M. (2003) 'Indexical order and the dialectics of sociolinguistic life', *Language and Communication*, 23: 193–299.

Silverstein, M. (2004) '"Cultural" concepts and the language-culture nexus', *Current Anthropology*, 45 (5): 621–652.

Slembrouck, S. (2001) 'Explanation, interpretation and critique in the analysis of discourse', *Critique of Anthropology*, 21: 33–57.

Tsosie, R. (2002) 'Symposium: cultural sovereignty: native rights in the 21st century. Introduction', *Arizona State Law Journal*, 34: 1–14.

van Dijk, T. (1993) '"Studies in critical discourse analysis', *Discourse and Society*, 4: 249–283 (special issue).

van Dijk, T. (2009) *Society and Discourse: How Social Contexts Influence Text and Talk*. Cambridge: Cambridge University Press.

van Dijk, T. (2010) 'Research in critical discourse studies'. Available online at http://www.discourses.org/projects/cda/ (accessed 29 October 2010).

Whorf, B. L. (ed.) (1956) *Language, Thought, and Reality: Selected Writings of Benjamin Lee Whorf*. Boston, MA: MIT Press.

13

Corpus-based discourse analysis

Lynne Flowerdew

Introduction

Discourse analysis covers a vast range of areas and is also one of the least clearly defined fields in applied linguistics (Stubbs, 1983; Aijmer and Stenström, 2004). Blommaert (2005: 2) notes that, traditionally, discourse has been treated in linguistic terms as 'language-in-use', informing areas such as pragmatics and speech act theory. However, for Blommaert discourse has a wider interpretation as 'language-in-action', i.e. 'meaningful symbolic behaviour'. Jucker *et al.* (2009b: 5) define this wider use of the term discourse as 'the totality of linguistic practices that pertain to a particular domain or that create a particular object'. A useful distinction is made by Gee (2001), who defines the 'language-in-use' aspect as 'discourse' (with a little 'd') and the more 'language-in-action' orientation as 'Discourse' (with a capital D), involving not only linguistic practices but other semiotic elements. Discourses are created through recognition work of 'ways with words, actions, beliefs, emotions, values, interactions, people, objects, tools and technologies' that constitute a way of being a member of a particular discourse community (ibid., p. 20).

Corpus linguistics is a field of enquiry whose essential nature, like that of discourse analysis, has also come under scrutiny. The main contention revolves around 'corpus-driven' vs. 'corpus-based' linguistics and whether corpus linguistics is a theory or a methodology. The field of corpus linguistics in the 'corpus-driven' sense is underpinned by a phraseological, syntagmatic approach to language data (see Sinclair, 2004), consisting of five categories of co-selection with the core lexical item and semantic prosody as obligatory elements, and collocation, colligation and semantic preference as optional categories. Proponents in the 'corpus-driven' camp regard corpus linguistics as essentially a theory with corpus enquiries revealing hitherto unknown aspects of language, thus challenging the 'underlying assumptions behind many well established theoretical positions' (Tognini Bonelli, 2001: 48). For this reason they oppose any a priori mark-up of the data, arguing that it would obscure the syntagmatic, lexico-grammatical patternings associated with the phraseological approach. However, most corpus linguists take a less extreme view, tending towards a more 'corpus-based' approach. For example, Aarts (2002) views corpus linguistics as a methodology for validating existing descriptions of language on which to make changes in the description where corpus data does not fit. While McEnery *et al.* (2006) conceive of corpus linguistics as a new philosophical approach to linguistic enquiry; they do not consider it to have the status of a theory (see also Biber *et al.*, 1998; Conrad, 2002). In spite of these different theoretical positions, corpus linguistics is generally regarded as a methodology, and 'corpus-based' is used as an umbrella term for a range of corpus enquiries, which is the sense adopted in this chapter.

Although discourse analysis and corpus linguistics both make use of naturally occurring attested data, they have intrinsically ontological and epistemological differences, as noted by Virtanen

(2009). Doing corpus analysis is not the same as doing discourse analysis (DA). Leech (2000: 678–680, cited in McEnery *et al.*, 2006) observes that there is a 'cultural divide' between the two: 'while DA emphasizes the integrity of the text, corpus linguistics tends to use representative samples; while DA is primarily qualitative, corpus linguistics is essentially quantitative; while DA focuses on the contents expressed by language, corpus linguistics is interested in language *per se*' (p. 111). Moreover, Biber *et al.* (1998) have noted that the software tools such as concordance packages for corpus analysis do not lend themselves to focusing on language characteristics extending across clause boundaries, or to semantic analysis, and are therefore not suitable for discourse analyses. The main epistemological differences, though, between the two fields lie in the fact that corpus analyses, by virtue of their methodological status, treat the text as product rather than as an unfolding discourse as process and social action: 'the computer can only cope with the material products of what people do when they use language. It can only analyse the textual traces of the processes whereby meaning is achieved' (Widdowson, 2000: 4).

As far back as 1998, I drew attention to the potential of corpus linguistics for 'doing' discourse analysis (Flowerdew, 1998). McEnery *et al.* (2006: 111) state that the aforementioned cultural divide 'is now diminishing', and Partington (2004) proposes that corpus and discourse methods are complementary. This chapter seeks to examine to what extent corpus and discourse approaches have now established a common meeting point, given their inherent differences in epistemologies and methodologies.

Studies of corpus-based discourse analyses will be discussed from the following three main approaches, adapted from categories proposed by Hyland (2009: 20). These have areas of overlap as, in reality, each approach also draws on aspects of the other approaches.

- **Textual**: approaches that focus on language choices, meanings and patterns in texts, including those based on the Swalesian (Swales, 2004) notion of genre and the problem-solution pattern. Also considered are various phraseological elements operating at the level of discourse.
- **Critical**: an approach that brings an attitude of criticality, such as critical discourse analysis (CDA), but also draws on other methods, e.g. systemic functional linguistics (SFL).
- **Contextual**: analyses that adopt a more sociolinguistic approach to the corpus data, where situational factors are also taken into account. This approach draws on conversation analysis, speech act theory and pragmatics.

Corpus-based discourse analyses can be viewed not only as adopting one of the main approaches above together with its attendant discourse area, e.g. the problem-solution pattern primarily associated with the textual approach, but also in terms of subject areas, i.e. workplace discourse, media discourse, academic discourse and so on, as a reflection of certain ideological positionings – discourses of racism, discourse of power – and mode – whether spoken or written or a 'hybrid' discourse, such as is emerging in the new technologies of blogs and chat rooms. Moreover, many of the discourse-based studies cited below implicitly subscribe to the 'corpus-driven' approach with their focus on the phraseological nature of language, in which the lexical item has primacy.

Corpus-based textual approach

The corpus studies discussed in this section have mainly a text-based – that is, 'language-in-use' – focus. However, at the same time many also address the interpersonal nature of language, so that the analyses are also reader- and/or writer-oriented.

Models of discourse

Handford's (2010a) overview article on the value of using specialized corpora for researching the discourse of particular genres reviews the operationalization of the Swalesian, new rhetoric and SFL approaches to genre across professional, academic and non-institutional genres. The Swalesian notion of genre as a goal-driven communicative event associated with particular discourse communities is the model that has been most widely applied in studies of written academic and professional texts, many previously hand-tagged for move structures. J. Flowerdew and Forest (2010) apply Swales' (1990: 141) CARS ('create a research space') model, originally posited for academic research article introductions, to PhD literature reviews, investigating the patterning of the keyword 'research' across different moves and steps (see also Gledhill, 2000; Upton and Connor, 2001; Flowerdew, 2008a for other genre-motivated corpus research). However, Bhatia *et al.*'s (2004) study of genre moves in law cases reveals the limitations of a purely corpus analytic approach: in order to make a pragmatic distinction between seemingly synonymous verbs, such as *dismiss* and *reject* in law cases, Bhatia *et al.* (ibid., p. 213) state that it would be necessary to 'look for evidence from institutional practices', as corpora cannot (usually) provide such information. Different from, yet complementing these genre analyses in the spirit of the Swalesian tradition, are those studies reported in Biber *et al.* (2007a) and Csomay (2005) on vocabulary-based discourse units (VBDUs), which are identified automatically through comparison of 50-word 'windows', i.e. segments, of text. Although this is not a functional approach, nevertheless it is another way of identifying topic or move boundaries in text.

The studies cited above all commence from a lexico-grammatical, bottom-up perspective. Kanoksilapatham's (2007) research, on the other hand, takes a rhetorical top-down perspective at the outset. In her study of biochemistry research articles Kanoksilapatham first develops an analytical discourse-based framework through the identification of rhetorical move types and then uses Biber's multi-dimensional analysis to determine the linguistic characteristic of each move (see Parodi, 2009 for application of Biber's model to disambiguating discourse variation across academic and professional genres in Spanish).

Another discourse model that has been applied to corpus investigations is the problem-solution (P-S) pattern (see Hoey, 2001). Flowerdew (2008b) used the appraisal system from systemic–functional linguistics (Martin and White, 2005) for classifying keywords for the P-S pattern in technical reports into different types of evaluative lexis, followed by micro-analyses of the semantic relation of cause and effect. Ali Mohamed (2007) investigated the problem element in another text type, Malaysian and British journalistic business texts, also applying Martin's appraisal system to categorizing interpersonal and evaluative meanings. A key feature of this study is her use of the WMatrix corpus tool (Rayson, 2008) to identify different semantic fields characteristic of the problem element. Development of such tools serves to address Biber's criticism, noted earlier, that discourse studies are not served well by the existing concordance tools. A corpus study investigating the P-S pattern in terms of a more reader- and writer-oriented perspective accompanying the textual analysis is that by Alonso Belmonte (2009), which investigates two corpora: newspaper editorials and op-eds. An interactional analysis of different communicative acts (e.g. justification, exemplification) associated with different elements of the pattern was complemented by an illocutionary analysis with the corpus coded for speech acts such as assertions, shared-knowledge assertions and so on, indicating how writers conduct interaction with their readers. Alonso Belmonte's interactional analysis involving various types of discourse relations shares some features with Thompson and Mann's rhetorical structure theory (RST), which Renkema (2009: 174–177), with reference to three small-scale RST corpora, has advocated as a starting point for further corpus linguistic research.

Linguistic devices with discourse functions

The focus of this section is on Hoey's theory of lexical priming as it operates at the textlinguistic level, and on three types of devices, namely lexical bundles, metadiscourse and metadiscoursal nouns. A key feature of the corpus studies reviewed below is that they are contrastive in nature, highlighting variation across different university disciplines, genres and registers.

Lexical priming

Hoey's (2004, 2005) theory of lexical priming maps out a theoretical relationship between lexis and textlinguistics, showing how semantic associations, collocation and colligation operate at a discoursal level. Hoey argues that some lexical items have a bias towards (or against) certain textual functions such as cohesion, theme choice and paragraph division and are also tied to particular genres and communities of users. For example, in the phrase *sixty years ago today*, all items, when they are the theme, have a preference for occurring in paragraph initial position (Hoey, 2004: 188).

Lexical bundles

Biber *et al.* (2004) classify bundles (contiguous sequences of (usually) three-, four- or five-word n-grams) into three main functional categories: discourse organizers, referential expressions and stance expressions, the latter consisting of epistemic stance bundles that comment on the knowledge status of the information (e.g. *I don't know if*) and attitudinal/modality stance bundles which express speaker attitude towards certain actions (e.g. *I want you to*). Hyland's (2008) categorization of lexical bundles is similar to that of Biber's, but differs in that, like his classification of metadiscourse, they are organized around categories that reflect either the writer or the reader involvement in the text. Both Biber's and Hyland's research studies on lexical bundles have been invaluable for highlighting the functional differences between spoken and written registers (Cortes, 2004; Biber, 2006) and disciplinary variation in the academy (Hyland, 2008).

Metadiscourse

Hyland's (2005) pioneering corpus research on metadiscourse is essentially interpersonal with its focus on those aspects of text that embody writer–reader interactions. On the basis of his model, which consists of an interactive (i.e. helping to guide the reader through the text) and interactional (involving the reader in the text) dimension, Hyland conducted corpus searches across various disciplines and levels of academic writing on the linguistic resources, realizing various functions subsumed under the two dimensions (see Hyland and Tse, 2004; Hyland, 2005). Bondi's (2001, 2004) quantitative and qualitative study of economics texts also examines the dialogic argumentative structure of academic text. Of interest is that Granger (1998) has found excessive the use of such signaling phrases for introducing arguments in learner academic writing. Likewise, Aijmer's (2009) study of 'I don't know' shows that this bundle is overwhelmingly used as a speech management function in learners' spoken English when compared with native speaker use.

Metadiscourse has also been investigated in the Michigan Corpus of Academic Spoken English (MICASE), most notably by Mauranen (2001, 2003) and Swales and Malczewski (2001). Mauranen's concept of metadiscourse differs somewhat from that of Hyland's, as she views this feature as fundamentally textual on account of its organization of ongoing discourse (*So let me just elaborate a little bit and then we…*). However, Mauranen argues that at the same time it is also interpersonally motivated, as it imposes the speaker's order on the discourse situation, thus socializing students into the discourse. Likewise, Crawford Camiciottoli (2007) assigns an expert to novice communication role to metadiscursive phrases in business lectures (e.g. *That is the main point, The key thing*).

Metadiscourse nouns

One area that has received a lot of attention is how certain nouns function at a discourse level. Drawing on Biber *et al.*'s distinction between epistemic and attitudinal markers, Charles (2003) compares the use of epistemic nouns, e.g. *assumption*, and stance nouns, e.g. *problem*, in post-graduate theses from the field of politics and materials science. Such metalinguistic nouns were found to function retrospectively, thus having an interpersonal function, as they indicate to the reader how the proposition is to be interpreted. Like Hyland, Charles (2006) also interprets her findings with reference to the different epistemologies and ideology of the discipline, noting that the higher frequency of metalinguistic nouns found in the politics corpus can be accounted for by the fact that knowledge construction in this discipline draws mostly on resources that are language-based, predominantly in written form (see J. Flowerdew, 2003 for research on nouns with discourse properties in a corpus of biology texts). A study examining the textlinguistic function of common nouns in a general corpus, i.e. the Bank of English, is that by Mahlberg (2003). Mahlberg notes the interactive nature of such nouns, identifying giving emphasis as one of their support functions: 'It would doubtless be too much to expect Spurs fans to suddenly express a sweetness for Alan Sugar, *a man* who's been subjected to more abuse and hate mail than the average child molester' (p. 102).

Corpus linguistic techniques have thus proved of great value in shedding light on how various language choices and patterns operate at a textlinguistic level, either at a level above the clause or sentence, or within the framework of discourse models, very often using a multi-pronged approach, for instance combining Biber's MDA with Swalesian genre move structures.

Corpus-based critical approach

In CDA the focus is on 'discourses' rather than on discourse per se. This notion refers to a broad range of linguistic and nonlinguistic social practices and ideological assumptions that co-construct, for example, 'discourses of power' or 'discourses of racism' – in other words, discourse with a capital 'D' (Gee, 2001). The techniques of CDA are multi-fold and vary. Text-analytic techniques draw on SFL, pragmatics and speech act analysis, and are integrated with concepts from contemporary social and cultural theory. Thus CDA is not a method as such in itself, but rather 'an academic movement', drawing on a kaleidoscope of methods increasingly those associated with corpus linguistics (Baker *et al.*, 2008). Two main approaches to CDA have developed since the 1960s. In the approach associated with Fairclough (2000) the analytical framework centres on a discursive event, an instance of language use, analysed not only as text, but also as discursive and social practice. The discourse–historical approach associated with the Viennese school (Wodak and Meyer, 2009) takes a more interdisciplinary, sociolinguistic perspective to the data, in which ethnography can also be a part of the analytical procedures.

What role do corpora play in these two approaches to CDA? Titscher *et al.* (2000: 158) state: 'Its [CDA's] point of departure is always the assumption that inequality and injustice are repeatedly reproduced in language and legitimized by it'. Corpus linguists working in CDA attempt to link recurring patterns in text with sociolinguistic features from the original contextual environment and vice versa. As Mautner (2009b: 124) points out: 'Doing so *critically* means unveiling and challenging taken-for-granted assumptions about language and the social, as well as recognizing discourse as a potentially powerful agent in social change'. Moreover, corpus-based CDA studies make use of both quantitative techniques, that is, frequency and keyword lists – complemented by more detailed qualitative textual analysis and combined in such a way so as to uncover the *non-obvious meaning*, unavailable to conscious awareness, in the discourse under investigation. Using corpora for CDA analysis would also help to offset Widdowson's (1995, 2004) criticism of CDA that ideological significance is assigned to co-textual relations on very scant evidence, thus helping to reduce researcher bias.

In fact corpus-based CDA is a relatively new field (see Hunston, 2002, and Mautner, 2009a for a review of key studies), put on the map by the pioneering work of Stubbs (1996, 2001) and Hardt-Mautner (1995). These studies have given rise to the newly emerging interdisciplinary field of corpus-assisted discourse studies (CADS), an approach underpinned by Fairclough's concept of CDA.

Corpus-Assisted Discourse Studies (CADS)

Some CADS case studies tend more towards the textual approach; such is Partington's (2003, 2007) research on the language strategies, metaphors and motifs used by journalists and spokes-persons in US press conferences and on how these reflect their respective world views. Others, for instance the study by Krishnamurthy (1996) on the construction of people and race, are positioned clearly in the critical discourse camp.

Many of these studies examine the pervasive phenomenon of evaluation (see Hunston and Thompson 2000), applying Martin and White's (2005) Appraisal system in systemic functional grammar (see Bednarek, 2006 for an in-depth study of evaluation in media text). Much work in this area has also been carried out under the auspices of the CorDis project, which examines, from an interactive discourse perspective, how the conflict in Iraq was discussed and reported in the Senate and Parliament and in various media outlets (Morley and Bailey, 2009; Haarman and Lombardo, 2009). Duguid (2007), for example, examines the dialogistic positioning of Tony Blair and of his two advisors in the Hutton enquiry, noting the frequency of the collective noun *people*, which Fairclough (2000) has also noted surfacing as a keyword in his corpus of Blair speeches. In the corpus extracts below, the use of *people* serves to make the interactive, dialogistic nature of the discussions explicit, illustrating 'the continuous inter-textual concerns of the team, where a constant second-guessing goes on about how actions or texts will be perceived by those outside' (Duguid, 2007: 91):

> You should not have gone to war – *people* can have a disagreement about that…

> to, as it were, offer the name, but on the other hand, not to mislead *people*

> but *people* would say, 'when did you know?'

Coffin and O'Halloran (2005) also make use of the Appraisal system, specifically of judgement, graduation and affect, first to carry out a detailed qualitative analysis of a report from *The Sun*. For example, in the sentence below, bold indicates graduation, underlining – judgement and italics – affect (adapted from Coffin and O'Halloran, 2005: 149):

> **Two million jobs** will be lost <u>if Tony Blair signs the EU treaty</u> (negative indirect judgement of Blair), it was *feared* last night.

They then used a 45-million word newspaper corpus, made up of *The Sun* and its Sunday version, *The News of the World*, to check any potential over-interpretation of their Appraisal analysis. Their concordances of *United States of Europe* reveal many of the local lexico-grammatical environments to indicate a negative evaluation.

towards their ambition of a	United States of Europe,	stretching from Shetland
could pave the wave for a	United States of Europe.	British people have made
leader's bleak plan for a	United States of Europe	came as a hammer blow to
the road towards a Federal	United States of Europe.	Hague has never tried to
forming into a giant	United States of Europe	–with the same tax and
for a hopeless dream of a	United States of Europe.	He is certain to pay the

Concordance lines for *United States of Europe* from the *sunnow* sub-corpus of the Bank of English (adapted from Coffin and O'Halloran, 2005: 157).

Because of the negative prosody of the *United States of Europe*, Coffin and O'Halloran argue that Sun readers will be potentially predisposed to evaluate related expressions negatively even when they occur in a seemingly neutral statement, as in the case of the last sentence (*Mr Blair will be expected to sign up to the constitution blueprint by the end of June*) in their text chosen for qualitative analysis (see also Coffin and O'Halloran, 2006; O'Halloran, 2009).

Corpus-informed critical discourse studies

Another perspective on corpus-based approaches to CDA, derived from the discourse-historical approach, is offered by the team of linguists working at Lancaster University on the project *Discourses of Refugees and Asylum Seekers in the UK press 1996–2006*. Their research is based on the analysis of a 140-million-word corpus of British news articles about refugees, asylum seekers, immigrants and migrants (collectively referred to as RASIM).

A key difference between CADS and this discourse-historical inspired study is that in the RASIM project a wide spectrum of background information on the social, political, historical and cultural context of the corpus data was used both to formulate hypotheses on which to base research questions and to inform interpretation of the corpus data. Key terms like 'refugee' were examined to see how they were conceptualized by 'official' sources such as dictionaries and organizations directly involved with these groups. Text-based analyses were also supported by official statistical information on the number of asylum applications.

The RASIM research has some affinity with the CADS approach through its focus on the identification of key words and collocation patterns, and of their underlying semantic preference and discourse prosodies (Baker and McEnery, 2005; Baker *et al.*, 2008), but it has less focus on SFL categories for linguistic analysis. It also differs from CADS in that these patterns were then mapped onto the discourse-historical CDA notions of *topos* and topic and also on the metaphors commonly employed in racist discourse, as a means of revealing elements of the underlying discourses relating to RASIM. For example, one of the common metaphors found to frame refugees was that of 'water', symbolizing the loss of control over immigration. Gabrielatos and Baker (2008: 15) point out: 'Statements employing this metaphor (e.g., *immigrants are flooding the country*) can very well utilize a *topos* of Number.' In assigning evaluative significance to various framing discourses for refugees and immigrants, Baker *et al.* (2008) also consulted the British National Corpus (BNC) to ascertain normative patterns of language use against which to compare the findings from the newspaper corpus (see Stubbs, 1996).

Corpus studies underpinned by the discourse-historical approach are few and far between, no doubt one reason being the intricate nature of the analyses drawing on a web of contextual strands at various stages of such a study as the one above. Contextual approaches are also the focus of the following section dedicated to various types of spoken corpora.

Corpus-based contextual approach

The analysis of spoken discourse through corpus linguistic techniques is largely concerned with how various rhetorical and pragmatic devices are operationalized by participants in specific social situations. This approach can be traced back to pioneering research carried out by Aijmer (1986) and others on the 500,000-word London-Lund Corpus (LLC) of spoken English of casual conversation. Stenström's (1994) application, on the basis of the Sinclair/Coulthard model, of the exchange sequence of questions and answers to this corpus is also a landmark in analyses of spoken discourse. Altenberg's (1998) study of the LLC was one of the first to explore phraseology in spoken corpora. His research shows that functional sequences often have a core with optional extensions (e.g., [oh/ yes] I see) and that sequences may overlap, being sometimes interrupted by non-formulaic language, in accordance with Sinclair's (1991) 'open-choice' principle.

Since the 1990s other studies making use of the LLC have adopted a more finely grained, integrative, multi-layered approach, also paying attention to prosodic elements of the discourse for meaning-making. Aijmer (2002) analysed the discourse particle actually by following Brazil's (1995) prosodic model of proclaiming and referring tones and by noting correlations between its prosody and discourse functions in different positions in the utterance. Other studies linking prosody with discourse function include Wichmann's (2004) study of please requests in the ICE-GB Corpus (the British contribution to the International Corpus of English) and Cheng and Warren's (2008) study mapping speakers' discourse intonation choices onto word association patterns in a corpus of public discourse, one of the four sub-corpora in the two-million-word Hong Kong Corpus of Spoken English (HKCSE). A CDA perspective on this corpus is given in Cheng (2004), who shows how prosodic choices can be exploited by speakers so that a politician might assert common ground where none exists (see also Warren, 2004).

The 5-million-word CANCODE (Cambridge and Nottingham Corpus of Discourse in English) marked a watershed in the era of computerized spoken corpora for its design and range of analytical procedures (McCarthy, 1998; Carter and McCarthy, 2004). As well as being marked up for demographic data, it has as its main organizing principle five genre contexts (transactional, professional, pedagogical, socializing and intimate) and focuses on three types of goal-oriented exchanges. These three interaction types cover information provision (e.g. commentary by museum guide), collaborative task (e.g. choosing and buying a television), and collaborative idea (e.g. chatting with hairdresser) (see Koester, 2006 whose analysis of workplace discourse, a part of which is based on CANCODE, adopts similar investigative procedures, with a focus on the analysis of transactional and relational goals). The multi-faceted sociolinguistic, analytical approach of the CANCODE data draws on praxis theory (meanings are negotiated face to face and emerge from the unfolding discourse), which itself implicates and extends, as context is taken into account, the notion of adjacency pairs, turn-taking, turn boundaries and sequencing associated with conversation analysis. Hughes and McCarthy (1998) also posit the notion of an interpersonal grammar, exemplifying how certain grammatical features, e.g. tags and amplificatory noun-phrases occupying the tail slot of a sentence – 'It's very nice that road up through Skipton to the Dales' – signal relationships between participants and their stance or attitudinal positioning towards the emergent discourse (see Leech, 2000 for a detailed discussion on discourse grammar).

The approach also draws on rational action (language as strategic motivated choices), encompassing Brown and Levinson's (1987) politeness theory. McCarthy (1998) reports that the CANCODE data show speech acts to be far more indirect and subtle in their unfolding than invented examples; the verb form *disagree* occurs mostly in contexts reporting disagreement with someone, or disagreeing with propositions rather than people. Adolphs' (2008) research on speech acts and pragmatic functions in CANCODE is primarily motivated by this 'language as rational action' perspective.

While corpus linguistics and discourse analysis have benefited from each other's strengths, there still remain some weaknesses to address. Widdowson (2000: 4) has remarked that corpus-based methods focus on the text as product and 'cannot account for the complex interplay of linguistic and contextual factors whereby discourse is enacted'. In a similar vein, Virtanen (2009: 62) remarks that 'the main problem on the road from discourse to corpora and back again remains the lack of contextual dynamism'. Furthermore, Lee (2008) notes the lack of non-verbal aspects of communication accompanying spoken corpora. The following section reviews some very recent endeavours that serve to address these issues, thereby investing corpus-based discourse analysis with more of a 'language in action' orientation. Yet at the same time the changing face of 'discourse' raises new challenges for corpus linguists.

Recent developments and new challenges

As Widdowson (2000: 4) has noted: 'It [the computer] cannot produce ethnographic descriptions of language use.' This fact, together with 'the lack of immediacy of the discourses vis-à-vis the analyst', which 'may be a hindrance for types of discourse analysis that rely on intimate knowledge of the data, participants and context' (Lee, 2008: 95) no longer remain such stumbling blocks as evidenced by Handford's (2010b) research of business meetings from CANBEC (Cambridge and Nottingham Corpus of Business English). Handford maps out a sophisticated set of practices (professional, social, discursive), including ethnographic data in the form of field notes and interviews, in order to understand professional practices of the genre. Through this multi-perspective lens Handford is able not only to capture the routinized aspects of the genre but also to tap into the 'contextual dynamism' of the communication to shed light on discourse features.

Until very recently corpora were analysed from a monomodal perspective, either written or spoken. Multimodal corpora are now being compiled with a view to aligning non-linguistic and linguistic aspects of spoken discourse. Pioneers in this field working in the Hallidayan tradition (Baldry and Thibault, 2006, and forthcoming) take a systemic–functional orientation to the discourse to determine how different semiotic resources (language, gaze, gesture, movement etc.) interact to create meaning. They propose the notion of 'visual collocation' to refer to the probability of constellations of visual items in a particular setting; for example, in car advertisements featuring test drivers, the car is often found as the phenomenon in a gaze transitivity frame, collocating with difficult testing terrains such as deserts. Another key initiative is that reported in Carter and Adolphs (2008) on a corpus of video-taped MA and PhD supervision sessions: the authors advocate the importance of taking a discourse-level perspective on the integration of verbal and visual elements of the corpus data, noting a correlation between different types of non-verbal backchanneling (head nods) and information structure and function. A third pioneering endeavour is that undertaken by Gu (2006), from a situated discourse perspective in which video streams and synchronized sounds take precedence over the orthographic transcription in the analysis. This type of multimodal analysis moves from the analytic unit of a situated discourse through several layers to a prosodic unit of illocutionary force. Gu's work, with its emphasis on language as a social phenomenon used in meaning-making, has some affinity with Halliday's SFL, and also draws on Kress' (2001) work on multimodality in its study of social action over time.

However, there is now a 'new modal order' emerging in this era of digital literacies, specifically computer-mediated communication involving e-mail, discussion groups, Internet relay chats (IRC) and weblogs (Beißwenger and Storrer, 2008; King, 2009; Ooi, 2009). Although some analyses have been carried out into weblogs (Ooi *et al.*, 2007), this is still a fledgling area as far as corpus-based discourse analysis is concerned, and one that poses enormous challenges. How can all the semiotic elements in a corpus of weblogs, with its manifold modalities (text, video, pictures, audio files, hypertextual links to other blogs,) be accommodated within a discourse-analytic framework? Even the written text alone will require new software for analysing discourse features of internet communication such as emoticons, which can have evaluative, expressive or regulative functions, and other conventions (such as upper case) for simulating prosodic features. Moreover, King (2009) notes the challenge for corpus linguists in analysing turn-taking in chat rooms, in which one turn can often be split into many in order to keep up with the real-time unfolding of conversation.

This review chapter of corpus-based discourse analysis has exemplified how the field has moved from single-pronged to more multi-pronged approaches, from a language in use to a more complex language in action perspective, and from monomodal to multimodal analyses. This complex synergy of methods, approaches and tools has enabled a rapprochement of the two fields, corpus linguistics no longer hovering on the periphery of discourse analysis but now assuming a central role. However, new forms of discourse are evolving that have thrown up new challenges for corpus linguistics, in the never-ending quest to get at the heart of what 'discourse' really entails.

Further reading

Aijmer, K. and Stenström, A.-B. (eds.) (2004) *Discourse Patterns in Spoken and Written Corpora*. Amsterdam: John Benjamins.

This edited collection contains a range of corpus-based studies on different aspects of discourse: cohesion and coherence, metadiscourse and discourse markers, and text and information structure.

Baker, P. (2006) *Using Corpora in Discourse Analysis*. London: Continuum.

This book provides a very reader-friendly introduction to how key words, frequency and dispersion, and collocational networks can inform discourse analysis, especially those studies of a CDA nature.

Charles, M., Pecorari, D., and Hunston, S. (eds.) (2010) *Academic Writing: At the Interface of Corpus and Discourse*. London: Continuum.

This volume contains a collection of articles that focus on different types of discourse: genre and disciplinary, interpersonal and learner discourse.

Paltridge, B. (2006) *Discourse Analysis*. London: Continuum.

Chapter 7 in this volume, 'Corpus Approaches to Discourse Analysis', presents a very useful overview of the relationship between corpus analysis and discourse analysis.

References

Aarts, J. (2002) 'Review of *Corpus Linguistics at Work*', *International Journal of Corpus Linguistics*, 7 (1): 118–123.

Ädel, A. and Reppen, R. (eds.) (2008) *Corpora and Discourse: The Challenges of Different Settings*. Amsterdam: John Benjamins.

Adolphs, S. (2008) *Corpus and Context: Investigating Pragmatic Functions in Spoken Discourse*. Amsterdam: John Benjamins.

Aijmer, K. (1986) 'Discourse variation and hedging', in B. Aarts and W. Meijs (eds.) *Corpus Linguistics II: New Studies in the Analysis and Exploitation of Computer Corpora*. Amsterdam: Rodopi, pp. 1–18.

Aijmer, K. (2002) *English Discourse Particles; Evidence From a Corpus*. Amsterdam: John Benjamins.

Aijmer, K. (2009) '"So er I just sort I dunno I think it's just because…": a corpus study of *I don't know* and *dunno* in learners' spoken English', in A. Jucker *et al.* (eds.) *Corpora: Pragmatics and Discourse*. Amsterdam: Rodopi, pp. 151–168.

Ali Mohamed, A. (2007) 'Semantic fields of problem in business English: Malaysian and British journalistic business texts', *Corpora*, 2 (2): 211–239.

Alonso Belmonte, I. (2009) 'Towards a genre-based characterization of the problem-solution textual pattern in English newspaper editorials and op-eds', *Text and Talk*, 29 (4): 393–414.

Altenberg, B. (1998) 'On the phraseology of spoken English: the evidence of recurrent word combinations', in A. Cowie (ed.) *Phraseology: Theory, Analysis and Applications*. Oxford: Clarendon Press, pp. 101–122.

Baker, P. (ed.) (2009) *Contemporary Corpus Linguistics*. London: Continuum.

Baker, P. and McEnery, T. (2005) 'A corpus-based approach to discourses of refugees and asylum seekers in UN and newspaper texts', *Journal of Language and Politics*, 4 (2): 197–226.

Baker, P., Gabrielatos, C., KhosraviNik, M., Krzyżanowski, M., Mcenery, T., and Wodak, R. (2008) 'A useful methodological synergy? Combining critical discourse analysis and corpus linguistics to examine discourses of refugees and asylum seekers in the UK Press', *Discourse and Society*, 19 (3): 273–306.

Baldry, A. and Thibault, P. (2006) "Multimodal corpus linguistics', in G. Thompson and S. Hunston (eds.) *System and Corpus; Exploring Connections*. London: Equinox, pp. 164–183.

Baldry, A. and Thibault, P. (forthcoming) *Multimodal Corpus Linguistics*. London: Routledge.

Bednarek, M. (2006) *Evaluation in Media Discourse*. London: Continuum.

Beißwenger, M. and Storrer, A. (2008) "Corpora of computer-mediated communication', in A. Lüdeling and M. Kytö (eds.) *Corpus Linguistics: An International Handbook. Vol. 1*. Amsterdam: Mouton de Gruyter, pp. 292–309.

Bhatia, V., Langton, N., and Lung, J. (2004) 'Legal discourse: opportunities and threats for corpus linguistics', in U. Connor and T. Upton (eds.), *Discourse in the Professions: Perspectives from Corpus Linguistics*. Amsterdam: John Benjamins, pp. 203–231.

Bhatia, V., Flowerdew, J., and Jones R. (eds.) (2008) *Advances in Discourse Studies*. London: Routledge.

Biber, D. (2006) *University Language: A Corpus-Based Study of Spoken and Written Registers*. Amsterdam: John Benjamins.

Biber, D., Connor, C., and Upton, T. (2007a) *Discourse on the Move: Using Corpus Analysis to Describe Discourse Structure*. Amsterdam: John Benjamins.

Biber, D., Conrad, S., and Cortes, V. (2004) '*If you look at…*: lexical bundles in university teaching and textbooks', *Applied Linguistics*, 25 (3): 371–405.

Biber, D., Conrad, S., and Reppen, R. (1998) *Corpus Linguistics: Investigating Language Structure and Use*. Cambridge: Cambridge University Press.

Biber, D., Csomay, E., Jones, J., and Keck, C. (2007b) 'Introduction to the analysis and identification of vocabulary-based discourse units', in D. Biber *et al.* (eds.), *Discourse on the Move*. Amsterdam: John Benjamins. pp. 155–173.

Blommaert, J. (2005) *Discourse*. Cambridge: Cambridge University Press.

Bondi, M. (2001) 'Small corpora and language variation: reflexivity across genres', in M. Ghadessy, A. Henry, and R. Roseberry (eds.) *Small Corpus Studies and ELT*. Amsterdam: John Benjamins.

Bondi, M. (2004) 'The discourse function of contrastive connectors in academic abstracts', in K. Aijmer and A.-B. Stenström (eds.) *Discourse Patterns in Spoken and Written Corpora*. Amsterdam: John Benjamins, pp.139–156.

Brazil, D. (1995) *A Grammar of Speech*. Oxford: Oxford University Press.

Brown, P. and Levinson, S. (1987) *Politeness*. Cambridge: Cambridge University Press.

Carter, R. and Adolphs, S. (2008) 'Linking the verbal and the visual: new directions for corpus linguistics', *Language and Computers*, 64: 275–291.

Carter, R. and McCarthy, M. (2004) 'Talking, creating: interactional language, creativity and context', *Applied Linguistics*, 25 (1): 62–88.

Charles, M. (2003) ' "This mystery…": a corpus-based study of the use of nouns to construct stance in theses from two contrasting disciplines', *Journal of English for Academic Purposes*, 2: 313–326.

Charles, M. (2006) 'The construction of stance in reporting clauses: a cross-disciplinary study of theses', *Applied Linguistics*, 27: 492–518.

Cheng, W. (2004) '//→ FRIENDS//↘↗ Ladies and GENtlemen//: Some preliminary findings from a corpus of spoken public discourses in Hong Kong', in U. Connor and T. Upton (eds.), *Discourse in the Professions: Perspectives from Corpus Linguistics*. Amsterdam: John Benjamins, pp. 35–50.

Cheng, W. and Warren, M. (2008) '//→ ONE country two SYStems//: The discourse intonation patterns of word associations', in A. Ädel and R. Reppen (eds.) *Corpora and Discourse: The Challenges of Different Settings*. Amsterdam: John Benjamins, pp. 135–153.

Coffin, C. and O'Halloran, K. (2005) 'FINDING THE GLOBAL GROOVE: Theorising and analyzing dynamic reader positioning using APPRAISAL, corpus, and a concordancer', *Critical Discourse Studies*, 2 (2): 143–163.

Coffin, C. and O'Halloran, K. (2006) 'The role of appraisal and corpora in detecting covert evaluation', *Functions of Language*, 13 (1): 77–110.

Connor, U. and Upton, T. (eds.) (2004a) *Applied Corpus Linguistics: A Multi-Dimensional Perspective*. Amsterdam: Rodopi.

Connor, U. and Upton, T. (eds.) (2004b) *Discourse in the Professions: Perspectives From Corpus Linguistics*. Amsterdam: John Benjamins.

Conrad, S. (2002) 'Corpus linguistic approaches for discourse analysis', *Annual Review of Applied Linguistics*, 22: 75–95.

Cortes, V. (2004) 'Lexical bundles in published student disciplinary writing: examples from history and biology', *English for Specific Purposes*, 23: 397–423.

Cowie, A. (ed.) (1998) *Phraseology: Theory, Analysis and Applications*. Oxford: Clarendon Press.

Crawford Camiciottoli, B. (2007) *The Language of Business Studies Lectures*. Amsterdam: John Benjamins.

Csomay, E. (2005) 'Linguistic variation within university classroom talk: a corpus-based perspective', *Linguistics and Education*, 15 (3): 243–274.

Duguid, A. (2007) 'Soundbiters bit. Contracted dialogistic space and the textual relations of the No. 10 team analysed through corpus-assisted discourse studies', in N. Fairclough, G. Cortese, and P. Ardizzone (eds.) *Discourse and Contemporary Social Change*. Frankfurt am Main: Peter Lang, pp. 73–94.

Fairclough, N. (2000) *New Labour, New Language?* London: Routledge.

Flowerdew, J. (2003) 'Signalling nouns in discourse', *English for Specific Purposes*, 22: 329–346.

Flowerdew, J. and Forest, R. (2010) 'Schematic structure and lexico-grammatical realization in corpus-based genre analysis: the case of research in the PhD literature review', in M. Charles, D. Pecorari, and S. Hunston (eds.) *Academic Writing at the Interface of Corpus and Discourse*. London: Continuum, pp. 15–36.

Flowerdew, L. (1998) 'Corpus linguistic techniques applied to textlinguistics', *System*, 26 (4): 541–552.

Flowerdew, L. (2008a) 'Determining discourse-based moves in professional reports', in A. Ädel and R. Reppen (eds.) *Corpora and Discourse: The Challenges of Different Settings*. Amsterdam: John Benjamins, pp. 117–131.

Flowerdew, L. (2008b) *Corpus-Based Analyses of the Problem-Solution Pattern*. Amsterdam: John Benjamins.

Gabrielatos, C. and Baker, P. (2008) 'Fleeing, sneaking, flooding. a corpus analysis of discursive constructions of refugees and asylum seekers in the UK press, 1996–2005', *Journal of English Linguistics*, 36 (1): 5–38.

Gee, J. P. (2001) *An Introduction to Discourse Analysis*. London: Routledge.

Gledhill, C. (2000) 'The discourse function of collocation in research article introductions', *English for Specific Purposes*, 19: 115–135.

Granger, S. (1998) 'Prefabricated patterns in advanced EFL writing: collocations and formulae', in A. Cowie, (ed.) *Phraseology: Theory, Analysis and Applications*. Oxford: Clarendon Press, pp. 145–160.

Gu, Y. (2006) 'Multimodal text analysis: a corpus linguistic approach to situated discourse', *Text and Talk*, 26 (2): 127–167.

Haarman, L. and Lombardo, L. (eds.) (2009) *Evaluation and Stance in War News*. London: Continuum.

Handford, M. (2010a) 'What can a corpus tell us about specialist genres?', in M. McCarthy and A. O'Keeffe (eds.) *The Routledge Handbook of Corpus Linguistics*. London: Routledge, pp. 255–269.

Handford, M. (2010b) *The Language of Business Meetings*. Cambridge: Cambridge University Press.

Hardt-Mautner, G. (1995) *Only Connect: Critical Discourse Analysis and Corpus Linguistics*. UCREL Technical Paper 6. Lancaster: University of Lancaster.

Hoey, M. (2001) *Textual Interaction: An Introduction to Written Discourse Analysis*. London: Routledge.

Hoey, M. (2004) 'Textual colligation: a special kind of lexical priming', in K. Aijmer and B. Altenberg (eds.) *Advances in Corpus Linguistics*, Amsterdam: Rodopi, pp. 171–194.

Hoey, M. (2005) *Lexical Priming: A New Theory of Words and Language*. London: Routledge.

Hughes, R. and McCarthy, M. (1998) 'From sentence to grammar: discourse grammar and English language teaching', *TESOL Quarterly*, 32 (2): 263–287.

Hunston, S. (2002) *Corpora in Applied Linguistics*. Cambridge: Cambridge University Press.

Hunston, S. and Thompson, G. (eds) (2000) *Evaluation in Text: Authorial Stance and the Construction of Discourse*. Oxford: Oxford University Press.

Hyland, K. (2005) *Metadiscourse*. London: Continuum.

Hyland, K. (2008) 'As can be seen: lexical bundles and disciplinary variation', *English for Specific Purposes*, 27 (1): 4–21.

Lynne Flowerdew

Hyland, K. (2009) *Academic Discourse*. London: Continuum.

Hyland, K. and Tse, P. (2004) 'Metadiscourse in academic writing: a reappraisal', *Applied Linguistics*, 25 (2): 156–177.

Jucker, A., Schreier, D., and Hundt, M. (eds.) (2009a) *Corpora: Pragmatics and Discourse*. Amsterdam: Rodopi.

Jucker, A., Schreier, D., and Hundt, M. (2009b) 'Corpus linguistics, pragmatics and discourse'. In A. Jucker *et al.* (2009a), pp. 3–9.

Kanoksilapatham, B. (2007) 'Rhetorical moves in biochemistry research articles', in D. Biber *et al.* (eds.), *Discourse on the Move*. Amsterdam: John Benjamins, pp. 73–119.

King, B. (2009) 'Building and analyzing corpora of computer-mediated communication', in P. Baker (ed.) *Contemporary Corpus Linguistics*. London: Continuum, pp. 301–320.

Koester, A. (2006) *Investigating Workplace Discourse*. London: Routledge.

Kress, G. (2001) *Multimodal Discourse: The Modes and Media of Contemporary Communication*. London: Arnold.

Krishnamurthy, R. (1996) Ethnic, racial and tribal: the language of racism? In R. Caldas-Coulthard, and M. Coulthard (eds.) *Texts and Practices: Readings in Critical Discourse Analysis*, pp. 129–149. London: Routledge.

Lee, D. (2008) 'Corpora and discourse analysis: new ways of doing old things', in V. Bhatia, J. Flowerdew, and R. Jones (eds) *Advances in Discourse Studies*. London: Routledge, pp. 86–99.

Leech, G. (2000) 'Grammar of spoken English: new outcomes of corpus-oriented research'. *Language Learning*, 50 (4): 675–724.

Mahlberg, M. (2003) 'The textlinguistic dimension of corpus linguistics', *International Journal of Corpus Linguistics*, 8 (1): 97–108.

Martin, J. and White, P. (2005) *The Language of Evaluation: Appraisal in English*. Basingstoke: Palgrave/Macmillan.

Mauranen, A. (2001) 'Reflexive academic talk: observations from MICASE', in R. Simpson and J. Swales (eds.) *Corpus Linguistics in North America*. Ann Arbor, MI: University of Michigan Press, pp. 165–178.

Mauranen, A. (2003) ' "But here's a flawed argument": socialization in and through metadiscourse', in P. Leistyna and C. Meyer (eds.) *Corpus Analysis: Language Structure and Language Use*. Amsterdam: Rodopi, pp. 19–34.

Mautner, G. (2009a) 'Corpora and critical discourse analysis', in P. Baker (ed.) *Contemporary Corpus Linguistics*. London: Continuum, pp. 32–46.

Mautner, G. (2009b) 'Checks and balances: how corpus linguistics can contribute to CDA', in R. Wodak and M. Meyer (eds.) *Methods of Critical Discourse Analysis*. London: Sage, pp. 122–143.

McCarthy, M. (1998) *Spoken Languages and Applied Linguistics*. Cambridge: Cambridge University Press.

McEnery, T., Xiao, R., and Tono, Y. (2006) *Corpus-Based Language Studies*. London: Routledge.

Morley, J. and Bailey, P. (eds.) (2009) *Corpus-Assisted Discourse Studies on the Iraq Conflict*. London: Routledge.

O'Halloran, K. (2009) 'Inferencing and cultural reproduction: a corpus-based critical discourse analysis', *Text and Talk*, 29 (1): 21–51.

Ooi, V. (2009) 'Computer-mediated language and corpus linguistics', in Y. Kawaguchi, M. Minegishi, and J. Durand (eds.) *Corpus Analysis and Variation in Linguistics*. Amsterdam: John Benjamins, pp. 103–120.

Ooi, V., Tan, P., and Chiang, A. (2007) 'Analysing personal weblogs in Singapore English: the Wmatrix approach', in *EVariEng (Journal of the Research Unit for Variation, Contacts, and Change in English). Volume 2: Towards Multimedia in Corpus Studies*. Finland: University of Helsinki.

Parodi, G. (2009) 'Academic and professional written genres in disciplinary communication', in J. Renkema (ed.) *Discourse, of Course: An Overview of Discourse in Research Studies*. Amsterdam: John Benjamins, pp. 93–110.

Partington, A. (2003) *The Linguistics of Political Argument*. London: Routledge.

Partington, A. (2004) 'Corpora and discourse, a most congruous beast', in A. Parrtington, J. Morley, and L. Haarman (eds.) *Corpora and Discourse*, Bern: Peter Lang, pp. 11–20.

Partington, A. (2007) 'Irony and reversal of evaluation'. *Journal of Pragmatics*, 39: 1547–1569.

Rayson, P. (2008) 'From key words to key semantic domains'. *International Journal of Corpus Linguistics*, 13 (4): 519–549.

Renkema, J. (2009) *The Texture of Discourse*. Amsterdam: John Benjamins.

Simpson, R. and Swales, J. (eds.) (2001) *Corpus Linguistics in North America*. Ann Arbor, MI: University of Michigan Press.

Sinclair, J.McH. (1991) *Corpus, Concordance, Collocation*. Oxford: Oxford University Press.

Sinclair, J.McH. (2004) *Trust the Text*. London: Routledge.

Stenström, A.-B. (1994) *An Introduction to Spoken Interaction*. London: Longman.

Stubbs, M. (1983) *Discourse Analysis*. Chicago, IL: University of Chicago Press.

Stubbs, M. (1996) *Text and Corpus Analysis*. Oxford: Blackwell.

Stubbs, M. (2001) *Words and Phrases: Corpus Studies of Lexical Semantics*. Oxford; Blackwell.

Swales, J. (1990) *Genre Analysis: English in Academic and Research Genres*. Cambridge: Cambridge University Press.

Swales, J. (2004) *Research Genres*. Cambridge: Cambridge University Press.

Swales, J. and Malczewski, B. (2001) 'Discourse management and new-episode flags in MICASE', in R. Simpson and J. Swales (eds.) *Corpus Linguistics in North America*. Ann Arbor, MI: University of Michigan Press, pp. 145–164.

Titscher, S., Meyer, M., and Vetter, E. (2000) *Methods of Text and Discourse Analysis*. London: Sage Publications.

Tognini Bonelli, E. (2001) *Corpus Linguistics at Work*. Amsterdam: John Benjamins.

Upton, T. and Connor, U. (2001) 'Using computerized corpus analysis to investigate the textlinguistic discourse moves of a genre', *English for Specific Purposes*, 20: 313–329.

Virtanen, T. (2009) 'Discourse linguistics meets corpus linguistics: theoretical and methodological issues in the troubled relationship', in A. Renouf and A. Kehoe (eds.) *Corpus Linguistics: Refinements and Reassessments*, Amsterdam: Rodopi, pp. 49–65.

Warren, M. (2004) 'A corpus-driven analysis of the use of intonation to assert dominance and control', in U. Connor and T. Upton (eds.), *Applied Corpus Linguistics. A Multi-Dimensional Perspective*. Amsterdam: Rodopi, pp. 21–33.

Wichmann, A. (2004) 'The intonation of *please*-requests: a corpus-based study', *Journal of Pragmatics*, 36: 1521–1549.

Widdowson, H. G. (1995) 'Discourse analysis: a critical view', *Language and Literature* 4 (3): 157–172.

Widdowson, H. G. (2000) 'The limitations of linguistics applied', *Applied Linguistics*, 21(1): 3–25.

Widdowson, H. G. (2004) *Text, Context, Pretext: Critical Issues in Discourse Analysis*. Oxford: Blackwell.

Wodak, R. and Meyer, M. (2009a) 'Critical discourse analysis: history, agenda, theory and methodology', in R. Wodak and M. Meyer (eds.) *Methods of Critical Discourse Analysis*. London: Sage, pp. 1–33.

R. Wodak, M. Meyer, (eds.) (2009b) *Methods of Critical Discourse Analysis*. London: Sage.

Part II
Register and genre

Part II

Register and genre

14

Register and discourse analysis

Douglas Biber

Introduction

One major approach to discourse analysis focuses on the study of language use, describing the ways in which lexical and grammatical features are used in texts (see Schiffrin *et al.*, 2001: 1; Biber *et al.*, 2007: 1–4). Different kinds of texts have different linguistic characteristics, representing systematic patterns of variation that can be investigated under the rubric of *register*: text varieties of a language associated with particular situations of use.

The description of a register includes three major components: the situational context, the typical linguistic features, and the functional relationships between the first two components (Biber and Conrad, 2009: 6–11). The situational context involves description of the circumstances of text production and reception, as well as the relationships among participants. For example: Is the text produced in speech or writing? Is the addressee present, and is communication interactive? What are the primary communicative purposes?

The linguistic analysis includes all lexical and grammatical characteristics that are typical of the text variety. These are usually core linguistic features like nouns, past tense verbs, relative clauses, and so on. The linguistic description of a register requires quantitative analysis to identify the features that are "typical." That is, these linguistic features can occur in any text from any variety. What makes them register features is that they are especially frequent and pervasive in some text varieties in contrast to other varieties.

To give a simple example, nouns and pronouns can be found in any text. However, nouns are extremely frequent in written academic texts but comparatively rare in spoken conversations, while pronouns have the opposite distribution (extremely frequent in conversation; rare in academic writing). Thus compare:

Text sample 1: academic research article

Nouns are underlined; **pronouns are marked in bold italics**

This paper reports an analysis of Tucker's central-prediction-system model and an empirical comparison of *it* with two competing models. *One* of these competing models is a modification of Tucker's model developed by Bashaw. The other is the standard linear-regression model. The term "central-prediction system" refers to any centralized statistical system for the prediction of academic success at a given educational level from achievement at a previous level. The most common application has been the prediction of college-freshman grade averages from high-school performance for a particular school system. The application of interest to the writer is the

Douglas Biber

prediction of (college) junior-year achievement from lower-division achievement—especially in
the case of the junior-college transfer student.

Text sample 2: conversation [two women with an infant]

Nouns are underlined; **pronouns are marked in bold italics**

A: **She** cut herself?
B: **I**'m not sure
A: Yeah, **she** cut her lip.
B: Okay. Oh my gosh—a big fat lip.
A: <sighing> Oh, oh.
B: Oh, **that** hurts. <sighing> oww
A: **You** want a little ice? a little paper towel?
B: Yeah, **that** would be great. This orange juice is not gonna feel good. **I**'m just gonna put
     some water in here. **It** won't feel good, **it** won't feel good, 'cause **it**'s orange juice.
A: Here, **it**'ll just help in a little.
B: Let**'s** put some water in, 'cause maybe **that** won't hurt your mouth. 'Cause if **I** give **her**
     that bit of orange juice **that** really hurts if **she** drinks **that**.
A: Um.

This sample from an academic research article uses only two pronouns (*it, one*), but it has
numerous nouns, which often occur in complex noun phrases (e.g., *the prediction of college-
freshman grade averages from high-school performance for a particular school system*). In contrast, nearly
every utterance in the conversational sample includes one or more pronouns (e.g., *I, you, she, it,
that*) but comparatively few nouns.

Linguistic differences of this type are the data that must be explained by the third component of a
register analysis: the functional interpretation. That is, one of the central assumptions of register analysis
is that linguistic features are always functional: linguistic features tend to occur in a register because
they are particularly well-suited to the purposes and situational context of the register.

The functional interpretation attempts to explain linguistic preferences in terms of the situational characteristics. In the above example, there are several important situational differences
between the registers, including:

Academic article	*Conversation*
written	spoken
separate physical setting	shared time/place
no interaction	interactive
professional background knowledge	personal background knowledge
time for planning/editing	real-time production
purposes: convey information;	purposes: on-going actions and
document past events	events; express feelings

With this many situational differences, it is easy to identify potential functional motivations for the
linguistic differences described above. That is, pronouns are very common in conversation (as
opposed to academic writing) because interlocutors make frequent reference to each other during
the interaction (*I, you*) as well as to objects and people in their shared time and place (e.g. *it, he, she,*

192

that). Pronouns are also used in expressions of personal stance (e.g. *that's great*). From a production point of view, it takes more effort to produce a noun phrase with specific reference than a pronoun with situated reference. For example, the situated pronoun in the utterance *Oh that hurts* would need to be replaced by a fuller noun phrase like *Oh that bad sore on your lip hurts* if the speaker wanted to achieve a more explicit situation-independent reference. Academic writing has the opposite characteristics (e.g. no shared time/place; no interaction or individual addressees; but extensive planning time and a much more "informational" purpose). As a result, we see the dense use of nouns rather than pronouns in academic writing.

The linguistic component of register analysis requires identification of the *pervasive* linguistic features in the variety: linguistic characteristics that might occur in any text but are especially common in the target register. It is these pervasive linguistic features that are clearly functional. As a result, registers can be identified and described based on analysis of either complete texts or a collection of text samples.

Text varieties can also be described by analyzing language features that characterize complete texts, referred to as the *genre* perspective (see Biber and Conrad, 2009: 15–19). Genre analysis corresponds to a second major approach to discourse analysis: consideration of linguistic structure "beyond the sentence" and of the ways in which texts are constructed (see Schiffrin *et al.*, 2001: 1; Biber *et al.*, 2007: 4–6).

Genre features are not pervasive; rather, they might occur only one time in a complete text, often at the beginning or ending of a text. An oft-cited example of genre features is the rhetorical sections that are conventionally used with construct an academic research article: abstract, introduction, methods section, results/discussion, and bibliography (see e.g. Swales, 1990). By convention, these sections are found in most research articles (at least in experimental studies), occurring in this fixed order. Unlike the distribution of nouns and pronouns, genre features often occur only once in a text, and thus they can only be identified through analysis of complete texts.

Genre features are often conventional rather than functional. That is, genre features conform to the social expectations of how a text of a particular type should be constructed, rather than having clear functional associations with the situational context. To give a simple example, by convention we expect the author/speaker to self-identify at the beginning of a text in many genres, including novels, textbooks, research articles, and even telephone conversations. However, in contrast, there is a strong conventional expectation that the author will self-identify at the *end* of a text in a personal letter, an e-mail message, or even a short note left for a friend. In cases like these it is not clear that the placement of the genre feature is directly functional. However, these are important aspects of textual structure.

The following sections will focus mostly on register analysis rather than genre analysis. Section "corpus-based analyses of registers" introduces corpus-based analysis as a research methodology that is particularly well suited for register studies. Section "e-mail messages as a register," then, presents a more detailed case study of a register analysis, focusing on email messages (adapted from Biber and Conrad, 2009, Chapter 7). This case study shows how registers can be investigated at different levels of generality. Thus emails as a general register are first compared to conversation and academic writing, but the case study also shows that it is possible to consider variation among sub-registers of email messages, depending on the relationship between the sender and recipient. This case study illustrates how even small situational differences among registers are associated with systematic linguistic differences.

Finally, section "multi-dimensional studies of register variation" describes the second major type of research question that arises in register studies: investigation of the overall patterns of register variation (rather than detailed descriptions of individual registers). Multi-dimensional analysis is introduced as a research approach designed for research questions of this type.

Douglas Biber

Corpus-based analyses of registers

Register analyses are often conducted using the methodologies of "corpus linguistics." There are several introductory textbooks that introduce this subfield of linguistics (e.g. McEnery *et al.*, 2006). According to Biber *et al.* (1998: 4), the essential characteristics of corpus-based analysis are:

- it is empirical, analyzing the actual patterns of use in natural texts;
- it utilizes a large and principled collection of natural texts, known as a "corpus," as the basis for analysis;
- it makes extensive use of computers for analysis, using both automatic and interactive techniques;
- it depends on both quantitative and qualitative analytical techniques.

Several of the advantages of the corpus-based approach come from the use of computers. Computers make it possible to identify and analyze complex patterns of language use on the basis of the consideration of a much larger collection of texts than could be dealt with by hand. Furthermore, computers provide consistent, reliable analyses—they don't change their mind or become tired during a register analysis. Taken together, these characteristics result in a scope and reliability of analysis otherwise not possible. However, the quantitative and computational aspects of corpus analysis do not lessen the need for functional interpretations in register studies. Rather, corpus-based analyses must go beyond simple counts of linguistic features to include qualitative, functional interpretations of the quantitative patterns. In this regard, all register studies follow the same major methodological steps, whether they are corpus-based or not.

In sum, the main contributions of corpus-based research are that it is based on the empirical analysis of a large sample of texts representing a register and, as a result, descriptions are more reliable and valid than analyses based on only a few texts. For these reasons, the case studies illustrated in the following sections all employ corpus-analysis techniques.

E-mail messages as a register

From a register perspective, e-mail messages are interesting because they share some situational characteristics with both conversational registers and written informational registers. For the case study I compiled a mini-corpus of 76 messages that I had received, with a total of 15,840 words. (All proper names except my own have been changed in the examples below.) Like face-to-face conversation, e-mail messages can involve single or multiple recipients, and they can be motivated by many communicative purposes. The corpus used here includes both professional/academic as well as social e-mail messages. However, the corpus was restricted to include only personal/individual e-mail messages: messages written to a single specific person by another person (excluding mass advertising, fraudulent attempts by an anonymous person to obtain money, etc.).

Like conversation, personal e-mail messages are interactive. Addressors normally expect the addressee of a message to respond (at least acknowledging receipt of the message). In addition, addressors in both personal e-mail and conversation convey personal feelings and attitudes. In the mini-corpus studied here, even the authors of workplace e-mails often expressed personal stance, as in:

It **would be great** to have a lesson on these structures.
Hope you have a **great** trip!
Well, I find our grammar discussions **very interesting** and **would love** to talk about Tom's writing sample …

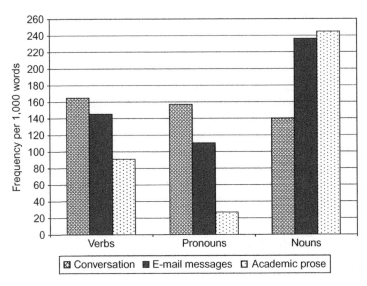

Figure 14.1 The use of major world classes in e-mail messages, compared with conversation and academic prose

At the same time, individual e-mail messages present some important differences from conversations. Conversation is spoken, while e-mail is written and then sent electronically. E-mail is therefore slower than conversation, but it has the potential to be more carefully planned, revised, and edited. In addition, time and space are shared to a lesser extent in e-mail messages than in face-to-face conversations. Physical space is rarely shared in e-mail messages, and an extended email interaction can occur over a period of many weeks, or even months.

In sum, e-mail messages are interpersonal and interactive (similar to conversation), but they are produced in writing, and the sender does not usually share time/place with the addressee (which makes e-mail more like other written registers). The linguistic characteristics of e-mail messages reflect this hybrid combination of situational characteristics.

Figure 14.1 compares the frequency of three basic grammatical features—lexical verbs (e.g. *run*, *want*), pronouns, and nouns—in e-mail messages, conversation, and academic prose. These three features were selected because they illustrate the range of distributions:

Linguistic feature	Characterization of e-mail messages
lexical verbs	similar to conversation
nouns	similar to academic prose
pronouns	intermediate

The frequency of lexical verbs in Figure 14.1 shows that e-mail messages incorporate frequent clauses, similar to conversation. For example, notice the relatively short clauses and numerous lexical verbs in the e-mail in Text sample 3:

Text sample 3: e-mail

Lexical verbs in bold

> Dr. Biber --
>
> I would love to meet with you in the afternoon on March 10. Anytime is fine. Just name the time and describe directions to your office. I appreciate all of your help in this. I have emailed Sandy Jackson to possibly meet about teaching placements and have been in contact with Andrea. See you in a few weeks!
>
> -- Dora

> This linguistic pattern is similar to the conversation sample (Text sample 2, repeated below), but dramatically different from the academic writing sample (Text sample 1, repeated below), which employs only three lexical verbs in a quite long passage:

Text sample 2 [repeated]: conversation

Lexical verbs in bold

> A: She **cut** herself?
> B: I'm not sure
> A: Yeah, she **cut** her lip.
> B: Okay. Oh my gosh – a big fat lip.
> A: <sighing> Oh, oh.
> B: Oh, that **hurts**. <sighing> oww
> A: You **want** a little ice? a little paper towel?
> B: Yeah, that would be great. This orange juice is not gonna **feel** good. I'm just gonna **put** some water in here. It won't **feel** good, it won't **feel** good, 'cause it's orange juice.
> A: Here, it'll just **help** in a little.
> B: Let's **put** some water in, 'cause maybe that won't **hurt** your mouth. 'Cause if I **give** her that bit of orange juice that really **hurts** if she **drinks** that.
> A: Um.

Text sample 1 [repeated]: academic research article

This paper **reports** an analysis of Tucker's central-prediction-system model and an empirical comparison of it with two competing models. One of these competing models is a modification of Tucker's model **developed** by Bashaw. The other is the standard linear-regression model. The term "central-prediction system" **refers** to any centralized statistical system for the prediction of academic success at a given educational level from achievement at a previous level. The most common application has been the prediction of college-freshman grade averages from high-school performance for a particular school system. The application of interest to the writer is the prediction of (college) junior-year achievement from lower-division achievement—especially in the case of the junior-college transfer student.

Fast production and a focus on specific tasks, activities, and personal stance (rather than concepts) all contribute to the high frequency of lexical verbs in e-mail messages. However, given those characteristics, the higher frequencies of nouns and pronouns in e-mails is surprising. Because e-mail messages are interactive, we might predict that pronouns would be used to the same extent as in conversation. Instead, we find more pronouns in conversation but more nouns in e-mail messages.

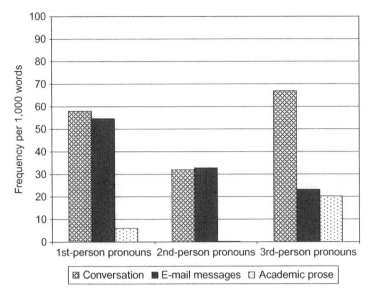

Figure 14.2 The use of pronoun classes, comparing conversation to e-mail messages

More detailed linguistic analyses help to explain these patterns. For example, Figure 14.2 considers the use of pronouns for each person separately: first, second, and third person.

Figure 14.2 shows that e-mail messages are actually very similar to conversations in the use of first-person pronouns (*I*, *we*) and second-person pronouns (*you*), indicating that these two registers are very similar in their overall interactivity. Text sample 3 above illustrates this dense use of *I* and *you*. In contrast, first-person pronouns are much less common in academic prose, while second-person pronouns are extremely rare in that register.

However, the pattern of use for third-person pronouns is completely different: common in conversation, but relatively rare in both e-mail messages and academic prose. Thus the conversation sample (Text 2) contains numerous occurrences of third-person pronouns (*she*, *it*, *that*), while there are few third-person pronouns in either the email or the academic writing passage (samples 1 and 3).

Instead of third-person pronouns, e-mail messages and academic prose both tend to rely on full nouns for third-person references. Sample 1 (above) illustrates this pattern for academic writing, while sample 3 is repeated below highlighting the dense use of nouns in everyday email messages:

Text sample 3 [repeated]: e-mail

nouns in bold

Dr. Biber --

I would love to meet with you in the **afternoon** on March 10. Anytime is fine. Just name the **time** and describe **directions** to your **office**. I appreciate all of your **help** in this. I have emailed **Sandy Jackson** to possibly meet about teaching **placements** and have been in contact with **Andrea**. See you in a few **weeks**!

--Dora

First- and second-person pronouns are common in conversation and individual e-mail messages because both registers have a specific addressor and a specific addressee, and the two interact directly with one another. However, the frequent use of third-person pronouns in conversation reflects a different situational characteristic: shared time and place. Participants usually do not share the same physical space in e-mail interactions, and often they do not share a temporal context either. As a result, these situated uses of third-person pronouns are much less common in e-mail messages, and full nouns are used instead. Text samples 3 (above) and 4 (below) both illustrate this pattern of use:

Text sample 4: professional e-mail

[third-person pronouns marked in **bold italics**; nouns underlined]

> Dear Professor Biber,
> Things are moving on for IALCC2004. The Program Committee met yesterday: we received 140 submissions and we have accepted around 90 papers for oral presentation. There will be also some poster presentations, but I do not know the number yet, because the "call for posters" is still open.
>
> I believe we have not talked about the proceedings yet. We plan to publish as usual two volumes of proceedings before the conference (Proceedings are usually distributed at the conference). **This** means that the delay is quite short for the editing work and we will have several people working on **it**. Of course, we would like to include the text of your talk in this book. Would it be possible for you to send us your text by the end of January? I am sorry I did not mention **that** to you earlier. I hope the delay will be ok for you.
> <...>

Notice first of all that this message incorporates numerous first- and second-person pronouns, referring directly to the writer (*I*) and the addressee (*you*). However, the message uses comparatively few third-person pronouns, and the ones that do occur are directly anaphoric, referring to the preceding proposition or a noun phrase in the preceding discourse. There are no third-person pronouns in this message that have a vague reference to the general situation or that refer directly to some entity in the writer's physical context. In contrast, there are numerous full nouns, referring to many entities and concepts in an explicit manner. The use of pronouns and nouns thus corresponds to the situational characteristics of high interactivity coupled with the lack of shared physical context.

Variation among sub-registers of e-mail messages

The linguistic characteristics described above apply generally to individual e-mail messages regardless of particular communicative purpose, because those messages are all interactive (with a specific addressor and addressee) but not produced in a shared physical context. In other respects, though, there are important situational differences among sub-registers of e-mail messages, and those differences correspond to systematic linguistic differences. Two parameters that are especially important in this case are the primary purpose/topic of communication, and the social relationship between the addressor and addressee.

To investigate these sub-registers, all e-mail messages in the mini-corpus were classified into three sub-categories: e-mails from friends and family on non-professional topics; e-mails from colleagues/friends on professional topics; and e-mails from "strangers" on professional topics. Table 14.1 shows the breakdown of messages across these categories:

One difference in these e-mail types is immediately clear from Table 14.1: text length. E-mail messages to friends and family on personal topics tend to be much shorter than e-mails on

Table 14.1. Composition of the mini-corpus of individual e-mail messages, classified according to addressee and purpose

Category	# of messages	Total words	Average length of message
friends and family; personal topics	23	2,852	124 words
colleagues/friends; professional topics	32	7,360	230 words
strangers; professional topics	21	5,628	268 words
Total	76	15,840	

professional topics; professional e-mails to strangers tend to be the longest. This difference exists in part because e-mails to friends can assume much more background knowledge, and therefore require much less explanatory prose. At one extreme, there are e-mail exchanges like the following—where people, places and contexts require no explanation:

Text sample 5: two e-mails between friends planning a social get-together

Doug, climbing gym tomorrow night, 6-ish, Scott
ok—see you then—Doug

In contrast, professional e-mails to strangers tend to be much longer, because the writers need to introduce themselves (or remind the recipient of who they are), state the reason for writing, provide any necessary background, and frame the whole discussion in a polite manner. Even a quick reminder about a meeting generally has more context than the exchange between friends, for example:

Text sample 6: e-mail from stranger confirming a meeting

Dr. Biber,

Just wanted to email and confirm that we were still on for meeting at 2:00 tomorrow. Hope to see you then. I don't know if I had CCd you, but I will be meeting with Dr. Bock at 1:30 and Dr. Edwards at 2:30, so it will be a whirlwind tour of the hallway!

If there are any problems, please call me at (111) 241–1925, as I will not have access to email until then. Thanks and I look forward to meeting with you.

Sincerely,
Donna Johansson

Not surprisingly, workplace e-mails between colleagues/friends tend to fall between these two extremes. Colleagues who interact regularly often write short messages that get directly to the point and assume a great deal of shared background, yet they still require more explanation than close friends continuing a social interaction.

Overall, there is a continuum of linguistic variation among these e-mail sub-registers. For example, Figure 14.3 repeats the information in Figure 14.1, but it distinguishes among the three e-mail sub-registers. Although the linguistic differences among the sub-registers are small, they are entirely consistent: "friends and family" emails are closest to conversation; "professional stranger" emails are closest to academic prose. Figure 14.4 plots the register distributions for a selection of other linguistic features, showing the same consistent patterns, but with the differences among email sub-registers

Douglas Biber

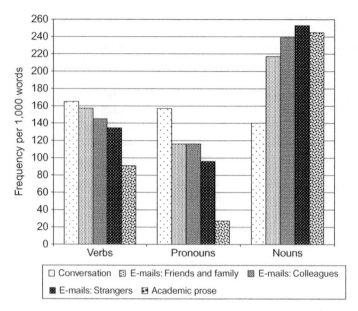

Figure 14.3 The use of major world classes, comparing conversation to e-mail sub-registers

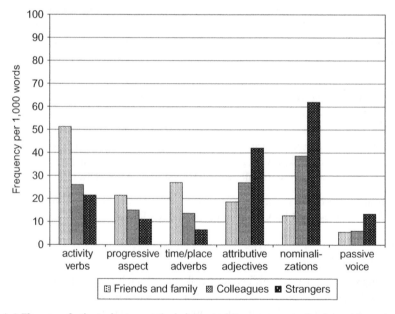

Figure 14.4 The use of selected grammatical characteristics across email sub-registers, depending on the relationship between addressor and addressee

being relatively large for some features. For example, activity verbs and time/place adverbs are much more common in the "friends and family" emails than in the other categories, reflecting the primary focus on everyday activities rather than conceptual discussions. In contrast, attributive adjectives and nominalizations are much more common in the professional emails, especially those written by "strangers," reflecting their informational focus (similar to academic prose).

In sum, the descriptions in this case study illustrate how register can be studied at any level of specificity. At the highest level, register differences can be studied between very general text categories, such as conversation versus academic prose. However, sub-registers can also be defined much more specifically, by focusing on particular situational parameters. The present case has shown how there are systematic patterns of linguistic variation among sub-registers within the general category of email message, depending on the role relation between sender and receiver, and depending on the primary communicative purpose of the message.

Multi-dimensional studies of register variation

The sections above have focused on the description of a particular register (and related sub-registers) with respect to both situational and linguistic characteristics. The second major type of research question that arises in register studies relates to the general patterns of register variation. That is, the distribution of individual linguistic features cannot reliably distinguish among a large set of registers: there are simply too many different linguistic characteristics to consider, and individual features often have idiosyncratic distributions. Instead, sociolinguistic research has argued that register descriptions must be based on linguistic co-occurrence patterns (see e.g. Ervin-Tripp, 1972; Hymes, 1974; Brown and Fraser, 1979: 38–39; Halliday, 1988: 162).

Multi-dimensional (MD) analysis is a corpus-driven methodological approach that identifies the frequent linguistic co-occurrence patterns in a language, relying on inductive empirical/quantitative analysis (see e.g. Biber, 1988, 1995). The set of co-occurring linguistic features that comprise each dimension is identified quantitatively. That is, on the basis of the actual distributions of linguistic features in a large corpus of texts, statistical techniques (specifically factor analysis) are used to identify the sets of linguistic features that frequently co-occur in texts.

The original MD analyses investigated the relations among general spoken and written registers in English, based on analysis of the LOB Corpus (15 written registers) and the London-Lund Corpus (6 spoken registers). Six/seven different linguistic features were analyzed computationally in each text of the corpus. Then the co-occurrence patterns among those linguistic features were analyzed using factor analysis, identifying the underlying parameters of variation: the factors or "dimensions." In the 1988 MD analysis, the 67 linguistic features were reduced to 7 underlying dimensions. (The technical details of the factor analysis are given in Biber, 1988, Chapters 4–5; see also Biber, 1995, Chapter 5.)

The dimensions are interpreted functionally, on the basis of the assumption that linguistic co-occurrence reflects underlying communicative functions. That is, linguistic features occur together in texts because they serve related communicative functions. For example, Table 14.2 lists the most important features on dimensions 1 and 2 in the 1988 MD analysis.

Each dimension can have "positive" and "negative" features. Rather than reflecting importance, positive and negative signs identify two groupings of features that occur in a complementary pattern as part of the same dimension. That is, when the positive features occur together frequently in a text, the negative features are markedly less frequent in that text, and vice versa.

On dimension 1, the interpretation of the negative features is relatively straightforward. Nouns, word length, prepositional phrases, high type/token ratio, and attributive adjectives all reflect an informational focus, a careful integration of information in a text, and precise lexical choice. Text sample 1 (above) illustrates these co-occurring linguistic characteristics in an academic article.

The set of positive features on dimension 1 is more complex, although all of these features have been associated with interpersonal interaction, a focus on personal stance, and real-time production circumstances. For example first- and second-person pronouns, WH-questions, emphatics, amplifiers, and sentence relatives can all be interpreted as reflecting interpersonal interaction and

Table 14.2. Summary of the major linguistic features co-occurring in dimensions 1 and 2 from the 1988 MD analysis of register variation

---

Dimension 1: involved vs. informational production

Positive features:
mental (private) verbs, *that* complementizer deletion, contractions, present tense verbs, WH-questions, 1st and 2nd person pronouns, pronoun *it*, indefinite pronouns, *do* as pro-verb, demonstrative pronouns, emphatics, hedges, amplifiers, discourse particles, causative subordination, sentence relatives, WH-clauses

Negative features:
nouns, long words, prepositions, high type/token ratio, attributive adjectives
Dimension 2: narrative vs. non-narrative discourse

Positive features:
past tense verbs, third-person pronouns, perfect aspect verbs, communication verbs

Negative features:
present tense verbs, attributive adjectives

---

the involved expression of personal stance (feelings and attitudes). Other positive features are associated with the constraints of real-time production, resulting in a reduced surface form, a generalized or uncertain presentation of information, and a generally "fragmented" production of text; these include *that*-deletions, contractions, pro-verb DO, the pronominal forms, and final (stranded) prepositions. Text sample 2 above illustrates the use of many positive dimension 1 features in conversation.

Overall, factor 1 represents a dimension marking interactional, stance-focused, and generalized content (the positive features in Table 14.1) versus high informational density and precise word choice (the negative features). Two separate communicative parameters seem to be represented here: the primary purpose of the writer/speaker (involved versus informational), and the production circumstances (those restricted by real-time constraints versus those enabling careful editing possibilities). Reflecting both of these parameters, the interpretive label "Involved versus Informational Production" was proposed for the dimension underlying this factor.

The second major step in interpreting a dimension is to consider the similarities and differences among registers with respect to the set of co-occurring linguistic features. To achieve this, *dimension scores* are computed for each text, by summing the individual scores of the features that co-occur on a dimension (see Biber, 1988: 93–97). For example, the dimension 1 score for each text was computed by adding together the frequencies of private verbs, *that* deletions, contractions, present tense verbs, etc. – the features with positive loadings (from Table 14.1)—and then subtracting the frequencies of nouns, word length, prepositions, and so on—the features with negative loadings.

Once a dimension score is computed for each text, the mean dimension score for each register can be computed. Plots of these mean dimension scores allow linguistic characterization of any given register, comparison of the relations between any two registers, and a fuller functional interpretation of the underlying dimension. For example, Figure 14.5 plots the mean dimension scores of registers along dimension 1 from the 1988 MD analysis.

The relations among registers shown in Figure 14.5 confirm the interpretation of dimension 1 as distinguishing among texts along a continuum of involved versus informational production. There is a large range of variation among spoken registers along this dimension, and an even larger range of variation among written registers. For example, expository informational registers, like

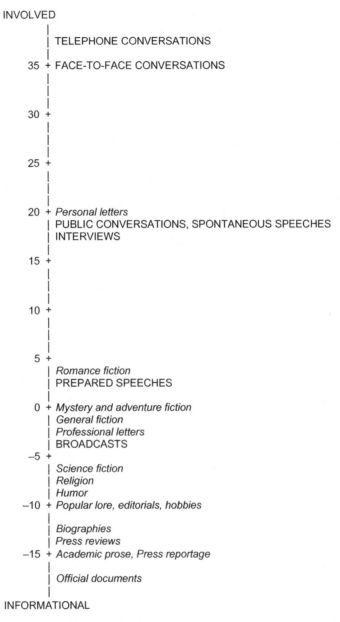

Figure 14.5. Mean scores of registers along dimension 1: involved vs informational production written registers are in *italics*; spoken registers are in CAPS. (F = 111.9, *p* <.0001, *r²* = 84.3%) (adapted from Figure 7.1 in Biber, 1988)

official documents and academic prose, have very large negative scores; the fiction registers have scores around 0.0; while personal letters have a relatively large positive score.

This distribution shows that no single register can be taken as representative of the spoken or written mode. At the extremes, written informational prose is dramatically different from spoken conversation with respect to dimension 1 scores. But written personal letters are relatively similar to spoken conversation, while spoken prepared speeches share some dimension 1 characteristics with written fictional registers. Taken together, these dimension 1 patterns indicate that there is extensive overlap between the spoken and written modes in these linguistic characteristics, while the extremes of each mode (i.e. conversation versus informational prose) are sharply distinguished from each other.

The overall comparison of speech and writing resulting from the 1988 MD analysis is actually much more complex, because six separate dimensions of variation were identified, and each of these defines a different set of relations among spoken and written registers. For example, dimension 2 is interpreted as "narrative vs. non-narrative concerns." The positive features—past tense verbs, third-person pronouns, perfect aspect verbs, communication verbs, and present participial clauses—are associated with past time narration. In contrast, the positive features—present tense verbs and attributive adjectives—have non-narrative communicative functions.

Each of the dimensions in the analysis can be interpreted in a similar way. Overall, the 1988 MD analysis showed that English registers vary along several underlying dimensions associated with different functional considerations, including: interactiveness, involvement and personal stance, production circumstances, informational density, informational elaboration, narrative purposes, situated reference, persuasiveness or argumentation, and impersonal presentation of information.

Many studies have applied the 1988 dimensions of variation to study the linguistic characteristics of more specialized registers and discourse domains. For example:

Present-day registers:	*Studies:*
spoken and written university registers	Biber *et al.* (2002)
AmE versus BrE written registers	Biber (1987)
AmE versus BrE conversational registers	Helt (2001)
student vs. academic writing (biology, history)	Conrad (1996)
direct mail letters	Connor and Upton (2003)
oral proficiency interviews	Connor-Linton and Shohamy (2001)
academic lectures	Csomay (2005)
conversation versus TV dialogue	Quaglio (2009)
female/male conversational style	Rey (2001); Biber and Burges (2000)
Historical registers:	*Studies:*
written and speech-based registers; 1650-present	Biber and Finegan (1989; 2001)
medical research articles and scientific research articles; 1650-present	Atkinson (1992, 1999)

Numerous other studies have undertaken new MD analyses, using factor analysis to identify the dimensions of variation operating in a particular discourse domain in English rather than applying the dimensions from the 1988 MD analysis (e.g. Biber, 2001, 2006, 2008; Reppen, 2001; Biber and Jones, 2005; Biber *et al.*, 2007; Friginal, 2009).

Given that each of these studies is based on a different corpus of texts, representing different registers, it is reasonable to expect that they would each identify a unique set of dimensions. This expectation is reinforced by the fact that the more recent studies have included additional linguistic features not used in earlier MD studies (e.g. semantic classes of nouns and verbs). However, despite these differences in design and research focus, there are certain striking similarities in the set of dimensions identified by these studies.

Most importantly, in nearly all of these studies the first dimension identified by the factor analysis is associated with an informational focus versus a personal focus (personal involvement/ stance, interactivity, and/or real time production features). This parameter of variation has emerged in the study of many different discourse domains, including general spoken and written registers (Biber, 1988), university spoken and written registers (Biber, 2006), and eighteenth-century speech-based and written registers (Biber, 2001). Surprisingly, a similar dimension has emerged in studies restricted to only spoken registers, such as White's (1994) study of job interviews and Biber's (2008) study of conversational sub-registers.

A second parameter found in most MD analyses corresponds to narrative discourse, reflected by the co-occurrence of features like past tense, third-person pronouns, perfect aspect, and communication verbs (see e.g. the Biber, 2006 study of university registers; Biber, 2001 on eighteenth century registers; and the Biber, 2008 study of conversation text types). In some studies a similar narrative dimension emerged, with additional special characteristics. For example, in Reppen's (2001) study of elementary school registers, "narrative" features like past tense, perfect aspect, and communication verbs co-occurred with once-occurring words and a high type/token ratio; in this corpus history textbooks rely on a specialized and diverse vocabulary to narrate past events. In Biber and Kurjian's (2007) study of web text types, narrative features co-occurred with features of stance and personal involvement on the first dimension, distinguishing personal narrative web pages (e.g. personal blogs) from the various kinds of more informational web pages.

At the same time, most of these studies have identified some dimensions that are unique to the particular discourse domain. For example, Biber's (2006) study of university spoken and written registers identified two specialized dimensions: "procedural vs. content-focused discourse" (distinguishing between classroom management talk and course syllabi versus textbooks), and "academic stance" (especially prevalent in classroom teaching and classroom management talk). A second example comes from Biber's (2008) MD analysis of conversational text types, which identified a dimension of "stance-focused versus context-focused discourse."

In sum, MD studies of English registers have uncovered both surprising similarities and notable differences in the underlying dimensions of variation. Two parameters seem to be fundamentally important, regardless of the discourse domain: a dimension associated with informational focus versus (inter)personal focus, and a dimension associated with narrative discourse. At the same time, these MD studies have uncovered dimensions particular to the communicative functions and priorities of each different domain of use.

These same general patterns have emerged from MD studies of languages other than English, including Nukulaelae Tuvaluan (Besnier, 1988), Korean (Kim and Biber, 1994), Somali (Biber and Hared, 1992), and Spanish (Biber *et al.*, 2006; Parodi, 2007). Taken together, these studies provide the first comprehensive investigations of register variation in non-Western languages.

Biber (1995) synthesizes several of these studies to investigate the extent to which the underlying dimensions of variation and the relations among registers are configured in similar ways across languages. These languages show striking similarities in their basic patterns of register variation, as reflected by:

- the co-occurring linguistic features that define the dimensions of variation in each language;
- the functional considerations represented by those dimensions; and
- the linguistic/functional relations among analogous registers.

For example, similarly to the full MD analyses of English, these MD studies have all identified dimensions associated with informational versus (inter)personal purposes and with narrative discourse.

At the same time, each of these MD analyses has identified dimensions that are unique to a language, reflecting the particular communicative priorities of that language and culture. For example, the MD analysis of Somali identified a dimension interpreted as "distanced, directive interaction," represented by optative clauses, first- and second-person pronouns, directional pre-verbal particles, and other case particles. Only one register is especially marked for the frequent use of these co-occurring features in Somali: personal letters. This dimension reflects the particular communicative priorities of personal letters in Somali, which are typically interactive as well as explicitly directive.

Conclusion

This chapter has surveyed the ways in which situational and linguistic differences distinguish among registers. Registers differ with respect to a wide array of situational characteristics relating to purpose, topic, physical setting, production circumstances, and the relations among participants. These situational differences are associated with important linguistic differences at the lexical, grammatical, and lexico-grammatical levels. Further, corpus-based analytical techniques can be employed to identify the linguistic co-occurrence patterns that regularly occur in texts from different registers, providing the basis for comprehensive analyses of register variation.

All language users adapt their language to different situations of use. It would be nearly impossible to spend an entire day using only one register – only participating in conversations, only listening to radio broadcasts, only reading a newspaper, or only writing an academic paper. Rather, switching among registers is as natural as human language itself. As a result, understanding register variation is not a supplement to the description of grammar, discourse, and language use; it is central.

Further reading

Biber, Douglas (1988). *Variation Across Speech and Writing*. Cambridge: Cambridge University Press.

This is the first major study of register variation to apply multi-dimensional analysis. The book identifies and interprets the major dimensions of variation among spoken and written registers in English.

Biber, Douglas and Susan Conrad (2009) *Register, Genre, and Style*. Cambridge: Cambridge University Press.

This book describes the most important kinds of texts in English and introduces the methodological techniques used to analyse them. Three analytical approaches are introduced and compared throughout the book, describing texts from the perspective of register, genre and style.

Friginal, Eric (2009). *The Language of Outsourced Call Centers*. Amsterdam: John Benjamins.

This is one of the first books to undertake a comprehensive linguistic description of an emerging register. The book describes the register of call-center discourse at multiple linguistic levels, including a survey of lexico-grammatical features, detailed descriptions of stance features, and a multi-dimensional analysis that captures the underlying parameters of variation.

Quaglio, Paulo (2009) *Television Dialogue: The Sitcom Friends versus Natural Conversation*. Amsterdam: John Benjamins.

This book presents a corpus-based description of the popular TV sitcom Friends compared to normal face-to-face conversations. The book offers a thorough linguistic description of the television sitcom register, including in-depth chapters that focus on vague language, the expression of personal emotion, informal language (including slang and expletives), and a comparison of narrative features in *Friends* versus natural conversation.

References

Atkinson, D. (1992) 'The evolution of medical research writing from 1735 to 1985: the case of the Edinburgh Medical Journal', *Applied Linguistics*, 13: 337–374.

Atkinson, D. (1999) *Scientific Discourse in Sociohistorical Context: The Philosophical Transactions of the Royal Society of London, 1675–1975*. Hillsdale, NJ: Lawrence Erlbaum Associates.

Besnier, N. (1988) 'The linguistic relationships of spoken and written Nukulaelae registers', *Language*, 64: 707–736.

Biber, D. (1987) 'A textual comparison of British and American writing', *American Speech*, 62: 99–119.

Biber, D. (1988) *Variation across Speech and Writing*. Cambridge: Cambridge University Press.

Biber, D. (1995) *Dimensions of Register Variation: A Cross-Linguistic Comparison*. Cambridge: Cambridge University Press.

Biber, D. (2001) 'Dimensions of variation among eighteenth-century speech-based and written registers', in S. Conrad and D. Biber (eds.) *Variation in English: Multi-Dimensional Studies*. London: Longman, pp. 200–214.

Biber, D. (2006) *University Language: A Corpus-Based Study of Spoken and Written Registers*. Amsterdam: John Benjamins.

Biber, D. (2008) 'Corpus-based analyses of discourse: dimensions of variation in conversation', in V. Bhatia, J. Flowerdew, and R. Jones (eds.) *Advances in Discourse Studies*. London: Routledge, pp. 100–114.

Biber, D., and Burges, J. (2000). 'Historical change in the language use of women and men: gender differences in dramatic dialogue', *Journal of English Linguistics*, 28: 21–37.

Biber, D., Connor, U., and Upton, T. A. (2007) *Discourse on the Move: Using Corpus Analysis to Describe Discourse Structure*. Amsterdam: John Benjamins.

Biber, D. and Conrad, S. (2009) *Register, Genre, and Style*. Cambridge: Cambridge University Press.

Biber, D., Conrad, S., and Reppen, R. (1998) *Corpus Linguistics: Investigating Language Structure and Use*. Cambridge: Cambridge University Press.

Biber, D., Conrad, S., Reppen, R., Byrd, P., and Helt, M. (2002) 'Speaking and writing in the university: a multi-dimensional comparison', *TESOL Quarterly*, 36: 9–48.

Biber, D., Davies, M., Jones, J. K., and Tracy-Ventura, N. (2006) 'Spoken and written register variation in Spanish: a multi-dimensional analysis', *Corpora*, 1: 7–38.

Biber, D. and Finegan, E. (1989) 'Drift and the evolution of English style: a history of three genres', *Language*, 65: 487–517.

Biber, D. and Finegan, E. (2001) 'Diachronic relations among speech-based and written registers in English', in S. Conrad and D. Biber (eds.) *Variation in English: Multi-Dimensional Studies*. London: Longman, pp. 66–83.

Biber, D. and Hared, M. (1992) 'Dimensions of register variation in Somali', *Language Variation and Change*, 4: 41–75.

Biber, D. and Jones, J. K. (2005) 'Merging corpus linguistic and discourse analytic research goals: Discourse units in biology research articles', *Corpus Linguistics and Linguistic Theory*, 1: 151–182.

Biber, D. and Kurjian, J. (2007) 'Towards a taxonomy of web registers and text types: a multi-dimensional analysis', in M. Hundt, N. Nesselhauf, and C. Biewer (eds.) *Corpus Linguistics and the Web*. Amsterdam: Rodopi, pp. 109–132.

Brown, P. and Fraser, C. (1979) 'Speech as a marker of situation', in K. R. Scherer and H. Giles (eds.) *Social Markers in Speech*. Cambridge: Cambridge University Press, pp. 33–62.

Connor, U. and Upton, T. A. (2003) 'Linguistic dimensions of direct mail letters', in C. Meyer and P. Leistyna (eds.) *Corpus Analysis: Language Structure and Language Use*. Amsterdam: Rodopi, pp. 71–86.

Connor-Linton, J. and Shohamy, E. (2001) 'Register variation, oral proficiency sampling, and the promise of multi-dimensional analysis', in S. Conrad and D. Biber (eds.) *Variation in English: Multi-Dimensional Studies*. London: Longman, pp. 124–137.

Conrad, S. (1996) 'Investigating academic texts with corpus-based techniques: an example from biology', *Linguistics and Education*, 8: 299–326.

Csomay, E. (2005) 'Linguistic variation within university classroom talk: a corpus-based perspective', *Linguistics and Education*, 15: 243–274.

Ervin-Tripp, S. (1972) 'On sociolinguistic rules: alternation and co-occurrence', in J. Gumperz and D. Hymes (eds.) *Directions in Sociolinguistics: The Ethnography of Communication*. New York: Holt, pp. 213–250.

Friginal, E. (2009) *The Language of Outsourced Call Centers*. Amsterdam: John Benjamins.

Halliday, M. A. K. (1988) 'On the language of physical science', in M. Ghadessy (ed.) *Registers of Written English: Situational Factors and Linguistic Features*. London: Pinter, pp. 162–178.

Helt, M. E. (2001) 'A multi-dimensional comparison of British and American spoken English', in S. Conrad and D. Biber (eds.) *Variation in English: Multi-Dimensional Studies*. London: Longman, pp. 157–170.

Hymes, D. (1974) *Foundations in Sociolinguistics: An Ethnographic Approach*. Philadelphia, PA: University of Pennsylvania Press.

Kim, Y. -J and Biber, D. (1994) 'A corpus-based analysis of register variation in Korean', in D. Biber and E. Finegan (eds.) *Sociolinguistic Perspectives on Register*. New York: Oxford University Press, pp. 157–181.

McEnery, A., Xiao, R., and Tono, Y. (2006) *Corpus-Based Language Studies*. London: Routledge.

Parodi, G. (2007) 'Variation across registers in Spanish', in G. Parodi (ed.) *Working with Spanish Corpora*. London: Continuum, pp. 11–53.

Quaglio, P. (2009) *Television Dialogue: The Sitcom Friends Versus Natural Conversation*. Amsterdam: John Benjamins.

Reppen, R. (2001) 'Register variation in student and adult speech and writing', in S. Conrad and D. Biber (eds.) *Variation in English: Multi-Dimensional Studies*. London: Longman, pp. 187–199.

Rey, J. M. (2001) 'Historical shifts in the language of women and men: gender differences in dramatic dialogue', in S. Conrad and D. Biber (eds.) *Variation in English: Multi-Dimensional Studies*. London: Longman, pp. 138–156.

Schiffrin, D., D. Tannen, and Hamilton, H. E. (eds.) (2001) *The Handbook of Discourse Analysis*. Oxford: Blackwell.

Swales, J. (1990) *Genre Analysis: English for Academic and Research Settings*. Cambridge: Cambridge University Press.

White, M. (1994). 'Language in job interviews: differences relating to success and socioeconomic variables', Ph.D. Dissertation, Northern Arizona University.

15

Genre in the Sydney school

David Rose

Genre and register: a stratal model of language in social context

Genre is the coordinating principle and starting point for discourse analysis in what has become known as the Sydney School (Martin, 2000, 2006; Martin and Rose, 2005). The approach has been designed over the past three decades with three major influences (among others): Halliday's (1975, 1994/2004) theory of language as a social semiotic (discussed by Schleppegrel in this volume; Martin, 1992; Martin and Rose, 2007, 2008); the sociological theory of Basil Bernstein (1990, 2000; see Christie and Martin, 1997); and a series of large-scale action research projects in literacy education (Martin, 1999, 2000; Rose, 2008; Rose and Martin, in press). The functional linguistic perspective on genre analysis distinguishes the Sydney School approach along several lines. With respect to linguistic models, its perspective is social rather than cognitive, its analysis of social contexts is social semiotic rather than ethnographic commentary, and it is designed along multiple dimensions as a stratified, metafunctional, multimodal theory of text in social context rather than eclectic. In relation to other fields, it is integrated in a functional theory of language rather than interdisciplinary, and its social goals are interventionist and focused on redistributing semiotic resources through education, rather than merely critical of those in power. With respect to the breadth and detail of its linguistic focus and its uniquely designed teaching strategies, Hyland (2007: 153) describes the Sydney School as 'perhaps the most clearly articulated approach to genre both theoretically and pedagogically' (see also Hyon, 1996; Johns, 2002).

As a working definition, genres have been characterized in this research tradition as staged, goal oriented social processes: social since texts are always interactive events; goal oriented in that a text unfolds towards its interactants' purposes; staged, because it usually takes more than one step to reach the goal. In functional linguistics terms this means that genres are defined as a recurrent configuration of meanings, which enact the social practices of a culture. Such a social semiotic interpretation necessitates going beyond individual genres, to consider how they relate to one another. For example, genres can be related and distinguished by recurrent global patterns. Thus story genres can be distinguished according to the presence or absence of sequence in time (news reports vs other stories) and the presence or absence of a complicating event (recount vs narrative); factual genres, according to whether they explain processes or describe things (explanation vs report); argument genres according to whether they argue for a point of view or discuss two or more points of view (exposition vs discussion). Secondly, the organization of each genre can be distinguished by recurrent local patterns, such as the narrative stages Orientation^Complication^ Resolution, or the exposition stages Thesis^Arguments^Reiteration.

The range of genres described in the Sydney School research is large and diverse, but it is still just a fraction of the repertoire of genres available to members of a culture. This chapter presents a brief introduction to the principles of analysis, exemplified with a few of the genres described to date, including types of stories, reports, explanations, arguments and text reponses. To begin with, the model of social context underpinning the approach is briefly outlined.

Modelling context

Halliday (1975: 5) described social context as 'the total environment in which a text unfolds' – building on Malinowski (1935), who interpreted the social contexts of interaction as stratified into two levels – 'context of situation' and 'context of culture'. Looked at from above, we can say that patterns of social organization in a culture are realized (manifested/ symbolized/ encoded/ expressed) as patterns of social interaction in each context of situation, which in turn are realized as patterns of discourse in each text.

Halliday links contexts of situation to three social functions of language – enacting speakers' relationships, construing their experience of social activity, and weaving these enactments and construals together into meaningful discourse. Accordingly, contexts of situation vary in these three general dimensions. The dimension concerned with relationships between interactants is known as *tenor*; that concerned with their social activity is known as *field*; and that concerned with the role of language is known as *mode*. In Martin's (1992) terms, the tenor, field and mode of a situation constitute the *register* of a text. As language realizes its social contexts, so each dimension of a social context is realized by a particular functional dimension of language. Halliday defines these dimensions as the 'metafunctions' of language: enacting relationships as the *interpersonal* metafunction, construing experience as the *ideational* metafunction, and organizing discourse as the *textual* metafunction. Relations between register variables and language metafunctions are as follows:

register		metafunction	
tenor	'kinds of role relationship'	interpersonal	'enacting'
field	'the social action that is taking place'	ideational	'construing'
mode	'what part language is playing'	textual	'organizing'

Genre is modelled by the Sydney School at the stratum of culture beyond register: as a config-uration of field, tenor and mode patterns. In this model, 'situation' and 'culture' are re-construed as social semiotic strata – *register* and *genre*. Following Hjelmslev (1961), language is thus a denotative semiotic realizing social context, and social context is a connotative semiotic realized through language, illustrated as nested circles in Figure 15.1.

The Sydney School approach is explicitly designed as interventionist, following Halliday's view of linguistics as an ideologically committed form of social action. In this respect its model of social context is influenced by Bernstein's 2000 analysis of symbolic control. Following Bernstein, ideology is understood in terms of relations within and between contexts, which permeate every level of semiosis. In everyday contexts within local kin and peer groups, power and control may be conditioned by age, gender and other status markers. In post-colonial societies, the range of genres in a culture is further differentiated by institutions such as science, industry and administration. Control over these genres depends on specialized educational pathways, and access to these pathways depends largely on our position in relation to socio-economic power. In this kind of social complex, the scope of our control over genres of power in turn conditions our status ranking in social hierachies,

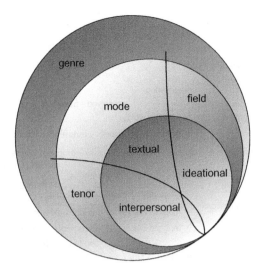

Figure 15.1 Genre and register in relation to metafunctions of language

our claim to authority in institutional fields and the prominence of our voice in public life. Within specific situations, these register variables translate into options to dominate or defer, to assert or concede authority, and to command attention or pay attention to others. Ideology thus runs through the entire ensemble of language in social context, differentiating social subjects into hierarchies of power, control, status, authority and prominence, for which we have used the following proportions:

ideology (access)	power
genre (management)	control
tenor (social hierarchy)	status
field (expertise and rank)	authority
mode (attention paid to us)	prominence

Genre relations

As flagged above, genres can be related to each other along various dimensions, such as a focus on entities vs activities, individual vs generic participants, recounting vs explaining events, explaining vs arguing, promoting vs rebutting an argument, and so on. In the context of school and academic curricula, one global perspective on written genres (by no means exhaustive) is provided by Figure 15.3. Here families of genres are grouped into four general categories, according to their most general social purposes and literacy teaching focus. First, a primary goal of stories is to engage and entertain, so a key focus of teaching is on the language resources that authors use for engaging readers. Another group of genres functions primarily to provide information, particularly in the context of educational curricula, and a third group is concerned with procedures for activities, so a teaching focus in these genres is on their field. A fourth group functions to evaluate – texts in the case of text responses, opinions or issues in the case of arguments; so a pedagogic focus here is on evaluative language resources. Of course any text will include multiple purposes, but the genre reflects its primary goal. In Figure 15.2, arrows indicate that engaging, informing, proposing and evaluating can be functions of various genres to some extent, but they are foregrounded more in some than in others.

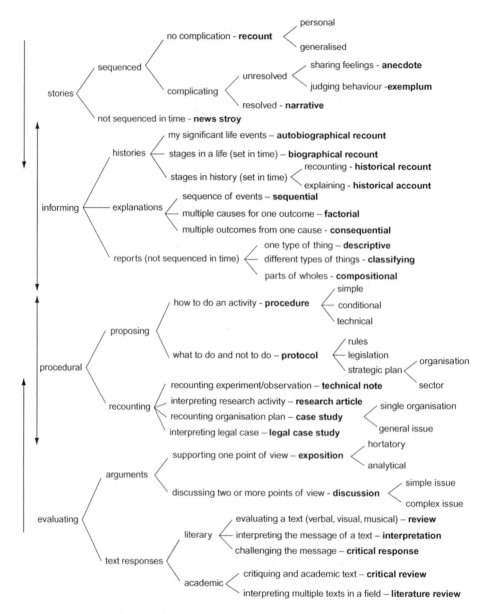

Figure 15.2 Common educational genres

Engaging listeners: story genres

An early starting point for work on genres was Labov and Waletzky's (1967) analysis of the Complication^Resolution structure of spoken narratives. Whereas variations from this pattern were dismissed by Labov and Waletsky as 'not well-formed', five distinct story genres are described in Sydney School research, which are found in oral stories (Martin and Plum, 1997), in children's written stories (Rothery, 1994; Rothery and Stenglin, 1997), in casual conversation (Eggins and Slade, 1997), in literary fiction (Macken-Horarik, 1996; Martin, 1996), in stories of illness and treatment (Jordens, 2002), and in traditional stories across language families (Rose, 2001, 2005a).

Table 15.1 Time structured story genres

staging	experience	response	experience	attitude
recount	Record	[prosodic]	–	variable
anecdote	Remarkable Event	Reaction	–	affect
exemplum	Incident	Interpretation	–	judgement
observation	Event Description	Comment		appreciation
narrative	Complication	Evaluation	Resolution	variable

Each story type begins (optionally) with an 'orientation' stage, which presents an expectant activity sequence, but varies in how this expectancy is disrupted and in how the disruption is responded to. Variations in the staging and type of attitude characteristic of each story genre are summarized in Table 15.1 (for attitude see Martin and Rose, 2007; Martin and White, 2005).

Staging and attitude in stories is exemplified here with an anecdote, from the novel *Follow the Rabbit-Proof Fence* by Indigenous Australian author Doris Pilkington (1996), about the epic journey of three girls who have been removed from their families and are returning to their home in the western Australian desert. In this extract, the policeman charged with removing the girls appears at the family campsite and announces his intention. The stages of 'remarkable event' and 'reaction' unfold in a sequence of intensifying problems and reactions, beginning with the appearance of the white man and the family's reaction of *fear and anxiety*; then the policeman's announcement and their reaction of *silent tears*; and finally the removal, followed by the family's intense grief. Each problem is thus evaluated by the emotional reaction that follows it. Anecdote stages are indicated with initial capitals, expressions of affect are in bold.

Orientation	Molly and Gracie finished their breakfast and decided to take all their dirty clothes and wash them in the soak further down the river. They returned to the camp looking clean and refreshed and joined the rest of the family in the shade for lunch of tinned corned beef, damper and tea.
Remarkable Event	The family had just finished eating when all the camp dogs began barking, making a terrible din. 'Shut up,' yelled their owners, throwing stones at them. The dogs whined and skulked away.
problem	Then all eyes turned to the cause of the commotion. A tall, rugged white man stood on the bank above them. He could easily have been mistaken for a pastoralist or a grazier with his tanned complexion except that he was wearing khaki clothing.
reaction	**Fear and anxiety swept over them** when they realised that the **fateful day** they had been **dreading** had come at last…
problem	When Constable Riggs, Protector of Aborigines, finally spoke his voice was full of authority and purpose… 'I've come to take Molly, Gracie and Daisy, the three half-caste girls, with me to Moore River Native Settlement,' he informed the family.
reaction	The old man nodded to show that he understood what Riggs was saying. The rest of the family just **hung their heads**, refusing to face the man who was taking their daughters away from them. **Silent tears welled in their eyes and trickled down their cheeks**.
problem	'Hurry up then, I want to get started. We've got a long way to go yet. You girls can ride this horse back to the depot,' he said, handing the reins over to Molly.
Reaction	Molly and Gracie sat silently on the horse, **tears streaming down their cheeks** as Constable Riggs turned the big bay stallion and led the way back to the depot. **A high pitched wail broke out**. The **cries of agonised** mothers and the women, and the **deep sobs** of grandfathers, uncles and cousins **filled the air**. Molly and Gracie looked

back just once before they disappeared through the river gums. Behind them, those remaining in the camp found sharp objects and **gashed themselves** and **inflicted deep wounds** to their heads and bodies as an **expression of their sorrow**.
The two **frightened and miserable** girls **began to cry, silently at first, then uncontrollably**; their **grief made worse** by the **lamentations** of their **loved ones** and the visions of them sitting on the ground in their camp **letting their tears mix** with the red blood that flowed from the cuts on their heads.

The stages of a genre are relatively stable components of its organization, but phases within each stage are more variable, and may be unique to the particular text. Common types of phases have been identified in a wide range of oral and literary stories in English and other languages (Rose, 2005b). Each phase type performs a certain function to engage the listener/reader as the story unfolds, by construing its field of activities, people, things and places, by evoking emotional responses or by linking it to common experiences and interpretations of life. These functions are summarized in Table 15.2.

Creative manipulation of story phases is a critical resource for achieving the social goals of story genres. For example, in the extract from *Rabbit-Proof Fence* above the author leads the reader's emotions through a seesaw of problems and reactions, to induce us to identify with the feelings of the family, and so to empathize with their resignation and grief at the invader's final act of barbarity.

Beyond this extract, *Follow the Rabbit-Proof Fence* is a long story whose overall purpose is to applaud the girls' tenacity, manifested in their returning to their family against all odds. But, like novels in general, this story is constructed as a series of smaller stories, which function in this case to engage the reader in sharing the protagonists' feelings, admiring the girls and their helpers and condemning their captors and pursuers. One way this is achieved is by building and releasing tension through series of problems and responses on the various scales of events, story stages and whole chapters. Longer texts such as novels are thus modelled as macro-genres (Martin, 1994; Martin and Rose, 2008).

While the deployment of phases in stories is highly variable, biographical recounts are more predictable. They also begin with an orientation, which typically charts the person's birth and early life, and perhaps the reasons for their fame; and they follow with 'life stages'. Each stage in the person's life is a phase of the text, and it is typically signalled by a time or place, as starting point of a sentence (technically a **Theme** in Halliday's 1994/2004 terms), underlined here.

Table 15.2 Common story phases

phase types	engagement functions
setting	presenting context (identities, activities, locations)
description	evoking context (sensual imagery)
events	expectant events
problem	counterexpectant creating tension
solution	counterexpectant releasing tension
result	material outcome
reaction	behavioural/attitudinal outcome
comment	intruding narrator's comments
reflection	intruding participants' thoughts

Orientation	Nganyintja is an elder of the Pitjantjatjara people of central Australia, renowned internationally as an educator and cultural ambassador. She was born in 1930 in the Mann Ranges, South Australia. Her early years were spent travelling through her family's traditional lands, living by hunting and gathering, and until the age of nine she had not seen a European.
Life stages	At that time her family moved to the newly established mission at Ernabella, 300km to the east of the family homeland. They were soon followed by most of the Pitjantjatjara people, as they were forced to abandon their Western Desert lands during the drought of the 1940s. At the mission, Nganyintja excelled at school, becoming its first Indigenous teacher. She married Charlie Ilyatjari and began a family that would include four daughters, two sons, 18 grandchildren and ever more great-grandchildren.
	In the early 1960s the family moved to the new government settlement of Amata, 100 km east of their traditional lands, which they visited with camels each summer holiday, renewing their ties to the land and educating their children in their traditions. Then in 1979 they were able to buy an old truck and blaze a track through the bush to re-establish a permanent family community at Nganyintja's homeland of Angatja.
	In those years the tragedy of teenage petrol sniffing began to engulf the Pitjantjatjara people. Nganyintja and Ilyatjari established a youth cultural and training program at Angatja, and worked for many years to get young people out of the settlements in the region and educate them, both in their cultural traditions and in community development skills. In addition, Nganyintja became a widely respected leader and spokesperson for her people.
	During the 1980s Nganyintja and Ilyatjari hosted many visits from students and organizations interested in learning about Indigenous Australian culture. In 1989 they established a cultural tourism venture known as Desert Tracks, that has brought hundreds of Australian and international visitors to Angatja, and provided income and employment to many Pitjantjatjara people, as well as winning major tourism awards.
	In 1993 Nganyintja was awarded the Order of Australia Medal for her services to the community.
	She is remembered for her vision and the love she gave unstintingly to her family and her people.

Historical recounts follow a remarkably similar pattern, with each phase typically signalled by time Themes, although their field is the life of institutions rather than individuals, and their first stage is typically an historical 'background'. Historical accounts are similar again, except that they introduce causal relations, explaining as well as recounting historical events. (For description of genres in history, see Coffin, 1996, 2003, 2007; Veel and Coffin, 1996; Martin, 2001; Martin and Rose, 2008.)

Informing readers: explanations, reports, procedures

Explanations, reports, procedures and protocols have evolved along with the institutional contexts of science, industry and administration. (Genres in the natural and social sciences are described in Painter and Martin, 1986; Halliday and Martin, 1993; Humphrey, 2008; Lemke, 1998; Martin and Veel, 1998; Unsworth, 2001, 2004; in science-based industries, in Rose et al., 1992/2008; Rose, 1997, 1998; and in administration, in Iedema, 2008.)

David Rose

Reports – classifying and describing things

Reports may classify an entity and then describe its features (descriptive), sub-classify a number of things with respect to a given set of criteria (classifying) or describe the components of an entity (compositional). The stages of reports include the 'classification' of the entity and its 'description', but the phases within the description vary with the type of report and the entity being described. For example, descriptive reports about animal species typically include phases such as appearance, behaviour, habitat, while descriptive reports about countries may include location, population, topography, economy, and so on. The potential is illustrated here with a classifying report. In this example organisms are classified as producers or consumers, so the text begins with the 'classification' system, which is followed by a 'description' of types. The phases describe each type (in bold) in terms of the criteria for their sub-classification (underlined).

Classification	**Producers and consumers**
	We have seen that organisms in an ecosystem are first classified as <u>producers or as consumers of chemical energy</u>.
Description type 1	**Producers** in ecosystems are typically photosynthetic organisms, such as plants, algae and cyanobacteria. These organisms <u>build organic matter</u> (food from simple inorganic substances by photosynthesis).
type 2	**Consumers** in an ecosystem obtain their energy in the form of chemical energy present in their 'food'. All consumers <u>depend directly or indirectly on producers for their supply of chemical energy</u>.
type 2a	Organisms that <u>eat the organic matter of producers or their products</u> (seeds, fruits) are called **primary consumers**, for example, leaf-eating koalas (*Phascolarctos cinereus*), and nectar-eating honey possums (*Tarsipes rostratus*).
type 2b	Organisms that <u>eat primary consumers</u> are known as **secondary consumers**. Wedge-tailed eagles that prey on wallabies are secondary consumers.
type 2c	Some organisms <u>consume the organic matter of secondary consumers</u> and are labeled **tertiary consumers**. Ghost bats (*Macroderma gigas*) capture a variety of prey, including small mammals.

The classification taxonomy realized in this text is represented in Figure 15.3. Left–right system networks are used for classification in systemic functional linguistics (SFL), in contrast to top-down 'tree' diagrams, which distinguish compositional taxonomies.

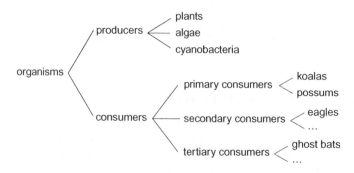

Figure 15.3 Classification taxonomy realized by a classifying report

In academic fields such as science, which take the form of a 'coherent, explicit, and systematically principled structure, hierarchically organised' (Bernstein, 2000), the global structure of textbooks is typically that of classifying reports, of types and their sub-types. In other words, the field as a whole is organized in the textbook macro-genre as a taxonomy of types, and the description of each type gives the criteria for its classification within the taxonomy.

Explanations – how processes happen

Explanations imply sequences of causes and effects: process x occurs, so process y results, which in turns causes process z, and so on. This kind of logical pattern has been termed an *implication* sequence (Halliday and Martin, 1993). The typical structure of explanations is to start by specifying the 'phenomenon' to be explained, which is followed by the implication sequence that explains it, i.e. by the 'explanation' stage. Explanation genres are of four general types: a sequence of causes and effects (sequential), multiple causes for an outcome (factorial), multiple effects from an input (consequential) and multiple conditions and effects (conditional). This potential is illustrated in Figure 15.4 below with a sequential explanation of steps in the cyclic burning and regeneration of the mallee eucalypt (Corrigan, 1991: 100). In Figure 15.4, logical relations between each step are made explicit with arrows, glossed as 'so' and 'but'.

Procedures, protocols and procedural recounts

The available space here precludes more than a brief outline of the diverse procedural genre family (see Figure 15.2 above). Procedures are of course endemic in everyday contexts, from recipes to appliance manuals, but also in industrial fields, from simple procedures on the factory floor, to those involving specialized operators or technicians (technical) and multiple choice points for action (conditional), often accompanied by complex flow charts. Protocols range from lists of rules and warnings that accompany appliances, to legislation (Martin and Rose, 2007) and strategic

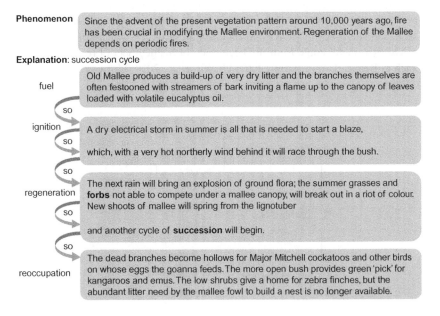

Figure 15.4 Fire – a natural process that is now significantly influenced by humans

plans developed in commercial and administrative contexts (Iedema, 2008). Procedural recounts range from experiment reports required of school students, through technical notes that recount the investigation of an industrial problem and recommend action, to academic research articles that recount a method of research and interpret its results, and case studies that interpret a wide range of activities in various institutional fields (Rose *et al.*, 1992/2008; Rose 1997, 1998).

Multimodal explanations, reports and procedures

Explanations, reports and procedures in science and technology frequently include diagrams, charts, photographs, line drawings or maps, which support the reader to interpret the verbal text. Conversely, such visual supports can rarely stand alone, without a verbal text to interpret them. Multimodal technical genres are described in Martin and Rose (2008) from three perspectives: types of ideational meanings construed by visual images; textual organization characteristic of visual images; and relations between visual and verbal genres in multimodal texts.

This potential is briefly exemplified here with the system of ideational meanings in technical images, in which the focus is either on entities – classifying or de/composing them – or on activities – either a single activity (simple) or a sequence (complex). Categories within an image may be either explicitly labelled, or implicit for the reader to infer from the accompanying verbal text or the reader's assumed knowledge of the field. Images may also be relatively iconic representations of an entity or activity, such as a photograph or realistic drawing, or they may be symbolic representations such as diagrams. In-between, indexical images such as outline drawings are neither realistic icons nor purely symbolic images, but indicate some recognizable features of the represented entity or activity. These three sets of features give the options in Figure 15.5.

An iconic classifying image is Figure 15.6, which classifies types of environment in Australia's Western Desert with realistic drawings. Each landscape type is explicitly labelled with its Indigenous Western Desert name: *puli* (rocky ranges), *kurku* (mulga plains), *pana* (grass plains), *tali* (sand ridges), *karu* (creeks and rivers) and *pantu* (salt lakes).

This iconic classifying image can be contrasted with symbolic classifying images such as the system networks in Figures 15.2, 15.3 and 15.5 above, the symbolic compositional diagram in Figure 15.1, and the indexical activity focus in Figure 15.4, in which arrows indicate logical relations. This is a small sample from the large body of Sydney School research in multimodal genres (such as Bednarek and Martin, 2009; Dreyfus *et al.*, 2010; Unsworth, 2004; Painter and Martin, 1986.)

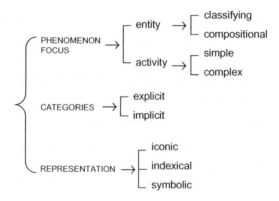

Figure 15.5 Options in technical images for ideational meanings

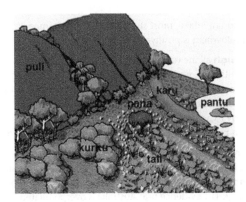

Figure 15.6 Types of western desert environment
Source: from Rose 2001

Evaluating discourses: arguments and text responses

Argument genres negotiate positions in public discourse. Perhaps the best known is exposition, in which a position is expounded, argued for and reiterated (Thesis^Arguments^Reiteration). Expositions vary in the number of supporting arguments (though commonly three) and reiterations of the thesis (typically one, after the arguments). While expositions are organized around arguments for a single position, discussions are scaffolded around competing positions: one position will be presented, then undermined by counter-arguments, and the discussion will be resolved in favour of the the latter (Issue^Sides^Resolution). They vary with the number of issues discussed: simple discussions present one issue, then sides for and against it; complex discussions include for and against sides for a series of sub-issues. And complementing these promotional genres is the challenge, which sets out to demolish an established position, effectively an anti-exposition (Position^Rebuttal). The potential is illustrated below with a complex discussion (from Rowe, 1998), in which the issues are scaffolded by means of **metadiscourse** (*reasons, argument, opposition* and the metaphor *political hot potato* – underlined below), and the author's counter-arguments, by **concession** and **negation** (in bold).

Issue	**Plus to immigration equation**
	Both before and since the White Australia policy of the 1950s, immigration has been a <u>political hot potato</u> – **yet** the economic evidence shows immigration has been extremely good for the nation. **In spite of the facts**, today's economic nationalist parties – One Nation, the Australian Democrats, Advance Australia, the Greens and Australia First – espouse policies of greatly reduced or zero net migration. They do so for <u>several reasons</u>.
Sides issue1 – economy	<u>The most common argument against</u> allowing migrants in numbers is based on a lopsided view of the impact on Australia's economy. The Advance Australia party wants to call a 'halt to all immigration until we have solved our unemployment problems' **as if the only** impact of migration is to take jobs which might otherwise be available to unemployed Australians.
	But the impact of immigration is determined **not only** by the number of jobs migrants take, **but also** by the jobs they create. Population growth through migration creates demand for housing, goods and services which is met through higher production which in turn leads to higher employment. Depending on the size and composition of

219

	the migrant intake, most studies show the net impact of immigration on unemployment is positive.
issue2 – environment	**Although** all the nationalist parties have some economic or cultural components to their anti-immigration policies, most of the bigger ones make the environment – **not** the economy – the <u>main plank of their opposition</u> to migration. The Australian greens argue that 'Australia's voluntary immigration program has to be reduced as part of a strategy to achieve eventual stabilisation of the Australian population.' Similarly One Nation proposes 'to cap population growth for environmental reasons'.
	Yet by the admission of most of the parties that espouse an end to population growth, there is **nowhere near** consensus on what Australia's sustainable population might be, **nor even** whether there is a single figure which represents Australia's carrying capacity. The evidence that Australia is overpopulated is **not** very persuasive. Australia has one of the lowest population densities in the world. It produces far more food than it consumes – we could double our agricultural consumption and still have a trade surplus in food.
issue3 – culture	<u>Perhaps even more important than the economic benefits</u> of migration is the contribution that immigration has made to our quality of life in the broadest sense – through cultural diversity, access to new ideas, and myriad everyday choices of foods, arts, clothes and so on which were **not on offer** to past generations of Australians.
Resolution	One of the most influential principles which environmentalists have introduced to economics is inter-generational equity. Our legacy to future generations should include sustainable economic growth and environmental quality. It would be a shame if we also bequeathed a cultural desert.

Beyond the scaffolding provided by metadiscourse, negation and concession, the author deploys a multitude of appraisals to promote his position and dismiss that of his opponents, including explicit or **inscribed** attitudes (*extremely good, positive, perhaps even more important, lopsided view, not very persuasive, shame*), but more often implicit or **invoked** attitudes (*economic nationalist, anti-immigration, admission, creates demand, contribution, quality of life, diversity, access, new ideas, influential, equity, sustainable, legacy, cultural desert*), and **graduation** (*greatly reduced or zero, most common, most of the bigger ones, one of the lowest, far more, could double, even more, broadest sense, myriad everyday choices*) (for these appraisal systems, see Martin and White, 2005; Martin and Rose, 2007). Manipulating such prosodies of appraisal within the overall scaffolding of argument genres is a highly complex skill, which potentially affords the adept writer a prominent voice in public discourse and a powerful weapon for promoting ideological positions (Hood and Martin, 2007; Martin and Wodak, 2003). But, aside from political contexts, deft manipulation of argument genres and appraisal prosodies is also an essential skill for academic writing, both for researchers promoting their work and for students demonstrating their acquisition.

Response genres – evaluating texts

Another major set of genres for exercising influence and demonstrating competence are text responses. Reviews of all kinds are endemic in post-colonial culture, describing and evaluating products from books and movies to cars and airlines. They typically include the elements Context^Description^Evaluation, although varying in their relative size and ordering. Beyond reviews, a key genre in the secondary school curriculum is interpretation. Mastery of the interpretation genre demonstrates 'that one is able to "read" the message of the text and hence is able to respond to the cultural values presented in the narrative' (Rothery, 1994: 156). Staging of interpretations include an **Evaluation** of both the text and its message, a **Synopsis** that selects certain elements of the text to illustrate the message, and a **Reaffirmation** of the evaluation, illustrated here with an interpretation of the movie *Rabbit Proof Fence* (Martin, 2005). Here **inscribed** attitudes are in bold, and **invoked** attitudes underlined.

Evaluation	It's **intriguing** how a **simple** story (originally released in 1996 with the title *Follow The Rabbit-Proof Fence*) could become such a **huge international success**. Aunty Doris had an **amazing** mother who undertook the **most incredible** journey of her life **against every single adversity** – both <u>natural and man-made</u> – and <u>still ended up losing</u> her own **precious** children to the <u>same government policy she thought she had conquered</u>. It <u>could only happen in Australia really</u>.
Synopsis message1 – stolen	For **those on another planet** for the last 12 months (or **in denial** of Australia's **terrible history of abuse** against Aboriginal people), *Rabbit Proof Fence* is the **true story** of Molly, born near Jigalong in the remote Pilbara region of Western Australia. **Forcibly stolen** as a child from her mother, along with her two sisters she is taken to the **penal like** Moore River Settlement near Perth – <u>a long way from home</u> and <u>virtually another world</u> for the trio.
political context	The policy makers of the time were **adamant** about the <u>'rescue of the native'</u> in Western Australia – that by integrating them into white society and <u>breeding them out</u> they could be <u>saved from their own 'primitive savagery'</u>. Moore River was a <u>testament to these scruples</u> in that it was <u>responsible for training</u> these half-caste children to be <u>servants for white families</u>, mainly in regional areas.
message2 – escape	**Treated harshly** at Moore River, Molly sees **only one option** for her and her siblings – to commence the journey back home to her mother and extended family on foot. <u>Escaping from their captors</u>, the girls had <u>no maps to guide them</u> on the <u>1600 kilometre journey</u>, just a long standing landmark to <u>man's battle against nature</u> – a north/south running rabbit-proof fence that stretched the length of the country to <u>lead them home</u>.
Reaffirmation	It's **gripping stuff really, full of adventure, tragedy and rejoices – prime material** for a feature length movie. It took the **bravery** of Australian director Phillip Noyce to see the **inner triumph** of this novel and turn it into a **much lauded** and **almost definitive** visual record of <u>this country's treatment</u> of Aboriginal people. And **every single** word is based on **truth**.

The interpretation begins by strongly evaluating both the film and its twin messages of tenacity and injustice. The Synopsis then presents the events that carry these messages – the initiating injustice and its political context; the girls' heroic escape – and the film and its messages are then strongly re-evaluated in the Reaffirmation. As with arguments, the play of appraisal is critical of the goals of the genre. The tenor enacted in this particular instance is one of solidarity, drawing the reader in by sharply excluding both *policy makers of the time* and *those on another planet … or in denial*, and proliferating explicit attitudes.

Where interpretation is the central genre in literature studies in the secondary school, critical responses are the domain of academic literary criticism, and they go beyond interpreting, to challenge the message of a text. They typically begin with an **Evaluation** that suggests the possibility of challenge, which is followed by a text **Deconstruction** that reveals how the message is constructed, and finally by the **Challenge**, which denaturalizes the message. Clearly, mastery of the interpretation genre is an essential foundation for this more complex and highly specialized task, but also for other response genres that are found across academic disciplines. Key genres are critical reviews that critique an academic text and literature reviews that discuss multiple positions taken by texts in a field. The latter are organized like complex discussions, starting with the **Topic** of study, followed by an **Issues** stage, that presents various writers' positions on each issue within the topic.

Apprenticing learners: genre-based literacy methodology

Inequalities in access to the privileged genres of modern institutional fields have been a central concern for the Sydney School program. The description of written genres has developed in tandem with a long-term literacy intervention designed to provide access for all the students to the linguistic resources required for educational success. There have been three major phases in the genre-based pedagogy's development: the initial design of the genre writing pedagogy in the 1980s, with a handful of genres in the primary school; the extension of the writing pedagogy in the 1990s, to genres across the secondary school curriculum and beyond; and the development of the reading pedagogy from the late 1990s, integrating reading and writing with teaching practice across the curriculum at primary, secondary and tertiary education levels.

The initial design of the pedagogy was influenced by Halliday's (1975) and Painter's (1984, 1998) work on language learning in the home, from which the principle of 'guidance through interaction in the context of shared experience' was adapted for classroom language learning contexts. On this principle, a teaching–learning cycle was designed by Rothery (1994, 1996) and her colleagues, with three main stages – **Deconstruction** (guiding students to recognize the cultural context, staging and key linguistic features in model texts), **Joint construction** (guiding the whole class to construct another text in the same genre), and **Individual construction** (in which students write a third text in the same genre). The success of this explicit research-based methodology has made it a standard literacy teaching practice in all Australian primary schools and increasingly internationally, as well as in English as a second language (ESL) and academic literacy programs.

Over the past decade, the principles of language learning through guided deconstruction and reconstruction of model texts has been extended in the Reading to Learn methodology. This methodology adds more intensive levels of support for students to recognize patterns of language in reading texts, and to appropriate them in their writing. In addition to a more detailed language focus, it uses highly designed cycles of teacher–class interaction in order to enable every student to read and write texts that are well beyond their independent competence (Rose, 2004, 2007, 2008, 2010; Martin, 2005; Martin and Rose, 2005, in press; www.readingtolearn.com.au). The *Reading to Learn* strategies have been consistently shown to accelerate literacy development at twice to over four times the expected rates, at the same time as they rapidly narrow the gap in any class between the most and the least successful students (McRae *et al.*, 2000; Culican, 2006; Rose *et al.*, 2008).

While there is no space to elaborate here on the pedagogy beyond a brief sketch of the rich variety of genre research that underpins it, we hope that discourse analysts and educators can use this contribution as a starting point in order to explore the areas that interest them in the Sydney School research.

Further reading

Martin, J. R. and Rose, D. (2008) *Genre Relations: Mapping Culture*. London: Equinox.

Provides a more detailed description of the genre families outlined in this paper. The volume describes genres associated with history, sciences, industry and stories, as well as relations with visual images and larger texts, or macro-genres, illustrated with texts from Indigenous and other Australian contexts.

Martin, J. R., and Rose, D. (2007) *Working with Discourse: Meaning Beyond the Clause*. London: Continuum.

Provides an accessible, practical introduction to analysing discourse semantics. The book outlines resources for construing experience, negotiating values and organizing discourse; and strategies for analysing texts by using examples from the South African liberation movement.

Rose, D. (2008) 'Writing as linguistic mastery: the development of genre-based literacy pedagogy', in D. Myhill, D. Beard, M. Nystrand, and J. Riley (eds.) *Handbook of Writing Development*. London: Sage, pp. 151–166.

Outlines the development of the genre pedagogy developed in the Sydney School, that draws on the genre analyses described above.

Rose, D. and Martin, J. R. (in press) *Learning to Write, Reading to Learn: Genre, Knowledge and Pedagogy in the Sydney School*. London: Equinox.

Elaborates the Sydney School genre pedagogy in more detail, from the initial design of the genre writing pedagogy, through the research in language across the curriculum, to the design of the reading pedagogy. This volume provides practical tools for classroom teaching and teacher education, along with the pedagogic and linguistic theory underpinning these tools.

Christie, F. and Martin, J. R. (eds.) (1997) *Genres and Institutions: Social Practices in the Workplace and School*. London: Cassell.

Comprises studies of school and workplace registers and genres, reporting the Sydney School research in language across the curriculum.

References

Bednarek, M. and Martin, J. R. (eds.) (2009) *New Discourse on Language: Functional Perspectives on Multimodality, Identity and Affiliation*. London: Continuum.

Bernstein, B. (1990) *The Structuring of Pedagogic Discourse*. London: Routledge.

Bernstein, B. (2000) *Pedagogy, Symbolic Control and Identity: Theory, Research, Critique*. London: Taylor and Francis.

Christie, F. and Martin, J. R. (eds.) (1997) *Genres and Institutions: Social Practices in the Workplace and School*. London: Cassell.

Coffin, C. (1996) *Exploring Literacy in School History*. Sydney: Adult Migrant English Service; Sydney: Metropolitan East Disadvantaged Schools Program.

Coffin, C. (2003) 'Reconstruals of the past – Settlement or Invasion? The role of JUDGEMENT analysis', in J. R. Martin and R. Wodak, R. (eds.) *Re/Reading the Past: Critical and Functional Perspectives on Discourses of History*. Amsterdam: Benjamins, pp. 219–246.

Coffin, C. (2007) 'Constructing and giving value to the past: an investigation into secondary School history', in F. Christie and J. R. Martin (eds.) *Knowledge Structure: Functional Linguistic and Sociological Perspectives*. London: Continuum, pp. 196–230.

Corrigan, C. (1991) *Changes and Contrasts: VCE Geography*. Units 1 and 2. Milton, QLD: Jacaranda Press.

Culican, S. (2006) *Learning to Read: Reading to Learn, a Middle Years Literacy Intervention Research Project*. Melbourne: Catholic Education Office. Availble at http://www.cecv.melb.catholic.edu.au/Research and Seminar Papers (accessed 21 January 2011).

Dreyfus, S., Hood, S., and Stenglin, M. (eds.) (2010) *Proceedings of the Semiotic Margins Conference, University of Sydney, Sydney, 2007*. London: Continuum.

Eggins, S. and Slade, D. (1997) *Analysing Casual Conversation*. London: Cassell.

Halliday, M. A. K. (1975) *Learning How to Mean: Explorations in the Development of Language*. London: Edward Arnold.

Halliday, M. A. K. (1994) *An Introduction to Functional Grammar*. Second Edition, 2004. London: Arnold.

Halliday, M. A. K. and Martin, J. R. (1993) *Writing Science: Literacy and Discursive Power*. Pittsburgh, PA: University of Pittsburgh Press.

Hasan, R. and G. Williams (eds.) (1996) *Literacy in Society*. London: Longman.

Hjelmslev, L. (1961) *Prolegomena to a Theory of Language*. Madison, WI: University of Wisconsin Press.

Hood, S. and Martin, J. R. (2007) 'Invoking attitude: the play of graduation in appraising discourse', in R. Hasan, C. M. I. M. Matthiessen, and J. Webster (eds.) *Continuing Discourse on Language*. London: Equinox, pp. 739–764.

Humphrey, S. (2008) *Exploring Literacy in School Geography*. Sydney: Metropolitan East Disadvantaged Schools Program. Sydney: Adult Migrant English Service.

Hyland, K. (2007) 'Genre pedagogy: language, literacy and L2 writing instruction', *Journal of Second Language Writing*, 16: 148–164.

Hyon, S. (1996) 'Genre in three traditions: implications for ESL', *TESOL Quarterly*, 30 (4): 693–722.

Iedema, R. (2008) *Literacy of Administration*. Sydney: Adult Migrant English Service. Sydney: Metropolitan East Disadvantaged Schools Program.

Iedema, R., Feez, S., and White, P. (2008) *Media Literacy*. Sydney: Adult Migrant English Service, Sydney: Metropolitan East Disadvantaged Schools Program.

Johns, A. M. (ed.) (2002) *Genres in the Classroom: Applying Theory and Research to Practice*. Mahwah, NJ: Lawrence Erlbaum.

Jordens, C. (2002) 'Reading spoken stories for values: a discursive study of cancer survivors and their professional carers', PhD thesis (Medicine), University of Sydney, Sydney.

Labov, W. and Waletzky, J. (1967) 'Narrative analysis: oral versions of personal experience', in J. Helm (ed.) *Essays on the Verbal and Visual Arts*. Seattle, WA: University of Washington Press, pp. 12–44.

Lemke, J. (1998) 'Multiplying meaning: visual and verbal semiotics in scientific text', in J. R. Martin and R. Veel (eds.), *Reading Science: Critical and Functional Perspectives on Discourses of Science*. London: Routledge, pp. 87–113.

Macken-Horarik, M. (1996) 'Construing the invisible: specialized literacy practices in junior secondary English', PhD thesis, University of Sydney, Sydney.

McRae, D., Ainsworth, G., Cumming, J., Hughes, P., Mackay, T., Price, K., Rowland, M., Warhurst, J., Woods, D., and Zbar, V. (2000) *What Has Worked, and Will Again: The IESIP Strategic Results Projects*. Canberra: Australian Curriculum Studies Association, pp. 24–26;.

Malinowski, B. (1935) *Coral Gardens and Their Magic*. London: Allen and Unwin.

Martin, J. R. and R. Wodak (eds.) (2003) *Re/Reading the Past: Critical and Functional Perspectives on Discourses of History*. Amsterdam: Benjamins.

Martin, J. R. (1992) *English Text: System and Structure*. Amsterdam: Benjamins.

Martin, J. R. (1994) 'Macro-genres: the ecology of the page', *Network*, 21: 29–52.

Martin, J. R. (1996) 'Evaluating disruption: symbolising theme in junior secondary narrative', in R. Hasan and G. Williams (eds.) *Literacy in Society*. London: Longman, pp. 124–171.

Martin, J. R. (1999) 'Mentoring semogenesis: "genre-based" literacy pedagogy', in F. Christie (ed.) *Pedagogy and the Shaping of Consciousness: Linguistic and Social Processes*. London: Cassell, pp. 123–155.

Martin, J. R. (2000) 'Grammar meets genre – reflections on the "Sydney school" ', *Arts: The journal of the Sydney University Arts Association*, 22: 47–95.

Martin, J. R. (2001) 'Writing history: construing time and value in discourses of the past', in C. Colombi and M. Schleppergrell (eds.) *Developing Advanced Literacy in First and Second Languages*. Mahwah, NJ: Erlbaum, pp. 87–118.

Martin, K. (2005) *Book Review: Rabbit-Proof Fence*. Available at: http://www.abc.net.au/message/blackarts/review/s773970.htm (accessed 15 January 2011)

Martin, J. R. (2006) 'Metadiscourse: designing interaction in genre-based literacy programs', in R. Whittaker, M. O'Donnell, and A. McCabe (eds.) *Language and Literacy: Functional Approaches*. London: Continuum, pp. 95–122.

Martin, J. R. and Plum, G. (1997) 'Construing experience: some story genres', *Journal of Narrative and Life History*, 7 (1–4): 299–308.

Martin, J. R. and Rose, D. (2007) *Working with Discourse: Meaning Beyond the Clause*. London: Continuum.

Martin, J. R. and Rose, D. (2005) 'Designing literacy pedagogy: scaffolding asymmetries', in R. Hasan, C. M. I. M. Matthiessen, and J. Webster (eds.) *Continuing Discourse on Language*. London: Equinox, pp. 251–280.

Martin, J. R. and Rose, D. (2007) 'Interacting with text: the role of dialogue in learning to read and write', *Foreign Languages in China*, 4 (5): 66–80.

Martin, J. R. and Rose, D. (2008) *Genre Relations: Mapping Culture*. London: Equinox.

Martin, J. R. and Veel, R. (1998) *Reading Science: Critical and Functional Perspectives on Discourses of Science*. London: Routledge.

Martin, J. R. and White, P. R. (2005) *The Language of Evaluation: Appraisal in English*. London: Palgrave.

Painter, C. (1984) *Into the Mother Tongue: A Case Study of Early Language Development*. London: Pinter.

Painter, C. (1998) *Learning Through Language in Early Childhood*. London: Cassell.

Painter, C. and Martin, J. R. (eds.) (1986) *Writing to Mean: Teaching Genres Across the Curriculum*, Occasional Papers 9, Applied Linguistics Association of Australia.

Pilkington, D. (1996) *Follow the Rabbit-Proof Fence*. St Lucia, QLD: University of Queensland Press.

Rose, D. (1997) 'Science, technology and technical literacies', in F. Christie and J. R. Martin (eds.) *Genres and Institutions: Social Practices in the Workplace and School*. London: Cassell, pp. 40–72.

Rose, D. (1998) 'Science discourse and industrial hierarchy', in J. R. Martin and R. Veel (eds.) *Reading Science: Critical and Functional Perspectives on Discourses of Science*. London: Routledge, pp. 236–265.

Rose, D. (2001) *The Western Desert Code: An Australian Cryptogrammar*. Canberra: Pacific Linguistics.

Rose, D. (2004) 'sequencing and pacing of the hidden curriculum: how indigenous children are left out of the chain', in J. Muller, B. Davies, and A. Morais (eds.) *Reading Bernstein, Researching Bernstein*. London: RoutledgeFalmer, pp. 91–107.

Rose, D. (2005a) 'Narrative and the origins of discourse: construing experience in stories around the world', *Australian Review of Applied Linguistics Series*, S19: 151–173.

Rose, D. (2005b) 'Reading genre: a new wave of analysis', *Linguistics and the Human Sciences*, 2 (2): 185–204.

Rose, D. (2007) 'Towards a reading based theory of teaching', Plenary paper in *Proceedings 33rd International Systemic Functional Congress 2006*. Available at http://www.pucsp.br/isfc/proceedings/ (accessed 19 January 2011).

Rose, D. (2008) 'Writing as linguistic mastery: the development of genre-based literacy pedagogy', in D. Myhill, D. Beard, M. Nystrand, and J. Riley (eds.) *Handbook of Writing Development*. London: Sage, pp. 151–166.

Rose, D. (2010) 'Meaning beyond the margins: learning to interact with books', in J. Martin S. Hood, and S. Dreyfus. (eds.) *Semiotic Margins: Reclaiming Meaning*. London: Continuum, pp. 177–208

Rose, D. and Martin, J. R. (in press, 2011) *Learning to Write, Reading to Learn: Genre, Knowledge and Pedagogy in the Sydney School*. London: Equinox.

Rose, D., McInnes, D., and Korner, H. (2007) *Scientific Literacy*. Sydney: Metropolitan East Disadvantaged Schools Program, Sydney: Adult Migrant Education Service.

Rose, D., Rose, M., Farrington, S., and Page, S. (2008) 'Scaffolding literacy for indigenous health sciences students', *Journal of English for Academic Purposes*, 7 (3): 166–180.

Rothery, J. (1994) *Exploring Literacy in School English (Write It Right Resources for Literacy and Learning)*. Sydney: Adult Migrant Education Service, Sydney: Metropolitan East Disadvantaged Schools Program (republished 2008).

Rothery, J. (1996) 'Making changes: developing an educational linguistics', in R. Hasan and G. Williams (eds.) *Literacy in Society*. London: Longman, pp. 86–123.

Rothery, J. and Stenglin, M. (1997) 'Entertaining and instructing: exploring experience through story', in F. Christie and J. R. Martin (eds.) *Genres and Institutions: Social Practices in the Workplace and School*. London: Cassell, pp. 231–263.

Rowe, L. (1998) 'Plus to immigration equation', *The West Australian*, 16 September 1998.

Unsworth, L. (2001) 'Evaluating the language of different types of explanations in junior high school science texts', *International Journal of Science Education*, 236: 585–609.

Unsworth, L. (2004) 'Comparing school science explanations in books and computer-based formats: the role of images, image/text relations and hyperlinks', *International Journal of Instructional Media*, 31 (3): 283–301.

Veel, R. and Coffin, C. (1996) 'Learning to think like an historian: the language of secondary school history', in R. Hasan and G. Williams (eds.) *Literacy in Society*. London: Longman, pp. 191–231.

16

Genre as social action

Charles Bazerman

Discourse arises among people, in interaction, and it is part of the means by which people accomplish social actions. Meanings arise within the pragmatic unfolding of events and mediate the alignment of participants to perceptions of immediate situations and relevant contexts (whether fictive or non-fictive) called to mind by language. Language is crafted, deployed, and interpreted by individuals in the course of social participation, even when individuals use language in a personally reflective mode, considering one's own identity, commitments, and actions while using received language. Language users (with particular neurophysiological capacities and individual histories of language experience) in the course of interaction call upon the resources of language that are socially and culturally available and that have been typified through histories of social circulation; nonetheless, individuals construct meanings and consequentiality from their perception of particular novel situations and of their participant action in those situations. Thus situated meaning is a negotiation between the public distribution and practices of language expected within the site of communication and the personal meaning systems of the receiving individuals, developed through a lifetime of socially embedded language use, as applied to the communicative issue at hand. These interactions over meaning may occur in the here-and-now in terms of material space, but they may also occur at a distance in time and space—a distance mediated through recorded language. We may use language both to cooperate in building a stone wall that is physically in front of us and to establish principles of chemical bonding in scientific publications (which, however, index and are accountable to the material chemical interactions in specialized experimental probes and in everyday life.) We may even use language to transport the imaginations of our audience into imagined events in a fictive galaxy where fundamental principles of the world we know are suspended.

The study of discourse, therefore, rightly begins with considering people in interaction, to locate the worlds of meaning they create in the pursuit of human ends. In investigating the meaning-making of cleverly creative people in variable circumstances (though not without constraints), we need to identify the processes by which language users create order and sense so as to align with each other for mutual understanding and coordination. These coordinations build on simple grounds but lead to the complexity of the discursive world as we know it.

The thinness of the written sign

In written language (the area of my primary concern), these themes of situated alignment over meaning are both highlighted and obscured. Because written texts often communicate with people at a distance of time and space, the here-and-now existence of one's interlocutor is typically invisible at the moment of writing or reading. If our interlocutors come to mind, they appear as acts of imagination based on limited clues obtained from prior texts or interactions, rather than as embodied presences. Without immediate interactive response we cannot rapidly repair, modify, or expand the utterance to increase alignment. (Of course the affordances of new communicative technologies change synchronicities and informational channels, but fundamental issues of communication at a distance remain.) The communicative clues for a successful alignment over meanings and actions must be carried through the arrangement of the few letters of the alphabet in words, sentences, and larger units—along with punctuation, graphic elements, and materialities of the medium.

The thinness of the written signs and the distance from the receiver often leave the writer uncertain whether the produced artifact will evoke the desired meanings and effects. On the receptive side, the reader may struggle with interpretation of what precise meanings could have been intended by the author or other presenter of the signs. The problem of alignment over limited clues is most poignant when the text is written in a hard-to-read script or in a language the reader has limited familiarity with. Then the reader may be left with just inkmarks on paper that cannot be animated into meanings and intentions. Even if the reader is highly literate in the language, ambiguous words, unfamiliar references, novel ideas, difficult syntax, or complex arguments can make an act of reading an imaginative and interpretive challenge. Even when only fully common words, genres, and constructions are used, the different associations, cognitive patterns, and interests of different readers can make reanimating another's meanings a challenge with only approximate results—otherwise there would be no fields of hermeneutics, literary criticism, legal disputation, and scriptural interpretation. Nor would reader response need theorizing.

Yet these thin symbols—only interpretable in an approximate way, at a different time and in a different place, by a different person, with different motives and mental contents—have proved remarkably robust in allowing communication of the complex thoughts of philosophy, accumulation of extensive interrelated knowledge and theories of science, planning and coordination of large architectural projects, and maintenance of large institutions such as legal systems and government bureaucracies. By what processes can these frail symbols bear so much weight of meaning and coordination?

The answer proposed in this chapter and in the kinds of work reported here is that the problem of the recognizability of meaning is in large part a matter of recognizing situations and actions within which the meanings are mobilized through the medium of the signs. Meaning is not fully available and immanent in the bare spelled words. Interactants' familiarity with domains of communication and relevant genres make the kind of communication recognizable: establishing roles, values, domains of content, and general actions that then create the space for more specific, detailed, refined utterances and meanings spelled out in the crafted words.

This perspective has helped me understand the nature of writing, particularly within organized systems of knowledge production and transmission—as found in the academy. As a teacher of college writing, I was faced with the practical task of improving students' literacy skills in order to increase their engagement and participation in the literate systems of the university. As I investigated how the highly specialized practices of scientific writing arose within the complex of evolving scientific activity (Bazerman, 1988), I began to see how the same principles of situated meaning making within activities applied to the classroom as well as to non-academic literate practice. I also came to appreciate the role of literacy in organizing the modern world (Goody, 1986; Bazerman, 2006). As I developed this perspective, I found many of the ordinary assumptions we have about written language turned inside out.

An interest in social processes, trajectories, patterns, and systems, has led some of us to put aside for a while the more traditional attention to language and meaning. Much of the work I will summarize considers what discourse analysts might consider context with a lesser focus on discourse proper. Nonetheless the traditional issues of signifying language remain and need to be rearticulated within the new activity based framework (Bazerman, 2003; Bazerman and Prior, 2005). Attentiveness to the words, choosing the right words, and being loyal to the words written by others supports the hard work of writing intelligibly and intelligently to readers and of sympathetically reconstructing the meanings other writers attempt to evoke. Attention to the details of each other's expressions is part of an ethics of interpersonal, social engagement. However, practical attention to language always occurs within situations that orient the participants and evoke particular expectations and knowledge worlds, even if only tacitly and habitually. Aiding student development to read and write in situations with which they are less familiar (such as those in research disciplines or professions) requires that we become explicit about the communicative situations, social organization, and activities they are engaging. Making explicit the organization and dynamics of communicative situations helps students know more concretely what their options are and how they might frame their goals, enhancing the potential for communicative success. The articulation of goals and repeated success in achieving them feeds back into increased motivation and engagement. Equally, in non-school settings, explicit analysis of communicative situations and options provides means to increase levels of practice, engagement and success of individual participants, and more effective organization of the social systems through redesigning genres and flows of documents. Finally an understanding of the relationship between school settings and other life settings can help align literacy education with the communicative opportunities and challenges students will face in their lives.

Activity, agency, and utterance at the start

Language exists in the utterances that bring it into being and in the evolving history of utterances that provide us with the resources for making new utterances and provide our interlocutors with the experiences needed for making sense of our utterances. Volosinov's (1973) critique of language points out that Saussure's (1986) simplifications—separating *la langue* from *la parole*, then diachrony from synchrony, and then limiting linguistics to dealing with one *langue*, considered synchronically (which is itself a fiction, out of time and place)—abstract the study of language from the concrete life of language. This critique has been rearticulated by Kristeva (1980), Harris (1981, 1987), Bazerman (1988), Todorov (1990), and Hanks (1996).

While linguistics has done well in creating abstracted accounts of language based on the regularized practices of groups of language users, we must take it seriously that these are only transient formations, constantly evolving, various in their local instantiations and used creatively and purposefully by each user in a specific set of circumstance. Accordingly, words are effective within the situation but do not have a timeless meaning in themselves. They serve as clues within a situation to align participants and achieve local actions. This view is consistent with theories of reading that suggest we make hypotheses about the meaning of texts on the basis of our previous knowledge and experience, of the encounter with the text prior to the current moment, and of our continuing monitoring in further reading for contradictory evidence, which might reassert meaning as an unsolved puzzle (Goodman, 1967; Rumelhart, 1977; Dole *et al.*, 1991).

Meaning-making, typification and genre

The complexity of meaning-making is visible when we see how fragmentary and indefinite utterances of young children are interpreted proleptically by the caregivers around (Cole, 1996; van Lier, 2004) or how people negotiate meanings and activities in high-noise environments; and it is also visible in the constant need for repair in spoken language as investigated by conversational analysts (Schegloff *et al.*, 1977; Sacks, 1995). The attempt at utterances is taken as completed when the parties decide that their needs/actions are met well enough, or when they give up the endeavor or accept lower degrees of approximation, good enough for all practical purposes, as phrased in phenomenology (Schutz, 1967; Schutz and Luckmann, 1973) and ethnomethodology (Garfinkel, 1967). All language is an approximate indicator of meaning, some situations having narrower tolerances for accuracy and alignment than others. Rather than taking transparency of language as the norm, we should rather take those situations that achieve high degrees of alignment, shared meaning, and reliability of co-reference as specific accomplishments, to be examined for the special means of achievement in their situation. While temporary woodland shelters may be impromptu constructions from materials at hand, skyscrapers are engineering marvels attentive not only to their sites, ambient weather, and materials available on the world market, but also to finances, client needs, and ideological climate of meanings that allow them to be constructed and used, as well as to the ongoing social and economic systems that allow them to be maintained. Likewise, powerful texts such as durable national constitutions and canonical works of philosophy require multiple dimensions of attention, work, and design in construction and ongoing social systems of meaning animation to stay alive and meaningful. (See Bazerman, 1999b, 2003 and Bazerman and Prior, 2005).

Available and familiar patterns of utterances (that is, genres) provide interpretable clues that allow people to make sense of each other's utterances and to frame utterances meaningful to one's interlocutors (Bazerman, 2003). Mead (1934) has in fact proposed that our sense of the self arises from our attempts to represent our meanings to be intelligible to others within a social field. The recent discovery of mirror neurons may provide neurological basis for the abilities to take the part of the other and to reconstruct what another's meaning might have been (Rizzolatti and Craighero, 2004). From a Vygotskian perspective we may say that the internalized words provide the means of regulating our cognitive and affective states as we orient towards social interaction (Vygotsky, 1987). Whatever the developmental, cognitive and neurological processes in aligning to social symbols, genre identifies the recognizable kind of utterance we believe we are producing or receiving.

Within the actual contexts of use, an utterance is the minimal unit, aimed at influencing others as part of our cooperative and competitive social interactions, minimally understandable as an act, an intention, a meaning to be transmitted. Its recognizability makes it perceivable as an intended act, an intended influence, an intended transformation of the interlocutor's attention and orientation. In a fundamental way, an utterance acts as the utterer's attempt to define the situation as a site of action for his or her utterance—what in rhetoric would be called the rhetorical situation (Bitzer, 1968) or *kairos* (Miller, 1992), and what Goffman might consider as footing or framing (Goffman, 1974, 1981). Miller (1984), following Schutz's concept of typification (1967), has associated genre with a typified response to a typified situation. In other words, the utterer sees the moment as similar to other moments in which certain kinds of utterances have been effective. Insofar as these typifications and their attendant instantiating moments are circulated and familiar within the group of interlocutors, they facilitate the mutual comprehension and intelligibity of an utterance within a shared and recognized context (Bazerman, 1994b).

Typification, social organization, and social change

Genre typifications result from a process of psycho-social category formation. The categories themselves have no permanent substance. Genre taxonomies, nonetheless, can be useful to map users' categories within a defined social historical space (such as Devitt's 1991 study of tax accountancy letters) and to define widespread functional patterns in robust social systems. Further, though human neurobiological organization may favor certain patterns of cognition (such as episodic memory) and perception (such as organization and salience in visual fields), which may in turn lead to preferences for certain sequencing of statements or recognition of text structures, these still operate below the level of organized social utterance within coordinated activity. Even in the short run, major changes in social relations, economic conditions, governmental regulations, disciplinary goals, communicative technologies or other situational dimensions can lead to a rapid genre change. Indeed the affordances of electronic search, rapid communication, and instantaneous access to wide ranges of information are currently changing genres in numerous social spheres vary rapidly, with further consequences for the social organization of activities, leading to further genre evolution.

What provides for communicative stability is not the genre in itself, but the system of activity that the genre is part of (Engestrom, 1987, 1990; Bazerman, 1994a; Russell, 1997a). Activity systems often give rise to larger institutions, in which the circulation of texts and literate activities are infrastructural (Giddens, 1984). For example Swales' (1990) "create a research space" model of scientific article introductions relies on a robust system of scientific communication supported by explicit intertextuality, tied to disciplinary specialization emerging in the eighteenth and nineteenth centuries, framed by a communal ethos of cooperative investigation, channeled through competitive individual contributions (Bazerman, 1991).

No matter how stabilized and defining genres may appear within some long enduring social systems, we must also remember that genre is a categorization of an utterance and is not a full account or description of any individual utterance itself and its meaning. Even if a text is widely and unproblematically attributable to a single genre (let us say, a bank cheque), it nonetheless carries out a specific communication in a specific context, identifying payer, payee, bank and account, and dates of transaction and will fail if there is some failure in these elements reported in the document. Further, these documents can circulate to different situations as parts of different activities, even if the original context is recognized. In a court proceeding, this checque (recognized as such) may turn into a piece of evidence of fraud (if it meets another very special set of criteria, drawn from legal rules of evidence). Fifty years from now it can become historical evidence of the financial dealings of a famous writer. That is, it may be viewed both variously and multiply in terms of genre. Genres facilitate interpretation of meaning or anticipation of interpretation, and may thereby guide production or reception, but they do not rule absolutely, nor do they displace local acts of meaning making that have evolutionary potential for the systems they are embedded in.

Speech acts, social facts, knowledge, and knowledge transitivity

An utterance noted and attended to is a speech act. What kind of speech act it is perceived to be and what the felicity conditions it must meet for success are very much a matter of typification, in terms of how the interlocutor sees the situation and the utterance as an intervention in the situation. We judge what is happening now on the basis of what has come before—what has been understood, what the consequence has been, how events have typically unfolded, what has seemed an adequate understanding of the utterance acceptable by relevant parties. (In tying speech acts to historically evolving social arrangements I follow the more open-ended definition of felicity conditions proposed by Austin, 1962 rather than the universalizing pragmatic grammar proposed by Searle, 1969.)

The successful speech act creates a social fact, both in the recognition of its accomplishment (e.g. we all agree you have made a bet, committed to a valid contract, etc.) and in terms of the contents represented and relied upon (e.g. a sports event is going to occur at a certain time and venue with certain participants, upon which the bet is placed). Social facts are those things that people believe in/believe to be the case and that, therfore, are true in their consequences, whatever their accountable relation to material events may be. In fact strong social facts that run up against an accountable contradiction with material events create their own set of consequences—perhaps a riot at the sports venue, when the gates are locked and the teams do not show despite the contract on the printed ticket.

Since utterances are the site for the creation and transmission of speech acts and social facts, the typification of utterances in genres is related to the recognizability of acts and the location of facts. Inversely, we can understand the effectiveness of texts in large part through their success in accomplishing speech acts and establishing social facts. Thus a successful bet or a successful court sentence or a successful scientific paper relies both on being enacted by the right participants in the appropriate situation, and on adopting a suitable form and meeting a series of expectations about the fact and reasoning presented within. In these differently genred utterances and associated acts, there are particulars presented and reasoned about that are also accountable to other, non-textual dimensions of the ambient worlds. These accountable relations are also structured through typified, genred understanding. Thus a court decision must appropriately index relevant laws, judicial rules, and precedents in such a way as to identify them persuasively as authoritative in this case; the decision, too, hangs on appropriate indexing and consideration of the evidence. Somewhat differently, the scientific paper must articulate with prior theory and findings as aggregated in the relevant literatures (relevancy here also being a negotiated construction), as well as with current evidence, gathered in ways that meet the evaluative criteria and expectations of the most influential peer readers. All these conditions must continue to stand for the text to be meaningful and consequential for the ongoing work of the court or scientific discipline.

Thus different genres are the origin, part of the validation system, and means of circulation, storage, and access of particular pieces of knowledge. Further, these or related genres are the means of reasoning about and responding to the facts established, as well as of applying knowledge to specific circumstances (Bazerman, 2000). Material, social, and textual universes surrounding each document are indexed and made relevant in the document by explicit representation or implicit assumption, establishing knowledge to be mobilized in reading the document. Thus we can say that knowledge is created and resides within specific genre and activity systems. Bakhtin's concept of chronotope (1981) provides a useful way of characterizing the expected knowledge and reasoning to be found in a genre. Bakhtin associates each genre with a particular space–time world that is represented in each text; moreover, within that space–time there are anticipated characters, landscapes, relations, and events. Fairy-tales happen long ago, in a kingdom far away, where kings, queens, princes, and princesses reside in castles while dragons and evil sorcerers threaten the countryside. The princes slay the dragons and overcome sorcerers to win the hearts of princesses. Similarly, papers in experimental psychology represent certain kinds of evidence produced through recognized methods, and then reasoned about in accepted ways, using a limited lexicon of expected concepts and terms. It would be shocking to the readers of such articles if dragons or psychoanalytic observations were to appear.

If some of the expectations were to be violated, that fact would be noticeable, hybridizing the genre and changing the ideological world—as in a feminist fairy-tale where the princess slays the dragon and creates an alliance with the evil sorceress, who turns out to have been the victim of sexist stigmatization. When accomplished speech acts in one domain travel to another, they both carry some of the assumptions and practices from the original domain and become transformed by the practices of the new domain. It is up to the readers to be convinced that this hybridization and change of the chronotope is legitimate. Thus bringing chemical evidence and physical reasoning into genetics in the middle of the last century required a great deal of preparation and argument for this combination to be accepted within the chronotopes of articles published in genetics journals (Ceccarelli, 2001).

This linkage between genres, speech acts, and social facts is visible when we, for example, seek to identify someone's citizenship. We know there are certain documentary locations where such information is established and kept—such as governmental records offices, where birth certificates are filed or passport records are kept. Further, the documents in question not only store the information but in fact establish the legitimacy and factuality of the information, entering it into a network of related documents that refer and respond to each other. The intertextual link with the originary record maintains the legitimacy of all the secondary documents. Genres are typified not only in the facts they use, but in the other genres they typically draw on, refer to, or otherwise use. Even the form of representation of the other text is generically typified. A news story can summarize and repeat prior reporting on the event without specific citation or quotation, while nonetheless it intentionally evokes previous reports, awaking the readers' memory of them. That same news story may need to be meticulous about identifying the exact words and venue of a politician's unsurprising public statement at the same time as attributing a significant revelation, paraphrased and attributed to "unidentified sources." This relationship among texts, or intertextuality, places every written utterance into a network of related utterances, whether explicitly mentioned, unmentioned but potentially mobilizable, or entirely implicit in the institutional and intellectual environment that forms the conditions for the current document.

Within activity systems, the intertext takes on an orderliness from the typical patterns of circulation, use, and sequence of texts. Within an activity system, texts circulate among a particular grouping of people who have specific action interests in the documents and who are bound together by some or all of the documents in the genre system. Thus a medical office has appointment records, patient appointment notices, patient intake forms, medical records, transmittal slips for tests and test results, billing records, bills, payments, insurance forms, authorizations for procedures that might involve patients, insurers, or hospital review boards. These documents follow each other in particular sequences as patients move through the system. There are specific sequences of documents that Swales (2004) has called "genre chains." Within each complex circulation of relation genres, or genre system, each person has a specific set of documents that he/she is responsible for preparing and has access to. This Devitt (1991) has called the genre set. These sets of documentary relations between participants (who gets to read what, written by whom) establish a series of genre roles and relationships that define a person's participation in the genre system. Further, as systems interact, sometimes genres move from one system to another or systems take on the character of others, in what Bhatia has a called genre colonization (2004).

The systematic circulation of genres among particular groupings serves to mediate communications within an activity system—that is, a group of people in systematic relations in pursuit of work or transformations of the environment (Bazerman, 1994a). The texts within these groups mediate communications (along with communications in other channels). The typification of message occasions and structures social and organizational relations in pursuit of the system's ends, providing a regularized communicative infrastructure. Within the genres of activity systems, the typified epistemic and ontological choices, as well as typical concepts, roles, stances, evaluations, lexicon, intertextuality, and other linguistic features serve in effect something like Foucault's (1970) episteme or discourse, inscribing an ideology and defining power relations. A genre/utterance/activity approach to this ideological/power process, however, provides a more articulated and realistic model of the specific circulation of linguistic tokens and associated meanings attached to specific actions within larger activity systems. Further, this model identifies specific actors with different roles and access to act within the communicative relations and the activity system. This model identifies more concretely where power lies, how it is exercised, and what it can accomplish, as well as how that power is associated with particular meanings and linguistic expressions, towards which different participants may have different access, stances, and uses.

Insofar as knowledge moves beyond its original genre and social ambit, there must be particular points of articulation as it moves from one genre and activity system to the next. Thus science gets into broader public spheres because journalists read certain scientific journals looking for findings they can turn into news stories, or because university public relations offices identify accomplishments with publicity value, or because a business enterprise has a commercial stake in exciting the public about some findings. Edison, for example, understood better than his competitors that the project of developing a system of electric and power required the enlistment of many groups of people. Edison needed to create presence, meaning, and value for electric light and power within their respective discursive systems. His prior experience as a childhood newsboy, as a freelance electrical inventor, as a patent holder, as a contractor to telephone and telegraph industrialists, and as a news celebrity following the invention of the phonograph prepared him to translate the meanings of his proposed project in order to seek support. Understanding how telegraphy, railroad distribution, and urbanization were creating a new kind of public forum, he saw the importance celebrity interviews and feature stories were taking to sell newspapers; he soon learned to become a good interview subject in order to publicize his new ventures. Understanding the rise of new financial markets to support large enterprises based on new technology, he was able to present his project as a potential financial bonanza to a cadre of elite investors and then later to financial markets. Understanding the patent system and the complexity of patent litigation, he and his attorneys were able to create a web of protections that maintained his ownership of a rapidly changing technology. Understanding how to draw on the skills of his inventive collaborators and communicate effectively with them, he was able to invent a new kind of industrial laboratory coordinated through a set of shared laboratory notebooks and other documents. Although an outsider to the European-based community of electrical scientists, he understood the importance of gaining their acknowledgment of the success of his system. With the help of his colleagues, he understood the importance of representing the electric light as an attractive enhancement to the new forms of urban domesticity. His energetic representations of the light in each of these forums were fundamental to his success. These representations were so important to him that he was willing to adopt unconventional means to make sure that he got the representations he needed—including bribing journalists, paying off city officials, packing scientific juries, and giving inside information to investors. His one major communicative failure—namely in turning the charismatic personal communications of his early companies into more regularized bureaucratic communications of a large corporation—contributed to his loss of ownership of General Edison, which became General Electric (Bazerman, 1999a).

A troubling example of the large barrier between the literatures of two domains is that of the circuitous paths by which the scientific literature does or does not get into the courts. The courts, intertextually linked to the legal code, prior judgments, legal opinions, and specific evidentiary documents, do not directly recognize the authority of scientific findings. Rather, in the United States, scientists are qualified through a process known as Daubert hearings to be expert witnesses, who can then express opinions about relevant issues in the case on the basis of their expertise. The scientific literature does not speak directly in the court, but only stands behind the expertise of the expert witness. The nature and quality of the scientific testimony in court is, then, a product of the procedures and contestations of the Daubert hearing (Bazerman, 2009b). Even between neighboring scientific specialties there are often barriers to communication, only overcome when the need for and the usefulness of each other's findings relax those barriers and bring greater acceptance of each other's procedures, as in the case of toxicology and ecotoxicology. Toxicology is a longstanding medical/pharmaceutically based specialty, which has done controlled laboratory studies on laboratory bred animals to determine safe versus lethal doses of specific substances; ecotoxicology is less than 40 years old and attempts to understand the impact of pollutants within naturally occurring ecosystems. It uses uncontrolled field studies and gathers results statistically. The founders of ecotoxicology felt toxicology's findings were not relevant for the environmental issues that concerned them, and practitioners of the traditional field looked on the new field as being too uncontrolled and imprecise to produce valid findings. Only over time, as they each needed each other's findings for their separate purposes, did some cross-citation begin to occur (Bazerman and De los Santos, 2005).

Genres, socialization, and cognitive development

From a Vygotskian perspective, it is worth noting that genres present the intersection between the socially organized interpersonal creation of knowledge and reasoning and the intrapersonal thought, as the individual learns to participate and contribute in those genres, activities, and knowledge systems (Vygotsky, 1987). This intersection involves both processes of internalization, making sense of the socially circulated knowledge and forms, and externalization of one's own thought by expressing it through the language and forms appropriate to the genres one practices (Bazerman, 2009a). Following Scribner and Cole (1981), cognitive development is not so much directly in the language as in the purposes that the languages are used for within the ambient social systems. Thus the relation of genre, utterance, activity, and social cultural forms all bear on how language and literacy affect cognition.

Studying the genres and discourses people are immersed in and how they take up the ambient linguistic tools within their own expressions and actions becomes a means to study the intersection of socialization and cognitive formation. Matching students' own forms of expression with those within the full corpus of the readings students gained in their professional training (such as reported by Parodi, 2009) might help us understand something of the process by which they are learning to think in the appropriate lines of their work. Similar in spirit is Berkenkotter et al.'s study (1991) of the uptake of disciplinary forms of citation by a graduate student in rhetoric and composition.

This approach also offers a framework for considering cognitive development as students engage in the communicative systems of their disciplines in higher education (Sternglass, 1997; Prior, 1998; Herrington and Curtis, 2000; Caroll, 2002; Thaiss and Zawacki, 2006; Rogers, 2010), as well as within occupational and professional settings (Russell, 1997b; Beaufort, 1999; Dias et al., 1999).

Implications for discourse analysis

The perspective presented here has several clear implications for the analysis of discourse.

First, discourse occurs within a social situation and should be understood and analyzed, as it operates meaningfully within that situation.

Second, discursive situations are understood by their participants as organized and structured so as to be meaningful and sensible to them. The mechanisms by which definitions of situation and action are shared among participants are at the heart of social systematicity and of the organization of discourse.

Third, the knowledge, thought, and meanings expressed within situated utterances then become part of the ongoing resources and definition of the situation for future utterances. Discourse is to be understood dynamically, within the construction of those situations and of the larger social activity systems within which those utterances occur.

Fourth, regularities of linguistic form usually accompany stabilizations of social groups and activities—so, to look for linguistic orders, we should look to social orders; and, to look for social orders, we should look to linguistic orders. While in the past geography may have been the dominant covariable of linguistic variation, with literacy and other communication-at-a-distance technology the social covariables of linguistic variation are increasingly tied to more extensive groupings—such as social and cultural institutions, disciplines and professions, work organizations, and media audiences.

Fifth, linguistic entrainment into particular discursive practices goes hand in hand with socialization into activity networks and with cognitive development into the forms of thinking associated with interacting in those activity systems. Internalization of linguistic action transforms into dispositions and orientations.

Sixth, when discourse travels outside of its original ambit, the mechanisms for that wider travel are themselves topics of examination. This includes study of the genres within which such discourses arise, the genres in which they travel, and the genres into which they are received, as well as the processes that occur at the translation border between genres. Those discourses that seem to circulate freely among multiple situations also deserve investigation for the mechanisms by which they appear meaningful at multiple sites and for the differential ways in which they are integrated into different discursive systems and their genres.

In sum, utterances are parts of social life, and the discourses produced within our social life are to be understood within all the dimensions of life. The signs we study are only the residue of complex psychosocial–cultural processes, in which they served as mediators of meaning. While we may study them as residues, for the regularities to be found in residues, their fundamental order is only to be found in their full animation as meaningful communication in the unfolding interactions of life. The orders of discourse are to be found in the dynamics of life processes.

Further reading

Bazerman, C. (1994a) 'Systems of genre and the enactment of social intentions', in A. Freedman and P. Medway (eds.) *Genre and the New Rhetoric*. London: Taylor & Francis, pp. 79–101.

Bazerman, C. (ed.) (1994b) 'Whose moment? the kairotics of intersubjectivity', *Constructing Experience*. Carbondale, IL: Southern Illinois University Press, pp. 171–193.

Bazerman, C. (2000) 'Singular utterances: realizing local activities through typified forms in typified circumstances', in A. Trosberg (ed.) *Analysing the Discourses of Professional Genres*. Amsterdam: Benjamins, pp. 25–40.

Bazerman, C. and Prior, P. (2005) 'Participating in emergent socio-literate worlds: Genre, disciplinarity, interdisciplinarity', in J. Green and R. Beach (eds.) *Multidisciplinary Perspectives on Literacy Research*. Urbana, IL: National Council of Teachers of English, pp. 133–178.

Bazerman, C. (2006) 'The writing of social organization and the literate situating of cognition: extending goody's social implications of writing', in D. Olson and M. Cole (eds.) *Technology, Literacy and the Evolution of Society: Implications of the Work of Jack Goody*. Mahwah, NJ: Erlbaum, pp. 215–239.

Bazerman, C. (2009a) 'Genre and cognitive development', in C. Bazerman, A. Bonini, and D. Figueiredo (eds.) *Genre in a Changing World*. West Lafayette, IN: Parlor Press and WAC Clearinghouse, pp. 279–294.

Miller, C. (1984) 'Genre as social action', *Quarterly Journal of Speech*, 70: 151–167.

Russell, D. R. (1997a) 'Rethinking genre in school and society: an activity theory analysis', *Written Communication*, 14: 504–554.

These elaborate the key theoretical issues of the perspective adopted here.

Bazerman, C. (1999b) 'Letters and the social grounding of differentiated genres', in D. Barton and N. Hall (eds.) *Letter Writing as a Social Practice*. Amsterdam: Benjamins, pp. 15–30.

Bazerman, C. (2006) 'The writing of social organization and the literate situating of cognition: extending goody's social implications of writing', in D. Olson and M. Cole (eds.) *Technology, Literacy and the Evolution of Society: Implications of the Work of Jack Goody*. Mahwah, NJ: Erlbaum, pp. 215–239.

Bazerman, C. (ed.) (2008a) *Handbook of Research on Writing: History, Society, School, Individual, and Text.* Mahwah, NJ: Routledge.

Russell, D. R. (1997b) 'Writing and genre in higher education and workplaces', *Mind Culture and Activity*, 4: 224–237.

These provide overviews of the relevant empirical studies.

Bazerman, C. (2008b) 'Theories of the middle range in historical studies of writing practice', *Written Communication*, 25 (3): 298–318.

Bazerman, C. and Prior, P. (eds.) (2004) *What Writing Does and How It Does It.* Mahwah, NJ: Erlbaum.

These provide the methodological guidelines for carrying out research and text analysis from this perspective.

References

Austin, J. L. (1962) *How to Do Things with Words.* Oxford: Oxford University Press.

Bakhtin, M. (1981) *The Dialogic Imagination: Four Essays* M. M. Bakhtin. Austin, TX: University of Texas Press.

Bazerman, C. (1988) *Shaping Written Knowledge: The Genre and Activity of the Experimental Article in Science.* Madison, WI: University of Wisconsin Press.

Bazerman, C. (1991) 'How natural philosophers can cooperate', in C. Bazerman and J. Paradis (eds.) *Textual Dynamics of the Professions.* Madison, WI: University of Wisconsin Press, pp. 13–44.

Bazerman, C. (1994a) 'Systems of genre and the enactment of social intentions', in A. Freedman and P. Medway (eds.) *Genre and the New Rhetoric.* London: Taylor & Francis, pp. 79–101.

Bazerman, C. (ed.) (1994b) 'Whose moment? the kairotics of intersubjectivity', *Constructing Experience.* Carbondale, IL: Southern Illinois University Press, pp. 171–193.

Bazerman, C. (1999a) *The Languages of Edison's Light.* Cambridge, MA: MIT Press.

Bazerman, C. (1999b) 'Letters and the social grounding of differentiated genres', in D. Barton and N. Hall (eds.) *Letter Writing as a Social Practice.* Amsterdam: Benjamins, pp. 15–30.

Bazerman, C. (2000) 'Singular utterances: realizing local activities through typified forms in typified circumstances', in A. Trosberg (ed.) *Analysing the Discourses of Professional Genres.* Amsterdam: Benjamins, pp. 25–40.

Bazerman, C. (2003) 'Textual performance: where the action at a distance is?', *Journal of Advanced Composition*, 23 (2): 379–396.

Bazerman, C. (2006) 'The writing of social organization and the literate situating of cognition: extending goody's social implications of writing', in D. Olson and M. Cole (eds.) *Technology, Literacy and the Evolution of Society: Implications of the Work of Jack Goody.* Mahwah, NJ: Erlbaum, pp. 215–239.

Bazerman, C. (ed.) (2008a) *Handbook of Research on Writing: History, Society, School, Individual, and Text.* Mahwah, NJ: Routledge.

Bazerman, C. (2008b) 'Theories of the middle range in historical studies of writing practice', *Written Communication*, 25 (3): 298–318.

Bazerman, C. (2009a) 'Genre and cognitive development', in C. Bazerman, A. Bonini, and D. Figueiredo (eds.) *Genre in a Changing World.* West Lafayette, IN: Parlor Press and WAC Clearinghouse, pp. 279–294.

Bazerman, C. (2009b) 'How does science come to speak in the courts? citations, intertexts, expert witnesses, consequential facts and reasoning', *Law and Contemporary Problems*, 72 (1): 91–120.

Bazerman, C. and De los Santos, R. (2005) 'Measuring incommensurability: are toxicology and ecotoxicology blind to what the other sees?', in R. Harris (ed.) *Rhetoric and Incommensurability.* West Lafayette, IN: Parlor Press, pp. 424–463.

Bazerman, C., and Prior, P. (eds.) (2004) *What Writing Does and How It Does It.* Mahwah, NJ: Erlbaum.

Bazerman, C. and Prior, P. (2005) 'Participating in emergent socio-literate worlds: Genre, disciplinarity, interdisciplinarity', in J. Green and R. Beach (eds.) *Multidisciplinary Perspectives on Literacy Research.* Urbana, IL: National Council of Teachers of English, pp. 133–178.

Beaufort, A. (1999) *Writing in the Real World.* New York: Teachers College Press.

Berkenkotter, C., Huckin, T., and Ackerman, J. (1991) 'Social context and socially constructed texts: the initiation of a graduate student into a writing research community', in C. Bazerman and J. Paradis (eds.) *Textual Dynamics of the Professions.* Madison, WI: University of Wisconsin Press, pp. 191–215.

Bhatia, V. (2004) *Worlds of Written Discourse.* London: Continuum.

Bitzer, L. (1968) 'The rhetorical situation', *Philosophy and Rhetoric*, 1: 1–14.

Caroll, L. (2002) *Rehearsing New Roles.* Carbondale, IL: Southern Illinois University Press.

Ceccarelli, L. (2001) *Shaping Science with Rhetoric: The Cases of Dobzhansky, Schrodinger and Wilson*. Chicago, IL: University of Chicago Press.

Cole, M. (1996) *Cultural Psychology: A Once and Future Discipline*. Cambridge, MA: Harvard University Press.

Devitt, A. (1991) 'Intertextuality in tax accounting: generic, referential, and functional', in C. Bazerman and J. Paradis (eds.) *Textual Dynamics of the Professions*. Madison, WI: University of Wisconsin Press, pp. 336–380.

Dias, P., Pare, A., Freedman, A., and Medway, P. (1999) *Worlds Apart: Acting and Writing in Academic and Workplace Contexts*. Mahwah, NJ: Erlbaum.

Dole, J. A., Duffy, G. G., Roehler, L. R., and Pearson, D. D. (1991) 'Moving from the old to the new: research on reading comprehension instruction', *Review of Educational Research*, 61: 239–264.

Engestrom, Y. (1987) *Learning by Expanding: An Activity-Theoretical Approach to Developmental Research*. Helsinki: Orienta-Konsultit.

Engestrom, Y. (1990) *Learning, Working and Imagining: Twelve Studies in Activity Theory*. Helsinki: Orienta-Konsultit.

Foucault, M. (1970) *The Order of Things; an Archaeology of the Human Sciences*. New York: Vintage Books (trans. anonymous).

Garfinkel, H. (1967) *Studies in Ethnomethodology*. Englewood Cliffs, NJ: Prentice-Hall, Inc.

Giddens, A. (1984) *The Constitution of Society*. Berkeley, CA: University of California Press.

Goffman, E. (1974) *Frame Analysis*. New York: Harper & Row.

Goffman, E. (1981) *Forms of Talk*. Philadelphia, PA: University of Pennsylvania Press.

Goodman, K. S. (1967) 'Reading: a psycholinguistic guessing game', *Journal of the Reading Specialist*, 6: 126–135.

Goody, J. (1986) *The Logic of Writing and the Organization of Society*. Cambridge: Cambridge University Press.

Hanks, W. (1996) *Language and Communicative Practices*. Boulder, CO: Westview.

Harris, R. (1981) *The Language Myth*. New York: St. Martin's Press.

Harris, R. (1987) *Reading Saussure: A Critical Commentary on the Cours de linguistique générale*. London: Duckworth.

Herrington, J. and Curtis, M. (2000) *Persons in Process: Four Stories of Writing and Personal Development in College*. Urbana, IL: NCTE.

Kristeva, J. (1980) *Desire in Language: A Semiotic Approach to Literature and Art*. New York: Columbia University Press.

Mead, G. H. (1934) *Mind, Self, and Society*. Chicago, IL: University of Chicago Press.

Miller, C. (1984) 'Genre as social action', *Quarterly Journal of Speech*, 70: 151–167.

Miller, C. (1992) '*Kairos* in the rhetoric of science', in S. P. Witte, N. Nakadate, and R. D. Cherry (eds.) *A Rhetoric of Doing*. Carbondale, IL: Southern Illinois University Press, pp. 310–327.

Parodi, G. (2009) 'Written genres in university studies: evidence from a Spanish corpus in four disciplines', in C. Bazerman, A. Bonini, and D. Figueiredo (eds.) *Genre in a Changing World*. West Lafayette, IN: Parlor Press and WAC Clearinghouse, pp. 483–501.

Prior, P. (1998) *Writing/Disciplinarity: A Sociohistoric Account of Literate Activity in the Academy*. Mahwah, NJ: Lawrence Erlbaum.

Rizzolatti, G. and Craighero, L. (2004) 'The mirror-neuron system', *Annual Review of Neuroscience*, 27: 169–192.

Rogers, P. (2010) 'The contributions of North American longitudinal studies of writing in higher education to our understanding of writing development', in C. Bazerman, R. Krut, K. Lunsford, S. McLeod, S. Null, P. Rogers, and A. Stansell (eds.) *Traditions of Writing Research*. New York: Routledge, pp. 365–377.

Rumelhart, D. E. (1977) 'Toward an interactive model of reading', in S. Dornic (ed.) *Attention and Performance IV*. New York, NY: Academic Press, pp. 573–603.

Russell, D. R. (1997a) 'Rethinking genre in school and society: an activity theory analysis', *Written Communication*, 14: 504–554.

Russell, D. R. (1997b) 'Writing and genre in higher education and workplaces', *Mind Culture and Activity*, 4: 224–237.

Sacks, H. (1995) *Lectures on Conversation*. Oxford: Blackwell, 2 vols.

Saussure, F. de (1986) *Course in General Linguistics*, ed. C. Bally and A. Sechehaye, trans. R. Harris. LaSalle, IL: Open Court.

Schegloff, E. A., Jefferson, G., and Sacks, H. (1977) 'The preference for self-correction in the organization of repair in conversation', *Language*, 53: 361–382.

Schutz, A. (1967) *The Problem of Social Reality*. The Hague: Martinus Nijhoff.

Schutz, A. and Luckmann, T. (1973) *The Structures of the Life-World*. Evanston, IL: Northwestern University Press.

Scribner, S. and Cole, M. (1981) *The Psychology of Literacy*. Cambridge, MA: Harvard University Press.

Searle, J. (1969) *Speech Acts*. Cambridge: Cambridge University Press.

Sternglass, M. S. (1997) *Time to Know Them: A Longitudinal Study of Writing and Learning at the College Level*. Mahwah, NJ: Erlbaum.

Swales, J. (1990) *Genre Analysis: English in Academic and Research Settings*. Cambridge: Cambridge University Press.

Swales, J. (2004) *Research Genres: Explorations and Applications*. Cambridge: Cambridge University Press.

Thaiss, C. and Zawacki, T. M. (2006) *Engaged Writers and Dynamic Disciplines: Research on the Academic Writing Life*. Portsmouth: Boynton/Cook.

Todorov, T. (1990) *Genres in Discourse*. Cambridge: Cambridge University Press.

van Lier, L. (2004) *The Ecology and Semiotics of Language Learning: A Sociocultural Perspective*. New York: Birkhäuser.

Volosinov, V. N. (1973) *Marxism and the Philosophy of Language*. Cambridge, MA: Harvard University Press.

Vygotsky, L. (1987) *Thinking and Speech*, ed. and trans. N. Minick. New York: Plenum.

17

Professional written genres

Vijay Bhatia

Written genres in academic and professional contexts have traditionally been the focus of much of ESP (English for specific purposes) inspired genre analysis.[1] However, the emphasis in this tradition has always been on the use of text-internal linguistic resources, in particular, on the use of formal properties of language, especially analysis of rhetorical 'moves' with relatively very little in-depth analysis of text-external resources, which play an important role in the socio-pragmatics of professional genres, whether written or spoken. This chapter will give a general overview of this approach to the analysis of professional written genres, and at the same, will also widen the scope of the construction, interpretation and use of professional written genres, focusing in particular, on the socio-pragmatic space within which such professional genres invariably function, and will also consider critically how expert professionals exploit this socio-pragmatic space to create new and hybrid forms across disciplinary, institutional, as well as cultural boundaries.

Analysing professional genres

One of the most popular frameworks for the analysis of professional written genres has been 'genre analysis', which initially was inspired by the studies of functional variation in language use as 'register' (Halliday *et al.*, 1964). The early analyses of genres focused on statistically significant features of lexico-grammar, used in a particular subset of texts, namely texts associated with a particular genre in a specific discipline. Barber's (1962) study was probably one of the earliest ones to identify significant lexico-grammatical features in a corpus of scientific texts. Similarly, Gustafsson (1975) focused on only one syntactic feature of legal discourse: binomials and multi-nomials. The trend continued with Bhatia and Swales (1983), who identified nominalizations in legislative discourse as their object of study. In all these preliminary attempts we notice two things: an effort to focus on the textualization of specific written professional genres; and an interest in the description of functional variation in discourse by focusing on statistically significant features of lexico-grammar. Both these concerns served well the cause of applied linguistics for language teaching, especially the teaching and learning of English for specific purposes (ESP). Gradually the emphasis shifted to the process of 'textualization', by focusing on the rhetorical values of specific features of lexico-grammar in the construction and interpretation of professional genres, though often within clause boundaries without much reference to the organizational properties of the genre in question (Selinker *et al.*, 1973; Swales, 1974; Oster, 1981; Dubois, 1982; Trimble, 1985). Bhatia (1992) extended the study of textualization of lexico-grammatical features to other genres by comparing their use across different genres. While investigating the use of nominals in professional genres such as advertisements, scientific research reports, and legislative provisions, he discovered that, although nominals were used overwhelmingly in all these genres, they were markedly different not only in their syntactic form, but also in their rhetorical function. In advertising, nominals typically take the form *(Modifier) Head (Qualifier)*, where modifiers are realized primarily through a series of linearly arranged attributes as *(Determiner) (Adjective) (Adjective) (Adjective) … Head (Qualifier)* – as exemplified in 'the world's smallest and lightest digital camcorder that's also a digital still camera'. Since one of the main concerns in advertising is to offer a positive evaluation of products or services being promoted, and since nominals, in particular noun phrases, are seen as carriers of adjectives, we are likely to find an above-average incidence of nominals in such genres.

On the other hand, nominals in academic research genres, especially in the sciences, are used to create and develop technical concepts. These nominals take the form of nominal compounds of the kind, *(Modifier) (Noun) (Noun) (Noun) … Head (Qualifier)*, where modifiers are typically realized in terms of a series of linearly arranged nouns functioning as classifiers and occasionally incorporating an adjective. A typical example of this phenomenon is (Bhatia, 1993: 149): 'nozzle gas ejection space ship attitude control'. In the case of legislative discourse, nominals are typically realized in the form of nominalizations, as these syntactic forms allow draftsmen to condense clauses for subsequent references in the same sentence, adding precision and unambiguity to legislative provisions (Bhatia, 1982, 1993), as illustrated in the following:

> No obliteration, interlineation or other alteration made in any will after the execution thereof shall be valid or have effect except so far as the words or effect of the will before such alteration shall not be apparent, unless such alteration shall be executed in like manner as hereinbefore is required for the execution of the will…
>
> *(Section 16: The Wills Act, 1970, Republic of Singapore)*

The next stage of development in the analysis of professional genres came as a result of several studies, particularly those of Widdowson (1973), Beaugrande and Dressler (1981), Brown and Yule (1983), Hoey (1983), and van Dijk (1985), who focused on developing a relationship between the choice of lexico-grammar and specific forms of discourse structures and paid special attention to regularities of organization in written genres, which triggered a serious interest in the analysis of complete genres rather than sections of discourses. In professional genres, these structures were seen in terms of socio-cognitive patterns called 'moves', as in Swales (1981, 1990) and Bhatia (1993).

This continual quest for more detailed descriptions of professional genres, primarily focusing on written forms, though equally relevant to spoken genres (see Handford, 2010, for instance), set the agenda for the next decade, without paying serious attention to the context in detail – either to the immediate context in the form of what surrounds a particular text or to context in the much broader sense of what makes a particular text possible and why most of the professionals from the same profession construct, interpret, and use language more or less the same way in specific professional contexts. The focus was centrally on the organization of genre in the form of move structures, which were seen as cognitive structures that professionals often use to make sense of the genres they habitually used. The seminal work by Swales (1990) was probably the most significant contribution to the development of genre theory in this direction; it was followed by Bhatia (1993), who extended the study of move structures in two ways: first, by applying it more generally to a number of other professional genres, most significantly from legal and business domains; and secondly by extending the role of context to bring in a number of other factors, particularly socio-cognitive, motivating discussion about issues related to the rationale for genres.

Genre analysis was, and still is, viewed as the study of situated linguistic behaviour in institutionalized academic or professional settings, whether defined in terms of *typification of rhetorical action*, as in Miller (1984), Bazerman (1994), and Berkenkotter and Huckin (1995); in terms of *regularities of staged, goal oriented social processes*, as in Martin *et al.* (1987), and Martin (1993); or in terms of *consistency of communicative purposes*, as in Swales (1990) and Bhatia (1993). Genre theory, in spite of these seemingly different orientations, covers a lot of common ground, some of which may be summarized on the basis of the analysis of these studies.

1. Genres have been viewed as recognizable communicative events, characterized by a set of communicative purpose(s) identified and mutually understood by members of the professional or academic community in which they regularly occur.
2. Genres are highly structured and conventionalized constructs, with constraints on allowable contributions in terms of the intentions one would like to give expression to, the shape they often take, and also in terms of the lexico-grammatical resources one can employ to give discoursal values to such formal features.
3. Established members of a particular professional community seem to have a much greater knowledge and understanding of the use and exploitation of genres than those who are apprentices, new members, or outsiders.
4. Although genres are viewed as conventionalized constructs, expert members of the disciplinary and professional communities often exploit generic resources to express their private organizational intentions within the constructs of professionally shared communicative purposes.
5. Genres are reflections of disciplinary and organizational cultures, and in that sense they focus on professional actions embedded within disciplinary, professional, and other institutional practices.
6. All disciplinary and professional genres have integrity of their own, which is often identified by reference to a combination of textual, discursive, and contextual factors.

As we can see, the most important feature of this view of language use is the emphasis on conventions that all the three manifestations of genre theory consider to be central to any form of generic description. To summarize, genre thus essentially refers to language use in a conventionalized communicative setting in order to give expression to the specific set of communicative goals of a disciplinary or social institution, which give rise to stable structural forms by imposing constraints on the use of lexico-grammatical as well as discoursal resources. Some of these constraints can also be attributed to variations in disciplinary practices.

The second important aspect of genre theory for the analysis of professional genres is that, although genres are typically associated with recurring rhetorical contexts and are identified on the basis of a shared set of communicative purposes, they are not static. As Berkenkotter and Huckin (1995: 6) point out,

> genres are inherently dynamic rhetorical structures that can be manipulated according to conditions of use, and that genre knowledge is therefore best conceptualized as a form of situated cognition embedded in disciplinary cultures.

Emphasis on conventions and propensity for innovation are therefore two important features of professional genres, and they seem to be contradictory in character. One the one hand, we view genre as a rhetorically situated and highly institutionalized textual activity, having its own generic integrity; on the other hand, we assign genre a natural propensity for innovation and change, which is often exploited by the expert members of the specialist community to create new forms in order to respond to novel rhetorical contexts or to convey private intentions within the context of socially recognized communicative purposes (Bhatia, 1993). How do we account for this seeming contradiction?

Although genres are associated with typical socio-rhetorical situations and in turn shape future responses to similar situations, they have always been 'sites of contention between stability and change' (Berkenkotter and Huckin, 1995: 6). We also know that situations, and more importantly rhetorical contexts, may not always recur exactly in the same way, though they may still be somewhat similar in certain aspects. It may be that a person is required to respond to a somewhat changing socio-cognitive need, which encourages him/her to negotiate his/her response in the light of recognizable or established conventions. It may also be that he or she may decide to communicate additional private intentions within the structure of a different genre (Bhatia, 1993). Established members of professional communities often need to manipulate institutionalized generic forms. Their experience and long association with the professional community give them tactical freedom to exploit generic resources to negotiate individual responses to recurring and novel rhetorical situations. However, such liberties, innovations, creativities, exploitations are invariably realized within rather than outside the genre conventions, whichever way one may draw them – in terms of recurrence of rhetorical situations (Miller, 1984) or in terms of consistency of communicative purposes (Swales, 1990). The nature of genre manipulation thus is invariably subtle, and the manipulation is realized within the broad limits of specific genres. Any serious disregard for these generic conventions leads to opting out of the genre and is noticed by the specialist community as odd. Genre theory as conceptualized in Swales (1990) and Bhatia (1993) thus became a favourite tool for the analysis of professional and academic discourses, as it had potential to go beyond textual analysis to explore specific institutional and disciplinary practices, procedures, and cultures in order to understand how members of specific discourse communities construct, interpret, and use these genres to achieve their community goals and why they write them the way they do. Referring to the works of Swales (1990) and Bhatia (1993) on the analysis of professional genres, Widdowson (1998: 7) points out:

> (Genre analysis) seeks to identify the particular conventions for language use in certain domains of professional and occupational activity. It is a development from, and an improvement on, register analysis because it deals with discourse and not just text: that is to say, it seeks not simply to reveal what linguistic forms are manifested but how they realize, make real, the conceptual and rhetorical structures, modes of thought and action, which are established as conventional for certain discourse communities.
>
> *(Widdowson, 1998: 7)*

To illustrate this kind of analysis, let me take the following letter, from a corporation chairperson, written to the shareholders, often as part of the annual report for the corporation.

Dear fellow shareholders,

I am pleased to present our interim results for the six months ended (date) on behalf of my fellow directors.

It is now two years since the merger of (Name of the Company 1) and (Name of the Company 2), and it is appropriate to address the progress we have made and the challenges ahead. Since the merger, we have concentrated on and successfully pursued three objectives.

First, we have responded to the poor economic environment and intense competition in our industry by driving operating efficiencies within our Company. Secondly, we have increased our financial flexibility, successfully reduced debt to a prudent level; extended the maturity of our remaining debt and reduced significantly our overall funding costs. Thirdly, we have brought together a world-class management team with broad industry experience and strong leadership qualities. Increased operating efficiencies and reduced funding costs are, in turn, driving strong and accelerating free cash flows to give the Company unprecedented flexibility going forward. Without diminishing our commitment to the objectives set during our first two years and, in particular, our commitment to find greater productivity gains and to reduce debt further, our management team is now concentrated on forming strategies to deliver sustained growth over the coming years.

Since the merger, (Name of the Company 1) has been positioned to prosper in extraordinarily difficult economic and operating conditions.

Accordingly, when our economy and operating environment turns round, (name of the Company 1) will be able to exploit opportunities to the benefit of our shareholders, customers and employees.

(Name) *Chairman*... Date....

A text like this can be analysed in terms of its statistically significant features of lexis and grammar. Two of the important aspects that become immediately obvious for lexico-grammatical attention are the pattern of verb tense and the pattern of nominals. The text contains a very high incidence of present perfect tense, such as *have concentrated, have responded to, have increased, have brought together, have concentrated, (have) reduced debt*. In addition, verb forms projecting future expectations are also very common. Typical examples include, *has been positioned to prosper, will be able to exploit opportunities*. Texts like this one also contain a very high incidence of various kinds of nominals, such as *the progress, the challenges, economic environment, intense competition* – including business terminology such as *operating efficiencies, financial flexibility, the maturity of our remaining debt, overall funding costs, free cash flows, productivity gains*, etc. Nominals associated with positive attributes leading to higher expectations of future business performance of the company are also favoured. Some examples may include: *a world-class management team, broad industry experience, strong leadership qualities, increased operating efficiencies, reduced funding costs, strong and accelerating free cash flows, unprecedented flexibility, commitment to the objectives*, and *commitment to find greater productivity gains* – to mention a few.

An above-average incidence of these features of lexico-grammar interestingly cooperates here to indicate that the text is embedded in a specific business context and that it strongly projects a positive and forward-looking image of the achievements of the specific organization in question. Depending on the typicality of use of such features of language, one may conclude that these features tend to help corporate writers in promoting the image of their respective companies. One may like to go further and explore the relationship between some of these features and the discourse action that is intended through this text; and, in order to investigate this, one may need to go beyond the typical use of these individual linguistic resources to see the whole text as a unit of discourse, its organization, and purpose. On the basis of the study of corporate discourses of 15 different Hong Kong stock-exchange listed companies, and especially of the annual reports over a specific period of five years, Bhatia (2004, 2008, 2010) assigned a 7-Move structure to the chairman's letter to the shareholders (see Table 17.1).

However, this is a minimal move-structure, based on the analysis of one example only. It is necessary to make it more generally valid by looking at a reasonably large representative corpus of several examples, which can give us a more generalized move-structure for the type of texts we are considering here. A more general move-structure looks like the following table (see Table 17.2).

Table 17.1 Analysis of a corporate chairman's letter to the shareholders

Dear fellow shareholders, I am pleased to present our interim results for the six months ended (date) on behalf of my fellow directors.	OPENING (Overview of the review period)
It is now two years since the merger of (Name of the Company 1) and (Name of the Company 2), and it is appropriate to address the progress we have made and the challenges ahead. Since the merger, we have concentrated on and successfully pursued three objectives.	ACHIEVEMENTS & MEASURES TAKEN TO ENSURE FUTURE GROWTH
First, we have responded to the poor economic environment and intense competition in our industry by driving operating efficiencies within our Company. Secondly, we have increased our financial flexibility, successfully reduced debt to a prudent level; extended the maturity of our remaining debt and reduced significantly our overall funding costs. Thirdly, we have brought together a world-class management team with broad industry experience and strong leadership qualities. Increased operating efficiencies and reduced funding costs are, in turn, driving strong and accelerating free cash flows to give the Company unprecedented flexibility going forward.	EVIDENCE (Claims to create value and foundation for growth)
Without diminishing our commitment to the objectives set during our first two years and, in particular, our commitment to find greater productivity gains and to reduce debt further, our management team is now concentrated on forming strategies to deliver sustained growth over the coming years.	EXPECTATIONS & PROMISES (Measures and actions taken in the preceding year)
Since the merger, (Name of the Company 1) has been positioned to prosper in extraordinarily difficult economic and operating conditions. Accordingly, when our economy and operating environment turns round, (name of the Company 1) will be able to exploit opportunities to the benefit of our shareholders, customers and employees. (Name) *Chairman*... Date....etc	CLOSING: LOOKING FORWARD (Positive and promising)

Multiperspective and multidimensional analysis of professional genres

Looking at the organization and layout of a particular genre text, one may notice that the text is a letter from the chairman of the company to its shareholders. It contains a number of conventional indicators that go with such a genre. As an example of a letter, it has all the typical signals such as the opening address, the closing, and of course the body of the letter. Moving more towards treating this as a genre, one may claim that the communicative purpose of this letter is to inform the readers, who are the stakeholders in the company, about the performance of the company in the past year. The rationale for writing this letter the way it has been written, in such a positive tone, is that businesses often downplay any indications of negative performance and instead highlight positive aspects for future growth. Letters like these are often accompanied by annual reports, which are supposed to contain more realistic and objective performance indicators, such as the facts and figures of growth and achievement, indicating profit or loss, past weaknesses and future

Table 17.2 Move-structure in a typical corporate chairman's letter to the shareholders

TIME	MOVE STRUCTURE	LEXICO-GRAMMAR
P	Move 1: OVERVIEW OF THE REVIEW PERIOD	Last year was ….
	Often positive, occasionally cautious	Year of value creation …
A	or negative mode	Year of considerable progress …
	Move 2: MAJOR THEMES	
S	Move 3: ACHIEVEMENTS-MEASURES	Weak economic environment …
	(ELABOTRATION & EXPLANATION	Dampening market demands …
T	OF THEMES)	Challenging environment …
	Major achievements, evidence and	
	detailing	Has enhanced our reputation …
	Major contributing factors (Often	Rapidly growing market …
	Inside the company for success or	
	outside factors for failures)	Strengthening our financial fundamentals …
F	Major steps or measure taken to	We expanded our coverage …
	ensure success	
U	Move 4: EXPECTATIONS AND PROMISES	Reshaped the cost base …
	Detailed accounts of future actions	Changes in our operating environment …
T	Measure to be taken	We expect further improvement
	Intended & expected outcomes	Potential to expand our various
U	Move 5: LOOKING FORWARD	businesses …
	Positive outlook	Prospects for 2004 are encouraging ….
R	Continued challenges (sometimes)	Alliance with China will strengthen our
	Grim outlook (rare)	ability …
E	Move 6: EXPRESSIONS OF GRATITUDE	
	(Optional)	Thanks to the quality and talent of our staff
	Appreciation to management team	and management team…
	Move 7: POSITIVE AND CONFIDENT	I wish to thank …. team…
	CLOSING	
	Revisiting themes from Move 1	As Chairman, I am diligently working… with
	Summarizing forward looking	the aim of making a significant and
	positive statements	positive impact on shareholder value.

strengths of the company in question. In order to get at the real picture, the stakeholders often need to go beyond the rhetoric and interpret the results carefully. All these factors, when analysed closely in the context of the rationale for the genre, of the lexico-grammatical features of the text, and also of the nature of participant relationship, are likely to disclose a number of other interesting interpretations of the genre. In order to be able to have such information, one may need to go beyond the text, look more seriously at what Bhatia (2004) calls the 'contextualization of discourse', and adopt a multiperspective and multidimensional approach to genre analysis (Bhatia, 2004) through an integration of a number of different methodologies (Bargiela–Chiappini and Nickerson, 1999), such as textography (Swales, 1998), interpretive ethnography (Smart, 1998), corpus analysis (Biber, 1995; Nelson, 2006; Fuertes-Olivera, 2007), participant perspectives on specialist discourses (Rogers, 2000), cross-cultural and intercultural perspectives (Scollon and Scollon, 1995; Gimenez, 2001; Vergaro, 2004; Planken, 2005), multimodal analysis (Brett, 2000), and observation analysis (Louhiala-Salminen, 2002) – to name only a few. The implication thus is that text-based analyses within register or genre analysis were found to be increasingly inadequate at explaining and accounting for the typical use of language in various

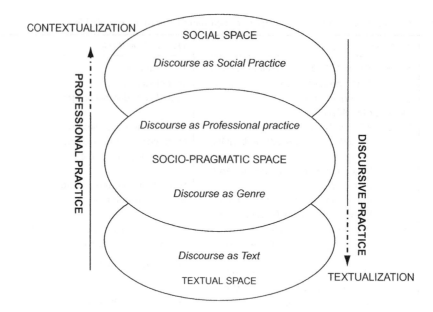

Figure 17.1 Multiperspective genre analytical framework
Source: adapted from Bhatia, 2004

professional contexts. There is an urgent need to study the context in all its multiple forms. This requires studies of how participants undertake these discursive tasks and what they achieve through these discursive activities, which I hope will make it possible for us to see 'as much of the elephant as possible', as the saying goes.

Bhatia (2004) proposed a multiperspective four-space model of genre analysis through the following figure (see Figure 17.1).

In this model, Bhatia uses 'discourse as text' to refer to the analysis of language use that is confined to the surface level properties of discourse, which include formal as well as functional aspects of discourse – that is, phonological, lexico-grammatical, semantic, organizational (including cohesion), and other aspects of text structure such as move structure and intertextuality (Devitt, 1991), not necessarily considering *context* in a broad sense but merely taking into account what is known as co-text. Although, as indicated earlier, discourse is essentially embedded in context, *discourse as text* often excludes any significant engagement with context, except in a narrow sense of intertextuality, to include interactions with surrounding texts. A typical example from research articles will include the use of quotes or citations from published sources to support one's claims or to dispute them by including references to such published sources. *Discourse as text* thus operates essentially within a *textual space* where the knowledge about language structure and its function, which may include the knowledge of intertextuality, is exploited in order to make sense of the text. The emphasis at this level of analysis is essentially on the properties associated with the construction of the textual product, rather than on the interpretation or use of such a product. It largely ignores the contribution often made by the reader on the basis of what he or she brings to the interpretation of the textual output, especially in terms of the knowledge of the world, including the professional, socio-cultural, and institutional knowledge as well as experience that one is likely to use to interpret, use, and exploit such a discourse.

Discourse as genre, in contrast, extends the analysis beyond the textual product to incorporate context in a broader sense to account not only for the way text is constructed, but also for the way it is often interpreted, used, and exploited in specific institutional, or more narrowly professional contexts to achieve specific disciplinary goals. The nature of questions addressed in this kind of analysis may often be not only linguistic, but also socio-cognitive and ethnographic. This kind of grounded analysis of the textual output is very typical of any framework within genre-based theory. Genre knowledge that makes sense of the text at this level includes, in addition to textual knowledge, the awareness and understanding of the shared practices of professional and discourse communities (Swales, 1990), their choice of genres in order to perform their everyday tasks. Genres often operate in what might be viewed as a *socio-pragmatic* (which includes tactical as well as professional) *space*, which allows established members of discourse communities to exploit generic resources to respond to recurring and often novel situational contexts. Closely related to this, one may find the concept of *discourse as professional practice*, which essentially extends the notion of genre use to relate it to professional practice. In order to operate effectively at this stage, one may require professional knowledge and experience of professional practice, in addition to genre knowledge. It operates with what could be regarded as *professional space*.

Discourse as social practice takes this interaction with the *context* much further in the direction of broader social context, where the focus shifts significantly from the textual output to the features of the context – such as the changing identities of the participants, the social structures or professional relationships the genres are likely to maintain or change, the advantages or disadvantages such genres are likely to bring to a particular set of readers. *Discourse as social practice* thus functions within a much broader *social space*, where one may essentially need social and pragmatic knowledge in order to operate effectively (Gee, 1999).

It is important to note that the three interacting views of discourse are not mutually exclusive, but essentially complementary to each other. It is possible to use the proposed framework in a number of ways, depending upon the objective one may decide to pursue. A typical sociolinguist interested in discourse analysis will perhaps begin from the top end, looking deeply and exhaustively into the social context, working her way downward, but not often getting seriously engaged in the textual space. An applied linguist, on the other hand, would find it more profitable to begin at the bottom end, exploring the textual space exhaustively, working toward social space, often using social context as explanation for the analysis of textualization of lexico-grammatical and discoursal resources. However, most users of the framework, whether interested in socio-cultural issues or in pedagogical ones, at some stage or the other will necessarily pay some attention to the socio-pragmatic space in order to consider strategic and tactical aspects of genre construction, interpretation, use, or exploitation of generic resources. Although the framework specifically refers to written genres, it can equally well be used to analyse spoken genres. Handford (2010) provides an excellent illustration of some of this when he applies it to business meetings.

One can also see the prominence of the socio-pragmatic space, which, again, incorporates two rather overlapping conceptualizations of tactical space and professional space in the proposed framework. These concepts seem to have a large degree of overlap because both of them work within the same socio-cognitive space, and also because genres are an integral part of professional practice, and hence both are closely related to each other in the context of professional cultures. More specifically, to look at professional written genres, we could say that all professional genres operate at least at four different yet overlapping levels and hence can be used as resources to explore all these levels, which can be represented as follows (see Figure 17.2).

In order to look beyond the textual genre within the multiperspective framework, the first thing we need to do is to look at the surrounding texts that seem to be part of the same genre, called 'annual corporate report'. Let us look at one such text, which is popularly known as disclaimer. The following is a typical example (see Figure 17.3).

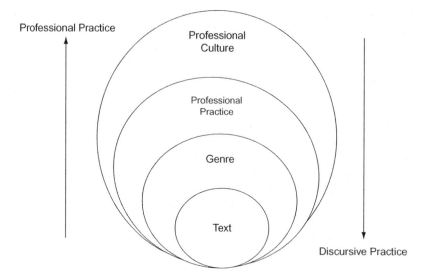

Figure 17.2 Perspectives on professional genres

THE NAME OF THE COMPANY

Disclaimer

FORWARD LOOKING STATEMENTS

This annual report contains forward-looking statements ... These forward-looking statements are not historical facts. Rather, the forward-looking statements are based on the current beliefs, assumptions, expectations, estimates and projections of the directors and management of (The name of the Company) ('the Company') about its business and the industry and markets in which it operates.

These forward-looking statements include, without limitation, statements relating to revenues and earnings. The words 'believe', 'intend', 'expect', 'anticipate', 'project', 'estimate', 'predict' and similar expressions are also intended to identify forward-looking statements. These statements are not guarantees of future performance and are subject to risks, uncertainties and other factors, some of which are beyond the Company's control and are difficult to predict. Consequently, actual results could differ materially from those expressed or forecast in the forward-looking statements.

Reliance should not be placed on these forward-looking statements, which reflect the view of the Company's directors and management as of the date of this report only. The Company undertakes no obligation to publicly revise these forward-looking statements to reflect events or circumstances that arise after publication...

Figure 17.3 A typical disclaimer in a corporate annual report

The disclaimer forms an interesting part of this genre. In the absence of such a disclaimer, one is likely to reach a misleading interpretation of the letter. If the letter is a claimer, in that it was designed to claim a positive and reassuring picture, the disclaimer makes it complete, in that it is meant to remedy any misleading impression it might have given to the shareholders about the future performance of the company. Ideally, the disclaimer, as the name itself suggests, seems to disclaim all that has been claimed in the letter. In addition to this second text, the annual report also contains two more kinds of discourse: 'the accounting discourse', which contains primarily numerical information – such as number and figures, charts and diagrams highlighting the performance of the company and signed by a certified public accounting firm, which gives an unmistakable impression to the reader that all the financial information given there is reliable and accurate, and the 'discourse of finance' in the financial review section of the report, which is generally written by the company's financial managers supposedly interpreting the accounting information in more reader accessible discourse. Once again, the assumption is that all the descriptions, explanations, and so on in the financial review section are accurately based on the accounting numbers, and hence are as reliable as the certified public accountants. If the reader believes this to be true, he or she may take the third step and think that, since the chairman's letter is part of the same reporting genre, whatever has been claimed in the letter is equally reliable and trustworthy, little realizing that the chairman's letter is a typical public relations job, often the work of the public relations department, and their main concern is not to give an accurate and honest interpretation of the figures, but to make an effort to stop any drastic share price movement at the time of weak performance by the company. This may seem a revelation to discourse analysts and to a number of uninitiated readers of annual reports, but it is seen as an established strategy in corporate culture.

It is also possible, and indeed often desirable, to explore other issues connected with contextualization, which will require a deeper understanding of context in addition to textualization and textual organization, and also a deeper understanding of the immediate context, including other relevant texts. One such aspect of contextualization could be the asymmetry in the role relationship between the participants, accompanied by the power distance between the company chairman and the shareholders, on the one hand, and social proximity between the chairman and the fellow directors, on the other. One may also notice the indications of one-way unequal interaction, with the writer providing general information to recipients who may not share the same awareness about the company's past performance. The social or professional context in which this text or genre plays an important role, the social action that this particular example of text represents, and the institutional, social, or professional culture it invokes when it is constructed and interpreted are some of the important issues that need to be investigated. It is not simply that a professional genre is constructed and used for a specific professional purpose; it may be that a specific genre is deliberately and consciously bent to achieve something more than just a socially accepted and shared professional objective, as we have discovered in the chairman's letter to shareholders. One may need to investigate how and to what extent this seemingly harmless genre can be used to disinform, if not deliberately misinform, minority shareholders and other stakeholders of the company about the real performance of the company. One may need to develop a much broader understanding not only of the context but also of corporate culture to answer some of these questions. Many of these questions can be explored through discourse and genre analysis, provided that we extend conventional genre analytical framework to a more multiperspective and multidimensional genre analytical framework, which explores a more socio-pragmatic space than just the textual space.

Towards critical analysis of professional genres

The foregoing account of analysis of professional genres, as illustrated through the analysis and discussion of the chairman's letter to shareholders as part of the annual corporate report, illustrates a quest for increasingly 'thicker' descriptions (Geertz, 1973) through detailed and insightful analyses of professional genres. In another way, it is also an effort to explore professional practices, rather than an end in itself. The most interesting part of the analysis is not the use of lexico-grammar, of intertextuality, or even of the move-structure, though it is very important to analyse the genre itself; it is that such analysis can and should be used as a tool to study and understand professional practice, and even professional culture. Only then we will be able to answer some of the questions often raised in the context of professional genres, some of the prominent ones of which may be:

- Why do the members of specific professional communities use language the way they do?
- How do these professionals manipulate professional genres to achieve their corporate objectives?
- How do these professionals 'bend generic norms' to achieve their 'private intentions' in addition to, and within, the framework of shared generic conventions?

It is therefore necessary to extend the analysis of professional genres beyond the textual space, and to explore more seriously the socio-pragmatic (tactical as well as professional) space within which all professional genres seem to operate. When we start doing this seriously, only then can we claim that we are on our way to look at professional written genres more critically, because only then our focus will extend beyond the genres to professional practice and professional culture, which should be the aim of all good analysis.

Further reading

Bhatia, V. K. (2004) *Worlds of Written Discourse – A Genre-Based View*. London: Continuum.
Bhatia, V. K. (2010) 'Interdiscursivity in professional communication', *Discourse and Communication*, 21 (1): 32–50.
Devitt, A. (1991) 'Intertextuality in tax accounting', in C. Bazerman and J. Paradis (eds.) *Textual Dynamics of the Professions*. Madison, WI: University of Wisconsin Press, pp. 336–355.
Handford, M. (2010) *The Language of Business Meetings*. Cambridge: Cambridge University Press.
Swales, J. M. (1990) *Genre Analysis: English in Academic and Research Settings*. Cambridge: Cambridge University Press.

Note

1 Some sections of this chapter draw on the first chapter of an earlier work of mine, published in *Worlds of Written Discourse – A Genre-Based View* by Continuum International.

References

Barber, C. L. (1962) 'Some measurable characteristics of scientific prose', in F. Behre (ed.) *Contributions to English Syntax and Phonology*. Stockholm: Almquist & Wiksell, pp. 1–23.
Bargiela-Chiappini, F. and Nickerson, C. (eds.) (1999) *Writing Business: Genres, Media and Discourse*. London: Longman.
Bazerman, C. (1994) 'Systems of genres and the enhancement of social intentions', in A. Freedman and P. Medway (eds.) *Genre and New Rhetoric*. London: Taylor & Francis, pp. 79–101.
Beaugrande, R. A. de and Dressler, W. U. (1981) *Introduction to Text Linguistics*. London: Longman.
Berkenkotter, C. and Huckin, T. N. (1995) *Genre Knowledge in Disciplinary Communication-Cognition/Culture/Power*. Hillsdale, NJ: Lawrence Erlbaum Associates, Publishers.
Bhatia, V. K. (1982) 'An investigation into the formal and functional characteristics of qualifications in legislative writing and its application to English for academic legal purposes', Ph.D. thesis, University of Aston in Birmingham, UK.
Bhatia, V. K. (1992) 'Pragmatics of the use of nominals in academic and professional genres, in pragmatics and language learning', in L. F. Bouton and Y. Kachru (eds.) *Monograph Series Volume 3*. Urbana-Champaign: University of Illinois, pp. 217–230.
Bhatia, V. K. (1993) *Analysing Genre –Language Use in Professional Settings*. London: Longman.
Bhatia, V. K. (2004) *Worlds of Written Discourse – A Genre-Based View*. London: Continuum.
Bhatia, V. K. (2008) 'Genre analysis, ESP and professional practice', *English for Specific Purposes*, 27: 161–174.
Bhatia, V. K. (2010) 'Interdiscursivity in professional communication', *Discourse and Communication*, 21 (1): 32–50.
Bhatia, V. K. and Swales, J. M. (1983) 'An approach to the linguistic study of legal documents', *Fachsprache*, 5 (3): 98–108.
Biber, D. (1995) *Dimensions of Register Variation: A Cross Linguistic Comparison*. Cambridge: Cambridge University Press.
Brett, P. (2000) 'Integrating multimedia into the business English curriculum: a case study', *English for Specific Purposes*, 19 (3): 269–290.

Brown, G. and Yule, G. (1983) *Discourse Analysis*. Cambridge: Cambridge University Press.

Devitt, A. (1991) 'Intertextuality in tax accounting', in C. Bazerman and J. Paradis (eds.) *Textual Dynamics of the Professions*. Madison, WI: University of Wisconsin Press.

Dubois, B. L. (1982) 'The construction of noun phrases in biomedical journal articles', in J. Hoedt *et al.* (eds.) *Pragmatics and LSP*. Copenhagen: Copenhagen School of Economics, pp. 49–67.

Fuertes-Olivera, P. A. (2007) 'A corpus-based view of lexical gender in written business English', *English for Specific Purposes*, 26 (2): 219–234.

Gee, J. (1999) *An Introduction to Discourse Analysis: Theory and Method*. London: Routledge.

Geertz, C. (1973) *The Interpretation of Culture*. New York: Basic Books.

Gimenez, J. C. (2001) 'Ethnographic observations in cross-cultural business negotiations between non-native speakers of English: an exploratory study', *English for Specific Purposes*, 20: 169–193.

Gustafsson, M. (1975) *Some Syntactic Properties of English Law Language*. Department of English, Turku: University of Turku.

Halliday, M. A. K., McIntosh, A., and Strevens, P. (1964) *The Linguistic Sciences and Language Teaching*. London: Longman.

Handford, M. (2010) *The Language of Business Meetings*. Cambridge: Cambridge University Press.

Hoey, M. P. (1983) *On the Surface of Discourse*. London: Allen & Unwin.

Louhiala-Salminen, L. (2002) 'The fly's perspective: discourse in the daily routine of a business manager', *English for Specific Purposes*, 21 (3): 211–231.

Martin, J. R. (1993) 'A contextual theory of language', in B. Cope and M. Kalantzis (eds.) *The Powers of Literacy – A Genre Approach to Teaching Writing*. Pittsburgh, PA: University of Pittsburgh Press, pp. 116–136.

Martin, J. R., Christie, F., and Rothery, J. (1987) 'Social processes in education: a reply to sawyer and watson (and others)', in I. Reid (ed.) *The Place of Genre in Learning: Current Debates*. Geelong: Deakin University Press, Australia, pp. 46–57.

Miller, C. R. (1984) 'Genre as social action', in *Quarterly Journal of Speech*, 70: 157–178. (Also published in A. Freedman and P. Medway (eds.) (1994) *Genre and the New Rhetoric*. London: Taylor and Francis, pp. 23–42.)

Nelson, M. (2006) 'Semantic associations in business English: a corpus-based analysis', *English for Specific Purposes*, 25 (2): 217–234.

Oster, S. (1981) 'The use of tenses in reporting past literature', in L. Selinker, E. Tarone, and V. Hanzeli (eds.) *English for Academic and Technical Purposes: Studies in Honor of Louis Trimble*. Rowley, MA: Newburg House, pp. 76–90.

Planken, B. (2005) 'Managing rapport in lingua franca sales negotiations: a comparison of professional and aspiring negotiators', *English for Specific Purposes*, 24 (4): 381–400.

Rogers, P. S. (2000) 'CEO presentations in conjunction with earning announcements: extending the construct of organizational genre through competing values profiling and user-needs analysis', *Management Communication Quarterly*, 13 (3): 426–485.

Scollon, R. and Scollon, S. (1995) *Intercultural Communication: A Discourse Approach*. Oxford: Basil Blackwell.

Selinker, L., Lackstrom, J., and Trimble, L. (1973) 'Technical rhetorical principles and grammatical choice', *TESOL Quarterly*, 7 (2): 127–136 (June 1972).

Smart, G. (1998) 'Mapping conceptual worlds: using interpretive ethnography to explore knowledge-making in a professional community', *The Journal of Business Communication*, 35 (1): 111–127.

Swales, J. M. (1974) *Notes on the Function of Attributive en-Participles in Scientific Discourse*, Papers for Special University Purposes No.1, ELSU, University of Khatoum, Sudan.

Swales, J. M. (1981) *Aspects of Article Introductions*, Aston ESP Research Report No. 1, Language Studies Unit, University of Aston in Birmingham, UK.

Swales, J. M. (1990) *Genre Analysis: English in Academic and Research Settings*. Cambridge: Cambridge University Press.

Swales, J. M. (1998) *Other Floors Other Voices: A Textography of a Small University Building*. London: Lawrence Erlbaum Associates, Publishers.

Trimble, L. (1985) *English for Science and Technology: A Discourse Approach*. Cambridge: Cambridge University Press.

van Dijk, T. (1985) *Handbook of Discourse Analysis*. London: Academic Press, Vol. 2.

Vergaro, C. (2004) 'Discourse strategies of Italian and English sales promotion letters', *English for Specific Purposes Journal*, 23 (2): 181–207.

Widdowson, H. G. (1973) 'An applied linguistics approach to discourse analysis', PhD thesis, University of Edinburgh, Scotland.

Widdowson, H. G. (1998) 'Communication and community: the pragmatics of ESP', *English for Specific Purposes Journal*, 17 (1): 3–14.

18

Spoken professional genres

Almut Koester and Michael Handford

Introduction

What do business meetings, job interviews and medical consultations have in common? The answer is that they are all examples of spoken professional interactions. However, arguably, these different types of professional interaction are defined more by what distinguishes them from one another than by what they have in common. Genre analysis is a particular type of discourse analysis that aims to identify the specific nature of such specialized types of interaction, whether they are written or spoken. However, as shown in previous chapters on genre in this volume, there is no uniform approach to deciding how genres should be defined and described. For some, a common communicative purpose is what all instances of a specific genre share (Swales, 1990), while for others it is the way a text or interaction is structured that determines whether it belongs to one genre or another (Hasan, 1985). In this chapter, two specific ways of seeing genre will be elaborated in detail: genre as communicative purpose and genre as staged practice. We begin with an overview of different approaches to describing and analysing genre and we discuss their relevance to the still developing field of spoken professional genre.

Describing spoken professional genres

Three main approaches to genre analysis have emerged over the last few decades, and while some have focused more on written than spoken genre, they are all relevant to a discussion of spoken professional genre.

Many descriptions of written academic and professional genres are influenced by Swales' (1990) pioneering work on the introduction section of academic articles. For Swales (1990: 58), it is communicative purpose that defines a genre:

A genre comprises a class of communicative events, the members of which share some set of communicative purposes.

Furthermore, he asserts that the shared communicative purpose of texts belonging to the same genre results in their having a similar 'structure, style, content and intended audience' (ibid., p. 58). Based on this premise, Swales developed a 'move' and 'step' analysis specifying the rhetorical functions of each element within the genre and where each element performs a more specific function, which serves the overall communicative purpose of the genre. Swales' approach lends itself well to describing specialized written genres such as sales promotional letters or legal cases (Bhatia, 1993), which follow quite sophisticated and complex, but also predictable, rhetorical patterns.

When it comes to spoken, dialogically constructed genres, the rhetorical strategies adopted by the speakers, and therefore the detailed structure of the genre, are much less predictable. This is probably the reason why descriptions of spoken genre tend to focus on global patterns at a general level of description, some of which are 'obligatory', whereas others are 'optional'. This approach was developed within systemic functional linguistics, originally by Hasan (1985), who studied service encounters and proposed that this genre could be described as consisting of the following obligatory and optional elements:

- Obligatory elements: sales request, sales compliance, sale, purchase, purchase closure
- Optional elements: greeting, sales initiation, sales enquiry, finis

While genre analysis in this tradition has examined written as well as spoken genre, the focus has been on general and 'everyday' genres such as narratives, explanations and procedures (Martin and Rothery, 1986; however, see Christie and Martin, 1997). This contrasts with the more specific descriptions of written academic and professional genres, carried out using the Swalesian approach.

Finally, the so-called 'social constructionist' approach does not focus on the formal properties of genres, but is interested in how genres are used by academic and professional discourse communities (Berkenkotter and Huckin, 1995). Devitt's (1991) much-cited study of the range of written genres used by tax accountants examines the ways in which these genres are linked to one another and 'essentially constitute and govern the tax accounting community, defining and reflecting that community's epistemology and values' (pp. 336–337).

In this tradition, genre is viewed as 'rhetorical action' (Miller, 1984), and Yates and Orlikowski (1992) adopt this approach to describe 'genres of organizational communication', which are defined as 'typified communicative action invoked in response to a recurrent situation' (p. 301). They see genre as being characterized by both 'substance' (which equates more or less to communicative purpose) and 'form', which includes structural and linguistic features but may also include elements of the context, for example the presence of an agenda and a chairperson for a meeting. As the situations within which genres occur are subject to socio-historical change, genres are seen as inherently dynamic, changing and evolving in response to the changing needs of the discourse community (Miller, 1984; Yates and Orlikowski, 1992; Berkenkotter and Huckin, 1995).

Written professional genre has received considerably more attention than spoken professional genre, although a wide range of institutional and professional interaction types – such as meetings, negotiations and interviews – have been examined using other analytical methods, for instance conversation analysis (e.g. Drew and Heritage, 1992) or ethnography (e.g. Duranti and Goodwin, 1992). Business meetings have been analysed as genre, starting with Bargiela-Chiappini and Harris' (1997) work comparing British and Italian corporate meetings, and more recently Handford (2010a) has proposed a generic structure for meetings based on a corpus of 64 meetings. Koester (2006) and Müller (2006) have identified and described a range of genres occurring across different workplace contexts, such as decision-making, planning/making arrangements, presentations, procedural encounters and training. Such recent work (e.g. Koester, 2006; Handford, 2010a) has shown that combining an analysis of the structural features of the genre, for example by identifying the different 'moves' or 'stages', with corpus analytical methods, whereby frequent linguistic features are investigated, can provide robust and multi-faceted accounts of spoken professional genre.

Genre and spoken corpora

Some of the earliest work on genre and corpora was conducted by Biber (e.g. 1988), who focused primarily on the pervasive linguistic patterns in different spoken and written genres (conversations and interviews; fiction and letters, respectively). While Biber's corpus-informed work (see Biber, this volume) continues to deepen our understanding of textual features of comparative genres and registers, it is primarily concerned with the linguistic aspects of the language/context relationship. The language/context relationship means the way language and other relevant features of the unfolding genre (such as the status of speakers, previous encounters or texts, the location, and so on) interact and constitute meaning. This section will briefly outline some other studies that have been concerned with exploring the relationship between text and context that go beyond the linguistic level.

In comparing developments in written and spoken genres and the language/context relationship, Bhatia (2004) draws the following distinction: while written genre analysis has moved from analysis of the language to the wider social context, particularly the reflexive relationship between genres and social practices, studies of spoken genres have progressed in the opposite direction and have only involved close analysis of the language used in the last two or three decades. Arguably, this is partly because the close analysis of spoken texts has only recently been possible: the development and availability of audio/video recorders have permitted the systematic study of individual speech events, and computers have enabled researchers to analyse and notice patterns across large collections of texts. The study of collections of machine-readable texts using computers is indeed one definition of corpus linguistics (Biber, 1988), and this approach has led to considerable developments and insights in the analysis of spoken genres. This is because corpus linguistics and genre analysis can complement each other: whereas corpora enable a fine grained analysis of language, their contextual interpretability can be insufficient; genres, on the other hand, are by definition contextual, but their linguistic features may not be adequately explored (Handford, 2010b).

Handford (2010b) discusses different types of corpora of specialized genres with specific reference to spoken discourse – specifically how smaller, specialized corpora, as opposed to more general, much larger corpora such as the British National Corpus (see Flowerdew, 2005), can inform the analysis of genre from all of the three perspectives discussed in section 'describing spoken professional genres'. For instance, work on the Michigan University MICASE corpus has shed considerable light on academic lectures, dissertation defences and meetings from a Swalesian perspective (Simpson, 2004; Swales, 2004).[1] Koester (2006, see below), also using a Swalesian definition of genre, shows that even a modest spoken corpus of under 50,000 words can be used to examine the occurrence of high frequency items in workplace genres. In her corpus of American and British office talk (ABOT), a number of interpersonal linguistic features, such as modal verbs, hedges and vague language, are compared across a range of workplace genres, including decision-making, procedural encounters and planning/making arrangements. Carter and McCarthy's work on CANCODE, the 5 million word corpus of spoken English, provides powerful insights into intimate, socializing, pedagogical, professional and transactional discourse (see McCarthy, 1998), not least in terms of the interpersonal aspects (Halliday, 1994) and fluidity (Bazerman, 1994) of various transactional and interpersonal genres (Carter, 2004; O'Keeffe et al., 2007). For example, McCarthy (2000) shows how, in a transactional service encounter in a hairdressing salon, over 90 per cent of the communication is interpersonal in nature. He concludes that our notions of transactional genres need to be able to account for such findings. Such findings also show that we need to be wary of attributing too rigid a framework to genres, which are by nature slippery and dynamic, as discussed in the next section. Handford's work on business meetings (2010a), discussed in the section on genre as staged practice, is an attempt, following Bhatia (2004), to account for both the regularity and dynamism that is apparent in CANBEC, a corpus of inter-organizational and intra-organizational meetings. As such, it draws on the three approaches to genre outlined above.

What counts as genre?

In the descriptions of genre surveyed in the section on spoken professional genres, both communicative goal and structural features emerge as important aspects of genre. And indeed, the notion of genre as staged, goal-oriented activity seems to provide a useful approach for trying to make sense of both the great diversity of interactions taking place in professional situations and also of their repetitive nature. But how does one decide what 'counts' as genre, and whether two spoken interactions are examples of the same genre or not? For example, are internal planning meetings within a company or department and external sales meetings (between two companies) both examples of the same genre – the business meeting – or do they constitute two different genres? This depends very much, of course, on the how genre is defined. If the communicative purpose is taken as the sole or main criterion for defining genre, then the business meeting would not constitute a genre, as different types of meetings will have different purposes. However, if other criteria, such as structure, are considered to be defining, then the business meeting is indeed as genre, as meetings tend to follow a particular pattern (see the section on genre as staged practice, below).

Yates and Orlikowski (1992) provide a useful perspective on the question of what counts as a genre. They hold that it is possible for genres to be either very general or very specific, as long as 'a recurrent situation, a common subject (either very general or more specific), and common formal features' can be identified. Genres thus exist at various levels of abstraction:

> the business letter and the meeting might at one point be genres, whereas at another point, these types of communication might be considered too general and the recommendation letter or the personnel committee meeting might better capture the social sense of recurrent situation.
>
> *(Yates and Orlikowski, 1992: 303)*

Yates and Orlikowski suggest that more general genres can be viewed as having sub-genres at various levels of specificity, for example the genre of business meetings could comprise more specific sub-genres, as shown in Figure 18.1.

Another useful view of the relationship between different genres comes from Bhatia's (2004: 57–84) description of 'colonies' of written genres. Besides including the idea that more general genres are composed of more specific sub-genres, the notion of 'genre colony' also deals with the phenomenon of related genres that have similar, but not necessarily identical, communicative purposes. Colonies are groupings of genres, some of which are very closely related ('primary members'), while others are not as central to the colony ('secondary' and 'peripheral' members). The genres in the colony all largely share a communicative purpose, but are different in a number of respects, such as discipline, profession, contexts of use or participant relationship. An example is the colony of promotional genres, which includes 'primary members' such as advertisements, promotional letters and job applications, as these have the primary communicative purpose of 'promoting a product or service to a potential customer' (Bhatia, 2004: 60). 'Secondary' members of the colony would not be considered advertisements, but nevertheless have a strong promotional concern, for example fundraising letters or travel brochures; whereas 'peripheral' genres will have other communicative purposes as well, and may be primary members in other genre colonies. For

business meeting

⇓

planning meeting

⇓

executive planning meeting

Figure 18.1 Genres and sub-genres

example, annual company reports belong primarily to the colony of reporting genres, but also have the purpose of promoting the company (ibid., p. 62).

Bhatia is concerned with written professional genres, but his idea of genre colonies can also be applied to spoken professional genres. The two genre colonies mentioned, promotional and reporting, also include spoken genres, for example:

- promotional: sales presentations, job interviews
- reporting: reporting back about a fair or convention, presentation of quarterly sales figures

In some contexts, presenting sales figures could also have a promotional dimension, and therefore this genre might be a peripheral member of the colony of promotional genres.

McCarthy (1998) proposes a corpus-based approach to exploring the overlap between related genres. Using data from CANCODE (see above), he examines how different variables or dimensions combine to form specific genres, and how small changes in these variables result in more or less subtle changes to the specific genre being performed (pp. 38–46). One dimension according to which all encounters in the corpus are categorized is 'goal type', for example 'collaborative task' or 'information provision'. Two of the encounters he compares involve decision-making or planning encounters (a sub-goal type of collaborative task). While the sub-goal type is the same, the two encounters differ in their 'context' (another key variable in the corpus referring to the relationship between the participants): one involves planning a family holiday ('intimate' context) and the other is a planning meeting in a publishing company ('professional' context). The two encounters are similar in a number of respects: they are both informal and there is a high degree of shared knowledge between the participants. However, the professional encounter has more indirect language, less deixis (i.e. use of deictics like *this, there, that* to refer to things in the immediate environment) and a slightly higher lexical density[2] than the intimate encounter. It is the subtle difference in the precise goals of the two encounters, in the relationship between the participants (including the degree of intimacy and shared knowledge) and in other contextual features that results in the somewhat different generic patterning of these two decision-making encounters. Most significantly, the participants in the planning meeting must orient to institutional deadlines and targets, which is obviously not the case in planning a family holiday. Balancing these goals with relational concerns (or 'face work') results in the use of more indirect language in the publisher's meeting.

From McCarthy's comparison of the family and company planning meetings, we can see that genres like 'decision-making' and 'planning' occur in social as well as professional situations. There is therefore no clear dividing line between 'everyday' and 'professional' spoken genres, but similar or related genres occur in social AND professional situations. As McCarthy's examples show, what distinguishes professional genres is the institutional goals and role relationships. This point will be developed more what follows.

Genre as communicative purpose

As the discussion above has shown, generic description can be either fairly general (e.g. 'meetings') or, alternatively, very specialized; for example, genres which are perhaps unique to specific professions or organizations can be described (e.g. weekly team meetings of the IT department). In order to compare genres across different organizations and workplaces, it is necessary to take a more broad-brush approach, focusing on genres that are widely used and not too specialized.

Two studies that have attempted to identify frequently occurring spoken genres across different workplace contexts are Koester (2006) and Müller (2006). In both studies, the genres have been

Table 18.1 Frequently occurring workplace genres

Müller's 8 genres (2006)	Koester's (2006) 10 genres ABOT
1) Private conversations	1) Small talk
2) Contact conversation	2) Office gossip
3) Presentation talks	3) reporting
	4) Briefing
–	5) Requesting
–	6) Service encounters
4) Training talks	7) Procedural and directive discourse
5) Evaluation (appraisal) conversations	–
6) planning conversations	8) Decision-making
7) Crisis conversations	
–	9) Making arrangements
8) Analysis talks	10) Discussing and evaluating

identified largely on the basis of the communicative goals of the interactions. Although the genre categories arrived at are not identical, there are clearly similarities and overlaps, as indicated in Table 18.1 (see also Koester, 2010).

Neither Koester nor Müller claim to present a complete taxonomy of spoken workplace genres, but rather a descriptive list of the genres identified in each corpus. It is interesting that there is, nevertheless, substantial overlap in the genres identified, although the data were collected in different countries (Koester's from the UK and US, and Müller's from Germany, France and Spain) and quite different workplace environments (Koester's from offices, and Müller's from factories). This seems to indicate that many of these genres are very widespread indeed in spoken workplace communication.

Basing a classification of genre on communicative purpose is, however, not unproblematic. Speakers may have more than one communicative goal in an interaction, and the goals of the speakers may not all be the same. Even more fundamental is the question of how speakers' communicative goals can be identified, as we cannot 'get inside' speakers' heads. Koester (2006) draws on the notions of 'contexualization cues' (Gumperz ,1982, 1992) and 'frames' (Goffman, 1974; Tannen, 1993), developed within interactional sociolinguistics in order to try to identify clues to speakers' communicative intentions in the discourse. According to Gumperz (1982, 1992), speakers and listeners use 'contextualization cues' to signal and make inferences about communicative goals. Contextualization cues are 'any feature of linguistic form that contributes to the signalling of contextual presuppositions' (1982: 131), and can be signalled through any aspect of linguistic or paralinguistic behaviour, from prosody to lexical forms through to choice of code or style. Frames are the participants' sense of what they are doing, or what activity they are engaged in (Tannen, 1993), and they are also signalled through a variety of surface level forms, including false starts, modals and hedges. This method, therefore, involves finding clues in what participants say or do to what genre they see themselves as 'doing'; it is not about trying to identify what their personal goals and motivations in the interaction are.

In order to demonstrate how generic frames can be inferred from what speakers say, an example of a decision-making encounter from the ABOT corpus will be examined (see also Koester, 2006: 35–41). Decision-making is the most frequently occurring genre in ABOT, and has also been identified as a key activity in other studies of workplace and professional discourse (Willing, 1992; Handford, 2010a). Previous studies have identified three stages in decision-making or problem-solving encounters (Willing, 1992; Hundsnurscher, 1986), following the general pattern of:

1) identifying or describing a problem or issue
2) discussion and problem-solving
3) deciding and agreeing on a course of action

The encounter to be examined is from the back office of an American food cooperative, and involves co-workers trying to decipher an item on a handwritten list on which co-workers in the 'deli' section of the co-op's shop must write down anything they take from the shop for cooking. Ann is the bookkeeper and Greta is a co-worker who shares the same office space:

Example 1 Deciphering Handwriting

1. <Ann>   Anyone wanna decipher handwriting?
2. <Greta> I will. I will.
3. <Ann>   What's *this*.
[3]
4. <Greta> Showy.
[3]
5. <Greta> i::ts a grocery, huh? sh:::::::: Well /broccoli/ certainly isn't grocery,
6. <Ann>   No:
7. <Greta> And… some kind of milk, isn't grocery,
8. <Ann>   Buttermilk,… but that was by a different person. So Shannon?
9. <Greta> ⌊ Oh ⌊ /She put-/
    <Ann>   ↓ Shannon's not /here/
10. <Greta> It looks like S-H.O-W-Y. showy.
11. <Ann>   ⌊ Mhm
12. <Ann>   or *soury*…. soury.
13. <Ann>   (sou:r /I think that's a G/)
14. <Greta> *Where.*
15. <Ann>   /Grewry/
16. <Greta> The first one?
17. <Ann>   Mhm,
18. <Greta> Mm. ↓ No. it's /a-/ Let's see. I'm usually really good at this. ↑ Oh I think it's a- S.
19. <Ann>   S-H, sh::: [4]
20. <Greta> sh:uzy. shorsy.
21. <Ann>   ⌊ That's definitely a Y:, it's *definitely* a Y at the end.
22. <Greta> ⌊ Yeah,
23. <Greta> Mm begins with an S, an' ends with a Y.
24. <Ann>   ⌊ Heheh
25. <Ann>   That's good.
26. <Greta> And it's some number of letters in between. for two–nineteen.
[10 turns ellipted]
27. <Ann>   I *would* say *sherry*, but I don't think we *have* sherry. Do we have *cooking* sherry?
[2.5]
28. <Greta> ↑Oh, maybe we do,
29. <Ann>   S-H-E, R-R-Y, that could be it, ↓ It's certainly /packaged grocery /??/… Think that might be sherry?
[12]
30. <Greta> S-H *somethin::'* somethin'… somethin' Y,
31. <Ann>   Mhm,

The word *decipher* in turn 1 signals a decision-making frame, as it indicates the existence of a problem (Ann cannot read a handwritten word) which needs to be solved (she needs to know what the word is). The formulation of this initial turn as a question is an indication of the interactive, collaborative nature of spoken genre; as Gumperz (1982: 167) notes, 'the signalling of speech activities is not a matter of unilateral action but rather of speaker–listener coordination'. Ann effectively makes a bid to 'do' decision-making, which is taken up by Greta, who sits next to her, and responds *I will. I will.* In the rest of the encounter, the speakers orient to the decision-making frame initiated in the first turn. Both speakers put forward guesses or make suggestions as to what they think the word or individual letters could be, for example (contextualization cues for generic activity are underlined):

Example 2
11. Greta   It <u>looks like</u> S-H.O-W-Y. showy.
12. Ann   ⌊ Mhm
13. Ann   or *soury*…. soury.
14. Ann   (sou:r <u>I think</u> that's a G)
15. Greta   *Where.*
16. Ann   /Grewry/
17. Greta   The first one?
18. Ann   Mhm,
19. Greta   Mm. ↓ No. it's /a-/ <u>Let's see</u>. I'm usually really good at this.
            ↑Oh <u>I think</u> it's a- S.

Both speakers use verbs that involve hypothesizing (*look like*, *I think,let's see*), and these contextualization cues are evidence of their engagement in the decision-making or problem-solving process. According to Willing (1992), hypothesizing or making suppositions often occurs in the second phase of problem-solving, which he calls 'deepening comprehension/interpreting'.

Analysis of all the decision-making conversations in the corpus showed that these usually follow a problem-solution pattern (Hoey, 1983, 1994), in which a problem is identified in a particular situation, and then a response or solution is proposed and then evaluated:

Situation → Problem → Response/Solution → Evaluation.

This pattern is also evident in the extract, with cyclical recurrence of the response and evaluation phases, as speakers make and reject various possibilities (e.g. *showy, soury, grewry*). For example, in turn 19 Greta disagrees that the first letter is a G, and in 25 Anna evaluates Greta's suggestions positively:

Example 3
24. Greta   Mm begins with an S, an' ends with a Y.
25. Ann   ⌊ Heheh
26. Ann   That's good.

In the end they seem to agree that the word is 'sherry'.

This brief analysis shows how evidence for participants' communicative goals, and thus the genre that is being performed, can be gleaned from the ways in which participants themselves 'frame' the encounter and the contextualization cues they provide through the language they use. This method of identifying genre is especially useful for a spoken genre, as many types of workplace interaction do not have 'labels', unlike written genres, which the discourse community has usually named (e.g. minutes, annual report, CV). The same method was applied to the other genres in the ABOT corpus listed above, and this meant that it was possible to track changes from one genre to a different one, or the mixing or blending of genres, within the same encounter.

Genre as staged practice

Whereas the approach outlined in the previous section permits the pinpointing and description of genres in spoken encounters that may not have clear labels or stages, this section will discuss how genre analysis can be applied to a type of spoken encounter that does have stages and a recognized label, namely business meetings. Using the 900,000 words of meetings in the CANBEC (Cambridge and Nottingham Business English Corpus) corpus, interpreted through reference to observation notes, interviews and expert informant comments, Handford (2010a) argues that meetings are genres that can be broken down into recurring stages and practices, and these stages and practices are invoked by recurring language items. However, like genre, practice is a slippery notion, and a certain degree of fuzziness is unavoidable when attempting to pin down practices.

As discussed in the section on what counts as a genre, interactions such as meetings can be categorized as genres if both the structure and the communicative purpose are considered, and Yates and Orlikowski's (1992) distinction between a general level of genre ('meeting') and sub-genres ('executive planning meeting') is a useful heuristic when attempting to define and describe such encounters. This section will first discuss the stages of business meetings, and then outline how discursive practices, which link speaker goals with the language used, play a central role in the construction and interpretation of genres. Finally, an extract from a meeting between on-site engineers will be analysed.

Previous research on business meetings has proposed a three-stage framework (Bargiela-Chiappini and Harris, 1996, 1997; Holmes and Stubbe, 2003): an opening stage, a discussion stage, and a closing stage. Through an analysis of 64 meetings, Handford (2010a) argues for a more complex structure, comprising these three stages (which are obligatory) plus a further three stages and three transition moves (see Figure 18.2).

Whereas stage pre-2 refers to relevant work preceding the meeting, stage 4 includes the repercussions and effects of the meeting. Both stages tend to occur some time (an hour, a month etc.) apart from the meeting proper, and indicate how meetings can link with and make reference to other written and spoken encounters. This is important because meetings, like other genres, form genre chains (Swales, 2004) with other meetings, preceding and successive, as well as with genre colonies (Bhatia, 2004, see above). Both stages – pre-2 and 4 – are potentially optional, pre-stage 2 because

---

Stage pre-2: Meeting preparation

Stage pre-1: Pre-meeting

      Transition move

Stage 1: Opening of meeting

      Transition move

Stage 2: Discussion of the agenda

      Transition move

Stage 3: Closing of meeting

Stage 4: Post-meeting effect

Figure 18.2 Structural aspects of the business meeting

some meetings occur spontaneously, and stage 4 because it is possible (although unlikely) to imagine a meeting that has no effects or repercussions. Similarly, the pre-meeting stage may be by-passed, especially in regular (daily or weekly) scheduled internal manager–subordinate meetings. However, it is common in internal meetings between managers and in external meetings, and it can involve 'work talk, meeting preparatory talk and shop talk' (Mirivel and Tracy, 2005: 1), as well as small talk. Stage 1 is usually enacted by the chair or the most senior person in internal meetings, but it may be less explicit in some meetings. The same can be said of stage 3.

Stage 2, the discussion of the agenda/topic, is usually made up of several 'phases' or 'clusters of activity' (Heritage, 1997: 167), each of which concerns a point of the (written or unwritten) agenda. Phases may be dealt with across turns in a linear fashion, or may be more cyclical, largely depending on the topic (Holmes and Stubbe, 2003). For instance, decision-making may be rather cyclical, with speakers referring to previous topics and introducing new points in an apparently haphazard way. Stage 2 is the most important part of the meeting genre as this is when the business gets done; therefore an extract from this stage of a meeting is discussed below.

Practices, in particular repeated discursive practices that can be pinpointed through the use of corpora of specialized genre (Handford, 2010b), form the other dynamic in Handford's (2010a) meeting-matrix genre. This is because discursive practices in a professional context are the local, goal-driven actions that members of a given community use to constrain and enable the unfolding genre through recognized language (for example, opening a meeting by saying 'OK, let's get started'). Drawing on work by Bhatia (2004, 2008) and Gee (2005; Gee *et al.*, 1996), Handford combines social, professional and discursive practices with Gee's notion of 'Discourses' (bundles of social practices[3]) to show how these layers of context constitute the text, addressing the transactional and interpersonal goals of the interlocutors through language. The importance of practices to meaningful communication cannot be overstated: there can be no meaning without practices (Gee, 2005: 8), and communities of speakers such as engineers or lawyers can share meaning because they interpret practices in recognizable ways. Figure 18.3 outlines the relations between

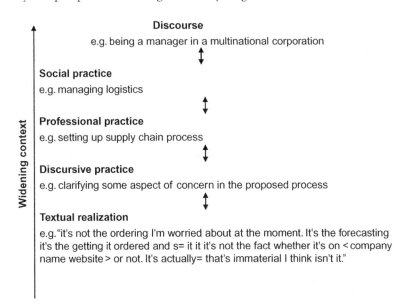

Figure 18.3 The relationship between discourses, practices, text and context
Source: CANBEC The Cambridge and Nottingham Business English Corpus, which is part of the Cambridge International Corpus © cambridge University Press

261

these levels of context through a brief extract from a logistics meeting (based on Handford, 2010a: 67). Discursive practices have the most direct relationship with the language produced, and the higher the level of context, the less direct the relationship.

A key question is how the discursive practices outlined above and the stages discussed here interact to construct the genre in question. The terms 'agreeing with a suggestion', 'referring to previous topics' and 'introducing new points' all refer to potential discursive practices typically found in stage 2, thus exemplifying how certain stages often feature recurrent practices (see Handford, 2010a: 77). Other examples include 'outlining the agenda' at the beginning of a meeting and 'bringing meeting to a close' at the end. Of course, several practices may not be so closely associated with particular stages, for instance 'summarizing' can occur at various points of a meeting.

An extract from an international professional meeting that is not from the CANBEC corpus will be analysed below, to show how the framework is relevant to other data sets. It is from a meeting between engineers on a tunnel construction project in Hong Kong (see Handford and Matous, 2010 for further details). The meeting is spontaneous and takes place in the office on site, immediately following the regular weekly meeting between the construction and engineering departments. The first speaker, Jimmy, is the head of the construction department (a 40–50-year-old male from Hong Kong); the second speaker, Alie, the head engineer from the engineering department (a 40–50-year-old male from Sierra Leone), is asking advice about certain problems concerning the part of the construction project he is managing. The meeting takes over 30 minutes, and this extract is from stage 2, discussion of the agenda/topic (in spontaneous meetings, the 'agenda' is usually unwritten, but at least one of the speakers will have a work-related topic or topics they want to discuss). This 'phase' concerns whether the position of one of the engineering job-sites can be moved. Jimmy is advising Alie about how to persuade the contractors (referred to as *they* in turn 3) to move the site.

Example 4

1. <Jimmy> Can you investigate this one [pointing with pencil at diagram] and then we propose to put it back here because it difficult to do it up there? (3)
2. <Alie> I I'll ask … I don't know if it can be [laughing] if (they can agree) –
3. <Jimmy> no but you can find a story why we change it
4. <Alie> Hmm
5. <Jimmy> and not argue (2)
6. <Alie> I I attempted to ask him the last time…he told me we've already agreed on the on this … relocation … so they … they- he don't wannadiscuss it because we already agreed on the relocation…so [laughs]
7. <Jimmy> [exhales] I think- (something and Ito) knows about this?
8. <Alie> I think so…or maybe we have to call in it … call him in … you know to just discuss this
9. <Jimmy> okay err
10. <Alie> because frankly speaking
11. <Jimmy> Mm hmm
12. <Alie> moving it up here is not to our advantage (1) unless if… we we've agreed…it definitely is going to change
13. <Jimmy> no I think from now on
14. <Alie> to come to this same level
15. <Jimmy> the design department and construction department must have co-… close coordination

16.	\<Alie\>	Yeah yeah…yeah
17.	\<Jimmy\>	Because…the the the the site condition … err… to which the engine- … your department
18.	\<Alie\>	Hmm
19.	\<Jimmy\>	[indecipherable]
20.	\<Alie\>	exactly
21.	\<Jimmy\>	so I maybe … err … um … you should go there from time to time
22.	\<Alie\>	yah
23.	\<Jimmy\>	maybe once a week or something you need
24.	\<Alie\>	yah
25.	\<Jimmy\>	to get familiar to
26.	\<Alie\>	yah I see
27.	\<Jimmy\>	there's ongoing changes yeah?
28.	\<Alie\>	Yah
29.	\<Jimmy\>	and think … err err err more advanced
30.	\<Alie\>	yah
31.	\<Jimmy\>	don't think of just now

As noted above, separating levels of discourses and practices is not a straightforward task, but the discourse (capital D 'Discourse' in Gee) here is arguably 'being an engineer'. In terms of practices, we could say that 'performing as an effective engineer' is the most relevant social practice in this meeting, 'advising' being the most pertinent professional practice (the whole meeting is concerned with advising). The act of advising in this extract is broken into two parts: turns 1–14 concern the specific issue of the particular site, whereas from turn 15 onwards Jimmy talks in more general terms about the need for better interdepartmental communication and for more active checking of progress by Alie. With the second piece of advice a far higher degree of hedging and indirect language is apparent (for instance, in turn 21 Jimmy says *maybe, er*, pauses and uses the idiom *from time to time*), whereas in the first Jimmy is far more abrupt (turns 3 and 5). One reason for the change in language may be the perceived face threat of Jimmy's advice: the second proposed action is a far greater imposition than the first. It is also interesting that, in the second part, Jimmy's syntax becomes noticeably more anomalous, which may be caused by the attention he is paying to achieving greater interpersonal sensitivity.

There are several discursive practices evident here that are found in meetings in CANBEC, such as suggesting, evaluating, clarifying and emphasizing, invoked through language items pinpointed in Handford (2010a). For instance there are several deontic modal verbs, used to suggest and recommend (*can* in turns 1 and 3, *must* in turn 15, *should* in turn 21 and *need to* in turn 23). According to Handford (2010a), deontic modals are a way speakers negotiate power, and we see the same here; the strongest modal form *must* is used to recommend changes at the organizational level, but when Jimmy is advising Alie the person, the modal forms are softer (*can, should, need to*). Idiomatic and metaphorical language (Handford and Koester, 2010) is also evident, for example the idioms *call him in, frankly speaking, to our advantage, from now on*, and the metaphor (*find*) *a story* (meaning to create an untrue reason for the change) and *think…more advanced*. As in other workplace encounters, metaphors and idioms are largely used to evaluate indirectly and mark the speaker's stance (see Koester, 2006; Handford and Koester, 2010).

Apart from deontic modal verbs, indirect language and metaphors and idioms, there are other items that are frequently used in business meetings, such as *if, I don't know if* and *I think*. Place deictics, however, such as *this one, back here* and *up there* in turn 1, are not statistically significant in business meetings, but have been shown to be very common in such construction-engineering interactions (Handford and Matous, 2010). In this meeting the speakers are constantly referring to the drawing in front of them to invoke the discursive practice of clarifying the position.

Conclusion

This chapter has outlined two contrasting approaches to the analysis of genre. Work by Koester (2006) and Müller (2006) strongly prioritizes the communicative purpose in defining the genre, for instance decision-making, which is seen as shaping the structure and lexico-grammatical characteristics of the genre. Handford (2010a), on the other hand demonstrates how certain genres, for instance business meetings, can have recurrent stages that tend to feature repeated discursive practices. While both approaches use spoken corpora and have helped to unearth the relationship between lexico-grammar and context, they diverge in terms of the relative primacy accorded to communicative purpose, on the one hand, and the recognizability and recurrence of stages, on the other, in identifying a genre. Also, whereas Koester draws on work in interactional sociolinguistics, Handford's approach is influenced by certain 'critical' scholars, such as Gee and Bhatia. Nevertheless, we do not think that the two approaches to spoken genres are mutually exclusive: genre provides considerable interpretative depth, and it is more a case of deciding which generic approach will better prize open the particular data at hand, than a case of stating, a priori, that one approach is more plausible or fruitful than the other. Indeed, Handford (2010a) states that the notions of discursive practices and certain of Gumperz's discourse strategies do overlap, and discursive practices may function as contextualization cues for the participants, signalling and negotiating the genre they are performing. Professional discourse is goal-driven, with speakers using language and genres to achieve these goals, and if a genre has clear stages then these should be described. As with other studies of genre, the challenge is how best to account for the dynamic and the recurrent in the unfolding context, and with spoken discourse that challenge is both more difficult and (we believe) more exciting.

One of the advantages of working with corpora when analysing genre is that it is possible to notice patterns that would be hidden from purely qualitative approaches. For example, Koester (2006) found that deontic modal forms are used with the same relative frequency across the ABOT, CANBEC and BNC spoken business sub-corpus. For instance, *need to* is far more frequent than *must*, which is best explained through reference to face issues. It is also worth briefly drawing attention to the language status of the speakers in the engineering extract. The use of clusters and metaphors/idioms is generally associated with L1 users of English, and yet in example 4 we see two L2 speakers using them successfully to index contextually appropriate discursive practices. Findings such as these suggest that we need more corpus-based studies in order better to understand expert users in different international English contexts and with different first languages (Firth, 2009).

In the future, more studies that explore the way genres change over time would be of great benefit, as would more studies on the inter-discursive nature of many newly formed genres (see Candlin and Maley, 1997 for work on mediation). Also, more research on intertextuality in and across genres would further our understanding of meaning-making. Multimodal research can show the importance of paralinguistic features in particular genres and can enable us to widen our understanding of interactional discourse: so much research on spoken communication is dependent on the written transcript, which inevitably means that important 'cues' (Gumperz, 1992) are missed during analysis. Finally, analysis of spoken professional genres in languages other than English (e.g. Parodi, 2010), would be of obvious benefit.

Transcription conventions

...   noticeable pause or break of less than 1 second within a turn

-   sound abruptly cut off, e.g. false start

italics   emphatic stress

→   speaker's turn continues without interruption

/ /   words between slashes show uncertain transcription

/?/   indicates inaudible utterances

[]   words in these brackets indicate non-linguistic information, e.g. pauses of 1 second or longer (the number of seconds is indicated), speakers' gestures or actions

()   parentheses around tone units spoken with 'sotto voce' (under one's breath)

Additional conventions for extract x, 'deciphering handwriting'

,   slightly rising in intonation at end of tone unit

?   high rising intonation at end of tone unit

.   falling intonation at end of tone unit

:   colon following vowel indicates elongated vowel sound

::   extra colon indicates longer elongation

↑   a step up in pitch

↓   a shift down in pitch

/ /   words between slashes show uncertain transcription

⌊   overlapping or simultaneous speech

Further reading

Bhatia, V. K. (2004) *Worlds of Written Discourse*. London: Continuum.

Although this book is concerned with the analysis of written professional discourse, it is highly relevant to the analysis of spoken professional discourse.

Handford, M. (2010a). *The Language of Business Meetings*. Cambridge: Cambridge University Press.

As discussed above, this book analyses a corpus of over 60 complete business meetings (CANBEC), and chapter 3 explicitly discusses the genre of the business meeting.

Koester, A. (2006) *Investigating Workplace Discourse*. Routledge: London.

This book describes and analyses 66 workplace conversations comprising the corpus of American and British Office Talk (ABOT) and compares a range of linguistic features across 11 spoken genres.

Koester, A. (2010). *Workplace Discourse*. London: Continuum.

This book provides an overview of and discussion of selected topics in workplace discourse, and includes a chapter (Chapter 2) on workplace genres, both written and spoken.

Notes

1 The British equivalent corpus is BASE, which contains video data, and both corpora are freely available online.

2 Lexical density refers to the proportion of lexical words (nouns, lexical verbs, adjectives) compared to grammatical words (articles, prepositions, auxiliary verbs etc.). Texts with a high proportion of lexical words have a high lexical density.

3 A Discourse is 'composed of ways of talking, listening, reading, writing, acting, interacting, believing, valuing, and using tools and objects, in particular settings and at specific times, so as to display or recognize a particular social identity' (Gee *et al.*, 1996: 10).

References

Bargiela-Chiappini, F. and Harris, S. (1996) 'Interruptive strategies in British and Italian management meetings', *Text*, 16 (3): 269–297.

Bargiela-Chiappini, F. and Harris, S. (1997) *Managing Language: The Discourse of Corporate Meetings*. Amsterdam: John Benjamins.

Bazerman, C. (1994) 'Systems of genres and the enhancement of social intentions', in A. Freedman and P. Medway (eds.) *Genre & New Rhetoric*. London: Taylor & Francis, pp. 79–101.

Berkenkotter, C. and Huckin, T. (1995) 'Rethinking genre from a sociocognitive perspective', *Written Communication*, 10: 475–509.

Bhatia, V. (1993) *Analysing Genre: Language Use in Professional Settings*. Harlow: Longman.

Bhatia, V. (2004) *Worlds of Written Discourse*. London: Continuum.

Bhatia, V. (2008) 'Towards critical genre analysis', in V. Bhatia, J. Flowerdew, and R. Jones (eds.) *Advances in Discourse Studies*. Abingdon: Routledge, pp. 166–177.

Biber, D. (1988) *Variation Across Speech and Writing*. Cambridge: Cambridge University Press.

Candlin, C. and Maley, A. (1997) 'Intertextuality and interdiscursivity in the discourse of alternative discourse resolution', in B. Gunnarsson, P. Linell, and B. Nordberg (eds.) *The Construction of Professional Discourse*. London: Longman, pp. 201–222.

Carter, R. (2004) *Language and Creativity: The Art of Common Talk*. London: Routledge.

Christie, F. and Martin, J. R. (eds.) (1997) *Genre and Institutions: Social Processes in the Workplace and School*. London: Continuum.

Devitt, A. (1991) 'Intertextuality in tax accounting: generic, referential and functional', in C. Bazerman and J. Paradis (eds.) *Textual Dynamics of the Professions*. Madison, WI: The University of Wisconsin Press, pp. 336–357.

Drew, P. and Heritage, J. (eds.) (1992) *Talk at Work*. Cambridge: Cambridge University Press.

Duranti, A. and Goodwin, C. (Eds.) (1992) *Rethinking Context: Language as an Interactive Phenomenon*. Cambridge: Cambridge University Press.

Firth, A. (2009) 'Doing not being a foreign language learner: English as a *lingua franca* in the workplace and (some) implications for SLA', *International review of Applied Linguistics in Language Teaching*, 47 (1): 127–156.

Flowerdew, L. (2005) 'An integration of corpus-based and genre-based approaches to text analysis in EAP/ESP: countering criticisms against corpus-based methodologies', *English for Specific Purposes*, 24: 321–332.

Gee, J. P. (2005) *An Introduction to Discourse Analysis*. Abingdon: Routledge.

Gee, J. P., Hull, G., and Lankshear, C. (1996) *The New Work Order*. London: Allen and Unwin.

Goffman, E. (1974) *Frame Analysis*. New York: Harper and Row.

Gumperz, J. J. (1982) *Discourse Strategies*. Cambridge: Cambridge University Press.

Gumperz, J. J. (1992) 'Contextualization and understanding', in A. Duranti and C. Goodwin (eds.) *Rethinking Context: Language as an Interactive Phenomenon*. Cambridge: Cambridge University Press, pp. 229–252.

Halliday, M. (1994) *An Introduction to Functional Grammar*. London: Edward Arnold.

Handford, M. (2010a) *The Language of Business Meetings*. Cambridge: Cambridge University Press.

Handford, M. (2010b) 'What corpora have to tell us about specialised genres', in M. McCarthy and A. O'Keeffe (eds.) *The Routledge Handbook of Corpus Linguistics*. Abingdon: Routledge.

Handford, M. and Koester, A. (2010) 'It's not rocket science': metaphors and idioms in conflictual business meetings', *Text and Talk*, 30 (1): 27–51.

Handford, M. and Matous, P. (2011) 'Lexicogrammar in the international construction industry: a corpus-based case study of Japanese–Hong-Kongese on-site interactions in English', *English for Specific Purposes*, 30: 87–100.

Hasan, R. (1985) 'The structure of a text', in M. A. K. Halliday and R. Hasan (eds.) *Language, Context and Text: Aspects of Language in a Social-Semiotic Perspective*. Cambridge: Cambridge University Press, pp. 52–69.

Heritage, J. (1997) 'Conversation analysis and institutional talk', in D. Silverman (ed.) *Qualitative Research: Theory, Method and Practice*. London: Sage, pp. 161–182.

Hoey, M. (1983) *On the Surface of Discourse*. London: Allen & Unwin.

Hoey, M. (1994) 'Signalling in discourse: A functional analysis of a common discourse pattern in written and spoken English', in M. Coulthard (ed.) *Advances in Written Text Analysis*. London: Routledge, pp. 26–45.

Holmes, J. and Stubbe, M. (2003) *Power and Politeness in the Workplace*. London: Longman.

Hundsnurscher, F. (1986) 'Dialogmuster und authentischer text', in F. Hundsnurscher and E. Weigand (eds.) *Dialoganalyse: Referate der 1. Arbeitstagung in Münster*. Tübingen: Niemeyer, pp. 35–49.

Koester, A. (2006) *Investigating Workplace Discourse*. Routledge: London.

Koester, A. (2010) *Workplace Discourse*. London: Continuum.

Martin, J. R., and Rothery, J. (1986) *Writing Project Report No. 4*, Working Papers in Linguistics. Linguistics Department, University of Sydney, Sydney.

McCarthy, M. (1998). *Spoken Language and Applied Linguistics*. Cambridge: Cambridge University Press.

McCarthy, M. (2000) 'Captive audiences: small talk and close contact service encounters', in J. Coupland (ed.) *Smalltalk*. Harlow: Pearson Education, pp. 84–109.

Miller, C. (1984) 'Genre as social action', *Quarterly Journal of Speech*, 70 (2): 151–167.

Mirivel, J. and Tracy, K. (2005) 'Premeeting talk: an organizationally crucial form of talk', *Research on Language and Social Interaction*, 38 (1): 1–34.

Müller, A. P. (2006) 'Some preliminaries for analysing communicative genres in organizational talk', in F. F. Ramallo, A. M. Lorenzo, and X. P. Rodríguez-Yañez (eds.) *Discourse and Enterprise: Communication, Business Management and Other Professional Fields*. Muenchen: LINCOM GmbH, pp. 277–286.

O'Keeffe, A., McCarthy, M., and Carter, R. (2007) *From Corpus to Classroom: Language Use and Language Teaching*. Cambridge: Cambridge University Press.

Parodi, G. (ed.) (2010) *Academic and Professional Discourse Genres in Spanish*. Amsterdam: John Benjamins.

Simpson, R. (2004) 'Formulaic expressions in academic speech in discourse', in U. Connor and T. Upton (eds.) *Discourse in the Professions: Perspectives From Corpus Linguistics*. Amsterdam: John Benjamins, pp. 37–64.

Swales, J. (2004) *Research Genres: Explorations and Applications*. Cambridge: Cambridge University Press.

Swales, J. M. (1990) *Genre Analysis: English in Academic and Research Settings*. Cambridge: Cambridge University Press.

Tannen, D. (1993) 'What's in a frame? surface evidence for underlying expectations', in D. Tannen (ed.) *Framing in Discourse*. Oxford: Oxford University Press, pp. 14–56.

Willing, K. (1992) 'Problem-solving discourse in professional work', *Prospect*, 7 (2): 57–65.

Yates, J. and Orlikowski, W. (1992) 'Genres of organizational communication: a structurational approach to studying communication and media', *Academy of Management Review*, 17 (2): 299–326.

Part III
Developments in spoken discourse

19

Prosody in discourse

Winnie Cheng and Phoenix Lam

Introduction to discourse intonation framework

This paper aims to examine the communicative value of discourse intonation by describing the four systems of discourse intonation (Brazil, 1985, 1997): prominence, tone, key and termination. The four systems of speaker intonational choices, each of which has a general meaning that takes on a local meaning within a particular context (Brazil, 1997: xi), are moment-by-moment judgments made by speakers on the basis of their assessment of the current state of understanding operating between the speakers. The paper begins with describing Brazil's (1985, 1997) discourse intonation framework as purpose-driven, speaker controlled, interactive, co-operative, context-referenced, and context-changing, followed by the description of each of the four systems illustrated with examples from naturally occurring speech. The data analysed in this paper come from the one-million-word Hong Kong Corpus of Spoken English (HKCSE) (prosodic) (Cheng et al., 2008) which is composed of the academic, business, conversation and public sub-corpora. The transcription notation used in the HKCSE (prosodic), as well as in this chapter, can be found in "Transcription conventions" at the end of this chapter.

Discourse intonation is based on the view that spontaneous speech is purpose-driven rather than sentence-oriented. It is speaker controlled, interactive, co-operative, context-referenced, and context-changing (Brazil, 1995: 26–39). Discourse intonation systems are motivated by real-time, situation-specific decisions taken by speakers to add extra layers of interpersonal meaning to words as they are spoken, and they are concerned with "the speakers' moment-by-moment context-referenced choices" (Cauldwell, 2007). The communicative value of intonation is concerned with the choices that speakers make and with their reactions to the ongoing task of making sense to their hearers in context in real-time (Cauldwell, 2002). Examining the choices of discourse intonation helps to determine the pragmatic and situated meanings of English utterances (Brazil, 1997: ix). The intonation choices that speakers make in relation to the four systems in the discourse intonation framework are independent. Altogether, thirteen intonation choices are available. Figure 19.1 summarizes the intonation choices available in the four systems of discourse intonation.

Tone units

Brazil (1995) states that, in purpose-driven talk, intonation and syntax are considered as "being separate areas of choice," and "there is no 'normal' relationship between tone units and clauses" (Cauldwell, 2007). In fact discourse intonation moves beyond the context of the single sentence and describes the rules that govern the pitch movement beyond and between the borders of tone

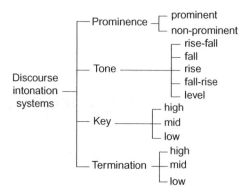

Figure 19.1 Map of the four systems of discourse intonation

units rather than sentences. Brazil (1985: 238) argues for a "need for stating the communicative value of intonation in terms of the projected contextual implications of the tone unit: only if we regard intonation as a 'situation-creating' device, … can we give proper recognition to its ability to carry independent meanings."

All of the thirteen intonation choices occur within the boundaries of a tone unit. In discourse intonation, a tone unit refers to "the stretch of language that carries the systematically-opposed features of intonation" (Brazil, 1997: 3). The internal organization of the tone unit in discourse intonation can be described in terms of three parts: non-prominent optional stretches (proclitic and enclitic segments) and the mandatory tonic segment delimited by the first and last prominent syllables, in which all the significant speaker-decisions are made (ibid., 15). A tonic segment typically comprises one or two prominent syllables, any of the five tones or pitch movements (fall, rise, fall–rise, rise–fall, level) carried by the final prominent tonic syllable; the three-term pitch-level system (high, mid and low) associated with the tonic syllable; and the three-term pitch-level system (high, mid and low) associated with the onset syllable.

A tonic segment can minimally consist of only one prominent syllable, which is the tonic syllable. Example 1 shows a one-word tone unit that contains only the mandatory tonic segment, with one prominent syllable (*so*) and no non-prominent stretches:

(1)
{= [< SO >]}

Alternatively, two prominent syllables, namely the onset and the tonic, may be found in the tonic segment. Example 2 shows a tone unit that contains only the mandatory tonic segment, with two prominent syllables (*so* and *have*) and no non-prominent stretches outside the tonic segment:

(2)
{= [SO] we < HAVE >}

An optional segment, namely the proclitic segment, may be present in front of the tonic segment. Examples 3 and 4 illustrate tone units that contain the mandatory tonic segment as well as the proclitic segment. Example 3 is a tone unit with one prominent syllable (*why*) in its tonic segment and the proclitic segment (*so I don't know*), and Example 4 shows a tone unit which contains two prominent syllables in its tonic segment (*may* and *please*) and the proclitic segment (*so*):

(3)
{\ so i don't know [< WHY >]}

(4)
{= so [MAY] i have your passport < ^ PLEASE >}

Instead of appearing in front of the tonic segment, an optional segment, named the enclitic segment, may be found after the tonic segment. Examples 5 and 6 illustrate tone units that contain the mandatory tonic segment as well as the enclitic segment but not the proclitic segment. Example 5 is a tone unit with one prominent syllable (*so*) in its tonic segment and the enclitic segment (*I have to*), and Example 6 shows a tone unit that contains two prominent syllables (*so* and *checked*) in its tonic segment and the enclitic segment (*with um it with*):

(5)
{= [< SO >] i have to}

(6)
{= [SO] i've already < CHECKED > with um it with}

In some cases, both proclitic and enclitic segments are found in addition to the tonic segment. Examples 7 and 8 show respectively one-prominence and two-prominence tone units that contain all the three parts:

(7)
{= i don't [< THINK >] so}

(8)
{\ so i [^ MADE] these < CHANges >}

Table 19.1 provides a schematic summary of the examples discussed above regarding the different internal structures of a tone unit.

The composition of tone units carries important information regarding the decisions made by speakers. Specifically, it indicates whether information is to be considered integrated or distinct. Tone unit boundaries, therefore, can function as a device of disambiguation (Cheng *et al.*, 2008). When the word *so* is in a separate tone unit, for example, it is very likely to be used as a discourse particle, as in Example 9:

(9)
{= [< SO >]} {= [WHERE] did you GET your < aMERican >} {\ [< ACcent >]}

On the other hand, the propositional uses of the word rarely constitute a separate tone unit on its own. In other words, when *so* is not a discourse particle, it is often in a tone unit with other items, as in Example 10:

(10)
{= er [ONE] three < A >} {= [ONE] three < B >} {= [ONE] three < C >} {\ and [SO] on and < SO > forth}...

Table 19.2 shows the frequency distribution of *so* in separate and shared tone units in the HKCSE (prosodic).

While there are more instances of *so* used as a discourse particle in the prosodic corpus regardless of whether the word is in a separate tone unit, it can be observed that there is a greater likelihood that this is the case when *so* is in a separate tone unit (Lam, 2008). Lam (2008) finds that of all the instances of *so* in a tone unit on its own, an overwhelming 98.1 percent, are discourse particles, and that only 1.9 percent of all instances of *so* in a separate tone unit express propositional content. In other words, tone unit boundaries help to disambiguate the discourse and propositional use of the

Table 19.1 Examples illustrating the three-part structure of a tone unit

(Proclitic segment)	Tonic segment	(Enclitic segment)
	{= [< SO >]}	
	{= [SO] we < HAVE >}	
{\ **so** i don't know	[< WHY >]}	
{= **so**	[MAY] i have your passport < ^ PLEASE >}	
	{= [< SO >]	i have to}
	{= [SO] i've already < CHECKED >	with um it with}
{= i don't	[< THINK >]	**so**}
{\ **so** i	[^ MADE] these < CHAN	ges >}

Table 19.2 The frequency distribution of so in separate and shared tone units in the HKCSE (prosodic)

Function of so	Total number of so	Shared	Separate
As a discourse particle	6,583 (81.6%)	4,160 (74.3%)	2,423 (98.1%)
Not as a discourse particle	1,487 (18.4%)	1,441 (25.7%)	46 (1.9%)
Total	8,070 (100%)	5,601 (100%)	2,469 (100%)

word. This is consistent with Cheng, Greaves, and Warren's (2008) observation that tone unit boundaries have an important function in disambiguation and help to indicate whether alternatives introduced by the vague expression *or something* are treated as distinct from each other or not. Further, the fact that many multi-word expressions such as phrasal verbs and idioms are often found within a tone unit provide evidence that speakers co-select words as a chunk instead of choosing individual words separately as information units (Sinclair, 1991).

Prominence

The communicative value of the utterance is affected by intonational variations on the basis of "a small set of either/or choices," which relates to "a set of meaningful oppositions that together constitute a distinctive sub-component of the meaning-potential of English" (Brazil, 1997: 2). The finite set of oppositions, or either/or choices, available to a speaker is "a binary prominent/non-prominent choice" (Brazil, 1997: 9). A prominent syllable is one that a hearer recognizes as being in some sense more emphatic than the others in the tone unit. The first (onset) and the last (tonic) prominent syllables in the tone unit constitute sub-sets of prominent syllables. Specifically, prominence determines the beginning and end of the tonic segment.

A tone unit may contain up to four prominent syllables, though tone units with one or two prominences are considered the norm (Brazil, 1997). This is supported by quantitative findings from the HKCSE (prosodic). In the corpus, tone units with one or two prominences constitute 91.49 percent of the total, tone units that contain one prominent syllable being the most frequently occurring ones (Cheng et al., 2008). Table 19.3 gives examples of tone units with different numbers of prominences.

In discourse intonation (Brazil, 1997), each prominent syllable gives prominence to a word. Prominent words, which contain prominent syllables, realize existential sense selections. A prominent word is presented as "a selection from a set of possibilities defined by the context of situation" (Brazil, 1997: 41). More correctly, a speaker's intonation projects a certain context of interaction, or projects the assumption that a particular word in the tone unit is selected, the assumption being understood as "part of the communicative value of the utterance" (p. 27). In

Table 19.3 Examples illustrating the number of prominences in a tone unit

Number of prominences in a tone unit	Examples
1	{? [< SO >] for example for}
2	{= [SO] it's < GOOD > to}
3	{\ [SO] we have a DAY < FREE >}
4	{\ [SO] you have to WEAR the rubber SHOES to < OFfice >}
Unclassified	{? er so it's}

other words, a speaker exploits the prominence system to project a context of interaction that suits his/her current conversational purposes.

In making a selection between prominence and non-prominence, speakers have available to them two paradigms: existential and general. The existential paradigm is "the set of possibilities that a speaker [*sic*] regard as actually available in a given situation," and the general paradigm is the set of possibilities that is "inherent in the language system" (p. 23), the words comprising the existential paradigm being a sub-set of those comprising the general one. The selection of prominence is "what a speaker does when he chooses from an existential paradigm" (p. 45). Brazil (1997: 22–23) exemplifies the two paradigms with his well-known *queen of hearts*, said in response to *which card did you play*. In this utterance, *of* is a product of the general paradigm, because the speaker is limited in this context to this word by the language system. Conversely, *queen* and *hearts* are choices limited by the contents of the pack of cards rather than by the language system, and they are therefore part of an existential paradigm as opposed to a general paradigm. The word *queen* is a selection from an existential paradigm of thirteen members, and *hearts* of four members.

(23) Q: What heart did you play? R: // the QUEEN of hearts //
(24) Q: What queen did you play? R: // the queen of HEARTS //

(Brazil, 1997: 23)

Non-prominent words or non-selection are due to shared extralinguistic factors, which have "a very wide currency," and to "shared experience of the immediate conversational environment of the response," which have a circumscribed currency (p. 25). In example 11, which is taken from an academic talk, a lecturer is making a contrast between two angles. Note that in the last two tone units prominence is given to the demonstratives *this* and *that*, to highlight this contrast. In addition, the values of the angles are also made prominent (*gamma/gamma* and *five*), to emphasize the difference between measurements of the two angles. The prominence selection in these tone units reflects the deliberate choices the speaker makes out of a number of possible alternatives in the existential paradigm in order to underline words that are considered situationally informative in this local context:

(11)
…{= [< THIS >] is} {V [< FIVE >]} {= [< AND >]} {V we [KNOW] that THIS angle is < GAMma >} {\ so [THAT] angle would be GAMma minus < FIVE >}…

While the selection of prominence emphasizes words that are more important or relevant in a particular context of interaction, words may be made non-prominent for phatic reasons. When disagreement or only partial agreement is expressed, for example, words that indicate divergence of views may not be chosen for prominence, in order to tone down the difference between interlocutors, for politeness purposes (Cheng *et al.*, 2008). In example 12, which is taken from a televised interview, the talk show host (speaker b1) is asking the guest (speaker b2) a declarative question based on the guest's previous response. Notice the guest's use of a non-prominent *well*, a typical marker of dispreferred response, to preface his partial agreement, followed by a prominent *yes* to highlight the convergence instead of the divergence between speakers:

(12)

b1: {\ so the [SEparate] rule you are TALking < _ aBOUT >} {\ is [< ACtually >]} {\ a [^ LOWer] < STANdard >}

b2: {\ well in [^ MAny] < CAses >} {\ [< YES >]} {= er [LET] me < SHOW > you} {= [< AN >]} {\ [< eXAMple >]} {\ [< _ HERE >]}...

Tone

The tone or pitch movement in the tone unit is associated with the final prominent syllable (the tonic syllable) in the tone unit, and so tone choices "attach additional meaning increments to tonic segments" (Brazil, 1997: 20). Speakers may choose from five tones: the rise, fall–rise, fall, rise–fall and level tones. Four of the tones are used to distinguish between information that is common ground, i.e. referring tones (R): rise (r+) and fall–rise (r), and information that is new, i.e. proclaiming tones (P): fall (p) and rise–fall (p+). Figure 19.2 gives a graphical representation of the referring and proclaiming tone choices available to speakers.

Any spoken discourse proceeds on the basis of a considerable amount of shared knowledge between discourse participants (Brazil, 1997: 109), and it is for the speaker to decide, moment by moment, whether what he/she is saying is shared or not. Table 19.4 describes the communicative functions of the proclaiming and referring tones (pp. 82–98).

Example 13 (reproduced from example 11), which is taken from a lecture, illustrates how the selection of tone indicates whether the information presented is considered by the speaker to be shared or not:

(13)

...{= [< THIS >] is} {∨ [< FIVE >]} {= [< AND >]} {∨ we [KNOW] that THIS angle is < GAMma >} {\ so [THAT] angle would be GAMma minus < FIVE >}...

At the beginning of this extract, the lecturer makes use of the fall–rise tones to signal that the values of the angles are in the common ground, as these values are already discussed earlier. The use of the referring tone and the words *we know that* make clear to the students that this part of the discourse is not presenting new information. On the other hand, the final tone unit in example 12 has fall tone. This is because the value of the angle concerned in this tone unit is unknown to the students up to this point. By using the proclaiming tone, the speaker is presenting new information.

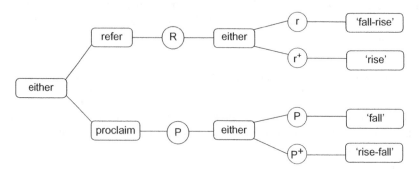

Figure 19.2 The referring and proclaiming tone choices available to speakers
Source: Brazil, 1997: 83

Table 19.4 Functions of proclaiming and referring tones

Tone	Functions
Referring tone:rise tone (r+)	To reactivate something which is part of the common ground
Referring tone: fall–rise tone (r)	To indicate that this part of the discourse is already present in the common ground, and therefore will not enlarge the common ground assumed to exist between the participants
Proclaiming tone: fall tone (p)	To indicate that this part of the discourse is not yet present in the common ground, and so will be news and world-changing. The area of speaker–hearer convergence is being enlarged
Proclaiming tone: rise–fall tone (p+)	• To indicate addition to the common ground and to the speaker's own knowledge at one and the same time • To indicate to the hearer that no feedback of either an adjudication or concurring kind is expected • To indicate that the speaker intends to continue to speak and so asserts control of the progress of the discourse

Its introduction enlarges the area of convergence, i.e. the knowledge in a particular academic discipline—in this context, between the lecturer and the students.

As shown by example 13 above, the proclaiming/referring opposition and the choices in the referring tone system contribute implications of common ground information or new information to the tonic segment. The selection of tones, as with other linguistic options, rests with the speaker, and the decision to present information as shared or as new is based on a subjective assessment of the state of shared knowledge between the participants, and is also open to exploitation, should the speaker choose to do so.

Tone selections are also accorded social significance, as there are tone selections that may be characterized as being participant-specific in specialized discourse types (i.e. discourse types other than conversation), and they imply a certain role relationship pertaining between the participants in a discourse (Brazil, 1997: 82–98). These participant-specific tones are the rise tone and the rise–fall tone. If a speaker selects a rise–fall (instead of a fall) in proclaiming something, or a rise (instead of a fall–rise) in referring to something, the speaker is considered to be exerting dominance and control additionally (Brazil, 1995: 243). In discourse types where one speaker is dominant in the sense of having greater responsibility for the discourse and greater freedom in making linguistic choices, that designated dominant speaker monopolizes the rise–fall/rise choice. Examples of specialized discourse types that involve an unequal power relationship between participants include teacher talk and job interviews. In academic lectures, for instance, it is the teacher who is mainly responsible for the content and process of the lesson. Accordingly, the teacher may exert his/her dominance in the discourse through a choice of tone. At the beginning of example 14 below, which comes from a lecture on count and mass nouns, a student (speaker a1) is asking the lecturer (speaker a2) whether "sheep" is considered a count noun or a mass noun on the basis of the ongoing discussion. The lecturer responds with the repeated selection of the rise tone:

> (14)
> a1: {/ then [< HOW >] about the word} {\ [< SHEEP >]} (.) {\ [< SHEEP >]}
> a2: {/ [< ^ SHEEP >]} (.) {/ [< SO >]} (.) {/ [DO] you think < SHEEP >} {= [< IS >] a} {\ [< COUNT >] noun or} {/ [MASS] < NOUN >}

The lecturer's choice of the rise tone asserts her dominance as the main speaker in the discourse and reminds the student that the answer to the question has already been established earlier in the discussion. In other words, it is perceived to be common ground between the participants.

The rise–fall tone is the least prevalent of the tones, according to Brazil (1997), and he claims that, in a discourse in which the participants are of unequal status, it tends to be the dominant speaker who alone makes this selection. In institutionalized discourse types such as classroom talk and medical consultation, for example, it is often the teacher or the doctor who uses the rise–fall tone to assert dominance and control (Cheng et al., 2008). The scarcity of the rise–fall tone in naturally occurring speech is supported by findings from the HKCSE (prosodic), which show that only a negligible 0.015 percent of all tone units (49 out of 313,340) carry the rise–fall tone (Cheng et al., 2008: 126). More examples of the rise–fall tone in a range of specialized discourse types are needed to investigate further the extent to which the use of this tone is confined to the dominant speaker.

In conversations, however, the selection of the rise and rise–fall tones is not restricted by the existence of institutionalized inequalities between the participants. In conversation, these tones are selected by all, some or none of the participants, depending on the moment-by-moment decisions of those involved and not, on the basis of a restrictive set of conventions. Brazil (1985: 131) argues that in conversation there is "an ongoing, albeit incipient, competition for dominance." However, he adds that this does not necessarily imply aggressiveness or rudeness on the part of speakers; rather, when a speaker selects the rise or rise–fall tone, this can be characterized as "to remind, underline, emphasize, insist or convey forcefulness" (Brazil, 1997: 98), and so overtly the speaker assumes the status of the dominant one. The important point is that dominant speaker status is neither predetermined nor fixed in conversation and is typically interchangeable among the participants as the discourse unfolds.

In asserting dominance in discourse through the use of the rise–fall tone, speakers may also modify their view of the world at the same time. In this respect, the rise–fall tone signals to the hearer that new information has been added to the speaker's own knowledge, as well as to the common ground between the speaker and the hearer at that moment of the talk. The addition of such new information often arises from a sudden realization by the speaker of the current state of affairs or of an unexpected event, which leads to the speaker's comment (Cheng et al., 2008). Example 15 below shows the use of the rise–fall tone in a conversation. In this extract the two speakers are talking about the number of universities in Hong Kong. The use of the rise–fall tone by speaker y in the first tone unit of the last utterance indicates that his view on this topic has suddenly changed and that he intends to assert his control of the talk through the continuation of speakership:

(15)
y:　{= [< _ THERE >] is} {= [YOUR] < uniVERsity >} {= [< THIS >] one} {? and the [< CHInese >] university} {\ [< THAT'S >] it}

b:　{= [< WHAT >]}

y:　{= [< _ THERE >] is} {\ [THREE] < uniVERsities >}

b:　{\ no there's [< SIX >]} {\ [< SIX >]}

y:　{∧ ah [< YEAH >]} {\ you [< _ TOLD >] me} {? because i} {\ i [DON'T] < reMEMber >} {= the [< eXACT >] er} {= [< NUMber >]}

The fifth tone—the level tone—is discussed in the context of the orientation or stance the speaker takes. The use of level tone projects neither a certain context of interaction nor any communicative value of the utterance. In fact this tone is used when the speaker does not intend to either proclaim or refer, and in so doing disengages from the immediate interpersonal, interactive context of interaction. In other words, the speaker does not make "either/or" choices of any kind, and presents the language with neutral projections as to the assumption made about the current state of understanding between the speaker and a hearer (Brazil, 1997: 132).

Instead of making the binary "either/or" selection, a speaker's choice of employing the level tone focuses on the linguistic properties or message organization of the utterance rather than on the truth of the assertion made in the utterance. Brazil (1997: 133–139) provides a detailed description of the two main contexts when speakers select the level tone. The first is when a speaker is adopting an "oblique presentation" (p. 133), or when a speaker is saying something, on paper or in the speaker's memory, that is either pre-coded or partially coded information (pp. 136–139). Example 16 (from a public speech) illustrates such a situation, when the speaker's continuous use of the level tone indicates that he is simply reading out pre-coded information and highlighting the words involved as an entity, which in this case is the name of a meeting. It is not until the end of the name has been reached that the speaker changes his tone choice to the fall tone:

(16)
…{/ i would [< LIKE >]} {= to [< exTEND >]} {∨ a [VEry] warm welcome to < ALL > of you} {= who have [COME] < HERE >} {= for the [< FOURteenth >]} {= [GENEral] < MEEting >} {= [< OF >]} {= [< paClfic >]} {= [< ecoNOmic >]} {\ [coOperation] < COUNcil >}…

The second context is one in which encoding has not yet been achieved, or it presents some kind of difficulty for the speaker (p. 139)—which is likely to happen when the speaker is telling a story (p. 140) or when the speaker is talking spontaneously, as in example 17 below, which comes from a conversation, where the speaker makes use of the level tone when he has yet to formulate what to say:

(17)
…{\ i [< GUESS >]} {= [< ^ SO >] ^ er} {= i [< THINK >] er} {? [< IT >] it} {= [< IT >]} {\ [I'M] < STUdying >} {\ [< HERE >]}

Brazil (1995: 244) describes another context where the level tone is used. It is not related to encoding problems, but found when a speaker says "incremental elements" that form part of a "telling increment." These elements are message fragments that have not yet reached the "target state" (Brazil, 1995: 165), namely the end of a discrete information unit. Typically, the incremental elements are said with level tones until the final tone unit which is said with the fall tone. Brazil states that a speaker's selection of tone signals her/his orientation to the ongoing talk at that moment in time. In example 18 (from a conversation), for instance, the speaker repeatedly makes use of the level tone to signal the development of the incremental elements until he comes to the end of the information unit, i.e. the construction of the complete question:

(18)
{= [< ER >]} {= [^ HOW] < aBOUT > the} {= [ecoNOmic] < situAtion >} {= [< _ IN >]} {\ u [< ^ K >]}

Figure 19.3 below shows the decisions the speaker has to make for each tone unit. Direct discourse refers to the discourse in process, which is hearer-sensitive and interactive, as opposed to oblique discourse such as reading and quoting, which briefly withdraws the speaker from interacting with the hearer (Cheng et al., 2008):

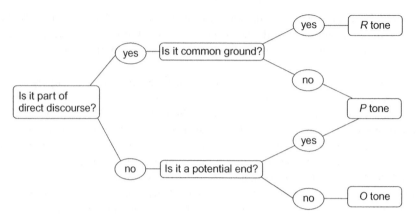

Figure 19.3 Tone choices available to speakers
Source: adapted from Brazil, 1997: 135–136

Key and termination

Key and termination refer to pitch-level choices available to speakers. Key is the pitch-level choice associated with the first prominent syllable (onset) in the tone unit. The high, mid and low pitch levels at which the onset is pitched are recognized in relation to the onset syllable of the previous tone unit. Termination is the pitch-level choice associated with the last prominent syllable in the tone unit. The high, mid and low levels at which the tonic is pitched are recognized in relation to the pitch level of the preceding prominent syllable in the same tone unit (i.e. the onset), or in the prior tone unit in the case of minimal tone units. Key and termination are therefore two systems with independent speaker choices for different meaning realizations. Key and termination choice in a particular tonic segment is "never more than one 'level' in the three-term system" (Cheng *et al.*, 2008: 62), namely one step above or one step below.

Brazil (1997) distinguishes between minimal and extended tonic segments, depending on whether the tonic segment contains one or more than one prominence. In tone units of both the minimal and extended types, pitch-level choices serve to determine the key and termination of the whole tonic segment. In the case of minimal tonic segments, however, it is not possible to make the selection of key and termination independently. In single prominence tone units without an onset syllable, "the first prominent syllable is also the last, so there can be no independent choices in the two systems" (p. 12), representing a simultaneous selection of key + termination. As an illustration, Table 19.5 shows some examples of tone units with different pitch-level choices of key and termination on the word *so*:

Table 19.5 Examples of key and termination pitch-level choices

Pitch-choice	Examples
high key	{∨ [^ SO] at this < MOment >}
mid key	{\ [SO] this is ONE < REAson >}
low key	{/ [_ SO] they have a DIfferent < SYStem >}
high termination	{\/ [BUT] < ^ SO > far}
mid termination	{= [THANK] you < SO > much}
low termination	{\ you [DON'T] THINK < _ SO >}
high key + termination	{\ and [< ^ SO >] you know}
mid key + termination	{\ okay [< SO >]}
low key + termination	{\ [< _ SO >]}

This method of analysis needs to be justified by showing that "the meaning increments derived from the two choices are compatible and both appropriate to the situation" (ibid.). The hearer then assigns communicative value to either key or termination in the local context. Nevertheless, there are conditions where a syllable in a tone unit that is not intended to realize a sense selection can be made prominent, simply in order to achieve a choice of key or termination, since "an intonation choice can be associated with a syllable only if it is prominent" (p. 65).

Key, defined as the pitch choice on the first prominent syllable, "affects the communicative value of the whole tonic segment" (p. 50). The selection of key projects the speaker's assumption about the hearer's expectations as the talk unfolds. High key, for example, has contrastive implications and may show surprise, pleasure, annoyance, alarm, and so on in the local context. "Contrasting" here refers to a selection that "projects a binary opposition upon the existential paradigm and explicitly denies an alternative" (p. 45). In other words, the speaker is indicating clearly a choice made out of two options (it is "a" NOT "b") through the use of high key. High key adds an increment of meaning to the effect that "this tone unit has a denial of expectation relations to what has preceded" (Brazil, 1997: 75–84; Cauldwell, 2007). In example 19 below (from a conversation between friends), the speaker is discussing the desserts in a foreign city that she has just visited. Notice the use of high key in the third tone unit on the word *so* to indicate a sharp contrast, and hence a surprise that the speaker feels at the variety of cakes available between the city she travelled to and her own city:

(19)
...{= [< ER >]} {= [< THERE >]} {= there are [< ^ SO >]} {= many different [< TYPES >] of um} {\ [< CAKES >]}...

The selection of low key in a tonic segment projects existential equivalence to the previous topic segment. Low key has equative value, adding an increment of meaning to the effect that "[t]his tone unit has an equative relationship with what has gone before" (Brazil, 1997: 75–84; Cauldwell, 2007). In other words, low key assumes that the hearer will perceive the content as following naturally upon what has gone before, and as "being entirely in line with what the hearer would expect" (Brazil, 1995: 245). In example 20 below (from a placement interview at a hotel), the interviewer is asking the student about the department that she would like to work in. The use of low key in the final tone unit, in combination with the lexical choice *you know*, signals the alignment of expectation to what has preceded, as the beginning of one's career is normally expected to follow one's graduation:

(20)
...{= [< ER >]} {/ [< ^ WHICH >]} {= department [THAT] < UM >} {/ you're [parTIcularly] interest < IN >} {= and would like [< TO >]} {V [emBARK] your < caREER >} {\ [_ YOU] know UPON < graduAtion >}

Mid-key attributes no special expectations to the hearer. It only has additive value, "merely adding its content to what has gone before" (Brazil, 1995: 245). In example 21, which is again taken from a placement interview, the student is explaining why she is interested in working in the hotel industry and studying hotel and management subjects at her university. Her repeated selection of mid-key shows that she is simply expanding on her reasons for her study and career choice:

(21)
...{= i [< THINK >] in} {V [THIS] < SUBject >} {= i [CAN] LEARN < aBOUT >} {= a [LOT] of er < PRACtical >} {= [< ER >]} {= [< ER >]} {\ [< KNOWledge >]} {= [SO] i THINK it is good for < ME >}...

Given the additive value associated with mid-key, it is perhaps not surprising that this key is found to be the most frequently occurring of all the pitch-level choices for key, more than 90 percent of all tone units in the HKCSE (prosodic) having been found to be produced with this key choice (Cheng *et al.*, 2008).

The selection of termination constrains the next speaker in his/her selection of key. This phenomenon is termed "pitch concord" (Brazil, 1995: 86). A speaker who conforms to pitch concord is likely to be giving a preferred response, and a speaker who does not is likely to be giving a dispreferred response (pp. 53–58).

TERMINATION
HIGH anticipates HIGH KEY response (i.e. adjudication)
MID anticipates MID KEY response (i.e. concurrence)
LOW sets up no particular expectations, and permits choice of high key, mid key or low key.

(Brazil, 1995: 246, 1997: 119)

Example 22 is taken from the beginning of a conversation. In this extract two friends are checking whether the recording has started.

(22)
a: {\ [< YES >]} {= i [THINK] it's < ER >} ★ {\ [STARTED] < alREAdy >}
A: ★★ {\ [< STARTED >]}
    {\ [< ^ YEAH >]}
A: ★ {\ [< ^ Okay >]} {\ [< ^ SO >]}
a: ★★ {\ [< YES >]}

At the beginning of the extract, speaker a selects high key + termination on *yeah* to seek adjudication from speaker A regarding whether the recorder is on. By providing a preferred response, which in this case is agreement with her friend's observation, speaker A also selects high key + termination on *okay* and *so*, hence achieving pitch concord.

On the other hand, example 23 shows a dispreferred response given in a televised interview:

(23)
b1: {\ [< _ NOW >]} {? [< K >] w} {? do you} {= do you [aGREE] with < THIS >}
b2: {\ [< ^ WELL >]} {? [< I >]} {? [< I >]} {\ i [< ^ THINK >]} {= [< ER >]} {= i
    [aGREE] < WITH > er} {\ er h [_ W] < BUT >} {= i [< ^ THINK >] we} {= we
    [NEED] to < LOOK > at the} {= [< THIS >] er} {= [< ISsue >] from a} {= from a [<
    BIGger >]} {\ [< CONtext >]}...

While speaker b1 selects mid-termination to seek concurrence, speaker b2 does not choose mid-key in his response. Instead he selects high key, to indicate a contrast, and suggests that he does not entirely agree with the other guest in the interview.

Conclusion

This paper has presented an overview of the discourse intonation systems and choices and has illustrated each of the four systems through discussions of examples from the HKCSE (prosodic) to show how the systems function in local contexts so as to add communicative value to what is said. It highlights the fact that intonation is situation-specific. For instance, it can be seen from the examples above that the discourse particle *so*, among other lexical items, can be used with a range of intonational choices. Instead of rigidly tying particular lexical or grammatical elements to intonation, the discourse intonation model thus argues that the use of intonation is context-sensitive and very much responsive to the communicative situation. While such intonational choices, consciously made by speakers, are not pre-determined, they can nonetheless be predicted to some extent through the detailed systematic observation, identification and description of general patterns. The study of the discourse intonation patterns observed in naturally occurring speech thus reveals to the analysts the intonational decisions that speakers have to make in real time interactions on a moment-by-moment basis, which reflect the rich layers of pragmatic and situated meanings expressed in speech. This is therefore an indispensable area of investigation for a deeper understanding of meanings in spoken discourse.

Transcription conventions

Transcription notation used in the HKCSE (prosodic)

Symbol	Remarks
...	parts of an utterance which have been omitted
★	onset of simultaneous speech produced by the current speaker
★★	onset of simultaneous speech produced by an interlocutor other than the current speaker
(.)	a brief, unfilled pause roughly lasts for the length of a syllable
(pause)	a unit, unfilled pause which is longer than a brief pause and normally lasts for a few seconds
(())	a non-linguistic feature such as laughter, coughing, throat clearing and applause
((inaudible))	unintelligible speech
A:	female native speaker of English
B:	male native speaker of English
a:	female Hong Kong Chinese
b:	male Hong Kong Chinese
x:	female speaker of a language other than English and Cantonese
y:	male speaker of a language other than English and Cantonese
u:	unknown speaker
{}	tone unit boundary
/	rise tone
V	fall-rise tone
\	fall tone
∧	rise-fall tone
=	level tone
?	unclassifiable tone
CAPS	prominent syllable
[]	key
< >	termination
∧	high pitch level
_	low pitch level

Further reading

Brazil, D. (1985) *The Communicative Value of Intonation*. Birmingham: English Language Research, University of Birmingham.

An important and original work on the study of discourse intonation, this book provides a detailed description of the discourse intonation framework.

Brazil, D. (1997) *The Communicative Value of Intonation in English*. Cambridge: Cambridge University Press.

This is the revised edition of Brazil's (1985) seminal work.

Cheng, W., Greaves, C., and Warren, M. (2008) *A Corpus-Driven Study of Discourse Intonation: The Hong Kong Corpus of Spoken English (Prosodic)*. Amsterdam; Philadelphia: John Benjamins.

This monograph discusses the discourse intonation patterns observed in the Hong Kong Corpus of Spoken English (Prosodic), one of the largest corpora of naturally occurring speech annotated with the discourse intonation framework.

References

Brazil, D. (1985) *The Communicative Value of Intonation*. Birmingham: English Language Research, University of Birmingham.
Brazil, D. (1995) *A Grammar of Speech*. Oxford: Oxford University Press.
Brazil, D. (1997) *The Communicative Value of Intonation in English*. Cambridge: Cambridge University Press.
Cauldwell, R. T. (2002) 'The functional irrhythmicality of spontaneous speech: a discourse view of speech rhythms', *Apples*, 2 (1): 1–24.
Cauldwell, R. T. (2007) SpeechinAction Research Centre (SPARC). Available online at: http://www.speechinaction.com (accessed 16 June 2007).
Cheng, W., Greaves, C., and Warren, M. (2008) *A Corpus-Driven Study of Discourse Intonation: The Hong Kong Corpus of Spoken English (Prosodic)*. Amsterdam, Philadelphia, PA: John Benjamins.
Lam, P. (2008) *Discourse Particles in an Intercultural Corpus of Spoken English*, PhD dissertation, The Hong Kong Polytechnic University, Hong Kong.
Sinclair, J. (1991) *Corpus, Concordance, Collocations*. Oxford: Oxford University Press.

20

Lexis in spoken discourse

Paula Buttery and Michael McCarthy

Introduction: lexis as a discourse phenomenon

More than a decade ago, McCarthy (1998) noted that the role of lexical patterns in written texts had been the object of detailed attention, especially within the study of lexical cohesion (Halliday and Hasan, 1976; Hasan, 1984). Similarly, the significance of multiple ties between words in written texts had been meticulously recorded by Hoey (1991). This, McCarthy asserted at the time, was not matched by anything like the same amount of research into lexical patterning in everyday spoken language. The present chapter can report some considerable progress since then, especially in light of the increased number of spoken corpus-based studies using large amounts of data and of growing interest in the study of collocation and chunking, which have in turn contributed to the methodology and findings of discourse analysis, as we demonstrate below. Chunking in particular has been examined in terms of its role in spoken interaction. In this chapter, we consider how the study of lexis using large amounts of spoken data can underpin the insights into lexical patterning already observed by keen-eyed discourse and conversation analysts in one-off extracts and can provide empirical support from a wide range of occurrences for statements concerning the regularity and recurrence of particular lexical phenomena at the level of discourse (Stubbs, 2001). The first question we address is whether there are differences between the spoken and written lexicon as a whole and what implications any differences might have for an understanding of spoken discourse. We then focus on how lexical patterns manifest themselves within and across speaker turns and their contribution to the unfolding discourse. We base our evidence on everyday, informal, spoken data, mostly social conversations, for it is there, we would argue, that patterns of negotiation and social convergence at the lexical level are most fruitfully observed. We take as uncontroversial the claim that the use of corpus data can offer considerable enhancements to discourse analysis, as demonstrated for example in Bublitz's (1988) use of corpus data in the study of cooperative conversations and, more recently, by Thornbury (2010), who argues that corpus linguistics, with its emphasis on the study of co-text, can powerfully supplement the discourse analyst's investigation of context, as well as providing large numbers of examples of given phenomena.

Lexis and register

One of the many features that mark out spoken language from written language is differences in the lexicon (Lee, 2001). Such differences are commonly described as differences of register, that is to say, lexical choices are made differently depending on, in Halliday's (1978) terms, the field, mode and tenor of the situation of utterance. In face-to-face spoken interaction, interpersonal constraints strongly influence the tenor of utterances, creating and maintaining social relations partly through lexical choices on the formal-to-informal cline (Scotton, 1985; Powell, 1992). By comparing large spoken and written corpora, it is possible quantitatively to isolate a lexicon whose probability of occurrence is much higher in, or almost exclusively confined to, spoken discourse modes, whether through the spoken medium itself, through modes that attempt to capture speech (such as fictional dialogue) or through hybrid modes such as real-time internet communications.

The lexical differences between spoken and written language may be broadly observed through a quantified comparison of word frequencies in spoken and written corpora. Distinctive items on the spoken side will then be examined in terms of their role in the creation and management of discourse. Here we consider the 2,000 most frequent items in the written (fiction) and spoken subsections of the British National Corpus (BNC, 2007). High-frequency items may be expected to form patterns at the discourse level more readily than the relatively low-frequency items that make up the rest of the English lexicon, and items that differentiate speech from writing may be analysed in terms of their roles in the creation of spoken discourse and the elaboration of social relations in conversational contexts.

We may first quantify the number of lexical items these two lists, the spoken and the written, have in common by calculating their intersection, where 'intersection' is calculated as twice times the number of items in both lists, divided by the number of items in the spoken list plus the number of items in the fiction list. For these two frequency lists we find the intersection to be 0.658. This indicates that some 65 per cent of all the lexical items are found in both lists, leaving 35 per cent unique to either the spoken or written data. In Figures 20.1 and 20.2 we also consider the order of the lexical items in the frequency lists by plotting their frequency in one corpus against their frequency in the other. These graphs are plotted as log frequencies rather than raw frequencies. The reason for plotting them this way is the tendency for lexical items in a corpus to follow a Zipfian distribution. According to Zipf (Zipf, 1935), the most frequent word in a corpus can occur twice as often as the second most frequent, and three times as often as the third most frequent, and so on.[1] A distribution such as this is difficult to plot readably on a graph, since it leads to an uneven spread of data points over a large range. On a base 10 log scale a lexical item

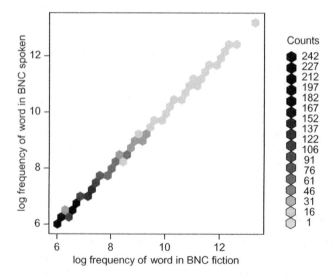

Figure 20.1 The 'null hypothesis' of lexical differences, spoken versus written

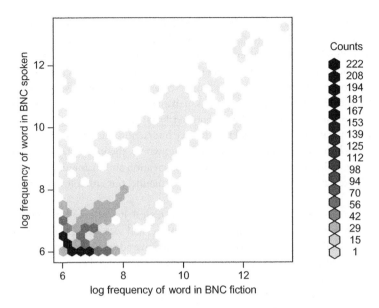

Figure 20.2 Actual variation in the data: spoken versus written frequency

occurring with a frequency of 1,000 words per million in the written corpus and 100 words per million in the spoken corpus could be plotted at point 3, 2. Since there are 2,000 points to plot on each graph, hexagonal areas in Figures 20.1 and 20.2, below have been shaded to indicate the density of points in that area. A darker hexagon indicates a greater density of points plotted. Figure 20.1 shows how the data would look if the ordering of lexical items in the two lists were equivalent (the 'null hypothesis' graph). Figure 20.2 shows the actual data as deviating considerably from the null hypothesis. In particular we notice a column of hexagons near the y-axis. This indicates high-frequency items found in the spoken corpus that occur with substantially lower frequency in the written corpus. Otherwise the wide spread of data points from the diagonal line shows how usage in general is different between the two corpora. That is, the ordering of lexical items in the frequency lists is quite distinct.

We can further express the differences that we have illustrated graphically above as a single numeric value such as the 'rank correlation coefficient'. This simple coefficient is calculated by considering the differences in ordering (ranking) between two lists.[2] The coefficient obtained will be within the range −1 to +1. A value of −1 indicates a complete reversal of ordering from one list to the other, whereas a value of +1 indicates an identical ordering. A value of 0, meanwhile, indicates that the two orderings are independent of each other. For our frequency lists, the rank correlation coefficient is approximately 0.5. This outcome indicates that, while on the whole the rankings are similar, there is some degree of distinctiveness between the two lists. We should note that rank correlation is a simple metric that treats all ranks with equal importance. Perhaps a more appropriate metric for long lists of lexical items would be one that punishes more heavily deviation between highly ranked items. The problem goes back to the Zipfian distribution described above: there will be many low-frequency items at the bottom of the list, which will tie for ranking. However, for shorter lists like ours, the rank correlation gives a good idea of important deviations of ordering.

What, then, is the nature of these differences between the spoken and written lexicons and what functions do the spoken elements carry out at the discourse level? McCarthy and Carter

(1997) showed how the top 50 most frequent words in a spoken corpus differed from the top 50 in a written corpus of the same size, and how discourse-marking items such as *know* (in its high-frequency chunked manifestation of *you know* – see below, section 'lexical items in discourse: chunks'), *right* and *well* featured in the spoken list but did not appear in the top 50 written list, giving further substance to the attention paid to these items by discourse analysts over a number of years. Equally, the very high frequency of items such as *just* and *think* (most commonly chunked as *I think*) in the spoken list pointed to the interpersonal strategies of hedging and politeness, which are central to cooperative and successful face-to-face interaction. Interpersonal exigencies seemed, therefore, to run high in the spoken lexicon. In other words, the items that are of unusually high frequency in the spoken corpus are implicated in the creation and maintenance of social relations and successful interaction; their roles are not merely semantic, but rather located in the pragmatics of discourse.

Further down our BNC frequency lists, many lexical items have overwhelmingly more occurrences in spoken discourse than in written discourse, and vice-versa. Certain morpohological types cluster on one list or the other. For example, evaluative adjectives ending in –*y* such as *yucky*, *stroppy*, *comfy* and *grumpy* have greatly differing distributions in the spoken and written components of the BNC (Figure 20.3).

Conversely, in the same corpora, a set of nouns indicating facial expressions (*grimace, scowl, smirk* and *pout*) are relatively rare in spoken discourse (Figure 20.4).

These different distributions are not absolutes; they are simply high probabilities which impart to spoken and written discourses their different lexical fingerprints and, in their institutionalized uses, have direct implications for the kinds of relationships projected and created among interlocutors.

But quantitative differences of register such as frequencies in speech versus writing are not enough to account for the contribution of lexis to discourse, albeit they may reveal something about the nature of informality in relationships among participants in banal, everyday conversations. Of greater interest to the discourse analyst is how lexical items are used in real contexts, so we now turn first to the discourse roles of lexical chunks (whose identification derives from quantitative measures) and then to how the use of lexical items unfolds in the developing discourse and to an exegesis of the functions of lexical choice within and across speaker turns. We still have recourse to our corpus of data, but our preoccupation is now with the local rather than the global, with the qualitative rather than the quantitative interpretation of spoken data.

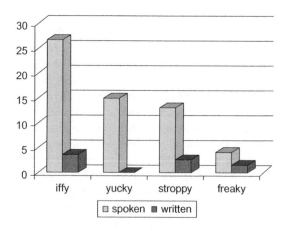

Figure 20.3 Frequency of –*y* adjectives (BNC) per 10m words

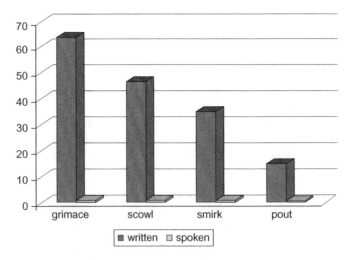

Figure 20.4 Frequency of facial expression nouns (BNC) per 10 m words

Lexical items in discourse: chunks

In this chapter we consider the discourse roles not only of single words, but of lexical chunks. The idea that strings of words may have integrated meanings and that such strings may develop specialized functions is not a new one (see Bolinger, 1976; Pawley and Syder, 1983). More recently, Sinclair (1987a, b, 1991) has proposed two basic principles that operate in the enactment of meaning. The first of these, the open choice principle, is the conventional notion that grammatical slots are 'filled' by lexical items. The second and more radical one is the *idiom principle*, which asserts that language users dispose of a huge repertoire of lexico-grammatical chunks whose form and meaning are pre-established and in a delicate relationship with each other. Chunks, as we shall refer to them in this chapter, have been extensively studied under different names, but with similar emphasis and preoccupations. Terms for the phenomenon, apart from widely used labels such as *fixed expressions* and *multi-word units*, include *routine formulae* (Coulmas, 1979), *lexicalized stems* (Pawley and Syder, 1983), *formulaic sequences* (Wray, 2002; Schmitt, 2004), *chunks* (O'Keeffe *et al.*, 2007) and *lexical bundles* (Biber and Conrad, 1999).

The significance of lexical chunks in spoken discourse is evidenced by the high frequency of items with interactive meanings, which are often as frequent as, or more frequent than, common, everyday single words. The most frequently occurring chunks in the five-million-word CANCODE[3] spoken corpus (for details of the corpus, see McCarthy, 1998) include items such as *you know, you know what I mean, (and) (all) that sort of thing, and all the rest of it* and various other items which project assumptions on the speaker's part and invite the listener to converge (see below). In this respect they play an important part in the creation of adjacency sequences; that is to say, for conversation to proceed normally and coherently, they invite listeners to respond as soon as possible after the utterance of the items (hence 'adjacency')(see also Chapter 9 in this volume). The high-frequency chunks also include discourse management items such as *so anyway*, which occurs more than 120 times in the CANCODE spoken corpus and is used to mark discourse boundaries, often a return to a series of narrative events after a descriptive or evaluative segment or an aside, or a shift to a new (sub-)topic. Extract 1 illustrates the narrative function.

1

[speaker is talking about making arrangements to view a house for a possible shared rental with friends]

... they rang me up, and I said look, you know, I've got, I've got my exams today and I really don't want to come up unless you see something, if you do, I will come up because they reckon it's a joint effort, if we're gonna live together, we've all got to see it and make a contribution to looking at the house. **So anyway**, they rang me up Friday night, and said, oh, seen this house, it's lovely and really nice. What's the arrangement? We'll meet you there at twelve o'clock Saturday, right. Right, I'll meet you at McDonald's blah blah blah. **So anyway**, we got down here,...

(BNC)[4]

Other chunks that have conversational-management functions include *talking of (x)*, *now you come to mention it*, *right then*, *now then*, *the thing is*, *there you go*, etc. These chunks may also be discontinuous, in that they may offer a slot within them that can be filled by an open choice. Such a chunk may be exemplified by *the x thing is*, where *x* is typically realized by an evaluative adjective phrase (frequent *x*-fillers in the spoken corpus include *best*, *worst*, *funny*, *silly*), or else an information-focus phrase such as *the (most) important thing is*, *the only thing is*, *the first thing is*, *the other thing is*. Extracts 2 and 3 exemplify this group.

2

<$1>   So if you go to London really **the best thing is** if you can get a research job and a contract and reasonable accommodation for six months.

<$2>   Er yeah. (CANCODE © Cambridge University Press)

3

<$1>   Cos it 's such er a light room.

<$2>   Mm.

<$1>   **The only thing is** with that radiator it still, it does get very cold in here. Because of all the glass. (BNC)

These lexical chunks have developed pragmatic specialisms in discourse with regard to organization and management and the signalling of stance, and operate outside of clause- and sentence-boundaries, as free-standing discourse items. *The only thing is* typically functions as a signal of a situation that may need attention or is problematic in some way. Such chunks function as 'long words' and co-exist with the many single words that have been recognized as having discourse-organizing or stance-signalling functions (e.g. *well*, *right*, *so*, *wow*, *anyway*, *absolutely*, *fine*, etc).

Lexical repetition and relexicalization

One of the most immediate and visible features of lexis beyond the sentence level in spoken interaction is the repetition of lexical items, which occurs both within and across speakers' turns. Persson (1974) used spoken and written data to examine repetition and included an examination of repeated modifiers and the friendly repetition of greetings and farewells. Persson's definition of repetition restricted itself to sequential repetition, that is to say, to the immediate repetition of identical lexical items by one speaker or writer (p. 11). Later work has stressed the importance of looking across turn boundaries to how repetition of lexis occurs between speakers in conversation. Bublitz (1988) used corpus data from the Survey of English Usage to look at a wide range of phenomena that manifest across speaker-boundaries in the creation and maintenance of supportive and cooperative conversations, within which he observed a number of examples of direct lexical repetition. In Bublitz's examples (p. 229), second speakers repeat one or more words used by first speakers to support the first speaker's utterance, further examples of which we provide below. Lindström (2001) (using Swedish data, though the same applies to English) notes how everyday greetings and other adjacency pair routines exploit lexical repetition (e.g. *Good morning – Good morning*) and comments on the range of interpretations that can be put on such examples, including the iconic nature of reduplication (see, for example, the type of phenomena attested in Wang, 2005) and considerations of politeness – for instance, how reduplicated routines may reinforce positive politeness (Brown and Levinson, 1987). Lindström (2001) also notes how reduplication in adjacency pairs can mark discourse boundaries; examples in English would include a second speaker repeating *right* or *fine* to mark a conversational (pre-)closure. Meanwhile, Carter (2004: 6–8) comments upon the role of repetition in everyday creativity in speaking (see also Chapter 22 in this volume).

Conversation analysis (CA) research has shed light on the functions of repetitions and on their place in sequences of turns. Schegloff (1997) argues that repetitions in conversation can raise the need for repair, can register receipt or can target a next action (see also Kim, 2002). A number of other studies have also taken a CA approach to lexical repetition and adjacency, explicating repetition in terms of focusing on items in a speaker's turn in order to acknowledge receipt and/or understanding, or to highlight a problem in the hearing or understanding of a highlighted item by a second speaker, to enact some organizational move in the talk, or to project stance (Wong, 2000; Svennevig, 2004; Koshik, 2005: ch. 5; Stivers, 2005). Tannen (1989) is an important study of repetition in which she examines a range of phenomena, including exact repetition and reformulation of the same ideas in different words, a feature we exemplify below.

McCarthy and Carter carried out research into patterns of lexis in spoken data, focusing on repetition and relexicalization (the repetition of content in modified lexical form – see below) within and across speaker turns in conversation (McCarthy, 1988, 1992; McCarthy and Carter, 1994: ch. 3). Their work was concerned with how speakers use repetition to create and sustain convergence or, on occasion, to signal resistance or divergence. They examined phenomena in conversation that included direct repetition, as in extracts 4 and 5:

4
<$1>   Yeah it's **nice** isn't it.
<$2>   Yeah. It is **nice**.
<$1>   **Nice nice** present. (CANCODE © Cambridge University Press)

5
<$2>   [Road name] Street's got so many houses on it that people won't move into even the homeless won't move into them because of the **crime**.
<$3>   **Crime problem**.
<$2>   **Crime problem**. But I mean whether that's exaggerated or not I don't know.
       (CANCODE © Cambridge University Press)

In extracts 4 and 5, speakers converge and create or maintain solidarity through repeating each other's words. In the case of extract 4, the sequence pivots around the repetition of *nice* across three turns. In extract 5, the first speaker's use of *crime* is incremented by the second speaker's adding *problem*, a collocation which is then taken up and repeated by the first speaker. Sometimes, however, the repetition of an entity may be realized by a relexicalized form, typically a (near-)synonym, as in extract 6, where the same speaker presents *fellow* and *chap* as synonymous.

6

… but he 's a very nice **fellow** now, very nice **chap**. (BNC)

A similar kind of solidarity to that in extracts 4 and 5 also seems to be achieved by rewording with near-synonymous expressions by a second or further speaker, as in extracts 7 and 8.

7

<$3>	I think he's a **brilliant** actor.
<$2>	Yeah. He is **very good**.
<$3>	He's a **really great** actor.
<$2>	Yeah. (CANCODE © Cambridge University Press)

8

<$2>	What what a **beautiful day**.
<$4>	It's **lovely** isn't it.
<$2>	Oh.
<$5>	Yeah. It's **fantastic**.
<$1>	A **great day** for the match. (CANCODE © Cambridge University Press)

Such patterns of relexicalization are commonplace in informal conversation. They serve a purpose in terms of content, in that they confirm understandings through negotiation of meanings, that is to say the local, contextual meaning of items is an achievement, arrived at through the proffering of terms by different speakers who converge with (extract 9) or renegotiate (extract 10) the use of particular items by their interlocutors.

9

[Speaker 1 addresses a cat, who has just greedily devoured a piece of chicken; the other speakers comment on the event]

<$1>	God have you eaten that already?
<$2>	Yeah.
<$1>	I'm surprised he didn't choke.
<$2>	I wouldn't say he **wolfed** it but he **lioned** it.
<$1>	**Catted** it.
<$2>	He **lioned** it.
<$1>	Yeah.
<$2>	**Tigered** it.
<$1>	Or something like that. (CANCODE © Cambridge University Press)

10

[discussing speaker <$1>'s new job]

<$1>	I've moved on and dealing with different things now.
<$2>	Mm.
<$1>	So erm-
<$2>	So you left us for something **better**. [laughs]
<$1>	**I wouldn't say better**. It's **different**. And I think you learn **different** things in each place that you go to. (CANCODE © Cambridge University Press)

In this way the establishment of lexico-semantic relations may be seen as interactive and, in the case of extract 9, creative (see Carter, this volume). The patterns also serve a relational purpose in that they create and consolidate social understandings and compacts. There are, of course, many occasions where speakers cannot or do not wish to converge lexically. In most such cases, in non-conflictual conversations, disagreements are hedged and counter-evaluations are downtoned rather than stated baldly, as in extracts 10 (above) and 11.

11
<$3>   Corfu is **awful** is it?
<$2>   Er **not really** no parts of it are **okay**. (CANCODE © Cambridge University Press)

Although syntax and phonology (see Ogden, 2006) clearly play a role in the construction of responsive turns, the lexical contribution to the preference organization of adjacency pairs is apparent, not just in formulaic sequences, but in the repetition and relexicalization we have exemplified here – a phenomenon underlined in the work of CA analysts such as Pomerantz (1984).

One aspect of repetition and relexicalization is manifested in the common practice of listeners to predict what a speaker is about to say, to utter the predicted words and then to receive confirmation of their prediction either through exact repetition or near-repetition or in the form of a relexicalization. By searching in a corpus for symbols denoting latched turns (typically a + sign), it is possible to observe the phenomenon as it unfolds. In a latched turn, a speaker is interrupted and then resumes his/her incomplete turn. The interruption is usually a cooperative act, perhaps designed to supply a word where there is evidence of hesitation, as in extract 10.

10
[<$?F>   = an unidentifiable female speaker]
<$6>   What was it in the little box?
<$?F>   Oh I dunno.
<$2>   Oh those little erm+
<$1>   The **charms**.
<$2>   +those little **charms**. (CANCODE © Cambridge University Press)

The latching may be more of an overlap than an interruption, providing an occasion for the almost simultaneous use of the same word(s), as in extract 11.

11
<$1>   Well quite honestly I said I despair coming down off the bus I thought well if this is the **future** | **generation**+
<$2> | **Future generation**. Yeah.
<$1>   +God help us. (CANCODE © Cambridge University Press)

Lexical triggers

Extracts 4–8 above consisted of short turns wherein an evaluative lexical item is taken up by another speaker and repeated or recast in a subsequent turn. The fact that the repeated or recast items are evaluative is important, in that evaluative claims lay the speaker open to contradiction or challenge, though by its very nature collaborative, non-conflictual conversation will tend towards supportive responses and, as we have seen, counter-evaluations may be downtoned or downgraded (Pomeratnz, 1984).

In conversational terms, evaluative claims are likely to trigger speaker change, in order for the subsequent speaker to be able to support (or challenge) the claim. Evison and McCarthy (in press) investigated this hypothesis in a 1-million-word sub-corpus of social and intimate conversations in the CANCODE corpus and found that a large proportion of utterances containing evaluations using the most frequent evaluative adjectives did indeed trigger speaker change. Evison and McCarthy found that, for the most frequent evaluative adjectives (which included, for example, *good, awful, true, nice, funny, lovely*), the percentages of the total occurrences that immediately preceded a listener response ranged from the lower 20s in the case of *good, bad* and *great*, to 34–37 per cent for *lovely, awful* and *horrible*, right up to 45 per cent and 49 per cent in the case of *brilliant* and *true*, respectively. Responses on occasion consist of no more than backchannels such as *mm* or *uhuh*, but they may also consist of more extended reactions. Examples of this phenomenon of lexical triggering abound in the CANCODE corpus and reveal another aspect of the role of lexis in the construction of discourse.

> 12
> <$1> I don't always agree the customer's always right I don't think that's **true**.
> <$1> No.
> <$2> But you've got to create an environment such as service level agreements, er monitoring meetings things like that.
> <$1> Yeah.
> <$2> Where you can have a dialogue with the customer. (CANCODE © Cambridge University Press)

> 13
> <$1> Right let's get on to the positive one then, your holiday.
> <$2> Yes it was **brilliant**.
> <$1> **Good**.
> <$2> We went on the fourth of June er for a fortnight and it was absolutely wonderful. (CANCODE © Cambridge University Press)

Evison and McCarthy (in press) also observed that vague language items such as *(and) things like that, or whatever, and so on, (and) that sort/kind of thing* regularly triggered speaker change – understandably, given the projection of shared knowledge that such items encode, inviting the listener(s) to concur with the assumed content, as in extracts 14 and 15.

> 14
> <$2> We also monitor complaints.
> <$1> Is this through Jim's | department?
> <$2> | Jim yeah. Yeah. And we also monitor er er capture er letters of praise and thank-yous **and things like that**.
> <$1> **Bouquets**.
> <$2> **Er yeah**. Em and of course we also have er the er Community Health Council drop in on us from time to time. (CANCODE © Cambridge University Press)

> 15
> <$5> You don't get private estates around factories **or whatever**+
> <$1> **Right**.
> <$5> +chemical plants, not in my experience. (CANCODE © Cambridge University Press)

It may also be noted that extract 12 above contained a further example of this phenomenon (*monitoring meetings things like that*).

Lexis and turn-openings

What we have attempted to show so far is the degree to which lexis is implicated in the successful construction of sequences of speaker turns, and we focused on how lexis is (a) taken up in subsequent turns and (b) may be a trigger for speaker change. A third dimension of turn construction is turn-opening. Tao (2003) investigated turn-openings in a spoken corpus and found that turn-initial items are mostly lexical and syntactically free-standing. Tao found in the turn-initial slot a high incidence of items such as *yes, well, right, okay* and of chunks such as *I think, you know, I mean, that's + adjective*. Tao's work underscores the way speakers attend to the prior turn and to relational concerns before they launch into their own message. Turn-initial items convey interactional meaning and maintain the flow of the talk by linking back to what has just been said. McCarthy (2010: 7–8), reinforcing Tao's work, shows that the top 20 turn-openers in the CANCODE corpus include common responsive items such as *yeah, yes, no, oh*, along with linking words such as *and, but* and *so*, backchannel items such as *mm*, and discourse-organizing words such as *well* and *right*. By far the most frequent word in a 5-million-word mixed written corpus, the definite article *the* occurs as sentence-initial in more than 23,000 written sentences (out of a total of 320,000, i.e. just over 7 per cent), yet only occupies the initial position in 4,300 of some 478,000 speaker turns (less than 1 per cent) in the 5 million words of the CANCODE corpus. Over 130 of these consist of chunks based around *the* such as *the thing is, the trouble is, the only thing is*, etc., which we examined above in section on lexis and register. The reason for dwelling on these numbers is that they underscore the lexical nature of turn openers and the way the free-standing lexical turn-openers 'push down' even such common words as the definite article, which might be expected to appear in almost any position in the speaker turn. In fact second, third, fourth and fifth position in the turn totals for the definite and indefinite articles all individually well exceed initial position totals for each of the articles. In other words, grammatical items such as the articles are dispreferred at the beginning of speakers' turns, in favour of the free-standing lexical turn-openers.

Response tokens as discourse items

As we have seen in the extracts presented so far, short responses are frequent in spoken discourse and may range from backchannels such as *mm* and *uhum*, through reactives such as *oh*, variations on *yes* and *no*, to fully lexical items such as *right* and *good*. This latter group of items, which in their grammatical identity belong mostly to the word class of adjectives and adverbs, includes single words such as *good, right, fine, lovely, wonderful, cool, marvellous, great, excellent, true, absolutely, definitely, certainly, exactly* – either used alone or along with *yes, yeah, no, okay* or with *that's*, as in extracts 16–18.

16
[talking about VAT, value added tax, a tax on goods and services]
<$1>   Really V A T's, I think, and I think it should only be paid when it, when the
             invoices+
<$2>   **Exactly**!
<$1>   +have been cleared, rather than always paying+
<$2>   **Exactly**!
<$1>   +for that quarter+
<$2>   Yeah.
<$1>   +even if you 've not got paid.
<$2>   Yeah. **Exactly**! (BNC)

17
[talking about someone who accepted an acting job]
<$1>   The thing is she couldn't have turned it down because she hadn't done any work for
             two years so she had to.

<$2>   **Oh yeah absolutely**.
<$1>   And she got to film on location in Majorca. (CANCODE © Cambridge University Press)

18
<$1>   Okay. Erm er you just want me to send these on presumably.
<$2>   Yeah. If you wouldn't mind.
<$1>   **That's fine**.
<$2>   Okay. Thanks.
<$1>   Okay then.
<$2>   Bye.
<$1>   Bye. (CANCODE © Cambridge University Press)

Some of these items are pragmatically specialized, for example the use of *fine* in (pre-)closing sequences (extract 18) or of *certainly* in response to a request, or of *right* to mark major discourse boundaries in longer events such as meetings and lessons (see Sinclair and Coulthard, 1975). The items may also be reduplicated, and it is not uncommon to find them repeated several times in one turn, expressing enthusiasm or extra engagement, as in extract 19.

19
[at an estate agent's: the customer is seeking a property in the stated locations]
<$1>   Two bedroomed, no? Round Arford, Johnston and Milford
<$2>   Yeah we 've got quite a few actually.
<$1>   Have you?
<$2>   Mm
<$1>   **Good good good good good**. Thank you. (BNC)

McCarthy (2002, 2003) calls such items 'non-minimal response tokens' (in the sense that they do more than the minimum requirement of acknowledgement or saying yes or no) and presents evidence of their widespread use. He attributes to them the function of displaying 'good listenership', in that they do more in both propositional and relational terms than bare *yes* or *no* and can display a high degree of involvement and interactivity without grabbing the floor and taking over the main speaker's role. Such items have almost shed their word-class identity as adjectives or adverbs and merit a separate classification as discourse items, displaying the full lexicality of discourse markers and free-standing, beyond-the-clause capabilities. Fries (1952: 49) long ago noted the responsive function of items such as *good*, while Duncan (1974) expanded the notion of backchannel (e.g. vocalizations such as *mm*) to include items such as *right* and *I see*. Pomerantz (1984), as we have noted, focused on the evaluative force of responses in second-pair parts of adjacency pairs. Öreström (1983) also broadened the purview of backchannel responses to examine fully lexical response items such as *quite* and *good*. Similarly, Tottie (1991) examines a range of responsive actions from body language, through vocalization, through single word responses, through phrasal/chunked responses, to short clauses and longer utterances, covering the whole cline to the point where a listener unequivocally takes over the speaker role. For our present purposes, though, it is the lexical nature of response tokens that is at the heart of their discourse roles.

Lexical chaining within and across speaker boundaries

In the section on lexical items in discourse (chunks), we considered repetition and relexicalization in relation to their role in the creation of adjacency sequences and interactional convergence.

However, uses of (near-)synonyms and relexicalized forms can carry over longer stretches of discourse to create lexical chains that allow us to follow both topical development and speakers' changing stances as they converge and occasionally diverge. Such chains may be developed both within an individual speaker's turn and across turn boundaries. In the examples below, the items contributing to chains are in bold. In example 20, the same speaker offers *fantastic, brilliant, nice* (x2) and boosted *really nice* to comment on a holiday just taken.

> 20
> \<\$2>   Ah well I went on holiday as you know.
> \<\$1>   Mhm.
> \<\$2>   That was **fantastic** that was. Oh dear it was **brilliant**. I didn't wanna come back at all. Oh it was **nice**. Mm. Beautiful sunshine beautiful beaches. Oh everything was **nice**.
> \<\$1>   Mm.
> \<\$2>   It was **really nice**.
> \<\$1>   Good. (CANCODE © Cambridge University Press)

Such relexicalizations over several turns are necessary insomuch as exact repetition of the initial evaluation *fantastic* four times in a row would be pragmatically odd and stylistically untypical (not to mention quite tedious for the interlocutors!). Where more than one speaker takes up an item, exact repetition seems more naturally allowable, as in extract 21.

> 21
> [In a shoe-shop: \<\$1> is the customer, \<\$2> is the assistant]
> \<\$2>   Probably needs adjusting but I'll check that.
> \<\$1>   Oh right. That's **lovely**.
> \<\$2> | Okay.
> \<\$1> | Yeah | that's **nice**.
> \<\$2> | They're **nice** aren't they.
> \<\$1>   Yeah they are **nice**.
> \<\$2>   **Very very nice**.
> \<\$1>   Thank you.
> \<\$2>   They feel **right**?
> \<\$1>   Yeah.
> \<\$2>   Does it?
> \<\$1>   That feels **pretty good** actually.
> \<\$2>   Yes **smashing fit**.
> \<\$1>   Yeah. (CANCODE © Cambridge University Press)

Extract 21 looks, on the face of it, to be a special and different case (a service encounter rather than a social conversation), but it underlines how social convergence can be exploited by servers and their clients to create good trading relations at the interpersonal level (see McCarthy (2000) for further examples).

9. Conclusion

Lexical patterning at the discourse level may be seen to be an important feature of spoken interaction. The choice of registers within the lexicon has important implications for the creation and maintenance of particular types of social relations and is a resource to be exploited or manipulated (a feature also noted and discussed by critical discourse analysts; see for example, Bhatia, 2006; Patrona, 2006). Beyond register, lexical patterns in spoken discourse are evidenced not only in the way speakers negotiate meanings through the trading and uptake of lexical items, but also in the ways social relations are projected, created and maintained through the sharing of lexical items and through the constant weaving and re-weaving of lexical meanings within and across turns. Indeed, we have attempted to show the centrality of lexis in turn-construction, in the sense of its role in effectively linking one turn to another and also in its function of responsiveness to incoming talk and in the part it plays in maintaining conversational flow or 'confluence' (McCarthy, 2010: 7–8) and in the projection of listenership.

Further reading

McCarthy, M. J. (1998) *Spoken Language and Applied Linguistics*. Cambridge: Cambridge University Press.

In this book McCarthy devotes a chapter to lexical patterning in spoken language, summing up work to date carried out in collaboration with Ronald Carter and others and adding evidence from the 5-million-word CANCODE corpus of everyday spoken English. The chapter shows corpus examples of repetition, relexicalization, negotiation of topic and listeners' contributions to lexical patterns in spoken discourse.

O'Keeffe, A., McCarthy, M. J. and Carter, R. A. (2007) *From Corpus to Classroom*. Cambridge: Cambridge University Press.

This book has several chapters in which lexical aspects of spoken language are dealt with. The authors use corpus evidence to illustrate the ubiquity of lexical chunks of spoken discourse as well as looking at the occurrence and functions of idiomatic expressions, the interrelationship between lexis and grammar, the role of listeners, hedging, vagueness and the use of discourse markers in everyday spoken language. The volume also includes sections on creativity in everyday discourse and special examples of spoken discourse such as academic talk and second-language classroom data.

Powell, M. J. (1992) 'Semantic/pragmatic regularities in informal lexis: British speakers in spontaneous conversational settings', *Text* 12 (1): 19–58.

Using the London–Lund spoken corpus, this study investigates the distribution and use of informal lexis in a database of conversations. An inventory of lexical items is drawn up and refined, which leads to the categorization of lexical items and their functions in spoken discourse. The principal functions discussed are evaluative and expressive ones, and idiomatic expressions, vague language and intensification are considered among and across different speakers.

Notes

1 Zipf actually suggested that an item's frequency is inversely proportional to its rank raised to a power close to 1.
2 For this calculation it is necessary that the compared orderings contain exactly the same set of items. The calculation was essentially carried out on the 65% intersection of the items that occur in both frequency lists.
3 CANCODE means Cambridge and Nottingham Corpus of Discourse in English. The corpus consists of five million words of informal conversations recorded across the islands of Britain and Ireland. Cambridge University Press is the sole copyright holder.
4 Where indicated, the data cited herein have been extracted from the British National Corpus Online service, managed by Oxford University Computing Services on behalf of the BNC Consortium. All rights in the texts cited are reserved.

References

Bhatia, A. (2006) 'Critical discourse analysis of political press conferences', *Discourse and Society*, 17 (2): 173–203.
Biber, D. and Conrad, S. (1999) 'Lexical bundles in conversation and academic prose', in H. Hasselgard and Oksefjell, S. (eds.) *Out of Corpora: Studies in Honor of Stig Johansson*. Amsterdam: Rodopi, pp. 181–190.
Bolinger, D. (1976) 'Meaning and memory', *Forum Linguisticum*, 1: 1–14.
Brown, P. and Levinson, S. (1987) *Politeness: Some Universals in Language Usage*. Cambridge: Cambridge University Press.

Bublitz, W. (1988) *Supportive Fellow-Speakers and Cooperative Conversations*. Amsterdam: John Benjamins.

Carter, R. A. (2004) *Language and Creativity: The Art of Common Talk*. London: Routledge.

Coulmas, F. (1979) 'On the sociolinguistic relevance of routine formulae', *Journal of Pragmatics*, 3: 239–266.

Duncan, S. (1974) 'On the structure of speaker-auditor interaction during speaker turns', *Language in Society*, 2: 161–180.

Evison, J. and McCarthy, M. J. (in press) 'Social talk', in A. Barron and K. Schneider (eds.) *Pragmatics of Discourse*. Berlin: Mouton de Gruyter.

Fries, C. C. (1952) *The Structure of English*. New York: Harcourt, Brace.

Halliday, M. A. K. (1978) *Language as Social Semiotic*. London: Edward Arnold.

Halliday, M. A. K., and Hasan, R. (1976) *Cohesion in English*. London: Longman.

Hasan, R. (1984) 'Coherence and cohesive harmony', in J. Flood (ed.) *Understanding Reading Comprehension*. Newark, Delaware: International Reading Association, pp. 181–219.

Hoey, M. P. (1991) *Patterns of Lexis in Text*. Oxford: Oxford University Press.

Kim, H. (2002) 'The form and function of next-turn repetition in English conversation', *Language Research*, 38 (1): 51–81.

Koshik, I. (2005) *Beyond Rhetorical Questions: Assertive Questions in Everyday Interaction*. Amsterdam/ Philadelphia, PA: John Benjamins.

Lee, D. Y. W. (2001) 'Defining core vocabulary and tracking its distribution across spoken and written genres: evidence of a gradience of variation from the British national corpus', *Journal of English Linguistics*, 29: 250–278.

Lindström, J. (2001) 'Testing Östman: iconicity and reduplicative politeness routines in Swedish', in V. Laakso, J. Leino, and J. Raukko (eds.) *Postcards, Implicitness, Constructions: Festschrift to Professor Jan-Ola Östman*. Vantaa: Tummavuoren kirjapaino, pp. 276–284.

McCarthy, M. J. (1988) 'Some vocabulary patterns in conversation', in R. A. Carter and M. J. McCarthy (eds.) *Vocabulary and Language Teaching*. London: Longman, pp. 181–200.

McCarthy, M. J. (1992) 'Interactive lexis: prominence and paradigms', in R. M. Coulthard (ed.) *Advances in Spoken Discourse Analysis*. London: Routledge, pp. 197–208.

McCarthy, M. J. (1998) *Spoken Language and Applied Linguistics*. Cambridge: Cambridge University Press.

McCarthy, M. J. (2000) 'Captive audiences: the discourse of close contact service encounters', in Coupland, J. (ed.) *Small Talk*. London: Longman, pp. 84–109.

McCarthy, M. J. (2002) 'Good listenership made plain: British and American non-minimal response tokens in everyday conversation', in R. Reppen, S. Fitzmaurice, and D. Biber (eds.) *Using Corpora to Explore Linguistics Variation*. Amsterdam: John Benjamins, pp. 49–71.

McCarthy, M. J. (2003) 'Talking back: "small" interactional response tokens in everyday conversation', in J. Coupland (ed.) Special issue of *Research on Language and Social Interaction* on 'Small Talk'. 36 (1): 33–63.

McCarthy, M. J. (2010) 'Spoken fluency revisited', *English Profile Journal*, 1 (1): 1–15. Availabe at http:// journals.cambridge.org/action/displayJournal?jid=EPJ (accessed 1 March 2011).

McCarthy, M. J. and Carter, R. A. (1994) *Language as Discourse: Perspectives for Language Teaching*. London: Longman.

McCarthy, M. J. and Carter, R. A. (1997) 'Written and spoken vocabulary', in N. Schmitt and M. J. McCarthy (eds.) *Vocabulary: Description, Acquisition, Pedagogy*. Cambridge: Cambridge University Press, pp. 20–39.

Ogden, R. (2006) 'Phonetics and social action in agreements and disagreements', *Journal of Pragmatics*, 38: 1752–1775.

O'Keeffe, A., McCarthy, M. J., and Carter, R. A. (2007) *From Corpus to Classroom*. Cambridge: Cambridge University Press.

Öreström, B. (1983) *Turn-Taking in English Conversation*. Lund: Gleerup.

Patrona, M. (2006) 'Conversationalization and media empowerment in Greek television discussion programs', *Discourse and Society*, 17 (1): 5–27.

Pawley, A. and Syder, F. (1983) 'Two puzzles for linguistic theory: nativelike selection and nativelike fluency', in J. Richards and R. Schmidt (eds.) *Language and Communication*. New York: Longman, pp. 191–226.

Persson, G. (1974) *Repetition in English: Part I, Sequential Repetition*. Uppsala: Acta Universitatis Upsaliensi.

Pomerantz, A. (1984) 'Agreeing and disagreeing with assessments: some features of preferred/dispreferred turn shapes', in J. Atkinson, and J. Heritage, (eds.) *Structures of Social Action*. Cambridge: Cambridge University Press, 57–101.

Powell, M. J. (1992) 'Semantic/pragmatic regularities in informal lexis: British speakers in spontaneous conversational settings', *Text*, 12 (1): 19–58.

Schegloff, E. (1997) 'Practices and actions: boundary cases of other-initiated repair', *Discourse Processes*, 23 (3): 499–545.

Schmitt, N. (ed.) (2004) *Formulaic Sequences*. Amsterdam: John Benjamins.

Scotton, C. (1985) 'What the heck, sir: style shifting and lexical colouring as features of powerful language', in R. Street, J. Capella, and H. Giles (eds.) *Sequence and Patterning in Communicative Behaviour*. London: Edward Arnold, pp. 103–119.

Sinclair, J. McH. (1987a) 'The nature of the evidence', in J. McH. Sinclair (ed.) *Looking up*. Glasgow: Collins, pp. 150–159.

Sinclair, J. McH. (1987b) 'Collocation: a progress report', in R. Steele, and T. Threadgold (eds.) *Language Topics: An International Collection of Papers by Colleagues, Students and Admirers of Professor Michael Halliday to Honour Him on His Retirement*. Amsterdam: John Benjamins, Volume 2, pp. 319–331.

Sinclair, J. McH. (1991) *Corpus, Concordance and Collocation*. Oxford: Oxford University Press.

Sinclair, J. McH. and Coulthard, R. M. (1975) *Towards an Analysis of Discourse*. Oxford: Oxford University Press.

Stivers, T. (2005) 'Modified repeats: one method for asserting primary rights from second position', *Research on Language and Social Interaction*, 38 (2): 131–158.

Stubbs, M. (2001) *Words and Phrases: Corpus Studies in Lexical Semantics*. Oxford: Blackwell.

Svennevig, J. (2004) 'Other-repetition as display of hearing, understanding and emotional stance', *Discourse Studies*, 6 (4): 489–516.

Tannen, D. (1989) *Talking Voices*. Cambridge: Cambridge University Press.

Tao, H. (2003) 'Turn initiators in spoken English: a corpus-based approach to interaction and grammar', in P. Leistyna and C. F. Meyer (eds.) *Corpus Analysis: Language Structure and Language Use*. Amsterdam: Rodopi, pp. 187–207.

The British National Corpus, version 3 (BNC XML Edition) (2007) Distributed by Oxford University Computing Services on behalf of the BNC Consortium. Available at http://www.natcorp.ox.ac.uk/.

Thornbury, S. (2010) 'What can a corpus tell us about discourse?', in A. O'Keeffe and M. J. McCarthy (eds.) *The Routledge Handbook of Corpus Linguistics*. Abingdon: Routledge, pp. 270–287.

Tottie, G. (1991) 'Conversational style in British and American English, the case of backchannels', in K. Aijmer and B. Altenberg (eds.) *English Corpus Linguistics*. London: Longman, pp. 254–271.

Wang, S.-P. (2005) 'Corpus-based approaches and discourse analysis in relation to reduplication and repetition', *Journal of Pragmatics*, 37 (4): 505–540.

Wong, J. (2000) 'Repetition in conversation: a look at "first and second sayings"', *Research on Language and Social Interaction*, 33 (4): 407–424.

Wray, A. (2002) *Formulaic Language and the Lexicon*. Cambridge: Cambridge University Press.

Zipf, G. (1935) *The Psychobiology of Language*. Boston, MA: Houghton Mifflin.

21
Emergent grammar

Paul J. Hopper

What is meant by emergent grammar?[1]

The initial premise of emergent grammar is that linguistic structure is a process that unfolds in real time. Emergent grammar therefore moves the focus of description to exemplifying the ongoing structuration of language as events of speech communication unfold. The fundamental temporality of spoken language implies the paradox that structure itself is unstable and intrinsically incomplete, and is constantly being created and recreated in the course of each occasion of use. This view is at odds with theories that presuppose a complete, fixed and stable grammatical system as a prerequisite to understanding and being understood through spoken language, and which view language use as distinct from and secondary to an a priori grammar. In this article I will present some of the arguments in its favor and discuss examples of usage that lend themselves to explanation along emergent grammar lines. I will also discuss the thinking behind emergent grammar that brings linguistics into alignment with current ideas in other language related and social science fields.

Emergent grammar has in the past two decades become absorbed into a general movement that arose in opposition to sentence-level approaches to linguistic structure. Since the opening statement of emergent grammar in Hopper (1987), some of its premises have been incorporated, either tacitly, explicitly, or independently, in other approaches, including conversational analysis (Ochs *et al.*, 1996) and interactional linguistics (Couper-Kuhlen and Selting, 2001).

Emergent grammar arose in the context of a perceived impasse in discourse and grammar studies in North America. During the 1970s and 1980s, mainstream grammatical theories denied the need or even the existence of language-external motivations for grammatical rules: rules generated grammatical sentences, and sentence-level grammaticality justified the rules. Grammar was autonomous—linguists did not investigate "performance" (what speakers *did* do) but rather "competence" (what speakers *could* do); competence so understood strongly implied that grammar was a self-contained, autonomous system. A leading defender of the autonomy of sentence grammar has been F. Newmeyer, whose view is summed up by Butler (2003: 21) as follows: "What the argument boils down to is this: the syntax of a language is a system in its own right, and in order to specify this system we do not need to (and, Newmeyer would claim, we should not) incorporate explanations of why it is the way it is."

In the 1970s a functionalist school made its appearance in North America and elsewhere that began to see the possibility for discourse explanations of grammatical facts established on the basis of isolated sentences. At first, this project supplemented rather than replaced structural grammar. Discourse provided an explanation for rules that were needed in any case. Functionalists pointed out many examples of linguistic phenomena that brought into question whether syntactic rules stated at the sentence level could exhaustively cover all the facts about sentences. Nonetheless, it was often assumed that discourse intruded on sentence structure only in minor ways, such as through the use of particles and sentence connectors, and that "nothing here denies the validity of sentence grammar within its own domain" (Grimes and Glock, 1970: 415). However, the sentence remained the site of core grammatical processes. Questions involving the relationship of discourse to sentences became especially cogent when a complete account of a sentence had to include semantic and pragmatic, that is, contextual, factors—a demand that, by the 1970s, was to a greater or lesser extent required of all theories.

The attention to texts highlights a second aspect of linguistics during the two decades in question: the issue of the appropriate data for the investigation of language. Syntacticians held firmly to individual sentence structure, validated by a criterion of grammaticality. Grammaticality was determined by introspection: a sentence was judged to be grammatical and therefore admissible as datum if the analyst declared it to be so. Introspection—the consultation of one's own inner grammatical knowledge—provided a ubiquitous and readily available source of data. Discourse linguists wishing to find and contextualize examples of grammatical constructions, on the other hand, were obliged to delve into long texts and count examples. Until electronically stored corpora and high-speed search software became available in the 1990s, doing discourse and grammar entailed working laboriously through book-length texts. Narrative appeared to exemplify the most neutral and concrete uses of language, and much early work along these lines was done on the basis of novels and stories in various languages. Later, precise transcripts of conversations became the standard source of natural language data.

By the mid-1980s a faultline had become apparent between two schools of thought that referred to themselves as *functionalists* (discourse-based linguists) and *formalists* (sentence-level syntacticians). In actual fact, the membership of both of these groups was quite diverse,[2] but a certain rivalry had sprung up, each school attempting to control how the other was to be defined. The alleged goal of functionalists was to replace grammatical rules with statements about discourse functions, indeed to establish that, once all the relevant facts about discourse pragmatics were known, grammatical rules would be redundant. This supposed agenda, formalists argued, was vulnerable to a *functionalist fallacy* (Newmeyer, 1983; Sadock, 1984): the match between sentence form and discourse function must be perfect. It was indisputable that syntactic facts often went in parallel with discourse ones. But functional statements could only successfully replace syntactic rules if it could be demonstrated that there were no autonomous syntactic facts. It would take only one instance of a syntactic fact that could not be replaced by a functional statement to bring down the entire theory.

Functionalists had never stated things in such radical terms. Still, the ongoing debate called for some way of reconciling two extreme positions: (1) grammatical rules were purely autonomous and insulated from discourse factors, and (2) syntactic rules could always be restated as functional principles that were secondary to strategies for building discourse. One response to this dichotomy was in fact already a standard assumption: language was partly functional and partly structural. This position has been restated by Givón (1999) on the axiological grounds that allegedly "extreme" (i.e. consistent) theoretical positions must be resolved through a compromise. Linguists would need to work both ends of the field in order to obtain a comprehensive view of language. But for many functionalists this was an uncomfortable concession, for it left the formalist agenda untouched. If grammatical rules were always needed, functional investigations could be indefinitely postponed, or even dismissed as irrelevant. In effect, there would be no motivation for linguists to study functions: this task could be left to psychologists and sociologists, or to one of the hyphenated fields (and indeed, discourse linguistics was often bundled with "sociolinguistics" in the catalogues of linguistics departments at this time). Moreover, the precise distribution of labor between formal rules and functional principles was never made clear.

Evidently, the problem lay not in the relationship between grammar and discourse but in the concept of grammar itself. Functionalists shared with formalists the standard view that speakers of a language communicate by virtue of a uniform common grammatical system. Disagreement only occurred over the source of this grammar—discourse pragmatics or mental structures. The validity of this assumption, which by some has come to be called the *fixed code* (Harris, 2003) or *a priori grammar* (Hopper, 1988) theory, was rarely questioned; yet, when examined, it was found to be full of paradoxes. One of these was that (as sociolinguists often pointed out) language variation in speech communities was normal and pervasive; how could this fact be reconciled with uniform grammatical representations? Another paradox was that the forms of fast interactive talk—the natural domicile of language—did not in any way resemble the stilted complete sentences of formal grammar. It had often been noticed that formal syntax took written forms as its model. Increasingly in the 1980s linguists began to realize that written language was not, as had previously been assumed, merely a graphic representation of speech, but was a specially developed artifact, whose rules of formation had evolved in exceptional cultural settings. A comprehensive statement of this observation by Per Linell, with the challenging title *The Written Language Bias in Linguistics* (Linell, 2005), arguing that the entire enterprise of linguistics as it had been formulated was derivative of the written representation of language, had been in circulation in an earlier form since the early 1980s. This recognition meant that linguists were obliged to take seriously a thesis to which many had previously paid lip service: the priority of speech over writing. Speech as it was normally encountered did not come in the form of planned solo monologues, but was *interactive*. The back-and-forth of normal conversation with its complexly signaled turn-taking placed quite different demands on theories from those offered by the solitary, thought up, decontextualized sentences that comprised the data of formal grammars.

The 1980s also saw increasing attention being paid to a facet of the study of language that had lain dormant for several decades. Grammaticalization, the process whereby new grammatical forms came into being, had long been the province of Indo-Europeanists and others concerned with historical changes. Interest in grammaticalization had receded before the resolutely synchronic orientation of post-war formalists. It now became a major project of functionalists. The study of grammaticalization pointed toward a more open-ended, diachronic conceptualization of grammar that undermined the synchronic fixed code idea and suggested that some provision had to be made for the fact that grammar was always changing, in fact that grammar was unstable and that the "system" was being constantly updated. In focusing on the interface between structure and usage, grammaticalization opened up the prospect that, if change was a constant feature of language, even ordinary spoken discourse would have to be seen as temporal (Hopper, 1992; Hopper and Traugott, 2003; Bybee, 2007).

Attention to fixed expressions was another theme that began to be developed strongly in the 1980s, in opposition to the idea that arrangements of words were governed solely by category membership, instead of by actual lexical preferences. A number of linguists recognized the important role of fixed phrases and formulae in the construction of discourse (Pawley, 2007 provides a helpful account of this trend). Again, this was not a new idea, but the increasing attention to corpus studies and usage moved it into a more empirical realm. Pawley and Syder (1983) argued that the sort of quick access required by fluent speaking presupposed that much of language is ready at hand in the form of prefabricated expressions. From the perspective of emergent grammar, speakers draw on previous experiences with other speakers in producing their own utterances, in the form of repeated phrases passed around among speakers in comparable social circumstances. These phrases are fragmentary sequences that may or may not conform to the structures devised by standard grammarians. Discourse proceeds by piecing together these fragments into forms prescribed by the norms that govern that particular interaction. These norms are not rules, but something much more flexible and negotiable. Speakers assemble utterances in the same way that they go through any other routine, in a culturally familiar process that is not precisely known in advance but also not blind, and is guided by the constant ratification of interlocutors.

To summarize, emergent grammar was conceived as an alternative to fixed-code grammar. Fixed-code grammar assumed that grammar logically preceded discourse. Emergent grammar inverted this premise by placing the fact of interactive communication first and seeing structure as a secondary by-product of the interaction. Emergent grammar was a Gordian knot solution to an impasse: since no agreement on the nature of a priori grammar and its relation to discourse is possible, let us *postulate* that grammar is not a priori at all, but is epiphenomenal to the primary fact of communication. Where would the adoption of this postulate lead linguistics? What advantages would it have over a priori assumptions about grammar?

Now a postulate is not a guess, not a mere stab in the dark. The emergent grammar position was supported, and indeed inspired, by much thinking outside of linguistics during the 1970s and 1980s. Later I will discuss some of the contemporary issues surrounding language and social structure that provide a historical and general intellectual context for emergent grammar.

Grammar from an emergent grammar perspective

When grammar is viewed from the perspective of its emergence in conversational texts transcribed from real time spoken interactions, significant differences from sentence-level grammar are apparent.

First, the grammatical structures that emerge out of discourse do not coincide with those developed from sentence-only observations. So one project is that of reformulating the already existing analyses in discourse terms. Actually spoken discourse is fragmentary and oriented towards the ad hoc communicative needs of the current interaction. The constructions characteristic of preformulated, preplanned utterances are longer, more complete and more consistent in shape than those found in spoken interactions. However, the resemblances between such "canonical" constructions and fragmentary sequences are partial and inconsistent from example to example.

Secondly, these sequences are themselves prelearned. They derive from interactive situations that are themselves part of the speakers' previous experience. To the extent that they are liberated from these situations, they may possess a certain, very limited provisional cognitive stability and cross-generic usefulness, properties that are sustained by artifacts such as prescriptive grammars and dictionaries and that may be mistaken for fixed grammar and morphology. However, this fixing is itself never uniform across all speakers in all situations. Real language is *distributed* over space and over occasions of use. It may be convenient to ignore variant styles, genres, places, situations, and speaker-groups in describing a language. But, if we are to take seriously statements about "the" language, it must be conceded that the wider the range of phenomena that must be accounted for, the smaller the inventory of forms common across all speech events must become— grammar contracts as texts expand. This fact makes the cataloguing of the entire inventory of rules and forms in a language a futile task. As Roy Harris has put it, we are not entitled to assume "that at any point in the ongoing diachronic flow we can in principle stop and draw up an inventory of the current linguistic facts" (Harris, 2004: 183). This in turn means that a language, and therefore its grammar, are essentially incomplete, a fact long recognized by anthropologists and anthropologically inclined linguists (see e.g. Grace, 1988). The intrinsic incompleteness of grammar is more than merely an inconvenient fact. It changes the nature of grammar, and therefore of the enterprise of linguistics. Emergent grammar is a proposal for "taking the temporality of spoken language seriously" (Auer, 2000).

Examples of emergent grammar

Since the hypothesis was first floated in the 1980s, a number of linguists have explored its possibilities in descriptive domains. The idea that structure follows rather than precedes ontologically the production of utterances might seem counterintuitive, and so a couple of examples will be presented and discussed.

Consider the well-studied English pseudocleft or *wh*-cleft construction (Quirk *et al.*, 1985: 1387–1389), which is standardly illustrated through sentences like:

What they dislike is the incessant rain.

Pseudocleft sentences consist of an initial clause, the *wh*-clause, and a follow-up clause introduced by *is* or *was*. It is generally held that such sentences are a version of a simpler transitive sentence:

They dislike the incessant rain.

In the pseudocleft version of such sentences the verb (here, "dislike") is assigned a strong secondary focus, and there is a primary focus on the direct object ("the incessant rain"):

what they `dislike* is the incessant ´RAIN.

In longer edited texts there is some justification for this analysis (Prince, 1978). However, when conversational discourse is examined, a different picture of the pseudocleft emerges. First, the contruction is no longer exclusively biclausal. Instead, the *wh*-clause is used alone in various interactive ways, for example to introduce a new theme, to claim a longer turn or to draw attention to an upcoming significant segment of discourse. The "second clause" (here:...*is the incessant rain*) now turns out to be no clause at all, but simply the continuation of the discourse opened by the *wh*-piece (*what they dislike*). In the following example (from the Santa Barbara Corpus),[3] a teacher named Sharon is talking about ways of dealing with large classes of children, in particular mixed third- and fourth-graders:

```
1   Sharon:   well,
2   →         what you do with those third-graders,
3             you know,
4             is you just like,
5             (H) take them,
6             and put them,
7             you know,
8             with one of the smarter fourth-graders,
9             who's very [ver]bal,
10  Carolyn:  [uh].
11  Sharon:   and (-) and well-beha=ved.
```

In line 2, Sharon introduces the theme of coping with third-graders, and then presents a solution. Notice that the follow-up, far from being the single clause required by the pseudocleft of sentence-level grammar, is an elaborate discourse segment. Significantly, there is no logical site for a focused element; instead Sharon has used the *wh*-clause "what you do with those third-graders" as a topic-introducer and launching pad for a recommendation. There are many examples of this sort of thing (e.g. Hopper, 2001; Günthner and Hopper, 2010). They require the standard grammatical analysis of the pseudocleft to be placed in an entirely new light, for the single clause follow-up can now be seen as simply one of a variety of possible continuations from the *wh*-clause. In the following example:

> ... But what they did bury in that freshly poured concrete,
> was one-inch steel water pipe

the pseudocleft appears in a form similar to that of the canonical pseudocleft, with the double focus on the verb (*did bury*) and the direct object noun phrase (*one-inch steel water pipe*). The speaker, the tour guide at a dam, is addressing the rumor that dead workmen were secretly buried in the concrete. This contrastive use of the pseudocleft, with a simple noun phrase as complement of *be*, is common in longer monologic texts. It is also especially prominent in writing, where the absence of phonetic stress removes the characteristic English means of signaling focus, and in rehearsed spoken texts. It is contexts of this kind that have made the noun phrase complement pseudocleft the prototype for the construction in syntactic studies; but in spoken language it is quite rare, being simply an unprivileged possibility. The biclausal pseudocleft is thus an emergent construction, one that owes its biclausality to a specific kind of discourse context.

Sentence-level approaches to grammar presuppose a holistic, bird's-eye view of a sentence in which the beginning, the middle and the end are apprehended simultaneously. Natural discourse rarely proceeds in this way, however. Discourse is rather an unfolding in time (Franck, 1985; Hopper, 1992; Auer, 2000, 2009; Günthner and Hopper, 2010). We see this in extended utterances like that of Sharon above. She submits her contribution piece by piece, taking care to establish her current utterance with her audience before proceeding to the next. Her previous experience with spoken interactions guides her and supplies her with the means to do this. These means include the appropriate use of *like* and *you know,* and also a use of the verb *take* that works in a way that can only be understood in discourse terms (Hopper, 2007). Semantically, Sharon's *you just like take them* is empty of content in sentence-level terms. But pragmatically it serves to delay the delivery of her main point *put them/you know/ with one of the fourth graders.* The delay serves more than one purpose: it creates a suspension that enhances the focus on the main point; it provides a space for ratification by the interlocutors; and it reinforces Sharon's claim to an extended turn at talk.

It can be seen from this example that the resources of sentence-level grammar are inadequate in either structural or pragmatic terms for the interpretation of the discourse. Furthermore, the total inventory of grammatical constructions in a language is only manifest in real-time interactions, from which they are inseparable, since it is in fact only in interactive discourse that they can *become* constructions at all. Sentence-level structures are only indirect and impoverished reflections of the interplay of linguistic forms that emerge in oral discourse. Under the aegis of emergent grammar, language is viewed from the double perspectives of *interaction* and *temporality.* Sharon's discourse is structured the way it is because she is unfolding it in real time, in obedience to the imperatives of an audience whose ongoing endorsement (manifested here by Carolyn's *uh*) is essential to her ability to go on. Her *like* and *you know* are addressive forms that appeal for ongoing approval and permission to continue. She cannot deliver her speech as if it were a whole and bounded entity, but must offer it to her audience one fragment at a time for their authorization.

However, although she repeatedly renews the bond with her audience, Sharon speaks in confidence that she will be allowed to continue. In deploying the *wh*-clause of a pseudocleft, she at once lays claim to an extended turn. There is an asymmetry to conversational interactions that reflects an unequal power relationship (Fairclough, 2001). Some speakers are entitled to extended turns and some are not. Very frequently we find the use of the *wh*-clause of the pseudocleft to be the prerogative of speakers who in some sense are wielders of local authority. In this case we have a more experienced teacher interacting with less experienced, perhaps younger, teachers. But the *wh*-construction also figures conspicuously in a variety of other asymmetrical scenes: salesperson and client, tour guide and audience, office chief and subordinate, and so on. Grammar is rarely an innocent participant. It makes its appearance in different ways, in harmony with the endless variety of human interactions, from which it is inseparable. In other words, it is emergent.

Incrementality

Oral discourses are built up out of *increments,* out of which structure emerges as an epiphenome-non (for a recent discussion, see Couper-Kuhlen and Ono, 2007). A crucial difference between the view of grammar as emergent from texts and grammatical schemata as an a priori set of rules and lexical items is that, in the former, speakers and hearers are not seen as referring to anything fixed or preformulated, but rather to something *improvised* (Breier *et al.*, forthcoming), loosely modeling their utterances on utterances previously used and heard, which thereby provide a potential model for other utterances. In effect, each new utterance creates a new grammatical fact. Consider, as an example, Sharon's relative clause *who's very verbal/... /and well behaved.* It might in more literate terms be seen as a restrictive modifier to a head noun phrase *one of the fourth graders.* Yet it is added on to an already complete noun phrase. Moreover, the clause is itself bipartite, with two predicates (*very verbal* and *well behaved*). But these two predicates are not formulated as a complete conjoined single predicate in the way a standard grammatical description would have it: *[[very verbal] and [well behaved]].* Rather, each predicate is delivered separately in a different turn, interrupted by Carolyn's reactive token *uh.* And, finally, whether the modifier(s) are restrictive or non-restrictive cannot be determined without reference to the specific point in the delivery of the whole utterance at which this determination is to be made. There is a compound predicate here, but it is not preconceived as such; it is present only retrospectively, for the analyst, as a product of Sharon's real-time action in incrementing her first predicate *very verbal* with a second one *and well behaved.* Again, the structure here is emergent.

The degree to which spoken language is incremental in this way is obscured by the evolution of written conventions, with their intricate embedded clauses. The study of discourse in preliterate or newly literate languages suggests that speech in such cultures is performed through the simple addition of formulaic phrases rather than through reference to complex grammatical rules.

Projection

The speaker and the hearer at the leading edge of an utterance have two perspectives: a recent memory of what has been said, and an anticipatory "pre-memory" of what is about to be said. The recovery of a previous referent from a current form—anaphora—is a process familiar to all students of grammar. It accounts for many uses of pronouns, for example. The corresponding forward-looking process known as cataphora has received less attention, as it is much less common and is often considered to be secondary to movement rules. (For example, in *Before he set off for Louisville, John bought a road atlas*, the cataphoric pronoun *he* is allegedly to be understood as an underlying anaphor: *John bought a road atlas before he set off for Louisville.*)

An important methodological concept in the analysis of spoken grammar has been *projection,* the ways in which speakers mold their utterances so that hearers can anticipate and thus prestructure a segment of discourse (Auer, 2005). The idea of projection is associated with the study of spoken language (Liddicoat, 2004). The term has its origin in conversation analysis,[4] where projection refers primarily to the combination of semantic, syntactic, and prosodic resources that alert listeners to the end of the current speaker's turn at talk. The term has been extended to a more general sense, the strategies for foreshadowing upcoming discourse. As such, projection plays a central role in discourse analysis. Without it, utterances would either be detached from a communicative event entirely, or utterance sequences would be predetermined and devoid of communicative value (Auer, 2005). Projection is what makes verbal communication an open and collaborative affair; as participants develop a sense of where the discourse is going, they can tacitly mold it, allow it to continue, harmonize with the speaker's goals, interrupt it with their own contribution, offer supportive tokens of various kinds, or predict when their turn will come.

The scope of a projection can be local, that is, short range, or more extensive. Short-range projections are quite exact, and they are made possible by idiomatization. The following exchange is quite typical. In it, Doris has told how the air was so thick during a dust storm that the car headlights were green:

1	DORIS:	… Yeah.
2		they just looked green.
3		… It was a wei=rd.
4		.. ugly.
5		.. ugly day.

In lines 1 and 2 Doris is winding down her story about the unsettling weather. She then sums up her story with three comments (lines 3–5) that are marked with utterance-final intonation (transcribed with a period/full stop). A standard sentence-level analysis would edit out the intonations and the turn-completions and present Doris's utterances as something like: *It was a weird, ugly, ugly day.*

But such an analysis would miss the point that *ugly* in line 4 replaces *weird* in line 3, and that *ugly* in line 5 confirms the replacement. The two adjectives do not belong in the same noun phrase (NP) because they are doing different work. They come in at different times and with different pragmatic assessments. Yet the indefinite article *a* in line 3 projects the noun *day* in line 5; that is to say, the interlocutor, on hearing *a* (or perhaps the sequence *a weird*), now anticipates the delivery of a noun that will resolve the projection and fulfill the formula *a^MODIFIER^day*.

Is there, then, an "NP" *[a weird ugly ugly day]* (Figure 21.1)? The answer to this question is yes, but it is an emergent NP, existing as a linguistic phrase only after the fact of its complete utterance, and retrospectively creating an ad hoc formula *[a^MODIFIERi^MODIFIERj^MODIFIERj^day]*. Clearly such formulae are not entirely novel. They are not thought up *de novo* in every instance. Rather, they are modeled on phrases that are actually remembered in a form that is identical or very similar to previously used and previously heard phrases, such as *a weird day* and *an ugly day*. The mechanism by which this is accomplished is analogy. As was maintained by Hermann Paul (1970 [1901]), analogy is the only mechanism needed to explain both novelty in

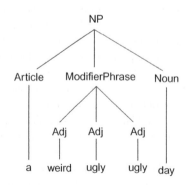

Figure 21.1 The 'noun phrase' *a weird ugly ugly day*

form and successful communication. Analogy also adequately explains projection, in that the anticipation of form relies on familiarity with that form on the part of both speaker and hearer. Familiarity does not have to be precise, any more than routine expectations of any kind between interactants are precise, nor does an experience have to be recalled exactly in order for it to be recognized as a repetition or a variant of some previous experience. But each variant of a formula can serve as the basis for a new formula. Such variants can consist of *substitutions* of words.

What key insights about grammar has the decision to focus on the emergent and temporal nature of structure brought to light?

The emergent grammar theory postulates an inversion of the usual relationship between a rule and a practice, one that is closer to Wittgenstein's analysis in the *Philosophical Investigations*. In this analysis, rather than speakers' practice being governed by rules, it would be more accurate to say that rules are created and sustained by agreement among speakers during acts of communication. "Rather than to say that we agree because we follow rules, it is more perceptive to say that our agreement fixes the meaning of the rules, defines their content" (Malcolm, 1967: 338). "Grammar" has its source in two very general linguistic processes: *repetition* and *routinization*. But repetition is a basic mechanism of speech, the appropriation of the discourse of others. As such, it may take the form of formulas and fixed expressions, as discussed above, as well as of macro–rhetorical moves. But, at a more minute level, repetition includes grammar (syntax) and morphology, which, being involved with essentially every utterance, are constantly being reintroduced into discourse and thus reappear insistently, to the point where they seem to form a necessary, a priori grammatical system. But the apparent system is in fact the result of what Coseriu (1974 [1958]) called the "constant restructuration" of language during usage.

   Not infrequently, when even quite robust grammatical patterns and constructions are examined in their detailed discourse contexts, they are found to be not so systematic as they seem in retrospect to be. A good case in point is Chatterjee's study of verbal aspect in several languages (Chatterjee, 1988): the "rules" that are formulated for the use of aspects are seen on close examination to be shot through with exceptions and indeterminacies (pp. 45–55). These cannot be dismissed with the facile observation that "grammars leak"; exceptions do not demonstrate the validity of a rule, rather they call the rule into question (that is, they "prove" the rule—"prove" in the older (Latin) sense of *probare* "put to the test").

   Language routines are subject to local cultural norms, that is, they are customs that differ from community to community. Moreover, because grammar is intertextual in a wide sense of "text," some of grammar belongs in the sphere of cultural uniformity. The emergent grammar perspective insists on the essential localness of linguistic forms and understands this wider uniformity as something more accidental and random, originating in small-scale detail, rather than as the overarching *langue* implicit in most other linguistic theories. Of course, there is widespread agreement among speakers concerning useful and acceptable forms of repetition. But, while mass media and standardized education may supply an increasing amount of new language to the wider population, new forms must first be ratified at the local level, in person-to-person interactions. This bottom–up approach to linguistic structure has many implications for well-known phenomena that have been inadequately explained in terms of a basic uniform grammatical system, such as applied linguistics and code-switching (see Linell, 2005). The ability to project upcoming discourse is tied closely to culturally informed expectations. H.-G. Gadamer noted:

"The anticipation of meaning that governs our understanding of a text is not an act of subjectivity, but proceeds from the communality that binds us to our own tradition ... Tradition is not simply a precondition into which we come, but we produce it ourselves, inasmuch as we understand, participate in the evolution of tradition and hence further determine it ourselves."

(quoted in Margolis, 1993: 185)

Projection has profound implications for the study of grammar. Indeed, we might view grammar as precisely the open-ended strategic routines that in certain discourse situations permit inferences about the future course of an utterance to be drawn (by hearers) or made (by speakers). Grammar is emergent because inferences are not rule-like or lexicon-like entities that are preformed and predetermined, and so the relationship between a projected inference and the form of an utterance is always a function of an interactive communicative situation. Speakers understand spoken discourse by virtue of a combination of inferences and familiarity, both guided by previous experiences. Like politics, all grammar is local.

One of the most striking manifestations of emergent grammar is the transitory, unstable nature of linguistic categories. An early study in emergent grammar (Hopper and Thompson, 1984) argued that the major categories noun and verb (NV) were not fixed entities as required by most linguistic theories, but that forms approached full categorial status according to the degree to which they fulfilled their prime discourse functions. For nouns, this function was to introduce a new, previously unspecified participant into the discourse. For verbs, it was to report a new, foregrounded event. Forms assumed the external attributes of noun or verb respectively only as they took on these functions. These attributes consisted of things like case, number, and gender suffixes for nouns, and tense, aspect, and modality markers for verbs. Thus it is not uncommon for nouns to appear in a base root or stem form when they made no specific reference, a situation common for example in English in the first part of NV compounds like *boat-building*, *dog-barking*. Verbs tended similarly to appear in an uninflected form when they referred to an event (as opposed to reporting it), as in *finding a bilingual inscription was an important step*, where *finding* is indifferent to tense, aspect, or modality. But specific reference and eventhood are not determined in advance of the discourse occasions. Again, category assignment is emergent rather than a priori.

Subsequent linguistic studies questioned the fixed status of other categories. The dividing line between definite article and demonstrative was fuzzy in many languages, and indeed in some languages that were alleged to lack a definite article a close analysis of the discourse contexts of the demonstrative showed that in the right contexts demonstratives could behave in ways that were indistinguishable from the definite articles of languages where article and demonstrative were morphologically different (see Laury, 1997, for Finnish; Huang, 1998, for Chinese). Similarly, under some discourse conditions, indefinite articles may emerge out of noun classifiers (Hopper, 1995, for Malay, Tao, 1999, for Chinese).

The principle of emergent structure has been extended from grammar to phonology (Hopper, 1990, 1994; Copeland, 1994; Bybee and Hopper, 2001), lexicon (Bybee, 1998), and semantics (Huang, 1998; Tao, 2003).

Emergent grammar in the context of recent language theory

While the theory of emergent grammar came about in response to a need to rethink the relationship between grammar and texts, this enterprise was not unaffected by completely parallel developments in other disciplines. The reinstatement of time was an especially significant common factor in this revisionist movement. Jacques Derrida's notion of *différance* (Derrida, 1982) captured the idea of a linguistic sign that is extended over time, and combined the notions of difference (contrast) and deferral (that is, the full meaning of a sign is constantly "deferred" to the next occasion of use). Michel Foucault pointed to the dangers of a too narrow definition of history: "We should avoid thinking of emergence as the final term of an historical development" (Foucault, 1977: 148). Foucault's comment was in line with the idea of linguistic structure as emergent, that is, as being intrinsically incomplete and unfinished; "history" normally refers to longer time spans, but there is no principled reason why it should not apply to periods measured in seconds rather than years. In the second chapter of *The Archeology of Knowledge* (1972), Foucault actually comments on grammar in terms that could be taken to anticipate emergent grammar directly:

> Must we admit therefore that grammar only *appears* to form a coherent figure; and that this group of statements, analyses, descriptions, principles and consequences, and deductions that has been perpetrated under this name for over a century is no more than a false unity? But perhaps we might discover a discursive unity if we sought it not in the coherence of concepts, but in their simultaneous or successive emergence, in the distance that separates them, and even in their incompatibility. We would no longer seek an architecture of concepts sufficiently general and abstract to embrace all others and to introduce them into the same deductive structure; we would instead try to analyse the interplay of their appearances and dispersion.

The influence of continental thought was also manifested in an interest in Heidegger and the idea of language as embodied (Fox, 1999).[5]

Another congener of emergent grammar was a group of linguists of the school of Roy Harris, whose ideological basis was an integrational view in which language was an inseparable component of communication rather than a "segregated" system (see Harris, 1998). Although this theory (known to its followers as integrationalism) went further than emergent grammar in refusing to recognize a discrete level of "language" at all, its promoters agreed with the emergentist position in seeing linguistic signs as ontologically secondary to the process of communication.

Further reading

Couper-Kuhlen, E. and Thompson, S. A. (2005) 'A linguistic practice for retracting overstatements: concessive repair', in A. Hakulinen and M. Selting (eds.) *Syntax and Lexis in Conversation: Studies on the Use of Linguistic Resources in Talk-in-Interaction*. Studies in Discourse and Grammar, vol.17. Amsterdam: John Benjamins, pp. 257–288).

This is a study of retraction—taking back something one has said. The article, while making a technical point about a single conversational tactic, well exemplifies the ideas, data and methods of conversation analysis. The authors conclude that "constructional formats emerge from interactional needs."

Weber, T. (1997) 'The emergence of linguistic structure: Paul Hopper's emergent grammar hypothesis revisited', *Language Sciences*, 19 (2): 177–196.

Weber places the emergent grammar hypothesis in the wider context of late twentieth-century post-structuralism, citing the deconstructivist school of Jacques Derrida and the idea of the temporal displacement of the sign. He argues that the formal schools of Chomsky, Searle, and others have so far failed to respond to the challenge offered by emergent grammar.

Linell, P. (2005) *The Written Language Bias in Linguistics*. London: Routledge.

This classic work had been in circulation in an earlier form since 1982. The revised and expanded form presents 101 topics arguing in each case when the way of thinking about language in "linguistics" is suffused with a more or less unconscious allegiance to written forms. Linell notes that emergent grammar supplies an alternative to theories that are grounded in written symbols (p. 217).

Auer, P. (2009) 'On-line syntax: thoughts on the temporality of spoken language', *Language Sciences*, 31: 1–13.

This influential paper, first published in German in 2000, was originally subtitled "Or: What it could mean to take the temporality of spoken language seriously." It presents an empirical study of the emergent grammatical structure of spoken language by using German conversational data. It is important for its method and for its insistence on three essential features of spoken language: that it is *transient, linear,* and *synchronous* (i.e. coordinated with other speakers).

Auer, P. and Pfänder, S. (eds.) (2010) *Emergent Constructions.* Berlin: Mouton de Gruyter.

An edited volume emanating from a conference held at the University of Freiburg in 2008. The papers illustrate a number of facets of Emergent Grammar focusing on the nature of the interface between grammatical constructions and usage.

Notes

1 I am grateful to the administration of the Freiburg Institute for Advanced Studies (FRIAS) for a Senior Fellowship in 2009 during which much of this article was written.
2 The internecine quarrels among formalists of different stripes at this time is described in Randy Harris's book *The Linguistics Wars* (1995).
3 Citations of data are from the Santa Barbara Corpus of Spoken American English (Du Bois *et al.*, 2000).
4 The prefiguring of actions has been studied under different names. Husserl's *protention*, a counterpart of *retention*, was central to his psychology of time-consciousness. Sinclair and his associates (e.g., recently, Mauranen and Sinclair, 2006) often refer to *prospection*, which is in concept identical to the conversation analysis school's *projection*.
5 The parallels between emergent grammar and late twentieth-century post-structuralist thought are laid out in Weber (1997).

References

Auer, P. (2000) 'On line-Syntax – oder: was es bedeuten könnte, die Zeitlichkeit der mündlichen Sprache ernst zu nehmen', *Sprache und Literatur*, 85: 43–56.
Auer, P. (2005) 'Projection in interaction and projection in grammar', *Text*, 25 (1): 7–36.
Auer, P. (2009) 'On-line syntax: thoughts on the temporality of spoken language', *Language Sciences*, 31: 1–13 (translation of Auer 2000).
Auer, P. and Pfänder, S. (eds.) (2010) *Emergent Constructions.* Berlin: Mouton de Gruyter.
Breier, T., Ehmer, O., and Pfänder, S. (forthcoming) 'Improvisation, temporality, and emergent constructions', in P. Auer and S. Pfänder (eds.) *Emergent Constructions.* Berlin: Mouton de Gruyter.
Butler, C. S. (2003) *Structure and Function: A Guide to Three Major Structural-Functional Theories. Part 1: Approaches to the simplex clause. Part 2: From clause to discourse and beyond.* Amsterdam and Philadelphia, PA: John Benjamins.
Bybee, J. (1998) *The Emergent Lexicon.* Chicago Linguistic Society 34: The Panels. Chicago, IL:Chicago Linguistics Society, pp. 421–435.
Bybee, J. (2007) *Frequency of Use and the Organization of Language.* Oxford: Oxford University Press.
Bybee, J. and P. Hopper (eds.) (2001) *Frequency and the Emergence of Linguistic Structure.* Typological Studies in Language, vol. 45. Amsterdam: John Benjamins.
Chatterjee, R. (1988) *Aspect and Meaning in Slavic and Indic.* Amsterdam Studies in the Theory and History of Linguistic Science, vol. 51. Amsterdam: John Benjamins.
Copeland, J. E. (1994) 'Unmotivated free alternation in Tarahumara: the principle of emergence in phonology', *Language Sciences*, 16 (1): 213–227.
Coseriu, E. (1974[1958]) *Synchronie, Diachronie, und Geschichte.* Munich: Fink (*Sincronia, diacronia, y historia: el problema del cambio linguistico.*, trans. H. Sohre), Montevideo: Universidad de la Republica, 1958.
Couper-Kuhlen, E. and Ono, T. (2007) ' "Incrementing" in conversation: a comparison of practices in English, German and Japanese', *Pragmatics*, 17 (4): 513–552.
Couper-Kuhlen, E. and M. Selting (eds.) (2001) *Studies in Interactional Linguistics.* Amsterdam: Benjamins.
Derrida, J. (1982) *Margins of Philosophy*, trans. A. Bass.Chicago and London: Chicago University Press.

Du Bois, J. W., Chafe, W., Meyer, C., and Thompson, S. A. (2000) *Santa Barbara Corpus of Spoken American English*. Part 1. Philadelphia, PA: Linguistic Data Consortium.

Fairclough, N. (2001) *Language and Power*. Second Edition. London: Longman.

Foucault, M. (1972) *The Archeology of Knowledge and The Discourse on Language*, trans. A. M. S. Smith. New York: Pantheon Books. (= *L'archéologie du savoir*, Gallimard 1969 and *L'ordre du discours*, Gallimard 1971.)

Foucault, M. (1977) *Language, Counter-Memory, Practice: Selected Essays and Interviews*, ed. and trans. D. Bouchard and S. Simon. Ithaca, IL and New York: Cornell University Press.

Fox, B. (1999) 'Directions in research: language and the body', *Research on Language and Social Interaction*, 32(1/2): 51–59.

Franck, D. (1985) 'Sentences in conversational turns: a case of syntactic 'double bind'' ', in M. Dascal (ed.) *Dialogue: An Interdisciplinary Approach*. Amsterdam: Benjamins, pp. 233–245.

Givón, T. (1999) 'Generativity and variation: the notion "rule of grammar" revisited', in B. MacWhinney (ed.) *The Emergence of Language*. Mahwah, NJ: Lawrence Erlbaum, pp. 81–109.

Grace, G. W. (1988) 'Why I don't believe that language acquisition involves the construction of a grammar.' *Ethnolinguistic Notes*, Series 4, No 1. Available at http://ww2.hawaii.edu/~grace/elniv1.html (accessed May 17, 2010).

Grimes, J. E. and Glock, N. (1970) 'A Saramaccan narrative pattern', *Language*, 46: 408–425.

Günthner, S. and Hopper, P. J. (2010) 'Die Pseudocleft-Konstruktion im Englischen und Deutschen', *Gesprächsforschung Online*. Available online at: http://www.gespraechsforschung-ozs.de/heft2010/heft2010.htm (accessed July 5, 2010).

Harris, R. A. (1995) *The Linguistics Wars*. Oxford: Oxford University Press.

Harris, R. (1998) *An Introduction to Integrational Linguistics*. Oxford: Pergamon Press.

Harris, R. (2003) 'On redefining linguistics', in H. Davis and T. J. Taylor (eds.) *Rethinking Linguistics*. London: Routledge, pp. 17–68.

Harris, R. (2004) *The Linguistics of History*. Edinburgh: Edinburgh University Press.

Hopper, P. J. (1985) 'A discourse function of noun classifiers in Malay', in Colette Craig (ed.), *Noun Classes and Categorization*. Typological Studies in Language, vol. 7. Amsterdam: John Benjamins BV, pp. 309–325.

Hopper, P. J. (1987) 'Emergent grammar', *Berkeley Linguistics Society*, 13: 139–157.

Hopper, P. J. (1988) 'Emergent grammar and the *A Priori* grammar postulate', in D. Tannen (ed.) *Linguistics in Context* (Collected General Lectures from the 1985 LSA Institute). Georgetown: Linguistics Institute, Georgetown University.

Hopper, P. J. (1990) 'Where do words come from?', W. Croft, K. Denning, and S. Kemmer (eds.) *Studies in Typology and Diachrony for Joseph Greenberg*. Amsterdam: John Benjamins, pp. 151–160.

Hopper, P. J. (1992) 'Times of the sign: on temporality in recent linguistics', *Time and Society*, 1 (2): 223–238.

Hopper, P. J. (1994) 'Phonogenesis', in W. Pagliuca and G. Davis (eds.) *Perspectives on Grammaticalization*. Amsterdam: John Benjamins, pp. 29–46.

Hopper, P. J. (2001) 'Grammatical constructions and their discourse origins: prototype or family resemblance?', in M. Pütz and S. Niemeier (eds.) *Applied Cognitive Linguistics: Theory, Acquisition, and Language Pedagogy*. Berlin: Mouton/De Gruyter, pp. 109–130.

Hopper, P. J. (2007) 'Emergent serialization in English: pragmatics and typology', in J. Good (ed.) *Language Universals and Language Change*. London: Oxford University Press, pp. 520–554.

Hopper, P. J. (forthcoming) 'Emergent grammar and temporality in interactional linguistics', in P. Auer and S. Pfänder (eds.) *Emergent Constructions*. Berlin: De Gruyter.

Hopper, P. J. and Thompson, S. A. (1984) 'The discourse basis for lexical categories in universal grammar', *Language*, 60 (4): 703–752.

Hopper, P. J. and Traugott, E. (2003) *Grammaticalization*. Second Edition. Cambridge: Cambridge University Press.

Huang, S.-F. (1998) 'Emergent lexical semantics', in Huang, S.-F. (ed.) *Selected Papers from the Second International Symposium on Languages in Taiwan*, pp. 129–150.

Huang, S.-F. (1999) 'The emergence of a grammatical category *definite article* in spoken Chinese', *Journal of Pragmatics*, 31 (1): 77–94.

Laury, R. (1997) *Demonstratives in Interaction: The Emergence of a Definite Article in Finnish*. Amsterdam: John Benjamins (Studies in Discourse and Grammar, 7).

Liddicoat, A. J. (2004) 'The projectability of turn constructional units and the role of prediction in listening', *Discourse Studies*, 6 (4): 449–469.

Linell, P. (2005) *The Written Language Bias in Linguistics*. London: Routledge.

Malcolm, N. (1967) 'Wittgenstein', in P. Edwards (ed.), *Encyclopedia of Philosophy*. Vol.8. New York: Macmillan, pp. 327–340.

Margolis, J. (1993) *The Flux of History and the Flux of Science*. Berkeley, CA: University of California Press.

Mauranen, A. and Sinclair, J.McH. (2006) *Linear Unit Grammar: Integrating Speech and Writing*. Amsterdam: John Benjamins (Studies in Corpus Linguistics 25).

Newmeyer, F. (1983) *Grammatical Theory: Its Limits and Possibilities*. Chicago, IL: University of Chicago Press.

Ochs, E., Schegloff, E., and Thompson, S. A. (1996) 'Introduction', in E. Ochs, E. Schegloff, and S. A. Thompson (eds.) *Interaction and Grammar*. Cambridge: Cambridge University Press, pp. 1–51.

Paul, H. (1970[1901]) *Principles of the History of Language*, trans. H. A. Strong. College Park: McGroth Publishing Company.

Pawley, A. (2007) 'Developments in the study of formulaic language since 1970: a personal view', in P. Skandera (ed.) *Phraseology and Culture in English*. Berlin: Mouton de Gruyter, pp. 1–43.

Pawley, A. and Syder, F. (1983) 'Two puzzles for linguistic theory: nativelike selection and nativelike fluency', in J. C. Richards and R. W. Schmidt (eds.) *Language and Communication*. New York: Longman, pp. 191–226.

Prince, E. (1978) 'A comparison of WH-clefts and IT-clefts in discourse', *Language*, 54: 883–906.

Quirk, R., Greenbaum, S., Leech, G., and Svartvik, J. (1985) *A Comprehensive Grammar of the English language*. Longman: London.

Sadock, J. (1984) 'Whither radical pragmatics?', in D. Tannen (ed.) *Round Table Conference on Linguistics*. Georgetown: Georgetown University Press, pp. 139–149.

Tao, H.-Y. (1999) 'The grammar of demonstratives in Mandarin conversational discourse: a case study', *Journal of Chinese Linguistics*, 27 (1): 69–103.

Tao, H.-Y. (2003) 'Toward an emergent view of lexical semantics', *Language and Linguistics*, 4 (4): 837–856.

Weber, T. (1997) 'The emergence of linguistic structure: Paul Hopper's emergent grammar hypothesis revisited', *Language Sciences*, 19 (2): 177–196.

22

Creativity in speech

Sarah Atkins and Ronald Carter

Creativity is a topic of contemporary interest across a range of fields. The focus of this chapter will be on linguistic creativity and how features of language that we might typically think of as occurring in literary, poetic or advertising discourses can also be identified in everyday spoken conversation. Much recent research suggests that linguistic creativity is a pervasive feature of everyday conversation; for example, these studies all look at the frequent creativity we find in spoken language (Cook, 2000; Carter, 2004 and Crystal, 1998). But what do we understand by 'creativity' when we make this claim about language use? The chapter will first outline, theoretically, what we might mean by 'creativity' and 'creative language'. We will then look at how this could be identified and analysed through textually focussed discourse analytic methods, discussing some specific examples of creativity in a spoken conversation between a group of friends. The analysis considers the functions that their creative language use might have in this particular social context, as well as the implications that such a close textual investigation might have on our understanding of creativity more generally.

What is creativity?

Defining creativity is a complex task. Social attitudes and understandings as to what it means to be 'creative' show considerable variation culturally and historically, and the word has undergone some semantic and morphological changes. Even contemporary approaches to researching the occurrence of creativity remain diverse in their theoretical points of departure and methodologies. One of the reasons for the difficulty in pinning down a precise definition or means of studying creativity is the mystical way in which it has been conceived:

> Creativity is a puzzle, a paradox, some say a mystery … many people assume that there will never be a scientific theory of creativity – for how could science possibly explain fundamental novelties.
>
> *(Boden, 1994)*

Pre-Christian views of creativity are interpreted as based in such mystical beliefs of divine inspiration, with the 'creative person … seen as an empty vessel that a divine being would fill with inspiration. The individual would then pour out the inspired ideas, framing an otherworldly product' (Sternberg and Lubart, 1999: 4–5). And, of course, the act of creation has associations with the creation of the world – the Latin words *creare* and *creatio*, from which the modern family of 'create'/'creation'/'creative' derives, were themselves used sometimes in late antiquity in the sense of 'divine creation'. In many creation stories language, in particular, has had deep associations with ideas of divine invention. For example, at Genesis 2: 19, the Christian notion of the origin of human language as a gift is expressed in Adam's being tasked by God to name the individual animals.

Modern conceptions of the agency of creation have shifted somewhat to emphasize its nature as a human source of art. Whether it be in the classical form of the 'Muse' and its modern invocations, or psychoanalytic theories of creativity as inspiration from the unconscious, the idea that the individual creative artist is seen as stimulated by a force larger than himself, external or internal, is pervasive:

> The 'other' that is 'dictating' might therefore be attributed to all sorts of agencies and influences; to a divinity or part of the psyche. ... to language and symbolic systems at large ... or to a historical moment, a political movement, an inner emotion or an outer motivation.
>
> *(Pope, 2005: 18)*

More recent theories on creativity present a problematized view of the privileged, autonomous creative subject. In contrast to traditional definitions of the mystical processes of creation, Marxist criticism has, for example, preferred to substitute the concept of literary production, emphasizing the material process of 'making' involved in creative work and deemphasizing this process as transcendental or the preserve of a single, individual subject. Further, a more democratized notion of creative agency emerges in recent theoretical work on creativity in terms of whose products we value in a society. For example, Willis *et al.* (1990) argues in *Common Culture* for an egalitarian aesthetic:

> In general the arts establishment connives to keep alive the myth of the special, creative, individual artist holding out against passive mass consumerism, so helping to maintain a self-interested view of elite creativity. Against this we insist that there is a vibrant symbolic life and symbolic creativity in everyday life, everyday activity and expression – even if it is sometimes invisible, looked down on or spurned. We don't want to invent it or propose it. We want to recognise it – literally re-cognise it.
>
> *(Willis et al., 1990: 1–2)*

The ability of communities, particularly youth subcultures in Willis's study, to create new forms and meanings from everyday spaces and practices is crucial to creating identity, as individuals and as groups (Willis *et al.*, 1990: 1). The question of what is 'valued' is key, though. Pope (2005) tentatively defines creativity as the capacity 'to make, do or become something fresh and valuable with respect to others as well as ourselves' (Pope, 2005: xvi). For an act to be understood as creative, then, it should be acknowledged and valued as such by a community, whether this be by an elite or a youth subculture as described by Willis *et al.* (1990).

To claim that valued creativity can be found in everyday conversation rather than being the preserve of high art and artistic 'otherness' is to make a case for a democratized notion of creativity. This is explicitly expressed by Carter (2004) as a feature of language use:

> linguistic creativity is not simply a property of exceptional people but an exceptional property of all people.
>
> *(Carter, 2004: 13)*

The ability to create new meanings and forms from everyday practices, here in the form of conversation, is an indication of how 'individuals and groups seek creatively to establish their presence, identity and meaning' (Willis *et al.*, 1990: 1). Further, since conversation is a collaborative activity, drawing on a shared system of communication, the notion of a privileged individual artistic subject is also problematized. Indeed, creativity can be seen as co-produced and locally evaluated within the belief and value system specific to the practices of a particular community's ways of writing and speaking. This means that creative language is seen as a shared activity, generated by a group as well as by an individual and as emergent within particular cultural or community norms. It also means that practices of creative language (co-)production are amenable to the techniques and practices of interactive spoken discourse analysis.

What is creative language?

In some sense, any of the language we use could be described as creative – there are very few fixed sentences that are used without variation (some examples of highly fixed sentences might be the formulaic utterances 'How are you?' or 'How do you do?') and we regularly create new words to account for new requirements in referencing the world around us. Good examples are the ways in which internet discourse has generated new language to meet newly evolving and emergent practices such as *download, wi-fi, blog* as well as the ways in which old words are given new meanings: *spam, virus, window, menu, wizard* (see Munat, 2007).

One of the creative resources of language involves the recursion of syntactic patterns in the construction of new meanings. Most of the language we use on an everyday basis is composed as we speak it and the particular text produced is likely to be new to the listener, but readily understood because of underlying rules for language choices that we share. This would seem to correspond the somewhat paradoxical idea that creativity needs to be novel but also appropriate. This is Chomsky's (1964) view on the generative creativity of all language users; a rule-governed linguistic competence, where a finite set of rules and elements enable an infinite set of outcomes. However, the generative approach to linguistic composition is restricted to looking at well-formed, often invented single sentences rather than at the naturally occurring conversational discourse we will be looking at later in the chapter.

What we are interested in here are the forms used in this particular conversational context that seem striking or innovative, which Chomsky's model does not address. This comes back to the issue of a particular artistic value ascribed to what we mean by 'creativity': when the word 'creative' is employed it entails uses which are marked out as striking and innovative. 'Conventionally, this involves a marked breaking or bending of rules and norms of language, including a deliberate play with its forms and its potential for meaning' (Carter, 2004: 9). What we are arguing then is that all speakers are linguistically creative, rather than this being the sole preserve of literary texts composed by skilled writers. But this democratized notion of 'literariness' occurring in spoken conversation does not in itself render our definition of creative language straightforward, since ideas about what constitutes 'literariness' similarly vary culturally and historically. Perhaps a good starting point for thinking about creative language is Jakobson's notion of the poetic function of language being 'a focus on the message for it's own sake', that is, where language draws attention to itself as a result of particular patterns being made especially salient (see Pratt, 1977; Maybin and Swann, 2007: 502; Ricoeur 2000 [1981]: 340).

The extent to which these linguistic features are highlighted can vary, determining a degree of creativity and aesthetic value. In this vein, Carter proposes a cline of literariness, suggesting that 'literary language' should not be thought of as a yes/no category and thus exclusive to particular artistic genres, but that we should consider 'a cline of literariness in language use with some uses of language being marked as more literary than others' (1987: 436–437). Thus attention to a particular linguistic organization such as repetitive patterning, or to lexical items deployed for their phonetic effect or associative meanings, could determine the place of a text, including conversational texts, along a cline of literariness. Certainly, some research seems to identify these kinds of literary patterns in spoken conversation. Coates notes 'patterns that could be called poetic' often occur in everyday conversational texts (1996: 230), and Carter too finds that 'ordinary language ... can involve ... the creation and interpretation of patterns which enjoy a family resemblance with those more usually designated literary' (2004: 24), such as irony, metaphor or hyperbole. These patterns are illustrated more fully below, and in the case study that follows in the section 'Creativity in context – a case study'.

The terminology we will be using in the following case study of creativity in context bases much of its analysis on Carter (2004), who proposes two levels of linguistically creative interaction: *pattern forming* and *pattern re-forming*. Pattern re-forming choices are 'more overt, presentational uses of language, open displays of metaphoric invention, punning, uses of idioms and departures from expected idiomatic formulations' (2004: 109), whilst pattern forming ones are 'less overt, maybe even subconscious' (2004: 109). The following study therefore differentiates between these creative forms and what functions these different levels of creativity fulfil.

In the context of a socially oriented discourse analysis, it is not unreasonable to ask what social functions these linguistically creative forms might be performing. Carter (2004: 8) proposes that, since creative language stimulates enjoyment, its occurrence in everyday talk can work to build an 'affective convergence or commonality between speakers'. Coates (1996) also addresses the idea of conversational language use as a pleasurable activity in maintaining close relationships. If linguistic creativity truly 'is a fundamentally egalitarian pastime' that 'brings people into a rapport with one another', (Crystal, 1998: 220), then we might expect to find it occurring frequently in the collaborative conversation of friends.

Creativity in context – a case study

We now move on to look at creative language use in the particular context of friendly conversation. We consider the function of creative language forms in this specific context as being to build collaborative relationships, but also to problematize the rather idealized and perhaps even stereotyped notion that all female friends converse creatively to establish solidarity. Coates, who argues strongly for talk being 'the central activity of women's friendship' (1996: 66), addresses the idea of their talk being a playful activity; 'talk is our [women's] chief form of recreation: we meet our friends to talk, and our talk is a kind of play. The conversations of women friends can be described as "jam-sessions"' (Coates, 1996: 1). In examining this 'play' she investigates a range of linguistic patterning in female conversations, such as repetition and simultaneous utterances, and considers them in terms of the kind of collaborative and egalitarian functions they perform.

This study therefore seeks to build on the work of Coates on the playful nature of conversation between female friends, but with a particular focus on its creativity and how creative strategies function within this social context. We assess whether spoken creativity can indeed be said to build an 'affective convergence or commonality between speakers' (Carter, 2004: 8) in all-female conversation or whether it performs a less collaborative function.

A group of three female friends, here named 'Helen', 'Laura' and 'Jess', were asked to record themselves talking with one another. The three women are close friends, what we could call in sociolinguistic terms 'a discourse community' (Swales, 1990). The particular mutual experiences of this small group include being students on the same university course and living together. The transcript comprises one hour of conversation and is given in extracts referred to below in the form *example number; line number*. One of us (Atkins) conducted a further interview with the three women, asking them to explain certain utterances that were difficult to understand and also questioning them about their own opinions of their conversation. This enabled the women to 'add their voices to mine (Coates's voice) in describing what was going on in friendly conversation' Coates (1996: 11). However, it also provided some tentative insights into what it is that they might value in their community in making linguistically creative utterances.

Pattern re-forming choices

Punning

Crystal suggests that speakers create puns 'as a source of enjoyment … And if someone was to ask why we do it, the answer is simply: for fun' (1998: 1). Certainly the amount of laughter elicited by these puns in the data would seem to indicate their entertaining quality, fulfilling a purpose of conversation identified in the women's interview to relax and 'just have a laugh' (Interview data). This fun 'brings people into a rapport with each other' (Crystal, 1998: 219): by laughing, the participants are signalling their enjoyment of the word-play and that they accept its socially cohesive function.

However, it is interesting that it should be the speaker Jess who produces most of the conversation's puns, a feature that might indicate that they have a function beyond entertainment. Puns draw attention to themselves and draw the attention of speakers and listeners in an overtly presentational verbal display (Carter, 2004: 97). This consciously presentational quality of puns would seem to suggest that the key user, Jess, is performing a particular role within the group by being their primary producer, perhaps signalling that she would like to be thought of as a speaker who is 'fun to be with' (Carter, 2004: 109). Eckert and McConnell-Ginet discuss the possible differing roles within a specific group of people who 'aren't all equally good friends with each other … Perhaps one of them has emerged as the leader, perhaps one of them is the joker' (2003: 58). Jess could be seen, through her overt language play, perhaps to be playing the role of 'the joker' in this group. This assertion of Jess's greater contribution to creativity would seem to contradict the traditional notion of the collaborative and egalitarian nature of women's conversation (see Coates, 1989; Maltz and Borker, 1982). To have a central creative speaker suggests an underlying power dynamic and hierarchy. However, this would also seem to complicate the more democratized notions of creativity discussed in the section 'What is creativity', since it does seem to be the case here that a more highly creative speaker emerges from the group. Whilst her creative language play is valued by the group and thus works to construct a more powerful position for her, it can be argued that it is in fact an already established powerful position that contributes to her ability to be more creative.

Re-forming lyrics

Both Tannen (1989) and Carter (2004) show speakers playing with formulaic utterances like proverbs and idioms deviating from expected patterns and creatively disfiguring them. However, rather than using formulaic utterances such as proverbs, what the speakers here often do is re-form lyrics from popular songs. For example, Jess adapts the lyrics of Tina Turner's 'Private Dancer', seen in Example 1:

Example 1

(Extract 6.32-39)	Tina Turner (1984): 'Private Dancer'
Jess: No no when you go on your private rambles	Chorus:
Helen: We don't go on many of [those though [I wish ((laughs))	
Jess: [((sings)) private ramble [ramble for	I'm your private dancer
money I'll do what you want me to do	a dancer for money
((laughter – 3.4 sec))	I'll do what you want me do
Jess: ((sings)) you're my private rambler	I'm your private dancer
((laughter))	a dancer for money

Like punning, this creative use of song lyrics elicits a great amount of laughter from the group, demonstrating their enjoyment of the creative adaptation. The cohesion it builds also stems from drawing on shared cultural knowledge of the original song. Intertextuality (reference to other texts) is a feature often discussed as occurring in literature (e.g. Coulmas, 2001: 234), but Bakhtin (1981: 338) also suggests that speakers in everyday conversations layer their texts with multiple voices and speaking styles, quoting other people and evaluating what they say. Within this particular conversation, it is the re-forming of song lyrics that seems to be particularly important to this creative layering of voices. The use of popular song lyrics in this manner occurs again elsewhere in the conversation, with the adaptation of Abba's 'Fernando' to refer a fern plant and 'Ooops upside the head' by Gap Band, which achieve much laughter and further cohesion through the other participants joining in the singing. Once again there is, hierarchically speaking, a central creative speaker, Jess, but the creative forms she produces still achieve group cohesion.

Repetition

Repeated patterns are often considered to be a basic foundation of certain literary language forms like metre or rhythm, or of stylistic features like alliteration or parallelism (Finnegan, 1992: 90). Repetition is also a feature of everyday conversation that has been analysed by Tannen (1989) and Carter (2004), who see it as a one of the innately literary features of casual talk. Internal repetition is what underlies many of the creative patterns and processes within this conversation. It occurs at various levels from very localized forms within a single utterance, to more global, macro-levels over many speaker turns and over the conversation a whole.

Repetitions within a single speaker's utterance occur regularly in what Tannen (1989: 54) terms self-repetition. One common characteristic of self-repetitions seems to be repeating construction so as to set up an echo:

Example 2. Examples of self repetition

EXAMPLE 1 Jess: ...with Will Smith it's one guy and you fancy that one guy
(1.14-15)

EXAMPLE 2 Laura: she's like a page three model and she's the perfect page three
(1.21-22) model by the way and she's..

EXAMPLE 3 Jess: ...once it becomes like semi your room and you're (.) you're
(1.36-37) doing stuff in your room

This double repetition establishes a pattern of sound and syntactic structure and serves to highlight non-repeated words (Tannen, 1989: 75), such as 'perfect', slotted in between the repetition of 'she's [...] page-three-model'. Repetition is thus used to create a framework around which emphatic meaning and expression can be produced, a resource that would seem to confer some degree of linguistic power on the speaker, since it stresses their turn of the conversational sequence. It is interesting, therefore, that once again Jess is the one who forms the greatest number of these echoes. This confers her a degree of influence over turns in the conversation and again suggests there might be a power dynamic within this intimate group.

Example 3. Pattern reforming repetition

```
       A  +  B   B  +  A
Jess: ( nice from far )( far from nice )
```

A particularly striking repetitive pattern is example 3. This displays an inverted repetition pattern similar to one described by Coates (1996) 'reversing the order … allows the speaker to give a slightly different emphasis the second time and tells the recipients of the message to process it in two slightly different ways' (206). This is the effect of the formation above; the word 'far' is understood in a literal sense in the first segment to mean distance and in a figurative sense in the second to mean the person's appearance is not 'close' to being attractive. This is a more overt, pattern re-forming repetition than the echo formations that is designed to explicitly draw attention to itself as word-play.

Example 4. Progression of creativity from pattern forming to pattern re-forming

Laura: =chubby as well

Helen: Oh he likes to chase after chubby girls does he

Jess: He's a chubby chaser!
         ((laughter))

Laura: Have you seen Catherine too she's like the [skinniest woman in the world=

Helen: [what did you call her a chubby chaser?
         ((laughs))]

Laura: =can you imagine her complexion there when ((quickly)) complex like with cos
         she's skinny [all over so she's] got ((pause)) she's not got Fat but she's not got a=

Jess: [yeah mhmm]

Laura: =[Figure at the same] time she's not got like a chubby big bum or anything

Jess: [yeah a figure]

In this extract the repetition of 'chubby' is performed collaboratively, and eventually it leads to the formation of the alliterative 'chubby chaser'. Tannen's (1989: 54) study differentiates this type of repetition from the self-repetiton we saw above as allo-repetition, the repetition of others. She finds that '[r]epetition is a resource by which conversationalists together create a discourse a relationship … a limitless resource for individual creativity and interpersonal involvement' (1989: 55). Carter too finds that it suggests 'high degrees of affective connection and convergence' (2004: 101). Certainly we can see this sense of convergence here through the occurrence of other cooperative forms, such as the minimal responses 'yeah mhmm', alongside the repetition. The repetition of words and syntactical structure here achieves a rhythm and coherence to the text the speakers are creating together.

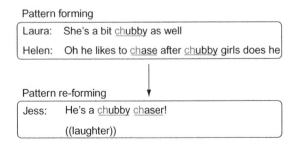

Whilst repetition across speaker turns is regarded as a less overt, pattern forming example of creativity, this often seems to progress to pattern re-forming creativity. For example, we saw this with the alliterative repetition of 'ch-' that led to the formation of 'chubby chaser' (see example 4).

It is remarkably frequent in this conversation, revealing perhaps that the two forms are intrinsically linked in this social context. Thus, whilst it is Jess who establishes most of the explicitly creative forms in the conversation, we can see that this accumulates from the less overt pattern forming creativity of previous speakers.

Example 6. Competitive repetition across speaker turns

However, pattern forming repetition is not always used for the purposes of collaboration. In this extract Jess and Laura have a disagreement on the topic of babies, using a repetitive pattern similar to that above.

Jess:	It's cute though, [any baby is cute
Helen:	[aww]
Laura:	I don't like it it looks like an old man baby
Jess:	Any kind of baby
Laura:	[I'm not with you on that one not any kind of- only cute babies are cute (.) and maybe if I have one my baby will [be cute regardless of
Jess:	[No but any kind of baby any kin any baby animal any baby

The two main speakers echo each other's statements but, rather than creating convergence, are expressing opposing opinions. This could be categorized as a mild form of verbal duelling, as in Gossen's (1976) study, where '[t]he rules of the contest are that each utterance must echo its predecessor phonologically' (Gossen, 1976 cited in Cook, 2000: 65). This is a more combative function of linguistic creativity, set within the conversation's collaborative forms, illustrating the close relationship between interactions of intimacy and competition (e.g. see Cook (2000) on Wolfson's 'bulge' model applied to creative language use). The duelling seems to be part of the women's entertainment. Nevertheless it still indicates a degree of power struggle within the group's apparently intimate and collaborative structure, displaying a characteristic that Pilkington (1998) recognizes – namely the fact that informal conversation 'enables members to 'covertly assert their status' (p. 256).

Establishing in-group language

What is striking is that a few of the women's creative forms begin to be repeated in a manner that suggests they are becoming formulaic, specific to this community of practice. Coulmas (2001: 234) notes that formulaic utterances can be specific to a particular community and may not be recognized outside that group. For example, Jess's pattern re-forming 'slap him upside the head', which manipulates a line from a song, requires an explanation on first encounter, but is then used later in the conversation with no explanation. The created form has thus become an established utterance within this particular conversation. This process of establishing phrases is not limited to a single conversation; utterances that have been created in previous conversations continue to be used later by the group. This is clearly apparent with references in the data to 'gardening with Britney Spears', the sexually euphemistic meaning of which must be explained to an outsider;

> it's something we came up with when we were watching [television]. ... he was interviewing
> Britney Spears ... she had these really red knees and then Laura said...that she'd been doing

lots of gardening … and we were like yeah right has Britney Spears been doing
GARDENING! … its kind of a phrase that's come to mean blow jobs.

(Interview with a member of the group)

The consequence of an originally creative euphemism like this becoming formulaic within the
group is that it develops a unique language for the women's community of practice. Only they are
likely to understand the phrase, because only they were present at the original formation. Such
unique language, inaccessible to outsiders, therefore signifies in-group membership (see also
Wenger, 1999 who has interesting things to say about a community's 'lore' and terminology).

Discussion and further directions

The study here contributes to the claims of recent research that finds casual talk to be inherently
and densely creative. Further it would seem to concur with the sense of group participation and
enjoyment by the speakers, and it relies much on this linguistic creativity. Identifying and
unpacking the creative features of conversation can therefore tell us much about how the group
of female friends here interact and perform particular roles within their social context. The relaxed
nature of the social context would seem to be what is fundamentally important here, since it is this
non-serious situation that allows word-play to take place and induces them to create a textually
coherent, convergent text. Most interestingly, the linguistic creativity seemed to establish a sense
of group membership among the women because its creative patterns established a language
unique to their community of practice, fitting with the notions of collaborative creation outlined
in the first two sections. Certainly it would seem to demonstrate that, linguistically at least,
'individuals and groups seek creatively to establish their presence, identity and meaning' (Willis
et al., 1990: 1). Nevertheless, the power dynamics at work here complicate our picture of
creativity, since it seems to be the case that there is a centrally creative speaker in the group and,
further, that the members use linguistic creativity to structure and win arguments amongst each
other at certain points in the conversation.

The focus of this chapter has been on casual conversation between friends, a context which
linguistic research has successfully demonstrated to be an important site of creativity. But the
importance of creative language in managing interpersonal relations extends to other contexts.
Especially important are the ways in which linguistic creativity is used in the workplace. Research
by Handford (2010) on the Cambridge and Nottingham Business English Corpus addresses how
creative problem solving and decision-making are managed in business meetings, looking in
particular at the linguistically creative forms of metaphor and idiom as part of this interpersonal
creativity. These features tended to be more frequent in internal meetings, since participants are
likely to have developed shared linguistic tools and discursive practices as a community internal to
the company. Frequently the creative forms are found to create convergence. However, as with
our analysis of casual conversation above, Handford (2010) and Handford and Koester (2010) find
metaphors and idioms also to be densely used in meetings involving disagreement and conflict.
The use of creative language forms in this context of business communication can, again, be seen
then to have the potential to foster intimacy, but also to assert power and status. Further research
into the transactional contexts of business interaction will therefore prove constructive in shaping
our understanding of the social purposes of creativity.

Another domain in which further research on linguistic creativity is proving fruitful is the
increasingly mobile and mediated modes of communication we now regularly use, such as the
Internet and mobile devices. These have drastically changed the mediating effects of physical
distance and require new linguistic competencies and creativities by participants to manage social

relationships. North (2007) looks at the ways in which wordplay and humour are used in online chatrooms to achieve social cohesion and to create a textually shared environment. This is crucially important in a context that, since it is online, is entirely textually co-constructed. Danet and Herring (2007: 27) note the drive for typographic innovation and linguistic play in computer mediated communication, across every language used online. As the platforms for interacting in virtual domains increase in uptake and variety, so the complex means by which people maintain social relations will shift too.

Research in these contexts extends the principle we began this chapter with: that is, researching creativity with a more democratized focus on the linguistically creative forms used between people in fostering social relations on an everyday basis. As research increases in this field of discourse analysis, our understanding of creativity in everyday language will become more nuanced and our understanding of what it means to be creative will necessarily be challenged.

Further reading

Carter, R. (2004). *Language and Creativity – The Art of Common Talk*. London: Routledge.

This book explores several approaches to creativity, and analyses creative uses of language in everyday interactions.

Handford, M. (2010). *The Language of Business Meetings*. Cambridge: Cambridge University Press.

Chapter 7 of this book deals specifically with 'interpersonal creativity' in a corpus of business meetings.

Cook, G. (2000). *Language Play Language Learning*. Oxford: Oxford University Press.

This book discusses how 'language play' can be observed in many contexts, and draws out the implications for language learning and teaching.

References

Bakhtin, M. (1981) 'Discourse in the novel', in M. Holquist (ed.) *The Dialogic Imagination*. Austin, TX: University of Texas Press.
Boden, M. (1994) *Dimensions of Creativity*. Boston, MA: MIT Press.
Carter, R. (1987) 'Is there a literary language?', in R. Steele and T. Threadgold (eds.) *Language Topics: Essays Presented to Michael Halliday*. Amsterdam: John Benjamins, Vol. 2, pp. 431–450.
Carter, R. (2004) *Language and Creativity – The Art of Common Talk*. London: Routledge.
Chomsky, N. (1964) *Current Issues in Linguistic Theory*. The Hague: Mouton.
Coates, J. (1989) 'Gossip revisited: Language in all-female groups', in J. Coates (ed.) *Language and Gender – A Reader*. Oxford: Blackwell, 1998, pp. 220–247.
Coates, J. (1996) *Women Talk*. Oxford: Blackwell.
Cook, G. (2000) *Language Play, Language learning*. Oxford: Oxford University Press.
Coulmas, F. (2001) 'Formulaic language', in R. Mesthrie (ed.) *The Concise Encyclopedia of Sociolinguistics*. Oxford: Elsevier, pp. 233–235.
Crystal, D. (1998) *Language Play*. Chicago: Chicago University Press.
Danet, B. and Herring, S. C. (2007) 'Introduction: welcome to the multilingual internet', in B. Danet and S. C. Herring (eds.) *The Multilingual Internet: Language, Culture and Communication Online*. Oxford: Oxford University Press.
Eckert, P. and McConnell-Ginet, S. (1998) 'Communities of practice: where language, gender and power all live', in J. Coates (ed.) *Language and Gender: A Reader*. Oxford: Blackwell, pp. 484–494.
Eckert, P. and McConnell-Ginet, S. (2003) *Language and Gender*. Cambridge: Cambridge University Press.
Finnegan, R. (1992) *Oral Poetry: Its Nature, Significance, and Social Context*. Bloomington: Indiana University Press.
Gossen, G. H. (1976) 'Verbal duelling in Chamula', in B. Kirschenblatt-Gimblett (ed.) *Speech Play*. Philadelphia, PA: Pennsylvania University Press, pp. 121–148. (Cited in Cook, 2000: 65).
Handford, M. (2010) *The Language of Business Meetings*. Cambridge: Cambridge University Press.
Handford, M. and Koester, A. (2010) ' "It's not rocket science": metaphors and idioms in conflictual business meetings', *Text and Talk*, 30 (1): 27–51.

Maltz, D. N. and Borker, R. A. (1982) 'A cultural approach to male-female miscommunication', in J. J. Gumperz (ed.) *Language and Social Identity*. Cambridge: Cambridge University Press, pp. 196–215.

Maybin, J. and Swann, J. (2007) 'Language creativity in everyday contexts', *Applied Linguistics*, 28 (4): 491–496 (special issue).

Munat, J. (ed.) (2007) *Lexical Creativity, Text and Contexts*. John Benjamins: Amsterdam.

North, S. (2007) ' "The voices, the voices": creativity in online conversation', *Applied Linguistics*, 28 (4): 538–555 (special issue).

Pilkington, J. (1998) ' "Don't try and make out that I'm nice!" – The different strategies women and men use when gossiping', in J. Coates (ed.) *Language and Gender – A Reader*. Oxford: Blackwell, pp. 254–267.

Pope, R. (2005) *Creativity: Theory, History, Practice*. Abingdon: Routledge.

Pratt, M. L. (1977) *Toward a Speech Act Theory of Literary Discourse*. London: Indiana University Press.

Ricoeur, P. (2000 [1981]) 'The creativity of language', in L. Burke, T. Crowley, and A. Girvin (eds.), *The Routledge Language and Cultural Theory Reader*. London: Routledge, pp. 340–344 (re-published 2000).

Sternberg, R. J. and Lubart, T. I. (1999) 'The concept of creativity: prospects and paradigms', in R. J. Sternberg (ed.) *The Handbook of Creativity*. Cambridge: Cambridge University Press.

Swales, J. (1990) *Genre Analysis*. Cambridge: Cambridge University Press.

Tannen, D. (1989) *Talking Voices: Repetition, Dialogue and Imagery in Conversational Discourse*. Cambridge: Cambridge University Press.

Wenger, E. (1999) *Communities of Practice: Learning, Meaning and Identity*. Cambridge: Cambridge University Press.

Willis, P., Jones, S., Canaan, J., and Hurd, G. (1990) *Common Culture: Symbolic Work at Play in the Everyday Cultures of the Young*. Milton Keynes: Open University Press.

Wolfson, N. (1988) 'The bulge: a theory of speech behaviour and social distance', in J. Fine (ed.) *Second Language Discourse*. Norwood: Ablex, pp. 174–196.

23

Spoken narrative

Mary M. Juzwik

Ms. Gomez (teacher):	Well, It's unfortunate, you know. As you get older, too, there are probably going to be things that come up, where people are going to try to take advantage of you, sometimes in a physical way. And will you be prepared for it? You know, I-my experience has been different growing up because I'm Mexican and I see the world through Mexican eyes. And I was taught that not everybody likes Mexican kids. And so I grew up being on guard around adults, around people. I have to watch out for that… Like let me give you an example. I was in the store the other day and the clerk was ignoring me. She was waiting on the person over here, and then she went to wait on the person over here, and after she did this twice and I had been there first, I spoke up. And I said, "Excuse me, am I invisible?"
Alice (student):	You said that?
Ms. Gomez:	Yes, to the clerk. And she looked at me. She said, "Oh I'm sorry." She said, I said, "I was waiting I was here first." And she wasn't going to acknowledge me until I spoke up…

This chapter overviews and illustrates methods, issues, and trends in discourse analytic approaches to spoken narrative such as this one, told by 7th grade teacher Susan Gomez[1] as part of literary discussion in an English language arts classroom.[2] The following questions organize the chapter: How do researchers entextualize a bit of discourse *as narrative*—that is, how do they make a selection from the infinite sea of discourse about what to designate as "narrative text," and so distinguish it from non-narrative discourse? How do researchers make decisions transcribing spoken narrative? What disciplinary approaches and constructs allow discourse analytic (DA) researchers of spoken narrative to conceptualize and approach analysis of narrative discourse such as this? How have approaches shifted and what new approaches are emerging?

Capturing and defining spoken narrative discourse

A challenge attendant on the very term "narrative" is that it tends to be used so pervasively in various research literatures and in everyday/ordinary language that many feel as though its meaning "goes without saying." If a discourse analyst hopes to focus analysis on spoken narratives in analysis, then defining that phenomenon is crucial for the credibility of the analysis. How, then, do narrative discourse analysts select what discourse counts as "narrative" from a data set inclusive of both narrative and non-narrative talk and texts? This question may initially seem arcane, trivial, or esoteric, but I believe its consideration is deeply practical for researchers who are new to the study of spoken narrative discourse.

Before addressing the technicalities and choices entailed in entextualizing a bit of spoken discourse as "narrative," it is useful to consider some broader distinctions related to the study of narrative. Scholars of oral and written narrative (e.g. Jakobson, 1971; Genette, 1980; Bauman, 1986; Wortham, 2001; Norrick, 2007) have distinguished between the referential content of the narrative (that is, the events that are being represented in a narrative text—such as the experience of being rendered invisible by a clerk in a store) and the interactional event of telling a narrative (the face-to-face or other interactional situation, in this case Ms. Gomez and her students sitting with their chairs arranged in a circle, doing "literary discussion"). We may refer to the former as "narrated event" and the latter as "narrative event." The discourse, or text, that takes shape in a narrative event, then, can be called a "narrative." But what distinguishes narrative discourse from other semiotic forms, functions, and activities?

A crucial tradition of defining narrative comes from the structuralist work of Labov (1972; Labov and Waletsky, 1967), who defines a minimal narrative as a series of at least two temporally sequenced, causally linked narrative clauses. Narrative clauses "recapitulate" an action event (often a simple noun/verb clause). Much of Ms. Gomez's narrative takes the form of an orientation that sets the scene for the confrontation described, but does not include narrative clauses. Following this logic, "Through Mexican eyes" does include the narrative or plot-driven clauses (with repetitions and elaborations excluded:

(a)   The clerk was ignoring me.
(b)   I spoke up.
(c)   And she looked at me.
(d)   She said, "Oh I'm sorry."
(e)   I said, "I was waiting, I was here first."

Clear temporal and causal movement connects (a) through to (e): as a result of the clerk ignoring her, Susan Gomez spoke up. This act of speaking caused the clerk to look at her and then to apologize. Ms. Gomez responded by stating her grievance: that an expectation for proper social behavior had been violated. It is useful to observe with this example how messy the process of parsing narrative identification can be, for example distinguishing between narrative clauses and other types of clauses within a narrative text.

Another complicated issue is determining where a narrative begins and ends. Why doesn't this particular narrative begin with the utterance "For example" rather than with "Well, it's unfortunate, you know"? I have demarcated the beginning of this narrative at different points for different analytic purposes. In the initial phase of narrative identification, colleagues and I identified its beginning as "I-my experience has been different." However, in re-visiting this narrative and a videotape of the narrative event for another analysis (Juzwik, 2010), I decided to rely on a phatic marker "Well" signaling a change in speaker (Bakhtin, 1986), but a continuation of an ongoing dialogue. This decision comported with the interactional focus of that analysis. For interactional researchers of spoken narrative, the change in speaking subject may be used as a satisfactory criterion for a narrative beginning; this is, however, a departure from the structuralist definition of narrative discussed above.[3]

To identify narrative beginnings (and endings) in the broader data set, we also relied on framing keys (Goffman, 1974)—discursive cues that narrative talk was beginning and ending. In fairy tales this is quite simple, as the phrase "Once upon a time" serves as a frame to signal a taleworld now beginning. In spoken narrative speakers often use abstracts to begin narratives. For example, after the initial phatic utterance, Ms. Gomez's warning to her 7th grade students introduces the topic of her narrative, "being taken advantage of," a theme from the literary text under discussion: "As you get older, too, there are probably going to be things that come up, where people are going to try to take advantage of you, sometimes in a physical way. And will you be prepared for it?" By cuing the gist of a narrative, an abstract can bring the audience immediately into the "so what" of a narrative. In conversational narrative events, openings can further function as bids for the floor, although teachers do not usually need to make such bids because they are typically assumed to have speaking rights most of the time, at least in classrooms. Students, however, often do need to make such bids. Some openings from the conversational narrative data set of which the opening narrative was part—which totals 145 narratives—include abstracts (e.g. "Well you think you can [tell if someone is pregnant],/ And you can't always tell"), conjunctive phrases (e.g. but, well, so, and), temporal locators (e.g. "One time I said," "I once babysat at a really dirty house"), and phatic phrases (e.g. "all right," "um," "see," "you know"). Further, because much narrative discourse is conversational and thus responds to prior narratives, narrators sometimes begin by repeating a word, phrase, or idea from a previous speaker/narrative (e.g. Ms. Gomez's "It's"). Other ways researchers discern endings of narratives are codas (Labov), which bridge between the narrated event and the narrative event and signal the narrative event is finished.

Beyond the structuralist criterion, it is difficult to set forth a definitive rule or procedure for identifying and demarcating narrative talk within all sets of spoken narrative data. However, the issue of identifying and defining narrative too often goes unaddressed in narrative discourse analytic research. Given the notional conceptions of story that circulate in public discourse and everyday language, and given the proliferating discussion about narrative analysis in the scholarly literature, a failure to define what one means by narrative can undermine analytic credibility. How narrative discourse was identified, for the purposes of a given narrative discourse analysis, should be addressed.

Transcribing spoken narrative discourse

The prose form of the narrative, such as the excerpt I presented above, is perhaps the most common way in which narratives are transcribed in my own field of educational research, and I suspect in other applied fields as well. But unbroken prose may not be the most useful way to transcribe narratives for discourse analyses of spoken narrative, unless the analysis focuses only on the lexical dimensions of the narrative. For most discourse analytic work (e.g. analyses beyond the word level), some level of breaking the transcript into smaller chunks is preferred in order to illuminate various discursive patterns.

Consider, for example, the following re-transcription of Ms. Gomez's "Through Mexican eyes."

Ms. Gomez
1. [WELL, It's] unfortunate,
2. you know.
3. As you get older too,
4. there are probably going to be things that come up
3. where people are going to try to take advantage of you
4. someTIMES in a physical way.
5. And will you be prepared for it?
6. You know,
7. I, my experience is dif-,
8. has been different growing up
9. Because I'm Mexican
10. And I SEE the world through Mexican eyes.
11. I was taught,
12. you know,
13. that not everybody LIKES Mexican kids.

14. And so I grew up being on guard around adults,
15. around people.
16. I have to WATCH OUT for that.
17. Because if I let my guard down,
18. and I've done that,
19. where I didn't think about it,
20. I wasn't paying any attention,
21. and somebody treated me unfairly.
22. And it,
23. then,
24. really makes me,
25. freaks me OUT
26. And it makes me uncomfortable,
27. when somebody's being prejudiced or something?
28. And I don't like not being ready for it
29. I'd RATHER,
30. I was explaining this to someone the other da:y,
31. I'd rather go into a situation EXPECTING to be treated unfairly
32. than go into a situation no-,
33. not expecting, thinking,
34. "Oh yeah, these are nice people,
35. Well, they're going to be nice to me."
36. Because,
37. when I'm not,
38. when I don't have my guard up,
39. I'm not prepared to answer back to somebody.
40. You know what I mean?
41. what I'm saying?
42. Like, let me give you an example
43. I was in the store the other day.
44. And the CLERK was ignoring me.
45. She was waiting on a person over here
46. And then she went to wait on a person over here
47. And after she did this TWICE
48. And I had been there FIRST,
49. I spoke up.
50. And I said,
51. "Excuse me,
52. Am I INVISIBLE?"
53. [And sh-
Alice: [You SAID that?
54. Yes, to the CLERK
55. And she looked at me.
56. She said,
57. "Oh, I'm sorry."
58. She said –
59. I said,
60. "I was WAITing,

61. I was here FIRST."
62. And SHE WASN'T GOING to acknowledge me
63. Until I spoke UP.
64. And it made me,
65. and it reminded me AGAIN
66. That there are people OUT there
67. That are going to try to take advantage of me,
68. and [be MEAN to me,
69. Being disrespectful to me.
Alice: [(That's like what happened to us too)]
Ms. Gomez: "Pardon?"

In this rendering I parse the narrative into small bits of language, what Chafe (1980) refers to as "idea units" (IUs) (cf. Scollon and Scollon, 1981; Gee, 1991). Idea units constitute "spurts of consciousness" that regulate the flow of information in discourse. To transcribe the narrative as shown above, I demarcated IUs by parsing them into lines. Relatively short (in Chafe's research, about six words on average), IUs are identified through (a) pauses: IUs are typically marked with a pause, sometimes brief and sometimes longer; (b) intonation: IUs typically constitute a single pitch glide ending with either a rise or a fall in pitch; (c) syntax: IUs tend to consist of a single clause, a verb with accompanying noun phrases. They also tend to begin with conjunctions (Chafe, 1980, p. 14): for example, Ms. Gomez relies heavily on "and" at places in the focal narrative excerpt, which I believe to be a characteristic of her "narrative style." Although Chafe argues that intonation is the chief most useful marker in identifying IUs, I along with Scollon and Scollon (1981) rely heavily on pauses. Stanzas are divided according to syntactic and thematic considerations (Hymes, 1981; Gee, 1989, 1991), analogous to paragraphs in prose. Stanzas mark shifts in perspective, topic, time, or dramatic shifts in intonation. Often, in the broader data set, temporal and orienting transitions signal the beginnings of stanzas, as do shifts in vantage point as indicated by shifting meanings of pronouns. Other features of the discourse—including volume or emphasis shifts, intonational features of the discourse, and transcriber uncertainty are shown in "Transcription conventions" at the end of this chapter.

Among scholars of spoken narrative, many lively debates about transcription have surfaced, particularly in folklore and anthropology (e.g. Tedlock, 1983; Hymes, 1996). Some have asserted that there is a single correct way to transcribe narrative discourse (e.g. Hymes, personal correspondence); my own position—and one taken by others in recent years—is that the method of transcription largely depends on (1) the focus of the study; (2) the body of theory and research informing the study; (3) the nature and qualities of data themselves; and (4) the current state of scholarship in the field in which the work is situated (cf. Ochs, 1979; Mishler, 1991). Some narrative analysts use transcription methods that follow conventions of conversation analytic (CA) transcripts (Juzwik et al., 2008; see also Chapter 20, this volume). Others do line-by-line transcription (such as the above) to highlight the performative, poetic, and structural features (Gee, 1991; Juzwik, 2009). Still others follow more prosaic conventions, for example to study story structure or lexical dimensions of narrative. CA transcripts are likely to represent disfluencies, hesitations, and repairs, because these moves are important to account for in analysis; however, more poetic transcription styles will often eliminate disfluencies to create an "ideal text" (Gee, 1989). It is commonly agreed that analysts of spoken narrative must determine which aspects of semiotic action are appropriate to foreground selectively in transcription for a given analytical project; for, as Ochs (1979) points out, a good transcript is a selective transcript. Analysts should further recognize that they are making rhetorical choices as they transcribe their data (Mishler, 1991).

A range of other factors can be taken into account when transcribing narrative discourse. Some researchers need to account for processes of *translation* in their transcription work: Blum-Kulka (2005), for example, presents transcripts of Israeli pre-schooler talk by using the Hebrew in the left column and the English translation in the right. What is essential is (a) the suitability of transcription choices for purpose of the research and (b) the explicit discussion on how and why narrative data were transcribed as they were—an argument that should not be neglected.

Disciplining spoken narrative discourse

As I observed already, narrative discourse analysis—like discourse analysis more generally—is an interdisciplinary enterprise. But what are some of the major disciplinary traditions informing narrative discourse analysis? And what different analytic or interpretive *concepts* do these traditions suggest/afford/offer? In what follows I discuss four major traditions informing current narrative discourse analytic work: 1(1) literary studies; (2) psychology; (3) folklore and anthropology; and (4) sociolinguistics. I am necessarily selective here, providing only cursory outlines of major disciplinary traditions informing narrative study in the past 40 years or so. In some cases it is difficult to distinguish or characterize certain scholars or collaborators within disciplinary boundaries because of the interdisciplinary cross-fertilization characterizing the study of spoken narrative.

Literary studies

Perhaps the greatest general influence on everyday and historical uses of the term "narrative," literary studies has seen a robust body of scholarship and terminology around "narratology" emerge in recent years. (For helpful summaries, see Mitchell, 1980; Herman and Vervaeck, 2001; Herman *et al.*, 2005; Phelan and Rabinowitz, 2005; Herman, 2007.) In the early 1970s a group of literary scholars and writers set out to redefine the parameters of American literature by including oral literature, such as Native American storytelling, within an intellectual project they called *ethnopoetics* (Quasha and Rothenberg, 1973). If secondary English classrooms today are any indication, this ambitious project was not successful; it did, however, provide a useful term for the comparative ethnographic study of oral literature (discussed in more detail in the section on folklore and anthropology, below).

More typically concerned with written and fictional narrative, the terminology and theory of literary study offer a rich set of theoretical resources for scholars of spoken narratives (even when, as is most usual, those narratives are non-fiction). Key themes and foci in literary scholarship work on narrative include (but are not limited to) story or plot (Chatman, 1978; Aristotle, 1992; Dannenberg, 2005), narration (Prince, 1980; Abbott, 2005), time (Genette, 1980; Ricoeur, 1984–1988), space–time (Bakhtin, 1981), character (Phelan, 1996; Margolin, 2007), dialogue (Bakhtin, 1981, 1984; Thomas, 2007), focalization (Jahn, 2005, 2007) genre (Bakhtin, 1986; Todorov, 1990; Beebee, 1994), audience and "the reader" (Rabinowitz, 1977; Iser, 1978; Phelan, 1996), and voice (Genette, 1980; Bakhtin, 1984; Aczel, 2005). An interesting body of work links literary narrative with rhetoric and ethics (Booth, 1983, 1988; Phelan, 1996), which is suggestive of the possibility for studying spoken narrative events as rhetorical situations with ethical reverberations (Juzwik, 2009).

Bakhtin's work on narrative deserves special mention, because it has traveled into and influenced virtually all of the disciplinary conversations discussed below. Organized by some critics around the comprehensive idea of "dialogism" (Holquist, 1990),[4] Bakhtin's work—which takes literary narratives, especially the novel (and precursors to the novel) as its data—interprets narratives as generic utterances within chains of communication. In the case of novels, the communicative chains to which authors respond span epochs. In great novels such as those of Dostoevsky—according to Bakhtin (1981, 1984)—characters and social voices get put into an "unfinalizable"

Table 23.1 A fuzzy-set definition of narrative

Dimension	Conditions for inclusion
Spatial (Semantic)	1. "Narrative must be about a world populated by individuated existents"
Temporal (Semantic)	2. "This world must be situated in time and undergo significant transformations."
	3. "The transformations must be caused by non-habitual physical events"
Mental (Semantic)	4. "Some of the participants in the events must be intelligent agents who have a mental life and react emotionally to the states of the world"
	5. "Some of the events must be purposeful actions by these agents."
Formal and Pragmatic	6. "The sequence of events must form a unified causal chain and lead to closure."
	7. "The occurrence of at least some of the events must be asserted as fact for the storyworld."
	8. "The story must communicate something meaningful to the audience".

Source: Ryan, 2007: 29

dialogue. Thus narratives can be said to be dialogic in two senses. First, they are dialogically linked to previous narratives; in Bakhtin's (1990) parlance, they are said to be "answerable" to previous texts. They also anticipate future responses; they are poised toward an "addressee" (Bakhtin, 1986). Second, they can be "internally dialogic" : within the utterance of a single speaker (e.g. a novelist or a character in a novel), multiple voices are dramatized and put into dialogue.

Scholars of literature have also developed nuanced definitions of narrative that analysts of spoken narrative may find generative. Ryan (2007) proposes defining narrative texts as belonging in a "fuzzy-set" across four dimensions, "allowing variable degrees of membership, but center[ing] on prototypical cases that everybody recognizes as stories" (p. 28). Table 23.1 details the "fuzzy-set" definition of narrative.

Returning to the data grounding this chapter, the "Through Mexican eyes" narrative, myriad directions could be pursued by an analyst equipped with the literary tools outlined above. One possibility involves comparing functions of oral and literary narrative in Ms. Gomez's classroom: Juzwik and Sherry (2007) show that the spoken narrative and literary discourse shared similar functional features at the levels of form, content, and narrator role.

Psychology

Bruner's (1985) distinction between "paradigmatic" and "narrative" modes of cognitive functioning has wielded extraordinary influence on narrative research and narrative theory in the social sciences. The paradigmatic mode, which Bruner argues has come to be more privileged and valued in Western culture, leads to "good theory, tight analysis, logical proof, and empirical discovery guided by reasoned hypothesis" (p. 98). The narrative mode, on the other hand, leads to "good stories, gripping drama, believable historical accounts" (ibid.). Drenched in value, the narrative mode relies on characters, actions, intentions, evaluations, and is essentially temporal in its logic. Moreover, the narrative mode depends on believability more than on "truth" and is evaluated on different grounds than the logico-scientific mode. Whereas the genre of "argument" corresponds with the paradigmatic mode, the "story" genre corresponds with the narrative mode (p. 106). More generally, Bruner advocates making narrative modes of knowing more central to social science inquiry and to educational processes.

While Bruner's paradigmatic/narrative distinction focuses on thinking, and therefore on the individual mind, some recent work in psychology has focused on the situated, relational, and interactional work that narratives do. In a rather strong statement about this line of work, M. Gergen (2004) writes: "a narrative comes into existence as a facet of relationship, not as a product of an individual" (p. 280). Much work from this perspective can be tied to an epistemology of "social constructionism." Such relational approaches to narrative have been further mobilized to reconsider women's ways of narrating (Gergen and Gergen, 1988; Bateson, 1989). Other researchers have turned to narrative to study human development, conceptualizing spoken (and written) narrative as a mediating device between unfolding sociohistoric processes and individual identity development (Nelson, 1989; Daiute, 2004; Thornborrow and Coates, 2005). Also from a sociohistoric perspective, researchers have studied spoken narratives as tools for collective remembering, for example in looking at how students in schools become socialized through textbook narratives and through oral talk about the past to interpret history according to nationally sanctioned storylines (Wertsch, 2002; Barton and Levstik, 2004; Juzwik, 2009).

To return to our excerpt, "Through Mexican eyes," this narrative could be explored from multiple angles by drawing upon contemporary psychological approaches to narrative. We might, for example, consider how the teacher's implied goal—helping her students prepare for situations when others try to take advantage of them—might be advanced through the narrative, as opposed to being advanced through the paradigmatic mode (e.g. through a treatise on racism or ethnic discrimination in American life). A further analytic direction might be to consider how—through oral narratives such as this—Ms. Gomez performs *ethos* over time, in her classroom conversations with students. Such an analysis might involve looking, for example, at how a teacher's short narratives (such as "Through Mexican eyes") accumulate and become sedimented over time, across a school year, to form a broader "life story." Finally, we might undertake a feminist analysis of how Ms. Gomez's narratives, over time, show her constructing a relational self—as indicated, for example, in line 30 of the narrative: "I was explaining this to someone the other da:y." This line further gives some indication of how she considers her literary discussions with students to be similar to her interactions with friends and family members beyond the classroom.

Folklore studies and anthropology

Although folklore studies and anthropology represent two distinct strands of scholarly activity, in the recent history of scholarship, which includes "spoken narrative" as data, these two approaches have been woven together—perhaps because of the considerable influence of Dell Hymes and Richard Bauman, scholars who seem to straddle both fields. Typically studies in folklore and anthropology situate the study of narratives within ethnographic descriptions of particular cultural groups (e.g. Bauman's (1986) study of oral storytelling among Texas dog traders) or comparative descriptions of multiple cultural groups (e.g. Heath's (1982) study of family narrative practices around bedtime in different communities in the southeastern United States or Scollon and Scollon's (1981) study of Athabaskan and English interethnic communication). Whereas anthropology has a considerable history of studying the narratives of "exotic others" (Boas, 1927), folklore studies has always been more focused on studying the narratives of groups of which scholars are part (Propp, 1968).[5] These disciplinary traditions have focused on the preservation of languages and oral storytelling traditions that are in danger of eradication due to industrialization or other forces of "modernity" (Shuman, 2005). In other cases scholars attempt to "give voice" to marginalized or neglected voices or narrators, in a populist aesthetic spirit.[6]

Folkloric and anthropological studies concerned with spoken narrative, many falling within the "ethnography of speaking" tradition, have shifted from comparative textual studies to comparative ethnographic studies of situated performances of narrative communication (Shuman, 2005). In fact, the construct of "performance" (laid out in Bauman, 1977) has been a key conceptualization informing studies of spoken narrative in folklore and anthropology. Bauman (1986) defines performance as:

> the assumption of responsibility to the audience for a display of communicative skill, high-lighting the way in which communication is carried out, above and beyond its referential content... the act of expression on the part of the performer is thus laid open to evaluation for the way it is done, for the relative skill and effectiveness of the performer's display. It is also offered for the enhancement of experience, through the present appreciation of the intrinsic qualities of the act of expression itself. Performance thus calls forth special attention to and heightened awareness of both the act of expression and the performer... performance may be understood as the enactment of the poetic function, the essence of spoken artistry.
>
> *(p. 3)*

Embedded in this notion of performance is a focus on narrative tellers and the sociocultural situations in which narratives are told. This does not, however, preclude attention to narrative texts themselves. Bauman and Briggs (1990) explain: "In order to avoid reifying 'the context' it is necessary to study the textual details that illuminate the manner in which participants are collectively constructing the world around them" (p. 69). Indeed, an important contribution of performance approaches to narrative study has been the careful ethnographic attention to *poetics* in the context of narrative performance (e.g. Hymes, 1981), an emphasis associated with the term *ethnopoetics* (Quasha and Rothenberg, 1973). Other points of comparison in performance studies of narrative include (but are not limited to) storytelling rights, or how the authorization to tell narratives in a particular cultural setting is negotiated and achieved by participants (Shuman, 1986), the ritualization and attendant social practices in which narrative tellings are embedded (Narayan, 1997), and the time–space of narrative performances (Heath, 1983).

More recent work on "context" in the cross-cultural study of oral narrative performance has moved away from a static approach to context (where context is comprised of a list of descriptors) to a more dynamic notion, focused on how texts come to be interactionally decontextualized, entextualized, and recontextualized by participants (Bauman and Briggs, 1990; Goodwin and Duranti, 1990; Silverstein and Urban, 1996). Bauman and Briggs detail how, in performances, texts come—through various signs, oftentimes poetic—to be cordoned off from the flow of discursive and semiotic activity (i.e. *decontextualized*) and then to be *recontextualized* in inventive ways for a narrator's performative purposes. This happens, for example, when a narrator recycles a "constructed dialogue," a bit of language whose authorship is attributed to someone other than the teller, for the purposes of her own story (e.g. to get a laugh, or to take a moral stance).

As a focus on narrative tellers and contexts of narrating has acquired prominence, so too folklorists and anthropologists have themselves become more reflexive about *who they themselves are* in relation to the persons whose stories they represent in their research. Narayan (1997), for example, collects and presents interpretations of Kangra folk narratives "in collaboration with" (so reads the cover of her book) storyteller Urmila Devi Sood, or "Urmilaji." In keeping with already discussed notions of researcher reflexivity, Narayan enlists Urmilaji to interpret the narratives she has recorded and transcribed in her field work, a process she describes as "oral literary criticism" (1995). Narayan identifies herself—an Indian American—as both insider and outsider in this work: While her (American-born) mother has lived in the Kangra community for many years (and Narayan reports living with her mother while doing her field work), she is herself an American professor who often feels like a "cultural other" in the village setting.

Through this disciplinary lens, we might consider the "Through Mexican eyes" narrative as a situated "performance," even though it is a "conversational narrative" (Georgakopoulou, 1998) rather than a "full performance" (Hymes, 1981). Juzwik (2010), for example, argues that Susan Gomez's narrative telling amounts to an (identifying) performance: She enacts being a person of color who speaks up in order to correct a violation of the social and moral order: being ignored by a clerk because she is Mexican. Showcasing her narrative virtuosity and drawing attention to herself as teller (and as protagonist), she recruits poetic and aesthetic performance keys. Poetic keys include the contrast between ONCE and TWICE (lines 47–48) and the trope of antanaclasis (the repetition of the same word with different meanings for each use), where "waiting" gets mobilized in multiple senses (lines 45–46 and line 60). Aesthetic keys include constructed dialogues (e.g. in lines 51–52) that revivify for her student audience the climactic event of *speaking up*. The analysis further explores how Ms. Gomez's constructed dialogue gets recontextualized by several students (including Alice) and by Ms. Gomez in subsequent (identifying) narrative performances. For example, Alice—who interjected what I interpret to be a *surprised* "You said that?" in response to Ms. Gomez's performed dialogue—responds immediately by telling a narrative in which an adult utters those same words—"Excuse me, I was here first"—to butt in front of her, a "kid" who is ignored by the clerk (the same scenario as in Ms. Gomez's narrative). Here she contests Ms. Gomez's storyline that "speaking up" (like Ms. Gomez) is necessarily the morally correct action by suggesting that an adult "speaking up" can also do wrong, at least according to "kids." This constructed dialogue gets recontextualized and recycled in two subsequent narratives, one told by Ms. Gomez and another by another student.

Sociolinguistics

Perhaps the most elaborated disciplinary perspective devoted to spoken narrative at present is sociolinguistics. This can perhaps be explained by the looming presence of William Labov in early, and defining, sociolinguistic research. Labov's (Labov and Waletsky, 1967; Labov, 1972) large-scale studies of narratives told in research interviews by African–American "inner-city" youth and by other groups of people pivotally shaped years of sociolinguistic research on spoken narrative. I mentioned above a key contribution of this research: a formalist strategy for defining minimal narrative discourse. Labov took as paradigmatic narrative data "fully-formed narratives" of personal experience, told by participants in structured research interviews. Vicarious narratives—that is, narrators narrating events that they themselves did not experience—were present in the data, but considered less artful or developed (Labov, 1972).

This work also influentially identified six features of "fully-formed narratives":

Abstract: opening clauses encapsulating the point of the narrative (lines 1–5 of Ms. Gomez's narrative)

Ms. Gomez (Teacher): Well, It's unfortunate, you know. As you get older, too, there are probably going to be things that come up, where people are going to try to take advantage of you, sometimes in a physical way. And will you be prepared for it? You know, I-my experience has been different growing up because I'm Mexican and I see the world through Mexican eyes. And I was taught that not everybody likes Mexican kids. And so I grew up being on guard around adults, around people. I have to watch out for that... Like let me give you an example. I was in the store the other day and the clerk was ignoring me. She was waiting on the person over here, and then she went to wait on the person over here, and after she did this twice and I had been there first, I spoke up. And I said, "Excuse me, am I invisible?"

Alice(student): You said that?

Ms. Gomez: Yes, to the clerk. And she looked at me. She said, "Oh I'm sorry."
   She said, I said, "I was waiting I was here first." And she wasn't going to acknowledge me until
   I spoke up...

Orientation: scene-setting descriptive clauses that locate the narrative—time, place, persons, situation (Ms. Gomez's narrative includes a lengthy orientation, which I locate from lines 6–43)

Complicating action: the clauses that form the action or plot of a narrative (see definition of narrative discussion in the section "Capturing and defining spoken narrative discourse" above)

Evaluation: "the means used by the narrator to indicate the point of the narrative" (Labov, 1972: 306). External evaluation is set apart from the narrated event, whereas embedded evaluation is (Labov believes, more artfully) placed within the narrated event. (Lines 62–63 in Ms. Gomez's narrative offer an example of external evaluation; the emphasis on the words "TWICE" and "FIRST," in lines 47 and 48, of embedded evaluation.)

Result or resolution: the termination, or result, of the complicating action (lines 55–61 of Ms. Gomez's narrative)

Coda: clauses signaling that the narrative is finished; may bridge the gap between the narrated event and the narrative event or show the effects of narrated events on narrator (lines 64–69 of Ms. Gomez's narrative)

Connected with formalist literary perspectives of the 60s and 70s (e.g. Genette, 1980), Labov's structuralist approach offered forth these touchstone concepts for the study of spoken narrative that have been developed, elaborated, and critiqued in recent years. Polanyi (1985), for example, further developed the concept of evaluation in a study of conversational American storytelling. This work argued that the temporally and causally sequenced narrative plot criteria alone were insufficient for defining a minimal narrative and, further, that some manner of narrator *evaluation* needed to be present in order for discourse to be labeled "narrative" (in contrast to the "annals" examined by White, 1980). In a related, but distinct, intellectual tradition, Halliday and Hasan's (1976) theorization of cohesion ties influenced a generation of researchers with an interest in spoken narrative: this work, although it pursued functional aims, was sometimes recruited for formalist narrative analyses.[7]
   Several trends in recent sociolinguistic narrative studies have resulted from the intellectual influences of interactional sociolinguistics (Goffman, 1974, 1981; Gumperz, 1982) and conversation analysis (see Clayman and Gill, this volume). First, contemporary scholars of spoken narrative have recognized that spoken narrative data need not be elicited in interviews, but that, in interview settings, analysts should account for the interactional work that narratives are doing (e.g. Wortham, 2001). Beyond research interviews, however, narratives abound in everyday conversation (Ochs and Capps, 2001), hence the term "conversational narratives" (Norrick, 2000) and an accompanying analytic focus on how narrative "talk in interaction" functions for participants in various social settings (Tannen, 1989; Georgakopoulou, 1998; Norrick, 2000; Bamberg, 2004). Ochs and Capps (2001), for example, outline five dimensions for analyzing conversational narrative data: (a) tellership (Is a narrative single or collaboratively told?); (b) tellability (High or low?); (c) embeddedness (relatively detached, i.e. more performative, or embedded, i.e. more dialogic in surrounding talk); (d) linearity (Is the temporal and causal ordering relatively closed or open?); and (e) Moral stance (Are the general point(s) about the teller or the world being conveyed certain and constant or are they uncertain and fluid in the telling?). Another key concept in the sociolinguistic literature, *constructed dialogue* (Tannen, 1989),

focuses attention on how narrators make use of reported speech (Volosinov, 1973) or animation (Goffman, 1981) in their narrative tellings. A further line of inquiry is the study of *response stories* (Norrick, 2007; Juzwik, 2010)—the study of how narratives are conversationally decontextualized, entextualized, and recontextualized to do identity and other social work.

Another contribution of recent sociolinguistic work on narrative is the idea that narrative discourse analysis ought to be expanded to include "small stories" (e.g. Bamberg, 2004, 2006; Georgakopoulou, 2007)—narratives that do not fit more "canonical" definitions of fully formed narratives, nor are they even necessarily even tales of once occurrent, personally experienced events. A narrative can, for example, be hypothetical or *irrealis* (Ochs and Capps, 2001; Juzwik, 2006), meaning that it narrates events that could happen or could have happened—but did not (yet) happen in the past, present, and/or future. "Small story" data are generally spoken and studied in contexts in and beyond research interviews, for example in everyday talk among friends, students and teachers in classrooms, families at the dinner table, and so on. Oftentimes conversational narratives are *co-authored* (Rymes, 2001), so that a single narrator is difficult to identify. Such co-authorship happened in Ms. Gomez's classroom, for example, when several students co-told a narrative about an unfair soccer coach whom many of them knew.

A sociolinguistic analysis of "Through Mexican eyes" might take a number of different directions. Sociolinguistic analyses often focus attention on a collection, or corpus, of narrative data generated in a particular context or by a particular participant or group of participants. Analysts might catalogue different types of narrative (e.g. personal experience, hypothetical) in the data set of which Ms. Gomez's "Through Mexican eyes" narrative was a part. An analysis might further compare the sorts of narratives that appear in classroom discussions of literature with those that occur in other disciplines (e.g. math, history). One sociolinguistically informed analysis (Juzwik *et al.*, 2008) explored several questions, including (1) the relationship between narrative and discussion and (2) how narratives—including this one—interactionally functioned in the classroom literary discussions. In the unit of which the "Through Mexican eyes" narrative event was a part, at least 40 percent of all discussion discourse was comprised of narrative discourse. In looking more closely at "conversational narrative discussion," we observed narratives serving to prime, sustain, ratify, and amplify discussion about the literature.

Shifting analytic approaches to spoken narrative data

As may be evident from my discussion of the four literatures above, narrative discourse analytic work appears to have shifted over time, with a general movement away from formalist approaches that dominated the 1970s and early 1980s to increasingly dialogic approaches that incorporate analysis of interaction and the situation of the narrative event, alongside attention to textual features and structures. Accompanying this trend toward more interactional analysis, some recent research on narrative tends to avoid grand claims about or evaluations of "narrative artfulness" (Labov, 1972) or the beneficence of narrative "modes of knowing" (Bruner, 1985). I conclude by noting one emerging direction for analysis of spoken narrative discourse: "multi-semiotic" analysis.

In a critical discourse analysis of "racial literacy" in teacher candidates' book club conversations, Rogers and Mosley (2008) categorize "multimodal" resources including pointing, motioning, using artifacts or bodies, eye contact/gaze, use of proximity, posture, use of print or images, facial expressions, head movements, use of air quotes, gestures, and reaching for artifacts (p. 128). This list offers one starting point for researchers wishing to consider narrative alongside other sign systems. Prior *et al.* (2006), however, prefer the term "multisemiotic" to "multimodal," because the former suggests a broader, more activity-oriented conception, beyond modes (e.g. image). Multisemiotic analysis of narrative seeks to capture, transcribe, and analyze the multiple, laminated sign systems at play when persons enact spoken narratives (Prior and Hengst, 2010). Hengst (2010), for example, offers an intriguing conversational narrative analysis of the successful communications of partners, one of whom has a diagnosis of the communicative disorder known as aphasia. Despite communicative challenges, such as "syntactic, semantic, phonemic, and articulatory errors and … false starts, long silences and prosodic disruptions" (pp. 109–110), partners with aphasia were able to communicate successfully with partners by using multisemiotic cues. Because of careful analytic attention to gesture, gaze, and other sign systems—beyond discourse—Hengst shows how overall communicative competence was far ahead of the linguistic competence for participants with aphasia. This insight would not be available through narrative discourse analysis alone.

Transcription conventions

ALL CAPS	The utterance is louder or otherwise emphasized, in comparison to surrounding words
[	Overlapping talk
(?)	unintelligible speech
(abc)	"best guess" transcription
(())	Additional information or description
:	Elongated vowel sound
?	Rising intonation and pause
.	Falling intonation and pause
,	Slight pause
- -	self-interruption/repair

Further readings

Bakhtin, M. M. (1981) *The Dialogic Imagination [1935]*, trans. M. Holquist, ed. C. Emerson and M. Holquist. Austin, TX: University of Texas Press and Bakhtin, M. M. (1986) *Speech Genres and Other Late Essays* [1953], ed. C. Emerson and M. Holquist, trans. V. W. McGee. Austin, TX: University of Texas Press. These have been enormously influential on discourse analytic work on spoken narrative, particularly from a dialogic perspective.
Bamberg, M. (ed.) (1997) 'Oral versions of personal experience: three decades of narrative analysis', *Journal of Narrative and Life History*, 7: 207–216 (special issue). Further commentary on and critiques of Labov's model, along with a re-print of Labov and Waletsky's (1967) seminal paper, are presented in this collection.
Halliday, M. A. K. and Hasan, R. (1976) *Cohesion in English*. London: Longman and Labov, W. (1972) 'The transformation of experience in narrative syntax', in W. Labov (ed.) *Language in the Inner City*. Philadelphia, PA: University of Pennsylvania Press, pp. 354–396. Both influenced formalist studies of spoken narrative.
Herman, D. (ed.) (2007) *The Cambridge Companion to Narrative*. New York: Cambridge University Press. This offers a helpful companion to the study of both spoken and written narrative. Norrick's chapter speaks specifically of conversational narrative analysis.
Ochs, E. and Capps, L. (2001) *Living Narratives: Creating Lives in Everyday Storytelling*. Cambridge, MA: Harvard University Press. Ochs and Capps, who themselves call upon Bakhtin, provide an overview and theoretical framework for conversational narrative analysis.

Notes

1 Pseudonym
2 For more detail about the project in which the narrative datum was generated, see Juzwik *et al.* (2008).
3 This change-in-speaker criterion, however, was not always helpful for identifying the boundaries of Susan Gomez's narratives or those of her students, because it did not allow for the back-and-forth narrative co-constructions that often characterize conversational narrative practices.
4 Although this interpretation is controversial: Bernard-Donals (1994) argues that Bakhtin's work does not neatly fall within a comprehensive theory, such as "dialogism," and that a philosophical tension between phenomenology and Marxism can be observed, especially if one turns to the lesser studied texts.

5 Scholars of spoken narrative whose work has made an impact on educational studies (e.g. Heath, 1983; Gee, 1985; Poveda, 2002) have often studied narratives and narrative practices in groups of which they are not members because of the illumination this work offers to educational practices.

6 Bourdieu (1998) critiques this effort as naïve (pp. 134–137).

7 For example, the work of Halliday and Hasan (1976) was enormously influential on narrative studies in literacy education in the 1980s.

References

Abbott, H. P. (2005) 'Narration', in D. Herman, M. Jahn, and M. L. Ryan (eds.) *Routledge Encyclopedia of Narrative Theory*. New York: Routledge, pp. 339–344.

Aczel, R. (2005) 'Voice', in D. Herman, M. Jahn, and M. L. Ryan (eds.) *Routledge Encyclopedia of Narrative Theory*. New York: Routledge, pp. 634–636.

Aristotle. (1992) 'Poetics', in R. McKeon (ed.) *Introduction to Aristotle*. New York: Modern Library, pp. 659–712.

Bakhtin, M. M. (1981) *The Dialogic Imagination* [1935], trans. M. Holquist, ed. C. Emerson and M. Holquist. Austin, TX: University of Texas Press.

Bakhtin, M. M. (1984) *Problems of Dostoevsky's Poetics* [1929], ed. and trans. C. Emerson. Minneapolis, MN: University of Minnesota Press.

Bakhtin, M. M. (1986) *Speech Genres and Other Late Essays* [1953], trans. V. W. McGee, ed. C. Emerson and M. Holquist. Austin, TX: University of Texas Press.

Bakhtin, M. M. (1990) *Art and Answerability: Early Philosophical Essays* by *M. Bakhtin* [1919–1986], trans. V. Liapunov and K. Brostrom. Austin, TX: University of Texas Press.

Bamberg, M. (ed.) (1997) 'Oral versions of personal experience: three decades of narrative analysis', *Journal of Narrative and Life History*, 7: 207–216 (special issue).

Bamberg, M. (2004) 'Talk, small stories, and adolescent identities', *Human Development*, 47: 331–353.

Bamberg, M. (2006) 'Stories: big or small? Why do we care?', *Narrative Inquiry*, 16: 147–155.

Barton, K. C. and Levstik, L. (2004) *Teaching History for the Common Good*. Mahwah, NJ: Lawrence Erlbaum.

Bateson, M. C. (1989) *Composing a Life*. New York: Plume.

Bauman, R. (1977) *Verbal Art as Performance*. Rowley, MA: Newbury House.

Bauman, R. (1986) *Story, Performance, and Event: Contextual Studies of Oral Narrative*. Cambridge, UK: Cambridge University Press.

Bauman, R. and Briggs, C. (1990) 'Poetics and performance as critical perspectives on language and social life', *Annual Review of Anthropology*, 19: 59–88.

Beebee, T. O. (1994) *The Ideology of Genre: A Comparative Study of Generic Instability*. University Park, PA: Pennsylvania State University Press.

Bernard-Donals, M. (1994) *Mikhail Bakhtin: Between Phenomenology and Marxism*. New York: Cambridge University Press.

Blum-Kulka, S. (2005) 'Modes of meaning making in young children's conversational storytelling', in J. Thornborrow and J. Coates (eds.) *The Sociolinguistics of Narrative*. Philadelphia, PA: Benjamins, pp. 149–170.

Boas, F. (1927) *Primitive Art*. Oslo: H. Aschehoug.

Booth, W. C. (1983) *The Rhetoric of Fiction*. Chicago, IL: University of Chicago Press.

Booth, W. C. (1988) *The Company We Keep*. Berkeley, CA: University of California Press.

Bourdieu, P. (1998) *Practical Reason*. Palo Alto, CA: Stanford University Press.

Bruner, J. (1985) 'Narrative and paradigmatic modes of thought', in E. Eisner (ed.) *Learning and Teaching the Ways of Knowing*. Chicago, IL: National Society for the Study of Education, pp. 97–115.

Chafe, W. (1980) 'The deployment of consciousness in the production of a narrative', in W. Chafe (ed.) *The Pear Stories*. Norwood, NJ: Ablex, pp. 9–50.

Chatman, S. (1978) *Story and Discourse: Narrative Structure in Fiction and Film*. Ithacy, NY: Cornell University Press.

Daiute, C. (2004) 'Creative uses of cultural genres', in C. Daiute and C. Lightfoot (eds.) *Narrative Analysis: Studying the Development of Individuals in Society*. Thousand Oaks, CA: Sage, pp. 111–133.

Dannenberg, H. P. (2005) 'Plot', in D. Herman, M. Jahn, and M. L. Ryan (eds.) *Routledge Encyclopedia of Narrative Theory*. New York: Routledge, pp. 435–439.

Gee, J. (1985) 'The narrativization of experience in the oral style', *Journal of Education*, 167 (1): 9–35.

Gee, J. P. (1989) 'Two styles of narrative construction and their linguistic and educational implications', *Discourse Processes*, 12: 287–307.

Gee, J. P. (1991) 'A linguistic approach to narrative', *Journal of Narrative and Life History*, 1 (1): 15–39.

Genette, G. (1980) *Narrative Discourse: An Essay in Method*. Ithaca, NY: Cornell University Press.

Georgakopoulou, A. (1998) 'Conversational stories as performances: the case of the Greek', *Narrative Inquiry*, 8 (2): 319–350.

Georgakopoulou, A. (2007) *Small Stories, Interaction, and identities*. Amsterdam: John Benjamins.

Gergen, M. (2004) 'Once upon a time: a narratologist's tale', in C. Daiute and C. Lightfoot (eds.) *Narrative Analysis: Studying the Development of Individuals in Society*. Thousand Oaks, CA: Sage, pp. 267–285.

Gergen, K. J. and Gergen, M. M. (1988) 'Narrative and the self as relationship', in L. Berkowitz (ed.) *Advances in Experimental Social Psychology*. San Diego, CA: Academic Press, pp. 17–56.

Goffman, E. (1974) *Frame Analysis*. New York: Harper.

Goffman, E. (1981) *Forms of Talk*. Philadelphia, PA: University of Pennsylvania Press.

Goodwin, C. and Duranti, A. (eds.) (1990) *Rethinking Context: Language as an Interactive Phenomenon*. New York: Cambridge University Press.

Gumperz, J. (1982) *Discourse Strategies*. Cambridge: Cambridge University Press.

Halliday, M. A. K. and Hasan, R. (1976) *Cohesion in English*. London: Longman.

Heath, S. B. (1982) 'What no bedtime story means: narrative skills at home and school', *Language in Society*, 11: 49–76.

Heath, S. B. (1983) *Ways with Words: Language, Life, and Work in Communities and Classrooms*. Cambridge: Cambridge University Press.

Hengst, J. (2010) 'Semiotic remediation, conversational narratives and aphasia', in P. Prior and J. Hengst (eds.) *Exploring Semiotic Remediation as Discourse Practice*. London: Palgrave McMillan, pp. 107–138.

Herman, D. (ed.) (2007) *The Cambridge Companion to Narrative*. New York: Cambridge University Press.

Herman, D., Jahn, M., and Ryan, M. (2005) *Routledge Encyclopedia of Narrative Theory*. London: Routledge.

Herman, L. and Vervaeck, B. (2001) *Handbook of Narrative Analysis*. Lincoln, NE: University of Nebraska Press.

Holquist, M. (1990) *Dialogism: Bakhtin and his World*. London: Routledge.

Hymes, D. (1981) 'Breakthrough into performance', in D. Hymes (ed.) *"In vain I tried to tell you": Essays in Native American Ethnopoetic* [1974]. Philadelphia, PA: University of Pennsylvania Press, pp. 79–141.

Hymes, D. (1996) *Ethnography, Linguistics, Narrative Inequality: Toward an Understanding of Voice*. London: Taylor and Francis.

Iser, W. (1978). *The Act of Reading: A Theory of Aesthetic Response*. Baltimore: Johns Hopkins University Press.

Jahn, M. (2005) 'Focalization', in D. Herman, M. Jahn, and M. L. Ryan (eds.) *Routledge Encyclopedia of Narrative Theory*. New York: Routledge, pp. 173–177.

Jahn, M. (2007) 'Focalization', in D. Herman (ed.) *The Cambridge Companion to Narrative*. New York: Cambridge, pp. 94–108.

Jakobson, R. (1971) 'Shifters, verbal categories, and the Russian verb', in R. Jakobson (ed.) *Selected Writings II: Word and Language* [1957]. Mouton: The Hague, pp. 130–147.

Juzwik, M. M. (2006) 'Performing curriculum: building ethos through narrative in pedagogical discourse', *Teachers College Record*, 108 (4): 489–528.

Juzwik, M. M. (2009) *The Rhetoric of Teaching: Understanding the Dynamics of Holocaust Narratives in an English Classroom*. Cresskill, NJ: Hampton Press.

Juzwik, M. M. (2010) 'Negotiating moral stance in classroom discussion about literature: Entextualization and contextualization processes in a narrative spell', in P. Prior and J. Hengst (eds.) *Exploring Semiotic Remediation as Discourse Practice*. London: Palgrave MacMillan, pp. 77–106.

Juzwik, M. M. Nystrand, M., Kelly, S., and Sherry, M. B. (2008) 'Oral narrative genres as dialogic resources for classroom literature study: a contextualized case study of conversational narrative discussion', *American Educational Research Journal*, 45 (4): 1111–1154.

Juzwik, M. M., and Sherry, M. B. (2007) 'Expressive language and the art of English teaching: theorizing the relationship between literature and oral narrative', *English Education*, 39 (3): 226–259.

Labov, W. (1972) 'The transformation of experience in narrative syntax', in W. Labov (ed.) *Language in the Inner City*. Philadelphia, PA: University of Pennsylvania Press, pp. 354–396.

Labov, W. and Waletsky, J. (1967) 'Narrative analysis: oral versions of personal experience', in J. Helms (ed.) *Essays on the Verbal and Visual Arts*. Seattle, WA: University of Washington Press, pp. 12–44.

Margolin, U. (2007) 'Character', in D. Herman (ed.) *The Cambridge Companion to Narrative*. New York: Cambridge, pp. 66–79.

Mishler, E. (1991) 'Representing discourse: the rhetoric of transcription', *Journal of Narrative and Life History*, 1 (4): 255–280.

Mitchell, W. J. T. (ed.) (1980) *On Narrative*. Chicago, IL: University of Chicago Press.

Narayan, K. (1995) 'The practice of oral literary criticism: women's songs in Kangra, India', *Journal of American Folklore*, 108: 243–264.

Narayan, K.in collaboration with Sood, U. D. (1997) *Mondays on the Dark Night of the Moon: Himalayan Foothill Folktales*. New York: Oxford University Press.

Nelson, K. (ed.) (1989) *Narratives from the Crib*. Cambridge, MA: Harvard University Press.

Norrick, N. (2000) *Conversational Narrative*. Amsterdam: Benjamins.

Norrick, N. (2007) 'Conversational storytelling', in D. Herman (ed.) *The Cambridge Companion to Narrative*. New York: Cambridge University Press, pp. 127–141.

Ochs, E. (1979) 'Transcription as theory', in E. Ochs and B. B. Schieffelin (eds.) *Developmental Pragmatics*. New York: Academic Press, pp. 43–72.

Ochs, E. and Capps, L. (2001) *Living Narratives: Creating Lives in Everyday Storytelling*. Cambridge, MA: Harvard University Press.

Phelan, J. (1996) *Narrative as Rhetoric: Technique, Audiences, Ethics, Ideology*. Columbus, OH: Ohio State University Press.

Phelan, J. and Rabinowitz, P. (2005) *A Companion to Narrative Theory*. Oxford: Blackwell.

Polanyi, L. (1985) *Telling the American Story*. Cambridge, MA: MIT Press.

Poveda, D. (2002) 'Quico's story: an ethnopoetic analysis of a Gypsy boy's narratives at school', *Text*, 22 (2): 269–300.

Prince, G. (1980) 'Introduction to the study of the narratee', in J. Tompkins (ed.) *Reader Response Criticism: From Formalism to Post-Structuralism*. Baltimore, MD: Johns Hopkins University Press, pp. 7–25.

Prior, P. and Hengst, J. (eds.) (2005) *Exploring Semiotic Remediation as Discourse Practice*. London: Palgrave Macmillan.

Prior, P., Hengst, J., Roozen, K., and Shipka, J. (2006) ' "I'll be the sun": from reported speech to semiotic remediation practices', *Text and Talk*, 26: 733–766.

Propp, V. (1968) *Morphology of the Folktale*, trans. L. Scott, ed. L. A. Wagner. Second Edition. Austin, TX: University of Texas Press.

Quasha, G. and Rothenberg, J. (eds.) (1973) *America a Prophecy: A New Reading of American Poetry from pre-Columbian Times to the Present*. New York: Random House.

Rabinowitz, P. (1977) 'Truth in fiction: a re-examination of audiences', *Critical Inquiry*, 4: 121–141.

Ricoeur, P. (1984–1988) *Time and Narrative*, trans. K. McLaughlin and D. Pelauer, 3 vols. Chicago, IL: University of Chicago Press.

Rogers, R. and Mosley, M. (2008) 'A critical discourse analysis of racial literacy in teacher education', *Linguistics and Education*, 19: 107–131.

Ryan, M. L. (2007) 'Toward a definition of narrative', in D. Herman (ed.) *The Cambridge Companion to Narrative*. New York: Cambridge, pp. 22–35.

Rymes, B. (2001) *Conversational Borderlands*. New York: Teachers College Press.

Scollon, R. and Scollon, S. B. K. (1981) *Narrative, Literacy and Face in Interethnic Communication*. Norwood, NJ: Ablex.

Shuman, A. (1986) *Storytelling Rights*. New York: Cambridge University Press.

Shuman, A. (2005) 'Folklore', in D. Herman, M. Jahn, and M. L. Ryan (eds.) *Routledge Encyclopedia of Narrative Theory*. New York: Routledge, pp. 177–179.

Silverstein, M. and Urban, G. (eds.) (1996) *Natural Histories of Discourse*. Chicago, IL: University of Chicago Press.

Tannen, D. (1989) *Talking Voices: Repetition, Dialogue, and Imagery in Conversational Discourse*. Cambridge, UK: Cambridge University Press.

Tedlock, D. (1983) *The Spoken Word and the Work of Interpretation*. Philadelphia, PA: University of Pennsylvania Press.

Thomas, B. (2007) 'Dialogue', in D. Herman (ed.) *The Cambridge Companion to Narrative*. New York: Cambridge, pp. 80–93.

Thornborrow, J. and Coates, J. (2005) 'The sociolinguistics of narrative: identity, performance, culture', in J. Thornborrow and J. Coates (eds.) *The Sociolinguistics of Narrative*. Philadelphia, PA: Benjamins, pp. 1–16.

Todorov, T. (1990) *Genres in Discourse*, trans. C. Porter. Cambridge: Cambridge University Press.

Volosinov, V. N. (1973) *Marxism and the Philosophy of Language* [1929], trans. L. Matejka and I. R. Titunik. Cambridge, MA: Harvard University Press.

Wertsch, J. V. (2002) *Voices of Collective Remembering*. New York: Cambridge University Press.

White, H. (1980) 'The value of narrativity in the representation of reality', in W. J. T. Mitchell (ed.) *On Narrative*. Chicago, IL: University of Chicago Press, pp. 1–24.

Wortham, S. (2001) *Narratives in Action: A Strategy for Research and Analysis*. New York: Teachers College Press.

24

Metaphor in spoken discourse

Lynne Cameron

What is metaphor in spoken discourse?

The historical context for metaphor in spoken discourse

To contextualize discourse approaches to metaphor, we can look back in time to the appearance of two earlier perspectives: the rhetorical and the cognitive. These earlier perspectives influence, inform and in some cases prefigure later ones.

The earliest ideas about metaphor seem to have come from Aristotle, in the *Poetics* and the *Rhetoric*, and might be labelled 'the rhetorical perspective'. In this perspective, metaphor is figurative use of language, the introduction of a strong and vivid expression that can create powerful images and change minds by comparing one thing with another.

> When the poet calls 'old age a withered stalk,' he conveys a new idea, a new fact, to us by means of the general notion of bloom, which is common to both things. (Aristotle's *Rhetoric*, Book III, Chapter 10, trans. Rhys)

Aristotle incorporated cognitive and discourse dimensions of metaphor within his major focus on the rhetorical function, and what he had to say about metaphor still makes for rich and relevant reading (Mahon, 1999).

In the more recent past, the arrival of a cognitive perspective took metaphor studies in a fresh direction after the publication of Lakoff and Johnson's *Metaphors We Live By* in 1980 and opened up interest in metaphor in disciplines far beyond the confines of literary studies, where it had been principally situated up to this point. From a cognitive perspective, metaphor is principally a matter of thought and not of language. A 'conceptual metaphor' is held to be a mapping between two conceptual domains that structures one of the domains in terms of the other. Metaphor in language, or 'linguistic metaphor', is then seen as the expression of metaphor in thought; a conceptual metaphor may give rise to many connected linguistic metaphors. By examining highly conventionalized metaphors in the same terms as strong or novel metaphors, the cognitive perspective reminded us that metaphor is ordinary and everyday as well as vibrant and striking. For example, the language contains many linguistic metaphors relating to the conceptual metaphor UNDERSTANDING IS SEEING, including *that's clear* and *I see what you mean*. (Small capitals are conventionally used to indicate conceptual metaphors and underlining to indicate linguistic metaphors.) Work in the cognitive perspective has led to development of the new field of 'cognitive linguistics' and produced a rich literature on metaphor that includes experimental psychological studies and theoretical development (for summaries of the field, see Gibbs, 1994, 2008).

The discourse perspective that has developed in the last decade views metaphor as discourse-based and, for some researchers, also as discourse-bound. It is inspired and informed by the cognitive perspective, but also reacts against it in seeking to re-establish the importance of the metaphorical use of language in context, which was downgraded in the cognitive emphasis on metaphor as mental mapping. From a discourse perspective, use of metaphor reveals something of a person's resources both for using language and for thinking, and studies based in this perspective tend to take a more holistic view of metaphor in the life of individuals and society than those based in the cognitive perspective. Technological advances in digital recording are now making discourse much more accessible for research, while advances in computer power facilitate automatic searches of large amounts of discourse data and enable researchers to investigate rigorously, for the first time in history, patterns of metaphor use across speech and discourse communities.

This chapter describes work on metaphor undertaken from a discourse perspective, and, in particular, metaphor in spontaneous spoken discourse activity, where speakers do not necessarily have the time to engage in thoughtful and deliberate construction of rhetorically striking metaphors but are obliged to use metaphors that 'come to mind' in the flow of talk – what I have also called 'prosaic use of metaphor', to contrast it with poetic use (Cameron, 2003).

The chapter discusses key issues, theoretical and methodological, raised by the discourse perspective and offers some solutions that have emerged from my own work. A summary of one method of metaphor analysis for spoken discourse is presented, and the chapter closes with items for future research agenda. First, however, an extract from the data is used to demonstrate something of the nature of metaphor in spontaneous spoken discourse.

Metaphor in spontaneous spoken discourse

The discourse perspective concerns itself with bringing together the local details of metaphor use with metaphor on more global or general levels. At the local level of talk, there is both regularity and variation, as the interaction of discourse participants produces varying patterns of metaphor dynamics. The amount of metaphor used varies according to what is being talked about and in relation with participants' attitudes towards the topic. Types of metaphors used by speakers vary in strength, conventionality, and frequency. Responses to the use of metaphor can produce chains of connected metaphors across episodes of talk.

The first extract is taken from a focus group discussion[1] in which eight Muslim women who live in a northern city in the UK were brought together and invited to respond to a series of questions about the effect of terrorism on their daily lives. At this point in talk, they had been discussing the question 'How do you think terrorists decide on their actions?' for several minutes, and Haifa had introduced the idea that Muslim extremism bears more resemblance to a *cult* than to a *religion*. Words and phrases identified as 'metaphorically used' are underlined.

Extract 1
1044 Haifa it's not even a religion at all.
1045 Haifa it's a cult.
1046 xxx yeah.
1047 Haifa and they're just doing,
1048 Haifa all the --
1049 Haifa [the things that a cult would do].
1050 Dina [and I think th-]--
1051 Dina they take them very young.
1052 xx [[vulnerable]]

1053	Aneesa	[[yeah.
1054	Aneesa	that's when you can start <u>brainwashing</u> them]].
1055	xxx	yeah.
1056	Dina	because they don't have their own opinions,
1057	Dina	and if they do,
1058	Dina	they are.. very <u>weak</u>.
1059	Dina	you know.
1060	Haifa	I think they're <u>putting</u> these young--
1061	Haifa	young boys,
1062	Haifa	<u>in the firing line</u>,
1063	Haifa	and probably,
1064	Haifa	<u>backing off</u> themselves,
1065	xx	[mastermind <X isn't going to be,
1066	xx	anywhere near X>
1067	Haifa	[and they're <u>taking</u> most of it],
1068	Haifa	well,
1069	Haifa	they're killing themselves,
1070	Haifa	aren't they,
1071	Haifa	really.
1072	Dina	X
1073	Dina	like,
1074	Dina	they don't <u>see</u> it like that,
1075	Dina	though,
1076	Dina	do they.8
1077	Dina	they don't <u>see</u> it like,
1078	Dina	they're killing themselves

The extract demonstrates features found to be typical of linguistic metaphor in spontaneous spoken discourse:

- metaphor occurs fairly frequently in talk, but with uneven distribution;
- metaphorical talk most commonly features vehicle terms that enter into the flow of topic talk rather than appearing as A IS B statements;
- frequent use occurs of conventional metaphors and rather rare use of novel or striking metaphors;
- conventional metaphors often use terms relating to the physical and perceptual world that also carry affect: e.g. movement metaphors to talk about actions and events, and seeing metaphors to talk about thinking and understanding;
- very frequently used words, particularly phrasal verbs, account for much metaphor use;
- distinctions between metaphorical and non-metaphorical uses are often blurred rather than clear-cut.

We now consider each of these features in more detail.

Metaphor occurs fairly frequently in talk, but with uneven distribution

The uneven distribution of metaphors across talk, and the occurrence of 'metaphor clusters', where many metaphors are produced in short episodes of talk, are phenomena now soundly established by empirical studies (Corts and Pollio, 1999; Corts and Meyers, 2002; Cameron and Stelma, 2004). Metaphor clusters sometimes signal critical points in discourse events, but they may also be produced by less dramatic features of talk. For example, we can see how the tendency of participants in spontaneous spoken discourse to repeat their own words or those of others when they emphasize, agree or dispute will increase the numbers of metaphors (e.g. 1074, 1077). There also seems to be a tendency for one use of metaphor to prime further metaphor, as may be happening in 1060–1064, when *putting in the firing line* is followed by *backing off*.

The metaphor density of this extract, calculated as the number of metaphorically used words or phrases per 1,000 words (Cameron, 2003), works out at 97 (11 underlined words and phrases in 113 words). Across the complete transcript, the metaphor density was 54, and this extract almost reaches the threshold for being considered as a metaphor cluster, which was set at 100 for this talk. Emotionally intense discourse events have been shown to have a much higher overall metaphor density (Cameron, 2007b), while more mundane talk such as classroom organization has a lower metaphor density (Cameron, 2003).

Metaphorical talk most commonly features vehicle terms that enter into the flow of topic talk rather than appearing as A is B statements

The Aristotelian example of metaphor: *old age as a withered stalk*, links two noun phrases and two ideas, old age and a withered plant stalk, to give a vivid way of thinking about the loss of vigour associated with age. What makes this a metaphor is that the two noun phrases and their related semantic fields are very different – humans and plants – and that joining them in metaphor adds extra meaning to the idea of *old age*. At the heart of metaphor is this kind of 'seeing one thing in terms of something else' (Burke, 1945); the impact of a metaphor comes from the contribution of the 'something else', here *withered stalk*, to the understanding of the 'one thing', *old age*. This type of noun metaphor can be put into the shorthand form 'A is B', where A stands for the topic/*old age* and B stands for the vehicle/*withered stalk*, and is stands for the metaphorical relation 'seeing in terms of'. When the concern of metaphor studies was principally with rhetorical or literary uses, this noun-based shorthand worked well; but when the concern is with spontaneous spoken discourse it works less well. None of the metaphorically used words and phrases in the extract has an explicit topic term in the talk; instead these vehicle terms enter the flow of talk, and their contextual meanings are, as far as we can tell from the absence of any explicit problematizing, effortlessly interpreted by other participants. Furthermore, many of the metaphors in talk occur in the verb phrase rather than as nouns.

Frequent use is made of conventional metaphors and rather rare use of novel or striking metaphors

The strongest metaphors in this extract are probably *brainwashing* (1054) and *putting them in the firing line* (1060–1062), both of which are conventional. In the first, the process of simplifying and intensifying someone's thinking is described in terms of washing; in the second, *the firing line* represents a dangerous position, not necessarily physical. Of course, those who become suicide bombers may literally be *put in the firing line*, although the scenario does not seem very convincing – bombers are more at risk from themselves than from finding people at the scene lined up ready to shoot them. If the topic of the conversation had been about redundancies at work, then being *put in the firing line* would clearly be only metaphorical.

Conventional metaphors often use terms relating to the physical and perceptual world that also carry affect

Backing off (1064) is identified as metaphor here because the idea of physical movement away from, and the implication of cowardice associated with such movement, is not appropriate to the discourse context; its contextual meaning is something like 'refusing to be near to terrorist action, on the part of the people in control of the terrorists'.

Towards the end of the extract, Dina uses and repeats *see* metaphorically, to mean 'understand', although, more precisely, she uses *don't see* metaphorically to mean 'don't understand'. We might also note that the *seeing* metaphor has an effect on the pronoun *it* that follows it: the idea that is misunderstood becomes an object that can be viewed. So, although it is clear that a metaphor is being used, deciding which words are used metaphorically is not completely straightforward, because of the way the metaphoricity spreads across the utterance.

The metaphoric linking of physical semantic fields or domains to non-physical fields produces systematic patterns of metaphors in language, which speakers use automatically or which sometimes they more deliberately select for affect, as with *backing off*, which does concern MOVEMENT but also carries a sense of cowardly retreat in a dangerous situation, rather than just 'moving away from'. It seems that our basic interactions with the physical world provide a rich source of metaphorical ways of talking and thinking about more abstract ideas, but they often come with emotions or attitudes that have become attached to them through sociocultural interaction.

Very frequently used words, particularly phrasal verbs, account for much metaphor use

Two uses of the verb *take* are marked as metaphorically used (1051, 1067). In the first case, extremists are described as *taking* young people into their 'cult'; this is metaphorical, since it does not involve physically moving people from one place to another but rather refers to convincing them of the new beliefs. In the second instance, *they're taking most of it* seems to refer to the young extremists bearing most of the risk and death or injury; this is a metaphor because the idea of physically moving something from one location to another is applied to the very different idea of bearing risk.

Another example of a highly conventionalized metaphor would be the word *things* in line 1049. The argument for including this as metaphor rests on the distinction between *things* as concrete objects and *things* in a non-concrete sense, here related to some kind of action.

Distinctions between metaphorical and non-metaphorical uses are often blurred rather than clear-cut

Identifying *taking* and *things* as metaphors might feel uncomfortable to readers more used to thinking of metaphor as active and novel. The cognitive shift in metaphor studies emphasized the ordinariness of metaphor, and the tendency to make metaphorical use of even the most common and mundane words. Rigorous operationalization of 'metaphor' in order to identify instances in spoken discourse and analyse use leads to the inclusion of such common lexical items (Cameron, 2003; pragglejaz, 2007). To exclude some frequent words, such as *do* or *have*, requires the researcher to impose boundaries on the category.

Even words with more semantic content can create problems in the identification of metaphor, as is exemplified by the adjectives *vulnerable* (1052) and *weak* (1058), here used to describe young people at risk from extremists and their opinions. The second is more clearly metaphorical, because the sense of physical weakness more strongly contrasts with the topic of emotional or spiritual weakness. The case for *vulnerable* rests on a similar contrast but is less obviously metaphorical because, in contemporary English, *vulnerable* is more frequently used in reference to susceptibility to emotional wounds than to physical vulnerability; it could be argued that this is not an instance of metaphor other than etymologically, and that the metaphorical meaning of the original Latin verb, *vulnerare* ('to wound'), has been lost as use has been extended from the physical to the emotional. The closeness of *weak* in the talk contributes to the decision here to include it as metaphor, as does finding both senses still included as active in a corpus-based dictionary. As a general principle, in my work on contemporary discourse metaphors that have become lexicalized and lost their historical connections to what was once a contrasting semantic field – what we might call 'etymological metaphors' – are not included. For example, the word *salary* has its origins in the Latin word for 'salt' and the convention of giving salt to Roman soldiers in lieu of payment. For the Roman soldiers, *salary* (in its Latin equivalent, *salarium*) was a metonymy; in earlier centuries, when the Latin origin was still generally available, *salary* would have been metaphorical because it retained the potential for connecting with salt; in the twenty-first century, connections with salt are so remote that *salary* would not count as metaphorical.

The blurring of the edges of the category 'metaphor' seems to be an inevitable outcome of the dynamic nature of language and of its evolution through use (Larsen-Freeman and Cameron, 2008), which forms a family resemblance category of phenomena we call 'metaphor'.

Metaphor in spoken discourse: summary

In summary, metaphor in spontaneous spoken discourse is occasionally striking but more often low key and conventionalized. However, the metaphors that speakers choose can be revealing of their ideas, attitudes and values. Ideas can be revealed by patterns of relations between the vehicles used and the topic ideas talked about: *brainwashing* as a metaphor for 'completely changing beliefs' and *weak* as a metaphor for 'not very entrenched' begin to build up a picture of Haifa's ideas about young Muslims and their thinking. Attitudes and values are particularly visible in metaphors: both of the above carry negative evaluations, and the metaphors of *putting in the firing line* and *backing off* carry a sense of disapproval from the speaker. This capacity for metaphor to reveal ideas, attitudes and values makes it an interesting proposition for use as a research tool as well as a research object (see the section 'The discourse dynamics approach').

What are the key issues that discourse analytic studies of metaphor have brought to light?

The discourse perspective on metaphor is producing several different approaches to data, including corpus linguistic approaches, critical discourse analytic approaches and, in my own work, the discourse dynamics approach. Each approach aims to find ways to combine analysis of the metaphors that people use with analysis of what they *do* with metaphors.

Issues around cognitive metaphor theory and discourse

Approaches vary in the strength of their allegiance to cognitive metaphor theory, and this needs to be appreciated as it reflects differing epistemologies. Strong adherence to a cognitive model of metaphor requires an assumption of 'conceptual metaphors' as large-scale, generalized mappings between concepts, established across the speakers of a language and brought 'ready made' to any specific discourse event. What is picked out of texts or transcripts is then assumed to be the verbal manifestation of a conceptual metaphor. Issues arise from this stance around connections between individual utterances and the 'concepts' that are said to underlie them. For example, if metaphorical mappings between concepts are held to exist in the minds/brains of individuals, then some account is needed of how they got there in development (Johnson, 1997). How active are such mappings in any discourse episode, and how do they actually produce specific linguistic metaphors? Ponterotto (2003), for example, claims that an underlying conceptual metaphor not only influences the linguistic metaphors that people use but also acts to create coherence across talk. How this might be evidenced remains unclear.

A more moderate view accepts that the examination of large amounts of discourse data reveals systematic patterns of metaphor in a language; these patterns are likely to shape the language resources of children as they grow up, while also being open to change in the processes of social interaction (Cameron and Deignan, 2006). As people grow up within social groups, they learn the language of conventionalized metaphors and their ways of thinking are channelled in certain ways, by language and by their embodied experiences in the physical world. In the course of a specific discourse event, metaphors may be produced or understood very swiftly, as lexicalized rather than as actively metaphorical items; connections across different concepts may be generated by metaphorical language, or there may be no active metaphorical processing by participants. A direct result of adopting this view is that researchers are usually assessing 'metaphorical potential' rather than evidence of active metaphoric processing when they examine discourse data.

Constraints on the language of metaphor

Corpus studies of metaphor patterns have shown that there is more specificity of language form and lexical choice attached to linguistic metaphors than would be predicted by the cognitive theory (Deignan, 2005). It appears that, over time, certain forms, such as singular rather than plural forms, or continuous tenses rather than others, come to be conventionally adopted for metaphorical usage, and different forms for non-metaphorical uses. For example, Deignan shows that the verb *blossom* is metaphorical in 98 per cent of its uses, as in *funds to help budding companies blossom*, while the noun is very rarely used metaphorically (Deignan, 2005: 178–179)

Using conventionalized metaphor in discourse thus appears to be quite constrained – in form, lexis and pragmatics. Constraints on the language of metaphor probably help participants to cope with the time demands of spontaneous spoken discourse by inhibiting non-metaphorical interpretations when these are not appropriate. Findings from discourse studies of metaphor have implications for the validity of test items selected for experimental studies.

Methodological issues from using spontaneous spoken discourse

Working with metaphor in spoken discourse data raises methodological issues, not the least of which is how to identify metaphorical, as distinct from non-metaphorical, uses of words and phrases. As we have already seen, identification depends on identifying metaphoric potential rather than on finding evidence of active metaphoric processing, and on making sound decisions on category boundaries.

To understand the purpose or impact of metaphor use in spontaneous discourse requires an analysis that takes account of discourse context, how metaphor shifts in the twists and turns of talk as it happens, and the movement of metaphor across participants as they respond to each other (Cameron, 2008a, b). A sociocognitive perspective on metaphor, which connects individual use of linguistic metaphor with the local discourse context and the broader social context, as well as with mental processing/thinking, becomes inevitable.

Discourse methods combine the analysis of metaphor patterns with some form of discourse analysis. Within the social sciences, combined methods include the use of metaphor analysis within critical discourse analysis, investigating for example how marketing discourse uses relational metaphor to relate to the public (Koller, 2008), and metaphor analysis alongside content analysis to investigate how media and medical experts talk about avian flu (Nerlich and Halliday, 2007, described in Todd and Low, 2010). In the humanities rather than in social sciences, Semino and Swindlehurst (1996) combine corpus analysis with metaphor analysis to show how mechanical metaphors are used in descriptions of mental illness in the novel *One Flew Over the Cuckoo's Nest*. The method that I have developed in my own work is called 'metaphor-led discourse analysis' and is detailed in the sections that follow.

The discourse dynamics approach

In my work I have tried to understand metaphor by examining it in spontaneous spoken discourse, and, more recently, I have used metaphor as a tool for researching social science problems, including the process of post-conflict reconciliation (Cameron, 2007b) and how the risk of terrorism affects people's everyday lives (Cameron *et al.*, 2009; Cameron and Maslen, 2010). This venture has involved developing tools and techniques of 'metaphor-led discourse analysis' that fit with validity into a coherent theoretical 'discourse dynamics' framework (Cameron, 2010a), described in this section.

The discourse dynamics theoretical framework

The discourse dynamics approach centralizes and starts from language use, seeing the language system as emerging from use in discourse (Larsen-Freeman and Cameron, 2008; Cameron, 2010a). It is inspired and informed by developments in cognitive psychology and cognitive metaphor theory, while resisting the latter's strong assumptions about the pre-existence of conceptual metaphors in the minds/brains of individuals, and it understands discourse as essentially a social and dialogic phenomenon (Bakhtin, 1981; Linnell, 1998). The interdependence of language and cognition in discourse is signalled by the hyphenated phrase 'talking-and-thinking', which refers to the processes speakers engage in while speaking (Cameron, 2003).

Complex dynamic systems theory provides an epistemology of, and a metatheory for, the discourse dynamics approach, understanding and theorizing human activity in terms of change over time. Activity occurs at different timescales and at different levels of social organization. Applied to spoken discourse, the timescale of the discourse event, such as a conversation or a lecture, is likely to be in the order of hours and minutes. Inside the discourse event, episodes of talk will be on a timescale of minutes and seconds, while individual utterances will be on a timescale of seconds. On a longer timescale, several discourse events may form a connected sequence, as when the same participants meet each other several times over a period of months or years. In a similar way, we can identify various levels of social organization related to spoken discourse, from the individual mind, through the dyad or small group, to larger social groups, some with tightly prescribed membership and others more loosely organized, including national or regional speech communities. The relations between timescales and levels can work both 'upwards', as when a small group of people develops a way of speaking that influences a larger group, or 'downwards', as when the language of a discourse community influences the discourse of a dyad. Interaction across timescales and levels in the discourse system sometimes leads to 'self-organization' and to the emergence of a new type of activity at a higher level or scale. Examples of emergence in discourse systems include speech genres that emerge as

349

a conventionalized way of using language (Bakhtin, 1986), accents and dialects that emerge within a regional social group, and, more relevant to this chapter, metaphorical idioms and proverbs that emerge with conventionalized forms and uses within speech and discourse communities. Emergence applied to metaphor theory helps to explain several empirical phenomena of spoken discourse:

Framing metaphors

When people talk together, they often converge on shared ways of referring to an idea or object. Brennan and Clark described these shared ways of referring as 'conceptual pacts' (1996), and Cameron (2007a) extended this to 'lexico-conceptual pacts', so as to include choice of language. Shared ways of talking-and-thinking are often metaphorical, as when 10-year-old pupils in a school classroom started using the phrase *lollipop trees* to refer to a way of drawing trees as a stick with a circle on top. Within the social group of the classroom, the phrase referred not only to the visual appearance, but also to the teacher's negative evaluation of this artistic style. The phrase emerged over a very short timescale, of several minutes, into the repertoire of the class (Cameron, 2003).

When shared metaphorical lexico-conceptual pacts emerge around thematically key topics, they become 'framing metaphors'. The reconciliation conversations produced several framing metaphors for the process of coming to understand another person in a post-conflict situation, including A JOURNEY and CHANGING A DISTORTED IMAGE OF THE OTHER (Cameron, 2007b).

Conventionalized metaphors

A similar emergent phenomenon on a larger level of social organization is the crystallization and conventionalization of metaphors across a discourse or speech community.

Discourse communities connected by shared occupations, beliefs or ways of living may develop metaphors that contribute to the cohesion and collective identity of the social group. For example, the Irish Republican Army, a paramilitary group previously active in Ireland and Britain, would refer to their conflict with the British and with loyalist activists as *the struggle*. Use of this metaphorical phrase came to mark a speaker as sympathizing with the group.

When metaphors are conventionalized, some stabilization occurs in form, meaning and pragmatics – as the corpus work mentioned above has shown, details of form become attached to particular meanings and uses. In the example of the noun phrase *the struggle*, the noun would always be preceded by the definite article as determiner and use of a modifier was very rare. Pragmatically, it would only be used by members of, or sympathizers with, the paramilitary group. This stabilization of a bundle of features – grammatical, lexical, pragmatic, referential – seems to occur at both local and global levels and applies to many conventionalized metaphorical ways of talking. It is difficult to predict exactly what kind of stabilization will occur, but that stabilization occurs seems to be predictable. These regularities of use not only help in marking social identity, but also assist the processes of discourse production and comprehension, which in spontaneous talk are strongly constrained by time pressures on participants. Cameron and Deignan (2006) suggested that such bundles of features, observed empirically, be recognized theoretically with the label 'metaphoreme'. Cameron (2010c) develops a theoretical explanation of the affective content of many metaphoremes, using the idea of mental simulations, in which the particular forms and reference come to be associated with particular attitudes or evaluations, and then evoke these in use (Gibbs, 2006; Ritchie, 2006, 2010).

Metaphor as research tool

Within the field of metaphors studies, metaphor has, quite understandably, been principally 'a research object', as researchers seek to understand the nature of metaphor by investigating how it is used. A further strand of work in the discourse perspective is less directly concerned with the nature of metaphor but instead uses metaphor as a research tool in exploring discourse data, and in this subsection I explain the method of analysis developed to do this.

Firstly, what makes metaphor suitable for use as a research tool in the social sciences or humanities? For various reasons, metaphor seems to offer particularly rich insights into people's ideas, attitudes and values. Novel metaphors can be striking and create impact in discourse, while much more frequent, conventionalized metaphors inform us about socialized and accepted ways of talking-and-thinking. Metaphors are used when talking about something emotionally charged, often in order to avoid explicit emotion. They are used when talking about something abstract, where the imagination needs some assistance. Metaphor is what we turn to when we have trouble expressing or capturing an idea in discourse; by making analogies or comparisons between what we are trying to express to someone else and something they are more familiar with, we try to get them to see the world as we do. Even the absence of metaphor can sometimes be very striking; in reconciliation conversations, talk about painful events was made highly direct by the absence of metaphor and shown to have a strong and lasting effect on the listener (Cameron, 2011). Highly conventionalized metaphors and the systematic patterns they fall into can illustrate ways of talking-and-thinking that have evolved in discourse communities. When people tell anecdotes or engage in narrative talk, metaphor often contributes to the coda, where content and feelings are summarized. Extract 2 shows an example of a coda to a stretch of talk in a focus group of Muslim men on the topic of terrorism; it comes from the same study as extract 1. The last two lines act as a coda, reformulating and summarizing what has been said in the preceding discourse, with a landscape metaphor describing how terrorism influences their lives:

Extract 2
315 it's   a subject which is <u>not far from</u>,
316 .. our daily..life.
317 it's--
318 ...(3.0) whether we discuss it or not,
319 .. it's <u>there</u> all the time,
320 <u>in the background</u>.

The small cluster of connected metaphors work together to construct a metaphorical view of *daily life* as situated on a sociocognitive landscape, with a foreground and a *background*. The *subject* of terrorism is discoursally placed on this landscape, firstly as *not far from our daily life* and then, in the coda, as *there … in the background*. Affective force is conventionally attached to nearness and distance, and, in this topic's context, nearness emphasizes the feeling of threat.

Metaphors like these offer neat ways of packaging a great deal of both information and affect into short phrases. Analysis of the metaphors that people invent or invoke can thus reveal something of their ideas, attitudes and values. Tracking and connecting metaphors across discourse events can reveal how ideas evolve in talk and how affective 'climate' is created and changed. The next section describes the method for doing this in more detail.

Metaphor-led discourse analysis

Identifying, grouping and tracking metaphors are the three core processes in the method of 'metaphor-led discourse analysis', complemented with analysis of the discourse dynamics of metaphors, i.e. their function in the ongoing discourse activity (Cameron, 2007b; Cameron *et al.*, 2009). It makes use of techniques from conversation analysis at local level, and from the discursive psychological approach (Edwards, 1997).

Identifying metaphor in spoken discourse

Cameron (1999, 2003) discussed many of the issues that have been already mentioned in respect of identifying metaphor, and offered, as a solution, a combination of necessary conditions for metaphor together with category boundaries to exclude/include less central examples. Identification procedures were further formalized by the 'pragglejaz group' (2007), in a method that works through a word-by-word transcript, testing for metaphorical use and using a corpus dictionary to help establish a 'basic' meaning of a word, which contrasts with but transfers meaning to the contextualized meaning of the word in the discourse. The pragglejaz article includes important discussion of reliability issues that researchers need to take seriously if empirical studies are to build on each other or to be comparative.

Investigation of metaphor patterns

Once metaphors have been identified, the discourse dynamics theoretical framework suggests searching for patterns in metaphor use across timescales and levels. For example, a framing metaphor (see 'The discourse dynamics theoretical framework' above) is a collection of connected metaphors, used over one or more discourse events to talk about a key idea in the discourse. More generally, Cameron (2003, 2007a) has used the phrase 'systematic metaphor' for a grouping together, by the researcher, of connected metaphors from one or more discourse events, to talk about connected ideas around a topic. While a systematic metaphor is given the form *A is B*, it must be remembered that it is not a single way of talking-and-thinking, but a collection of related metaphors produced in the stream of talk. The collection may also be thought about dynamically, as a 'metaphor trajectory' in the discourse system, and examining its evolution through adaptation and shifting across speakers can provide useful information as to how participants use metaphor in discoursally constructing ideas, attitudes and values.

Research questions may relate to a longer timescale or to a larger level of social organization than that of individual discourse events, for example asking how metaphors contribute to building social identity. The data set will correspondingly need to be much larger. Techniques developed within corpus linguistics can then assist in finding patterns of metaphor use (Deignan and Semino, 2010). To compare individual use of metaphor with socially accepted norms, a small context-rich dataset can be compared with a larger reference corpus (e.g. Cameron and Deignan, 2003).

Analysing the discourse dynamics of metaphors

Metaphor alone cannot cover all that happens in a discourse event; some complementary method of discourse analysis is required. Participants' goals (conscious or not), such as wanting to justify an opinion, disagreeing with other participants or answering a question, create dynamic forces that influence the unfolding activity of the discourse event. In metaphor-led discourse analysis, metaphors are examined within their discourse dynamics; temporal segments of the discourse event are inspected for the functions that metaphors play in the discourse activity.

Analysis of discourse dynamics proceeds by segmenting transcriptions into smaller episodes of discourse action. For example, a classroom lesson may begin with an opening segment in which the teacher organizes students and materials, followed by a teacher fronted segment that introduces and gives an overview of the topic and tasks coming up in the lesson; the major section of the lesson then follows, as students carry out their assigned tasks, and the lesson closes with a summary of work done and more organizational logistics. Each of these lesson segments can be broken down further, perhaps by topic or by the actions of students or teacher into smaller episodes: for example, the opening may start with a greeting and organization of logistics; the teacher fronted segment is likely to contain sequences of questions and answers (Cameron, 2003).

The discourse activity analysis is mapped onto the analysis of linguistic metaphor in a detailed and recursive process, which requires close attention to lexis, grammar and rhetorical patterning, in order to reveal how metaphors contribute to discourse activity. There is no single template for the process of combining analyses of metaphors and discourse activity, since it has to be sensitive to the specific research goals (Cameron, 2010b). In moving between the metaphors and discourse activity, the researcher comes to understand how participants use metaphors to frame and elaborate ideas, and how the choice of metaphors contributes to the expression and construction of attitudes and values (Cameron and Maslen, 2010). At this stage, the method moves from analysis to interpretive synthesis, and it becomes important here to guard against unwarranted interpretations or too much idealization of the complexity and messiness that characterize spontaneous talk.

Looking to the future

Exploiting the potential for metaphor as a research tool in the social sciences is still only in its infancy. Metaphor analysis has shown its promise, but there is much room for further extending its range and for investigating how metaphor influences other aspects of the research process. My own work in the immediate future will examine metaphor in data collection and in reporting findings to research users.

I suspect too that we will see interest reviving in poetic, rhetorical and other creative uses of metaphor (Cameron, 2010c). Metonymy in discourse has received little attention to date. Its overlaps and interplay with metaphor makes it ripe for deeper investigation. Multimodal metaphor has a sound base in published work on gesture (Cienki and Müller, 2008) and on visual images (Forceville, 1994), but also promises extensive development in the near future, in its own right and as part of the development of multimodal discourse analysis.

Further reading

Cameron, L. and Maslen, R. (eds.) (2010) *Metaphor Analysis: A Guide to Research Practice in Applied Linguistics, Social Sciences and the Humanities*. London: Equinox.

An edited collection demonstrating how metaphor can be used as a tool in discourse-based research studies.

Gibbs, R. (ed.) (2008) *Cambridge Handbook of Metaphor and Thought*. Cambridge: Cambridge University Press.

A recent collection of writings by key scholars in metaphor studies, covering all major areas of work.

Semino, E. (2008) *Metaphor and Discourse*. Cambridge: Cambridge University Press.

An introductory guide to metaphor for undergraduate and postgraduate students.

Journals:

Metaphor and the Social World, John Benjamins. Available online at: http://www.benjamins.com/cgi-bin/ t_seriesview.cgi?series=MSW (accessed 21 April 2009).

Metaphor and Symbol, Taylor & Francis. Available online at: http://www.tandf.co.uk/journals/titles/1092- 6488.asp (accessed 21 April 2009).

Lynne Cameron

Note

1 The focus group was one of 12 which were organized as part of a research project 'Perception and communication of terrorist risk', funded by the UK Economic and Social Research Council and carried out at the University of Leeds.

References

Aristotle, *Rhetoric*, trans. W. Rhys Roberts. Available at http://www.public.iastate.edu/~honeyl/Rhetoric/rhet3-10.html (accessed 22 December 2009).

Bakhtin, M. (1981) *The Dialogic Imagination: Four Essays*. Austin, TX: University of Texas Press.

Bakhtin, M. M. (1986) *Speech Genres and Other Late Essays*. Austin, TX: University of Texas Press.

Brennan, S. and Clark, H. (1996) 'Conceptual pacts and lexical choices in conversation', *Journal of Experimental Psychology: Learning, Memory, and Cognition*, 22 (6): 1482–1493.

Burke, K. (1945) *A Grammar of Motives*. New York: Prentice Hall.

Cameron, L. (1999) 'Identifying and describing metaphor in spoken discourse data', in L. Cameron and G. Low (eds.) *Researching and Applying Metaphor*. Cambridge: Cambridge University Press, pp. 105–132.

Cameron, L. (2003) *Metaphor in Educational Discourse*. London: Continuum.

Cameron, L. (2007a) 'Confrontation or complementarity: metaphor in language use and cognitive metaphor theory', *Annual Review of Cognitive Linguistics*, 5: 107–135.

Cameron, L. (2007b) 'Patterns of metaphor use in reconciliation talk', *Discourse and Society*, 18 (2): 197–222.

Cameron, L. (2008a) 'Metaphor and talk', in R. Gibbs (ed.) *Cambridge Handbook of Metaphor*. Cambridge: Cambridge University Press, pp. 197–211.

Cameron, L. (2008b) 'Metaphor shifting in the dynamics of talk', in M. S. Zanotto, L. Cameron and M. Cavalcanti (eds.) *Confronting Metaphor in Use*. Amsterdam: John Benjamins, pp. 45–62.

Cameron, L. (2010a) 'The discourse dynamics framework for metaphor', in L. Cameron and R. Maslen (eds.) *Metaphor Analysis: Research Practice in Applied Linguistics, Social Sciences and the Humanities*. London: Equinox, pp. 77–94.

Cameron, L. (2010b) 'Metaphors and discourse activity', in L. Cameron and R. Maslen (eds.) *Metaphor Analysis: Research Practice in Applied Linguistics, Social Sciences and the Humanities*. London: Equinox.

Cameron, L. (2010c) 'Metaphor in physical-and-speech action expressions', in A. Deignan, L. Cameron, G. Low, and Z. Todd (eds.) *Researching and Applying Metaphor in the Real World*. Amsterdam: John Benjamins, pp. 45–62.

Cameron, L. (2011) *Metaphor and Reconciliation*. New York: Routledge.

Cameron, L. (in press) 'Metaphor in prosaic and poetic creativity', in J. Swann, R. Carter and R. Pope (eds.) *Language and Creativity: The State of the Art*. London: Palgrave Macmillan.

Cameron, L. and Deignan, A. (2003) 'Using large and small corpora to investigate tuning devices around metaphor in spoken discourse', *Metaphor and Symbol*, 18 (3): 149–160.

Cameron, L. and Deignan, A. (2006) 'The emergence of metaphor in discourse', *Applied Linguistics*, 27 (4): 671–690.

Cameron, L. and Maslen, R. (2010) 'Using metaphor analysis to compare expert and public perceptions of the risk of terrorism', in L. Cameron and R. Maslen (eds.) *Metaphor Analysis: Research Practice in Applied Linguistics, Social Sciences and the Humanities*. London: Equinox, pp. 248–256.

Cameron, L., Maslen, R., Todd, Z., Maule, J., Stratton, P., and Stanley, N. (2009) 'The discourse dynamics approach to metaphor and metaphor-led discourse analysis', *Metaphor & Symbol*, 24 (2): 63–89.

Cameron, L. and Stelma, J. (2004) 'Metaphor clusters in discourse', *Journal of Applied Linguistics*, 1 (2): 7–36.

Cienki, A. and Müller, C. (eds.) (2008) *Metaphor and Gesture*. Amsterdam: John Benjamins.

Corts, D. and Meyers, K. (2002) 'Conceptual clusters in figurative language production', *Journal of Psycholinguistic Research*, 31 (4): 391–408.

Corts, D. and Pollio, H. (1999) 'Spontaneous production of figurative language and gesture in college lectures', *Metaphor and Symbol*, 14 (1): 81–100.

Deignan, A. (2005) *Metaphor and Corpus Linguistics*. Amsterdam: John Benjamins.

Deignan, A. and Semino, E. (2010) 'Corpus techniques for metaphor analysis', in L. Cameron and R. Maslen (eds.) *Metaphor Analysis: Research Practice in Applied Linguistics, Social Sciences and the Humanities*. London: Equinox, pp. 161–179.

Edwards, D. (1997) *Discourse and Cognition*. London: Sage Publications.

Forceville, C. (1994) 'Pictorial metaphor in advertising', PhD thesis, Vrije Universiteit, Amsterdam.

Gibbs, R. W. (1994) *The Poetics of Mind: Figurative Thought, Language and Understanding*. Cambridge: Cambridge University Press.

Gibbs, R. W. (2006) *Embodiment and Cognitive Science*. New York: Cambridge University Press.

Gibbs, R. W. (ed.) (2008) *The Cambridge Handbook of Metaphor and Thought*. Cambridge: Cambridge University Press.

Johnson, C. (1997) 'Metaphor vs. conflation in the acquisition of polysemy: the case of see', in M. K. Hiraga, C. Sinha, and S. Wilcox (eds.) *Cultural, Typological and Psychological Perspectives in Cognitive Linguistics*. Amsterdam: John Benjamins.

Koller, V. (2008) 'Brothers in arms: Contradictory metaphors in contemporary marketing discourse', in M. Zanotto, L. Cameron, and M. Cavalcanti (eds.) *Confronting Metaphor in Use: An Applied Linguistic Approach*. Amsterdam: John Benjamins.

Lakoff, G. and Johnson, M. (1980) *Metaphors We Live By*. Chicago, IL: University of Chicago Press.

Larsen-Freeman, D. and Cameron, L. (2008) *Complex Systems and Applied Linguistics*. Oxford: Oxford University Press.

Linnell, P. (1998) *Approaching Dialogue*. Amsterdam: John Benjamins.

Mahon, J. (1999) 'Getting your sources right: what Aristotle didn't say', in L. Cameron and G. Low (eds.) *Researching and Applying Metaphor*. Cambridge: Cambridge University Press, pp. 69–80.

Nerlich, B. and Halliday, C. (2007) 'Avian flu: the creation of expectations in the interplay between science and the media', *Sociology of Health and Illness*, 29: 46–65.

Ponterotto, D. (2003) 'The cohesive role of cognitive metaphor in discourse and conversation', in A. Barcelona (ed.) *Metaphor and Metonymy at the Crossroads*. Berlin: Mouton de Gruyter, pp. 283–298.

pragglejaz (2007) 'MIP: a method for identifying metaphorically-used words in discourse', *Metaphor and Symbol*, 22 (1): 1–40.

Ritchie, D. (2006) *Context and Connection in Metaphor*. Basingstoke: Palgrave Macmillan.

Ritchie, D. (2010) 'Between mind and language: a journey worth taking', in L. Cameron and R. Maslen (eds.) *Metaphor Analysis: Research Practice in Applied Linguistics, Social Sciences and the Humanities*. London: Equinox, pp. 57–76.

Semino, E. and Swindlehurst, K. (1996) 'Metaphor and mind style in Ken Kesey's one flew over the Cuckoo's nest', *Style*, 30 (1): 143–166.

Todd, Z. and Low, G. (2010) 'A selective survey of research practice in published studies using metaphor analysis', in L. Cameron and R. Maslen (eds.) *Metaphor Analysis: A Guide to Research Practice in Applied Linguistics, Social Sciences and the Humanities*. London: Equinox.

25

From thoughts to sounds

Wallace Chafe

A fundamental property of language is its ability to associate thoughts with sounds. Those who are producing language are experiencing thoughts. Those thoughts are somehow associated with sounds that pass through the air and strike the ears of listeners, whose brains then interpret the sounds with thoughts that partially resemble those of the speaker, or at least take some account of the speaker's thoughts. The resemblance can never be more than partial, because the contents of different minds are inevitably very different. New thoughts entering someone's mind are always interpreted in terms of thoughts that are already there. But language at least permits separate individuals to know something of each others' thoughts, whatever use they make of such knowledge.

Stages from thoughts to sounds

The first thing to notice is that thoughts and sounds are very different in nature, so it is impossible for them to be in any one-to-one correspondence. Thoughts pass through several stages of filtering and adjustment before a representation in sounds is achieved. Those stages can be described in terms of a progression from thoughts to a semantic structure, from a semantic structure to a syntactic structure, and then to phonology and sounds. I will focus here on reasons why the path from thoughts to sounds involves both a semantic and a syntactic organization.

These stages are by no means self-contained. Thoughts are already shaped in major ways by language, and especially by a language's semantic structuring. Semantic structures and syntactic structures also have much in common. Ultimately we would like to know what the *brain* is doing, and certainly it does not assign these stages to isolated modules. Nevertheless, it is useful up to a point to discuss thoughts, semantic structures, and syntactic structures separately, since each has its own properties and its own reasons for existence.

There is an important sense in which thoughts are where the action is. The flow of language is determined by the flow of thoughts, which constitute the force that drives language forward. Semantics, syntax, and ultimately sounds exist in service to the thoughts. Linguists who focus their attention on syntax may pretend that syntax is the creative, driving force of language, but that cannot possibly be true. Speakers and listeners are primarily, if not exclusively, conscious of the flow of their thoughts. If one hears a language that is unfamiliar, one can only be conscious of its sounds; but that is not the way language functions. The biggest step in learning a new language is to acquire the ability to experience thoughts while hearing sounds, largely ignoring the sounds themselves. The discussion here will proceed from thoughts to semantic structures to syntactic structures, asking why the latter two stages exist and why sounds cannot be associated with thoughts directly.

Linguists have seldom given thoughts the attention they deserve. The reason is clear. Sounds have physical properties that anyone can observe, whereas thoughts can be observed directly only by the thinker. Thoughts are "subjective" rather than "objective." If one's goal is to be "scientific," one may find it necessary to remain safely with phenomena that are publicly observable. That can be a hindrance, however, if thoughts have the priority just described. We need to deal with them in spite of their subjectivity, and language can help.

How, then, can we learn more about thoughts? It seems that there are at least three general pathways that can and have been followed. One is introspection, another language, and a third experimentation. Systematic introspection was more popular in the nineteenth century than in the twentieth, when behaviorism, logical positivism, and other philosophical trends saw introspection as next to useless. Properties of thoughts were discussed insightfully by William James in his *Principles of Psychology* (1890), but the twentieth century turned its attention elsewhere. It was an unfortunate development, because introspection can tell us important things about thoughts, a few of which will be mentioned here. The focus here, however, will be on ways we can learn about thoughts through language. The third pathway, experimentation, may offer greater objectivity, but usually it suffers from the artificality of experimental data. In the end, the best insights should come from combining introspection, language, and experimentation in order to expand the total picture from multiple directions.

Introspection suggests that thoughts have perceptual, evaluative, and verbal components. Perceptual experiences enter thoughts, directly or indirectly, through the senses. They fall into two major subclasses. First, there are immediate experiences derived from seeing, hearing, touching, tasting, and smelling aspects of the immediate environment—whatever is present at the very time and place of those experiences. But many perception-based thoughts are displaced, appearing in consciousness as imagery, a kind of attenuated perception. Thoughts of that kind may result from past contacts with some immediate environment, in which case we say they are remembered, or they may be more or less invented by our minds, in which case we say they are imagined. There is no sharp division between remembering and imagining. Memories are to some extent imaginatively constructed, and imagination depends heavily on remembered experiences. The general point is that thoughts consist in part of experiences that are perception-based. Thoughts also exhibit an evaluative component. We experience emotions, attitudes, and moods, to which I will return at the end of this discussion. The third component of thoughts that is introspectively obvious is inner language. We are conscious of talking silently to ourselves. More is involved than just auditory imagery. Sounds constitute part of this inner language, but we also experience language-based ways of organizing thoughts, or composing ideas.

How can language add to introspection by shedding light on the nature of thoughts? One might at first suppose that it could tell us only how thoughts are organized by language itself, excluding experiences that lie outside of language. There are reasons to believe, however, that examining the way people talk can shed important light on the nature of thoughts as a whole, beyond just the ways in which they are verbalized.

An example

It is important to be able to refer to some data. Here I will take advantage of a project that began in Berkeley in the mid-1970s, when we made a short film that was carried around the world and shown to speakers of different languages, who were asked to tell what happened in it (Chafe,

1980). Our main purpose was to use the experience of watching this film, something that was relatively constant across languages, as a basis for examining ways in which that common experience was expressed in different languages. In addition, we could also observe ways in which the experience was verbalized by different speakers of the same language, or even by the same speaker at different times. The film involved a man picking pears and a boy stealing some of the pears, and so it came to be called the Pear Film, and the narratives based on it, the Pear Stories. An extensive collection of those narratives, 68 in all, was recorded in German in Berlin in 1978 by Swantje Ehlers, later a professor at the Justus-Liebig University in Giessen, whose contribution to this chapter is gratefully acknowledged.

Early in the film one sees a man picking pears and then descending a ladder to empty the pears into a basket. When one of the German speakers who saw the film talked about this sequence, she said the following. (The sequences of dots show pauses, whose length corresponded roughly to the number of dots.)

.... Dieser Mann sammelt seine Birnen in der.. Schürze,
und wenn die Schürze voll ist,
... geht er,
... steigt er mm die Leiter herunter,
um diese Birnen in einen Korb zu werfen.
.... Werfen ist eigentlich übertrieben,
ich.. hatte also wirklich stark den Eindruck,
wie sorgfältig der.. Mann mit den Birnen umgeht.
... Und dazu.. mm.. ja.. nahm sogar ne Hals- sein Halstuch.. vom... ab,
... um.. wenigstens die zwei oberen.. Birnen damit... blankzuputzen.
Und ich hab' eigentlich darauf gewartet,
daß er sich... wenigstens also eine davon... nimmt,
.. und reinbeißt.
... Die sa- die Birnen sahen eben auch sehr... frisch und knackig und grün aus.
.... Also ich hätt's gemacht.
... Mm (laugh).
.... Der Mann.. tat es aber nicht,
... sondern stieg wieder auf die Leiter um weiterzupflücken.

This man is gathering his pears in his apron,
and when the apron is full,
he climbs down the ladder,
to throw these pears into a basket.
Throw is actually exaggerated,
because I was really impressed
with how carefully the man handles the pears.
And then he took off his kerchief,
to polish at least the two top pears with it.
And I actually waited
for him at least to take one of them
and bite into it.
The pears looked so fresh and crisp and green.
I would have done it.
But the man didn't do it,
but climbed back up the ladder to pick some more.

The (partial) independence of thoughts from language

The fact that thoughts consist of more than just language is evident in disfluencies—pauses, pause fillers, and changes of wording. If thoughts were only verbal, there should be no difficulty in verbalizing them; they would have been verbalized already. But people often do experience difficulty in verbalizing their thoughts. The following line is a good example:

> … Und dazu.. mm.. ja.. nahm sogar ne Hals- sein Halstuch.. vom… ab,

There are pauses, the pause filler *mm*, the change from some feminine noun, perhaps *Halsbinde*, to the neuter noun *Halstuch* "neckerchief," and the abandonment of some prepositional phrase, perhaps *vom Hals* "from his neck," followed by a longer pause before the final particle *ab*, part of the verb *abnehmen* "take off."

Sometimes a speaker will talk overtly about a difficulty in matching thoughts with words, saying perhaps *it's hard to put this into words* or *that's not exactly what I meant*. There is a good example here, when this speaker expressed dissatisfaction with her choice of the word *werfen* "throw":

> Werfen ist eigentlich übertrieben,
> *Throw is actually exaggerated,*

The same speaker talked about the film on two later occasions, and we can look at the three ways she expressed her thoughts about the man emptying the pears into the basket. The first time, as shown above, she said this:

> …. Dieser Mann sammelt seine Birnen in der.. Schürze,
> und wenn die Schürze voll ist,
> … geht er,
> … steigt er mm die Leiter herunter,
> um diese Birnen in einen Korb zu werfen.
> *This man is putting his pears in his apron,*
> *and when the apron is full,*
> *he climbs down the ladder,*
> *to throw these pears into a basket.*

The second time she said:

> …. Er stieg (cough)…. mm… von der… Leiter herunter,
> nachdem er etliche Birnen in seiner Schürze,
> … gesammelt hatte und schüttet sie in 'n Korb.
> *He climbed down from the ladder,*
> *after he had collected some of the pears in his apron,*
> *and shook them into a basket.*

And the third time:

> …. wenn seine Schürze voll ist,
> dann.. steigt er die Leiter herunter,
> …. füllt die Äpfel in einen Korb.
> … Vor der Leiter.
> *when his apron is full,*
> *then he climbs down from the ladder,*
> *puts the apples into a basket.*
> *In front of the ladder.*

The language of each of these three excerpts differed in various ways, but the thoughts remained very similar, although between the second and third versions her memory had transformed the pears into apples. She must have remembered what was essentially the same event when she said any of the following:

> um diese Birnen in einen Korb zu werfen,
> und schüttet sie in einen Korb,
> füllt die Äpfel in einen Korb.
> *to throw these pears into a basket,*
> *and shook them into a basket,*
> *puts the apples into a basket.*

People quickly forget the exact language they used. Thoughts, as thoughts, are not necessarily tied to any particular language that is used to express them on a particular occasion.

Linguistic evidence for the nature of thoughts

What can language tell us about the nature of thoughts themselves? Introspection shows that thoughts are in constant change. What we are thinking right now is not what we were thinking a few seconds ago, or what we will be thinking a few seconds from now. Language reflects this restlessness, constantly changing language expressing constantly changing thoughts. Restlessness is apparent in these examples, but any example of speech will show the same. Language is produced in brief segments that typically extend over a second or two and are segmentable prosodically. Each line of the above examples represents a separate prosodic phrase or intonation unit, and each phrase reflects a separate focus of consciousness. Thoughts proceed through time by constantly activating new foci, one at a time (Chafe, 1994, cf. Pöppel, 1994).

If we look more closely at how these phrases function, we find that many of them express ideas of events or states along with their participants. The beginning of this excerpt consisted of:

> .... Dieser Mann sammelt seine Birnen in der.. Schürze,
> *This man is gathering his pears in his apron,*

The idea of an event is captured with the word *sammelt* "is gathering," in which there are three participants, expressed with the words *dieser Mann* (the one who did the gathering), *seine Birnen* (what was gathered), and *in der Schürze* (where it was gathered). The next phrase,

> und wenn die Schürze voll ist,
> *and when the apron is full,*

expresses the idea of a state, being full, which has only one participant, expressed as *die Schürze* "the apron." The organization of experience into ideas of events or states and their participants appears repeatedly in every language, and is thus a good candidate for a fundamental and universal property of thought organization, basic to the way our minds interpret experience.

Ideas are positioned within a complex web of orientations. The idea of an event or state may be located in time, space, epistemology, evaluation, social interaction, and the context of the ongoing stream of thought. Ideas are expressed with so-called content words, while orientations are usually expressed with affixes or particles. *Dieser (Mann)*, for example, orients the man within the ongoing context, the tense suffix on *sammelt* orients the event in time, and so on.

Language, in short, gives evidence of the following properties of thoughts, whose expression in all languages suggests their universality. First, thoughts are dynamic, constantly changing. Second, thoughts consist of a succession of foci of consciousness. Third, thoughts focus on ideas of events and states and their participants. Fourth, those ideas are oriented in a multidimensional web of time, space, epistemology, evaluations, interaction, and context. Understanding the basic structure of thoughts in this way, we can return to the question of why they should be organized into semantic structures and why those semantic structures should in turn be represented by syntactic structures. Why is it not possible for thoughts, as thoughts, to be represented directly by sounds?

From thoughts to semantic structures

As thoughts are organized into semantic structures, there are at least four processes at work, identifiable as selection, categorization, orientation, and combination. To begin with selection, thoughts have a rich content, which extends well beyond anything language can express. The time and resources available to speakers are too limited to let them verbalize everything they are thinking, and much of what they are thinking is likely to be irrelevant to the interests of others. People select what to say in part on the basis of what they judge will resonate in the minds of their listeners. Language attempts to select from thoughts those ideas that are judged of mutual interest. On different occasions the selections may be different. As one small example, the third time this speaker talked about the film she described the location of the basket as *vor der Leiter* "in front of the ladder," but she omitted that location in her other narratives.

A second essential adjustment is categorization. In addition to their rich content, thoughts contain ideas that are particular and idiosyncratic. What we experience from one moment to the next is something we never experienced before and will never experience again in the same way. It would obviously be impossible for language to associate every particular idea with a unique sound. Even if it were possible, there would be no way a listener could know what particular idea was associated with whatever sound might have been assigned to it. The association of thoughts with sounds must be shared by speaker and listener. It follows that particular elements of thought need to be interpreted as instances of shared categories.

Categorization accomplishes two things. First, it provides expectations regarding unique experiences by associating them with already familiar experiences, so that one can know something of their nature and what might be done with them. Knowing the *Birne* or *pear* category lets one expect of an instance of that category that it can, for example, be eaten. But at the same time the category provides a word or phrase that can be used for verbalizing the particular idea, for example the words *Birne* and *pear*. Some ideas lend themselves easily to categorization. Such "highly codable" ideas (Brown, 1958) are likely to be categorized the same way at different times, as was true of *die Leiter* "the ladder" or of the event that was categorized as an instance of *heruntersteigen* "climb down." Other ideas fit less well into any easily available category and are likely to be categorized differently at different times, as with *werfen* "throw," *schütten* "shake," and *füllen* "fill up." In such cases a speaker may at times show dissatisfaction with the categorization, as in *werfen ist eigentlich übertrieben* "throw is actually exaggerated." In short, in addition to selecting from their thoughts, speakers also interpret particular ideas as instances of categories, something they may accomplish more or less easily.

A third adjustment of thoughts to semantic structures is orientation. If, as suggested above, thoughts are positioned in space, time, epistemology, evaluation, interaction, and the context of other thoughts, and if we express ideas in order to communicate them, some of these orientations may be necessary, so that listeners can position ideas within their own store of thoughts. Comparing different languages shows that the orientations present in thought may be too many and too diverse for all of them to be verbalized. Every language makes it easy or even obligatory to express certain orientations while ignoring others. Different languages make these choices in different ways.

In these examples we can note a complex interplay of tenses and aspects. The man's activities were first expressed with the present tense: *er sammelt die Birnen* "he is gathering the pears," *er steigt die Leiter herunter* "he climbs down the ladder." But then came a shift to the past: *er nahm sein Halstuch ab* "he took off his neckerchief," *er stieg wieder auf die Leiter* "he climbed back up the ladder." The speaker's own thoughts were oriented first with a simple past: *ich hatte also wirklich stark den Eindruck* "I had the really strong impression," but then there was a switch to *haben* with the past participle, a switch impossible to reproduce in English: *ich hab' eigentlich darauf gewartet* "I actually waited for it." The man's hypothetical future action was captured with the present tense: *daß er sich wenigstens also eine davon nimmt, und reinbeißt* "that he would at least take one of them and bite into it." But then the speaker's own, more hypothetical action was expressed with the subjunctive: *ich hätt's gemacht* "I would have done it." These shifts in orientation had subtle effects on thought transmission.

The fourth adjustment is combination. The ideas and orientations that are chosen for verbalization do not float in the air like disconnected bubbles. Obviously they must be combined, but the ideas and orientations themselves do not always dictate unique patterns of combination. Different languages offer different *constructions* from which a speaker can choose. The ways semantic elements are combined is open to dispute and is too large an issue to be addressed here, but obviously combining them in some way is a necessary fourth step in the adjustment of thoughts to language.

Thoughts, in summary, are adjusted to language in the four ways described. Every language provides its speakers with ways of selecting, categorizing, orienting, and combining thoughts as ways of shaping them, so that they can be associated with sounds. Every language provides its own unique semantic resources, its own ways of accomplishing these adjustments in order to yield a semantic structure.

The resulting semantic structure bears some resemblance to a syntactic structure. The categorized events share properties with verbs, the categorized participants with nouns. The orientations resemble inflections on verbs and nouns, as well as function words of various types. The ways in which these elements are combined resemble syntactic constructions. The fundamental difference between a semantic structure and a syntactic structure is that semantic elements and their combinations are all directly related to thoughts, whereas syntactic elements may not be.

From semantic structures to syntactic structures

The fact that a syntactic structure is not a semantic structure is hardly a new idea. Linguists have explored many ways of describing syntactic structures, but the latter always contain some elements, patterns, and processes that depart from a direct association with thoughts. Why should that be? Why are semantic structures not associated with sounds directly? A syntactic structure is in essence a semantic structure that has been modified by language change and, specifically, by the twin historical processes of lexicalization and grammaticization.

To begin with lexicalization, we can focus on the formation of idioms (Chafe, 1968). An example is an idiom that was used by another German speaker to express the idea of an event that occurred toward the end of the film. Early in the film one saw a boy steal some pears. Later he gave three of the pears to some other boys. At the end of the film, those boys walked by the man who had been picking the pears, who looked as if he was wondering how the boys obtained the pears they were carrying and eating. Some speakers said that he was *verblüfft* "perplexed" or *verdutzt* "bewildered," but one speaker described his state of mind by saying *er kann sich keinen Vers daraus machen*, literally "he can't make himself any verse out of it."

Let us suppose that among this speaker's thoughts was the idea of the man's puzzlement, and that she chose to interpret it as an instance of a certain semantic category provided by the German language. In semantic terms, it was a unitary category in the same way that *verblüfft* or *verdutzt* expressed unitary categories. The category in question was activated when one heard *er kann sich keinen Vers daraus machen*. In order to be associated with sounds, it needed first to be converted from a semantically unitary category into something else: something *quasi-semantic*, in the sense that it behaved as if it were composed of semantic elements although it was not. What was realized in the sounds *er kann sich keinen Vers daraus machen* was no longer directly semantic but the result of idiom formation. English has a semantic category that is quite similar, although it is associated with a different syntactic structure: *he can't make head or tail of it*.

This processing of thoughts through intermediate, quasi-semantic syntactic structures must have been a major step in the evolution of language, something uniquely human. Other animals have signaling systems that allow their thoughts to be selected and categorized and expressed through sounds or smells or visual displays. But only in humans, apparently, do we find this intermediate stage in which some semantic elements are first symbolized with other, quasi-semantic elements before they proceed to be expressed with sounds.

Idiomaticization leads to the indirect expression of ideas of events or states and their participants. But something similar occurs with the semantic elements that orient those ideas. The term *grammaticization* already suggests converting something into grammar that was not grammar to begin with. Like idiomaticization, grammaticization leads to the intermediate expression of semantic elements by quasi-semantic elements, but in this case the semantic elements are not ideas but orientations.

How grammaticization occurs can be illustrated with an example from English. It is an example that has been frequently discussed (e.g. by Hopper and Traugott, 1993), but its familiarity can make it easy to appreciate. I refer to the use of the construction *be going to* as a way of expressing futurity. In the beginning there were expressions such as *I'm góing to éat* (that is, *I'm going for the purpose of eating*), where there were two events, a *going* event and an *eating* event. Now there is only the eating, and the language has acquired a new way of expressing a future orientation. The going event, its orientation with the progressive aspect (*I'm going*), and its purposive relation to the eating event (*I'm going for the purpose of eating*), were all left as quasi-semantic elements of English syntax, no longer directly associated with the thought of going somewhere for a purpose. Semantically there is only the future orientation, but before it is passed on to sound it must first be converted into this quasi-semantic syntactic form.

Speakers sometimes exhibit a tendency to simplify this picture by reducing the distinction between syntax and semantics. Quasi-semantic elements, just because they are not directly tied to thoughts, have a tendency to dissipate over time. The reduction of *going to* to *gonna* illustrates nicely this drive toward a more direct expression of thoughts. Speakers have lost direct awareness of the semantic origin of *be going to*, and by eroding it to *gonna* they have created a simpler auxiliary. The need for a separate syntactic structure has been to that extent reduced.

Returning to German, we can ask how this way of viewing language applies to a brief segment from the narrative we have been examining. This speaker alternated between two points of view. Sometimes she talked about what was happening in the film—*er sammelt Birnen* "he's gathering pears," *er nahm sein Halstuch ab* "he took off his neckerchief," *er tat es nicht* "he didn't do it"—and sometimes she stepped outside the film and talked about her own reactions to it—*werfen ist übertrieben* "throw is exaggerated," *ich hab' darauf gewartet* "I waited for it," *die Birnen sahen frisch und knackig und grün aus* "the pears looked fresh and crisp and green."

We can examine one of those places where she stepped outside the film. As her thoughts moved forward, she arrived at a thought she verbalized as follows:

Und ich hab' eigentlich darauf gewartet daß er sich,
… wenigstens also eine davon,
… nimmt,
.. und reinbeißt.
And I actually waited for him
to take at least one of them,
and bite into it.

But this is not the only way she might have verbalized this thought, and in fact on another occasion she said:

…. man dachte oder erwartete daß er,
…. nun eine nimmt,
und kräftig reinbeißt,
one thought or expected that he,
would take one,
and vigorously bite into it.

On still another occasion she said:

…. und man hat den Eindruck,
… daß er… eigentlich jeden Moment,
wenigstens in einem Mal hineinbeißen müßte,
and one had the impression,
that he actually at any minute,
at least at some point had to bite into it,

Focusing on the first phrase of her first version, we can note for comparison the corresponding phrases in her second and third versions:

(1)   und ich habe eigentlich darauf gewartet *and I actually waited for it*
(2)   man dachte oder erwartete *one thought or expected*
(3)   und man hat den Eindruck *and one has the impression*

The phrase in (1) is centered on the idea of an event that is categorized as an instance of the *warten* "wait" category, or more precisely the derived, transitive category *warten auf* "wait for." In (2) she had trouble deciding whether to categorize this idea as *denken* "think" or *erwarten* "expect." In (3) she changed the categorization to *den Eindruck haben* "have the impression."

The event idea in (1) was oriented as something that happened in the past. It included as a participant the idea of the person who waited—the speaker herself. Perhaps she felt a more personal involvement just after seeing the film, because later she changed it to the more impersonal *man* "one." She gave this idea an epistemic orientation with the word *eigentlich* "actually," which implied something a little unexpected about the man taking a bite out of a pear. There was nothing corresponding to *eigentlich* in (2) or (3). Connections with other thoughts were evident in the word *und* "and" at the beginning, attaching this thought to the chain of preceding thoughts, and the *da* of *darauf* "for it," anticipating what was to come, her idea that the man would take a bite. Everything mentioned so far had a direct relation to her thoughts. But the construction consisting of *haben* "have" with the past participle (*habe… gewartet*), literally "have waited," shows a mismatch between syntax and semantics, as does the agreement of *haben* with its subject: *ich habe* (obscured in *ich hab' eigentlich*).

Does all of this really matter? Why should syntacticians concern themselves with the relation of syntax to thought? In the most general terms, there is a need to refocus our attention in order to understand language and languages more realistically, with syntactic structure understood, not as the centerpiece of language, but as a modification of semantic structure that mixes semantic and quasi-semantic elements. Such a perspective should motivate us, first, to pay more attention to the nature of semantics and the historical processes that convert it into syntax, abandoning attempts to treat syntax as self-contained. It should lead us ultimately to see the fundamental question to be the nature of thoughts and their relation to semantics. But there are two specific areas where a change in perspective can be especially useful. One is the familiar question whether the speakers of different languages think differently. The other is the nature of translation.

Do speakers of different languages think differently?

Is it true that people who speak different languages think differently? The question goes back at least to German scholars like Johann Gottfried von Herder, Wilhelm von Humboldt, and Heymann Steinthal. At present one often hears heated disputes over whether Benjamin Lee Whorf was on the right track or totally misguided. Strong opinions exist on both sides. If the question is whether different languages provide their speakers with different *semantic* resources, it is obvious that they do. No one doubts that different languages organize *sounds* in different ways, and surely they differ at least as much, and probably more, in the ways they organize *thoughts*. If the question is whether *syntactic* structures influence thinking, we have seen how lexicalization and grammaticization distort semantic structures in ways that increase their distance from thoughts. Asking whether syntactic structures influence thoughts is a pointless question.

To what extent, then, do the different *semantic* structurings imposed by different languages feed back into thoughts? Dan Slobin has described what he calls "thinking for speaking" (Slobin, 1996), and he and others have shown convincingly that the way one thinks *when one speaks* does differ across languages. We are left with the question of how much *all* of thinking—not just its verbal component—is affected by the different semantic resources of different languages. However that may be, an important component of thoughts is unquestionably verbal—we think much of the time with inner language—and certainly that much of thought cannot avoid being affected by language differences. The aspects of thought that are not verbal but perceptual and emotional may be freer to go their own ways regardless of one's language. It is likely that the influence of verbalized thought on all of thought differs with different situations, different individuals, and different cultures, some cultures encouraging verbal thinking or nonverbal thinking more than others. Language necessarily influences how we think when we are speaking aloud, and also to a considerable extent when we are speaking to ourselves; but that is only part of thinking.

The translation paradox

If the semantic structures of different languages organize thoughts in different ways, how is it possible for the thoughts that are expressed in one language to be expressed adequately in another? There is a paradox here (Chafe, 2003). We find people translating from one language to another all the time, and the results seem reasonably successful, at least for practical purposes. How can that be?

The essentials of translation can be understood in the following way. We begin with the thoughts of the source: someone who is either speaking or writing in the source language. Those thoughts are processed in accordance with the semantic and syntactic resources of that language, yielding the sound or writing that provides the input for the translator. That sound or writing leads to thoughts in the mind of the translator, thoughts that resemble those of the source, as they were filtered through the semantic choices that were made. The translator must then pass those thoughts through the semantic and syntactic resources of the target language, so that in the end they can enter the thoughts of the consumer of the translation. The success of the translation might be measured by the degree to which the consumer's ultimate thoughts resemble those of the source. But because there is an inevitable unconformity between the semantic and syntactic resources of the source language and the target language, the source thoughts and the target thoughts can never be identical.

Looking again at the beginning of our example, we can ask how it might be translated into English, a closely related language, as was attempted above. Languages that are not as similar as German and English can create larger problems. Here, once again, is the German source:

.... Dieser Mann sammelt seine Birnen in der.. Schürze,
und wenn die Schürze voll ist,
... geht er,
... steigt er mm die Leiter herunter,
um diese Birnen in einen Korb zu werfen.
.... Werfen ist eigentlich übertrieben,
ich.. hatte also wirklich stark den Eindruck,
wie sorgfältig der.. Mann mit den Birnen umgeht.

The following was suggested as a possible English translation:

This man is gathering his pears in his apron,
and when the apron is full,
he climbs down the ladder,
to throw these pears into a basket.
Throw is actually too strong,
because I was really impressed
with how carefully the man handles the pears.

Attempting to translate the third word of the German, *sammelt*, calls attention to the fact that the semantic resources of English include a durative or so-called *progressive* orientation that is absent from the semantic resources of German. This speaker used the simple present tense with *sammelt*. To say in English *this man gathers his pears* would be awkward, and the progressive *is gathering* is the obvious choice.

Such subtle differences are very common. There is a different problem with *werfen ist eigentlich übertrieben*. In English it is certainly possible to say *throw is actually exaggerated*, but it is probably more natural to use a noun: *throw is actually an exaggeration*, whereas it might be less natural in German to say *werfen ist eigentlich eine Übertreibung*. In fact, *exaggeration* in any form may not be the ideal choice in English, where it might be more natural to say *throw is actually too strong*. Translation is thus an art where subtle choices come frequently into play.

The need for rephrasing is more obvious in the last line, where *wie sorgfältig der Mann mit den Birnen umgeht* exhibits another German idiom. No one would expect to translate it literally: *how carefully the man goes around with the pears*. The most natural phrasing in English might be *how carefully the man handles the pears*, but that is a choice with other connotations. The literal meaning of *damit umgehen* "go around with" may be experienced as a shadow meaning by German speakers, and shadow meanings are particularly resistant to translation (Chafe, 2008).

These have been a few brief illustrations of how a translation, even between such closely related languages, cannot reproduce everything in the source. At the same time it is important to keep in mind that people do not remember very long the specific language they chose to express their thoughts in. The thoughts themselves, the ideas of events and their participants, may remain in memory longer, but the way they happen to have been verbalized on a particular occasion quickly dissipates.

We are thus left with the following question. Although translations cannot capture the full richness of the semantic choices made in a particular verbalization, if those specific choices quickly fade from memory and if the translation does succeed in capturing more grossly the ideas of events and their participants, does that mean that, whatever differences there may have been at first, what remains in memory can be more or less the same in the mind of the original language producer and the hearer or reader of the translation? Is it in the end only a question of how well the translation succeeds in conveying the *ideas* expressed by the original—the ideas themselves, and not the ways in which they happen to have been categorized and oriented and combined on a particular occasion? If specific semantic categorizations and orientations quickly fade, how much is the memory for thoughts affected in the long run by whatever language happened to express those thoughts on a particular occasion?

It is an important question, which has no clear answer at present. To carry the question further, it may sometimes be the case that the thoughts conveyed by language pass through three stages in people's minds. During the first stage, the moment when language is produced and received and for a short time thereafter, people are conscious not only of the ideas and the emotions that were expressed, but also of the rich flavoring that was added by the ways in which those ideas were categorized, oriented, and combined. Within a short time, however, at least some of those categorizations, orientations, and combinations will have faded from memory, whereas the ideas themselves, along with associated emotions, will remain much longer. That is stage two. It is during that stage that we might say that a translation has been successful, because the ideas—as ideas—that were in the mind of the source language speaker or writer were successfully transmitted through the target language.

But sometimes there may be a third stage. If stage two retains the ideas and also the emotions of the original, at stage three the ideas may fade and little may be remembered except the emotions. After sufficient time, all that is remembered are the emotions or attitudes that were at first just one component of the thoughts. People may remember little more than how they felt about something, and no longer what that something was.

If we are sometimes left with only this stage three, there is a final question of interest. To what extent are emotions, apart from the ideas with which they are associated, affected by language differences? In this speaker's third narrative, she ended her description of the pear-picking scene as follows:

> Das ist alles sehr… tsch anschaulich,
> oder sehr.. hmm…. ja einprägsam sinnlich.
> *All that is very vivid,*
> *or very impressively sensual.*

She clearly had trouble expressing her feeling, as shown by her hesitations and changes of wording. Now, if events are processed as perceptual experiences, presumably the processing takes place in the neocortex. That is also where the segmental aspects of phonology—the vowels and consonants and syllables—are processed. But emotions are processed in the older brain, where connections to the segmental aspects of language are less direct. Hence, people often find it difficult to express emotions in words. Could it be that languages differ most in the ways they express and communicate emotions, and that this kind of difference is in the end the most difficult of all challenges for translations to solve? Language has an aesthetic component in which emotions are heavily involved, and that component is widely recognized as the most difficult translation problem of all.

Summary

My main points have been, first, that thoughts are where the action is: where language begins for the speaker and where it ends for the listener. Thoughts are what people are conscious of, as language is created and received and remembered. Second, when thoughts are expressed in language, they must be filtered through processes of selection, categorization, orientation, and combination, and those processes lead to semantic structures. Third, because languages change through lexicalization and grammaticalization, what is passed on to sounds is not a semantic structure directly, but a kind of distorted semantic structure replete with quasi-semantic elements, what we know as syntax. Finally, both thoughts and the language that expresses them are dynamic, constantly changing through time as people think and talk. It follows that static representations of isolated sentences leave much to be desired.

Further reading

Chafe, W. (1994) *Discourse, Consciousness, and Time: The Flow and Displacement of Conscious Experience in Speaking and Writing*. Chicago, IL: The University of Chicago Press.

References

Brown, R. (1958) *Words and Things*. Glencoe, IL: The Free Press.
Chafe, W. (1968) 'Idiomaticity as an anomaly in the Chomskyan paradigm', *Foundations of Language*, 4: 109–127.
Chafe, W. (ed.) (1980) *The Pear Stories: Cognitive, Cultural, and Linguistic Aspects of Narrative Production*. Norwood, NJ: Ablex.
Chafe, W. (1994) *Discourse, Consciousness, and Time: The Flow and Displacement of Conscious Experience in Speaking and Writing*. Chicago, IL: The University of Chicago Press.
Chafe, W. (2003) 'The translation paradox', in N. Baumgarten, C. Böttger, M. Motz, and J. Probst (eds.) *Übersetzen, Interkulturelle Kommunikation, Spracherwerb und Sprachvermittlung: das Leben mit mehreren Sprachen. Festschrift für Juliane House zum 60. Geburtstag. Zeitschrift für Interkulturellen Fremdsprachenunterricht*, 8(2/3): 1–10. Available online at: http://www.ualberta.ca/~german/ejournal/Chafe1.htm.
Chafe, W. (2008) 'Syntax as a repository of historical relics', in A. Bergs and G. Diewald (eds.) *Constructions and Language Change*. Berlin: Mouton de Gruyter, pp. 259–266.
Hopper, P. J. and Traugott, E. C. (1993) *Grammaticalization*. Cambridge: Cambridge University Press.
James, W. (1890) *The Principles of Psychology*. New York: Henry Holt (reprinted in 1950 by Dover Publications).
Pöppel, E. (1994) 'Temporal mechanisms in perception', in O. Sporns and G. Tononi (eds.) *Selectionism and the Brain: International Review of Neurobiology*, vol. 37. San Diego, CA: Academic Press, pp. 185–201.
Slobin, D. I. (1996) 'From "thought and language" to "thinking for speaking"', in J. J. Gumperz and S. C. Levinson (eds.) *Rethinking Linguistic Relativity*. Cambridge: Cambridge University Press, pp. 70–96.

Part IV
Educational applications

26

Discourse and "the New Literacy Studies"

James Paul Gee

The New Literacy Studies and the New Literacies Studies

The new literacy studies (hereafter "NLS") is a name that arose "after the fact." In the 1980s a number of scholars from different disciplines (see citations below, in the next section) began to critique the traditional view of literacy as "the ability to read and write" (a largely individual and mental phenomenon) and to argue for a social and cultural approach to literacy. In the late 1980s I referred to this work, in which I was myself engaged, as "the New Literacy Studies" (Gee, 1989), because I believed that the work shared some common themes and was converging on a new interdisciplinary field of study. The people I included under this label did not necessarily see themselves at the time as being in the same "movement." Brian Street, one of the earliest and leading scholars in the NLS, has since done more than anyone to institutionalize the NLS and to get it recognized as a consistent approach to literacy studies (Street, 1997, 2003, 2005).

The NLS is today accompanied by a related, but different movement, with a name that sounds very close to the NLS: the new literacies studies (Lankshear, 1997; Gee, 2004; Lankshear and Knobel, 2006, 2007). The NLS was about a new approach to print literacy and the oral language practices that surrounded it. The new literacies studies is about new "literacies" involving digital media or popular-culture practices, and thus it goes beyond print literacy. However, the NLS itself stressed the plurality of literacy in terms of different socially and culturally defined practices connected to print (different "literacies"). With such a stress on multiplicity, it is natural that people have extended the plurality of literacy practices to practices involving technologies other than print (such as digital technologies). Thus arose the new literacies studies, which shares with the NLS a social and cultural rather than a psychological approach.

There is yet another wrinkle to this story. In the mid-1990s a group of scholars from the United States, Australia, England, and South Africa met several times, calling themselves "the New London Group" (because their first meeting was in New London, New Hampshire, in the United States). The New London Group (1996) introduced the term "multiliteracies" and stressed the multiplicity of "literacies" in terms of (a) multiple practices using print literacy; (b) practices around multimodal texts that incorporate both images and language; and (c) practices around new digital literacies (just really starting at the time). The New London Group argued, in regard to literacy in all these senses, that people use "signs" (including "grammar") to produce and "design" their own meanings within communities of practice (Lave and Wenger, 1991). They do not just "follow rules." They actively invent the resources necessary for the meanings they wish to communicate. This idea anticipated, by some years, the current focus in areas like the new media studies (or new media literacy studies) on production and "participant culture" (Jenkins, 2006). Furthermore, the New London Group applied this production and participation focus to oral language and print literacy, and not just to digital media.

The NLS and the new literacies studies have always had close ties to discourse analysis. They both stress the fact that "technologies" like print or digital media do not have fixed and universal meanings or universal effects on people. Rather, the meaning and effects a "text" (oral, print, or digital) has are always produced in, and vary with, specific contexts of use within practices connected to specific social and cultural groups. Discourse analysis—sometimes extended to the analysis of multimodal texts and images as well—is the tool most used to analyze the production of meanings in context (Gee, 2005). In fact, the NLS can be viewed—though no one put the matter this way—as a discourse analytic (meaning in context) approach to literacy rather than as the traditional "structures in the head" approach. In the examples of NLS work I detail below, we will see discourse data or aspects of the nature of "language in use" that are often used as evidence for NLS claims.

The NLS: the basic argument

Traditionally, literacy was looked at as primarily a mental phenomenon—the mental "ability" to read and write. In fact, traditionally, all knowledge was viewed as "mental," and literacy itself was just a form of knowledge, namely knowing how to read and write (Snow *et al.*, 1998).

The traditional view saw both literacy and knowledge in terms of mental representations stored in the head ("mind/brain"). These representations are the way in which information from the world is stored and organized in the mind/brain and in terms of which it is then processed or manipulated. Such a perspective leads to focusing on questions about how information gets into the head, how exactly it is organized in the head, and how it gets back out of the head when people need to use it. And indeed these questions have played a central role in much psychological and educational research.

The NLS attacked (or, at times, simply ignored) this mental view of literacy in favor of a historical and sociocultural approach to literacy. Further, the NLS was part of a larger "social turn" in the 1980s, in which work in a variety of areas began to look at language, literacy, knowledge, and learning in social and cultural terms (Gee, 2000). Sociocultural viewpoints look at knowledge and learning not in terms of representations in the head, but in terms of *relationships* between individuals (with both minds and bodies) and physical, social, and cultural environments in and through which individual think, feel, act, and interact with others (Gee, 2004).

In the 1980s a group of scholars, who would later be seen as foundational to the NLS (Graff, 1979, 1987a, b; Hymes, 1980; Michaels, 1981; Scollon and Scollon, 1981; Scribner and Cole, 1981; Gumperz, 1982a, b; Heath, 1982, 1983; Street, 1984, 1993; Gee, 1985, 1987, 1988, 1989; Kress, 1985; Cook-Gumperz, 1986; Wells, 1986; Barton, 1994; Barton and Hamilton, 1998; Cazden, 2001), began seriously to question traditional mental views of literacy as well as the "literacy myth," the idea that literacy, universally and decontextually, leads to more intelligent, modern, humane, and successful people (Graff, 1979). They did this by asking anew the questions: What is literacy? and What is it good for?.

The NLS hit on a seeming paradox: It will not work to define literacy simply as the ability to write and read, though that seems to be the everyday meaning of the word. To see why this is so we need to run through a rather simple argument (Gee, 1989, 2007). The argument has something of the structure of a *reductio ad absurdum*. Our little argument starts with the assumption that reading (or writing) is central to literacy, only to show that this very assumption leads to a view of literacy in which reading or writing (ironically, perhaps) plays a less central role than one might have thought. We will sketch the argument as it has to do with reading. There is an obvious analogue of the argument that starts with writing, rather than reading.

Here's the argument. Literacy surely means nothing unless it has something to do with the ability to read. At the level of meaning, "read" is a transitive verb, since it always implies that the reader can read *something*. So literacy must have something to do with being able to read something. And this something will always be a text of a certain type. Different types of texts (e.g. newspapers, comic books, law books, physics texts, math books, novels, poems, advertisements, etc.) call for different types of background knowledge, require different skills to be read meaningfully, and can be and are read in different ways.

To go one step further: no one would say anyone could read a given text if he or she did not know what the text meant. But there are many different levels of meaning one can give to or take from any text, many different ways in which any text can be read. You can read a friend's letter as a mere report, an indication of her state of mind, a prognosis of her future actions; you can read a novel as a typification of its period and place, as vicarious experience, as "art" of various sorts, as a guide to living, and so on and so forth.

Let me elaborate a bit further on this notion of reading texts in different ways by giving a concrete example. Consider the following sentences from a little story in which a man named "Gregory" has wronged his former girl friend Abigail: "Heartsick and dejected, Abigail turned to Slug with her tale of woe. Slug, feeling compassion for Abigail, sought out Gregory and beat him brutally." In one study (Gee, 2007), some readers (who happened to be African–Americans) claimed that these sentences "say" that Abigail told Slug to beat up Gregory. On the other hand, other readers (who happened not to be African–Americans) claimed that these sentences "say" no such thing. These readers claim, in fact, that the African–Americans have mis-read the sentences.

The African–Americans responded with remarks like the following: "If you turn to someone with a tale of woe, and, in particular someone named "Slug," you are most certainly asking him to do something in the way of violence and you are most certainly responsible when he's done it."

The point is that these different people read these sentences in different ways and think that others have read them in the "wrong" ways. Even if one thinks that the African–Americans (or the others) have read the sentences "incorrectly," the very act of claiming that their reading is incorrect admits that there is a way to read the sentences and that we can dispute how (in what way) the sentences ought to be read (and we can ask who determines the "ought" here and why). If we say that the African–Americans have gone too far "beyond" the text (or that other readers who do not follow them have not gone "far" enough), we still are conceding that there is an issue of "how far" to go, what counts as a way (or the way) of reading a text.

Thus, so far, we have concluded that, whatever literacy has to do with reading, reading must be spelled out, at the very least, as multiple abilities to "read" texts of certain types in certain ways or to certain levels. There are obviously many abilities here, each of them a type of literacy, one of a set of literacies.

The next stage of the argument asks: How does one acquire the ability to read a certain type of text in a certain way? Here proponents of a sociocultural approach to literacy argue that the literature on the acquisition and development of literacy is clear (Heath, 1983; Gee, 2004): a way of reading a certain type of text is only acquired when it is acquired in a "fluent" or "native-like" way, by one's being embedded (apprenticed) as a member of a social practice wherein people not only read texts of this type in this way, but also talk about such texts in certain ways, hold certain attitudes and values about them, and socially interact over them in certain ways.

Thus, one does not learn to read texts of type X in way Y unless one has had the experience of settings where texts of type X are read in way Y. These settings are various sorts of social institutions, like churches, banks, schools, government offices, or social groups with certain sorts of interests, like baseball cards, comic books, chess, politics, novels, movies, or what have you. One has to be socialized into a practice to learn to read texts of type X in way Y, a practice other people have already mastered. Since this is so, we can turn literacy on its head, so to speak, and refer crucially to the social institutions or social groups that have these practices, rather than to the literacy practices themselves. When we do this, something odd happens: the practices of such social groups are never just literacy practices. They also involve ways of talking, interacting, thinking, valuing, and believing.

Worse yet, when we look at the practices of such groups, it is next to impossible to separate anything that stands apart as a literacy practice from others practices. Literacy practices are almost always fully integrated with, interwoven into, constituted as parts of, the very texture of wider practices that involve talk, interaction, values, and beliefs. You can no more cut the literacy out of the overall social practice, or cut away the non-literacy parts from the literacy parts of the overall practice, than you can subtract the white squares from a chess board and still have a chess board.

People who take a sociocultural approach to literacy believe that the "literacy myth" (Graff, 1979, 1987a, b)—the idea that literacy leads inevitably to a long list of "good" things—is a "myth" because literacy, in and of itself, abstracted from historical conditions and social practices, has no effects, or at least no predictable effects. Rather what has effects are historically and culturally situated social practices, of which reading and writing are only bits, bits that are differently composed and situated in different social practices. For example, school-based writing and reading leads to different effects than reading and writing embedded in various religious practices (Scribner and Cole, 1981; Kapitzke, 1995). And, further, there are multiple school-based practices and multiple religious practices, each with multiple effects. Literacy has no effects (though, of course, it may well have certain affordances or tendencies)—indeed, no meaning—apart from particular cultural contexts in which it is used, and it has different effects in different contexts (Graff, 1979; Scollon and Scollon, 1981; Scribner and Cole, 1981, 1987a, b; Gee, 2004).

Examples of founding work in the NLS: Scollon and Scollon

Three founding works that helped initiate the contemporary project of looking at literacy in the context of the social practices and world views of particular social groups were Ronald and Suzanne Scollon's *Narrative, Literacy and Face in Interethnic Communication* (1981); Shirley Brice Heath's *Ways with Words* (1983); and Brian Street's *Literacy in Theory and Practice* (1984). What I want to make clear in my discussion below of these three founding works—all now "old"—is the ways in which, from the outset, work in the NLS melded the study of culture, discourse, language, literacy, and often history and politics.

Scollon and Scollon

The Scollons believe that discourse patterns—ways of using language to communicate, whether in speech or in writing—in different cultures reflect particular reality sets or world views adopted by these cultures. Discourse patterns are among the strongest expressions of personal and cultural identity. The Scollons argue that changes in a person's discourse patterns—for example, in acquiring a new form of literacy—may involve change in identity. They provide a detailed study of the discourse practices and world view of Athabaskans in Alaska and northern Canada and they contrast these with the discourse patterns and world view in much of Anglo-Canadian and Anglo-American society (see also Wieder and Pratt, 1990).

Literacy as it is practiced in European-based education ("essay-text literacy" in the Scollons' phrase) is connected to a reality set or world view that the Scollons term "modern consciousness."

This reality set is consonant with particular discourse patterns, ones quite different from the discourse patterns used by the Athabaskans. As a result, the acquisition of this sort of literacy is not simply a matter of learning a new technology, it involves complicity with values, social practices, and ways of knowing that conflict with those of the Athabaskans.

Athabaskans differ at various points from mainstream Canadian and American English speakers in how they engage in discourse. A few examples: (1) Athabaskans have a high degree of respect for the individuality of others and a careful guarding of their own individuality. Thus they prefer to avoid conversation, except when the point of view of all participants is well known. On the other hand, English speakers feel that the main way to get to know the point of view of people is through conversation with them. (2) For Athabaskans, people in subordinate positions do not display their capacities or show off, rather they observe the person in the superordinate position. For instance, adults in the capacity of parents or teachers are supposed to display abilities and qualities for the child to learn. However, in mainstream American society, children are supposed to show off their abilities for teachers and other adults. (3) The English idea of "putting your best foot forward" conflicts directly with an Athabaskan taboo. It is normal for an English speaker, in situations of unequal status relations, to display oneself in the best light possible. One will speak highly of the future as well. It is normal to present a career or life trajectory of success and planning. This English system is very different from the Athabaskan system, in which it is considered inappropriate and bad luck to anticipate good luck, to display oneself in a good light, to predict the future, or to speak badly of another's luck.

The Scollons list many other differences, including differences in systems of pausing that ensure that English speakers select most of the topics and do most of the talking in interethnic encounters. The net result of these communication problems is that each group ethnically stereotypes the other. English speakers come to believe that Athabaskans are unsure, aimless, incompetent, and withdrawn. Athabaskans come to believe that English speakers are boastful, sure that they can predict the future, careless with luck, and far too talkative.

The Scollons, as I mentioned above, characterize the different discourse practices of Athabaskans and English speakers in terms of two different world views or "forms of consciousness": bush consciousness (connected with survival values in the bush) and modern consciousness. These forms of consciousness are "reality sets" in the sense that they are cognitive orientations toward the everyday world, including learning in that world.

Anglo-Canadian and American mainstream culture has adopted a model of literacy based on the values of the essayist prose style, a model that is highly compatible with modern consciousness. In essayist prose, the important relationships to be signaled are those between sentence and sentence, not those between speakers, nor those between sentence and speaker. For a reader, this requires a constant monitoring of grammatical and lexical information. With the heightened emphasis on truth value rather than social or rhetorical conditions comes the necessity to be explicit about logical implications.

A further significant aspect of the essayist prose style is the fictionalization of both the audience and the author. The "reader" of an essayist text is not an ordinary human being, but an idealization, a rational mind formed by the rational body of knowledge of which the essay is a part. By the same token the author is a fiction, since the process of writing and editing essayist texts leads to an effacement of individual and idiosyncratic identity. The Scollons show the relation of these essayist values to modern consciousness by demonstrating that they are variants of the defining properties of the modern consciousness as given by Berger *et al.* (1973).

For the Athabaskan, writing in this essayist mode can constitute a crisis in ethnic identity. To produce an essay would require the Athabaskan to produce a major display, which would be appropriate only if the Athabaskan was in a position of dominance in relation to the audience. But the audience, and the author, are fictionalized in essayist prose, and the text becomes decontextualized. This means that a contextualized, social relationship of dominance is obscured. Where the relationship of the communicants is unknown, the Athabaskan prefers silence.

The paradox of prose for the Athabaskan, then, is that, if it is communication between a known author and an audience, it is contextualized and compatible with Athabaskan values, but not good essayist prose. To the extent that communication becomes decontextualized, and thus good essayist prose, it becomes uncharacteristic of Athabaskans to seek to communicate. The Athabaskan set of discourse patterns is to a large extent exclusive of the discourse patterns of essayist prose.

Examples of founding work: Shirley Brice Heath

Shirley Brice Heath's classic *Ways with Words* (1983) is an ethnographic study of the ways in which literacy is embedded in the cultural context of three communities in the Piedmont Carolinas in the US: Roadville, a white working-class community that has been part of mill life for four generations; Trackton, a working-class African–American community whose older generation was brought up on the land, but which now is also connected to mill life and other light industry; and mainstream middle-class urban-oriented African–Americans and whites (see also Heath, 1994).

Heath analyzes the ways these different social groups "take" knowledge from the environment, with particular concern for how "types of literacy events" are involved in this taking. A literacy event is any event involving print, such as group negotiation of meaning in written texts (e.g. an ad), individuals "looking things up" in reference books, writing family records in the Bible, and dozens of other types of occasions when books or other written materials are integral to interpretation in an interaction.

Heath interprets these literacy events in relation to the larger sociocultural patterns that they may exemplify or reflect, such as patterns of care giving roles, uses of space and time, age and sex segregation, and so forth. Since language learning and socialization are two sides of the same coin (Schieffelin and Ochs, 1986), Heath concentrates on how children in each community acquire language and literacy in the process of becoming socialized into the norms and values of their communities.

As school-oriented, middle-class parents and their children interact in the pre-school years, adults give their children, through modeling and specific instruction, ways of using language and of taking knowledge from books that seem natural in school and in numerous other institutional settings such as banks, post offices, businesses, or government offices. To exemplify this point, Heath analyzes the bedtime story as an example of a major literacy event in mainstream homes (Heath, 1982; all page references below are to this article).

The bedtime story sets patterns of behavior that recur repeatedly through the life of mainstream children and adults, at school and in other institutions. In the bedtime story routine, the parent sets up a "scaffolding" dialogue (Cazden, 1979) with the child by asking questions like "What is X?" and then supplying verbal feedback and a label after the child has vocalized or given a nonverbal response. Before the age of two, the child is thus socialized into the "initiation–reply–evaluation" sequences so typical of classroom lessons (Mehan, 1979).

In addition, reading with comprehension involves an internal replaying of the same types of questions adults ask children of bedtime stories. Further, "What is X?" questions and explanations are replayed in the school setting in learning to pick out topic-sentences, write outlines, and answer standardized tests. Through the bedtime story routine and similar practices, in which children learn not only how to take meaning from books, but also how to talk about it, children repeatedly practice routines that parallel those of classroom interaction: "Thus, there is a deep continuity between patterns of socialization and language learning in the home culture and what goes on at school" (p. 56).

Children in both Roadville and Trackton are unsuccessful in school despite the fact that both communities place a high value on success in school. Roadville adults do read books to their children, but they do not extend the habits of literacy events beyond book reading. For instance they do not, upon seeing an event in the real world, remind children of similar events in a book, or comment on such similarities and differences between book and real events.

The strong religious fundamentalist bent of Roadville tends to make parents view any fictionalized account of a real event as a lie; reality is better than fiction, and they do not encourage the shifting of the context of items and events characteristic of fictionalization and abstraction. They tend to choose books that emphasize nursery rhymes, alphabet learning, and simplified Bible stories. Even the oral stories that Roadville adults tell, and that children model, are grounded in the actual. The sources of these stories are personal experience. They are tales of transgression, which make the point of reiterating the expected norms of behavior.

Thus Roadville children are not practiced in decontextualizing their knowledge or fictionalizing events known to them, shifting them about into other frames. In school they are rarely able to take knowledge learned in one context and shift it to another; they do not compare two items or events and point out similarities and differences.

Trackton presents a quite different language and social environment. Babies in Trackton, who are almost always held during their waking hours, are constantly in the midst of a rich stream of verbal and nonverbal communication that goes on around them. Aside from Sunday School materials, there are no reading materials in the home just for children; adults do not sit and read to children. Children do, however, constantly interact verbally with peers and adults.

Adults do not ask children "What is X?" questions, but rather analogical questions, which call for non-specific comparisons of one item, event, or person with another (e.g. "What's that like?"). Though children can answer such questions, they can rarely name the specific feature or features that make two items or events alike.

Parents do not believe they have a tutoring role, and they do not simplify their language for children, as mainstream parents do, nor do they label items or features of objects in either books or the environment at large. They believe children learn when they are provided with experiences from which they can draw global rather than analytically specific knowledge. Heath claims that children in Tracton seem to develop connections between situations or items by gestalt patterns, analogs, or general configuration links, not by specification of labels and discrete features in the situation. They do not decontextualize, rather they heavily contextualize nonverbal and verbal language.

Trackton children learn to tell stories by rendering a context and calling on the audience's participation to join in the imaginative creation of the story. In an environment rich in imaginative talk and verbal play, they must be aggressive in inserting their stories into an ongoing stream of discourse. Imagination and verbal dexterity are encouraged.

Indeed, group negotiation and participation constitute a prevalent feature of the social group as a whole. Adults read not alone but in a group. For example, someone may read from a brochure on a new car while listeners relate the text's meaning to their experiences, asking questions and expressing opinions. The group as a whole synthesizes the written text and the associated oral discourse to construct a meaning for the brochure.

At school, most Trackton children not only fail to learn the content of lessons, they also do not adopt the social interactional rules for school literacy events. Print in isolation bears little authority in their world, and the kinds of questions asked of reading books are unfamiliar (for example, what-explanations). The children's abilities to link metaphorically two events or situations and to recreate scenes are not tapped into at school. In fact these abilities often cause difficulties, because they enable children to see parallels teachers did not intend to—and indeed may not—recognize until the children point them out. By the time in their education, after the elementary years for the most part, when their imaginative skills and verbal dexterity could really pay off, they have failed to gain the necessary written composition skills they would need in order to translate their analogical skills into a channel teachers could accept.

Heath's characterization of Trackton, Roadville, and Mainstreamers leads us to see, not a binary (oral/literate) contrast, but a set of features that cross-classifies the three groups in various ways. The groups share various features with each other, and differ from each other in yet other regards. The Mainstream group and Trackton both value imagination and fictionalization, while the Roadville does not; the Roadville and the Trackton group both share a disregard for decontextualization that is not shared by Mainstreamers. Both Mainstreamers and Roadville, but not Trackton, believe parents to have a tutoring role in language and literacy acquisition (they read to their children and ask questions that require labels), but Roadville shares with Trackton, not with the Mainstream, an experiential, non-analytic view of learning (children learn by doing and watching, not by having the process broken down into its smallest parts). As we added more groups to the comparison, e.g. the Athabaskans (which share with the Trackton group a regard for gestalt learning and storage of knowledge, but differ from it in the degree of self-display they allow), we would get more complex cross-classifications.

Heath suggests that, in order for a non-mainstream social group to acquire mainstream, school-based literacy practices, with all the oral and written language skills this implies, individuals, whether children or adults, must "recapitulate," at an appropriate level for their age, of course, the sorts of literacy experiences the mainstream child has had at home. Unfortunately, schools as currently constituted tend to be good places to practice mainstream literacy once you have its foundations, but they are often not good places to acquire those foundations (for example, to engage in the sorts of emergent literacy practices common in many middle-class homes).

Heath also suggests that this foundation, when it has not been set at home, can be acquired by apprenticing the individual to a school-based literate person, for example the teacher, in a new and expanded role. Heath has had students, at a variety of ages, engage in ethnographic research with teachers, studying for instance the uses of language or languages, or of writing and reading, in their own communities. This serves as one way for students to learn and practice, in a meaningful context, the various sub-skills of essay-text literacy (e.g. asking questions, note-taking, discussion of various points of view, as well as writing discursive prose and revising it) with feedback, often from non-present readers.

This approach fits perfectly with Scribner and Cole's (1981) practice account of literacy. And, in line with Street's ideological approach to literacy (see below), it claims that individuals who have not been socialized into the discourse practices that constitute mainstream school-based literacy must eventually be socialized into them if they are ever to acquire them. The skills component of this form of literacy must be practiced, and one cannot practice a skill one has not been exposed to, or engage in a social practice one has not been socialized into—which is what most non-mainstream children are expected to do in school. But at the same time we must remember the Scollons warning that, for many social groups, this practice may well mean a change of identity and the adoption of a reality set at odds with their own at various points. There is a deep paradox here, and there is no facile way of removing it, short of changing our hierarchical social structure and the school systems that by and large perpetuate it.

Examples of founding work: Brian Street

The work of Scribner and Cole–another founding work in the NLS—calls into question what Brian Street, in his book *Literacy in Theory and Practice* (1984), calls "the autonomous model" of literacy: the claim that literacy (or schooling, for that matter) has cognitive effects apart from the context in which it exists and the uses to which it is put in a given culture. This is also sometimes called "the literacy myth." Claims for literacy, in particular for essay-text literacy values, whether in speech or writing, are thus "ideological." They are part of an armory of concepts, conventions, and practices that privilege one social formation as if it were natural, universal, or at least the end point of a normal developmental progression (achieved only by some cultures, thanks either to their intelligence or to their technology).

Street proposes, in opposition to the "autonomous model" of literacy, an "ideological model." The ideological model attempts to understand literacy in terms of concrete social practices and to theorize it in terms of the ideologies in which different literacies are embedded. Literacy—of whatever type—only has consequences as it acts together with a large number of other social factors, including political and economic conditions, social structure, and local ideologies.

Any technology, including writing, is a cultural form, a social product whose shape and influence depend upon prior political and ideological factors. Despite Eric Havelock's (1976) brilliant characterization of the transition from orality to literacy in ancient Greece, for example, it now appears that the Greek situation has rarely if ever been replicated. The particular social, political, economic, and ideological circumstances in which literacy (of a particular sort) was embedded in Greece explain what happened there. Abstracting literacy from its social setting in order to make claims for literacy as an autonomous force in shaping the mind or a culture simply leads to a dead end. This is so because literacy's effects always flow from its social and cultural contexts and vary across those contexts.

There is, however, a last refuge for someone who wants to see literacy as an autonomous force. One could claim that essay-text literacy and the uses of language connected with it lead, if not to general cognitive consequences, to social mobility and success in the society. While this argument may be true, there is precious little evidence that literacy in history or across cultures has had this effect either.

Street discusses, in this regard, Harvey Graff's (1979) study of the role of literacy in nineteenth-century Canada. While some individuals did gain through the acquisition of literacy, Graff demonstrates that this was not a statistically significant effect and that deprived classes and ethnic groups as a whole were, if anything, further oppressed through literacy. Greater literacy did not correlate with increased equality and democracy, nor with better conditions for the working class, but in fact with continuing social stratification.

Graff argues that the teaching of literacy in fact involved a contradiction: illiterates were considered dangerous to the social order, thus they must be made literate; yet the potentialities of reading and writing for an underclass could well be radical and inflammatory. So the framework for the teaching of literacy had to be severely controlled, and this involved specific forms of control of the pedagogic process and specific ideological associations of the literacy being purveyed.

While the workers were led to believe that acquiring literacy was in their benefit, Graff produces statistics to show that, in reality, this literacy was not advantageous to the poorer groups in terms of either income or power. The extent to which literacy was an advantage or not in relation to job opportunities depended on ethnicity. It was not because you were "illiterate" that you finished up in the worst jobs, but because of your background (e.g. being Black or an Irish Catholic rendered literacy much less efficacious than it was for English Protestants).

The story Graff tells can be repeated for many other societies, including Britain and the United States (Donald, 1983; Levine, 1986). In all these societies literacy served as a socializing tool for the poor; but it was seen as a possible threat if misused by the poor (toward an analysis of their oppression and to make demands for power), and it served as a technology for the continued selection of members of one class for the best positions in the society. Yoshio Sugimoto (2003) talks about a parallel situation in Japan, where social class strongly dictates "success" in society, despite the nation's high literacy rates and the mainstream acceptance of Japan as an egalitarian society with equal opportunities.

Conclusion

I have concentrated in this paper on three founding documents in the NLS, in order to give readers a feel for the basic ideas and approaches that formed the NLS. There are, of course, other equally important pieces of early work that I could have surveyed. Also, the work I have surveyed is now dated, though it still incorporates the core arguments for and approaches to literacy as social and cultural that are the foundations of the NLS. For another discussion of the foundations of the NLS and for some more current applications, see Hull and Schultz (2001). Current work has continued along the lines of the foundational work I have surveyed (e.g. Larson and Marsh, 2005; Pahl and Rowsell, 2005, 2006; Gee, 2007), though today NLS work commonly combined with the new literacies studies, to incorporate new forms of literacy, forms that often use not just (or not even) the technology of print, but digital media (e.g. Gee, 2004; Lankshear and Knobel, 2007). Finally, the NLS shows us that, when we move from a psychological approach to a sociocultural approach to something like literacy (or knowledge, the emotions, or problem solving, for example), then discourse analysis and ethnography become the favored methods of research.

References

Barton, D. (1994) *Literacy: An Introduction to the Ecology of Written Language*. Oxford: Blackwell.

Barton, D. and Hamilton, M. (1998) *Local Literacies: Reading and Writing in One Community*. London: Routledge.

Berger, P., Berger, B., and Kellner, H. (1973) *The Homeless Mind: Modernization and Consciousness*. New York: Random House.

Cazden, C. (1979) 'Peekaboo as an instructional model: discourse development at home and at school', *Papers and Reports in Child Language Development* 17: 1–29. (Stanford, CA: Department of Linguistics, Stanford University.)

Cazden, C. (2001) *Classroom Discourse: The Language of Teaching and Learning*. Second Edition. Portsmouth, NH: Heinemann.

Cook-Gumperz, J. (ed.) (1986) *The Social Construction of Literacy*. Cambridge: Cambridge University Press.

Donald, J. (1983) 'How illiteracy became a problem (and literacy stopped being one)', *Journal of Education*, 165 (1): 35–52.

Gee, J. P. (1985) 'The narrativization of experience in the oral style', *Journal of Education*, 167 (1): 9–35.

Gee, J. P. (1987) 'What is literacy?', *Teaching and Learning*, 2 (1): 1–11.

Gee, J. P. (1988) 'Legacies of literacy: from Plato to Freire through Harvey Graff', *Harvard Educational Review*, 58 (2): 195–212.

Gee, J. P. (1989) 'Literacy, discourse, and linguistics: essays by James Paul Gee', *Journal of Education*, 171 (C. Mitchell, ed., special issue).

Gee, J. P. (2000) 'The new literacy studies: from "socially situated" to the work of the social', in D. Barton, M. Hamilton, and R. Ivanic (eds.) *Situated Literacies: Reading and Writing in Context*. London: Routledge, pp. 180–196.

Gee, J. P. (2004) *Situated Language and Learning: A Critique of Traditional Schooling*. London: Routledge.

Gee, J. P. (2005) *An Introduction to Discourse Analysis: Theory and Method* (1999). Second Edition. London: Routledge.

Gee, J. P. (2007) *Social Linguistics and Literacies: Ideology in Discourses* (1990). Third Edition. London: Taylor & Francis.

Graff, H. J. (1979) *The Literacy Myth: Literacy and Social Structure in the 19th Century City*. New York: Academic Press.

Graff, H. J. (1987a) *The Labyrinths of Literacy: Reflections on Literacy Past and Present*. New York: The Falmer Press.

Graff, H. J. (1987b) *The Legacies of Literacy: Continuities and Contradictions in Western Culture and Society*. Bloomington, IN: University of Indiana Press.

Gumperz, J. J. (1982a) *Discourse Strategies*. Cambridge: Cambridge University Press.

Gumperz, J. J. (ed.) (1982b) *Language and Social Identity*. Cambridge: Cambridge University Press.

Havelock, E. (1976) *Preface to Plato*. Cambridge, MA: Harvard University Press.

Heath, S. B. (1982) 'What no bedtime story means: narrative skills at home and at school', *Language in Society*, 11: 49–76.

Heath, S. B. (1983) *Ways with Words: Language, Life, and Work in Communities and Classrooms*. Cambridge: Cambridge University Press.

Heath, S. B. (1994) 'The children of Tracton's children: spoken and written language in social change', in R. B. Ruddell, M. R. Ruddell, and H. Singer (eds.) *Theoretical Models and Processes of Reading*. Fourth Edition. Newark, DE: International Reading Association, pp. 208–230.

Hull, G. A. and Schultz, K. (2001) *School's Out: Bridging Out-of-School Literacies with Classroom Practice*. New York: Teachers College Press.

Hymes, D. (1980) *Language in Education: Ethnolinguistic Essays*. Washington, DC: Center for Applied Linguistics.

Jenkins, H. (2006) *Convergence Culture: Where Old and New Media Collide*. New York: New York University Press.

Kapitzke, C. (1995) *Literacy and Religion: The Textual Politics and Practice of Seventh-Day Adventism*. Amsterdam: John Benjamins.

Kress, G. (1985) *Linguistic Processes in Sociocultural Practice*. Oxford: Oxford University Press.

Lankshear, C. (1997) *Changing Literacies*. Berkshire, UK: Open University Press.

Lankshear, C. and Knobel, E. (2007) *A New Literacies Sampler*. New York: Peter Lang.

Lankshear, C. and Knobel, M. (2006) *New Literacies*. Second Edition. Berkshire, UK: Open University Press.

Larson, J. and Marsh, J. (2005). *Making Literacy Read: Theories for Learning and Teaching*. Thousand Oaks, CA: Sage.

Lave, J. and Wenger, E. (1991) *Situated Learning: Legitimate Peripheral Participation*. New York: Cambridge University Press.

Levine, K. (1986) *The Social Context of Literacy*. London: Routledge.

Mehan, H. (1979) *Learning Lessons*. Cambridge, MA: Harvard University Press.

Michaels, S. (1981) ' "Sharing time": children's narrative styles and differential access to literacy', *Language in Society*, 10: 423–442.

New London Group (1996) 'A pedagogy of multiliteracies: designing social futures', *Harvard Education Review*, 66 (1): 60–92.

Pahl, K. and Rowsell, J. (eds.) (2005). *Literacy and Education: Understanding the New Literacy Studies in the Classroom*. Thousand Oaks, CA: Paul Chapman Educational Publishing.

Pahl, K. and Rowsell, J., (eds.) (2006). *Travel Notes from the New Literacy Studies: Instances of practice*. Clevedon: Multilingual Matters.

Schieffelin, B. B. and Ochs, E. (eds.) (1986) *Language Socialization Across Cultures*. Cambridge: Cambridge University Press.

Scollon, R. and Scollon, S. W. (1981) *Narrative, Literacy, and Face in Interethnic Communication*. Norwood, NJ: Ablex.

Scribner, S. and Cole, M. (1981) *The Psychology of Literacy*. Cambridge, MA: Harvard University Press.

Snow, C. E., Burns, M. S., and Griffin, P. (eds.) (1998) *Preventing Reading Difficulties in Young Children*. Washington, DC: National Academy Press.

Street, B. (1984) *Literacy in Theory and Practice*. Cambridge: Cambridge University Press.

Street, B. (ed.) (1993) *Cross-Cultural Approaches to Literacy*. Cambridge: Cambridge University Press.

Street, B. (1997) 'The implications of the "New Literacy Studies" for literacy education', *English in Education*, 31 (3): 45–59.

Street, B. (2005) 'At last: recent applications of new literacy studies in educational contexts', *Research in the Teaching of English*, 39 (4): 417–423.

Street, B. (2003) 'What's new in new literacy studies?', *Current Issues in Comparative Education*, 5 (2): 1–14.

Sugimoto, Y. (2003) *An Introduction to Japanese Society*. Cambridge: Cambridge University Press.

Wells, G. (1986) *The Meaning Makers: Children Learning Language and Using Language to Learn*. Portsmouth, New Hampshire: Heinemann.

Wieder, D. L. and Pratt, S. (1990) 'On being a recognizable Indian among Indians', in D. Carbaugh (ed.) *Cultural Communication and Intercultural Contact*. Hillsdale, NJ: Lawrence Erlbaum, pp. 45–64.

27

Ethnography and classroom discourse

Amy B. M. Tsui

Classroom discourse research has always been central to educational research. As Cazden (2001) pointed out, the basic purpose of schools is achieved through communication. By studying discursive activities in the classroom, researchers gain insights into the complex and dynamic relationships between discourse, social practices, and learning. An ethnographic approach to L1 (first language) classroom discourse studies was first adopted in the 1960s. However, the use of this approach in L2 (second language) classroom discourse studies is a relatively recent development. This chapter provides a brief account of the nature of ethnography and of the characteristics of ethnographic approaches to classroom discourse, along with a discussion of the major themes that have emerged in the studies so far and some of the issues that the field needs to address.

What is ethnography?

Ethnography originated in Western anthropological studies of non-Western human societies and cultures in the nineteenth century, and is primarily concerned with field research. The word "ethnography" is derived from the Greek words *ethnos* (race, people, or cultural groups) and *graphe* (writing or representation). In order to produce representations or descriptions of cultural groups, events, or phenomena, the ethnographic researcher usually spends an extended period of time in the community under investigation, participating either overtly or covertly in people's lives, observing, listening, and asking questions in the data collection process to gain insights into the issues being studied. This approach to research has been adopted in social sciences and educational research as a reaction against positivistic research, which emphasizes the importance of rigorous measurement and highly structured empirical research, where extraneous variables are controlled for hypothesis testing. Ethnographic researchers have argued that positivism fails to recognize the complexity of human social life and the importance of meaning and interpretation in the research process.

However, since ethnography has been used in different disciplinary contexts in association with, as well as in opposition to, different methodological approaches, there is no standard definition of the term. LeCompte and Preissle (1993) pointed out that, apart from being a product, ethnography is a process—a way of studying human life. They emphasized the fluidity of the ethnographic process and cautioned against rigidifying it as a specific research model. Nevertheless, they also outlined four characteristics of its investigative strategies. First, ethnography aims to represent the worldview of the participants; second, it is empirical and naturalistic;

third, it aims to construct a holistic description of a phenomenon in its context; and, fourth, its data collection strategies are eclectic. Hammersley and Atkinson (2007) observed that ethnography "plays a complex and shifting role in the dynamic tapestry that the social sciences have become in the twenty-first century" (p. 2). Therefore, instead of defining ethnography, they outlined the characteristics of what ethnographers do, which largely converge with the characteristics outlined by LeCompte and Preissle (1993): first, the investigation is conducted in naturalistic, as opposed to experimental or highly structured, settings; second, data are collected through a range of sources, including documentary evidence, but mainly through participant observation and informal conversations with participants in the study; third, the data collection process is largely unstructured in that it does not involve following a rigid predetermined design or using a set of pre-determined categories; fourth, the analysis of data is mainly qualitative (quantitative analysis plays a supplementary role), involving the interpretation of meaning in context; and, finally, the data set usually consists of only a small number of cases, sometimes even a single case, so that in-depth analysis can be made.

In other words, one could say that ethnographic studies are exploratory in orientation and, as such, typically adopt a relatively open-ended approach to investigation. Instead of having a *definitive* set of well-defined research questions with associated hypotheses to be confirmed or disconfirmed, ethnographers typically refine and even change their research questions as they respond to the data collected, and this, in turn, directs them to collect further data to address these refined questions.

Despite the variations in the interpretation of ethnography, one major feature that distinguishes it from other research approaches is the role of the researcher as a participant in the lives of people and a community, one who immerses him- or herself in a specific cultural setting in order to gain an understanding of the phenomenon under investigation. The phrase "participant observation," as Wolcott (2008) has pointed out, is used to capture the first-hand experience of the researcher in naturally occurring events. It should be noted, however, that this expression has been used in some cases as an umbrella to encompass all the activities that the researcher performs in the field, whereas in other cases a distinction has been made between "participant" and "non-participant" observations, the latter referring to instances in which the researcher acts as an observer rather than as a participant and collects data mainly through interviews. For example, Wolcott (2008) distinguishes between participant observation, interviewing, and archival research and describes what the researcher needs to do to accomplish each of them as, respectively, experiencing, enquiring, and examining.

Characteristics of ethnographic approaches to the study of classroom discourse

As I have mentioned, an ethnographic approach to L2 classroom discourse studies is a relatively recent development. Early L2 classroom discourse studies, in the 1970s and 1980s, focused mainly on observable linguistic behaviors in the classroom. A plethora of classroom observational schedules and discourse analysis tools were devised and the analysis was done largely from an *etic* (outsider) perspective. However, since the late 1980s, the importance of interpreting the data from an *emic* (insider) perspective has been pointed out by a number of researchers. Kumaravadivelu (1991), for example, made a good case for this by showing the mismatches between the teacher's intended meaning and the learner's interpretation, as well as between the teacher's and the learner's intention and the observer's interpretation. The inadequacies of using a decontexualized approach to classroom discourse analysis to understand the complexities of classroom interaction have also become clear. In the late 1980s and 1990s, a number of studies pointed out that several dimensions come into play in the process of interaction, including students' cultural backgrounds and learning styles, their psychological states such as motivation, attitudes and beliefs, and classroom cultures, along with teachers' conceptions of teaching and learning, and their lived experiences of L2 teaching and learning (see for example Allwright and Bailey, 1991; Johnson, 1995; Tsui, 1996). Subsequently, research methodologies in neighbouring disciplines have been appropriated for analysis (see Tsui, 2008 for a review of these studies).

Many of the classroom discourse studies since then have been inspired by ethnography of communication, founded by Hymes (1962, 1974), in which studies of language are situated in specific social and cultural settings and are central to the study of culture and communities (see Smart, this volume). The initial focus of ethnography of communication was spoken language, but the discipline was subsequently broadened to include nonvocal forms such as written and sign languages and nonverbal forms such as silence, laughter, and paralinguistic gestures. In the 1970s and 1980s, when issues of language socialization and the literacy development of linguistic and ethnic minorities at home and in schools became a growing concern (Heath, 1982; Philips, 1983), the site of study extended from communities to schools. These studies identified the cultural discontinuity between the home and the school for minority children as a major cause of educational failure and called for a better understanding of the linguistic and social practices in these communities and a better transition from home to school learning environments. They also showed how educational practices reproduced socioeconomic and political practices and called for the need to link micro classroom processes to macro social processes (Toohey, 2008). Since then, a number of studies have been conducted in schools, initially in L1 classrooms (see for example Cazden, 2001; Mehan, 1979) and subsequently in L2 classrooms as well (see for example Watson-Gegeo, 1988; Harklau, 1994; Duff, 1995; Johnson, 1995).

Ethnographic studies of classroom discourse are characterized by the researcher spending an extended period of time in the classroom, either as an observer or as a participant, taking on the role of a teacher or a teacher assistant. Typically, the lessons observed are audio or videorecorded and supplemented by field notes. As it is not always practicable to be a participant researcher, many classroom researchers obtain an *emic* perspective on classroom processes through the collection of a variety of qualitative data, such as teachers' and learners' journals, interviews, and stimulated recalls. The researcher also spends time in the school, outside the classroom, gathering data on the wider sociocultural and political contexts that are relevant to the research focus and throw light on the interpretation of classroom discourse data, such as educational policy documents, the school curriculum, the socioeconomic background of learners, and the school culture (van Lier, 1988; Duff, 1995; Johnson, 1995; Bailey and Nunan, 1996). In other words, the classroom researcher, as an ethnographer, is engaged in "watching what happens, listening to what is said, asking questions through informal and formal interviews, collecting documents and artefacts—in fact, gathering whatever data are available to throw light on the issues that are the emerging focus of inquiry" (Hammersley and Atkinson, 2007: 3).

An ethnographic approach that focuses on one part of the situation, or a slice of everyday life, and analyzes in great detail how interaction is organized and managed socially and culturally at the micro-level in particular settings, has been referred to as "ethnographic microanalysis of interaction" or "microethnography" (see Garcez, 2008 for a summary of micro-ethnographic studies). Ethnographic studies of classroom discourse are essentially micro. Face-to-face interaction in the classroom is taken as a site for studying cultural production and reproduction (Mehan, 1998), and the focus is the description and interpretation of detailed interactional processes. As such, the discipline has close affinity with ethnomethodology, which examines the reflexivity of spoken interaction and the management of the interactional process by participants as they make sense of each other's actions in real time (Garfinkel, 1967) (see Clayman, this volume).

Micro-ethnographical studies of classroom discourse have been criticized for offering a "limited and limiting perspective," on the grounds that they treat the classroom as a self-contained unit rather than as part of the larger society, and largely ignore the sociocultural and political structures that have a bearing on classroom discourse (Kumaravadivelu, 1999: 453). This criticism is perhaps not entirely well founded, because many of the studies that have emerged since the mid-1990s did involve a combination of micro- and macroethnography (Duff, 2002; Garcez, 2008; Toohey, 2008) (see also Jasper, this volume). That is, data are collected from both the larger social context and the classroom context. Data reduction is done by selecting sample data sets that are considered to reflect the general patterns observed in the larger data set, or specific data sets that are relevant to the research question, and by conducting interviews with selected participants who are able to provide an *emic* perspective on the phenomenon under investigation. Hence, ethnographic studies typically identify a case, or several cases, for in-depth investigation. For example, Duff (1995) conducted a study in which she explored the impact of language socialization on students' learning opportunities from a transmission mode to an open enquiry mode of learning in Hungary in early 1990, when the country was going through significant social changes. She selected history lessons because history was a very popular and important subject in the Hungarian curriculum. These lessons dealt with issues that were relevant to the sociopolitical changes at the time, and therefore rich discursive activities could be found in the classroom. Similarly, to investigate problems generated by the transition of English as second language (ESL) learners to mainstream classroom learning, Harklau (1994) identified a small number of Chinese immigrant students and investigated the differences in their patterns of participation in the different learning environments in ESL and mainstream classrooms.

For the case(s) identified, the researcher usually observes a large number of lessons in order to get a sense of the general interaction patterns, routines, norms of practice, and participant relationships. In many cases, most, if not all, of these lessons are recorded. As it would not be possible for the researcher to transcribe and analyze in detail such voluminous data, typically activities or speech events that are representative of the overall patterns observed, or illustrative of the phenomenon under investigation, are chosen for detailed analysis. For example, in the study of history lessons in Hungarian classrooms cited above (Duff, 1995), instead of analyzing all 36 hours of lesson recordings, Duff selected for detailed analysis a total of 16 hours of a speech event, "Student Lectures" involving extensive student talk. According to Duff, an activity, or a speech event, is "simply a way of framing culturally organized behavior in order to consider what is being done, how it is being done, and what it entails and signifies" (p. 513). Focusing on one speech event, she argued, facilitates the deconstruction of the event and comparisons across contexts. As in all ethnographic studies, the choice of a case, or cases, and the selection of the units within a case for detailed analysis are critical. This point will be elaborated further in the penultimate section.

Major themes in ethnographic studies of classroom discourse

Ethnographic approaches to L2 classroom discourse started in the late 1980s and began to attract attention in the 1990s (see for example McKay 1995; Lantolf, 2000). They are often adopted in conjunction with discourse analysis methodologies, to investigate how educational processes and practices are co-constructed by the teacher and the students and how discourse processes and practices shape learning, what opportunities for learning are opened up, and what is being learnt (Gee and Green, 1998; see Richland, this volume). In the rest of this section I shall outline some of the key issues that have been addressed so far and the methods of investigation that have been adopted.

Language socialization of ESL learners

One important theme has been the socialization of ESL learners into different learning environments and the difficulties and opportunities that they encounter in the transition. For example, Harklau (1994) conducted a three-and-a-half-year ethnographic study on the transition of four Chinese immigrant students from ESL to mainstream classrooms in a Californian high school. She investigated the differences in the learning environments in mainstream and ESL classrooms and the learners' performance. Patterns of spoken and written language use displayed by the students, as well as language instruction and feedback in the classroom, were examined together with the content and goals of ESL and mainstream curricula. Harklau was an observer and, at times, a participant playing a similar role as the two aides in the class. She found that one important difference in the learning environments was the interactional routines used in ESL and mainstream classes. While the ESL learners were very quiet in the mainstream classes, they participated actively in ESL classes, initiated more questions, and received more feedback on phonological and grammatical accuracy. Interviews with the learners revealed that in the mainstream classes, where the teacher was a native speaker of English, the teacher's use of unmodified speech, digression into the teacher's own personal experiences, and the use of sarcasm were a source of frustration because the learners could not understand the input. Consequently, the ESL learners "tuned out" and preferred to interact with the written text, which they considered more important than the spoken text. On the basis of these findings, Harklau argued for the integration of the curricula and instructional practices in ESL and mainstream classrooms, so that ESL learners would not be disadvantaged.

On the same theme, Duff (1995) explored the socialization of students from a traditional transmission mode of teaching to an open enquiry mode of learning, which she found resulted in very different patterns of interaction in the classroom and opened up new opportunities for learning. Duff investigated the classroom discourse of an English-medium history classroom in an experimental dual-language (i.e. foreign language immersion) school in Hungary, in the context of sociopolitical changes in the late 1980s that also encompassed educational changes. The Soviet model of teaching, which had been adopted previously, involved recitation (*felelés*), which required students to present formally to the teacher, in front of the whole class, an oral summary of particular aspects or themes covered in the previous lesson, and to respond to questions subsequently posed by the teacher. At the end of the performance a grade was announced. In the 1980s, this Soviet model was replaced by short student lectures and open discussions. Duff observed history lessons in both non-dual language (Hungarian-medium) and dual language (English-medium) lessons, and the former was used as the baseline for analyzing the latter. Over the span of a year, in lessons taught by six Hungarian teachers, Duff observed and recorded almost 40 hours of English-medium teaching. Out of this data set, rather than analyzing the entire lesson, she selected a total of 16 hours of speech events taught by one of the best teachers and containing extended student talk for closer analysis. The speech event was "Student Lectures," which had replaced "Recitation" in the Hungarian-medium lessons. The focus of the study was not, however, the difficulties encountered by the students, but the impact that a more open mode of inquiry had on learning. The findings showed that the introduction of a more democratic form of teaching, one that provided space for students to participate in the co-construction of knowledge, resulted in very different interactional patterns, in which students freely voiced their views and challenged each other and even the teacher. The significance of the discourse, and the socialization of students into the use of a foreign language for a democratic exchange of ideas, could not have been fully appreciated without grounding it in the political changes that were taking place in Hungary at that time.

On a much smaller scale, Morita (2000) conducted a longitudinal ethnographic study on the socialization of L1 and L2 English speaking graduate students into academic spoken discourse. The focus of the study was oral presentation, an "activity" or speech event that occurred frequently and was highly routinized. To understand the academic culture of graduate study at the university, Morita conducted interviews with students and professors, classroom observation, and questionnaire surveys. The findings of the study suggested that the socialization into oral academic presentation, a commonplace feature of graduate studies, is a complex process that involves negotiation between the instructor, the student, and his or her peers.

(Co)-Construction of social relationships, identities and ideologies

Another important theme that has attracted much attention is the conception of ESL learning as not only involving the development of linguistic competence in L2 but also the development of identities, social relationships, and ideologies. For example, Willet (1995) conducted a year-long study of a first grade classroom as part of a larger four-year study of a community of international graduate students and their families. Grounded in the conception of learning as changing participation (Lave and Wenger, 1991; Gee and Green, 1998), the study focused on the changing participation of four children, officially labeled as learners of limited English proficiency (LEP), in activities designed for mainstream classes as their L2 competence developed over time. As a participant–observer, Willet acted as a teacher's aide and collected extensive data through audio-taping the interactions in the classroom and the participation of the children, taking field notes of critical as well as of daily events in the classroom, the school, and the community, conducting casual conversations with the children to obtain their understanding of classroom events, and conducting interviews with teachers and parents. Classroom discourse data, including both teacher–pupil and pupil–pupil interactions collected at different junctures during the longitudinal study, were analyzed in great detail by drawing on the ethnographic data of each participant, their ethnic and family backgrounds, and the micropolitics of the classroom, which became evident after lengthy and sustained involvement in the classroom and community culture. Questions that guided the analysis of data pertained to the structure of events, the spoken and written discourse structures, the participant roles played by the children, the contextual cues they used, and the social relations, identities, and ideologies that were indexed. Willet observed that the interactional routines and strategies used by the children were sites for constructing their relationships with peers, their identities as competent learners, and their ideologies about the dignity and value of work that were sanctioned in the classroom. These, in turn, affected the children's access to the language and culture of the classroom. Hence, according to Willet, the question that was addressed was not what interactional routines and strategies led to successful language acquisition but how the learners locally defined the meanings of the interactional routines and strategies that enabled them to construct positive relations and identities in the classroom.

Another example is the study conduced by Duff (2002) on how knowledge, identities, and cultural differences were co-constructed and manifested in the interactions in an ethnically heterogeneous mainstream classroom, which consisted of what she referred to as the newcomers, mostly ethnic Chinese immigrants, the old-timers, and the "local" English-speaking Canadian students. The research question she addressed was how the classroom could provide opportunities for the creation of a cohesive learning community among culturally heterogeneous students where knowledge and identities are negotiated in a culturally respectful manner. She examined both the micro- and the macro-contexts of communication in a content classroom, the interactional features, and the implicit and explicit references to cultural differences and identity. Over a period of two years, she attended two mainstream social studies classes offered by two teachers.

These two classes were selected on the basis of their ethnic mix and of the content of instruction, social studies, which involved issues of Canadian culture, national identity, and current social issues. The data reported in Duff (2002) pertained to classes taught by one of two teachers whom she observed weekly. To gain a better understanding of both the school culture and the individual teachers, she attended other school activities and other lessons taught by the same teacher. She focused on the discourse generated by discussion (a format used by the teacher to explore the history curriculum), during which students were encouraged to express their views about social issues with the goal of creating an inclusive classroom. Duff examined the relational and experiential dimensions of the students' identity construction. The former refers to how the students were perceived by others and the latter refers to how the students experienced and negotiated their own identities. She found that, notwithstanding the good intention to cultivate respect for cultural differences and diversity and to engage local and non-local students in discussions of culture, the teacher inadvertently widened rather than bridged the cultural gap, as a result of the way she positioned the students culturally through the turns she allocated to certain students and through her attempts to get these students to relate the course content to their own cultural backgrounds. The findings problematized the received view of language socialization as a process of the novice learning to participate in the discourse like an expert. They showed that it is a complex process, in which students may or may not socialize into the mainstream discourse, depending on whether they have other multilingual repertoires and identities to draw on, whether they have communities other than the classroom with which they can identify, and what their personal preference for the manner of their participation in the discourse is.

Social positioning, power and gender in classroom discourse

Closely connected to the theme of the co-construction of identities in classroom discourse are the themes of social positioning, power relationships, and gender. Studies engaging with such themes have generally adopted critical approaches to discourse, examining the implications of discourse practices for power, status, distribution of resources, and their relationship with the achievement of desirable social, political, and ethical goals (Hammersley, 2002; Gee, 2004). Kumaravadivelu (1999) suggested critical discourse analysis as the research tool to unravel the "hidden meanings and underlying connections" in classroom discourse "through posing questions relating to ideology, power, knowledge, class, race, and gender" (p. 476) (see Fairclough, this volume). Ethnographic studies with such an orientation have been referred to as critical ethnography. In fact, many of the recently published ethnographic studies in classroom discourse have adopted critical perspectives, and have engaged with issues of equality of access to opportunities for learning, power relationships, gender, social positioning, and identities (see Coates, this volume; Blackledge, this volume). For example, Menard-Warwick (2008) explored the issue of gender and social positioning in an ESL course for adult immigrants as part of an ethnographic study on immigrant women and L2 learning. By examining the linguistic and interactional structures in the classroom, she showed the tension between the identities that the female immigrant learners claimed for themselves as competent members of the community and the gendered social identities that were assigned to them by their teacher. She argued that teachers should listen for and support learners' reflexive positioning in order to facilitate their reconstruction of L2 identities and voices. Another example is the work of Bloome *et al.* (2005), which investigated the social construction of identities and power relationships in two primary classrooms, one being a language arts classroom and the other a social studies classroom, through a detailed analysis of classroom discourse data.

Teacher and learner agency in the co-construction of knowledge

Another prominent theme has been the shift from a deterministic view of classroom discourse being shaped by the context to a view of classroom discourse and context being mutually constitutive. The agency of the teacher and of the learners in co-constructing knowledge and in creating opportunities for learning has been emphasized. For example, over one year, as part of a large-scale research program, spanning ten grades, on how everyday life in the classroom was constructed by members and how opportunities for learning were opened up by these construc-tions, Tuyay *et al.* (1995) studied the face-to-face interactions of two teams of third-grade bilingual children, a pair of female students, and a group of three male students who were completing a writing task in the classroom. The aim of the study was to investigate the opportunities for learning and the co-construction of knowledge through both spoken and written discourse. The study focused on analyzing the discourse of the two teams of students as they struggled to complete a writing task—a 30-minute student-initiated task called the "planet story," in which students first listened to a student reading aloud a book on extraterrestrials and then wrote their own stories. This key event was selected because it was typical of the discourse patterns, collaborative tasks, and co-construction of knowledge that could be found throughout the school year, and because it clearly illustrated the roles of both the students and the teacher in the knowledge construction process. Detailed analysis of segments of discussions from both teams was provided, drawing on the ethnographic data on classroom life. The findings showed how the two teams of students negotiated, shaped, and reshaped the task through interaction. The researchers concluded that, while a common task does not entail common opportunities to learn, it nevertheless opens up possibilities for students to construct their own learning through negotiation and renegotiation.

The importance of the agency of the teacher in using creative discursive practices that are appropriate for the students was highlighted in Lin (1999), an ethnographic study of four ESL classrooms in Hong Kong. Drawing on Bourdieu's concepts of habitus, cultural capital (1973), and symbolic violence (1991), Lin analyzed excerpts of discourse in these classrooms. She showed that, when the teacher refused to use L1 to help the students to transition to English-medium learning, students from low socioeconomic families who had not been socialized into English-medium communication at home were not only disadvantaged but also alienated from learning English. However, when the teacher was able to use L1 judiciously as a bridging tool, ESL learning became meaningful to students.

The above brief review is an attempt to outline only some of the prominent themes that have emerged so far and is by no means exhaustive. It shows that ethnographic studies of classroom discourse have yielded immensely rich data, which have illuminated our understanding of the multi-faceted nature of interaction in the classroom, tof he role of the teacher and learners, and of the challenges faced by them. Nevertheless, there is a number of issues that the field needs to address, most of which are methodological, to which I now turn.

Issues to be addressed in future research

Research design and theoretical motivation

Methodological issues in ethnographic research have generated much debate. Walford (2005: 1) observes that "what counts as ethnography and what counts as good ethnographic methodology are both highly contested." On the one hand, ethnographic researchers have criticized positivistic research for failing to recognize the complexity of human social life and the importance of a qualitative approach to the interpretation of data. Positivistic researchers, on the other hand, have questioned ethnographic research for not adequately attending to the two cannons of scientific enquiry, namely reliability and validity, and for neglecting the importance of quantitative analysis, generalizability, and hypothesis-testing. Hammersley (2002) points out that, as a result of the growing influence of ethnography and qualitative research in the past few decades, quantitative research has been marginalized in some areas of social sciences research. He argues that quantitative and qualitative approaches should be seen as complementary rather than mutually exclusive (see also LeCompte and Goetz, 1982; Hammersley, 1990). He further observes that most ethnographic studies do not go beyond the stage of putting into question what has been taken for granted and providing plausible explanations for the identified puzzling phenomenon (see also Hammersley and Atkinson, 2007). He suggests that there is a need for ethnographic research to advance theory through explicit theorizing and hypothesis testing. The latter requires the selection of cases that are theoretically motivated, referred to by Glaser and Strauss (1967) as theoretical sampling, and the partial control of extraneous variables that are relevant to the research question under investigation.

While the ethnographer should adopt an entirely open approach when conducting the study and refrain from imposing his or her own views or a conceptual framework in data analysis and interpretation (LeCompte and Preissle, 1993), this does not mean that the ethnographer should not have any theoretical assumptions that he or she wishes to investigate. In the studies reviewed above, the selection of cases for detailed investigation was motivated by theoretical assumptions or hypotheses rather than being random. The important point is that the researcher should have an open mind and allow the data to refute whatever theoretical assumptions he or she may have. If ethnographic studies were to advance theory, there should be more explicit articulation of the theoretical motivation in the design of the studies.

Etic *and* emic *perspectives*

As outlined at the beginning of this chapter, an essential characteristic of ethnographic research is the investigation of a phenomenon from the world view of the participants. In fact, participant constructs should be used to structure the research. While the majority of the ethnographic studies of classroom discourse reviewed here have been based on interviews or informal conversations conducted with participants to construct the larger context in which the classroom discourse data are situated, there are not many that demonstrate an analysis of the classroom discourse data from the participants' perspective. In a number of cases, the analysis of the data presented by the researcher appears to be *etic* rather than *emic*, because there is little or no triangulation between the discourse data, the participants' intentions when they participated in the discourse, and their interpretation of the discourse at the time. (For an example of an explicit triangulation of classroom discourse data with the participation interview data, see Duff, 2002). What Duff has demonstrated by such triangulation is that the participants' perceptions of the discourse in which they are engaged are central to the elucidation of the relationship between social practices of language use and issues of identity, social positioning, power, and gender.) The apparent *etic* perspective could well be due to the fact that the ethnographic studies reported in journal papers are typically part of a larger, long-term study, often lasting over one year and involving the collection of a larger data set than reported in the cited publication. The restricted word limits of most journal papers tend to prevent the author from providing a detailed account of the entire data collection and analysis processes, hence giving the impression that analysis was done entirely from the researcher's perspective. As a number of researchers have pointed out, it is difficult for a journal article of limited length to do justice to the thick description typical of ethnographic research (Lazaraton, 1995; Green and Dixon, 2002; Rampton *et al.*, 2002). Nevertheless, it should be cautioned that truncated reports in journal articles may mislead novice researchers in the field in terms of methodology.

Macro- and micro-analysis of classroom discourse

Earlier studies of classroom discourse typically attended to the micro-analysis of classroom discourse, providing detailed descriptions of linguistic features of utterances and interactional features. These analyses, however, were decontextualized, as pointed out before. With the growing emphasis on situating the analysis of classroom discourse in the larger social context, the pendulum now seems to have swung the other way. Many of the more recent ethnographic studies have provided rich descriptions of the social context and interaction in the classroom without giving an account of the micro-analytic method adopted, or of the actual data analysis (Green and Dixon, 2002). Frequently, although a few excerpts from the classroom discourse data set were selected and narratives were provided to describe what was happening in these excerpts, the actual micro-analysis of the classroom discourse data was not reported. Zuengler and Mori (2002) observed that there has been little meta-methodological discussion on the micro-analytic frameworks for classroom discourse. The special issue in *Applied Linguistics* Volume 23 (3) was the first attempt. Three exemplars were presented illustrating three different methodologies, ethnography of communication, conversational analysis (CA), and systemic functional linguistics, grounded in three respective disciplines, anthropology, sociology, and functional linguistics (see Duff, 2002; Mori, 2002; Young and Nguyen, 2002). As pointed out by both Rampton *et al.* (2002) and Green and Dixon (2002), who were respondents to the three exemplars, no one micro-analytic framework can independently provide a full picture of language in use in the classroom. The collection of papers showed that merely focusing on the analysis of language produced in one type of text or task, without linking it to the broader context and without accessing the interpretive frames and procedures that participants draw on during the interaction, is insufficient to illuminate what constitutes language in use in the classroom and the factors that come into play as the discourse unfolds. Access to participants' interpretative frames is particularly important in the adoption of CA for analyzing classroom discourse, because of the different assumptions about the conversationalists' linguistic and conversational competence and the shared knowledge between them in natural conversational contexts and in ESL classroom contexts (Rampton *et al.*, 2002). However, detailed turn-by-turn analyses of the discourse, such as those reported in Mori (2002), were necessary to reveal how an intended classroom task (a discussion meeting) was transformed into another unintended task (an interview). As Green and Dixon (2002) observed, it is the interweaving of macro- and micro-levels of analysis that provides the basis for making grounded claims about the interpretation of data. In other words, to gain a better and broader understanding of the multi-faceted nature of the classroom discourse and the challenges faced by teachers and students, it is necessary to use a combination of macro- and micro-analytic frameworks and methodologies.

Classroom as a bounded unit and a unit of inquiry

The basic assumptions of ethnography are that there exists distinct culturally and geographically bounded units and that cultural practices are transmitted from "oldtimers" to "newcomers." These two assumptions, however, have been challenged in the last two decades, as the impact of globalization, typified by the breaking down of boundaries and the emergence of hybridization on all fronts, has become increasingly strong (Toohey, 2008). Rampton *et al.* (2002) questioned whether labels such as "oldtimers," "newcomers," "locals," and "non-locals" continue to be relevant in a postmodern world where cultural, political, and geographical boundaries are much more porous and fluid than before and cultural hybridity has become the norm. As Toohey (2008) pointed out, new methods of inquiry may be necessary for an investigation that allows the ethnographer to access the multiple contexts and realities in which learners are located (see also Eisenhart, 2001). The question that needs to be considered is whether it is sufficient to take the classroom as the site of inquiry or whether the focus of inquiry needs to "shift from local to broader contexts and back again, as the effects of practices in other contexts are keenly felt at the local level" (Toohey, 2008: 184). The accomplishment of the latter not only requires a much closer link between macro- and micro-levels of research, but also imposes a greater demand on the researcher's ability to perceive the part–whole relationship among the phenomena being investigated.

Concluding remarks

Ethnographic studies of classroom discourse have provided immensely rich insights into classroom discourse as a mediational tool, not only for learning but also for the negotiation and (co)-construction of identity, power, and social relationships. These studies situate classroom discourse in the wider context and have provided a better understanding of the ways in which micro-processes in the classroom are profoundly influenced by and interconnected with the macro-processes, social and political, that occur beyond the immediate context of the classroom (Erickson, 2004). Studies of this kind help to raise teachers' awareness of the complexities of the discourse that is generated in their classrooms and of the agency required from them in order to create opportunities for learning. It also helps teachers to understand the learners' agency—in their constructing knowledge, in their positioning themselves in relation to other members of the community, and in their negotiating their identities as competent members of the learning community.

As ethnographic micro-analysis of classroom discourse, or micro-ethnography, is time-consuming and labor-intensive and comprehensive analysis of classroom discourse data is onerous, the selection of data within a case is very important (Hammersley and Atkinson, 2007). Most of the studies outlined in this chapter have selected for detailed analysis specific speech events, or activities that are typical and relevant to the research question rather than the whole lesson. The deep analysis of the phenomenon under investigation, through repeated reading and reviewing of the data, enables the researcher to gain insights that may not be immediately apparent during participant observation (see also Garcez, 2008).

The issues outlined in this section that need to be further addressed are mostly methodological ones, pertaining to ethnography as a whole rather than just to classroom discourse studies. These are, nevertheless, fundamental issues that are likely to undermine the significance of studies in this area, if they are not addressed properly.

Further reading

Zuengler, J. and Mori, J. (eds.) (2002) *Applied Linguistics*, 23 (3) (special issue).

This special issue contains three papers reporting on studies adopting different perspectives in the micro-analyses of classroom discourse and two papers which critiqued these three studies. The exemplars provided an excellent context for the reader to appreciate the issues raised in the critiques.

Hammersley, M. (1990) *Classroom Ethnography*. Milton Keynes: Open University Press.

This book provides an excellent account of some of the earlier but important debates on methodological issues in ethnography.

Amy B. M. Tsui

Hammersley, M. and Atkinson, P. (2007) *Ethnography: Principles in Practice*. Third Edition. London and New York: Routledge.

This book will serve as an excellent guide for those who are interested in conducting ethnographic studies.

References

Allwright, D. and Bailey, K. (1991) *Focus on the Language Classroom*. New York: Cambridge University Press.
Bailey, K. and Nunan, D. (eds.) (1996) *Voices from the Language Classroom*. New York: Cambridge University Press.
Bloome, D., Carter, S. P., Christian, B. M., Otto, S., and Shuart-Faris, N. (2005) *Discourse Analysis and the Study of Classroom Language and Literacy Events: A Microethnographic Approach*. Mahwah, NJ: Lawrence Erlbaum Associates.
Bourdieu, P. (1973) 'Cultural reproduction and social reproduction', in R. Brown (ed.) *Knowledge, Education and Cultural Change*. London: Tavistock, pp. 71–112.
Bourdieu, P. (1991) *Language and Symbolic Power*, trans. G. Raymond and M. Adamson. Cambridge, MA: Harvard University Press.
Cazden, C. (2001) *Classroom Discourse: The Language of Teaching and Learning*. Second Edition. Portsmouth, NH: Heinemann.
Duff, P. A. (1995) 'An ethnography of communication in immersion classrooms in Hungary', *TESOL Quarterly*, 29 (3): 505–537 (Qualitative Research in ESOL).
Duff, P. A. (2002) 'The discursive co-construction of knowledge, identity, and difference: an ethnography of communication in the high school mainstream', *Applied Linguistics*, 23 (3): 289–322.
Eisenhart, M. (2001) 'Educational ethnography past, present and future: ideas to think with', *Educational Researcher*, 30 (8): 16–27.
Erickson, F. (2004) *Talk and Social Theory: Ecologies of Speaking and Listening in Everyday Life*. Cambridge: Polity Press.
Garcez, P. M. (2008) 'Microethnography in the classroom', in K. A. King and N. H. Hornberger (eds.) *Encyclopedia of Language and Education*. Vol. 10. Second Edition. New York: Springer, pp. 257–271.
Garfinkel, H. (1967) *Studies in Ethnomethodology*. Englewood Cliffs, NJ: Prentice-Hall.
Gee, J. P. (2004) 'Discourse analysis: what makes it critical?', in R. Rogers (ed.) *An Introduction to Critical Discourse Analysis in Education*. Mahwah, NJ: Lawrence Erlbaum Associates, pp. 19–50.
Gee, J. P. and Green, J. L. (1998) 'Discourse analysis, learning, and social practice: a methodological study', *Review of Research in Education*, 23: 119–169.
Glaser, B. G. and Strauss, A. L. (1967) *The Discovery of Grounded Theory: Strategies for qualitative research*. New York: Aldine Publishing Company.
Green, J. L. and Dixon, C. N. (2002) 'Exploring differences in perspectives on microanalysis of classroom discourse: contributions and concerns', *Applied Linguistics*, 23 (3): 393–406.
Hammersley, M. (1990) *Classroom Ethnography*. Milton Keynes: Open University Press.
Hammersley, M. (2002) 'Ethnography and the disputes over validity', *Debates and Development in Ethnographic Methodology*, 6: 7–22.
Hammersley, M. and Atkinson, P. (2007) *Ethnography: Principles in Practice*. Third Edition. London and New York: Routledge.
Harklau, L. (1994) 'ESL versus mainstream classes: contrasting L2 learning environments', *TESOL Quarterly*, 28 (2): 241–272.
Heath, S. B. (1982) 'What no bedtime story means: narrative skills at home and school', *Language in Society*, 11 (1): 49–76.
Hymes, D. (1962) 'The ethnography of speaking', in T. Gladwin and W. C. Sturtevant (eds.) *Anthropology and Human Behavior*. Washington, DC: The Anthropology Society of Washington, pp. 13–53.
Hymes, D. (1974) *Foundations in Sociolinguistics: An Ethnographic Approach*. Philadelphia, PA: University of Pennsylvania Press.
Johnson, K. (1995) *Understanding Communication in Second Language Classrooms*. New York: Cambridge University Press.
Kumaravadivelu, B. (1991) 'Language learning tasks: teacher intention and learner interpretation', *ELT Journal*, 45: 98–107.
Kumaravadivelu, B. (1999) 'Critical classroom discourse analysis', *TESOL Quarterly*, 33: 453–484.
Lantolf, J. P. (2000) 'Introducing sociocultural theory', in J. P. Lantolf (ed.) *Sociocultural Theory and Second Language Learning*. Oxford: Oxford University Press, pp. 1–26.

Lave, J. and Wenger, E. (1991) *Situated Learning: Legitimate Peripheral Participation*. New York: Cambridge University Press.

Lazaraton, A. (1995) 'Qualitative research in applied linguistics: a progress report', *TESOL Quarterly*, 29 (3): 455–472.

LeCompte, M. D. and Goetz, J. P. (1982) 'Problems of validity and reliability in ethnographic research', *Review of Educational Research*, 52 (1): 31–60.

LeCompte, M. D. and Preissle, J. (1993) *Ethnography and Qualitative Design in Educational Research*. Second Edition. San Diego, CA: Academic Press.

Lin, A. (1999) 'Doing-English-lessons in the reproduction or transformation of social worlds?', *TESOL Quarterly*, 33 (3): 393–412.

McKay, S., Davis, K. A., and Lazaraton, A. (eds.) (1995) *TESOL Quarterly*, 29 (3): 419–626 (special issue).

Mehan, H. (1979) *Learning Lessons: Social Organization in the Classroom*. Cambridge, MA: Harvard University Press.

Mehan, H. (1998) 'The study of social interaction in educational settings: accomplishments and unresolved issues', *Human Development*, 41 (4): 245–269.

Menard-Warwick, J. (2008) ' "Because she made beds every day," social positioning, classroom discourse, and language learning', *Applied Linguistics*, 29 (2): 267–289.

Mori, J. (2002) 'Task design, plan, and development of talk-in-interaction: an analysis of small group activity in a Japanese language classroom', *Applied Linguistics*, 23 (3): 323–347.

Morita, N. (2000) 'Discourse socialization through oral classroom activities in a TESL graduate program', *TESOL Quarterly*, 34 (2): 279–310.

Philips, S. U. (1983) *The Invisible Culture: Communication in Classroom and Community on the Warm Springs Indian Reservation*. New York: Longman.

Rampton, B., Roberts, C., Leung, C., and Harris, R. (2002) 'Methodology in the analysis of classroom discourse', *Applied Linguistics*, 23 (3): 373–392.

Toohey, K. (2008) 'Ethnography and language education', in K. A. King and N. H. Hornberger (eds.) *Encyclopedia of Language and Education*. Vol. 10. Second Edition. New York: Springer, pp. 177–187.

Tsui, A. B. M. (1996) 'Reticence and anxiety in second language learning', in K. Bailey and D. Nunan (eds.) *Voices from the Language Classroom*. New York: Cambridge University Press, pp. 145–167.

Tsui, A. B. M. (2008) 'Classroom discourse: approaches and perspectives', in J. Cenoz and N. H. Hornberger (eds.) *Encyclopedia of Language and Education*. Vol. 6. New York: Springer, pp. 261–272.

Tuyay, S., Jennings, L., and Dixon, C. (1995) 'Classroom discourse and opportunities to learn: an ethnographic study of knowledge construction in a bilingual third-grade classroom', *Discourse Processes*, 19 (1): 75–110.

van Lier, L. (1988) *The Classroom and the Language Learner*. London: Longman.

Walford, G. (2005) 'Introduction: methodological issues and practices', in G. Troman, B. Jeffrey, and G. Walford (eds.) *Methodological Issues and Practices in Ethnography*. Vol. 11. Amsterdam, New York, Oxford: Elsevier, JAI, pp. ix–xiii.

Watson-Gegeo, K. (1988) 'Ethnography in ESL: defining the essentials', *TESOL Quarterly*, 22 (4): 575–592.

Willet, J. (1995) 'Becoming first graders in an L2: an ethnographic study of L2 socialization', *TESOL Quarterly*, 29 (3): 473–503.

Wolcott, H. (2008) *Ethnography: A Way of Seeing*. Lanham, MD: AltaMira Press.

Young, R. F. and Nguyen, H. T. (2002) 'Modes of meaning in high school science', *Applied Linguistics*, 23 (3): 348–372.

Zuengler, J. and Mori, J. (eds.) (2002) 'Microanalyses of classroom discourse: a critical consideration of method', *Applied Linguistics*, 23 (3): 283–288 (special issue).

28

Education and bilingualism

Karen Thompson and Kenji Hakuta

Introduction

Given the multilingual contexts in which the majority of the world's population lives, educational systems have in some cases implemented instructional programs using multiple languages, sometimes in response to pressure by activists, sometimes as a means for spreading the national language among language minority groups, and sometimes as part of effort to promote economic competitiveness. After briefly reviewing the links between bilingual education and larger issues of ideology and political discourse, we will describe a variety of frameworks that researchers have used to analyze talk among bilinguals and we will discuss the value that a discourse analysis approach provides. We will then turn to bilingual classrooms specifically and provide an overview of empirical studies that have looked at talk in such classrooms, focusing particularly on code-switching. Finally, we will sketch some directions for future research in which discourse analysis could continue to serve as a tool for deepening our understanding of bilingual education and power relations in multilingual contexts.

Political discourse and macro-sociolinguistics

The multiracial, multicultural, and multilingual peoples of the United States have long engaged in battles—both literal and metaphorical—about how to balance unity and diversity. Such conflicts are mirrored in many other contexts around the world. One arena in which these battles have been waged is that of contests about the appropriate language of instruction for educating children. In these language wars, individuals have fought over what the balance should be between learning a common, national language and preserving multiple primary languages. Bilingual education is one attempt to balance the need for a common language with the benefits of maintaining individuals' primary languages.

Although bilingual education in the US and around the world is widely perceived as a recent phenomenon, its history dates back centuries. In the United States, for example, Ohio was the first state to officially adopt a bilingual education law. In 1839 the state legislature explicitly authorized bilingual education in German and English at parents' request (Sanchez and Sanchez, 2008). While German was the second most commonly used language of instruction in the nineteenth century (after English), children were also schooled in French, Dutch, and Spanish among other languages (U.S. Department of Education, 1991).

Much has been written about different models of bilingual education (see Romaine, 1995; García, 1997). Despite the sometimes bewildering proliferation of labels for these models, at the most basic level bilingual education simply refers to the use of two languages for classroom instruction. Bilingual programs differ on a variety of dimensions. First, they differ in the composition of their student population, some programs enrolling only speakers of the minority language, some enrolling only speakers of the majority language, and others enrolling some combination of the two. Programs also differ in the amount of time and the purposes for which each language is used. Some programs devote 50 percent of instructional time to each language throughout all grade levels, while others devote a decreasing amount of instructional time to the minority language over time. Programs also differ in their overall goals, some viewing the minority language as a temporary bridge for learning the majority language while others aim for the full development of both languages. These different goals for bilingual education programs often reflect different underlying language ideologies.

In countries with substantial immigrant populations, struggles around bilingual education closely parallel struggles around immigrant rights. Bilingual education typically becomes more common during upswings in immigration, but resistance to it also tends to peak during these upswings. In the United States, the multilingual reality of the nation's peoples stands in stark contrast to a political discourse that emphasizes English monolingualism. For example, President Theodore Roosevelt, during a time of heavy immigration from southern and eastern Europe, stated: "We have one language here, and that is the English language, and we intend to see that the [assimilation] crucible turns our people out as Americans, of American nationality, and not as dwellers of a polyglot boarding house" (Roosevelt, 1919). Thirty states currently have policies declaring English their official language (U.S. English, 2009), yet federal and state laws mandate that many government documents, such as voter guides, be printed in multiple languages.

Since 1970, immigration from Latin America and Asia to the United States has increased dramatically (Terrazas and Batalovo, 2009), with a corresponding increase in attempts to formalize the dominance of English in the public sphere. Three states with large Spanish-speaking immigrant populations passed propositions severely restricting bilingual educations programs—California in 1998, Arizona in 2000, and Massachusetts in 2002. The percentage of non-native English speakers who participate in bilingual programs in California has dropped from approximately 30 percent prior to the proposition's passage to less than 5 percent today (authors' calculations, based on California Department of Education DataQuest statistics). Yet similar English-only propositions have failed in two other states—Colorado in 2002 and Oregon in 2008. The tension between the long-standing emphasis on English monolingualism and the multilingual reality of the nation continues to play out at the ballot box as voters are asked to decide questions of language policy.

Many other countries around the globe are also engaged in debates to determine the language(s) in which their linguistically diverse populations should be educated. Consider the case of Guatemala. In this country of 12.7 million people that has Spanish as its official language, 24 languages are spoken, 21 of which belong to the Mayan linguistic family (López, 2006). Approximately 40 percent of the population speaks a Mayan language, though only 13.5 percent of the population is monolingual in one of these languages. The Mayan population has historically had lower literacy rates, worse health outcomes, and higher rates of poverty than the non-indigenous population. López (2006) describes these disparities in extreme terms: "The Guatemalan governmental neglect of indigenous children and adolescents was an outcome of a hierarchically and racially structured society, which in many cases resembled Apartheid" (p. 240).

In 1979 experiments with bilingual education began in Guatemala: the government established ten schools in each of the four most commonly spoken Mayan languages (Kiche, Mam, Kachiquel, and Qeqchi). These schools used students' primary Mayan language as the medium of instruction in the earliest grades while gradually increasing the amount of instruction conducted in Spanish in later grades (Dutcher, 2004). After early evaluation studies showed better educational outcomes for students in the bilingual schools than in traditional Spanish-language schools, the number of bilingual schools expanded, as did the number of languages in which bilingual education was provided. By 1999, these bilingual schools were "providing instruction in 14 languages for 230,000 rural children in 1200 schools" (Dutcher, 2004: 5). Meanwhile, Guatemala's three-decades-long civil war came to an end in 1996, and a variety of laws, passed during this time period, increased rights of the country's indigenous population, including linguistic rights. The National Language Act of 2003, while declaring Spanish the official language, provided not only recognition of indigenous languages, but advocated their use in education as well as in other spheres. The law states, "[t]he national education system, both public and private, must foster in all processes, modalities, and levels, the respect, promotion, development, and use of the Mayan, Garifuna, and Xinka languages, conforming to the particulars of each linguistic community" (El Decreto Número 19–2003, 2003, authors' translation).

Despite the expansion of bilingual education in Guatemala, a shortage of qualified teachers and a lack of appropriate curriculum materials have plagued bilingual schools in the country (Dutcher, 2004; López, 2006). Furthermore, leaders within some indigenous communities found fault with the form that bilingual education took in these government-operated schools. As one indigenous leader stated: "We are against a model of development that misinterprets our thoughts and knowledge, a model which only pursues economic accumulation as well as assimilation into the hegemonic Western way of life" (López, 2006: 254). Thus, in recent years, Mayan communities have established their own network of bilingual schools that teach not only Mayan languages but Mayan history, cosmology, and philosophy. By 2005, 56 such schools existed across Guatemala, striving to develop bilingualism and biculturalism in students rather than using Mayan languages as a bridge to learning Spanish.

India, in contrast, has seen a decreasing use of minority languages in schools across the country, but increased instances in which English and an Indian language serve as the medium of instruction. A 1991 language census identified 216 primary languages with more than 10,000 speakers in India; an additional 900 languages had fewer than 10,000 speakers. Of these languages, the national Constitution recognizes 22 as official languages, and 41 are used in educational settings, down from 81 in 1970 (Mohanty, 2006). As Mohanty states, "[m]ost of the tribal and minority mother tongues have no place in the educational system of India" (p. 268). In 2009, the Indian Parliament passed a landmark Right to Education Act providing for free and compulsory education for all children in India between 6 and 14 years of age, but the Act has come under fire from some quarters because it makes no explicit provisions for educating students in their primary languages (Sarva Shiksha Abhiyan Right to Education Committee, 2009).

This is not to suggest that India's educational system aims to foster monolingualism. In fact, while instruction in minority languages has been declining in India in recent decades, instruction in English has been increasing. A 1964 decree, still in force, directs Indian schools to teach three languages: (1) the regional or mother tongue; (2) either Hindi or English; and (3) an additional modern Indian language or foreign language. However, as a recent government report found, the three language formula "has not been uniformly implemented across the country," and issues such as a lack of educational materials in particular languages, a shortage of adequately trained teachers, and the multiplicity of linguistic backgrounds found in many communities have hampered efforts to make mother tongue education available to India's students (Sarva Shiksha Abhiyan Right to Education Committee, 2009: 30). Today, English (not Hindi) has become the most common second language subject in all states. Furthermore, given the importance of English fluency in the global economic sphere, members of the elite are increasingly sending their children to expensive private schools in which English is the medium of instruction from the earliest grades (Mohanty, 2006).

Across these three contexts—the United States, Guatemala, and India—we see that larger power asymmetries manifest themselves in struggles over linguistic rights and the language(s) in which schooling is to be conducted. As we turn to examining talk in bilingual classrooms, we must remember that talk in such classrooms is a microcosm in which societal struggles about language and national identity play out.

Key theoretical perspectives that bear on classroom discourse

Before examining discourse in bilingual classrooms specifically, we will describe models that have been developed for examining discourse in multilingual settings more generally. In 1959, Charles Ferguson proposed an influential framework for such settings. Ferguson noted that, in communities in which distinct varieties of a language co-existed, speakers used particular varieties for particular domains. For example, in Cairo, a professor would likely deliver a university lecture in classical Arabic but discuss the day's events with family members in Egyptian Arabic, listen to a news broadcast in classical Arabic but buy coffee from a local merchant in Egyptian Arabic. Ferguson used the term *diglossia* to describe such communities. In these communities, Ferguson argued, context almost completely determined language variety: "In one set of situations only H [the high or standard variety] is appropriate and in another only L [the low or vernacular variety], with the two sets overlapping only very slightly. ... The social importance of using the right variety in the right situation can hardly be overestimated" (2000/1959: 68).

Many linguists contested Ferguson's claims, arguing that diglossic situations in which two varieties of the same language were dedicated to specific domains within society were actually quite rare. For example, Fishman (2000/1967) argued that multilingual communities could take one of several forms: bilingualism with diglossia, bilingualism without diglossia; diglossia without bilingualism; or neither diglossia nor bilingualism. Fishman also argued that diglossia represented a useful concept for understanding language use at a broad, societal level, but other frameworks were necessary for understanding individuals' language choices within particular interactions. He suggested that the concept of language domains guide this latter type of analysis. Domains such as family, friends, religious institutions, and the government, Fishman explained, "designate the *major clusters of interaction situations that occur in particular multilingual settings*" (p. 93; emphasis in the original), and within particular multilingual communities interactions within particular domains will tend to be carried out in particular languages. Therefore, using domain analysis, individual language use within a particular domain can be compared to overall societal trends for language use within that particular domain, Fishman urged. Despite his emphasis on domains of language use, Fishman did acknowledge that other factors, particularly role relations and topic, might influence language choice, and he urged these factors be considered alongside domain.

From social psychology came another approach that has been influential in analyzing discourse among bilingual speakers. In a series of studies beginning in the 1970s, Howard Giles and his associates demonstrated that speakers had a tendency to accommodate to one another on a variety of dimensions, from rate of speech to phonological features. Giles himself and linguists studying interactions in multilingual communities applied Giles' accommodation theory, as it was named, to explain speakers' language choices in these communities, where speakers tended to converge to what they perceived to be the preferred language of interlocutors by whom they wanted to be liked, but diverged from the preferred language of interlocutors they wanted to resist (Giles *et al.*, 1991). In what could be considered an expansion of the accommodation theory, sociolinguist Douglas Bell (1984) proposed audience design theory, asserting that speakers formulate their utterances on the basis of their perceptions of their audience. In some ways, both Giles' and Bell's theories could be viewed as extensions of Grice's well-known cooperative principle, which, he argued, underlay speakers' pragmatic behavior in interactions: "Make your contribution such as it is required, at the stage at which it occurs, by the accepted purpose or direction of the talk exchange in which you are engaged" (Grice, 1989: 26). Thus we would expect bilingual speakers to speak in the language that their interlocutor would not only understand but prefer.

Building on the notion of accommodation, Carol Myers-Scotton (1983) proposed yet another model to analyze discourse in multilingual settings, which she termed the "markedness model." In multilingual communities, Myers-Scotton argued, factors such as domain, topic, and role relations combine to create societal expectations about the language in which a particular interaction will occur; use of this language is unmarked—in other words, expected. However, individual speakers may violate these expectations by choosing to use the marked or unexpected language for all or some portion of a particular interaction. In a revision of Grice's (1975) cooperative principle, Myers-Scotton proposed that bilingual speakers observed the following principle in their inter-actions with other bilingual speakers: "Choose the *form* of your conversation contribution such that it indexes the set of rights and obligations which you wish to be in force between speaker and addressee for the current exchange" (1983, cited in Myers-Scotton, 2006: 160; emphasis in the original). If a speaker makes a marked choice, using a language that is unexpected for a particular interaction (if the professor in Cairo mentioned above delivered a lecture in Egyptian Arabic rather than in Classical Arabic, for example), this speaker is signaling a particular set of rights and obligations that he wishes to be in effect for that interaction, Myers-Scotton asserts.

Linguists working within the discourse analysis tradition criticized Ferguson's framework of diglossia, Fishman's framework of language domains, Giles' accommodation theory, and Myers-Scotton's markedness model as overly deterministic and speculative and argued that it imposed a reified view of social categories, which is removed from the behavioral realities of discourse. Under these frameworks, all talk in classrooms might be considered to fall within a single domain, that of education; researchers might presume a tendency for utterances in bilingual classrooms to be conducted in a particular language and view utterances in another language as marked. Empirical evidence does not support these assumptions. Researchers have found that both Spanish and English are used by teachers and students for a wide variety of purposes in bilingual classrooms in the United States, for example (cf. Legarreta, 1977; Zentella, 1981; Freeman, 1998).

John Gumperz (1982), Li Wei (1994, 1998), and Peter Auer (1998), among others, have argued that actual conversations in bilingual communities should be analyzed in detail, so as to provide information about how bilingual speakers use their linguistic repertoires within particular interactions to wield power, manage interactions, indicate preferences, index identity, and build alliances. As Li Wei (1998) explains, rather than speculating about the motivation for speakers' language choices and linking these choices to broader societal factors, a discourse analysis approach to analyzing talk in multilingual communities "dispenses with motivational speculation, in favor of an interpretative approach based on detailed, turn-by-turn analysis of language choices" (p. 169). From the fine-grained analysis of conversational turns, discourse analysts can describe the ways that Gee (2005) has termed the "little-d discourses," or "language-in-use" that operates within multilingual communities generally and bilingual classrooms specifically. Building from this analysis of the "little-d discourses," then, researchers can describe the "Big D Discourses," the "ways of acting, interacting, feeling, believing, valuing" (Gee, 2005: 7) operating in these contexts.

Ana Celia Zentella is one example of a sociolinguist who has used discourse analysis to connect talk in bilingual communities to larger social structures and ways of being. In her landmark study *Growing Up Bilingual: Puerto Rican Children in New York*, Zentella (1997) analyzes language samples mainly from seven girls growing up on a particular block, over a period of 14 years. Zentella finds that children in this community do not restrict Spanish and English "to specific settings and/or purposes .... [Rather] codes are switched by the same speaker in the same setting" (p. 80). While acknowledging that the underlying reasons motivating code-switches are complex and impossible to determine definitively, Zentella finds that speakers' switches between English and Spanish serve a variety of conversational functions. She categorizes code-switches by conversational strategy and finds switches that coincide with a topic shift, mark a quotation, mitigate or aggravate a request, and clarify or emphasize information, among many other functions. Zentella also analyzes differences in the code-switching behavior of individual speakers on the basis of their age and language preferences. From this analysis, Zentella concludes: "In addition to serving as their badge of membership in *el bloque* [the block], the girls' code switching enabled each one to fulfill crucial communicative functions in ways that joined her to others similar in age or language profile, as well as to construct and display her unique self" (p. 114).

Empirical studies of language, power, and code-switching in bilingual education settings

Up to this point we have discussed various frameworks, including discourse analysis, that have been used to analyze speech in bilingual communities generally. Now we will move to a discussion of work that analyzes discourse in bilingual classrooms specifically. Basic questions about the implementation of bilingual education programs in the United States motivated an early wave of research analyzing talk in bilingual classrooms during the 1970s. With the passage of the Bilingual Education Act in 1968, which provided federal funds for districts to establish bilingual programs, such programs began to spring up around the United States in areas with substantial immigrant populations. Researchers investigated basic questions about the balance of Spanish and English use by teachers and students in these new bilingual classrooms. For example, Legarreta (1977) analyzed Spanish and English use in six bilingual kindergarten classrooms in California, finding that language use varied by type of bilingual program. Although all programs had a goal of 50 percent Spanish and 50 percent English use, in programs using a concurrent translation model, in which material was presented alternately in each language, teachers used English approximately 70 percent of the time and native Spanish-speaking students seemed to mirror teachers' language choices, also using English approximately 70 percent of the time. In these classrooms English dominated teachers' language use across a variety of functions, including directing students, evaluating and elaborating students' responses, and correcting students. However, in one classroom using an alternate days model, in which Spanish was used for the entire morning and English for the entire afternoon one day and English for the morning and Spanish for the afternoon on the following day, there was greater parity in both teacher and student language use. Nonetheless, Legarreta concluded that, in most classrooms, "[d]espite a sincere and conscious commitment to bilingual teaching by the teachers/aides, they seem overwhelmed by the pull of the dominant language and the dominant culture, with the result that English again becomes the classroom language" (1977, p. 15).

In another early study of language use in bilingual classrooms, Zentella (1981) analyzed the language choices of two native Spanish-speaking teachers and their students in a third and sixth grade bilingual classroom in New York City. Zentella made audio-recordings of classroom interactions and conducted interviews with the teachers and their students. As Legarreta's (1977) work might lead us to predict, Zentella found that teachers' language choices exerted considerable influence over students' language choices. "Despite the often unpredictable changes in the teachers' language, children in both grades usually responded in the language in which they were addressed during formal sessions, particularly the younger ones," Zentella wrote (p. 119). Instances in which a student responded in a different language from that used by the teacher "usually reflected [the student's] language proficiency and, especially with sixth graders, their degree of linguistic security and language preference" (p. 120). Despite similarities in patterns of language choice across the two classrooms, Zentella noted that the third grade teacher was much more likely to code-switch, using both English and Spanish within a single conversational turn, than the sixth grade teacher. However, Zentella concluded, "[s]ince these teachers differ in language dominance, teaching style, and personality variables, it is difficult to attribute the differences in their patterns to anything but a complex configuration of variables" (p. 129). And, although bilingualism is the goal for students in the bilingual program, Zentella noted that English seemed to "dominate school life" (p. 112).

A separate strand of research has investigated how teachers' language choices impact students' content-area learning. For example, Setati and Adler (2000) analyzed teachers' language use during mathematics instruction in multilingual classrooms in both urban and rural areas of South Africa. In these classrooms, English was the principal language of instruction, but Setati and Adler documented numerous instances in which teachers code-switched into students' native languages for a variety of purposes such as to provide translations for certain unfamiliar vocabulary words, to clarify a concept, or to press students to elaborate their thinking. Nonetheless, teachers felt conflicted about how much to use students' native language(s) and how much to use English:

> On the one hand as teachers they needed to switch languages in order to reformulate a question or instruction, or to reexplain a concept, and they needed to encourage their learners to use their main [native] language in order to facilitate communication and understanding. At the same time however, it was their responsibility to induct their learners into mathematical English and hence it was important to use English in the mathematics classroom as much as possible.
>
> *(Setati and Adler, 2000: 255)*

Teachers in rural areas felt particular pressure to use English because, unlike students in urban areas, their students were unlikely to be exposed to any English outside of school.

Contemporary researchers using discourse analysis to analyze interactions in bilingual classrooms in the United States have also noted the pull that English exerts, despite teachers' stated intentions. Freeman (1998) spent two years as a participant–observer at a dual-language elementary school in the Washington DC area, recording classroom interactions and conducting open-ended interviews with a variety of stakeholders. Dual-language programs enroll native speakers of two different primary languages, in this case Spanish and English, and aim to develop students' fluency in both. Freeman found that "observations of the students talking informally among themselves ... at lunch or at recess or during Storywriting time in kindergarten, ... suggest that the students attribute more prestige to English than Spanish, despite the ideal that these languages be distributed and evaluated equally throughout the school" (1998, p. 197). Through a fine-grained analysis of transcripts from a particular "opening" activity in a kindergarten classroom, Freeman demonstrates one way in which teachers contribute to messages about the status of Spanish and English. Although the "opening" activity was carried out in Spanish and English on alternating days, more sophisticated contributions were required of students on days when the activity was conducted in English. During the "opening" activity, the teacher always led the students in a song and then guided them in completing a variety of statements about the date and the number of students present. Compare the written statements the students were asked to complete when the activity took place in English and when it took place in Spanish:

English	Spanish
Today is _____	Hoy es _____
	(*today is*)

We have ___ girls	las niñas
	(the girls)
We have ___ boys	los niños
	(the boys)
We have ___ students	los estudiantes
	(the students).

(Freeman, 1998: 197)

Although the format is almost identical in both languages, the English version requires students to complete full sentences, while the last three items in the Spanish version of the activity contain phrases rather than full sentences. This pattern of more skills being required of students in the English version of the activity plays out in other ways, as well. The teachers ask students to supply spelling information about the day of the week in English but not in Spanish, for example. Freeman concludes: "The kindergarten analysis … provides concrete evidence of a more general pattern that I observed throughout the school. Although students are expected to develop academic skills in both Spanish and English, there are higher standards in English" (1998: 209).

Palmer (2008) also served as a participant–observer in a dual-immersion classroom and found evidence of the pull that English exerts, despite teachers' intentions. Reflecting on her own experience as a teacher in a dual-immersion classroom, Palmer writes: "in my own classroom Spanish was not as high status a language as English. Despite my daily efforts to use exclusively Spanish when expected, to discuss with students the value of knowing the language, and even to openly reward use of Spanish, I was daily challenged by students refusing to respond to me in Spanish, even though I knew they were capable" (p. 650). Palmer explicitly chose to collect data in the classroom of a teacher who seemed "able to strike a more equitable linguistic balance in her classroom" (p. 651). Through discourse analysis, Palmer provides evidence of ways in which this teacher explicitly communicates the value she places on the contributions of her native Spanish-speaking students. When students have gathered in a circle to read essays they each have written in response to a novel, the teacher interrupts the first reader, a native Spanish speaker who is reading very softly, saying: "'Perdón la interrupción pero no escucho' *(pardon the interruption but I cannot hear you well)*. This sends a clear message to the entire class: it is not only important to have the chance to read your own essay, but also to have the chance to hear your classmates' essays" (p. 658). When the student still cannot be understood clearly, another native Spanish speaker interrupts him, repeating the teachers' words. Later in the activity, a native English speaker interrupts a native Spanish speaker, using a variation of the teacher's original phrase.

However, Palmer concludes that the linguistic parity that the teacher seems to have achieved within her classroom is quite fragile and does not extend to instances in which she herself is not present. Palmer provides transcripts of two interactions, one when a substitute teacher is instructing the class and another when the librarian is leading the class in a read-aloud. In both interactions, native Spanish speakers become disengaged when their questions are not fully answered by their native English-speaking interlocutors. For example, after the substitute teacher instructs students to begin playing a subtraction game in small groups, Oswaldo, a native Spanish speaker, initially expresses his confusion, saying: "I don't understand." He continues to try to clarify his understanding in the following interaction but disengages as his confusion persists:

James: You rolled a one, then take out nine ones.
Nancy: Nine ones?
James: Yea. So it's [One two three four five six seven eight.

Roberto: [I take one of these (ten-sticks) and I get one of these (cubes).
James: OK, then you—no you take nine ones.
Oswaldo: Whaa?
Roberto: Nine ones? I didn't have –
James: You put nine of those in there.
Roberto: I took one of these (ten-sticks) out then I put one of these (cubes).
James: No, you need to put nine of those!
Oswaldo: One. [Two. Three.

(Palmer, 2008: 662)

Shot down by native English-speaking James, Oswaldo resorts to counting cubes rather than thinking about the subtraction processes the game is designed to highlight and ultimately starts building with the manipulative materials rather than participating. On the basis of this and other interactions, Palmer concludes:

> One classroom teacher and the lessons and conversations she manages form only a small part of the discourses/Discourses that youngsters encounter as they undertake the ongoing process of dialogue involved in developing their identities as learners. It is impossible to limit students' exposure to dominant discourses. This study demonstrates that, even while attempting to engage students in a struggle to change their discourse patterns, we will find students slipping back repeatedly into inequitable patterns drawn from the expectations of the larger society
>
> *(2008: 663–664)*

In our own work, we have found that, even within interactions in which all participants are native Spanish speakers, those with greater English fluency may use their English fluency as one of a set of resources to exert power. We have been recording interactions in a first and third grade bilingual classroom in an elementary school in Northern California. All students in both classrooms are native Spanish speakers, with varying degrees of English fluency. Students receive instruction primarily in Spanish during their first years in this school, with the amount of English increasing each year. We have recorded interactions during a "free time" period that happens in each classroom once a week. During free time, students may interact in whichever language they wish. We have been analyzing the language choices of students during free time over the course of eight weeks, noting when students use Spanish, English, or a mixture of both languages.

In the following transcript, two first grade girls, Perla and Monica, are playing a game with marbles, using a large plastic structure, which serves as a racetrack for the marbles.[1] The winner is the person whose marble completes the course first. The first part of the interaction (lines 1–36), before Perla runs off to look for her missing marble, takes place almost entirely in Spanish, with two brief exceptions. The teacher uses English to clarify that the bell that is ringing applies only to older students (lines 5–6), and Perla makes a quick switch to English to ask: "Where's my ball?" (line 9). This pattern of language use, long stretches of Spanish punctuated by occasional phrases in English, is typical of this first grade classroom during free time. Students in this classroom have only been receiving instruction in English for a little over one year; most of their day is still spent learning in Spanish, and their teacher typically uses Spanish as the default language for a wide range of functions, including giving instructions during free time, making informational announcements, and disciplining students (though she breaks from this pattern and uses English for an announcement during this interaction). Utterances in English are the exception rather than the rule during free time in this classroom. However, in this particular interaction, once Perla goes to retrieve her marble, she speaks predominantly in English for the remainder of the exchange (lines 40–57), except for a single turn (lines 54–55) when she is again admonishing Monica to give her marble back to her. In this second portion of the interaction, Monica's turns consist entirely of squeals or laughter, except for her final turn, when, following the admonition Perla gives in Spanish, she exclaims simply in English, "Yes! I win!" Note the balance of power between the two girls throughout the interaction.

1	Perla:	Aaaaah! ((singing)) Te estoy ganando, te estoy ganando, te estoy ganando, te estoy
2		ganando!
3		*Aaaaah! I'm beating you, I'm beating you, I'm beating you, I'm beating you!*
4	((bell rings))	
5	Teacher:	No, no, it's for big kids ((in other words, the bell does not mean free time is over
6		for the first graders)). Keep playing.
7	Perla:	Whe:[ee!] ((as they let their marbles go))
8	Monica:	[Whe:ee!]
9	Perla:	Te gané, yo te gané, te voy a ganar. (4.8) ((ball rolls onto the floor)) Where's my ball?
10		*I beat you, I beat you, I'm going to beat you.*
11	Monica:	Yo no te las tiré.
12		*I didn't throw them to you.*
13	Perla:	O, ¡cuida:do, Monica!
14		*Oh, careful, Monica!*
15	(7.0) ((more racing the marbles with no dialogue))	
16	Perla:	((in a very high-pitched voice)) Ee:w! (15.2) ((marble racing continues)) ¡Ya:y! ¡Mi
17		pelota está ganando!
18		*Ee:w!(15.2) Yay! My ball is winning!*
19	Monica:	O, ¡yo gané! ((laughs))
20		*Oh, I won!*
21	Perla:	¡No:! (1.4) ¿Dónde fue mi pelota? (1.5) ¿Dónde fue mi pelota? ((looks for it on the
22		floor))
23		*No! Where did my ball go? Where did my ball go?*
24	Monica:	((laughs))
25	Perla:	¡Mi pelota, mi pelota, la pelota!
26		*My ball, my ball, my ball!*
27	Monica:	((laughs))
28	Perla:	¿Dónde está mi pelota? ((deepens her voice)) ¿Dónde está la pelota, Monica? (3.6)
29		(Ay, Monica,) estabas cheatiando, ¿sabías?
30		*Where is my ball? Where is the ball, Monica? (Ay, Monica,) you were cheating, you know?*
31	Monica:	Ay, ¡ew!
32		*Ay, ew!*
33	Perla:	O, da:me la pelota mí:a:. Ya sé me estás cheatiando. (5.6) Yo te gané prime:ro. (17.6)
34		*Give me my ball. I know that you're cheating me. I beat you first.*
35	((marble racing continues))	
36	Monica:	¡Ah!
37	Perla:	Hey! ((laughs))
38	Monica:	((laughs))
39	((Perla's marble rolls off across the room))	
40	Perla:	Oh no you—((goes to retrieve marble)) Oh no you **di:dn't**! (4.5) Thank you (?) for
41		saving my little ball.
42	Monica:	((squeals as marble racing continues))
43	Perla:	Yay!
44	Monica:	((squeals again))

45 Perla: No, baby! No! ((ball goes onto the floor again)) Where's my little
46   ball?
47 Monica: ((squeals))
48 Perla: (What you did) with my little ball?
49 ((marble races continues without talking for 22.4 seconds))
50 Perla: ((to Monica)) Hey, (1.5) you cheater! (7.9) ((addressing her marble)) Hey, you win!
51   You won, my little ball!
52 Monica: ((squeals))
53 ((more marble racing))
54 Perla: ¡Da:me mi pelo:ta:! ¡Da:me mi pelo:ta:! (4.7)
55   *Give me my ball! Give me my ball!*
56 Monica: ((in a very high-pitched voice)) Yes! I win!
57 ((Clean up begins.))

Perla clearly dominates this interaction. Not only does she exuberantly proclaim that she is winning (as in lines 1–3) or has won (line 9), she also taunts Monica, as well, stating that she is going to beat her (line 9). Furthermore, Perla repeatedly chides Monica, accusing her of cheating (lines 28–30, lines 33–34, line 50), questioning her about the whereabouts of her missing marble (lines 21–23), and demanding that she return the marble (lines 54–55). Throughout this interaction, to the best of our knowledge, we observed no evidence of Monica cheating. Instead, Perla simply seemed frustrated when her marble rolled away out of sight or did not complete the course first, and she seemed to blame Monica, somewhat jokingly, for her bad luck. In contrast, Monica never questions or chides Perla. Also note the differences in the girls' utterances when their marbles are victorious or about to be victorious. (When a literal translation would differ from a gloss, we first provide the literal translation from Spanish into English, followed by the gloss.)

(1) Monica: O, ¡yo gané! (lines 19–20)
              Oh, I won!
(2) Monica: I win! (line 56)
(3) Perla: ...te estoy ganando. (line 1)
              ...you I am winning.
              ... I'm beating you.
(4) Perla: Yo te gané. (line 9)
              I you won.
              I beat you.
(5) Perla: Yo te gané primero. (line 33)
              I you won first.
              I beat you first.

Monica never specifies over whom she has been victorious. In contrast, when claiming victory, Perla specifies that she has beaten Monica by including the pronoun *te* (*you*) in her utterances.

Although Monica is clearly capable of speaking English (see line 56), according to the state's testing, Monica's English skills are at the beginning stage, whereas Perla's are considered intermediate. Although we lack sufficient evidence to prove this claim, it may be that Perla's switch to English for lines 40–57 has the effect of silencing Monica somewhat if she feels less able to interact in this language. Perla's use of English for an extended period of time may serve as one more way in which she can dominate the interaction.

From our preliminary data, it appears that it is not just students' English skills but their abilities to switch between Spanish and English that facilitate their ability to exercise power in the interactions we observed. However, students with beginning English skills sometimes use the English they do command in order to refuse requests made of them. Consider this very brief exchange between two third grade students, Eduardo and Yesenia. Eduardo is a tall, outgoing boy born in the US. Though Spanish is his native language, Eduardo has already been formally redesignated by the school as fluent in English on the basis of high standardized test scores in second grade. Such redesignation by the beginning of third grade is quite unusual for students in the bilingual program, who receive the majority of their instruction in Spanish during their first years of school. Eduardo is almost always at the center of activity in the classroom, establishing the rules for games, giving out Pokemon cards that other students proceed to trade during free time, or proposing bets with other students. He is a clear leader and other students seem to want to be his friends. He almost always speaks in English, but he will use Spanish on occasion. Yesenia, on the other hand, is a shy, slight girl. Though she was born in the United States, Yesenia's English skills lag behind those of many of her peers, and she typically chooses to use Spanish, unlike most other students in the class. She tends to interact primarily with a girl, Lizbeth, who immigrated from Mexico at the end of second grade.

During free time one Friday, Yesenia has been sitting at a table in the back of the classroom with Lizbeth working on her own art project. Eduardo approaches. He has just been speaking in English to another student, but he switches to Spanish to address Yesenia.

Eduardo: ((to Yesenia)) Agarras otra hoja mismo, trata de colorearlo otros mismo, y luego los cortas los dos para afuera, y luego lo doblas y lo pegas más.
Get another of the same sheets of paper, try to color the other ones in the same way, and then cut out two of them, and then fold it, and glue it more.
Yesenia: I don't wanna do that.

Eduardo made a suggestion in Spanish, his dispreferred language, and Yesenia refused his suggestion in English, her dispreferred language. Both went against their general language preferences here. Eduardo seemed to be trying to accommodate to his perception of Yesenia's language preference, making his suggestion more appealing by couching it in the language she preferred. Yet Yesenia responded in English, seemingly marking not just her refusal of his suggestion but also her refusal of his language choice. This fits with Li Wei's (1994) finding that bilingual children may use code-switching to mark dispreferred second turns in conversation, such as refusing a request. In addition to marking her refusal of Eduardo's request and her refusal of his language choice, Yesenia may also be claiming an identity as an English speaker, since, as Legarreta (1977), Zentella (1981), Freeman (1998), and Palmer (2008) have found, even in bilingual programs English typically has higher status. Meanwhile, though Eduardo was rebuffed in this interaction, he found other ways to exercise power in the classroom. After Yesenia rejected his suggestion, Eduardo simply left and went back to being a ringleader of the Pokemon trading activity nearby.

Looking to the future

Despite the insights into bilingual education settings that discourse analysis has provided, as we hope to have illustrated in this chapter, its use as a research method has dwindled in recent decades, particularly within the United States. The major funding mechanism for research related to bilingual education in the US was Title VII, the Bilingual Education Act, which was enacted in 1968 to support the education of language minority students and reauthorized at regular intervals through to 2002. Title VII accepted and enabled basic research on classroom language use, especially through the mid-1980s (Moran and Hakuta, 1995). However, the 1980s ushered in the standards movement, an effort to raise student achievement by defining a set of rigorous academic standards, to which all students would be held accountable, and then testing students' proficiency in these standards. This movement created an overwhelming emphasis on academic achievement, and in this climate educational research focusing on student outcomes and program evaluation has increasingly overshadowed research such as discourse analysis, which focuses on the processes through which education occurs. Meanwhile, the focus on academic achievement has been accompanied by a focus on measuring the effects of specific interventions on student achievement, and research designs that constitute or approximate randomized field trials are now considered the gold standard, in spite of recommendations by authorities such as the National Research Council to look more broadly at the scientific basis of educational research (Shavelson and Towne, 2002). In a recent report to Congress describing the research agenda of the Institute of Education Sciences, the branch of the federal government that provides the bulk of education research funding, the word "discourse" appears only once, in a project unrelated to discourse analysis (Institute of Education Sciences, 2008).

Discourse analysis does not lend itself easily to the current education research paradigm. Yet understanding the nested relationship between how language is used in the classroom and how bilinguals use languages in different ways is basic to understanding how language mediates academic learning. Although many academics and practitioners readily recognize the importance of academic language and academic vocabulary, little attention is currently paid to the discourse within which this language occurs. While the current research paradigm offers limited possibilities for research using discourse analysis, we see several lines of research that might prove fruitful, all of which are currently being explored by small numbers of researchers but could be expanded. First, building on work conducted by Schleppegrell (2003, 2004), researchers could use discourse analysis to explore the differing demands of discourses across academic disciplines, with an ultimate goal of developing methods to support students in becoming successful users of the unique discourses of science, mathematics, social studies, and so on. Second, more research on ways in which peers support one another's academic learning through language brokering could be explored as well. One example of such work is Bayley *et al.*'s (2005) study of the ways in which bilingual students served as language brokers for recent immigrants in an English-medium middle school science class. Given the increasing geographic spread of the language minority population, an increasing percentage of teachers are responsible for educating students not yet fluent in English, and often such teachers do not speak the primary languages of these students. By better understanding the kinds of language brokering in which students within linguistically diverse classrooms engage, educators could potentially develop methods for encouraging such brokering when necessary. Finally, numerous researchers have expressed concerns about the achievement of language minority students within dual-immersion classrooms (cf. Valdés, 1997). In such classrooms equal numbers of majority and minority language speakers are educated together, with the goal of building students' fluency in both the majority and the minority language; yet the language minority students often lag behind the language majority students in academic achievement. Given the increasing popularity of dual-immersion classrooms, research such as Palmer's (2008) and Freeman's (1998) could be expanded by using discourse analysis to explore the relative status of the majority and minority languages and their speakers in such classrooms and to identify ways in which the academic identities of the language minority students within such classrooms could be supported. We remain hopeful that the powerful tools within discourse analysis can serve as a valuable resource for improving educational outcomes for language minority students.

Transcription conventions

(())   Information between double parentheses represents contextual, extra-linguistic information, such as who is being addressed or actions that are occurring.

(guess)   Words between parentheses represents the transcriber's best guess for a stretch of talk that was difficult to hear.

[A square bracket marks where overlap by another speakers begins.

?   An initial question mark indicates a conversational turn by a speaker whose identity cannot be determined.

(0.5)   Numbers between parentheses represent the duration of pauses, given in seconds and tenths of seconds.

ti:me   A colon after a vowel indicates that the duration of the vowel lengthened.

italics   Italics are used for English translations of Spanish utterances.

bold   Bold is used to indicate words that were given particular emphasis by the speaker.

Further reading

For those interested in learning more about the application of discourse analysis to understanding bilingualism and bilingual education settings, there are numerous possibilities for further reading.

Zentella, A. C. (1997) *Growing up Bilingual: Puerto Rican Children in New York.* Malden, MA: Blackwell.

At a micro-level, Zentella's classic uses discourse analysis to provide a fascinating, in-depth portrait of how seven Puerto Rican girls growing up in New York City use English and Spanish across multiple dimensions of their lives, including schooling.

Dutcher, N. (2004). Expanding educational opportunity in linguistically diverse societies. Washington DC: Center for Applied Linguistics. Available online at: http://www.cal.org/resources/pubs/ford report_040501.pdf (accessed 14 November 2009).

At a macro-level, this report by Dutcher, on behalf of the Center for Applied Linguistics (2004), describes distinctive multilingual education programs in 13 different counties, providing insight into the variety of forms that multilingual education can take depending on the linguistic context and the resources necessary for programs to succeed.

Myers-Scotton, C. (2006) *Multiple Voices: An Introduction to Bilingualism.* Malden, MA: Blackwell.

Finally, for those particularly interested in theory, Myers-Scotton offers a broad introduction to key topics in bilingualism, including an overview of competing theoretical perspectives on language use in multilingual settings. It is our hope that coming years will see a resurgence of work that applies discourse analysis to multilingual educational environments.

Note

1 All names are pseudonyms.

References

Auer, P. (ed.) (1998) *Code-Switching in Conversation: Language, Interaction and Identity.* New York: Routledge.

Bayley, R., Hansen-Thomas, H., and Langman, J. (2005) 'Language brokering in a middle school science class', in J. Cohen, K. T. McAlister, K. Rolstad, and J. MacSwan (eds.) *ISB4: Proceedings of the 4th International Symposium on Bilingualism.* Somerville, MA: Cascadilla Press, pp. 223–232.

Bell, A. (1984) 'Language style as audience design', *Language in Society,* 13 (2): 145–204.

Dutcher, N. (2004). Expanding educational opportunity in linguistically diverse societies. Washington DC: Center for Applied Linguistics. Available online at: http://www.cal.org/resources/pubs/ford report_040501.pdf (accessed 14 November 2009).

El Decreto Número 19–2003. (2003). Available online at: http://www.almg.org.gt/UserFiles/File/LEYES%20DE%20IDIOMAS%20MAYAS/LeyIdiomasNacionales%2019–2003.pdf (accessed 14 November 2009).

Ferguson, C. (2000/1959) 'Diglossia', in L. Wei (ed.) *The Bilingualism Reader*. New York: Routledge, pp. 65–80. (Reprinted from *Word 15*, 325–340.)

Fishman, J. (2000/1965) 'Who speaks what language to whom and when?', in L. Wei (ed.) *The Bilingualism Reader*. New York: Routledge, pp. 89–106. (Reprinted from *La Linguistique 2*, 67–88.)

Fishman, J. (2000/1967) 'Bilingualism with and without diglossia; diglossia with and without bilingualism', in L. Wei (ed.) *The Bilingualism Reader*. New York: Routledge, pp. 81–88. (Reprinted from *Journal of Social Issues* 23 (2): 29–38.)

Freeman, R. D. (1998) *Bilingual Education and Social Change*. Philadelphia, PA: Multilingual Matters; Malden, MA: Blackwell.

García, O. (1997) 'Bilingual education', in F. Coulmas (ed.) *The Handbook of Sociolinguistics*. Malden, MA: Blackwell, pp. 405–420.

Gee, J. P. (2005) *An Introduction to Discourse Analysis: Theory and Method*. Second Edition. New York: Routledge.

Giles, H., Coupland, J., and Coupland, N. (eds.) (1991) *Contexts of Accommodation: Developments in Applied Sociolinguistics*. New York: Cambridge University Press.

Grice, H. P. (1975). 'Logic and conversation'. In P. Cole and J. L. Morgan (eds), *Syntax and Semantics*. Vol. 3: *Speech Acts*. New York: Free Press, pp. 41–58.

Grice, H. P. (1989) *Studies in the Way of Words*. Cambridge, MA: Harvard University Press.

Gumperz, J. J. (1982) *Discourse Strategies*. New York: Cambridge University Press.

Institute of Education Sciences (2008) *Rigor and Relevance Redux: Director's Biennial Report to Congress (IES 2009–6010)*. Washington, DC: US Department of Education.

Legarreta, D. (1977) 'Language choice in bilingual classrooms', *TESOL Quarterly*, 11 (1): 9–16.

López, L. E. (2006) 'Cultural diversity, multilingualism and indigenous education in Latin America', in O. García, T. Skutnabb-Kangas, and M. E. Torres-Guzmán (eds.) *Imagining Multilingual Schools: Languages in Education and Glocalization*. Buffalo, NY: Multilingual Matters, pp. 238–261.

Mohanty, A. K. (2006) 'Multilingualism of the unequals and predicaments of education in India: mother tongue or other tongue?', in O. García, T. Skutnabb-Kangas, and M. Torres-Guzmán (eds.) *Imagining Multilingual Schools: Languages in Education and Glocalization*. Buffalo, NY: Multilingual Matters, pp. 262–283.

Moran, C. and Hakuta, K. (1995) 'Bilingual education: broadening research perspectives', in J. Banks (ed.) *Handbook of Multicultural Education*. New York: MacMillan Publishing Co, pp. 445–462.

Myers-Scotton, C. (1983) 'The negotiation of identities in conversation: a theory of markedness and code choice', *International Journal of the Sociology of Language*. 44: 115–136.

Myers-Scotton, C. (2006) *Multiple Voices: An Introduction to Bilingualism*. Malden, MA: Blackwell.

Palmer, D. K. (2008) 'Building and destroying students' "academic identities": the power of discourse in a two-way immersion classroom', *International Journal of Qualitative Studies in Education (QSE)*, 21 (6): 647–667.

Romaine, S. (1995) *Bilingualism*. Second Edition. Malden, MA: Blackwell.

Roosevelt, T. (1919, January 3). [Letter to Mr. Hurd]. Library of Congress, Manuscript Division. Washington DC. Available at http://msgboard.snopes.com/politics/graphics/troosevelt.pdf (accessed 14 November 2009).

Sanchez, H. T. and Sanchez, M. A. (2008) 'The politics of illegal immigration, bilingual education, and the commodity of the post-technological society', *Educational Forum*, 72 (4): 329–338.

Sarva Shiksha Abhiyan Right to Education Committee (2009) Sarva Shiksha Abhiyan Final Report on Right to Education Act. Available online at: http://www.indg.in/primary-education/policiesandschemes/rte_ssa_final_report.pdf (accessed 14 November 2009).

Schleppegrell, M. J. (2003) *Grammar for Writing: Academic Language and the ELD Standards*. Santa Barbara, CA: University of California Linguistic Minority Research Institute.

Schleppegrell, M. J. (2004) *The Language of Schooling: A Functional Linguistic Perspective*. Mahwah, NJ: Lawrence Erlbaum.

Setati, M. and Adler, J. (2000) 'Between languages and discourses: language practices in primary multilingual mathematics classrooms in South Africa', *Educational Studies in Mathematics*, 43: 243–269.

Shavelson, R. and Towne, L. (2002) *Scientific Research in Education*. Washington, DC: National Academy Press.

Terrazas, A. and Batalovo, J. (2009) Frequently requested statistics on immigrants and immigration in the United States. Washington, DC: Migration Policy Institute. Available online at: http://www.migrationinformation.org/Feature/display.cfm?ID=747 (accessed 14 November 2009).

U.S. Department of Education. (1991) The condition of bilingual education in the nation: a report to the Congress and the President. Available online at: http://www.eric.ed.gov/ERICWebPortal/content delivery/servlet/ERICServlet?accno=ED335945.

U.S. English. (2009). Official English – States with official English laws. Available online at: http://www. us-english.org/view/13 (accessed 14 November 2009).

Valdés, G. (1997) 'Dual-language immersion programs: a cautionary note concerning the education of language-minority students', *Harvard Educational Review*, 67 (3): 391–429.

Wei, L. (1994) *Three Generations, Two Languages, One Family: Language Choice and Language Shift in a Chinese Community in Britain*. Bristol, PA: Multilingual Matters.

Wei, L. (1998) 'The "why" and "how" questions in the analysis of conversational code-switching', in P. Auer (ed.) *Code-Switching in Conversation: Language, Interaction, and Identity*. New York: Routledge, pp. 156–179.

Zentella, A. C. (1981) '*Tá bien*, you could answer me *en cualquier idioma*: Puerto Rican codeswitching in bilingual classrooms', in R. P. Durán (ed.) *Latino language and Communicative Behavior*. Norwood, NJ: ABLEX Publishing Corporation, pp. 109–132.

Zentella, A. C. (1997) *Growing up Bilingual: Puerto Rican Children in New York*. Malden, MA: Blackwell.

29

English for academic purposes
and discourse analysis

Ken Hyland

Introduction

English for academic purposes (EAP) is an activity at the forefront of language research and teaching today, with a distinctive focus on the particular linguistic preferences, discourse features and communicative practices used in specific academic contexts. Driven by the globalization of higher education and by the emergence of English as the international lingua franca of scholarship, EAP has crucially depended for its growth on its ability to identify accurately what these features and practices are, so that they may be taught to students and relayed to academics seeking to publish in English. In this enterprise discourse analysis, particularly text-based forms of genre analysis, has become established as perhaps the most widely used and productive methodology. It has helped to describe texts within textual and social contexts and has provided insights into the ways rhetorical choices are related to social and epistemological practices in the disciplines. This chapter will offer an overview of the importance of discourse analysis in this area of research and pedagogy, outline something of my own contribution to the area, and make some predictions about future research directions.

What is EAP?

EAP is usually defined as teaching English with the aim of assisting learners' study or research in that language (e.g. Flowerdew and Peacock, 2001). In this sense it is a broad term, covering all areas of academic communicative practice such as pre-tertiary, undergraduate and post-graduate teaching, classroom interactions, academic publishing and curriculum issues, as well as research, student and instructional genres (e.g. Hyland, 2009a). The emergence of EAP in the 1980s, as a response to growing numbers of second language (L2) students in university courses and in a framework informed by English for specific purposes, originally produced an agenda concerned with curriculum and instruction rather than with theory and analysis. EAP was then largely a materials and teaching-led movement focusing on texts and on the search for generic study skills, which could be integrated into language courses to make students more efficient learners.

Since then, a developing research base in EAP has emphasized the rich diversity of texts, contexts and practices in which students must now operate. While it continues to be heavily involved in syllabus design and it needs analysis and materials development, EAP has moved away from purely pedagogic considerations to become a much more theoretically grounded and research informed enterprise. The communicative demands of the modern university involve far more than simply controlling linguistic error or polishing style. In fact international research, experience, and practice provide evidence for the heightened, complex, and highly diversified nature of such demands. Supported by an expanding range of publications and research journals, there is a growing awareness that students, including native English speakers, have to take on new roles and engage with knowledge in new ways when they enter university. They find that they need to write and read unfamiliar genres and participate in novel speech events, and that communication practices are not uniform across academic disciplines but reflect different ways of constructing knowledge and engaging in teaching and learning.

The role of EAP has therefore changed in response to changing conditions in the academy. The huge expansion of university places in many countries, together with an increase in full fee-paying international students to compensate for cuts in government support, has resulted in a more culturally, socially and linguistically diverse student population than ever before. Moreover, with the rapid rise in refugee populations around the world and the consequent increase in international migration, it is common for teachers find non-native users of English in their high school classrooms for whom the concept of 'academic language' (expressed in any language) is an unfamiliar one. In other words, students bring different identities, understandings and habits of meaning-making to their learning, which means that teachers can no longer assume that their students' previous learning experiences will provide appropriate schemata and skills to meet the demands of their subject courses.

In addition, students now take a broader and more heterogeneous mix of academic subjects. In addition to traditional single-subject or joint-honours degrees, we now find complex modular degrees and emergent 'practice-based' courses such as nursing, management and social work. These new course configurations are more discoursally challenging for students who have to move between genres, departments and disciplines. Further, while in the past the main vehicles of academic communication were written texts, now a broad range of modalities and presentational forms confront and challenge students' communicative competence. They must learn rapidly to negotiate a complex web of disciplinary specific text-types, assessment tasks and presentational modes (both face to face and online) in order first to graduate, and then to operate effectively in the workplace. The diverse learning needs of students are therefore focused on the challenges to communicative competence presented by disciplinary-specific study, by new modes of distance and electronic teaching and learning, and by changing circumstances, both within the academy and in society at large.

As a result, EAP has assumed greater prominence and importance in the academy, forcing it to evolve and to ask new questions. Instead of focusing on why learners have difficulties in accessing academic discourses, EAP now addresses the influence of culture and the demands of multiple literacies on students' academic experiences. These questions, moreover, accompany new challenges, which centre on the increased concern with the English language skills of non-native English speaking academics. The ability to deliver workshops in English, to participate in meetings, to make presentations at international conferences and, above all, to conduct and publish research in English are all demanded as part of such lecturers' competence as academics. This group's needs are now beginning to be noticed and analysed, and programmes are emerging which cater to their particular requirements.

Current EAP aims, therefore, at capturing thicker descriptions of language use in the academy at all age and proficiency levels, incorporating and often going beyond immediate communicative contexts to understand the nature of disciplinary knowledge itself. It employs a range of inter-disciplinary influences for its research methods, theories and practices to provide insights into the structures and meanings of spoken, written, visual and electronic texts, into the demands placed by academic contexts on communicative behaviours, and into the pedagogic practices by which these

413

behaviours can be developed. It is, in short, specialized English language teaching grounded in the social, cognitive and linguistic demands of academic target situations and informed by an understanding of texts and of the constraints of academic contexts. Discourse analysis is a key resource in this research agenda and has made an enormous contribution to our understanding of academic communication.

What has discourse analysis told us about EAP?

Discourse analysis is a collection of methods for studying language in action, looking at texts in relation to the social contexts in which they are used. Because language is an irreducible part of social life, connected to almost everything we do, this broad definition has been interpreted in various ways across the social sciences. In EAP it has tended to be a methodology which gives greater emphasis to concrete texts than to institutional social practices, and has largely taken the form of focusing on particular academic genres such as the research article, the conference presentation, and the student essay. Genre analysis can be seen as a more specific form of discourse analysis, which focuses on any element of recurrent language use, including grammar and lexis, that is relevant to the analyst's interests. As a result, genre analysis sees texts as representative of wider rhetorical practices and so has the potential to offer descriptions and explanations both of texts and of the communities that use them.

Genres are the recurrent uses of more or less conventionalized forms through which individuals develop relationships, establish communities and get things done using language. Genres can thus be seen as a kind of tacit contract between writers and readers, which influence the behaviour of text producers and the expectations of receivers. By focusing on mapping typicality, genre analysis thus seeks to show what is usual in collections of texts, and so it helps to reveal underlying discourses and the preferences of disciplinary communities. These approaches are influenced by Halliday's (1994) view of language as a system of choices that link texts to particular contexts through patterns of lexico-grammatical and rhetorical features (Christie and Martin, 1997) and by Swales' (1990) observation that these recurrent choices are closely related to the work of particular discourse communities, whose members share broad social purposes.

A range of spoken and written academic genres have been studied in recent years. These include student dissertations (Bunton, 2002; Hyland, 2004c), research articles (Lewin *et al.*, 2001), scientific letters (Hyland, 2004a), book reviews (Hyland and Diani, 2009), conference presentations (Carter-Thomas and Rowley-Jolivet, 2001) and PhD theses (Swales, 2004)–as well as various 'occluded' (or hidden) genres such as the Master of Business Administration (MBA) 'thought essay' (Loudermilk, 2007), grant proposals (Connor and Upton, 2004) and editors' responses to journal submissions (Flowerdew and Dudley-Evans, 2002). This research demonstrates the distinctive differences in the genres of the academy where particular purposes and audiences lead writers to employ very different rhetorical choices (e.g. Hyland, 2004a). Table 29.1, for example, compares frequencies for different features in a corpus of 240 research articles and 56 textbooks.

We can see considerable variation in these features across the two genres. The greater use of *hedging* underlines the need for caution and opening up arguments in the research papers

Table 29.1 Selected features in research articles and textbooks

per 1000 words	Hedges	Self-mention	Citation	Transitions
Research articles	15.1	3.9	6.9	12.8
University textbooks	8.1	1.6	1.7	24.9

compared with the authorized certainties of the textbook, while the removal of *citation* in textbooks shows how statements are presented as facts rather than as claims grounded in the literature. The greater use of self-mention in articles points to the personal stake that writers invest in their arguments and to their desire to gain credit for claims. The higher frequency, in textbooks, of transitions, which are conjunctions and other linking signals, is a result of the fact that writers need to make connections far more explicit for readers with less topic knowledge.

Perhaps the most productive application of discourse analysis in EAP has been to explore the lexico-grammatical and discursive patterns of particular genres in order to identify their recognizable structural identity. Analysing this kind of patterning has yielded useful information about the ways in which texts are constructed and the rhetorical contexts in which such patterns are used, as well as providing valuable input for genre-based teaching. Some of this research has followed the move analysis work pioneered by Swales' (1990) which seeks to identify the recognizable stages of particular institutional genres and the constraints on typical move sequences. Moves are the typical rhetorical steps which writers or speakers use to develop their social purposes, and recent work on academic genres has produced descriptions of the methods sections in research articles (Bruce, 2008) and the peer seminar (Aguia, 2004).

While analysing schematic structures has proved an invaluable way of looking at texts, analysts are increasingly aware of the dangers of oversimplifying by assuming blocks of texts to be monofunctional and ignoring writers' complex purposes and 'private intentions' (Bhatia, 1999). There is also the problem of validating analyses to ensure they are not simply products of the analyst's intuitions (Crookes, 1986). Transitions from one move to another in a text are always motivated outside the text, as writers respond to their social context, but analysts have not always been able to identify the ways these shifts are explicitly signalled by lexico-grammatical patterning.

One feature of academic genres to receive attention is writers' use of *evaluative that* constructions in articles and dissertations (Hyland and Tse, 2005), a structure that allows a writer to thematize evaluative meanings by presenting a complement clause following *that* (as in *We believe that this is an interesting construction*). Other recent studies have looked at circumstance adverbials in student presentations (Zareva, 2009), interactive features of undergraduate lectures (Morrell, 2004), and the common four-word collocations, or lexical bundles, which are typical of student dissertations (Hyland, 2008). A recurrent feature in much recent work has been to show how persuasion in various genres is not only accomplished through the ways ideas are presented, but also through the construction of an appropriate authorial self and the negotiation of participant relationships.

Academic discourse analysis research has also pointed to cultural specificity in rhetorical preferences (e.g. Connor, 2002). Although 'culture' is a controversial term, one influential interpretation regards it as an historically transmitted and systematic network of meanings that allow us to understand, develop and communicate our knowledge and beliefs about the world. Culture is seen as inextricably bound up with language (Kramsch, 1993), so that cultural factors have the potential to influence perception, language, learning and communication. Although it is far from conclusive, discourse analytic research suggests that the schemata of L2 and L1 (first language) writers differ in their preferred ways of organizing ideas that can influence academic writing (e.g. Hinkel, 2002). These conclusions have been supported by a range of studies over the past decade comparing the features of research articles in various countries (e.g. Duszak, 1997), in student essays (Kubota, 1998) and conference abstracts (Yakhontova, 2002).

Much of this contrastive rhetoric research assumes a 'received view of culture' that unproblematically identifies cultures with national entities and emphasizes predictable consensuality *within* cultures and differences *across* them (e.g. Atkinson, 2004). However, it is fair to say that, compared with many languages, academic writing in English tends to:

- be more explicit about its structure and purposes with constant previewing and reviewing of material
- employ more, and more recent, citations
- be less tolerant of digressions
- be more cautious in making claims, doing it with considerable use of mitigation and hedging
- use more sentence connectors to show explicitly how parts of the text link together.

While we can't simply predict the ways people are likely to write on the basis of assumed cultural traits, discourse studies have shown that students' first language and prior learning come to influence ways of organizing ideas and structuring arguments when they write in English at university.

Research into academic discourse has not been entirely focused on the printed page, however. As Fairclough (2003: 3), among other, observes: 'text analysis is an essential part of discourse analysis, but discourse analysis is not merely the linguistic analysis of texts'. A number of studies have sought to show how academic discourses are firmly embedded in the cultures and activities in which their users participate. One example is Prior's (1998) study of the processes of graduate student writing at a US university. This draws on transcripts of seminar discussions, student texts, observations of institutional contexts, tutor feedback and interviews with students and tutors to give an in-depth account of the ways students negotiate their writing tasks and so became socialized into their disciplinary communities. Swales (1998), on the other hand, offers a 'thick' description of the literate cultures of academics themselves. Combining text analyses with extensive observations and interviews, he provides a richly detailed picture of the professional lives, commitments and projects of individuals in three diverse academic cultures: a computer centre, a herbarium and a university's English language centre.

Finally, studies conducted from a critical perspective have focused on how social relations, identity, knowledge and power are constructed through written and spoken texts in disciplines, schools and classrooms. Distinguished by an overtly political agenda from other kinds of discourse analysis, CDA has attempted to show that the discourses of the academy are not transparent or impartial means for describing the world; they work in order to construct, regulate and control knowledge, social relations and institutions. Particular literacy practices possess authority because they represent the currently dominant ideological ways of depicting relationships and realities, and these authorized ways of seeing the world exercise control of academics and students alike. Studies by Ivanic (1998) and Lillis (2001) show how this can create tensions for students in coping with university literacy demands, while Flowerdew's (1999) research suggests similar concerns among non-Native English scholars.

The findings produced by discourse analysis applied to academic texts have not only contributed to our understanding of such texts and practices, but have also had a major impact on EAP teaching. Analyses have provided teachers, materials designers and students with an understanding of how target texts are structured and the reasons they are written as they are. EAP practitioners draw on the findings of discourse analytic studies to determine what is to be learned and to organize instruction around the genres that learners need and the social contexts in which they will operate. Texts and tasks are therefore selected according to learners' needs and genres are modeled explicitly to provide learners with something to aim for: an understanding of what readers are likely to expect.

What has my work contributed to this area?

My own contribution to this research has mainly addressed two broad areas: the role of interpersonal aspects of academic persuasion and disciplinary variations in academic literacy practices.

First, my research has helped to establish that written texts embody interactions between writers and readers. While this view is not now news, it was once considered self-evident that academic writing was an objective, faceless and impersonal form of discourse, simply reporting the 'real' academic work that was done in the lab, the library or the field. It is now fairly well established, however, that academic writing is a persuasive endeavour, so academics are not seen as simply producing texts that plausibly represent an external reality, but as using language to acknowledge, construct and negotiate social relations. Discourse analysis can help show how writers seek to offer a credible representation of themselves and their work by claiming solidarity with readers, evaluating their material and acknowledging alternative views.

As this view gains greater currency, considerable attention has turned to the features that help towards realizing this interpersonal and evaluative dimension of academic texts, and much of my own work over the past decade or so has been devoted to this. Beginning with work on hedges (Hyland, 1996, 1998), I have explored various interpersonal resources such as personal pronouns (2001a, 2002a), reporting verbs (2004a), questions (2002b) and directives (2002c), as well as looking at the ways particular genres such as acknowledgements (2004b) and journal descriptions (Hyland and Tse, 2009) function to engage readers and convey the writer's position.

In addition to studying individual features, I have attempted to offer a framework, or rather two frameworks, for analysing the linguistic resources of intersubjective positioning. This has consolidated much of my earlier work and collected together a range of features under the headings of 'stance and engagement' (Hyland, 2005a) and of 'metadiscourse' (Hyland and Tse, 2004; Hyland, 2005b). The first of these attempts to capture how discoursal choices help construct both writers and readers. *Stance* is an attitudinal dimension, which includes features that refer to the ways writers present themselves and convey their judgements, opinions and commitments, either intruding to stamp their personal authority onto their arguments or stepping back to disguise their involvement. *Engagement* (Hyland, 2001a), in contrast, is an alignment dimension where writers acknowledge and connect to others, recognizing the presence of their readers, pulling them along through their argument, focusing their attention, acknowledging their uncertainties, including them as discourse participants. *Metadiscourse*, on the other hand, seeks to offer a more comprehensive and integrated way of examining interaction in academic argument, broadening the scope of interactional resources to include also features such as conjunctions, framing devices and glosses on content. While these are often considered as simply helping to tie texts together, they have an important role in relating a text to a community.

Interaction in academic writing thus involves 'positioning', or adopting a point of view in relation to both the issues discussed in the text and to others who hold points of view on those issues. When they claim a right to be heard and to have their work taken seriously, writers must display competence as disciplinary insiders. This writer–reader dialogue therefore occurs in a disciplinary context, and attempting to map the rhetorical preferences that help to identify these communities is the second main area of my work.

Essentially, we can see disciplines as language-using communities that provide the context within which students learn to communicate and to interpret each other's talk, gradually acquiring the specialized discourse competencies to participate as group members. Texts are influenced by writers' memberships of disciplinary groups, which have objectified in language certain ways of experiencing and talking about phenomena. Assumptions about what can be known, how it can be known and with what degree of certainty all help to shape discourse practices, so that what counts as convincing argument, appropriate tone, persuasive interaction and so on is managed for a particular audience (Hyland, 2004a). This emphasis on what is 'shared' by a community has led to criticisms that the concept is too structuralist, static and deterministic (e.g. Prior, 1998). But, like any community, disciplines are composed of individuals with diverse experiences, expertise and commitments, so that actions and understandings are influenced by the personal and biographical as well as by the institutional and sociocultural.

Successful academic writing, however, depends on the individual writer's control of the epistemic conventions of a discipline—that is, of what counts as appropriate evidence and argument—and my research has contributed to the growing body of work now devoted to elaborating upon the considerable differences in these conventions across disciplines. This body has explored both student and professional academic genres and has discovered rhetorical variation in, for example, the extent of self-mention (Hyland, 2001a), citation practices and reporting verbs (Hyland, 2004a), hedges and boosters (Hyland, 1998), sub-technical lexis (Hyland and Tse, 2007), metadiscourse (Hyland, 2005b) and lexical bundles (Hyland, 2008).

One of the most striking differences in how language differs across fields is the use of hedges. These function to withhold complete commitment to a proposition, implying that a claim is based on plausible reasoning rather than on certain knowledge. They indicate the degree of confidence the writer thinks it might be wise to give a claim while opening a discursive space for readers to dispute interpretations (Hyland, 1996). Because they represent the writer's direct involvement in a text, something that scientists generally try to avoid, they are twice as common in humanities and social science papers as in the hard sciences. One reason for this is that in the humanities there is less control of variables, more diversity of research outcomes and fewer clear bases for accepting claims than in the sciences. Writers can't report research with the same confidence of shared assumptions, so papers rely far more on recognizing alternative voices. Arguments have to be expressed more cautiously by using more hedges. In the hard sciences positivist epistemologies mean that the authority of the individual is subordinated to the authority of the text and facts 'speak for themselves'. The implication is that writers often disguise their interpretative activities behind linguistic objectivity. They downplay their personal role so as to suggest that results would be the same whoever conducted the research. The less frequent use of hedges is one way of minimizing the researcher's role.

This variation is also apparent in student essays (Hyland, 2009b) and dissertations (Hyland, 2004c) and in the *kinds* of writing that students are asked to do: even students in fairly cognate fields, such as nursing and midwifery, are given very different writing assignments (Gimenez, 2009). In fact the failure to recognize that discourse conventions are embedded in the epistemological and social practices of the various disciplines means that writing is a black box to students, particularly as lecturers themselves have difficulty in explaining what they mean. Entering the academy means making a 'cultural shift' in order to take on identities as members of those communities.

An example analysis of an EAP genre

Discourse analyses of academic texts takes a variety of forms, tending towards the textual, the critical or the contextual, but there have been two main ways of studying interactions in writing. Researchers have examined the actions of individuals as they create particular texts (Bosher, 1998), or they have studied the distribution of different genre features to see how they cluster in complementary distributions (Biber, 2006). The approach I illustrate here steps back from particular authors or readers to reveal interaction as a collection of rhetorical choices rather than as specific encounters of people with texts. To see how writers behave as members of social communities means going beyond the decisions of individual writers to explore the regularity and repetition of the socially ratified forms which represent preferred disciplinary practices. Writers are oriented to more than an immediate encounter with their text when composing; they also conjure up institutional patterns that naturally and ideologically reflect and maintain such patterns. These can only be seen by viewing their activity as a socially and culturally constituted mode of praxis.

One example of this is a study of *self-mention*, which concerns how far writers want to intrude into their texts though use of '*I*' or '*we*', or avoid it by choosing impersonal forms. The use of self-mention is a rather vexed issue in academic writing and remains a perennial problem for students, teachers and experienced writers alike; the extent to which one can reasonably assert one's personal involvement remains highly controversial. While claims have to be warranted by appropriate support and reference to existing knowledge by fitting novelty into a community consensus, success in gaining acceptance for innovation also involves demonstrating an *individual contribution* to that community and establishing a claim for recognition for *academic priority*. To some extent this is a personal preference, determined by seniority, experience, personality and so on (Hyland, 2010), but the study illustrated here shows that the presence or absence of explicit author reference is a conscious choice by writers to adopt a particular community-situated authorial identity (Hyland, 2001b).

This study employed both qualitative and quantitative approaches, comprising frequency counts and text analysis of a corpus of published articles and a series of interviews with academics from the same fields. The text corpus of 240 research articles consisted of three papers from each of ten leading journals in eight disciplines selected to represent a broad cross-section of academic practice in the fields of engineering, physical sciences, social sciences and humanities. The texts were scanned to produce an electronic corpus of 1.5 million words and searched for expressions of self-mention using WordPilot, a text analysis programme. The search items were the first person pronouns *I*, *me*, *my*, *we*, *us* and *our*; cases of self-citation and references to work conducted elsewhere by the same authors; and examples of self-mention terms such as *this writer* or *the research team*.

The most immediately striking features of the text analysis was the saliency of self-mention in the articles and the variety of its disciplinary and formal expressions. While research articles may well be characterized by abstraction and high informational production (Biber, 2006), human agents are integral to their meaning. There are sufficient cases of author-reference to suggest that writers have conspicuous promotional and interactional purposes, every article containing at least one first person reference. Overall, there were roughly 28 expressions of self-mention in each paper; 81 per cent of these were pronouns and 16 per cent self-citations. There were considerable differences between the disciplines (Table 29.2): an average of 44 cases per article in marketing, and only 7 in mechanical engineering.

Perhaps the most obvious form of self-mention is to refer to one's earlier research, but the extent of self-citation in these papers was surprising, about 70 per cent of the papers in the study containing a reference to the author. This was particularly frequent in biology, where an average

Table 29.2 Average frequency of self-mention per paper

Discipline	Totals	Self-citations	Pronouns	Other
Biology	26.9	10.8	15.5	0.5
Physics	21.0	2.8	17.7	0.5
Electronic eng	15.9	3.8	11.6	0.5
Mechanical eng	6.8	3.7	2.6	0.5
Average hard fields	17.6	5.3	11.9	0.5
Marketing	43.9	4.9	38.2	1.0
Philosophy	36.7	2.2	34.5	0.0
App Ling	36.5	3.2	32.3	1.0
Sociology	35.3	5.1	29.4	0.8
Average soft fields	38.1	3.9	33.6	0.7
Overall	27.8	4.6	22.7	0.6

of 11 citations per paper was registered, and it was particularly prominent in the sciences and engineering, where it made up almost 11 per cent of all references (compared with only 5 per cent in the soft fields). These broad variations indicate the underlying differences in the research practices of these communities that I noted above. References in sciences and engineering tend to be tightly bound to a particular research topic and contribute to a sense of linear progression in these areas. Because of the heavy financial investment in technical equipment on which scientific research often depends and because of the sheer volume of knowledge generated, scientists tend to participate in highly discrete and specialized areas of research from where they can follow defined paths and make precise contributions. Research on particular issues is therefore often conducted at a restricted number of sites and by a limited number of researchers, allowing writers to draw on their own work to a greater extent than in the soft knowledge fields.

The high proportion of personal pronouns in the soft knowledge articles, on the other hand, suggests quite different research and rhetorical practices. Establishing an appropriately authorial persona and maintaining an effective degree of personal engagement with one's audience are valuable strategies for probing relationships and connections between entities that are generally more particular, less precisely measurable, and less clear-cut than in the hard sciences. Writers in the sciences are seeking to establish empirical uniformities through research that involves precise measurement of a limited number of controlled variables. There are familiar procedures and relatively clear criteria of acceptability, so that writers can downplay their personal role in order to highlight the phenomena under study, the replicability of research activities and the generality of the findings. By electing to adopt a less intrusive or personal style, writers can strengthen the objectivity of their interpretations and subordinate their own voice to that of nature. In the soft knowledge fields, in contrast, successful communication depends to a larger extent on the author's ability to evoke a real writer in the text. The first person assists authors to make a personal standing and to demarcate their own work from that of others.

In all disciplines, writers' principal use of the first person was to explain the work that they had carried out by way of representing their unique role in constructing a plausible interpretation for a phenomenon. In the hard knowledge corpus and in the more quantitative papers in the soft fields, this mainly involved setting out methodological procedures so that self-mention helped to underline the writer's professional credentials through a familiarity with disciplinary research practices. In addition, it acts to highlight the part the writer has played in a process that is often represented as having no agents at all, reminding readers that, in other hands, things could have been done things differently. In more theoretically oriented articles writers sought less to figure as practical agents than as builders of coherent theories of reality. Explicit self-mention here establishes a more personal form of authority, one based on confidence and command of one's arguments.

It has to be said that the relationships between knowledge, the linguistic conventions of different disciplines and personal identity are fuzzy and complex. Yet it is equally true that these broad differences suggest that self-mention varies with different assumptions about the effects of authorial presence and rhetorical intrusion in different knowledge-making communities. These are issues worth addressing and exploring further with students, for only by developing a rhetorical consciousness of these kinds of features can they gain control over their writing in academic contexts.

Looking to the future

Predictions are always difficult to make, but it is clear that the influential role of discourse analysis in assisting teachers to prepare students for their language-related experiences is unlikely to diminish any time soon. The findings of discourse analytic studies have replaced intuitions about academic writing based on impressions of scientific discourse, revealing that texts are highly persuasive and interactive and that writers in different disciplines represent themselves, their work and their readers in very different ways. There are, however, a number of areas where research is likely to make an increasing impact on EAP.

The first is the area of clarifying the interdisciplinary complexities of the modern academy. Many student genres remain to be described–for instance counselling case notes, reflexive journals and clinical reports–while analyses of more occluded research genres would greatly assist novice writers in the publication process. We also know little about the ways genres form 'constellations' with neighbouring genres (Swales, 2004); or about the 'genre sets' that a particular individual or group engages in; or about how spoken and written texts cluster together in a given social activity. In addition, as I have mentioned earlier, the mix of academic subjects now offered to students impacts on the genres they have to participate in, compounding the challenges of writing in the disciplines with novel literacy practices that have barely been described. Discourse analyses have much to contribute in all of these areas.

Second, it is also clear that much remains to be learnt and considerable research undertaken before we are able to identify more precisely the notion of 'community' and how it relates to discipline and the discoursal conventions that it routinely employs. Nor is it yet understood how our memberships of different groups influence our participation in academic discourses. For now, the term *discipline* might be seen as a shorthand form for the various identities, roles, positions, relationships, reputations, reward systems and other dimensions of social practices constructed and expressed through language in the academy, but these concepts need to be refined through the analyses of academic texts and contexts.

A third broad area is that of understanding the increasing role of multimodal and electronic texts in academics contexts. Academic texts, particularly in the sciences, have always been multimodal, but textbooks and articles are now far more heavily influenced by graphic design than ever before and the growing challenge to the page by the screen as the dominant medium of communication means that images are ever more important in meaning-making. Analytical tools developed by Kress and van Leeuwen (2006) and others, for example, provide a starting point for researchers and teachers to explain how visuals have been organized for maximum effect, while considerably more work needs to be done to understand the role of multimedia and hypertext in EAP classrooms.

Conclusions

While EAP is a practically oriented activity committed to demystifying prestigious forms of discourse, unlocking students' creative and expressive abilities and facilitating their access to greater life chances, it is grounded in the descriptions of texts and practices. By providing teachers with a way of understanding how writing is shaped by individuals who make language choices in social contexts, it contributes to both theory and practice. In particular, it shows that it has nothing to do itself with topping up generic language skills, but involves developing new kinds of literacy: equipping students with the communicative skills to participate in particular academic cultures. While these ideas have been around for some time, it is only through discourse analysis that we have been able to specify more clearly what this actually means.

Further reading

Flowerdew, J. (ed.) (2002) *Academic Discourse*. London: Longman.

A collection covering key approaches to academic discourse analysis and illustrated by empirical studies.

Hyland, K. (2004) *Disciplinary Discourses*. Ann Arbor, MI: University of Michigan Press.

An argument for disciplinary variation drawing on a range of features and genres.

Hyland, K. (2009) *Academic Discourse*. London: Continuum.

A non-technical orientation to a wide range of spoken and written academic genres.

Swales, J. (2004) *Research genres*. New York: Cambridge University Press.

A rich and accessible account of research genres.

References

Aguia, M. (2004) 'The peer seminar, a spoken research process genre', *Journal of English for Academic Purposes*, 3 (1): 55–72.

Atkinson, D. (2004) 'Contrasting rhetorics/contrasting cultures: why contrastive rhetoric needs a better conceptualization of culture', *Journal of English for Academic Purposes*, 3 (4): 277–289.

Bhatia, V. K. (1999) 'Integrating products, processes, and participants in professional writing',, in C. N. Candlin and K. Hyland (eds.) *Writing: Texts, Processes and Practices*. Harlow: Longman, pp. 21–39.

Biber, D. (2006) *University Language: A Corpus-Based Study of Spoken and Written Registers*. Amsterdam: Benjamins.

Bosher, S. (1998) 'The composing processes of three southeast Asian writers at the post-secondary level: an exploratory study', *Journal of Second Language Writing*, 7 (2): 205–233.

Bunton, D. (2002) 'Generic moves in PhD thesis introductions', in J. Flowerdew (ed.) pp. 57–74.

Carter-Thomas, S. and Rowley-Jolivet, E. (2001) 'Syntactic differences in oral and written scientific discourse: the role of information structure', *English for Specific Purposes*, 31: 19–37.

Christie, F. and Martin, J. R. (eds.) (1997) *Genre in Institutions: Social Processes in the Workplace and School*. New York: Continuum.

Connor, U. (2002) 'New directions in contrastive rhetoric', *TESOL Quarterly*, 36: 493–510.

Connor, U. and Upton, T. (2004) 'The genre of grant proposals: a corpus linguistic study', in U. Connor and T. Upton (eds.) *Discourse in the Professions*. Amsterdam: Benjamins, pp. 235–255.

Crookes, G. (1986) 'Towards a validated analysis of scientific text structure', *Applied Linguistics*, 7: 57–70.

Duszak, A. (1997) ' "Analyzing", "digressiveness in Polish academic texts" ', in A. Duszak (ed.) *Culture and Styles of Academic Discourse*. Berlin: Mouton de Gruyter, pp. 323–341.

Fairclough, N. (2003) *Analyzing Discourse*. London: Routledge.

Flowerdew, J. (1999) 'Problems of writing for scholarly publication in English: the case of Hong Kong', *Journal of Second Language Writing*, 8 (3): 243–264.

Flowerdew, J. and Dudley-Evans, T. (2002) 'Genre analysis of editorial letters to international journal contributors', *Applied Linguistics*, 23: 463–489.

Gimenez, J. (2009) 'Beyond the academic essay: discipline-specific writing in nursing and midwifery', *Journal of English for Academic Purposes*, 7 (3): 151–164.

Halliday, M. A. K. (1994) *An Introduction to Functional Grammar*. Second Edition. London: Edward Arnold.

Hinkel, E. (2002) *Second Language Writers' Text*. Mahwah, NJ: Lawrence Erlbaum.

Hyland, K. (1996) 'Writing without conviction? hedging in scientific research articles', *Applied Linguistics*, 17 (4): 433–454.

Hyland, K. (1998) *Hedging in Scientific Research Articles*. Amsterdam: John Benjamins.

Hyland, K. (2001a) 'Bringing in the reader: addressee features in academic articles', *Written Communication*, 18 (4): 549–574.

Hyland, K. (2001b) 'Humble servants of the discipline? self-mention in research articles', *English for Specific Purposes*, 20 (3): 207–226.

Hyland, K. (2002a) 'Authority and invisibility: authorial identity in academic writing', *Journal of Pragmatics*, 34 (8): 1091–1112.

Hyland, K. (2002b) 'What do they mean? questions in academic writing', *TEXT*, 22, 529–557.

Hyland, K. (2002c) 'Directives: argument and engagement in academic writing', *Applied Linguistics*, 23 (2): 215–239.

Hyland, K. (2004a) *Disciplinary Discourses*. Ann Arbor, MI: University of Michigan Press.

Hyland, K. (2004b) 'Graduates' gratitude: the generic structure of dissertation acknowledgements', *English for Specific Purposes*, 23 (3): 303–324.

Hyland, K. (2004c) 'Disciplinary interactions: metadiscourse in L2 postgraduate writing', *Journal of Second Language Writing*, 13: 133–151.

Hyland, K. (2005a) 'Stance and engagement: a model of interaction in academic discourse', *Discourse Studies*, 6 (2): 173–191.

Hyland, K. (2005b) *Metadiscourse*. London: Continuum.

Hyland, K. (2008) 'As can be seen: lexical bundles and disciplinary variation', *English for Specific Purposes*, 27 (1): 4–21.

Hyland, K. (2009a) *Academic Discourse*. London: Continuum.

Hyland, K. (2009b) 'Corpus informed discourse analysis: the case of academic engagement', in M. Charles, S. Hunston, and D. Pecorari (eds.) *At the Interface of Corpus and Discourse: Analysing Academic Discourses*. London: Continuum.

Hyland, K. (2010) 'Community and individuality: performing identity in Applied Linguistics', *Written Communication*.

Hyland, K. an Diani, G. (eds.) (2009) *Academic Evaluation: Review Genres in University Settings*. London: Palgrave MacMillan.

Hyland, K. and Tse, P. (2004) 'Metadiscourse in academic writing: a reappraisal', *Applied Linguistics*, 25 (2): 156–177.

Hyland, K. and Tse, P. (2005) 'Evaluative that constructions: signalling stance in research abstracts', *Functions of Language*, 12 (1): 39–64.

Hyland, K. and Tse, P. (2007) 'Is there an "academic Vocabulary"?' *TESOL Quarterly*, 41 (2): 235–254.

Hyland, K. and Tse, P. (2009) ' "The leading journal in its field": evaluation in journal descriptions', *Discourse Studies*.

Ivanic, R. (1998) *Writing and Identity: The Discoursal Construction of Identity in Academic Writing*. Amsterdam: Benjamins.

Kramsch, C. (1993) *Context and Culture in Language Teaching*. Oxford: Oxford University Press.

Kress, G. and van Leeuwen, T. (2006) *Reading Images: The Grammar of Visual Design*. Second Edition. London: Routledge.

Kubota, R. (1998) 'Ideologies of English in Japan', *World Englishes*, 17: 295–306.

Lewin, B., Fine, J., and Young, L. (2001) *Expository Discourse*. London: Continuum.

Lillis, T. (2001) *Student Writing: Access, Regulation, Desire*. London: Routledge.

Loudermilk, B. (2007) 'Occluded academic genres: an analysis of the MBA thought essay', *Journal of English for Academic Purposes*, 6 (3): 190–205.

Prior, P. (1998) *Writing/Disciplinarity: A Sociohistoric Account of Literate Activity in the Academy*. Hillsdale, NJ: Lawrence Erlbaum.

Swales, J. (1990) *Genre Analysis: English in Academic and Research Settings*. Cambridge: Cambridge University Press.

Swales, J. (1998) *Other Floors, Other Voices: A Textography of a Small University Building*. Mahwah, NJ: Erlbaum.

Swales, J. (2004) *Research Genres*. New York: Cambridge University Press.

Yakhontova, T. (2002) ' "Selling" or "telling"? The issue of cultural variation in research genres', in J. Flowerdew (ed.) *Academic Discourse*. London: Longman, pp. 216–232.

Zareva, A. (2009) 'Informational packaging, level of formality, and the use of circumstance adverbials in L1 and L2 student academic presentations', *Journal of English for Academic Purposes*, 8 (1): 55–68.

Part V
Institutional applications

30

Advertising and discourse analysis

Elsa Simões Lucas Freitas

Introduction: advertising messages as samples of social interaction and activities

Ads are wonderful examples of the diverse roles discourse can fulfil in society. To consider them as discourse types can prove very enlightening about the ways people communicate and relate to each other within the different spheres where they perform their daily activities. This exemplary character is intrinsically connected with the very nature of ads: advertising is one of the liveliest and most representative forms of discourse when it comes to displaying its own inner functioning, since it not only enhances its status as a linguistic form of communication but also foregrounds the need for context when it comes to the full understanding of the overall message – which is the cornerstone of discourse analysis as a method of discursive interpretation (Cook, 1992: 2).

As a discourse type, advertising has always suffered the consequences of a perceived marginal status, at different levels. This marginality has to do with the very nature of ads. In fact, one of the outstanding characteristics of this relatively young form of discourse is its ability to raid successfully desirable elements from other, more clearly defined discourses in order to borrow credibility from others or enhance some of its own features (Williamson, 1978: 165). The resulting restlessness and ambiguity contribute to a feeling of mistrust towards it: its features are not its own, and ad discourse might even threaten to replace others, which are more firmly established, because of this ability to draw inspiration from all possible sources (Freitas, 2010: 259), even when ads are able to incorporate criticism to themselves as useful material for creation (Myers, 1999: 209). On account of not enjoying the status of a fully established discourse, advertising has consistently been a target for attacks aimed at its lack of intrinsic and defining characteristics (Geis, 1982: 159). This elusiveness would then account for the difficulty of establishing boundaries on which to base effective standards for assessing and evaluating this form of communication.

In addition to this charge of lack of credibility, advertising has also been denied seriousness of purpose on the grounds of its ultimate commercial aims (Myers, 1999: 4). Broadly speaking, these aims would include the sales promotion of a given product or service, the firm establishment of the presence of a given brand in the public's mind, or even the reassurance of the public as to the quality of the product in the event of rebranding strategies (Brierley, 1995: 45–47; Wells *et al.*, 1998: 14–15, Yeshin, 2006: 8–11). This kind of socially oriented criticism attacks advertising on moral grounds: the hidden agenda behind advertising discourse introduces a financial element in this communication process that taints it and causes it to be seen as less worthy of serious attention (Freitas, 2010: 260). After all, ads consist in messages that are paid for, conveyed in a space or time that I bought (Belch and Belch, 2004: 16) and that mercantile inception robs of whatever purity they might possess as a discourse type. This socially critical perspective also relates to another marker of marginality, since advertising is often accused of creating an opposition between two worlds: one that is real (where we all in fact live in) and an illusory one – created for us by ads (see, among others, Williamson, 1978: 207; Geis, 1982: 122; Cortese, 2004: 13). The postulation of two opposite realms, that of reality and that of fiction – whose relevance is challenged by other authors (Cook, 1992; Myers, 1994; MacRury, 1997 and 1999; Freitas, 2008) – implies that advertising might ultimately be responsible for a serious threat to social values, in that it would propose a deliberately deceitful and delusional universe to the consumers, causing them to be permanently dissatisfied with the factual world they are condemned to inhabit in everyday life and thereby to seek refuge in a substitute kind of reality (Williamson, 1978: 47). According to some critics to the advertising system, this could ultimately lead to the consumers' alienation, since, on to this reasoning, they have fallen into the ad-induced habit of identifying what should merely be a factual (and real) commodity with unreal emotions. This perspective implies, as will be later discussed, a preconception about the identities and values of the receptors of the discourse of advertising (they are easily deluded), as well as a didactic perspective on the part of these critics: it would seem that this specific discursive practice must be handled with care, because of its corruptive seductiveness, although it is possible to decipher it, provided you are in possession of the appropriate hermeneutical tools to do it.

A third kind of marginality embedded in advertising discourse could be called situational insofar as it is related to the way ads are consumed by their viewers: they are marginal in that they are never what people really want to look at or listen to: 'An ad is never the programme they are watching, never the letter they are waiting for, never the part of the newspaper they are reading' (Cook, 1992: 13) – their status as intruders in other communication processes is deeply imbued in their very structure, and it also functions as an important part of their effectiveness. By nature, they are meant to be understood at a glance (hence their extreme condensation of meaning), and they are expected to be broadcast with a fair amount of repetitions, having their message replicated in several media over a given period of time – which explains the often redundant layers of meanings simultaneously conveyed by the different channels available in the media used in a specific campaign (Freitas, 2004: 294). Due to its peculiar circumstances of conception, production and reception, advertising is, therefore, a type of discourse that, unlike many others, cannot claim its public's undivided attention for a long time (Cook, 1992: 217): it is easily disposed of, often scorned, criticized and belittled; and it thrives in spite of (or maybe because of) these seemingly adverse circumstances, always managing to make the most of its status as an outsider, using it to its advantage as a creative resource among many others.

It is the purpose of this chapter to undertake a reflection on ads as a rewarding object of study for the discipline of discourse analysis, taking into consideration the special characteristics of advertising discourse and their great relevance as an ever-changing, perpetually dynamic and continuously updated source of information as to past and present prevalent social values and beliefs (Cook, 1992: 3). Such as they are, and also because of their omnipresence in contemporary western societies, ads constitute forms of discourse that strongly influence the construction of their viewers' social and cultural identities (Goddard, 1998: 4) and demand a proper macro-contextualisation in order to be conveniently integrated in that wider set of values, as well as a micro-context within which they will acquire their full significance as fully functional elements of an advertising campaign. For that purpose, a recent campaign for a language school will be analysed – by taking into consideration its linguistic elements as well as non-linguistic features and by stressing the importance of contextual material, so as achieve a balanced interpretation of the meanings intended, as befits a multi-semiotic process of communication such as advertising (Yuen, 2004: 163).

The academic background: key studies in the analysis of advertising discourse

Advertising, as far as we know, has been in existence approximately since the nineteenth century, although its earlier origins can be traced back to ancient Rome, or even Egypt (Wells *et al.*, 1998: 23). Although ads from previous eras often seem quaint and old-fashioned to contemporary publics, the essence of their discourse has not altered in a substantial manner (Myers, 1994: 17). The kind of claims contemporary ads make and the seduction strategies they use do sound more sophisticated nowadays; however, viewers are able to pinpoint specific decades in ads not so much due to the presence or absence of sophistication of the strategies used as due to the form in which power relationships between the actors portrayed in an ad are depicted – which mimic real social connections (Goffman, 1979: 7); the kind of values that are upheld by the ad and those that are implicitly or explicitly rejected; or even the forms of behaviour deriving from consensually accepted gender roles (Freitas and Tuna, 2010: 18).

The evolution of advertising discourse throughout the ages has accompanied social evolutions, as befits a discourse that can only survive its eternally peripheral status by keeping up to date with the latest social developments and by integrating references to them in its inner structure (Cunha and Freitas, 2010: 30). As the main focus of the ad's message shifts from the factuality of the goods or services promoted to meanings that were associated with them by means of a number of seductive strategies, it has become increasingly common for commercial advertising to encompass reality in a way that, once again, can easily generate attacks on the opportunism of this ever polemical discourse:

> Many people also feel confused by advertising's apparent change of attitude towards contemporary problems. Some ads make a show of ecological concern, of support for women's rights, of recommending a healthy diet to prevent disease. This apparent social conscience may give rise to three very different judgements. According to the first, [...] it is possible for advertising to influence society: for good as well as for bad. In the second view, advertising is amoral, and merely reflects states and changes in society, whether good or bad [...]. In the third view, the apparent social concern and progress professed in some ads is simply fraudulent, and ads are always bad [...].
>
> *(Cook, 1992: 17)*

Advertising has very often been analysed from the point of view of the effects it might have on the social and cultural status quo, because of the way in which it appears to depict daily life and lifelike situations. According to this perspective, this apparently faithful depiction is, however, particularly pernicious to the public's mentality, since what is being shown has previously undergone a careful process of selection and transformation, whereby scenes are refined, relationships are stylized, people and sets are beautified and perfected – thus becoming versions of everyday reality in disguise. According to this reasoning (which can be found in more or less acrimonious forms in authors such as Williamson, 1978; Geis, 1982, or even Dyer, 1982), this would correspond to a dangerous veneer that unduly 'cooks' – i.e. civilizes – whatever should remain natural and pure – 'raw' (Williamson, 1978: 121).

Such a perspective, which is partially shared by more recent authors such as O'Barr (1994), Vestergaard and Schroder (1985) or Cortese (2004), presupposes up to a point the existence of a 'correct' interpretation of the ad's ultimate message, a message that would only be totally accessible to the detached interpreter who, thanks to a superior knowledge, remains immune to the negative influence of the pervasive advertising phenomenon (Cook, 1992: 205). This kind of reasoning clearly throws the analysis off balance, since it attributes near magical powers to advertising

(Williams [1960] 1997: 170), singling it out and attributing to it a more central role than it really has, blaming it *in toto* for the constant state of dissatisfaction and wishful thinking the public reputedly hovers in, overlooking the fact that the forging of people's identity is necessarily the result of amalgamated and extremely varied social and cultural influences. Also, as we have seen, at the base of such reasoning is the premise thatthere is on the one hand a safe, factual world ruled by logic and, on the other hand, a dangerous world created by ads, where illogicalness and falsehood rule. This distorted mirror would be responsible for the appearance of 'false needs'. However, how do we decide which of our needs are real and which are false? Later critics have looked at advertising and consumption in a less rigid form:

> It is not easy […] to decide what is a socially necessary commodity. At its simplest there are clothes, heat, food and shelter […]. The problem becomes more complicated when discriminating between different cuts of coat, different styles of housing or different kinds of food. At what point does a decision based on a principle of style, taste, or fashion move from the necessary to the excessive? Is the 'aesthetic' arguably as important a consideration as the 'function'?
>
> *(Myers, 1986: 129–130)*

In accordance with this view, contemporary authors such as Greg Myers refuse this rigid distinction between two sets of needs, based on the difference between 'real wants' and 'imaginary needs': '[…] I will argue that the distinction between what we want and what we need cannot be so easily made: the values added by advertising can be real values' (1999: 8).

When that kind of judgement is being passed on what should rightfully be acquired (because it is necessary) and what is superfluous – and is therefore only being bought for consumption's sake – the burden of condemnation is being placed on the underlying advertising system but also, rather heavily, on the misguided viewers, who, in Geis's words, '[…] get the commercials they deserve, that is, commercials to which they respond' (1982: 110). It is important to stress at this point that this equation is, in fact, leaving out one of its most important factors, which is the audience for this kind of discourse. Excessive attention paid to the text will, once again, distort the experience of being exposed to ads in our daily lives. As we have seen, ads very seldom get undivided attention; they are not meant, or functionally prepared, to deal with that. As audiences become increasingly more advertising-literate, claims made by ads become more and more relative in their minds. Very often, apparently factual claims are meant to be read as tongue-in-cheek, or the explicit message of the ad seems to be totally unrelated to whatever is being promoted. It is also common to present contradictory inner layers of meaning within the same ad, where some of the channels are conveying one message while simultaneously being undermined or denied by others (Freitas, 2008: 174). Sophistication of this kind is easily grasped by the publics, briefly commented on, transiently gratifying, or downright refused or overlooked (Myers, 1999: 203). The advertising process is never univocal: even when the ad is not received by its intended public, it elicits a reaction, even if that is one of refusal of the message proposed. This reaction expands far beyond the mere acquisition of the product, which is related to the way ads project an image of their intended audiences and, perhaps even more importantly, to the way audiences accept the proposed image or refuse to comply with it (Myers, 1999: 221–222). In fact, we can say with Myers that audiences do talk back when confronted with ads (1994: 88–89), in other words they establish a dialogic relationship with the ad's message, its surroundings and the role ads ask us to assume as viewers, whether or not we are members of their intended target audience. On the one hand, publics are never passive; on the other hand, interpretations can never be entirely predicted – and that margin of unpredictability is embedded in the ad's inner workings.[1]

The concentration on the perceived impact of advertising on capitalist societies, as well as the oversimplification of audiences' reactions to ads, was, as we have seen, a recurring feature of many works that, mainly in the 1980s, took an interest in advertising and its social consequences. More recently, academic interest has been focussed rather on the way viewers actively interact with the meanings and associations proposed by ads, as well as with the form the worlds created by ads are, themselves, integrated with other cultural aspects that constitute contemporary societies.

Examining ads in context: advertising seen through the eyes of discourse analysis

Accompanying these alterations in the focus of analysis, and perhaps as one of its logical consequences, the form of exploring the actual discourse developed by ads has been evolving as well. In fact, in many of the earlier works that took an interest in looking at a real corpus of ads, the preference for print ads is clear (Baldry, 2004: 83). One of the reasons for that choice is the fact that it is easier with a print ad to immobilize the object of analysis, since it is possible to reproduce it on a book page with relative fidelity to its original version.[2] That restriction of the corpus chosen to only one medium (which already implied a bias of some kind) was often accompanied by analytical concentration on the linguistic features of the ad (see Preston, 1967; Preston and Scharbach, 1971; Grunig, 1990; Pons-Ridler, 1994), which was involving analytical distortions once again. As is the case very often with ads appearing in all the media, the most relevant meanings are commonly conveyed non-linguistically, through channels such as image or sound (Cook, 1992: 38), where emotions and subjectivity are more easily triggered and activated, and where their interplay creates different layers of interpretation:

> Mere semantic description and univocal semiotic approaches […] are not sufficient to account for connotation and emotion. That is the ad's ultimate battlefield […] This area of indeterminacy and appeal to emotion which ads play upon contributes to the creation of an atmosphere of shared knowledge and assumed intimacy between the *I* in the ad and the *I* of the viewer […].
>
> *(Freitas, 2008: 46)*

In fact, in print ads, it is often up to the linguistic part to establish the factual part of the message, whereas the pictorial features introduce indeterminacy and ambiguity. A combination of both is also possible, as in the case of pictorial metaphors, where it is common for the image to suggest the transference of characteristics from secondary to primary domain, thus achieving the desired conflation between different 'systems of things' (Forceville, 1995: 38), with the textual part merely guiding readings towards the intended interpretation (Barthes, 1977; Pateman, 1980).

If serious distortion in interpretation is a major threat when we isolate linguistic matter from the other elements in a print ad, that threat becomes even more real when we consider television commercials as a corpus for discourse analysis. How do we stabilize meanings in such a corpus long enough to undertake analysis, when their most salient characteristic is the dynamism of their fluxes of meaning? (O'Halloran, 2004: 109). This difficulty of a very practical order is still commonly dealt with by ignoring their dynamic nature (Cook, 1992: 38), either by sidestepping television ads altogether or, when they are referred to, by singling out their most stable features – the linguistic elements.[3]

Instability is not the only problem when dealing with the pictorial or musical mode in ads. Although target viewers can be relied on to understand their role within the framework of a particular ad, the meanings they convey are hard to conceptualize (Kress and van Leeuwen 1996:

1; van Leeuwen, 1998: 26; Rose 2001: 48–52). This makes them a very useful tool in the hands of advertisers (how do we criticize their use when it is so difficult to express their meaning verbally?) but also a major challenge for academics who want to attribute to those modes the same importance that is normally given to linguistic features. How to solve this difficulty? As Cook would put it:

> I do not see a way of overcoming these problems – but neither do I believe they should be ignored. The obstacle which they pose enables advertising to keep analysis at bay, for it can shift its ground constantly, emphasizing now one mode and now another. There is a danger of dilution in an analysis which attempts to tackle too much, and no individual analyst will feel equally at home in all modes and all media; but I believe that the converse fault – of fragmentation and incompleteness – is worse. Advertising, unlike analysis, operates in all modes and media at once, and must be treated accordingly.
>
> *(Cook, 1992: 38)*

This kind of analysis, although it is still relatively infrequent, has been lately attempted by a number of authors within the field of discourse analysis (see, among many others, Cook, 1992; Myers, 1994 and González Requena and Ortiz de Zárate, 1995, 1999; Freitas, 2004 and 2008), which seems to indicate that 'discourse' has started to be equated with modes other than the strictly linguistic, and that it is not possible to analyse one mode in isolation, since various communicative competences are always at stake in every interpersonal interaction – of which ads are wonderful examples: since none of them is reducible to 'plain text', they should rightfully be treated as interactional phenomena (Heller, 2001: 253).

Lack of clear discourse boundaries: multimodality and overall coherence in advertising messages as addressed by discourse analysis [4]

Ads are good examples of why communication processes should be analysed in a global manner. Although a complete analysis that encompasses every element is not possible for the reasons mentioned above, analysis should strive, nonetheless, to take as much as possible into account: 'Actual analyses, of course, develop in detail only a small part of the full picture. However, any discourse analysis needs, at least, to give some consideration, if only as background, to the whole picture' (Gee, 2005: 110).

In the specific case of multimedia advertising campaigns, the 'whole picture' should doubtlessly be the main focus of analysis. This is where the message effectively lies, since 'each medium presents its own obvious advantages for advertisers, but also some disadvantages. Multimedia campaigns offer one way of compensating for the weaknesses of one channel by using the strong points of others' (Freitas, 2004: 295). In that manner, the intended 'advertising pressure' can be exerted upon the viewers (Brochand *et al.*, 1999: 356), guaranteeing that, in one way or another, they will be exposed to at least a part of the divulgation effort.

A possible way of undertaking the analyses of such a campaign is by bearing in mind a number of building tasks and discourse analysis questions that are at stake when we assess any sample of 'language in use': they have to do with (1) the significance that a piece of language can lend to certain situations and the way the way this happens; and (2) what situations this piece of language is creating in such a way that they are recognized by the others. Another important issue is related to the establishment of (3) specific identities and (4) relationships by means of this language sample (Gee, 2005: 11–13). A given piece of language will also indicate some sort of (5) assessment on social values, will (6) establish connections with other utterances, making them relevant to the present one, as well as (7) attribute prevalence to a given sign system over others (Gee, 2005: 11–13).

The ad corpus chosen to illustrate the application of the points above to advertising messages is the most recent multimedia campaign for the Wall Street Institute (WSI). These ads were specifically produced for WSI Portugal, and are not part of an international campaign for this institution. They were broadcast in Portugal in 2008 and involved media such as television, banners and leaflets, window display material, outdoor ads and an interactive website. The generic name for the campaign was 'linguspresus' (a mock Latin expression that would roughly translate as 'tongue-tied'), which is close enough to the Portuguese expression 'língua presa' to be easily understood by the target audience and at the same time to achieve a humorous effect right from the start.

This campaign is based on a rather simple concept, which is afterwards expanded to different media with the help of the different channels technically available to each of them, and also by means of different advertising strategies such as pictorial metaphors, intertextuality, humour and music – which are, in their turn, adapted and translated into the characteristics of each medium used in the campaign.

As befits a language institute, the focus is on the tongue itself: the difficulties felt by many in achieving an adequate level of fluency in the English language are equated with health problems with their tongue, namely with a virus ('linguspresus') that attacks their skills in speaking the English language. Although it is being done in a humoristic form,[5] this concept establishes a number of assumptions on social values right from the start: in fact, it starts from the notion that having English language skills is highly desirable and even indispensable for an adequate social and professional life (as the situations depicted in the television commercials illustrate); it also conveys the notion that language skills are a commodity that can be bought just like any other – in this case, as easily and quickly as taking a vaccine boost. This assumption carries with it at least three implications, both for the service that is being offered and for prospective students: classes at WSI are value for money and cost-effective, and (perhaps even more importantly) viewers who do nothing to improve their skills in English will eventually be demeaned in a number of social situations.[6] This campaign proposes a worldview where these values are taken for granted and address viewers according to these assumptions. Although many viewers would probably question the assumptions if they were clearly verbalized, many others will probably accept the worldview proposed and step into the role the ad (and the expert in the ad) proposes to them, seemingly in a personal manner:

> Ads can create a sense of addressing a person whether they are on target in that particular case or not. […] For some ads I do step into the position offered. [but] the address in ads can also be effective even when I don't step in. Just by understanding the question 'Shamed by your English?', by recognising that some people could or should be ashamed, I am accepting the advertiser's view of language as a commodity that can be sold by mail, and as a personal attribute like halitosis.
>
> *(Myers, 1994: 78–79)*

– or like a disease or a virus, as in the WSI case.

The WSI campaign: the print ads

For practical reasons (which correspond to the ones mentioned in the previous section), only some samples of the printed material will be reproduced here.

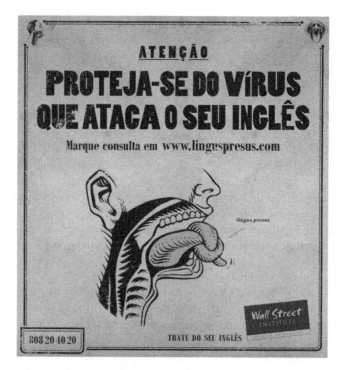

Figure 30.1 Image of outdoor ad *Linguspresus* (more general approach)

The outdoor material either identifies the problem ('Protect yourself from the virus', Figure 30.1) with the help of a vaccine (i.e. classes at the WSI) or offers quick means for diagnosing the disease by asking people quickly to translate to English some sentences with rather unusual words or grammatical constructions in Portuguese (see Figures 30.2, 30.3 and 30.4). Those who are unable to do it (as most would be) have indeed the virus and are offered specialised help – at WSI centres. Although the linguistic part of the ad is crucial for transmitting the concept (NOT POSSESSING LANGUAGE SKILLS = VIRUS and VACCINE FOR THE VIRUS = WSI CENTRES), the images in these ads are responsible for firmly establishing the pictorial metaphor that lends wit and originality to the campaign, namely LANGUAGE SKILLS = HEALTHY TONGUE. The layout and the old-fashioned drawings that illustrate these out-doors also lend them an air of mock credibility and incongruity that contributes to the humorous effect (Gulas and Weinberger, 2006: 23–24), as if they had been taken from a derelict copy of Gray's Anatomy.

The WSI campaign: the television commercials

In the television ads (available for consultation at the Handbook's Website), an equivalent effect to this quaint tone is rendered by the presence of a prototypical middle-aged doctor cum scientist, Dr E. P. Glote (Dr E. P. Glottis), who, with a slightly pedantic intonation, speaking Portuguese with a markedly foreign accent and using a direct address form, explains to an invisible audience the nature of the problem. Under the form of a lecture, he points at several diagrams to clarify the physical problem of 'linguspresus' and uses a number of short films to illustrate embarrassing situations where people become tongue-tied due to their lack of

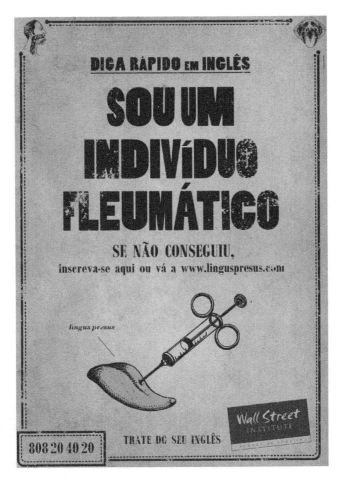

Figure 30.2 Image of outdoor ad *Linguspresus* ('Say it quickly in English!')

fluency – literally, they are left with their tongues hanging out, which makes the situation all the more ridiculous. In the case of the television ads, it is the bassoon musical theme that emphasizes the risible consequences of the prototypical situations depicted: it sounds goofy-like, although it is slow and portly. The pictorial metaphor that is conveyed by the visual features in the printed material (the tongue) is now present in the doctor's surgery, under the form of a tongue-shaped sofa and a number of trophy-like framed tongues on the walls, reinforcing the notion that this man is indeed an expert in tongue-related problems and has been hunting them all his life. The idea of big game hunting is further stressed by another element that is contextual in nature: the narrator's voice belongs to a TV presenter who used to be the Portuguese voice-over of National Geographic animal life documentaries, and it is immediately recognizable to Portuguese native speakers.

Although it is used in a self-parodic manner, the easily recognizable format of a lecture delivered by an expert creates a prototypical simulation (Gee, 2005: 75) of a lesson in a classroom or a doctor–patient consultation, where a number of assumptions and judgements on social values are put forward by someone in a position of authority – which would be the television equivalent of the expert position assumed by the old anatomy diagrams of the print and outdoor ads. Once

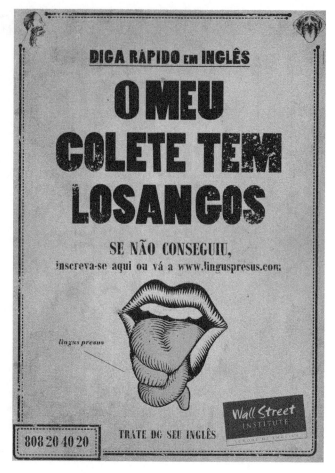

Figure 30.3 Image of outdoor ad *Linguspresus* ('Say it quickly in English!')

again, the underlying paratextual message could be verbalized as: 'this is meant to be funny, and we know that you will identify the game, but deep down you know that we are right, and English is important for you'.

The WSI campaign: the website material

The website material for this campaign opens a large number of interactive possibilities to the viewers. The link to the WSI campaign website is mentioned in the printed material and also in the television ads. Although it is still rather unusual to use websites as an extension to the campaign, in this particular instance it makes sense that such a strategy is used, since teaching methods at WSI centres involve the frequent use of computers. This site maintains the same witty tone, by providing mock factual elements about the disease and about the doctor's personal and professional life. This is clearly an invitation to the viewer to join the game and have fun with the cornerstone concept of the campaign. The interactivity that is expected of all ad viewers is made evident here through the exhibition of the ad's fictional devices.

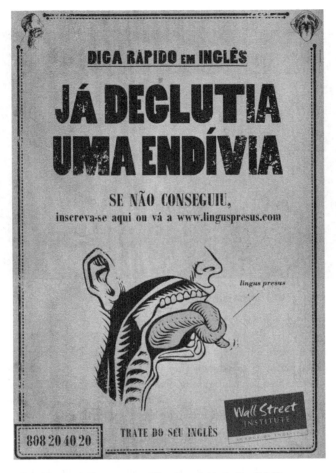

Figure 30.4 Image of outdoor ad *Linguspresus* ('Say it quickly in English!')

Further developments in the reading of advertising discourse(s) and concluding remarks

In contemporary society, advertising is a pervasive and omnipresent cultural form (Myers, 1999: 212), and it might be particularly disturbing and disconcerting to deal with a discourse that thrives on restlessness, whose features are undefined and unclear, and which refuses to become stable so as to provide a clearly focused corpus for analysis. As we have seen in the previous sections, in spite of their characteristic restlessness, ads are readily recognized for what they are, mainly because of the position they occupy in relation with other discourses (Cook, 1992: 224). Their ultimate purpose is clear for everyone involved in the process, so it is often understated, this causing a good part of the ad messages in advertising nowadays to appear unrelated with the product or service proposed. For critics of advertising, this margin of free time or space is where its danger lies: unencumbered by the necessity to define themselves as specific discourse types, ads can associate their product with whatever social values they see fit or acceptable:

Figure 30.5 Image of WSI *Linguspresus* website

It is worth considering that ads, despite the belief of manufacturers and advertisers that they exist solely to promote goods, may do many other things as well, and that these other activities are extremely revealing about the needs of contemporary society. Debate about the morality of ads tends to focus on the use of time and space to sell. This, however, may be only a small part of ads' function and attractiveness.

(Cook, 1992: 225)

Although they are, by nature, resistant to detailed analysis, ads are indeed valuable documents on how society evolves and what we, as viewers, tolerate as acceptable. It is perhaps within this sphere that DA analysis may prove more relevant and rewarding – and not so much in the close attention to minute detail, which would, after all, deny the form in which ads are consumed in everyday life.

Further reading

There is a number of works on advertising written under a DA perspective.

Myers, G. (1994) *Words in Ads*. London: Edward Arnold.

This is an excellent introduction to detailed analysis of this kind, with an innovative focus on the way ads are received by the audiences.

Cook, G. (1992) *The Discourse of Advertising*. London and New York: Routledge.

First published in 1992, followed by a new updated edition in 2001, this is a classic work on the DA of ads and is consistently referred to in subsequent writings in this area. Apart from focussing on the characteristics of ads themselves, it explores the issue of the intertextuality and contextualization of ads in contemporary society and in connection with other discourses.

Freitas, E. S. L. (2008) *Taboo in Advertising*. Amsterdam, Philadelphia, PA: John Benjamins.

This also applies DA analysis to a corpus of ads, especially in multimedia campaigns, taking into account the different modes that can be used to convey meanings in ad messages.

Forceville, C. (1995) *Pictorial Metaphor in Advertising*. London and New York: Routledge. *Pictorial Metaphors in Advertising* (1995).

This has become a reference book in ad analysis and is particularly useful for providing a methodology for the study of the visual components of ad messages.

Rose, G. (2001) *Visual Methodologies*. London, Thousand Oaks, CA, New Delhi: Sage Publications.

Although not specifically focussed on advertising, this also provides excellent discussions on DA as applied to meaning-making processes, especially in Chapters 4 and 7.

Notes

1 This is one of the reasons why criticism based on literal readings of textual features of ads might be targeting the wrong conveyor of meaning. Very often, the intended meaning is being conveyed non-textually, i.e. through channels whose interpretation might not be challenged on the basis of literalness (for example, music or, to a lesser degree, some images).

2 Even though it is virtually impossible to reproduce accurately the context where the print ad has been reproduced.

3 Due to the complexity of the dynamic flux of information in television ads, multimodal transcription systems have been developed of late, in order to try to account for all the elements conveyed by the different modes (among others, cf. Baldry, 2004).

4 The author would like to thank Sandra Coelho, Marketing Assistant at Wall Street Institute, for kindly allowing the reproduction of parts of their ad campaign (Advertising agency: Brandia Central) in this chapter, as well as for providing clearance for the uploading of their advertising material onto the Handbook's Website.

5 The humorous approach (established on the basis of incongruity and surprise) had already been used in a previous WSI campaign, under the concept *a língua dos bifes* ('the steak language'), where raw steaks were depicted talking to each other, by means of superimposed speech bubbles. This concept was based on a cultural-specific pun: the Portuguese word *bife* ('steak') can be slang for 'English person'; therefore the 'steak language' would be English. One of the print ads from this campaign is reproduced in the Handbook's website.

6 At this point it is important to notice that the stress is on the 'improvement' of existing but insufficient language skills, which might also mean that the mere idea of not speaking English at all would be totally outrageous – another judgement on social values.

References

Baldry, A. P. (2004) 'Phase and transition, type and instance: patterns in media texts as seen through a multimodal concordancer', in K. L. O'Halloran (ed.) *Multimodal Discourse Analysis: Systemic-Functional Perspectives*. London and New York: Continuum, pp. 83–108.

Barthes, R. (1977) *Image Music Text*, trans. S. Heath. London: Fontana Press.

Belch, G. E. and Belch, M. A. (2004) *Advertising and Promotion: An Integrated Marketing Communication Perspective*. New York: McGraw-Hill.

Brierley, S. (1995) *The Advertising Handbook*. London and New York: Routledge.

Brochand, B., Lendrevie, J., and Rodrigues, J. V. (1999) *Publicitor*. Lisboa: Dom Quixote.

Cook, G. (1992) *The Discourse of Advertising*. London and New York: Routledge.

Cortese, A. J. (2004) *Provocateur: Images of Women and Minorities in Advertising*. Lanham, MD: Rowman & Littlefield.

Cunha, C. and Freitas, E. S. L. (2010) 'Uma análise dos novos média e a criação de conteúdos como estratégia publicitária para o sucesso das marcas' [An analysis of the new media and content development as an advertising strategy for brand success], in E. S. L. Freitas and S. Tuna (eds.) *Cadernos de Estudos Mediáticos 7 [Dossier of Media Studies 7]*. Porto: Edições Universidade Fernando Pessoa, pp. 29–42.

Dyer, G. (1982) *Advertising as Communication*. London and New York: Routledge.

Forceville, C. (1995) *Pictorial Metaphor in Advertising*. London and New York: Routledge.

Freitas, E. S. L. (2004) 'Similar concepts, different channels: intersemiotic translation in three Portuguese advertising campaigns', in B. Adab and C. Valdés (eds.) *Key Debates in the Translation of Advertising Material*, 10 (2). Manchester: St Jerome Publishing, pp. 291–311.

Freitas, E. S. L. (2008) *Taboo in Advertising*. Amsterdam, Philadelphia, PA: John Benjamins.

Freitas, E. S. L. (2010) 'Advertising the medium: on the narrative worlds of a multimedia promotional campaign for a public service television channel', in M.-L. Ryan and M. Grishakova (eds.) *Intermediality and Storytelling*. The Hague: Walter de Gryuter, pp. 258–284.

Freitas, E. S. L. and Tuna, S. (2010) 'Comunicação publicitária em tempos de crise: análise discursiva de estratégias de honestidade em duas campanhas "estilo de vida" ' [Advertising communication in times of economic crisis: a discursive analysis of honesty strategies in two "lifestyle" advertising campaigns], in E. S. L. Freitas and S. Tuna (eds.) *Cadernos de Estudos Mediáticos*, 7 [*Dossier of Media Studies*, 7]. Porto: Edições Universidade Fernando Pessoa, pp. 15–27.

Gee, J. P. (2005) *An Introduction to Discourse Analysis: Theory and Method*. London and New York: Routledge.

Geis, M. L. (1982) *The Language of Television Advertising*. New York: Academic Press.

Goddard, A. (1998) *The Language of Advertising: Written texts*. London and New York: Routledge.

Goffman, E. (1979) *Gender Advertisements*. London and Basingstoke: Macmillan.

González Requena, J. and Ortiz de Zárate, A. (1995) *El Espot Publicitario: Las metamorfosis del deseo. [Television Commercials: The Metamorphoses of Desire]*. Madrid: Cátedra.

Grunig, B. -N. (1990) *Les Mots de la Publicité*. Paris: Presses du CNRS.

Gulas, C. S. and Weinberger, M. G. (2006) *Humour in Advertising: A Comprehensive Analysis*. New York: M.E. Sharpe.

Heller, M. (2001) 'Discourse and interaction', in D. Schiffrin, D. Tannen, and H. E. Hamilton (eds.) *The Handbook of Discourse Analysis*. Oxford: Blackwell, pp. 250–264.

Kress, G. and van Leeuwen, T. (1996) *Reading Images: The Grammar of Visual Design*. London and New York: Routledge.

MacRury, I. (1997) 'Advertising and the modulation of narcissism: the case of adultery', in M. Nava, A. Blake, I. MacRury, and B. Richards (eds.) *Buy This Book: Studies in Advertising and Consumption*. London ad New York: Routledge, pp. 239–254.

Myers, G. (1994) *Words in Ads*. London: Edward Arnold.

Myers, G. (1999) *Ad Worlds: Brands, Media, Audiences*. London: Arnold.

Myers, K. (1986) *Understains: The Sense and Seduction of Advertising*. London: Commedia.

O'Barr, W. M. (1994) *Culture and the Ad: Exploring Otherness in the World of Advertising*. Boulder: Westview.

O'Halloran, K. L. (2004) 'Visual semiosis in film', in K. L. O'Halloran (ed.) *Multimodal Discourse Analysis: Systemic–Functional Perspectives*. London and New York: Continuum, pp. 109–130.

Pateman, T. (1980) 'How to do things with images: an essay on the pragmatics of advertising', *Theory and Society: Renewal and Critique in Social Theory*, 9 (4), Amsterdam: 603–622.

Pons-Ridler, S. (1994) 'Nier pour convaincre', in *La Linguistique – Langage, sujets, lieu social*, 30 (2) 30, Paris: PUF: 93–104.

Preston, I. L. (1967) 'Logic and illogic in the advertising process', *Journalism Quarterly*, 44 (2): 231–239.

Preston, I. L. and Scharbach, S. E. (1971) 'Advertising: more than meets the eye?', *Journal of Advertising Research*, 11(3): 19–24.

Rose, G. (2001) *Visual Methodologies*. London, Thousand Oaks, CA, New Delhi: Sage Publications.

van Leeuwen, K. (1998) 'Music and ideology: notes towards a socio-semiotics of mass media music', *Popular Music and Society*, 22: 21–54.

Vestergaard, T. and Schroder, S. (1985) *The Language of Advertising*. Oxford: Basil Blackwell.

Wells, W., Burnett, J., and Moriarty, S. (1998) *Advertising: Principles and Practice*. London, Sidney, Toronto: Prentice-Hall International Editions.

Williams, R. ([1960] 1997) 'Advertising: the magic system', *Problems in Materialism and Culture*. London: Verso Books, 170–195.

Williamson, J. (1978) *Decoding Advertisements*. London and Boston, MA: Marion Boyars.

Yeshin, T. (2006) *Advertising*. London: Thompson.

Yuen, C. Y. (2004) 'The construal of ideational meaning in print advertisements', in K. L. O'Halloran (ed.) *Multimodal Discourse Analysis: Systemic-Functional Perspectives*. London and New York: Continuum, pp. 163–195.

31

Media and discourse analysis

Anne O'Keeffe

What is media discourse?

Media discourse refers to interactions that take place through a broadcast platform, whether spoken or written, in which the discourse is oriented to a non-present reader, listener or viewer. Though the discourse is oriented towards these recipients, they very often cannot make instantaneous responses to the producer(s) of the discourse, though increasingly this is changing with the advent of new media technology, as we shall explore. Crucially, the written or spoken discourse itself is oriented *to* the readership or listening/viewing audience, respectively. In other words, media discourse is a public, manufactured, on-record, form of interaction. It is not ad hoc or spontaneous (in the same way as casual speaking or writing is); it is neither private nor off the record. Obvious as these basic characteristics may sound, they are crucial to the investigation, description and understanding of media discourse.

Because media discourse is manufactured, we need to consider how this has been done – both in a literal sense of what goes into its making and at an ideological level. One important strand of research into media discourse is preoccupied with taking a critical stance, namely critical discourse analysis (CDA). It is important that we continually appraise the messages that we consume from our manufactured mass media. The fact that media discourse is public means that it also falls under the scrutiny of many conversation analysts who are interested in it as a form of institutional talk, which can be compared with other forms of talk, both mundane and institutional. The fact that media discourse is on record makes it attractive for discourse analysts and increasingly so because of the online availability of newspapers, radio stations, television programmes and so on. Advances in technology have greatly offset the ephemerality factor that used to relate to media discourse, especially radio and television (where it used to be the case that, if you wanted to record something, it had to be done in real time).

It is a time of great change in media discourse, and this chapter aims to capture this moment, especially in the final section, where traditional notions of media discourse are challenged, in this time of opening up of the medium through Web 2 technologies.

How have print media been studied?

Linguistic analysis of the newspaper media is very often sceptical, and linguists sometimes see themselves as policing the subtle manipulation of language to distort reality. White (1997), for example, claimed that, by 'severely' circumscribing subjective interpersonal features in hard news reports, journalists can, through 'objective' language, purport to be neutral, essentially where formal language provides the veneer of neutrality. White suggests that the use of such an

441

impersonal register is but 'a rhetorical stratagem to aid the obfuscation of a reporter's subjectivity' (p. 130). However, quantitative measuring of media bias has largely been left to other disciplines, such as content analysis.

Of note, Biber *et al.* (1999) identify the language of newspapers as one of the four major registers in the English language, along with spoken conversation, academic writing and fiction. Much attention is given to 'genre analysis' (see Swales, 1990) in the linguistic study of newspapers. That is where the language used in print media is described in terms of what makes it different from other 'genres' of language, and in so describing it linguists aim to arrive at a better understanding of individual genre characteristics. For example, Toolan (1988) examines the language of press advertising. Other studies have examined sports reporting in newspapers (Wallace, 1977; Ghadessy, 1988; Bhatia, 1993). Register variation is covered in depth by Biber (1988); (1995) and Biber and Finegan (1994). In-depth treatments of the language of newspapers are relatively few. The most comprehensive, from a linguistic perspective, come from Reah (2002, a reprint of 1998 edition) and Bednarek (2006a, b). Reah (2002) comprehensively characterizes what newspapers are, as well as providing a detailed treatment of newspaper headlines and their 'manufacture' through what is left in and what is left out and how words are ordered. Reah also takes a detailed look at newspaper audiences and their role and relationship with and for newspapers. Linguistically, Reah looks bottom-up at the impact of both lexical choice and syntax and discourse on the building and manipulation of meaning, using case studies from the press. Bednarek (2006a, b) present a corpus-based study of evaluation in newspapers based on a corpus of 100 newspaper articles comprising a 70,000 word corpus, from both tabloid and broadsheet media. Bednarek's work is quantitative and she provides detailed explanations and justifications of her framework of evaluation and bias in newspapers. Given the superfluity of newspapers and the daily role they have in meaning-making, it is surprising how few linguistic studies there are, proportionally, of how they use language. The area of critical discourse analysis offers more potential as a framework for the analysis of newspapers and there has been a number of substantial works in this area. When coupled with corpus linguistics, it offers a very powerful tool for the analysis of how newspaper texts frame topics over time. We shall explore this further below. Overall, we can say that the discourse of newspapers has not been studied in any concerted way. We have learnt a lot from different perspectives, but so much more could be done in this respect, and perhaps with the easier availability of texts in electronic form more concerted progress will be made.

How have spoken media been studied?

Conversation analysis (CA) has been the prevailing methodology in the study of spoken media discourse, that is, radio and television. CA is a research tradition that has grown out of ethno-methodology, an area within sociology rather than linguistics. The influential work of Sacks, Schegloff and Jefferson has contributed to and strongly influenced research into spoken media discourse (for example Schegloff, 1968; Sacks *et al.*, 1974; Schegloff *et al.*, 1977; Sacks, 1992). CA takes a 'bottom-up' approach to the study of the social organization of conversation, or 'talk-in-interaction', by means of a detailed inspection of recordings and transcriptions (Have, 1986). That is, it focuses in on how conversations are structured and organized locally turn by turn, and from this it makes inductive comments about social organization. As Scannell (1998) notes, the object of study for CA is social interaction rather than language. As McCarthy (1998) points out, this field offers the possibility of fine-grained descriptions of how participants orient themselves towards mutual goals and negotiate their way forward in highly specific situations. This makes it suitable for the study of many social situations, including media interactions. In the area of media discourse quite a substantial amount of CA research has amassed around news interviews, talk shows and radio phone-ins. By comparing turn sequential order in media interactions with those in mundane talk, much can be revealed. Moving above the level of individual turns or adjacency pairs, conversation analysts are also interested in identifying the 'canonical' structure of interactions, that is, the sequential norms of interaction in particular settings. Telephone call openings have received particular attention (Schegloff, 1968; Godard, 1977; Schegloff, 1986; Whalen and Zimmerman, 1987; Hopper, 1989, 1992; Cameron and Hills, 1990; Hopper *et al.*, 1991; Hutchby, 1991, 1996a, 1996b, 1999; Halmari, 1993; Drew and Chilton, 2000 – among others). This has proven a very powerful comparative tool in the analysis of institutional interactions, including media discourse, because 'baseline' sequences of interaction from mundane conversation can be compared with interactions in institutional or other settings.

By way of example, Schegloff (1986) characterized the canonical structure for a phone call opening between 'unmarked forms of relationships' (that is, among people who are not particularly intimate, but who are not strangers) as having the following structural organization (Figure 31.1):

Summons-answer:	0. Phone rings	
	1. Answerer:	**Hello**
Identification-recognition:	2. Caller:	**Hello Jim?**
	3. Answerer:	**Yeah**
	4. Caller:	**'s Bonnie**
Greetings:	5. Answerer:	**Hi**
	6. Caller:	**Hi**
'How are you?' sequences:	7. Caller:	**How are yuh**
	8. Answerer:	**Fine, how're you**
	9. Caller:	**Oh, okay I guess**
	10. Answerer:	**Oh okay**
First Topic:	11. Caller:	**What are you doing New Year's Eve?**

Figure 31.1 Canonical call opening between 'unmarked forms of relationships'
Source: Schegloff 1986

Hutchby (1991) provides these typical examples of radio phone-in openings:

1)

1. Presenter: John is calling from Ilford good morning
2. Caller: .h good morning Brian (pause: 0.4) .hh what I'm phoning up is about the cricket.

(Hutchby, 1991: 120–121)

2)

1. Presenter: Mill Hill is where Gloria calls from good morning
2. Caller: Good morning Brian hh erm re the Sunday opening I'm just phoning from the point of view hh as an assistant who actually does do this…

(Hutchby, 1991: 120–121)

By comparing the canonical turn structure of telephone opening (that is, what typically happens in a normal call between callers who are neither very intimate nor strangers) with a call opening from a radio phone-in, we can immediately see how the stages or turn sequential order differs. We can see that the identification and recognition is carried out by the institutional power role holder, the

Anne O'Keeffe

presenter. We can see that the presenter's first turn not only performs the function of summons and identification, it also includes the greeting. There is therefore a contracting, or attenuation, of turns as a function of the institutional interaction. However, this attenuation could also be referenced against work by Drew and Chilton (2000) who look at call openings between intimates, drawing on a corpus of calls made between a mother and daughter over a three two-month period, where they found the attenuation of turns to be a function of the close relationship and regularity of the calls over time.

Most of the calls analysed by Drew and Chilton were for the purpose of 'keeping in touch', in other words there is normally no express purpose for calling other than to maintain contact. Mother and daughter call each other once a week, around the same time every week (Figure 31.2).

Summons	0.	Phone rings
Answer + Identification-recognition +	1. Answerer:	**Hello**
Greetings ('How are you?' also possible)	2. Caller:	**Hello**
	3. Answerer:	**Oh hello**
First Topic:	4. Answerer:	**I've been waiting for you**

Figure 31.2 Call openings between intimates after Drew and Chilton (2000)

Again, here we see attenuation of call stages. As Drew and Chilton point out, the relationship of the callers allows for the attenuation of the canonical stages because the callers are intimates, and because they are expecting the call. The voice sample provided by *hello* achieves all Schegloff's stages of answering, identification/recognition and greeting in this interaction. O'Keeffe (2006) argues that radio-in presenters, in their public personae, build a pseudo-intimate relationship with their audience and, like in the mother–daughter calls, there is both an intimacy and a regularity about the interaction. The show is on at the same time every day or week, callers 'know' the presenter and they call him or her. This pseudo-intimacy and pseudo-familiarity is borne out in the way that presenters talk about themselves as ordinary friends with ordinary lives, as exemplified in this example from an Irish radio chat show:

3)

Presenter: It's Wednesday morning Anna good morning to you.
Caller: Good morning Gerry how are you?
Presenter: Oh well [yawning] I'm good a little bit of sunshine this morning.
Caller: Oh well that's good.
Presenter: It's had a positive effect on me anyway dunno about every.
Caller: Well I think it has on everybody hasn't it?
Presenter: It took me feckin well half an hour to put out the bins this morning that was the only thing that depressed me and then do you know do you ever have one of these ones where you know everything is going well Ryan then decides that he is going to put five or six of plastic sacks up on top of one bin that I'm wheeling right?
Caller: Yeah.
Presenter: And then puuff.
Caller: And they all fall.
Presenter: No one of them explodes all over me
Caller: Stop. [laughter] That's horrible.

Presenter:	[laughter] and I know you know that one or two of me neighbours are looking out at going 'look at the big ejitt I knew that was going to happen to him'.
Caller:	Yeah but they'd be looking at you y'see they wouldn't look at me doing that.
Presenter:	Ah well who knows.
Caller:	Well I hope they wouldn't anyway.
Presenter:	Okay what do you want to talk to us about? (The Gerry Ryan Show RTÉ 2fm radio)

Markers of pseudo-intimacy in extract 3 are:

- First name reciprocation: *Anna – Gerry*
- Informal non-verbal behaviour: presenter yawning
- Chit-chat and badinage: *how are you/ I'm good a little bit of sunshine this morning/Oh well that's good … I'm good a little bit of sunshine this morning*, etc; reciprocation and repetition of discourse markers *oh well* by both presenter and caller; collaborative laughter.
- Use of taboo language not normally associated with talk radio discourse: *feckin* and other non-standard language: the Irish English for *ejitt* meaning idiot.
- Talk about mundane domestic chores from the private life of the presenter (moving from public to private persona): talking about putting out the rubbish bins and the story of what went wrong.

Using corpus linguistics in tandem with other methodologies

The study of turn structure and organization is the main means of looking at spoken media discourse within the framework of CA. Its main limitation is that it only allows for the close analysis of small amounts of interaction, and so it is more difficult to make generalizations about findings. A growing number of studies are using small corpora, however. O'Keeffe (2006) shows how a corpus-based approach can work well with CA as a means of analysing larger amounts of data. Let us take for example openings and closings. If we look at a small corpus of radio phone-ins – 55,000 words, all from the same show, *Liveline*, an afternoon show broadcast on Irish radio (RTÉ 1) – and we look at all of the closings across the corpus, we can make more general points than by looking closely at one or two alone. In all, there are 21 closings in the data and in 100 per cent of these we find discourse markers and *thanks*. The discourse markers operate as linguistic brackets to accompany the discourse markers symbiotically in many of the openings. These again are liminal items marking the boundary where the presenter shifts footing from the transient caller back to the relatively stable audience, to bring about the closing of the call in a collaborative manner. The opening patterns are the opposite. We find that the audience is addressed first, then the footing is changed to the caller by use of discourse markers and vocatives. For example:

4) Opening

1. Presenter:	And next we head west Colm good afternoon to you.
2. Caller:	Am good afternoon Marian.
3. Presenter:	Colm McCarthy now you're involved can you tell me how you got involved in Inis Mór and what you're doing there?
4. Caller:	Well we're opening up a new heritage centre on on Inis Mór the largest of the Aran Islands am based on the story of the Aran sweater…

In turn 1, the presenter addresses the audience: *And next we head west*, giving them a deictic orientation as to the location of the next caller. Also in turn 1, the presenter changes footing to address the caller. The vocative becomes the footing pivot *Colm good afternoon to you*. The repetition of the vocative in line 3, followed by the discourse marker *now*, moves into 'business of the call' phase. In the closing, we see a reversal of the footing pattern whereby the presenter typically uses discourse markers to signal closing (*well* in the extract 5) and finally uses a discourse marker plus the vocative to introduce the thanking phase. Notice the use of the pronoun *us* in turn 1 (extract 5) to signal the change of footing back to the audience. The presenter does not say 'thank you very much indeed for talking to *me*':

5) Closing

1. Presenter: **Well well** I suppose one way or the other I I I've a suspicion that people want certain things to go away but some things just won't <laughs> am some things have to be faced anyway there you go. **Ah listen** Bishop Donal Murray thank you very much indeed for talking to **us**.
2. Caller: Not at all. Thank you very much.
3. Presenter: ⌊**Okay** all the best cheers bye bye.

In turn 1, the discourse marker *well* draws a line in the discourse and orients the caller and the audience to the forthcoming closing. The use of *ah listen* later in the same turn consolidates this process. On closer analysis, we find that in 67 per cent of all closings *us* is used, and *we* (presenter + audience) is used in 24 per cent of all closings. Here are some more examples:

6)

1. Presenter: …Obviously that's what on your mind **anyway** Breda **we**'ll see what advice **we** can get I imagine people are going to say that you have an excessive prejudice against tattoos but **we**'ll see **we**'ll see **okay**?
2. Caller: …Thank you very much Marian.
3. Presenter: **OK** all the best Breda thanks a lot cheers thank you bye bye.
4. Caller: OK many thanks bye bye now.

7)

Presenter: **Right. Okay okay well** I can tell you this much you could talk until the cows came home and you would not convince our first caller that it was a good idea however am there you go. Nora Donnelly thank you very much indeed for talking to **us** and thank you Una. Thank you. All the best. Bye bye.

8)

Presenter: **Okay** Catherine it's a cautionary tale and of course it <unintelligible utterance> applies to the pill obviously and applies to other medication I mean to actually know what the side effects could be and to take steps as soon as you do and thank you very very much indeed for talking to **us**.

In the closings, we also notice another common feature, which collaboratively closes the call and ensures common ground for all the participants, namely the use of a coda, formulation or evaluation of the state of affairs. We find that these occur in 67 per cent of all closings. For example in the above extracts we find:

1) we'll see what advice we can get I imagine people are going to say that you have an excessive prejudice against tattoos but we'll see we'll see

2) I can tell you this much you could talk until the cows came home and you would not convince our first caller that it was a good idea however am there you go

3) it's a cautionary tale and of course it <unintelligible utterance> applies to the pill obviously and applies to other medication I mean to actually know what the side effects could be and to take steps as soon as you do.

Table 31.1 provides a summary of the quantitative analysis of presenter–audience address features in closings.

By using a corpus we can also examine the consistency and pragmatic specialization of certain patterns. Such evidence of lexico-grammatical systematicity at routines of openings, transitions and closings gives us a strong sense of a programme and its familiar and repeated structure. The routineness, created, repeated and sustained by the presenter, brings stability and familiarity to this mediated form of communication and thus simulates the kind of pseudo-intimacy that we find in the mother–daughter calls (cf. Drew and Chilton, 2000). One can illustrate this by using a concordance search for the high-frequency pattern of: 'Right. Okay.' We find that it clusters within the routine of call closings in the radio phone-in corpus and it is uttered by the presenter, very often being followed by a vocative (see Figure 31.3) to signal that the call is drawing to a close.

Table 31.1 A breakdown of the discourse features of presenter–audience features in closings

Feature	Occurrence	Percentage
discourse marker	21	100%
thank	21	100%
us	14	67%
coda/formulation/evaluation	13	62%
bye	16	62%
we	5	24%

1	<$1> **Right. Okay**. Listen thank you very much
2	<$1> **Right. Okay James** thank you very much
3	<$1> **Right Okay Joe**. Okay thanks a million
4	<$1> **Right okay**. <$2>
5	<$1> <$E "Laughing"> **Right okay**. Okay all sorts of spin off
6	<$1> **Right. Okay**. Okay well that's a good a
7	<$1> **Right okay**. <$2> <$1> Okay C
8	<$1> **Right okay** <$E "chuckles"> <$2>
9	<$1> **Right okay**. <$2>
10	<$1> **Right okay** good to hear it nice to tal
11	<$1> **Right. Okay Áine Ní Chiarán** thank you
12	<$1> Denis? <$2> <$1> **Right. Okay** thank you very much indeed
13	<$1> **Right okay** so you're opperating stricl
14	<$1> **Right okay** so let people be beware of
15	<$1> **Right okay Michael McDowell** thank you
16	<$1> **Right okay** so basically you want to kn
17	and I'd recommend it to anyone. <$1> **Right. Okay** okay well I can tell you t
18	<$1> **Right okay Teresa** thank you very much
19	<$1> **Right okay** eh just before I let you go
20	<$1> Um **right right okay David**. What are you
21	<$1> Um right **right okay David**. What are you doing
22	<$1> <$E laughs> **Right okay** okay </$E > right **Emmett** tha
23	<$1> <$O2> Okay **right okay Noel**. All the best </$O2> b
24	<$1> **Right okay** Thank you very much indeed

Figure 31.3 Presenter's systematic use of *right + okay* [+ vocative] in call closings

In the brief example above we mentioned the use of a vocative. This brings us into the area of pragmatics. The field of pragmatics also provides a worthwhile complement to corpus linguistics. O'Keeffe (2006) illustrates in detail how it can play a key role as an analytical framework within the study of spoken media discourse. Issues of power and politeness are fundamental to this institutional context where the power role holder, the presenter on radio or television, is keen to downplay power through hedging and other politeness devices. O'Keeffe (2006) also highlights the importance of looking at deixis ('pointing', i.e. words and phrases that we use to point to people, things, time and place). In political interviews, it is always worthwhile exploring the use of pronouns, as exemplified in this extract from an interview, conducted in February 2003 as part of a special BBC *Newsnight* programme in the lead up to the invasion of Iraq. The interview was between the British prime minister at the time, Tony Blair, and BBC presenter Jeremy Paxman. It was held in front of a live public audience in Gateshead. In the later stages of the programme, the audience asked the prime minister questions. The transcript and video clip are available online. Notice how the pronoun *we* is used and re-appropriated. What the audience use of *we* refers to is 'the people of Britain who are against an invasion of Iraq', while the prime minister's use, to the contrary, refers to 'we the people of Britain who must invade Iraq':

9)

Male:	What are **we** going to accomplish with war?
Tony Blair:	Disarmament of Iraq, of the weapons of mass destruction.
Male:	And then **we** move round the world?
Tony Blair:	No, **we** don't move round the world creating war on everyone, but what **we** do do is **we** do confront those countries that have this material and if **we** can do it through partnership and by agreement with them, **we** have to reduce the threat that they pose. Because otherwise this stuff will carry on proliferating and it will be traded round the world and that causes a threat to us….

(South Africa. 6 February 2003. Full transcript and actual interview available at: http://news.bbc.co.uk/1/hi/programmes/newsnight/2732979.stm)

Another bedfellow of corpus linguistics in the study of media discourse is critical discourse analysis. One of its main exponents in relation to media discourse is Fairclough (1989, 1995a, b, 2000). CDA, according to van Dijk (2001: 352), is a type of discourse analytical research that primarily studies the way social power abuse, dominance and inequality are enacted, reproduced and resisted by text and talk in the social and political context. Van Dijk (2009) observes that critical studies of discourse are problem-led rather than discipline or theory oriented. Obvious examples of problems that relate to abuses of power and injustice are in relation to gender, race and class. Critical scholars, according to van Dijk, are interested in the way 'discourse (re)produces social domination, that is the power abuse of one group over others, and how dominated groups may discursively resist that abuse' (van Dijk, 2009: 63). However, the impact of CDA in the study of the discourse of media may have been lessened by the largely qualitative nature of CDA, whereby single texts were often the basis for analysis and hence limited the scope for generalization of findings. CDA studies looked at how single texts framed issues. The wider availability of newspaper texts in electronic form has allowed for the merging of the more quantitative approach from corpus linguistics with CDA to provide a very sharp analytical tool. As O'Halloran (2010: 563) comments:

> Before corpus linguistics became mainstream, CDA examined such framings in single texts at a particular point in time, or over a very short period. One of the advantages of the abundance of media texts in electronic form … is the ease with which corpora can be assembled for

revealing the following: how media texts might be *repeatedly* framing issues or events which are reported over a significant period of time.

CL has proved a boon for CDA. As O'Halloran (2010) notes that, increasingly, critical discourse analysts employ corpora in their investigations of media discourse and points out that, by using corpus investigation, critical discourse analysts can now gain insight into the kinds of cultural and ideological meanings being circulated regularly.

Looking to the future: new frameworks

Let us return to the definition of media discourse. At the outset, we said that it refers to interactions that take place through some broadcast platform, whether spoken or written, in which the discourse is oriented to a non-present reader, listener or viewer. We also said that, though the discourse is oriented towards these recipients, they very often cannot make instantaneous responses to the producer(s) of the discourse. However, at the time of writing, we are in the midst of a major change in terms of how and who mediates the discourse. Our traditional paradigms are rapidly becoming outmoded by virtue of their limited view of the scope of audience participation. The change is driven by new media, their opening up of how to broadcast your thoughts far and wide and how audiences can respond to what they see, hear or read, instantly. This throws up in the air our traditional notions of the institutional participation framework of media discourse, both spoken or written. Let us consider in detail this changing notion of participation frameworks of media discourse.

The phrase 'participation framework' comes from Goffman (1981). Essentially, it refers to the communicative environment within which media discourse happens, and core to that context is not only the producer(s) of the discourse but also the consumers – the audience. In the case of written discourse, the participation framework comprises an author or authors (the media persona) who broadcasts through the written medium to a reader or readers. What is produced may be read at any time after it is published (Figure 31.4).

In the case of spoken media discourse, the participation framework is made up of a studio-based media person, often interacting with a guest or another media person, in the studio, on location or on a phone line, and their interaction is broadcast either though an audio channel alone or through an audio-visual channel. It is consumable as soon as it is broadcast, or it may be recorded or downloaded and listened to at a later stage (Figure 31.5).

Up until the advent of Web 2 technologies (internet, social networking, blogs, wikis, video-sharing and more) and other advances (mobile phone technologies, advances in hardware), these

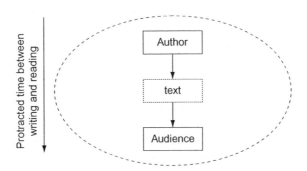

Figure 31.4   Basic participation framework for written discourse

Anne O'Keeffe

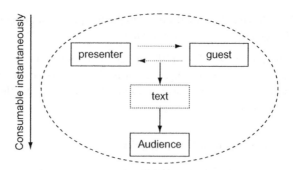

Figure 31.5   Basic participation framework for spoken discourse

two basic participation formats would have covered most possible forms of media discourse. Now, however, media discourse is at a new stage and the participation frameworks have altered in a number of ways. There are greater levels of intertextuality and a blurring of the lines between spoken and written media. Newspapers have web and video links as well as sound clips and opinion polls. Television programmes have text on screen, websites to follow up on, chatrooms and so on. Radio programmes can talk about pictures and visual items and post them on their website for listeners to see; they can have a webcam in their studio so that audiences can 'see' them on the radio. The advent of social networking sites means that television and radio programmes can be 're-broadcast' within micro-participation frameworks. The social networking sites themselves have the potential to connect with larger audiences than some television, radio or newspaper articles. Facilities such as twitter allow individuals to generate broadcast thoughts to which others can respond to. In summary, we can say that:

1)   the reader is no longer reading an article in protracted isolation; s/he can comment on it via a website, email it to a friend, post it on a social network for others to discuss it. Journalists and commentators often respond to the comments posted in reaction to their articles, thus creating an extension of the process–product–process–(product–process) ...;
2)   the audience is no longer a passive recipient or eavesdropper in the case of radio and television; its members can very often text the programme and have that text read out, they can join a chat with each other, they can post a link to the programme on a social network or blog and have others listen/view it and comment. They can take part in audience opinion polls via text message or weblink;
3)   the ephemerality of the spoken and written media is lessened by the ripple effect that email, websites and social networks can have; when a consumer reads/listens to/views something that s/he wants to react to, s/he can spread it around over time to others, who will then consume it, possibly comment on it at a later date and pass it on further, and so on.

This calls for a new understanding of media participation frameworks. The following figures are proposed as a starting point for new ways of looking at the participation frameworks of new written and spoken media (Figures 31.6 and 31.7).

The opening up of the feedback channel from the audience means that we find new patterns of interaction; for example, we regularly hear presenters say things like 'A text in from Peter in Warwick says ...' or 'we have a number of texts suggesting ...'. Our news broadcasts can have ticker tapes running with text responses to what viewers are watching in real time. Whereas before we might get a colour piece giving us a random recording of the *vox populi* in some streetscape on

450

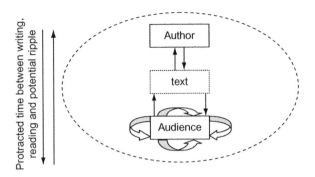

Figure 31.6 New participation framework for written discourse

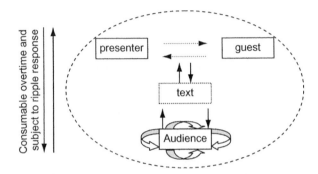

Figure 31.7 New participation framework for radio and television discourse

some issue of the day (e.g. a *vox pop* piece within a radio or television programme on what people stopped in the street think of X), this has now become much more spontaneous and instantaneous. Social networking sites, twitter, discussion boards and blogs are just some of the formats that allow anyone to broadcast from the profound (*what's the meaning of life?*) to the practical (*anyone know how to fix an ipod?*) and even to the minute (*I'm off to bed now*).

The discourse of social networking sites is an exciting area, waiting to be substantially researched and described. Here are some typical interactions from social networking sites:

10)

Post 1 A: Back in Melbourne, Canberra wouldn't just set my world on fire …

Post 2 B: Hey [nickname] were you trying to skype me per change? I am an hour ahead here. I am off today, it's a bank holiday definately [*sic*] chat soon x

Post 3 C: that's [*sic*] what you get for going there when everything is happening in Melbourne – see you next week

11) (this post was spread over a 28-hour period)

Post 1 A: [name] is waiting for furniture …

Post 2 B: it's still here, sorry!

Post 3 A: Hmm. Some of it is here, just not mine … The wireless is work, though!

Post 4 C: where (and what) did you order?!?!

Post 5 A: Ha! I didn't really order anything, [name of C]. My department is moving to a different building on campus and I'm just waiting for my desk, bookcases, crates and filing cabinets to arrive. I like the new space – it's just a little empty right now …

Post 6 D: a bit too much space then;) have you tried out the acoustics before all the stuff comes in?

Post 7 A: Ha, yes, the acoustics are good!
All my furniture and crates are here now. Anyone wanna help me unpack??:)

Post 8 E: Any time, if you help me get rid of the fridges in my living-room.

Post 9 A: Oh dear … sounds painful but then having a fridge in the living-room may actually be quite convenient. Nobody has to go far from the soda to get refreshments and snacks … I'm done with the crates and will start decorating now!

Post 10 E: I can see the possible bright side – but now the fridges (two) are gone! So little space feels like so much!

These interactions push us into new ground as discourse analysts. On initial perusal, the following are noteworthy in terms of their description:

- the language use is closer to spoken than written discourse,
- the language is informal and marked by emoticons and exclamations to create a sense of non-verbal communication and co-presence,
- however, these interactions, though they appear to simulate face-to-face interaction, do not always happen in real-time. The ten posts in extract 11 happened over 28 hours,
- posts roughly equate to turns,
- sequences of posts roughly equate to an exchange,
- posts are not ephemeral; they remain to be read and responded to at an indefinite time after they have been written. They are therefore much more 'on record' than a spoken interaction,
- conventions of written grammar can be flouted with relative impunity (especially spelling, punctuation and grammar).

In summary, it is an exciting time in the study of media discourse because all of the parameters are changing; all of the modes of communication are opening up to the *vox populi*. It is the challenge of discourse analysts to come up with new paradigms and appropriate methodologies to encapsulate and describe all of these new frontiers of communication.

Related topics

Conversation analysis
Critical discourse analysis
Creativity in discourse
Multimedia analysis
Discourse and knowledge

Further reading

Durant, A. and Lambrou, M. (2009) *Language and Media: A Resource Book for Students*. London: Routledge.

This book gives a comprehensive introduction to the study of media genres. It also collates key readings and is accompanied by a supporting website. Of particular use to research students is the section on exploring examples of language data.

O'Halloran, K. (2010) 'How to use corpus linguistics in the study of media discourse', in A. O'Keeffe and M. J. McCarthy (eds.) *The Routledge Handbook of Corpus Linguistics*. London: Routledge, pp. 563–577.

This article provides a very good insight into the application of corpus linguistics to critical discourse analysis, using a corpus of articles from the UK newspaper *The Sun* as a case study.

Bednarek, M. (2006) *Evaluation in Media Discourse: Analysis of a Newspaper Corpus*. London: Continuum.

This is a very thorough corpus-based study of evaluation in newspapers on the basis of a corpus of 100 newspaper articles comprising a 70,000 word corpus, from both tabloid and broadsheet media. Methodologically, it is a good example of the use of corpus linguistics in the study of newspaper texts.

O'Keeffe, A. (2006) *Investigating Media Discourse*. London: Routledge.

This volume provides an exploration of spoken media discourse using a combination of approaches including conversation analysis, discourse analysis and pragmatics in the exploration of a corpus of over 200,000 words of spoken media interactions.

Reah, D. (2002) *The Language of Newspapers*. Second Edition. London: Routledge.

A detailed treatment of newspaper discourse and its wider context, including a detailed look at audiences and their role and relationship with newspapers. It looks at the impact of language and discourse on the building and manipulation of meaning, using case studies from the newspapers.

References

Bednarek, M. (2006a) *Evaluation in Media Discourse: Analysis of a Newspaper Corpus*. London: Continuum.

Bednarek, M. (2006b) 'Evaluating Europe – parameters of evaluation in the British press', in C. Leung and J. Jenkins (eds.) *Reconfiguring Europe – the Contribution of Applied Linguistics*. London: BAAL/Equinox (British Studies in Applied Linguistics), pp. 137–156.

Bhatia, V. K. (1993) *Analysing Genre: Language Use in Professional Settings*. London: Longman.

Biber, D. (1988) *Variation Across Speech and Writing*. Cambridge: Cambridge University Press.

Biber, D. (1995) *Dimensions of Register Variation: A Cross-Linguistic Comparison*. Cambridge: Cambridge University Press.

Biber, D. and Finegan, E. (1994) *Sociolinguistic Perspectives on Register*. Oxford: Oxford University Press.

Biber, D., Johansson, S., Leech, G., Conrad, S., and Finegan, E. (1999) *Longman Grammar of Spoken and Written English*. Essex: Longman.

Cameron, D. and Hills, D. (1990) ' "Listening in": negotiating relationships between listeners and presenters on radio phone-in programmes', in G. McGregor and R. White (eds.) *Reception and Response: Hearer Creativity and the Analysis of Spoken and Written Texts*. London: Routledge & Kegan Paul, pp. 53–68.

Drew, P. and Chilton, K. (2000) 'Calling just to keep in touch: regular and habitual telephone calls as an environment for small talk', in J. Coupland (ed.) *Small Talk*. London: Longman, pp. 137–162.

Fairclough, N. (1995a) *Media Discourse*. London: Arnold.

Fairclough, N. (1995b) *Critical Discourse Analysis*. London: Longman.

Fairclough, N. (1988) 'Discourse representation in media discourse', *Sociolinguistics*, 17: 125–139.

Fairclough, N. (1989) *Language and Power*. London: Longman.

Fairclough, N. (2000) *New Labour, New Language*. London: Routledge.

Ghadessy, M. (1988) 'The language of written sports commentary: soccer – a description', in Ghadessy, M. (ed.) *Registers of Written English: Situational Factors and Linguistic Features*. London and New York: Pinter Publishers Ltd, pp. 17–51.

Godard, D. (1977) 'Same setting, different norms: phone call beginnings in France and the United States', *Language in Society*, 6: 209–219.

Goffman, E. (1981) *Forms of Talk*. Oxford: Basil Blackwell.

Halmari, H. (1993) 'Intercultural business telephone conversations: a case of Finns vs. Anglo-Americans', *Applied Linguistics*, 14 (4): 408–430.

Hopper, R. (1989) 'Sequential ambiguity in telephone openings: "what are you doin" ', *Communication Monographs*, 56 (3): 240–252.

Hopper, R. (1992) *Telephone Conversation*. Bloomington, IN: Indiana University.

Hopper, R., Doany, N., Johnson, M., and Drummond, K. (1991) 'Universals and Particulars in Telephone Openings', *Research on Language and Social Interaction*, 2 (4): 369–387.

Hutchby, I. (1991) 'The organisation of talk on talk radio', in Scannell, P. (ed.) *Broadcast Talk*. London: Sage, pp. 119–137.

Hutchby, I. (1996a) *Confrontation Talk – Arguments, Asymmetries, and Power On Talk Radio*. Mahwah, NJ: Lawrence Erlbaum Associates.

Hutchby, I. (1996b) 'Power in discourse: the case of arguments on a British talk radio show'. *Discourse and Society* 7(4): 481–497.

Hutchby, I. (1999) 'Frame attunement and footing in the organisation of talk radio openings', *Journal of Sociolinguistics*, 3: 41–64.

McCarthy, M. J. (1998) *Spoken Language and Applied Linguistics*. Cambridge: Cambridge University Press.

O'Halloran, K. (2010) 'How to use corpus linguistics in the study of media discourse', in A. O'Keeffe and M. J. McCarthy (eds.) *The Routledge Handbook of Corpus Linguistics*. London: Routledge, pp. 563–577.

O'Keeffe, A. (2006) *Investigating Media Discourse*. London: Routledge.

Reah, D. (2002) *The Language of Newspapers*. Second Edition. London: Routledge.

Sacks, H. (1992) *Lectures on Conversation*. Oxford: Blackwell.

Sacks, H., Schegloff, E. A., and Jefferson, G. (1974) 'A simplest systematics for the organisation of turn-taking for conversation', *Language*, 50 (4): 696–735.

Scannell, P. (1998) 'Media – language – world', in A. Bell and Garrett, P. (eds.) *Approaches to Media Discourse*. Oxford: Blackwell, pp. 251–267.

Schegloff, E. A. (1968) 'Sequencing in conversational openings', *American Anthropologist*, 70: 1075–1095.

Schegloff, E. A. (1986) 'The routine as achievement', *Human Studies*, 9: 111–152.

Schegloff, E. A., Jefferson, G., and Sacks, H. (1977) 'The preference for self-correction in the organization of repair in conversation', *Language*, 53: 361–382.

Swales, M. (1990) *Genre Analysis*. Cambridge: Cambridge University Press.

ten Have, P. (1986) *Issues in Qualitative Data Interpretation*, Paper read at the International Sociological Association, XIth World Congress of Sociology, New Delhi, August 1986. Available online at: http://www.paultenhave.nl/mica.htm (accessed 23 October 2010).

Toolan, M. (1988) 'The Language of Press Advertising', in Ghadessy, M. (ed.) *Registers of Written English*. London: Pinter Publishers, pp. 52–64.

van Dijk, T. A. (2001) 'Critical Discourse Analysis', in D. Schiffrin, D. Tannen, and H. Hamilton (eds.) *The Handbook of Discourse Analysis*. Oxford: Blackwell.

Wallace, W. D. (1977) 'How registers register: a study in the language of news and sports', *Studies in the Linguistic Sciences*, 7 (1): 46–78.

Whalen, M. R. and Zimmerman, D. H. (1987) 'Sequential and institutional context in calls for help', *Social Psychology Quarterly*, 50 (2): 172–185.

White, P. (1997) 'Death, Disruption and the Moral Order: the Narrative Impulse in Mass-Media "Hard news" Reporting', in F. Christie, and J. R. Martin (eds.) *Genre and Institutions*. London: Cassell, pp. 101–133.

32

Asian business discourse(s)

Hiromasa Tanaka and Francesca Bargiela-Chiappini

Situating the new discourses

This chapter engages with some of the issues and challenges raised by a new body of research on interactional practices in business contexts in East and Southeast Asia, which has been conveniently subsumed under the banner of Asian business discourse(s)—or ABDs. The discussion first situates the development of the 'new discourses' both historically and geographically, and then moves on to identify some salient debates that ABDs have brought to the attention of interpretive researchers and business practitioners. It will be argued that the multi-perspectival nature of business discourse (analysis) benefits from an intersubjective epistemology, according to which interpretation of the manifold relations informing business practice can eventually only emerge through deployment of several analytical tools and in dialogue with a number of co-interpreters, situated practices and ideological traditions. An illustration of the interpretive processes involved in the analysis of a Japanese business meeting is offered before concluding the chapter with reflections on future directions.

Space constraints are inevitably guiding and limiting our discussion of ABDs, therefore in this chapter we will not deal with conceptual and ideological issues which are examined elsewhere (Bargiela-Chiappini, 2011). Instead, the aim is to provide an accessible and informative introduction to a new development in the discourse studies tradition, which thus far has been dominated by Western scholarship. (The field of politeness research is probably a notable exception and one that has potentially a great deal to offer to ABDs.)

In choosing illustrative material inspired by Japanese business interaction we are aware that there are several other 'local realities' that space prevented us from representing here; we refer keen readers to the analyses of and references to business discourse in Malaysia, Korea, China, Vietnam (and Japan) included in the *Handbook of Business Discourse* (Bargiela-Chiappini, 2009).

Before embarking on the discussion of ABDs proper, a brief historical introduction is in order. In the early stages of business discourse research, in the seventies and eighties, linguists, especially but not exclusively in Europe and the US, focused on the study of English as the most widely used language of business. Although local languages have been analysed in various business contexts, English continues to be seen as the dominant or official business language even among Asian countries.

In the early days, lexis and genres of written business English were the main concern of linguistic research, which was based on the assumption that language encodes a decontextualized and static body of knowledge. Mizutani (1994), for example, argues that business people's language reflects organizational views and values; a perspective such as this prioritizes transactional over relational exchange. Linguistic studies were driven by pedagogic priorities and therefore were largely prescriptive in nature; many business communication textbooks have been published in this tradition. The notion of 'business communication' as a set of arbitrary prescriptions also raised researchers' interest in quantitative methods that tested and measured business language competencies (Nakasako, 1998). Such studies were fuelled by the conviction that English language competence is a crucial element of business success.

Following increased intercultural contact, management scholars have sought to address the complex issues affecting culturally diverse teams. A large body of attitudinal research was undertaken in the eighties and nineties using self-reporting questionnaires; this method was employed to capture the views and perceptions of business actors within specific work sites. One such study in Japan was carried out by Daiichi Kangyo Bank (1986). Using questionnaire data from 300 foreign business practitioners in Japan, it unveiled that many respondents used Japanese in the workplace as well as English. Although English is frequently used in international trade documents and intercultural business encounters, more and more non-Japanese use Japanese in business activities (Lee, 2002). Arguably a more significant finding was that taken-for-granted Japanese meeting procedures and decision-making systems, rather than language competence, were problematic for non-Japanese participants. A number of other studies followed that employed large-scale questionnaire-based surveys. However, since then such studies have been criticized for assuming accuracy in participants' self-understanding and self-perceptions and honesty in self-reporting (Du-Babcock, 2005).

More ambitious studies have tried to analyse specific components of organizational culture such as differences attributable to local management philosophies and business customs. So ideological and procedural differences in Asian business practices such as decision-making (Takahashi and Takayanagi, 1985), human resource management (Huang, 1998) and career development systems (Uhl-Bien *et al.*, 1990) have come under the spotlight. Even though largely based on survey data, cultural approaches to business practices are less likely to oversimplify or ignore the interplay of management and communication strategies, emotions, politics and power relations that manifest themselves in verbal interaction.

Globalization and technological development has led to diversification in business communication; in turn, multimedia communication has forced researchers to pay more attention to intermodal meaning-creation in business situations. The diversification of business roles and functions also requires that we regard business interaction as more than just transactional communication; 'doing business' is now viewed as a process of meaning-making infused with cultural and ideological influences. Single-method research approaches are no longer sufficient to grasp communication phenomena taking place at the intersection of language and managerial systems and informed by indigenous philosophies, cultural values and first language (L1) pragmatic transfer. Moreover, conventional research approaches have tended to overlook the complexity and sophistication of intercultural communication practices. More recently, alternative multimethod approaches, focusing on actual organizational practice, have become less rare in spite of the difficulties related to accessing authentic interactional data for use in research projects and publications.

(Asian) business discourse (analysis)

Researchers applying a combination of discourse methods to the analysis of business interaction have probably been more successful than their predecessors at ferreting out some of the intricate issues underlying business interaction, especially when communication takes place across cultures. Thanks to qualitative, interpretive approaches, business discourse researchers have been able to appreciate, describe and analyse communication practices as they happen, be they intercultural or intracultural meetings (Emmet, 2003; Fujio, 2004), intraorganizational written communication

(Kong, 2001; Chakorn, 2006), corporate communication (Jung, 2005) or interaction at training and development sites (Nair-Venugopal, 2006).

Elsewhere (Bargiela-Chiappini, 2009a; Tanaka, 2009) we have engaged with the concept of 'business discourse' (BD) and the advantages and limitations of a multi-disciplinary approach to the analysis of human interaction in business and organizational settings. Rather than claiming that BD is a well-defined field of study with a distinctive methodological profile, we have opted for a definition that emphasizes the dynamic, unbounded and eclectic nature of BD as a 'a metaphor for dialogue' (Bargiela-Chiappini, 2009a: 2). This characterization is especially important in light of the wide-ranging (Western) disciplinary interests that BD is accommodating while at the same time fostering the smaller but growing body of research that is now going under the acronym of ABDs. The use of shorthand to encompass a myriad of distinct countries, communities and languages has not come to pass without a good measure of self-critical reflection (Bargiela-Chiappini, 2006, 2011).

The plural form of the ABDs acronym is intended to alert us to the dangers of essentialist, totalizing ethnocentric labels. In its current form, ABDs acknowledge the distinctiveness of indigenous voices, which in the past tended to be incorporated in scholarly traditions ideologically rooted in the West (e.g. business communication, discourse studies). At the same time, ABDs challenge us to recognize and move on from persistent and often pernicious conceptual dichotomies such as East v. West (Hendry and Wong, 2006), which have hampered collaborative research for too long. In this sense, ABDs is a first step towards an enlarged, truly international business discourse community, which values the original contribution of its newer members and encourages the inclusion of world views other than those that have dominated research and scholarship up until recently.

The role of English in international business interaction also comes under scrutiny. If English is used as a lingua franca (ELF) in intercultural business encounters, the working assumption may be that Anglophone business and management norms apply, even in an Asian setting. This in turn may give rise to serious misunderstanding, which can degenerate into tension and conflict. ABDs recognize the practical value of ELF but are also aware of the politics surrounding the choice of a former colonial language that is still often taught according to the norms imposed by the centre (Britain, US; see Bargiela-Chiappini, 2006). On the other hand, observation of business practices shows that local Englishes, and at times also local languages, are in fact adequate for performing a whole range of tasks in the workplace (Nair-Venugopal, 2009).

Reflecting the mood in critical organization and management studies, postcolonial studies and anthropological theory, Asian business discourse(s) apply a poststructuralist notion of discourse in order to glimpse the dynamics of verbal interaction in Asian business sites. They combine insight from socio-economic, socio-political and critical theory with multi-method analyses of discursive practices. Researchers working under this banner draw from various methodologies and disciplinary traditions, including conversation analysis, ethnography, organizational studies, management studies, pragmatics, and politeness studies (see e.g. Bargiela-Chiappini and Gotti, 2005; JAPC, 2005, 2006). Discourse analytical approaches, of which there are several (Stubbe *et al.*, 2003; Glynos *et al.*, 2009), can be effective in highlighting the interplay of contextual, situational and interpersonal factors in power-laden, strategic communication. For example, Boden (1994) applied conversation analysis to the interpretation of interaction in organizational settings, and Cooren (2001) documented the realization of organizational practices through speech acts.

Within ABDs, discourse strategies that have been documented by both intercultural and intracultural research have been shown to be attributable to interpersonal, situational and contextual factors, but also to underlying management, educational and historical ideologies that, once brought to the surface, can provide a much richer, situated understanding of business practices.

457

In order to engage more fully with the multi-dimensionality of business discourse, ABDs researchers are increasingly moving towards social constructionist and interpretive approaches designed to face the epistemological issues raised by the field. In so doing, they inevitably tangle with issues of power, gender and 'culture' that underlie practice in actual job sites. In this sense, ABDs, like business discourse (BD), are inherently critical in their approach to the analysis of communication, even though analysis does not always translate into transformative action.

The process of 'seeing' in which discourse analysts are implicated is a political one, especially when it entails cognizance of phenomena that were previously ignored, dismissed, or silenced (Parker and Grimes, 2009). 'Seeing' as an epistemological stance also entails engagement with the manifestations of affect in human interaction, a long-neglected yet pervasive aspect of organizational life (Iedema and Scheeres, 2009; Samra-Fredericks, 2004). The analysis in Section 4 shows how affect permeates a business meeting, for example in the way speakers show discernment for listeners' sensitivities while tactically positioning themselves and others in response to the seemingly conflicting demands of hierarchy and harmony.

The contribution of Asian business discourse(s) to discourse analysis—and vice versa

For a deeper understanding of work practices that can be subsumed under ABD, the study of local business discourses points to the influence of indigenous philosophies and management traditions that in turn affect both intracultural and intercultural encounters. As an illustration of the advantages and challenges of a multi-perspectival discourse analytic approach to ABDs, Section 4 charts the interpretive process implicated in the analysis of a business meeting held in a Japanese company.

If several large-scale quantitative surveys uncovered foreign business practitioners' unease with Japanese business communication norms (Chikyu Sangyo Bunka Kenkyujo, 1993; Akiyama, 1994; Dowa Kasai Kaijo Hoken, 1988), qualitative studies of naturally occurring data also concluded that Japanese communication style is often perceived as ambiguous, if not downright inaccessible (e.g., Marriot and Yamada, 1991; Marriott, 1995). Yamada's comparative study of Japanese and American meetings (1992) points to several interactional style differences, including linear versus circular logic development and group versus individual orientation; these are factors deeply rooted in different value systems and manifested in conversational routines. Intercultural management studies indicate that 'culture-bound' discourse potentially excludes foreigners (Kopp, 1999). At the same time, Japanese are also constrained by their business discourse and may potentially end up being excluded from other discourses; for example, research has shown how Japanese are marginalized in meetings conducted in English (Tanaka, 2006).

A normative management approach such as the Japanese one, inspired by indigenous philosophies claiming to emphasize interpersonal relations over atomistic individuals (Hamaguchi, 1985), clashes with business discourses developed in other parts of the world, in particular in Western countries and countries heavily influenced by Western values. Because of Japan's extensive business contact with such countries, appreciation of the differences in management styles and of their practical consequences is critical. Intercultural management research points to two fundamental principles in Japanese business discourse that potentially clash with Western capitalist discourse: hierarchy and harmony. Kleinberg (1999) notes the importance of conforming to a vertically graded social order and the great concern for social harmony that characterizes Japanese societal culture. Ybema and Byun (2009) describe the uneasiness experienced by Dutch managers employed by a Japanese company's subsidiary in the Netherlands, who perceive Japanese organizational communication to be inherently hierarchical. Similarly, Kopp (1999) writes about the invisible power wall in Japanese organizations that segregates natives from non-natives.

While hierarchy is considered as a critical element in Japanese business, several researchers point to 'egalitarianism' as one of the basic concepts underpinning harmony in Japanese organizations (e.g. Aoki and Dore, 1996; Washimi, 2004). These researchers dwell on the ways in which Japanese organizations practice egalitarianism, the shared work space being one of them: in many companies, executive managers including presidents, use the same cafeteria, lavatories and parking lot as lower-ranking employees. The seemingly conflicting notions of hierarchy and harmony based on egalitarianism are reified in the practice of *Omikoshi* management. The *Omikoshi* is a portable shrine carried on the shoulders of perhaps a dozen men. It is impossible to identify the leader or those who are, or are not, carrying their fair load. All are anonymous contributors to the group's effort (Anderson, 2009). This management style is often seen in Japanese businesses, in which top management may seem to be aloof (Goto, 2004). In this system it is not clear who is actually in charge. In an earlier study (Tanaka, 2001), the first author observed a Japanese general manager who took no turns in an important inter-organizational meeting—in fact he remained completely silent—a good example of a manager engaging in *Omikoshi* management by letting his subordinates attend to the discussion.

Studies of Japanese local business discourse reveal that Japanese communication often becomes ambiguous due to participants' attempts to avoid potential conflict and maintain harmony (e.g. Kondo, 2007). In Japanese business interactional data, topic shifting is used as a strategy to avoid conflict in both inter-firm meetings (Kondo, 2007) and internal meetings (Yamada, 1997). Other studies have concentrated on the strategic use of honorifics in Japanese meetings, a complex linguistic system absent in English (e.g. Tanaka, 2011).

The data analysed in the next section are extracted from what could be defined as a hierarchical, yet harmony-oriented and egalitarian, Japanese business meeting. As already mentioned, the two seemingly conflicting elements of hierarchy and harmony co-exist in the value system of Japanese management discourse. Suzuki (2007) argues that showing consideration for others is crucial to achieving social equilibrium. It is thus essential for interlocutors to demonstrate discernment (*wakimae* in Japanese). Discernment is, according to Ide (1989), the acknowledgment of one's sense of vertical and horizontal place and role in a given situation, as prescribed by social convention. Yamada (1997) found that some Japanese speakers tend to value reticence and orderly turn-taking and are less inclined to claim the floor. This could be interpreted as a demonstration of discernment on the speakers' part, which affects their approach to conversational engagement.

In Japan, talk and behaviour based on discernment rather than self-centred motivation is of the essence for hierarchically ordered, harmonious work relations. When we investigate business discourse using individuals as the basic unit of analysis, harmony and hierarchy appear as conflicting values. If, on the contrary, one applies the notion of 'relation' as a minimum unit of analysis, harmony and hierarchy emerge as two important and complementary tenets of business interaction in Japan—and possibly in other Asian contexts.

The multi-dimensionality of ABDs requires a commensurate epistemological and methodological response. The emphasis on relation-building and maintenance, which characterizes many Asian societies, is an epistemological stance that underpins the analysis in Section 4. Meeting participants are seen as operating within a complex relational network predicated upon age, seniority of employment, experience and expertise, which are some of the factors that determine a person's status and hierarchical position in a Japanese organization. Meeting participants will have been educated to show sensitivity to matters of hierarchy and status; arguably, the latter can only go unchallenged if the status quo is maintained. Personal interests and preferences may be required to be set aside for the sake of preserving good, that is, harmonious interpersonal and group relations.

This vivid awareness of one's own position in the system and of the interdependence of individuals and groups, forged through painstaking relational work, seems to us to call for a multi-perspectival discourse analytical approach, couched in an intersubjective interpretive epistemology. Intersubjectivity has been conceptualized as 'the variety of relations between perspectives. Those perspectives can belong to individuals, groups, or traditions and discourses, and they can manifest as both implicit (or taken for granted) and explicit (or reflected upon)' (Gillespie and Cornish, 2009: 19–20). Intersubjectivity is more than a 'situation in which two or more persons share knowledge reflexively' (Reich, 2010: 41): it describes the human condition of being 'connected' and dependent, of being a 'node' in a web of relations with individuals and groups in contact with which we reflexively make sense of our own being as 'related'. The analytical focus then is not the individual and her self-reflexivity, but her 'relatedness' (to others), the processes through which such relatedness is effected and their outcomes, for example co-constructed knowledge. Intersubjectivity is performed in situated interaction and often expressed in attributions of intentions and feelings to others; a discursive approach is well suited to capture the manifold perspectives animating the intersubjective condition in which we are immersed.

This epistemology is particularly useful in charting the multiplicity, dynamics and characteristics of relational traffic in organizational settings, but it is also useful as a way of expressing and mapping the conditions that make 'discernment' (*wakimae*) possible. Intersubjectivity is central to social science, but methodological approaches to its study have suffered from a marked individualistic bias, so that relations between people and groups have escaped analysis. Within ABDs intersubjectivity inscribes not only the relations between academic researchers and their collaborating business partners but also between business practitioners situated in their locales and the wider societal contexts, as well as between the disciplines and epistemologies called upon in the research and the local traditions and values in which business practices are embedded. In the illustrative analysis that follows, specific discourse analytic tools, multi-party interpretation and ethnographic knowledge are drawn upon to make sense of situated meeting behaviour cast against the complex web of (Japanese) intersubjectivity.

Data and interpretation

The data

The excerpts are taken from a regular monthly meeting held at Toyoko Network, a consulting company with 12 employees located in Yokohama, Japan. The meeting was held on 25 June, 2008. The first author asked Kasai, one of the participants, to record the non-confidential part of the meeting (22 minutes and 38 seconds).

Below is the list of the meeting participants, all men ages between 26 and 65, whose real names have been replaced by pseudonyms:

Company President: Hanawa, 65
Senior Vice President, Research: Nojima, 59
Senior Vice President, Sales: Kasai, 54
Sales Director: Umemoto, 48
Sales Associate Director: Taneda, 44
Sales Representative: Ochiai, 26
Intern from Local Board of Education: Tsuda, 50

Given the intersubjective epistemology adopted here, personal narratives, historical accounts, local management philosophies, contextual knowledge and so on, as well as interviews, email exchanges and the meeting agenda are all considered as 'data'. At the same time, they all contribute to the ongoing interpretive process that, given native language and extensive contextual knowledge, has centred mainly on the first author, with a later dialogic stage where both authors were involved in extensive email discussions.[1]

Interpreting intersubjectively: mapping the relations

Personal stories, corporate trajectories

This section of the article illustrates the extent to which interpersonal relations matter to this meeting and to its interpretation. The narration begins in the first person because it involves the first author and several of Toyoko's members as well as two of his postgraduate students.

About ten years ago Hanawa, Nojima and Kasai quit a large consultation institute (of which I was also an associate) and started Toyoko Network. The reason Kasai gave me for quitting was that they wanted to work for themselves rather than for the institute's owners. Kasai's annual income suffered a drop but he is happier because in his new role as vice-president he can provide leadership for the new company. Kasai left the institute two years after I did and then contacted me to share some business; he sells training and consultation programmes and I currently act as an external consultant for his company for 15–20 days a year. Toyoko only has one internal consultant in its company, Nojima, and uses external consultants for most of its business.

The company is a small business, therefore the travel expenses issue raised by President Hanawa in the meeting in question is an important matter. Hanawa is always worried about Toyoko's financial status. I have known him for 12 years, since he was a general manager in the company we used to work for, and he is known to be attentive to detail. Umemoto and Taneda also quit the same institute, after which they worked for two different companies for a couple of years before joining Toyoko. The fact that most of the meeting participants are former colleagues and have long-standing relations means that they consider team harmony as extremely important.

Kasai and I were both *Kacho*, middle managers, in the institute we worked for; it is on the basis of this long-standing relationship that I have been granted access to the company's meetings. Having been in the consultation business for 20 years, I also share Toyoko's values and norms. All meeting participants were informed of the purpose of the recording and I promised to use pseudonyms throughout; only the part of the meeting which did not contain sensitive personal material was used for this article.

Negotiating multiple interpretations

I conducted a preliminary analysis of the data, then I listened to the audio-recording again, first with two of my postgraduate students and later with an American colleague and consultant. They all contributed new insights such as the observation that low-status employees appear to start a turn after significant pauses.

Within the company, I talked to Kasai and exchanged emails with him about the data. For example, I wanted to find out why he dared take the chair's role when it was not him who called the meeting (in Japan the meeting host usually also acts as chair). I also discussed the *Omikoshi* management approach with him, and he was comfortable with the idea that it applied to how business was conducted at Toyoko. Finally, I exchanged emails on data interpretation with the second author, on the basis of the English translation and of Francesca's listening to the original recording. Bearing in mind that she does not understand Japanese, her role was to catch instances of simultaneous and overlapping talk. In spite of the overall relaxed and even informal register of

Table 32.1 Meeting turn distribution and topics

Topics	Finance	Tsuda	Seminar Review	A New Client	Next Meeting	Total
Hanawa	42	1	18	9	20	90
Kasai	50	8	26	11	19	114
Nojima	17	2	20	0	13	52
Umemoto	25	2	8	0	2	37
Taneda	10	0	1	0	1	12
Ochiai	11	0	18	13	0	42
Tsuda	0	10	24	1	1	36

the meeting, a native speaker embedded in Japanese business practice will not fail to perceive a strong sense of hierarchy in the interaction.

A further and more important finding of the multiple interpretation effort is that the participants' topic shifting and development seem influenced by hierarchical power relations, concern for harmony within the organization and an egalitarian view of topic management. It is therefore unsurprising that the participants responsible for the highest numbers of turns were company President Hanawa and Vice-President Kasai (see Table 32.1).

Omikoshi management in action

On a close examination of turn distribution topic by topic, it appears that participants' turn-taking patterns were mainly topic-related.

As Table 32.1 shows, the top three scores in the total column correspond to the three higher-status managers. The frequency of participation of two of the managers was particularly high when their individual expenditures were discussed. On the other hand, lower-status employees took a comparable number of turns to the higher-status participants when the topic under discussion concerned employees' responsibility. For example, when the topic was Tsuda's learning experience through his internship, Tsuda took ten turns, the largest single turns count for topic 3.

In the post-meeting interview, Kasai mentioned that the last part of the meeting, from which the excerpts were taken, was '*yuuzuu muge*', which in Kasai's vocabulary means 'flexible'. Many of the topics discussed were not on the agenda, or at least Hanawa, the formal meeting chair and host, was not informed of them prior to the meeting. Kasai reported: '*Kaigi no shusaisha wa tooji Shacho no Hanawa san desu. Hanawa san ga ajenda wo sakusei shi toojitsu haifu simasu.*' ('The meeting was called by Hanawa, who was president at that time. Hanawa drew up the agenda and distributed it.') However, Kasai took the largest number of turns. He also voluntarily took on the role of facilitator. Kasai later explained the reason for his frequent interventions thus: '*Kasai*[2] *ga debaru no wa omo ni eigyo kaigi no shikisai ga tsuyoi tame.*' ('The reason why Kasai talked a lot was that the topics were related to sales.')

This phenomenon can be interpreted as *Omikoshi* management practice. President Hanawa could be seen as the shrine on the shoulders of his men—sacred and respectable. Thus Kasai took it on himself to act as facilitator, to avoid inconvenience to the meeting's host. As Kasai wrote to the first author: '*Gutai teki na katsudo nitsuite hanashiai no shikiri wa shosei ga tantoo.*' ('I facilitated the discussion on our actual activities.') Kasai also added that in order to emphasize his (Hanawa's) position as the meeting's host, Hanawa formally declared the meeting open. Kasai's description of Hanawa's role sounds like that of a god controlling the world from his shrine. According to Kasai,

Hanawa's role is '*sore wo mimamori karini yappari fukuzatsu na baai wa Hanawa san ga hyooka saitei suru katachi ni narimasu*' ('to watch over the whole meeting and intervene, evaluate, and judge when issues become complex'). Kasai demonstrates his discernment as a vice-president whose role is to support Hanawa by voluntarily taking on the role of facilitator or 'acting chair', inviting lower-status participants to initiate their topics. Not only does turn-taking reflect the hierarchical order, it also shows the participants' concern for relations maintenance in terms of confirming relative positionings within the interaction.

Silent moves

The participants' topic opening strategies in the current meeting appear to contradict Yamada's (1992) findings: according to which, in an American meeting, the person responsible for a deal initiates his or her own topic, while in a Japanese meeting there is no person in charge of a topic; any employee can initiate one. In the present meeting, topic initiation depends on whether the formal chair had been notified in advance of the topics. In the interview, Kasai confirms that Hanawa had been made aware of some topics while others were raised without prior notice being given to him. In the case of 'advised' topics, it was Kasai who raised them and invited the relevant speakers to take the floor:

> Excerpt 1
> 112. (3.0) Kasai: *Eeto. koko made ii desuka. ja. shucchouhi no ken.* (3.0) Well. Are we okay so far? So, on to travel expenses.
>
> 113. Hanawa: *Aa. korewa desu ne. ichioo uchi wa shucchoo kitei tte no wo. oozappa na mono wo kimete run desu kedo.* Er. That is, for the present, we have, a so-called a travel expense regulation. A very simple one.

In the interview, Kasai disclosed that he and Hanawa had already discussed the issue of travel expenses and had planned to inform the meeting of the change in the company's reimbursement system. In this sense, then, the meeting has a rubber-stamping function for a new policy that senior management are set on introducing regardless.

As excerpt 1 shows, topic shifts tend to take place after a relatively long silence, in this case of three seconds. This finding resonates with Yamada's observations (1992). She points out that Japanese use silence to signal the end of a topic. Participants in the Toyoko meeting similarly use silence as a postlude to a topic discussion. In the interview Kasai explained that he uses silence to find out whether anyone else in the meeting has anything to say. A pause of three seconds is sufficient to confirm that nobody wishes to speak, so the chair moves on to the next topic. There were three instances of junior managers opening a topic. According to Kasai, these topics had not been agreed with management prior to the meeting. Since Kasai knew that a couple of such topics could be raised, he intentionally used silence to give the opportunity to lower-status employees to initiate them. The transcript indicates that lower-status employees read his silence as confirmation that the previous topic is closed and that they can initiate a new one. In contrast with junior managers, senior managers open new topics without waiting for a significant pause; in so doing, they use the privileges afforded by their hierarchical status.

The role of silence in meetings has been the focus of several studies that investigate interaction involving Japanese (Yamada, 1992; Fujio, 2004; Nakane, 2007). The agreement seems to be that Japanese speakers send a message by not talking. Our interpretation of the current meeting suggests that the participants use silence to express consideration for others and to show discernment. Silence may also contribute to maintaining equilibrium in social relations; while this function may not be apparent to non-Japanese meeting participants, the harmony achieved as a result of significant pauses is instrumental for Japanese to achieve a productive synergy. When a person sends a message by keeping silent, others interpret the message and react accordingly. This kind of silent exchange is based on individuals showing discernment and is believed to play a vital role in facilitating 'friction free' communication among insiders in Japanese business organizations (Ray and Little, 2003).

When Japanese transfer this normative behaviour to intercultural meetings conducted in English, they might come across as inscrutable to non-Japanese participants. On the other hand, Japanese find Anglo-Saxon-style meeting management difficult to operate in, because tolerance for longer silent pauses is low, and thus the opportunities to initiate a new topic or to voice their ideas are considerably reduced. Consequently, in intercultural meetings Japanese are usually set apart by their low participation, following self-marginalization (Tanaka, 2006; Nakane, 2007).

Mitigating bad news

In excerpt 1, Hanawa tentatively prefaces the announcement of the new policy and then moves on to state that the company is now going to reimburse only those travel costs actually incurred. Employees potentially stand to lose financially because they will no longer be able to take advantage of the price difference between a standard ticket and a discount ticket. Immediately after Hanawa's announcement, Kasai intervenes with a personal anecdote of his experience of travelling with an economy airline, thus apparently deviating from the main topic (excerpt 2). Kasai explains how uncomfortable the experience was, a stance which he reinforces in turn 68. Umemoto and Ochiai bolster the argument against cheap flights in short, empathetic turns:

Excerpt 2

114. (2.0) Kasai: *Konkai ano sukai maaku ano mukoo to no okyaku san tono settingu no jikan mo atta nde sukai maaku maaku ni shitan desu yo. moo katte atta ndesu kedo mo ano kekkyoku ne. nyuusu ni atta yooni futari pairotto ga inain'de sorede nanbin mo kekkoo shiteiru wake desu yo. (2.0).* This time, Skymark. I used Skymark because of the time set for the other party, the client. I had already bought a ticket but eventually as you saw in the news, they were short of pilots and cancelled some flights.

115. Umemoto: *Un.* Yeah.

116. Kasai: *De soreni ataru kanoosei mo attanda.* I could be on one of such flights.

117. Umemoto: *Uun a soka soka.* Yeah. right right

118. Kasai: *De. Sukai maaku ni denwa shitan desu yo. zen zen tsuuji nain desu yo. maa demo hoomu peeji mitara dore to dore ga kekkoo ni narutte noga atta kara. de. kinoo kinoo Jaru de kaette kitan desu kedo ne. Jaru wa niman nisen happyaku en nan dakedo ano yappari ne suchuwaadesu wa ippai iru wa ano juusu wa deru wa de Sukai maaku wa hajimete nottanda keredo suchuwaadesu wa nisan nin datta shi seibi in wa tarinaitte iwareteru shi pairotto wa nisanwari futsuuno pairotto yorimo yobun ni yatteru shi de juusu nanka derukato omottara uruni ikun dayone are hyaku en toka* (laughter) And I called Skymark. Never connected. But their webpage informed of which flights were cancelled. And, yesterday, yesterday, I came back by JAL. JAL cost 22,800 yen. Well, you know, there were many flight attendants and they served me juice. I used Skymark for the first time and there were only a few flight attendants and it is said that Skymark lacks sufficient maintenance and I thought they'd served me juice but they sell juice, like 100 yen (laughter).

119. Umemoto: *Aa* Ah.

120. Kasai: *Anmari kimochi no ii mon ja nai.* It was not so comfortable.

121. Umemoto: [*Nanka kowai yo ne.* [It's kind of scary.]

In line with Kondo's (2007) findings, Kasai's temporary digression from a potentially controversial topic can be interpreted as a strategy to avoid friction among employees. The personal touch and humor detectable in excerpt 2 are directed towards mitigating the negative impact of Hanawa's announcement. Having provided a temporary buffer between Hanawa and junior employees, Hanawa confirms the new policy (128) before Kasai moves on to the next topic (133):

Excerpt 3

128. Hanawa: *Hikooki ni noru shucchou tte soo nai shi ne*. Business trips on airplanes do not take place so often.

129. Umemoto: *Nai Un*. No. Right.

130. Hanawa: *Ii desu ka jippi shugi toyuu koto de* Okay with this refund for the amount paid.

131. Kasai: *Hikooki ni tsuite wa*. About airplanes.

1322. Hanawa: *Hikooki ni tsuite wa*. About airplanes.

133. Kasai: *Hai. Yoroshii desu ka. Ja hoomu peeji no mentenansu* Er. Okay. Then, on to the maintenance of our webpage.

As sales director, Umemoto supplies positive if short comments on the policy change to which other employees and lower-status managers react with silence, thus showing discernment of their superiors' position. Once again, managers and employees collaborate to preserve organizational equilibrium. Had non-Japanese participants attended this meeting, the strategic use of silence and the (apparent) circularity of topic development might have possibly confused them, even if they were highly competent in Japanese. As the non-Japanese respondents in Kondo's survey (2007) noted, outsiders might think of meetings such as the current one as ambiguously structured, time-consuming and producing 'unclear decisions'.

Ybema and Byun (2009) discuss cultural differences and reactions to them among employees of Dutch and Japanese companies' overseas subsidiaries in Japan and the Netherlands. In their study, the participants' identity talk reflects different perceptions of power relations: Japanese employees think that Japanese management is egalitarian, while Dutch employees think that Japanese managers are hierarchical. The multi-perspectival interpretation illustrated in this chapter shows how Japanese can in fact be both hierarchical and egalitarian, but these apparently contradictory positionings only become obvious with substantial contextual and situational knowledge. Ethnographic diachronic knowledge accumulated through participation in a dense network of relevant relations, as well as direct personal experience and observation of business practices, proved essential in order to recover the pragmatic meanings from the contextual and situational embeddedness of a particular fragment of human interaction. The value of an intersubjective epistemology extends to co-interpretation as an act that blurs the boundaries of authorship in research findings presented as a multi-authored 'text'.

ABDs: where we are now and where we may be going

This chapter has sought to frame the recent development of Asian business discourse(s) within a context of intensified contact between the West and Asia, where the promotion of English as a lingua franca of international business and of Anglo-Saxon-style management often belie ignorance of, or resistance to, local practices and preferences. And on this note we should perhaps also add that the authors do not subscribe to the view of much prescriptive literature that intercultural communication is inherently problematic and more likely to generate conflict than intracultural communication. Instead, the underlying assumption of our work is that the meeting of 'cultures', for want of a better word, is rich with opportunities for knowledge of both self and other in the respect of differences.

In representing both 'East' and 'West' in this chapter, we are aware of the ideological dominance of the latter over the former in international business practice, but also of the ethnocentric bias of the related vocabularies of management and business. Elsewhere (Bargiela-Chiappini and Tanaka, 2012) we have been exploring some of the historical and ideological cross-currents underpinning the development of Japanese management thought and practice, and in so doing we have uncovered patterns of mutual influence between Europe, the US and Japan—a reminder of the longevity of intercultural contact.

Discourse analytic approaches to business and organizational practices in Asia have a distinct place in ABDs research, where an eminently Western set of methodologies is being deployed to 'get close' to business practice as it unfolds; a growing number of Asian scholars have been able to access work sites and to write about their experience. It would be unwise to attempt any generalization on the basis of the illustrative material discussed in this chapter. Instead, we offer a few observations for reflection and further research, but also as an antidote to the enduring prescriptivism of influential scholarship on intercultural (business) communication.

First, in ABDs analysis 'what we see is not what we get.' An analysis of meeting interaction based on a Western conceptualization of sociological categories such as hierarchy and egalitarianism would have yielded a different (and probably misguided) interpretation of Japanese business relations and practices. The delicate mechanisms implicated in the negotiation of power, hierarchy and egalitarianism in Japanese corporate settings must be understood against participants' pervasive concern with maintaining (organizational) harmony. In turn, such interpretation is only recoverable as a multi-authored text that reflects the microcosm of the researcher's experiential and relational world. Far from engaging in 'objective', detached analysis, the researcher is able to exploit his closeness to the phenomenon under observation through an epistemology that prizes intersubjectivity.

Second, the tool-kit provided by discourse analytical approaches, deployed against an epistemology of intersubjectivity, allows the analyst to zoom into the interaction as it unfolds, and to zoom out into contextual, situational and interpersonal dimensions that illuminate local practice. As the multiple interpretive effort described in this chapter has shown, ethnographic and native knowledge are required to unlock deeper layers of meaning. Once again, the researcher is able to exploit his closeness to the phenomenon under observation in ways that are not available to an outsider looking in.

Third, while East–West collaborative research is important for the development of ABDs, what is urgently needed is more inter-Asian collaboration concentrating on interpreting the use of local languages in business, with or without English as a lingua franca, and including Asian Englishes. Finally, future Asian-based research should also aim at exploring the contribution of indigenous philosophies, religions, and traditions to business practice as well as taking on board local developments in the social sciences that can lead to a deeper appreciation of human interaction, and therefore also of business interaction.

Transcription conventions

[interruption or
[overlap
(1.0)   one second pause
(.)   micro pause
=   immediate latching on

Acknowledgements

We are very grateful to Sandra Harris and to the volume editors for their insightful comments on an earlier version of the chapter.

Further reading

The bibliography on (Asian) business discourses is still quite small but growing. Listed below are indicative titles:

Bargiela-Chiappini, F. and Gotti, M. (eds.) (2005) *Asian Business Discourse(s)*. Bern: Peter Lang.

The first collection of essays on Asian business discourse under one cover.

Tanaka, H. and Fujio, M. (forthcoming) '"Harmonious disagreement" in Japanese business discourse', in J. Aritz and R. Walker (eds.) *Discourse Perspectives on Organizational Communication*. Madison, NJ: Fairleigh Dickinson University Press.

An illustration of business discourse analysis of an inter-firm meeting held in a Japanese company.

Journal of Asian Pacific Communication (2005–2006), 15:2 and 16:1 (special double issue on Asian business discourse(s)).

Journal of Business Communication (2014), 51:1, (special issue on 'Crossing Boundaries: Working and Communicating in East Asia').

Notes

1 The agenda only included a selection of the topics eventually discussed: (1) figures of the company's turnover, expenses, and profits for 2005–2008, and sales and profit objectives for 2009; (2) actual sales results for April–May, 2009; (3) current market situation; (4) other issues. For reasons of confidentiality, the data recorded and analysed refer to the last part of the meeting only.
2 In the email exchange, Kasai refers to himself by his last name.
3 Tsuda is a high school in-service teacher. The area board of education sends teachers to local business corporations for training for a whole academic year. Tsuda was placed at Toyoko Network as an intern. In the interview, Kasai speaks of his concern about Tsuda's learning progress.

References

Akiyama, K. (1994) 'Bijinesu komyunikeeshon ni okeru "hanashi kotoba" no yakuwari to kadai', *Nihongo gaku*, 13 (2): 38–45.
Anderson, R. V. (2009) Japanese and American management: a contrast of styles. *Management World*. March/April. Available at http://cob.jmu.edu/icpm/management_world/CMartMar09.pdf (accessed 20 January 2010).
Aoki, M. and Dore, R. (1996) *The Japanese Firm: The Sources of Competitive Strength*. New York: Oxford University Press.
Bargiela-Chiappini, F. (ed.) (2009) *The Handbook of Business Discourse*. Edinburgh: Edinburgh University Press.
Bargiela-Chiappini, F. and Gotti, M. (eds.) (2005) *Asian Business Discourse(s)*. Bern: Peter Lang.
Bargiela-Chiappini, F. (2006) '(Whose) English(es) for Asian business discourse(s)?' *Journal of Asian Pacific Communication*, 16 (1), 1–24.
Bargiela-Chiappini, F. (2011) 'Asian business discourse(s)', in J. Aritz and R. Walker (eds.) *Discourse Perspectives on Organizational Communication*. Fairleigh Dickinson University Press.
Bargiela-Chiappini, F. (2009a) 'Introduction: business discourse', in F. Bargiela-Chiappini (ed.) *The Handbook of Business Discourse*. Edinburgh: Edinburgh University Press, pp. 1–17.
Bargiela-Chiappini, F. and Tanaka, H. (2012) 'The mutual gaze: Japan, business management and the West', in S. Nair-Venugopal *et al.* (eds.) *The Gaze of the West: Framings of the East*. Palgrave Macmillan, 139–155.
Boden, D. (1994) *The Business of Talk: Organizations in Action*. Polity Press: Cambridge.
Chakorn, O. (2006) 'Persuasive and politeness strategies in cross-cultural letters of request in the Thai business context', *Journal of Asian Pacific Communication.*, 16 (1): 103–146.

Chikyu Sangyo Bunka Kenkyujo (Global Industrial and Social Progress Research Institute) (1993) *Bijinesu komyunikeeshon no sogai yooin to nihongo no juyoo jittai. (Language Barriers in Business Communication and Actual Demand for Japanese Language)*. Tokyo: Chikyu Sangyo Bunka Kenkyujo.

Cooren, F. (2001) 'Acting and organizing: how speech acts structure organizational interactions', *Concepts and Transformation*, 6 (3): 275–293.

Daiichi Kangyo Bank. (1986) *Zainichi gaikoujin no mita nihon no bijinesu* [*Japanese Business Viewed by non-Japanese Living in Japan*]. Tokyo: Daiichi Kangyo Bank.

Dowa Kasai Kaijo Hoken (1988) *Zainichi gaikokujin bijinesu man no Nippon fureaido chosa* [*A Survey of non-Japanese Business Men's Contact to Japan*]. Tokyo: Dowa Kaijo Kasai.

Du-Babcock, B. (2005) 'Communication behaviors in intra- and inter-cultural decision making meetings', *Journal of Asian-Pacific Communication*, 29: 147–170.

Emmett, K. (2003) 'Persuasion strategies in Japanese business meetings', *Journal of Intercultural Studies*, 24 (1): 65–79.

Fujio, M. (2004) 'Silence during intercultural communication: a case study', *Corporate Communications*, 9 (4): 331–339.

Gillespie, A. and Cornish, F. (2009) 'Intersubjectivity: towards a dialogic analysis', *Journal of the Theory of Social Behaviour*, 40 (1): 19–46.

Glynos, J., Howarth, D., Norval, A., and Speed, E. (2009) Discourse analysis: varieties and methods. ESRC National Centre for Research Methods Review paper, National Centre for Research Methods, NCRM/014, University of Essex, UK, document available at http://eprints.ncrm.ac.uk/796/1/discourse_analysis_NCRM_014.pdf.

Goto, T. (2004). 'Stakeholder dialogue'. *Global Reporting Initiative*. Available online at: http://www.daiwa-grp.jp/english/pdf/2004_Sustainability_Report/04_report_42-49_e.pdf) Daiwa Securities Group Inc.

Hamaguchi, E. (1985) 'A contextual model of the Japanese: toward a methodological innovation in Japan studies', *Journal of Japanese Studies*, 11 (2): 289–231.

Hendry, J. and Wong, H. W. (eds.) (2006) *Dismantling the East-West Dichotomy: Essays in Honour of Jan van Bremen*. London and New York: Routledge.

Huang, T. (1998) 'The strategic level of human resource management and organizational performance: an empirical investigation', *Asia Pacific Journal of Human Resources*, 36: 59–72.

Ide, S. (1989) 'Formal forms and discernment: two neglected aspects of linguistic politeness', *Multilingua*, 8 (2/3): 223–248.

Iedema, R. and Scheeres, H. (2009) 'Organisational discourse analysis', in F. Bargiela-Chiappini (ed.) *The Handbook of Business Discourse*. Edinburgh: Edinburgh University Press, pp. 80–91.

Iedema, R. and Scheeres, H. (2005–2006), *Journal of Asian Pacific Communication*, 15 (2), and 16 (1) (special double issue on Asian business discourse(s)).

Jung, Y. (2005) 'The rhetorical structure in Korean business writing', in M. Gotti and P. Gillaerts (eds.) *Genre Variation in Business Letters*. Bern: Peter Lang, pp. 347–368.

Kleinberg, J. (1999) 'Negotiated understanding: the organizational implication of a cross-national business negotiation', in S. L. Beechler and A. Bird (eds.) *Japanese Multinationals Abroad: Individual and Organizational Learning* New York: Oxford University Press, pp. 62–91.

Kondo, A. (2007) *Nihonjin to gaikokujin no bijinesu komyunikeishon ni kansuru kenkyuu* [*Research on Business Communication Between Japanese and Foreigners*]. Tokyo: Hitsuji Shobo.

Kong, K. C. C. (2001) 'Marketing of belief: intertextual construction of network marketers' identities', *Discourse and Society*, 12 (4): 473–503.

Kopp, R. (1999) 'The rice paper ceiling in Japanese company: why it exists and persists', in S. Beecher, and A. Bird (eds.) *Japanese Multinationals Abroad*. New York: Oxford University Press, pp. 107–128.

Lee, J. (2002) 'Bijinesu Nihongo wo kangaeru' ['A study on Japanese language education for business']. *Gengobunka to Nihongo Kyoiku* (May): 245–260.

Marriot, H. and Yamada, H. (1991) 'Japanese discourse in tourism shopping situations', *Japan and the World*, 3: 155–168 (The Japanese Studies Association of Australia).

Marriott, H. (1995) 'Deviations in an intercultural business negotiation', in A. Firth. (ed.) *The Discourse of Negotiation*. Oxford: Pergamon Press, pp. 247–268.

Mizutani, O. (1994) 'Bijinesu nihongo wo kangaeru: kooteki na kotoba wo motomete', *Nihongogaku*, 13 (12): 14–20.

Nair-Venugopal, S. (2006) 'An interactional model of English in Malaysia: a contextual response to commodification', *Journal of Asian Pacific Communication*, 16 (1): 51–76.

Nair-Venugopal, S. (2009) Malaysia, in F. Bargiela-Chiappini (ed.) *The Handbook of Business Discourse*. Edinburgh: Edinburgh University Press, pp. 387–399.

Nakane, I. (2007) *Silence in Intercultural Communication: Perception and Performance*. Amsterdam/Philadelphia, PA: John Benjamin Publishing.

Nakasako, S. (1998) 'Japan (business communication) (Forum: International Perspectives on Business Communication Research)', *Business Communication Quarterly*, 61 (3): 101–106.

Parker, P. S. and Grimes, D. S. (2009) ' 'Race' and management communication', in F. Bargiela-Chiappini (ed.) *The Handbook of Business Discourse*. Edinburgh: Edinburgh University Press, pp. 292–304.

Ray, T. and Little, S. (2003) 'Communication and context: collective tacit knowledge and practice in Japan's workplace', *Creativity and Innovation Management*, 10 (3): 154–164.

Reich, W. (2010) 'Three problems with intersubjectivity – and one solution', *Sociological Theory*, 28 (1): 40–63.

Samra-Fredericks, D. (2004) 'Managerial elites making rhetorical and linguistic 'moves' for a moving (emotional) display'. *Human Relations*. 57(9): 1103–1143.

Stubbe, M., Lane, C., Hilder, E., Vine, B., Marra, M., Holmes, J., and Weatherall, A. (2003) 'Multiple discourse analyses of a workplace interaction', *Discourse Studies*, 5 (3): 351–388.

Suzuki, T. (2007) *A Pragmatic Approach to the Generation and Gender Gap in Japanese Politeness Strategies*. Tokyo: Hitsuji Shobo.

Takahashi, N. and Takayanagi, S. (1985) 'Decision procedure models and empirical research: the Japanese experience', *Human Relations*, 38 (8): 767–780.

Tanaka, H. (2001) *Business English Needs Analysis*, Paper presented at the 14th Annual Conference of International Association of Japanese Business Studies, Seinajoki Polytechnic University, Finland.

Tanaka, H. (2006) 'Corporate language policy change: the trajectory of management discourse in Japan, the oppressed or the oppressor?', *Quaderns de Filologia. Estudis Lingüístics*, 11: 279–288.

Tanaka, H. (2009) 'Japan', in F. Bargiela-Chiappini (ed.) *The Handbook of Business Discourse*. Edinburgh: Edinburgh University Press, pp. 332–344.

Tanaka, H. (2011) 'Politeness in a Japanese intra-organizational meeting: honorifics and socio-dialectal code switching', *Journal of Asian Pacific Communication*, 21(1): 60–76.

Uhl-Bien, M. P., Tierney, S., Graen, G. B., and Wakabayashi, M. (1990) 'Company paternalism and the hidden-investment process: identification of the 'right type' for line managers in leading Japanese organizations', *Group and Organization Management*, 15: 414–430.

Washimi, J. (2004) Guroobaruka to Nippon no jidoosha sangyo. *The Japan Institute of Labor Policy and Training*. Available online at: http://www.jil.go.jp/institute/discussion/2004/04-009.html (accessed 16 January 2010).

Yamada, H. (1992) *American and Japanese Business Discourse: A Comparison of Interactional Styles*. Norwood, NJ: Albex.

Yamada, H. (1997) 'Organization in American and Japanese meetings: talk versus relationship', in F. Bargiela-Chiappini and S. Harris (eds.) *The Languages of Business*. Edinburgh: Edinburg University Press, pp. 117–135.

Ybema, S. and Byun, H. (2009) 'Cultivating cultural differences in asymmetric power relations', *International Journal of Cross Cultural Management*, 9 (3): 339–358.

33

Discourse and healthcare

Kevin Harvey and Svenja Adolphs

Introduction

In this chapter we explore the interrelation between discourse and healthcare. Health communication is a broad field of enquiry and practice, and so we will restrict our focus to health communication research that is concerned with naturally occurring linguistic routines (as opposed to more abstract, theoretical approaches to health communication and approaches which seek to identify and describe, if possible, what constitutes effective health communication). We take the phrase 'discourse' to refer to stretches of 'contextually sensitive written and spoken language produced as part of the interaction between speakers and hearers and writers and readers' (Candlin *et al.*, 1999: 321). Thus our focus is on discourse as a linguistic practice rather than on discourse as conceived by social theorists–that is, on discourse 'as ways structuring areas of knowledge and social/institutional practices' (p. 323). Like other linguistic practitioners who interrogate discourse (Kress, 1988; Fairclough, 1992), we, too, conceive of language as not merely reflecting 'entities and relations in social life' but actively contributing to their construction and constitution (Candlin *et al.*, 1999: 323). With regard to healthcare and health communication, language plays a significant part in constituting practices that take place within a range of medical settings, and, as we seek to demonstrate in this chapter, discourse can be seen as a central activity within the context of healthcare that helps to determine successful (or otherwise) outcomes and patient satisfaction.

What is health communication?

Health communication, by definition, refers to all aspects and modes of communication that take place within medical contexts or broadly relate to the subject of health and illness. Accordingly, health communication is an all-embracing concept, which takes into account a huge and diverse range of communicative activities touching on health and healthcare, ranging from personal accounts of health and illness and encounters with medical professionals through to health policy documentation and side effects information presented on drug packaging. Notwithstanding its broad subject matter, health communication also constitutes various modes of communicative practice, including spoken and written language, as well as new and emerging forms of communication, such as email, electronic bulletin boards and online health forums: electronic modes of communication that could be characterized as being 'hybrid' or 'centaur' (Baron, 1998), discursive forms that possess textual characteristics of both the spoken and written modes.

Alongside the sheer amount of discursive activities that potentially fall under the umbrella of health communication, it is also important to note that healthcare (and, concomitantly, the communication that takes place within healthcare contexts) is constantly in flux, and it is through discourse that it is possible to see exactly what changes are taking place and in which direction. For example, in the context of US and UK medicine, the last decade has witnessed some profound changes in healthcare policy and practice, changes, in particular, stemming from the concepts of patient empowerment and patient-centred medicine (Brown *et al.*, 2006: 30), and such changes are realized in shifts in contemporary discursive practices. For instance, the term 'client' has, in some domains of healthcare, supplanted the more traditional, if paternalistic, appellation 'patient', a linguistic shift that reflects the consumerist and choice-inspired ideology at the heart of much western healthcare practice. Similarly, although the GP-patient consultation is, by necessity, restricted to a short period of time (in the UK, for instance, the average time is typically no more than 10 minutes), counselling-based approaches to medical interaction are being adopted by a range of health professionals. Such approaches place emphasis on the autonomy of the patient (or 'client') and on shared decision-making, involving, in some instances, the practitioner's use of open questions that allow the patient to take the floor and set the topical agenda and the professional's showing of empathy towards the patient (Fairclough, 1995: 192; Babaul-Hirji *et al.*, 2010). Contemporary healthcare, then, can be seen to be moving from a paternalistic model of medical practice, in which the healthcare professional is seen as responsible for the health of patients/clients, to a patient-centred practice, in which the patient shares in the decision-making process. These changes can be examined with regard to how communication actually takes place in clinical settings.

Whatever the changes that are affecting contemporary medical practice may be, the very nature of healthcare unavoidably involves communication between various participants. As Sarangi (2004: 1) observes, the clinical encounter between professionals and patients is a communicative relationship. Communication is a central aspect of health and healthcare provision, especially, as Sarangi points out, in terms of how discourse produces a cause and effect, given that the professional causes the patient to adopt or modify certain behaviours. The contemporary focus on discourse and communication in healthcare (both from practitioner and scholarly perspectives) has witnessed a 'communicative turn' in medical practice, which recognizes the limitations of a biomedical model of health and illness (Sarangi, 2004: 3). Consequently, rather than emphasizing the technical, scientific assumptions of medicine, much contemporary research in health communication now emphasizes patients' voices and perspectives, personal narratives of health and illness. Such research prioritizes the role of discourse in patients' accounts of health and illness, exploring the discursive means by which people articulate and make sense of their condition. In this chapter we will consider some of this discourse-based research, examining the function and significance of discourse in medical exchanges.

What are the key studies in the area?

There exists a wide-range of discourse-based research into health communication. Consequently, in this section we will confine our attention to identifying a limited number of studies, studies nonetheless that aim to provide a representative survey of the type of research that is currently being conducted in the field. We conclude this section by providing a more in-depth overview of a specific example of health communication in the context of mental health, illustrating the practical relevance of discourse-based research in contemporary healthcare.

Health communication has attracted attention from a wide range of disciplines such as health services, ethics, psychology, social sciences, anthropology, media studies and linguistics–to cite but a few. In particular, research on communication in healthcare settings has, over the last 30 years, contributed significantly to the study of health practitioners and patients (Sarangi, 2004: 2). Although, as many commentators have pointed out, the analytical focus of a substantial amount of this research has been exclusively on doctor–patient interaction (ten Have, 1995; Atkinson,

1999; Candlin, 2000), there exists a diverse and ever-increasing body of enquiry into medical discourse. Such diversification, for example, has considered the verbal routines of a variety of non-physician personnel, including nurses (Crawford *et al.* 1998), physiotherapists (Parry, 2004) and pharmacists (Pilnick, 1999)–as well as exploring written medical discourse in various communicative contexts such as medical note taking (Van Naerssen, 1985; Hobbs, 2003), case histories (Francis and Kramer-Dahl, 2004) and patient information leaflets (Clerehan and Buchbinder, 2006). Though these discourse-based studies are diverse and wide-ranging, what they have in common is a close focus on language *in situ* and the consequent pointing up of the role of discourse in the practice of medicine and health care (Sarangi, 2004: 2).

Methodologically, much of the aforementioned research has taken, broadly, an applied linguistic perspective (featuring conversation analysis, text analysis and critical discourse analysis). These perspectives have provided promising points of entry into the interrogation of medical practice. Moreover, many health discourse studies have combined perspectives, utilizing theoretical eclecticism in order to understand complex human communication better (Jeffries, 2000). There has been, for example, as McHoul and Rapley (2001) observe, a recent tendency for conversational analysis and interactional sociolinguistic methodologies to be supplemented by a strain of critical discourse analysis, the research impetus being as much to criticize and change practices in healthcare settings as to describe and understand them (e.g. Lobley, 2001; McCarthy and Rapley, 2001; Francis and Kramer-Dahl, 2004).

A good illustration of this strain of research, which seeks to alter clinical practice, can be found in discourse-based studies that interrogate mental health communication, particularly in psychiatric and counselling-based contexts (e.g. Telles Ribeiro, 1996; Palmer, 2000; Madill *et al.*, 2001). Given that a number of key therapeutic activities such as assessment, diagnosis and intervention within mental health are conducted through face-to-face interaction, analysis of spoken discourse is well suited to empirically examining the verbal exchanges that constitute these various activities. Indeed both researchers working outside mental health and practitioners within have increasingly utilized discourse approaches to provide descriptions of a broad range of interactional routines, as well as addressing specific practical problems in order to promote smooth and effective practice (ten Have, 2001: 3).

A seminal and often cited discourse-based study in psychiatric discourse is that conducted by Bergmann (1992), who examines the discourse of psychiatric intake interviews. The purpose of such interviews is to assess whether candidate patients, interrogated by psychiatrists, should be hospitalized on the basis of their 'observable behaviour during the interview' (1992: 137). Bergmann reveals how psychiatrists, apart from using questions to assess formally the mental well-being of candidate patients, also frequently present interviewees with information about themselves in order to elicit further responses from them. Bergmann, after Pomerantz (1980), describes this process of psychiatric exploration as 'fishing', an interactional phenomenon whereby a speaker, in this case the psychiatrist, does not construct a direction question but produces an assertion, referring to the patient's personal state of affairs (state of health, mood) to which s/he, as an outside observer, has only limited access (1992: 142). Such 'fishing' or 'information-eliciting telling' (1992: 142) invites the patient to 'formulate private problems, to disclose personal feelings, and to talk about their troubles' (p. 155). Psychiatrists' use of this type of rhetorical strategy avoids questioning patients directly and obliging them to answer; instead patients are gently solicited to give authentic descriptions–and to talk about issues they would have been reluctant to broach in the first place (ibid.).

However, this interactional strategy on the part of the psychiatrist is far from equitable, trapping patients in what Bergmann describes as a 'double-bind'. If patients provide information voluntarily, then that is to accept what the psychiatrist is insinuating in their (typically negative) assertions concerning the patient's personal predicament. Yet to reject the insinuation is to risk confronting the psychiatrist and being assessed as requiring treatment, and ultimately being hospitalized. Bergmann, therefore, identifies the contradictory meaning structure of psychiatric discretion, relating such contradiction to the institutional character of psychiatry itself. He powerfully concludes by contending that psychiatry as an institution is (as are the candidate patients it assesses) 'caught and twisted between medicine and morality' (1992: 159). This essential underlying tension, or contradictory structure, exhibits itself at the level of discourse, the moment-by-moment unfolding of interaction and, consequently, is only exposed through detailed attention to the participants' use of language *in situ*.

To summarize this section, then, discourse-based research in health communication is extensive, covering a wide range of health and health communication themes. Most research has clustered in the area of professional–patient relations, in particular consultations between doctors and patients. In the following section we offer a detailed exposition of the function in such encounters, as well as considering the discursive routines of personnel (which are often overlooked in health communication research).

What can discourse analysis tell us about health communication?

As mentioned in the section 'What is health communication?' above, much discourse-based research in the field has sought to highlight patients' perspectives. In the case of the medical encounter, researchers such as Mishler (1984), Fisher (1991) and Fairclough (1992) critically expose the interactional asymmetries that arise between doctors and patients, in particular how the perspective of the patient (the personal and social context of their illness) is marginalized by the doctor in pursuit of a medico-technical understanding of the patient's condition. In order to illustrate the type of analyses emblematic of these seminal and often dramatic discourse studies, we will consider a sample of discourse analysis conducted by Fairclough (1992) on the basis of clinical data first presented and discussed by Mishler in his 1984 pioneering work *Discourse of Medicine: Dialectics of Medical Interviews*. Fairclough's analysis serves as a fine illustration of how attention to discourse structures can expose power and dominance at work in the medical consultation.

P = Patient; D = Doctor
1   D: Hm hm (.3) now what do you mean by a sour stomach?
2   P: (1.1) What's a sour stomach? A heartburn
3   like a heartburn or someth[ing.
4   D: [Does it burn over here?
5   P: Yeah
6   It li- I think- I think it like- If you take a needle
7   and stick [ya right [....there's a pain right here [
8   D: [Hm hm [Hm hm   [Hm hm
9   P: and and then it goes from here on this side to this side.
10 D: Hm hm does it [go into the back?
11 P: [It's a:ll up here. No. It's all right
12   [Up here in the front.
13 D: [Yeah And when do you get that?
14 P: (1.3) Wel:l when I eat something wrong
15 D: How- how soon after you eat it?
16 P: Wel:l probably an hour maybe [less.
17 D: [About an hour?

18	P:	Maybe less I've cheated and I've been
19		drinking which I shouldn't have done.
20	D:	Does drinking make it worse?
21	P:	Ho ho uh ooh Yes (1.0) especially the carbonation and the alcohol.
22	D:	Hm hm how much do you drink?
23	P:	(1.5) I don't know enough to make me
24		sleep at night and that's quite a bit.
25	D:	One or two drinks a day?
26	P:	O:h no no no humph it's more like ten [at night
27	D:	[How many drinks – a night.
28	P:	At night.
29	D:	Whaddya ta- What type of drinks? I [((unclear))
30	P:	[Oh vodka yeah vodka
31		and ginger ale.
32	D:	How long have you been drinking that heavily?
33	P:	(1.4) Since I've been married.
34	D:	How long is that?
35	P:	((giggle)) Four years. ((giggle)). (Mishler, 1984)

As Fairclough (1992: 140) observes in his commentary on this medical consultation, the encounter is organized around the doctor's questions, to which the patient then responds, and thus the doctor closely controls the organization of the dialogue by opening and closing each interactional cycle while acknowledging/accepting the patient's answers. Consequently the doctor is controlling the turn-taking system. The patient's contributions are therefore restricted, since she talks only when the doctor prompts her – for example by asking her a question. The doctor, conversely, is not granted turns at talk but takes them when the patient has finished her answers or when she has provided sufficient information to answer the doctor's query.

Another feature of the interview is the introduction, maintaining and changing of topic. The doctor sets the topical agenda since, typically, it is he who introduces new subjects or chooses whether to ignore the pursuit of new topics initiated by the patient. For instance, at line 18, the patient mentions that she has 'cheated' – that is 'drinking', which she 'shouldn't have done'. The doctor, however, does not follow up this potentially revealing and significant personal admission, instead concentrating on the medical details of the patient's alcohol consumption. Fairclough suggests (1992: 141) that, given his narrow focus on medical aspects as opposed to the patient's social and personal concerns, the doctor is limiting topics in accordance with a pre-set agenda, which the patient is prevented from disrupting. Moreover, as well as severely restricting the patient's access to new topics, the doctor further constrains her turns through the consistent use of closed questions. Such questions (e.g. 'Does it burn over here?' and 'Does it go into the back?') produce only information-limited 'yes/no' responses and do not allow the patient to take the floor in the same way that question such as 'Tell me about your concern' would do. Yet, for all that, the doctor does employ a number of more open questions that, in theory, would provide more substantial access to the floor: 'How many drinks a night?', 'What type of drinks?'. But these questions are tightly focused on specific details (e.g. the type and quantity of alcohol) in relation the patient's drinking and do not encourage her (as her responses demonstrate) to introduce new topics germane to the personal and social context of her troubles.

It is also telling how the doctor's questions often interrupt and overlap the patient's as still incomplete prior turns. This would seem to indicate that the doctor has received all the information he considers necessary from the patient's particular reply and is simply cleaving to the pre-set agenda or routine mentioned above, an agenda through which he passes swiftly and efficiently (at least in terms of speed and verbal economy). According to Fairclough, this routine, from the patient's point of view, can appear as a series of disjointed and unpredictable questions, a strategy of interrogation that might well account for the patient's hesitations before she produces her answers.

This analysis is, as Fairclough himself concedes, one-sided in its focus upon interactional authority and control. Nevertheless, it insightfully and powerfully demonstrates how the doctor interactionally dominates the encounter, limiting the conversational resources of the patient in order to pursue a pre-determined medical agenda. The doctor's authority is manifested in linguistic features (such as turn-taking or topic shifts) that are used to enact interactional control. Controlling the discourse in this way allows the doctor to respond to the scientific, medical aspects of the patient's complaint, without appealing to the condition in the context of other aspects of the patient's personal, social life. In this sense the doctor manifests the voice of medicine (Mishler, 1984), whereas the patient's responses mix the voice of medicine with the voice of 'the lifeworld' (Habermas, 1984), the voice of ordinary experience. The voice of medicine, according to Fairclough (1992: 144), 'embodies a technological rationality which treats illness in terms of context-free clusters of physical symptoms, whereas the lifeworld embodies a "common sense" rationality which places illness in the context of other aspects of the patient's life'.

Critical analysis of the doctor–patient relationship (for example research by Mishler, 1984 and Todd, 1989) has commonly characterized the exchange as an asymmetrical encounter between the two parties, the doctor exhibiting almost exclusive concern for medical topics at the expense of attending to the social, biographical context of patients' lives (Fisher, 1991: 158). According to Fisher, this medical relationship rests on a medical model of health and illness which sees disease as the organic pathology of the individual patient. The problem to be targeted exists in the patient's body – organs and body parts malfunction in mechanistic fashion – and, accordingly, non-organic problems and hence the social contexts of patients' lives do not fit comfortably into this medical account of illness (ibid.).

What discourse analytic interrogations of provider–patient exchanges are able to expose, then, is how diverse and contrasting perspectives are commonly brought into being during the health care interaction. As Fairclough (1992: 144) concludes close critical analysis of the doctor's controlling medical interaction and the ideological voices that shape it are means by which to grasp routine, standardized health practices at a micro-analytical level, affording penetrating insights into health care as a mode of professionalism and social practice.

Although the doctor is undoubtedly a central figure in the healthcare system, many other personnel play a crucial, if less public and authoritative, part in the delivery of healthcare. At the expense of other medical staff, discourse studies interrogating the practitioner–patient encounter have tended to focus on the doctor–patient relationship. Yet the range of discursive practices that takes place in healthcare settings is diverse indeed and, of course, no less significant than the communicative routines of physicians. To illustrate the point, let us consider a stretch of discourse featuring a hospital chaplain interacting with a patient who had recently suffered a stroke. The exchange, taken from a study into the discourse of spiritual and pastoral care (Harvey *et al.*, 2008), aimed, among other things, to illustrate the role that members of non-physician personnel play in the healthcare system. The extract represents just one of the many routine conversations conducted by the chaplain with patients during the course of the priest's regular spiritual and pastoral duties at a British hospital.

C=Chaplain; P=Patient

1　C　You were saying that you were er feeling a bit bored today.
2　P　((unclear)) that's right yeah.
3　C　Uh uh.
4　P　Because it's pretty boring in the hospi
5　C　Yeah. Just lying in in in the
6　P　Bed fed up
7　C　Uh hu yeah.
8　　　　　silence
9　C　You finding it a bit frustrating to be
10　P　Yeah because I had a stroke.
11　C　Yes.
12　P　That makes it a lot worse.
13　C　Yes uh uh.
14　C　Would you be able to tell me a little bit about how that affects you?
15　　　　　How having this
16　P　((unclear))
17　C　having had this stroke affects you?
18　P　It affects in just about everything honest.
19　C　Yeah.
20　P　I can't talk properly ((unclear)) speech got brain damage
21　　　　　so I can't explain just like that.
22　C　Yes uh uh. I understand. But it has always seemed to me
23　　　　　that you you you explain things very well.
24　P　Oh if you say so ((laughs))
25　C　Uh hu. Yeah.
26　P　I try to
27　C　Yes.
28　P　explain as best I can.
29　C　Uh hu.
30　P　((unclear))
31　C　Yes.
32　P　See what happens.
33　C　Yes.

Unlike the somewhat predictable structure of physician–patient discourse, the patterns and dynamics of interaction here resemble those of everyday conversation more than a predetermined, institutional exchange. There doesn't appear to be an obvious pre-allocated sequence or agenda, which character-istically informs the more standardized doctor–patient consultation. Indeed, looking at this stretch of discourse without recourse to precise contextual details, it would be difficult to identify precisely the genre (and consequently the participants) of the extract; it could relate to a range of communicative situations, for instance a lay visitor (such as a family member or friend) speaking to a patient. The interaction has a more informal, less institutional flavour–an observation borne out by the regular and relatively equal distribution of turns at talk. Moreover, though the chaplain appears to be in a position from which to ask questions and focus on particular topics in relation to the patient's wellbeing, he nevertheless takes on a 'relaxed' listening role, seemingly encouraging further free, expansive responses from the patient (note the backchannelling at lines 3, 7, 11, 13, 19, etc.–those minimal utterances such as 'yeah' and 'uh uh', which indicate listenership and encourage further disclosure).

Yet, for all its discursive uniqueness, the above extract nonetheless overlaps with other forms of spoken interaction. For instance, the sequence contains properties of discourse common in counselling discourse (for example, the emphasis on encouraging personal disclosure), as well as in everyday informal conversation. However, chaplain–patient interaction, though displaying properties of various genres, is still a form of institutional discourse, and therefore is organized towards a specific end (Telles Ribeiro, 1996); and there are interactional features present that evince an institutional character. Note, for instance, how the chaplain, apart from orienting to his official roles (through his eliciting personal disclosures from the patient and the patient responding accordingly), encourages the patient to talk about his illness, specifically the syntactical structure of elicitation: 'Would you be able to tell me a little bit about how that affects you?' (line 14). Taking the grammatical form of a question, this utterance is, though indirectly constructed, a request for the patient to disclose personal information. Its indirect, polite form presupposes some distance between the participants and potentially displays awareness that it is a face-threatening request, an imposition on the patient that requires his disclosing personal information that is almost certainly uncomfortable and intimate. Such a tentative, attenuated request would most likely be out of place or unnecessary between intimates in everyday non-institutional conversation, where requests for information typically take a more direct, less polite form. If, for example, the chaplain were conversing with a friend at home who was ill, a marked polite request for details concerning his or her wellbeing (such as 'Would you be able to tell me how that affects you') would most certainly be inappropriate, or at the very least somewhat unusual.

What kind of/how much data do you need to study health communication?

Many studies in health communication are purely qualitative in their approach to analysis, and are based on relatively small databases and do not originate in large collections of data. This has led to another recent development in health language research, which has seen a number of researchers calling for studies to make greater use of more substantial datasets, while at the same time recognizing that quantitative inquiries alone, which deprive linguistic data of context, are unlikely to be sufficient for providing an understanding of communication (Skelton and Hobbs, 1999a, b). Consequently there has been an increase in health language studies that integrate both qualitative and quantitative approaches to data analysis, employing, in the first analytical instance, corpus tools as their primary methodology, supplementing these approaches with a range of theoretical and methodological perspectives (Thomas and Wilson, 1996; Skelton and Hobbs, 1999a, b; Skelton et al., 1999, 2002; Adolphs et al., 2004).

Adolphs et al. (2004) provide a detailed illustration of how a combined quantitative and qualitative methodology that draws on corpus technology can enhance our understanding of a particular healthcare setting. Their research is based on a sub-sample of the Nottingham Health Communication Corpus (NHCC). The NHCC is a one million word corpus comprising of a variety of different communication contexts and including a number of different groups of health professionals and patients. The corpus is unique in that it contains both written and spoken (though mainly spoken) modes of communication and represents the communicative routines of non-physician personnel: pharmacists, nurses, midwives, mental health workers and chaplains. Since doctor–patient discourse studies have dominated health communication research, with the consequence of helping to contribute to the marginalization of certain non-physician service providers (Hak, 1999), the NHCC aims to represent the neglected communicative routines of such providers and describe their contribution to health care. Adolphs et al. (2004) investigate the language used in a 50,000 word sample of the NHCC that features transcribed recordings of interactions between health advisors for the UK National Health Service telephone helpline NHS-Direct and callers to this service. A corpus linguistics approach is used in the first instance to develop a profile of the sub-corpus. An analysis of keywords, or words that occur with a significantly higher frequency in the target corpus when compared to a reference corpus reveals the following 10 most significant keywords in the NHS-Direct data:

1. OK/Okay
2. Your
3. Antibiotics
4. Diarrhoea
5. Call
6. Direct
7. NHS
8. Information
9. You
10. Help

The comparison was carried out with a 5-million-word corpus of mainly casual conversation (see also Adolphs, 2006). The list of keywords contains references to medication (*antibiotics*), ailments (*diarrhoea*), the nature of the discourse (*information*), the mode of the discourse (*call*) and the medical context (*NHS, Direct*). All of these items contribute to the characterization of this corpus. At the same time, we find keywords that mark listener responses in an advice-giving setting (*ok, okay*) and the pronouns *you* and *your*, which indicate the 'other-oriented' nature of the discourse, in this case towards the patient. Subsequent analysis of extended stretches of discourse confirms this tendency in the text through the health advisor's carefully explaining the interactive process and eliciting information from the caller [HA = health advisor and C = caller].

HA:	Yeah, you see you have to do the whole course, you see. Right. What I'm gonna do is just take some details of you for our confidential files.
C:	Eh ha
HA:	If I may, and then get a nurse to call you back it will be
C:	OK
HA:	Approximately around about 40, 45 minutes at the moment. Or, a little later
HA:	[…] Thank you very much. Right, have you called us before about yourself?

This extract also illustrates the need for the health advisor to strike a balance between the almost mechanical elicitation of information and putting the caller at ease with the advice giving process (Adolphs *et al.*, 2007). The latter is achieved through the use of modal markers and mitigating devices (just, may, little, approximately) and a series of politeness strategies. Modal terms such as 'just' and 'may' introduce optionality and tentativeness into the conversation, giving the appearance of allowing the patient to make their own decision on whether or not to follow the advice that is given. In the NHS-Direct exchanges 'may' is used mainly to soften the more or less categorical listing of side effects of certain treatments or conditions, or to suggest further action on the part of the patient. As such, it serves a dual role—as an epistemic softener and, perhaps less obviously, as a politeness device. It also worth noting that 'may' is also used in conjunction with other modalizers which encode further politeness and help to prevent the operative from sounding too authoritative, a consequence that would probably distance the two parties interpersonally.

Using a corpus-based approach as a way into the data, or indeed (subsequently) into discourse analysis at any level, can thus provide interesting insights that neither of the two approaches could generate when used in isolation. The question about the size of the data set thus has to be answered in relation to the research question that is being pursued. Given the difficulties associated with gathering health communication data due to privacy, confidentiality and ethical issues that often arise from such an endeavour, it is reassuring to know that the analysis of even very small data sets, both in terms qualitative and quantitative approaches, can be very revealing and can lead to new insights about this particular domain of discourse. Indeed patterns of communication are liable to emerge from interrogating only very small corpora, particularly if such corpora represent a very a unique and specific area of discourse (O'Keeffe *et al.*, 2011).

Conclusion

This chapter has aimed to provide an overview of some of the key studies that examine the inter-relation between discourse and healthcare. This exciting field of enquiry is broad indeed, as the reader will hopefully appreciate by now, and still continues to expand rapidly, as discourse analysts (and in some instances professionals themselves) interrogate ever refined and marginal spheres of health communication and thereby shed light on discursive practices that have hitherto avoided linguistic scrutiny. What a number of the studies examined in this chapter demonstrate is that use of discourse in healthcare is not simply a means of conveying information and representing particular states of affairs. Discourse in fact constitutes medical procedures and hence helps determine certain clinical outcomes, outcomes that are liable in some instances to have a profound impact on patients (consider, for example, the role of discourse in the psychiatric intake interview and how some specific, negatively evaluated linguistic responses may lead to patients' being hospitalized).

Accordingly, analysing medical discourse not only contributes to our knowledge and under-standing of the various social and clinical activities that take place in healthcare settings–not to mention the role that discourse plays in conveying and shaping individuals' personal experiences of health illness–but also has very practical consequences with regard to engendering more equitable and humane practices in healthcare. Among its many functions, the discourse analysis of healthcare affords rich opportunities for exploring the situated routines of health professionals and is thereby able to draw attention to potential asymmetries between professionals and patients–asymmetries and other interactional tensions that might not be apparent to the participants at the time of interaction. It is revealing that a number of health professionals themselves are showing increasing interest in discourse analysis and in the insights it offers, conducting their own discourse-based research (often in conjunction with discourse analysts) to help improve clinical communication and to enhance patient satisfaction in a range of medical contexts.

Further reading

Adolphs, S., S., Atkins S., and Harvey, K. (2007) 'Caught between professional requirements and inter-personal needs: vague language in healthcare contexts', in J. Cutting (ed.), *Vague Language Explored*. Basingstoke: Palgrave Macmillan, pp. 62–78.

Babaul-Hirji, Hewson, S. and Frescura, M. (2010) 'A sociolinguistic exploration of genetic counselling discourse involving a child with a new genetic diagnosis', *Patient Education and Counselling*, 78: 40–45.

Brown, B., Crawford, P. and Carter, R. (2006) *Evidence Based Health Communication*. Buckingham: Open University Press.

Gwyn, R. (2002) *Communicating Health and Illness*. Sage: London.

Sarangi, S. (2004) 'Towards a communicative mentality in medical and healthcare practice', *Communication & Medicine*, 1 (1): 1–11.

Skelton, J. (2008) *Language and Clinical Communication: This Bright Babylon*. Oxon: Radcliffe Publishing.

Kevin Harvey and Svenja Adolphs

References

Adolphs, S. (2006) *Introducing Electronic Text Analysis*. Abingdon: Routledge.

Adolphs, S., Brown, B., Carter, R., Crawford, C., and Sahota, O. (2004) 'Applying corpus linguistics in a health care context', *Journal of Applied Linguistics*, 1 (1): 9–28.

Atkinson, P. (1999) 'Medical discourse, evidentiality and the construction of professional responsibility', in S. Sarangi and C. Robert (eds.) *Talk, Work and Institutional Order: Discourses in Medicine, Mediation and Management Settings*. Berlin: Mouton de Gruyter, pp. 75–107.

Baron, N. (1998) 'Letters by phone or speech by other means: the linguistics of email', *Language and Communication*, 18: 133–170.

Bergmann, J. R. (1992) 'Veiled morality: notes on discretion in psychiatry', in P. Drew and J. Heritage (eds.) *Talk at Work: Interaction in Institutional Settings*. Cambridge: Cambridge University Press, pp. 137–162.

Brown, B., Crawford, P., and Carter, R. (2006) *Evidence Based Health Communication*. Buckingham: Open University Press.

Candlin, S. (2000) 'New dynamics in the nurse-patient relationship?', in S. Sarangi and M. Coulthard (eds.) *Discourse and Social Life*. London: Longman, pp. 230–245.

Candlin, C. N., Maley, Y., and Sutch, H. (1999) 'Industrial instability and the discourse of enterprise bargaining', in S. Sarangi and C. Roberts (eds.) *Talk, Work and Institutional Order: Discourse in Medical, Mediation and Management Settings*. Berlin: Mouton De Gruyter, pp. 323–349.

Clerehan, R. and Buchbinder, R. (2006) 'Towards a more valid account of functional text quality: the case of the patient information leaflet', *Text and Talk: An Interdisciplinary Journal of Language, Discourse, and Communication Studies*, 26 (1): 39–68.

Cobb, M. (2001) 'Walking on Water? the moral foundations of Chaplaincy", in H. Orchard (ed.), *Spirituality in Health Care Contexts*. London: Jessica Kingsley Publishing.

Crawford, P., Brown, B., and Nolan, P. (1998) *Communicating Care: The Language of Nursing*. Cheltenham, Gloucester: Stanley Thornes.

Fairclough, N. (1992) *Discourse and Social Change*. Cambridge, England: Polity Press.

Fairclough, N. (1995) *Critical Discourse Analysis: The Critical Study of Language*. New York: Longman.

Fisher, S., (1991) 'A discourse of the social: medical talk/power talk/oppositional talk?', *Discourse and Society*, 2(2): 157–182.

Francis, G. and Kramer-Dahl, A. (2004) 'Grammar in the construction of medical case histories', in C. Coffin, A. Hewings, and K. O' Halloran (eds.) *Applying English Grammar: Functional and Corpus Approaches*. London: Arnold, pp. 172–196.

Habermas, J. (1984) *Theory of Communicative Action*. London: Heinemann.

Hak, T. (1999) 'Text? and con-text? Talk bias in studies of health care work', in S. Sarangi and C. Roberts (eds.) *Talk, Work and the Institutional Order*. Berlin: Mouton De Gruyter, pp. 427–451.

Harvey, K., Brown, B., Crawford, P., and Candlin, S. (2008) ' "Elicitation hooks": a discourse analysis of chaplain-patient interaction in pastoral and spiritual care', *The Journal of Pastoral Care and Counseling*, 62: 43–62.

ten Have, P. (1995) 'Disposal negotiations in general practice consultations', in A. Firth (ed.) *The Discourse of Negotiation: Studies of Language in the Workplace*. Oxford: Pergamon, pp. 319–344.

ten Have, P. (2001) 'Applied conversation analysis', in A. McHoul and M. Rapley (eds.) *How to Analyse Talk in Institutional Settings: A Casebook of Methods*. London: Continuum, pp. 3–11.

Hobbs, P. (2003) 'The use of evidentiality in physician's progress notes', *Discourse Studies*, 5: 451–478.

Jeffries, L. (2000) *Don't Throw Out the Baby with the Bathwater: In Defence of Theoretical Eclecticism in Stylistics*. Working Paper. Poetics and Linguistics Association, Huddersfield, UK.

Kress, G. (1988) *Linguistic Processes in Sociocultural Practice*. Oxford: Oxford University Press.

Lobley, J. (2001) 'Whose personality is it anyway? The production of "personality" in a diagnostic interview', in A. McHoul and M. Rapley (eds.) *How to Analyse Talk in Institutional Settings: A Casebook of Methods*. London: Continuum International, pp. 113–123.

Madill, A. L., Widdicombe, S., and Barkham, M. (2001) 'The potential of conversation analysis for psychotherapy research', *The Counseling Psychologist*, 29 (3): 413–434.

McCarthy, D. and Rapley, M. (2001) 'Far from the madding crowd: psychiatric diagnosis as the management of moral accountability', in A. McHoul and M. Rapley (eds.) *How to Analyse Talk in Institutional Settings: A Casebook of Methods*. London: Continuum International, pp. 159–167.

McHoul, A. and Rapley, M. (2001) *How to Analyze Talk in Institutional Settings: A Casebook of Methods*. London and New York: Continuum.

Mishler, E. G. (1984) *The Discourse of Medicine Dialectics in Medical Interviews.* Norwood, NJ: Ablex.

O'Keeffe, A., Clancy, B., and Adolphs, S. (2011) *Introducing Pragmatics in Use.* Abingdon: Routledge.

Palmer, D. (2000) 'Identifying delusional discourse: issues of rationality, reality and power', *Sociology of Health and Illness,* 22 (5): 661–678.

Parry, R. (2004) 'Communication during goal-setting in physiotherapy treatment sessions', *Clinical Rehabilitation,* 18: 668–682.

Pilnick, A. (1999) ' "Patient counselling" by pharmacists: advice, information or instruction?', *The Sociological Quarterly,* 40: 613–622.

Pomerantz, A. (1980) 'Telling my side: "limited access" as a "fishing" device', *Sociological Inquiry,* 50, 186–198.

Sarangi, S. (2004) 'Towards a communicative mentality in medical and healthcare practice', *Communication & Medicine,* 1 (1): 1–11.

Skelton, J. R. and Hobbs, F. (1999a) 'Descriptive study of cooperative language in primary care consultations by male and female doctors', *British Medical Journal,* 318: 576–579.

Skelton, J. R. and Hobbs, F. (1999b) 'Concordancing: the use of language-based research in medical communication', *The Lancet,* 353: 108–111.

Skelton, J. R., Murray, J., and Hobbs, F. (1999) 'Imprecision in medical communication: study of a doctor talking to patients with serious illness', *Journal of the Royal Society of Medicine,* 92: 620–625.

Skelton, J., Wearn, A., and Hobbs, F. (2002) 'A concordance-based study of metaphoric expressions used by GPs and patients in consultation', *British Journal of General Practice,* 52: 114–118.

Telles Ribeiro, B. (1996) 'Conflict talk in a psychiatric discharge interview: Struggling between personal and official footings', in C. R. Caldas-Coulthard and M. Coulthard (eds.) *Texts and Practices: Readings in Critical Discourse Analysis.* London: Routledge, pp. 179–193.

Thomas, J. and Wilson, A. (1996) 'Methodologies for studying a corpus of doctor-patient interaction', in Thomas, J. and Short, M. (eds.) *Using Corpora for Language Research.* London: Longman, pp. 92–109.

Todd, A. D. (1989) *Intimate Adversaries: Cultural Conflicts Between Doctors and Women Patients.* Philadelphia, PA: University of Pennsylvania Press.

van Naerssen, M. (1985) 'Medical records: one variation of physician's language', *International Journal of the Sociology of Language,* 51: 43–74.

34

Discourses in the language of the law

Edward Finegan

The most dramatic and most often dramatized stage for displaying and observing legal discourse is the courtroom. There judges preside over criminal and civil trials in which the task is to determine the facts and, in light of them and the application of relevant law, to render a verdict or decision. Courtroom trials are witness to opening and closing statements, to direct examination and cross-examination with objections by counsel and rulings by the court, and to jury instructions; they are preceded by examination of prospective jurors under oath, a process known as *voir dire*, and may be peppered by in-chambers discussions between judge and attorneys; and they often draw to a close with jury deliberations. Television shows treating the law emphasize courtroom drama in criminal cases, and some semi-judicial civil law courtroom shows have large followings, for instance the US program "Judge Judy," which has been the focus of professional discourse analysis (van der Houwen, 2005). Some domains of legal discourse exercise their strongest impact on litigants, some on jurors, some on attorneys, some on judges, and so on. Appellate court (i.e. court of appeals) opinions exert extraordinary impact on judges and attorneys and are the most widely influential discourses in common law theory and practice. The role of legislation—the literal "language of the law"—is overshadowed insofar as its interpretation by appellate courts constitutes the precedents of common law. Such appellate opinions also suffuse law school classrooms and teach prospective lawyers what it means to use discourse in a lawyerly fashion, to think like a lawyer—indeed, to be a lawyer (Mertz, 2007).

Although some domains of legal discourse are better researched than others, legal discourse in general is understudied, and no domain is yet well understood. Among the most important but least studied forms of discourse, jury deliberations remain largely immune to analysis because of their secrecy (but see Conley and Conley, 2009); the same holds for face-to-face interaction between attorneys and clients (but see Sarat and Felstiner, 1995). Legislation itself has been examined, but little is known about the negotiations that underlie legislative drafting (see e.g. Bhatia *et al.*, 2003 and about cross-linguistic and cross-cultural perspectives Gotti and Williams, 2010). Still, the importance of the various forms of legal discourse cannot be exaggerated, and the growing interest in them is to be applauded.

What is discourse in the language of the law?

Given the wide scope of the law and its reach beyond courts and attorneys, most kinds of legal discourse cannot be addressed in a chapter. This chapter notably excludes statutory language, the language of legal consultation and arbitration, jury deliberations, and all non-public discourses. Far more legal work and dispute resolution takes place orally and in private between attorneys and clients, attorneys and attorneys, attorneys and prosecutors, and attorneys and officers of the court than the record of published research might suggest. Conclusions from these interactions may be memorialized in writing, and some forms of interaction, such as police interviews of suspects, are increasingly video-recorded, but we lack sufficient substantive information about the discourse of such consequential interactions (but cf. Berk-Seligson, 2009 and Eades, 2009). Neither can we address certain registers of courtroom interaction such as jury instructions, by which jurors are instructed in the law as it relates to the issue before them. Likewise for the comprehensibility of legal documents and the plain English movement—important matters to which discourse analysts still have much to contribute. Nor can certain complex arenas in legal language even be noted beyond citing bibliographies (Levi, 1994), standard works on legal language (Tiersma, 1999), textbooks and handbooks about forensic linguistics (Coulthard and Johnson, 2010; Eades, 2010), and the *International Journal of Speech, Language and the Law*. In those arenas there are adequate and accurate transcriptions of courtroom trials and other oral proceedings, courtroom interpretation, second and foreign language speakers, non-standard dialect speakers and speakers of dialects unfamiliar to the courts, and an increasing range of forensic matters, including discourse analysis of interrogations, confessions, or accounts of conspiring and defamation (Shuy, 1998, 2010). Indeed, what might be understood even in a narrow interpretation of legal discourse includes so many registers and discourse-related questions that even a superficial analysis would be impossible here.

Centrally, the phrases "language of the law" and "legal discourse" refer to (a) language that arises in statutory law; (b) the interpretation of statutory law in judicial opinions; (c) various forms of courtroom language, including opening statements and closing arguments, direct examination and cross-examination of witnesses, and jury instructions; (d) written contracts that create legal obligations, including rental agreements, insurance policies, wills, and liability waivers. Less central perhaps, but crucially important in people's lives and a frequent topic of analysis by forensic linguists, is the wide array of registers representing interaction between institutional operatives and ordinary citizens, including police interviews of persons of interest and criminal suspects; ordinary electronic and other correspondence examined in connection with possibly illegal communication; and face-to-face and telephone conversations (for example, surreptitiously recorded interaction between persons suspected of conspiring to commit a crime).

I focus here on three kinds of legal discourse: the formal talk of lay litigants in small claims courts; the language of attorneys and witnesses in cross-examination, as illustrated in a brief excerpt from a rape trial; and certain aspects of the discourse of appellate court opinions. The first forcefully illustrates how the ordinary discourse of some social groups, when deployed in a courtroom setting, can place members of those groups at a disadvantage before the law, as compared with other social groups. Both the first and the second kinds demonstrate the conflict between views of fairness and justice held by ordinary citizens and the enormous power of institutionalized and structural superiority. The third kind is examined here because appellate court opinions exercise such a powerful effect at so many levels, from law school students, who are in turn the main players in propagating the social structures imposed by and through the law, to attorneys and lower court judges and the litigants and other participants in their courtrooms, and out on to the streets, where such opinions ultimately have their most important effects. In all three arenas—and all those not touched on here—"the details of legal discourse matter because language is the essential mechanism through which the power of the law is realized, exercised, reproduced, and occasionally challenged and subverted" (Conley and O'Barr, 2005: 129). This chapter is written with that observation in mind.

Demographics and lay litigants' talk in court

In small claims or magistrates' courts, litigants aim for dispute resolution over relatively small economic matters (as compared to ordinary civil suits), but the disputes in small claims courts often represent matters of social importance and quotidian views of fairness and justice. In such courts, litigants represent themselves, usually without guidance or assistance from attorneys. Extensive work in the 1980s revealed the extent to which different forms of lay discourse can affect the internal workings of litigation in small claims courts, and in particular whether characteristic discourse practices of speakers from different social groups and genders influence the outcome of their claims. Conley and O'Barr (1990) present a distilled analysis of 466 small claims court cases in six US jurisdictions. Their ethnography is rich in detail and we focus on only one aspect: the rule-oriented accounts and relational accounts identified as the two principal kinds of discourse characteristic of lay litigants.

Rule-oriented accounts are characterized by a tendency to: (1) base claims for relief on violations of specific rules, duties, obligations (as in contracts); (2) follow a sequential order in a straight-line narrative telling; (3) deal with cause and effect and human agency; (4) be highly factual in ways that are relevant to the law; (5) report names, dates, content of conversation in detail and as relevant to a specific alleged violation; (6) describe documents in detail; and (7) assume no prior knowledge. They are, in other words, just what a judge needs to know in order to address the legal matter at issue, just what a judge is pleased to hear. Put otherwise, rule-oriented accounts tend to honor Grice's maxims of relevance, manner, quantity, and quality.

Below is an example of *a rule-oriented account*, as presented in a small claims court case in which an employee (Dan Webb) sued his employer (represented by Lynn Hogan) in connection with a promotional bonus for a spectrometer sale that the employee felt entitled to but did not receive.

> JUDGE: Let's turn over to you ma'am. We do need your name, business address, and connection with the uh, Instrument Supply Company.
> [...]
> HOGAN: Okay, thank you. Um, as uh Dan stated, uh, Instrument Supply is a scientific distributor. Uh, we represent over 1500 manufacturers and we sell over 60,000 products. Um, we are continuously being exposed to gimmicks from our manufacturers to boost the sale of their products. Uh, the only control that management has, um, over these prod-, over these promotions, is to pick and choose the ones that uh, best support our local selling programs, where we want the local emphasis to be. Um, then it is my responsibility, as well as the district manager, to assist the sales reps in focusing on these sanctioned programs. Uh, in order to keep track of what we have sanctioned, we have a calculation sheet that specifically shows the sales representative what we are sanctioning. I have highlighted that that particular promotion for spectrometers was on the first half, from March until August of 1984, giving the particular payouts, and as you'll see there is a $200 payout there for 1001 Spectrometer.

[there follows additional testimony by Hogan, a question from the judge, and a further lengthy reply from Hogan; then...]

> JUDGE: Go right ahead.
> HOGAN: For the second half, and this goes with that one other thing that I gave you, this is the second half PIP calculation sheet, and you will see on there is no Diller and Macy payout for the second half.

(Conley and O'Barr, 1990: 64–66)

In her testimony, witness Hogan makes no reference to any personal relationship with Mr. Webb or to irrelevant past history but focuses on whether Instrument Supply Company had a contractual obligation to pay certain monies to employee Webb, as he claimed. In other words, her testimony addresses the particular issue in dispute and does so with appropriate details of dates, monetary amounts, and agency. In that sense, her testimony honors the Gricean cooperative principle as they apply to this legal proceeding.

In contrast to rule-oriented accounts, relational accounts tend to identify claims for legal relief (1) based on general rules of social conduct; (2) focused on personal status and social position; (3) displaying a view that decent folks who meet their social obligations are entitled to fair treatment; (4) relying on details about the personal life of the speaker and other matters that are irrelevant to the law's concerns; and (5) displaying idiosyncratic treatment of time and of cause and effect. Relational litigants focus on "status and social relationships," believing "that the law is empowered to assign rewards and punishments according to broad notions of social need and entitlement"; they "strive to introduce into the trial the details of their social lives [and] emphasize the social networks in which they are situated, often to the exclusion of the contractual, financial, and property issues that are typically of greater interest to the court"; as Conley and O'Barr (1990: 58) note, "the courts tend to treat such accounts as filled with irrelevancies and inappropriate information, and relational litigants are frequently evaluated as imprecise, rambling, and straying from the central issues."

The account below exemplifies the characteristics of *relational discourse*. Conley and O'Barr characterize the testimony as that of "an unsuccessful plaintiff (Rawls) who has sued her next-door neighbor (Bennett) for removing a hedge on her side of the property line, failing to control the growth of his shrubbery onto her property, and generally harassing her."

JUDGE: You're alleging that these trees and, and the shrubs and apparently the hedge included were removed. When did this happen?

RAWLS: Oh, well now that happened this year. At, uh—

JUDGE: And how did it happen?

RAWLS: Well I can, well, well I have to jump back because, uh, for three years when Mr. Bennett moved back—because he was there once before and then he moved and then he come back into that house—and all the time before—I have to say this though Judge—because all the time before everybody took care of that hedge and they wouldn't let me take care of it. They trimmed it and I even went to Mr. Bennett when he was there before—

JUDGE: Wait a moment. Now the question that I asked you—and I would like to have you answer it—and that is how did the hedge get removed?

RAWLS: Well, um, Mr. Bennett said he told me when he moved back in, uh, because I was taking care of my trees coming up through the hedge, I was cutting them off and he told me not to do that. He said, "Don't do it," he said, [...] And that's when I told him, and he said he would do it, "I and the church would take them out," and I, that's when I told him, "If you need, uh, money for a tool or something to help you. I'll pay for the tool or whatever." And he told, didn't do it, and so then I just had a, the Milehigh, uh, Tree Service come uh, uh, and um, a, and Mr., I had his name here—Mr., uh, Cook come and he come in the house and sat down with me and he looked at that and he said well he surely should help in the shrubbery in the back because there's shrubbery in the back that was over on my line that I've got to take out and I've got pictures of that too, sir. And he said he didn't know what the man or what the man was because the tree was dead why didn't he take it out? Well all he wants to do is harass me so he leaves it there so I have to keep taking the stuff out and bending over and using my trashcan, you know. This is something else. I only got one can. Why don't he pick up his own trash? <u>And so I went ahead and paid it</u>. He told me he would come if I need. He says, "I'll cut it when you need me." Yet I could never get this man. I tried to have him subpoenaed, yet I could never get him because I think Bennett got to him first. But, anyway <u>I got the Milehigh Tree Service here for 275</u>, and I got his mess in the backyard—if you want the pictures here—that's what I took them for.

(Conley and O'Barr 1990: 61–63)

I have underscored the judge's question and what seem the relevant facts in response to it. All the rest—and it is a good deal more than here included, as represented by the bracketed ellipsis points— seems non-responsive or extraneous to the judge's question. In particular, there are details completely irrelevant to the issues in the case (*I only got one can. Why don't he pick up his own trash?*). There are direct quotes of earlier exchanges between Rawls and Bennett (Bennett: *"I and the church would take them out."* Rawls: *"If you need, uh, money for a tool or something to help you. I'll pay for the tool or whatever."*). Supporting statements from third parties are offered and details about the circumstances surrounding those statements (he sat down with me and he said well he surely should help in the shrubbery because…). From first-hand reports by judges who regarded "relational litigants as hard to follow, irrational, and even crazy," Conley and O'Barr (2005: 73) conclude that such litigants "have a harder time gaining access to justice than do their rule-oriented counterparts."

Rule-oriented and relational litigants fall along a continuum, the kinds of discourse exemplified above representing discourse at either end of the spectrum. In an important observation that cannot be pursued here, Conley and O'Barr take the position that relational litigants are more typically women than men and conclude that, if rule-oriented discourse, "powerful discourse," is patriarchal, then

> the law's preferences for it both reflects and reinforces the essential patriarchy of legal discourse.

> When the law, as personified by judges, reacts more favorably to rule-oriented accounts, it is granting privileged status to linguistic practices that historically have been more associated with men than with women … the law is preferring the abstract, rule-driven logic typical of men to the more contextual reasoning that characterizes women. … In this way, the law's linguistic practice reveals its fundamental patriarchy. The details of the interactions between judges and rule-oriented litigants comprise the mechanics of translating patriarchy into social action.

> *(Conley and O'Barr 2005: 74)*

Whether the intervening decades since this research was carried out have made a significant difference in the realization of relational and rule-oriented discourse between men and women is an important question. A broader point useful to underscore is that a system of justice that privileges one style of discourse over another, whether the discourse is based in gender or any other social category, is fundamentally unjust to the extent that members of some groups have greater access to the privileged discourse style than members of other groups. "Over and over," Conley and O'Barr (2005: 74) report, sociolegal analyses "have shown the gap between the claims of law-in-theory and the realities of law-in-action."

Patriarchy in cross-examination of rape victims

Next, in order to exemplify other challenges laypersons face in their efforts to tell a story in their own words and on their own terms, I rehearse a couple of aspects of the character of cross-examination in a rape trial. Instead of the simple, informal procedures of a small claims court, a formal courtroom trial with judge, jury, prosecutor, and defense attorney are in play in an adversarial system, in which cross-examination is inherently hostile. In the original analysis by Matoesian (1993), several aspects of cross-examination are explored in which the plaintiff, the rape victim, is being cross-examined by the defendant's attorney. Matoesian explores the examining attorney's use of topic management and commentary, as well as other phenomena. Here we focus on questions and the forms of the answers they constrain a witness to give. The aim is to illustrate and highlight the following contention: "Cross-examination is an adversarial war of words, sequences, and ideas, a war in which the capability to finesse reality through talk represents the ultimate weapon of domination" (Matoesian, 1993: 1).

In his compelling analysis, Matoesian contrasts the locally managed turn-taking of ordinary conversation with the institutionally structured turn-taking of cross-examination. He notes that, in trial talk,

> the scope of opportunity to talk is both differentially and asymmetrically distributed across social structure [and] nonconversational speech exchange systems preallocate… the opportunities for action. Differential access to the procedures of talk is prestructured or built into the social organization of particular speech exchange systems, constituting a major resource of power and constraining the form of the interaction.
>
> *(Matoesian, 1993: 98–99)*

Like Conley and O'Barr, Matoesian emphasizes the patriarchy of legal discourse, arguing that in a rape trial the accuser is subjected to a discursive rape. In the slightly adapted excerpt below, DA stands for defense attorney; V for victim (the accuser); J for judge; and PA for prosecuting attorney. Underlining indicates stress or emphasis; capital letters indicate raised volume; a degree symbol ° represents speech delivered in a "considerably lowered volume compared with surrounding talk"; (.) represents a gap of a tenth of a second or less; punctuation represents intonation rather than grammatical features. I have normalized spellings (e.g. replacing *did'ju* with *did you*) and omitted most marked time lapses and the attorney's false starts.

DA: Did you know Brian's last <u>name</u>? when you left the parking lot that night?

V: °No

DA: Did you know where Brian was <u>from</u>? when you left the parking lot- that night?

V: °From Illinois.

[two similar exchanges between DA and V are omitted here]

DA: Did you know where Brian <u>worked</u>? when you left the parking lot that night?

V: °No

DA: Did he force you to get in- to his automo<u>bile</u> in the parking lot?

V: °No

DA: How did you wind up in his automobile?

V: I got in.

DA: <u>WHY</u>:::::.

V: Because he said we were going to a party at a friend of his house.

DA: But you didn't kno::w (.) <u>his last name</u> (.) <u>where he worked</u> (.) or <u>where he was from</u> correct?

V: °Yes.

DA: You didn't know a <u>thing about him</u> did you?

V: °No.

(Matoesian, 1993: 131–132)

Several contrasts between ordinary conversational interaction and the asymmetrical rules of turn-taking that govern cross-examination are painfully apparent even in so brief an excerpt. For example, while in face-to-face conversation the speaker holds the floor and can designate the next speaker, in a cross-examination the floor belongs to the examining attorney once the judge so assigns it. In the course of the examination, once an answer is given, the floor automatically returns to the attorney, who thus generally controls topics, timing, and the form of questions. The cross-examining attorney asks questions of the witness, who answers and is constrained to yield back the floor. Other than for a request to clarify, in which the tables are briefly turned as the witness asks a question of the attorney, control of the speech exchanges belongs to the attorney. As a consequence, the institutional norms of turn-taking in courtroom testimony create a greatly imbalanced interaction as compared with ordinary conversation, and only attorneys are practiced in this kind of highly structured exchange. Even a glance at a transcript of an ordinary conversation will reveal how differently structured a cross-examination is. A scarcity of overlapped turns, lengthy pauses between turns (omitted in the transcript above), rhythmic patterns of question and answer, and the brevity and volume of the attorney's questions, and especially the witness's answers, are among other notable characteristics of cross-examination. Five of the witness's eight answers in the excerpt are monosyllabic, and six of eight are marked as of distinctly lowered volume, risking a suggestion of shame to jurors. In addition, the attorney invokes rhetorically persuasive moves such as the three-part list (*last name, where he worked, where he was from*), the "puzzle sequence" (*How did you wind up in his automobile?/I got in./WHY::::.*), and the attempted knock-out punch (*You didn't know a thing about him did you?*). With all the patriarchal assumptions built into such a question, Matoesian argues, a jury could readily believe that the victim is at fault. Whereas, in ordinary conversation, floor and topic selection are locally managed, in cross-examination the defense attorney manages the floor throughout and lends the floor to the witness solely to answer the questions asked. Those questions, as we will see, are generally of the most constraining kind. Judges, of course, may take the floor at any time for any reason, and opposing counsel may object when an objection is warranted; in case of an objection, the interaction between defense attorney and witness is put on hold until the judge rules on the objection.

In the excerpt above, which has equally apportioned turns, the defense attorney speaks about four times as many words as the witness. This imbalance results directly from the structure of the questions, nearly all of which are closed questions that constrain the witness to minimal "yes" or "no" answers in five of her eight turns. Tag questions in particular—"correct?" and "did you?"—are even more powerful: they compel an answer and constrain its form while enabling the defense attorney to enter statements into the record (and jurors' ears) in the attorney's words, not those of the witness, as in the two below:

(1) But you didn't kno::w (.) <u>his last name</u> (.) <u>where he worked</u> (.) or <u>where he was from</u>
(2) You didn't know a <u>thing about him</u>

Such questions differ importantly from open questions, which permit a witness to choose her own words, as in *Because he said we were going to a party at a friend of his house.* But open questions in cross-examination are scarce, the only one in this excerpt (*WHY::::*) being highly accusatory in volume (upper case letters), stress (underscore), and length (four colons). Closed questions and tag questions exert powerful constraints on a witness who is attempting to relate her story. By contrast, open questions leave a witness some latitude in answering. In cross-examination, however, such "open" questions are highly constrained and strategically directed to arenas where an open question is difficult to respond to.

In rehearsing some of Matoesian's findings, Conley and O'Barr view revictimization as having little to do with rules about introducing evidence about a victim's prior sexual history, as is commonly believed. Instead, they urge us to look at "the linguistic details of common cross-examination strategies that are taken for granted in the adversary system," and they argue persuasively as follows:

> Rape victims are ... revictimized ... not by any legal rules or practices peculiar to rape [but by] the ordinary mechanics of cross-examination that, in this extraordinary context, simultaneously reflect and reaffirm men's power over women. The basic linguistic strategies of cross-examination are methods of domination and control.
>
> *(Conley and O'Barr, 2005: 37)*

Appellate court opinions, appellate court briefs, adverbs and intensifiers

Solan (1993: 1) has observed that serious judges struggle with the balance between making what is often a very tough decision and the presentation of an opinion that depicts the decision as logical, even inevitable. In this section I focus on appellate court opinions, including those of the United States Supreme Court. I also report some findings about the discourse of legal briefs submitted by attorneys in appellate cases.

Appellate courts, including state and federal supreme courts in the US, establish jurisprudential precedent. They are thus the most important courts in terms of jurisprudence, but, because they are not trial courts, citizens whose understanding of the legal system derives from film and television dramatizations of courtroom trials in criminal cases may infer a fundamentally skewed view of the justice system. Limiting their scope to the trial record of a court below, augmented by written pleadings and very brief oral presentations from each side, interrupted freely by questions from appellate judges, it is appellate court opinions—majority, minority, concurring, and dissenting—that enshrine jurisprudence. From appellate courts come decisions and opinions that, as much as statutory law, constitute the theoretical and practical jurisprudence of a common law judicial system.

Partly as a consequence of researchers' recognizing the importance of such opinions in supporting a law-abiding society, appellate court decisions have been attracting increasing attention from analysts. Partly, too, scholars have taken an interest in the discourse of appellate cases because technology and the Internet have enabled faster and more complete access to briefs submitted on appeal, to oral arguments offered in appellate court hearings, and to the ensuing decisions and opinions. While discourse analysts have until recently paid little attention to appellate court opinions and less to the briefs submitted in appellate cases, social psychologists and other social scientists are examining them from perspectives likely to disappoint discourse analysts.

In one recent study, specialists in government and political science assessed complexity of thought and language in US Supreme Court opinions solely on the basis of lexical items used in the opinions. What, to a discourse analyst, may seem a mechanical (even naïve) tool for gauging complexity of thought and language is nevertheless a tool whose validity is supported by impressive published credentials in the scholarly literature of social psychology. While this is not the appropriate venue in which to critique such methods, it is useful to highlight selected findings so as to illustrate the kinds of questions social scientists are asking about legal discourse.

Using a content analysis program called Linguistic Inquiry and Word Count (LIWC), which is "designed to parse the complexity of words and cognitive thought" in various kinds of discourse, Owens and Wedeking (2010) explored such complexity in US Supreme Court opinions, aiming to measure the clarity of opinions by examining their "cognitive complexity." Fundamental to their enterprise is the assumption that objective linguistic measurements of (ostensibly) greater cognitive complexity in an opinion reflect less clarity. Relying on a train of work by social psychologists (see e.g. Tausczik and Pennebaker, 2010), they claim: "Less cognitive complexity may highlight an 'ability to penetrate to the essence of key issues' while, conversely, increasing levels of cognitive complexity may represent 'muddled, confused, and vacillating thought' " (Owens and Wedeking, 2010: 14). From more than 2,700 cases decided over a 25-year period ending in 2007, they examined nearly 5,800 opinions (majority, concurring, dissenting, and mixed), each one treated as an independent observation. Focusing solely on lexicon, LIWC tabulates "indicators" of causation (e.g. *because, effect, hence*), insight (*think, know, consider*), tentativeness (*maybe, fairly, perhaps*), certainty (*always, absolutely, clearly*), negation (*no, never*), and others, along with the percentage of words containing six or more letters. Such indicators are assumed to represent a range of psychological and intellectual content, matters that discourse analysts might investigate principally using textual micro-analyses. An exploratory factor analysis gave the researchers the "confidence that all ten [of their] indicators are part of the same underlying dimension that [they] theorize to be cognitive complexity" (p. 28). From their provocative findings, they conclude that ideology and clarity are not correlated (liberal and conservative Supreme Court justices are equally clear or unclear), but that dissenting opinions are clearer than majority opinions, and those in criminal procedure cases are clearer than those in civil procedure cases. Furthermore, the greater the number of justices joining an opinion, the less clear it is likely to be. This finding is ascribed to the necessity of accommodating the increasingly diverse views of a larger number of joiners to the opinion. The researchers also identified justices who systematically crafted clearer and less clear opinions than those of others.[1]

In a study of nearly 900 briefs submitted in appellate cases, Long and Christensen (2011: 1) found that readability as measured by popular formulas relying solely on word length and sentence length (Flesch Reading Ease scale and Flesch–Kincaid Grade-Level scale) could not be correlated with successful outcomes on appeal. This finding, they concede, affords little encouragement to "legal writing professionals who may want to believe that the likelihood of success on appeal can be increased by writing a more 'readable' brief and that a computerized readability formula can provide a basis for determining readability."

Another study of appellate court briefs examined intensifying adverbs, which are commonly lambasted in legal writing guides and have been accused of conveying meanings exactly the opposite of the intended ones. In a study of more than 400 federal and state appellate court cases concluded between 2001 and 2003, Long and Christensen (2008) examined adverbs such as *very, clearly, obviously, patently,* and *plainly* and found that in certain situations excessive intensifier use is associated with a statistically significant increase in *adverse* outcomes for the "offending" party, as one might expect, but in other situations it is associated with a significant increase in *favorable* outcomes. Perhaps not surprisingly, "the odds of reversal [i.e., success] can actually be higher for appellants who have high intensifier usage rates ... when the judge writing the opinion is also a prodigious user of intensifiers" (p. 185).

Adverbial expressions in appellate cases have received notable attention from linguists. In legal contexts, potential ambiguities of adverbial scope carry a certain notoriety because adverbial scope in English can be ambiguous and, consequently, interpretation of such ambiguity has figured prominently in litigation. Solan (1993) discusses a case in which the scope of the expression *knowingly and willfully* in a section of the US Criminal Code was at issue. The defendant's conviction was overturned when the appellate court disagreed with the trial court's interpretation, but upon further appeal the US Supreme Court reversed the appellate court on the matter of scope. Schane (2006) discusses wide and narrow adverbial scope in another US Supreme Court case.

Finegan (2010), comparing adverbial use in a 900,000-word corpus of state and federal supreme court opinions with similar use in standard reference corpora of written English, found that supreme court opinions deploy much higher rates of certain adverbs and adverbial types than other registers of written English. Especially in expressing emphasis, appellate court judges exploit the semantic polysemy and word-order flexibility of adverbs to accomplish multiple goals simultaneously—as in this example (internal citations silently omitted), in which a California Supreme Court justice wrote:

> By doing so, a defendant alerts the trial court to a possible error and provides the opportunity for correction. This defendant <u>clearly</u> did.
>
> *(People v. Carasi, 44 Cal. 4th 1263)*

In the sentence above, *clearly* serves simultaneously as a manner adverb ("This defendant did that clearly") and as an emphatic ("It is clear that this defendant did that"). Whether a distinct advantage is afforded to judges tasked with drafting appellate opinions by the word-order flexibility, polysemic character, and ambiguous scope of many adverbials remains to be thoroughly investigated.

As in the example above, adverbs serve commonly as one vehicle for jurists to express stance, though they are by no means the only such vehicle available to them. Especially in dissent, appellate court justices rely heavily on adverbial expression not only to intensify and emphasize but also to express disdain. As an example, consider this excerpt from a 2008 dissenting opinion (*Boumediene v. Bush*) issued by Justice Antonin Scalia of the US Supreme Court, in which the underscoring of adverbial and other markers of stance has been added for present purposes:

> Today the Court <u>warps</u> our Constitution in a way that goes beyond the narrow issue of the reach of the Suspension Clause, invoking <u>judicially brainstormed</u> separation-of-powers principles to establish a <u>manipulable "functional"</u> test for the extraterritorial reach of habeas corpus (and, <u>no doubt</u>, for the extraterritorial reach of other constitutional protections <u>as well</u>). It <u>blatantly misdescribes</u> important precedents, <u>most conspicuously</u> Justice Jackson's opinion for the Court in *Johnson v. Eisentrager*. It <u>breaks a chain of precedent</u> as old as the common law that prohibits judicial inquiry into detentions of aliens abroad absent statutory authorization. And, <u>most tragically</u>, it sets our military commanders <u>the impossible task</u> of proving to a civilian court, under <u>whatever</u> standards this Court <u>devises</u> in the future, that evidence supports the confinement of <u>each and every</u> enemy prisoner.

Thus, in choice of verbs (*warps, misdescribes, breaks*, perhaps *devises*), adjectivals (*brainstormed, manipulable, impossible, each and every*), adverbials (*judicially, no doubt, as well, blatantly, most conspicuously,* and *most tragically*), and perhaps quotation marks, stance finds expression. Little in the excerpt is free of disdain, and no one reading it could wonder how its author *feels* about the majority's decision. Still, while Scalia's writing is more dramatic in its expression of stance than that of his fellow justices, he is not alone in marking opinions with unmistakable stance.

It may be useful briefly to point out that this excerpt does not exhibit many of the characteristics widely associated with the language of the law, broadly conceived. Its sentences, while not short, are not overly long (they average 34 words each); the passage contains no passive voice verbs and little repetition of nouns where pronouns might occur—the pronoun *it* appears three times, referring to the Court. The characteristic of the language of the law that is most apparent in the excerpt is its comparatively long words and the Latin expression *habeas corpus*.[2] Other than excessive internal citation and quotation from earlier opinions, the discourse of appellate court opinions characteristically reflects the struggle for balance between decision making and a clear presentation referred to at the head of this section.

Conclusion

We have examined three of the many arenas in which legal discourse and its institutional instantiation have a significant impact on the lives of ordinary people: the discourse of lay litigants in small claims courts; the discourse of cross-examination by a defense attorney of a witness who has accused someone of rape; and the discourse of appellate court opinions. Much of what is discussed in this chapter has application in other domains of law and, of course, in jurisdictions other than those in the United States. While more discourse analysts are taking an interest in the various registers within the language of the law, much of their work arises in forensic contexts and, perhaps inevitably, does not find its way into the ordinary vehicles of scholarly dissemination other than the journal of the International Association of Forensic Linguists. Much of the work of forensic linguists (e.g. Shuy, 1993, 1998, 2010; Gibbons, 2003; Olsson, 2004; Coulthard and Johnson, 2007) and other linguists (Solan and Tiersma, 2005) provides useful insight into cases before the law, but additional work displaying more fundamental or systematic discourse analysis of spoken and written texts in law's many registers is still needed, not purely for scholarly reasons but in the interest of fairness and social justice.

Further reading

Conley, J. M. and O'Barr, W. M. (2005) *Just Words: Law, Language, and Power*, Second Edition. Chicago, IL: University of Chicago Press.

This second edition of a classic rehearses work by its authors in small claims courts and by Matoesian and others; in separate chapters it also treats mediation, patriarchy, a natural history of disputing, cross-cultural and historical perspectives, ideology, and forensics.

Coulthard, M. and Johnson, A. (eds.) (2010) *The Routledge Handbook of Forensic Linguistics*. Abingdon: Routledge.

Nearly forty chapters, authored by respected scholars, organized into sections on legal language in the legal process, the linguist as expert, and new debates and directions (multimodality and terrorism, among others).

Eades, D. (2010) *Sociolinguistics and the Legal Process*. Bristol: Multilingual Matters.

A rich and thoughtful treatment of many sociolinguistic aspects of discourse in the legal process by a scholar deeply involved in these issues in Australia.

Mertz, E. (2007) *The Language of Law School: Learning to "Think Like a Lawyer."* New York: Oxford University Press.

Awarded the Herbert Jacob Book Prize by the Law & Society Association, Mertz explores the role of discourse in law school in shaping how students learn to think and talk as lawyers.

Tiersma, P. M. (2010) *Parchment, Paper, Pixels: Law and the Technologies of Communication*. Chicago, IL: University of Chicago Press.

An exploration of the relationship between speech and writing in the law and the effects of modern technologies on the law's textualization.

Notes

1 By these indicators, Antonin Scalia and Stephen Breyer, coincidentally representing the conservative and liberal wings of the Court, wrote the clearest opinions, Ruth Bader Ginsburg the least clear opinions.
2 Other Latin and Anglo-Norman/French phrases such as *post, ante, per se, voir dire*, and *stare decisis* also appear regularly in recent Supreme Court opinions.

References

Berk-Seligson, S. (2009) *Coerced Confessions: The Discourse of Bilingual Police Interrogations*. Berlin: Mouton de Gruyter.

Bhatia, V., Candlin, C. N., and Gotti, M. (eds.) (2003) *Legal Discourse in Multilingual and Multicultural Contexts: Arbitration Texts in Europe*. Bern: Peter Lang.

Conley, J. M. and O'Barr, W. M. (1990) *Rules versus Relationships: The Ethnography of Legal Discourse*. Chicago, IL: University of Chicago Press.

Conley, J. M. and O'Barr, W. M. (2005) *Just Words: Law, Language, and Power*. Second Edition. Chicago, IL: University of Chicago Press.

Conley, R. H. and Conley, J. H. (2009) 'Stories from the jury room: how jurors use narrative to process evidence', *Studies in Law, Politics and Society*, 49: 25–56. UNC Legal Studies Research Paper No. 1510290. Available at http://papers.ssrn.com/sol3/papers.cfm?abstract_id=1510290 (accessed 4 November 2010).

Coulthard, M. and Johnson, A. (2007) *An Introduction to Forensic Linguistics: Language in Evidence*. Abingdon: Routledge.

Coulthard, M. and Johnson, A. (eds.) (2010) *The Routledge Handbook of Forensic Linguistics*. Abingdon: Routledge.

Eades, D. (2009) *Courtroom Talk and Neocolonial Control*. Berlin: Mouton de Gruyter.

Eades, D. (2010) *Sociolinguistics and the Legal Process*. Bristol: Multilingual Matters.

Finegan, E. (2010) 'Corpus linguistic approaches to "legal language": adverbial expression of attitude and emphasis in Supreme Court opinions', in M. Coulthard and A. Johnson (eds.) *The Routledge Handbook of Forensic Linguistics*. Abingdon: Routledge, pp. 65–77.

Gibbons, J. (2003) *Forensic Linguistics: An Introduction to Language in the Justice System*. Malden, MA: Blackwell.

Gotti, M. and Williams, C. (eds.) (2010) *Legal Discourse across Languages and Cultures*. Bern: Peter Lang.

Levi, J. N. (1994) *Language and Law: A Bibliographic Guide to Social Science Research in the USA*, Chicago, IL: American Bar Association Commission on College and University Legal Studies: Teaching Resource Bulletin No. 4.

Long, L. N. and Christensen, W. F. (2008) 'Clearly, using intensifiers is very bad – or is it?', *Idaho Law Review*, 45: 171–189.

Long, L. N. and Christensen, W. C. (2011) 'Does the readability of your brief affect your chance of winning an appeal? An analysis of readability in appellate briefs and its correlation with success on appeal', *Journal of Appellate Practice and Process*, 12. Available at: http://works.bepress.com/lance_long/2.

Matoesian, G. M. (1993) *Reproducing Rape: Domination through Talk in the Courtroom*. Chicago, IL: University of Chicago Press.

Mertz, E. (2007) *The Language of Law School: Learning to "Think Like a Lawyer."* New York: Oxford University Press.

Olsson, J. (2004) *Forensic Linguistics: An Introduction to Language, Crime and the Law*. London: Continuum.

Owens, R. J. and Wedeking, J. (2010) 'Justices and legal clarity: analyzing the complexity of supreme court opinions'. Available at: http://ssrn.com/abstracts=1695775 (accessed 18 November 2010).

Sarat, A. and Felstiner, W. L. F. (1995) *Divorce Lawyers and Their Clients: Power and Meaning in the Legal Process*. New York: Oxford University Press.

Schane, S. (2006) *Language and the Law*. London: Contiuum.

Shuy, R. W. (1998) *The Language of Confession, Interrogation, and Deception*. Thousand Oaks, CA: Sage.

Shuy, R. W. (2010) *The Language of Defamation Cases*. New York: Oxford University Press.

Solan, L. M. (1993) *The Language of Judges*. Chicago, IL: University of Chicago Press.

Solan, L. M. and Tiersma, P. M. (2005) *Speaking of Crime: The Language of Criminal Justice*. Chicago, IL: University of Chicago Press.

Tauszik, Y. R. and Pennebaker, J. W. (2010) 'The psychological meaning of words: LIWC and computerized text analysis methods', *Journal of Language and Social Psychology*, 29: 24–54.

Tiersma, P. M. (1999) *Legal Language*. Chicago, IL: University of Chicago Press.

van der Houwen, F. (2005) *Negotiating disputes and achieving judgments on Judge Judy*, unpublished dissertation, University of Southern California.

35

Ethnicity and humour in the workplace

Janet Holmes and Julia de Bres

Humour is a very broad and well-researched area.[1] Studies of humour range from those attempting to explain what we find amusing and why, through those examining the functions of humour, to those providing typologies identifying different categories of humour.[2] There is also a considerable amount of research examining linguistic features of humour (e.g. Attardo, 1994, 2001; Görlach, 2000; Norrick, 2003; Kotthoff, 2006; Morreall, 1991; Raskin, 1985, 1987; Ross, 1998). However, relatively little research has focussed on the way humour is interactionally achieved in spoken discourse; even less has examined humour in workplace discourse, and very few researchers have examined the way different ethnic groups use humour in the workplace, which is the focus of this chapter.

In this chapter, we first review research that has explored the social functions of humour in workplace discourse. We next consider what constitutes ethnic humour, focussing in particular on Māori humour in the New Zealand context. We then turn to the analysis of spoken discourse, approaching humour as an interactional achievement and illustrating it with data from New Zealand workplaces. Finally, we consider what further research is needed to extend our understanding of some of the issues raised in this chapter.

Humour in the workplace[3]

As many researchers have noted, humour serves a wide range of functions besides its core function of providing amusement. Focussing just on its social functions, humour can create, maintain and strengthen solidarity between family members, friends, and colleagues; it may emphasize or attenuate power relationships, provide tension release in social groups, and contribute to the construction of a particular type of social identity, including ethnic or cultural identity (e.g. Duncan, 1985; Hay, 1995; Holmes, 2000; Rappoport, 2006). Unsurprisingly, all these functions prove relevant in workplace interaction.

Research on humour in the workplace is steadily increasing, but much of it has been undertaken from a management perspective rather than from a sociolinguistic or discourse analysis point of view.[4] One strand of this research presents the argument that workplace humour benefits employment relationships, job satisfaction, creativity, and even productivity (e.g. Morreall, 1991; Caudron, 1992; Clouse and Spurgeon, 1995). Humour, it has been argued, can increase employees' morale by reducing tension, defusing conflict and spicing up routines, and may help them deal with stress and change (Morreall, 1991; Ehrenberg, 1995; Plester and Orams, 2008). In contexts as diverse as hospitals (Pizzini, 1991), paramedical departments (Rosenberg, 1991), hotel kitchens (Brown and Keegan, 1999), police departments (Pogrebin and Poole, 1988) and IT companies (Plester and Sayers, 2007), humour has been shown to have beneficial effects.

On the other hand, while humour may promote 'a healthy exchange of ideas' (Barsoux, 1993: 112), it may also serve to 'bring [...] people back into line' (Barsoux, 1993: 95) and help to control subordinates' behaviour (Clouse and Spurgeon, 1995; Terrion and Ashforth, 2002). Pizzini (1991), for example, found that doctors used humour in consultations to control their patients' discourse. (See also Linstead, 1985; Ackroyd and Thompson, 1999.) Humour may thus be an effective means for asserting authority or 'doing power' in the workplace. Taking an explicitly critical perspective to the analysis of workplace humour in a lorry producing factory, Collinson (1988, 2002) also identifies humour as a control mechanism, encouraging conformity to group norms, but also as a strategy for expressing resistance to management. Similarly, in a white-collar, commercial context, Rodrigues and Collinson (1995) demonstrate that telecommunications employees in Brazil not only used humour (and particularly cartoons) as a safety valve for channelling emotions and expressing dissatisfaction, but also as a weapon of contestation and a means to effect change. These studies indicate how different types of humour contribute to the construction of particular kinds of workplace cultures and to enhancing particular aspects of an organisation's culture (see also Berger, 1976; Duncan and Feisal, 1989).

Our own previous research supports the view that humour is an important feature of workplace culture, which may contribute to distinguishing different communities of practice. Holmes and Marra (2002a) compared the amount of humour, the type of humour (supportive or contestive in content) and the style of humour (collaborative or competitive in expression) in four different workplaces; the results suggested that each workplace had its own distinctive mix of features. Each workplace team created its own particular combination from the discursive resources available, within the parameters acceptable at that workplace. So, for example, meetings of a team within a large commercial organization produced a high level of sparky humour, which was frequently contestive and expressed in a competitive style more often than in other workplaces – possibly one enactment of the more individual values and orientations, as well as of the pressure on team members to perform in these meetings. By contrast, the more formal meetings of teams in a government organization had the least amount of humour of all those analysed, and the humour was predominantly supportive in content and collaborative in style. Our analysis of humour thus provided another layer of support for our ethnographic observations regarding the different 'systems of shared understandings' and ways of doing things which obtained in the different communities of practice. Using these dimensions, the Māori workplace on which we focus in section 4 under the pseudonym 'Kiwi Consultations' was characterized by a high frequency of humour that was often collaborative and overall supportive in content, though a considerable amount of contestive humour also occurred.

One further strand of research that adopts a discourse analysis approach to humour in the workplace focuses on its role in constructing leadership identity. Holmes (2007a) and Schnurr (2009) examine how effective leaders use humour in white-collar professional New Zealand organizations. Humour provides a team leader with a valuable discursive resource for interactively achieving workplace goals, since it makes it possible to 'do' both power and politeness, and accomplish both transactional and relational objectives, often simultaneously (Holmes, 2000; Holmes and Stubbe, 2003; Holmes and Marra, 2006). In sum, as an interactive strategy involving all participants, humour is often an important component contributing to the construction and maintenance of a particular type of workplace culture or community of practice, as well as to the construction of a type of leadership identity appropriate to that culture. These points are illustrated in the analyses in this chapter.

Ethnic humour and Māori humour

The appreciation and enjoyment of humour generally requires, among other things, shared cultural values and assumptions: different cultural backgrounds and beliefs influence what is perceived as amusing. There is an extensive literature on the relationship between ethnicity and humour, which involves the analysis of ethnic jokes (e.g. Davies, 1990; Nilsen and Nilsen, 2000) or of different cultural styles of humour (e.g. Ziv, 1988, 1997). Most relevant from our perspective in this chapter, however, is the spontaneous interactional humour which arises naturally in informal conversational contexts.

In New Zealand, there are significant differences between Māori and Pākehā culture, and hence it is not surprising that there are also differences in the ways in which Māori and Pākehā use humour. Pākehā culture, a culture derived from Europe, and from Britain in particular, is the dominant one. The indigenous Māori people constitute only 14 per cent of the New Zealand population, and over the past 150 years their language and culture have been steadily eroded (Metge, 1976, 1986). The Māori language is in very real danger of disappearing (Benton, 1996; Te Puni Kokiri, 2007; Bauer, 2008), and, despite some improvement over the last three decades, the culture of the indigenous Māori people is still much less prominent than Pākehā culture, so that it is not well understood by many Pākehā New Zealanders.[5] More specifically, and especially of greater relevance in relation to the analysis of the functions of humour, Māori culture emphasizes the group over the individual and places a high value on humility and avoidance of self-promotion (Metge, 1995), points we return to in section 4.

The research most relevant to our concern in this chapter examines the function of humour in maintaining and reinforcing ethnic boundaries and constructing solidarity and cultural identity in social interaction (Lowe, 1986; Holmes and Hay, 1997; Holmes and Marra, 2002b; Holmes, 2007a; Kell et al., 2007). An analysis of 259 examples of everyday humour in conversations between Māori and Pākehā participants (Holmes and Hay, 1997) indicated that Māori participants were much more likely than Pākehā to engage in both boundary-marking humour (constructing and maintaining group boundaries) and in solidarity-building humour (emphasizing cultural identity and similarities between members of a group). These findings suggested that the ethnic boundary between Māori and Pākehā is more salient to Māori as a minority group than to the dominant Pākehā. By constructing those who fall outside the group boundary as 'other' and as outsiders, the beliefs and values that the speakers share are emphasized, enhancing solidarity among the group. Conversely, the Māori participants often also used humour to highlight similarities between themselves, establishing connections and explicitly emphasizing shared interests, ideas and values. Moroever, Māori participants in conversation with each other used many more items of Māori vocabulary, and made more frequent reference to Māori cultural concepts than Pākehā participants did. While closely related, the two functions of maintaining boundaries and constructing solidarity can be distinguished in the data we have analysed in our corpus of New Zealand workplace interaction, as illustrated below. First, however, we provide a brief overview of research on ethnicity and humour in the workplace.

Ethnicity and humour in the workplace

As mentioned in the introduction, relatively little research has explicitly focussed on the variable of ethnicity in the analysis of workplace humour. Rogerson-Revell's (2007) analysis of how humour contributes to the power play in business meetings in intercultural contexts provides useful insights into the potential contribution of ethnicity to intercultural misunderstanding. She analysed meetings between Anglophone expatriates and ethnic Chinese employees in a south-east Asian airline corporation and found that humour was a recurring interactive strategy that characterized the style of particular groups of speakers and was used by them in a range of ways. Specifically, she demonstrates an interesting contrast between two meetings: in one, humour was used positively and collaboratively by a group of Anglophones; in the other, the same group used humour to collude against the (Chinese) chair. Despite attempts to align with the Anglophones, the chair was clearly uncomfortable with their contestive, adversarial style and 'highly-contextualised humour' (Rogerson-Revell, 2007: 18–19), characterized by witty quips that interrupted or subverted the on-going talk, by exaggeration, by prosodic intensity and highly contextualized lexis, including metaphors, and by frequent swearing (2007: 20–21). Her analysis thus demonstrates how humour can be used 'subversively to mask aggression or frustration and also to signal distance between the focus or butt of the humour (in this case the [Chinese c]hair) and the in-group' (2007: 20). Clearly, humour can simultaneously serve to construct in-group cohesion for members of one ethnic group, while distancing another.

The disharmony illustrated in Rogerson-Revell's analysis of intercultural meetings in a southeast Asian context provides an interesting contrast with the way humour functions in meetings in the New Zealand multicultural communities of practice that we have analysed. Marra and Holmes compared the use of humour in two different workplaces, and, while the preferred styles of humour differed, it was notable that both workplaces illustrated the significance of 'the shared cultural knowledge, values, and beliefs which underlie the appropriate use and interpretation of humour …' (2007: 153). In one workplace, where the organization was committed to the promotion of Māori objectives, Māori ethnicity was foregrounded: Māori ways of behaving and interacting were the norm, and there was considerable use of the Māori language (Marra and Holmes, 2007: 157). In this workplace self-deprecating humour was often used to manage the pressures of conforming to Pākehā business norms while incorporating Māori values into workplace interaction. In the second workplace, a team comprising employees from four ethnic groups formed a particularly cohesive community of practice with a strong sense of group identity, 'a strong orientation to team morale, and a very distinctive sparky communicative style' (Marra and Holmes, 2007: 161). Expletives and jocular abuse, in particular, distinguished this team as a community of practice from others, both within the organization and outside. Given that a third of this team identified as Samoan and that Ginette, the team leader, was Samoan, it is unsurprising that Samoan styles of humour appeared to predominate (Marra and Holmes, 2007: 162). Overall, Marra and Holmes point to the contrast between the direct, robust and confrontational nature of the style of this community of practice and the much lower-key humour of the Māori team. While workplace culture is clearly a contributing factor, ethnicity also seems a crucial component in the 'interactive mix', which results in different styles of humour (Rogerson-Revell, 2007: 23).

Drawing on data gathered in two Māori communities of practice, Holmes (2007a) examined the ways in which humour serves as a useful strategy to enable Māori leaders to manage workplace conflict. Most relevantly, this involved conflict between the need to demonstrate leadership by being authoritative and decisive on the one hand, and the need to behave in a modest, humble and self-deprecating way, in conformity with Māori values, on the other. The analysis demonstrates how humour enables Māori leaders to 'walk a tightrope between the demands of their position and the need to demonstrate their *mana*, on the one hand, and the requirement of modesty or *whakaiti* on the other' (Holmes, 2007a: 20–21).[6] In sum, this research illustrates how humour can be a valuable discourse strategy enabling minority group members to 'do' ethnicity, while nevertheless operating successfully according to norms that are not always in line with traditional ethnic values.

This potential for humour to serve a range of functions simultaneously is illustrated further below, where we examine how humour functions to construct, maintain and reinforce ethnic boundaries at a New Zealand workplace, whilst also constructing solidarity by emphasizing shared aspects of cultural identity in social interaction.

Using a discourse analysis approach to analyse humour

In this section we first describe our data collection method, then we provide the definition of humour used in our analysis, and finally we illustrate our approach with data from participants in one particular Māori workplace.

Collecting workplace data

The data used to analyse workplace humour in the various studies undertaken by the Wellington Language in the Workplace Project (LWP) team has been collected from a wide range of New Zealand workplaces, including government departments, commercial companies, small businesses and factories. Our ethnographic methodology was designed to give participants maximum control over the data collection process, whilst also allowing workplace interactions to be recorded as unobtrusively as possible (Holmes and Stubbe, 2003). Typically, after a period of participant observation by one of our research assistants to establish how the workplace operates, a group of volunteers from the workplace record a range of their everyday work interactions over a period of two to three weeks. Some keep the recorder and microphone on their desks, while others carry the equipment around with them. In addition, where possible, a series of regular workplace meetings is video-recorded.

Over the recording period, people increasingly ignore the microphones and the video cameras (which are relatively small and fixed in place), and consequently we have collected some excellent examples of workplace interaction that are as close to 'natural' as one could hope. This database provides a rich resource for analysing humour in the workplace. The analysis below focuses on interactions recorded during work time in a Māori organization which we refer to using the pseudonym 'Kiwi Consultations' – a place where Māori cultural values, attitudes and beliefs are regarded as fundamental to the work being undertaken, Māori ways of doing things are the norm, and the objectives of the organization encompass achieving good outcomes for Māori people in general. Since humour is the focus of the analysis, a definition of what counts as an instance of humour is a necessary starting point.

Defining humour

Even if we focus exclusively on verbal humour and exclude practical jokes and non-verbal humour, defining humour is not straightforward. Workplace humour is often extremely context-embedded, and evaluating an utterance as amusing frequently depends on shared experience, assumptions and values. For our purposes, humorous utterances have been defined as those identified by the analyst, on the basis of paralinguistic, prosodic and discoursal clues, as intended to be amusing by the speaker(s) and perceived to be amusing by at least some participants. (See Holmes, 2000, for a fuller discussion of this issue.) We use a wide range of linguistic as well as contextual clues to identify instances of humour, including the speaker's tone of voice and the audience's auditory and discoursal responses. Laughter, and, where video recording is available, facial expression, including smiles, are also helpful indicators. When more than one person contributes to humour on a single topic, we generally treat this as one collaborative sequence of humour, i.e. one instance of humour for the purposes of quantitative, comparative analysis. In the next section, however, we illustrate a qualitative approach to workplace humour by using discourse analysis.

Analysing Māori humour in the workplace

Workplace humour functions to construct, maintain and reinforce boundaries between Māori and Pākehā, whilst also constructing different aspects of Māori identity in social interaction, as we will illustrate. First, however, we provide a very brief summary of some salient distinguishing features of Māori culture.

For Māori people, establishing connections and areas of shared cultural knowledge is a core dimension of communication.[7] This is especially evident in Māori views of the value and function of talk, which is often oriented to sharing knowledge and achieving consensus (Metge and Kinloch, 1978; Metge, 1995). Moreover, in general, verbal interaction is other-oriented and characterized by high involvement between speakers and their addressees. This is an aspect that Māori culture shares with other Polynesian cultures, and more generally with cultures based on an oral tradition (e.g. Ito, 1985; Besnier, 1989; Edwards and Sienkewicz, 1990). Researchers investigating pragmatic features of New Zealand English have suggested that this emphasis on connection provides one explanation for a preference in the speech of Māori New Zealanders for pragmatic features which serve to construct solidarity. These include more frequent use of the pragmatic tag *eh* (Meyerhoff, 1994), and high-rising terminals (HRTs) among Māori than among Pākehā speakers (Britain, 1992). These pragmatic devices are means by which Māori express rapport in New Zealand society. As they become associated with Māori ethnicity, they may also be used as social indexes of Māori identity and indicate positive attitudes to Māori values. Another means of expressing rapport and solidarity is humour. Our analyses suggest that, like other pragmatic devices, humour may be used to express a distinctive ethnic identity, both by drawing clear-cut ethnic boundary lines and by dynamically constructing in-group solidarity and ethnic identity.

Boundary-marking humour

Our first example focuses around humour arising from a very explicit acknowledgement of the differences between Māori and Pākehā formal meeting behaviour. In Pākehā meetings, people are usually silent while someone is contributing to the floor; in Māori meetings, however, it is common to hear quiet background talk and regular affirmatory feedback while someone is talking (Metge and Kinloch, 1978; Kell *et al.*, 2007). Background talk can be heard in most of the larger meetings in our Māori organizations. For Māori participants, this functions as a signal of engagement and attention. In other words, this Māori communicative norm typically overrides the expectation of silence as a signal of attention where Māori participants are involved.

Familiarity with this norm provides the basis for a humorous exchange between Frank and Steve, two Pākehā participants in this excerpt from a meeting at Kiwi Consultations.

Example 1 [For transcription conventions see below, p. 505]

Context: Regular staff meeting of 16 participants in a Māori workplace. All but three are Māori. The Chief Executive Officer, Daniel, and senior manager Frank have been talking quietly, and on topic, in the background while Steve is making his presentation.

1.	Steve:	one of the important things in communication is
2.		not to talk when others are talking
3.	Group:	[loud laughter]
4.	Steve:	I hope that the cameras picked up (that)
5.	Group:	[loud laughter]
6.	Frank:	Steve this indicates a need for you to be out in hui ['meetings']
7.	Group:	[laughter]
8.	Frank:	one of the things that you learn very quickly
9.		is that a sign of respect is that other people are talking about
10.		what //you're saying while you're saying it\

11.   Group: /[laughter]\\ [laughter]
12.   Steve: I see I see
13.   Caleb: //good recovery Frank good recovery\
14.   Dan: /that's right Steve Frank is\\ bicultural
15.   Group: [laughter]

During Steve's extended contribution to the meeting many participants make quiet remarks to each other, but, when Frank makes a comment to Daniel, Steve reacts by humorously reprimanding them, *one of the important things in communication is not to talk when others are talking* (lines 1–2). For the participants, this is amusing since Steve is reprimanding his superiors. Furthermore, Steve is inappropriately asserting the Pākehā communicative norm in a workplace where Māori ways of speaking obviously prevail, as is evident from the fact that others have been talking quietly during Steve's contribution.

Frank responds (line 6) by challenging Steve's rebuke as inappropriate, implying that Steve is not yet familiar enough with Māori interactional norms: *Steve this indicates a need for you to be out in hui* (i.e. to attend more Māori meetings). Frank then spells out the Māori communicative norm: *a sign of respect is that other people are talking about what you're saying while you're saying it* (lines 9–10). Caleb laughingly compliments Frank on his riposte to Steve's scold, using a repetitive pattern, very typical of Māori discourse (Metge, 1995; Stubbe and Holmes, 2000), *good recovery Frank good recovery* (line 13), and Daniel adds *that's right Steve, Frank is bicultural* (line 14), a comment that is almost certainly contestively ironic, since Frank's very self-conscious Pākehā identity is something that Daniel is very aware of, as he has indicated in interview.

Paradoxically, as a result of drawing attention to the quiet side conversation, Steve causes an even bigger interruption to his presentation and attracts (good-humoured) critical attention to his own cultural ignorance and insensitivity. Ethnicity is suddenly a workplace issue influencing what is considered effective and appropriate communication. This excerpt thus provides a clear example of boundary-marking humour, and, interestingly, it is a Pākehā who draws attention to the different interactional norms of the two ethnic groups, demonstrating that Māori-related humour may be used to good effect by Pākehā in appropriate contexts.

Our second example again makes very explicit reference to ethnic boundaries, but also illustrates the very collaborative style typical of in-group humour. This group of senior Māori managers jointly constructs a humorous fantasy that indicates its members' attitudes to being patronized by those they regard as well-to-do and hypocritical Pākehā.

Example 2

Context: Meeting of senior management team in a Māori organization

1.   Cal: multimillion dollar properties up //( )\
2.   Dan: /[laughs]\\ oh they'll have a happy weekend then won't they
3.   Har: yeah
4.   Dan: [laughs]: the neighbours hey:
5.   Cal: //[laughs]\
6.   Har: /that's good\\ they love it eh
7.   Dan: [laughs]: yeah: I bet they love it
8.   Har: they love they love that stuff //that Māori dynamic\
9.   Dan: /that cultural colour\\
10. Har: yeah
11. Hin: [name] was //saying that they've been\

12.	Har:	/the property values go up\\
13.	Hin:	coming round to offer offer what they can do
14.		whether they can bake or
15.	Dan:	//[laughs] [laughs]: yeah yeah choice\:
16.	Har:	/yeah oh yeah yeah straight up eh\\
17.		Māori is the new black eh Caleb?
18.	Cal:	yeah it is
19.	Group:	[laughter]
20.	Cal:	it is it is the new black bro [laughs]
21.	Group:	[laughter]

At the beginning of this excerpt, Daniel makes explicit fun of rich Pākehā who find they have new Māori neighbours: *they'll have a happy weekend then … I bet they love it that cultural colour* (lines 2, 7, 9). Hari's comment that *the property values go up* (line 12) is especially telling, since the traditional cultural stereotype entails depressed house prices in Māori neighbourhoods. He follows this up with another witty comment: *Māori is the new black eh Caleb* (line 17), which gains its effect not only from the enduring fashionability of the colour black in the clothing industry and the associated expression 'X is the new black', but also from the irony of the fact that Māori, who are a brown-skinned people, have long been perceived and labelled as 'black' in Pākehā eyes. The contributors in this example are all Māori, with Daniel leading the humour and encouraging his team in mocking Pākehā hypocrisy. The example is marked discursively as Māori interaction through features such as the pragmatic tag *eh* (lines 6, 16, 17), which, as mentioned above, is strongly associated with Māori ethnicity, and the address term *bro*, which is also associated with Polynesian identity. Again, there is repetition (lines 6, 7, 8, and lines 17, 20), a well-recognized characteristic of Māori discourse. And the syntactic apposition evident in Daniel's comment, *they'll have a happy weekend then won't they … the neighbours*, is another feature that tends to typify Māori English discourse.

In this example, the humour is generated by Māori people's awareness of Pākehā's discomfort when Māori 'invade' well-to-do suburbs and by their ignorance of Māori ways of doing things. The group fantasize and satirize Pākehā attempts at polite behaviour in such a situation. Similarly, in example 1, culturally different norms are the basis of the humour, which focuses on the Pākehā employee's ignorance of Māori speaking norms, and their appropriateness in this Māori organization. These examples of humour, generated from awareness of different interactional norms, testify to the salience of the ethnic boundary between Māori and Pākehā for participants in this Māori workplace.

Constructing in-group solidarity and reinforcing Māori identity

Boundary-marking humour focuses on the differences between groups and emphasizes ways in which norms, attitudes and behaviours can be distinguished. Another type of humour very characteristic of the Māori organizations with whom we worked was humour that instantiated and enacted norms, attitudes and values associated with Māori people. This kind of humour can be regarded as contributing to the construction of a specific and distinctive kind of Māori identity, and typically served to maintain and reinforce solidarity between Māori participants. We illustrate two distinct but related ways in which this was evident in the data from Kiwi Consultations: first self-disparaging humour, and secondly group-disparaging humour.

Self-disparaging humour

Individually directed, self-disparaging or self-deprecating humour is very apparent in the data from all the Māori organizations with whom we have worked. The extensive influence of the

Māori concept of *whakaiti* (appropriate modesty and humility) has been discussed in some detail in our recent research (Holmes, 2005; Marra and Holmes, 2005; Holmes, 2007b), and it is particularly evident in the prevalence of this type of humour. Māori leaders, for instance, are very aware of the need to avoid being seen as boastful or self-promoting. The late Sir Robert Mahuta, a much respected leader of his people and a major figure in national life, refers to 'the whole spirit of whakaiti … being very humble' (Diamond, 2003: 141).

In his interactions with his staff, Daniel, the Chief Executive Officer at Kiwi Consultations, uses self-deprecating humour with skill, as one means of enacting the egalitarian ethics he likes to promote. Near the start of one meeting, for example, he refers to a training course on speed-reading that he has just attended, and he deliberately downplays his level of achievement. The others respond to this by teasing him in turn, illustrating how this kind of humour reinforces in-group solidarity.

Example 3

Context: Meeting of senior management team in a Māori organization discussing a speed-reading course attended by some of their members, including Daniel, the CEO and chair.

1.	Daniel:	I brought my certificate I brought my
2.		um we grad- [seriously]: I graduated on Friday:
3.	Caleb:	oh ka pai ['well done'] what was that for
4.	Daniel:	certificate of attendance
5.	Albert:	so at least we know you attended
6.	Group:	[laughter]
7.	Albert:	we have no idea how you performed
8.		but we know that you were there
9.	Caleb:	no no we've got to chuck him this report
10.	Hine:	no I got dux of the class he got attendance
11.	Daniel:	certificate of attendance but this is just terrible
12.		am I going to put this on the wall //certificate of attendance\
13.	Caleb:	/I hope so\\
14.	Hari:	go on
15.	Caleb:	I hope you do
16.	Hari:	I think you should
17.	Caleb:	we're gonna throw this report at you
18.		and we're gonna time you thirty seconds
19.		and you can tell us exactly what's going on

Daniel sets up the humour in this excerpt by stating that he has brought along his certificate and informing people he has graduated (lines 1–2), with the implication that these are substantial achievements. Caleb then congratulates Daniel with a frequently heard Maori phrase, *ka pai* ('well done'), and feeds him a question (line 3), which sets Daniel up for his punchline, delivered in a deadpan style, *certificate of attendance* (line 4). This clearly subverts people's expectations and generates laughter, and the group then proceed to tease Daniel. He responds with more humour, repeating and elaborating with an explicitly self-deprecating comment: *but this is just terrible am I going to put this on the wall certificate of attendance* (lines 11–12). This excerpt again includes a good deal of repetition, as well as some parallel syntactic structures (e.g. lines 7–8, line 10), stylistic features which emphasize the collaborative discursive interactional style of this group.

Other Maori leaders in our data also use witty, self-directed quips that downplay their abilities and skills and enable them to conform to cultural expectations of good leadership (Marra *et al.*, 2008).

Group-disparaging humour

Group-disparaging humour is more complex. When Māori people make fun of their own group, they obviously emphasize in-group solidarity; the same comments from an outsider would cause great offence (see Nilsen and Nilsen, 2000: 117). But in some cases the Māori target group appears to be treated as 'other' by the speakers, as a sub-group to be ridiculed. It is important to bear in mind that this may be tongue-in-cheek, an echo of the views of the wider society, rather than the actual views of those involved. Example 4 illustrates this ambiguity: it is implicitly rural, less educated Māori who are the specific target of the ridicule and portrayed as relatively illiterate – a view of rural Māori that is prevalent in the wider society.

Example 4

Context: Meeting of senior management team in a Māori organization. They are discussing the issue of mailing out a consultation document to different *iwi* (tribal groups) around the country. Albert is Pākehā, Hari is Māori.

1.	Albert:	um so there'll be seven hundred and fifty go out
2.		ten to each iwi I sort of tossed up
3.		whether to send five to only smaller ones
4.		and I thought no
5.		it's probably likely to cause more trouble
6.		even though for some of them
7.		they'll be getting two each [laughs]
8.	Hari:	not all of them can read
9.	Albert:	[laughs]

In this excerpt Albert comments that differently sized *iwi* will be offended if they don't get the same number of documents. Competitiveness between *iwi* is a common theme and source of humour when dealing with Māori groups, so Albert is here demonstrating understanding of Māori inter-group dynamics, and his comment therefore functions to construct in-group solidarity. Hari's deadpan response *not all of them can read* (line 8) elicits laughter. It is perceived as amusing because it is so outrageous and insulting to out-of-town Māori. It breaks the norms and expectations that Māori should be treated with respect, especially by other Māori. Another similar example involves a member of this team referring to a need to use *tom tom drums* instead of cellphones when out visiting Māori in remote areas. This outrageous comment, which portrays rural Māori as technologically backward and out of touch, also elicits laughter, and again may parody societal views rather than expressing the views of the speaker.

Finally, it is important to note that the strong ethnic dimension in the humour used in such workplaces is further reinforced by being encoded in linguistic features associated with Māori participants and Māori domains.[8] These include the non-standard second person plural pronoun *yous* (e.g. *and um would yous be driving there*), the pragmatic particle *eh* (discussed above), use of Māori phrases (e.g. *ka pai*) and lexical items (e.g. *hui*), as well as items associated with Māori varieties of English, such as *fellas* and *bro*, as illustrated in example 5 below (and example 2 above).

Example 5

Context: Meeting of senior management team in a Māori organization. Daniel is in the chair.

1.	Caleb:	oh they're still going
2.	Daniel:	yeah another three weeks after this I think
3.	Caleb:	oh okay I thought it was all over last week

4. Daniel: no I think they're trying to capture
5.   your communication styles eh bro
6. Caleb: oh bugger

At the start of a meeting, Caleb, a Māori staff member, makes reference to the continued presence of our recording equipment, and Daniel responds by teasing Caleb that his *communication styles* are the focus of the research. So here, interestingly, Daniel both explicitly refers to and uses (*eh bro*) features of a specifically Māori communication style, actively constructing his identity as ethnically Māori.

In this section we have illustrated two broad categories of ethnic humour: first, boundary-marking humour, which draws attention to differences between Māori and Pākehā interactional norms; and, secondly, humour that enacts or constructs a shared ethnic identity or a shared understanding of ethnically distinctive cultural values, thus building solidarity between participants. Our analyses suggest that both these types of humour are particularly characteristic of the discourse of Māori in New Zealand organizations.

Future research in ethnicity and humour

Many aspects of the interaction of ethnicity and humour in the workplace context remain to be explored. In particular, the complexities of perspective and attitude suggested in example 4 deserve further examination. Members of minority groups who succeed by the criteria of the wider society (education, occupation, wealth) often find themselves in a difficult position ideologically and politically. They tread a tricky pathway, balancing the demands of integrity against the values of their ethnic group, whilst also taking account of rules that ensure continued success in the wider society. Humour is a classic means of blending disparate identities and yoking together incompatible concepts. Research exploring the role of humour in accomplishing this feat in everyday workplace interaction would be very illuminating.

It also seems worth considering a wider range of types of workplace humour. Practical jokes and tricking people are further common themes in Māori humour, and recent research on humour in New Zealand IT organizations (Plester and Sayers, 2007; Plester and Orams, 2008) identifies the same types of humour as endemic in these organizations. There are clearly interesting opportunities for exploring similarities and differences in the types of humour prevalent in different occupational areas, especially those heavily populated by particular ethnic groups. From a discourse analysis perspective, this presents an interesting challenge, namely how to integrate and satisfactorily analyse non-verbal aspects of humour. Multimodal analysis may be required (Kress and Van Leeuwen, 2001; Jewitt, 2009), as advocated by researchers in areas such as the discourse of advertising (Cook, 2001).

This chapter has also suggested the importance of cultural values as contributing factors in accounting for preferences in styles of humour, using the example of the Māori concept of *whakaiti* and relating it to disparaging humour in a Māori context. There is scope for research on the use of humour to accomplish the complementary process of 'cutting people down to size' and reminding them of their place in the wider group – a type of humour that has been reported as commonly heard in Māori contexts and is also associated with other ethnic groups (Davies, 1990, but also see Billig, 2001; Laineste, 2005).

Finally, there is scope for further research on the role of narrative in ethnic humour in the workplace. In the New Zealand context, comedians often make use of narratives that create distinctive, stereotypical Māori characters and draw to a greater or lesser extent on Māori oral traditions (e.g. stories passed down over time and delivered in a characteristic style of oratory). This is a theme associated with, among others, the late Māori comedy icon, Billy T James (born William James Taitoko), who for many New Zealanders represents the quintessential style of

Māori humour. Our research suggests that traces of this style are evident in workplace humour recounting stories about colleagues (Marra and Holmes, 2008). Thus humorous narratives with an ethnic theme are another potential area for further research, not only in New Zealand but in other contexts where oral narrative is a feature of ethnic discourse.

Transcription conventions

All names used in the examples are pseudonyms.

[laughs]	Paralinguistic features and editorial comments in square brackets
: :	Colons indicate start/finish of paralinguistic feature
+	Pause of up to one second
// \,/\\	Simultaneous speech
(hello)	Transcriber's best guess at an unclear utterance
( )	Unintelligible utterance
[' ']	Translations of Māori words
?	Questioning intonation
–	Incomplete or cut-off utterance

Further Reading

There are no books specifically on ethnic humour in the workplace from a discourse analysis perspective. We recommend two articles and two books that we consider will prove useful for those interested in this area.

Holmes, J. (2000) 'Politeness, power and provocation: how humour functions in the workplace', *Discourse Studies*, 2 (2): 159–185. Reprinted in Teun van Dijk (ed.) 2007. *Discourse Studies*. Vol. III. London: Sage, pp. 76–101.

Although this paper does not focus on ethnicity, it provides a useful starting place for those interested in using a discourse analysis approach for analysing workplace humour. It has been widely referred to because it provides useful definitions and categories for analysis.

Holmes, J. and Hay, J. (1997) 'Humour as an ethnic boundary marker in New Zealand interaction', *Journal of Intercultural Studies*, 18 (2): 127–151.

Although this paper does not focus on workplace discourse, it provides some very useful categories for analysing ethnic humour, with examples that illustrate the concepts discussed. It also includes a useful literature review.

Davies, C. (1990) *Ethnic Humor Around the World: A Comparative Analysis*. Bloomington, IN: Indiana University Press.

While this book does not involve discourse analysis, it earns its place because of its extensive influence in humour research. Davies is the main proponent of a widely cited theory, which explains ethnic humour according to general characteristics of industrial societies, involving oppositions such as stupid–clever and stereotypical cultural characteristics. While the approach has been critiqued, it is important for researchers in the area of ethnic humour to be familiar with it.

Rappoport, L. (2005) *Punchlines: The Case for Racial, Ethnic, and Gender Humor*. Westport, CT: Prager.

Building on Davies' research, Rappoport discusses the social functions and benefits of stereotype humour. In Chapter 3, in particular, he surveys possible reasons for minority group humour in some detail, as well as examining the powerful role of irony and satire in ethnic humour.

Notes

1 This chapter has benefited from considerable research assistance from Sharon Marsden, which we gratefully acknowledge. It makes extensive use of the research of the Language in the Workplace Project and has benefited from comments from other team members, and in particular Meredith Marra.

2 See Nilsen (1993), Hay (1995), Nilsen and Nilsen (2000), Schnurr (2010) for overviews.
3 This section draws on Holmes (2007a).
4 See Schnurr (2008, 2010) for a thorough review.
5 Metge (1976, 1986, 1995) provides a very thorough description of characteristics of Māori culture and society, including the significance of inherited land, the cultural significance of *te reo Maori*, the Maori language, and the fundamental importance of *whanaungatanga* or kinship in Maori society.
6 'Mana' can be roughly translated as 'prestige' or 'standing', though its meaning in Maori culture is much richer than these words suggest.
7 This section draws on Holmes and Hay (1997).
8 See Bell (2000), Stubbe and Holmes (2000), Holmes (2005) for a discussion of these features.

References

Ackroyd, S. and Thompson, P. (1999) *Organizational Misbehaviour*. London: Sage.
Attardo, S. (1994) *Linguistic Theories of Humor*. Berlin, Germany: Mouton de Gruyter.
Attardo, S. (2001) *Humorous Texts: A Semantic and Pragmatic Analysis*. Berlin, Germany: Mouton de Gruyter.
Barsoux, J. -L. (1993) *Funny Business: Humour, Management and Business Culture*. London: Cassell.
Bauer, W. (2008) 'Is the health of te reo Māori improving?', *Te Reo*, 51: 33–73.
Bell, A. (2000) 'Māori and Pākehā English: a case study', in A. Bell and K. Kuiper (eds.) *New Zealand English*. Wellington: Victoria University Press, pp. 221–248.
Benton, R. A. (1996) 'The Māori language in New Zealand', in S. A. Wurm, P. Muhlhausler, and D. T. Tyron (eds.) *Atlas of Languages of Intercultural Communication in the Pacific, Asia and the Americas*. Berlin: Walter de Gruyter, pp. 161–171.
Berger, A. A. (1976) 'Anatomy of the joke', *Journal of Communication*, 26 (3): 113–115.
Besnier, N. (1989) 'Information withholding as a manipulative and collusive strategy in Nukulaelae gossip', *Language in Society*, 18: 315.
Billig, M. (2001) 'Humour and hatred: the racist jokes of the Ku Klux Klan', *Discourse and Society*, 12 (3): 267–289.
Britain, D. (1992) 'Linguistic change in intonation: the use of high rising terminals in New Zealand English', *Language Variation and Change*, 4 (1): 77–104.
Brown, R. B. and Keegan, D. (1999) 'Humor in the hotel kitchen', *Humor*, 12 (1): 47–70.
Caudron, S. (1992) 'Humor is healthy in the workplace', *Personnel Journal*, June, 63–68.
Clouse, R. W. and Spurgeon, K. L. (1995) 'Corporate analysis of humor', *Psychology: A Journal of Human Behavior*, 32 (3/4): 1–24.
Collinson, D. L. (1988) ' "Engineering humour": masculinity, joking and conflict in shopfloor relations', *Organizational Studies*, 2: 181–200.
Collinson, D. L. (2002) 'Managing humour', *Journal of Management Studies*, 39 (3): 269–289.
Cook, G. (2001) *The Discourse of Advertising*. Second Edition. New York: Routledge.
Davies, C. (1990) *Ethnic Humor around the World: A Comparative Analysis*. Bloomington, IN: Indiana University Press.
Diamond, P. (2003) *A Fire in Your Belly: Māori Leaders Speak*. Wellington: Huia.
Duncan, W. J. (1985) 'The superiority theory of humor at work: joking relationships as indicators of formal and informal status patterns in small, task oriented groups', *Small Group Behaviour*, 16 (4): 556–564.
Duncan, W. J. and Feisal, J. P. (1989) 'No laughing matter: patterns of humour in the workplace', *Organizational Dynamics*, 17 (4): 18–30.
Edwards, V. and Sienkewicz, T.J. (1990) *Oral Cultures: Past and Present*. Oxford: Blackwell.
Ehrenberg, T. (1995) 'Female differences in creation of humor relating to work', *Humor: International Journal of Humor Research*, 8 (4): 349–362.
Görlach, M. (2000) 'Linguistic aspects of jokes', in Elżbieta Mańczak-Wohlfeld and Władysława Bulsza (eds.), *Tradition and Postmodernity: English and American Studies and the Challenge of the Future*, Proceedings of the Eighth International Conference on English and American Literature and Language. Kraków, 7–9 April 1999. Kraków: Jagiellonian University Press, pp. 53–67.
Hay, J. (1995) 'Gender and humour: beyond a joke', MA thesis, Victoria University of Wellington.
Holmes, J. (2000) 'Politeness, power and provocation: how humour functions in the workplace', *Discourse Studies*, 2 (2): 159–185.
Holmes, J. (2005) 'Using Māori English in New Zealand', *International Journal of the Sociology of Language*, 172: 91–115.
Holmes, J. (2007a) 'Humour and the construction of Māori leadership at work', *Leadership*, 3 (1): 5–27.

Holmes, J. (2007b) *Relativity rules: Politic Talk in Ethnicised Workplaces*. Closing plenary at the Third International Symposium on Politeness, University of Leeds, 2–4 July 2007.

Holmes, J. and Hay, J. (1997) 'Humour as an ethnic boundary marker in New Zealand interaction', *Journal of Intercultural Studies*, 18 (2): 127–151.

Holmes, J. and Marra, M. (2002a) 'Having a laugh at work: how humour contributes to workplace culture', *Journal of Pragmatics*, 34: 1683–1710.

Holmes, J. and Marra, M. (2002b) 'Humour as a discursive boundary marker in social interaction', in A. Duszak (ed.) *Us and Others: Social Identities across Languages, Discourses and Cultures*. Amsterdam: John Benjamins, pp. 377–400.

Holmes, J. and Marra, M. (2006) 'Humor and leadership style', *Humor*, 19 (2): 119–138.

Holmes, J. and Stubbe, M. (2003) *Power and Politeness in the Workplace: A Sociolinguistic Analysis of Talk at Work*. London: Longman.

Ito, K. (1985) 'Affective bonds: Hawaiian interrelationships of the self', in G. White and J. Kirkparrick (eds.) *Person, Self, and Experience: Exploring Pacific Ethnopsychologies*. Berkeley, CA: University of California Press, pp. 301–307.

Jewitt, C. (ed.) (2009) *The Routledge Handbook of Multimodal Analysis*. London: Routledge.

Kell, S., Marra, M., Holmes, J., and Vine, B. (2007) 'Ethnic differences in the dynamics of women's work meetings', *Multilingua*, 26 (4): 309–331.

Kotthoff, H. (2006) 'Gender and humor: the state of the art', *Journal of Pragmatics*, 38 (1): 4–25.

Kress, G. and Van Leeuwen, T. (2001) *Multimodal Discourse*. London: Arnold.

Laineste, L. (2005) 'Targets of Estonian ethnic jokes within the theory of ethnic humour (Ch. Davies)', *Electronic Journal of Folklore*, 29: 7–24.

Linstead, S. (1985) 'Jokers wild: the importance of humour and the maintenance of organizational culture', *Sociological Review*, 33 (4): 741–767.

Lowe, J. (1986) 'Theories of ethnic humor: how to enter, laughing', *American Quarterly*, 38 (3): 439–460.

Marra, M. and Holmes, J. (2005) 'Constructing ethnicity and leadership through storytelling at work', in C. Mills and D. Matheson (eds.) *Communication at Work: Showcasing Communication Scholarship. Refereed Proceedings of the Annual Meeting of the Australia and New Zealand Communication Association*, Christchurch. Available online at: http://www.mang.canterbury.ac.nz/ANZCA/FullPapers.shtml (accessed 27 April 2011).

Marra, M. and Holmes, J. (2007) 'Humour across cultures: joking in the multicultural workplace', in H. Kotthoff and H. Spencer-Oatey (eds.) *Handbook of Intercultural Communication*. Berlin: Mouton de Gruyter, pp. 153–172.

Marra, M. and Holmes, J. (2008) 'Constructing ethnicity in New Zealand workplace stories', *Text and Talk*, 28 (3): 397–420.

Marra, M., Vine, B., and Holmes, J. (2008) 'Heroes, fathers and good mates: leadership styles of men at work', in *Proceedings of the Australia and New Zealand Communication Association 2008*, pp. 1–15. Available online at: http://www.massey.ac.nz/massey/research/conferences/australian-new-zealand-communication-association-conference/anzca08-refereed-proceedings.cfm (accessed 27 April 2011).

Metge, J. (1976) *The Māoris of New Zealand: Rautahi*. London: Routledge & K. Paul.

Metge, J. (1986) *In and Out of Touch: Whakamaa in Cross-Cultural Context*. Wellington, NZ: Victoria University Press.

Metge, J. (1995) *New Growth from Old: The Whanau in the Modern World*. Wellington, NZ: Victoria University Press.

Metge, J. and Kinloch, P. (1978) *Talking Past Each Other: Problems of Cross-Cultural Communication*. Wellington: Victoria University Press.

Meyerhoff, M. (1994) 'Sounds pretty ethnic, eh? A pragmatic particle in New Zealand English', *Language in Society*, 23 (3): 367–388. Morreall, J. (1989) 'Enjoying incongruity', *Humor: International Journal of Humor Research*, 2: 1–18.

Morreall, J. (1991) 'Humor and work', *Humor*, 4: 359–373.

Nilsen, A. P. and Nilsen, D. L. F. (2000) *Encyclopedia of 20th Century American Humor*. Westport, CT: Greenwood.

Nilsen, D. L. F. (1993) *Humor Scholarship: A Research Bibliography*. Westport, CT: Greenwood.

Norrick, N. (2003) 'Issues in conversational joking', *Journal of Pragmatics*, 35 (9): 1333–1359.

Pizzini, F. (1991) 'Communication hierarchies in humour: gender differences in the obsterical/gynaecological setting', *Discourse and Society*, 2 (4): 477–488.

Plester, B. A. and Orams, M. (2008) 'Send in the clowns: the role of the joker in three New Zealand IT companies', *Humor, International Journal of Humor Research*, 21 (3): 253–281.

Plester, B. A. and Sayers, J. (2007) 'Taking the piss: the functions of banter in three IT companies', *Humor, International Journal of Humor Research*, 20 (2): 157–187.

Pogrebin, M. R. and Poole, E. D. (1988) 'Humor in the briefing room: a study of the strategic uses of humor among police', *Journal of Contemporary Ethnography*, 17 (2): 183–210.

Rappoport, L. (2006) *Punchlines: The Case for Racial, Ethnic, and Gender Humor*. Westport, CT: Prager.

Raskin, V. (1985) *Semantic Mechanisms of Humor*. Dordrecht, Netherlands: D. Reidel.

Raskin, V. (1987) 'Linguistic heuristics of humor: a script-based semantic approach', *International Journal of Society and Language*, 65: 11–25.

Rodrigues, S. B. and Collinson, D. L. (1995) ' "Having fun?" Humour as resistance in Brazil', *Organization Studies*, 16 (5): 739–768.

Rogerson-Revell, P. (2007) 'Humour in business: a double-edged sword: a study of humour and style shifting in intercultural business meetings', *Journal of Pragmatics*, 39(1): 4–28. Available online at: http://www.sciencedirect.com/science?_ob=ArticleURL&_udi=B6VCW-4M81C4H-1&_user=10&_coverDate=01%2F31%2F2007&_rdoc=2&_fmt=high&_orig=browse&_origin=browse&_zone=rslt_list_item&_srch=doc-info%28%23toc%235965%232007%23999609998%23637124%23FLP%23display%23Volume%29&_cdi=5965&_sort=d&_docanchor=&view=c&_ct=13&_acct=C000050221&_version=1&_urlVersion=0&_userid=10&md5=db2241ac9930c4514b33f80ca77d29b6&searchtype=a.

Rosenberg, L. (1991) 'A qualitative investigation of the use of humor by emergency personnel as a strategy for coping with stress', *Journal of Emergency Nursing*, 17 (4): 197–202.

Ross, A. (1998) *The Language of Humour*. London: Routledge.

Schnurr, S. (2008) 'Surviving in a man's world with a sense of humour: an analysis of women leaders' use of humour at work', *Leadership*, 4 (3): 299–319.

Schnurr, S. (2009) 'Constructing leader identities through teasing at work', *Journal of Pragmatics*, 41: 1125–1138.

Schnurr, S. (2010) 'Humour/laughter', in M. Locher and S. Graham (eds.) *Handbook of Pragmatics*. Volume 6: *Interpersonal Pragmatics*. Berlin: de Grutyer, pp. 307–326.

Stubbe, M. and Holmes, J. (2000) 'Talking Māori or Pākehā in English', in A. Bell and K. Kuiper (eds.) *New Zealand English*. Wellington: Victoria University Press, pp. 249–278.

Te Puni Kokiri (2007) *Survey of the Health of the Māori Language in 2006. Wellington: Te Puni Kokiri.*

Terrion, J. L. and Ashforth, B. E. (2002) 'From "I" to "we": the role of putdown humor and identity in the development of a temporary group', *Human Relations*, 55 (1): 55–87.

Ziv, A. (1988) *National Styles of Humor*. Westport, CT: Greenwood.

Ziv, A. (ed.) (1997) *Jewish Humor*. London: Transaction publishers.

36

Discourse, gender and professional communication

Louise Mullany

Introduction

Research investigating the interplay between discourse, gender and professional communication has grown rapidly over the last decade in a wide range of geographical locations. Professional communication is defined here as spoken and written communication, including all electronic forms, that takes place with at least one person occupying a professional role. Following Gunnarsson (2009: 5), 'professional' is defined in general terms as 'paid-work related', and therefore applies equally to skilled/non-skilled workers and to white-collar/blue-collar workers.[1] Professional communication should thus be viewed as an overarching category, which incorporates more specific terms in discourse analysis research within its definition. This includes workplace discourse (Koester, 2010), business discourse (Bargiela-Chiappini *et al.*, 2007) and institutional discourse (Sarangi and Roberts, 1999).

One of the best known and most influential projects focusing on gender and discourse in professional communication is the *Language in the Workplace* project in New Zealand (Holmes and Stubbe, 2003; Holmes, 2006a; Schnurr, 2009). Other discourse and gender researchers have investigated professional communication in locations such as Brazil (Ostermann, 2003), Germany (Thimm *et al.*, 2003), Greece (Angouri, forthcoming), Hong Kong (Schnurr, 2010; Schnurr and Mak forthcoming), India (Iyer, 2009), Japan (Saito, 2009), Kenya (Yieke, 2005), Malaysia (Mohd Jan, 2008), Spain (Martin-Rojo and Gómez Estaban, 2005), the UK (Mullany, 2007, 2010a; McRae, 2009; Baxter, 2010) and the US (Ashcraft and Mumby, 2004; Kendall, 2004).

Professional communication research on discourse and gender thus far has tended to be dominated by a focus on spoken discourse, though studies of written discourse have also recently emerged (Koller, 2004; Iyer, 2009). Early research in the field of spoken discourse tended to examine professional–lay person encounters, for example courtroom interaction between lawyers and witnesses, or doctor–patient interactions (see Kendall and Tannen, 1997 for an overview). More recently, there has been an increased emphasis on studying discursive interactions *between* professionals. This includes encounters between people of equal status and interactions where there are power differences between interactants.

Both inter-professional and professional–lay person communications need to be examined if gender and discourse studies are to be as inclusive and wide-ranging as possible. Written discourse analysts, including Koller (2004) and Iyer (2009), have produced fruitful investigations of professional communication texts created by the mass media, and the development of new technologies using written electronic communication has opened up new contexts where professional discourse can be analysed. For example, Schnurr and Mak (forthcoming) examine the discourse of a woman manager through her email discourse style as well as through a more traditional analysis of her spoken discourse.

A number of different approaches to discourse analysis have been adopted by researchers – including critical discourse analysis, interactional sociolinguistics, discourse analysis, conversation analysis, corpus-based discourse analysis and narrative analysis.[2] The boundaries between some of these approaches are fluid, and researchers will often blend together different discourse analytical approaches with the aim of providing thorough and varied analyses. Detailed researcher reflexivity is crucial when one integrates approaches in order to ensure that researchers present a legitimately accountable case for combining discourse analytic frameworks.

For example, Mullany (2007) places interactional sociolinguistics at the centre of her approach, though her analysis includes techniques more commonly associated with conversation analysis, critical discourse analysis and pragmatics. The *Language in the Workplace* data have been successfully examined from a range of perspectives that include critical discourse analysis (Holmes, 2005), interactional sociolinguistics (Holmes and Marra, 2004) narrative (Holmes and Marra, 2005) and pragmatics (Holmes, 2006b); and often these approaches are integrated (Holmes and Stubbe, 2003; Holmes, 2006a; Schnurr, 2009). McRae (2009) investigates meetings in UK companies by combining conversation analysis with evidence from the broader sociocultural context, more akin to techniques from critical discourse analysis. This includes background information from companies, meeting participant feedback and employment statistics. In the area of written discourse, Koller (2004) integrates critical discourse analysis with corpus-based discourse analysis in her examination of media business texts in the US and the UK. Mullany (forthcoming) combines corpus-based discourse techniques with interactional sociolinguistics to examine how gender and professional identities are enacted in spoken inter-professional business interactions and in written electronic healthcare interactions between adolescents and general practitioners (GPs).

Combining different approaches has proved fruitful in contemporary gender and language research. However, some researchers align themselves with one particular paradigm and are not open to integration. This often depends upon the intellectual tradition of the discipline and on how researchers position themselves in relation to this background. For example, researchers who take a 'pure' approach to conversation analysis do not integrate it with any other approach; in this they differ from McRae's study outlined above. For example, Stokoe's (2008: 151–154) analysis of professional–lay person communication during police–suspect interviews focuses solely on the transcriber's version of talk in interaction. No approach or evidence from any other data source is used. 'Pure' conversation analysts only investigate gender when it becomes the topic of conversation through directly indexicalized lexical items (Ochs, 1992), defined as items where gender is explicitly encoded within the lexis, such as *woman/man* (see the section on key concepts for further discussion).[3]

Approaches to gender and discourse that integrate different elements can arguably be seen as more adaptable when researchers are engaged in jointly negotiated, reciprocal investigations that aim to be of practical relevance to those in the professional world who are being researched. According to Sarangi (2006), this should be the aim of all professional communication research. The flexibility and adaptability of the researcher is key to the success of any such jointly negotiated projects. Having a varied discourse analytical toolkit to draw upon can be a distinct advantage when producing jointly negotiated questions and topics. For example, the *Language in the Workplace* researchers have produced a range of written material and hosted events such as workshops and training sessions for their research participants (see Mullany, 2008 for further discussion).

Whatever approaches are taken, it is crucial that the focus remains on exploring social and political gender-based problems in professional settings, which require analysis from a discourse-based perspective. While debates between proponents of different paradigms can be useful if they are well intentioned, it is important for researchers not to get side-tracked by situating themselves in 'armed camps' (Silverman, 2000: 10). This runs the risk of infighting about whose paradigm is 'better' or 'superior', at the expense of exploring continued and persistent gender inequalities.

The next section of this chapter will give an overview of gender and discourse issues that have been examined thus far in professional communication research. 'Key concepts' then details key theoretical concepts that have been used to conceptualize gender and discourse, including specific discourse contexts where professional communication takes place. An analysis section then provides a series of examples of analysis, illustrating a variety of approaches in action. The final section will focus on future lines of enquiry.

Exploring gender issues

A good deal of research thus far has focused on women working in professional roles traditionally occupied by men. For example, in law enforcement, McElhinny (1998) examines the discourse of women police officers in Pittsburgh in the US and Ostermann (2003) analyses how women police officers interact with female members of the public in Cidade do Sudeste, Brazil. Walsh (2001) examines the interplay between discourse and gender when women occupy male-dominated roles within politics, as members of parliament in Northern Ireland and as priests in the Church of England.

A key area of exploration has been that of the persistent gender inequalities that exist within professions and the role that discourse may play in maintaining and perpetuating such inequalities. A focus has been given to women attempting to break through the 'glass ceiling', the persistent barrier faced when aiming to reach the higher echelons of power in businesses and organizations. This has led, in part, to a focus on the discourse of women who occupy leadership positions (Baxter, 2010). In blue-collar workplaces, attention has also been given to women who occupy supervisory/managerial positions, running teams of shop-floor workers in factories (Holmes and Stubbe, 2003; Holmes, 2006a). For low-paid, unskilled professional positions, Cameron (2003) has examined the gendering of spoken discourse in call centres and how this can work to disadvantage both women who occupy these low-paid, low-status roles and men who may not gain employment in such workplaces, as they are perceived to lack the required communication skills for the job (see 'Key concepts' below).

In addition to producing studies that examine women's professional discourse, it is also important for researchers to produce empirical studies of the discourses of men and masculinities. In the late 1990s researchers commented that, although a good deal is written about men and masculinities, often this is not based on empirical evidence (Johnson, 1997), partly due to the understandable initial desire to focus on women's discourse in early research. Within the field of professional communication some researchers have investigated the discourse of both women and men simultaneously, in a range of mixed-sex settings (Baxter, 2003; Holmes, 2006a; Mullany, 2007; Schnurr, 2009). Research on the discourses of men and on masculinities in the professions is still lacking, though data analysis looking solely at this issue has emerged. Holmes (2009) focuses on men, masculinities and leadership. She demonstrates how leaders enact masculinities through their discourse strategies, which include the themes of leader as hero, leader as father and leader as a good bloke/mate. Work has also started to emerge on men in blue-collar professions. Baxter and Wallace (2009) examine the discourse strategies of British builders and Mullany (2010b) examines the discourse styles of Canadian truckers.

Key concepts

The majority of contemporary professional communication researchers view gender as a fluid, active concept, something that we *do* through language as opposed to something that we inherently have (see also Coates, this volume). Butler's (1990, 2004) concept of gender as a performative social construct has played an influential role. Butler advocates that gender is a process that constantly has to be enacted. From her perspective, gender is a 'doing, an incessant activity performed' (Butler, 2004: 1).

In professional communication research the conceptualization of gender as socially constructed is frequently integrated with the communities of practice (CofP) approach. CofPs have been used to investigate how gender and discourse practices are related to specific groups and contexts of interaction. CofPs are conceptualized as follows:

> An aggregate of people who come together around mutual engagement in an endeavor. Ways of doing things, ways of talking, beliefs, values, power relations – in short – practices – emerge in the course of this mutual endeavor.
>
> *(Eckert and McConnell-Ginet, 1992: 464)*

Wenger (1998) argues that a CofP must have the three following components in order to exist: (1) mutual engagement; (2) a jointly negotiated enterprise; and (3) a set of negotiable resources accumulated over time. This 'resources' category includes discourse styles. The CofP approach has proved to be a particularly productive framework, serving as a concept that enables the nuances of individuals' gendered linguistic practices to be accounted for in different professional settings. Holmes and Stubbe (2003) have adapted the CofP framework from a specifically gender-based perspective for investigations of professional communication. They demonstrate how particular workplace contexts can be usefully categorized on a continuum from 'more feminine' to 'more masculine' CofPs.

In addition to gender as a socially constructed concept and to the CofP approach, gender and professional communication researchers have also emphasized the importance of looking not just at the micro context but also at the macro, overarching social context in terms of societal power structures. One effective way to do this is to follow Foucault (1972: 49) in conceptualizing discourses as pluralized and as 'practices that systematically form the objects of which they speak'. When defined in this manner, 'discourses' can be seen as *carrying* ideology' (Sunderland, 2004: 6; see Mills, 1997 for further discussion). The concept of gendered discourses governed by gender ideologies enables researchers to focus upon systems that regulate gendered norms and govern our judgements and evaluations of one another through analyses of discursive content and production.

Gendered discourses will vary from society to society, though one globally consistent discourse is 'the discourse of gender difference' (Sunderland, 2004: 52). This is an all-encompassing discourse, which operates upon the stereotypical precept that women and men will interact and behave in inherently different ways due to biological differences alleged to exist between them. Such perceptions are based upon stereotypical notions of biological essentialism regarding gender and language use, according to which women and men are biologically programmed to speak differently – a myth frequently perpetuated by the mass media and popular culture publications (see Cameron, 2007 for a detailed critique).

Another approach that has been influential in discourse and gender work on professional communication is Ochs' (1992) theory of indexicality. Direct indexicality has already been explained in reference to 'pure' conversation analysis (see 'Introduction' and endnote 3). It is Ochs' theory of indirect indexing of gender that has been used more frequently in professional discourse research thus far. Indirect indexicality of gender is characterized by the fact that interactional styles come to be encoded, and thus indexed, with specific gendered meanings. Individuals' speech styles are viewed and evaluated in light of these gendered norms and expectations. Each society has a range of normative gendered speech styles, held in place by powerful gender ideologies, including the discourse of gender difference, which govern how professionals evaluate one another on the basis of gender. In Western cultures, this includes expectations from men to be assertive, competitive speakers who will dominate the talking time, will be direct and will interrupt aggressively, whereas women will be collaborative and co-operative, will speak minimally, will give supportive feedback and will use indirectness (see Holmes, 2006a: 6 for further details).

Research has shown that, if women stray too far beyond the boundaries of normative feminine discourse styles when enacting professional identities, they may well be negatively evaluated for being too bossy or overly aggressive. On the other hand, if women in positions of authority favour normatively feminine speech styles, they may be negatively evaluated for being weak and ineffective (Crawford, 1995; Lakoff, 2003; Mullany, 2007). This persistent problem, faced by numerous women professionals, is termed the 'double bind'.

Some time will now be spent demonstrating these concepts in practice, as the chapter moves on to present a series of analytical examples of professional discourse in action.

Analysis

There is a wide range of spoken discourse features, taken from various sub-disciplines such as conversation analysis, critical discourse analysis, interactional sociolinguistics and pragmatics, which have proved to be beneficial categories to use when analysing gender and professional communication in stretches of talk. When different analytical paradigms are integrated, this can include (but is by no means limited to) the following: turn-taking techniques, including interruptions and supportive simultaneous talk; contextualisation cues; managing the discourse of disagreement and conflict, including the speech act categories of criticisms, warnings and refusals; giving directives; the role of narrative; and the use of humour and small talk (see Holmes, 2006a; Mullany, 2007 for overviews). In the interests of space, this chapter will focus upon one area specifically: that of managing disagreement and conflict. However, as an integrated analytical approach is adopted here, other discourse elements will be observable within these stretches of discourse: the multi-layered analysis will also highlight the importance of turn-taking, interruptions, contextualization cues, humour, speech acts, and the overall importance of the enactment of power, status and solidarity.

The analysis will examine how the articulation of disagreement and conflict can bring different gendered discourse norms into focus in the societal contexts where professional communication takes place, drawing upon the theoretical concepts outlined in the previous section. From a normatively feminine perspective, disagreement and conflict would be delivered in a way that 'entails damage control, mitigating potentially threatening behaviour, minimizing conflict, and negotiating consensus' (Holmes, 2006a: 171). From a normatively masculine perspective, disagreement and conflict would be articulated in a direct, competitive way, with unmitigated refusals, disruptive interruptions and instances of threatening behaviour.

The first two examples are taken from a meeting recorded as part of an ethnographic case study within a UK-based manufacturing company (Mullany, 2007). This is a company-wide CofP whose main jointly negotiated enterprise is the regular task of reviewing company products. There are ten participants present – six males and four females. Rob is the meeting's Chair and one of the company's directors. All other participants are at a middle-management level apart from Julie, who is at a lower–middle level. (Transcription conventions are at the end of the chapter.)

Example 1

The group is discussing a problem with surplus stock

1.	Carl:	I didn't realise we had (-) fifteen pallets worth
2.	Julie:	hh.
3.	David:	/It's not true to say but\
4.	Julie:	/and I can't believe\ you're saying that I told you
5.		/lot about it\ [laughs]
6.	David:	/oh right\
7.		[laughter from many]
8.	Carl:	I think that must have been before you're saving that for
9.		cust/omers\
10.		/[continued laughter]\
11.	Julie:	hh.
12.	Mark:	So erm Wayne and Paul (xxxx) are looking at (.)
13.		sorting forklift out (.) erm (-).

(Mullany, 2007: 143)

Example 1 illustrates Julie, the most junior member of the CofP, challenging her superiors Carl and David. She begins by exhaling sharply (line 2) in response to Carl's statement (line 1). She then disruptively interrupts David and takes the floor to challenge him, Carl, and by implication all other CofP members at the meeting. Her challenge is mitigated only by her use of *you lot* as a colloquial, collective form of address, in conjunction with her laugh at the end of her utterance (line 5), both of which operate as contextualisation cues of humour. David overlaps the end of her utterance ambiguously (*oh right*), and this is directly followed by laughter from many of the meeting participants. Julie engages in normatively masculine jocular abuse here, using metadiscourse to strengthen her challenge (*saying, told*). Her challenge operates as a form of 'subversive' humour (Holmes and Marra, 2002), where the power of one's superiors can be subverted and challenged with the protection of humour's ambiguity: perlocutionary force can always be denied under the guise that the speaker was not being serious.

Julie successfully challenges her superiors for failing to listen to her at an earlier meeting, but protects herself somewhat through humour and a colloquialism, to ensure that her challenge is not completely unmitigated. Carl adds to this with his humorous comment to Julie (lines 8–9) and laugher continues, with humour operating as a tension releaser. Although Julie laughs along, she then exhales sharply again (line 11), which appears to signal her continued exasperation at information not being retained by her superiors. Mark then takes the floor and brings the topic to a conclusion (lines 12–13).

Example 2 also focuses on Julie's discourse strategies. On this occasion, she performs a refusal that results in disagreement when her superior, David, prompts her to retake the conversational floor. Example 2 takes place after example 1, and Julie and Carl have just been involved in a lengthy process of negotiation regarding the storage space of further stock that has been over-ordered:

Example 2

Julie and Carl have just finished discussing other stock storage space problems. This is followed by a lengthy pause

1.		(-)
2.	David:	You got another one Julie?
3.	Julie:	No get lost
4.		[laughter from many]
5.	Sharon:	No you have

6.	David:	monitors and {product name}
7.	Julie:	[smile voice] what about the one in the
8.		middle that Rob's meant to be
9.		/doing exp\lore opportunity of using
10.	Rob:	/me again?\
11.	Julie:	/{company name}\ samples there [points at agenda]
12.	Rob:	/oh right\ okay well I have sent a note

(Mullany, 2007: 144)

Julie issues a direct, on-record dispreferred response (line 3) to David's indirect directive, mitigated in the form of a request for Julie to take the floor again, after a lengthy pause (lines 1–2). David briefly adopts the role of Chair here, but Julie challenges him in the form of a refusal, followed by a direct command (*get lost*), which functions as an insult. Her challenge is again mitigated by humour, this time through her adoption of a register most typically associated with children's discourse. Uttering direct insults is at odds with the interactional norms of this CofP, and thus results in laughter from many of the meeting participants. Julie has again used subversive humour to challenge her superiors, demonstrating her use of normatively masculine discourse styles.

Sharon then continues by issuing a direct, unmitigated, normatively masculine disagreement with Julie (line 5), and David again attempts to get Julie to take the floor by reading out the agenda item listed with Julie's initials next to it: this is designed to act as a turn-taking prompt. However, Julie is right. There is another agenda item in-between, which belongs to the meeting's Chair, Rob, and he has overall responsibility for turn-allocation in this meeting. Julie draws all participants' attention to this by questioning the item, using a smile voice to give at least some mitigation to her challenge. Rob overlaps, questioning whether it is his turn (line 10), and finally takes the floor after Julie physically points to the place on the agenda by using the deictic 'there' to prove to Rob that she is right. Julie's challenge and refusal, mitigated by humour functioning subversively, highlight how Rob has been neglecting his chairing role.

The next two examples also include a female employee issuing refusals and are taken from Holmes' (2006a) work. Instead of being taken from white-collar meetings, both of these extracts are taken from the interaction of blue-collar employees working in a factory. They involve Ginette, who occupies the position of team manager. The first example takes place on the factory floor, where Ginette is with her subordinate Russell. Russell needs a piece of equipment to carry out his task:

Example 3

Ginette is the team manager of a factory production team, and Russell is a packer in her team on the factory floor

1.	Russ:	can you get me one please [in Samoan] :fa'amolemole: ['please']
2.	Gin:	you get one
3.	Russ:	ah you're not doing anything
4.	Gin:	you go and get one
5.	Russ:	fuck it +++ fuck you go and get your fucking legs out here (fatters)
6.	Gin:	why didn't you get one before I talked to you about that yesterday
7.	Russ:	because we're busy + I got to get all that out of the way

(Holmes, 2006a: 165)

Ginette gives a direct, unmitigated refusal to Russell's request (line 2). Holmes (2006a) details how these participants have a close working relationship and Russell's originally seeming polite request, where he code-switches into Samoan, should be interpreted as rather tongue-in-cheek, as opposed to genuine, politeness (line 1). Politeness in requesting is not a norm in this team, and thus stands out as non-genuine. Russell then issues an explicit challenge to Ginette in response (line 3) and she repeats her earlier unmitigated refusal (line 4). Russell then uses a succession of expletives, commonplace within this team's interaction. Ginette's response shows that she has neither taken offence nor is surprised by Russell's expletives. Instead, Holmes (2006a: 165) observes how she shifts from normatively masculine, direct, on-record refusals to a more normatively feminine strategy, issuing a '"motherly" reprimand', as Russell's superior, that he should have already done this himself.

Holmes contrasts Ginette's interactional refusal of Russell with another of Ginette's refusals, this time in interaction with non-team member Francie:

Example 4

Ginette is talking to Francie, the quality assurance checker. (An NCR is 'a sheet filled out when a product is not up to standard', 2006a: 173):

1. Fra: do you have an NCR for that (box) over there?
2. Gin: yeah I've I'm waiting for a number + +
3.   I need to see Vicky about the NCR thing
4.   I haven't got a number for it yet
5. Fra: oh how would you get it
6. Gin: when I get to see Vicky +++
7. Fra: oh how's about you just give it to me now +
8.   take a copy of that + so I can compare it
9.   and I'll take the number then+++
10. Gin: (where are they) + do you want it right now
11. Fra: if it's possible [laughs]
12. Gin: it's just I've left a + I've got um Jennifer's working +
13.   going through it as well
14. Fra: oh okay is it possible tomorrow then?
15. Gin: I'll get it to you tomorrow morning yeah.

(Holmes, 2006a: 166)

Holmes draws attention to how Ginette displays very different strategies in refusing Francie's request. Ginette does not have the number that is needed, but on this occasion she uses lengthy strategies of conventional politeness to refuse Francie. Ginette starts off in response to Francie's initial request with 'yeah', a 'conventionally polite agreement marker' (Holmes, 2006a: 166). Ginette then provides Francie with a full explanation of why she does not have a number (lines 2–4). Holmes then draws attention to three further attempts by Francie to get the information she needs from Ginette (line 5, 7–9 and 14), and Ginette shows reluctance to respond by pausing on each occasion. She also uses other politeness strategies including hesitations, offering another explanation and engaging in avoidance strategies (lines 2–4, 10, 12–13). Both speakers negotiate with each other and come up with a compromise (lines 14–15) – both parties are satisfied by the end of the interaction.

In contrast to the normatively masculine strategies that Ginette uses with Russell, she displays a range of normatively feminine strategies when needing to issue a refusal to non-team member Francie. Ginette thus draws on a wide range of strategies in her discourse style. Holmes concludes that it is commonplace within the production team for masculine strategies to be used, with on-record, direct refusals being given, but, when interacting with a member of the factory CofP outside the production team, Ginette uses more conventionally feminine strategies.

Coming back to meeting discourse, the final analytical example is taken from an ethnographic study of a retail company in the UK (Mullany, 2007). Example 5 is from a regular departmental managerial meeting, though all managers also work on the shop floor. There are six participants present – four females and two males. The meeting is chaired by Amy, an upper-middle level manager who is the direct superior of all present. Kirsty and Eddie are trainee managers. This is their first meeting. Karen is at a middle-management level:

Example 5

Amy is explaining departmental policy to Kirsty and Eddie

1. Amy: we're going to be carrying it for more than fifteen weeks=
2. Karen: =yeah it's ten weeks for stock and it will be calculated
3.   on how many sales within five weeks
4. Amy: No it's longer than that Karen
5. Karen: Oh (.) right
6. Amy: It's longer

In example 5, Amy issues a direct, on-record, unmitigated disagreement (line 4), which challenges her subordinate Karen's declarative (lines 2–3). Amy thus adopts a normatively masculine style to correct Karen's mistake. Karen's response (line 5) is rather ambiguous, and Amy responds to it by reiterating her point (line 6). Amy decides not to protect Karen's face needs at the expense of ensuring that trainee managers Kirsty and Eddie have the correct information they need in order to carry out their roles successfully.

All analytical examples presented here demonstrate that, in contrast to early discourse and gender findings that catalogued distinct gender differences in professional discourse styles (see Kendall and Tannen, 1997), more recent studies have found ample evidence of women using normatively masculine strategies as well as normatively feminine strategies, even when the speaker occupies the lowest position on the institutional hierarchy, as was the case in examples 1 and 2. Julie was very strategic in how she issued her challenges, which arguably prevented her from being reprimanded by her superiors. Ginette's discourse provides evidence of a 'wide verbal repertoire' (Marra *et al.*, 2006), where a speaker strategically adopts normatively masculine and feminine strategies. Although space prevents further illustrations, it is notable that Julie and Amy can also be witnessed using features of a wide verbal repertoire, in addition to the normatively masculine strategies they have been shown to use above (see Mullany, 2007).

The discourse strategies selected will depend in part upon workplace cultures, the type of CofP where the discourse has taken place, the specific discourse setting and the conversational topic. However, the crucial point is that women and men may not be evaluated and assessed in the same manner as professionals, even if they use remarkably similar discourse styles. Marra *et al.* (2006) draw attention to the fact that exactly the same linguistic strategies can be evaluated very differently depending upon whether they are used by a woman or a man, women often being subject to the double bind, particularly when they try to enact authority.

With the two women leaders introduced above, Ginette provides a good example of a successful woman leader who is positively evaluated by her colleagues and is not subject to the double bind. However, in contrast, when interviewed as part of the retail ethnographic study, Karen made the following comment about Amy:[4]

> Amy (.) is a very strong character very straightforward erm says
> what she means is very direct (.) and it can be quite an overpowering
> experience talking to her.

Lucy, another of Amy's subordinates, made the following comment:

> Amy is very domineering…she's quite abrupt you know as a woman (.)
> I can be quite honest with her though sometimes she scares the pants off me.

These evaluations typify a series of negative comments made about Amy on the basis of her gender and interactional style from both women and men, status equals and subordinates (Mullany, 2007: 169–176). These evaluative instances illustrate the importance of looking for evidence of the double bind and how the discourse of gender difference can result in a negative evaluation of women in professional positions if they stray outside of expectations for gendered speech norms. Although Amy's interactional style displayed many features of normatively feminine discourse (2007: 106–124), it is the less frequent instances of normatively masculine talk that get focused upon in evaluations of her as a manager. Commentators have illustrated that men are not subject to the same negativity if they stray outside the boundaries for acceptable masculine behaviour:

> When women attempt to prove their competence by 'acting like a man' they are considered to be less than women. When there seems to be some merit in what would normally have been considered a 'female' approach, men adopt it as their own. What was seen as weak is now thought of as flexible; what was emotional now combines with the rational to bring balance.
>
> *(Appelbaum et al., 2002: 45)*

This rather pessimistic scenario is not the case in all professional communicative settings, as evidenced by Ginette's success in her factory. However, it is crucially important to look for any evidence of the double bind when examining discourse and gender in professional communication, and, as part of this, to ensure that broader social–cultural practices of the societal context where the discourse is taking place are also analysed.

Towards the future

It is the intention that this chapter has demonstrated the importance of conducting studies of discourse, gender and professional communication. In particular, there was a focus upon how discourse and gender have been theorized and analysed in recent professional communication research. However, although investigations in this area have grown significantly in recent years, there is still a range of topics and a plethora of different professional groups whose discourse remains underexplored from a gender perspective. For instance, much more research is required on what Banyard (2010) refers to as the five 'Cs', where women in countries all over the world dominate the professions of *cleaning, caring, clerical work, cashiering* and *catering*. These are all low-paid posts with minimal status. Banyard (2010: 85–86) argues that, as there is so little opportunity for career development within these professions, this forms a 'sticky floor', which prevents women from 'getting anywhere near the glass ceiling, let alone smashing it'.

Although research on gender, discourse and sexualities has grown in a range of other contexts (Saunston and Kryatzis, 2007), the interplay between discourse, sexualities and professional identities remains underexplored in professional contexts (though see Morrish, 2002). This should include a focus on the influence of sexual orientation on the performance of professional identities and also on the study of sexual desires/sexual behaviour in professions. As a part of this, in addition to issues of gender inequality (including the 'glass ceiling' and the 'sticky floor'), other gender-based social and political problems, such as instances of sexual harassment and sexual harassment legal cases, would benefit from a discourse-based analysis. Access to such data may be far more difficult to obtain, but, nevertheless, research of this nature would be invaluable. The research field would also be more inclusive if a range of different ethnic groups and more varied age ranges were investigated. In overall conclusion, discourse and gender studies of professional communication are currently at an exciting stage of development. All indications are that this area of discourse analysis research will continue to thrive in future years.

Transcription conventions

A combined version of Holmes (2006a: 223) and Mullany (2007: xii):

+	Pause of up to one second
(.)	Pause of two seconds or less
(-)	Pause of over two seconds
(xxx)	Material that was impossible to make out
(fatters)	Transcriber's best guess at an unclear utterance
{xxx}	Material that has been edited out for the purposes of confidentiality
xx/xxx\xx	Simultaneous speech
[laughs]	Paralinguistic features in square brackets
[*comments*]	Editorial comments italicized in square brackets
=	No discernible gap between speakers' utterances

Further reading

Baxter, J. (2010) *The Language of Female Leadership*. Basingstoke: Palgrave.

This volume presents an up-to-date perspective on gendered discourses and how they affect the spoken discourse strategies that female leaders use. Baxter defines three corporation types: male-dominated, gender-divided and gender-multiple. She identifies different gendered discourses that go along with each type. The book includes advice on how women leaders can achieve effective leadership language.

Holmes, J. (2006) *Gendered Talk at Work*. Oxford: Blackwell.

Holmes' work brings together a plethora of spoken data analyses from the *Language in the Workplace* corpus. These include interactions from government departments, corporate organizations, factories, medical settings and IT companies. She covers a range of areas of analysis including gender and leadership talk, relational practice, humour, disagreement and complaint and narrative analysis.

Mullany, L. (2007) *Gendered Discourse in the Professional Workplace*. Basingstoke: Palgrave.

This monograph is based upon ethnographic studies in UK manufacturing and retail companies. Its overarching aim is to provide a discourse-based investigation of why women managers still cannot break through the glass ceiling. A number of different approaches to discourse are explored and analyses of the interactions of women and men managers are presented to explore this complex and persistent area of gender inequality.

Iyer, R. (2009) 'Entrepreneurial identities and the problematic of subjectivity in media-mediated discourses', *Discourse and Society* 20: 241–264.

This article presents a written textual analysis of media discourses authored by women entrepreneurs, taken from Indian newspapers and popular magazines. Iyer takes a critical discourse analysis approach, which draws upon a range of different analytical features. She explores dominant gender discourses in her texts including dominant discourses of femininity and patriarchy. She characterizes a newer, oppositional discourse of 'being/becoming', which signifies a shift in representations of women, echoing shifts in gender relations and wider social changes.

Notes

1 The terms 'white collar' and 'blue collar' originate from a tradition of different colours of workplace clothing, depending upon occupation type. 'Blue collar' refers to blue shirts/overalls worn by those

engaged in manual labour. 'White collar' refers to white shirts worn by those in offices, engaged in non-manual work.

2 An additional approach to professional communication research is 'feminist post-structuralist discourse analysis' (FPDA, Baxter, 2003). According to Baxter, FPDA is a supplementary approach. It aims to examine 'the continuously fluctuating ways in which speakers, within any discursive context, are positioned as powerful or powerless by competing social and institutional discourses' (2003: 44). Baxter suggests that these aspects of spoken discourse analysis have not been given enough focus by researchers of conversation analysis or critical discourse analysis.

3 From a 'pure' conversation analysis perspective, lexis that directly indexes gender is known as a categorization device. Advocates of this approach argue that this is the only way to see if gender is relevant in a conversation. In contrast, many others argue that gender is omnirelevant within discourse (Eckert and McConnell-Ginet, 2003; Holmes, 2005). An approach that relies upon instances where gender is directly indexed is limiting, particularly as direct indexicality of gender occurs very infrequently within professional (and everyday) discourse (see Swann, 2009).

4 The interviews where these stretches of talk occurred were dyadic encounters collected as part of a mixed-methods approach. For a detailed account of the interview process, see Mullany (2007).

References

Angouri, J. (forthcoming) 'Doing gender in a consortium of two multinational engineering companies situated in Greece', *Gender and Language*, 5 (2).

Appelbaum, S., Audet., L., and Miller, J. (2002) 'Gender and leadership? Leadership and gender? A journey through the landscape of theories', *Leadership and Organization Development*, 24: 43–51.

Ashcraft, K. and Mumby, D. (2004) 'Organizing a critical communicology of gender and work', *International Journal of the Sociology of Language*, 166: 19–43.

Banyard, K. (2010) *The Equality Illusion*. London: Faber.

Bargiela-Chiappini, F., Nickerson, C., and Planken, B. (2007) *Business Discourse*. Basingstoke: Palgrave.

Baxter, J. (2003) *Positioning Gender in Discourse: A Feminist Methodology*. Basingstoke: Palgrave.

Baxter, J. (2010) *The Language of Female Leadership*. Basingstoke: Palgrave.

Baxter, J. and Wallace, K. (2009) 'Outside in-group and out-group identities? Constructing male solidarity and female exclusion in UK builders' talk', *Discourse & Society*, 20: 411–430.

Butler, J. (1990) *Gender Trouble: Feminism and the Subversion of Identity*. New York: Routledge.

Butler, J. (2004) *Undoing Gender*. New York: Routledge.

Cameron, D. (2003) 'Gender and language ideologies', in J. Holmes and M. Meyerhoff (eds.) *The Handbook of Language and Gender*. Oxford: Blackwell, pp. 447–467.

Cameron, D. (2007) *The Myth of Mars and Venus*. Oxford: Oxford University Press.

Crawford, M. (1995) *Talking Difference: On Gender and Language*. London: Sage.

Eckert, P. and McConnell-Ginet, S. (1992) 'Think practically and look locally: language and gender as community-based practice', *Annual Review of Anthropology*, 21: 461–490.

Eckert, P. and McConnell-Ginet., S. (2003) *Language and Gender*. Cambridge: Cambridge University Press.

Foucault, M. (1972) *The Archaeology of Knowledge*. London: Routledge.

Gunnarsson, B.-L. (2009) *Professional Discourse*. London: Continuum.

Holmes, J. (2005) 'Power and discourse at work: is gender relevant?', in M. Lazar (ed.) *Feminist Critical Discourse Analysis*. Basingstoke: Palgrave, pp. 31–60.

Holmes, J. (2006a) *Gendered Talk at Work*. Oxford: Blackwell.

Holmes, J. (2006b) 'Sharing a laugh: pragmatic aspects of humour and gender in the workplace', *Journal of Pragmatics*, 38: 26–50.

Holmes, J. (2009) 'Men, masculinities and leadership: different discourse styles at work', in P. Pichler and E. Eppler (eds.) *Gender and Spoken Interaction*. Basingstoke: Palgrave, pp. 186–210.

Holmes, J. and Marra, M. (2002) 'Having a laugh at work: how humour contributes to workplace culture', *Journal of Pragmatics*, 34: 1683–1710.

Holmes, J. and Marra, M. (2004) 'Relational practice in the workplace: women's talk or gendered discourse?', *Language in Society*, 33: 377–398.

Holmes, J. and Marra, M. (2005) 'Narrative and the construction of professional identity in the workplace', in J. Thornborrow and J. Coates (eds.) *The Sociolinguistics of Narrative*. Amsterdam: Benjamins, pp. 193–213.

Holmes, J. and Stubbe, M. (2003) ' "Feminine" workplaces: stereotype and reality', in J. Holmes and M. Meyerhoff (eds.) *The Handbook of Language and Gender*. Oxford: Blackwell, pp. 573–600.

Iyer, R. (2009) 'Entrepreneurial identities and the problematic of subjectivity in media-mediated discourses', *Discourse and Society*, 20: 241–264.

Johnson, S. (1997) 'Theorizing language and masculinity: a feminist perspective', in S. Johnson and U. H. Meinhof (eds.) *Language and Masculinity*. Oxford: Blackwell, pp. 47–64.

Kendall, S. (2004) 'Framing authority: gender, face and mitigation at a radio network', *Discourse & Society*, 15: 55–79.

Kendall, S. and Tannen, D. (1997) 'Gender and language in the workplace', in R. Wodak (ed.) *Gender and Discourse*. New York: Longman, pp. 81–105.

Koester, A. (2010) *Workplace Discourse*. London: Continuum.

Koller, V. (2004) *Metaphor and Gender in Business Media Discourse: A Critical Cognitive Study*. Basingstoke: Palgrave.

Lakoff, R. (2003) 'Language, gender and politics: putting "women" and "power" in the same sentence', in J. Holmes and M. Meyerhoff (eds.) *The Handbook of Language and Gender*. Oxford: Blackwell, pp. 161–178.

Marra, M., Schnurr, S., and Holmes, J. (2006) 'Effective leadership in New Zealand workplaces', in J. Baxter (ed.) *Speaking Out: The Female Voice in Public Contexts*. Basingstoke: Palgrave, pp. 240–260.

Martin Rojo, L. and Gómez Esteban, C. (2005) 'The gender of power: the female style in labour organizations', in M. Lazar (ed.) *Feminist Critical Discourse Analysis*. Basingstoke: Palgrave, pp. 66–89.

McElhinny, B. (1998) '"I don't smile much anymore"', in J. Coates (ed.) *Language and Gender: A Reader*. Oxford: Blackwell, pp. 309–327.

McRae, S. (2009) 'It's a blokes' thing: gender, occupational roles and talk in the workplace', in P. Pichler and E. Eppler (eds.) *Gender and Spoken Interaction*. Basingstoke: Palgrave, pp. 186–210.

Mills, S. (1997) *Discourse*. London: Routledge.

Mohd Jan, J. (2008) Euphemisms at work: a linguistic inquiry of men's discourse at the workplace. Paper presented at IGALA5, Victoria University of Wellington, New Zealand, 3 July.

Morrish, L. (2002) 'The case of the indefinite pronoun: discourse and the concealment of lesbian identity in class', in L. Litosseliti and J. Sunderland (eds.) *Gender Identity and Discourse Analysis*. Amsterdam: Benjamins, pp. 177–192.

Mullany, L. (2007) *Gendered Discourse in the Professional Workplace*. Basingstoke: Palgrave.

Mullany, L. (2008) 'Negotiating methodologies: making language and gender relevant in the professional workplace', in K. Harrington, L. Litosseliti, H. Sauntson, and J. Sunderland (eds.) *Gender and Language Research Methodologies*. Basingstoke: Palgrave, pp. 43–55.

Mullany, L. (2010a) 'Gendered identities in the professional workplace: negotiating the glass ceiling', in C. Llamas and D. Watt (eds.) *Language and Identities*. Edinburgh: Edinburgh University Press, pp. 179–191.

Mullany, L. (2010b) '(Im)politeness, rapport management and workplace culture: truckers performing masculinities on Canadian ice-roads', in F. Bargiela-Chiappini and D. Kadar (eds.) *Politeness Across Cultures*. Basingstoke: Palgrave, pp. 61–184.

Mullany, L. (forthcoming) *The Sociolinguistics of Gender in Public Life*. Basingstoke: Palgrave.

Ochs, E. (1992) 'Indexing gender', in A. Duranti and C. Goodwin (eds.) *Rethinking Context: Language as an Interactive Phenomenon*. Cambridge: Cambridge University Press, pp. 335–358.

Ostermann, A. C. (2003) 'Communities of practice at work: gender, facework and the power of habitus at an all-female police station and a feminist crisis intervention center in Brazil', *Discourse & Society*, 14: 473–505.

Saito, J. (2009) 'Are they always direct? Male superiors' directive strategies in a Japanese workplace', in J. De Bres, J. Holmes, and M. Marra (eds.) *Proceedings of the 5th Biennial IGALA Conference*. Wellington: Victoria University of Wellington, pp. 195–210.

Sarangi, S. (2006) 'The conditions and consequences of professional discourse studies', in R. Kiely, P. Rea-Dickens, H. Woodfield, and G. Clibbon (eds.) *Language, Culture in Applied Linguistics*. London: Equinox, pp. 199–220.

Sarangi, S. and Roberts, C. (1999) 'The dynamics of interactional and institutional orders in work-related settings', in S. Sarangi and C. Roberts (eds.) *Talk, Work and Institutional Order: Discourse in Medical, Mediation and Management Settings*. Berlin: Mouton, pp. 1–57.

Saunston, H. and Kryatzis, S. (eds.) (2007) *Language, Sexualities and Desires*. Basingstoke: Palgrave.

Schnurr, S. (2009) *Leadership Discourse at Work*. Basingstoke: Palgrave.

Schnurr, S. (2010) ' "Decision made, lets move on": negotiating gender and professional identity in Hong Kong workplaces', in M. Bieswanger *et al.* (eds.) *Language in Its Socio-Cultural Context: New Explorations in Global, Medial and Gendered Uses*. Berlin: Peter Lang, pp. 111–136.

Schnurr, S. and Mak, B. (forthcoming) 'Leadership and workplace realities in Hong Kong: Is gender really *not* an issue?', *Gender and Language*, 5 (2).

Silverman, D. (2000) *Doing Qualitative Research: A Practical Guide*. London: Sage.

Stokoe, E. (2008) 'Categories, actions and sequences: Formulating gender in talk-in-interaction', in K. Harrington, L. Litosseliti, H. Sauntson, and J. Sunderland (eds.) *Gender and Language Research Methodologies*. Basingstoke: Palgrave, pp. 139–157.

Sunderland, J. (2004) *Gendered Discourses*. Basingstoke: Palgrave.

Swann, J. (2009) 'Doing gender against the odds', in P. Pichler and E. Eppler (eds.) *Gender and Spoken Interaction*. Basingstoke: Palgrave, pp. 18–41.

Thimm, C., Koch, S., and Schey, S. (2003) 'Communicating gendered professional identity: competence, cooperation, and conflict in the workplace', in J. Holmes and M. Meyerhoff (eds.) *The Handbook of Language and Gender*. Oxford: Blackwell, pp. 528–549.

Walsh, C. (2001) *Gender and Discourse: Language and Power in Politics, the Church and Organisations*. Harlow: Pearson.

Wenger, E. (1998) *Communities of Practice*. Cambridge: Cambridge University Press.

Yieke, F. (2005) Gender and discourse: topic organisation on workplace management committee meetings in Kenya. Paper presented at Theoretical and Methodological Approaches to Gender BAAL/CUP Seminar, University of Birmingham, 18 November.

Part VI

Identity, culture and discourse

37

Politics as usual

Investigating political discourse in action

Ruth Wodak

Introduction: discourse and/about politics

In our daily lives we are confronted with many genres of political discourse: political speeches of all kinds, televised press conferences, broadcast or televised interviews with politicians, snippets on the Internet (e.g. YouTube) or reports on political events in the press.[1] Moreover, slogans and advertisements confront us when we are walking down the street, leaflets from political parties or interest groups are delivered by mail and during election campaigns, we are able to listen to politicians campaigning at election rallies. Political parties have their own home pages, logos and brands; we are thus able to download relevant documents and photos as well as party programmes. If we wish to contact members of parliament, or even the president of the United States, we are able to email them or chat with them on discussion forums specifically constructed for such purposes (Wodak and Wright, 2007).

The above examples all shed light on the life and work of politicians from the outside. These are official genres, designed for the public and demonstrating the many ways in which politicians like to present themselves, stage their work and 'perform', and therefore how they like to be perceived by their various audiences (on 'frontstage', see below). These activities follow specific norms and rules, are part of the 'field of politics' (in Pierre Bourdieu's sense) and are ritualized, as Murray Edelman claimed in his seminal book *The Symbolic Use of Politics* (Edelman, 1967). We rarely (if ever), though, have access to the backstage, to the politics *du couloir*, and to the many conversations and gossip in the corridors when politicians meet informally.[2] Indeed, research provides ample evidence that such interactions on backstage influence political decision-making in much more salient ways than (the more easily accessible) frontstage performances (Wodak, 2011).

The notion of *performance* is necessarily and inherently related to the metaphor of being in the theatre and on stage. Goffman distinguishes between *frontstage* and *backstage*; these two concepts are central for the analysis and understanding of politicians' behaviour. Frontstage is where the performance takes place and the performers and the audience are present.

> Front, then, is the expressive equipment of a standard kind intentionally or unwittingly employed by the individual during his performance. For preliminary purposes, it will be convenient to distinguish and label what seem to be the standard parts of the front.
>
> *(Goffman, 1959: 17)*

Backstage is where performers are present but the audience is not, and the performers can step out of character without fear of disrupting the performance; 'the back region is the place where the impression fostered by the performance is knowingly contradicted as a matter of course' (Goffman, 1959: 112). It is where facts suppressed in the frontstage or various kinds of informal actions may appear which are not accessible to outsiders. The backstage is completely separate from the frontstage. No members of the audience can or should appear in the back. The actors adopt many measures to ensure this; thus access is controlled by gate-keepers. It is, of course, much more difficult to perform once a member of the audience is in the backstage; politicians would not want the audience to see when she or he is practising a speech or being briefed by an advisor (see Wodak, 2009a: 7–11, 2011 for an extensive overview of Goffman's approach).

Before, however, turning to this specific aspect of 'doing politics', I would like to – at least briefly – point to salient issues that currently determine the field of language and/in politics:

a) How broad or narrow should 'political action' (or 'political language behaviour') be defined? Do we restrict ourselves to the study of the traditional political genres (like speeches, slogans, debates), or are all everyday actions in some way 'political'?

b) What is the role of the political elites? Who determines political issues? What is the role of grassroot movements?

c) How do ideologies and belief systems manifest themselves in various genres of political discourse? What is the relationship between media and politics?

d) What are the main functions of political discourses? How do power structures relate to decision-making strategies?

e) Finally, what are the main settings where political practices take place (*doing politics*)? How do the structures of various organizations and institutions influence political discourses?

There are certainly many more and related questions, like the influence of globalizing processes or the change of political rhetoric and its functions over time (Chilton *et al.*, 2010).

In this chapter, it is, of course, impossible to answer all these questions. I will thus mainly explore one particular dimension of political discursive practices in more detail: *politics as usual* on the *backstage*. This implies investigating the daily work of politicians in their respective workplace – national and transnational political institutions. Hence, many relevant aspects of *organizational discourse studies* have to be accounted for as well. In sum, I ask the question: what do politicians actually *do*? How is the *profession* of politics organized, apart from the scarce impressions that are accessible to laypeople? The opacity of *politics as usual* has severe consequences, as Colin Hay (2007) has rightly pointed to: des-information and non-information about the work of politicians might be some of many factors leading to disillusionment and depoliticization – or to what in the European Union is labelled as 'democratic deficit' (see also Abélès, 1992; Koller and Wodak, 2008; Wodak, 2009a, b, 2010, 2011).

In the following, I will first summarize some relevant approaches to the study of discourse and politics and discuss the development of the field of 'language and politics'. Thereafter I will present my own interdisciplinary theory to 'performing politics' and illustrate it with some examples of recent ethnography in European Union institutions. Finally, the contribution and the limitations of discourse analysis to the study of language and/in politics will be discussed.

'Grand/symbolic politics' and 'politics in everyday life' – theoretical approaches

The meanings of 'politics' – characteristics of 'grand politics'

The approaches of Aristotle and Machiavelli can be regarded as the two primary roots for the many and diverse meanings of politics: ethics and morals, on the one hand, violence and hegemony, on the other:

Our purpose is to consider what form of political community is best of all for those who are most able to realize their ideal in life. We must therefore examine not only this but other constitutions, both such as actually exist in well-governed states, and any theoretical forms which are held in esteem, so that what is good and useful may be brought to light.

(Aristotle, 1999: Book II, Ch. 1, pp. 30–31)

The Aristotelian goal, to discover the best form of government, is thus clearly linked to definitions of ethics and morals, i.e. values for a given society: what is believed to be 'good' or 'bad'. The definition of values always depends on the context and the political system: what might have been 'good' for a totalitarian state like Nazi Germany was certainly experienced as 'bad' for democratic systems. On the other hand, we find 'the dark view of political power'. All politics is of necessity driven by a quest for power, but power is inherently unpredictable, irresponsible, irrational and persuasive. This view has been articulated most prominently by Michel Foucault, yet its roots can be detected in many authors, from Niccolò Machiavelli to Antonio Gramsci.

Research in the field of language and politics has expanded enormously in recent years (see Wodak and de Cillia, 2006 for an overview). Although this kind of research may seem to be quite 'young', rhetoric is one of the oldest academic disciplines and was already concerned with aspects of political communication in ancient times. After the Second World War, Harold Lasswell and Nathan Leites (1949) published one of the most important studies on quantitative semantics in the field of language and politics, developing approaches from communication and mass media research. In the late 1940s, research on the intricate links between language and politics began throughout Central Europe, though mainly in Germany. The novel *1984* by George Orwell (1949) was a significant point of departure for the development of the entire field. Of course, all this research was influenced by the massive use of propaganda during the Second World War and in the emerging Cold War era, in the 1950s.

Political linguistics (*Politolinguistik*) was the first attempt to create an academic discipline for the research of political discourse. Critical linguistic research began in the wake of National Socialism and was conducted primarily by Victor Klemperer (1947, 2005) and Rolf Sternberger (Sternberger *et al.*, 1957) who both paved the way for the new discipline. Both Klemperer and Sternberger sampled, categorized and described the words used during the Nazi regime: many words had acquired new meanings, other words were forbidden (borrowed words from other languages, like *cigarette*), and neologisms (new words) were created; similar language policies were adopted by former communist totalitarian regimes (Wodak and Kirsch, 1995). Controlling language in this way implies an attempt to control the (minds and thoughts of) people.

Burkhardt (1996: 79) proposed the use of 'political language' as the generic phrase comprising 'all types of public, institutional and private talks on political issues, all types of texts typical of politics as well as the use of lexical and stylistic linguistic instruments characterizing talks about political contexts'. He lists four different procedures as being particularly promising methods and techniques to be used for 'ideological reconstruction': *lexical-semantic techniques* (analysis of catch-words and value words, of euphemisms and of ideological polysemy); *sentence and text-semantic procedures* (analysis of tropes, of semantic isotopes and of integration and exclusion strategies); *pragmatic text-linguistic techniques* (analysis of forms of address, speech acts, allusions, presuppositions, argumentation, rhetoric, quotations, genres and intertextuality); and finally *semiotic techniques* (icon, symbol and semiotic analysis).

From 1990 onwards research on *political discourse* expanded (Wilson, 1990). Research was carried out into communication within political organizations (European Union committees and decision-making processes: Krzyżanowski and Oberhuber 2007; the United Nations: Holzscheiter, 2005 the European Parliament: Wodak, 2009a, 2010, 2011), as well as on the unique (charismatic) style of politicians (Tony Blair: Fairclough, 2000; US senators: Duranti, 2006), on political speeches (commemorative speeches: Ensink and Sauer, 2003; Herr *et al.*, 2008), on right wing political rhetoric (Wodak and Pelinka, 2002), on strategies of manipulation and persuasion (the 2003 Iraq war: Chouliaraki 2006), on interviews with politicians in the media (Clayman and Heritage, 2002), and so forth. Nowadays many refereed journals publish research from this area (e.g. *Discourse and Society; Journal of Language and Politics; Discourse and Communication*).

Politics on 'backstage'

It is much more difficult to explore the 'backstage', the everyday life of politicians, than the staging of 'grand politics'. Once we enter the backstage, for example in the European Parliament (see below), we encounter the routines of political organizations that are – at first sight – non-transparent and seem as chaotic as in any organization. Hence, ethnographic research is needed, such as participant observation in organizations, in-depth and narrative interviews, shadowing of insiders, and so forth to be able to grasp the processes of political strategizing and decision-making. Focussing only on typical frontstage activities (such as political speeches, for example) does not suffice to understand and explain the complexity of 'politics'. This is why the organizational contexts (structures, rules, regulations, and constraints) have to be accounted for in detail.

Issues of *power, hegemony* and *ideology* have been reconceived as central to social and linguistic practices in all organizations, since all organizational forms can be translated into language and communication and because, as Deetz (1982: 135) concluded, talk and writing 'connect each perception to a larger orientation and system of meaning'. The distinction between structure and agency is useful, since it moves us away from a preoccupation with individual motivations and behaviours to the discursive practices through which organizational activity is performed in ritualized in ever new ways. Four prominent linguistic–discursive approaches have proven particularly influential in organizational research to date: ethno-methodology; conversation analysis (CA); sociolinguistic analysis; and (critical) discourse analysis (CDA).

Pre-eminent in this regard is *critical discourse analysis* (CDA), which integrates a range of discourse analytic approaches and methodologies with theoretical concerns by drawing on key approaches in social theory (Wodak and Meyer, 2009). Arguably, CDA has gained ground because it provides researchers with the requisite ontological and methodological traction to look at the processes that render semiotic devices 'objective', and therefore provide the basis for logics to be mobilized, (re)contextualized and made manifest through hierarchy, values, symbols, strategies and discursive as well as social practices within organizations.

Ethnomethodology, whilst technically rooted in sociology, emphasizes the conditions that have to be satisfied for certain actions to be perceived as signifying a recognized sanction (Garfinkel *et al.*, 1981). *Conversation analysis* (CA) identifies the very detailed aspects of members' turn-taking strategies that are critical to performance and membership (Schegloff, 1987; Drew and Heritage, 1992) and deals with relatively short stretches of interaction as being revealing and representative of, the organizations' interactional principles. *Sociolinguistic analysis* has a basis in the tradition of correlating sociological parameters (e.g. age, class and gender) with variations in organizational discourse (Bernstein, 1987). *Interactional sociolinguistics* has its origins in symbolic interactionism (Goffman, 1959) and is further developed in the broad domain of discourse studies, and responds to the criticism that the first approach underplays the effect of context on organizational discourse.

Studies in this domain are not only labour-intensive due to the required ethnography, but they are usually organized as case studies that are not easy to generalize from. Nevertheless, Holzscheiter's investigation into decision-making procedures about legal requirements of child protection on the UN level allows important insight into the debates of NGOs and their impact on government officials (2005). Duranti's participant observation of a US senator's election campaign trail raised awareness about the many discursive practices and persuasive devices required to keep on track such a huge campaign and related persons (2006). Decision-making processes involving both written materials (such as minutes, statements and programs) and debates in committees lie at the core of qualitative political science research into Israeli community centres (Yanow, 1996) and of text-linguistic and discourse analytic investigations into EU committees such as the Competitiveness Advisory Group (Wodak, 2000a, b; Wodak *et al.* 2011). The interdependence of frontstage and backstage becomes truly apparent in these studies; moreover, it becomes obvious how much is decided on backstage and how negotiations and compromises are staged and enacted thereafter on frontstage.

Pragmatic–linguistic expertise becomes salient in the discourse analysis of daily (political) interactions: much knowledge is regularly *presupposed* in every interaction (Goffman, 1981; Wodak, 2009a: 45ff.). Misunderstandings occur when presuppositions or other indirect pragmatic devices either are not available or differ significantly. Sharing presupposed and inferred meanings and hence including or excluding others in strategic ways is, I believe, constitutive of political power play and of achieving one's aims in the political arena (Jäger and Maier 2009).

The discourse-historical approach in CDA (DHA)

Developed in the field of *critical discourses studies*, the DHA provides a vehicle for looking at latent power dynamics and the range of potential in agents, because it integrates and triangulates knowledge about historical, intertextual sources and the background of the social and political fields within which discursive events are embedded. Moreover, the DHA distinguishes between three dimensions that constitute textual meanings and structures: the *topics* that are spoken/written about; the *discursive strategies* employed; and the *linguistic means* that are drawn upon to realize both topics and strategies (e.g. argumentative strategies, *topoi*, presuppositions – see below for an extensive discussion).

Systematic qualitative analysis in the DHA takes *four layers of context* into account: the *intertextual and interdiscursive relationships* between utterances, texts, genres and discourses; the extra-linguistic social/sociological variables; the *history and archaeology of texts and organizations*; and institutional frames of the specific *context of a situation* (the specific episodes under investigation). In this way we are able to explore how discourses, genres and texts change due to socio-political contexts, and with what effects (see Wodak, 2001).

Furthermore, two concepts are salient for analysing the *backstage* of politics: *intertextuality* refers to the linkage of all texts to other texts, both in the past and in the present. Such links can be established in different ways: through continued reference to a topic or to its main actors; through reference to the same events as the other texts; or through the reappearance of a text's main arguments in another text. The second important process is labeled *recontextualization*. By taking an argument, a topic, a genre or a discursive practice out of context and restating/realizing it in a new context, we first observe the process of de-contextualization, and then, when the respective element is implemented in a new context, of recontextualization. The element then acquires a new meaning, because, as Wittgenstein (1967) demonstrated, meanings are formed in use.

When analysing micro-linguistic patterns of persuasive rhetoric, *topoi* and forms of argumentation in Toulmins' sense (1956) are relevant. *Topoi* are the content-related warrants or 'conclusion rules' that connect the argument or arguments with the conclusion or the central claim. They appeal to commonsense knowledge, frequently without providing any evidence for establishing the warrant. As such, they justify the transition from the premise to the conclusion: *topoi* are thus central to the analysis of seemingly convincing fallacious arguments that are widely adopted in all political discourses (Kienpointner, 1996: 562). As I illustrate below, the concept of *topos* can be adequately employed when analysing everyday political discourse. Reisigl and Wodak (2001) also draw on Van Eemeren and Grootendorst (1992) when providing a list of common fallacies, which includes the following frequently employed argumentative devices: *argumentum ad baculum*, i.e. 'threatening with the stick', thus trying to intimidate instead of using plausible arguments; *argumentum ad hominem*, which can be defined as a verbal attack on the antagonist's personality and character instead of discussing the content of an argument; and *the fallacy of hasty generalization*, when one makes generalizations about characteristics attributed to a group without providing any substantial evidence. When presenting some aspects of 'politics as usual' by drawing on my ethnography of the European Parliament and members of the European Parliament's (MEP) daily lives, I will employ the DHA and the categories listed above.

Investigating 'politics as usual': an integrative and interdisciplinary approach

In studying the *performance of politicians*, while conducting a case study on MEPs' daily work in the European Parliament (Wodak, 2009a, 2009c, 2011, for extensive discussion of the theoretical concepts), I draw on several different approaches from a range of disciplines, in addition to CDA and the DHA. Apart from interviewing many MEPs about their socialization into the EP, their motives, their daily work routines and their visions for the European Union, I was able to follow MEPs throughout their daily life, from morning to evening and tape record all instances of talk which occurred. In conceptualizing and analysing this huge range of data, I necessarily had to draw on a number of linguistic and extra-linguistic social theory approaches, which I can only briefly discuss in the following. In the next section I will present a few examples of the many challenges politicians are confronted with in their daily work and in this way I will illustrate the *backstage* of politics.

Thus I make use of symbolic interactionism and of Goffman's concepts of *frontstage* and *backstage* (1959; see above); of Bourdieu's theory of habitus, social fields and capitals (1991); of Lave and Wenger's notion of 'community of practice' (1991); of various approaches to the construction of individual and collective identities (Wodak *et al.*, 2009 [1999]); and of Weber's approach to legitimacy and authority (2003). These approaches conceptualize different aspects of politicians' everyday *performances* and activities and allow analysing their socialization into the rules and conventions of the field of politics and thus the dynamics of acquiring the habitus of a politician. Individual politicians construct their *identities* in different, typical and unique ways, depending on the *communities of practice* to which they belong, the various organizational contexts in which they move, their personal biographies and their national, regional and local histories. Moreover, they possess different amounts of *symbolic capital*, as expressed in their *expert, organizational,* and *political knowledges*. Importantly, they are also attributed with varying degrees and forms of *legitimacy*; in the case of the European Parliament, this is largely based in legal–rational authority, although charisma certainly also plays a role, particularly in the rhetoric and persuasion used to convince other politicians, bureaucrats and the electorate.

A further aspect of my analysis examined the rules, norms, routines and constraints that structure MEPs' daily working environment and thus shape the *social order* (Gioia, 1986) of the European Parliament. In other words, I investigated the order behind the apparent chaos of the *backstage* by drawing on organizational studies, combining my *ethnography* of MEPs daily lives with the analysis of interviews with MEPs and other written and spoken genres. In all organizations there exist power struggles for hegemony. These can be more or less explicit and express themselves, *inter alia*, in the distribution of resources (Bourdieu, 1991). In our case, the primary resources at stake are different types of knowledge, which makes the backstage of politics an ideal arena in which to study the power–knowledge dynamic at the heart of Foucault's concept of governmentality (Dreyfus and Rabinow, 1982; Jäger and Maier, 2009). These knowledges manifest themselves in material and discursive practices and in forms of *knowing* that depend on context-specific agenda, necessities, interests and strategic intentions. Forms of power and knowledge and types of discourses, genres and texts are therefore dialectically linked to each other in the material, social and discursive practices that MEPs engage in. Thus critical ethnography allows documenting the daily struggles for power in which competing voices and interests come together in the negotiation, construction, implementation and eventual sedimentation of knowledge in the world of (EU) politics.

Knowledge-making struggles are operationalized through, and can only fully be understood by analysing, an extensive repertoire of linguistic and interpersonal strategies. A systematic analysis includes discursive strategies of positive self- and negative other presentation, rhetorical tropes (metaphors, metonymies, personifications), indirect pragmatic devices (insinuations, implicatures, presuppositions), sociolinguistic–discursive means (forms of address, pronouns, footing, and deixis) and argumentative strategies (*topoi*, fallacies and so forth). From the range of potentially relevant linguistic strategies, the necessarily selective analytical focus will depend on the *immediate context* (which is determined on the basis of the 'four-level model of context'; see above). The linguistic repertoire is also, of course, inherently linked to specific genres in the field of politics, each serving important and quite specific functions in the backstage and frontstage. Thus it should be clear that an important part of being a successful politician implies acquiring effective and functionally appropriate linguistic and rhetorical knowledge, and genre competence (Scollon, 2008).

Moreover, as argued at the outset, politics and the media have always, to some degree, been interdependent: boundaries are blurred between entertainment and information, between private and public domains, between politicians and celebrities, between traditional media and new media and so forth (Wodak, 2009a, c, 2010). Like never before, people are networked together, communicating opinions and consuming information on a global basis, and at unprecedented speeds. In this way politics has become increasingly innovative, and a strategic understanding of the media and its effects is now an essential aspect of being a successful politician. This kind of political participation is, of course, dependent on affordable and easy access to the Internet and on computer literacy. Paradoxically, therefore, this form of 'e-democracy' is a mechanism both for increasing democratic participation and for reproducing forms of social inequality and exclusion.[3]

Figure 37.1 (below) provides a heuristic (and thus necessarily crude) summary of the theoretical cornerstones of 'politics as usual' (adapted from Wodak, 2009a: 192).

Examples from European Union institutions – one day in the life of a MEP

In what follows, I analyse two brief episodes which occurred during one day in the life of an Austrian MEP – we name him Hans – a member of the Social–Democratic Party and an expert on matters related to trade unions and social affairs, to illustrate backstage activities of politicians (see Wodak, 2009a: 120ff. for the analysis of an entire day at the EP).

Hans wore a tiny microphone attached to his jacket and a tape-recorder in his pocket. He invited us to follow him to meetings inside and outside of the European Parliament, and to sit and observe when he spent time in his tiny office cubicle, preparing, phoning or talking to his personal assistant M or to other visitors and colleagues. Moreover, he frequently commented on the encounters and explained his behaviour towards other MEPs or elaborated on the statements he had made during a committee meeting. In this way we gained access to the many latent norms, functions and rules in the various communities of practice, to coded and shared knowledges, and to the otherwise inaccessible subtext of many conversations. To take a typical example, on 20 May

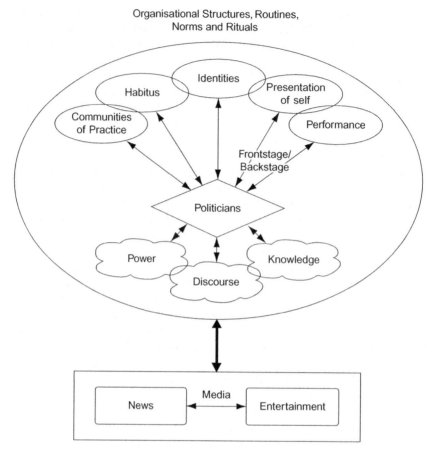

Figure 37.1 'Theoretical cornerstones of "politics as usual"'

2008, 17 different items from 6 standing committees (including the Committee on the Environment, Committee on Transport and Tourism, Committee on legal Affairs, and the Committee on Employment and Social Affairs[4]) were discussed and put to motion in the plenary, starting at 9 am and scheduled to end at midnight. Of course, most MEPs do not primarily spend their days attending plenary debates; they only participate if their own agenda from the committees to which they belong are to be discussed. Otherwise they have their own schedules, which may periodically overlap with the official agenda or run in parallel. Below, when I present two episodes of having shadowed one MEP throughout his day, readers will encounter the many appointments and small meetings which typically 'overfill' the tight schedule that characterizes 'politics as usual' or – perhaps even more accurately – 'politics as business' or 'political business as usual'.

Episode 1: Starting the day

At 8 am, MEPs usually start their official day. Hans meets M in his small office (a cubicle with a desk, computer, a few book shelves, telephone, *in toto* about 8–10 square meters) for a quick briefing and organization of upcoming events. M has prepared all the relevant documents for the day and organized them neatly into specific folders. Hans mainly poses quick questions; the dialogue takes on a staccato form; quick, often elliptic, and abrupt – thus rapid question and answer sequences conveying urgency and pressure. If we regard the whole day as an entire genre or activity, then this *orientation* in the morning would serve as introduction and overall structuring device and frame for all upcoming events:

> Text 1
> H: hey social security systems are included
> M: I have already contacted (xxx)
> H: We haven't received any answer yet (huh)?
> M: no obviously I'm glad I sent that off
> H: on Friday?
> M: no no I sent it off last week -   no Sunday I sent it
> H: Sunday
> M: yes
> H: they're coming
> M: Sunday the 14th of November
> H: in fact they're coming again with the social security systems we would have needed that for today
> M: no we don't have that

Text 1 offers an insight into the sort of rapid-fire exchange, relying on shared language and organizational knowledge, which is typical of an MEP and his/her personal assistant, impatiently chasing up on the whereabouts of some document or letter urgently needed for a committee meeting. In this exchange, both M and Hans have obviously forgotten on which day Hans' letter was actually sent off, and the inferred argument consists of the following sequence:

If the letter had already been sent off the previous week, then it is reasonable to expect that they should have had a response by now. If, however, the letter hadn't been sent until Sunday or Monday, then they can't really expect an answer yet. Hans' questions also imply an indirect accusation: that M might have sent the letter too late. In any case, it seems obvious that the response to this letter is crucial for a meeting on insurance and social security systems, for which Hans is now preparing. Hans emphasizes quite clearly that he needed this response to his letter, which – by analysing the various existential and counterfactual presuppositions – we can infer must have contained some salient information. Already in this brief sequence, we thus encounter the reliance on shared organizational knowledge and the overall responsibility of the personal assistant, who has to take the blame if something doesn't go according to plan.

In Text 2, the quick dialogue continues with a frame-shift: the search for the document ends because – as M reveals – he has found the relevant document. Hence, Hans and M start discussing and preparing the statement for the committee later on that day, and switch to a dense strategy debate about the wording of the statement: what to change, to amend, to include or delete, and so forth. At the same time, we encounter another frame and change of footing: the collegial, friendly relationship where Hans asks M to give him a cigarette (6). M complies but in a humorous way (7), with a joke. This brief interlude eases the tension by re/producing the good interpersonal relationship and by shifting, in line 10, to a discussion of content after the frantic search for the missing document.

> Text 2
> 1. H: that (would be) bad
> 2.   uh
> 3. M: I have (xxxx) our paper there
> 4. H: oh you have (xxxx) our paper there too?

 5. M: yes
 6. H: (c'mon gimme one)
 7. M: alright fine (because it's you)
 8. H: do you have a (xxxxx)
 9. M: no (a German)
10. H: what does a sixteen mean
11. M: for the ÖGB
12. H: okay
13. M: also, in the mean time I'm supposed to put his ethical work with your
14. H: yes
15. M: next to your hundredth
16. H: social clause on the WTO last paragraph
17. M: WTO social clause is in there?
18. H: yes (xxx social clause xxxxxxxx)
19. M: where where in here?
20. H: of course last paragraph
21. M: which last paragraph?
22. H: WTO social clause (xxxx) that belongs
23. M: where where?
24. H: yes
25. M: no not there in that paper there
26. H: in that (xx) paper
27. H: yes
28. M: in that one there?
29. H: yes
30.   linguistic confusion
31. M: WTO social clause
32. H: yes there there WTO social clause
33.   (can you remember)
34. M: yes oh yes yes yes yes yes yes
35. H: that's currently the established discussion
36. M: sub subsume
37. H: yes yes nobody understands it like this
38.   if we don't add the social clause
39.   ah, and the other part is naturally an awful exaggeration
40. M: a terrible one, as usual
41. H: but seriously
42.   we can't do something like that I think we can't do that
43.   this is really in width
44.   it's like this so that I
45.   (xxxxxxxx give me)
46. M: hehehe
47. H: (I've) noted that there
48.   but that's always the same
49. H: there's nothing useful there

This hectic and elliptical discussion continues for more than 20 minutes. Hans and M read through the draft statement together and stop at various points while questioning specific formulations that

Hans eventually labels 'linguistic confusions' and that could be interpreted as typical organizational ambiguities (30, 38, 42). The two of them support and acknowledge each other's suggestions and comments through brief interjections and supportive comments (backchannels), or laughter (34, 47). The quick turn-taking illustrates the shared routines of their community of practice, and they do not interrupt each other but automatically sense when transition-relevant points occur, or when support is needed to reassure the other. The interaction also builds solidarity between the two, notably through jokes, allusions to shared experiences, elliptical comments and more generally through evaluative language. On the one hand, the document is defined as 'useless' (49), the ongoing discussion about social benefits and the WTO are believed to be totally 'exaggerated' (39), or even 'terrible' (40). The meta-comments and assessments oscillate between evaluating the committee, the ongoing debates themselves and particular parts, sentences or even words in the draft document. In line 32, Hans briefly checks if M still remembers the genesis of the discussion; after M asserts (33) that he indeed does share the same memories, their rapid exchange continues with highly truncated utterances, which presuppose much expert knowledge (existential presuppositions).

Finally, this part of the day comes to an end: the first appointment is scheduled for 9.15 am. M also informs Hans of a photo appointment at 12.45 pm, which becomes a prominent feature of this particular day because it has to be rescheduled several times, requiring the afternoon's schedule to be repeatedly renegotiated. This final intimate exchange, involving the banter over the cigarette, is interpersonal talk that serves primarily as a transition and frame shift from the formal discussion of the draft document, onto the 'time and organizational talk' that they launch into while walking to their first official appointment.

Episode 2: Statement by Hans in the Committee for Social Affairs

Hans rushes down the stairs and arrives just on time for his presentation to the Committee of Employment and Social Affairs. On the way, M hands him the documents they have just discussed. Hans now has to deliver his statement, which he just finished preparing half an hour ago and which he practised with M. Thus one can experience yet another frame shift, namely to Hans' official performance and identity construction as the politically experienced social democratic Austrian MEP in this committee.

At this point I would like to emphasize that both Hans' statement and his role in the committee illustrate clearly that MEPs actually '*do politics*' during their day in very involved and engaged ways, drawing on their political, organizational and expert knowledges. Although many routines in such a large organization are necessarily bureaucratic, the essence remains political, albeit it shows in employing strategies and tactics to convince other MEPs of seemingly small aspects of larger issues. This fact relates well to the discussion about MEPs' legal–rational authority. Their day is, of course, mostly filled with organizational and ritualized events; however, parts of their day are dedicated to a substantial political agenda: to formulating their positions, to working on resolutions and promoting their ideological agenda, to formulating a common understanding with party colleagues and so forth. Hence the profession of MEPs (or, more generally, of politicians) integrates 'real' political work and is not merely confined to public performances or media interviews on frontstage – even though these are also important constitutive symbolic elements in the construction and representation of politics in action (see Edelman, 1967).

In what follows I analyse the beginning of Hans' statement, which manifests his official and public rhetoric as well as his ideological and political position on the EU enlargement proposed for 2004. In this case, the larger socio-political context relates to the debates on the costs and benefits of the proposed EU enlargement, the so-called 'big bang' 2004, where ten countries joined the EU. The Employment and Social Affairs Committee has to prepare a resolution and is currently discussing a document, proposed by a group of political scientists and other experts, on the possible implications and consequences of enlargement. This resolution will be put forward to the commission if it is approved in the plenary session of the parliament. Hans is particularly concerned that the enlargement countries are not helped enough when creating and protecting their social institutions. Furthermore, Hans rejects the 'myth' that enlargement can take place at no additional cost to the union (*topoi* of burden and costs prevail). Hans quite openly criticizes the policy strategies of the commission and the member states as being unprofessional and inadequate and as failing to take into account the particular circumstances faced by Eastern European countries. Hans speaks German as German is one of the three official working languages adopted for the committee's internal use. German is translated, for other members of the committee, into English and French; this necessarily implies that MEPs who have a different native language might be discriminated against when having to speak in a foreign language.

Text 3: Introduction, justification and critique of status quo, explicit declaration of intent
Given the statements' function in presenting a MEP's position on a strategic policy issue, the committee meeting statement is an inherently argumentative and persuasive genre, although one that has thus far not been systematically analysed.

> uhm I am very thankful for this working paper of the (xxx) science directorate
> we probably could have used that much earlier, for example when we began the
> Eastern enlargement discussions on a parliamentary level....
> in reality we would have had better management at the European level
> then we could have like at the time of the single market
> when we began with the single market concept [and] thoroughly discussed what the possibilities
> [and] chances are then we could have xxx very very differently in terms of Eastern enlargement

At the beginning of this short statement Hans presupposes that everybody knows and has read the document he is referring to; he also presupposes that every committee member is well informed about the problems related to enlargement and about the many debates and decisions which have already taken place. He employs the discursive strategy of painting an 'unreal scenario' in the function of rhetorical contrast – 'what would have happened if' – in order to highlight how much better it would have been had the debate on management of the enlargement issue begun much earlier. He also refers intertextually to past debates on the 'single market', where he claims that better procedures had been used. By drawing on this as a *shared* past experience ('when *we* began with … and thoroughly discussed') as a model of how things should have been done in relation to enlargement (topos of history), he is assuming not only that this event is shared knowledge but also that everybody agrees with his evaluation of it. The macro-argumentative strategy consists of a justification for missed opportunities and (in Hans' view) obviously wrong decisions and policies. He shifts the blame onto the commission (a typical fallacy), which serves to unite the committee members and also relieves them of responsibility. In this way the introduction sets the ground for more detailed criticism and for some constructive proposals, which cannot be presented due to issues of space (see Wodak, 2009a: 126ff, 2011).

Politics as usual: perspectives and limitations

Common sense presupposes that politicians are very well organized, in spite of the many urgent and important events they must deal with, which have an impact on all our lives. We all have cognitive models (*event models, experience models, context models*: van Dijk, 2008), which quickly and automatically update, perceive, comprehend and store such events. From this we might assume that politicians also routinely access their own set of cognitive models for 'doing politics' in order to respond rapidly,in a rational and quite predictable way, to the various events they encounter.[5] However, this is in fact not the case: the everyday life of politicians is as much filled with accident, coincidence and unpredictability as it is filled with well-planned, strategic and rational action. Chaotic situations are a necessary feature of 'politics as usual'; experienced politicians simply know how to cope with them better – thus there is '*order in the disorder*' (Wodak, 1996, 2009a), established *inter alia* through routines, norms and rituals. Politicians have acquired strategies and tactics to pursue their agenda more or less successfully. The 'success' depends on their position in the field, on their power relations and, most importantly, on what I label *knowledge management*: much of what we perceive as disorder depends on inclusion in shared knowledge or exclusion from shared knowledge.

Shadowing one MEP, Hans, through his entire day provides some important answers to the questions posed above which, again, could be generalized to other political realms. Hans employs both strategic and tactical knowledge when trying to convince various audiences of his political agenda. These discursive strategies and tactics also structure his day, which might otherwise seem totally chaotic from the outside, or very ritualized and bureaucratic – oriented, for example, solely towards the drafting and redrafting of documents. Hans knows the 'rules of the game', he oscillates between a range of communities of practice in very well planned and strategic ways, he employs a wide range of genres suited to the immediate context in order to push his agenda, and thus possesses a whole repertoire of genres and modes which he applies in functionally adequate ways (see also Scollon, 2008: 128–137 for the range of multimodal modes employed in bureaucracies and political institutions).

In Hans' case, different genres are used to convince members of various committees, other MEPs of various political parties, visitors and diverse audiences outside of the institution and 'at home' of his mission: in this particular case, to enable EU enlargement in a rational way; to be honest about the likely costs, however politically unpopular, and to support the social agenda and the trade unions in the accession countries. Hans' entire day (and, of course, many following months) is dedicated to this mission, which he pursues in statements, written resolutions, conversations at lunch, lectures, and in the politics *du couloir* – as well as 'at home' (in his local community), when trying to convince his electorate and national political party. In this way Hans is an example of what I call a *small-scale policy entrepreneur*, one of many MEPs, all of whom are striving to push their various and very diverse agendas, with varying degrees of success.

In sum: *This, I argue, is how politics works; that is, how politicians work*. Hans, as a small-scale policy entrepreneur, does political work; however – as citizens are excluded from the backstage and the many communities of practice where Hans implements his strategies and pushes his agenda – these activities and practices remain invisible. Of course, this is not only the case for one MEP; this is generally true for the field of politics as a whole. To challenge the *democratic deficit*, at the very least, information about daily political work would need to be made more publicly accessible to a certain degree.

Further reading

Chilton, P. (2004) *Analyzing Political Discourse* London: Routledge.
Krzyżanowski, M. (2010) *The Discursive Construction of European Identities* Bern: Peter Lang.
Muntigl, P., Weiss, G., and Wodak, R. (eds.) (2000) *European Union Discourses on Un/Employment*. Amsterdam: Benjamins.
Okulska, U. and Cap, P. (eds.) (2010) *Political Discourse: New Perspectives*. Amsterdam: Benjamins.
Wodak, R. (2009) *The Discourse of Politics in Action: Politics as Usual* Basingstoke: Palgrave (second revised edition, 2011).

Notes

1 E.g. Chilton, 2004; Reisigl, 2008a, b; Wodak, 2009a, b, 2010, 2011; Okulska and Cap, 2010.
2 E.g. Duranti, 2006; Wodak, 2009a.
3 At this point, I must introduce a *caveat:* integrated interdisciplinary frameworks (and the related research) bring a number of risks alongside the value they add. On the one hand, interdisciplinarity opens up new perspectives and allows for novel ideas and innovative approaches; on the other hand, one risks accusations of superficiality if viewed from narrow disciplinary perspectives. It is obvious that critical problem-oriented research in the social sciences is obliged to transcend disciplinary boundaries, because social phenomena themselves are highly complex and certainly cannot be explained by one discipline (Weiss and Wodak, 2003). For this reason, I have consulted extensively with experts in the relevant neighbouring fields, in order to bridge some of the inevitable knowledge gaps encountered by all interdisciplinary researchers.
4 See http://www.europarl.europa.eu/sides/getDoc.do?pubRef=-//EP//TEXT+AGENDA+20080521 +SIT+DOC+XML+V0//EN&language=EN (downloaded 1 May 2008).
5 Van Dijk (2008: 84) defines *experience* (or *event*) *models* as 'a construction of what is relevant in the ongoing situation for the (inter) actions of the participants'. Moreover, van Dijk (p. 74) stresses that context is not something primarily 'objective'; he maintains that '[s]ettings, participant roles or aims of communicative events are not relevant *as such*, but are *defined* as such by the participants themselves'. This is, of course, also relevant where actors, agency, their perceptions and expectations, i.e. their socialization into a habitus become salient.

References

Abélès, M. (1992) *La Vie Quotidienne au Parlement Européen.* Paris: Hachette.
Aristotle (1999) *The Politics and The Constitution of Athens,* trans. S. Everson. Cambridge: Cambridge University Press.
Bernstein, B. (1987) 'Social class, codes and communication', in U. Ammon, N. Dittmar, and K. J. Mattheier (eds.) *Sociolinguistics: An International Handbook of the Science of Society.* Volume 1. Berlin: de Gruyter, pp. 563–579.
Bourdieu, P. (1991) *Language and Symbolic Power.* Cambridge: Polity Press.
Burkhardt, A. (1996) 'Politolinguistik. Versuch einer Ortsbestimmung', in J. Klein and H. Diekmannshenke (eds.) *Sprachstrategien und Dialogblockaden. Linguistische und politikwissenschaftliche Studien zur politischen Kommunikation.* Berlin: de Gruyter, pp. 75–100.
Chilton, P. (2004) *Analysing Political Discourse: Theory and Practice.* London: Routledge.
Chilton, P., Tian, H., and Wodak, R. (2010) ' "Critical" in the east and west', *Journal of Language and Politics,* 9(4): 489–507.
Chouliaraki, L. (2006) *The Spectatorship of Suffering.* London: Sage.
Clayman, S. and Heritage, J. (2002) *The New Interview: Journalists and Public Figures on Air.* Cambridge: Cambridge University Press.
Deetz, S. (1982) 'Critical interpretive research in organizational communication', *Western Journal of Speech Communication,* 46: 131–149.
Drew, P. and Heritage, J. (1992) *Talk at Work: Interaction in Institutional Settings.* Cambridge: Cambridge University Press.
Dreyfus, H. L. and Rabinow, P. (1982) *Michel Foucault: Beyond Structuralism and Hermeneutics.* Sussex: The Harvester Press.
Duranti, A. (2006) 'The struggle for coherence: rhetorical strategies and existential dilemmas in a campaign for the US congress', *Language in Society,* 35: 467–497.
Edelman, M. (1967) *The Symbolic Uses of Politics.* Second Edition. Urbana, Chicago, IL: University of Illinois Press.
Ensink, T. and Sauer, C. (eds.) (2003) *The Art of Commemoration.* Amsterdam: Benjamins.
Fairclough, N. (2000) *New Labour, New Language?* London: Routledge.
Garfinkel, H., Lynch, M., and Livingstone, E. (1981) 'The work of discovering science construed with materials from the optically discovered pulsar', *Philosophy of the Social Sciences,* 11: 131–158.
Gioia, D. A. (1986) 'Symbols, Scripts, and Sensemaking', in H. P. Sims and D. A. Gioia (eds.) *The Thinking Organisation.* San Francisco, CA: Jossey-Bass Publishers, pp. 49–74.
Goffman, E. (1959) *The Presentation of SELF in Everyday Life.* Garden City, NY: Doubleday, Anchor Books.

Goffman, E. (1981) *Forms of Talk*. Philadelphia, PA: University of Pennsylvania Press.

Hay, C. (2007) *Why We Hate Politics*. Polity Short Introductions. Cambridge: Polity Press.

Heer, H., Manoschek, W., Pollak, A., and Wodak, R. (eds.) (2008) *The Discursive Construction of History. Remembering the Wehrmacht's War of Annilihation*. Basingstoke: Palgrave.

Holzscheiter, A. (2005) 'Power of discourse and power in discourse: an investigation of transformation and exclusion in the global discourse of childhood', Unpublished PhD Thesis, FU Berlin.

Jäger, S. and Maier, F. (2009) 'Theoretical and methodological aspects of critical discourse analysis', in R. Wodak and M. Meyer (eds.) *Methods of Critical Discourse Analysis*. Second Edition. London: Sage, pp. 34–61.

Kienpointner, M. (1996) *Vernünftig argumentieren. Regeln und Techniken der Diskussion*. Hamburg: Rowohlt.

Klemperer, V. (1947) *LTI. Lingua Tertii Imperii. Die Sprache des Dritten Reiches*. Leipzig: Reclam.

Klemperer, V. (2005) *The Language of the Third Reich: LTI. Lingua Tertii Imperii*. London: Continuum.

Koller, V. and Wodak, R. (2008) 'Introduction: shifting boundaries and emergent public spheres', in R. Wodak and V. Koller (eds.) *Communication in the Public Sphere*. Berlin: De Gruyter, pp. 1–21.

Krzyżanowski, M. and Oberhuber, F. (2007) *(Un)Doing Europe: Discourses and Practices of Negotiating the EU Constitution*. Bern: Peter Lang.

Lasswell, H. D. and Leites, N. C. (1949) *Language of Politics: Studies in Quantitative Semantics*. New York: G. W. Stewart.

Lave, J. and Wenger, E. (1991) *Situated learning: Legitimate peripheral participation*. Cambridge: Cambridge University Press.

Okulska, U. and Cap, P. (2010) *Political Discourse: New Perspectives*. Amsterdam: Benjamins.

Orwell, G. (1949) *1984*. London: Harcourt Brace & Company.

Reisigl, M. (2008a) 'Analyzing political rhetoric', in R. Wodak and M. Krzyżanowski (eds.) *Qualitative Discourse Analysis in the Social Sciences*. Basingstoke: Palgrave, pp. 96–120.

Reisigl, M. (2008b) 'Rhetoric of political speeches', in R. Wodak and V. Koller (eds.) *Communication in the Public Sphere: Handbook of Applied Linguistics*. Volume 4. Berlin: De Gruyter, pp. 243–271.

Reisigl, M. and Wodak, R. (2001) *Discourse and Discrimination. Rhetorics of Racism and Antisemitism*. London: Routledge.

Schegloff, E. (1987) 'Between micro and macro: contexts and other connections', in J. Alexander, B. Giesen, R. Munch, and N. Smelser (eds.) *The Micro-Macro Link*. Berkeley, CA: University of California Press, pp. 207–236.

Scollon, R. (2008) *Analyzing Public Discourse*. London: Routledge.

Sternberger, D., Storz, G., and Süßkind, W. E. (1957) *Aus dem Worterbuch des Unmenschen*. Hamburg: Claassen.

Toulmin, S. (1958) *The Uses of Argument*. Cambridge: Cambridge University Press.

van Dijk, T. A. (2008) *Context*. Cambridge: Cambridge University Press.

van Eemeren, F. and Grootendorst, R. (1992) *Argumentation, Communication and Fallacies*. Hillsdale, IN: Erlbaum.

Weber, M. (2003) *Political Writings*. Third Edition. Cambridge: Cambridge University Press.

Weiss, G. and Wodak, R. (eds.) (2003) *Critical Discourse Analysis: Theory and Interdisciplinarity*. Basingstoke: Palgrave.

Wilson, J. (1990) *Politically Speaking: The Pragmatic Analysis of Political Language*. Oxford: Blackwell.

Wittgenstein, L. (1967) *Philosophische Untersuchungen*. Frankfurt: Suhrkamp.

Wodak, R. (1996) *Disorders of Discourse*. London: Longman.

Wodak, R. (2000a) 'From conflict to consensus? The co-construction of a policy paper', in P. Muntigl, G. Weiss, and R. Wodak (eds.) *European Union Discourses on Unemployment*. Amsterdam: Benjamins, pp. 73–114.

Wodak, R. (2000b) 'Recontextualization and the Transformation of Meaning: a critical discourse analysis of decision making in EU-meetings about employment policies', in S. Sarangi and M. Coulthard (eds.) *Discourse and Social Life*. Harlow: Pearson Education, pp. 185–206.

Wodak, R. (2001) 'The discourse-historical approach', in R. Wodak and M. Meyer (eds.) *Methods of Critical Discourse Analysis*. London: Sage, pp. 63–94.

Wodak, R. (2011[2009a]) *The Discourse of Politics in Action: Politics as Usual*. Basingstoke: Palgrave.

Wodak, R. (2009b) 'Language and politics', in J. Culpeper *et al.* (eds.) *English Language: Description, Variation and Context*. Basingstoke: Palgrave, pp. 576–593.

Wodak, R. (2009c) 'Staging politics in television: fiction and/or reality?', in S. Habscheid and C. Knobloch (eds.) *Discourses of Unity: Creating Scenarios of Consensus in Public and Corporate Communication*. Berlin: De Gruyter, pp. 33–58.

Wodak, R. (2010) 'The glocalisation of politics in television: Fiction or reality?', *European Journal of Cultural Studies*, 13 (1): 43–62.

Wodak, R. and de Cillia, R. (2006) 'Politics and language: overview', in K. Brown (Editor-in-Chief) *Encyclopedia of Language and Linguistics*. Volume 9. Second Edition. Oxford: Elsevier, pp. 707–719.

Wodak, R., de Cillia, R., Reisigl, M., and Liebhart, K. (2009 [1999]) *The Discursive Construction of National Identity*. Edinburgh: Edinburgh University Press.

Wodak, R., Krzyzanowski, M. and Forschtner, B. (2011) 'The interplay of language ideologies and contextual cues in multilingual interactions: Language choice and code-switching in European Union institutions', *Language in Society* (in press).

Wodak, R. and Kirsch, P. (eds.) (1995) *Langue du Bois*. Vienna: Passagen Verlag.

Wodak, R. and Meyer, M. (2009) 'Critical discourse analysis: history, agenda, theory, and methodology', in R. Wodak and M. Meyer (eds.) *Methods of CDA* (Second Revised Edition). London: Sage, pp. 1–33.

Wodak, R. and Pelinka, A. (eds.) (2002) *The Haider Phenomenon in Austria*. New Brunswick, NJ: Transaction Press.

Wodak, R. and Wright, S. (2007) 'The European Union in cyberspace: democratic participation via online multilingual discussion boards', in B. Danet and S. C. Herring (eds.) *The Multilingual Internet: Language, Culture, and Communication Online*. Oxford: Oxford University Press, pp. 385–407.

Yanow, D. (1996) *How Does a Policy Mean?* Georgetown: Georgetown University Press.

38

Discourse geography

Yueguo Gu

Introduction: discourse, space and time

This chapter deals with the relation between discourse on the one hand, and space and time on the other. It is helpful from the outset to spell out how the terms *discourse, space,* and *time* will be used so as to avoid potential misinterpretations. "Discourse," Blommaert (2005: 2) observes, "is language-in-action." Specifically, it "comprises all forms of meaningful semiotic human activity seen in connection with social, cultural, and historical patterns and developments of use. ..." (p. 3). Blommaert approaches such discourse by critically examining *voice*, i.e. "the way in which people manage to make themselves understood or fail to do so" (p. 4). Gu (2002a) looks at discourse (qua language-in-action) by adopting the perspective of human geography, in which discourse is viewed as a web of trajectories constructed by human actors' movements over space and time, while carrying out their daily routine activities. In this perspective, discourse (qua language-in-action) is regarded as being equivalent to social activity, and occurrences of such discourse are prototypically here-and-now, spatially–temporally bounded events, situated in specific *behavior settings* (Barker's 1968 terminology) and related to the performance of specific social actors.

Space and time are so fundamental to human existence, and we are so immersed in them, that everyone seems to have an intuitive grasp of what they are and to take them for granted. Philosophers, scientists, sociologists, anthropologists, geologists, theologians, and of course linguists all have invested interest in space and time. In the literature of mainstream linguistics space is traditionally associated with dialectology, time with historical linguistics. Various positions taken by linguists on space and time will be reviewed below. In this chapter space and time will be dealt with in terms of the spatial–temporal behavior displayed by individual social actors as well as by social systems (e.g. by a family, a city, a nation–state). This treatment subscribes to a position advanced in human geography—time geography in particular (see e.g. Hägerstrand, 1996 [1982], Carlstein *et al.* 1978a, 1978b). The phrase *discourse geography* is coined after *human geography* (see e.g. Fellmann *et al.* 1995; Agnew *et al.* 1996).[1]

The bulk of the chapter will address what is called the *land-borne situated discourse* (LBSD for short), in other words, the core of discourse geography. In what follows we shall first explain why this new terminology is necessary and useful. Then we shall review linguists' studies of space and time. The remaining part will deal with (1) the LBSD and human spatial–temporal behavior from the social actor's viewpoint, including (a) spatial–temporal behavior and trajectory-mediated chain of LBSDs, (b) the actor's activity zone and its impact on the LBSD, and (c) an ecological chain of discourse; and (2) the LBSD and human spatial–temporal behavior from the system's viewpoint, including (a) temporal structuring of LBSDs in present-day China, (b) urbanization and spatial concentration of LBSD types, and (c) power, spatial–temporal behavior, and the LBSD's interactive order. The chapter concludes with a note on some theoretical issues.

All the data cited in this paper are taken from the Spoken Chinese Corpus of Situated Discourse (SCCSD; see Gu, 2002b, and www.multimodalgu.com for details).

The LBSD: the usefulness of this concept

Discourse (qua language-in-action), at its most concrete level and since the very beginning of speaking in *Homo sapiens*, always occurs in a particular spatial–temporal setting, as an oral–aural–visual event produced by one or more particular speakers. *It is an embodied form of discourse* in the following sense. First, it involves what Goffman calls "bodily activity" on the speaker/performer's side, and "naked senses" on the addressee/receiver's side. "When one speaks of experiencing someone else with one's naked senses, one usually implies the reception of embodied messages. This linkage of naked senses on one side and embodied transmission on the other provides one of the crucial communication conditions of face-to-face interaction" (Goffman, 1963: 15). As emphasized by Goffman, ordinarily in using the naked senses to receive embodied messages from others one also makes oneself available as a source of embodied messages for others. In other words, in face-to-face co-present interaction, one is both a giver and receiver of embodied messages via natural multimodality.

Physical co-presence, situated in a particular and specific spatial–temporal setting in a two-way embodied interaction, serves as the basis for proposing the phrase (and the concept of) "land-borne situated discourse." The compound *land-borne* is coined to highlight the fact that face-to-face co-presence makes it obligatory that the social actors (in Giddens' sense, see Giddens, 1981) must converge physically to a particular behavior setting. The physical convergence, on the other hand, demands that the social actors move over physical space and time. In addition, the fact that no one physically can be present simultaneously in two different places at a time, the LBSD therefore is both framed and enabled by human movements over space and time.

In the Chinese context, the LBSD had remained the only mode of discourse for over 390,000 years,[2] before the invention of oracle bone scripts in Shang Dynasty (1765–1122 BC), when the written word-borne discourse (WWBD) came into existence. The WWBD did not replace the LBSD, but only provided an extra dimension for discourse production, reproduction, and consumption. China witnessed the emergence of the air-borne situated discourse (ABSD) in the middle of the nineteenth century, when the telecommunications technology was used to air messages in the oral–aural mode. Towards the end of the twentieth-century China witnessed the emergence of still another mode of discourse, the web-borne situated discourse (WBSD). Elsewhere (Gu, 2009a) I have adopted Wittgenstein's metaphorization of language as an ancient city and explored, conceptually as well as demonstratively, how the cityscape of the Chinese language has been constructed through the four-borne discourses over its long evolutionary history. The Chinese language is shown to be a multi-dimensional city of historicity and mystery (for its future path is yet to be unfolded, and no one is able to predict with confidence how it will evolve).

Space and time in linguistics and discourse studies: a brief review of the literature

Space and time in everyday experience

No experience probably can be more elementary than that of space and time. Space in everyday experience of it is typically associated with *room* and *distance*, and time with *change*, *cycle* and *sequence*. It seems that there would have been no way to detect time, or simply no sense of its existence, if everything, no matter what, had remained the same from beginning to end. *Cycle* involves changes with some regularity. The Chinese lunar calendar is based on cyclic changes due to the effects the moon has on the climate of the earth. Note that time, measured in terms of clock time and coordinated by the Universal Time or the Greenwich Mean Time, is a modern invention, not a natural occurrence such as *change* and *cycle* in the Chinese lunar calendar. Finally time is experienced when a series of events occur one after another.

Space and language

Space and language, as mentioned above, are traditionally associated in dialectology, and in dialect geography in particular. Nowadays the connections between the two are far more varied than ever before. Space, particularly the human usage of space, is conceptualized in term of language, as *space as language* (e.g. Lawson, 2001). Conversely, language, particularly conceptual constructs of linguistic meaning, is conceived of in terms of "mental spaces," as *language as space* (e.g. Fauconnier, 1985, Brandt, 2004, Dancygier and Sweetser, 2005). In the former, the term "space" literally refers to physical space, the term "language" being used figuratively. In the latter, "language" is literary, "space" figuratively. In other words, *space as language* and *language as mental spaces* show the conceptual supports between space and language.

Space as language, and language as space, are different from *language and space* as analyzed in Bloom *et al.* (1996), Pütz and Dirven (1996), Zee and Slack (2003), Levinson (2003), Levinson and Wilkins (2006), and Hickmann and Robert (2006). In these works, language and space are not conceptually connected, but are related to each other as the former encoding the latter. That is, the research question is: How does space get encoded in language? Lastly, there is research on *space in language*, in other words, sign language (Emmorey and Reilly, 1995). In *language and space*, space is considered to lie *externally* to language, whereas in *space in language* space is an *intrinsic element* of sign language.

Of the varied connections discussed above, *dialect geography* and *language and space* are the most pertinent to the current chapter. Dialect geography maps the relations between linguistic items such as sound, lexical variations, and human habitats. Language and space, as represented by Levinson (2003), is especially concerned with spatial cognition, e.g. *frames of reference* as expressed in spatial language and everyday thinking. Levinson's approach can be demonstrated by the examination of his sentence: "The statue by Giambologna is in front of the cathedral" (Levinson, 2003: 67). The Leibnizian notion of *space as relation* (see Urry, 1985: 21) is adopted here. The analyses go as follows. The statue is the *figure*, with the cathedral as the *ground*. The figure (i.e. the statue) is identified by way of adopting an *intrinsic frame of reference* (i.e. the front of the cathedral as an angle of reference, the front being an intrinsic facet of the cathedral).

It is important to note that space, in both dialect geography and *language and space*, is considered as being external to language. That is, it serves as a context or a container in which language is located. This chapter will depart from this traditional way of approaching space. We shall look at space in terms of *human spatial behavior*, and the research question is: In what ways does human spatial behavior frame and enable discourse production and reproduction? Before we dwell upon the notion of human spatial behavior (see pp. 00–00 below), let me use Levinson's sentence quoted above to illustrate the difference between the current study and Levinson's. The key questions we are concerned with are:

> What human activity is prototypically associated with the statue, and/or the front of the cathedral, and/or the cathedral itself?—This is the question about the *potential behavior pattern* associated with the three *behavior settings*;

What *activities* are visitors actually doing when they converge on the three behavior settings? How are the actual activities *framed* and *enabled* by the behavior settings?

Levinson and his associates often use such labels as "spatial language," "grammar of space," "language and space" to characterize their research. The present study uses the land-borne situated discourse as an umbrella term for easy reference. The fundamental difference between the two research frameworks lies in the fact that the cognitive approach takes language as a given, particularly as a coding system, whereas *our framework, labeled as "ecological approach," does not take language as given, but as an unfinished, open system constantly being produced and reproduced by human activities, of which the temporal and spatial behaviors are the two fundamental ones.*

Time and language

It is a truism that language changes over time, which has long been the subject matter of historical linguistics (about 200 years old; see Trask, 2000: 52). As is generally acknowledged, modern linguistics owns its inauguration to Saussure, one of whose "main achievements is the distinction between the diachronic (historical) study of language and the synchronic study of the language state (or *état de langue*) at any one particular moment" (Sanders, 2006: xx). Hale (2007: 4–6) observes that neogrammarian doctrine represented an attempt to implement diachronic generalizations about language directly, without a coherent synchronic theory of the nature of language as an object of study. To Saussure, such an attempt "is doomed from the outset: diachronic generalizations must hold over what are, in fact, a series of synchronic stages."

At this point it is worth noting that in the Saussurean theorization time is external to language. Similarly to space, it is regarded as a context, or a container in which language changes take place. This leads to the conceptualization of the relation between language and time as that of coding vs. being encoded, the view that underpins works such as Richards and co-authors' (1989) study of temporal representation, Arche's (2006) examination of how language encodes individuals in time, Sattig's (2006) exploration of temporal predication.

The linguistic encoding of time is generally represented in the tense system of the grammar that describes the states and events in the deictic world, i.e. the space–time world of the speaker. Besides the deictic world, there are of course other imaginable worlds, e.g. the worlds of desire, necessity, or possibility. These other imaginable worlds are represented in what is known as the modality system of the grammar. Guéron and Lecarme (2008) show that, in actual natural languages, the two systems are often intertwined and inseparable. They attempt to account for both the morpho-syntactic inseparability and the interpretive independence of tense and modality.

Time, however, can be argued to be an intrinsic property of language, namely time found in speech production.[3] Siegman and Feldstein (1979), for example, treat time as an integral dimension of speech. Similar views are also found in e.g. Chafe (1994). Moreover, time allocation (e.g. turn-taking) is a very important principle of organization in conversation (in this connection see the latest study by Auer *et al.* 1999).

Time, narrative and written discourse

This brief review of the literature cannot be complete with mentioning Ricoeur's study of narrative. Ricoeur is concerned with historical and fictional narrative. Historical narrative involves truth claims, while fictional narrative does not. But both narratives share some major presuppositions which in turn "have a common core."

[W]hat is ultimately at stake in the case of the structural identity of the narrative function as well as in that of the truth claim of every narrative work, is the *temporal character of human experience*. The World unfolded by every narrative work is always a temporal world. Or, as will often be repeated in the course of this study: time becomes human time to the extent that it is organized after the manner of a narrative; narrative, in turn is meaningful to the extent that it portrays the features of temporal experience.

(1984: 3; italics mine)[4]

What is insightful is that Ricoeur draws our attention to the temporal character of human experience that is the common core bridging humans' real-life experience, historical narrative and fictional narrative. Written discourses, narrative and non-narrative, produced by writing systems act, as it were, like time-freezing devices.

To wrap it up, this chapter will approach time, just like space, in terms of *human temporal behavior*, a concept that is associated with Ricoeur's temporal character of human experience and with speech production time (mentioned above).

Human agency, memory-dependent time, and Hägerstrand's time geography

Human agency, and Firth's "whole man"

To treat time and space as human spatial–temporal behavior puts human agency as the pivotal point of theorization. In linguistics as well as discourse analysis, theorization is almost universally being made without explicit reference to human agency. Statements such as "language does such and such ...," "discourse or text does such and such ..." are the norm. In this chapter, however, we shall depart from this tradition. Human agency plays a pivotal role in the theorization of the LBSD and of time–space.

Following Firth (1957: 19), we treat "human agency" as "the whole man, thinking and acting as a whole, in association with his fellows." Further, recall that, as discussed above, when the whole person interacts with her/his fellows, s/he interacts in a naturally multimodal way. Note also that the whole person is not a static one either. She has a personality that is both stable and changing over space and time, as initially discussed in Firth (1957: 177–189) and in sociology (e.g. Ewen, 1993). So, when the compound "social actor" is used in this chapter, that will be a short-hand phrase for this notion of "the whole person."

Memory-dependent time

As pointed out above, time in terms of clock or calendar (i.e. time-reckoning) is the modern invention. To human agency, what is more fundamental is what I propose to call memory-dependent time. This notion can be demonstrated by a 75-year-old man afflicted with Alzheimer's disease. Some of his daily activities in the hospital have been video-taped and included in the SCCSD.[5] He has lost his long-term memory almost completely, except for a few episodic memories still surviving. He cannot even recognize his own image in the mirror. His working and short-term memories are much weaker than in the normal person of his age. His experience of living (or his being) is almost all "present." This is a real-life case demonstrating Giddens' observation, based on Heidegger (1962), that "Being exists in the coming-to-be of presence" or simply in *presencing* (Giddens, 1995: 32).

It is important to note that Gidden's notion of "Being" (i.e. the coming-to-be of presence) is equally applicable to normal social actors. The difference between the normal and the Alzheimer's disease patient lies in the fact that the normal actor's working, short-term, and long-term memories function normally. Thanks to this normal functionality of memory systems, the ongoing here-and-now presencing (*situated presencing* hereafter) is constantly being saved in memories, thus generating the past, i.e. memory traces of what has happened. Situated presencing advances in response to human intentionality (including motive, desire, wish, affect, etc.), thus generating the sense of incoming future. As Bergson (1991: 78) vividly points out, the human body is

> an ever advancing boundary between the future and the past, as a pointed end, which our past is continually driving forward into our future. Whereas my body, taken at a single moment, is but a conductor interposed between the objects which influence it and those on which it acts.

The whole interactive process between intentionality (i.e. the future), situated presencing (i.e. the here-and-now action), and memory systems integrating the past, the present, and the future is graphically represented in Figure 38.1.

It is important to note that the tripartite division between the past, the present, and the future above is memory-dependent, and is constantly alternated and updated.

The human actor's situated presencing always has a duration, which extends from birth to death: simply, the life-span. All the things s/he has done during the life-span make up the contents of situated presencing. Think about this individual who happens to have remained illiterate across the life-span (note that there are about 116,000,000 such individuals in the present-day China alone: Gu, 2009a: 103). The life-span presencing is integrated crucially by the human memory, particularly by the long-term memory. Once the long-term memory is lost, the past, and probably the future too, will be erased. What is left is only the *situated presencing*, mediated by perceptual and working memories alone—we are back to the being of the Alzheimer's disease patient mentioned above.

Hägerstrand's time geography

Note that the human actor's situated presencing is not just temporal, but also spatial. Human actors are mobile agents. This leads us to very insightful studies known as Hägerstrand's time geography.

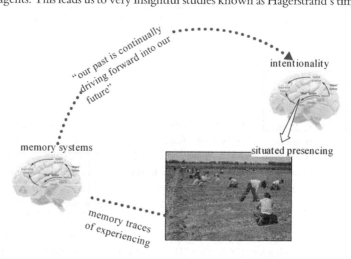

Figure 38.1 The interaction involving intentionality, the body and memory

Time geography studies human action, first and foremost, in terms of humans' movements over space and time. An individual's existence is seen as consisting of trajectories of space–time movements at varied scales, such as daily, weekly, monthly, yearly, or in life-long paths, involving travels from one "station" (i.e. a workplace, home, etc.) to another. This applies to the study of collective existence of a whole population, which is a *web* interwoven by all the individual members' trajectories. The interweaving of the web is framed by three major classes of constraint: (1) *capability constraints*, (2) *coupling constraints*, and (3) *authority constraints*. The capability constraints build on the fact that time is a valuable but limited resource. For instance large chunks of everyday time must be allocated to physiological necessities, e.g. sleeping and eating. For another person, given the means of transportation available, certain amounts of time must be spent on traveling from one station to another. The coupling constraints refer to the fact that the majority of human activities (what Hägerstrand calls "activity bundles") demand the co-presence of a group of individuals at a particular station together for a certain period of time. Finally, the authority constraints include the rights of access to space and time for given activities. There are laws, rules, economic barriers, power relationships, etc. that regulate who does or does not have access to some activities in some stations at specific times.

There are two points about time geography worth highlighting here. First, time and space are fundamentally treated as scare resources (in this connection see also Carlstein, 1982). The constraints imposed on the formation of human activity due to scarcity are rightly pointed out and given their theoretical importance. The enabling capability of time–space resources, however, is very much underplayed. It is very important to note that the memory-dependent time discussed above is totally compatible with the notion of time and space as scarce resources, found in time geography. *The memory-dependent time is intrinsically a human internal experience at the individual actor's level. The time and space as scare resources are at the social, collective level, playing dual roles of both constraining and enabling the actor's memory-dependent behavior.* (Remember that whether or not time and space are valuable is a social–cultural variable.)

Second, the term *constraint*, negative as it may sound, does not mean that Hägerstand regards an individual as a passive actor. On the contrary, in time geography, an individual is an active pursuer of a life-long "project." The three classes of constraint constitute in fact the necessary (though not sufficient) conditions in order for individuals to implement their projects. The preference of constraint to necessary condition analysis is consistent with Hägerstrand's contention that there is a need to be "able to pinpoint the reasons for 'non-events,' that is, to trace barriers which prevent certain types of events and stages from occurring" (cited in Pred, 1996: 640).

The LBSD and the individual actor's spatial–temporal behavior

The LBSD is a mode of discourse that is embodied in humans' natural multimodality and is being produced by human actors along the spatial–temporal paths, starting at the point of birth and ending at the point of death. This does not mean that the LBSD is a study of actors' individualistic discourse. On the contrary, human agents' spatial–temporal behavior is always interwoven, as emphasized by time geography. The LBSD is in essence a web of trajectories pursued by actors over space and time.

The trajectory-mediated LBSD

Gu (2002a) reports a study of Mr. X's trajectories on a week-path by audio-recording all his wakeful activities from the moment he got up in the morning to the time he went to bed at night. Adopting the same time–space notation scheme of Hägerstrand's, this study can be graphically represented as in Figure 38.2.

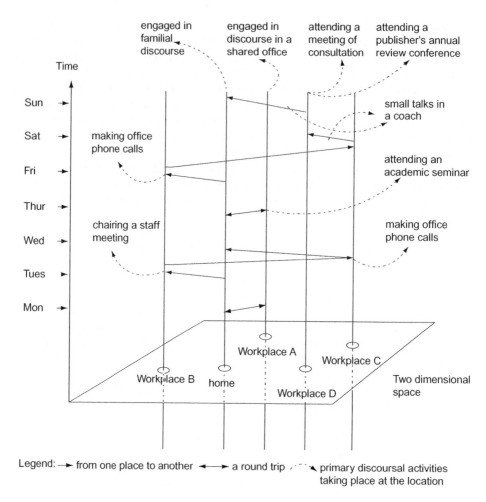

Figure 38.2 Mr. X's weekly trajectory of activities

Figure 38.2 clearly shows that Mr. X's week-path was very mobile. On Monday and Thursday he commuted from home to Workplace A. On Tuesday he left home for Workplace B, from which he traveled to Workplace C, and returned home afterwards. On Wednesday he stayed at home. On Friday he went to Workplace B, then to Workplace C, where he joined a coach trip to Workplace D. There he stayed for two days, Saturday and Sunday, before returning home on the Sunday evening.

This log of Mr. X's whereabouts, appearing quite mundane if not trivial, is significant to discourse studies and to discourse geography in particular, namely in the following ways. First, the spatial–temporal movements of actors count for one of the fundamental motor forces that maintain the dynamism of all the LBSDs in China (it is perhaps also true of all other languages in the world). Second, discoursal activities taking place at particular behavior settings, appearing to be independent and self-contained events by themselves, are in fact not isolated or disconnected ones. *The actors' spatial–temporal movements from one discoursal activity to another provide embodied cognitive links and connections, thus producing a chain of LBSDs mediated by an actor's trajectories of activity paths.* For ease of reference, this kind of chain will be referred to as *trajectory-mediated chain of LBSD.*

Third, the LBSD's trajectory-mediated chain is framed by what Carlstein calls "human time," i.e. "a temporal portion of a person" (Carlstein, 1982: 27), which in everyday parlance means a person's availability for a given activity.[6]

The actor's activity zone and its impact on the LBSD

Although modern transportations enable people to be more mobile than ever before, their accessibility and affordability are extremely varied from actor to actor. A CEO, for example, may spend most of his time on airplanes, whereas a herdsman (e.g. in Inner Mongolia) is found hardly going beyond a walking distance from home. The term *activity zone* is used to refer to the behavior settings an actor regularly visits. Urban commuters' activity zone includes workplace, transportation station, home, and local markets. Rural farmers' activity zone, on the other hand, includes the land being farmed, home, vegetable plots, and local markets. The activity zone impacts the LBSD in several ways. First, it routinizes the LBSD. Second, it makes some types of LBSD more frequent to the actor than others, e.g. workplace discourse, familial discourse, local market discourse thus becoming more frequent than others. Third, it may reserve or make loss of dialects or languages. The Inner Mongolian herdsmen of grandpa and grandma generation, thanks to their constrained activity zones, reserve the spoken Mongolian language. The mum/dad generation, on the other hand, thanks to their much broader activity zones, become bilingual, speaking Putonghua (the national standard language) at the workplace and Mongolian at home. The grandchildren generation, however, due to their activity zones in schools and close to the county town, have almost lost their spoken Mongolian, and have become monolingual like their grandpa and grandma—only not in Mongolian, but in Putonghua. Millions of Chinese migrant workers, for another instance, pour into major cities. Their activity zones become seasonal: when they find work, the host cities become their activity zones. When they go home for the Chinese New Year break or because they have lost their job, their former hometowns become their activity zones again. Many of them, particularly women migrant workers (as domestic helpers) become bidialectal as a result.

An ecological chain of discourse with the LBSD as its node

The LBSD's trajectory-mediated chain captures the interconnectivity between discourses that occur in different places. There is another interconnectivity forged by what I propose to call *ecological chain of discourse* with the LBSD as its node. This can be demonstrated by the ensuing chain of events (reconstructed on the basis of a real-life case).

A certain individual, let's call him Mr. Y, suffers from hay fever (as the result of his interaction with the physical environment). He sneezes like mad (non-verbal physiological behavior of an individualistic kind). He takes bus to go to a drug store. He enters into a node on the web of spatial–temporal trajectories, framed and enabled by the community. In the drug store—another node on the web of spatial–temporal trajectories—he talks about his hay fever to a girl assistant, who shows him a few choices and offers him some advice. He makes a choice and pays. This whole transaction would have been impossible without a drug manufacturer producing the drug. The latter, on the other hand, would never have been produced without research on anti-allergic drugs. Anti-allergic drug research, in turn, is motivated by the fact that Mr. Y is not the only one who sneezes on exposure to the pollen of flowering plants. Figure 38.3 is a graphic representation of Mr. Y's hay fever's ecological chain.

The LBSDs of a community consist of many such ecological chains. The significance of such ecological chains lies in the fact that it gives coherence and integrity to all the LBSDs as a whole.

Yueguo Gu

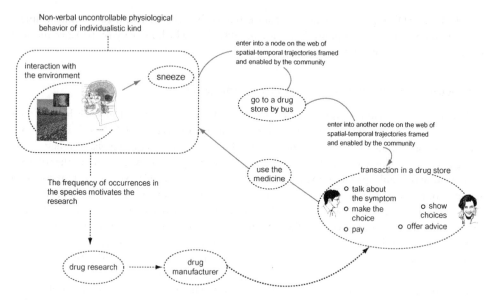

Figure 38.3 An ecological chain of activities

The LBSD and human spatial–temporal behavior from the system's point of view

The section above discussed the correlation between the social actor's spatial–temporal behavior and the LBSD. As shown in Hägerstrand's theory of time geography, the social actor's spatial–temporal behavior is under three major constraints. The third one, "authority constraints," regulates actors' individual behaviors in such a way that a spatial–temporal order for collectivities results from them. In this section we examine the correlation between a collective spatial–temporal order and the LBSD.

Temporal structuring of LBSDs in present-day China

There are two general types of temporal structuring in the present-day China. One is by adopting the Western calendar,[7] and the other by using the traditional Chinese lunar calendar. Both are officially valid, and citizens are free to choose one or both. But, in practice, the two types of calendar have divided the population into two types of actors: salary earners, and farmers. Salary earners' temporal behavior is structured by using the Western calendar, whereas farmers' by the lunar calendar. This is so because the lunar calendar is primarily based on the seasonal and climatic behavior of nature, which is crucial for farming. So the salary earner's temporal patterns of discourse are quite different from the farmer's. The former can be characterized as artificial temporality of workplace discourse, whereas the later is natural temporality of subsistence discourse. Table 38.1 tabulates the major differences between the two.

There are three points worth mentioning. First, there is no official monthly structuring for salary earners (as there is a yearly, seasonal, weekly, and daily structuring). An exception is perhaps to be found in the Muslim holy month of fasting and prayer. Second, farmers' agricultural activities are mainly consulted with the 24 jieqi (节气), lasting 15 days each. These represent weather patterns found mainly in the areas of the Yellow and Yangtze River. Third, at the bottom part of the table, attached are the potential hours for speaking per annum, and the estimated amount of

Table 38.1 Temporal patterns

	Salary Earners	Farmers	
	the Western calendar	the Chinese lunar calendar	
Yearly structuring	29-day discourse for public holidays	the same	
Seasonal structuring	no classroom discourse for 3 months	Seasonal structuring	subsistence discourse structured by the natural laws regarding the growth of crops or animals
Monthly structuring	?	Structuring by the weather patterns (24 jieqi)	
Weekly structuring	5-day workplace discourse		
Daily structuring	8-hour workplace discourse	Daily structuring	field labour discourse timed mainly by the solar behavior

potential hours for speaking per annum, and their estimated amount of syllables (equal to Chinese characters) that might be produced at normal tempo
7-hour sleep per day x 365 = 2,555 hours; 17 waking hours per day x 365 = 6,205 hours per annum
(1 minute x 45 syllables) x 60 = 2,700 syllables per hour; 17 waking hours x 2700 = 45,900 syllables per day; 6205 x 2700 = 16,753,500 syllables per annum

syllables that might be produced at normal tempo.[7] Since Chinese characters are mostly mono-syllabic, the amount of syllables is equivalent to the amount of spoken characters.

Gu (2002a) examines some workplace discourses over a time span running from 7 a.m. to 24 p.m. The home discourse is included, for contrast (see Figure 38.4). Four salient changes are noted. (1) People in private enterprises work much longer hours than those in state owned ones. (2) It is only in recent years that street markets in Beijing offer early morning service. This is in sharp contrast with street markets in southern parts of China, which have a long tradition of early morning service. (3) It is also quite a recent phenomenon that supermarkets in Beijing have long non-stop opening hours, from 8:00 a.m. to 8:30 p.m., or even to 10 p.m. (4) Evening classes are now taught at primary, secondary and tertiary levels. The practice used to be rare, but is now widespread. All these changes mean, with regard to workplace discourse, that Beijing citizens spend more time/space in workplace discourse than they used to do. In other words, they would spend less time/space in home discourse than they would do.

In view of physical time, Figure 38.4 shows an important feature of *discourse timetabling* at various degrees of strictness. At certain times of the day in a given region, the LBSD web can be extremely busy with all sorts of face-to-face discourses hotly being engaged in.

Urbanization, and spatial concentration of LBSD types

One of the biggest changes that China has recently witnessed is rapid urbanization, the scope of which is unprecedented in the whole Chinese history. Regarding the LBSD, this means that the country has increased its urban space and lost its former rural space. Demographically speaking, there

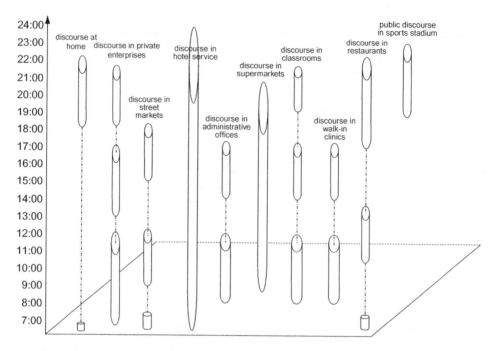

Figure 38.4 Temporal patterns of workplace discourse
Source: quoted from Gu (2002: 150)

are more people engaged in workplace discourse than in subsistence discourse. Thus their temporal patterns of discourse have also been changed as a result of their spatial migration into cities.

There is another phenomenon, to be called *cheng*-phenomena[9] in Chinese or "city-phenomenon" in English, co-occurring with urbanization. This label depicts the fact that areas are exclusively allocated for activities of similar types. In other words, the LBSD of a particular type gets densely concentrated at a particular zone of a city. Take Beijing for example. There are (1) such-and-such *cheng*, e.g. daxue cheng (大学城, university city), qipei cheng (汽配城，automobile city), yule cheng (娱乐城, fun city), jiaju cheng (家具城, furniture city), cha cheng (茶城，tea city), shiji cheng (世纪城, millennium city), keji cheng (科技城, technology city)；(2) such-and-such *zhongxin*, e.g. shangmao zhongxin (商贸中心，trade center), shimao zhongxin (世贸中心, global business center); (3) such-and-such *chang*, e.g. youle chang (游乐场，recreation ground), yundong chang (运动场, sports ground); (4) such-and-such *yitiaojie*, e.g. shipin yitiaojie (食品一条街，food and catering street), jinrong yitiaojie (金融一条街, bank and finance street), guwan yitiaojie (古玩一条街，antique street), dianzi yitiaojie (电子一条街，electronics street); and (5) such-and-such *qu*, e.g. waijiao qu (外交区，diplomatic quarters), junshi qu (军事区, military zone), lüyou qu (旅游区，tourist area), kaifa qu (开发区, development area).

These *cheng, chang, zhongxin, yitiaojie,* and *qu are* large-scale behavior settings where LBSDs of certain types are clustered for easy access. Nowadays, with the help of GoogleEarth, these clusters can be mapped to minute details.

Power, spatial–temporal behavior and the LBSD's interactive order

Time in everyday understanding is linear, that is, there is a sequential order. In time-reckoning, time is divided into units and made measurable (i.e. quantifiable). Space, on the other hand, is three-dimensional—it has length, width, and height. In this section we examine the ways the Chinese social–cultural systems make use of these features of spatiality and temporality in framing and enabling social actors' spatial–temporal behaviors in the LBSD. The examination will be focused on the interaction between political–administrative power and spatiality/temporality.

Of all forms of power, the political–administrative form is granted dominating position in present-day China. That is, it overpowers all the other forms of power (for detailed discussion about Chinese power, see Gu, in press). Everything else being equal, its incumbents will be given priority in temporal sequences of events: to speak first, to walk in front of everybody else, and so on. A greater amount of time will be given to them too, if they wish to have it. The social use of three-dimensional space with regard to political–administrative power, as shown in Gu (2009b), is organized in terms of prominence. The center of the front row is considered as the most prominent position, and the degree of prominence decreases from this central reference point sidewise and row-wise. The Chinese spatial order framing the spatial behaviors between the incumbents of political-administrative power and those holding other forms of power is graphically represented in Figure 38.5.

It is interesting to note that, while in mainland China the spatial order is rather universal, this is not the case in Taiwan. In other words, the political–administrative power does not always enjoy priority in the local spatial–temporal behaviors of Taiwan. For instance, in an international conference I attended in 2009, the head of the department sat at the most important seat, as president of the conference—and not the university's vice-president. This would have been a serious breakdown of the spatial order, should it have happened on the mainland.

The Chinese temporal sequential order can be shown by contrasting it with the British. In the Hong Kong handover in 1997, on the British side, it was Chris Pattern who took the lead and first walked onto the stage with Prince Charles at the rear. On the Chinese side, it was President Jiang Zemin who took the lead and first walked onto the stage with Dong Qianhua at the rear. Should Dong Qianhua as Chris Pattern's counterpart have done the same, that would have been a totally unacceptable breakdown of temporal order.

Social space–time vs. social space–time

The phrase "*social space–time*" will be used by the author to conceptualize two interrelated phenomena. One sense refers to the scope of social mobility and to the freedom a social system provides for its members by way of laws, decrees, regulations, control of resources, values, and so

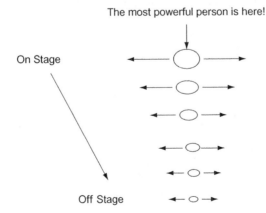

Figure 38.5 The Chinese spatial order
Source: quoted from Gu (2009b: 136)

on (recall Hagerstrand's third authority constraints). This sense will be marked through initial capital letters, "Social Space–Time." The other sense refers to the chances of making a living a social system offers its members. This sense is to be signaled through the usual spelling, "social space–time."

The previous section has shown the coupling of human bodily movement in physical space and time with individual members' everyday activities. This coupling provides a bridge linking bodily movements in physical space and time with Social Space–Time. The concept can be demonstrated with the age-old household registration practice, the earliest written record of which was found in West Zhou Dynasty (1121–771 BC). In Ming Dynasty (AD 1368–1644) there was a law with the ensuing article: "Farmers must remain within one *li* [a unit of distance]. Go out to labour in the morning and return home in the evening. Whereabouts must be made known to one another."[10] Whoever wants to leave beyond one hundred *li* must obtain a travel certificate (*luyin* 路引). While "one hundred *li*" is physical space, and from morning to evening is physical time, the fact that farmers and their behavior are bound by the law to this physical space–time is Social Space–Time. The farmers' chances for making a living within this Social Space–Time will be their social space–time.

In twenty-first-century China the law about household registration still remains in effect, although it is much less restrictive. Its consequences however are quite substantial. The fact that millions of migrant workers pour into cities to make a living shows that their Social Space–Time is thus made much broader than that of their non-migrant countryside compatriots. This does not improve their social space–time, since they cannot become registered as regular household members in their host cities, thus being denied access to the benefits the urban citizens enjoy. Migrant workers bring their LBSDs with them to the host cities. Their LBSDs are automatically made inferior to the urban LBSDs, and physically evaporate the moment they are being produced.

The delicate interaction between the Social Space–Time, and the social space–time can be shown in the following anecdote. In Beijing there are many street hawkers selling petty goods in streets and on flyovers. They hide themselves from 8 a.m. to 6 p.m., since during this time span the market control police is at work. They appear as if from nowhere after 6 p.m. Figure 38.6a is a photo picture of a flyover at 4:30 p.m, and Figure 38.6b a photo picture of the same flyover at 6:30 p.m.

The rules and regulations give no Social Space–Time to street hawkers, which is supposed to be reinforced by the market control police during its office hours. Once the police officers are off duty, there is no reinforcement for a certain period of time, which becomes the street hawkers' social space–time, granted by themselves.

(a)

(b)

Figure 38.6 Social Space–Time vs. social space–time

Summing up

Discourse geography, as discussed so far, is a study of the correlation between discourse qua language-in-action and human spatial–temporal behaviors. This correlation is crystallized in the conceptualization of the land-borne situated discourse (LBSD). The LBSD, being both framed and enabled by human spatial–temporal behaviors, has several intrinsic properties: (1) it is a web interwoven by life-path trajectories of human activities; (2) it is regionalized by actors' activity zones; (3) the web of life-path trajectories is criss-crossed by an ecological chain of discourse/activities; (4) it is temporally structured by calendars and timetables; (5) it is spatially concentrated into clusters due to urbanization; and (6) it exhibits patterns of sequential and spatial order thanks to actors' differences in power relations.

Discourse geography: a final note

In this last section we explore some theoretical issues related to the conceptualization of discourse geography in terms that the LBSD has brought up.

As mentioned above, on top of the LBSD there are three more modes of discourse: the WWBD, the ABSD, and the WBSD. These four modes of discourse are not evenly distributed among cultures. The LBSD is prototypical of oral–aural cultures, i.e. of what Ong (1982) calls "primary orality cultures." There is no shortage of such cultures in the world, and in China alone there still exist a few dozen. Since these cultures do not have writing systems, the LBSD is the dominant mode of discourse.

Of the four modes of discourse, the LBSD, being interwoven, structured, and organized by human spatial–temporal behaviors over physical space and time, is not only the oldest, but also the most basic. We tend to be blind to the fact that language is first and foremost our mode of living, i.e. "the coming-to-be of presence." It is therefore fruitful to look at language as a multi-dimensional city, which is built by us and in which we live.

Further reading

Agnew, J., Livingstone, D. N. and Rogers, A. (eds.) (1996), *Human Geography: An Essential Anthology*, Oxford: Blackwell Publishers Ltd, and Carlstein, T. (1982) *Time Resources, Society and Ecology*. London: George Allen and Unwin Ltd.

For human geography and time geography, these books provide a scholarly treatment of the subject.

Gu, Y. (2009a) 'Four-borne discourses: towards language as a multi-dimensional city of history', in L. I. Wei and V. Cook (eds.) *Linguistics in the Real World*. London: Centinuum, pp. 98–121.

This paper has a preliminary discussion about the four-borne discourses.

Notes

1 Gu (2002a) tentatively introduced the term in this sense for the first time.
2 The Peking Man (Homo erectus, 400,000–200,000 BP; see Fairbank, 1997: 31) who was excavated in a Beijing suburb in 1929, was taken here as the landmark of pre-history. See Gu, 2009a: 99.
3 Saussure's notion of linearity (2001 [1983]: 103), being closely associated with speech production, can be argued to treat time as an intrinsic property of language. This sense of time is obviously different from the one that underlies his dichotomy between synchrony and diachrony, as discussed in 3.3 above.
4 It is obvious, as admitted by Ricoeur, that the relation between narrativity and temporality thus defined is circular. But it is argued that it is "not a vicious but a healthy circle, whose two halves mutually reinforce one another" (Ricoeur, 1984: 3).
5 Thanks to Dr. Liu Hongyan, who made the recording.

6 Carlstein (1982: 28–30) argues against using "convenient ways of obfuscating human time" such as using "labour," "effort," "energy," "convenience," etc., which are in essence time notions. Here I quite subscribe to Carlstein's position. The advantage of preferring "human time" to other expressions lies in the fact that it explicitly highlights the organizing as well as the integrating functions of time in human activities.

7 The Western calendar was officially adopted in 1949, the year the New China was founded. The traditional lunar calendar goes back as early as Xia Dynasty 2207–1766 BC, hence it is often called *xia li* 夏历.

8 The figure of 45 syllables per minute is based on a sample of four activities from the SCCSD. It is subject to fine-tuning when the sample population is increased. At this stage the figure is only suggestive at best.

9 Cheng 城 literally means city in English.

10 "农业者不出一里之间，朝出暮入，作息之道相互知," see 江立华，"中国户籍制度的历史考察。载《人口学与计划生育》2002 (01) .

References

Agnew, J., Livingstone, D. N., and Rogers, A. (eds.) (1996) *Human Geography: An Essential Anthology.* Oxford: Blackwell Publishers Ltd.

Arche, M. J. (2006) *Individuals in Time: Tense, Aspect and the Individual/Stage Distinction.* Amsterdam: John Benjamins Publishing Company.

Auer, P., Couper-Kuhlen, E., and Müller, F. (1999) *Language in Time: The Rhythm and Tempo of Spoken Interaction.* New York: Oxford University Press.

Barker, R. G. (1968) *Ecological Psychology.* Stanford: Stanford University Press.

Bergson, H. (1991) *Matter and Memory*, trans. Nancy Margaret Paul and W. Scott Palmer. New York: Zone Books.

Blommaert, J. (2005) *Discourse: A Critical Introduction.* Cambridge: Cambridge University Press.

Bloom, P., Peterson, M. A., Nadel, L., and Garrett, M. F. (eds.) (1996) *Language and Space.* Cambridge, MA: The MIT Press.

Brandt, P. A. (2004) *Spaces, Domains and Meanings.* Bern: Peter Lang.

Carlstein, T. (1982) *Time Resources, Society and Ecology.* London: George Allen and Unwin Ltd.

Carlstein, T., Parkes, D., and Thrift, N. (eds.) (1978a) *Human Activity and Time Geography.* London: Edward Arnold Ltd.

Carlstein, T., Parkes, D., and Thrift, N. (eds.) (1978b) *Making Sense of Time.* London: Edward Arnold Ltd.

Chafe, W. (1994) *Discourse, Consciousness, and Time.* Chicago, IL: The University of Chicago Press.

Dancygier, B. and Sweetser, E. (2005) *Mental Spaces in Grammar: Conditional Constructions.* Cambridge: Cambridge University Press.

Emmorey, K. and Reilly, J. S. (eds.) (1995) *Language, Gesture, and Space.* Hillsdale, NJ: Laurence Erlbaum Associates, Publishers.

Ewen, R. B. (1993) *An Introduction to Theories of Personality.* Fourth Edition. Hillsdale, NJ: Lawrence Erlbaum Associates, Publishers.

Fairbank, J. K. (1997) *China: A New History.* London: The Belknap Press of Harvard University Press.

Fauconnier, G. (1985) *Mental Spaces: Aspects of Meaning Construction in Natural Language.* London: The MIT Press.

Fellmann, J., Getis, A., and Getis, J. (1995) *Human Geography.* Dubuque: Wm. C. Brown Communications, Inc.

Firth, J. R. (1957) *Papers in Linguistics 1934–1951.* London: Oxford University Press.

Giddens, A. (1981) 'Agency, institution and time-space analysis', in K. Knorr-Cetina and A. V. Cicourel (eds.) *Advances in Social Theory and Methodology: Toward an Integration of Micro- and Macro-Sociologies.* London: Routledge & Kegan Paul, pp. 161–174.

Giddens, A. (1995) *A Contemporary Critique of Historical Materialism.* Second Edition. London: MacMillan Press Ltd.

Goffman, E. (1963) *Behavior in Public Places.* New York: The Free Press.

Gu, Y. (2002a) 'Towards an understanding of workplace discourse: A pilot study for compiling a spoken Chinese corpus of situated discourse', in C. Candlin (ed.) *Research and Practice in Professional Discourse.* Hong Kong: City University of Hong Kong Press, pp. 137–186.

Gu, Y. (2002b) 'Sampling and representativeness in compiling SCCSD (written in Chinese)', in the World Economics Research Centre and the Chinese Academy of Social Sciences (eds.), *Globalization and the 21st Century.* Beijing: Social Sciences and Archive Press, pp. 484–500.

Gu, Y. (2009a) 'Four-borne discourses: towards language as a multi-dimensional city of history', in L. I. Wei and V. Cook (eds.) *Linguistics in the Real World.* London: Centinuum, pp. 98–121.

Gu, Y. (2009b) 'An institutional anniversary ceremony as systemic behavior in Chinese context', in K. Turner and B. Fraser (eds.) *Language in Life, and a Life in Language: Jacob Mey —A Festschrift*. Bingely: Emerald Group Publishing Limited, pp. 121–129.

Gu, Y. (in press) 'Approaching Chinese Power in Situated Discourse: From Experience to Modeling', in Y. Pan and D. Kador, (eds.), *Chinese Discourse and Interaction*. London: Equinox.

Guéron, J. and Lecarme, J. (eds.) (2008) *Time and Modality*. Berlin: Springer.

Hägerstrand, T. (1996 [1982]) 'Diorama, path and project', in J. Agnew, D. N. Livingstone, and A. Rogers (eds.), *Human Geography: An Essential Anthology*. Oxford: Blackwell Publishers Ltd, pp. 650–674.

Hale, M. (2007) *Historical Linguistics: Theory and Method*. Malden: Blackwell Publishing.

Heidegger, M. (1962) *Being and Time*, trans. John Macquarrie and Edward Robinson. Oxford: Basil Blackwell.

Hickmann, M. and Robert, S. (eds.) (2006) *Space in Languages*. Amsterdam: John Benjamins Publishing Companay.

Lawson, B. (2001) *Language of Space*. Oxford: Architectural Press.

Levinson, S. C. (2003) *Space in Language and Cognition*. Cambridge: Cambridge University Press.

Levinson, S. C. and Wilkins, D. P. (eds.) (2006) *Grammars of Space: Explorations in Cognitive Diversity*. Cambridge: Cambridge University Press.

Ong, W. J. (1982) *Orality and Literacy*. London: Methuen.

Pred, A. (1996) 'The choreography of existence: Comments on Hagerstrand's time-geography and its usefulness', in J. Agnew, D. N. Livingstone, and A. Rogers (eds.), *Human Geography: An Essential Anthology*. Oxford: Blackwell Publishers Ltd, pp. 636–649.

Pütz, M. and Dirven, R. (eds.) (1996) *The Construal of Space in Language and Thought*. Berlin: Mouton de Gruyter.

Richards, B., Bethke, I., van der Does, J., and Oberlander, J. (eds.) (1989) *Temporal Representation and Inference*. London: Academic Press.

Ricoeur, P. (1984) *Time and Narrative*, trans. Kathleen McLaughlin and David Pellauer. Volume 1. Chicago: The University of Chicago Press.

Sanders, C. (2006) *Introduction to Ferdinand de Saussure's Writings in General Linguistics*. New York: Oxford University Press, pp. xv–xxx.

Sattig, T. (2006) *The Language and Reality of Time*. Oxford: Clarendon Press.

Saussure, Ferdinand de (2001 [1983]) *Course in General Linguistics*, translated by Roy Harris. Beijing: Foreign Language Teaching and Research Press.

Siegman, A. W. and Feldstein, S. (eds.) (1979) *Of Speech and Time: Temporal Speech Patterns in Interpersonal Contexts*. Hillsdale, NJ: Lawrence Erlbaum Associates, Publishers.

Trask, R. L. (2000) *Historical Linguistics*. Beijing: Foreign Language Teaching and Research Press and Edward Arnold (Publishers) Ltd.

Urry, J. (1985) 'Social relations, space and time', in D. Gregory and J. Urry (eds.), *Social Relations and Spatial Structures*. London: Macmillan, pp. 20–48.

Zee, E. and Slack, J. (2003) *Representing Direction in Language and Space*. Oxford: Oxford University Press.

39

Queer linguistics, sexuality, and discourse analysis

William L. Leap

Queer linguistics is a relatively recent academic formation, but one that has quickly become firmly embedded in the current conversations about language, gender, and sexuality. As is also the case in language and gender studies (see Coates, this volume), queer linguistics refuses to frame discussions of linguistic practices in terms of an assumed male/female binary (or on a limited set of identities based solely on erotic practices and preferences). Instead, queer linguistics exposes the assumptions that lead researchers to view gender in terms of a predetermined, static framework.

The term 'queer' is an especially suitable focus for such an inquiry. Here as elsewhere in queer theory,

> queer does not name some natural kind of referent to some deterministic object; it acquires its meaning from its oppositional relation to the norm.
>
> *(Halperin, 1995: 62)*

Queer linguistics posits that gender is the normative reference in this discussion, recognizing that a society's statements about 'who men and women are' are ideological formations; they constitute 'a representation of the imaginary relationship of individuals to their real conditions of existence' whose outcome of representation is 'the "constituting" [of] concrete individuals as subjects' (Althusser, 1971: 162, 171). These relationships are represented to individuals through discursive practices, but they are represented variously given how the particulars of race and ethnic background, class position, age, dimensions of (dis)ability, and attendant locations of citizenship, nationality, and diasporic flow shape discussions about gender in the social moment. Under such circumstances, while the persuasive power of the ideological formations remains, the everyday understandings of 'who men and women are' are unlikely to follow a uniform pathway and often become sources of disagreement and conflict.

By paying attention to the discursive practices through which these understandings, disagreements and conflicts unfold, queer linguistics confirms the limits of gender as an explanatory category in linguistic analysis and forces studies of 'who men and women are' to look beyond those discourses of certainty. The terrain of sexuality becomes an alternative space for inquiry at this point, since the 'oppositional relations' associated with gendered norms are often located and mediated in the form of in sexual desires, practices, and identities. But queer linguistics cannot be concerned solely with sexuality as its subject matter, just as it could not be concerned solely with gender. Sexual desires, practices and identities are also inflected variously across the social terrain, and in some cases they are inflected privately or silently rather than as components of public discourse. As a general task that is mindful that certain ideological messages about 'who men and women are' circulate widely in the social moment, queer linguistics explores the discursive inflections of the sexual – desires, practices, and identities – as they unfold in the context of that circulation, and often (as Halperin suggests) in opposition to it.

To summarize: if, following Judith Butler, we think of gender as 'repeated acts within a highly rigid regulatory frame that congeals over time to produce the appearance of substance' (1990: 33), then 'what kind of subversive repetition might call into question the regulatory practice of identity itself ?' (1990: 32). Queer linguistics looks to discursive practices to provide answers to Butler's question.

Reading the discourses of sexuality queerly: an example

I turn now to an example that shows what a queer linguistics-based analysis of discursive practices – sexuality, gender, identity, and related themes – might entail. The narrative in this example is extracted from a life story narrative that I collected during a four-year-period of field work (1995–1999) in the metropolitan area of Cape Town, South Africa. Of interest to that project were the changes in urban sexual geography that were unfolding during the transition away from policies of 'strict apartheid' and into the beginnings of democratic rule. During the research period, I interviewed same-sex identified white men living in the city centre and suburbs and same-sex identified coloured and black men living in the townships on the Cape Flats.[1] I learned from these stories that gay life had been deeply segregated in Cape Town during the days of apartheid rule. But I also learned that, as early as 1990, apartheid regulations had begun to be relaxed in some city centre commercial venues, to accommodate the need of international travellers. Under the strict letter of the law, Cape Town area persons of colour were now granted access to these sites, and some of them attempted to make use of those opportunities. But strict apartheid remained preferred practice throughout the city centre business community, and some club owners found ways to maintain racial exclusion regardless of the change in legal policy.

Comments in life-story narratives like example 1 below suggest that some same-sex identified coloured and black men were aware of the contradictory conditions that emerged within this context. They understood that practices of exclusion positioned them as *refused subjects* at the same time as these initial changes in apartheid policy had finally made freedom from discrimination more attainable. Jameson, the narrator in example 1, was 35 years old at the time of our interview (1996) and was in his late twenties when he first encountered these contradictions. He grew up in one of Cape Town's coloured townships, and was still living at home with his parents and working for a township-based social services agency when he told me this story. We were introduced by a mutual friend, who had told him about my interests in Cape Town sexual geography. Jameson was happy to speak with me, since he had many stories to tell about sexual sameness and spatial practices related to the townships and the city centre. Example 1 is one of those stories.

Example 1

001 J: … and eventually I started going [to the Rondebosch Train Station] regularly, and then

002 I met someone there. At the station. And I knew him from the university, and uh we

003 started chatted, and every Friday we saw each other at the place, gave him my telephone

004 number and gave me his, told him I'll meet you Rondebosch that time. We used to cruise

005 around the area, lucky some nights, unlucky other nights.

006 Until he said what he heard about this gay bar in Cape Town. He said let's go, I
007 said no way I'm going to go into a gay bar. I had cold feet at that stage as well, being very
008 tired, coming out at 11:00 and going to the station.
009 And then one evening he said, let's go and see what it's like. We got there, it was
010 packed ! [said in whispered excitement] *with men!* And as you walked past people looked
011 at you and rubbed against you, and I thought, this is really for me. And we left. And the
012 next week we said, OK now we know the place and are we going backthere again? We
013 got there and it was closed.

(WLL: Which place was it?)

014 J: It was the [location 1.] It was closed. I though Oh no, where is this place now
015 now. And my friend, of course, inquired from other people, said now anew place opened
016 up called [location 2.], and then eventually we found [location 2] and we
017 went there .The first night we went inside and we had a drink inside, westayed there for
018 about an hour and we left.
019 And the next week we came back and they said, you can't go it,it's only for
020 members. And we asked, you know how, members? We were here lastweek. No, only
021 for members. The bar in front is for the public, and the inside bar. At that stage, we
022 realized that it was a race thing, uhm, went to the bar and sat there the front bar feeling
023 really rejected because we'd had a good time the week before. And we asked the barman
024 how come we can't get in, and he asked, are you gay? At that stage, both of us did not
025 want to admit to anybody that we were gay, so we said, does it matter ? He said, it's a
026 gay bar so it matters a lot.
027 We left, and the next week we came back again, and we decided to go into the
028 members' bar, and we walked in, and uhm no one stopped us again.
029 And the barman said [names location 3], that was the bar we should go to. So
030 that's how I discovered the bar scene.

(W. Leap field notes)

Taken at face value, example 1 falls within a familiar genre of gay narrative: it is a coming out story, nested within a story of sexual/spatial discovery. Initially, according to the storyline, Jameson was unfamiliar with the city's gay commercial resources and is forced to meet people by cruising the cottages (public restrooms) and the parking lot at the Rondebosch train station.[2] Through this process he confirmed the same-sex identity of a man he had met while at the university, someone who became his partner in this urban exploration. The friend suggested the initial foray downtown, and through a process of trial and error they located several clubs, negotiated access, and thereby 'discovered the bar scene' (1:030). There was a difficult moment in the process of discovery. Jameson and his friend were excluded from a club because of what they 'realized was a race thing' (1:021–022). But the bartender saw things differently. He asked Jameson, 'Are you gay?', asking him to make a coming out declaration, which he was not yet prepared to make. Hence Jameson reworked the anticipated adjacency pairing – 'Does it matter?' – And abruptly departed the site, returning at a later time to seek entrance under different circumstances, this time successfully.

Reading example 1 as a coming out story emphasizes the story's events prompted the formation of the subject's sexual identity. Not fully acknowledged in that reading is the significance of the racial question or the extent to which apartheid authority, even at the beginning of transition, may have framed sexual formation in racial terms. Jameson and his friend being denied entrance to the private club because of 'a race thing' (1:021–022) is an important reference in this regard, of course. But denied entrance has to be read beside the fact that Jameson and his friend had previously been granted entrance to the private club, and were allowed entrance to the private club on their next visit. Apparently, at this point in Cape Town's history, the apartheid practice of racial exclusion was no longer a matter of categorical denial, but involved a more arbitrary and unpredictable process of refusal. If so, then example 1's discussion of coming out and special/ sexual discovery becomes a story of refused subject formation as well as a story explaining how two such subjects engaged the contradictory conditions of refusal once subject formation in those terms began to unfold.

The bartender's question: 'Are you gay?' (1: 024) assumes a particular significance under this reading. As Jameson explained:

… [we] sat there the front bar feeling really rejected because we'd had a good time the week before. And we asked the barman how come we can't get in.

(1: 022–024)

Jameson's response to the bartender's question reflected a reluctance to make a public statement about their sexuality, as he explained:

At that stage, both of us did not want to admit to anybody that we were gay, so we said, does it matter? He said, it's a gay bar so it matters a lot.

(1:024–026)

But Jameson's response says more than that: the bartender's question implied that Jameson and his friend could gain access to the private club if they admitted that they were gay. Saying 'yes' to the barman's question would not change the fact that they had previously been refused on racial grounds, but it would give them admission to the private club and terminate their status as refused subjects. At the same time, saying 'yes' to the barman's question would also admit that sexual sameness erases racial differences in the city centre's gay terrain, that gay men of colour are now allowed to 'pass for white' in the context of late apartheid. By saying 'no' to the bartender's question, Jameson and his friend maintained the integrity of their racial status even if they also remained in the status of refused subjects and at distance from the sexual venues initially of great interest to them. And by endorsing this status, Jameson and his friend also underscored the ideological stance expressed in the doorman's act of refusal: 'gay' is implicitly a white person's status, and persons of colour acquire that status only under context-specific and other exceptional circumstances.

So there is nothing inappropriate about discussing example 1 as a coming out story, but making such an appeal to genre predetermines the references that are relevant to the storyline and, as a more careful reading of the text reveals, the scope of relevant references proves to be much more complex than a trajectory of self-discovery. Similarly, example 1 could be called a 'gay' narrative in the sense that the narrator is same-sex identified, defines himself as a gay man, and is telling a story about experiences (coming out, discovery) that are familiar to same-sex identified men in any number of locations worldwide. But, here again, the term 'gay' can not have a predetermined meaning within the context of this narrative. In fact one of the components of the 'bar scene' that

Jameson 'discovered' (1:030) through this experience in the city centre commercial terrain was what the category 'gay' could mean for him in this particular moment of Cape Town's social and political history.

Queer linguistics as a part of a broader 'queer project'

Finally, example 1's continual weaving of sexuality, race, and responses to apartheid regulation can also be read as instances of 'subversive repetition' whose effects 'call into question the regulatory practice of identity' (Butler, 1990: 32). Importantly, repetition and subversion are not properties 'of' text but reflect the engagements of speakers and audiences with text production and reception: Jameson and his friend, the doorman, the bartender, as well as the researcher – and now the reader of this article – become deeply invested in the process of refused subject formation as described in this text. This is another reason for arguing that example 1 is not just a story about coming out, sexual/spatial discovery, or some other form of gay narrative. What is at stake here are uneven inflections between discursive practice and structures of power, with sexuality so often used as the signpost to indicate the critical points of intersection: 'we realized it was a race thing ... [but] the bartender asked, are you gay ?' (1:021–022, 024).

Queer theory as a whole is also interested in the uneven inflections between sexuality, discursive practices and structures of power. And, like queer linguistics, queer theory pays attention 'not just what is said, but also the context within which narratives unfold' (Giffney, 2009: 7). In fact, as Giffney explains, queer theory itself can be described as 'an exercise in discourse analysis' in the sense that '[i]t takes very seriously the significance of words and the power of language' (2009: 7).

For example, in the opening of *The Epistemology of the Closet*, one of the anchoring texts in the queer canon, Eve Sedgwick wrote:

> Modern Western culture has placed what it calls sexuality in a more and more distinctively privileged relation to our most prized constructs of individual identity, truth and knowledge ... (and) the language of sexuality not only intersects with but transforms the other languages and relations by which we know.
>
> *(Sedgwick, 1990: 3)*

Not content merely to produce discussions of 'the sexual', queer theory began by taking note of the ways that 'sexuality', as a named category, imposes meaning on, and thereby helped to regulate, other dimensions of human experience. In this sense, a long-standing goal of queer inquiry has been to provide

> a deepened understanding of the discursive structures and representational systems that determine the production of sexual meanings and that micromanage individual perceptions, [and to show how they] maintain and reproduce the underpinnings of heterosexist privilege.
>
> *(Halperin, 1995: 32)*

Admittedly, and the discussion of example 1 had confirmed this, there are forms of discursive practice outside of language, which help to 'determine the production of sexual meanings and ... micromanage individual perceptions' related to sexuality and heterosexist privilege. For that reason, and

> [g]iven its commitment to interrogating the social processes that not only produced and recognized but also normalized and sustained identity, the political promise of [queer] resided specifically in its broad critique of multiple social antagonisms, including race, gender, class, nationality and religion, in addition to sexuality.
>
> *(Eng et al., 2005: 1)*

As time passed, the 'broad critique' engaging the 'production of sexual meanings' and its attendant 'multiple social antagonisms' has assumed a variety of formats, including critical race theory and the queer critique of colour, crip theory (queer disability studies), transgender studies, new statements of post-colonial theory, migration/diaspora studies, studies of (homo)phobia/ hate speech. Queer linguistics is adding its own insights to this 'broad critique', and in the following sections I examine some of these insights and the projects on which they are based.

Queer linguistics on its own trajectory: beyond identity to performativity and desire

Work in queer linguistics began in the late 1990s by as a critique of studies 'that conflates what some (again, usually white, middle-class, educated) gay men says in some contexts with a general "Gay English" ' (Kulick, 1999: 616) and of other studies that assumed that linguistic practices indexed the fact of gendered identity and/or sexed body. Rather than asserting that gay language had certain indexical properties in such instances, queer linguistics problematized those properties. As Livia and Hall explained, it was not enough to argue that certain forms of utterance not only describe the world but act on it – a way of 'doing things with words' (1997: 11). What makes the performative effect possible in every instance cannot always be named, and attempts to pinpoint linguistic features designating texts or speech acts as uniquely queer usually proved unsuccessful. The 'queerness' of linguistic practices derives as much from the audience response to linguistic practice as from any formal representation that speakers give to intended message or meaning.

Example 2, extracted from the verbal monologue of an African American drag queen while performing on stage in a drag bar in Austin, Texas, shows how the construction of a sexual message depends on a subtle interplay of speaker intention and audience recognition.

Example 2

001   Are you ready to see some muscles [audience yells] … Some dick?
002   Excuse me I'm not supposed to say that …
003   Words like that in the microphone …
004   Like shit, fuck, and all that, you know?
005   I am a Christian woman.
006   I go to church
007   I'm always on my knees.

(Barrett, 1999: 324)

As Barrett notes, the performer has adopted a 'white-woman style of speaking' (hereafter WL), modelled after the white female behaviour and its attendant discursive practices described in Lakoff (1975: 53–56). Use of WL discourse while in drag persona encodes the performer's intention to present herself as a woman of middle-class refinement while on the stage (Barrett, 1999: 321). But part of the point of drag is to be larger than life, to surpass and critique rather than imitate the object of performance. The contradiction between the performer's African American embodiment and her white-lady verbal practice reflect this point: if a black man can 'be' a white woman on the drag club stage, than someone else can 'pass for white', and thus the category 'white woman' begins to lose its appearance of authority. Also underscoring this point is the performer's introduction of an oppositional discursive stance. In line 2:001, the performer uses a vernacular term for the male genitalia that a woman of middle-class refinement might not employ in a public setting. In lines 2:004, the performer adds additional expletives, equally incongruous with her WL assertions. WL discourse returns in 2.005–006, using a reference that situates WL refinement within a performative Christianity, while line 2:007 either extends or subverts that references, depending on whether the audience aligns the remark with piety or erotic posture.

The point is that, the performer has including nothing within the textual detail that states, explicitly, 'I am a drag queen.' That message is encoded through the peformer's accumulation of discursive materials within the indicated passage, but that accumulation has to be read in relation to the embodiment of the performer within the context of performance site and against the contradictory statements that the discursive materials themselves display. As in example 1, sexuality is one component through which the work of queerness is expressed and, as in example 1, the text has to be read broadly and not in a foreclosed fashion.

Under such conditions, discussions of linguistic practices closely tied to sexual identity – e.g. the discussion of 'gay English' in Leap (1996) and related writings – had to be retheorized, if not rejected entirely. Cameron and Kulick (2003b: 74–105, and see also Kulick, 2000) offered especially strong proposals to that end. They were critical of studies of gay and lesbian language, or of any project that 'remains invested in the idea that "queer language" is somehow linked to queer (i.e. non-heterosexual) identities' (2003: 102): the focus on sexual identity, whatever its orientation, 'leaves unexamined everything that arguably makes sexuality sexuality: namely fantasy, repression, pleasure, fear and the unconscious' (2003: 105). Alternatively, Cameron and Kulick proposed that 'language and desire' become the entry point for studies of language and sexuality. This shift in emphasis 'acknowledges that sexuality is centrally about the erotic' and indicates 'the extent to which our erotic lives are shaped by forces which are not wholly rational and of which we are not fully conscious' (2003: 106, 107).

Equating sexuality and 'desire', where desire is a cover-term reference for 'fantasy, repression, pleasure, fear and the unconscious', opened a broad terrain for studies of queerness as an identity-free 'becoming'. But whether queer linguistics could operate within this framework was another question. Some scholars argued that dedicating linguistic analysis entirely to such decontextualized inquiry artificially segregates sexuality from political economy and history, yielding what Penelope Eckert termed 'the mystification' of the study of sexuality (2002: 100).

> The challenge then is to adopt an approach that focuses on the social mediation of desire: to construct a view of desire that is simultaneously internal and individual and eternal and shared
>
> *(Eckert, 2002: 100).*

Cameron and Kulick's discussion of language and desire spoke directly to Eckert's 'challenge'.[3]

> Although we may experience sexual desire as uniquely personal and intensely private, their form is shaped by social and verbal interaction.
>
> *(2003b: 131)*

Recognizing that that desire is a 'socially mediated' formation revealed two things about the relationship between language and desire (and about language and sexuality, more broadly framed). First, desire is specifically

> made intelligible [in language] because it draws on codes of signification that circulate within the wider society – in Eckert's terms, they are 'external and shared' [Secondly], 'individuals cannot chose *not* to have their desires understood in terms of prevailing social norms'.
>
> *(Cameron and Kulick, 2003b: 132)*

While not directly referenced, this statement acknowledges the interest in language and ideology that had been central to discourse analysis for some years (see Fairclough and Van Dijk chapters, this volume), but was now becoming integral to the explorations of language and sexuality in other areas of queer theory. But the ideological processes that were of interest there could not be described simply in terms of the interpolation or 'hailing' of the subject form. Sexual ideologies promote obedient subjects in some cases, but sexual ideologies also prompt conditions of 'disidentification' (Muñoz, 2000: 11–34) in which speakers step outside of the normative terrain and 'work' the subject form imposed on them by ideology, thereby forcing ideology to 'operate in reverse, i.e. on and against itself through the overthrough-rearrangement of ...[its] formations (and of the discursive formations ... imbricated with them)' (Pêcheux, 1982: 159).

Because transgender subjects are so frequently caught up in the work of disidentification, relationships between transgender and language became an especially productive research area in queer linguistics. In earlier times, studies of 'transgender language' were concerned with assessing how closely transgender subjects conformed to linguistic norms of their gender of choice. Queer linguistic inquiry immediately called into question the limited vision of language that such research displays and became even more critical of the assumed obligations of conformity that motivate it.

As Valentine (2007) shows, part of the problem lies with the growing popularity of the term 'transgender' itself. While this term purports to designate subjects according to their 'gender of identification not their ascribed birth gender', it has also become 'a useful shorthand for describing non-normative genders as a whole', and thereby 'a way of describing a diverse group of people both in the United States and beyond its borders' (2007: 23, 19). In this sense 'transgender' is an artificial formation, imposing a single description onto a range of experiences whose details are now obscured by the unifying effects of the category. And, while a range of linguistic practices can be associated with transgendered experience, it is equally artificial to suggest that these practices constitute a single 'transgender language', since transgender subjects draw variously on a range of linguistic practices along with other kinds of discursive encodings to encode their claims to a gender or sexual identity different from that assigned to them at birth.

For example, some linguistic practices allow speakers to mark a transgender status in a speech event by 'bending the rules' that ordinarily govern the gender-marking functions of adjectives, pronouns, and verb-endings, playing with metaphoric references, or manipulating other elements of linguistic surface structure (Kulick, 1998: 206–211; Morial, 1998; Hall, 2002). But there is also 'stealth', a creative synthesis of word choice and intonation, posture and gesture, clothing style, and other markers by means of which post-operative trans-subjects encourage a normative rather than transgendered reading of their embodiment, thereby deflecting potentially awkward questions about their birth gender ('Is he or isn't he?') before they arise in the public arena (Edelman, 2009).[4] Queer linguistics explores how speakers employ these practices, when they employ them, and which speakers do so. Queer linguistics also examines the forms of audience reception that these practices engage and the messages about gender (local and ideological) that become validated and/or contested through these processes.

Intentionality, (inter)subjectivity, belonging, and citizenship

Implied in these discussions of transgender and language was some degree of speaker intentionality. This was a fundamental theme in early discussions of language and gay identity (Leap, 1996: 24–73), and in the initial queer critique of performativity as well (Livia and Hall, 1997: 11). But intentionality was anathema to the interrogation of language and desire as Cameron and Kulick originally proposed it, since the wilful decisions that the individual speaker might make during textual practice can always be upstaged by failure, forgery, misuse, or other ensuing feature of iteration (Cameron and Kulick, 2003a; Kulick, 2003: 112–122).

To resolve this problem, Bucholtz and Hall (2004) looked beyond the work of the individual speaker and considered 'identity, sexual and otherwise' as 'the outcome of intersubjectively negotiated practices and ideologies' (2004: 469).[5] Linguistic practices are deeply embedded within every level of these intersubjective negotiations. But, rather than being drawn from some predetermined inventory, the form that these practices assume and the functions that they serve are shaped through the dynamic engagement of speakers and interlocutors.

Barrett's discussion of African American drag queen performance (example 2 above) provides a rich illustration of how 'tactics of intersubjectivity' unfold, particularly how tactics of intersubjectivity gain representation in linguistic practice through polyphonous connections between specific forms of linguistic genre, including African American vernacular and 'white woman speech'. Brian King (2008) makes a similar point when showing how same-sex desire encouraged the learning of English as a second language among some Korean men in New Zealand. The men that King interviewed reported feelings of discomfort when talking English with 'white people' generally, but also noted that discomfort disappeared when they started talking English with gay white men. For example, King cites comments like the following from Hyoung, a 35-year-old middle-class self-identified gay man, who reported consciously attempting to maintain his distance from the local Korean community because 'especially being GAY they wanted to know where am I and so detail' (2008: 241), and therefore spending his time interacting with his (non-Korean) boyfriend's social network. King asked if Hyoung was 'comfortable with all of those people? speaking //English?' and example 3 shows Hyoung's reply.

Example 3

```
001   … mmm actually straight people is like a little more difficult really … it's very
002   difficult sometimes and not very much comfortable and then we talk like much
003   comfortable is like GAY people like they know our LIFE and they … know the
004   y'know experience and we can SHARE.
```

(King, 2008: 242, histranscription retained)

Hyoung refers here to a discursive sexuality shaped in response to tensions between social sameness and difference, which Bucholtz and Hall (2004: 494) term 'tactics of adequation and distinction'. Here, however, sameness and difference do not coincide with the broader English vs. Korean linguistic contrasts, but indicate a more nuanced struggle to establish claims to place within each linguistic and social terrain. That is, by his report, Hyoung struggles with others in the local Korean community to demonstrate conformity with the expectations of heteronormative ideology, and his own sense of difference is heightened when he finds himself in those settings even if the (Korean) discursive practices are otherwise familiar. When he is with 'Gay people', any uncertainties that he and others might have about his sexual status are swept away by the expectations of shared gay experience and by the assumed familiarity with linguistic practices through which those expectations are encoded. These are English-based linguistic skills, however, and skills that Hyoung has just begun to master. So here is a different kind of linguistic difficulty, but this time a difficulty made less serious by the cordiality of the social setting.

English becomes a kind of 'gay language' in Hyoung's example, but it does so in a fashion that is very different from the linguistic playfulness encoding 'gay identity' in English (Leap, 1996: 12–23) or the more carefully mediated encoding that allows 'yan daudu in Northern Nigeria to integrate a 'feminine male' identity in colloquial Hausa (Gaudio, 2009: 89–116). Similarly, given the complex negotiation of public and private identities that Hyoung confronts, but also the relative freedom he has to move between the indicated locations, what 'gay' means as a discursive inflection of sexual identity in Hyoung's example is very different from what 'gay' meant in the context of Jameson's experience in late apartheid Cape Town's city centre (example 1).

Other work in queer linguistics has looked beyond tactics of intersubjectivity and has situated individual formations of desire within an even broader social dynamic. Particularly important has been the work that examines sexuality, social responsibility and 'good citizenship', asking how subjects who claim a non-conforming sexuality are also able to minimize an appearance of threat to mainstream governance. For example, as Puar and Rai (2003) explain, when US-based messages about terrorism during the years immediately after 9/11 demonized homosexuality, those messages also opened a space for US 'homosexuals' to condemn terrorist acts by showing that their loyalty to the state took precedence over commitments to sexual sameness.[6] Such responses have not offset a noticeable increase in anti-gay verbal or physical assault in the US and other national settings since that time.

Understandably, discourses related to homophobia are rapidly becoming a site of interest in queer linguistics. Like nationalism, these discourses are broadly cast, in this case assigning meanings of disdain, disgust, or hatred to certain experiences of sexual sameness that immediately draw connections with other forms of social marginality. Thus Murray defines homophobia as 'a socially produced form of discrimination located within relations of inequality' (2009: 3), making no reference to its connections to sexuality at all. For Bryant and Vidal-Ortiz, such an erasure of the sexual may be a problematic move. They find that violent acts directed against identified same-sex subjects are sometimes described as homophobia, other times described as assault or robbery, and sometimes not reported at all. Contrary to its 'taken-for-granted under-standings and uses', homophobia is not a static, predetermined formation, but a discursive position whose uses have 'unintended and sometimes less than libratory consequences' and often carry their 'own forms of violence' (discursive and material) (2008: 391).

Visibility and tacit subjects

A particularly important new direction in queer linguistics has emerged from Carlos Decena's discussion of tacit subject formation, a discursive position evidenced in narratives of same-sex identified Dominican men living in New York City. Tacit subject formation speaks directly to the assumption that, to be same-sex identified, the subject must be 'out of the closet', visible, and explicit about sexual sameness. In the Dominican Republic and in settings of the Dominican diaspora, such public statements are unnecessary and unwanted, because anything about a person's sexuality that is worth knowing publicly is already known by family members and other relatives already bound together by ties of dependence and respect. Unlike in the US gay mainstream, the Dominican same-sex identified men that Decena interviewed faced a normative obligation to 'exercise ownership of their sexual identities by negotiating the degree to which their sexual and romantic lives become (or not) points of discussion in family settings' (Decena, 2008: 340). Part of their response to that obligation invoked the rules of tacit subject formation in Spanish grammar. 'The sujeto tácito is the subject that is no spoken but can be ascertained through the conjugation of the verb' or through some other linguistic means, Decena explains. 'What is tacit is neither secret nor silent', although it may already be understood or assumed and, 'if people have the requisite skills to recognize and decode [the] behavior', the tacit message may not require explicit statement (2008: 340).

'Tacit subject' formations are attested among Spanish-speaking subjects elsewhere in Latin America (Wright, 2000). Similar discursive principles guide the 'coming out' process in urban and rural France (Provencher, 2007: 85–149), where same-sex identified men and women do not just tell their parents and friends that they 'are gay' (since parents and friends may already suspect this fact and do not need to have it articulated). Instead, they tell about their involvement in a committed relationship with a same-sex partner – information that parents and friend may not have grasped (or been willing to grasp) through other means. For example, Gabriel, a 29-year-old self-identified gay man, described the following 'coming out' experience with his father. Gabriel lives in Paris and keeps his personal life separate from any interaction that he had with his natal family. But one weekend he was visiting his father (his parents are divorced) and during an evening discussion his father raised the topic of marriage, family life, and children. Gabriel continues the story in example 4, where, rather than stating explicitly, 'I am gay', he adds a statement to an ongoing discussion that forces his father to make the desired inference: 'No, dad, you do not understand. I will not have any children because two men cannot have children' (4:004–005).

Example 4

001 … I was saying 'well, I don't believe in marriage … I don't think I will ever have
002 children' and he said, he didn't understand, he didn't want to understand, he looked at
003 me and said: 'Why? You seem s sure, I do not understand, why, you don't know,
004 perhaps you will have some' 'No but dad, you don't understand. I will not have any
005 children because two men cannot have children'. And it was there that
    he understood.
006 And since I'd had a bit to drink it was a bit easier to tell him. And I asked him if I had
007 shocked him' I asked he if he resented me and he said 'no' And he said to me, 'you
008 know, I have always left you to live the way you wanted, do what you wanted … I
009 would have preferred it if you were heterosexual instead of homosexual but that is
010 the way it is. I cannot stop you.'

(Provencher, 2007: 127)[7]

It is tempting to think of Gabriel's reluctance to name to his social status explicitly as an enduring allegiance to 'the closet'. But what is at stake here is an entirely different discursive stance, one that sets the French example apart from the mainstream US-based expectations of 'out and proud' sexual subject and aligns it with the public mediation of sexual sameness associated with a responsible Dominican sexual sameness in diaspora.

Paradoxes of visibility: a queer linguistics of colour, globalization and shame

Until recently, queer linguistics has largely been predicated on discursive practices that were visible and accessible to audiences and to researchers, or on discursive practices that, for particular reasons, were deliberately withheld. Growing interest in electronic media as formats for communicating 'queer messages' both locally and throughout the global circuit (e.g. Berry et al., 2003; Mowlabocus, 2010) has required new ways of discussing turn-taking, identity-management, language socialization and other properties traditionally associated with face-to-face, spoken language use. New studies of visibility have extended these interests, by reminding us that discursive processes relevant to textuality need not be explicit displayed. Hence, in queer linguistics as in queer theory as a whole, 'unpacking the latent content is as important a task [for queer theory] as understanding that which is stated directly' (Giffney, 2009: 7). Under these circumstances, statements like 'if we can't say it, how can we be it?' – for years, the informal motto of the American University Lavender Languages and Linguistic Conference[8] – assume an entirely new meaning: what does 'being' entail, when access to the attendant discursive practices of 'saying' is mediated or foreclosed, rather than unproblematically accessible?

This is not a question to be debated in the abstract, but must be explored 'at the site'. Here emerging work in queer linguistics overlaps with new projects in radical cartography and experimental geography (Paglen, 2008). Here, also, queer linguistics intersects with the body of work associated under the general rubric, the *queer of colour critique* (Ferguson, 2004: 1–30). Even more than in queer theory, queer of colour critique notes how long-standing ascriptions of whiteness and privilege dominate the categories of reference in vernacular and scholarly discourses, especially so where discourses pertain to sexual sameness. That 'queer' 'acquires its meaning from its oppositional relation to the norm' (Halperin, 1995: 62) has additional significance, if the 'norm' is a privileged discursive terrain embracing heterosexuality as well as whiteness, and if the 'oppositional relation' includes a range of positions only some of which are explicitly articulated in discursive practice (in the sense of Decena's argument).

Strengthening the queer of colour critique are arguments from two other areas of queer linguistic inquiry: studies examining the movement of North Atlantic-based 'gay English' discourse within the global circuit and studies examining how diasporic subjects encounter 'gay English' discourses when the diaspora brings them into the North Atlantic terrain (Manalansan, 2003; Peña, 2004; Boellstorff, 2005; Leap, 2008). As in the domestic arena, these globalized discourses of sexual sameness and privilege underscore 'race's imbrications with sexuality'. Further, the speed with which these discourses travel within the global circuit points to the 'great evasions, silences and distortions of nationalist formations' (Ferguson, 2009: 114) even as the national, like the racial, becomes deeply embedded within linguistic intersubjectivity and even as yearnings of desire remain unaddressed, in spite of those negotiations.

Work in queer linguistics is also exploring these yearnings of desire through studies that connect textual practices with broader discourses of 'gay shame' (Mundt, 2007; Halperin and Traub, 2009) and 'queer trauma' (Cvetkovic, 2003). Such research engages forms of popular culture, pulling the inquiry even further from a traditional linguistic interest in verbalized discourse, and engaging more fully forms of message-making that work with, through, and in spite of the spoken language and its attendant expression of sexual norms.

Further reading

Cameron, D. and Kulick, D. (2003) *Language and Sexuality*. Cambridge: Cambridge University Press.

A useful, if at times partisan, review of twentieth-century studies of language and sexuality, and a persuasive argument in favour of using a desire-centred paradigm to remedy the shortcomings of earlier work.

Gaudio, R. (2009) *Allah Made Us: Sexual Outlaws in an Islamic City*. Malden, MA: Wiley-Blackwell.

Explores the linguistic and social practices associated with two forms of non-normative Hausa masculinity: '*yan daudu* (primarily same-sex identified, and often feminized men) and masu *harka* (the more masculine, sometimes married men, with families, who 'do the deed' with *yan daudu*). Shows how Hausa/ Islamic nationalism is reshaping language, sexuality and citizenship in northern Nigeria.

Kulick, D. (2003) 'No!', *Language and Communication*. Special issue on Language and Desire. D.Cameron and D.Kulick (eds.), 23 (2): 139–151.

How the act of 'saying "no"' in the context of a hetero-erotic encounter confirms the subject position 'woman' – or confirms a subject position 'man' whose masculinity is now suspect.

Leap, W. (2008) 'Queering gay men's English', in K. Harrington, Lia Litosseliti, H. Sauntson, and J. Sunderland (eds.) *Language and Gender Research Methodologies*. Basingstoke: Palgrave, pp. 408–429.

An analysis of a coming-out story, where the analysis treats identity as a 'product of the speaker's linguistic practices rather than the foundation on which they are based' (2008: 285).

Notes

1 The city centre includes the central business district and adjacent residential and commercial areas. These areas were 'proclaimed' white space under apartheid rule. Coloured and black residents were removed to township communities on the Cape Flats, the vacant lands extending to the east of the city centre.

2 During strict apartheid, several train stations were popular cruising areas for same-sex identified men, particularly because, being heterotopic locations, train stations were places where men from different racial/ethnic backgrounds could meet in relative safety. This tradition continued into the democratic period.
3 See also the research agenda outlined in Kulick (2003: 130).
4 Edelman writes: 'within the academic literature, stealth is most commonly defined as the non – disclosure of one's trans history or present … The narratives collected in this project show that stealth is a dynamic and situated practice of ideological negotiation …' (2009: 168–169).
5 Bucholtz and Hall organize their tactics of intersubjectivity in three pairs: adequation and distinction, 'processes by which subject construct and are constructed within social sameness and difference' (2004: 494); authentication and denaturalization, having to do with 'truth … vs. pretense and imposture in identity positioning' (2004: 498); and authorization and illegitimation, which distinguish uses of power to legitimate or withhold legitimacy from social identities (2004: 503).
6 Similarly, the bar-tender in the Cape Town city centre gay club (example 1) opened a similar space for Jameson and his friend when he asked: "Are you gay?"
7 Provencher (2007: 126–127) cites the French (original) version of Gabriel's text as well as this translation. I have renumbered the English translation in the presentation of this example.
8 www.american.edu/lavenderlanguages.

References

Althusser, L. (1971) 'Ideology and ideological state apparatus (Notes toward an investigation)', in *Lenin and Philosophy and Other Essays*. New York City: Monthly Review Press, pp. 127–186.
Barrett, R. (1999) 'Indexing polyphonous identity in the speech of African American drag queens', in M. Bucholtz, A. Liang, and L. Sutton (eds.) *Reinventing Identities: The Gendered Self in Discourse*. New York City: Oxford University Press, pp. 313–332.
Berry, C. Martin, F., and Yue, A. (eds.) (2003) *Mobile Cultures: New Media in Queer Asia*. Durham: Duke University Press.
Boellstorff, T. (2005) *The Gay Archipelago: Sexuality and Nation in Indonesia*. Princeton NJ: Princeton University Press.
Bryant, K. and Vidal-Ortiz, S. (2008) 'Introduction to retheorizing homophobias', *Sexualities* (Special Issue on Retheorizing Homophobias), 11: 387–396.
Bucholtz, M. and Hall, K. (2004) 'Theorizing identity in language and sexuality research', *Language in Society*, 33: 469–515.
Butler, J. (1990) 'Subjects of sex/gender/desire', in *Gender Trouble: Feminism and the Subversion of Identity*. New York: Routledge, pp. 1–34.
Cameron, D. and Kulick, D. (2003a) 'Introduction: language and desire in theory and practice', Language *and* Communication', *Language and Communication* (Special Issue on Language and Desire), 23: 93–105.
Cameron, D. and Kulick, D. (2003b) *Language and Sexuality*. Cambridge: Cambridge University Press.
Cvetkovic, A. (2003) 'Introduction: the everyday life of queer trauma', in *An Archive of Feelings: Trauma, Sexuality and Lesbian Public Cultures*. Durham: Duke University Press, pp. 15–48.
Decena, C. (2008) 'Tacit subjects', GLQ', *A Journal of Lesbian and Gay Studies*, 14: 339–359.
Eckert, P. (2002) 'Demystifying sexuality and desire', in K. Campbell-Kibbler, R. Podesva, S. Roberts, and A. Wong (eds.) *Language and Sexuality: Contesting Meaning in Theory and Practice*. Stanford: Center for the Study of Language and Information, pp. 99–110.
Edelman, E. (2009) 'The power of stealth: (in)visible sites of female-to-male transsexual resistance', in E. Lewin and W. Leap (eds.) *Out in Public: Reinventing Lesbian/Gay Anthropology in a Globalizing World*. Malden, MA: Wiley-Blackwell, pp. 164–179.
Eng, D., Halberstam, J., and Muñoz, J. (2005) 'Introduction: what's queer about queer studies now?', *Social Text: Special Issue on What's Queer about Queer Studies Now ?*, 23: 1–17.
Ferguson, R. (2004) 'Introduction: queer of color critique: historical materialism and canonical sociology', in *Aberrations in Black: Toward a Queer of Color Critique*. Minneapolis, MN: University of Minnesota Press, pp. 1–31.
Ferguson, R. (2009) 'The relevance of race for the study of sexuality', in G. Haggerty and M. McGarry (eds.) *A Companion to Lesbian, Gay, Bisexual, Transgender, and Queer Studies*. Malden, MA: Blackwell, pp. 109–123.
Gaudio, R. (2009) *Allah Made Us: Sexual Outlaws in an Islamic African City*. Malden, MA: Wiley-Blackwell.
Giffney, N. (2009) 'Introduction: the "q"word', in N. Giffney and M. O'Rourke (eds.) *Ashgate Research Companion to Queer Theory*. Farnham, UK: Ashgate Publishing Ltd, pp. 1–13.

Hall, K. (2002) ' "Unnatural"gender in Hindi', in M. Hellinger and H. Bussman (eds.) *Gender Across Languages: The Linguistic Representation of Women and Men*, Volume 2. Amsterdam: John Benjamins, pp. 133–162.

Halperin, D. and Traub, V. (eds.) (2009) *Gay Shame*. Chicago, IL: University of Chicago Press.

Halperin, D. (1995) *Saint Foucault: Toward a Gay Hagiography*. New York: Oxford University Press.

King, B. (2008) ' "Being gay guy, that is the advantage": queer Korean language learning and identity construction', *Journal of Language, Identity and Education*, 7: 230–252.

Kulick, D. (1998) 'Travestí gendered subjectivity', in *Travestí*. Chicago, IL: University of Chicago Press, pp. 191–238.

Kulick, D. (1999) 'Transgender and language', *GLQ: A Journal of Lesbian and Gay Studies*, 5: 605–622.

Kulick, D. (2000) 'Gay and lesbian language', *Annual Review of Anthropology*, 29: 243–285.

Kulick, D. (2003 'Language and desire', in J. Holmes and M. Meyerhoff (eds.) *The Handbook of Language and Gender*. Malden, MA: Blackwell, pp. 119–142.

Lakoff, R. (1975) *Language and Women's Place*. New York: Harper and Row.

Leap, W. (1996) *Word's Out: Gay Men's English*. Minneapolis, MN: University of Minnesota Press.

Leap, W. (2008) ' "True thing that binds us": Globalization, US language pluralism and gay men's English', in M. Bertho (ed.) *The Impact of Globalization on the United States: Culture and Society*. Westport, CT: Praeger Publishers, pp. 183–209.

Livia, A. and Hall, K. (1997) ' "It's a girl!": bringing performativity back into linguistics', in *Queerly Phrased: Language, Gender and Sexuality*. New York: Oxford University Press, pp. 3–18.

Manalansan, M. (2003) *Global Divas: Filipino Gay Men in the Diaspora*. Durham: Duke University Press.

Morial, L. (1998) 'Diva in the promised land: a blueprint for newspeak?', *World Englishes: Symposium on Creativity in LGBT Discourse*, 17: 225–238.

Mowlabocus, S. (2010) *Gaydar Culture: Gay men, Technology and Embodiment in the Digital Age*. Aldershot: Ashgate.

Mundt, S. (2007) *Queer Attachments: The Cultural Politics of Shame*. Aldershot: Ashgate Publishing.

Murray, D. (2009) 'Introduction', in D. Murray (ed.) *Homophobias: Lust and Loathing across Time and Space*. Durham: Duke University Press, pp. 1–15.

Muñoz, J. (2000) 'Introduction: performing disidentifications', in *Disidentifications: Queers of Color and the Performance of Politics*. Minneapolis, MN: University of Minnesota Press, pp. 1–35.

Paglen, T. (2008) 'Experimental geography: from cultural production to the production of space', in N. Thompson (ed.) *Experimental Geography*. Brooklyn, NY: Melville House Publishing, pp. 27–33.

Peña, S. (2004) 'Pájaration and transculturation: Language and meaning in Miami's Cuban American gay worlds', in W. L. Leap and T. Boellstorff (eds.) *Speaking in Queer Tongues: Globalization and Gay Language*. Urbana, IL: University of Illinois Press, pp. 231–250.

Provencher, D. (2007) *Queer French: Globalization, Language and Sexual Citizenship in France*. Aldershot: Ashgate.

Puar, J. and Rai, A. (2003) 'Monster-terrorist-fag: the war on terrorism and the production of docile patriots', *Social Text*, 72: 117–148.

Pêcheux, M. (1982) 'The subject-form of discourse in the subjective appropriation of scientific knowledges and political practice', *Language, Semantics and Ideology* [1975], trans. Harbans Nagpal. New York: St. Martins Press, pp. 155–170.

Sedgwick, E. (1990) 'Introduction: Axiomatic', in *Epistemology of the Closet*. Berkeley, CA: University of California Press, pp. 1–66.

Valentine, D. (2007) *Imagining Transgender: An Ethnography of a Category*. Durham: Duke University Press.

Wright, T. (2000) 'Gay organizations, NGOs and the globalization of gay identity: the case of Bolivia', *Journal of Latin American Studies*, 5: 89–111.

40

Intercultural communication

Helen Spencer-Oatey, Hale Işık-Güler and Stefanie Stadler

What is intercultural communication?

The term 'intercultural' literally means 'between cultures', and so, at one level, 'intercultural communication' could refer to all communication between members of two (or more) different social/cultural groups. This, in fact, is how the term has traditionally been used. Difference in nationality or mother tongue has typically been taken as the criterion for membership of different social/cultural groups, and communication between people of different nationalities or different mother tongues has then automatically been classified as intercultural. However, there are several problems with this. If culture is associated with social groups, then nationality and mother tongue are not the only social groups we each belong to. We are all simultaneously members of numerous other groups, such as regional, professional and religious, and so, if communication between members of different social groups is classified as intercultural, virtually all communication would thereby be defined as intercultural. Such a broad definition is clearly unsatisfactory – not simply because it is too all-encompassing, but also because, as Hartog (2006: 185) points out, discourse is not necessarily intercultural just because people from two different cultures meet. In other words, cultural factors do not necessarily impact on the communication process at all times. Žegarac (2007: 41) distinguishes between intracultural and intercultural communication from a cognitive point of view, and identifies an intercultural situation as one in which 'the cultural distance between the participants is significant enough to have an adverse effect on communicative success, unless it is appropriately accommodated by the participants'. In this chapter, we adopt Spencer-Oatey and Franklin's (2009: 3) slightly revised version of Žegarac's definition:

> An intercultural situation is one in which the cultural distance between the participants is significant enough to have an effect on interaction/communication that is noticeable to at least one of the parties.

Verschueren (2008: 23) makes the important point that intercultural communication should not be treated as 'something "special" and different from other forms of communicative interaction', but rather should be viewed first and foremost as communication. So our study of intercultural communication needs to focus on the processes by which communicative intentions are produced and (mis)interpreted and on the ways in which meanings are negotiated and co-constructed. Throughout this endeavour, we need to explore the ways in which contextual and situational factors impact on these processes, including cultural ones.

In this chapter we discuss four main issues in relation to intercultural discourse: achieving understanding, managing rapport, sense of identity and intercultural competence. All of the issues are closely intertwined, but for convenience sake, we treat them sequentially here.

Achieving understanding in intercultural discourse

In this section we concentrate on the 'content' aspect of understanding; in other words, on the (co-)construction of message meaning. The vast majority of this body of research has focused on the difficulties and misunderstandings that have occurred; however, more recently there have been calls (e.g. Bührig and ten Thije, 2006; Verschueren, 2008) for a shift towards the study of communicative success.

It should be remembered, of course, that understanding is not an 'all or nothing' phenomenon. As Roberts (1996: 12) points out, there is

> a continuum from, at one end, sufficient understanding for both parties to continue to, at the other end, total lack of understanding. In addition, many interactions are characterized by the illusion of understanding [...] in which both sides believe, at least for a while, that they have understood each other.

It should also be remembered that misunderstandings obviously do not only occur in intercultural interactions. Quite the contrary; as Coupland *et al.* (1991: 3) point out, 'Language use is pervasively and even intrinsically flawed, partial and problematic.' Nevertheless, the less participants have in common (linguistically, culturally or personally), the greater the expected difficulty in achieving mutual understanding (Gass and Varonis, 1991: 122), and hence the more noticeable the occurrence of misunderstanding in intercultural communication.

Factors that can make communication problematic

A number of factors influence how well participants of an intercultural interaction are likely to understand each other's messages, and one of the most fundamental of these is use of the linguistic code. If people cannot speak a given language fluently and/or if proficient speakers use it in 'unhelpful' ways, it will be very difficult for them to understand each other. For example, Bremer (1996), who carried out extensive research into the discourse of intercultural encounters, provides examples of comprehension problems that were triggered by the following linguistic code factors: mispronunciation or mishearing of a lexical item; unfamiliarity with a lexical item; structural complexity; ellipsis.

However, even when there are no language code problems of this kind, achieving understanding can still be extremely difficult. This is because, even though human communication to a large extent exploits a linguistic code, it is not feasible for everything to be expressed explicitly in the code. Much has to be left for the participants to work out, and in intercultural interaction this can be particularly problematic, because people may focus on different clues when inferring meaning and/or they may arrive at different meanings from the same clues.

A number of researchers (e.g. Gumperz, 1982; Marriott, 1990; Gumperz and Roberts, 1991; Bunte and Franklin, 1992; Tyler, 1995; Cook-Gumperz and Gumperz, 2002; Miller, 2008) have focused on such matters and analysed the difficulties that participants have experienced in interpreting meaning when the challenges are not simply related to language code problems. We illustrate this type of analysis with an example from Miller (2008), who recorded naturally occurring talk at two advertising agencies in Tokyo. The agencies had both Japanese and American staff, and all of the participants spoke each other's language with various degrees of proficiency.

Example 1: Problems of understanding in workplace interaction (from Miller, 2008: 233)

In this extract, an American copywriter named Ember (E) and one of his Japanese co-workers named Nakada (N) are reviewing some advertisements for which Ember has provided the English copy. They are talking about one advertisement in particular.

```
 1   E   I mean yuh can see through it right
 2       you don't have to use your imagination you can
 3       see every little thing so–(it's?) right
 4       (it?) plays off of the–the visual
 5       (leaves?) nothing <<wh> to the imagination>
 6       (0.5)
 7   N   (.hss) Is that so?
 8       (0.2)
 9   N   idea is cl-very clear to me [now]
10   E                               [no:w]
11   N   this video can do everything=
12   E   =do everything
13       (0.8)
14   N   But too much pitch for the vi(hihi)sual
15   E   too (hihi) much? [No no no no]
16   N                    [too much visual]no?
17   E   no (.) no I don't think so
18       (0.2)
19   N   {smacks lips} (.hhh) maybe
20   E   (maybe?)
21   N   ye [ahh]
22   E      [I thin] I think it's okay
```

Ember starts by describing what the advertisement is about (lines 1–5), and after this we would normally expect Nakada to provide some sort of evaluative comment. Instead there is a silence (line 6), followed in line 7 by Nakada giving an inbreathed fricative or <.hss>, and a repair initiator 'Is that so?' Nakada than provides two weak agreement comments (lines 9 and 11), after which he gives an explicit negative assessment in line 14. At the conclusion of this conversation (not transcribed here), Nakada tells Ember to 'think about' this ad copy a little longer, using the Japanese phrase *kangaete okimashô* ('let's think about it'). A few days later Ember finds out that this particular copy has been excluded from the campaign and is very surprised to hear this. He had clearly misunderstood the evaluation Nakada had made. What, then, are the reasons for this?

One explanation is that Ember failed to notice two clues that Nakada used that are commonly associated in Japanese with negative evaluations. According to Miller (1991; 2008: 229), the inbreathed fricative <.hss> (Line 7) is a Japanese paralinguistic hesitation marker that generally indicates an inability to agree with something or an unwillingness to express one's negative opinion. Similarly, the Japanese phrase *kangaete okimashô* ('let's think about it') is, according to Miller (2008: 233), 'a formulaic preface in Japanese for a negative assessment that, when used alone, signals that something "won't do" or "isn't right" '. Nakada uses this English phrase as if it had the same communicative function as it does in Japanese, and presumably assumes that Ember will interpret it accordingly (i.e. as a rejection). Thus one possible reason for the misunderstanding is that Ember failed to pick up on the Japanese-style cues for interpretation that Nakada was using. Nakada probably thought he was being very clear and did not realize that the cues were less obvious to Ember.

Gumperz (1982) proposes the notion of 'contextualization cues' to account for this phenomenon. He defines these as 'constellations of surface features of message form … the means by which speakers signal and listeners interpret what the activity is, how semantic content is to be understood and how each sentence relates to what precedes or follows' (p. 131). Communication is likely to be particularly problematic if the participants of an interaction pay attention to different cues, as happened in the conversation between Ember and Nakada.

Another way of accounting for Ember's failure to pick up on Nakada's cues is to draw on the concepts of high-context and low-context communication styles. This is a dimension of cultural difference proposed by the anthropologist Edward Hall (1976). Ting-Toomey and Chung (2005) explain it as follows:

> Low-context communication (LCC) refers to communication patterns of direct verbal mode: straight talk, nonverbal immediacy, and sender-oriented values (i.e. the sender assumes the responsibility to communicate clearly). In the LCC system, the speaker is expected to be responsible for constructing a clear, persuasive message that the listener can decode easily. In comparison, high-context communication (HCC) refers to communication patterns of indirect verbal mode: self-humbling talk, nonverbal subtleties, and interpreter-sensitive values (i.e. the receiver or interpreter of the message assumes the responsibility to infer the hidden or contextual meanings of the message) ... In the HCC system, the listener or interpreter of the message is expected to 'read between the lines', to accurately infer the implicit intent of the verbal message, and to decode the nonverbal subtleties that accompany the verbal message.
>
> *(Ting-Toomey and Chung, 2005: 172)*

So another interpretation of the misunderstanding is that Nakada's style of communication was more 'high-context' than Ember's. He was thus less explicit than Ember was expecting; conversely, Ember was insufficiently aware of the need to pay close attention to any subtle signals of disapproval that Nakada might give.

Further insights into the misunderstanding can be gained by considering the nature of the communicative event; and the nature of the relationship between Nakada and Ember also needs to be considered. Nakada had a position of authority in the company, and when Miller spoke to him after the interaction, he explained that he regarded the meeting as an opportunity for a senior (himself) to tell a subordinate (Ember) which ad copy had been selected for use and which had been retracted. When Miller spoke to Ember, on the other hand, he maintained that the purpose of the meeting was for him to explain to Nakada his ideas for the ads. He thus gave his personal opinions freely, disagreeing with Nakada's negative assessment and producing his own assessment (see line 22, 'I think it's okay'). From Nakada's perspective, Ember's expression of a differing opinion was inappropriate; he regarded it as an uncooperative reluctance to accept his decision and thus churlishly argumentative. Ember, on the other hand, thought Nakada had deliberately misled him by not stating his wishes clearly.

Through this example we can also see that various types of background knowledge (e.g. knowledge of linguistic conventions, knowledge of role relations and communicative events) play a major role in the communication process. Leech (1983: 10–11) uses the terms 'pragmalinguistic' and 'sociopragmatic' to refer to the pragmatic knowledge that participants draw on to interpret language. Some aspects of pragmatic knowledge are more linguistic in nature, whereas others are more social in nature. Pragmalinguistics is at the linguistic end and is concerned with the linguistic resources available and conventionally used for conveying a given pragmatic meaning in a given context. Sociopragmatics is at the social end and is concerned with social appropriateness in language use. Thomas (1983) uses the terms pragmalinguistic failure and sociopragmatic failure to refer to the mismatches that may occur between a speaker's intended meaning and the hearer's constructed meaning.

In the extract, the conventional use of both an inbreathed fricative to convey hesitation and lack of approval and the direct translation of the Japanese phrase *kangaete okimashô* ('let's think about it') to convey a negative assessment are examples of pragmalinguistic transfer and failure. On the other hand, Nakada's and Ember's differing interpretations of the purpose of the communicative event and Ember's 'right' to freely give his views are an example of sociopragmatic failure.

Strategies that can help to promote mutual understanding

Compared with the number of studies that have analysed communication problems in inter-cultural interaction, relatively few have focused on the positive elements – the factors or strategies that can help to prevent misunderstandings or can promote mutual understanding. Most of those that have (e.g. Bremer *et al.*, 1996; Sunaoshi, 2005; Mauranen, 2006; Chiang, 2009a, b) have concentrated on the management of the linguistic code. This relates quite closely to work carried out in the field of second language acquisition in the 1980s and 1990s on communication strategies (see Dörnyei and Scott 1997 for a review) and the negotiation of comprehensible input (e.g. Long, 1983; Varonis and Gass, 1985). For example, Chiang (2009a) analyses the corrective and pre-ventative strategies that international teaching assistants and American college students use when interacting with each other, and identifies and illustrates the following: clarification requests, confirmation requests, self-reformulations and other-reformulations.

Bremer and Simonot (1996: 159–175) take a slightly broader perspective and explain and illustrate a number of ways in which fluent speakers can maximize mutual understanding when interacting with less fluent speakers. Spencer-Oatey and Franklin (2009: 83–86) and Spencer-Oatey and Stadler (2009: 20–21) also discuss this phenomenon, labelling it respectively as 'linguistic accommodation' and 'language adjustment'. Spencer-Oatey and Stadler give the following authentic example to illustrate its successful use, and also to point out that effective language adjustment is not always as easy to carry out as it might superficially appear. The extract comes from a meeting between some British and Chinese academics who were meeting for the first time at a British university to discuss the potential for collaborative research.

Example: 2 Language Adjustment at the start of a meeting (Spencer–Oatey and Stadler, 2009: 21)

Adjusting one's use of language to the proficiency level of the recipient(s) is vital for effective communication; however, it is sometimes easier said than done. Consider the following interaction that took place at one of our meetings:

Chair:	I'm going to ask everybody to speak very clearly and uh without heavy accents if possible
Everyone:	Laughter [as the Chair speaks with a Scottish accent]
Chair:	and we may take some pauses just to make sure everybody uhm uh is keeping up with the conversation cause we can sometimes each of us speak very quickly when we get excited. Uh this afternoon is a chance for us really to explore the research issues ## tell each other what we're doing ## tell each other what we hope to achieve what we're aspiring to ### and it would be wonderful if we could perhaps focus on the use of technology in learning ## if that was of interest to you ##### so what I I'd like to do is I think it would be very helpful for one of our colleagues to volunteer to <as we say in Scotland: start the ball rolling cause we really love football>. Uh I think I think it would be fair to ask one of our colleagues to start the ball rolling and [name of British colleague] if you would like to kick off for us. (An audio clip of this extract is available at http://www.globalpeople.org.uk/)

This excerpt demonstrates a number of adjustment practices. The Chair clearly shows a high level of awareness of this competence by asking participants to speak clearly, to avoid accents, to avoid fast speech and to pause regularly in order to ensure that all participants have the chance to follow the conversation. The Chair then goes on to put her insights into practice by speaking slowly and clearly, by pausing regularly (signalled by #) and by trying to avoid the use of a heavy Scottish accent. However, only seconds later she speeds up (signalled by < >), falls into a more pronounced Scottish accent, uses an idiomatic expression ('to start the ball rolling') that leaves all but one of the Chinese participants with blank faces, and then goes on to repeat the idiom and to use complex vocabulary ('kick off'), which is unlikely to be understood and could easily have been replaced by a more simple word, such as 'start' or 'begin'.

Spencer-Oatey and Stadler (2009: 24–25) also use this example to illustrate another strategy that they identify as being very important for promoting mutual understanding: the building of shared knowledge. The Chair did not immediately focus on the main task (discussing what joint research project they might be able to work on), but rather made sure first that everyone learned about each other's research interests.

Spencer-Oatey and Stadler (2009) report that, in their study of international teams, the establishment of shared knowledge was particularly crucial; and Spencer-Oatey and Franklin (2009: 82–88) provide a detailed case study that illustrates it. The same also emerges in studies by Sunaoshi (2005) and Marriott (1990), although it is not labelled as such.

Varonis and Gass (1985: 341) point out that '[t]he most conversationally "dangerous" situation arises when interlocutors lack shared background, linguistic system and specific beliefs, yet do not seek to negotiate meaning'. Use of the various strategies discussed in this section can be valuable tools to help in this process; but, needless to say, they cannot guarantee success. Equally dangerous (if not more so) is the situation in which none of the interlocutors is aware of their differing background knowledge and assumptions and of the impact of this on the meanings they are each constructing. No strategy can easily address such challenges, but the careful establishment of shared knowledge can play an important role.

Managing rapport in intercultural discourse

In this section we turn to the management of rapport. Many studies of intercultural discourse (e.g. Bailey, 1997, 2000; Tyler, 1995; Spencer-Oatey and Xing, 2003, 2004; Ryoo, 2005, Ginthner, 2008) have analysed how people manage their relationships in social/professional encounters. A large number of theoretical frameworks have been used for such purposes, and one of the most influential concepts has been the notion of 'face'. This was defined by Goffman (1967: 5) as 'the public self-image that every member wants to claim for himself'. Brown and Levinson (1987) built on this concept in their classic theory of politeness, in which they attached central importance to the notion of face-threatening acts (FTAs). These are acts that risk damage to speakers' and hearers' face wants: their negative face wants that their actions are not impeded by others and their positive face wants that their qualities/characteristics are desirable to others. In social interaction, people are said to manage their social relationships by avoiding imposition on and threat to each other's positive and negative face wants. The example from House (2000: 155) illustrates the problems that can occur when face concerns are not addressed.

Example 3: Problems of rapport in social interaction (from House, 2000: 155–156)

Brian, an American student spending a year in Germany, has cooked a meal for Andi, a German friend, who has recently helped him with his German seminar paper. Andi has just arrived.

01 Brian: hallo Andi how are you?
02 Andi: yeah fine oh fine really yea;
03 Brian: so everything's ready now (.) I hope you like it I have cooked it myself [so because]
04 Andi: [yeah fine]
05 Brian: that's what we eat in the South
06 Andi: {in a loud voice} but that's so much that is FAR TOO MUCH rice
07 Brian: that doesn't MATTER I have paid for it and I have INVITED you (.) [you have]
08 Andi: [no it] DOES matter it DOES it DOES think of the many poor people who go hungry and would like to eat something like that [well I]
09 Brian: [I I]believe I (0.1) I [find]
10 Andi: [I find] one should in this common world in which we do all live (0.2) the world in which we are all endowed with material goods so UNequally we should at least on a small scale try to produce no waste no useless [waste]
11 Brian: [well Andi] I am not I (0.2) [don't believe]
12 Andi: produce [no waste] and always in our consciousness think that we in the rich western world … {monologue continues for 1½ minutes}

In the retrospective interview that I conducted with each interactant, Brian said that in his role as host he felt unpleasantly 'talked at' by his friend, who in his view acted like a 'know-all' teacher figure. He was disappointed that his friend did nothing to keep a 'real conversation' going, and he felt overrun by the monologue. In fact he said he often felt in interactions with German friends that they did not want to, or were unable to, engage in any sort of small talk. He had got the impression that it often happened in German conversations that the topic was more important than the human beings discussing it, and that discussions therefore often turned out to be serious, 'deep' and controversial. Andi said he thought they had reflected well on the problems of the so-called 'Third World' and on the way structural problems in the economies of the developing countries might be resolved. He said he was often surprised that Americans had a different outlook on the resources available in different countries and that this kind of 'overly generous' handling of the resources was also reflected in their often rather irresponsible behaviour vis-à-vis food and possessions. He was surprised that Brian had said so little and suspected that he was not interested in the topic.

According to Brown and Levinson's (1987) face theory, Andi's disagreement with Brian (turn 8) and his implicit criticism of Brian (turns 8, 10 and 12) both threaten Brian's positive face and are a fundamental reason for his discomfort with the interaction.

Brown and Levinson's (1987) theory has been hugely influential, but, despite its many strengths, it has been particularly criticized for its lack of applicability in different cultural contexts (e.g. Ide 1989; Mao 1994; Matsumoto 1988). It is not very suitable for analysing intercultural discourse because it takes a universalist approach and thus cannot provide an intercultural perspective on rapport management issues. For example, in relation to example 3, it cannot explain why Brian and Andi evaluated the interaction (and its typicality) so differently.

Another theory of politeness, Leech's (1983, 2007) Politeness Principle, is much more suited to the analysis of intercultural discourse. Leech argues that human communicative behaviour is constrained by a number of politeness maxims or constraints (e.g. modesty, agreement) and that the relative importance of these constraints can vary across cultures; for instance, that modesty is of greater importance in Asian cultures than in Western cultures (e.g. Leech, 1983; Gu, 1990; Chen, 1993). If Leech's framework is used to analyse example 3, the rapport management problems could be explained in terms of the 'agreement constraint' – that 'agreement' is of greater importance to Brian than to Andi, and that, because of this, Brian forms a negative evaluation of Andi's behaviour, as well as of the interactional behaviour of other Germans.

Yet another perspective is provided by House (2000). She argues that 'Andi and Brian have different conceptions of what communicative conventions hold in a conversational opening phase, of the topics appropriate for a dinner table conversation, and of the appropriateness of turn allocation and floor holding during dinner conversation' (2000: 157), and she links this with underlying cross-cultural differences in communicative style preferences. She identifies several dimensions of potential difference, including two that seem particularly applicable to example 3: directness–indirectness and orientation-towards-content versus orientation-towards-other.

Spencer-Oatey (2008) integrates these various perspectives in her 'rapport management' model, arguing that there are three fundamental, interrelated bases to rapport: face sensitivities, behavioural expectations, and interactional goals, each of which can be subject to individual and cultural variation. With respect to behavioural expectations, she gives the following explanation:

> People typically form expectations (conscious or unconscious) as to the behaviour that will occur in a given context, based on the norms, conventions, principles, legal agreements and protocols that are associated with that context. They may then develop a sense that others should or should not perform that behaviour, and prescriptive and proscriptive overtones become associated with that behaviour. As a result, people start perceiving sociality rights and obligations in relation to them, and may feel annoyed if the expected behaviour does not occur
>
> *(Spencer-Oatey and Franklin, 2009: 111).*

With respect to example 3, Spencer-Oatey's (2008) rapport management model yields multiple interpretive perspectives. There were clearly differences in the participants' preferred communicative styles (in line with House's 2000 perspective), especially in terms of directness–indirectness and of orientation-towards-content versus orientation-towards-other. These gave rise to differing behavioural expectations, such as in the likelihood of 'content talk' versus 'small talk' among acquaintances in a social gathering. Breach of the expectations resulted in several negative emotions, especially on Brian's part, who felt disappointment, sadness and anger (House, 2003). However, these emotions may not only have been due to unfulfilled expectations – it is also quite likely that face sensitivities were at stake. Andi's explicit disagreement with Brian over the amount of food served and his insistence that food quantity is an important matter were probably face-threatening to Brian, and Brian's comments that he felt 'talked at' and treated like an ignorant underling suggest that his self-image had been challenged. Yet another angle is offered by considering Brian and Andi's interactional goals. Although House provides little explicit data on this, the background note implies that Brian's invitation to dinner may have been a 'thank you' gesture for the help that Andi had given, and a retrospective interview comment by Brian indicates that he wanted to establish common ground with Andi (House, 2003: 47). For Andi, however, the upholding of ethical values and principles was a more important interactional goal than the building of common ground on the basis of small talk.

As this discussion implies, it is impossible to gain in-depth insights into rapport management issues by only looking at conversational transcripts and without having access to retrospective interview comments from the participants. The key to understanding (and anticipating) how people perceive face threat/loss, how they react to perceived breaches of sociality rights and obligations, and how they deal with differing interactional goals (and hence how smooth or turbulent their interpersonal rapport is) is not only to analyse the discourse in detail, but also to interview the participants themselves. This can reveal valuable additional insights into how the participants dynamically perceive their relationship, and perhaps how different their perceptions may be.

Strategies that can help to promote positive rapport

Just as relatively little research has investigated strategies that can promote mutual understanding of 'content' (see the section 'Achieving understanding in intercultural discourse'), similarly, relatively few studies have focused on the effective management of rapport. This is a weakness of much current research, and it is something that needs to be rectified. Ryoo (2005), for example, maintains that, in relation to African American–Korean interactions, there has been a disproportionate focus on the negative and conflictive aspects of interactions. In her study of service encounters between African-American customers and Korean shopkeepers, she found that there are many positive aspects to the interactions. She illustrates how the participants used a number of specific rapport-building strategies: (1) in-group identity markers; (2) attitude sharing and support giving; (3) compliments; (4) initiation of personal, phatic communication; and (5) joking and laughing. These interactional rapport-building moves helped create positive and harmonious encounters.

Spencer-Oatey and Franklin (2009) and Spencer-Oatey and Stadler (2009) have also taken a positive approach and have developed an intercultural competency framework, which includes a cluster of competencies for managing rapport. These include contextual awareness, interpersonal attentiveness, social information gathering, social attuning, emotion regulation and stylistic flexibility. They provide authentic examples to illustrate each of these competencies.

Identity and intercultural discourse

There are many definitions of identity, and they foreground different perspectives on the concept. Some definitions emphasize the reflection, understanding and positioning of self and others in 'doing identity'; other definitions underscore the partly cognitive, partly social schemas through which we sort information and reach meaning to interpret our experiences. For example, Bucholtz and Hall (2005: 586) define identity as 'the social positioning of self and other', and Jenkins (2004: 5) argues that 'identity is our understanding of who we are and of who other people are, and, reciprocally, other people's understanding of themselves and of others (which includes us)'.

Traditional theories of group identity recognize two types of group identity (Collier, 1997): (a) *ascribed identity*: the set of demographic and role descriptions that others in an interaction assume to hold true for you; and (b) *avowed identity*: the group affiliations that one feels most intensely. For example, if an individual is assimilated into a new culture, then the values and practices of that destination culture will figure importantly in his/her avowed culture. The concepts of ascribed and avowed identity are important for understanding intercultural communication, because, if a person moves to another culture, others will usually communicate with him/her in accordance with his/her ascribed identity. However, sometimes a person's avowed identity (the groups with which s/he really feels a sense of comfort and affiliation) may differ from that person's ascribed identity. In such cases the interaction is bound to be frustrating for both parties.

The post-modern understanding of identity is intertwined with social constructivism (Burr, 1995). According to post-modern beliefs, the self is fragmented and contains multiple, often contradictory identities, which do not constitute a coherent self (Fornäs, 1995: 222, 233). In the post-modern tradition, identity is considered a social construction. Correspondingly, Carbaugh (1996: 23) emphasizes that identities are something one does. They are invoked, applied and implemented in social scenarios (Carbaugh, 1996: 25–27). The changing nature of identities allows certain individual identities to be of more significance in some situations than in others. Thus in certain contexts an individual will view himself or herself first as a national of a certain country, then as a member of a given profession, then as a member of a religious group and so on.

The relative salience of one's identities is dependent upon context and varies over time; for example, in a national rally demonstration, national identity will be prioritized over professional identity or religious identity.

Recently, some identity theorists have moved toward a 'communication theory of identity' (see Hecht et al., 2005). This theory characterizes identity as the interactional achievement of four interpenetrating layers: personal (identity as an individual's self-concepts or self-images), enacted (identity as performed or expressed in communication), relational (identity as a jointly negotiated through communication, including identifying oneself through one's relationships with others) and communal (identities that emerge from groups and networks) (Hecht et al., 2005: 263–264). According to this perspective, a person's cultural group membership is not a static label or fixed attribute. Rather, cultural identities are enacted or performed through interaction. One enacts identity through choice of language, nonverbal signs such as gesture and clothing, discourse strategy, and even dress (Spreckels and Kotthoff, 2007). People may enact identity in very different ways, depending on the situation and on their goals.

Many linguistic studies of identity concentrate on the negotiation of identity through features of language use, focusing on issues such as identity and race, language and gender, and language choice in multilingual environments (Valeš, 2007). Other studies focus on choice of language, demonstrating that choice of language and the use to which language is put are central to a person's definition of himself or herself in relation to his or her natural and social environment. With regard to intercultural discourse, Bucholtz and Hall's (2005) sociocultural and linguistic framework is helpful for the analysis of identity as it emerges in linguistic interaction. Their framework regards identity as the *product* rather than the *source* of linguistic and other semiotic practices, and therefore as a social and cultural phenomenon rather than primarily an internal psychological one. As such, identities encompass macro-level demographic categories, temporary and interactionally specific stances and participant roles, and local, ethnographically emergent cultural positions. Moreover, identities may be linguistically indexed through labels, implicatures, stances, styles, or linguistic structures and systems and are relationally constructed through several, often overlapping, aspects of the relationship between self and other, including similarity/difference, genuineness/artifice and authority/delegitimacy (p. 585). Bucholtz and Hall (2005) maintain that identity may be in part intentional, in part habitual and less than fully conscious, in part an outcome of interactional negotiation, in part a construct of others' perceptions and representations, and in part an outcome of larger ideological processes and structures.

By using language in one way rather than another, people establish their identities in relation to others. A growing area of research examines ways in which people 'do' identity work in intercultural discourse, and much notable work in this area has emerged from Holmes' project on language in the workplace. This research has examined Māori and Pākehā leadership styles, with 'doing identity' as a major research focus. The researchers were interested in how people's identities (their culture, gender, age, education and previous experiences) affect how they interact in the workplace environment. Analyses of the corpus of workplace recordings demonstrate the dynamic and intersubjective nature of workplace talk: conversational participants realign their identities and goals in the course of interactions through a range of devices, including borrowing and intentional code-switching, style shifting, type of verbal feedback, pauses and use of silence. Stubbe and Holmes (2000: 276–277) explain: 'Rather than viewing Māori and Pākehā communicative styles as given, this approach problematizes ethnic identity and examines it as a social construction with discourse playing a crucial role in the process.' Such an approach is most fruitful for intercultural discourse analysis.

An increasing trend in the pragmatics literature on intercultural communication is to examine the interconnections between face and identity (e.g. Spencer-Oatey and Ruhi, 2007) and to conceptualize face in the context of a more general concern for identity in interaction (Locher,

2008). In intercultural studies more broadly, there is an important focus on identity and personal growth. When people move into culturally unfamiliar contexts, such as when they go abroad to live or study, or when they take up a job in a very different type of organization, they often experience some challenges to their senses of identity. For example, they may find that their perception of themselves as 'competent persons' is brought into question, they may be unsure how to fulfil their role, and/or they may feel unsure which group they 'really' belong to. Although this can be deeply unsettling, it can also lead to development and growth and to journeying towards 'intercultural personhood' (Kim, 2001). Fougère (2008: 200), for example, speaking of one of his research participants who was in an intercultural situation and quoting from Kim (2001: 196), notes: 'His journey is far from over, and he seems to be on his way to developing an intercultural personhood through "a 'working through' of all cultural experiences, so as to create new constructs – that is, constructs that did not exist previously".'

Competence in intercultural interaction and the need for new research directions

Underlying much research into intercultural communication is a concern with 'effectiveness' or 'appropriateness'. Yet the concept of intercultural communicative competence has attracted very little explicit attention from linguists, despite their long-term interest in communicative competence (Spencer-Oatey and Franklin, 2009). Most theorizing has been carried out in the fields of psychology, business and management, communication studies, and foreign language education. However, intercultural competence is now identified as an objective in many national foreign language curricula, and it is thus very important that linguists (including discourse analysts) take up the challenge of researching this area. There are several important contributions that the field can make.

Most conceptualizations of intercultural competence include communication as one of the key components (Spencer-Oatey, 2010), and yet few of them offer any detailed unpacking of what this entails. Scholars working in the fields of psychology, communication studies, and business and management have provided a large number of frameworks of intercultural competence (for an overview, see Spencer-Oatey and Franklin, 2009 and Spitzberg and Changnon, 2009), and yet they nearly all fail to provide detailed descriptions of the component competencies of intercultural communication. Even fewer provide authentic examples to illustrate their generalized descriptions. Linguists and discourse analysts, on the other hand, typically publish very detailed analyses of specific examples of authentic interaction, but rarely link their analyses to higher-level conceptualizations of intercultural competence. Two recent exceptions are Spencer-Oatey and Franklin (2009) and Spencer-Oatey and Stadler (2009). There is thus, currently, a massive gap between the worlds of psychology, communication studies, and business and management on the one hand, and the world of linguistics and discourse analysis on the other. All fields are the weaker for this, and there is an urgent need for more crossings of these disciplinary boundaries, so that new insights may be gained from synergistic collaborations.

As explained above, within linguistics (including pragmatics and discourse analysis) there has been a tendency to focus on problematic intercultural interaction and to conduct detailed analyses of the problems that occur in achieving understanding and/or in managing rapport in particular encounters. Despite some recent calls for a greater focus on the nature of successful intercultural communication (see the section 'Achieving understanding in intercultural discourse'), as yet there have been relatively few intercultural discourse studies that have taken this approach (Ryoo, 2005 is an exception). If we are to understand the nature of intercultural communicative competence more fully, this is insufficient. We need far more studies of effective intercultural interaction, as well as of problematic encounters.

A further challenge for linguists who analyse intercultural discourse is to make their research more relevant to professionals. As Chick (1996) points out, linguists have been slow to draw on their research insights into intercultural (mis)communication in order to help improve the practice of intercultural communication in the future. He implies that this slowness is due to a reluctance to 'meddle' (p. 331) with the cultures under study. However, he asserts that, in an increasingly interdependent intercultural world, it is vital that those who know so much about intercultural communication should contribute to its improvement. Roberts (2003: 132) proposes a more fundamental shift. Referring to medical discourse research and publications, she argues as follows:

> If applied linguistics research is to be practically relevant and to have some kind of intervention status, then the design and implementation of the research needs to be negotiated from the start with those who may be affected by it. And since with discourse-based research the insights are in the analytic writing rather than in the results which can be implemented, how applied linguists and health professionals can present and write together is also an issue.

The same can be said for research into intercultural discourse. There is a great need for analysts of intercultural discourse to work closely with professionals who are regularly engaged in intercultural interaction and who feel they could benefit from insights into the communication processes. Currently much intercultural discourse research is initiated for academic reasons and is disseminated within independent silos. As a result, it is barely read by academics working on this topic in related disciplines, and virtually never read by professionals. This needs to change. Linguists need to cross disciplinary and professional boundaries, so that we can all achieve greater insights into the processes of intercultural interaction and reap practical benefits from doing so.

Further reading

Bremer, K., Roberts, C., Vasseur, T., Simonot, M., and Broeder, P. (1996). *Achieving Understanding. Discourse in Intercultural Encounters*. London: Longman.

This book offers an in-depth analytic study of the discourse of intercultural encounters among adult immigrants in several European countries, focusing particularly on the challenge of achieving understanding.

Deardorff, D. (ed.) (2009) *The Sage Handbook of Intercultural Competence*. Thousand Oaks, CA: Sage.

This book provides a detailed exploration of intercultural competence from a multidisciplinary point of view, but with little input from linguists.

Spencer-Oatey, H. and Franklin, P. (2009) *Intercultural Interaction: A Multidisciplinary Approach to Intercultural Communication*. Basingstoke: Palgrave Macmillan.

This book takes a multidisciplinary approach to the study intercultural interaction and provides a useful overview of theoretical conceptualizations and research findings in this broad area.

References

Bailey, B. (1997) 'Communication of respect in interethnic service encounters', *Language in Society*, 26 (3): 327–356.

Bailey, B. (2000) 'Communicative behavior and conflict between African–American customers and immigrant Korean retailers in Los Angeles', *Discourse and Society*, 11 (1): 86–108.

Bremer, K. (1996) 'Causes of understanding problems', in K. Bremer, C. Roberts, T. Vasseur, M. Simonot, and P. Broeder (eds.) *Achieving Understanding: Discourse in Intercultural Encounters*. London: Longman, pp. 37–64.

Bremer, K. with Simonot, M. (1996) 'Preventing problems of misunderstanding', in K. Bremer, C. Roberts, T. Vasseur, M. Simonot, and P. Broeder (eds.) *Achieving Understanding: Discourse in Intercultural Encounters*. London: Longman, pp. 159–180.

Bremer, K., Roberts, C. Vasseur, T., Simonot, M. and Broeder, P. (1996) *Achieving Understanding. Discourse in Intercultural Encounters*. London: Longman.

Brown, P. and Levinson, S. C. (1987) *Politeness. Some Universals in Language Usage*. Cambridge: Cambridge University Press. Originally published as 'Universals in language usage: politeness phenomenon', in E. Goody (ed.) (1978) *Questions and Politeness: Strategies in Social Interaction*. New York: Cambridge University Press.

Bucholtz, M. and Hall, K. (2005) 'Identity and interaction: a sociocultural linguistic approach', *Discourse Studies*, 7 (4–5): 585–614.

Bührig, K. and ten Thije, J. D. (eds.) (2006) *Beyond Misunderstanding*. Amsterdam: John Benjamins.

Bunte, P. and Franklin, R. (1992) ' "You can't get there from here": Southern Paiute testimony as intercultural communication', *Anthropological Linguistics*, 34 (1–4): 19–44.

Burr, V. (1995) *An Introduction to Social Constructionism*. London: Routledge.

Carbaugh, D. (1996) *Situating Selves: The Communication of Social Identities in American Scenes*. New York: State University of New York Press.

Chen, R. (1993) 'Responding to compliments: a contrastive study of politeness strategies between American English and Chinese speakers', *Journal of Pragmatics*, 20: 49–75.

Chiang, S.-Y. (2009a) 'Dealing with communication problems in the instructional interactions between international teaching assistants and American college students', *Language and Education*, 23 (5): 461–478.

Chiang, S.-Y. (2009b) 'Mutual understanding as a procedural achievement in intercultural interaction', *Intercultural Pragmatics*, 6 (3): 367–394.

Chick, J. K. (1996) 'Intercultural communication'. In S. McKay and N. H. Hornberger (eds.), *Sociolinguistics and Language Teaching*. Cambridge: Cambridge University Press, pp. 329–348.

Collier, M. J. (1997) 'Cultural identity and intercultural communication', in L. A. Samovar and R. E. Porter (eds.) *Intercultural Communication: A Reader*. Eighth Edition. Belmont, CA: Wadsworth Press, pp. 36–44.

Cook-Gumperz, J. and Gumperz, J. J. (2002) 'Narrative accounts in gatekeeping interviews: intercultural differences or common misunderstandings', *Language and Intercultural Communication*, 2 (1): 25–36.

Coupland, N., Wiemann, J. M., and Giles, H. (1991) 'Talk as "problem" and communication as "miscommunication": an integrative analysis', in N. Coupland, H. Giles, and J. M. Wiemann (eds.) *"Miscommunication" and Problematic Talk*. Newbury Park: Sage, pp. 1–17.

Dörnyei, Z. and Scott, M. L. (1997) 'Communication strategies in a second language: definitions and taxonomies', *Language Learning*, 47 (1): 173–210.

Fornäs, J. (1995) *Cultural Theory and Late Modernity*. London: Sage Publications.

Fougère, M. (2008) 'Adaptation and identity', in H. Spencer-Oatey (ed.) *Culturally Speaking: Culture, Communication and Politeness Theory*. Second Edition. London: Continuum, pp. 187–203.

Gass, S. and Varonis, E. M. (1991) 'Miscommunication in non-native speaker discourse', in N. Coupland, H. Giles, and J. M. Wiemann (eds.) *"Miscommunication" and Problematic Talk*. Newbury Park, CA: Sage, pp. 121–145.

Günthner, S. (2008) 'Negotiating rapport in German–Chinese conversation', in H. Spencer-Oatey (ed.) *Culturally Speaking: Culture, Communication and Politeness Theory*. Second Edition. London: Continuum, pp. 207–226.

Goffman, E. (1967) *Interaction Ritual: Essays on Face-to-Face Behavior*. New York: Anchor.

Gu, Y. (1990) 'Politeness phenomena in modern Chinese', *Journal of Pragmatics*, 14: 237–257.

Gumperz, J. J. (1982) *Discourse Strategies*. Cambridge: Cambridge University Press.

Gumperz, J. and Roberts, C. (1991) 'Understanding in intercultural encounters', in J. Blommaert and J. Verschueren (eds.) *The Pragmatics of International and Intercultural Communication*. Amsterdam: John Benjamins, pp. 51–90.

Hall, E. T. (1976) *Beyond Culture*. New York: Doubleday.

Hartog, J. (2006) 'Beyond "misunderstandings" and "cultural stereotypes": analysing intercultural communication', in K. Bührig and J. D. ten Thije (eds.) *Beyond Misunderstanding*. Amsterdam: John Benjamins, pp. 175–188.

Hecht, M. L., Warren, J. R., Jung, E., and Krieger, J. L. (2005) 'The communication theory of identity: Development, theoretical perspective, and future directions', in W. B. Gudykunst (ed.) *Theorizing about intercultural communication*. Thousand Oaks, CA: Sage, pp. 257–278.

House, J. (2000) 'Understanding misunderstanding: a pragmatic-discourse approach to analysing mismanaged rapport in talk across cultures', in H. Spencer-Oatey (ed.) *Culturally Speaking. Managing Rapport through Talk across Cultures*. London: Continuum, pp. 145–164.

House, J. (2003) 'Misunderstanding in intercultural university encounters', in J. House, G. Kasper, and S. Ross (eds.) *Misunderstanding in Social Life: Discourse Approaches to Problematic Talk*. London: Longman, pp. 22–56.

Jenkins, R. (2004) *Social Identity*. Second Edition. London: Routledge.

Kim, Y. Y. (2001) *Becoming Intercultural: An Integrative Theory of Communication and Cross-Cultural Adaptation.* Thousand Oaks, CA: Sage.

Leech, G. (2007) 'Politeness: is there an East-West divide?', *Journal of Politeness Research: Language, Behaviour, Culture*, 3 (2): 167–206.

Leech, G. N. (1983) *Principles of Pragmatics.* London: Longman.

Locher, M. (2008) 'Relational work, politeness and identity construction', in G. Antos, E. Ventola, and T. Weber (eds.) *Handbook of Interpersonal Communication.* Berlin: Mouton de Gruyter, pp. 509–540.

Long, M. (1983) 'Native speaker/non-native speaker conversation and the negotiation of comprehensible input', *Applied Linguistics*, 4 (2): 126–141.

Marriott, H. E. (1990) 'Intercultural business negotiations: the problem of norm discrepancy', *ARAL Series S*, 7: 33–65.

Mauranen, A. (2006) 'Signaling and preventing misunderstanding in English as lingua franca communication', *International Journal of the Sociology of Language*, 177: 123–150.

Miller, L. (1991) 'Verbal listening behavior in conversations between Japanese and Americans'. In J. Blommaert and J. Verschueren (eds.), *The Pragmatics of Intercultural and International Communication.* Amsterdam: John Benjamins, pp. 110–130.

Miller, L. (2008) 'Negative assessments in Japanese–American workplace interaction', in H. Spencer-Oatey (ed.) *Culturally Speaking: Culture, Communication and Politeness Theory.* Second Edition. London: Continuum, pp. 227–240.

Roberts, C. (1996) 'A social perspective on understanding: some issues of theory and method', in K. Bremer, C. Roberts, T. Vasseur, M. Simonot, and P. Broeder (eds.) *Achieving Understanding. Discourse in Intercultural Encounters.* London: Longman, pp. 9–36.

Roberts, C. (2003) 'Applied linguistics applied', in S. Sarangi and T. van Leeuwen (eds.) *Applied Linguistics and Communities of Practice.* London: Continuum, pp. 132–149.

Ryoo, H. -K. (2005) 'Achieving friendly interactions: A study of service encounters between Korean shopkeepers and African-American customers', *Discourse and Society*, 16 (1): 79–105.

Spencer-Oatey, H. (2008) 'Face, (im)politeness and rapport', in H. Spencer-Oatey (ed.) *Culturally Speaking: Culture, Communication and Politeness Theory.* Second Edition. London: Continuum, pp. 11–47.

Spencer-Oatey, H. (2010) 'Intercultural competence and pragmatics research: Examining the interface through studies of intercultural business discourse', in A. Trosborg (ed.) *Handbooks of Pragmatics (HOPS).* Volume 7: Pragmatics across Languages and Cultures. Berlin: Mouton de Gruyter, pp. 189–216.

Spencer-Oatey, H. and Franklin, P. (2009) *Intercultural Interaction: A Multidisciplinary Approach to Intercultural Communication.* Basingstoke: Palgrave Macmillan.

Spencer-Oatey, H. and Ruhi, S. (2007) 'Identity, face and (im)politeness' (Editorial)', *Journal of Pragmatics*, 39 (4): 635–638.

Spencer-Oatey, H. and Stadler, S. A. (2009) *The Global People Competency Framework. Competencies for Effective Intercultural Interaction.* Warwick Occasional Papers in Applied Linguistics, #3. Available online at: http://www.globalpeople.org.uk/ (accessed January 2010).

Spencer-Oatey, H. and Xing, J. (2003) 'Managing rapport in intercultural business interactions: A comparison of two Chinese-British welcome meetings', *Journal of Intercultural Studies*, 24 (1): 33–46.

Spencer-Oatey, H. and Xing, J. (2004) 'Rapport management problems in Chinese- British business interactions: A case study', in J. House and J. Rehbein (eds.) *Multilingual Communication.* Amsterdam/Philadelphia: Benjamins, pp. 197–221.

Spitzberg, B. H. and Changnon, G. (2009) 'Conceptualizing intercultural competence', in D. Deardorff (ed.) *The Sage Handbook of Intercultural Competence.* Thousand Oaks, CA: Sage, pp. 2–52.

Spreckels, J. and Kotthoff, H. (2007) 'Communicating identity in intercultural communication', in H. Kotthoff and H. Spencer-Oatey (eds.) *Handbook of Intercultural Communication.* New York: Mouton de Gruyter, pp.415–439.

Stubbe, M. and Holmes, J. (2000) 'Signalling Māori and Pākehā identity through New Zealand English discourse', in A. Bell and K. Kuiper (eds.) *New Zealand English.* Amsterdam: Benjamins, pp. 249–278.

Sunaoshi, Y. (2005) 'Historical context and intercultural communication: interactions between Japanese and American factory workers in the American South', *Language in Society*, 34: 185–217.

Thomas, J. (1983) 'Cross-cultural pragmatic failure', *Applied Linguistics*, 4 (2): 91–112.

Ting-Toomey, S. and Chung, L. C. (2005) *Understanding Intercultural Communication.* Los Angeles, CA: Roxbury Publishing Company.

Tyler, A. (1995) 'The coconstruction of cross-cultural miscommunication', *Studies in Second Language Acquisition*, 17 (2): 129–152.

Valeš, M. (2007) 'Lakhota language and identity in Pine Ridge, SD', *Language Design*, 9: 35–60.

Varonis, E. M. and Gass, S. (1985) 'Non-native/non-native conversations: a model for negotiation of meaning', *Applied Linguistics*, 6 (1): 71–90.

Verschueren, J. (2008) 'Intercultural communication and the challenges of migration', *Language and Intercultural Communication*, 8 (1): 21–35.

Žegarac, V. (2007) 'A cognitive pragmatic perspective on communication and culture', in H. Kotthoff and H. Spencer-Oatey (eds.) *Handbook of Intercultural Communication*. Berlin: Mouton de Gruyter, pp. 31–53.

41

Discourse and knowledge

Teun A. van Dijk

Introduction

Both *knowledge* and *discourse* are fundamental notions in the humanities and social sciences. It is therefore surprising that so little detailed research has been done on the equally fundamental relationship between these two notions.

Epistemology has generally ignored discourse, and linguistics and discourse analysis only marginally deal with knowledge, for instance as old or given 'information' in the study of topic and focus. The social sciences have dealt with knowledge (especially scientific or medical knowledge), but again barely do so in terms of the discourses expressing or regulating such knowledge. It is therefore the task of this chapter to summarize a theory of 'natural' knowledge and of its fundamental relevance for the study of text and talk. Since cognitive and social psychology are the only disciplines that have paid extensive attention to the role of knowledge in discourse processing, our general perspective on this relationship will generally be sociocognitive.

Elements of a theory of natural knowledge

As a summary of epistemology, both historically and more recently in the relation to the humanities and social sciences, is not possible, the following properties of knowledge that are relevant to this chapter will be discussed (for classical as well as modern theories of knowledge, see, e.g., Stehr and Meje, 1984; Wilkes, 1997; Goldman, 1999; Bernecker and Dretske, 2000).

- Knowledge is justified belief shared by the members of an (epistemic) community.
- *Justification* (validation, etc.) of beliefs is based on the epistemic *criteria* or *standards* of the knowledge community (K-community), such as reliable observation, sources or inference. Different K-communities may have different K-criteria. K-criteria may be formulated by recognized organizations, institutions or experts of the community.
- Knowledge is *relative* to the K-community: what is knowledge for one K-community may be mere or false belief of another community. In other words, we do not deal with absolute, 'true' beliefs, independent of K-communities and of people who know and believe (see also García-Carpintero and Kölbel, 2008).
- *Truth* is an attribute of assertions (talk or text) and not of beliefs, which we assume correspond to, or to represent, facts or states of affairs in some situation or possible world.
- Knowledge is *contextual*: what counts as (justified) belief in one context (e.g. in everyday life) may not be justified in another context (e.g. in a specialized context); and what may be

accepted as knowledge today may be rejected as false belief or superstition later (see also Preyer and Peter, 2005).

- Knowledge is routinely *presupposed* or *taken for granted* in the public discourses of a community. This is one of the fundamental basic relationships between discourse and knowledge.
- There are different *types* of knowledge. The knowledge we here deal with is also called *declarative* knowledge (knowledge *that*), as distinct from *procedural* knowledge or ability (knowledge *how* …). Also, in this chapter we deal mostly with *social* (shared) knowledge of a community, and not with *personal* knowledge. Similarly, we may distinguish between *general* (or generic) and *specific* knowledge (as between knowledge about wars or knowledge about the Second World War), between *abstract* (e.g. logical or mathematical) and *concrete* knowledge, between *fictional* (about the characters of a novel) and *real* knowledge, and so on – depending on the category of knowers, the relation between knowledge and the world, and the kind or level of the knowledge in question.
- Social knowledge is *represented* as *distributed cognition* in the *semantic memory* (part of long-term memory) of the members of a K-community (Salomon, 1993; Kronenfeld, 2008).
- Knowledge consists of a system of *concepts* organized by *categorical* relationships (chair is a kind of furniture, etc.) and by more complex *schemata* or *scripts* (e.g. what a kitchen or a person looks like; what to do when one goes to the movies) (Schank and Abelson, 1977).
- Knowledge is *grounded in the neurological structure* of the brain and its *modal* specialization derived from our repeated everyday experiences with our environment (e.g. the visual information about a car, the auditory noise of a car relate to the neural motor areas that allow us to drive a car, to the emotional part of our brain that enable us to love or hate cars, etc.; Barsalou, 1999, 2003, 2008).
- Knowledge is traditionally *represented* or *described* in terms of *propositions* that can be expressed in natural or formal languages. For practical purposes this may do, since we need a natural language to talk about knowledge. However, it is doubtful that the mind features propositions to represent knowledge (such as 'a car is a means of transport'). It seems more plausible to conceive of knowledge in terms of specific *networks* or *schemata* that might be related to the neurological structure of the brain.
- Knowledge may be *acquired* from (reliable) discourse, as we shall see below, or by abstraction and decontextualization from concrete personal experiences represented as subjective *mental models* in episodic memory (also part of long-term memory).
- *Mental models* are subjective representations of *events* or *situations* in which a person participates at a certain *moment of time*, at a certain *place*, with other participants (with variable *identities* and social *roles*), engaged in a specific *action* and with specific *goals*. Beside personal opinions, these models may feature emotions. Conversely, we use and apply our knowledge to interpret and represent our daily experiences and *construct* them as mental models. As we know from novels, movies and fantasies, people may construe mental models that do not correspond to reality.

Mental models in communication and interaction

Mental models play a central role in the *understanding and production of discourse*. Since they represent the events as we have experienced them (or heard about), they are the basis of all discourse genres based on the representation of specific events, such as conversations, stories or news. And, conversely, when understanding text or talk, recipients typically construe or update a semantic mental model of the situation or events referred to by that discourse: a *situation model*, stored in the episodic memory (see Johnson-Laird, 1983; Van Dijk and Kintsch, 1983; Kintsch, 1998; Zwaan and Radvansky, 1998; Van Oostendorp and Goldman, 1999).

However, it should be repeated that such models of personal beliefs are construed not only on the basis of personal experiences (perception, discourse, etc.), but also by the *application* or *instantiation* of more general, socially shared knowledge and beliefs. It is also for this reason that we are able to express and communicate our mental models to other people, and hence this is why discourse is *meaningful* and *understandable* in the first place. That is, through discourse, communication and interaction, other language users of the same language and knowledge community are able to reconstruct (at least more or less) *what we had in mind* – namely a mental model. In sum, *understanding text or talk means construing a mental model for such discourse, or of the intentions (mental models) of the speaker*. And, vice versa, planning a discourse or action means construing a mental model for such communicative verbal activity.

With the theory of mental models we have the crucial interface between discourse and knowledge on the one hand, communication and interaction in general on the other: human beings are able to 'read the mind' of others through plausible and often reliable reconstructions of the mental models of others.

Context models

Language users not only form *semantic* situation models of the events referred to in a discourse, but also reflexively construe dynamic *pragmatic* models of (each moment of) the very communicative situation in which they participate themselves, and these are called *context models* (Van Dijk, 2008a; see also Givón, 2005). These models are crucial for the management of discourse, because they represent the way language users interpret their current environment as relevant for the current discourse. Context models enable language users to adapt their discourse to the communicative situation, which is a crucial condition for their discourse to be *appropriate*. Such context models typically feature the self in various communicative roles (speaker, recipient, author, etc.), social roles or identities (professor, journalist), social categories (gender, class, age, etc.), relationships (friend, enemy, assistant), as well as the current goals, intentions and knowledge state of the participants at each moment of interaction. Since at least the time, the knowledge and the intentions of the context model change permanently during discourse processing (production, comprehension), context models are fundamentally *dynamic*.

One of the crucial functions of context models is the *management of knowledge in interaction*. That is, language users, using strategies of 'audience design', need to adapt their discourse and actions to the assumed knowledge of the other participants. Speakers generally need not assert what they know to be well known by the recipients, and hence they may *presuppose* that information in discourse. Because general sociocultural knowledge is shared by members of the same knowledge community (culture, society, country, city, profession, etc.), language users often know that the recipients know what they themselves know. Membership of the same epistemic community is the basis of a powerful and simple strategy for the pragmatic management of shared, general sociocultural knowledge, and it is essential for the construction of semantic mental models that represent the understanding of discourse. Among many other functions, context models contribute to the construction of the *common ground* of participants in an interaction (Clark, 1996).

Context models not only feature a knowledge device to handle epistemic strategies. They also represent the mutual *intentions* of the participants. Recognizing the intentions of others is a basic condition of all human interaction (Tomasello, 2008). To understand an action, and hence also a communicative action, people need to attribute an intention to the observed conduct of an actor/speaker. But, since such intentions themselves cannot be directly observed, people need to do what is called 'mind reading', that is, they have an implicit 'theory of mind' that allows them to make inferences about the intentions of co-participants, for instance on the basis of their *simulation of other minds* in their own mind (Givón, 2005; Goldman, 2006; Barsalou, 2008), using their observations of the current conduct, eye contact, and so on. It has recently been found that human brains are specially equipped with special 'mirror neurons' that are able to perform such simulation.

Strategies of discourse processing

With the theoretical notions introduced above we now are able to briefly summarize how discourse is (mentally) produced and what role knowledge plays in this process. It is important to realize that such processes are *strategic*, that is, fast but based on assumptions and inferences that may be misguided, so that errors may ensue. Here are some of these strategies of discourse processing (for detail, see e.g. Van Dijk and Kintsch, 1983; Britton and Black, 1985; Britton and Graesser, 1996; Graesser *et al.*, 1997; Kintsch, 1998; Graesser *et al.*, 2003; McNamara and Magliano, 2009) – beginning with discourse production (most psychological studies of discourse deal only with comprehension, which is easier to control in the laboratory):

Formation of an experience model

In a given social situation (a conversation, giving a talk, visiting a doctor, etc.) an actor forms a mental model of this situation or experience (an experience model), including a mental representation of the current *setting* (time, place) her *self* (and of her current roles and identities), her *co-participants* (and their current roles and identities), her current *goal(s)*, current *intention + conduct (action)*, as well as the current *knowledge* and *intentions* of the co-participants. This experience model controls all (inter) action in a situation.

Formation of the context model

If the situation currently represented requires verbal communication, the actor forms a context model with the same overall structure as the experience model, but with specific communicative roles (e.g. speaker or author, recipient), goals, intentions of communicative actions as well as relevant knowledge that is presupposed, and knowledge (wishes or opinions) that must be communicated. It is this context model that dynamically and ongoingly controls all further discourse production, so as to make sure that the discourse, at all levels, be appropriate in the current situation.

Formation/selection of situation model

If knowledge about an event is to be communicated, as in a story or news report, the (subjective) situation model of that event is activated, and the context model will strategically select the information that is now important, relevant and appropriate (and as yet unknown) in the current communicative situation, for the current audience.

Genre selection

Under the influence of the context model, and hence depending on the current setting, participants, communicative activity (e.g. conversational storytelling, parliamentary debate, news writing, etc.), goals and intentions, a relevant genre is being selected to organize the discourse, for instance a conversational story, a parliamentary speech or a news report in the press. Depending on the communicative event, this genre selection may take place at the same time as the construction of a context model. Indeed genres are conventional discourse practices largely defined in terms of the context.

Semantics

Under the general control of the context model and on the basis of the situation model, the selected relevant (interesting, etc.) information is introduced into the semantics module of discourse production, which controls the production of meaningful discourse. This module first of all construes the macro-propositions that define the overall topics of the discourse and may directly give rise to the production of titles, summaries and leads. Under the control of these global topics (macro-propositions) there follows, on line, the linear production of the discourse, proposition by proposition, word by word, selecting from the situation model the relevant details of the situation talked about and linearized according to various strategies – e.g. chronological sequence in storytelling or relevance, recency and genre schema of news reports – under the control of the rules of local (sequential) coherence between propositions. Propositions that – according to the information about the recipients in the context model – are already known to the recipients need not (or may not) be included in the semantic representation of the discourse or may only be marked as presupposed (e.g. by being put in initial subordinate clauses).

Syntax and lexicon

The propositions (sentence meanings) thus produced are sequentially introduced, one by one, into the syntax and lexicon modules for expression, in ordered sequences of lexical items, and in the relevant syntactic patterns that are most suitable for the contextually appropriate expression of the propositions (for details, see Levelt, 1989).

Expression

At the same time, these syntactically organized strings of lexical items (clauses, sentences) are being introduced in any of several multimodal expression modules, such as those of phonology, visual or other articulation, still under the overall control of the context model, so that also the pronunciation, typography, images, and the like are situationally appropriate.

Cross level

All expressions (formats, syntactic forms, lexical items, sounds, visuals, etc.) are selected not only as a function of the underlying model of the events talked about, and of the global and local discourse meanings selected from this model, but also as a function of the pragmatic context model that conditions the appropriate realization of the discourse in the current communicative situation.

Of course, this is merely a general summary of very general and complex strategies involved in discourse production. The process of *discourse comprehension* more or less follows these strategies in a different order, beginning with the same interactional situation, experience model and context model, but now language users assume the role of the recipient and represent themselves as such in their own context model. That is, given the current goals as represented in their own context model, recipients construe a subjective situation model (an interpretation) of the discourse they strategically understand, word for word, sentence by sentence, turn by turn, etc. Again, they are able to construe the model that represents their understanding by *activating relevant fragments of their general social knowledge,* by *instantiating* or *applying* this general knowledge to a specific event and often by reactivating or updating previous models – construed during previous communicative events. This also means that a mental model is much richer than the text itself, because it may feature propositions that are *inferred* by recipients from their general knowledge but not expressed in the discourse itself – such as plausible causes or consequences of action.

Knowledge and the structures of discourse

We have argued that, within our sociocognitive approach, the role of context in the production and understanding of discourse is fundamental. Since knowledge is part of the context, each level of discourse structure depends on the knowledge of the participants, as explained above. In this section we analyse how the structures of discourse are controlled by the knowledge of the language users.

This is first of all obvious for the knowledge of the language itself. Yet there is no clear boundary between knowledge of the language and knowledge of the world. This is especially clear for our *lexical* knowledge, which combines knowledge of words and their meanings with our conceptual knowledge of the 'world'. Thus it is not likely that the meaning of the word *terrorism* is very different from what we know about terrorism as a social or political phenomenon.

The important implication of the contextual approach to discourse is that participants already know much about each other, the intentions, the goals and much of the meaning of discourse even before producing or understanding the first words. Thus the degree of detail and explicitness of a discourse depends on the mutual knowledge of the participants.

In order to examine in more detail the ways knowledge is related to the structures of discourse, we shall examine how knowledge is presupposed, implied, expressed or signalled in a concrete example.

Example: the inaugural speech of President Obama

As example in the rest of this chapter we will use some fragments of President Obama's inaugural address of 20 January 2009 (the complete text of this address can easily be downloaded from the Internet). The reason why we choose this example is that it presupposes the shared knowledge of most US citizens, as well as of many other people in the world. It has some of the properties of spoken language, but its formal style at the same time is close to written texts.

Phonology: knowledge, information and the role of focus

We must be brief about the way knowledge is expressed or presupposed by the sound structure of discourse, also because we cannot show the actual recording of Obama's speech here. However, let me mention at least one way knowledge (or 'information') is typically signalled in text and talk, namely in what is called the *focus* (or *comment*) (see Lambrecht, 1994; Erteschik-Shir, 2007). This functional part of sentences usually receives special stress, and in English and many other languages it tends to occur at the end of the clause (or intonation unit). Relevant for our discussion here is that focus generally manifests that part of the 'information' of the clause or sentence that is 'new' and less predictable than other parts of the sentence – e.g. as compared to the initial or 'topic' part of the sentence. This sentence topic typically continues previous parts of the discourse or of the context, for instance with a pronoun or definite description, say the deictic pronoun *I* (referring to the speaker in most discourse). Consider, for example, the opening lines of President Obama's speech:

(1) I stand here today humbled by the task before us, grateful for the trust you have bestowed, mindful of the sacrifices borne by our ancestors.

Contextually shared knowledge in this fragment is expressed by the pronoun *I* referring to the current speaker – as well as by the formal plural pronoun *us*, typically used by heads of state – by the pronoun *you* referring to the audience and more generally to the people of the USA, by the present tense of the verb *stand*, by the deictic adverb *today* referring to the temporal dimension of the setting category of Obama's context model, and by the possessive adjective *our* referring to the people of the United States (again, represented by Obama as recipients in his context model).

Also contextually (visually) known, for those present or those watching TV, is that the president is standing while delivering his address and that he is now assuming the presidency, and hence assuming a very important task, facts that refer to the political meaning and function of his speech.

In other words, the first clause is nearly entirely an expression of the context model of Obama when he delivers his address. Part of this clause is the less stereotypical expression of the current mood of the president – also part of the context model – when he describes this as *humbled*, a well-known modesty move that is part of the overall pragmatic strategy of positive self-presentation.

So the contextually 'new' information in this fragment (information not yet known or inferable by the audience) is what Obama says about himself and his current state of mind or emotions. Hence the main focus in this fragment is carried by the words *humbled*, *grateful* and *mindful*. In this case, the focus is not only generated by the functional nature of the new information conveyed by these words, namely as implementing a modesty move as part of a self-presentation strategy, but also by the rhetorical parallelism between three mind descriptions. This means that in this fragment focus is not necessarily expressed in the last part of the clauses but precisely by the first words of the last clauses, so as to give extra emphasis to the current state of mind of the president.

These persuasive moves, performed through the use of these discourse structures, have as their first goal to influence positively the context models of the recipients, a process that in classical rhetoric was called *captatio benevolentiae* and in more contemporary social psychological jargon is called *impression management* (Tedeschi, 1981).

Syntax

Word order, topic functions, pronouns, definite descriptions, nominalizations, passive structures and many other syntactic properties of discourse are variously based on the availability or accessibility of information in current situation and context models (for details, see e.g. Givón, 1983; Lambrecht, 1994; Partee and Sgall, 1996).

In the first sentence of Obama's speech we already have seen an example when he refers to *the trust* and *our ancestors*, that is, information about discourse actors that can be derived from the contextually activated information about the 'people of the USA' he is now addressing.

Thus in the speech of Obama we find the following passive sentences, gerunds and nominalizations whose actors significantly remain implicit, that is, they are not irrelevant, simply inferable from preceding or following discourse or from world knowledge:

(2) (i) Homes have been lost; jobs shed; businesses shuttered.
   (ii) (…) a sapping of confidence (…)
   (iii) false promises, the recriminations (…)

These phrases do not say who lost homes, shed jobs or shuttered businesses, or who is sapping our confidence or making false promises. Sometimes this is obvious, while inferable from our social knowledge (those who lose homes), sometimes it is not easily identifiable who does what (as in sapping our confidence), and sometimes a specific political accusation is avoided, as in (iii), which may be referring to the previous administration. In general though, Obama's speech is quite explicit with its agents, especially his positive agents, first of all himself. Also, in this speech, his slogan 'Yes we can' appears in many ways in sentences referring to all the energetic actions he, his administration and the American people are going to engage in. Hence in this slogan there is no agent obfuscation through passives or nominalizations. More generally, the ideological strategy of ideological discourse is to emphasize *our* good things and *their* bad things (and to de-emphasize *our* bad things and *their* good things) (Van Dijk, 1998). Thus our positive agency is emphasized through explicit self-reference to the agents of these acts. On the other hand, the conciliating and diplomatic policy of Obama is shown by the way in which he does not emphasize and make explicit the bad things of the opponents or the enemies, referring to them only in quite abstract phrases.

Meaning: From lexical items to propositions

Once we have construed the first phase of a dynamic context model for a communicative event, as the members of the audience do when starting to listen to Obama's speech, the first step in the complex strategy of discourse comprehension is the decoding and interpretation of *words*. We have seen above that 'looking up' the meaning of words in our mental lexicon is inextricably related to the world knowledge associated with the things talked about. Thus we know that words such as *humbled* and *grateful* are about the opinions or emotions of people. Probably not part of the lexical definition of these words is the conventional, cultural association or connotation that these are 'positive' feelings. Using them when referring to oneself, as Obama does, thus has the political communicative implicature of positive self-presentation, in order to make a good impression from the start, that is, a mental model of the recipients featuring a positive opinion or an emotion of liking.

However, these words do not appear alone, but are part of clauses, which themselves are part of a complex sentence. Hence, we do not only need to make sense of these words, but also to make sense of the clauses and of the sentence, namely by construing *propositions*. Though propositions are traditionally defined in philosophy as units that may be true or false, in a linguistic and discursive framework we rather regard them as units that define *meaningfulness* (Saeed, 1997).

> Propositions as we know them from logic and philosophy—consisting of a predicate and some arguments, and modified by various modalities – may not be the most adequate ways to represent the sometimes subtle and complex sentence meanings in natural language. Probably some kind of schematic structure representing events or states of affairs, with various categories (e.g. for Settings, Events or Actions, various Participants with different roles, some Event or Action, Goals, etc.), would be more adequate, and closer to the structure of the mental models we form when we understand discourse. However, mostly for practical and formal reasons (propositions are easier to express in natural language and can be formalized), for the moment we represent local and global discourse meanings as propositions.

For instance, when construing a proposition or event schema, when Obama thanks ex-president Bush, the role of Bush in the sentence is that of an addressee of the action of thanking. Propositions may be modified by modal expressions such as 'It is possible (probably, necessary) that ...', or 'It is permitted (obligatory) that ...', as we see in the expressions *surely* and *must* in the following fragment of Obama's speech, both expressing conviction and necessity:

(3) But our time of standing pat, of protecting narrow interests and putting off unpleasant decisions – that time has *surely* passed. Starting today, we *must* pick ourselves up, dust ourselves off, and begin again the work of remaking America.

Indeed, throughout Obama's speech we find not a single modality involving possibility or probability, only assessments that are formulated in quite affirmative modalities.

Sequences of propositions: Local coherence

In the propositions subsequent to his first sentence, Obama refers to his various states of mind, his tasks as president, the people of the USA and their ancestors, and former President Bush. All these propositions make sense within the political knowledge script of the ritual of assuming the presidency, a presidential speech, recipients and so on. In that sense, the first sentence is both semantically and pragmatically meaningful.

In other words, this is not an arbitrary sequence of propositions, but a *locally* (or *sequentially*) *coherent* sequence of propositions that may be interpreted as a mental model of the current feelings and actions of Obama (Van Dijk, 1977). One way to define meaningfulness in a proposition and in a sequence of propositions is by reference to their defining a possible situation model for the recipients. And we have seen above that such models activate and integrate instantiations of general knowledge as well as necessary inferences in order for discourses to be understood as coherent.

Note that the mere repetition or continuity of discourse referents, for instance as expressed by pronouns (*Obama ... he ... he*), is neither necessary nor sufficient for such local discourse coherence. What is needed is that the *whole propositions*, including predicates, argument roles and modalities are thus related according to the mental model. Indeed, it is not primarily the *meaning* of propositions that defines the local coherence of discourse, but rather their *reference* to situations, events or actions as construed by the mental models of the discourse participants. Again, we witness the fundamental role of knowledge-based mental models for the production and comprehension of coherent discourse.

Consider the next paragraph of Obama's speech:

(4) (i) Forty-four Americans have now taken the presidential oath. (ii) The words have been spoken during rising tides of prosperity and the still waters of peace. (iii) Yet, every so often, the oath is taken amidst gathering clouds and raging storms. (iv) At these moments, America has carried on not simply because of the skill or vision of those in high office, but because We the People have remained faithful to the ideals of our forebears, and true to our founding documents.

In order for this sequence of sentences/propositions to be coherent, we need general and political knowledge about the US presidency, taking the presidential oath, and pronouncing an inaugural speech. We need to know that taking the oath is a type of discourse, and that discourses consist of words and are spoken. Thus the second sentence is coherent with the first, because it continues to characterize the event referred to (taking the presidential oath) in the first sentence, namely the social circumstances in which these oaths were taken in the past of the USA. At the same time, good and bad periods may be coherently referred to through various mutually coherent NATURE metaphors, such as rising tides with prosperous moments, still water with peace, and raging clouds and raging storms with difficult periods. Finally, the coherence is established by the mental model fragment about the qualities and ideals of the American people and their leaders – itself part of the main mental model of Obama's speech, namely the current difficult period of the world and of the USA in particular, and how to meet that challenge. At the beginning of sentence (iv) we observe a temporal phrase (*at these moments*) that makes explicit the temporal coherence (as events in the past) of the paragraph.

Although sequential discourse coherence is largely based on reference and hence to model of the participants of the situation talked about, local coherence may also be *intensional* (based on meaning), for instance when one proposition has a *functional relation* to other propositions – as a generalization, specification, example, contrast and so on. In our example the second sentence and the third sentence and their propositions are related as specifications of the first, because they say something more specific about the (circumstances) of the presidential oath. Again, we need to activate our general knowledge of such oaths to be able to infer what possible properties they may have, including what counts as the relationship of specification – which presupposes a hierarchical underlying organization of knowledge.

Implications

Discourses are like icebergs. Only a minor part of their meaning is 'visible' as *explicit* propositions expressed in their sentences. The major part of their meaning remains implicit, namely as *implied* propositions (Bertuccelli-Papi, 2000). Language users know or assume that recipients are able to *infer* these implied propositions on the basis of generally shared knowledge, and thus construe a mental model for the discourse. This means that mental models are much more detailed than the discourses based on them. The definition of implications (implied propositions of a discourse) is thus very straightforward: all the propositions of a situation model that are not expressed in the discourse itself. Despite the common ground of shared sociocultural knowledge, there are differences between epistemic communities even within the same culture (nation, society, etc.), and also differences between individual members. Those recipients who know more about Obama, presidential addresses, the USA and its history or the current social, economic and political situation of the world will be able to infer more propositions from Obama's speech, and hence are able to build richer mental models (interpretations) for that speech. Take for instance the next paragraph of Obama's speech:

> (5) (i) That we are in the midst of crisis is now well understood. (ii) Our nation is at war, against a far-reaching network of violence and hatred. (iii) Our economy is badly weakened, a consequence of greed and irresponsibility on the part of some, but also our collective failure to make hard choices and prepare the nation for a new age. (iv) Homes have been lost; jobs shed; businesses shuttered. (v) Our health care is too costly; our schools fail too many; and each day brings further evidence that the ways we use energy strengthen our adversaries and threaten our planet.

This passage is quite general and abstract in its formulations. To know what Obama talks about, more concretely, one needs to activate and apply much general knowledge about the social, political and economic situation in the world and in the USA. Thus sentence (ii) will be understood by many as referring to the wars in, for instance, Iraq and Afghanistan, and 'far-reaching network of violence and hatred' as referring especially to Al Qaeda (among other terrorist groups). Similarly, the vague expression 'greed and irresponsibility on the part of some' in sentence (iii) may be understood as referring to banks or other financial institutions that have been blamed for the current economic crisis, whereas 'collective failure to make hard choices' may be construed as referring to specific national policies to control the market. And so on.

There are of course various strategic reasons for this kind of vagueness and indirectness; this is not just a question of style in such high-level presidential addresses. Thus Obama is able to avoid accusing Muslim fundamentalists, because such specific accusations might be resented in the world of Islam. Accusing bankers and the market more concretely may not sit well with large parts of the financial and economic elites. Specifying the reference to the failure to make hard choices would probably mean accusing the Bush administration. Yet knowledgeable recipients are able to make these inferences for themselves and hence know whom Obama is referring to. In many situations of political and diplomatic communication, but also in everyday conversation, one function of abstractness and implicitness is *deniability*. Against counter-accusations, Obama may always claim that he did not actually *say* what many people understand he *meant*.

Presuppositions

One of the central features of the knowledge management engaged in during the production of discourse is the use of presuppositions, that is, propositions that must be known (or accepted as true) for other propositions to be meaningful (true or false, etc.) (Krahmer, 1998). One might say that, whereas implications, as discussed above, are inferred as *consequences* of propositions in a discourse, presuppositions are like the *conditions* of propositions, as is the case for all prior knowledge. Thus presuppositions are implied propositions following from earlier parts of the discourse, the situation model, the context model or by inferences from general knowledge, thus making following expressions (words, phrases, clauses, sentences, etc.) meaningful. Pragmatically speaking, presuppositions are propositions that are implied by such expressions without being explicitly asserted. This may also have the function of deniability, as we have seen for all implications.

Presuppositions may be detected and interpreted by language users because they are often signaled by specific grammatical structures, so called presupposition 'triggers', such as special ('factive') verbs and adverbs, definite articles, initial that-clauses, and so on. Well-known examples are factive verbs such as *stop, end, remain, know, realize*, and *discover*, or adverbs such as *even, not only, again, and too*, among many others. Some of the presuppositions in these initial paragraphs of Obama's speech are for instance the following (with the expressions that trigger the presuppositions between parentheses).

- Bush has served the nation (*was generous, cooperated*)(*to thank for*)
- Those in high office were skilled and had vision (*not simply, because*)
- We are now in the midst of a crisis (Initial that-clause of *It is understood that*)
- Our ways to use energy strengthen our adversaries (*evidence that*)
- The stale political arguments that have consumed us for so long no longer apply (*fail to understand that*)
- Our power alone cannot protect us, nor does it entitle us to do as we please (*they understood that*)

Presuppositions are not always propositions that are assumed by the speaker to be known to the recipients. They may be used to state, indirectly or obliquely, what was not known or stated before – again, as a well-known strategic means to make (deniable) statements without explicitly asserting them. Thus the press and politicians may typically state that 'the delinquency of immigrants worries them', thus presupposing, with the use of the definite article, that immigrants are delinquent (Van Dijk, 1993). See also the following fragment of Obama's speech:

(6) On this day, we come to proclaim an end to the petty grievances and false promises, the recriminations and worn-out dogmas, that for far too long have strangled our politics.

In this fragment, to proclaim and 'end to' petty grievances, false promises and recriminations presupposes that there actually were such grievances, promises and recriminations. He does not actually assert this, but presents this information as if everyone knows what he is talking about. On the other hand, presupposed may be those propositions that are taken for granted within a cultural community or ideological group, as is the following presuppositions in Obama's speech:

- In reaffirming the greatness of our nation (…)
- We remain the most prosperous, powerful nation on Earth (…)

Descriptions

Another important semantic property of a discourse controlled by underlying knowledge is the way discourse *describes* the 'world', that is, situations, events, actions, objects, people, etc. Although this dimension of text and talk is quite crucial in discourse semantics, we know as yet quite little about it, but let us summarize some properties of descriptions.

Granularity. The first element of a description we may pay attention to is what may be called, with a metaphor borrowed from photography, *granularity*. That is, all situations and events (and their components objects, people, etc.) may be described more finely or more coarsely, with more or less detail. Granularity may be defined for a discourse as a whole, but may also vary within the same discourse. Obama speaks about the current situation of the USA and the world, as well as about his own planned actions and policies, with very coarse granularity:

(7) For everywhere we look, there is work to be done. The state of the economy calls for action, bold and swift, and we will act – not only to create new jobs, but to lay a new foundation for growth. We will build the roads and bridges, the electric grids and digital lines that feed our commerce and bind us together. We will restore science to its rightful place, and wield technology's wonders to raise health care's quality and lower its cost. We will harness the sun and the winds and the soil to fuel our cars and run our factories. And we will transform our schools and colleges and universities to meet the demands of a new age. All this we can do. And all this we will do.

Obviously, in a general speech and policy document, no details of this future 'work' and 'action' are specified – how job will be created, roads and bridges built, etc. Each of these actions may in the future give rise to so many policy documents.

Level. Related to, but different from, granularity is the *level* of a description. That is, we may describe events at a very high level of abstraction and in very *general* terms, but also at lower, more *specific* levels. And for each level we may provide more or less details, that is, enhance or diminish granularity. Thus in headlines we generally find a high-level, general description of an event that will be specified in the rest of the news report. This is also because headlines typically express the macro-structure or topic of a discourse (see below). See the following passage from Obama's speech:

(8) For us, they packed up their few worldly possessions and traveled across oceans in search of a new life. For us, they toiled in sweatshops and settled the West; endured the lash of the whip and plowed the hard earth. For us, they fought and died, in places like Concord and Gettysburg; Normandy and Khe Sahn. Time and again, these men and women struggled and sacrificed and worked till their hands were raw so that we might live a better life. They saw America as bigger than the sum of our individual ambitions; greater than all the differences of birth or wealth or faction.

Note how in this passage there are high-level action descriptions (travelled across oceans, etc.), but also more specific descriptions that emphasize hard work (packed up, endured the lash of the whip, plowed the hard earth, worked until their hands were raw). This semantic feature of description also has overall rhetorical functions, namely to emphasize the importance or relevance of some event or action described.

Perspective. Events, actions and situations may be described from different perspectives, for instance from the perspective of onlookers or participants, with or without access to their thoughts, from far or from close by, and so on – again, as we would describe the way cameras are used to record visual images.

Action. Many discourse types are about action, as is the case for storytelling, news reports and historical documents. Such actions may also be described in many ways – first of all, as seen above, with coarser or finer granularity or at more or less general or specific levels. But actions have many other properties that are attended to in a description, namely whether something was planned or intended, or more or less spontaneous, more or less conscious, as an action from a different kind of actor (see below), as more or less successful, and so on (see e.g. Van Leeuwen, 1995).

Actors. Similarly, there are many ways to describe actors, namely as a collective or institution, as anonymous, named or described, as personal or impersonal, as generic or specific, as individual persons or as members of a category, as an aggregate or collective and so on (see Van Leeuwen, 1996).

Similar remarks may be made for the descriptions of events, situations, objects, places, nature and so on.

Relevant, for us, of these various types, modes and properties of description is that they presuppose both a general knowledge of the world and the mental models underlying discourse. Coarse descriptions lead to the formation of coarse mental models when recipients are unable or unwilling to supply the finer details of events or action. Fine descriptions not only tend to lead to finer mental models of a situation, but also signal to the recipients that the current passage of a discourse is especially relevant or important, slowing down the reading and promoting deeper processing of the information provided – and hence, most likely, better memory of the events for later recall. The same is true for high level and specific level descriptions. Actor and action description also presuppose and form specific mental models, for instance in order better to understand and explain actions, reasons, goals and outcomes of action. Describing a person merely as member of a group or category, such as 'immigrant', has a very different effect on the mental model than when we describe her or him by a name, or by a name and a role (father, mother, friend, etc.), for instance to promote identification and empathy, and hence the emotional dimension of mental models (Van Dijk, 1984, 1987). See for instance the following actor descriptions in a passage from Obama's speech:

> (9) In reaffirming the greatness of our nation, we understand that greatness is never a given. It must be earned. Our journey has never been one of shortcuts or settling for less. It has not been the path for the fainthearted – for those who prefer leisure over work, or seek only the pleasures of riches and fame. Rather, it has been the risk-takers, the doers, the makers of things – some celebrated, but more often men and women obscure in their labor – who have carried us up the long, rugged path toward prosperity and freedom.

Actors are described here hardly by category (at the end only as men and women), and neither by name, group or other usual way of actor description by the nature of their actions and by their character (fainthearted, risk-takers, doers, makers of things) and the results of their actions (the famous vs. the obscure). Obama thus abstracts from the very actors themselves and focuses on the *character* of the actors that built America. Such a description barely results in a specific mental model

599

Teun A. van Dijk

of specific actors and actions, but rather in a very general, if not generic image of the history of the USA.

Evidentiality

In many discourse genres language users account for the *sources* of their knowledge – a property that has been called *evidentiality* (Chafe and Nichols, 1986). In everyday conversations, storytellers may justify or legitimate their knowledge as being acquired from reliable sources, ranging from friends, experts, the mass media or own, personal observation. Scholarly discourse is replete with references that provide the required warrants to assertions that are not the result of own research.

As with all semantic properties of discourse, evidentiality may come in many forms and may have several pragmatic and other social functions. We may provide such evidence for our current assertions in terms of our personal experiences or investigations or of those of others, of lay people or experts, in generic terms ('experts have found that …') or by specific or named sources, as we have seen for the description of authors. In the same way, we may describe the situations or contexts in which the knowledge was acquired, e.g. in a conversation yesterday with a friend, or by looking up information in Google or in an encyclopedia, or having heard it in a lecture, and so on. As always, more detail generally conveys the impression of more reliability or credibility of sources or the acquisition of knowledge, and hence is more persuasive. Obama makes many very general sweeping statements in his address when he describes, in very broad strokes (rough granularity), the current political and social situation of the world. Of course, presidential addresses have and need no footnotes. It is assumed that these discourses are written by experts and based on reliable political information of state agencies. On the other hand, we also know, for instance from the analysis of the discourses of Bush and Blair, that statements may be made whose evidentiality is at best tenuous (Van Dijk, 2008b). Obama pronounces the following brief (and quite vague) passage about the sources or his knowledge about the current situation:

(10) These are the indicators of crisis, subject to data and statistics. Less measurable but no less profound is a sapping of confidence across our land – a nagging fear that America's decline is inevitable, and that the next generation must lower its sights.

Macrostructures: topics

Finally, discourse semantics not only accounts for the local meanings of clauses and sentences, but also for larger parts of discourse or whole discourses. Strangely, this level of description is ignored in much linguistics and even in many forms of linguistically based discourse studies, despite the crucial importance of this macro-level of discourse description. Semantic macrostructures consist of a hierarchical schema of macro-propositions that 'summarize' lower level sequences of (micro-) propositions. Macro-structures are crucial for the establishment of global coherence, the identification of global discourse topics, the planning and recall of discourse in processing, as well as the description of many genre properties of text and talk – such as headlines and leads in news reports, titles and abstracts in scholarly papers, conclusions in many kinds of discourse (for detail, see Van Dijk, 1977, 1980).

In discourse, macropropositions not only organize underlying meanings but may also be explicitly expressed and thus precede or follow lower level descriptions, namely as headlines, introductory thematic sentences or as conclusions. Thus paragraphs may start with high-level propositions that will be specified in the rest of the paragraph, as in the following fragment in Obama's speech:

(11) For everywhere we look, there is work to be done. The state of the economy calls for action, bold and swift, and we will act – not only to create new jobs, but to lay a new foundation for growth. We will build the roads and bridges, the electric grids and digital lines that feed our commerce and bind us together. We will restore science to its rightful place, and wield technology's wonders to raise health care's quality and lower its cost. We will harness the sun and the winds and the soil to fuel our cars and run our factories. And we will transform our schools and colleges and universities to meet the demands of a new age. All this we can do. And all this we will do.

Thus this paragraph starts with the very high-level call for action, then specifies the actions (create jobs, etc.), and then returns to the high level by describing our ability and determination to do so – implementing again the general Obama slogan *Yes, we can!*

Speech acts

Beyond the grammar of discourse, we also need to account for the role of knowledge in the appropriate performance of (speech) acts and for the participation in talk in interaction. Thus context models have been introduced as a sociocognitive basis for the theory of pragmatics, and hence also account for the well-known appropriateness conditions of speech acts. For instance, the condition of an assertion is that the speaker assumes that the hearer does not know *p*. (Searle, 1969). It is this epistemic condition that must characterize the knowledge component in the context model of the speaker. Similar conditions should be formulated for questions, accusations and other speech acts – and to be accounted for in the context model that represents the mutual (lack of) knowledge of the participants. We have seen in the examples above that much of Obama's speech is a (macro-)assertion, which presupposes that the recipients do not know what he affirms. This may be true for some of his emotional states and future plans, but many of the things he affirms are already generally known – as is the case in much public discourse, which has the function of recalling or emphasizing what is already generally known.

Talk in interaction

Finally, what has been outlined above for discourse in general, also holds for conversation and other forms of talk in interaction. Whereas earlier epistemic studies of discourse focused on such topics as topic-comment structure, focus, presupposition, implicatures or evidentials, also conversation analysis – so far seldom interested in more 'cognitive' aspects of talk – has now begun to study the subtle ways in which (mutual) knowledge and ignorance is managed in talk, for instance what speaker has the 'authority' or access to knowledge, and hence may make truthful claims (Heritage and Raymond, 2005; Raymond and Heritage, 2006; see also Sidnell, 2005).

Concluding remarks

From the analysis of some of the properties of Obama's speech we have seen that the role of knowledge is ubiquitous in the production, the structures and the comprehension of discourse. Discourse presupposes (semantic) situation models of events talked about, as well as (pragmatic) context models of the communicative situation, both construed by the application of general, socially shared knowledge of the epistemic community. These models control the production and comprehension of all levels of text and talk, from intonation, syntax and the lexicon, to the many types of semantic structures, notably those of implication, presupposition and description, as well as the strategies of conversation. It is therefore crucial that a theory of discourse also feature a central epistemic component that explains how language users are able to manage knowledge in discourse processing, e.g. by appropriately adapting their discourse to what they assume the recipients to know (or not yet to know) as members of the same knowledge community. Although philosophy, cognitive science, neuroscience and the social sciences still need to be develop a coherent, integrated theory of knowledge, what we do know today already offers a framework that enables us to provide quite detailed *epistemic analyses* of text and talk.

Further reading

Unfortunately, there is as yet no general introduction to the epistemic analysis of discourse. For further reading about the topics of this chapter, the following books may be recommended:

Bernecker, S. and Dretske, F. I. (eds.) (2000) *Knowledge: Readings in Contemporary Epistemology*. Oxford: Oxford University Press.
Erteschik-Shir, N. (2007) *Information Structure: The Syntax-Discourse Interface*. Oxford New York: Oxford University Press.
Graesser, A. C., Gernsbacher, M. A., and Goldman, S. R. (eds.) (2003) *Handbook of Discourse Processes*. Mahwah, NJ: L. Erlbaum.
Van Dijk, T. A. (2008a) *Discourse and Context: A Socio-Cognitive Approach*. Cambridge, New York: Cambridge University Press.

References

Barsalou, L. W. (1999) 'Perceptual symbol systems', *Behavioral and Brain Sciences*, 22 (4): 577–660.
Barsalou, L. W. (2003) 'Situated simulation in the human conceptual system', *Language and Cognitive Processes*, 18: 513–562. (Reprinted in H. Moss and J. Hampton, *Conceptual Representation*).
Barsalou, L. W. (2008) 'Grounded cognition', *Annual Review of Psychology*, 59: 617–645.
Bernecker, S. and Dretske, F. I. (eds.). (2000) *Knowledge: Readings in Contemporary Epistemology*. Oxford: Oxford University Press.
Bertuccelli-Papi, M. (2000) *Implicitness in Text and Discourse*. Pisa: ETS.
Britton, B. K. and Black, J. B. (eds.) (1985) *Understanding Expository text: A Theoretical and Practical Handbook for Analyzing Explanatory Text*. Hillsdale, NJ: L. Erlbaum Associates.
Britton, B. K. and Graesser, A. C. (eds.) (1996) *Models of Understanding Text*. Mahwah, NJ: Lawrence Erlbaum Associates.
Chafe, W. L. and Nichols, J. (eds.) (1986) *Evidentiality: The Linguistic Coding of Epistemology*. Norwood, NJ: Ablex Corp.
Clark, H. H. (1996) *Using Language*. Cambridge, England: Cambridge University Press.
Erteschik-Shir, N. (2007) *Information Structure: The Syntax-Discourse Interface*. Oxford, New York: Oxford University Press.
Garcia-Carpintero, M. and Kölbel, M. (eds.) (2008) *Relative Truth*. Oxford: Oxford University Press.
Givón, T. (ed.). (1983) *Topic Continuity in Discourse: A Quantitative Cross-Language Study*. Amsterdam, Philadelphia, PA: J. Benjamins Co.
Givón, T. (2005) *Context as Other Minds: The Pragmatics of Sociality, Cognition and Communication*. Amsterdam: Benjamins.
Goldman, A. I. (1999) *Knowledge in a Social World*. Oxford, UK, New York: Clarendon Press Oxford University Press.
Goldman, A. I. (2006) *Simulating Minds: The Philosophy, Psychology, and Neuroscience of Mindreading*. Oxford: Oxford University Press.
Graesser, A. C., Gernsbacher, M. A., and Goldman, S. R. (eds.) (2003) *Handbook of Discourse Processes*. Mahwah, NJ: L. Erlbaum.
Graesser, A. C., Millis, K. K., and Zwaan, R. A. (1997) 'Discourse comprehension', *Annual Review of Psychology*, 48: 163–189.
Heritage, J. and Raymond, G. (2005) 'The terms of agreement: Indexing epistemic authority and subordination in talk-in-interaction', *Social Psychology Quarterly*, 68 (1): 15–38.

Johnson-Laird, P. N. (1983) *Mental Models: Towards a Cognitive Science of Language, Inference, and Consciousness*. Cambridge, MA: Harvard University Press.

Kintsch, W. (1998) *Comprehension: A Paradigm for Cognition*. Cambridge: Cambridge University Press.

Krahmer, E. (1998) *Presupposition and Anaphora*. Stanford, CA: Center for the Study of Language and Information, Leland Stanford Junior University.

Kronenfeld, D. B. (2008) *Culture, Society, and Cognition: Collective Goals, Values, Action, and Knowledge*. New York: Mouton de Gruyter.

Lambrecht, K. (1994) *Information Structure and Sentence Form: Topic, Focus, and the Mental Representations of Discourse Referents*. Cambridge, New York: Cambridge University Press.

Levelt, W. J. M. (1989) *Speaking: From Intention to Articulation*. Cambridge, MA: MIT Press.

McNamara, D. S. and Magliano, J. (2009) 'Toward a comprehensive model of comprehension', *Psychology of Learning and Motivation*, 51: 297–384.

Partee, B. H. and Sgall, P. (eds.) (1996) *Discourse and Meaning: Papers in Honor of Eva Hajicova*. Amsterdam: John Benjamins Publishing Co.

Preyer, G. and Peter, G. (eds.) (2005) *Contextualism in Philosophy: Knowledge, Meaning, and Truth*. Oxford, New York: Clarendon Press, Oxford University Press.

Raymond, G. and Heritage, J. (2006) 'The epistemics of social relations: owning grandchildren', *Language in Society*, 35 (5): 677–705.

Saeed, J. I. (1997) *Semantics*. Cambridge, MA: Blackwell Publishers.

Salomon, G. (ed.) (1993) *Distributed Cognitions: Psychological and Educational Considerations*. Cambridge, England and New York: Cambridge University Press.

Schank, R. C. and Abelson, R. P. (1977) *Scripts, Plans, Goals and Understanding*. Hillsdale, NJ: Erlbaum.

Searle, J. R. (1969) *Speech Acts: An Essay in the Philosophy of Language*. London: Cambridge University Press.

Sidnell, J. (2005) *Talk and Practical Epistemology: The Social Life of Knowledge in a Caribbean Community*. Amsterdam, Philadelphia, MA: J. Benjamins.

Stehr, N. and Meja, V. (eds.) (1984) *Society and Knowledge: Contemporary Perspectives in the Sociology of Knowledge*. New Brunswick, NJ: Transaction Books.

Tedeschi, J. T. (ed.) (1981) *Impression Management Theory and Social Psychological Research*. New York: Academic Press.

Tomasello, M. (2008) *Origins of Human Communication*. Cambridge, MA: MIT Press.

Van Dijk, T. A. (1977) *Text and Context: Explorations in the Semantics and Pragmatics of Discourse*. London, New York: Longman.

Van Dijk, T. A. (1980) *Macrostructures: An Interdisciplinary Study of Global Structures in Discourse, Interaction, and Cognition*. Hillsdale, NJ: L. Erlbaum Associates.

Van Dijk, T. A. (1984) *Prejudice in Discourse: An Analysis of Ethnic Prejudice in Cognition and Conversation*. Amsterdam, Philadelphia, PA: J. Benjamins Pub. Co.

Van Dijk, T. A. (1987) *Communicating Racism: Ethnic Prejudice in Thought and Talk*. Newbury Park, CA: Sage Publications, Inc.

Van Dijk, T. A. (1993) *Elite Discourse and Racism*. Thousand Oaks, CA: Sage Publications.

Van Dijk, T. A. (1998) *Ideology: A Multidisciplinary Approach*. London, England UK: Sage Publications.

Van Dijk, T. A. (2008a) *Discourse and Context: A Socio-Cognitive Approach*. Cambridge, New York: Cambridge University Press.

Van Dijk, T. A. (2008b) *Discourse and Power*. Houndmills, UK: Palgrave.

Van Dijk, T. A. and Kintsch, W. (1983) *Strategies of Discourse Comprehension*. New York, Toronto: Academic Press.

Van Leeuwen, T. J. (1995) 'Representing social action', *Discourse and Society*, 6 (1): 81–106.

Van Leeuwen, T. J. (1996) 'The representation of social actors', in C. R. Caldas-Coulthard and M. Coulthard (eds.) *Texts and Practices: Readings in Critical Discourse Analysis*. London, England: Routledge, pp. 32–70.

Van Oostendorp, H. and Goldman, S. R. (eds.) (1999) *The Construction of Mental Representations During Reading*. Mahwah, NJ: Lawrence Erlbaum.

Wilkes, A. L. (1997) *Knowledge in Minds: Individual and Collective Processes in Cognition*. Hove: Psychology Press.

Zwaan, R. A. and Radvansky, G. A. (1998) 'Situation models in language comprehension and memory', *Psychological Bulletin*, 123 (2): 162–185.

42

Narrative, cognition, and rationality

David R. Olson

Discourse and rationality

Rationality, the giving of reasons, is the hallmark of the human mind, a native endowment, a universal human trait. Cognitive psychologists analyze the processes involved in reasoning and propose mechanisms to explain these processes, sometimes appealing to the relation between language and rationality (Dennett, 1978; Carruthers, 1996). I propose to examine the relation between language and rationality in terms of modes of discourse or *genre* in which distinctive ways of thinking and reasoning are called for. Although the genres of literature are both very diverse and ill defined, I shall focus on two general classes of extended discourse that Bruner (2002) described as narrative and paradigmatic—what we may think of as literary and scientific modes of discourse. The claim is that the invention of distinctive modes of discourse and, equally, their mastery by children entail distinctive modes of thought. Thus, if the claim is true, there is not one way of thinking but as many ways as there are distinctive modes of discourse. And the task of this chapter is to sketch out these distinctive ways.

The view linking rationality to modes of discourse stands in sharp contrast to general cognitive processing models of rationality such as that proposed by Stanovich (2009), building on the influential work of Tversky and Kahneman (1974) and of Kahneman and Tversky (1996). Like in the case of other "two tier" models of cognitive processing, Stanovich distinguishes low-level, automatic "algorithmic" processes from "higher level" reflexive processes, further claiming that failures on such high-level tasks indicate that people are often, if not basically, irrational. Such information processing models pay little attention to what in fact subjects are thinking, and they overlook the possibility that deviant answers are actually a rational solution to a different problem. By appeal to the understanding of the alternative modes of discourse mentioned above, we may be able to fill in that gap. Specifically, it is proposed that a class of reasoning failures occur when formal reasoning tasks are disguised as conventional narratives. Narratives, like ordinary informal oral discourse, are radically open to context and to prior knowledge in determining the meaning of a word or expression; paradigmatic discourse, of which reasoning tasks are exemplary, require attention to a narrowed and specialized "literal" or logical meaning of terms. Which terms and how they are interpreted remains to be determined. While such specialized knowledge of the meaning of terms is important for science and philosophy, it can also easily mislead the innocent, as noted by the Lone Ranger's partner Tonto when he said: "White man speaks with forked tongue."[1]

That people are largely irrational contrasts sharply with the view advanced by Locke (1690/1961), which I largely endorse (while, with Locke, granting a place for logic):

But God has not been so sparing to men, to make them barely two-legged creatures, and left it to Aristotle to make them rational … He has given them a mind that can reason without being instructed in methods of syllogizing; the understanding is not taught to reason by these rules, it has a native faculty to perceive the coherence or incoherence of its ideas, and can range them right without any such perplexing repetitions.

(pp. 264–265)

While reasoning and rationality are manifest characteristics of the human species, humans have developed more specialized modes of thought, suitable to particular social and intellectual functions. The modes of discourse of concern here are the literary and the scientific, what Bruner (1986) first distinguished as the narrative and the paradigmatic modes.

The place of narrative

Whereas stories are both ancient and universal, non-fictional prose is the more refined instrument of science and philosophy, not to mention the primary discourse, at least in the West, of the dominant society and its schools. Stories are commonly seen as works of the imagination, whereas non-fictional prose is seen as serious discourse, uniquely suited to issues of truth, validity, and rationality more generally. Indeed, some classical Greek philosophers disparaged all artistic uses of language, including poetry and narrative, Plato going so far as to suggest he would banish users of such language from his ideal republic.

While scientific, academic prose remains relatively unchallenged as an instrument of science and philosophy and as an important goal of schooling (Snow and Uccelli, 2009), the position of the narrative remains more controversial. Bruner describes two contrasting attitudes to story. In one camp he places the "fabulists," those who point out the importance of story in understanding ourselves, others, and the world, and in the other, the "antifabulists," who worry about the ways that stories mislead (Bruner, 2002: 11–12). Fabulists, Bruner claims, describe the virtues of story not only for its power to entertain, but also for its ability to "subjunctivize" experience, to bring experience out of the ordinary world of doings and happenings into the world of the possible, the hypothetical. It is to enter the world of the imagination and to learn to see that what happens is only one out of a large number of possible outcomes. In a word, stories allow one to adopt a more reflective and self-conscious attitude to experience, thereby liberating the mind. Given his attitude to the exploration of the possible through stories, it is easy to understand Bruner's commitment to the "process" of education, the invitation to speculative thinking (Bruner, 1960)—in contrast to the more rigid attainment of specific, fixed goals.

But the imagination gives rise to error as often as to truth. Modern critics are equally suspicious of stories, claiming that people spin themselves into stories that are clearly at odds with scientific and logical truths. As an example, in America much ink is spent in the science versus religion debate between the biblical account of creation and the Darwinian account of evolution, one side insisting that creationism is a scientific theory, the other that it is rather a religious "Biblical narrative," that is, a story; one side, that Darwin's account is just another story, the other, that it is a rigorous scientific theory. The frontier between story and theory has become a much contested one. When does a story become a theory?

We find much the same difficulties in advancing psychological laws, in that they often rely on an inexhaustible list of possible exceptions that may be better explored in narrative than set out in truly causal laws (Allport, 1937). Hence some psychologists have begun to turn from the causal theories offered by standard cognitive science and to adopt, with Bruner, "the narrative stance," the attempt to understand thought and action in terms of the consciousness, the beliefs, and the intentions of actors. As novelist Julian Barnes (NYRB, June 11/2009: 10) suggested, "human consciousness always insists on narrative and meaning."

Similarly, in other disciplines such as medicine, some researchers have begun to advocate a narrative approach (Greenhaigh, 1998). This approach treats patients not as objects, but as agents who are attempting to deal with their illness and its consequences. Economists, too, despair of finding causal laws for economic growth and may be more inclined to providing narrative accounts. Nobel laureate Robert Solow said: "In real life it is very hard to move the permanent growth rate; and when it happens. … The source can be a bit mysterious even after the fact" (Easterly, 2009).

The increasing importance of narrative discourse and narrative modes of explanation has undermined the monopoly on knowledge, truth and rationality currently held by scientific discourse. A recognition of narrative as a mode of thought opens the possibility of at least two modes, appropriate to different contexts and uses, and each dependent upon particular uses of language. Put simply, one cannot ordinarily think of science without appealing to notions of hypotheses, evidence, facts, and theories (see Snow and Uccelli, 2009). And one cannot think in terms of narrative discourse without appeal to notions of agency, intentionality, and, most importantly, disruptions to the expected.

As mentioned, in his earlier writing on narrative Bruner saw narrative as one out of two equally important modes of representation: the more scientific and logical form, which he dubbed the "paradigmatic mode," and the less formal mode, which he called the "narrative mode." Both were seen as essential to understanding the mind—one tied more to the sciences, the other to the humanities. In more recent writing (Bruner, 2002) he acknowledged that the contrast between and comparison of the two modes "has been left behind," adding "for better or worse" (p. 115, n. 19), and he concentrated on the diverse uses of story in literature, law, and life.

But what Bruner has "left behind," the scraps from the table, so to speak, provide sufficient nourishment for the less adventurous; and in the remainder of the chapter I shall employ the distinction between narrative and paradigmatic discourse and show how the failure to recognize the rational uses of these alternative modes of discourse leads to misleading conclusions about reason and rationality.

What is a story?

The critical centre of a story is what Aristotle called *peripateia* ("adventure," "reversal"): the violation of expectation, the event that upsets the ordinary, taken for granted, everyday happenings, what I shall call "exceptionality." Kenneth Burke (1945) in *The Grammar of Motives* referred to this violation of expectation as "Trouble" with a capital T. "In the still of the night, there is a knock at the door. And in comes a stranger." The unexpected, exceptional event is at the heart of the story. That exceptionality is what makes stories endlessly entertaining.

But stories are said to contain other features as well, including a cast of characters, a setting that provides the basis our expectations as to what normally occurs—a restaurant, a beach, a post-office, a bar, a market, a home, or the like—the *peripeteia*, as Aristotle called the unexpected and the exceptional—sometimes a resolution to the trouble, and finally a narrator to tell it and an audience to listen. The understanding of stories has generated a vast literature that shows that readers and listeners are well aware of these distinctive properties (Cooper, 1985). The telling and the understanding of stories is further embedded within the general discourse constraints deriving from Grice's "cooperative principle" (Grice, 1989): to honor what he called the maxims of quantity and quality, that is, to tell what is necessary for the listener to grasp the meaning and to exclude information that is irrelevant and distracting. This point is expressed in the formal convention known to every reader and spelled out in every manual of story writing: "The invariable rule should be, put in nothing that has not a bearing on the catastrophe of the story, and omit nothing that has" (Cody, 1894: 37). It is a convention recognized by children as young as nine years. In one study (Winner *et al.*, 1986) children were asked to select one out of two endings for a story, one of which adverted to as incident mentioned in the introduction, the other not. Whereas the choices of 7-year-olds were made at chance, 9- and 12-year-olds chose the ending that picked up the earlier mentioned incident.

It is the trouble, Burke's "Trouble," the violation of the reliable expectations of the listener, that is central to narrative and distinguishes narrative from more paradigmatic modes. There is a phrase in logic that captures, so as to exclude or at least to manage, the notion of trouble. It is the Latin expression *ceteris paribus*, which means "all other things being equal." A scientific law, for example Charles' law relating temperature and the volume of a gas, claims that an increase in temperature causes a linear increase in volume, *ceteris paribus*, all other things being equal. The law does not hold if the pressure changes or, worse still, if there is a hole in the container. Scientific laws assume that all the other conditions excluded by the *ceteris paribus* clause can be systematically controlled, if necessary by creating an artificial world known as a laboratory (Hacking, 1983). If these conditions cannot be stipulated, narrowly defined, and brought under some degree of control, one cannot formulate a causal theory. In literature, and arguably in the social sciences, there is no way to exhaust all the possibilities excluded by that clause. In a story, as in real life, when there is a knock at the door, it is someone who is expected; when "in comes a stranger," that *ceteris peribus* condition has been violated. In a story, things are conspicuously not equal, nor can they be systematically ruled out as they may be in a scientific laboratory. In a story the unexpected occurs. The more unexpected, the better the narrative. It is, after all, the unexpected event that makes the story worth telling, thereby creating a link between the narrator and the audience. But this is also the reason why narrative is so important to explanation, in everyday life as well as in the psychological and other social sciences, and in the study of the human mind. This is a world in which it may be unrealistic to expect strictly causal laws; it is impossible to assume, for any real, naturally occurring event, that all other things are equal. Explanation will be local and contextual. Let us explore this issue more fully.

Ceteris paribus

Ceteris paribus is a Latin phrase, literally translated as "if other things are equal/of the same weight." It is commonly rendered in English as "all other things being equal." A prediction, or a statement about causal or logical connections between two states of affairs, is qualified by *ceteris paribus* in order to acknowledge, and to rule out, the possibility of other factors that could override the relationship between the antecedent and the consequent (Schlicht, 1998).[2]

Put another way, *ceteris paribus* marks the limits of generalization. "I'll meet you for lunch tomorrow *ceteris paribus*," that is, unless something completely unforeseen comes up. My grandmother always guarded her promises by adding "Lord willing," thereby acknowledging that not everything was under her control. Nor could her, or anyone else's, actions be predicted by purely causal laws; the unexpected may, and often did, intervene; conspicuously, all other things are not equal. The history of science is replete with cases in which scientists were misled or confused about which factors had to be listed as having to be held equal. Prior to the invention of astronomy, astrologers sought to influence the motion of planets by prayer and ritual. Astronomy became a science when the factors relevant to celestial motion could be enumerated. In this way the *ceteris paribus* conditions could be sufficiently contained to allow the formulation of strictly causal laws. As suggested above, whether or not the social sciences can formulate such laws remains an open question.

In literature there is no way to limit these conditions. A defining feature of narrative is the open-ended opportunities it provides for exploring the exceptional events that violate expectation. Narrative is the primary means for exploring the possible, for linking unlikely events into a coherent, comprehensible story. To do so, it expands or stretches not only the imagination but the language as well. Literature relies on the openness of the meaning of the terms it employs, allowing meaning to be more context and situation sensitive. Consider what the word *word* means when we say "I give you my word," or what *all* means in "All men are created equal" or in "I gave it my all." Or consider what the word *and* means in literary contexts such as "love and marriage," where *and* means something like "leads to," or in expressions such as "he ate and left," where *and* means "and then" and yet in other, more specialized contexts, where it means something like *plus*. Words cover diverse situations by allowing context to specify their appropriate interpretation.

Rationality and modes of discourse

The distinction between narrative and scientific and philosophical discourse may be drawn on the basis of assumptions about *ceteris paribus* conditions. Discourse that restricts these conditions in a manageable way, so as to allow the formation of lawful relations, defines the paradigmatic genres, the discourses of science and philosophy; discourse that treats these conditions as essentially open ended defines the narrative genres. Neither has a monopoly on rationality; both offer distinctive advantages and uses. Problems arise when the boundary between these classes of genre is unacknowledged, as in the current debates on rationality. Let us examine this claim by appeal to literary and non-literary examples.

Let us begin with a literary example. Consider poor Mary Barton, the central character in Mrs. Gaskell's nineteenth-century novel of the same name, about life in a textile mill-town in England a century earlier (Gaskell, 1848). Mary Barton is the beautiful and dutiful daughter of a struggling weaver who is courted by the mill owner's son, Harry. A reader, reading this novel, may think: Is it more likely that Mary Barton will marry the mill-owner's son, or is it more likely that she will marry the mill-owner's son *and* use her newly acquired status to relieve her family from oppressive poverty? Most readers will choose the latter, but, if current research on rationality and summarized by Stanovich (2009) is to be believed, those readers would be irrational. We shall return to Mary Barton presently.

So-called failures of rationality of this sort have become a favored topic in the psychology of reasoning in the past few years, largely because of the discovery by Kahneman and Tversky (1996) of what they called "cognitive illusions": cases in which adults are routinely distracted into making invalid decisions. Even well educated persons often draw conclusions that are formally invalid, particularly if they rely on naïve statistical intuitions. Stanovich (2009) reviewed this rich literature on invalid reasoning, what he calls "irrationality." The reasons people base their invalid conclusions on are often bad ones, and when recognized as such may be held in check—or so, at least, educators hope. The list of types of errors in reasoning include anchoring bias, confirmation bias, hindsight bias, self-serving bias, base rate neglect and other failings. These errors are not all of the same type, some being caused by ego-centrism, some by cognitive overload, some by ignorance of statistics, and yet others, the ones I consider here, by—I suggest—a conflation of genre, namely, of narrative with more scientific–philosophical discourse. I shall attempt to show that narrative, far from being the cause of errors in reasoning, is an alternative and valid mode of thought.

The most famous of the problems studied by cognitive psychologists is that of a certain fictional character named Linda. The story continues: "Linda is a 31 years old, single, outspoken, and very bright. She majored in philosophy. As a student, she was deeply concerned with issues of discrimination and social justice, and also participated in anti-nuclear demonstrations." The reader is then asked to "[r]ank the following statements by their probability," and the statements to be ranked included:

1. Linda is a bank teller.
2. Linda is an insurance salesperson.
3. Linda is a bank teller and is active in the feminist movement.

Most adults commit the logical error of thinking that (3) is more probable, whereas, by necessity, the probability of (1) is greater. Rather than see the problem in terms of probabilities, thereby choosing (1), 80 percent of subjects see it in terms of what Stanovich refers to as "similarity assessment"—it seems like a good description of Linda—and choose (3). And they are thereby judged by the psychologists as irrational.

In fact, readers are not blind to probabilities. In Tolstoy's celebrated novel *War and Peace*, the Czar asks General Kutuzov why he has decided to abandon Moscow to the invading armies of Napoleon. Kutuzov replies: "Which is worse? To lose Moscow? Or to lose Moscow and the entire Russian army?" The Czar concedes that the general is right not to try to defend Moscow; a double loss is greater than a single one. And, as every reader knows, although Moscow was burned, the army survived to destroy the retreating French troops. So, if simple probabilities are not the problem for readers, what is?

Subjects are judged as irrational in the Linda problem because they fail to apply a formal, statistical model. Indeed, they were asked "Which is more probable?" and so they should, perhaps, be alerted to the type of problem they were facing. If we apply a statistical model to the Linda problem, it would be represented thus. Is she more likely to satisfy condition A, that she become a banker, say, with probability of 0.5, or that she satisfy both condition A, that she be a banker with a probability of 0.5, and B, say, also with a probability of 0.5, that she becomes a feminist, which results in a joint probability of $0.5 \times 0.5 = 0.25$ (assuming that the two conditions are independent)? Obviously 0.25 is less than 0.5, so A is more probable than A and B together. Readers are misled by their over-reliance on their literary intuitions about Linda. For good reason, as we see when we return to poor Mary Barton.

Consider again, then, the narrative model carefully constructed by Mrs. Gaskell. The likelihood of Mary Barton (1) marrying the mill-owner's son is zero, unless (2) she is granted the right to benefit her impoverished family. Consequently, the probability of her meeting both conditions (1) and (2) is equal to, if not greater than, that of her meeting the single condition (1), namely that she marry the mill-owner's son. The narrative model would seem to predict just the opposite of what is predicted by the statistical model. And it is the one most frequently chosen by readers and by subjects in experiments on rationality. The narrative model allows scope for all sorts of possibilities; one cannot assume "all things being equal," the *ceteris paribus* clause. Specifically, in this narrative context, *and* is not treated as conjoining independent conditions but as meaning something more, like *unless*; and in order to understand Mary Barton's decision a reader must grasp that relation. That is what narrative rationality requires.

Or consider a more famous case, the biblical story of Esther. Esther is a Jewess admired by the non-Jewish king. Esther knows that only the king could save her father, and her people, from the evil plot of the king's servant Haman. Which is more likely: That Esther marry the king? Or that Esther marry the king *and* thwart Haman's threat? The latter, because she would marry the king only if he frustrated Haman's evil plot. And a reader is not irrational if s/he judges the latter as more likely. Here *and* means something like *if only*. A reader, to understand her decision, would have to interpret *and* in this contextually more appropriate way.

Again, statistically, the probability of meeting two criteria is the diminished product of the probability of each of the two independent criteria, so the "rational" answer is that it is more likely that Esther will marry the king than that she will marry the king and plead for her people. However, the narrative context makes the latter alternative the more likely one, because if she could not defend her people she would not consider marrying the foreign king at all.

But this is not the whole story. Technically speaking, it is not possible that the joint probability of being a banker and a feminist is greater than the probability of simply being a banker, because the part cannot exceed the whole; she is a banker in both cases. Again, even if Mary Barton marries to help her family, she still marries the mill-owner's son. So in both cases the likelihood of the specific claim cannot exceed the general one. This is why most subjects in such experiments eventually come around to agreeing that being a banker is more likely than being a banker and a feminist.

But, again, we suspect a linguistic trick. Technically speaking, the category "banker" is an inclusive category that includes "banker and feminist," just as the category "animal" is an inclusive category that includes "rabbits." But in informal discourse, including in narrative, categories are ordinarily used contrastively, such that, if one category is "banker and feminist," the contrasting category is "banker and not feminist." Or if one category is "rabbit" the contrasting category would conventionally be something like "dog" or "duck," members of the same class. If asked to compare "animal" with "rabbit," the reader or listener is likely to infer that "animal" is to be interpreted as "animal *other than* rabbit." Piaget (1962) reported just this pattern in young school-age children. Children are told: "There are three rabbits and two ducks." When asked "Are there more rabbits or animals?," children typically reply, "Rabbits." When asked "Why?," they reply "Because there are only two ducks." That is, they treat the question as "Are there more rabbits or *other* animals?" This phenemonon has been studied extensively in children (Ford, 1976; French and Nelson, 1985; Macnamara, 1986).[3] Children, like unwary adults, assume that *or* conjoins mutually exclusive classes, as it does in ordinary and in literary contexts. They succeed only if they are forewarned that they are to treat the expressions strictly, literally, or technically and if they have been schooled in just these formal conventions. The technical conventions involved in this case have to do with treating terms of ordinary language as if they were logical or mathematical expressions. One is taught that *and* is to be treated as equivalent to the mathematical operator *plus* and *or* is to be treated as logical disjunction.

The discourse in which the meaning of terms is to be constrained to their stipulated, defined meanings is the discourse of modernism (Reiss, 1982). It is the use of language with, as the Secretary to the Royal Society of London put it, a "mathematical plainness of style" (Sprat, 1966). It is the language of science and philosophy, the formal language that is referred to as "schooled" or "academic" language, an end product of a literate tradition (Olson, 1977, 1994; Snow and Uccelli, 2009). It is a discourse in which the text is treated as if complying with the *ceteris paribus* convention—the convention of "all other things being equal."

Narrative, on the other hand, is literary genre appropriate for coping with human contexts in which the logical demands of *ceteris paribus* cannot be assumed. There is no formal computational rule for determining the actions of unique persons in unique situations. Mary Barton is a uniquely human person in which feelings of concern, values, and goals temper every decision. The writer, Mrs. Gaskell, plays on the reader's knowledge of these personal characteristics and on their ability to anticipate the actions of Mary Barton and their consequences. Narrative, consequently, provides a frame for probing into the vicissitudes of everyday life as well as of literature.

Narrative is not only an alternative to more formal and statistical models of rationality, it is by far the more universal mode of thought. Indeed, it takes several years of schooling for reasoning to be brought under the more austere forms of rationality essential to the kinds of tasks confronted in more formal contexts. The issue is not one of rationality, but of learning to recognize and cope with alternative genres of literature.

The Linda problem is in the narrative genre. It is clearly fictional, and the reader recognizing it as a narrative knows that the mentioned details are essential to the story (to mention irrelevant details is to violate Grice's cooperative principle). In spite of this, researchers require the reader to read it in the paradigmatic, that is, in the scientific–philosophical genre, and to treat as irrelevant the detail that Linda is committed to social justice. When the reader fails to comply with the assumptions of the test giver, he or she is judged irrational.

On the contrary, it may be argued that what is at stake is the experimenter's insensitivity to the conventions of genre. Indeed Stanovich, citing Kahneman and Tversky, describes these different interpretive stances (i.e. ways of reading) as "framing effects." Framing effects are "basic violations of the strictures of rational choice" (2009: 88), as they are responses to surface variants or "trivial rewordings" of formally identical problems. As I have indicated above, narrative is closely attuned to surface variants and readers of narratives know that those surface variants cannot be ignored. Conditions of "formal identity" occur only in logic and mathematics. Gigerenzer (1996) criticized Kahneman and Tversky on just these grounds, claiming that the questions asked did not make sense and that "the conjunction rule is [not] a universally applicable norm for sound reasoning" (p. 593). Hertwig and Gigerenzer (1999) provided evidence that people assume non-mathematical meanings for the terms in such tasks, basing their judgments on semantic and pragmatic rather than strictly mathematical meanings. More generally, even such logically equivalent expressions as active and passive sentences are not semantically equivalent, as they carry different presuppositions (e.g. "John chased Mary" is logically equivalent to "Mary was chased by John," although one is about John, the other about Mary). The notion of descriptive invariance is defensible only by reference to some specified criterion and cannot be assumed to be a general property of language.

In fact there is a long history of confusing the rationality of persons with their culturally conventional ways of using language. Researchers were early drawn to what appeared to be conspicuous failures of reasoning demonstrated by members of traditional societies who had had limited access to modern society, and in particular to a formal education. Luria (1976), in collaboration with Vygotsky, conducted a series of studies in Central Asia, in an area undergoing rapid social change under the collectivization programs of the Soviet government in the 1930s. Luria was able to give a series of psychological tests, including classification and reasoning tests, to a group of traditional non-literate farmers and to a comparable group from the same villages who had some formal schooling. The least literate tended to treat tasks in a concrete, context-bound way, whereas those more educated treated them in a more formal, logical way. No doubt the educated subjects had learned something important. However, it is the responses of the uneducated subjects that are more informative. In a typical, widely cited example, subjects were told the following story:

> In the far North, where there is snow, all the bears are white. Novaya Zemlya is in the far North and there is always snow there. What color are the bears there?

> Literate subjects, of course, answered "White." The non-literate subjects tended to reply as "I don't know… there are different sorts of bears."

(Luria, 1976: 108–109)

Luria called such responses failures to infer from the syllogism. Kahneman, Tversky, and Stanovich would presumably agree and claim further that these more traditional subjects are irrational. A more charitable explanation would be to say that these subjects are perfectly rational, but that they are unfamiliar with the required genre and treated the narrative as a narrative with an unknown and unspecified set of alternative conditions and consequently as open to interpretation. The subject, it appears, treated the story not as a set of logical premises but as a set of ordinary assertions forming the kind of narrative from which one is free to draw one's own conclusion depending on the possible contexts of interpretation. To advert to the earlier argument, subjects fail to treat the story as implying that all other things are equal. Schooling, in large part, is learning to manage paradigmatic discourse systematically, to the point of learning to read even narratives in a formal, logical manner. And possible problems are particularly difficult to detect when logical tasks are disguised as narrative, as Kahneman, Tversky, Stanovich, and Luria have done.

A discourse model of reasoning

What requires analysis, then, is not the rationality of persons but the distinctive properties of genres of literature, in particular the narrative and the paradigmatic. Narrative forms are both extremely ancient and universal. Paradigmatic modes are special in ways that require examination. Lyotard (1993) described paradigmatic, what he called scientific discourse, as a specific type of language game, in that it restricted itself to denotative statements. As noted earlier, these are statements with precise meanings from which valid inferences may be drawn. Learning to read and think paradigmatically is slow to develop in children and requires extensive schooling (Olson, 1977, 1994, 2009). Furthermore, there is considerable evidence to suggest that the development of extended paradigmatic discourse is a relatively recent historical development, set in motion by Aristotle's logic and given rigorous form only by the Renaissance humanists and the early modern scientists.

Linguist Roy Harris (2009) has traced the development of logic to the Aristotelian attention to "sentences" rather than to "utterances." Sentences are treated as autonomous artifacts with stipulated meanings, which may be examined for their semantic values quite independently of how they are used in context by persons. Harris writes:

> With the arrival of 'the sentence', a new forum is created for the discussion of human thinking, and along with that comes the concomitant demand or expectation that all thinking (reasoning) worth bothering about has to be presented in sentential form. (This expectation is already realized by the time of Aristotle, because the sentence is the basis of the Aristotelian syllogism.)
>
> This new forum, however, is also an intellectual cage or enclosure imposing its own limitations. It cannot accommodate non-sentential modes of thought.
>
> *(Harris, 2009: 51)*

In his study of the history of the understanding of metaphor, Leezenberg (2001) similarly concluded that "literal meanings, then, are not the start of the life of the language, but rather the end product of a long social and historical process ... Literal meanings depend on the stabilization and codification of linguistic norms; these are achieved with the aid of literacy, education, standardization of language and lexicography" (p. 302). The literal meanings of particular relevance to the reasoning tasks I have considered are those of the connectives *and* and *or* and quantifiers such as *all*. Presumably these terms have, among their possible meanings, the narrow meanings seized upon by logicians; but the meaning in such cases depends upon context. It requires a tradition of defining, refining, and clarifying terms to make one of these meanings the normative standard. Stipulated definitions develop as a historical process, a part of a literate or written tradition passed on through systematic schooling. It is the special, indeed peculiar form of this formalized genre that students of rationality have failed to recognize in imputing irrationality to anyone who fails to honor it. This is to confuse rationality with a particular use of language.

Non-sentential modes of thought are what I have been describing as narrative modes of thought, thought in which both premises and inferences are open to redefinition in the context. Or, more precisely, statements for which one cannot safely make the *ceteris paribus* assumption.

Such expressions are best treated as the manifestation of a human mind subject to equivocation and re-interpretation rather than as formal objects for which "other things being equal" may be assumed.

The narrative and paradigmatic simply distinguish two great classes of the genres of literature. All of the ways of using and understanding language are grounded in ordinary spoken discourse. Metaphor and simile are common in all speech, any expression may be quoted and commented on, statements may be judged true or false, assertions agreed or disagreed with, intentions and feelings discussed. Ways of writing and reading exploit these linguistic resources in extended discourse, in part taking expressions out of the ordinary oral context of direct speech and creating a written record, thus displacing language from its immediate context of use and opening it to re-reading and design for particular purposes. The result is literature, with its diverse ways of reading and its models of rationality. In fact, defenders of the humanities often bemoan the monopoly of rationality held by the "maths and sciences." Slouka (2009) argues that the neglect of the humanities has a seriously distorting effect on defining the goals of education.

Conclusion

Many of our arts and sciences are devoted to creating such formal expressions, whether in science, philosophy, or law. The advance of true statements from which valid inferences may be drawn is the goal of all of our sciences. Such laws hold by virtue of the condition known as *ceteris paribus*, the assumption that all other things may be equal. Narrative is called for when all the conditions cannot be assumed to be equal, when human purposes, fears, hopes, beliefs, and desires come into play. Which is to say, most of the time other than when we are doing our science—and perhaps even then. Different genres have been invented to handle these differences, the narrative and paradigmatic being two of these clusters of genre. And the study of thinking and reasoning will take an important step forward when thinking is set in the context of discourse genres that have been invented for ordering our world and our minds. What psychologists treasure as rationality is merely a special way of using language. It is using language in a mathematical kind of way that has given us our modern scientific world. Not to be disparaged, of course, but to be recognized for what it is. And to restore to narrative its privileged place in the human sciences.

Further reading

Havelock, E. (1982). *The Literate Revolution in Greece and its Cultural Consequences*. Princeton, NJ: Princeton University Press.

Havelock was the first to state, one could say overstate, the role of writing in the invention of philosophical discourse in classical Greece. He thought the alphabet critical, a view that must be tempered by new understandings of the importance of other scripts. But he was correct, I believe, in emphasizing the importance of the fixed text and of its availability to the common as opposed to the elite reader.

Goody, J. (1987). *The Interface between the Oral and the Written*. Cambridge: Cambridge University Press.

Goody uses his extensive knowledge of traditional oral culture to reflect on social changes produced by the agricultural and urban revolutions and on the role of writing in intellectual and social changes that accompanied them.

Eisenstein, E. (1979). *The Printing Press as an Agent of Change*. Cambridge: Cambridge University Press.

Eisenstein documents the increasing reliance on printed documents in social, political and intellectual life in the sixteenth and seventeenth centuries, when modern thought evolved. Her important emphasis on the availability of texts, in my view, somewhat understates the importance of the new authority of the common reader and the waning authority of king and church during that period.

McLuhan, M. (1962). *The Gutenberg Galaxy*. Toronto: University of Toronto Press.

David R. Olson

McLuhan, often disparaged for his overstatement and universal popular appeal, was nonetheless the first to insist that the medium of communication mattered and that writing invited a new mentality.

Notes

1 The unscrupulous often take advantage of the gap between explicit and implied meaning, that is, between what is said and what is meant, a distinction critical to modern literacy (Olson, 1977). Reasoning tasks that involve "trick" questions are subject to Tonto's charge.
2 Philosophers who worry about *ceteris paribus* analyses do *not* worry about cases in which the "other factors" can be systematically evaluated; their worries are focused on *ceteris paribus* clauses that are not even eliminable *in principle*. For example, in the philosophy of science, it is common to say that there is a natural law that events of kind A cause events of kind B *if and only if* an event of type A, *ceteris paribus*, is always followed by an event of kind B—in order to rule out the possibility of other causal phenomena overriding the ordinary effect of the event of type A. But, in order to eliminate the *ceteris paribus* clause in *this* analysis, a philosopher would need to know *every* sort of causal event that could possibly override *any other* sort of causal event—and, even if there is *in principle* some finite list that exhausts all of these possibilities (a philosophically controversial claim), that list is, for certain, *not* known to the person claiming to be giving a definition of causality. So there is no one who can say just what is being ruled out by the *ceteris paribus* clause in this analysis. (Even if an omniscient physicist *could* spell it all out in a finite period of time, *we* are the ones purporting to understand how to use the words, and *we* see these things only through a glass, darkly.) *Wikipedia, On-line*, 2009.
3 Piaget took children's failure as indicating a logical failure, others as a failure to recognize the special nature of language involved.

References

Allport, G. (1937) *Personality*. New York: Holt.
Barnes, J. (June 11, 2009) *New York Review of Books*, 56.
Bruner, J. S. (1960) *The Process of Education*. Cambridge, MA: Harvard University Press.
Bruner, J. S. (1986) *Actual Minds, Possible Worlds*. Cambridge, MA: Harvard University Press.
Bruner, J. S. (2002) *Making Stories: Law, Literature, Life*. New York: Farrar, Strauss & Giroux.
Burke, K. (1945) *A Grammar of Motives*. New York: Prentice-Hall.
Carruthers, P. (1996) *Language, Thought and Consciousness*. Cambridge, UK: Cambridge University Press.
Cody, S. (1894) *The Art of Writing and Speaking the English Language*. New York: Funk & Wagnalls.
Cooper, C. R. (ed.) (1985) *Researching Response to Literature and the Teaching of Literature: Points of Departure*. Norwood, NJ: Ablex.
Dennett, D. (1978) *Brainstorms: Philosophical Essays on Mind and Psychology*. Cambridge, MA: MIT Press.
Easterly, W. (October 8, 2009) 'The anarchy of success', *New York Review of Books*, 56: 28–30.
Ford, W. G. (1976) *The Language of Disjunction*. Unpublished PhD Dissertation. OISE/University of Toronto.
French, L. and Nelson, K. (1985) *Young Children's Understanding of Relational Terms*. New York: Springer Verlag.
Gaskell, M. (1848) *Mary Barton*. London: Dent.
Gigerenzer, G. (1996) 'On narrow norms and vague heuristics: a reply to Kahneman and Tversky (1996)', *Psychological Review*, 103: 592–596.
Greenhaigh, T. (ed.) (1998) *Narrative Based Medicine: Dialogue and Discourse in Clinical Practice*. London: BMJ Books.
Grice, H. P. (1989) *Studies in the Ways with Words*. Cambridge, MA: Harvard University Press.
Hacking, I. (1983) *Representing and Intervening: Introductory Topics in the Philosophy of Natural Science*. New York: Cambridge University Press.
Harris, R. (2009) 'Speech and writing', in D. R. Olson and N. Torrance (eds.) *The Cambridge Handbook of Literacy*. New York: Cambridge University Press, pp. 46–58.
Hertwig, R. and Gigerenzer, G. (1999) 'The "Conjunction Fallacy" revisited: how intelligent inferences look like reasoning errors', *Journal of Behavioral Decision Making*, 12 (4): 275–305.
Kahneman, D. and Tversky, A. (1996) 'On the reality of cognitive illusions', *Psychological Review*, 103: 582–591.
Leezenberg, M. (2001) *Contexts of Metaphor*. New York: Elsevier.
Locke, J. (1690/1961) *An Essay Concerning Human Understanding*. Vol. 2. London: Dent/Everyman's Library.

Luria, A. R. (1976). *Cognitive Development: Its Cultural and Social Foundations*. Cambridge: Cambridge University Press.

Lyotard, J.-P. (1993) *The Postmodern Condition: A Report on Knowledge*. Minneapolis, MN: University of Minnesota Press.

Macnamara, J. (1986) *A Border Dispute: The Place of Logic in Psychology*. Cambridge, MA: MIT Press.

Olson, D. R. (1977) 'From utterance to text: The bias of language in speech and writing', *Harvard Educational Review*, 47: 257–281.

Olson, D. R. (1994) *The World on Paper: The Conceptual and Cognitive Implications of Writing and Reading*. Cambridge, UK: Cambridge University Press.

Olson, D. R. (2009) 'A theory of writing/reading: From literacy to literature', *Writing Systems Research*, 1: 51–64.

Piaget, J. (1962) *The Psychology of Intelligence*. New York: Routledge.

Reiss, T. J. (1982) *The Discourse of Modernism*. Ithaca, NY: Cornell University Press.

Schlicht, E. (1998). *On Custom in the Economy*. Oxford: Clarendon.

Slouka, M. (2009) 'Dehumanized: when math and science rule the school', *Harper's Magazine*, 319 (1912): 32–40.

Snow, C. and Uccelli, P. (2009) 'The challenge of academic language', in D. R. Olson and N. Torrance (eds.) *The Cambridge Handbook of Literacy*. New York: Cambridge University Press, pp. 112–133.

Spratt, T. (1966[1667]) *History of the Royal Society of London for the Improving of Natural Knowledge*. Ed. J. I. Cope and H. W. Jones. St. Louis: Washington University Press.

Stanovich, K. (2009) *What Intelligence Tests Miss: The Psychology of Rational Thought*. New Haven, CT: Yale University Press.

Tversky, A. and Kahneman, D. (1974) 'Judgment under uncertainty: Heuristics and biases', *Science*, 185: 1124–1131.

Winner, E., Rosenblatt, E., Windmueller, G., Davidson, L., and Garnder, H. (1986) 'Children's perception of "aesthetic" properties of the arts: Domain-specific or pan-artistic?', *British Journal of Developmental Psychology*, 4: 149–160.

43

Discourse and power

Adrian Blackledge

Introduction

Research on discourse and power focuses on the ways in which language is central in constituting and reproducing relations of power that result in forms of inequality. This chapter begins by summarizing some of the key studies in this emergent research tradition, focusing on the development of critical discourse analysis (CDA). I also review critical perspectives on research on discourse and power. The chapter goes on to propose that recent studies have paid detailed attention to interactional patterns of language use, as researchers take ethnographic approaches to analysis of discourse and power. The chapter further considers perspectives that engage with the notion of 'voice'. Data from current research offer exemplification of the concept of 'voice' in a brief episode of interactional speech. Here I finally argue that the analysis of voice offers critical insight into processes of discourse and power in contemporary societies, and that such an analysis has great potential to illuminate objects of investigation across subject territories and disciplines.

Key studies in discourse and power

A relatively recent progression in research on discourse and power has been the development of CDA. As CDA is discussed elsewhere in this volume, I will only briefly summarize these developments. There is no single theory or method that is uniform and consistent throughout CDA (Meyer, 2001; Fairclough, 2003a, b; Weiss and Wodak, 2003). Martin and Wodak (2003) point out that CDA has never been one single specific theory or methodology. Titscher, Meyer, Wodak and Vetter suggest that this plurality is born out of the concern of CDA with the social rather than the purely linguistic:

> CDA is concerned with social problems. It is not concerned with language or language use per se, but with the linguistic character of social and cultural processes and structures.
>
> *(Titscher et al., 2000: 146)*

It is this concern with social life, and with the role of discourse in social life, that is most characteristic of CDA. Fairclough (2003c) points out that CDA developed as a response to the traditional divide between linguistics and areas of social science such as sociology. Van Dijk (2001) presents a harder edge to the claim that CDA is concerned with social problems, representing it as 'discourse analysis with an attitude' (p. 96). In van Dijk's view, CDA emphatically opposes those who abuse text and talk in order to establish, confirm or legitimate their abuse of power: 'CDA does not deny, but explicitly defines and defends its own sociopolitical position. That is, CDA is biased – and proud of it' (p. 96). CDA is fundamentally political in its orientation, interdisciplinary in its scholarship and diverse in its focus. However, there are a number of identifiable characteristics of theoretical positions adopted in CDA research.

First, CDA sees language as social practice. Social life can be seen as networks of diverse social practices, including economic, political, cultural, familial practices and so on. Social practices are more or less stable forms of social activity, which always, or almost always, include discourse. The role of discourse in social practices cannot be taken for granted, but must be established through analysis. Second, CDA takes a particular interest in language and power, and argues that 'the language element' of critical social research has become more salient, more important, and a crucial aspect of making sense of changes and transformations in societies (Fairclough, 2003a: 203). CDA is centrally interested in language and power because it is usually in language that discriminatory practices are enacted, in language that unequal relations of power are constituted and reproduced, and in language that social asymmetries may be challenged and transformed. Third, the shared perspective of approaches to CDA relates to the understanding that language is not powerful on its own, but gains power through the use powerful people make of it. An important perspective in CDA is that a text is rarely the work of any one person, but often shows traces of different discourses contending and struggling for dominance (Weiss and Wodak, 2003: 15). That is, texts relate to other texts, and they relate to the social and historical conditions of their production.

The notion of intertextuality does not suggest that just any voice has equal opportunity to inform authoritative and powerful discourse. To develop an understanding of how the voices of social actors are shaped in the process of their transformation, we turn to the work of Russian theorists Bakhtin and Voloshinov.[1] Bakhtin emphasized the dialogicality of language, in the sense that a text is always aware of, responding to, and anticipating other texts, and also in the sense that discourse is at times 'double-voiced'. In Bakhtin's theory of language as responsive to the social world, discourse is dialogic, shaped and influenced by the discourse of others. For Bakhtin, dialogical relationships are possible not only between entire utterances; the dialogical approach can be applied to any meaningful part of an utterance, even to an individual word, 'if we hear in that word another person's voice' (1973: 152). That is, the way in which speech is constructed is determined by awareness of, and reaction to, the speech of the other. Dialogical relationships can penetrate an utterance, or even an individual word, so long as two voices collide within it. In dialogic discourse more than one voice is evident in a single utterance, shaping and re-shaping the word, so that the author's thought no longer completely dominates, and it responds to the voice of the other. This is a *social* model of language – that is, the relation between the various voices within an utterance is subject to relations of power within society. The authority of the authorial voice is likely to be maintained where it belongs to those in powerful positions in society. Its discourse may nevertheless be double-voiced, where it dismisses or deletes voices that contradict its perspective.

Critical perspectives on discourse and power

A number of criticisms have been made of research on discourse and power, and of CDA in particular. Schegloff (1997) takes the position that text analysts should produce description of texts first, and only then should critical analysis be conducted. Schegloff's concern is that in CDA the researcher can introduce into the analysis pre-ordained categories, which arise from the bias of the researcher rather than from the text itself. Widdowson (1995, 1998, 2000) also warns against the dangers of bias in CDA, as researchers may start from a particular ideological position, then select for analysis only those texts that support this position. Slembrouck (2001) expresses his concern that, far from diminishing unequal relations of power, CDA potentially ignores the voices of those subject to inequalities. By erasing the messiness and complexity of the voices of social actors, CDA potentially offers a view from above rather than from below. Whereas an ethnographic approach represents the perspective of social actors, CDA may limit its gaze to structures of power in society. Blommaert (2005) acknowledges that CDA offers considerable potential in conducting research on discourse and power, but proposes that there are three main problems. First, he argues that CDA is guilty of 'linguistic bias', privileging systemic–functional linguistics over other available means of analysis. Second, Blommaert argues that 'CDA overlooks sociolinguistics' (2005: 36). That is, much of the research hitherto undertaken in CDA is situated in late modern, post-industrial, Western contexts, and has rarely ventured into developing world contexts. Third, there is an absence of historical analysis in CDA. Blommaert argues that a critical analysis of discourse must transcend the present and address the historical. In relation to this third point, though, we might reflect again that there is no *single* CDA. Wodak and her colleagues have developed a 'discourse-historical approach' (Wodak *et al.*, 1999; Reisigl and Wodak, 2001; Martin and Wodak, 2003), which insists that discourse analysis is firmly situated in its historical context.

Current research on discourse and power

In recent times researchers investigating discourse and power have turned to ethnographic approaches. Heller (2008: 250) suggests that doing ethnographic research allows us to tell our story of someone else's experience, 'a story which illuminates social processes and generates explanations for why people do and think the things they do'. Blommaert (2005: 16) suggests that in an ethnographic approach the analysis of small phenomena is set against an analysis of big phenomena, in which 'both levels can only be understood in terms of one another'. Ethnography is discussed elsewhere in this volume. For the purposes of this discussion, however, I will dwell briefly on recent developments in 'linguistic ethnography' and on its potential as a means of understanding discourse and power.

Linguistic ethnography is a theoretical and methodological development orienting towards particular established traditions, but defining itself in the new intellectual climate of late modernity and post-structuralism. Traditions combined in linguistic ethnography include interpretive approaches from anthropology, applied linguistics, cultural studies and sociology. Linguistic ethnography has been shaped by developments in linguistic anthropology in the mid-twentieth century in the US (Rampton *et al.*, 2004; Rampton, 2007; Creese, 2008). Particular strands of linguistic anthropology that have influenced linguistic ethnography are the ethnography of communication (Hymes, 1974, 1980), interactional sociolinguistics (Gumperz, 1982, 1999) and micro ethnography (Erickson, 1990, 1996). Oriented towards these traditions, linguistic ethnography argues that ethnography can benefit from the analytical frameworks provided by linguistics, while linguistics can benefit from the processes of reflexive sensitivity required in ethnography. In linguistic ethnography, linguistics offers an ethnographic analysis of a wide range of established procedures for isolating and identifying linguistic and discursive structures. In linguistic ethnography, ethnographic analysis offers linguistic analysis a non-deterministic perspective on data. Because ethnography looks for uniqueness as well as for patterns in interaction, it 'warns against making hasty comparisons which can blind one to the contingent moments and the complex cultural and semiotic ecologies that give any phenomenon its meaning' (Rampton *et al.*, 2004: 2). A linguistic ethnographic analysis, then, attempts to offer close detail of local action and interaction embedded in a wider social world. It draws on the relatively technical vocabularies of linguistics to do this. Rampton suggests two tenets which underpin the development of linguistic ethnography: (1) 'meaning takes shape within specific social relations, interactional histories and institutional regimes, produced and construed by agents with expectations and repertoires that have to be grasped ethnographically'; and (2) 'meaning is far more than just an "expression of ideas", as biography, identifications, stance and nuance are extensively signalled in the linguistic and textual fine-grain' (2007: 585). It is precisely the linguistic and textual fine-grain of multilingual urban settings to which linguistic ethnography attends.

Like CDA, linguistic ethnography has found Bakhtin's notion of dialogic discourse and his focus on 'voice' to offer a valuable perspective on discourse and power. Bailey (2007: 269) argues that a Bakhtinian perspective 'explicitly bridges the linguistic and the sociohistorical, enriching analysis of human interaction', as it is 'fundamentally about intertextuality, the ways that talk in the here-and-now draws meanings from past instances of talk'. Rampton (2006: 364) adopts Bakhtin's analysis to understand the linguistic practices of students in an inner-city high school, and especially the 'spontaneous moments when these youngsters were artfully reflexive about the dichotomous values that they tacitly reproduced in the variability of their routine speech, moments when they crystallized the high-low structuring principles that were influential but normally much more obscure in their everyday variability'. Lin and Luk (2005: 86) engage with Bakhtin's notion of 'carnival laughter' to understand the creative linguistic practices of English language learners in Hong Kong schools. They demonstrate that students are able to resist the routines of regular classroom practice by populating prescribed utterances with playful, ironic accents.

Linguists have increasingly turned to the works of Bakhtin and Voloshinov because their theories of language enable connections to be made between the voices of social actors in their everyday, here-and-now lives and the political, historical and ideological contexts they inhabit. As we saw in the earlier discussion of CDA, Bakhtin argued that voices relate to other voices by representing within their own utterance the voices of others. In doing so, a voice may be hostile to other voices or may be in complete harmony with them, or it may suppress them, leaving only a suggestion that they are in any way present. Luk (2008: 129) suggests that, according to Bakhtin, 'our speech, that is all our utterances, comes to us already filled with the words of others'. Discourse bears the traces of the voices of others, is shaped by them, responds to them, contradicts them or confirms them, in one way or another evaluates them (Bakhtin, 1981: 272). Bakhtin argued that language is 'historically real, a process of heteroglot development, a process teeming with future and former languages … which are all more or less successful, depending on their degree of social scope and on the ideological area in which they are employed' (Bakhtin, 1981: 357). Rampton (2006: 27) notices in the speech of students in British secondary schools that young people at times break into 'artful performance', when the act of speaking itself is put on display for the scrutiny of an audience. Rampton refers to a particular kind of spoken performance, 'stylization', in which 'accent shifts represent moments of critical reflection on aspects of educational domination and constraint that become interactionally salient on a particular occasion'. That is, in producing an artistic image of another's language (in Rampton's study, 'posh' or 'Cockney' accents), speakers position themselves interactionally in relation to certain ideologies. Bakhtin argued that the importance of struggling with another's discourse, and its influence in the 'individual's coming to consciousness' (1981: 348), are enormous.

In his seminal work *Rabelais and His World* (1968), Bakhtin analysed three arenas of significance in what he called the language of carnival (Bakhtin, 1994: 196): (1) festivities; (2) parody; and (3) the language of the market-place. For Bakhtin, carnivalesque language is full of 'the laughter of all the people' (1994: 200) and includes ritual spectacles, festive pageants, comic shows, parodies, curses and oaths. In medieval Europe, carnival festivities were characterized by comic parodies of serious official, feudal and ecclesiastical ceremonies. Carnival was 'the feast of becoming, change, and renewal' (Bakhtin, 1986: 10). The notions of change and renewal, and of 'becoming', are crucial to Bakhtin's understanding. The festive laughter of carnival is ambivalent, at one and the same time triumphant and mocking, asserting and denying, burying and reviving. Parody was a widespread feature of these festivities. Bakhtin demonstrated that carnivalesque parody was often tolerated by the powerful, as it was no more than a temporary representation of the usurping of traditional hierarchies. Bakhtin pointed out that the language of carnival was the language of degradation, a language that, in its debasement, debased power and was at the centre of all that was unofficial. At once positive and negative, speaking both of decay and renewal, 'the beginning and end of life are closely linked and interwoven' (Bakhtin, 1994: 234), as each image creates a 'contradictory world of becoming' (Bakhtin, 1968: 149).

Approaches to analysing discourse and power

In order to exemplify the potential of Bakhtin's thought for research on discourse and power, in this section I present a small fragment of interactional classroom data. The research reported here is from a comparative sociolinguistic study of complementary ('heritage language', 'community language', 'supplementary') schools in four cities in the UK (ESRC-RES-000-23-1180). These are non-statutory schools, run by their local communities, which students attend in order to learn the language normally associated with their ethnic heritage. The study focused on Gujarati schools in Leicester, Turkish schools in London, Cantonese and Mandarin schools in Manchester and Bengali schools in Birmingham. The children were audio-recorded during the classes observed – in all, we collected 192 hours of audio-recorded interactional data, wrote 168 sets of field notes, made 16 hours of video-recordings, and interviewed 66 key stakeholders, as we investigated how the linguistic practices of students and teachers in these language schools are used to negotiate young people's multilingual and multicultural identities (Creese et al., 2008; Blackledge and Creese, 2010, 2009a, b, 2008). In this chapter I focus on just one key classroom episode, which reveals something of the ways in which the participants' linguistic practices constituted and were constituted by their social, political and historical contexts and extended our understanding of discourse and power in the young people's linguistic (and other semiotic) meaning-making. The classroom activity was recorded in one of the Turkish schools in London.

In this episode the teacher is teaching Turkish through content related to a traditional Mother's Day celebration. The participants are the teacher (T); a student (S1) who wears a digital audio-recorder; and other students (Ss). The episode begins with the teacher dictating to the students the lyrics of a traditional song. S1 is engaged in conversation with other students, inaudible to the teacher.[2]

Example 1

T: başlık yazın annenize başlık. evet yazıyoruz < *write the title. for your mother. yes we are writing*>yazıyoruz annenize <*we are writing to your mother*> bu şarkıyı ben söylicem siz yazıyorsunuz <*I will tell you the lyrics you'll write it*> [some of the students are playing with their mobile phones]

S1: [to a student] yea you dickhead (.) suck my balls man suck my balls suck it no I'm not accepting it suck my balls

T: çocuklar yazdığınızı okuyorum. < *kids, I am reading the lyrics that you were trying to write*> yani anlayacağınız o kadar çok zahmet çekiyor ki kimsenin güleceği yok. Bunu yazdınız mı? <*that is to say that she is toiling away to such an extent that nobody feels like smiling. Have you written this?*>

Ss: yazdık <*yes, we have*>

T: ikinci kıtaya geçiyoruz. <*now we are going to the second verse*>
     [plays music on cd system. some students are talking]

S1: I bet it's a man who's high (.) yani gelin çiçek toplayalım [sings, exaggeratedly imitating the high-pitched voice of the singer] ey he's taken helium he's taken helium the person singing is a man who's taken helium man

T:	dinliyoruz < *we are listening*> [stops the music] Yazmaya devam edeceğiz. <*we will continue writing*>
S1:	[to a student] shut the (.) s-t-f-u (.) you know what s-t-f-u means?
T:	[reading the lyrics of a song] yollarına serelim. Yani gelin çiçek toplayalım. <*let's cover her way with flowers. So let's collect some flowers*> kimin yollarına seriyorlar? <*whose way are they covering with flowers?*>
Ss:	annelerinin <*their mother*>
T:	annelerinin <*their mother*>
S1:	exactly it means shut the fuck up
T:	çok önemli anneler gününde. <*it is very important especially on Mother's Day*>
S1:	[to a student] I am not accepting man
T:	sevgi dolu türkülerle. < *and with songs full of love*> Melis yazıyor musun? annesini sevenler yazıyor. sevgi dolu türkülerle. annemize verelim. <*are you writing Melis? If you love your mother you will write this. And give the flowers to your mother*>
S1:	I don't like my mum (.) I love her
T:	seni annene şikayet edeceğim. <*I will complain to your mother about you*>
S1:	eh fat boy eh the one who sucks your dad's dick eh the one that sucks dick the one that's not gay I want the one that's not gay.

(classroom audio-recording, Turkish school)

The teacher dictates the lyrics of a traditional Turkish song. As he speaks, some of the students continue to use their mobile phones to send songs to each other. S1 uses abusive language to insist on his negotiating position in relation to swopping music files with another student. He is 'not accepting' the file the other student wants to send, and argues this emphatically, in what Bakhtin called the language of the market-place, three times repeating 'suck my balls'. The teacher appears to be unaware of this interaction, or else judiciously ignores it. He continues with the dictation and plays a traditional Turkish song to the class on an audio system. The 'official' activity of the classroom continues, with the complicity of most of the students. S1 immediately takes up the opportunity to ridicule the song, joining in with the singer in a mocking, high-pitched voice. He argues that the voice of the female singer is probably that of a man 'who's taken helium', further ridiculing the song. However, this is double-voiced discourse, as, in order to exaggerate and mock the voice of the singer, he also participates and becomes at least minimally involved in the celebration of Mother's Day. The student on the one hand does what he is supposed to do, while on the other hand he simultaneously makes space for activities more to his liking. The teacher stops the music and tells the class that they will continue writing. S1, denied his opportunity for subversion, again invokes the language of curses and oaths. His discourse appears to be quite literally that of the 'market-place', the language in which to negotiate the swopping of sound files on his mobile phone. S1's language creates a second, unofficial world, a discursive space in which to do business quite unrelated to the official activity of the classroom. At the same time he is able to move between the two floors, at one moment negotiating with oaths and curses that distinguish the discourse of the market-place, and are only for the ears of other students, and in the next re-joining the more public discussion of the Mother's Day celebration. Ironically in the context of the planned activity, the teacher now uses S1's mother as a threat. S1, having made his brief incursion into the official, public world of the classroom, returns to his semi-private space of oaths, curses and degradation, again invoking ribald reference to genitals and sexual activity. This is discourse at the centre of all that is unofficial. It is discourse that, in its grotesque imagery, creates a second life, one that opposes power without opposing it, that undermines the official activity without undermining it. This is the language of the market-place, in its debasement debasing power, if only ephemerally.

The next excerpt is from the same class, recorded two minutes later. Now other students, S2 and S3, become audible. The teacher switches on the music again.

Example 2

T: [switches music on again] dinliyorsunuz. sizde söyleyin dans yapabilirsiniz <*you are listening. you can sing along too, you can dance*>

S1:   hadi <*let's do it*>

S2:   hey dance Turkish style. Turkish style 'düğün' <*wedding ceremony*> [laughs]

S1:   hadi halay çekelim. halay çekelim <*let's do folk dancing.. let's do folk dancing*> do you know how to halay çek? hadi halay çekelim <*do you know how to do folk dancing? let's do folk dancing.*> whoever is doing it with me? Halay çekelim.<*let's do folk dancing*> hey just come, just come, just come man. fuck you. it's gonna be joke. hey, hey [dancing] I know how to do it. AAHH MY PENIS!

S3:   [laughs uncontrollably]

T: [switches music off. wants students in two groups so that they can sing together. switches music on again]

S1:   wait. shush I'm gonna sing [coughs to clear his throat] evet <*right*>

T: söylüyoruz. <*we are singing*>

S1:   hoy Ismet, let's sing. kimsenin güleceği yok kimsenin güleceği yok [singing along to music] LA LA LA LA LA LA LA [exaggerated, loud] yeah. [to a student] give me that ball please. please

[T is singing, some students are singing and clapping]

T: Gökhan dışarı. <*Gokhan get out*> sen dışarı. <*you get out*> Hakan dışarı.. <*Hakan get out*> başkanın yanına gidiyorsunuz. annelerinize söyleyin beni görsün. <*you are to see the principal.. tell your mother to see me*>.

(*classroom audio-recording, Turkish school*)

S1 again seizes an opportunity to subvert the activity, bursting with enthusiasm when the teacher suggests that the students can dance to the traditional music. The second student picks up on S1's intonation and suggests that they should dance 'Turkish style', in the way that would be typical at a Turkish wedding. The Turkish word *halay* refers to a folk dance performed in a circle. Here S2 invokes the wedding, appropriating one traditional ritual (the wedding) in order to mock and subvert another (celebration of Mother's Day). S1 continues in English and Turkish, inviting all to 'just come'. At this point S1 is shouting loudly, while S3 is laughing uncontrollably. Our field notes for this session read as follows: 'The music plays and the boys rap dance, make odd faces and produce funny noises. S2 is now setting the tone in the group of boys. They are imitating folk dance movements'. The students here introduce elements of popular culture ('rap dance'), and at the same time parody traditional folk dance. By both means, hostility to the official, traditional, authorized activity is constituted. It is an act of sameness and difference, based in the traditional, in traditional music, but at the same time creating something new, making change through recontextualization. This is not mere repetition but appropriation, the subversion of ritual by presentation of a new version of the traditional, which creates a momentary suspension of conventional hierarchies. The introduction of 'rap dance' is comic, not least because it is anachronistic – an element of the 'folk-culture' of the people that impinges on the authorized heritage of school activity. The mockery of the traditional dance (odd faces and funny noises) becomes a comic parody of the official discourse. Notwithstanding this, there is again a sense in which the creation of the parody partakes of the activity that the teacher is seeking to create. This is very different from non-participation. It is participation, but on the terms of the students rather than of the teacher. They use the tradition, the heritage, to create their own order, to challenge the existing hierarchy and to claim their freedom, however ephemeral. They populate traditional discourse with their own local social languages and voices for their own purposes (Lin and Luk, 2005: 89). In mocking the dance they mock tradition, but at the same time they mock themselves. This is ambivalent laughter, at once positive and negative, creating a 'contradictory world of becoming' (Bakhtin, 1968: 149). It is as if the students will only participate in the 'heritage' they are offered if they can put their own stamp on it, taking it as their own and usurping it. S1 dances, but ends the dance with a cry of 'AAH MY PENIS!' as reference to the genitals becomes once again the centre of the unofficial world. S1's cry subverts the formality of the dance, but at the same time he mocks himself and, perhaps, all males. This is an inclusive joke, a laugh at the expense of the people, but also with the people. At this point the teacher attempts to organize the students to sing the Mother's Day song. Again taking his cue for subversive action, S1 is quick to take the floor. He clears his throat with a cough which exudes seriousness and respect. Here 'evet' is stylized, adopting the voice of a professional singer, as he prepares to sing. At first he calls on another student (Ismet) to help him with the song, just as he had called on others to help him with the dance. Ismet does not join in, but S1 goes ahead, at first singing the song rather hesitantly, but apparently respectfully. After a few moments he changes tone, singing 'LA LA LA LA LA LA LA' in a comic, grotesque, exaggerated voice, which serves to undermine the activity. It may be that S1 did not know the words of the song very well, and so lost confidence and reverted to the comic. Whatever the reason, there is more than one voice evident here: the voice that attempts to participate in singing the Mother's Day song, and the voice that subverts the celebration and exudes hostility to the authorized heritage. Although some students are engaged in the activity, the teacher breaks off from this to admonish the group of boys who have treated Mother's Day as an opportunity for carnivalesque humour, and dispatches them from the classroom with another threat to involve their mothers.

Rampton (2006: 31) builds on Bakhtin's (1986) notion of 'speech genres' in arguing that, in classrooms as elsewhere, certain roles and relationships, certain patterns of activity come to be expected, but 'generic expectations and actual activity seldom form a perfect match, and the relationship between them is an important focus in political struggle'. In the classroom we investigated there appeared to be more than one set of expectations for the students: the 'official' genre of teacher-directed discourse, and the 'unofficial', carnivalesque genre of the market-place. The discourses of the students parodied 'cultural/heritage' practices. In the complementary schools, while teachers and administrators often believe that teaching 'language' and 'heritage' is a means of reproducing 'national' identity in the next generation, the imposition of such identities is often contested and re-negotiated by the students, as classroom interactions became sites where the students occupied subject positions that were at odds with those imposed by the institutions. In the brief episode examined in this chapter we saw students in the Turkish classroom parody 'heritage' songs associated with a traditional festival and engage in a parodic, mocking version of a traditional Turkish wedding-dance. The students moved between subject positions, or maintained more than one subject position simultaneously, as they both participated in the activity and derided it. The students' discourse became a battleground on which to play out oppositions between the 'heritage' identity imposed by the school and the students' contestation and re-negotiation of such impositions. Their clowning and laughter, hostile to the reified, 'immortalized and completed' (Bakhtin, 1968: 10) version of heritage, created a moment of freedom from the school's imposed ideological position. Contrary to the official world of teaching and learning, the student's grotesque realism was an accepted discourse in the second life in the classroom. At the same time positive and negative, this was a language that was hostile to all that was completed,

Adrian Blackledge

immortalized and official, but a language that generated a world of creativity and laughter in which unofficial business could be transacted. These negotiations are not simply between a 'dominant' and a 'dominated' group. They are altogether more subtle and nuanced interactions, which can be described at the 'micro/macro' dimension, as students and teachers use discourse to move in and out of more and less powerful subject positions.

Future directions in discourse and power

There are many approaches to the study of discourse and power, many of them represented in this volume. In this chapter I argue for an analysis of *voice* because, in Blommaert's words, '[v]oice is the issue that defines linguistic inequality (hence, many other forms of inequality) in contemporary societies' (2005: 5). Analysing voice means analysing the effects of power and the conditions of power. A Bakhtinian analysis enables us to identify how meaning-making emerges as an ongoing dialogic process at a number of different interrelated levels. The voices of the students in the examples here are common: mocking voices, complicit voices, parodic voices, voices that clash with each other and are hostile to each other, voices that represent and recontextualize other voices, voices of oaths, curses and abuses, and voices of what Bakhtin calls the 'bodily lower stratum' (1968: 20). Adopting a theoretical and analytical perspective that combines the ethnographic with the linguistic and engages the dialogic thought of Bakhtin, we are able to tell a story that connects a cacophony of linguistic practice with histories and territories, with traditions and heritages, with pedagogies and ideologies, and with the changing worlds of digital communication and globalization.

Analysis of voice offers an opportunity to take a perspective on language as intrinsically tied to social context. For Bakhtin, the utterance

> is entangled, shot through with shared thoughts, points of view, alien value judgements and accents, weaves in and out of complex interrelationships, merges with some, recoils from others … and having taken meaning and shape at a particular historical moment in a socially specific environment, cannot fail to brush up against thousands of living dialogic threads.
>
> *(Bakhtin, 1981: 276)*

That is, to analyse voice requires us to look not only synchronically, but also diachronically, to look in all directions at once, including to the future and to the past. This is an approach that incorporates intrinsically historical concepts. Terms such as intertextuality, interdiscursivity and entextualization, especially in their rich Bakhtinian interpretation, explain the textual present in relation to textual histories (Blommaert and Huang, 2009). Entextualization refers to 'the process by means of which discourses are successively or simultaneously decontextualised and metadiscursively recontextualised' (Blommaert, 2005: 47). Original bits of discourse are lifted out of their original context and inserted into a new context. In the example from the Turkish classroom, as the traditional wedding-dance is first performed, then parodied, then replaced with a 'rap' dance, and as the traditional song is first performed and then mocked, our analysis looks to the historical space and time of tradition and the homeland; to the globalized popular cultural form; to classroom norms and peer-group expectations; and to family practices. These links are made intertextually – through concepts introduced by Bakhtin, developed in CDA and elaborated upon in an ethnographic approach that takes language as its focus.

It is the interdisciplinary nature of linguistic ethnography that allows us to look closely and locally, while tying our observations to broader relations of power and ideology. Rampton argues that linguistic ethnography is 'a site of encounter where a number of established lines of research interact, pushed together by circumstance, open to the recognition of new affinities, and sufficiently familiar with one another to treat differences with equanimity' (2007: 585). Recent research into linguistic interaction has begun to emphasize the advantages of combining analytical approaches rather than relying on only one approach or framework (Rampton *et al.*, 2002; Zuengler and Mori, 2002). Stubbe *et al.* (2003) also consider the benefits of using different discourse analytic approaches to interpret talk in interaction. They conclude that each approach provides 'a different lens with which to examine the same interaction' (p. 380), noting that different approaches are not necessarily in conflict with each other, but may be used in complementary ways.

Tusting and Maybin (2007: 576) argue that linguistic ethnography, in particular, lends itself to interdisciplinary research and offers a practical and theoretical response to 'the turn to social constructionism and to discourse across the social sciences', in its ability to probe in depth the interrelationship between language and social life. According to Blommaert, the autobiographical–epistemic dimension of ethnography lends itself to interdisciplinary engagement:

> This 'deeper' dimension allows ethnography to be inserted in all kinds of theoretical endeavors, to the extent of course that such endeavors allow for situatedness, dynamics and interpretive approaches. Thus, there is no reason why ethnography cannot be inserted e.g. in a Marxist theoretical framework, nor in a Weberian one, nor in a Bourdieuan or Giddensian one.
>
> *(Blommaert, 2001: 3)*

Tusting and Maybin (2007) argue that in recent years, alongside a broadening and diversifying of interests among sociolinguists, the boundaries between the traditional variationist, sociological and ethnographic branches of sociolinguistics have become more blurred. Rampton (2006: 22) proposes that sociolinguistics should be able to participate in broader debates about the contemporary world, and, since post-structuralist perspectives in social science attach special importance to discourse, sociolinguists may be able to use their specialist expertise to make a distinctive contribution.

In this chapter I have commented on the value of CDA as a means of analysing discourse and power, and I have argued that an ethnographic approach, which takes language as its focus of analysis, also offers a valuable means of understanding language and inequality. These paradigms rarely intersect, being often separated by territorial borders. My argument is that, in taking an approach that places analysis of *voice* at the centre of our investigations of discourse and power, we can see the interactional in the ideological and the ideological in the interactional. This dynamic is always present, of course, but at times we lack the means to make it visible. If CDA potentially ignores the perspective of those subject to inequalities, and ignores the messiness and complexity of the voices of social actors, offering a view from above rather than from below, it is in engaging with *voice* that these perspectives can be heard. And, by the same token, if ethnography potentially misses the historical (Blommaert and Huang, 2009), it is in engaging with *voice* that the threads of history become visible in interaction. I propose that the analysis of voice may enable us to take at least a tentative step forward in the analysis of discourse and power.

Further reading

Blackledge, A. and Creese, A. (2010) *Multilingualism: A Critical Perspective*. London: Continuum Books.
Blommaert, J. (2010) *The Sociolinguistics of Globalization*. Cambridge, Cambridge University Press.
Pennycook, A. (2010) *Language as a Local Practice*. London, Routledge.

Notes

1 Some scholars have suggested that the works of Voloshinov were in fact written by Bakhtin. Others disagree. In the absence of irrefutable evidence either way, I am adopting the usual convention of citing Voloshinov's works separately.

2 Transcription conventions followed in this chapter are as follows:

Plain font: original speech

Italicized font: translated speech

[brackets]: comment or 'stage directions'.

References

Bailey, B. (2007) 'Heteroglossia and boundaries', in M. Heller (ed.) *Bilingualism: A Social Approach.* Basingstoke: Palgrave, pp. 257–276.
Bakhtin, M. M. (1968) *Rabelais and His World,* trans. H. Iswolsky. Indiana: Indiana University Press.
Bakhtin, M. M. (1973) *Problems of Dostoevsky's Poetics,* trans. R. W. Rotsel. Ann Arbor, MI: Ardis.
Bakhtin, M. M. (1981) *The Dialogic Imagination: Four Essays,* ed. Michael Holquist, trans. C. Emerson and M. Holquist. Austin, TX: University of Texas Press.
Bakhtin, M. M. (1986) *Speech Genres and Other Late Essays,* ed. C. Emerson and M. Holquist. Austin, TX: University of Austin Press.
Bakhtin, M. M. (1994) 'Problems of Dostoevsky's poetics', in P. Morris (ed.) *The Bakhtin Reader: Selected Writings of Bakhtin, Medvedev, Voloshinov.* London: Arnold, pp. 110–113.
Blackledge, A. and Creese, A. (2008) 'Contesting "language" as "heritage": negotiation of identities in late modernity', *Applied Linguistics,* 29 (4): 533–554.
Blackledge, A. and Creese, A. (2009a) 'Meaning-making as dialogic process: official and carnival lives in the language classroom', *Journal of Language, Identity, and Education,* 8 (4): 236–253.
Blackledge, A. and Creese, A. (2009b) ' "*Because tumi Bangali*": inventing and disinventing the national in multilingual communities in UK', *Ethnicities,* 9 (4): 451–476.
Blackledge, A. and Creese, A. (2010) *Multilingualism: A Critical Perspective.* London: Continuum Books.
Blommaert, J. (2001) Reflections from overseas guests. Linguistic ethnography in the UK. A BAAL/CUP seminar. University of Leicester 28–29 March 2001. Available online at: http://www.lancs.ac.uk/fss/organisations/lingethn/leicesteroverseasreflections.rtf (accessed 23 April 2010).
Blommaert, J. (2005) *Discourse: A Critical Introduction.* Cambridge: Cambridge University Press.
Blommaert, J. and Huang, A. (2009) 'Historical bodies and historical space', *Journal of Applied Linguistics,* 6(3): 267–282.
Creese, A. (2008) 'Linguistic ethnography', in K. A. King and N. H. Hornberger (eds.) *Encyclopedia of Language and Education. Second Edition. Volume 10: Research Methods in Language and Education.* New York: Springer Science+Business Media LLC, pp. 229–241.
Creese, A., Baraç, T., Bhatt, A., Blackledge, A., Hamid, S., Wei, Li., Lytra, V., Martin, P., Wu, C.-J., and Yağcıoğlu-Ali, D. (2008) *Investigating Multilingualism in Complementary Schools in Four Communities.* Final Report. RES-000-23-1180. Birmingham: University of Birmingham.
Erickson, F. (1990) 'Qualitative methods', in R. L. Linn and F. Erickson (eds.) *Research in Teaching and Learning.* Volume 2. New York: MacMillan Publishing Company, pp. 77–195.
Erickson, F. (1996) 'Ethnographic microanalysis', in S. L. McKay and N. H. Hornberger (eds.) *Sociolinguistics and Language Teaching.* New York: Cambridge University Press, pp. 283–306.
Fairclough, N. (2003a) *Analysing Discourse: Textual Analysis for Social Research.* London: Routledge.
Fairclough, N. (2003b) 'The dialectics of discourse', *Textus,* 14 (2): 231–242.
Fairclough, N. (2003c) 'Semiotic aspects of social transformation and learning', in R. Rogers (ed.) *An Introduction to Critical Discourse Analysis in Education.* Mahwah, NJ: Lawrence Erlbaum, pp. 225–236.
Gumperz, J. (1982) *Discourse Strategies.* Cambridge: Cambridge University Press.
Gumperz, J. J. (1999) 'On interactional sociolinguistic method', in S. Sarangi and C. Roberts (eds.) *Talk, Work and Institutional Order.* Berlin: Mouton de Gruyter. pp. 453–471.
Heller, M. (2008) 'Doing ethnography', in W. Li and M. Moyer (eds.) *The Blackwell Guide to Research Methods in Bilingualism and Multilingualism.* Oxford: Blackwell, pp. 249–262.
Hymes, D. (1974) *Foundations in Sociolinguistics: An Ethnographic Approach.* Philadelphia, PA: University of Pennsylvania Press.
Hymes, D. (1980) *Language in Education: Ethnolinguistic Essays.* Washington, DC: Center for Applied Linguistics.
Lin, A. M. Y. and Luk, J. C. M. (2005) 'Local creativity in the face of global domination: insights of Bakhtin for teaching English for dialogic communication', in J. K. Hall, G. Vitanova, and L. Marchenkova (eds.)

Dialogue with Bakhtin on Second and Foreign Language Learning: New Perspectives. Mahwah, NJ: Lawrence Erlbaum, pp. 77–88.

Luk, J. C. M. (2008) 'Classroom discourse and identities', *Encyclopedia of Language and Education. Second Edition. Volume 3: Discourse and Education*. New York: Springer Science+Business Media LLC, pp. 121–134.

Martin, J. and Wodak, R. (2003) 'Introduction', in J. Martin and R. Wodak (eds.) *Re/reading the Past: Critical and Functional Perspectives on Time and Value*. Amsterdam: John Benjamins, pp. 1–18.

Meyer, M. (2001) 'Between theory, method, and politics: positioning of the approaches to CDA', in R. Wodak and M. Meyer (eds.) *Methods of Critical Discourse Analysis*. London: Sage, pp. 14–31.

Rampton, B. (2006) *Language in Late Modernity*. Cambridge: Cambridge University Press.

Rampton, B. (2007) 'Neo-Hymesian linguistic ethnography in the United Kingdom', *Journal of Sociolinguistics*, 11 (5): 584–607.

Rampton, B., Tusting, K., Maybin, J., Barwell, R., Creese, A., and Lytra, V. (2004) *UK Linguistic Ethnography*, A discussion paper. Available online at: www.ling-ethnog.org.uk (accessed 23 April 2010).

Reisigl, M. and Wodak, R. (2001) *Discourse and Discrimination: Rhetorics of Racism and Antisemitism*. London: Routledge.

Schegloff, E. (1997) 'Whose text? whose context?', *Discourse and Society*, 8 (2): 165–187.

Slembrouck, S. (2001) 'Explanation, interpretation and critique in the analysis of discourse', *Critique of Athropology*, 21: 33–57.

Stubbe, M., Lane, C., Hilder, J., Vine, E., Vine, B., Marra, M., Holmes, J., and Weatherall, A. (2003) 'Multiple discourse analyses of a workplace interaction', *Discourse Studies*, 5 (3): 351–388.

Titscher, S., Meyer, M., Wodak, R., and Vetter, E. (2000) *Methods of Text and Discourse Analysis*. London: Sage.

Tusting, K. and Maybin, J. (2007) 'Linguistic ethnography and interdisciplinarity: opening the discussion', *Journal of Sociolinguistics*, 11 (5): 575–583.

van Dijk, T. A. (2001) 'Multidisciplinarity CDA: a plea for diversity', in R. Wodak and M. Meyer (eds.) *Methods of Critical Discourse Analysis*. London: Sage, pp. 95–120.

Weiss, G. and Wodak, R. (2003) 'Introduction', in G. Weiss and R. Wodak (eds.) *Theory, Interdisciplinarity and Critical Discourse Analysis*. London: Palgrave, pp. 1–34.

Widdowson, H. (1995) 'Discourse analysis: a critical view', *Language and Literature*, 4 (3): 157–172.

Widdowson, H. (1998) 'The theory and practice of critical discourse analysis', *Applied Linguistics*, 19 (1): 136–151.

Widdowson, H. (2000) 'Critical practices: on representation and the interpretation of text', in G. Weiss and R. Wodak (eds.) *Theory, Interdisciplinarity and Critical Discourse Analysis*. London: Palgrave, pp. 155–169.

Wodak, R., de Cillia, R., Reisigl, M., and Liebhart, K. (1999) *The Discursive Construction of National Identity*. Edinburgh: Edinburgh University Press.

Zuengler, J. and Mori, J. (2002) 'Microanalyses of classroom discourse: a critical consideration of method', *Applied Linguistics*, 23 (3): 283–288.

44
Literary discourse

Peter K. W. Tan

Is there such a thing as literary language?

One of the difficulties in trying to discuss literary discourse is that it is in dispute whether there is such a thing as a form of discourse that is *intrinsically* literary in nature. This is not to say that the notion of literary language in itself is denied. What is in contention is whether literariness resides in the language or whether it is a function of something outside the language such as the readers, their expectations or the cultural norms of the time. There is, for the moment, no agreed position on this, and in this section it might be worth our while to consider the various positions that we could take.

One popular notion is that language and, in particular, words can have literary qualities. Dictionaries conventionally label particular words as being *literary*. Here is the second edition of the *Oxford English Dictionary* (1989):

> the English vocabulary contains a nucleus or central mass of many thousand words whose 'Anglicity' is unquestioned; some of them only literary, some of them only colloquial, the great majority at once literary and colloquial – they are the *common words* of the language.

And, in diagrammatic representation (see Figure 44.1), the *literary* is still within the common core.

The label therefore finds its way into various dictionaries together with various other register labels such as *technical, formal* or *humorous*. The *Longman Dictionary of Contemporary English*, for example, labels words like *anew* and *asunder* as 'literary'. We also find discussions about items of English vocabulary based on their source:

> The simultaneous borrowing of French and Latin words led to a highly distinctive feature of modern English vocabulary .... The Old English word ... [e.g. *kingly, ask*] is the most colloquial, the French ... [e.g. *royal, question*] is the more *literary*, and the Latin word ... [e.g. *regal, interrogate*] more learned.
>
> *(Jackson and Amvela 2000: 35, my emphasis)*

Probably a couple of things need to be said: literariness appears to be a gradable feature – in that a comparative form (*more* literary) is available rather than a distinctive one. The other is that the feature of literariness is not clearly defined. Ikegami (2005), who examined these labels in dictionaries, concluded that '"literary" tends to be a highly uncertain label throughout'.

It might be worthwhile then to consider a well-known account of this (gradable) literariness, given by Jakobson – although his label is the 'poetic function'. In this, Jakobson shared the views of the group known as 'the Russian formalists', who held that art, including literary works, should draw attention to itself: in other words, readers should look *at* the text rather than look *through* the

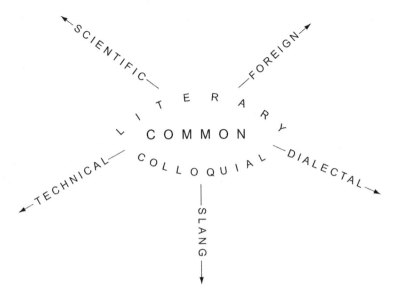

Figure 44.1 English vocabulary, according to the *Oxford English Dictionary*

text. In his well-known essay 'Linguistics and poetics' (1960), he describes six functions of language, but he maintains that verbal messages are diverse not because they take on different functions but because they assign different hierarchical orders of function. The poetic function of language is said to be in operation when there is 'focus on the message for its own sake' and forms the 'dominant, determining function' in verbal art (Jakobson, 2000 [1960]: 337). This is expressed in a more complex fashion when Jakobson says:

> *The poetic function projects the principle of equivalence from the axis of selection into the axis of combination.*
> (p. 339, original italics)

This simply means that, in 'normal' discourse, the discourse producer makes choices between similar or roughly equivalent items; whereas in verbal art these are put together so that there is evidence of additional patterning there.

For example, in employing a word or a phrase, the user normally has to make the choice of a particular sense of the word or phrase. Yet in literary discourse ambiguity or multiple meanings might be desirable. Here is the beginning of Act 3, Scene 1 of *Romeo and Juliet*, where Tybalt (from Juliet's clan of the Capulets) confronts Mercutio (from Romeo's clan of the Montagues), their two clans being rivals.

TYBALT: Gentlemen, good den [= good evening]: a word with one of you.

MERCUTIO: And but one word with one of us? couple it with something; make it a word and a blow.

TYBALT: You shall find me apt enough to that, sir, an [= if] you will give me occasion.

MERCUTIO: Could you not take some occasion without giving?

TYBALT: Mercutio, thou consort'st with Romeo, –

MERCUTIO: Consort! what, dost thou make us minstrels? An thou make minstrels of us, look to hear nothing but discords: here's my fiddlestick; here's that shall make you dance. 'Zounds, consort!

Peter K. W. Tan

Mercutio deliberately ignores the idiomatic phrases said by Tybalt. He deliberately chooses not to accord 'a word' its conventional sense, 'a short conversation', but takes in its literal sense. He chooses not to understand 'to give occasion' to mean 'provide a reason' but 'unbleaches' the meaning of *give* from the expression. (I use 'unbleaching' to mean restoring the full meaning to the word.) He also chooses not to focus on the sense of 'consort' to mean 'to accompany', but instead focuses on the sense 'a musical group' and therefore refers to minstrels, discords, fiddlesticks and dancing. This kind of talk draws attention to itself as talk and is surely an instance where Jakobson's poetic function is dominant. Obviously, the patterning could be at different linguistic levels, not just the semantic or the lexical. There could be patterning at the level of orthography, phonology, morphology or syntax. The fact that the text is from an avowed literary work that is part of the canon of English literature might cause us not to be surprised at its presence here.

The question that arises is how this is different from what David Crystal's (1998) example of a conversation between two couples where the coinage *cat*-frontation (a confrontation involving a cat) was followed by a comment about how the event was to have been a *cat*-astrophe, a *cat*-alyst for something and so on. This, together with instances of punning and word play, he describes as fulfilling the ludic function of language; this is roughly what Sherzer (2002) calls speech play. The answer to that question must be that the poetic function is as much in operation and dominant in spontaneous word play as in the *Romeo and Juliet* extract, and both could in fact be labelled 'literary' – although the spontaneous word play could be called 'literature with a small "l"' (McRae, 1994).

Some empirical work done on readers (e.g. Miall and Kuiken, 1999) suggests that a model of literariness needs to continue to include the notion of foregrounded textual or narrative features. The term 'foregrounding' is of course borrowed from visual art and applied to verbal art to refer to all that is thrust into prominence for the reader or the audience. This is also in line with the poetics of the Russian formalists mentioned earlier, in that literary discourse is seen as that which disorientates through manipulating the language, and by doing so it gives prominence to Jakobson's poetic function.

These approaches continue to emphasize the textual distinctiveness of literary discourse. This needs to be balanced with the view that the distinctiveness is not of the text or of the language. Particular texts are elevated to literary status as a result of the social conditions in which they were produced or received.

> In this view there is nothing distinctive about either the language of literary discourse or its representations of the world; it is rather that some texts become literary when presented as such by institutions or when read in certain ways by readers, and that is all. Which texts these are will thus always be relative to a specific social milieu.
>
> *(Cook, 1994: 1)*

A well-known and prominent proponent of this view is the American literary critic Stanley Fish. His book *Is There a Text in This Class?* (1980) launched the interest in reader–orientated research and the notion of the interpretive community. His essay 'How to recognize a poem when you see one' best illustrates his point. In it he describes how he tells his class that a series of names on the blackboard (which was actually the reading list from the previous class) was a poem to be interpreted. The students, well armed with a familiarity with Christian symbolism and biblical allusions, gamely pulled apart the names and interpreted their 'message'. So what was originally a reading list can be treated like a 'found poem' (*un poème trouvé*).

> Skilled reading is usually thought to be a matter of discerning what is there, but if the example of my students can be generalized, it is a matter of knowing how to *produce* what can

thereafter be said to be there. Interpretation is not the art of construing but the art of constructing. Interpreters do not decode poems; they make them.

(Fish, 1980: 327, original italics)

It therefore follows that the acceptability of any interpretation is not dependent on textual support, but on the status accorded to the interpreters by the community. As the community is bounded by space and time, there can be no universal meaning for all time. If that is the case, the notion of literary discourse is like a will o' the wisp.

It will probably be possible to manoeuvre around the more entrenched positions taken up and we might want to consider whether those positions are only supported by the 'literary' texts that are less prototypical in nature.

How is the discourse situation different in literary texts?

Another way to consider literary discourse is to examine it from the point of view of fictionality. Literary discourse has been characterized by the use of 'duplicitous' communication. For example, from early on Widdowson (1975, 1992) has pointed out that, when one reads poetry, the pronoun system must be understood to behave differently from what it does in non-literary systems. Poetry readers have long known not to equate the 'I' in the poem with the author and will have been trained to talk about the *persona* (the word originally means 'mask') of the poem. In prose, outside of reported speech, the 'I' is also not to be identified with the author: this is the *narrator*.

Short (1996) also points out that communication in dramatic texts is marked out by the presence of multiple discourse layers, as illustrated in Figure 44.2. The author has normally no way of communicating directly with the reader or the audience except indirectly, through the mediation of the characters. The Shakespearian term is the *dramatis personae*: the masks of the drama. The only occasion when the author might be able to communicate directly, in a manner of speaking, is through the use of the chorus in Greek plays (the device is also employed in Shakespeare). There are at least two levels of discourse and it might be necessary to include more for play-within-a-play situations (Figure 44.3).

Literary texts cannot be taken at face value, because the reliability of the character, persona or narrator can be held in question. Some literary works continue to be unresolved in their interpretation because of this question of reliability. A notable example is Henry James's novella *The Turn of the Screw*: did the governess really see ghosts, or was the narrator neurotic, or something else? Cook (1994) calls this the hearsay principle: because communication is indirect, there must always be consciousness that distortion is possible.

The layered and embedded nature of literary discourse also opens up the possibility of other worlds that partly resemble the world as known by the reader, to a greater or lesser extent. The concept of 'possible worlds' is one that continues to attract the attention of philosophers and

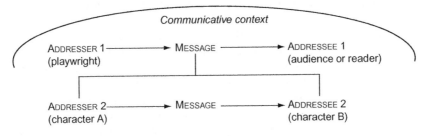

Figure 44.2 The dramatic communicative situation
Source: from Short 1996: 169

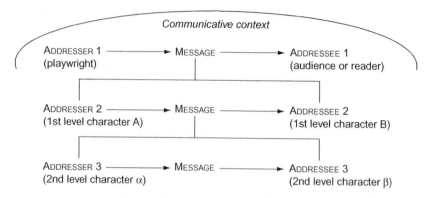

Figure 44.3 The play-with-a-play situation

semanticists. This concept is clearly exploited in genres such as science fiction or fantasy. We accept the possibility of the alternative magical world of witches, wizards and other creatures existing alongside the Muggle (human) world in the Harry Potter books.

An early response to fictionality in speech act terms came from one of the main proponents of speech act theory, John Searle. The account that is given in a novel, for instance, would seem to fit into one of his five categories of speech acts: representative or assertive, whose function is to represent a state of affairs in the world. In Searle's terms, this category has a word-to-world fit; in other words, the language maps onto a pre-existing state of affairs in the world. To describe a journalist's account as an assertive would seem to be unproblematic, but to describe a novelist's account as such would certainly be highly problematic. Searle's (1975) solution is the describe fiction as the author's pretence at performing speech acts: the author only makes a pretence at asserting, promising, and so on. For him/her, the vertical relationship between the language and the world are cancelled, and this is replaced by horizontal rules. (This particular conception bears some resemblance to Short's representation above.)

Many have been dissatisfied with an account of fictionality in literary texts that is based on pretence:

> the author is performing a genuine communicative act that is not merely the pretense of some other act, assertive or otherwise. … At best the pretense theory is incomplete. The author of fiction must be doing something more than merely pretending to assert.
>
> *(Currie 1990: 13, 18)*

Currie suggests instead that a different kind of act is being performed, perhaps something akin to make-believe: 'make-believe allows us to achieve in imagination what we are denied in reality' (p. 19). Currie uses the phrase 'fictive communication' and describes what an author produces as fictive utterances.

A seminal account of how a literary work should be regarded as performing its own speech act is the one by Mary Louise Pratt (1977). Her work develops the notion of the literary text as being an extended 'display' text. For a successful rendition, it must demonstrate the key feature of *tellability* (borrowed from Labov's (1972) account of oral narratives), which would be seen as an appropriateness condition (or felicity condition) of performing this speech act. A tellable story is simply one that is worth telling, with sufficient interesting parts, in a style that is engaging. Readers do not expect to have their time wasted on a pointless or badly written story! She also argued that literary texts were *detachable* from the immediate context, and in this manner she confirms what was mentioned earlier in this section.

The concern about the distinctive nature of the author-to-audience communication, with it particular functions and constraints, eventually gave rise to what Roger Sell calls *literary pragmatics* (e.g. Sell, 1991): his particular focus was on the politeness pragmatics of literary communication. More broadly speaking, we could ask how general pragmatic constraints that apply to ordinary communication expressed in terms of Grice's cooperative principle (CP) or in terms of politeness or face constraints could be applied to literary communication. There is clearly an expectation for authors to be sensitive to their audience and that the literary text will be in an appropriate style and contain sufficient information for interpretation; in other words, authors are expected to demonstrate some level of cooperation (in Grice's sense) and politeness. Where there are deviations, we could expect these to be instances of *flouting* rather than *violation* of maxims. (Flouting refers to the deliberate and open breaking of the maxims of the CP, whereas violation refers to their surreptitious and misleading breach.)

When Muriel Spark disrupts the chronology of the narrative in *The Prime of Miss Jean Brodie* (1961) by frequently resorting to prolepsis, when future events are included sporadically in the novel, we assume that this is a case of the flouting of the maxim of manner, and we consider the effects intended (see for example Bridgeman 2005).

In the case of detective fiction or whodunits, it is almost standardly the case that a crucial bit of information – the identity of the murderer – is omitted and only revealed at the end, and therefore the natural order is disrupted. So it is that, in Agatha Christie's *The Murder of Roger Ackroyd* (1926), the narrator, Dr James Sheppard, does not reveal that he is indeed the murderer until the last chapter, which constitutes his suicide note. In such a case, this omission of information is expected, as it characterizes the genre, and it might be more helpful to consider this not a case of *flouting* but of which Jenny Thomas (1995) calls the *suspension* of a maxim. A suspension comes into effect, according to Thomas, when special cultural circumstances or genres prescribe a norm that is different from the prevailing norm of cooperation. In the case of detective fiction, some aspects of the maxims of quantity (providing the right amount of information) and manner (providing the information at the appropriate time) are suspended. It might be worth considering how literary texts and genres of literary texts might suspend particular maxims. For example, ambiguity is sometimes prized in literary texts rather than seen as a problem. It might be worth considering the ambiguous nature of *The Turn of the Screw* (mentioned above) a case of maxim suspension as well.

Do the different literary genres require different approaches?

In order to answer this question, I would like to invite us to consider the discourse levels mentioned above. If we consider the topmost level of discourse and the features of literary communication, we could be reasonably comfortable about pointing out features that are special to literary texts. However, there are features of literary texts that seem to be derived from other texts. One of the most important features of literary texts is that it borrows, manipulates or transforms other kinds of discourse. One way it does this is by quoting or alluding to some other text, a phenomenon usually referred to as *intertextuality*, so that 'literature is nothing but a re-writing or recycling of other texts, and has of necessity to be parasitic' (Broich, 1997: 252). However, literary texts can be considered parasitic in the way in which they make use of, or redeploy, other kinds of discourse – the most notable among them being conversation in its widest sense. It is of course not only literary discourse that can be parasitic; advertisements can take on features of conversations, or news articles and recipes can include characteristics of a travelogue. Texts were said to contain *residual register features* of other texts (the expression is from Ellis and Ure, 1976).

As mentioned above, the conversation was the most common genre that was reproduced in literary texts, notably in drama and novels, but it is not infrequent in poetry. In fact the representation of conversational dialogue is an area that has generated much interest, and in particular the use of the *free indirect speech* is said to be prevalent in novels. Known in French as *discours indirect libre*, this was said to characterize the novels of Flaubert in the nineteenth century. And in England 'Jane Austen is generally acknowledged to be the first English novelist to make sustained use of free indirect discourse in the representation of figural speech and thought' (Gunn, 2004: 35). Here is an extract from Chapter 22 of *Northanger Abbey* that illustrates its use.

> And when they had gone over the house, he promised himself moreover the pleasure of accompanying her into the shrubberies and garden. She curtsied her acquiescence. 'But perhaps it might be more agreeable to her to make those her first object. The weather was at present favourable, and at this time of year the uncertainty was very great of its continuing so. Which would she prefer? He was equally at her service. Which did his daughter think would most accord with her fair friend's wishes? But he thought he could discern. Yes, he certainly read in Miss Morland's eyes a judicious desire of making use of the present smiling weather. But when did she judge amiss? The abbey would be always safe and dry. He yielded implicitly, and would fetch his hat and attend them in a moment. [He left the room.]

General Tilney is represented as speaking to Catherine Morland here, but his speech is in free indirect speech in that the original first and second personal pronouns have been turned into third-person pronouns ('he promised himself ... the pleasure of accompanying her' as opposed to 'I promised myself ... the pleasure of accompanying you'). But this is not indirect speech, because the interrogative form is left intact ('Which would she prefer?' rather than 'He wondered which she would prefer').

The use of free indirect speech becomes significant in the light of other available choices: free direct speech, direct speech, indirect (or reported) speech. Against the norm of direct speech, the use of free indirect speech creates a distancing effect and positions General Tilney, the speaker here, further away from the reader.

Speech and thought presentation have also become the subject of a number of corpus studies with the setting up of the Lancaster Speech, Writing and Thought Presentation (SW&TP2) Spoken Corpus. (See, for example, McIntyre, 2004.) It is also an important component in the investigation into point of view or perspective in literature.

When conversations are represented in literary texts, we would also generally not expect them to be exactly like real-life conversations. There are of course different tolerances for the gulf between them and this depends on the author's perspective on realism, in particular mimetic realism. Even if the author had a good ear for dialogue and wanted to represent it faithfully, the constraints of tellability (the need to render something interesting and worth listening to, as mentioned above) might mean that the tedious repetitions, false starts and reformulations that characterize spontaneous conversations will not be fully represented in literary conversations. The constructed nature of literary conversations, which undergoes several rounds of editing, will also cause it to be different from unplanned speech. It would not be surprising to expect literary conversations to be neater and to fulfil Grice's conversational maxims more fully than real-life conversations.

Carter and McCarthy (2006) note the following features in their extract of everyday informal conversation:

1. Sentences can be difficult to identify
2. There are many short units of communication
3. The minimal unit of communication is the tone unit
4. Turns can be untidy

5. Back-channelling behaviour (*mm, yes*) is normal
6. There are abandoned or incomplete structures
7. References (e.g. pronouns like *he*) are not explicit
8. Subordinate clauses might be unconnected to main clauses
9. Structures can be difficult to label
10. Ellipsis is common
11. Some words have uncertain status: they could be discourse markers or interjections
12. The grammar can share many features of written English (pp. 165–167).

In poetry, the dramatic monologue is a form that is derived from conversation, although usually only the speech from one party in the conversation is represented. The most well known, arguably, is Browning's 'My Last Duchess'. Here is a portion of the poem.

She thanked men, – good! but thanked	1
Somehow – I know not how – as if she ranked	2
My gift of a nine-hundred-years-old name	3
With anybody's gift. Who'd stoop to blame	4
This sort of trifling? Even had you skill	5
In speech – (which I have not) – to make your will	6
Quite clear to such an one, and say, 'Just this	7
Or that in you disgusts me; here you miss,	8
Or there exceed the mark' – and if she let	9
Herself be lessoned so, nor plainly set	10
Her wits to yours, forsooth, and made excuse,	11
– E'en then would be some stooping; and I choose	12
Never to stoop. Oh sir, she smiled, no doubt,	13
Whene'er I passed her; but who passed without	14
Much the same smile? This grew; I gave commands;	15
Then all smiles stopped together. There she stands	16
As if alive. Will't please you rise? We'll meet	17
The company below, then.	18

The poem successfully imitates the style of someone talking, and it does this through the use of short, loosely connected clauses (points 2 and 3 above). There is some ellipsis (point 10: [*that is*] *good!*, line 1), and there is an exclamation (point 11: *Oh*, line 13; perhaps also *good!*, line 1). However, the sentence structures are clear and complete: there are no abandoned or incomplete structures. In addition to this, we might also notice features associated with poetry: there is a pattern of rhyming couplets (*thanked/ranked, name/blame* etc.).

We might also note the use the flouting of conversational maxims, designed to generate implicatures (roughly: what is suggested in an utterance rather than said explicitly). For example, the Duke says, 'Who'd stoop to blame/This sort of trifling?' (lines 4–5). This is literally a question. Such a question would, however, seem irrelevant in the context, and we could assume that it *flouts* the relevance maxim to generate at least two implicatures: (a) nobody in these circumstances would deign to lower himself to reprimand the Duchess; and (b) he himself did not stoop to blame her. (This would, of course, be a 'rhetorical question' in traditional terminology.)

We might also notice, similarly, that the Duke seems to give incomplete information later: 'I gave commands;/Then all smiles stopped together' (lines 15–16). *What* did he command? *Why* did the smiles stop? These break the quantity maxim relating to the amount of information. One interpretation is that he ordered his wife to be killed; another is that all his strictures caused her to sicken and die. Nothing is explicitly said. Is the implicature to threaten the hearer (an emissary of his prospective new wife)?

The poem therefore exploits the features of conversation so that we are able to have some access to the character of the Duke from a close perspective.

Browning does not use all the features of conversation, and it is possible to include more, as in some modernist works like T. S. Eliot's *The Wasteland*.

> When Lil's husband got demobbed, I said –
> I didn't mince my words, I said to her myself,
> HURRY UP PLEASE IT'S TIME
> Now Albert's coming back, make yourself a bit smart.
> He'll want to know what you done with the money he gave you
> To get yourself some teeth. He did, I was there …

(T. S. Eliot, The Wasteland III)

Here we see the use of colloquialism (*demobbed* rather than *demobilized*), non-standardism (*what you done* with the money rather than *what you did* with the money) and interruption (HURRY UP PLEASE IT'S TIME).

Apart from informal conversation, literary texts can also be parasitic upon discourses such as institutional discourses, including doctor–patient discourse – as in the play *Equus*:

> *Nurse goes out and back to her place. Dysart sits, opening a file.*
> DYSART So did you have a good journey? I hope they gave you lunch at least. Not that there's much to choose between a British Rail meal and one here.
> *Alan stands staring at him.*
> DYSART Won't you sit down?
> *Pause. He does not. Dysart consults his file.*
> Is this your full name? Alan Strang?
> *Silence.*
> And you're seventeen. Is that right? Seventeen? … Well?
> ALAN (*singing low*) Double your pleasure
> Double your fun
> With Doublemint, Doublemint
> Doublemint gum.
> DYSART (*unperturbed*) Now, let's see. You work in an electrical shop during the week.
> You live with your parents, and your father's a printer. What sort of things does he print?
> ALAN (*singing louder*) Double your pleasure
> Double your fun
> With Doublemint, Doublemint
> Doublemint gum.

(Peter Shaffer, Equus, Act 1, Scene 3: pp. 5–6)

In this extract, the play is doubly parasitic in that it not only employs doctor–patient discourse, with its use of a question-and-answer sequence, but it also includes an advertising jingle, and the incongruous juxtaposition should cause us to interpret the extract more carefully.

This parasitic relationship between literary texts and other kinds of discourse means that it is possible to discuss general linguistic and pragmatic phenomena through examining literary texts: for example, Rudanko (2006) examines the phenomenon of impoliteness through examining Shakespeare. Literary texts have also been used for a long time to teach the language.

It is appropriate now to return to the original question. Different literary texts are parasitic on different kinds of discourses: this should be clear from our examination of Austen, Browning, Eliot and Shaffer. The discourse methods for analysing these discourses, which the literary text exploit, must be the ones that can be used as well. It must therefore follow that there cannot be a standard, single method of analysing different literary texts. Much depends on the lower levels of discourse. If there is much dialogue involved, it might make sense to examine dialogue structure and ask questions like 'Who initiates the exchanges?' or 'Are supportive responses given?'. If, however, there is a long soliloquy or confessional, examining dialogue structure is less likely to be helpful.

We also noted features of the discourse that could be attributed to the topmost level of discourse (i.e. to the author rather than narrator, persona or character) – features such as the use of rhyme in 'My Last Duchess'. These would be non-parasitic elements of literary discourse and discussion about these elements has been developed within literary criticism: we can think about metre and rhyme in poetry; characterization, plot and setting in prose and drama.

What work in discourse analysis is useful for analysing literary discourse?

Almost the whole gamut of approaches used in discourse analysis can potentially be appropriated for analysing literary discourse. A lot of the discussion about literary discourse that examines the language with some degree of rigour comes under the rubric of stylistics. (Initially, the label 'literary stylistics' was also used for contrast with the study of style in non-literary texts.) Stylistics is sometimes seen as an approach within discourse analysis, although what really happens is that stylistics employs a range of approaches, including (but not restricted to) those in discourse analysis.

The work on functional grammar, especially the systemic functional grammar as developed by Michael Halliday and continued by Jim Martin and others, remains significant. A functional grammar has been seen to be useful because in this model form is related to function and meaning. One of the earliest landmark works has been Halliday's (1971) analysis of Golding's *The Inheritors*, which focuses on the different transitivity choices made by the Neanderthals and the humans. This also opens an important entry to the discussion of point of view. Functional grammar continues to be an important framework for analysing prose in particular, and a lot of textbooks on stylistics in the 1990s devote a lot of attention to the use of systemic functional grammar for analysis, for example that by Toolan (1998).

The work on the ethnography of communication, with its emphasis on norms within speech communities establishing the culture, is also significant in turning the attention of literary scholars to the production and reception of literary texts. Sell's (1991) literary pragmatics has clear links to this. Indeed, the initial, gut reaction, inherited from new criticism, to trust only the text has largely been abandoned, and aspects of the conditions under which literary texts are published are readily incorporated, as in Cooper's (1998) discussion of whether the ending of *The Taming of the Shrew* is ironic or not.

The Birmingham school of discourse analysis, a development from systemic functional grammar, has also generated some interest in stylistics. Discourse is conceived of as having a hierarchical structure, with moves combining to form exchanges. An early application can be found in Nash's (1989) analysis of the change of guard in *Hamlet*. It will be noticed that there is a greater focus on the lower levels of discourse – in other words on interactions between characters.

In so far as the lower discourse levels in literary texts, particularly but not only dramatic texts, resemble 'ordinary' discourse, it would seem obvious that any framework developed to deal with that can be appropriated. A lot of the developments within pragmatics (speech act theory, Grice's cooperative principle, relevance theory) are readily applied to that level of discourse. This is also the case with work in conversation analysis (e.g. the work on turn-taking). Much of this can be seen in Cooper (1998) and in Black (2006).

The work on cognitive psychology also provided the impetus for much of the more recent work on stylistics; but more of that below.

Looking to the future

What kinds of developments in the investigation of literary discourse can we look forward to? I shall only highlight two areas, which are not brand new, but have attracted recent attention.

The first is the investigation of literary discourse involving the corpus – corpus stylistics. The developments in corpus linguistics, including software that can retrieve more and more complex information from the corpus, have meant that it is increasingly possible to get more nuanced information from a corpus of literary texts. The Lancaster Speech, Writing and Thought Presentation (SW&TP2) Spoken Corpus has already been mentioned. In this case, though, the analysis had to be done by hand.

The second area is that of developments that involve marrying an interest in the close study of literary texts with 'a systematic and theoretically informed consideration of the cognitive structures and processes that underlie the production and reception of language' (Semino and Culpeper, 2002: ix). This enterprise is sometimes labelled 'cognitive poetics' (Stockwell 2002; Gavins and Steen 2003), in recognition of the fact that the emphasis is on *explaining* how interpretations are derived (as is the case with the enterprise of poetics) on the basis of cognitive theories, rather than on *producing* new interpretations. On other occasions, this field is known as cognitive stylistics. (Some might make a subtle distinction between them; others don't.) The earlier work based on reader-response theories (including those by Fish mentioned above) and the empirical study of literature (Miall and Kuiken 1999 mentioned above) paved the way. Prominent focal points include those that apply the notion of schema or the conceptual metaphor.

Cook links the notion of schema to readers' expectations: 'the essence of schema theory is that discourse proceeds and achieves coherence by successfully locating the unexpected within a framework of expectations' (1994: 130). The schema can involve expectations about how things typically operate or the objects typically found and there can be world, text and language schemata. Walsh (2008) employs schema theory, among other things, to highlight the contrast in perspective between a narrator with Asperger's syndrome and the reader, because the narrator lacks the schemata that we take for granted. (She focuses on *The Curious Incident of the Dog in the Night-Time*, 2003, by Mark Haddon.) The contrast can also be used for comedic effect. We can consider the beginning of the third act of Wilde's *The Importance of Being Earnest*. Gwendolen and Cecily have gone back into the house in a huff because they discovered that their suitors Jack and Algernon have been lying to them.

> GWENDOLEN: The fact that they did not follow us at once into the house, as anyone else would have done, seems to me to show that they have some sense of shame left.
> CECILY: They have been eating muffins. That looks like repentance.

There could be a variety of appropriate behaviour accompanying repentance, so the schema could vary between cultures. We might, for example, be familiar with the biblical wearing of sackcloth and application of ash. It might be just a matter of adopting a hangdog look. Whatever it is, it would not involve consuming pleasurable food; the eating of muffins would, instead, be interpreted as self-indulgent behaviour. The girls' schema contradicts our schema; and it is the ludicrous contrast that generates humour here.

Another way of separating the way 'our' world works and the way the text-internal world works is through the text world theory, developed by Gavins (for example, Gavins 2003). (This is related to the notion of 'possible worlds', discussed above in relation to the Harry Potter books.) A text world analysis would distinguish between the *discourse world* where participants engage in a language event (in this case, the author communicating with the reader or audience), where general discourse principles such as cooperation and face operate. Participants also need to construct a *text world*: this is a mental representation constructed in order to understand the discourse through the use of textual cues (in the case of our example, 'eating muffins'). There could be numerous text worlds created by participants or characters.

Work on conceptual metaphor, first initiated by Lakoff and Johnson (1980), continues to garner interest. Arguments are often expressed, for example, in terms of warfare. These are Lakoff and Johnson's (1980: 4) examples.

> Your claims are *indefensible*.
> He *attacked every weak point* in my argument.
> His criticisms were *right on target*. (Original italics)

Semino (2008: 5) defines conceptual metaphors as

> systematic sets of correspondences, or 'mappings', across conceptual domains, whereby a 'target' domain (e.g. our knowledge about arguments) is partly structured in terms of a difference 'source' domain (e.g. our knowledge about war).

Lakoff and Johnson's examples therefore generate the conceptual metaphor ARGUMENT IS WAR.

Semino (2002) makes use of the conceptual metaphors employed by the protagonist of John Fowles's first novel, *The Collector*, as a way into the mind of the character. This character, Frederick Clegg, is a clerk who also collects butterflies. He kidnaps Miranda Grey, an art student, who eventually dies after two months. Evident in much of the book is the construction of Miranda as BUTTERFLY. Semino shows a systematic mapping between the BUTTERFLY source domain and the MIRANDA target domain, such as the following:

> I watched the back of her head and her hair in a long pigtail. It was very pale, silky, like burnet cocoons.
>
> *(p. 9)*

> Seeing her always made me feel like I was catching a rarity, heart-in-mouth, as they say. A Pale Clouded yellow, for instance.
>
> *(p. 9)*

It is these correspondences that account for much of Clegg's behaviour. The persistence of the metaphor in the parts of the novel told from Clegg's point of view also establish his peculiar preoccupation and his mental illness.

The work on cognitive poetics – including the schema theory, text worlds theory and the conceptual metaphor – is very likely to continue to attract attention.

Further reading

Rather than reinventing the wheel and give a list of reading items, I will refer the reader who wants to explore this area to two volumes.

Carter, R. and Stockwell, P. (eds.) (2008) *The Language and Literature Reader*. London: Routledge.

This volume contains 28 chapters and is organized around three main periods. The section entitled 'Foundations' presents work from the 1960s and 1970s and contains chapters that employ grammatical analysis of literary texts (and includes the Halliday (1971) study mentioned above). 'Developments' covers work from the 1980s and 1990s (such as Nash's study on *Hamlet*). 'New Directions' showcases more recent work, including work in cognitive and corpus stylistics. The volume also contains a reprinted version of Gavins (2003) and Semino (2002).

Lambrou, M. and Stockwell, P. (eds.) (2008) *Contemporary Stylistics*. London: Continuum.

This volume of 20 chapters is organized around the three main literary genres of prose, poetry and drama and provides a very wide range of approaches to literary texts. It includes the chapter on schema poetics by Walsh mentioned above.

References

Black, E. (2006) *Pragmatic Stylistics*. Edinburgh: Edinburgh University Press.

Broich, U. (1997) 'Intertextuality', in H. Bertens and D. Fokkema *International Postmodernism: Theory and Literary Practice*. Amsterdam: Benjamins, pp. 249–256.

Bridgeman, T. (2005) 'Thinking ahead: a cognitive approach to prolepsis', *Narrative*, 13 (2): 125–159.

Carter, R. and McCarthy, M. (2006) *Cambridge Grammar of English*. Cambridge: Cambridge University Press.

Cook, G. (1994) *Discourse and Literature*. Oxford: Oxford University Press.

Cooper, M. (1998) 'Implicature, convention and *The Taming of the Shrew*', in J. Culpeper *et al.* (eds.) *Exploring the Language of Drama: From Text to Context*. London: Routledge, pp. 54–66.

Crystal, D. (1998) *Language Play*. Harmondsworth: Penguin.

Currie, G. (1990) *The Nature of Fiction*. Cambridge: Cambridge University Press.

Ellis, J. and Ure, J. N. (1976) 'Registers', in C. S. Butler and R. R. K. Hartman (eds.) *A Reader on Language Variety*. Exeter: University of Exeter, pp. 32–40.

Fish, S. (1980) *Is There a Text in this Class? The Authority of Interpretive Communities*. Cambridge, MA: Harvard University Press.

Gavins, J. (2003) 'Too much blague? An exploration of the text worlds of Donald Barthelme's *Snow White*', in J. Gavins and G. Steen (eds.) *Cognitive Poetics in Practice*. London: Routledge, pp. 129–144.

Gavins, J. and G. Steen (eds.) (2003) *Cognitive Poetics in Practice*. London: Routledge.

Gunn, D. P. (2004) 'Free indirect discourse and narrative authority in *Emma*', *Narrative*, 12 (1): 35–54.

Halliday, M. A. K. (1971) 'Linguistic function and literary style: an inquiry into the language of William Golding's *The Inheritors*', in S. Chatman (ed.) *Literary Style: A Symposium*. Oxford: Oxford University Press, pp. 330–368.

Ikegami, Y. (2005), 'Register specification in the learner's dictionary'. Available online at: http://www.pearsonlongman.com/dictionaries/pdfs/register-specification.pdf (accessed 15 January 2010).

Jackson, H. and Amvela, E. Zé. (2000) *Words, Meaning, and Vocabulary: An Introduction to Modern English Lexicology*. London: Cassell.

Jakobson, R. (1960) 'Closing statements: linguistics and poetics', in T. A. Sebeok (ed.) *Style In Language*. Cambridge, MA: MIT Press, pp. 350–377.

Labov, W. (1972) *Language in the Inner City*. Philadelphia, PA: University of Pennsylvania Press.

Lakoff, G. and Johnson, M. (1980) *Metaphors We Live By*. Chicago, IL: University of Chicago Press.

McIntyre, D. (2004) 'Investigating the presentation of speech, writing and thought in spoken British English: a corpus-based approach', *ICAME Journal*, 28: 49–76.

McRae, J. (1994) *Literature with a small 'l'*. Basingstoke: Macmillan.

Miall, D. S. and Kuiken, D. (1999) 'What is literariness? Three components of literary reading', *Discourse Processes*, 28: 121–138.

Nash, W. (1989) 'Changing the guard at Elsinore', in R. Carter and P. Simpson (eds.) *Language, Discourse and Literature*. London: Unwin Hyman, pp. 23–41.

Oxford English Dictionary (1989) 'Preface to the second edition', *OED Online*. Oxford: Oxford University Press. Second Edition. Available at http://dictionary.oed.com/archive/oed2-preface/general.html (accessed 15 January 2010).

Pratt, M. L. (1977) *Toward a Speech Act Theory of Literary Discourse*. Bloomington, IN: Indiana University Press.

Rudanko, J. (2006) 'Aggravated impoliteness and two types of speaker intention in an episode of Shakespeare's *Timon of Athens*', *Journal of Pragmatics*, 28: 820–841.

Searle, J. R. (1975) 'The logical status of fictional discourse', *New Literary History*, 6: 319–332. (Reprinted in John R. Searle, *Expression and meaning*, Cambridge: Cambridge University Press, 1979.)

Sell, R. (1991) *Literary Pragmatics*. London: Routledge.

Semino, E. (2002) 'A cognitive stylistic approach to mind style in narrative fiction', in E. Semino and J. Culpeper (eds.) *Cognitive Stylistics: Language and Cognition in Text Analysis*. Amsterdam: Benjamins, pp. 95–122.

Semino, E. (2008) *Metaphor in Discourse*. Cambridge: Cambridge University Press.

Semino, E. and J. Culpeper (eds.) (2002) *Cognitive Stylistics: Language and Cognition in Text Analysis*. Amsterdam: Benjamins.

Sherzer, J. (2002) *Speech Play and Verbal Art*. Austin, TX: University of Texas Press.

Short, M. (1996) *Exploring the Language of Poems, Plays and Prose*. London: Longman.

Stockwell, P. (2002) *Cognitive Poetics: An Introduction*. London: Routledge.

Thomas, J. (1995) *Meaning in Interaction: An Introduction to Pragmatics*. London: Longman.

Toolan, M. (1998) *Language in Literature: An Introduction to Stylistics*. London: Arnold.

Walsh, C. (2008) 'Schema poetics and crossover fiction', in M. Lambrou and P. Stockwell (eds.) *Contemporary Stylistics*. London: Continuum, pp. 106–117.

Widdowson, H. G. (1975) *Stylistics and the Teaching of Literature*. London: Longman.

Widdowson, H. G. (1992) *Practical Stylistics: An Approach to Poetry*. Oxford: Oxford University Press.

45

A multicultural approach to discourse studies

Shi-xu

Introduction

On the current international scene of discourse studies, the mainstream traditions of research often prize themselves on their joining with one or the other discipline – or with more – say, linguistics, psychology, sociology, anthropology, political science and/or media studies. This cross- or multi-disciplinarity is held out as the best, if not the only, method of guaranteeing knowledge, because such disciplines are presupposed to share the same universality of rationality and reason: fundamentally, they all represent the human world in some neutral, objective way, and therefore they are simply true and hence applicable across all cultures; culture itself is but an epiphenomenon. There is rarely any reflection over, or passing discussion of, where they come from historically and culturally, or whether there might be culturally other, different systems of theory and methods.

The presumed universality of the multi-disciplinarity is further elevated in certain critical approaches to discourse studies. That is, the values and norms assumed in them, and ultimately by the agents of those approaches, are taken to be universal, too. As the knower of the true, good and right – and, for that matter, of justice, freedom and democracy – the critical practitioner passes muster as a judge of the false, bad, wrong discourses, and so discourses of injustice, human rights abuse, corruption, prejudice and domination, whether it comes to Asian cultures, African cultures or Latin American cultures. Little is thought of the fact that, although many human norms and values – say, human rights – are universal, their understanding and practice are historically and culturally conditioned, hence complex, so that the locally appropriate perspectives need to be taken into consideration as well.

From a broader cultural perspective and on closer inspection, however, it will become clear that the disciplinary discourses mentioned above, including their agents/authors, have all Western European/American origins and orientations, as we shall discuss below. As they become globalized and globally dominant through the powerful Western machinery of international marketing, distribution and circulation, they hardly attend to culturally other philosophies, perspectives and practices of language and communication research, let alone engage in dialogue with them. Indeed the tendency to over-generalize, and consequently to neglect the cultural context, has been identified as one of the central and debilitating problems in contemporary social science (Hollinger, 1994; Flyvbjerg, 2001; Smart, 2003).

It is against this culturally blind attitude of discourse studies that I shall outline, in this chapter, an alternative – multicultural – approach to discourse studies. 'Multicultural', as will be described in detail below, is the overarching principle that is integrated into the formation and use of a discourse research system, or paradigm, of epistemology, theory, methods and questions – which, beyond the ethnocentric monopoly of truths and values, places cultural diversity, co-existence and prosperity at the centre of the research process. The upshot of this multicultural re-orientation of discourse studies is that it overcomes the limits of the cultural imperialism on the one hand and maintains multicultural dynamics on the other hand (Shi-xu, 2005, 2006).

In what follows I shall first examine, through intercultural dialogue and critique, the case of 'critical discourse studies'. Next I shall canvass an alternative multicultural discourse research system. In conclusion I shall suggest a range of action strategies for accomplishing the envisaged paradigm.

The cultural nature of discourse studies

Before I present a multicultural approach, I should like to examine the current mainstream mode of discourse research, because this not only is a point of departure and reference for the present proposal, but also constitutes an important motivating reason for it. I shall focus on critical discourse analysis, as this is one of the prominent streams of the discipline (Van Dijk, 1993; Wodak 2005; Fairclough 1997). The discipline in question will be considered as a scholarly *discourse*, which is composed of particular agents, forms and contents, media, consequences, and it will be examined from a historical and intercultural perspective (Shi-xu, 2005). It is hoped that, when analysed and assessed in this holistic and dialectic way, the seen but otherwise obscured properties of the discipline will become highlighted. But, for my present purposes, it will not be necessary to go through all these components and processes; it will suffice to make mention of some of the salient facts.

It should be cautioned and stressed here that the present examination does not presuppose or imply an internally homogeneous, coherent and monolithic discourse within. My purpose is merely to identify certain discursive characteristics and tendencies.

(1) Critical discourse analysis (CDA henceforth) has still a *structuralist* tendency. That is, modelled upon 'language' as conceptualized in structural linguistics, discourse is often, to all practical purposes, treated as a static unit of elements in systematic relations, which is different in kind and separable from the world/context. This is manifested in such common binary conceptions of 'discourse' as 'being influenced by', 'reflecting', 'constructing' the world/context. But, historically, this linguistic structuralism comes from the nineteenth-century science-oriented European and American linguistics flowing from Ferdinand de Saussure. In Asian/ Chinese culture, by contrast, language is understood as unfolding and evolving in constant and complex interaction with the world, where not two, but many elements being dialectically interconnected, multi-relational and so holistically considered.

(2) More recently, CDA stresses its inter-, cross- or multi-disciplinary approach to discourse, incorporating the disciplinary knowledge of – for example – sociology, psychology, political science, anthropology or some other science as the foundational apparatus for knowledge. Underlying such multi-disciplinarity is the belief that these disciplines are all grounded in universal rationality. However, little thought is given to the same cultural origin of the European Enlightenment tradition. In Asian/Chinese culture, scholarship has been holistic and, further, is guided morally by concerns of social harmony rather than of 'pure knowledge'.

(3) Related to the above credo in multi-disciplinarity, CDA takes its theory and methods to be universal and fails to recognize the culturally different realities and approaches. Discourse is

often assumed to have *the same*, or *similar*, kinds of structures and functions across cultures, such that they can be analysed through uniform methods. Consequently, standard research topics, questions, issues and types of data are replicated and answers rehearsed. Significantly, silence is kept about possible culturally alternative forms of texts and contexts, including local, native concerns and questions and broader historical and contemporary ways of thinking.

(4) CDA practitioners usually portray themselves, implicitly or explicitly, as being knower and judge of the true (rational and neutral), the right, the good and therefore rarely reflect on their own possible cultural bias. Their identity, position and background as members of, or trained in, some particular historical and cultural – usually Anglo-Saxon – community are presumed to be irrelevant to their academic discourse. Similarly, a particular set of cultural–intellectual – normally white male American/European – scholars are cited as the standard authorities for warranting knowledge and values and for settling arguments. Hardly ever are there non-Western scholars or non-Western academic and philosophical heritages recognized or acknowledged.

This aculturalist discourse has a host of unfortunate, though inadvert, theoretical and cultural consequences. On the one side, since theories always arise from a particular culture and history and deal with particular relevant problems, the current West-originating and West-oriented discourse analysis begs the question of how it comes to have access to universality. Moreover, as such, it may fail to reflect local, particular and perhaps mutually incommensurable discourses from the non-Western world, including their particular issues, concerns, rules, histories, circumstances, power positions etc. Further, since contemporary culture has become increasingly globalized and hence interconnected, diversified yet alienated (Appadurai, 1996; Bauman, 1998), the received approach may fail to represent the new, complex, hybridized, polyglossic, multicultural and contested processes of human discourses. More seriously, as the current mainstream discourse analysis has rested on culturally exclusive intellectual traditions with the result of their being recreated as the standard and norm, opportunities are missed not only for learning from other different cultural-intellectual heritages, but also for intercultural critique and ultimately for genuine theoretical innovation. Think of the large and rich scholarly and intellectual heritages in language and communication from non-Western and Third-World cultures (e.g. Kincaid, 1987; Dissanayake, 1988; Gumperz and Levinson, 1996; Silverstein and Urban, 1996; Asante, 1998; Heisey, 2000; Shen, 2001).

On the side of the wider cultural impact, it may be suggested that, when the West-turned aculturalist discourse reigns over the international discourse scholarship, one of the obvious consequences is that the intellectual traditions embodied in other languages, in other cultures, in other parts of the world, become marginalized or ignored, excluded and denigrated. It has already been registered that certain intellectual communities have become academically and intellectually 'aphasic' (e.g. Wang, 2002, 2003). The practice of the aculturalist theoretical discourse has critical scholarly effects on non-Western discourses, too. It is now a common occurrence in the field that Western standard frameworks are applied to discourses from non-Western cultures. This may perhaps reveal some interesting features, but it will fail to see many other important properties at the same time and arrive very likely at a negative evaluation. Finally, just as the predominance of the British/American English language overshadows other multilingual and multicultural experiences and realities (Ngũgĩ, 1986; Pennycook, 1998), so the monocultural scholarship of discourse analysis will become a monopoly on truths, legitimating and re-producing the existing hegemonic scientific disorder. Consequently, as science becomes impoverished, academic dialogue is replaced by scientific war.

Of course I do not mean that there has been no reflexive, self-critical and constructive effort on the cultural issue of theoretical discourse (see e.g. Newmeyer, 1986; Sherzer, 1987; Urban, 1991; Cameron, 1992; Carey, 1992; Bazerman, 1998; Milhouse *et al.*, 2001; Blommaert, 2005 as well as the journal *Discourse and Society*). Nor do I suggest that there has been no theoretical attempt to take note of non-Western, non-white or Third-World discourses (see e.g. Ngũgĩ, 1986; Young, 1994; Gumperz and Levinson, 1996; Silverstein and Urban, 1996). But I do want to stress that endeavours such as these are few and far between and often come from the margins (e.g. Asian communication studies, area studies), or have origins from outside the discipline. Indeed, given the current international cultural imbalance and disorder in the social sciences and humanities, the struggle against cultural hegemony in general and theoretical imperialism in particular will be a gradual, long and arduous process and much more effort is needed.

Towards a multicultural mode of research

The important lessons from the above critique should become clear now. We must refrain from (a) knowing from culturally exclusive perspectives and (b) producing universalistic knowledge from ethnocentric vantage points. To avoid such pitfalls, we must then try to find a different cultural attitude and, more specifically, an alternative conceptual strategy. Such a strategy, as I shall argue in this section, should be characterized by a *multicultural* stance on knowledge and knowledge reproduction. This refers to the strategy of knowing and knowledge reproduction that, other than from just one cultural tradition, one draws eclectically, critically and creatively upon culturally diverse – especially Western *and* Eastern (see below) – perspectives. This implies that one will need to locate oneself between the Eastern and Western traditions of knowledge-seeking and to form a non-oppressive, synthetic and holistic viewpoint. To put it more broadly, the present epistemological attitude may be said to be oriented towards 'outward' learning, 'helpful' innovation and reaching out to the hitherto unexplored, unfamiliar or marginalized ways of seeing, understanding and meaning-making.

Firstly, such a multicultural–epistemological stance is necessary because human culture is possessed of not just one, but different and possibly mutually complementary ways of looking at and understanding the world. The Western pattern of thinking has been heavily influenced by the Cartesian tradition, the Enlightenment philosophy and individualism and is consequently largely analytic, individualistic and instrumental. The world is then often divided up into fragments and dimensions and social science then compartmentalized into separate departments or disciplines. People, action or events are accordingly analysed, isolated and abstracted from context into smaller, 'controllable' units, components or levels and explained in terms of individualistic purposes. The Eastern way of thinking, in contrast, being penetrated by Confucianism, Taoism, Buddhism, Hinduism and so on is more intuitive, synthetic, holistic and dialectic, social–relational and collectivist, where man and nature, self and other, subject and object, language and context, and all other things are seen as interconnected, interpenetrated and interdependent.

If we appropriately combine culturally diverse ways of knowledge-seeking, we might be able to see things that we would otherwise fail to see. The awareness of the diversity of cultural ways of knowledge-seeking and making will also encourage us to learn not just from the mainstream, established, dominant Western systems of knowledge, but more widely and more inclusively, from culturally different ways of thinking and knowing, and, especially now, from the non-Western, non-white and Third-World heritages. In this way, we may reach more widely informed, sophisticated and innovative understanding. In addition, we may become more reflexive on and critical of our own cultural ways of knowing as well as of those of others. This kind of multicultural stance will allow us an opportunity to intervene personally upon culturally shared systems of knowledge, Eastern and Western. For we must make a personal choice from more than one cultural way of knowing.

Secondly, a multicultural stance is much needed now also because, historically, the Eastern and Western different worldviews and value systems have not enjoyed an equal relation to each other. Rather, knowledge, history and power are intermeshed and bound up specifically with the historically situated colonialism and continued cultural imperialism (Habermas, 1972; Said, 1978, 1993; Foucault, 1980; Young, 2001). Our earlier analysis of the discipline of discourse studies is a case in point. To offset the current cultural asymmetry in knowledge-seeking and knowledge-making and to redress the resultant cultural hegemony (Gramsci, 1971) in norms, values and standards involved in international scientific research, a culturally more balanced and pluralist strategy, mindful especially of non-Western ways of knowing is therefore called for.

In terms of theoretical benefit, then, the multicultural stance may compel us to seek the co-existence of, and cohesion between, different and competing cultural–intellectual traditions. The multicultural position renders it possible for them to transcend cultural boundaries and break out of cultural confinements. Consequently, theoretical self-reflection, dialogue and negotiation will be facilitated and the space for transforming existing theory and creating genuinely new frameworks opened up.

Thirdly, still another consideration behind the present proposal is that contemporary culture is becoming increasingly globalized. This means that cultures are being interconnected, hybridized and diversified. Cultural ways of thinking, speaking and acting are becoming more complex, pluralist, varied and dynamic. Traditional, singular and closed ways of knowing are no longer adequate for theorizing about the new globalized condition of discourse. It will be important then to seek all the culturally relevant ways of knowing and to apply them to the understanding of particular cultural settings.

When we take a multicultural stance in discourse theorizing, we become more sensitive to the new complexities and dynamic changes taking place in globalized contemporary culture and discourse. In particular, we may be able to observe how local culture/discourse responds to global influences.

It should be stressed that the present references to Eastern and Western cultures, their ways of thinking and the relevant power relations must not be misunderstood as ways of reifying and homogenize human cultures. Rather these distinctions are meant as a heuristic, for one to try to go beyond one's familiar scholarly traditions and learn from other cultural ways of knowing and the historically situated relations of power between them, especially those between East and West (e.g. overlapping, complimenting or excluding each other). Therefore, the understanding that cultures are not pre-given, homogeneous or static must not be (ab)used as rhetoric or as an excuse not to pay attention to cultures outside the West, not to learn from intellectual heritages from the non-Western world and not to recognize the continued repression and subjugation of Third/Fourth-World cultures.

The multicultural stance on knowledge construction is designed specifically for the transformation of current aculturalist theoretical practice and for the reconstruction of new and alternative forms of discourse theory. In the remainder of this chapter, I shall accordingly turn to drawing out the implications of this multicultural stance for practical theory-building. By doing this I hope to show how the conceptual strategy works in practice. The implications I shall discuss involve the theorist in terms of his/her principles of action on the one hand and of the characteristics of the resultant theory on the other hand. The two sides of the theoretical activity are interrelated, but for the sake of exposition I shall treat them separately.

The multicultural researcher

In line with the historically conscious, culturally pluralist stance outlined above, the theorist should first of all decide on some particular, culturally specific discourse as a starting point and focus for theory reconstruction. This will help to overcome the general universalizing tendency and to avoid its negative consequences, which we saw earlier. For the features, functions, relations and so on of a discourse are inextricably bound up with context, and context is always defined by particular culture and history, including the whole way of life of the relevant group of people. Therefore the chosen object has to be grounded in some particular, historically concrete context. Thus, for example, one can theorize the discourse of Great Britain, of Europe, of the West, or of the non-Western world, or of somewhere in-between. Of course such a decision also depends on one's intended research objective and scope. To theorize Asian discourse or Chinese discourse are intellectually equal choices and matters of research aims. At the same time, practically speaking, the decision must be made in proportion to one's breadth of knowledge and experience with regard to the discourse in question.

Immediately I must add that I am fully aware of the diversities, hybridities and other dynamics within such particular categories of discourse. And I am all for attempts at genuinely inclusive understandings of all human discourse. But these must not become the reasons (or excuses) for not paying attention to particular, locally relevant and context-specific concepts, practices and theoretical legacies, which at the present stage have continued to be marginalized from the 'centre' (Kincaid, 1987; Asante, 1998; Dissanayak, 2003; Shi-xu et al., 2005). Attention to these traditions has not been too much but too little, and if we continue to (re)produce general theory with no regard to such particularities we do it at our own peril. The general and the particular, the global and the local, the universal and the individual are dialectic opposites of holistic unities. More importantly, there may be – and many would claim there are – rich intellectual heritages, notions and actual activities from which new and useful theories may be derived or reconstructed, in Asia, Africa and Latin America, for example.

Secondly, in theorizing a particular cultural discourse, the theorist should not be constrained by local perspectives, but must try to seek dialogue and cross-fertilization between different, relevant cultural theories, whether they are Eastern and Western, Asian and European, Chinese and German and so on. Traditions of language studies from different cultures may contain insights that will help one to ask new questions, beyond one's familiar cultural pattern of thinking, or to shed light on aspects of language and communication that would otherwise go unheeded. Notions and theories of language and communication from such other cultures may also give one inspirations and resources for genuine theoretical innovation (Shi-xu, 2005). Indo-European languages are inflexional; partly due to this fact, theory tends to be formal, analytic and low-context, for example – whereas the Chinese language relies on meaning agreement and is characterized by high context; consequently theory tends to be culture-specific and holistic (Shen, 2001). It would be a form of strength and resourcefulness to learn from culturally different theories such as these through comparison and contrast, and, on that basis, to create new and more sophisticated theories, suitable for local use. This leads to my next point.

Thirdly, the multicultural theorists should constantly monitor and reflect on their own theoretical discourse in order to produce innovative and effective theoretical ideas. Just as they should be critical of the object of their enquiry, they must be continuously critical of themselves. For one thing, they have a social role to play in the theoretical production, and they have cultural responsibility for the international scholarly community. For another, the context of discourse and its theorizing are not static but changing; the changes have been accelerated at the threshold of the twenty-first century. Therefore the theorist ought to try to keep his/her theory relevant and useful. If notions of discourse are themselves products of scholarly construction, the theorist must refrain from totalizing them. Instead, s/he should pay attention to other cultural intellectual traditions, even if they may be unfamiliar ones. In this respect the theorist must take seriously 'race', ethnicity and cultural imperialism in discourse. For the same reason, s/he must also attend especially to hitherto silenced, repressed or otherwise marginalized forms of discourses.

A multicultural paradigm

Given the complexities of human discourses and the diversities of cultural scholarly heritages – and, above all, perhaps, the innovativeness of intellectual individuals – a multicultural theory, as now may become apparent, can and will take a variety of forms. However, following from the principles of theoretical articulation laid out above, the new theories may also share some starting points and objectives. In this section I shall then try to sketch them out. To show clearly the concrete effects of the multicultural theoretical orientation, I shall make use of the case of Chinese discourse for illustration.

Firstly, a culturally pluralist theory should represent the distinctiveness and identity of particular, local discourses, thereby contributing to the understanding of the heterogeneity and equality of human discourses. For, on the one hand, the world cultures have different histories, conditions, problems, issues, aspirations and so on, and consequently would have not only different objects of construction or topics, but also different concepts and categories, perspectives, norms and values and so on. On the other hand, the corresponding cultural discourses embody different symbols, rules and strategies for constructing meaning. In Western cultures, for instance, people often use language as an expression of valued individual reason and self-identity (Bellah *et al.*, 1985; Carey, 1992; Carbaugh, 1993). But in Eastern cultures people generally hold speech communication as a tool for maintaining social relationships (Young, 1994; Liu, 1996; Chen, 2005). Similarly, women and men may be said to possess and use different discourses (Tannen, 1990). In fact, it has long been recognized that human discourses are not unified or universal; they consist in a diversity of language-games, voices, intertextualities and so on (Bakhtin, 1981; Kristeva, quoted in Moi, 1986; Wittgenstein, 1968). Concepts, theories and methods will no longer be assumed as universal and applied dogmatically across all cultures; rather they will have to be re-oriented to local, concrete and particular situations. In such a multicultural perspective, discourses from non-Western, non-white or Third-World cultures and communities cannot be 'contained' in a general, comprehensive and integrated theory, but must first be treated in their own right and as different orders of things from Western discourses (in terms of language philosophy, power relations, communities of speakers, issues and concerns, etc.) and as requiring a culturally nuanced and historically conscious perspective. Regarding apparently the 'same' issue, Chinese media, for example, can have very different notions, topics, values and strategies of communication from those of its Anglo-American counterpart. If a discourse framework originating from a Western tradition were dogmatically applied to the analysis of this article, not only would important aspects and characteristics be missed, but also a necessarily negative evaluation would result.

Secondly, a multicultural theory should feature the internal discursive complexities, hybridities and even conflicts or contradictions of an otherwise unified cultural discourse, and consequently the porosity and openness of its boundary. Human discourses are not univocal but polyglossic. There may be internal variations, or even contradictions (Sherzer, 1987). In the age of globalization, facilitated by transnationalism, digital media and human migration (Appiah, 1992; Appadurai, 1996; Bauman, 1998), different discourses meet and mix, so that different elements of discourse co-exist and new discourses take shape (Chouliaraki and Fairclough, 1999).

A language as 'uniform' as Chinese has been multilingual and multicultural since its inception (Shen, 2001; Li, 2003). Contemporary Chinese, too, especially since the opening up and reform in the 1980s, also contains discursive elements from the West, but puts them to different uses. So my point here is that contemporary Chinese is not entirely different from, or opposed to, non-Chinese discourses; it has connections and hybridities with Western discourse.

Thirdly, a multicultural discourse theory should take note of the historicity of human discourses, especially the more recent particular world histories of colonialism, global capitalism and neo-expansionism. Any discourse has a particular past; cultural traditions provide context, resources and reasons for change. The predominance of English as a world language, together with its peculiar traits, concepts, categories and evaluations, has everything to do with the erstwhile imperialist aggression of Britain and its contemporary cultural hegemony (Pennycook, 1998). The consequential repression, marginalization or even extinction of other (aboriginal) languages (along with their relevant concerns, issues and aspirations) can be understood only in terms of this historical context, too. Contemporary Chinese discourse on nationalism, similarly, cannot be properly understood without recourse to the particular context of Old China as a semi-colonial and semi-feudal society and to the related Western imperialist history.

It is easy but mistaken to degrade, from an imperialist point of view, such non-Western discourse of nationalism as shear Nazism, or to brand it with the label 'communist ideology against the Western world'. For Western culture and its media have always demeaned and tried to repress nationalism from the non-Western world. But in this Western action and representation there is no regard for the *historical* oppression of European/American/Japanese imperialism, nor for *contemporary* unilateralism, neo-conservatism and neo-colonialism. As a matter of fact, for the past hundreds of years, China has been the victim of foreign aggression and exploitation. Now, when it is gaining breathtaking ascendancy in economy, it is clouded by 'anxieties' and 'concerns' about its 'future expansion' from countries far and near. Taking a historical perspective, then, we shall realize that this discourse of nationalism is a product and process of this particular local and global history.

Fourthly and importantly, closely related to the historicity of discourse, a culturally pluralist theory should pay attention to cultural power relations and practices involved in and through discourse (as text and context) – tensions, domination, exclusion, resistance and so on between and upon different cultures, East and West. Different cultural groups or communities have not enjoyed the same access to voice and communication (Van Dijk, 1993; McQuail, 2000) and discourses of different cultures have not treated one another with tolerance and forbearance (e.g. Said, 1978, 1993; Spivak, 1988; Hall, 1990, 1997; Bhabha, 1994). Such cultural inequality in discourse, as may be pointed out, typically occurs along the borders of 'race', ethnicity, gender, class and nation. Thus, through demeaning metaphors, narratives, arguments on the one hand and ethnocentric norms and values on the other, dominant Western discourses often discredit, ignore and exclude non-Western and Third-World discourses (and consequently their experiences and realities). As a result, the discourses of non-Western and Third World communities are suppressed, dismissed, discredited or silenced, but at the same time their discourses of resistance are growing as well. Just as Western discourse has always opposed the nationalist discourse from the non-Western and Third World, as I said above, so there is also a discourse to resist it, which should also be taken into account.

Finally, a multicultural theory of discourse should attempt to illuminate what might be called the 'self-critical consciousness' of discourse – the intrinsic ability of a discourse community to re-create and transform its own discourse and so its own culture. Discourse, i.e. texts and their contexts, do not stay the same through time. Nor will a dominant communal discourse continue to repress alternative discourses unopposed and unchanged. Each speaking community, hence its discourse, has the internal spirit to reflect upon itself critically in order to create a historically better discourse. The rise and spread of feminist discourse, anti-racist discourse and anti-imperialist discourse within Western society are a case in point. A multicultural theory should then be able to reveal such historically conscious change in discourse.

Strategies for constructing and practising multicultural paradigms

Below I will go on suggesting some interrelated principles for the construction, choice and utilization of theory and methods for discourse research. Culturally irrelevant or inappropriate frameworks of research may lead to not just misleading conclusions but also counter-productive to what social scientific work is supposed to achieve. These would share certain aspects with the existing paradigms, but also bear characteristics of their own. On the whole, they favour a cultural–critical attitude towards theory and methodology for the sake of human cultural knowledge innovation and common cultural prosperity.

Our first proposed principle is to be culturally conscious and in particular *multicultural* in the formation, selection and application of theory and methods, which of course also implies the same attitude with regard to the underlying ontological and epistemological stances. This means, specifically, that we stress cultural pluralism, diversity and egalitarianism and oppose cultural imperialism. So, in examining the discourse of any culture, we must not be contented with culturally singular or exclusive or even imperialist theoretical lens and methodological apparatus, but perforce attempt to draw on diverse cultural resources.

Secondly, we should strive to be *holistic* in conceptualizing and theorizing discourses of human cultures. This means, in particular, that we take into account not only the present, but also the past and the future, and further that we also consider the intercultural connections. For human cultural discourses are neither historically unrelated nor culturally separable. In other words, the historical and intercultural dialectics of discourses must be recognized. In addition, the interpenetration of the researched discourse and discourse researcher must be reckoned with, too.

Thirdly, given the multicultural and holistic nature of human cultural discourses, we should, methodologically, make use of historical and cross-cultural examination, comparison and contrast, as necessary and effective tools for the understanding and critique of human cultural discourses. Only in this way can we have a comprehensive, penetrating and sympathetic understanding and critique of the differences, similarities, changes, agencies, creativity, and so on of the peoples and cultures that we attempt to study, and indeed of their discourses.

Last but not least, we need also to be reflexive throughout the research process. Because we cannot be separated from the object we study or from the cultural milieu we are in, and because our research results can be consequential for the people or the phenomena we choose to study, we should be conscious of our own roles in the research process and the outcomes on the one hand and on the other hand attempt to render our research useful and helpful to the groups of people under investigation.

In this essay I have argued for a multicultural approach to the theoretical articulation of discourse. That means, in sum, that the multicultural theorist, on the one side, must try first and foremost to integrate culturally diverse intellectual traditions of language, communication and discourse, secondly ground his/her theory in a concrete, particular cultural setting whilst maintaining a global vision and, last but not least, through personal critical and reflexive mediation, create a relevant, novel and helpful understanding of the discourse in question. The resultant multicultural theory itself, on the other side, must represent the basic properties of the local discourse of interest and, given the current theoretical imbalance and bias, pay special attention to cultural particularity, internal complexity, cultural historicity, cultural inequality and critical consciousness.

The multicultural approach has a number of advantages. Firstly, the practising theorist becomes culturally more widely informed and as a result his/her chances of achieving genuine theoretical innovation are increased. Seen from another perspective, as a result of the required reflection on and integration from divergent cultural–intellectual heritages, there arises an opportunity for the individual theorist to intervene personally in culturally shared traditions, thereby transforming intellectual culture. Secondly, the resultant culturally pluralist and therefore more sophisticated theory might help to reveal properties that might otherwise go unheeded. Thirdly, the less familiar and marginalized discourses, especially from the non-Western and Third/Fourth-World communities, including their concerns, issues, questions and aspirations, may be given more attention and legitimacy in their own right. Finally, the positivist, essentialist, universalist tendencies, which have been impoverishing discourse studies, may become neutralized or curbed.

There is a formidable difficulty facing the theorist, however. Namely, the requirement and expectation of the practitioner to be abreast of not merely one's own intellectual tradition, but also of culturally other, unfamiliar, paradigms, to develop a global perspective beyond one's comfortable sphere of vision, and, inevitably, to be versed in other relevant foreign languages and cultures (cultural discourses) in addition to one's own are all very challenging demands. Theoretical multiculturalism will be a matter of degree, and for individuals this means that it will be a life-long process. There is no other way of getting over this, than by mustering the willpower to continue to learn.

Further reading

Blommaert, J. (2005). *Discourse: A Critical Introduction*. Cambridge: Cambridge University Press.
Briscoe, F., G. Arriaza, and R. C. Henze (2009). *The Power of Talk: How Words Change our Lives*. Thousand Oaks, CA: Cowin.
Shi-xu (2005). *A Cultural Approach to Discourse*. Houndmills/New York: Palgrave Macmillan.
Scollo, M. (forthcoming) 'Cultural approaches to discourse analysis: a theoretical and methodological conversation with special focus on Donal Carbaugh's cultural discourse theory', *Journal of Multicultural Discourses*.

References

Appadurai, A (1996) *Modernity at Large: Cultural Dimensions of Globalization*. Minneapolis, MN: University of Minnesota Press.
Appiah, K. A. (1992) *In My Father's House: Africa in the Philosophy of Culture*. London: Methuen.
Asante, M. K. (1998) *The Afrocentric Idea*. Revised and Expanded Edition. Philadelphia, PA: Temple University Press.
Bakhtin, M. M. (1981) *The Dialogic Imagination: Four essays*, ed. M. Holquist, trans. C. Emerson and M. Holquist. Austin, TX: University of Texas Press.
Bauman, Z. (1998) *Globalization: The Human Consequences*. Cambridge: Polity Press.
Bazerman, C. (1998) 'Emerging perspectives on the many dimensions of scientific discourse', in J. R. Martin and R. Veel (eds.) *Reading Science: Critical and Functional Perspectives on Discourses of Science*. London: Routledge, pp. 15–28.
Bellah, R. N., Madsen, R., Swindler, W. M., and Tipton, S. M. (1985) *Habits of the Heart: Individualism and Commitment in American life*. Berkeley, CA: University of California Press.
Bhabha, H. K. (1994) *The Location of Culture*. London: Routledge.
Blommaert, J. (2005) *Discourse: A Critical Introduction*. Cambridge: Cambridge University Press.
Bourdieu, P. (1990) *In Other Words: Essay Towards a Reflexive Sociology*. Cambridge: Polity Press.
Bourdieu, P. (1998) *Acts of Resistance: Against the New Myths of Our Time*. Cambridge: Polity Press.
Cameron, D. (1992) *Feminism and Linguistic Theory*. Second Edition. London: Macmillan.

Carbaugh, D. (1993) 'Communal voices: an ethnographic view of social interaction and conversaion', *The Quarterly Journal of Speech.*, 79: 99–113.

Carey, J. W. (1992) *Communication as Culture: Essays on Media and Society.* New York: Routledge.

Chen, G.-M. (2005) 'The two faces of Chinese communication', *Human Communication.*

Chouliaraki, L. and Fairclough, N. (1999) *Discourse in Late Modernity: Rethinking Critical Discourse Analysis.* Edinburgh: Edinburgh University Press.

Dissanayak, W. (2003) 'Asian approaches to human communication: retrospect and prospect', *Intercultural Communication Studies*, 12 (4): 16–37.

Dissanayake, W. (ed.). (1988) *Communication Theory: The Asian Perspective.* Singapore: Asian Mass Communication Research and Information Center.

Flyvbjerg, B. (2001) *Making Social Science Matter: Why Social Inquiry Fails and How it can Succeed Again.* Cambridge: Cambridge University Press.

Foucault, M. (1973) *The Order of Things: An Archaeology of the Human Sciences.* New York: Vintage Books.

Foucault, M. (1980) *Power/Knowledge: Selected Interviews and Other Writings 1972–1977.* Ed. Colin Gordon. New York: Pentheon Books.

Foucault, M. (1986) *The Care of the Self: The History of Sexuality.* Volume 3. London: Penguin.

Geertz, C. (1973) *The Interpretation of Cultures: Selected Essays.* New York: Basic Books, Inc. Publishers.

Giddens, G. (1990) *The Consequences of Modernity.* Cambridge: Polity Press.

Gramsci, A. (1971) *Selections from the Prison Notes of Antonio Gramsci*, ed. and trans. Q. Hoare, G. N. Smith. London: Lawrene and Wishart.

Gumperz, J. J. and Levinson, S. (eds.) (1996) *Rethinking Linguistic Relativity.* Cambridge, NY: Cambridge University Press.

Habermas, J. (1972) *Knowledge and Human Interests*, trans. and intr. T. McCarthy. Cambridge: Polity Press.

Hall, S. (ed.) (1997) *Representations: Cultural Representation and Signifying Practices.* London: Open University.

Hall, S. (1990) 'Cultural identity and diaspora', in J. Ruterhford (ed.) *Identity: Community, Culture, Difference.* London: Lawrence & Wishart, pp. 222–237.

Hall, S. (1999) 'Cultural studies and its theoretical legacies', in S. During (ed.) *The Cultural Studies Reader.* London: Routledge, pp. 97–109. (Also in L. Grossberg *et al.* (eds.) 1992, *Cultural Studies.* London: Routledge.)

Heisey, D. R. (ed.) (2000) *Chinese Perspectives in Rhetoric and Communication.* Stamford, CT: Ablex.

Hollinger, R. (1994) *Postmodernism and the Social Sciences: A Thematic Approach.* London: Sage Publications.

Kincaid, D. L. (ed.) (1987) *Communication Theory: Eastern and Western Perspectives.* San Diego, CA: Academic Press.

Li, B.-J. (2003) *Zhongguo Yuyan Wenhua Shi (Chinese Linguistic and Cultural History).* Nanjing: Jiangsu Jiaoyu Chubanshe (Jiangsu Educational Press).

Liu, Y. (1996) 'To capture the essence of Chinese rhetoric: anatomy of a paradigm in comparative rhetoric', *Rhetoric Review*, 14 (1): 318–334.

Lu, X. (1999) 'An ideological/cultural analysis of political slogans in communist China', *Discourse and Society*, 10 (4): 487–508.

McQuail, D. (2000) *Mass Communication Theory.* Fourth Edition. London: Sage Publications.

Milhouse, V. H., Asante,, M. K. and Nwosu, P. O. (eds.) (2001) *Transculture: Interdisciplinary Perspectives on Cross-Cultural Relations.* Thousand Oaks, CA: Sage.

Moi, T. (1986) *The Kristeva Reader.* Oxford: Basil Blackwell.

Newmeyer, F. J. (1986) *The Politics of Linguistics.* Chicago, IL: The University of Chicago Press.

Ngũgĩ, W. -T. (1986) *Decolonising the Mind: The Politics of Language in African Literature.* London: James Currey.

Pennycook, A. (1998) *English and the Discourses of Colonialism.* London: Routledge.

Said, E. (1978) *Orientalism.* London: Routledge & Kegan Paul.

Said, E. W. (1993) *Culture and Imperialism.* New York: Alfred A. Knopf.

Shen, X. -L. (2001) *Hanyu Yufa Xue (Chinese Syntax).* Nanjing: Jiangsu Jiaoyu Chubanshe (Jiangsu Educational Press).

Sherzer, J. (1987) 'A discourse-centred approach to language and culture', *American Anthropology*, 89: 295–309.

Shi-Xu (2005) *A Cultural Approach to Discourse.* Houndmills/New York: Palgrave Macmillan.

Shi-Xu (2006). 'Editorial: multicultural discourses', *Journal of Multicultural Discourses*, 1: 1.

Shi-Xu, Kienpointner, M., and Servaes, J. (eds.) (2005) *Read the Cultural Other.* Berlin: Mouton de Gruyter.

Silverstein, M. and Urban, G. (eds.) (1996) *Natural Histories of Discourse*. Chicago, IL: University of Chicago Press.

Smart, B. (2003) *Economy, Culture and Society: A Sociological Critique of Neo-Liberalism*. Buckingham and Philadelphia, PA: Open University Press.

Spivak, G. C. (1988) *In Other Words: Essays in Cultural Politics*. New York: Routledge.

Stanley, L. and Wise, S. (1983) *Breaking Out: Feminist Consciousness and Feminist Research*. London: Routledge and Kegan Paul.

Tannen, D. (1990) *You Just Don't Understand: Women and Men in Conversation*. New York: Ballantine.

Urban, G. (1991) *A Discourse-Centered Approach to Culture: Native South American Myths and Rituals*. Austin, TX: University of Texas Press.

Van Dijk, T. A. (1993) *Elite Discourse and Racism*. London: Sage Publications.

Wang, N. (2003) 'How can Chinese social science journals join rank with prestigious international journals?', *China Readers*, 3 September.

Wang, S. -r (2002) 'China: how to cure its aphasia?', *Social Science Weekly*, 17 October.

Wittgenstein, L. (1968) *Philosophical Investigations*. Oxford: Basil Blackwell.

Young, L. W. L. (1994) *Crosstalk and Culture in Sino-American Communication*. New York: Cambridge University Press.

Young, R. (2001) *Postcolonialism: A Historical Introduction*. Oxford: Blackwell Publishing Ltd.

46

World Englishes and/or English as a lingua franca

Andy Kirkpatrick and James McLellan

Introduction

As many chapters in this handbook illustrate, the phrase 'discourse analysis' can carry a range of meanings. Most scholars agree, however, that discourse analysis involves the study of the way language is used in a variety of sociocultural contexts. The study of discourse is an 'enquiry into how people make meaning, and make *out* meaning'. Meanings are 'socio-cultural constructs of reality' (Widdowson, 2007: xv–xvi). Paltridge defines discourse analysis as 'an approach to the analysis of language that looks at patterns of language across texts as well as the social and cultural contexts in which the texts occur' (2010: 1). Gee (1999: 6) has made a distinction between discourse with 'a big D' and discourse with 'a little d'. 'Little d' discourse refers to the way languages are used 'to enact activities and identities' (1999: 6). But we cannot rely solely on language to establish identities and complete activities. We also need what Gee refers to as 'non-language stuff' to establish successfully our identity/ies and complete actions. This non-language stuff includes such things as clothing, manner, gestures, tools and technologies. And when this non-language stuff combines with language in use, then we have 'big D' discourse (1999: 7).

In this chapter we shall use forms of discourse analysis to analyse representative samples of world Englishes (e.g. Malaysian English and Nigerian English) and English as a lingua franca (e.g. the English used in interactions between Malaysians and Nigerians). We shall use discourse analysis to test the following interrelated hypotheses.

(i) Any variety of world English is, by definition, primarily concerned with establishing an identity and membership of a particular speech community. As such it will be characterized by lexical items and idioms that refer to specific items and beliefs that are of particular importance to the local culture and environment. As the great majority of speakers of a particular world English are multilinguals who have learned English as an additional language and who share a linguistic repertoire (that is to say, they speak the same languages), a world English may also be characterized by frequent use of code-mixing and code-switching. This use of code-mixing serves to establish identity and belonging to a speech community. Finally, a world English will also be characterized by the reflection of cultural values and pragmatic norms specific to its speakers. Needless to say, these cultural values and pragmatic norms will differ across different world Englishes.

(ii) As the major function of English as a lingua franca (ELF) is to act as a common medium of communication between people who do not share the same first language and culture, its role is primarily one of ensuring successful communication between people of different linguistic and cultural backgrounds. As such, ELF will be characterized by the relative absence of lexical items and idioms that refer to culturally and locally specific items and beliefs – for the simple reason that such lexical items and idioms are unlikely to be understood by people from outside the culture. As mutual communication is the goal of English as a lingua franca, the latter will also be characterized by a lack of code-mixing and code-switching, as participants in lingua franca communication are unlikely to share the same linguistic repertoire. Finally, English as a lingua franca will not normally reflect cultural values and pragmatic norms specific to a particular culture, as these may also interfere with successful cross-cultural communication.

(iii) In world Englishes and in English as a lingua franca, communicative success does not depend on the use of standard native-speaker forms. World Englishes can develop their own standard forms, which may well differ from those of standard British English, for example. This includes the many vernaculars of native-speaker varieties of English (Britain 2010). English as a lingua franca will be similarly characterized by the use of forms that would traditionally be classified as non-standard but do not necessarily interfere with communication.

In short, we argue that a world English is primarily, though not exclusively, concerned with identity and membership of a speech community, while English as a lingua franca is primarily, though not exclusively, concerned with cross-cultural communication (Kirkpatrick, 2010a). We therefore also suggest that it will be easier to undertake a study of 'big D' discourse with excerpts from world Englishes than with excerpts from English as a lingua franca.

In the next section we provide a brief introduction to world Englishes and then conduct a discourse analysis on authentic texts of world Englishes. We then provide a comparable introduction to the use of English as a lingua franca and conduct a discourse analysis on naturally occurring examples of English as a lingua franca. Finally we summarize our findings on the basis of the discourse analysis and consider whether the hypotheses outlined above are supported or not.

Background to world Englishes (WE)

While many scholars have developed theories and models of world Englishes (e.g. McArthur, 1998; Schneider, 2007), the discipline 'world Englishes' owes a great deal to Braj Kachru, who, along with Larry Smith, can be called the founders of the discipline. Kachru's great insight was to see that many different varieties of English were developing throughout the world and that many of these were able to be independent in the sense that they could derive their own linguistic and sociolinguistic norms from within, rather than being dependent on traditional 'native-speaker' Englishes. Kachru's 'circles' model has been particularly influential.

> The current sociolinguistic profile of English may be viewed in terms of three concentric circles … The Inner Circle refers to the traditional cultural and linguistic bases of English *(e.g. Britain, USA, Australia)*. The Outer Circle represents the institutionalized non-native varieties (ESL) in the regions that have passed through extended periods of colonization *(e.g. Singapore, India, Nigeria)* … The Expanding Circle includes the regions where the *performance* varieties of the language are used essentially in EFL contexts *(e.g. China, Japan, Egypt)*.
>
> *(Kachru, 1992: 356–357)*

In the next section we analyse samples of both 'inner' and 'outer circle' varieties of world Englishes (WE), with an initial focus on idioms.

Examples from WE

Before proceeding, it is important to stress that idiom has been defined in a number of ways, to include two-word phrases (such as 'of course') and strong collocations (such as 'hard facts') as well as proverbs and idiomatic expressions (Pitzl, 2009: 299). In our analysis here, we focus on idioms that can be defined as expressions whose meaning is more than, or distinct from, the sum of its individual components. That is to say, we are interested here in expressions whose meanings cannot be derived from the meaning of each individual word in the expression. To give a simple example, the meaning of 'to kick the bucket' cannot be derived from ideas of 'kicking' and of 'buckets'.

(i) 'a different kettle of fish'

The text 'Aussies will be a different kettle of fish' (5 October 2009) was published in the Dominion Post newspaper, based in Wellington, both in print and in online editions. It is taken to represent a sports opinion ('op-ed') text in an inner-circle variety, New Zealand English (NZE).

One characteristic discoursal feature of this genre is the frequent use of idioms and figurative expressions (Grant, 2005: 436). Writers often choose expressions which are clichés, rather than original or creative turns of phrase, in order to invoke a sense of solidarity and to appeal to readers, who have come to expect idiomatic phrases as a stylistic feature of sports reports and opinion texts.

The wider context is the build-up to an international cricket match between New Zealand and Australia, part of a competition staged in South Africa, in which the New Zealand team had managed to advance to the final stages by defeating three teams normally considered stronger in this form of the sport.

The text of 540 words contains a total of 32 idiomatic expressions (77 words), giving a ratio of idiom to total words of 1: 7.01, which is very high when contrasted with other written genres, including comparable subgenres in media discourse.

The core idiomatic expression in the title ('Aussies will be *a different kettle of fish*') is found to occur frequently in New Zealand sports media texts, as is evident from a search of the webpages of the Dominion Post newspaper, which shows eight uses of this exact expression relating to New Zealand's premier national sport, rugby, two relating to soccer, and one in a political rather than a sports story. A further example – 'A different kettle of kai moana' (where 'kai moana' [Te Reo Māori] means 'food sea', thus 'sea food') – also occurs in a rugby text, illustrating how idioms can cross language boundaries.

Table 46.1 lists the expressions deemed to be either idiomatic or figurative, or to have one non-compositional element (ONCEs), according to the definitions proposed by Grant and Bauer (2004).

This sample text of NZE sports journalism, whilst locally situated in terms of its content and informal style, includes a wide range of mostly clichéd idioms, which are arguably intelligible across most of the inner-circle varieties of English, with the exception of those of Canada and of the USA, where cricket is not a major national sport. Whilst it is monolingual, unlike the other world Englishes texts discussed in this chapter, it can be considered as borderline deviant in terms of the high frequency of idiomatic expressions, yet at the same time representative of media text in this genre, as can be established through the investigation of a corpus of comparable texts from the New Zealand print media.

The online edition of the Dominion Post newspaper allows for readers to submit comments on the article and thus to participate in the processes of print media news and opinion dissemination. In the 19 comments submitted by readers in response to this piece on 5–6 October 2009, none referred to any stylistic aspects of language use or to the surfeit of idiomatic expressions. From this

Table 46.1 Idioms, figuratives and ONCEs in a sports opinion article

	Category	Text
Headline	Core idiom	*Aussies will be a different kettle of fish*
1.	ONCE	On paper it is a win to Australia …
2.	ONCE	a dropped catch like the howler by Younis Khan yesterday …
3.	Fig.	… can all turn a big game on its head
4.	ONCE	a team on a winning roll …
5.	ONCE	can be hard to peg back …
6.	Fig	that is a big tick for New Zealand …
7.	Fig.	With their patched up squad, …
8.	Fig.	New Zealand have defied the odds …
9.	ONCE	… with three sudden-death victories …
10.	ONCE	Sri Lanka choked …
11.	Fig./Fig.	England toppled in a lottery … (x2)
12.	Core idiom	Australia will be a different kettle of fish.
13.	Fig.	They have the all-conquering Ricky Ponting in vintage form
14.	Fig.	… favoured to do a similar demolition job on New Zealand
15.	ONCE	Australia's firepower is vastly superior.
16.	Fig.	For decades scrapping has been a forte of New Zealand sides
17.	Fig.	But rolling their sleeves up might not be enough here
18.	Fig.	… that a couple of blokes in black uniforms have to play out of their skins otherwise New Zealand will finish second
19.	Fig.	Bond has been a mixed bag at the tournament …
20.	Core idiom	… his opening spell against Pakistan yesterday morning was top drawer
21.	ONCE	… the final may hinge on whether …
22.	ONCE	… he can get an early crack at Ponting
23.	Fig.	… for the seventh time in 10 clashes ..
24.	Fig.	… Australia has been content to milk Vettori for 30–40 runs
25.	Core idiom	… they can fill their boots against the other bowlers.
26.	Fig.	But Bond is back in the mix, …
27.	ONCE	They can't sit on two bowlers.
28.	Core idiom	McCullum has pulled finger at the Champions Trophy …
29.	ONCE	… a niggle in Vettori's lower back or hamstring
30.	Fig.	Hats off to Vettori's men for making it this far.
31.	ONCE	… if they were able to stun the cricketing world …

Source: Millmow, 2009, 5 October

we can draw the opposite conclusion, that the text is not deemed deviant or exceptional as an exemplar of the sports opinion article genre in New Zealand English.

Thus one stylistic feature of this text, the high frequency of clichéd idiomatic expressions, signals both conformity to local discoursal norms and deviation and distinctiveness within inner-circle varieties of English in a specific genre.

(ii) Advertisements in the print media in East Malaysia

Despite sharing a number of pan-Malaysian cultural features, the East Malaysian states of Sabah and Sarawak, on Borneo Island, are ethnically, linguistically and culturally distinct from the states of the Malay Peninsula (West Malaysia). Many research studies on Malaysia assume the situation in West Malaysia to be the default norm, and marginalize or ignore Sabah and Sarawak.

Andy Kirkpatrick and James McLellan

As noted by Azirah Hashim (2010: 525–526), there have been studies of the discourse of advertising in the Malaysian media covering radio, television and the print media. However, in terms of their data sources and focus, these have all been oriented towards West Malaysia. In Sarawak and Sabah the greater ethnic and linguistic diversity, allied to higher levels of multi-lingualism, means that advertising text authors need to make choices that reflect their target market, both in terms of which language or languages to use and in terms of which style or variety to choose for maximum appeal and impact. Newspapers are published in English, Malay and Chinese. The *Sabah Daily Express* newspaper has separate English, Malay and Kadazandusun sections. *Utusan Borneo*, a Malay newspaper published in Sarawak, has a section in Iban. Kadazandusun and Iban are the major indigenous languages of Sabah and Sarawak respectively. Particularly in Sarawak, where English-medium education was maintained into the 1980s prior to switching to mainly Malay-medium, English is frequently used for both inter- and intra-ethnic communication. This is especially true in private sector business organizations, where English is used alongside Chinese and both the local Sarawak and the national standard varieties of Malay.

For analysis of language choice and use, a corpus was collected, comprising 174 classified advertisements (CAs) in the *Borneo Post* edition of Tuesday 27 July 2010, and a further 76 that appeared in the Malay-language *Utusan Borneo* on the same day. Tables 46.2 and 46.3 give background details about the languages used in these. Public service announcements, for instance tender notices and court proceedings, were not included, nor were family announcements such as obituaries.

Almost 80 per cent of the CA texts in the *Borneo Post* are in monolingual English, although 15.5 per cent show some measure of code-switching with either Malay or Chinese, and 4.6 per cent are in monolingual Malay.

Whilst we might normally expect all CAs to be in the same language as that of the newspapers' news content, this turns out not to be the case, 43 out of the total of 76 advertisements in the

Table 46.2 Borneo Post, language use in 174 classified advertisements published on 27/7/10

Language	Number of CAs	Remarks
English only	139	79.8% of total
English/Malay	15	8.6% of total
English/Chinese	12	6.9% of total
English/Malay/Chinese	—	
Malay only	8	4.6% of total
Other languages	—	

Table 46.3 Utusan Borneo, language use in 76 classified advertisements published on 27/7/10

Language	Number of CAs	Remarks
English only	43	56.6% of total
English/Malay	10	13.1% of total
English/Chinese	3	3.9% of total (Chinese for names of companies, hotel and dish being promoted)
English/Malay/Chinese	2	2.6% of total
Malay only	17	22.4% of total
Other languages	1	Iban (job vacancy advertisement)

658

Malay language *Utusan Borneo* being in monolingual English. Only 17 (22.4 per cent) are in monolingual Malay, and 15 (19.7 per cent) have text in more than one language (i.e. they use code-switching). In terms of the discourse of world Englishes, this is significant, as it shows that advertisers are conscious of the multilingual capabilities of their target readership. Code-switching is thus a prominent feature of these CA texts, English and Malay being the most frequent combination in single advertisements. Examples of code-switching include the following:

[1] Borneo Post

(a) *Lori di sewa. Pengangkutan Barang-Barang. Pindah rumah, ofis, kedai dan lain-lain.* Services all the way in Sarawak

(b) Waiter (*mesti ada pengalaman*) … Cook–Malay/Western/Chinese (*mesti ada bukti pengalaman kerja*)

(c) *staff hostel dan staff meal disediakan; lelaki sahaja*

(d) *Berth at Kuching* _____ *Wharf,* _____. *Kargo ringan diterima dan penghantaran boleh di buat pada hari yangsama'*

Translations: (a) Lorry for hire. Transport of goods. Move house, office, shop etc.

(b) (must have experience) (must have proof of work experience)

(c) staff hostel and staff meals available; male only

(d) …Light cargo taken and delivery can be made the same day

Utusan Borneo

(e) '黑鸡人参汤. Double boiled black chicken. Ginseng soup with dried seafood'

(f) Outstation/*Semenanjung Malaysia* (*menawarkan semua jenis pekerjaan*)

(g) We supply wrought iron material, hollow section, flat bar … *Harga Termurah*

(h) *Emas boleh tukar wang.* One stop service. (*Jual, Tukar, Trade in dan lain-lain*)

(i) *Cagaran tanah*: Native Land and Mixed Zone Land

(j) *Terdapat jawatan kosong di cawangan Miri:*
Office boy cum delivery driver (*lelaki*)
Cashier (*perempuan*)

Translations: (e) (the English is a direct parallel translation of the Chinese here)

(f) Outstation/ Malay Peninsula (offering all types of work)

(g) … Lowest prices.

(h) Gold can be exchanged for cash… (Sell, exchange, trade-in and others)

(i) Security for land:…

(j) There are vacancies at Miri branch:
Office boy cum delivery driver (male)
Cashier (female)

Along the predictable dominance of English CAs in the English newspaper, English is also encroaching into the Malay newspaper, where CAs in monolingual Malay are a minority. Other instances of code-switching with Chinese involve the advertiser's name and are therefore not included in this set of examples.

In terms of deviation from international standard English norms, a few examples occur in both the English and Malay newspaper CAs:

[2]   Examples of non-standard English usage

Borneo Post

Show time are subject to change without prior notice (*Cinema advertisement*)

Check this professional service provided as follow: … (*Housing repair advertisement*)

Hands-on site experiences in construction is an advantage … (*Job vacancy*)

____ Plumbing Service … specialized in toilet problem, blocked, pipes leakages …
(*Plumbing company advertisement*)

5 working days, working hour 8.00 a.m. to 5.30 p.m. (*Job vacancy*)

We provided various cloth & uniform for company, association, school, kindergarten …
    (*Clothing company advertisement*)

Gold can exchange with cash. One stop service (*Gold trader's advertisement*)

Utusan Borneo

Show times are subject to change without prior notice (*Cinema advertisement*)

Show times are subjected to change without prior notice (*Cinema advertisement*)

Never suppress your dream, the _____ **Music Studio** has made it **Easy** and **Fun**

to achieve. Even start with **ZERO** musical background, you'll be able to **play your favorite songs** from ballads, the latest hits, Oldies, Worship, etc.

(*Music Studio advertisement, original emphasis*)

A proviso about guarding against 'incidentalism' is important here: these examples do not show serious deviations from standard English, a point also emphasized by Gupta (2006) in her discussion of standard English and Borneo. Nor can any of these deviations be deemed to affect intelligibility. They do, however, reflect commonly attested syntactic features of both world Englishes and ELF, including zero plural marking and free variation between past and present tense verb morphemes.

Through their language choices, especially in the genre-specific moves and strategies of product promotion, naming of the advertiser, location of the business premises, listing of goods or services offered, these texts display high levels of conformity with the communicative norms of the discourses of advertising globally, whilst adhering to local norms and expectations in terms of language choice (see discussion in Bhatia, 2009: 166).

In terms of the main analytical framework for this chapter, the advertisement texts present a challenge to the identity-communication continuum. The CA texts, aimed at English- and Malay-knowing multilingual Malaysians who form the majority of the readership, contain textual reflections of the shared identity of advertisers and their addressees. At the same time the particular nature of advertising text as discourse ensures that communication is also a key factor, as is shown by the obligatory and optional generic features of this small corpus of advertisements.

(iii) Extract from Brunei public online discussion forum posting:

[3]

(1)Thats why drg should to hangout and chill somewhere. (2).Salah   kah?
            ABBR. 'diaorang', 3P★   *Wrong DM?*
(3)Jgn   salahkan urg   lepak.. (4)Pls read ur alls
ABBR 'jangan' NEG IMP accuse   ABBR 'urang', people loaf
minds thats kmu   ato over negetive thinking. (5)Tau   sudah country ane
        ABBR 'kamu', 2P DEM   *Know already   DEM*
very low entertainment cuba try to make a new place for chill. (6)Tantu kan! (7)About this

try   Sure NEG

probs jua byk   urg   tane run away from another
    also ABBR 'banyak', many ABBR 'urang', people 1pI

country for release theirs tension and go vacation frm ths place.. (8)Pls concern about this
probs before got a bad respond from other people. (9)Don't make our town like a haunted
place. We need to make a best decision about this probs. (10)Indeed. (11)Just for help our
people in this country felt satisfied and confidence about from this bad thinking for budaya

culture

lepak d'brunei   tane   ah.
loaf ABBR 'di', in   1PI   DM

(★ See 'Transcription conventions' at the end of this chapter for key to interlinear gloss
abbreviations.)

(Free translation, by second author: That's why they should have somewhere to chill and
hang out. Is that wrong? Don't accuse those who loaf around. Please look into your own
minds and get over the negative thinking. We know that this country of ours has little in
the way of entertainment, so let's provide a place to chill. Sure, let's do that. Many of our
people get round this problem by going out of the country on vacation to release their
tension. Please be concerned about this problem before others give a bad response. Don't
make our town like a haunted place. We need to make the best possible decision about this
problem. Indeed. We just want to help our people in this country to feel satisfied and
confident and overcome this bad thinking about the loafing culture in our country Brunei.)

This extract, from a text posted on the Brudirect HYS (Have Your Say) public online discussion
forum in August 2010, represents a genre previously analysed in greater detail by Chitravelu and
Rosnah (2007), by McLellan (2005, 2009), and by McLellan and Noor Azam (2007). These
in-depth studies, drawing on larger corpora, help to eliminate the risk of 'incidentalism' in relation
to this single text. It is a mixture of informal Brunei English and informal Brunei Malay,
representative of the spoken and text messaging communication patterns of many younger
bilingual Bruneians.

In this extract there is a predominance of English over Malay, 97 words as against 26, although
the whole text is more balanced with 182 English words (60.9 per cent) and 117 Malay (39.1 per
cent). Analysis of the extract by phrase/clause shows a total of 35, with 24 in English only, 6 in
Malay only, and 5 mixed. Surface features include deviant grammar and spelling, and the use of
abbreviations caused in part by the prevalence of text messaging conventions and the need for
brevity. However, this keyboarded text also shows additions to standard English forms: 'should
to', 'alls', 'theirs' as adjective, 'confidence'. These perhaps reflect the way these words are spoken
by Bruneians.

The code-switching in this text is both inter- and intra-sentential, with a single-word
pronominal switch to Malay (drg – diaorang – 'they') in sentence 1, but also a sentence
(no. 5) that shows Malay and English contributing to both the grammatical frame and to the
propositional content. The sentence begins in Malay ('Tau sudah'), then has a mixed noun
phrase, 'country ane' with English head and Malay modifier, following Malay constituent
structure, and functioning as subject of a proposition with Malay zero-copula but English lexis,
'very low entertainment'. This is immediately followed, without punctuation, by the code-mixed
stock phrase 'cuba try', heard very often in the speech of Bruneians as an exponent of the speech act
of encouragement or suggestion, in which 'cuba' and 'try' are translation equivalents. The final
clause of the sentence is in English only: 'to make a new place for chill'. Thus a sentence that begins

with a dominant Malay grammatical frame ends with English supplying both the grammatical frame and the lexical content.

From a broader, 'big D Discourse' perspective, we need to realize that such texts of Brunei English have maximal communicative efficiency, since they reflect the bilingual competence and strategic code choices of the producer and are addressed to similar proficient bilinguals. They can therefore be compared with the code-mixed CA texts from the Sarawak newspapers, as texts of world Englishes that are locally appropriate but are not fully accessible to those not familiar with Brunei or Malaysian English.

This section has demonstrated the application of DA to world Englishes' texts from three separate contexts. In the inner-circle NZE sports text, the frequent use of figurative idiomatic expressions has been highlighted. The Sarawak CA and the Brunei discussion forum texts display varying degrees of deviation from inner-circle Englishes and the use of other languages within the repertoires of the text producers and their readers. The NZE sports text and the Brunei online forum posting both support the idea that WE texts can be analysed along an identity–communication continuum, since they reflect the discourse communities to which they all belong.

The Sarawak CA texts, however, because of the nature of advertising texts, reflect aspects of both communication and identity.

Background to English as a lingua franca (ELF)

English as a lingua franca is a 'contact language between persons who share neither a common native tongue nor a common (national) culture and for whom English is the chosen foreign language of communication' (Firth, 1996: 240). A major development with regards to English in recent years has been its rapidly increasing role as a regional and international lingua franca. It is now commonly accepted that far more people use English as a lingua franca than as a first language. Indeed, Xu (2010) has suggested that there are now more learners and users of English in China alone than there are native speakers of it worldwide. When one considers that the BRIC political grouping, comprising the countries of Brazil, Russia, India and China, primarily uses English as a lingua franca as its medium of communication, the scale of this role of English becomes clear. English is also the sole official working language of the Association of Southeast Asian Nations (ASEAN) (Kirkpatrick, 2010b). Thus, if we want to understand the use of English in today's world, 'ELF must be one of the central concerns in this line of research' (Mauranen, 2006: 147).

Examples from ELF

The examples of ELF analysed below are primarily taken from the Asian Corpus of English, a corpus of spoken English currently being collected by a number of teams throughout Asia (Kirkpatrick, 2010c). Examples from the Vienna Oxford Corpus of International English (VOICE) will also be used. VOICE is a corpus of more than 1 million words of naturally occurring spoken ELF usage, which has been collected by Seidlhofer and her team at the University of Vienna (Seidlhofer, 2009; see http://www.univie.ac.at/voice/).

In order to test the hypotheses presented above, we shall first analyse the corpus for use of idioms. We predict that there will be relatively few of these in ELF communication, as their use is thought to be culturally specific and thus likely to hinder communication. However, that is not to say that they don't occur and, as we shall see from the first example, the same idiom can occur in different languages. The first example is from the VOICE corpus (and adapted from Pitzl, 2009: 308). The participants are in business and, in this short excerpt, comprise two Koreans (S1 and S2) and an Austrian (S4). (There is a total of five participants at the meeting.)

[4]
S4:   you have in the stores since when since a couple of months
S1:   only er one and a half month
S2:   months
S4:   yeah then I think in that case *we should not wake up any dogs any dogs* by going now

The interesting point to note is that, while the idiom used here varies significantly from the native English 'let sleeping dogs lie', its meaning in its new formulation or 're-metaphorization' (Pitzl, 2009: 306) is perfectly clear. What is also interesting is that this idiom also exists in German and Korean, which would suggest that the participants here would have no problem interpreting the meaning of the metaphor, and this would, in turn, suggest that there may be more room than originally anticipated for the use of idiom and metaphor, especially those which undergo this process of re-metaphorization. However, this turns out not to be the case in the ACE data, where idioms and metaphors are used sparingly. In one way, this is disappointing, as the use of 'new' metaphors from a speaker's first language would add spice and freshness to the language. For example, the Chinese expression that describes people who are very close but up to no good as 'breathing through the same nostril' and the Japanese expression that describes adult children who still live off their parents as 'chewing on their parents' shins' are both evocative and, while they may take initial explanation, would, we argue, be easily memorized after one hearing. But these don't occur in the ACE data.

The following two excerpts represent the only two occasions in a two-hour meeting when idioms or metaphors are used and, on both occasions, the speaker was the same person, a Chinese male. The meeting was held in Hong Kong. The ten participants, comprising three Chinese males, two Chinese females, a Nepalese male, a Filipina female, a Pakistani female, an Indian female and a Pakistani male, discussed ways of providing assistance to ethnic minorities in Hong Kong.

[5]
S1:   er yes *I buy your second point* and I think that we can create a regular system....'
S1:   yes, okay then I think there's no harm in try but of course they just want to meet just meet to know about some perspectives of some Muslim's communities they think er *this is not their cup of tea* or this is not allowed but of course....

In answer to any possible charge of incidentalism here, we point out that in some 14 hours of ACE data which has already been collected and analysed, there are only 4 uses of idiom and metaphor, two of which are described above.

We now turn to incidences of code-switching in the ACE data. In a 20-minute discussion involving a Singaporean female – whose first language is Malay (SM) – an Indonesian male (I) and a Cambodian male (C), there was this single instance of the use of the Malay/Indonesian word *rojak*. Rojak is a Malay/Indonesian word that literally refers to a special type of mixed salad. Here the particpants are using the term metaphorically, to describe the colloquial variety of Singapore English, Singlish.

[6]
SM: ... all the English and Singlish are all mixed together like *rojak*
I: oh like *rojak* like that
SM: yes you know *rojak* right
I: yes, it's fruits mixed
SM: all up together.

(Kirkpatrick, 2007: 168)

Not speaking Malay, the Cambodian will not have been able to understand the meaning of this term on its own. This may explain why the Singaporean and Indonesian participants discuss the meaning of the term explicitly: they do it in order not to exclude the Cambodian. In any event, code-mixing is extremely rare in the data, and this contrasts markedly with the world Englishes' CA and discussion forum texts, as we have illustrated above.

In the Hong Kong excerpt, use of code-mixing is extremely rare, as it is throughout the data. One occasion when Cantonese (the first language of the Chinese participants) is used occurs when the name of a particular educational scheme, *yijin*, is used. *Yijin* is an educational programme that gives a second chance to children from lower socio-economic backgrounds who have not done well in the standard school system. In this excerpt, S1 and S7 are both Chinese males, S2 is a Nepalese male and S3 an Indian female. When it becomes clear to S1 that some of the participants do not understand the meaning of *yijin*, he explains it to them.

> [6]
> S1: yeah anyway okay so yes anyways just for your information yes (.) er::m (3) er yes m- I'd like to share about my my er last week I had the training erm (.) at er (.) *yijin*
> S7: *yijin yijin*
> S2: *yijin*
> S1: *yijin* I don't know if you know about *yijin yijin* programme
> S3: *yijin* it's English?
> S1: er: er last week I h- I gave I gave two talks together with er [first name] er our former staff she's a volunteer on that day *yijin* er *yijin* college is for those who want to study form five again after some time so er because of their poor schooling beforehand (.) and they like to go back to school and er er if they got pass they it's equivalent to form five level …

On another occasion S1 also uses Cantonese, but this is because he can't think of the appropriate English word. His Cantonese-speaking colleagues help him out and they agree on 'consistent', but the word SI was really looking for is probably 'unanimous', if his use of 'anonymous' is a clue.

> [7]
> S1: but er on that day I was very surprised that er the the opinions was (.) how how should I say *ho yat zee* anonymous not anonymous er very
> S7: consistent
> S5: consistent
> S1: consistent yes
> S6: mhm

On another occasion Cantonese is used by the Cantonese speakers after the Nepalese male asks what the next item on the agenda is. The Cantonese speakers are surprised at this, as the agenda items are clearly marked, and they talk briefly to each other in Cantonese, saying the equivalent of 'It's the next item on the list isn't it?'. The misunderstanding is swiftly repaired.

Part of hypothesis (ii) above was that ELF, in contrast to world Englishes, would see few uses of specific cultural and pragmatic norms. This hypothesis is also borne out, but in the Hong Kong excerpt there is evidence that the participants know and respect the cultural norms of their fellow participants. In the following excerpt the Nepalese male thanks a fellow participant, the Pakistani Muslim male, and addresses him by using the formula Mister + First Name.

> [8]
> S1: he did pay the fee
> S2: yeah he paid eighty one people they paid fifty eight (.) er fifty five enjoyed including

children
S1:   okay
S2:   and thank you mister [first name] thank you for thank you for having us
S6:   it's a pleasure also one of my duties

Through the rest of the discussion, people are routinely referred to by their first names. Only the Muslim male is addressed in this more formal way, despite being around the same age as many of the other participants. As he is also addressed in this way by other participants, this would suggest that the speakers are aware of Muslim naming patterns and adopt them accordingly.

To turn now to the discourse analysis of ELF in search of so-called non-standard forms, any analysis of ELF discourse shows a range of these forms. There is some debate as to the cause of these distinctive forms. On the one hand, it seems obvious that the first language of the speakers influences the English they speak (see Mesthrie and Bhatt, 2008). However, the results of discourse analysis have shown a remarkable number of linguistic features that, while being distinctive in that they differ from standard British or American English, are shared across many varieties of world English (Kortmann, 2010). These also occur in ELF. This has led people to argue for the existence of vernacular universals, made up of non-standard forms that occur in all colloquial varieties of English (Chambers, 2004; and see Filppula *et al.*, 2009). We don't have the space to enter this debate in any depth here, but Thomason's advice in cautioning against drawing a line between contact-induced change and vernacular universals seems wise, as 'many linguistic changes involve both kinds of processes – that is various processes of contact-induced change and also universal tendencies of various kinds' (2009: 349). What the analysis of ELF data clearly shows (Mauranen and Ranta, 2009, Kirkpatrick, 2010b) is that so-called non-standard forms are common, that many of them are shared and that they seldom interfere with cross-cultural communication. Here we offer two examples. The first comes from the Hong Kong meeting, and the non-standardness has more to do with overall sentence structure than with grammatical marking, which is exemplified in the second extract. Non-standard forms or structures are indicated in bold. Both speakers are Chinese males whose first language is Cantonese.

[9]
S1:   okay thank you I I er know they they must they must have a good time er er all over there yes and er I think of course we play our role to recruit people *just wondering er we can learn from experience how can secure the better commitment* from the communities especially we'll be given (.) nine- ninety free ticket *agains hope* the tickets will not be abused er by some members (.) anyway thank you yes so (.) anymore
S7:   er somehow for the community
S1:   participation
S7:   participation and we will er we just talked about we will have er other than flag day hh we will arrange some maybe erm still discussing *two possible* one is cleaning the street or bridges

Ellipsis, the apparent deletion of items, characterizes this excerpt. We have added the apparently elided items in italics in the version below. A native speaker of English might say something like,

[10]
I was just wondering er *whether* we can learn from experience *about* how *we* can secure (the) better commitment from the communities especially *as* we'll be given nine- ninety free tickets ....

665

Ellipsis of this type is, to a certain extent, predictable, as the speaker's first language is Cantonese – which allows, for example, subjectless sentences. The incidence of elision does not appear to affect the intelligibility of what is being said, however, as S7 immediately offers the suggestion, 'community participation'.

The other non-standard form here is 'agains'. It is hard to be sure about the cause of this form, but the insertion of a sibilant sound after nasals such as /n/ and dentals such as /t/ is common in the speech of many participants in the ACE.

Despite the use of these non-standard forms, S1's anticipation of the word 'participation' is evidence that the conversation is flowing freely. S7 also appears to 'delete' a word like 'ideas' after 'two possible', but this may also be simply explained by a change of mind, a common phenomenon in unplanned spontaneous discourse of this type.

The second example is of an Indonesian female recounting to a Burmese colleague what had happened to her when she arrived at Singapore airport and was waiting to be collected. Here we focus on the non-marking of the past tense; the unmarked verbs are bolded and the marked ones are in italics.

> [11]
> I2:   I waited for the official who **pick** me up OK and then I *tried* to look for the official but because ere r the plane you know *landed* early so early so the official *hadn't come* yet
> B2:   what a pity
> I2:   I *had* to stay in the airport and then *did* nothing just **sit** and I **check** the placard of RELC ok and I *couldn't* see that's why I just **sit** and **take** a rest … what about you what time.

(Kirkpatrick, 2007:160)

This is of particular interest, because it illustrates that the non-marking of a form does not necessarily mean that the speaker does not know the rule. With regard to past tense marking in the extract above, there are 11 verbs that could be marked for past tense. Of these, the speaker fails to mark only five. However, as the non-marking of 'pick' in line 1 is almost certainly due to the phonological environment (no one would actually say picked /pikt/ in this context), only the verbs 'sit', 'check' and 'take' are unmarked. It may also be that the non-marking of 'check' has a phonological cause, as 'checked' is not easy to pronounce. But the non-marking of 'sit' and 'take' cannot be explained in this way. This apparently random marking of forms is common in ELF (see Breiteneder, 2009) and illustrates that the non-use of a particular form does not necessarily mean that the form is not available to the speaker. What this also shows is that the non-use of tense markers in these contexts does not interfere with communication.

Conclusion

We posited three hypotheses at the beginning of this chapter, which we then tested by conducting forms of discourse analysis on excerpts of world Englishes and ELF. On the basis of the results of our findings from the discourse analysis, we now conclude that:

(i)   The world Englishes data from Malaysia and Brunei support the hypothesis that world Englishes are by definition code-mixed varieties, on account of the availability of languages other than English, as resources on which speakers and writers can draw, knowing that their readership or audience share similar multilingual capabilities. The East Malaysian classified advertisements, by virtue of the generic properties of advertising texts, signal aspects of both communication and shared identity of sellers and potential buyers. The Brunei online forum posting, by contrast, very much reflects Bruneian identity being negotiated through language choices, including micro-level intra-sentential code-switching. The inner-circle New Zealand sports text illustrates shared cultural and pragmatic norms in terms of the stylistic feature of rich and frequent figurative idiomatic language.

(ii) The ELF examples analysed above show a strong orientation towards communication rather than expression or negotiation of identities. The relative absence of both idiomatic expressions and of recourse to other languages (i.e. code-switching) supports this contention. However, there is evidence, especially in the Hong Kong ELF examples, of interactive negotiation that is aimed at maintaining clear communication and at showing respect for interlocutors from other linguacultural backgrounds.

(iii) The third hypothesis, relating to 'native-speaker' or 'inner-circle' norms, is supported by both the WE and the ELF examples. Evidence of inner-circle varieties showing non-standard or idiosyncratic features is found in both the New Zealand sports media text discussed above and in Britain (2010). In all the examples analysed, except the Brunei discussion forum text, the deviations from standard norms are minor and certainly do not impede communication.

Transcription conventions

Interlinear glossing conventions used in codemixed text extract [3]

1PI 1st person plural inclusive pronoun
2P 2nd person plural pronoun
3P 3rd person plural pronoun
ABBR Abbreviation
DEM Demonstrative adjective
DM Discourse marker
IMP Imperative
NEG Negative

Further Reading

Honna, Nobuyuki (2008) *English as a Multicultural Language in Asian Contexts: Issues and Ideas*, Tokyo: Kurosio Publishers.

This gives a very useful account of recent developments concerning the roles and status of English in Asia.

Jenkins, Jennifer (2007) *English as a Lingua Franca: Attitude and Identity*. Oxford: Oxford University Press.

The author provides a review of the development of ELF as a field of study and presents the results of empirical research into attitudes towards ELF.

Kirkpatrick, Andy (2010) *The Routledge Handbook of World Englishes*. London: Routledge.

A companion volume in the Routledge Handbook series, this gives a comprehensive overview of the field of world Englishes, along with an up-to-date account of recent developments and debates.

Mauranen, Anna and Ranta, Elina (2009) (eds.) *English as a Lingua Franca: Studies and Findings*, Newcastle: Cambridge Scholars Publishing.

This edited volume contains a collection of articles detailing the latest ELF research findings.

Texts discussed as data sources

Classifieds (27 July 2010). *The Borneo Post*, Kuching, Sarawak, Malaysia, pp. C1–C10.
Iklaneka (27 July 2010). *Utusan Borneo*, Kuching, Sarawak, Malaysia, pp. B1–B4.

Millmow, J. (5 October 2009). Aussies will be *a different kettle of fish*. Wellington, New Zealand, The Dominion Post. Available online at: http://www.stuff.co.nz/sport/opinion/2929974/Aussies-will-be-a-different-kettle-of-fish (accessed August 13, 2010).

'Positive thinking' (pseudonym) (11 August 2010) 'Relex sha okay'. Public discussion forum posting on Brunei Have No Fear/Have Your Say. Available online at: http://www.bruneihys.net/newhys/2010/08/11/ (accessed 30 August 2010).

References

Bhatia, T. (2009) 'English in Asian advertising and the teaching of World Englishes', in K. Murata and J. Jenkins (eds.) *Global Englishes in Asian Contexts: Current and Future Debates*. Basingstoke, England: Palgrave Macmillan, pp. 154–171.

Breiteneder, A. (2009) 'English as a lingua franca in Europe: an empirical perspective', *World Englishes*, 28 (2): 256–269.

Britain, D. (2010) 'Grammatical variation in the contemporary spoken English of England', in A. Kirkpatrick (ed.) *The Handbook of World Englishes*. London: Routledge, 37–58.

Chambers, J. (2004) 'Dynamic typology and vernacular universals', in B. Kortmann (ed.) *Dialectology Meets Typology: Dialect Grammar from a Cross-Linguistic Perspective*. Berlin: Mouton de Gruyter, pp. 124–1245.

Chitravelu, N. and Rosnah, H. R. (2007) 'English–Malay border crossings: a study of code-switching in Brunei Darussalam', in S. K. Lee, S. M. Thang, and K. S. Lee (eds.) *Border Crossings: Moving between Languages and Cultural Frameworks*. Subang Jaya, Malaysia: Pelanduk Publications, pp. 23–55.

Filppula, M., Klemola, J., and Paulasto, H. (eds.) (2009) *Vernacular Universals and Language Change*. London: Routledge.

Firth, A. (1996) 'The discursive accomplishment of normality: on "lingua franca" English and conversation analysis', *Journal of Pragmatics*, 26: 237–259.

Gee, J. P. (1999) *An Introduction to Discourse Analysis*. London: Routledge.

Grant, L. (2005) 'Frequency of "core idioms" in the British National Corpus (BNC)', *International Journal of Corpus Linguistics*, 10 (4): 429–451.

Grant, L. and Bauer, L. (2004) 'Criteria for defining idioms: are we barking up the wrong tree?', *Applied Linguistics*, 25 (1): 38–61.

Gupta, A. F. (2006) 'Standard English and Borneo', *Southeast Asia: A Multidisciplinary Journal*, 6 (1): 79–94.

Hashim, A. (2010) 'Englishes in advertising', in A. Kirkpatrick (ed.) *The Handbook of World Englishes*. London: Routledge, pp. 520–534.

Kachru, B. B. (1992) *The Other Tongue*. Urbana, IL: University of Illinois Press.

Kirkpatrick, A. (2007) *World Englishes: Implications for International Communication and ELT*. Cambridge, England: Cambridge University Press.

Kirkpatrick, A. (2010a) 'English as an Asian lingua franca and the multilingual model of ELT', *Language Teaching*, 43 (3): 1–13.

Kirkpatrick, A. (2010b) *English as a Lingua Franca in ASEAN: A Multilingual Model*. Hong Kong: Hong Kong University Press.

Kirkpatrick, A. (2010c) 'Researching English as a lingua franca in Asia: the Asian corpus of English (ACE) project', *Asian Englishes*, 13 (1): 4–18.

Kortmann, B. (2010) 'Variation across Englishes: syntax', in A. Kirkpatrick (ed.), *The Handbook of World Englishes*. London: Routledge, pp. 400–424.

Mauranen, A. (2006) 'A rich domain of ELF: the ELFA corpus of academic discourse', *Nordic Journal of English Studies*, 5 (2): 145–159.

McArthur, T. (1998) *The English Languages*. Cambridge: Cambridge University Press.

McLellan, J. (2005) 'Malay–English language alternation in two Brunei Darussalam online discussion forums'. Unpublished thesis, Curtin University of Technology.

McLellan, J. (2009) 'When two grammars coincide: Malay–English code-switching in public on-line discussion forum texts'. *International Sociological Association RC25 Newsletter*, 5. Available online at: http://www.crisaps.org/newsletter/summer2009/ (accessed 30 August 2010).

McLellan, J. and Noor Azam Haji-Othman (2007) 'The changing ecology of language in Negara Brunei Darussalam'. Paper presented at International Convention of Asian Scholars (ICAS5), Kuala Lumpur, Malaysia, August.

Mesthrie, R. and Bhatt, R. (2008) *World Englishes*. Cambridge, England: Cambridge University Press.

Paltridge, B. (2010) *Discourse Analysis*. London: Continuum.

Pitzl, M.-L. (2009) ' "We should not wake up any dogs": idiom and metaphor in ELF', in A. Mauranen and E. Ranta (eds.) *English as a Lingua Franca: Studies and findings*. Newcastle: Cambridge Scholars Publishing, pp. 298–322.

Schneider, E. (2007) *Postcolonial Englishes: Varieties around the World*. Cambridge, England: Cambridge University Press.

Seidlhofer, B. (2009) 'Orientations in ELF research: form and function', in A. Mauranen and E. Ranta (eds.) *English as a Lingua Franca: Studies and Findings*. Newcastle, England: Cambridge Scholars Publishing, pp. 37–59.

Thomason, S. (2009) 'Why universals versus contact-induced change', in M. Filppula, J. Klemola and H. Paulasto (eds.) *Vernacular Universals and Language Contacts: Evidence from Varieties of English and Beyond*. London: Routledge, pp. 349–364.

Widdowson, H. (2007) *Discourse Analysis*. Oxford, England: Oxford University Press.

Xu, Zhichang, M. (2010) *Chinese English: Features and Implications*. Hong Kong: Open University Press.

Index

www.routledge.com/linguistics

Also available...

An Introduction to Discourse Analysis

4th Edition

By James Paul Gee

Discourse analysis considers how language, both spoken and written, enacts social and cultural perspectives and identities. Assuming no prior knowledge of linguistics, *An Introduction to Discourse Analysis* examines the field and presents James Paul Gee's unique integrated approach which incorporates both a theory of language-in-use and a method of research.

The fourth edition of this bestselling textbook has been extensively revised and updated, with new examples and activities. While it can be used as a stand-alone text, this edition has also been fully cross-referenced with the practical companion title *How to do Discourse Analysis: A Toolkit* and together they provide the complete package for students studying discourse analysis. A new companion website provides additional resources for students and instructors.

Clearly structured and written in a highly accessible style, *An Introduction to Discourse Analysis* includes perspectives from a variety of approaches and disciplines, including applied linguistics, education, psychology, anthropology and communication to help students and scholars from a range of backgrounds to formulate their own views on discourse and engage in their own discourse analysis.

2014 | 224 Pages | HB: 978-0-415-72125-7| PB: 978-0-415-72556-9
Learn more at: www.routledge.com/9780415721257

Available from all good bookshops

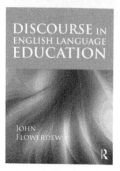

How to Do Discourse Analysis

A Toolkit, 2nd Edition

By James Paul Gee

How to do Discourse Analysis: A Toolkit is the essential guide to doing discourse analysis, from James Paul Gee, bestselling author of *An Introduction to Discourse Analysis: Theory and Method*.

Using a practical how-to approach, Gee provides the tools necessary to work with discourse analysis, with engaging step-by-step tasks featured throughout the book. Each tool is clearly explained, along with guidance on how to use it, and authentic data is provided for readers to practice using the tools. Readers from all fields will gain both a practical and theoretical background in how to do discourse analysis and knowledge of discourse analysis as a distinctive research methodology.

This second edition includes new examples, especially from digital media, a more user-friendly and accessible layout and a website, including online activities, podcasts and weblinks, which links the book with *An Introduction to Discourse Analysis*.

How to do Discourse Analysis: A Toolkit is the ideal text for all those taking courses in discourse or text analysis , to be used either as a companion to Gee's *An Introduction to Discourse Analysis: Theory and Method* or as a stand-alone book.

2014 | 224 Pages | HB: 978-0-415-72557-6| PB: 978-0-415-72558-3
Learn more at: www.routledge.com/9780415725576